CRIMINAL LAW

CRIMINAL LAW

10th Edition

Joycelyn M. Pollock

John C. Klotter Justice Administration Legal Series

AMSTERDAM • BOSTON • HEIDELBERG • LONDON
NEW YORK • OXFORD • PARIS • SAN DIEGO
SAN FRANCISCO • SINGAPORE • SYDNEY • TOKYO

Anderson Publishing is an imprint of Elsevier

ELSEVIER

Acquiring Editor: Sara Scott
Project Manager: Danielle S. Miller
Designer: Kristen Davis

Anderson Publishing is an imprint of Elsevier
225 Wyman Street, Waltham, MA 02451, USA

Library of Congress Cataloging-in-Publication Data
Application submitted

British Library Cataloguing-in-Publication Data
A catalogue record for this book is available from the British Library.

ISBN: 978-1-4557-3052-0

Printed in the United States of America
12   13   14   15   16   17   10 9 8 7 6 5 4 3 2 1

For information on all Anderson publications visit our website at www.elsevierdirect.com

Table of Contents

Sample Case Citations

Gideon v. Wainwright, 372 U.S. 335 (1963). This case is located in volume 372 of the *United States Reports*, beginning on page 335. It was decided in 1963.

Gideon v. Wainwright, 83 S. Ct. 792 (1963). Gideon v. Wainwright is published in volume 83 of the *Supreme Court Reporter*, beginning on page 792.

Gideon v. Wainwright, 9 L. Ed. 2d 799 (1963). Gideon v. Wainwright is also published in volume 9 of *Supreme Court Reports, Lawyers' Edition*, Second Series, beginning on page 799.

Phillips v. Perry, 106 F.3d 1420 (9th Cir. 1997). This case is located in volume 106 of *Federal Reports*, Third Series, beginning on page 1420. It was decided by the Ninth Circuit Court of Appeals in 1997.

Brockway v. Shepherd, 942 F. Supp. 1012 (M.D. Pa. 1997). This case is located in volume 942 of *Federal Supplement*, beginning on page 1012. It was decided in 1997 by the Federal District Court for the Middle District of Pennsylvania.

Preface

I was deeply honored to be asked to take over John Klotter's *Criminal Law*. I have used the book in teaching and believe it to be an excellent resource. It combines the best features of a traditional law casebook with those of a textbook, in that it explains the law, but also offers the student a chance to read cases. One of the best features of a casebook is that students learn how to identify the issues and holdings from court decisions. Hopefully, this will help students learn how to find these elements themselves. Note that federal crimes are still discussed separately in Chapters 12 and 13. Because students seem to have trouble grasping the different jurisdictional issues in federal jurisprudence, moving all federal cases to their own chapters make it more clear how federal laws are created and enforced.

In this edition the following changes have been made:

- Chapters 8 and 9 have been consolidated into one chapter covering all forms of theft and deception.
- The last two chapters, covering federal crimes, were also consolidated (now Chapter 13) so that federal crimes are now discussed in two chapters instead of three.
- The following cases have been added: *McDonald v. City of Chicago* (2010), *Dean v. U.S.* (2009); *Graham v. Florida* (2010), *Tison v. Arizona* (1987); *Washington et al. v. Glucksberg et al.* (1997); *Norris v. Morgan* (2010); *Pruneyard Shopping Center v. Robins* (1980); *Brown v. Entertainment Merchants Assoc.* (2011); *Skilling v. U.S.* (2010), *U.S. v. Williams* (2008); *Holder v. Humanitarian Law Project* (2010).
- News boxes or expanded discussions have been added on violent video games, virtual child pornography, honest services fraud, insider trading investigations, First Amendment challenges to the Patriot Act, and other current legal news.

I want to thank Mickey Braswell and the staff at Lexis/Nexis for giving me the opportunity to make the changes to John Klotter's text that I think will help ensure its continued success. I also appreciate, as always, their incredible assistance in its preparation. Of course, I also thank John Klotter for producing a well-researched, comprehensive, well-written text; it is a pleasure and honor to be associated with it.

As always, I want to thank Eric and Greg for putting up with me.

Joycelyn M. Pollock

Online Instructor and Student Resources

Thank you for selecting Anderson Publishing's *Criminal Law,* 10th edition. To complement the learning experience, we have provided a number of online tools to accompany this edition. Two distinct packages of interactive resources are available: one for instructors and one for students.

Please consult your local sales representative with any additional questions. You may also email the Academic Sales Team at textbook@elsevier.com.

For the Instructor

Qualified adopters and instructors can access valuable material for free by registering at http://textbooks.elsevier.com/web/manuals.aspx?isbn=9781455730520.

- **Test Bank** Compose, customize, and deliver exams using an online assessment package in a free Windows-based authoring tool that makes it easy to build tests using the unique multiple choice and true or false questions created for *Criminal Law,* 10th edition. What's more, this authoring tool allows you to export customized exams directly to Blackboard, WebCT, eCollege, Angel, and other leading systems. All test bank files are also conveniently offered in Word format.
- **PowerPoint Lecture Slides** Reinforce key topics with focused PowerPoint slides, which provide a perfect visual outline with which to augment your lecture. Each individual book chapter has its own dedicated slideshow.
- **Lesson Plans** Design your course around customized lesson plans. Each individual lesson plan acts as a separate syllabus and contains a content synopsis, key terms, directions to supplementary websites, and more open-ended critical thinking questions designed to spur class discussion. These lesson plans also delineate and connect chapter-based learning objectives to specific teaching resources, making it easy to catalog the resources at your disposal.

For the Student

Students can access all the resources below by simply following this link: http://www.elsevierdirect.com/companion.jsp? ISBN=9781455730520.

- **Self-Assessment Question Bank** Enhance review and study sessions with the help of this online self-quizzing asset. Each question is presented in an interactive format that allows for immediate feedback.
- **Case Studies** Apply what is on the page to the world beyond with the help of topic-specific case studies, each designed to turn theory into practice and followed by three interactive scenario-based questions that allow for immediate feedback.

PART I

Defining Crime

1

Chapter Outline

Cases

Constitutional Challenge (Vagueness): *City of Chicago v. Morales,* 527 U.S. 41 (1999)

Constitutional Challenge (Second Amendment): *McDonald v. City of Chicago*, 561 U.S. __ (2010)

§ 1.1   Introduction

Why are some acts defined as crimes and punished? Who has the power to define crime? In this first chapter, we discuss

- the definition of crime and criminal law,
- the purpose, objective, and sources of criminal law, and
- the limitations placed upon those who make and enforce such laws.

We will also discuss the approach taken in interpreting criminal laws and the **burden of proof** (the responsibility of the prosecution to prove the various elements of the crime charged).

§ 1.2   Definitions of Crime and Criminal Law

What is a "crime?" Blackstone, a famous English jurist, defined **crime** as "an act committed or omitted in violation of public law, either forbidding or commanding it."[1] In a broad sense, the word "crime" includes every violation of law, including treason, felonies, and misdemeanors.[2] In its narrow sense, it does not include petty offenses that were triable without a jury at common law.[3] Among the many other definitions are these:

---

[1] 4 Blackstone, Commentaries 15.

[2] Schick v. United States, 195 U.S. 65, 24 S. Ct. 826, 49 L. Ed. 99 (1904).

[3] Callan v. Wilson, 127 U.S. 540, 8 S. Ct. 1301, 32 L. Ed. 223 (1888).

5

- "A crime may be generally defined as the commission or omission of an act which the law forbids or commands under pain of punishment to be imposed by the state by a proceeding in its own name."[4]
- "A crime is a violation or a neglect of legal duty, of so much public importance that the law, either common or statute, provides punishment for it."[5]

Criminal law is the branch or division of law that defines crimes and provides for their punishment.[6] In a criminal case, the sovereign, or state, is the plaintiff, and the purpose of the prosecution is to preserve the public peace, or redress an injury to the public at large.

Substantive criminal law declares what acts are crimes and prescribes the punishment for committing them. **Procedural criminal law** regulates the steps by which one who commits a crime is to be punished. Substantive criminal law, for instance, is concerned with the definition of homicide and the elements that distinguish homicide from manslaughter. Procedural criminal law is concerned with whether or not the due process steps required during the pretrial period and during trial were followed before a conviction.

Specifically, the objectives of criminal law in a free society are to

- make it possible for individuals to coexist in society,
- define the wrongs that are considered necessary to protect the individuals,
- define the method of determining guilt or innocence, and
- designate the type of punishment or treatment following conviction for violating the laws of society.

§ 1.3   The Purpose of Criminal Law

The purpose of criminal law is to protect society so that members of that society can be reasonably secure in carrying out their constructive activities. Only behaviors that are detrimental to the welfare of society should be made criminal. There is always a balance to be achieved between the rights of the individual and the protection of society. In the **social contract**, a concept originating with Thomas Hobbes and John Locke, individuals give up certain liberties in return for being protected by society. We give up the "right" to steal what we want in return for society's protection against our being victimized by others. We also give up other liberties as members of a lawful society, but, in return, that society must impose only laws that have a purpose consistent with protection and that are minimally intrusive on our individual liberties.

---

[4]   MARSHALL, LAW OF CRIMES § 201 (7th ed. 1967).
[5]   MILLER, CRIMINAL LAW 16 (1934).
[6]   22 C.J.S. *Criminal Law* § 2 (1989).

There are three forms of harm that criminal law protects against:

- protection from the harm caused by others;
- protection from the harm caused by ourselves; and
- protection of societal morals.

The most obvious protection that the criminal law provides is protection against harm caused by others. Laws against homicide, rape, theft, and arson offer obvious protections. We feel reasonably secure that most people, most of the time, will not harm us in these or other ways, and that if we are harmed, the offender will be caught and punished.

The second form of protection that the law provides is protection against harm caused by ourselves. So-called **paternalistic laws** protect us against ourselves—a seat belt law is one example of a paternalistic law. Although you may prefer to drive your car without such a restraint, you will be punished with a fine if you do so because your duly elected representatives have determined that such behavior is so potentially harmful that it must be criminalized (albeit in a fairly minor manner). Other paternalistic laws include those that punish

- drivers for not having children restrained in child safety seats,
- drivers for not having chains while going over mountain passes, and
- motorcycle drivers for not wearing a helmet

LEGAL NEWS: CELL PHONE USE LAWS

The dangers involved in using cell phones, especially the act of texting while driving, has led many states to enact laws that criminalize such behavior. Laws exist in some jurisdictions that prohibit the use of cell phones to text while driving, or, in some cases, prohibit their use entirely, except with the use of hands-free devices. Some states restrict the ban to school zones, others have a blanket prohibition while driving, and still others have enacted bans on only some drivers, for example, bus drivers and those under 21 years old. The rationale for such laws is certainly paternalistic, but it is also to protect harm against others, even if the proof that cell phones are more likely than other distractions to cause accidents is not clear at this time. For a complete review of such laws, go to http://www.ghsa.org/html/stateinfo/laws/cellphone_laws.html.

The third form of protection the law provides is protection of societal morals. This purpose of law is as old as the others and is as legitimate. In fact, we used to have many more laws that protected societal morals. For instance, laws against businesses operating on Sunday, laws against blasphemy, and laws against adultery may all be relics of the past, but the major purpose of some of our current laws (gambling, pornography, prostitution) continues to be enforcing society's morals.

In 1933, authors Michael and Adler listed three factors that should be considered when deciding whether a harmful behavior should be made criminal:

1. the *enforceability* of the law,
2. the *effects* of the law, and
3. the *existence of other means* to protect society against undesirable behavior.[7]

If the law is *unenforceable*, then the act probably should not be criminalized. A lesson learned during the Prohibition Era was that enacting unenforceable laws only breeds contempt for the law. Another example of a law that proved difficult to enforce was the 55 miles-per-hour speed limit.

If the *effects* of the law are more disadvantageous than advantageous, it may not be a good law. For instance, in the mid-1980s at the height of the "crack epidemic," some prosecutors advocated passing laws that made it a crime to ingest drugs while pregnant (in addition to existing drug laws). The purpose of the proposed law was to protect unborn fetuses. Health professionals argued, on the other hand, that when drug-using pregnant women were prosecuted, the effect was that women simply stopped going to doctors for prenatal care in order to avoid detection. Lack of prenatal medical care was an extremely negative effect of the new law (or new use of existing laws). Thus, the effect (worse birth outcomes) may have been just the opposite of what was intended (protection of the unborn).

The final consideration is whether *other means exist* to control or restrict negative behavior. In protecting society and public interests, the criminal law approach is a negative one. Because there are more positive approaches to change behavior, punishment for engaging in certain acts should be a last resort. For example, perhaps better education would limit the need for so many criminal laws. Also, emphasizing ethical and religious codes that distinguish between good and evil conduct might reduce the need for the enactment and enforcement of criminal laws.

Even if the informal social controls of family, church, community, and education have been unsuccessful in controlling behavior, there are still other alternatives that are less stigmatizing than criminal law. Some of the possible alternatives include

- tort law,
- administrative sanctions, and
- regulations.

§ 1.4 Common Law Crimes

The system of laws in the United States is especially complex in that our criminal law is derived from English common law, statutory law, and our own case law tradition, split into 50 different state jurisdictions and the federal system.

---

[7] Michael & Adler, The Law and Society 353 (6th ed. 1997).

Most of the present-day crimes in the various states have their origins in the so-called **"common law"** of England. This was the law that developed in the early English case decisions. While formal laws were developed in England as early as the reign of King Aethelbert in the seventh century, William the Conqueror (1066) and his son, Henry I (1100-1135), are generally accepted as responsible for the development of a national court system that involved judges who traveled across England and provided guidance to local magistrates. The effect was a gradual consistency in court decisions that led to the establishment of common decisions in similar cases—thus, the "common law." By 1400, judges held themselves bound to decide the cases that came before them according to established principles and, as new combinations of circumstances arose, the principles were more fully developed. Even though, eventually, legislation supplemented common law, it still continued as a body of authoritative material. In 1765, William Blackstone published *Commentaries on the Laws of England*. This series of reports on the law of England is still widely cited as a legal source and was the most comprehensive written source of the common law at the time. This body of English law, except that which was not applicable in the American colonies because of different circumstances and conditions, was brought to our shores by colonists when they emigrated from England, and it became the starting point for American criminal law.[8]

In referring to "common law," some authorities hold that the common law, strictly speaking, is the case law of England as it existed during the American colonial period, and does not include changes by the courts of this country. Other authorities are convinced that the common law includes changes brought about by early court decisions in the United States.[9] Regardless of which approach is more persuasive, the study of the common law is still important. In states that retain the common law, common law definitions are still enforced until they are supplanted by new statutes. For instance, in *Keeler v. Superior Court* in 1970, the defendant was prosecuted for intentionally killing his wife's unborn child by kicking her in the stomach. However, because the California statute in question defined homicide as the killing of a person, and the common law definition of "person" did not include the unborn, Keeler could not be prosecuted.[10] This led to California and other states passing statutes that redefined "person" to include fetuses or creating a new crime of "feticide." Even in states that have replaced the common law crimes with a state penal code (which is an organized set of statutes that fully defines the law for the state), a study of the common law still serves a practical, useful purpose because it illustrates the origin of modern-day statutes.

---

[8]   Patterson v. Winn, 5 Pet. 233 (1831).

[9]   State v. McElhinney, 80 Ohio App. 431, 100 N.E.2d 273 (1950).

[10]   Keeler v. Superior Court, 470 P.2d 617 (Cal. 1970).

LEGAL NEWS: DEFINITION OF LIFE

Mississippi voters were asked in November 2011 to vote on whether to change the statutory definition of life to conception. A bill to amend the state constitution to define the word person or persons to include "every human being from the moment of fertilization, cloning, or the functional equivalent thereof" was presented to the voters. Critics argued that the amendment would outlaw all forms of abortion and some forms of birth control, as well as cause other legal difficulties. The voters rejected the amendment. For further information, go to http://jurist.org/paperchase/2011/11/mississippi-voters-reject-personhood-amendment.php.

§ 1.5 Statutory Crimes

While most of the present-day crimes in the various states have their origin in the common law of England, it can be safely said that most state law is now **statutory law** rather than common law. Some states have completely replaced the common law with statutory law; for instance, Kentucky's law states: "Common law offenses are abolished and no act or omission shall constitute a criminal offense unless designated a crime or violation under this code or another statute of this state."[11] Where such provisions have been adopted, a person's act or omission may go unpunished, despite the basic seriousness or undesirability of such behavior, unless the legislature has specifically decreed it to be criminal in nature. In the federal system, there are no common law crimes, because the federal government has only the power that is delegated to it by the Constitution.

When a legislative body (federal or state) determines that certain conduct is undesirable and should be forbidden, a bill is prepared describing what conduct should be prohibited. This is introduced in the House of Representatives or the Senate, and is voted upon by the elected members of the legislative body. If both houses of the legislature approve the bill, it then goes to the governor or president for consideration and approval. If the chief executive officer signs the legislation, it then becomes a law to be enforced by those involved in the justice process. Even if the chief executive officer vetoes the bill, the bill may become law if enough members of the legislative body approve it, overriding the veto.

The legislature is permitted to define criminal offenses and the elements of criminal offenses in any way it chooses, as long as its decision is not arbitrary or violative of the Constitution. Some of these challenges are discussed in Section 1.6.

---

[11]   KY. REV. STAT. § 500.020(1).

A. State Legislation

Police power, which is the primary authority to enact and enforce legislation to protect the health, welfare, morals, and safety of the people, lies with the state. This "police power" is inherent in the government of the state and is a power that the state did not surrender by becoming a member of the Union.[12] When the First Congress met, the Tenth Amendment to the Constitution was added to make clear that the powers not delegated to the United States by the Constitution would remain in the states, respectively, and the people. The Tenth Amendment states

> The powers not delegated to the United States by the Constitution, nor prohibited by it to the States, are reserved to the States respectively, or to the people.

According to the Supreme Court, the police power of the state is one of the most essential powers and is one that the federal government cannot usurp. Under this power, states have passed laws defining crimes, regulating traffic, and providing for criminal procedural rules. Courts still emphasize that the primary authority to make and enforce laws to protect the health, welfare, and morals of the people resides in the state.

State legislative bodies do have limitations when enacting laws, however. First, the laws must comply with the state constitution. Second, the laws must also comply with the federal Constitution as interpreted by the U.S. Supreme Court. However, the state is still primarily responsible for enacting and enforcing criminal laws to protect the health, welfare, safety, and morals of the people.

B. Federal Legislation

Strictly speaking, the federal government has no inherent police power. However, Congress may exercise a similar power, incident to the powers expressly conferred upon it by the Constitution.[13] The validity of any statute enacted by Congress depends upon whether it directly relates to one of the powers delegated to the federal government by the Constitution. The enumerated powers granted to the federal government are found primarily in Article I, Section 8 of the Constitution. Although these powers are stated specifically and succinctly in these clauses, their interpretation has been a matter of debate for two centuries.

LEGAL NEWS: HEALTH CARE AND IMMIGRATION

A current controversy concerning federal power revolves around the Patient Protection and Affordable Care Act of 2010, an expansive health care bill that continues to be highly controversial. Several states have challenged the federal

---

[12]   Jacobson v. Massachusetts, 197 U.S. 11, 25 S. Ct. 358, 49 L. Ed. 643 (1904).

[13]   United States v. DeWitt, 76 U.S. 41, 19 L. Ed. 593 (1869).

law and the Supreme Court will hear and decide one of these cases, *Florida v. Sebelius,* in 2012. The challengers argue the Act is outside the enumerated powers of the federal government. The opposing argument is that the powers vested to the federal government under the commerce clause also covers the power to require health care coverage. For further information, go to http://healthcarereform.procon.org/view.resource.php?resourceID=004134.

Another area where the separation of powers between the federal government and states is debated is with immigration laws. Recently several states have passed laws that criminalize being in this country illegally. Federal prosecutors have challenged laws in Pennsylvania, Arizona, and Alabama as intruding upon the federal power to "establish uniform rules of naturalization." The 9th Circuit Court of Appeals found that some provisions of the Arizona law were unconstitutional in that they usurped the federal government's role. Another Arizona law that would make it a state crime to hire illegal immigrants is also under a constitutional challenge. For further information on state immigration legislation, go to http://www.ncsl.org/default.aspx?tabid=22529.

In Article I, Section 8, Congress was delegated 17 specific powers and one power of a general nature.[14] An abbreviated list of the powers is offered here:

- To borrow money;
- To regulate commerce with foreign nations, and among the several States, and with the Indian Tribes;
- To establish uniform rules of naturalization and bankruptcies;
- To coin money;
- To provide for the punishment of counterfeiting;
- To establish post offices and post roads;
- To offer and protect copyrights;
- To create inferior courts to the Supreme Court;
- To define and punish "piracies" and "felonies committed on the high seas";
- To declare war;
- To raise and support armies;
- To provide and maintain a navy;
- To regulate land and naval forces;
- To call forth the militia to execute the laws of the union, suppress insurrections, and repel invasions;
- To provide for organizing, arming, and disciplining the militia;

---

[14]   *See generally* Kanovitz & Kanovitz, Constitutional Law (12th ed. 2010).

- To exercise exclusive Legislation in [the district of Columbia];
- To make all laws which shall be necessary and proper for carrying into execution the foregoing powers.

Certain crimes, such as treason, counterfeiting, crimes against the law of nations, and crimes committed on the high seas are specifically enumerated. Other crimes are consistent with other powers. For instance, federal smuggling crimes derive from the power of the federal government to protect the country's borders. These powers have been broadly interpreted and other crimes have been enacted that are not so obviously connected to the powers assigned to the federal government. For example, under the power to regulate interstate and foreign commerce, Congress has created federal crimes such as interstate transporting of stolen vehicles, kidnapping (if the victim is taken across state lines), and drug trafficking. All have been made federal crimes because of some connection to interstate commerce. Similarly, the 1964 Civil Rights Act, which made it illegal to discriminate on the basis of race, religion, ethnicity, or sex, was predicated on the commerce clause under the rationale that all businesses participate in interstate commerce. There are limits, however, to how far Congress can take its authority under the commerce clause. In *United States v. Lopez*, the Supreme Court held that the Gun-Free School Zones Act passed by Congress under the power of the commerce clause was an unconstitutional overreach of federal power.[15] The rationale of the Act was that the presence of guns made it difficult to learn, which affected the economic productivity of the nation. The Supreme Court rejected this line of reasoning and held that the Act was beyond federal powers to enact. Basically, Congress has the power to create a law based on the commerce clause when (a) the activity affects instrumentalities used in interstate commerce (i.e., arson of a railroad); (b) when it affects persons or things involved in interstate commerce (i.e., bank robbery of an FDIC-insured bank); or (c) when it has a substantial effect on interstate commerce (monopolies).

Congress is limited by the provisions of the Constitution and especially by the **Bill of Rights**, the first 10 amendments, which were added specifically to limit the power of Congress. We will discuss some constitutional challenges in Section 1.6.

C. Legislation by Political Subdivision

Legislative bodies of political subdivisions, including cities, counties, townships, and municipal corporations, also have limited authority to make and enforce rules and regulations prohibiting acts or penalizing the failure to act in certain situations. After the American Revolution, the state legislature became the depository for all legislative power and took over the granting of power to political subdivisions. These units of government have been invested by the state legislature with subordinate legislative powers to enact legislation that does not conflict with the Constitution or laws of the state.

---

[15]   United States v. Lopez, 514 U.S. 549 (1995).

The state may withhold, grant, or withdraw powers and privileges as it sees fit. However great or small its sphere of action, the political subdivision remains a creature of the state, exercising and holding powers and privileges subject to the sovereign will of the state.[16]

The states have delegated certain authority to political subdivisions, either specifically, or by way of broad general authority, to enact ordinances to protect the safety and welfare of their inhabitants and to preserve good order within their limits. Unlike states, however, the police powers of political subdivisions are not inherent and the police power of the municipality exists solely by virtue of a legislative or constitutional grant of powers.[17] Thus, a city's right to enact ordinances that make it illegal to ride a skateboard on a sidewalk or be out in public past 11 p.m. if you are below the age of 18 derives from state "police power" that has been delegated to the municipality. Cities now and in the past have prohibited everything from crossing the street outside a crosswalk to spitting on a sidewalk. Often the "dumb laws" websites that purport to show ridiculous laws still on the books utilize city ordinances (see, for instance, http://www.dumblaws.com).

Municipal ordinances and the laws of other political subdivisions (such as counties) are subject to the same state and federal constitutional limitations and restrictions as state laws. Specifically, the police power of a municipality, broad as it may be, cannot justify the passage of a law or ordinance that runs counter to any of the limitations of state constitutions or the federal Constitution.[18]

D. Model Penal Code

Promulgated by the American Law Institute, The Model Penal Code is not the law in any state, but rather serves as a guide to state lawmakers. The American Law Institute is an association of judges, lawyers, and law professors and they created the Model Penal Code (MPC) in 1962 with revisions and commentary being added through 1985. The MPC is helpful to students as a general outline of modern criminal law because the specific criminal statutes of the 50 states and the federal government are different enough that it is impossible to comprehensively discuss them all. Some provisions of the Code are not followed in some states, and some are not followed in the majority of states; however, no one disputes that the general approach to the construction of law and some substantial changes to the common law have taken place largely through the influence of the MPC. For this reason, we offer provisions of the Model Penal Code throughout this book, along with examples of state statutes, to represent modern criminal law.

---

[16] Bissell v. Jeffersonville, 66 U.S. 287, 16 L. Ed. 664 (1861).
[17] Salt Lake City v. Young, 45 Utah 349, 145 P. 1047 (1915).
[18] Spann v. Dallas, 111 Tex. 359, 235 S.W. 513 (1921).

§ 1.6   Constitutional Challenges

The federal government does not have the power to pass a law that violates one of the rights granted by the United States Constitution. Specifically, protections are most often found in the first 10 amendments that make up the Bill of Rights. We are protected against laws that are vague, that punish behavior after the fact (**ex post facto laws**), or that infringe upon our freedom of expression, association, or religion. It should be noted that the Bill of Rights protected citizens against laws or actions of the federal government. As written, it did not apply to the states. A summary of the rights granted in the Bill of Rights below.

Bill of Rights

First Amendment—Freedom of religion, expression, association, press

Second Amendment—Right to bear arms

Third Amendment—Right not to have soldiers quartered in peoples' homes

Fourth Amendment—Right to be free in person and home from unreasonable governmental search and seizure (must have probable cause and define item with specificity)

Fifth Amendment—Right to be free from compulsory self-incrimination, federal right to grand jury, protection against double jeopardy, due process

Sixth Amendment—Right to an impartial jury trial that is speedy and public with specified due process elements

Seventh Amendment—Right to trial in suit at common law, jury to be trier of fact

Eighth Amendment—Right against excessive bail, right to be free from cruel and unusual punishment

Ninth Amendment—States "The enumeration in the Constitution, of certain rights, shall not be construed to deny or disparage others retained by the people."

Tenth Amendment—Reserves all other powers not specifically delegated in the Constitution for the states

A. Incorporation

While the Bill of Rights protected American citizens against actions of the federal government, they had almost no protection from violations of rights by state actors or laws until after the Civil War. The Fourteenth Amendment, ratified in 1868, was passed to detail how representation was to be apportioned among the states, but also to protect newly freed slaves from state laws that withheld the rights to vote, own property, or contract. It reads:

> Amendment XIV. Section 1. All persons born or naturalized in the United States and subject to the jurisdiction thereof, are citizens of the United States and of the State wherein they reside. No State shall make or enforce any law which shall abridge the privileges or immunities of citizens of the United States; **nor shall any State deprive any person of life, liberty, or property, without due process of law;** nor deny to any person within its jurisdiction the equal protection of the laws.

The due process clause in the Fourteenth Amendment (above, in bold) is virtually the same as that found in the Fifth Amendment but has been more broadly applied, in that it acts as the vehicle by which some of the rights recognized in the Bill of Rights have been "incorporated" to protect citizens against state actions. Thus, the federal government cannot pass laws or act in ways that violate the rights enumerated in the Bill of Rights, and, if the right has been "incorporated" through a Supreme Court holding, neither can state (or local) governments encroach upon the right. In effect, the Fourteenth Amendment has applied most of the Bill of Rights to you as a state citizen against state actions that violate one or more of the Bill of Rights.

B. *Due Process and Vagueness Challenges*

One element of due process is *notice*. Legislation must not be vague and must not be so uncertain as to leave doubt as to its meaning. For example, the Court of Appeals of New York, in the case of *People v. Munoz*, held that a statute that made it unlawful for any person under 21 to "carry on his person or have in his possession, in any public place, street, or park any knife or sharp-pointed or edged instrument which may be used for cutting or puncturing" was unconstitutional because it was too broad and vague in its definition of cutting instruments.[19] In this case, the proscribed action (carrying any type of cutting instrument) was just as likely to be consistent with harmless behavior (carrying scissors) as harmful behavior (carrying a switchblade knife), and thus was overbroad in its scope.

On the other hand, a federal statute that proscribes "mailing pistols, revolvers and other firearms capable of being concealed on the person" was upheld by the U.S. Supreme Court. The court agreed that the law intelligibly forbids a definite course of conduct: the mailing of concealable firearms. It held that the drafting of a law did not have to be foolproof and even if the language could have been more clear, that fact alone does not make a statute unconstitutionally vague.[20]

In 1991, in the case of *Chapman v. United States*, the U.S. Supreme Court considered the "vagueness" rule in determining the validity of a drug possession statute.[21] In this case, the defendant argued that a statute calling for a five-year mandatory minimum sentence for the offense of distributing more than one gram of a "mixture or substance containing a detectable amount of LSD" was unconstitutionally vague. The court held that although there may have been plausible arguments against describing blotter paper impregnated with LSD as a "mixture or substance" containing LSD for purposes of determining the appropriate sentencing, this statute was not unconstitutionally vague, given the fact that any debate would center on the appropriate sentence rather than the conduct's criminality.

In *City of Chicago v. Morales*, the Supreme Court struck down an anti-gang law that prohibited those believed to be criminal street gang members from loitering in any

---

[19]   9 N.Y.2d 51, 172 N.E.2d 535 (1961).
[20]   United States v. Powell, 423 U.S. 87 (1975).
[21]   Chapman v. United States, 500 U.S. 453 (1991).

public place.[22] Some members of the court objected to the vague manner in which loitering and the identity of street gang members was defined, and the majority objected to the fact that it was solely within the police officer's discretion to define when loitering was occurring. The language of the court indicated that there may be anti-gang laws that could pass the vagueness test, but they needed to be written in a way that definitely stated what actions would be defined as criminal.

> **CASE NOTE:** *City of Chicago v. Morales*, 527 U.S. 41 (1999)
> What was the holding of the Court? Where does the right to not have vague laws enforced upon individuals come from? What could the city of Chicago do to prevent gangs from intimidating neighbors and passersby?

Other courts, in explaining the vagueness doctrine, have used these terms:

- The void-for-vagueness doctrine requires that a penal statute define the criminal offense with sufficient definiteness that ordinary people can understand what conduct is prohibited, and in a manner that does not encourage arbitrary and discriminatory endorsement.[23]
- While a state statute need not be so precise as to enable a person in every case to determine in advance what conduct is within reach of the statute, a reasonable degree of certainty is required to avoid unconstitutional vagueness.[24]

Basically, the right to be free from vague and overbroad laws comes from the Fifth and Fourteenth Amendments. Both amendments provide that an individual should receive "due process of law" before being deprived of life, liberty, or property. The Fifth Amendment provision has been interpreted to provide protection from federal actors and the Fourteenth Amendment provision protects us from state governmental actors. **Due process** includes the right to notice (to know what we are being accused of). Obviously, in order to have notice, a law must be certain and not subject to arbitrary definitions.

C. Equal Protection Challenges

Laws that treat "similarly situated" people differently also violate the Fourteenth Amendment's "equal protection" clause. The government must have a very good reason for treating a certain group of people differently under the law. If a law that is neutral on its face differentially affects only one group of people, it would also be scrutinized.

In 1967, the Supreme Court struck down Virginia's miscegenation laws, which made it a crime to marry someone of a different race.[25] The groups at issue were those who wished to marry a person from the same race compared to those who wished to

---

[22]   527 U.S. 41 (1999).
[23]   United States v. Sun, 278 F.3d 302 (4th Cir. 2002).
[24]   State v. Ausmus, 37 P.3d 1024 (Or. Ct. App. 2001).
[25]   Loving v. Virginia, 388 U.S. 1 (1967).

marry someone of a different race. The Court held that the state did not have a reason that was sufficiently important to justify treating these groups differently and the holding invalidated all miscegenation laws in not only Virginia, but also the other states that had them.

LEGAL NEWS: SAME SEX MARRIAGE

Today, the issue of same sex marriage is as controversial as interracial marriages were when *Loving v. Virginia* was decided. The Defense of Marriage Act (Pub. L. 104-199, 110 Stat. 2419) was enacted by Congress in 1996. This federal law defines marriage as a legal union between one man and one woman and ensures that no state or other political subdivision may be required to recognize a same sex marriage legally, even if it is considered a marriage in another state. The law also allows ignoring such marriages for purposes of federal insurance, survivor's benefits, and social security. Certain parts of the law are under appeal as unconstitutional and the Obama administration has indicated in 2011 that it will not defend the law in court. For more information, go to http://www.cbsnews.com/8301-504564_162-20035495-504564.html.

In the case of *Craig v. Boren*, the Supreme Court struck down a law that prohibited the sale of beer to girls under the age of 18 and boys under the age of 21 on the grounds that boys and girls were "similarly situated" and there was no reason to treat them differently. On the other hand, in the case of *In re Michael M.*, a California statutory rape law was upheld, even though it treated male and female actors differently by defining a crime with only male perpetrators and female victims.[26] In this case, the Supreme Court upheld the law because the parties were not considered similarly situated in that only female victims could become pregnant and the law's imputed purpose was to prevent teenage pregnancy. Other laws that treated the sexes differently have been struck down because the Court did not see any reason for the different treatment.

D. Ex Post Facto Challenges

The U.S. Constitution and provisions of the constitutions of the various states specifically prohibit ex post facto laws. The two sections of the federal Constitution that relate to ex post facto laws are Article I, Section 9, which provides that "no bill of attainder or ex post facto law shall be passed," and Section 10, which provides that "[n]o state shall . . . pass any ex post facto law."[27]

These provisions were added to the Constitution of the United States and similar provisions have been added to the constitutions of the respective states to prohibit

---

[26]   Craig v. Boren, 429, U.S. 190 (1976); In re Michael M., 450 U.S. 464 (1981).
[27]   U.S. CONST. art. I, §§ 9 and 10, cl. 1.

legislative bodies from punishing a person for an act that was neither a crime nor punishable when the act was committed, or from increasing the punishment after the fact. A bill of attainder is a special legislative act that declares a person or group of persons guilty of a crime and subjects them to punishment without trial. An ex post facto law, within the meaning of these constitutional provisions, is "one which, in its operation, makes that criminal which was not so at the time the action was performed, or which increases the punishment, or, in short, which in relation to the offense or its consequences, alters the situation of a party, to his disadvantage."[28]

Two critical elements are necessary to establish an ex post facto claim:

1. The law must be retrospective—that is, it must apply to events occurring before its enactment.
2. It must disadvantage the offender affected by it.[29]

A mere procedural change in the law, not increasing punishment or changing the elements of the offense, does not result in an ex post facto violation. Statutes that delay or postpone the eligibility of an inmate for parole have also generally been upheld and found not to be a violation of the ex post facto provision.[30] However, a statute that created a new term of supervised release was ruled retroactive and, thus, unconstitutional. The imposition of a new term of supervised release increased the punishment and thus violated the ex post facto clause.[31]

It should be noted that the fact that a law is ex post facto as to a person who committed an act before its enactment does not affect its validity generally. A legislative body may make an act a crime through legislation; such legislation would be ex post facto in relation to a person who committed the act prior to the enactment of the legislation, but would not be considered ex post facto when applied to persons who commit the same act after the legislation.

Ex post facto provisions apply if legislation relates to substantive criminal law or the rules of evidence. For example, a change in a rule of evidence that would allow a conviction on less evidence or proof than one previously required is considered ex post facto and unenforceable.[32] When a criminal sentencing statute is amended, generally the punishment cannot be enhanced for those who committed their crimes prior to the change in statute.

Recently, sex offender registration laws have proliferated and enhanced the requirements for those subject to registration. Such statutes have been subject to ex post facto challenges when they require those who committed crimes before their enactment to register. The Jacob Wetterling Crimes Against Children and Sexually Violent

---

[28]   Duncan v. Missouri, 152 U.S. 377 (1894).
[29]   United States v. Abbington, 144 F.3d 1003 (6th Cir. 1998); Myers v. Ridge, 712 A.2d 791 (Pa. 1998).
[30]   Jones v. Georgia State Board of Pardons and Paroles, 59 F.3d 1145 (11th Cir. 1995); Allison v. Kyle, 66 F.3d 71 (5th Cir. 1995), and Kruger v. Erickson, 875 F. Supp. 583 (D. Minn. 1995). For a thorough discussion of ex post facto law and parole hearings, *see* California Dept. of Corrections v. Morales, 514 U.S. 499, 115 S. Ct. 1597, 131 L. Ed. 2d 588 (1995).
[31]   United States v. Lominac, 144 F.3d 308 (4th Cir. 1998).
[32]   Duncan v. Missouri, 152 U.S. 377 (1894).

Offender Registration Act (SORA), passed in 1994, required the states to adopt sex offender registration laws within three years of the Act's passage to receive federal law enforcement funding. Megan's Law, in 1996, amended the Jacob Wetterling Act to include the dissemination of registration information to the community (Sex Offender Registration and Notification Act, SORNA). Since then, registration laws have proliferated in number and comprehensiveness.

The earliest sex offender registration laws applied to those convicted of sexual molestation or assault against a child. Today, many states have expanded such laws to include registration requirements for any sexual offense (even consensual sex if one partner is underage), and even offenses (such as kidnapping) that involve children, but have no sexual motive. Restrictions on where offenders can live and work have been added and the amount of personal information posted in sex offender registration lists has been expanded, along with who can access such information. Further, the registration statutes are more likely to require lifetime registration and cover those who were convicted and served out their sentence decades before the registration law was passed. The latter provision has been challenged as being in violation of ex post facto. In *Smith v. Doe* in 2003, the Supreme Court held that Alaska's sex offender registration statute was not an ex post facto law, even though it required those who had been convicted and punished before the enactment of the statute to register as a sex offender. The reason was that the sex offender registration requirement was determined to be civil in nature, not criminal punishment. It was for the protection of society, not to punish the offender. The Court held that in order to determine whether something is punitive or purely administrative, one must look to whether it was punitive in nature, that is, banishment, stigma, loss of freedom, or shaming. Some argue that, even if the early sex offender registration statutes did not meet the definition of punishment, more recent ones certainly do, especially those with travel and housing restrictions.

In *Carr v. United States* (2010), the Supreme Court asked and answered a very narrow question of Congressional intent to find that the provision of SORNA, which required a sex offender to register when traveling, did not apply to those who failed to register while traveling before the statute was enacted. With the increasingly punitive and onerous nature of such statutes, it is possible that the Supreme Court will be called upon in the coming years to more squarely address whether newer sex offender registration statutes that are applied to those who committed their crime before the statute's enactment violate ex post facto prohibitions.[33]

E. First Amendment Challenges

In drafting criminal legislation, the legislative body is also limited by other constitutional restrictions. A federal or state criminal statute may be clear yet unenforceable if it violates constitutionally protected activities. This is especially true if the First Amendment to the federal Constitution is in question. If the legislation infringes on

---

[33] Smith v. Doe, 538 U.S. 84 (2003); Carr v. United States 130 S. Ct. 2229 (2010).

rights protected by the First Amendment, the legislation is unconstitutional and unenforceable.[34]

As you know, the First Amendment protects our freedom of speech, association, and religion, as well as ensures the freedom of the press. The government has the right to pass laws that do not unduly interfere with these rights. Thus, if our speech creates an imminent danger to others it can be prohibited and punished. For instance, one does not have the right to incite a riot. On the other hand, an ordinance that makes it criminal to simply *verbally* (not physically) object to the arrest of another has been ruled as unconstitutional in that it infringes upon free speech.[35] Generally, "fighting words," "obscenity," and "commercial speech" can be prohibited, punished, or regulated.

In *Texas v. Johnson,* the Supreme Court in 1989 ruled that the state could not create a crime that punished flag burning. Gregory Lee Johnson was part of a demonstration that involved burning the American flag. Texas had a statute that made it a crime to "desecrate" a flag. He was convicted and appealed on the basis that the Texas statute was a violation of the First Amendment. The Supreme Court, first, had to find that the burning of the flag was "speech." Their conclusion was that because the act was symbolic and carried a message, it could be defined as speech. The Court also had to determine whether or not the statute was suppressing expression, that is, the act was illegal for the reason of the message itself rather than for some other reason. They determined that it was not "fighting words" (which could be prohibited) because there was no strong evidence to assume that violence would be imminent or certain: further, such a statute was "underinclusive" in that protesters could do many other things that might incite violence as well as those that were not criminalized. Following are excerpts from the opinion.

> In deciding whether particular conduct possesses sufficient communicative elements to bring the First Amendment into play, we have asked whether "[a]n intent to convey a particularized message was present, and [whether] the likelihood was great that the message would be understood by those who viewed it.". . . . Hence, we have recognized the expressive nature of students' wearing of black armbands to protest American military involvement in Vietnam, . . . ; of a sit-in by blacks in a "whites only" area to protest segregation, . . . ; of the wearing of American military uniforms in a dramatic presentation criticizing American involvement in Vietnam, . . .
>
> Especially pertinent to this case are our decisions recognizing the communicative nature of conduct relating to flags. Attaching a peace sign to the flag, . . . ; refusing to salute the flag, . . . ; and displaying a red flag, . . . , we have held, all may find shelter under the First Amendment. . . . That we have had little difficulty identifying an expressive element in conduct relating to flags should not be surprising. The very purpose of a national flag is to serve as a symbol of our country; it is, one might say, "the one visible manifestation of two hundred years of nationhood." . . .
>
>   . . .
>
> Pregnant with expressive content, the flag as readily signifies this Nation as does the combination of letters found in "America." . . .
>
>   . . .

---

[34]   Miller v. California, 413 U.S. 15, 93 S. Ct. 2607, 37 L. Ed. 2d 419 (1973).
[35]   City of Houston v. Hill, 482 U.S. 451 (1987).

Texas claims that its interest in preventing breaches of the peace justifies Johnson's conviction for flag desecration. However, no disturbance of the peace actually occurred or threatened to occur because of Johnson's burning of the flag.

. . .

. . . a principal "function of free speech under our system of government is to invite dispute. It may indeed best serve its high purpose when it induces a condition of unrest, creates dissatisfaction with conditions as they are, or even stirs people to anger." . . . It would be odd indeed to conclude *both* that "if it is the speaker's opinion that gives offense, that consequence is a reason for according it constitutional protection," . . . , *and* that the government may ban the expression of certain disagreeable ideas on the unsupported presumption that their very disagreeableness will provoke violence.

Thus, we have not permitted the government to assume that every expression of a provocative idea will incite a riot, but have instead required careful consideration of the actual circumstances surrounding such expression, asking whether the expression "is directed to inciting or producing imminent lawless action and is likely to incite or produce such action." . . .

. . .

Nor does Johnson's expressive conduct fall within that small class of "fighting words" that are "likely to provoke the average person to retaliation, and thereby cause a breach of the peace." . . . No reasonable onlooker would have regarded Johnson's generalized expression of dissatisfaction with the policies of the Federal Government as a direct personal insult or an invitation to exchange fisticuffs. . . .

. . .

. . . If there is a bedrock principle underlying the First Amendment, it is that the government may not prohibit the expression of an idea simply because society finds the idea itself offensive or disagreeable. . . .

We have not recognized an exception to this principle even where our flag has been involved. . . .

"If there is any fixed star in our constitutional constellation, it is that no official, high or petty, can prescribe what shall be orthodox in politics, nationalism, religion, or other matters of opinion or force citizens to confess by word or act their faith therein." . . .

. . .

. . . In short, nothing in our precedents suggests that a State may foster its own view of the flag by prohibiting expressive conduct relating to it.

. . .

There is, moreover, no indication — either in the text of the Constitution or in our cases interpreting it — that a separate juridical category exists for the American flag alone. Indeed, we would not be surprised to learn that the persons who framed our Constitution and wrote the Amendment that we now construe were not known for their reverence for the Union Jack. The First Amendment does not guarantee that other concepts virtually sacred to our Nation as a whole — such as the principle that discrimination on the basis of race is odious and destructive — will go unquestioned in the market-place of ideas. . . . We decline, therefore, to create for the flag an exception to the joust of principles protected by the First Amendment.

. . .

We are tempted to say, in fact, that the flag's deservedly cherished place in our community will be strengthened, not weakened, by our holding today. Our decision is a reaffirmation of the principles of freedom and inclusiveness that the flag best reflects, and of the conviction that our toleration of criticism such as Johnson's is a sign and source of our strength. Indeed, one of the proudest images of our flag, the one immortalized in our own national anthem, is of the bombardment it survived at Fort

McHenry. It is the Nation's resilience, not its rigidity, that Texas sees reflected in the flag — and it is that resilience that we reassert today.

The way to preserve the flag's special role is not to punish those who feel differently about these matters. It is to persuade them that they are wrong. "To courageous, self-reliant men, with confidence in the power of free and fearless reasoning applied through the processes of popular government, no danger flowing from speech can be deemed clear and present, unless the incidence of the evil apprehended is so imminent that it may befall before there is opportunity for full discussion. If there be time to expose through discussion the falsehood and fallacies, to avert the evil by the processes of education, the remedy to be applied is more speech, not enforced silence." . . . And, precisely because it is our flag that is involved, one's response to the flag burner may exploit the uniquely persuasive power of the flag itself. We can imagine no more appropriate response to burning a flag than waving one's own, no better way to counter a flag burner's message than by saluting the flag that burns, no surer means of preserving the dignity even of the flag that burned than by — as one witness here did — according its remains a respectful burial. We do not consecrate the flag by punishing its desecration, for in doing so we dilute the freedom that this cherished emblem represents.[36]

This issue continues to be controversial and a large number of people believe that burning the flag should be criminalized. More recent cases challenging laws under First Amendment grounds exist as well. In *Brown v. Entertainment Merchants Association*, the Supreme Court examined a California law that made it illegal to sell or rent violent video games to youth. This case will be discussed again in Chapter 9 and excerpted for that chapter in Part II of this textbook.

LEGAL NEWS: FREE SPEECH IN THE NEWS

Several First Amendment challenges have been heard by the Supreme Court recently, including a 2011 case that upheld the free speech rights of offensive protestors at a funeral for a Marine who died in Iraq. The protestors held up signs saying "Thank God for Dead Soldiers," in an effort to relay their message that God is punishing the United States by allowing gay soldiers to serve (*Snyder v. Phelps,* 131 S. Ct. 1207 [2011]). The court ruled that the speech cannot be suppressed just because it is offensive. In another case, the Court struck down a federal statute that made it illegal to distribute video depicting animal cruelty (*U.S. v. Stevens*, 130 S. Ct. 1577 [2010]).

In 2012, the Supreme Court will decide whether the federal "Stolen Valor" law, which makes it a crime, punishable by up to a year in jail, to lie about receiving a war medal, is unconstitutional. The federal law has been enforced but offenders have usually received community service. In most cases, there was no financial gain. Several circuits have ruled the law an unconstitutional infringement upon free speech. Opponents of the law argue that the speech does not fall into any of the prohibited areas of speech (i.e., "fighting words" or obscenity). Proponents of the bill argue that there is proof the founders meant to punish those who lied about military service.

---

[36]   491 U.S. 397 (1989).

Other constitutional challenges may involve the First Amendment's protections of religion, speech, or association. Can one's freedom of religion, for instance, include the freedom to sacrifice children at midnight? (Obviously not.) What about sacrificing goats? (Maybe. According to the Supreme Court in one case, a city could not fashion an ordinance prohibiting animal slaughter in religious ceremonies because it was overly broad in the conduct it prohibited and discriminatory because it targeted one religion.)[37] What if your religion allowed you to have multiple wives, would you still be subject to bigamy laws? (Yes.) If your religion uses peyote, are you exempt from drug laws that criminalize the use and possession of this controlled substance? (Yes. After the Supreme Court upheld the right of states to enforce drug laws against Native Americans using peyote in *Employment Division, Oregon v. Smith* in 1990, Congress passed the American Indian Religious Freedom Act Amendments in 1994 that protects the right of Native Americans to use peyote in religious ceremonies despite federal or state drug laws.)[38]

In all cases, federal and state courts must weigh the individual's rights against the need for the law.

F. Second Amendment

Strangely, even though the Second Amendment specifically identified rights related to the possession of firearms, it has been only recently that gun control laws have been successfully challenged. In 2008, in *District of Columbia et al. v. Heller*, the Supreme Court for the first time recognized that the right to firearms as described in the Second Amendment was an individual right and that the government could not unduly infringe upon that right by onerous handgun control laws.[39] The Supreme Court ruled that the District of Columbia handgun law that required owners of handguns to have their guns totally dysfunctional or have trigger locks installed was an unconstitutional burden on their Second Amendment right to bear arms. Because this was a District of Columbia law, this case was decided under the Supreme Court's direct jurisdiction; however, in McDonald v. City of Chicago, a case in Part II of this text, the Court incorporated the 2nd Amendment right to bear arms to state citizens and ruled that Chicago's gun control law was unconstitutional.

CASE NOTE: *McDonald, et al. v. City of Chicago,* 130 S. Ct. 3020 (2010)
What was the holding of the Court?
Explain incorporation and the test for incorporating the Second Amendment to the states.
What restrictions on gun possession might the Supreme Court feel are acceptable?

---

[37] Church of Lukami Babalu Aye v. City of Hialeah, 508 U.S. 520 (1993).
[38] Employment Division, Oregon v. Smith, 494 U.S. 872 (1990).
[39] District of Columbia et al. v. Heller, 554 U.S. 570 (2008); McDonald v. City of Chicago 130 S.Ct. 3020 (2010).

G. Privacy Challenges

The right to privacy is not identified specifically in the Constitution, but has been recognized by the Supreme Court as existing based on their interpretation of what the framers meant by such rights as those previously discussed. One of the most important cases that established the protected right of privacy against governmental interference was *Griswold v. Connecticut*.[40] In that case, the Supreme Court struck down Connecticut's criminal law that punished the distribution of information regarding birth control to married couples. According to Justice Douglas, the First, Third, Fourth, Fifth, Ninth, and Fourteenth Amendments can be read to construe a privacy right that restricts the government from interfering with private decisions on procreation by a married couple. This case eventually became the precedent to overturn abortion laws as described in Chapter 10 and in the Legal News box that follows.

LEGAL NEWS: ABORTION LAW

The act of voluntary abortion has been an extremely controversial issue before and after the landmark case of *Roe v. Wade*, 410 U.S. 113 (1973). Abortion had been illegal in this country until the Supreme Court held that laws criminalizing abortion infringed upon women's privacy rights, at least in the first and second trimesters. Several cases came after *Roe v. Wade* that further refined individual rights and constitutional restrictions in this area. The latest case concerning fetal rights and a woman's right to choose was *Gonzales v. Carhart*, 550 U.S. 12 (2007). In this case, the Supreme Court upheld the constitutionality of the federal law titled the Partial Birth Abortion Ban Act of 2003. The federal law defined as criminal any and all procedures of abortion that involved inducing a partial birth and destroying the fetus after it had been removed from the womb. This procedure occurred in a very small number of cases during late-term abortions. Challenges to *Roe v. Wade* will continue to be addressed by the Supreme Court.

Another right of privacy case was *Stanley v. Georgia* in 1969, in which the Supreme Court held that states could not criminalize the mere possession of obscene materials, although states could prohibit and punish any distribution or sale of such materials (and states could criminalize the mere possession of child pornography).[41] In later chapters, especially Chapter 10, which deals with gambling, some sexual behaviors, drugs, and prostitution, we will see that some laws have been struck down as violative of protected privacy rights, but other laws are upheld as legitimate safeguards of societal morals.

---

[40]   381 U.S. 479 (1965).
[41]   381 U.S. 479 (1965).

§ 1.7   Construction of Criminal Law Statutes

Criminal law statutes are not always clear to those who interpret them. In fact, many who are charged with criminal violations are released when their attorney convinces the court that the construction given to the statute by the state is inaccurate. As indicated, it is a fundamental principle of criminal law that legislation must not be vague and must not be so uncertain as to leave doubt as to its meaning. If persons of ordinary intelligence must guess at the meaning of a statute, it is unenforceable.

When the meaning of a statute is doubtful, the court may take into consideration the purpose of its enactment when construing it and give effect to the intent of the legislature. However, if the wording is clear and the statute is clear on its face, it is not permissible to add or vary the provisions of the statute to accomplish a supposed legislative purpose.

Finally, in construing a statute, the intent of the legislature is not to be ascertained from any particular expression or section but from the whole act. All the words used in the act are to be given force and meaning rather than any one section of the statute.

§ 1.8   Classification of Crimes

Crimes may be statutory or common law, but in either case they fall into various categories or grades.

A. Classification According to the Nature of the Crime

Crimes have been divided according to their nature into *mala in se* and *mala prohibita*.

Mala in se: These are acts that are immoral or wrong in themselves, or acts that are naturally evil. *Mala in se* crimes are considered wrong in any society and include the common law crimes of murder, rape, arson, burglary, and larceny.

Mala prohibita: These crimes are not naturally evil, but are prohibited by statute because they infringe upon the rights of others. This type of act is not wrong in some societies, but is wrong in other societies. It is wrong because it is prohibited by statute. Generally, *mala in se* crimes involve moral turpitude, while *mala prohibita* crimes do not. Examples would include all traffic offenses, as well as some laws regarding "gray" areas of crime, such as pornography and gambling. Also, regulatory offenses are generally *mala prohibita* crimes.

Some crimes are difficult to classify. Individual or subjective beliefs involving religion, politics, and ethics create diverse views as to whether activities such as gambling and prostitution are *mala in se* or *mala prohibita*. Cultural norms weigh heavily in any attempt to classify sexual offenses.

B. Classification According to Degree

All crimes are classified as felonies, misdemeanors, or treason. These classifications become important not only in determining the degree of punishment, but also when determining the authority of justice personnel to take action. For example, in some states, law enforcement officers may not make misdemeanor arrests unless the offense was committed in their presence (or they have a warrant).

1. Felonies

According to most authorities, crimes punishable by death or imprisonment in a state prison or penitentiary are felonies. A crime may be made a **felony** by a statute that specifically says that it is a felony. When an offense is not designated by statute as either a felony or a misdemeanor, but a specific punishment is prescribed, then the grade, or class, of the offense is determined by the punishment. Generally, felonies are punishable by at least one year in prison, but this is not a requirement if the statute provides that the crime is a felony and sets the punishment at less than one year.

2. Misdemeanors

Crimes or offenses not amounting to felonies are **misdemeanors**. Another definition is that misdemeanors are offenses for which the punishment is other than death or imprisonment in a state prison, or that have not been designated felonies by statute. A person convicted of a misdemeanor will ordinarily be incarcerated in a local jail or be required to pay a fine, but will not be sent to a state penitentiary.

Although there is apparent consensus in the technical definitions of felony and misdemeanor, what is regarded as a felony in one state may constitute a misdemeanor in another. Except for the most serious crimes, such as murder, robbery, and rape, generalizations in the area of what crimes are felonies or misdemeanors are unreliable. Therefore, the legislative designations in the particular jurisdiction must be carefully examined.

3. Treason

Treason is the only crime that is described in the Constitution.[42] Because those who commit treason threaten the very existence of the nation, it is given a higher classification than a felony.

Also, the Constitution provides that no person shall be convicted of treason unless on the testimony of two witnesses to the same overt act, or on confession in open court.

---

[42]   U.S. CONST. art. III, § 3.

C. Classification Based on Punishment

States often choose to distinguish, or classify, their criminal statutes based on the range of possible sentences available upon conviction. For example, in Kentucky, any offense for which the legislature has authorized a sentence of one to five years in prison is classified as a Class D felony. Misdemeanors are also often classified by the states into degrees based on their range of punishments.

§ 1.9   Distinction between Crimes and Torts

When one person is wronged by another, he or she may seek a remedy against the wrongdoer by bringing what is known as a civil action. The process by which a person initiates an action against another is known as the law of torts. A function of tort law is to compensate an injured person for the harm he or she has suffered. For example, if Henry is struck by Sophia, causing him bodily injury, Henry may bring an action in court for recovery of expenses and for compensation for losses incurred. The state may also initiate an action against Sophia for assault and battery and prosecute the case in criminal court. The most famous example of this is the successful civil suit against O.J. Simpson for wrongful death after his 1994 acquittal for murder in criminal court. It is entirely possible for a defendant to win in one court and lose in the other.

Civil law resolves the conflicting interests of individuals. Criminal law deals with public wrongs and views a crime as a violation of the public's rights and as an injury to the whole community. In spite of the differences between tort law and criminal law, there are many ideas and concepts common to both areas. For example, some of the defenses that will be discussed in Chapter 3 are available to a defendant in a civil case as well as a defendant in a criminal case. The differences between tort law and criminal law are illustrated in Table 1.1.

§ 1.10   Burden of Proof—Prosecution

In a criminal case, the state has the burden of proving the guilt of the accused beyond a reasonable doubt. That means that the prosecution has the responsibility to prove each element of the crime with which the accused is charged. For example, the common law crime of burglary has six elements:

Table 1.1

Distinctions between Torts and Crimes

Torts	Crimes
Private wrong	Public wrong
Action initiated by an individual	Action taken by the state
Private attorney represents plaintiff	Prosecutor represents the state
Action for money damages	Punishment by fine or imprisonment
Unanimous verdict of jury not usually required	Unanimous verdict of jury usually required
Proof by a preponderance of evidence	Proof beyond a reasonable doubt

1. breaking,
2. entering,
3. the dwelling,
4. of another,
5. at night,
6. with intent to commit a felony therein.

These elements must be proved in accordance with the definition of each element as described by the court. If the prosecution fails to prove one element of the crime beyond a reasonable doubt but proves the other elements, the accused may sometimes be found guilty of a lesser crime. But ordinarily, if any element is not proved beyond a reasonable doubt, the person charged cannot be convicted of the crime. Failure of those involved in the criminal justice process to gather and introduce sufficient evidence to meet this burden will result in an acquittal or, at least, in the conviction of a less serious crime.

While in a civil case the degree of proof is a "preponderance of the evidence," in a criminal case the degree of proof is "beyond a reasonable doubt." In some states, the exact wording of the charge to the jury dealing with the standard of proof is stated by statute. In other states, there is no such requirement and, in fact, the judge does not have to explain the term at all.[43] When a statute specifically includes the charge that the judge is to read to the jury, it must be read as stated. An example of such a statute is that of California, which provides

> It (reasonable doubt) is not a mere possible doubt; because everything relating to human affairs is open to some possible or imaginary doubt. It is that state of the case which, after the entire comparison and consideration of all the evidence, leaves the minds of the jurors in that condition that they cannot say that they feel an abiding conviction of the truth of the charge.[44]

The "beyond a reasonable doubt" standard is a constitutional requirement. In 1970, the Supreme Court left no doubt about the requirement in its holding in *In re Winship*:

> Lest there remain any doubt about the constitutional stature of the reasonable-doubt standard, we explicitly hold that the Due Process Clause protects the accused against conviction except on proof beyond a reasonable doubt of every fact necessary to constitute the crime with which he is charged.[45]

Referring to the *In re Winship* decision and reiterating that the government must prove beyond a reasonable doubt every element of a charged offense, the United States Supreme Court in 1994 acknowledged that this ancient and honored aspect of our criminal justice system defies easy explanation.[46]

---

[43] McCORMICK, EVIDENCE 684 (2d ed. 1972).
[44] CAL. PENAL CODE § 1096 (1995).
[45] In re Winship, 397 U.S. 358, 90 S. Ct. 1068, 25 L. Ed. 2d 368 (1970).
[46] Victor v. Nebraska, 311 U.S. 1, 114 S. Ct. 1239, 127 L. Ed. 2d 583 (1994).

§ 1.11   Burden of Proof—Defendant

The previous section makes it clear that the prosecution has the duty to prove the defendant's guilt beyond a reasonable doubt, as well as every element of the crime charged. However, when claiming an affirmative defense such as coercion, self-defense, entrapment, mistake, alibi, or insanity, all of which would absolve the defendant of culpability, the defense has the responsibility of "going forward with the evidence."

To warrant submission of the defense to the jury, the defendant must produce substantial evidence. The burden to prove an affirmative defense such as insanity or self-defense is by a *preponderance of the evidence* and not by evidence beyond a reasonable doubt. Legislative bodies may enact legislation modifying the burden of proof where this does not violate constitutional principles.

An example of laws relating to the burden of proof are those that define the insanity defense. Evidence of the defendant's insanity must be brought forward by the defendant and meet some minimum threshold, but then, if he is successful in meeting the burden of proof, the prosecution has the ultimate burden of proving sanity. The United States Supreme Court, in several instances, has determined that placing the burden on the defendant does not violate the Constitution. In 1984, as part of the Comprehensive Crime Control Act, Congress enacted legislation titled the Insanity Defense Reform Act of 1984. This section of the Code defines the scope of the insanity defense for the federal offenses and shifts the burden of proof to the defendant. The section provides

> (a) Affirmative Defense—It is an affirmative defense to the prosecution under any federal statute that, at the time of the commission of the acts constituting the offense, the defendant, as a result of a severe mental disease or defect, was unable to appreciate the nature and quality of the wrongfulness of his acts. Mental disease or defect does not otherwise constitute a crime.
>
> (b) Burden of Proof—The defendant has the burden of proving the defense of insanity by clear and convincing evidence.[47]

The standard of proof—clear and convincing evidence—is a higher standard than a mere preponderance of the evidence, but is less than beyond a reasonable doubt. The federal courts have been consistent in holding that the provisions of the Insanity Defense Reform Act that shift to the defendant the burden of proving the affirmative defense by clear and convincing evidence do not violate due process.

In other situations in which the defendant claims an affirmative defense, the state may require that the defense be proven by either a preponderance or clear and convincing evidence. The Supreme Court in 1987 upheld an Ohio law that required the defendant to prove self-defense by a preponderance of the evidence.[48] Although the defendant may be required to meet the preponderance or clear and convincing burden

---

[47]   Title 18 U.S.C. § 17.
[48]   Martin v. Ohio, 480 U.S. 228, 107 S. Ct. 1098, 94 L. Ed. 2d 267 (1987).

to submit the defense to the jury, it is still up to the prosecutor to prove beyond a reasonable doubt that the defendant is guilty of each element.

§ 1.12   Summary

When someone causes harm to another or to the property of another, not only is the victim harmed, but society and the state also are considered victimized. Criminal law, then, is the branch or division of law that defines crimes, their elements, and provides for their punishment. In a criminal case, the sovereign, or state, is the plaintiff, and the purpose of the prosecution is to preserve the public peace or address an injury to the public at large. The protections of law fall into the three areas of

1. protection from harm from others,
2. protection from harm from oneself, and
3. protection of society's morals.

Since the beginning of time, various societies have been faced with the problem of determining what standards of conduct must be established. In determining what acts should be made criminal, at least three factors should be given weight:

1. the enforceability of the law,
2. the effects of the law, and
3. the existence of other means to protect society against the undesirable behavior.

Once the legislative or judicial branch of government decides that certain conduct is prohibited or required, criminal justice personnel are charged with enforcing those laws, and have the responsibility to do so until the laws are repealed or declared unconstitutional.

Most of the present-day crimes in the various states had their origins in the common law of England. This was the law developed in the early English court decisions and modified by English legislative bodies. All of this body of English law, except that which was not applicable in the American colonies, was brought by the colonists when they emigrated from England. This became the starting point for our criminal law. While most present-day crimes have their origin in the common law of England, no state currently follows the common law without modification.

Criminal laws (either federal or state) can be created and enforced only if they do not violate the constitutions of the various states and the Constitution of the United States, as interpreted by the courts. Some of the more common constitutional challenges include vagueness, equal protection, ex post facto, First Amendment, and privacy challenges.

Crimes are classified according to the nature of the crime, such as *mala in se* and *mala prohibita*. Crimes are also classified as felonies, misdemeanors, and treason. According to most authorities, crimes punishable by death or imprisonment in a state prison are felonies, while crimes not amounting to felonies are classified as misdemeanors. What is regarded as a felony in some states may constitute only a misdemeanor in others, although the more serious crimes, such as murder, robbery, and rape, are classified as felonies in all jurisdictions.

When one person is wronged by another, that person may seek a remedy against the wrongdoer by bringing a civil, or tort, action. With torts, the emphasis is on adjusting the conflicting interests of individuals to achieve a desirable social result, while a crime is a public wrong that affects public rights and is an injury to the entire community. When a crime is committed, attorneys and judges look to statutes, codes, constitutions, and case decisions to determine what conduct has been prohibited by law and for procedures to be followed in proving guilt.

In the criminal law system in the United States, the prosecution has the heavier burden of proof. The prosecution has the responsibility to prove each element of the crime with which the accused is charged beyond a reasonable doubt. If one element is not proved beyond a reasonable doubt, the person charged cannot be convicted of that particular crime. Although it is unconstitutional to shift the burden of proof of guilt, or any element of the crime, to the defendant in a criminal case, the defendant may be required to prove an affirmative defense by a preponderance or clear and convincing evidence in order to submit the defense to the jury.

Our legal system protects us by defining harmful behavior and setting punishments. The government is not free to declare any act criminal, however, and the federal and state constitutions protect us from laws that violate our protected liberties. Further, the state must prove each element of the crime beyond a reasonable doubt in order to find us guilty.

REVIEW QUESTIONS

1. What is a crime? What is the difference between substantive and procedural law?
2. What are the three forms of harm that criminal law protects against? What are paternalistic laws?
3. What are the three factors that should be considered before making certain acts a crime?
4. What are some alternatives to controlling behavior besides criminal law?
5. What is common law? What is the importance of William Blackstone?
6. What is the difference between statutory law and common law?
7. What is police power? Where does it primarily lie? What does the 10th Amendment to the Constitution say?

8. When can the federal government pass criminal laws? When can political subdivisions pass laws?

9. What is the Model Penal Code?

10. When can a law be challenged?

11. What are the rights guaranteed by the Bill of Rights and the Fourteenth Amendment?

12. What do we mean when we say most of these rights have been incorporated to your rights as a state citizen?

13. Describe the vagueness challenge.

14. Describe the ex post facto challenge.

15. Describe the equal protection challenge.

16. Describe First Amendment challenges.

17. Describe privacy challenges.

18. What are *mala in se* crimes versus *mala prohibita* crimes? What are the differences between felonies and misdemeanors?

19. What are the differences between crimes and torts?

20. Who has the burden of proof? When does it shift? What are affirmative defenses?

Principles of Criminal Liability

2

Chapter Outline

Cases

Actus Reus of Crime: *Powell v. Texas,* 392 U.S. 514 (1968)
Strict Liability: *Dean v. United States*, 556 U.S. __ (2009)

accessory before the fact	negligence
accessory after the fact	principal in the first degree
actus reus	principal in the second degree
concurrence	proximate causation
criminal facilitation	specific intent
criminal omission	strict liability
filial responsibility laws	superseding intervening factor
general intent	transferred intent
Good Samaritan laws	vicarious liability
mens rea	

§ 2.1   Introduction

In this chapter, we will discuss some general principles of criminal responsibility and liability. Obviously, those people who actually commit a criminal act are legally culpable; however, others who *encourage, assist,* or *hinder apprehension* may also be liable under the law. The prosecution must prove that there was, in fact, a criminal act (*actus reus*) and that the persons charged committed the act or participated to the extent that they shared culpability with the primary actor. The law specifies the level of participation necessary in order to find criminal culpability. We will discuss these levels of culpability in Section 2.2.

We will also explain the elements of a crime. Before there can be a finding of guilt, the following elements of any crime must be proven:

- parties to the crime (at least one),
- the criminal act or omission (*actus reus*),
- the criminal state of mind (*mens rea*),
- causation, and
- concurrence.

Thus, the general "formula" for criminal liability becomes

$$\text{Act/Omission} + \text{Requisite State of Mind} + \text{Causation} + \text{Concurrence of Act and State of Mind} = \text{Crime}$$

For example, when one or more human beings (parties) take the life of another human being (act) with a plan or design to take that life (intent), absent a break in the chain of events (causation) they will be liable for the crime of murder (assuming there is no justification or excuse). These and other principles are discussed in Sections 2.3 through 2.8.

§ 2.2 Parties to the Crime

When a crime is committed, one or several persons may be involved. For example, if one person pulls the trigger that results in the firing of a handgun and the bullet injures or kills another person, the person who fired the handgun might be the only participant in the felony crime. However, many others could be involved. For example, some may have been involved in planning the crime, the weapon may have been purchased from a person who knew it was going to be used to commit a crime, other people may have been present when the weapon was fired, and still others could have helped the person who fired the weapon to escape justice after the crime was committed.

A. Common Law

According to common law concepts of "parties to the crime," it was accepted that one incident could result in four different categories of individuals being found guilty of a crime. They might be, respectively

1. principals in the first degree,
2. principals in the second degree,
3. accessories before the fact, or
4. accessories after the fact.

1. Principals in the First Degree

One who actually commits the act that causes a crime to occur is a **principal in the first degree**. One who is actually or constructively present during the commission of the crime and participates in a *substantial* way is also a principal in the first degree, provided that the offense is attempted or completed by at least one party.

One may perpetrate a crime, not only with his or her own hands, but through an agency of mechanical or chemical means, as by instruments, poisons, or powder, or by an animal, child, or other innocent agent acting under his or her direction.[1] Therefore, there may be joint principals in the first degree, such as when two or more cause the death of another by beating, stabbing, shooting, or other means, in which both, or all, participate.

---

[1]   Agresti v. State, 2 Md. App. 278, 234 A.2d 284 (1967); Beausoliel v. United States, 107 F.2d 292 (D. C. Cir. 1939).

2. Principals in the Second Degree

One who *aids* or *abets* a principal in the first degree as he or she commits the criminal act, or *incites* the commission of the crime, and who is actually or constructively present at the time of the commission, is a **principal in the second degree**. A principal in the second degree differs from a principal in the first degree only in that he or she does not commit the offense personally or with an innocent agent, but instead *aids* or *encourages* the principal in the first degree to commit the crime; for example, a person who acts as a lookout or is the driver of the getaway car in a robbery situation is a principal in the second degree.

In order for a person to be a principal in the second degree, he or she must be present at the scene of the crime; however, presence may be either actual or constructive. A person is constructively present when he or she assists the principal in the first degree at the very time the offense is committed, but from such distance that he or she is not actually present.[2]

In a joint trial in Virginia, a man was found guilty of raping his wife's 15-year-old niece, and the wife was found guilty as a principal in the second degree, even though she was not actually present. The Supreme Court of Virginia agreed that the wife was guilty of rape as a principal in the second degree because she *procured, encouraged, countenanced,* and *approved* the husband's having sexual intercourse by intimidation with the victim against her will.

> To establish Virginia as a principal in the second degree, the Commonwealth was required to prove that she was present, either actually or constructively, when the rape was committed. . . .Presence alone, however, is not sufficient to make Virginia a principal in the second degree. It must also be established that she procured, encouraged, countenanced, or approved Raymond's commission of the crime; she must have shared his criminal intent or have committed some overt act in furtherance of the offense. . . . Virginia Sutton's actions meet these requirements for a principal in the second degree to rape as that crime is now defined by Code § 18.2-61.
>
> The trial judge found, from undisputed evidence, that Virginia solicited Beverly to have sexual intercourse with Raymond. The judge also found that both Virginia and Raymond knew that Beverly was afraid to go back to her father. By preying on that fear, Virginia applied relentless pressure on Beverly to submit to Raymond. Shortly before July 23, Virginia reproached Beverly for refusing to submit to Raymond and threatened to return her to her father if she maintained the attitude that she was "too good to go to bed with [her] uncle." On July 22, Virginia and Raymond took Beverly to get birth control pills and paid for the purchase. When Raymond and Beverly had intercourse the following night, Beverly testified, she was afraid that Virginia would send her back to North Carolina.
>
> During the rape, Virginia was not physically present but was in bed in another room. Nevertheless, her malevolent, intimidating influence on her niece was present and continued unabated. This evidence is sufficient to establish Virginia's constructive presence during the commission of the crime. Long ago, this Court said in Dull's Case. . . . of constructive presence:

---

[2]   State v. Sauls, 29 N.C. App. 457, 224 S.E.2d 702 (1976); State v. Wade, 11 N.C. App. 169, 180 S. E.2d 328 (1971).

the presence need not be a strict, actual, immediate presence, such a presence as would make [the defendant] an eye or ear witness of what passes, but may be a constructive presence. So that if several persons set out together. . . . upon one common design, be it murder or other felony, or for any other purpose unlawful in itself, and each takes the part assigned him; . . . they are all, provided the fact be committed, in the eyes of the law, present at it. . . . "

In this case, Virginia and Raymond discussed Raymond's desire to have intercourse with Beverly and Beverly's resistance. They embarked on a common purpose of inducing Beverly by intimidation to submit to Raymond's advances. Virginia's part in the scheme was to so overcome Beverly with the prospect of returning to North Carolina and a life of physical abuse that she would no longer refuse Raymond's demands. By her reprimands of Beverly and her warning about the consequences of continued resistance, Virginia executed her part in the crime and helped ensure the success of their common enterprise.[3]

In a 1986 case, a Maryland court reaffirmed the rule that "a principal in the second degree is one who actually or constructively was present when the felony was committed, and who aids or abets in its commission." In this case, the defendant was convicted as a principal in the second degree even though the defendant did not actively participate in the acts but was present when the acts occurred.[4] The prosecution must prove that that person *aided, abetted, advised, assisted,* or *encouraged* the actual perpetration of the crime. Mere presence would not be sufficient to create criminal culpability; however, the level of participation is not extremely high; for instance, "encourage" may be proven by a simple statement of support for the offender to engage in the criminal act.

Generally, the prosecution must prove that a crime was committed by the principal in the first degree and that the defendant aided and abetted him or her in order to obtain a conviction of that person as a principal in the second degree. It makes no difference, however, if the principal in the first degree is found not guilty by another jury as long as the jury that convicts the principal of the second degree finds, as a matter of fact, that the principal in the first degree is guilty beyond a reasonable doubt.[5]

3. Accessory before the Fact

Accessories before the fact are persons who *counsel, procure,* or *command* the principal in the first degree to commit a criminal offense, yet who are too far away to have participated in the felonious act. Accessories before the fact are distinguished at common law from principals in the second degree (aiders and abettors) by the fact that the latter must be present during the commission of the offense, but accessories do not need to be present at all.[6]

To be guilty as an accessory before the fact, the defendant must have acted in some manner as a participant in the scheme of events in preparation for, or commission of,

---

3   Sutton v. Commonwealth of Virginia, 228 Va. 654, 324 S.E.2d 665 (1985).

4   Smith v. State, 66 Md. App. 603, 505 A.2d 564 (1986).

5   Forbes v. State, 513 S.W.2d 72 (Tex. Crim. App. 1974).

6   State v. Mower, 317 A.2d 807 (Me. 1974); Huff v. State, 23 Md. App. 211, 326 A.2d 198 (1974).

the offense. Mere knowledge that a crime is to be committed is insufficient to support a guilty verdict; the defendant must provide some assistance or encouragement. It is immaterial that such participation is small, as long as it has the effect of inducing the principal to commit the crime.

In the case of *State v. Walden*, the court noted that at common law one who encouraged or aided another in committing a crime but who was not present at the commission of the crime was classified as an accessory before the fact.[7] Concluding that this test was met in this case, the court indicated that the state had offered substantial evidence of each and every element of, and the judge properly instructed the jury on, accessory before the fact, i.e., that (a) the defendant *counseled*, *procured*, or *commanded* the principal to commit the offense; (b) the defendant was not present when the principal committed the offense; and (c) the principal committed the offense. This was sufficient to find the defendant guilty as an accessory before the fact under the common law rule that existed in North Carolina at the time.

4. Accessory after the Fact

An **accessory after the fact** is one who *receives*, *comforts*, or *assists* another, knowing that the other has committed a felony, in order to hinder the perpetrator's arrest, prosecution, or conviction.[8] In order to convict a party charged as an accessory after the fact, it is essential to prove that

- a felony was committed,
- the defendant *knew* the felony had been committed, and
- he or she intended to shield the perpetrator from the law.

If an act of assistance is offered to enable a felon to escape justice after the crime has been committed, the assistance is rendered with the knowledge that the crime has been committed, and the person assisted did in fact commit the crime, this constitutes the crime of accessory after the fact. The fact that the person who gave the assistance discontinues the assistance at a later date, and notifies the authorities, does not relieve that person of criminal liability for the acts committed before notification.

B. Model Penal Code

Under modern statutes and the Model Penal Code, the trend has been to reduce the number of categories of culpability. The liability of those who participate in any way in the crime is equal to the primary actor under many state statutes today. The Model Penal Code provides that a person is guilty of an offense if it is committed by his or her own conduct or by the conduct of another person for whom he or she is "legally

---

[7]   State v. Walden, 330 S.E.2d 271 (N.C. 1985). *See also* Duke v. State, 137 Fla. 513, 188 So. 124 (1939), which held that presence, actual or constructive, is the determining factor in the distinction between a principal in the second degree and an accessory before the fact.

[8]   Whorley v. State, 45 Fla. 123, 33 So. 849 (1903).

accountable." One is "legally accountable" for the conduct of another if he or she causes an innocent person to engage in conduct constituting a crime or if he or she is an accomplice to the crime of the other person. An accomplice is one who *solicits* the commission of an offense, *aids* in its commission or, having a legal duty to prevent the commission of the offense, *fails to make proper effort to prevent it*, or his or her conduct is expressly declared by law to establish complicity.

§ 2.06 Liability for Conduct of Another; Complicity[9]

(1) A person is guilty of an offense if it is committed by his own conduct or by the conduct of another person for which he is legally accountable, or both.
(2) A person is legally accountable for the conduct of another person when:
    (a) acting with the kind of culpability that is sufficient for the commission of the offense, he causes an innocent or irresponsible person to engage in such conduct; or
    (b) he is made accountable for the conduct of such other person by the Code or by the law defining the offense; or
    (c) he is an accomplice of such other person in the commission of the offense.
(3) A person is an accomplice of another person in the commission of an offense if:
    (a) with the purpose of promoting or facilitating the commission of the offense, he:
        (i) solicits such other person to commit it; or
        (ii) aids or agrees or attempts to aid such other person in planning or committing it; or
        (iii) having a legal duty to prevent the commission of the offense, fails to make proper effort so to do; or
    (b) his conduct is expressly declared by law to establish his complicity.

The Model Penal Code has done away with the distinctions of second-degree principals and accessories before the fact—these individuals would now be considered and punished as principals. One other important change occurred in the Model Penal Code as compared to common law regarding accomplice liability. Prosecutors must prove that accomplices had the *mens rea* attached to the crime(s). Under the MPC, accomplices are not liable for natural and foreseeable acts of the principal unless they also intended those acts. In cases where the *mens rea* is reckless, the prosecutor need only show a reckless *mens rea* on the part of the accomplice.

Accessories after the fact, those who knowingly harbor or help offenders but do not directly assist or encourage the crime, are still distinguished. The Model Penal Code, which has been adopted by some states, is specific in stating that a person commits the offense of accessory after the fact if he or she

1. harbors or conceals another;
2. provides aid;
3. conceals, destroys, or tampers with evidence;
4. warns of impending discovery or apprehension; or
5. volunteers false information to a law enforcement officer.[10]

---

[9]   MODEL PENAL CODE § 2.06(1), (2), and (3) (1985).
[10] MODEL PENAL CODE § 242.3 (1985).

C. State Statutes, Codes, and Cases

Most state statutes have simplified the concept of culpability and no longer follow the common law principles identifying four types of actors. Instead, the "law of parties" in modern criminal law states that anyone who participates, procures, aids, or assists a criminal act is equally culpable. Further, unlike common law, an accomplice can now be tried and convicted for their part in an offense even if the principal party was acquitted or even if the principal was never prosecuted at all. The Alabama and California statutes provide the following:

Alabama Criminal Code § 13A-2-23

—Criminal Liability Based upon Behavior of Another—Complicity. A person is legally accountable for the behavior of another constituting a criminal offense if, with the intent to promote or assist the commission of the offense:
1. He procures, induces or causes such other person to commit the offense; or
2. He aids or abets such other person in committing the offense; or
3. Having a legal duty to prevent the commission of the offense, he fails to make an effort he is legally required to make.[11]

Cal. Penal Code § 30-33

—32. Who are Principals. All persons concerned in the commission of a crime, whether it be felony or misdemeanor, and whether they directly commit the act constituting the offense, or aid and abet in its commission, or, not being present, have advised and encouraged the commission, and all persons counseling, advising, or encouraging children under the age of fourteen years, or persons who are mentally incapacitated, to commit any crime, or who, by fraud, contrivance, or force, occasion the drunkenness of another for the purpose of causing him to commit any crime, or who, by threats, menaces, command, or coercion, compel another to commit any crime, are principals in any crime so committed.

A Wisconsin court, in determining the application of that state's statute, explained that there are three alternative ways in which a defendant can be found liable for the commission of an offense under the party-to-a-crime theory:

• by aiding and abetting,
• by conspiracy, or
• by direct commission of a crime.[12]

In interpreting the "aids and abets" provision of a similar statute, a Louisiana court held that a person who aids and abets another in a crime is just as liable as the person who directly commits it. Explaining the scope of the term *principal*, a Louisiana court held that this term is broadly defined to include the actual perpetrator of the crime as well as one who assists in the perpetration. The court noted, however, that only those persons who *knowingly* participate in the planning or execution of the crime are principals; mere

---

11   ALA. CODE § 13A-2-23 (1998).
12   State v. Hamm, 586 N.W.2d 5 (Wis. 1998).

presence at the scene is not enough to involve an individual in the crime. In addition, the court noted that an individual may only be convicted as a principal for those crimes for which he personally has the requisite mental state.[13] There have been some cases in which presence plus "implicit encouragement" have been sufficient to find culpability.[14] Generally, states require that accomplices have criminal intent, that is, they share the same criminal purpose as the primary actor. Some states also hold all parties responsible for the natural and probable consequences of the crime. For example, an accomplice might agree to act as a look out for someone robbing a bank but only on the condition that the robber use a fake gun. During the robbery, if the robber has lied to his accomplice and actually brings a real gun and shoots the victim, the accomplice may be guilty of murder, even though he specifically intended otherwise. A different example would be if kidnappers had agreed that the victim would not be harmed, all parties will still be guilty of murder if the victim dies during the kidnapping because it is a foreseeable and probable event.

LEGAL NEWS: THE LAW OF PARTIES IN TEXAS

Ansel Abdygapparova was tried and convicted for rape and first-degree homicide in Texas, even though she did not actively participate in either the rape or the murder of the victim by her boyfriend and another man. Abdygapparova did participate to the extent that she purchased a shovel to bury the body. She argued that she was merely present and anything she did was under duress because her boyfriend physically abused her and she was afraid of him. She was convicted and sentenced to life in prison.

In 2009, Robert Lee Thompson was executed for his part in an armed robbery where a store clerk was killed. Thompson's crime partner killed the clerk and the jury in his trial sentenced him to life in prison, but the jury in Thompson's trial sentenced him to death. Steven Michael Woods was executed in 2011 in a similar case whereby his crime partner confessed to killing a young couple. Even though the other man confessed, Woods' jury sentenced him to be executed while the other jury sentenced the murderer to life in prison.

Source: *San Antonio Express News*, February 13, 2005 at A48; March 3, 2005 at A20; retrieved December 20, 2011 from http://standdown.typepad.com/weblog/law_of_partiesfelony_murder_rule/.

An accessory after the fact is generally treated as a separate offense and is accorded different treatment in modern codes. To establish the crime of accessory after the fact, the state must establish

- the completed felony was completed by another party prior to any acts engaged in by the defendant,

---

[13]   State v. Cayton, 721 So.2d 542 (La. 1998); State v. Arnold, 801 So.2d 408 (La. 2001).
[14]   State v. Doody, 434 A.2d 523 (Me 1981), *but see* State v. Vaillancourt, 453 A.2d 1327 (N.H. 1982).

- the accessory was not a principal in the commission of the felony,
- the accessory had knowledge of the felony, and
- the accessory acted personally to aid or assist a felon to avoid detection or apprehension for the crime or crimes.[15]

There is disagreement between states as to whether or not to hold parties liable when they knew their actions may assist in a crime, but did not intend the crime to occur. Some states hold such persons liable, others require the prosecutor to prove the accomplice had the same level of *mens rea* as the primary party. Some states solve the problem by creating a new statute. **Criminal facilitation** statutes impose liability for providing aid to someone, knowing that he or she is about to commit an offense. Typical of these statutes is that of Kentucky, KRS § 506.080(1), which states

> A person is guilty of criminal facilitation when, acting with knowledge that another person is committing or intends to commit a crime, he engages in conduct which knowingly provides such person with means or opportunity for the commission of the crime and which in fact aids such person to commit the crime.

The major difference between being charged under a complicity statute or being charged under a facilitation statute is the intent of the actor. If the aid is provided with the intent to commit the same crime as the person being assisted, the offense is charged under the complicity statute and both the "doer" and the one providing assistance are guilty of the substantive crime. However, if aid is offered only "with knowledge" that the recipient is committing a crime, then the aider is guilty of the offense of facilitation, not the substantive offense committed by the one who was assisted. In most jurisdictions, the penalty for facilitation is one level, or class, lower than the substantive offense for which the aid was offered.

LEGAL NEWS: HINDERING APPREHENSION

Laura Hall was convicted in 2007 of tampering with evidence and "hindering apprehension," a charge similar to accessory after the fact. The conviction stemmed from the murder of Jennifer Cave by Colton Pitonyak, a former University of Texas student, in 2005. After the murder, Pitonyak sought help from Hall, another university student, who helped him partially cut off the victim's head and hands in the bathtub of Pitonyak's apartment where the murder took place. Then, Hall drove them both to Mexico where they were apprehended. Hall originally received a five-year sentence. She appealed that sentence and received a new sentencing hearing. The second jury sentenced her to ten years for evidence tampering and one year, to be run concurrently, for hindering apprehension.

Retrieved December 20, 2011 from http://www.statesman.com/blogs/content/shared-gen/blogs/austin/courts/entries/colton_pitonyaklaura_hall/.

---

[15]   Little v. United States, 709 A.2d 708 (D.C. 1998).

D. *Summary*

In sum, the liability of an actor is categorized according to proximity to the offense and the level of participation. In most modern statutes, the only two types of criminal parties are

1. party (includes principals and accomplices), and
2. accessory after the fact.

However, in some jurisdictions, there is also the lesser crime of

3. criminal facilitation.

§ 2.3   Criminal Act Requirements

In order to find someone guilty of a crime, every element of this formula must be proven:

Criminal Act (*Actus Reus*) + Requisite State of Mind (*Mens Rea*) + Causation + Concurrence (of Act and State of Mind) = Crime

If the prosecution is unable to prove all of the elements, there can be no conviction. Before a person may be convicted of a crime, the prosecution must show that the person committed an act prohibited by some law, or failed to act when he or she had a legal obligation to do so. Often this principle is referred to as the ***actus reus***. The law does not punish mere criminal thoughts, nor does it punish a person for his or her status. As a rule, legal liability is typically based upon an affirmative physical act by the person charged, but in some instances liability can rest upon a failure to act, if it is determined that a person had a legal obligation to act under the circumstances. In this section, the *criminal act* requirement is discussed. Omission is analyzed in § 2.4.

The Model Penal Code describes criminal acts and omissions as follows:

§ 2.01 Requirement of Voluntary Act; Omission as Basis of Liability; Possession as an Act[16]

(1) A person is not guilty of an offense unless his liability is based on conduct which includes a voluntary act or the omission to perform an act of which he is physically capable.
(2) The following are not voluntary acts within the meaning of this Section:
    (a) a reflex or convulsion;
    (b) a bodily movement during unconsciousness or sleep;
    (c) conduct during hypnosis or resulting from hypnotic suggestion;
    (d) a bodily movement that otherwise is not a product of the effort or determination of the actor, either conscious or habitual.

---

[16] MODEL PENAL CODE § 2.01 (1985).

(3) Liability for the commission of an offense may not be based on an omission un-accompanied by action unless:
    (a) the omission is expressly made sufficient by the law defining the offense; or
    (b) duty to perform the omitted act is otherwise imposed by law.
(4) Possession is an act, within the meaning of this Section, if the possessor knowingly procured or received the thing possessed or was aware of his control thereof for a sufficient period to have been able to terminate his possession.

Criminal culpability generally occurs through some act or conduct. The act or the conduct may consist of the physical movement of a person, such as pulling the trigger of a gun or breaking into a house to commit theft, or it may consist of verbal acts—for example, making verbal threats that induce fear in a victim. Possession can also form the basis of criminal liability even though it does not seem like an act, as long as the prosecutor can prove that the defendant knowingly had custody or control over the contraband.

As discussed in Chapter 1, the statute or law cannot be vague in its description of the act or conduct that would create criminal culpability. The test as to whether the law is vague or not is reasonableness (whether reasonable people would know whether or not their conduct violates the law).

A. Voluntary Act

The act must be voluntary. There have been a few cases in criminal law in which the act was deemed to be not "volitional" or voluntary on the part of the perpe-trator. Examples of acts that are not considered voluntary include epileptic seizures or spasms, reflexive actions, or actions taken while sleepwalking or in some other form of "unconscious" state. In cases of sleepwalking, for instance, any acts carried out by the sleepwalker are held to be not voluntary for purposes of criminal liability. Note that this is not a mental illness or capacity defense, nor is it a question of *mens rea*—rather, because the action is not under the volition of the actor, the first element of the crime (a voluntary act) is missing.

One example of this type of situation was the case of a man who killed his mother-in-law while sleepwalking. He drove 14 miles to her home and beat her to death with a tire iron. Medical experts testified that this behavior was indeed possible and, in fact, dozens of cases exist in which sleepwalkers have killed someone. In this case, the man had a very good relationship with his mother-in-law and there was no apparent reason for the killing. The jury acquitted him and the appellate court upheld the acquittal.[17]

Other possible situations that might raise the argument that the defendants' acts are not voluntary might be individuals who suffer epileptic seizures while driving and kill innocent bystanders. In these cases, the question of voluntariness typically turns on whether the individual knew that they were subject to loss of control, and knew that they posed a risk to others. If they had had seizures before and drove anyway, they

---

[17]   The Queen v. Parks [1992] 2 S.C.R. 871 (Can.); *but see* Sallee v. State, 544 P.2d 902 (Okla. Crim. App. 1975).

typically are held liable under some form of gross recklessness or negligence.[18] The act in those cases is not the involuntary seizure that led to the automobile accident, but rather, the act of starting to drive the car in the first place.

What about brainwashing or hypnosis? Is it possible for someone to have no control over their actions because their will has been compromised by some form of mind control? The courts have not been open to such defenses, but there may be situations in which a defendant might successfully argue that they not only did not have *criminal intent,* but also that they did not even perform a *criminal act* because the action was not voluntary.

B. *Act versus Status*

The criminal law does not punish thoughts, emotions, personality, or character. Following this reasoning, the courts have determined that a statute that punishes someone for "who" or "what" they are, rather than "what they've done" violates the Eighth Amendment, which prohibits cruel and unusual punishment. For example, statuses, such as "vagrancy," "being a common drunkard," or "being addicted to the use of narcotics," cannot be the basis of criminal culpability because there is no act involved.

In the case of *Robinson v. California*, the Supreme Court of the United States declared that a California law that provided "no person shall use, or be under the influence of, or be addicted to the use of narcotics . . ." was unconstitutional because making the status of being an addict a crime violated the Eighth Amendment as applied to the states by way of the Fourteenth Amendment.[19] The justices made clear, however, that this interpretation did not prohibit punishment for the *use of* narcotics, because use is prohibited conduct. The Court summarized with this paragraph:

> We hold that a state law which imprisons a person thus affected as a criminal, even though he has never touched any narcotic drug within the state or been guilty of any irregular behavior there, inflicts a cruel and unusual punishment in violation of the Fourteenth Amendment.[20]

However, a statute that prohibits being in public while drunk was held to be constitutional. In *Powell v. Texas*, the U.S. Supreme Court distinguished the two cases.[21] They held that California punished someone for the mere *status* of being an addict, but the Texas statute against public drunkenness punished the *act* of being drunk in public, a behavior that may create substantial health and safety hazards. The Supreme Court held that the Texas law was quite different from convicting a

---

[18]   People v. Decina, 138 N.E.2d 799 (N.Y. 1956).
[19]   Robinson v. California, 370 U.S. 660, 82 S. Ct. 1417, 8 L. Ed. 2d 758 (1962).
[20]   *Id.*
[21]   Powell v. Texas, 392 U.S. 514, 88 S. Ct. 2145, 20 L. Ed. 2d 1254 (1968).

person for simply being an addict, a chronic alcoholic, a leper, or someone who is mentally ill.

C. Possession

"Possession" offenses sometimes pose problems because it is claimed that, in some instances, the possession of property often involves no physical action to gain control of the contraband item. Although in some of the early cases the courts held that mere possession was not a crime because no "act" was involved, modern statutes, which make possession of contraband (such as narcotics or stolen goods) a crime, have been upheld. The rationale is that the "act" requirement is complied with because the defendant either actively procured or received the items, or violated the legally imposed duty to divest him- or herself of control as soon as possible upon discovering the illegal nature of the possession.[22] In this sense, possession crimes might be considered crimes of omission because the individual did not divest themselves of contraband once they had knowledge, and this omission created criminal culpability.

> **CASE NOTE:** *Powell v. Texas*, 392 U.S. 514 (1968)
> What was the holding of the Court?
> What was the appellant's argument as to why Powell should not be punished for being drunk in public?
> Explain what the "act" is in the crime of public drunkenness.
> Are there any circumstances in which punishing an alcoholic might be ruled unconstitutional? Explain.

D. Summary

In order to be convicted of a crime, the accused must have committed a criminal act (or omission as will be explained in § 2.4). The act may involve an actual physical movement, or it may consist of verbal acts. One cannot be punished for evil intent alone, nor for any status (such as being an addict or an alcoholic). When criminal liability is based upon the defendant's affirmative act, there usually must be a showing that he or she made some conscious movement. However, "possession" crimes have been upheld even if there is no proof of a conscious movement related to the contraband.

§ 2.4 Criminal Omission

Although in the usual case an affirmative act is required for criminal culpability, in some instances, liability can rest on the failure to act. This is referred to as "**criminal omission**," "acts of omission," or in some instances, "failure to act."

There are many statutes that make failure to act a violation of the law; for example, failure to register for the draft or failure to prepare income tax returns. Although the cases concerning failure to act generally arise in homicide cases in which the

---

22   MODEL PENAL CODE § 2.01(4) (1985).

defendant's conviction is predicated on the theory that the defendant failed to take steps to save the victim's life, the rationale also applies in other cases. The rule is that the defendant's omission will support a finding of criminal liability when it is shown that he or she was under a legal duty to act and that it would have been possible for him or her to act. In the case of *Jones v. United States*, the court held that a person who failed to act may be found guilty of homicide, if there existed a duty, declaring

> There are at least four situations in which the failure to act may constitute a breach of legal duty. One can be held criminally liable: first, where a statute imposes a duty to care for another; second, where one stands in a certain status relationship to another; third, where one has assumed a contractual duty to care for another; and fourth, where one has voluntarily assumed the care of another, and so secluded the helpless person as to prevent others from rendering aid.[23]

LEGAL NEWS: FAILURE TO RENDER ASSISTANCE = MURDER

In 2002 Chante Mallard (27) hit Gregory Biggs (37), a homeless man, on her way home from a night of drinking and using drugs. Her car hit him with such force that he was lodged headfirst in her windshield. After she hit him, she drove home, parked the car in the garage with Biggs still impaled on the windshield, and went into her house. She admitted later that she went out to the garage several times to apologize to Biggs, but did nothing to help him. He died an unknown number of hours later from shock and loss of blood. Mallard and two friends dumped his body in a nearby park. The death would have remained unsolved if she hadn't explained to a friend why she wasn't driving her car anymore, laughing about the incident in the telling. Someone overheard her and tipped off police who found hair and blood from Biggs in her car's windshield and other evidence. She was convicted of murder and sentenced to 50 years in prison. If she had immediately sought assistance, Biggs might be alive today; but, even if he had died, she would not have faced a murder charge. Her duty to seek assistance was created by her causing the accident. Now she will spend most of the rest of her life in prison.

Retrieved December 20, 2011 from http://articles.cnn.com/2003-06-27/justice/windshield.death_1_chante-mallard-brandon-biggs-mallard-family?_s=PM:LAW.

A. Duties

The four types of duty that might create liability if there is an omission or failure to act are statutory duties, duties derived from relationships, contractual duties, and failure to continue care duties.[24]

---

[23] Jones v. United States, 308 F.2d 307 (D.C. Cir. 1962). *See also* Commonwealth v. Kellam, 719 A.2d 792 (Pa. 1998).

[24] Jones v. United States, 308 F.2d 307 (D.C. Cir. 1962).

1. Statutory Duty

Where a statutory duty is imposed, criminal liability could result if the person charged had the opportunity and ability to perform the act and did not. Examples of statutory duties are, for instance, the duty to file tax returns and the duty (of convicted sex offenders) to register in sex-offender registries. Failure to perform these duties is a crime in itself. Another example of a statutorily created duty is the duty to provide safe working conditions.

Other statutory duties may create the potential for criminal liability if their omission results in a death or injury. For instance, a parent has a duty to provide care to their child; thus, the failure to act when someone else is hurting the child creates criminal liability. Statutory duties may include

- The duty to stop and render assistance if involved in a traffic accident
- The duty to care for a minor child
- The duty of "mandated reporters" to report child abuse to law enforcement
- The duty to render assistance to someone in danger ("Good Samaritan" statutes)

It should be noted that, although they are fairly common in Europe, most states do not have **"Good Samaritan" laws** that create a duty to render assistance when one citizen sees another in distress. Actually, all states have what are called Good Samaritan laws, but these types of laws protect citizens from civil liability if they stop and render assistance to a victim and are sued as a result of their actions. Few states have the European type of law that requires one to step in and help when someone else is the victim of a crime.

In 1964, when 28-year-old Catherine Genovese was murdered in New York, 37 people who witnessed the attack did not call the police, yet there was no criminal liability on the part of those who refused to help. A newspaper article expressed shock that we, in this country, are not interested enough in our fellow humans to take action under such circumstances.[25] However, as a federal court explained, in the United States, a breach of a legal duty—rather than a mere moral command—is necessary to impose criminal liability for failure to assist one in need.[26] Only a few states have a legal duty to render assistance, including Rhode Island, Wisconsin, Minnesota, and Vermont. For instance, Vermont's statute specifies that

> A person who knows that another is exposed to grave physical harm shall, to the extent that the same can be rendered without danger or peril to himself or without interference with important duties owed to others, give reasonable assistance to the exposed person unless that assistance or care is being provided by others.[27]

Note that the statute creates a duty to act only to the extent that the citizen can do it without danger to self; further, the law would only require intervention to the extent of

---

[25]   N.Y. TIMES, Mar. 28, 1964.
[26]   *See generally Culpable Non-Intervention: Reconsidering the Basis for Party Liability by Omission*, 18 CRIM. L.J. 90-107 (1994); *The Efficient Duty to Rescue*, 15 INTER. REV. of l. & ECON. 141-150 (1995); *Cal. Penal Code § 654 and the Neal Doctrine*, 26 UNIV. OF W. L.A. L. REV. 335-363 (1995); *see also* FRENCH PENAL CODE, ART. 63 and United States v. Bonetti, 277 F.3d 441 (4th Cir. 2002).
[27]   VT. STAT. ANN. Tit. 12, Sec. 519.

one's abilities. This means, for instance, that if a passerby could not swim, they would not be obligated to jump in the river to save a drowning person; they would have a duty, however, to alert others or to help the drowning victim by throwing in a life ring or doing some other affirmative act.

Slightly different are statutes that require one to report a crime. Fewer than 10 states have such laws. For instance, Massachusetts has a statute that requires someone to report certain enumerated crimes (aggravated assault, rape, murder, manslaughter, and armed robbery) if they are witnessing it and can report it without danger to themselves or others. They must report it as soon as is reasonably practicable. Violation of this law is a misdemeanor.[28] Other states may have statutes against false reports to police, but do not require citizens to report a crime.

LEGAL NEWS: A DIFFERENT KIND OF GOOD SAMARITAN LAW

In 2011 New York passed a law that would bar prosecution for personal possession of drugs, paraphernalia, or underage drinking of individuals who helped save the life of an overdose victim. The law's proponents argued that overdoses are one of the leading causes of accidental deaths and many can be prevented with early intervention, but bystanders typically fail to call 911 because of fear of prosecution. This Good Samaritan law will remove that fear and, hopefully, lead to lives saved.

Retrieved December 20, 2011 from http://healthland.time.com/2011/07/29/new-york-state-passes-good-samaritan-law-to-fight-overdose/.

---

2. Relationship Duties

At common law, certain affirmative duties were placed upon persons with designated relationships. For example, a parent has the duty to prevent physical harm to his or her children. Today, there is disagreement in case decisions regarding the duty of a stepparent to stepchildren, but generally, if the adult has been acting in the role of a parent, a duty has been created. On the other hand, there is no such duty (at least recognized in common law) to provide for the care of one's parent. Thus, an adult child may have no duty (depending on the state) to see that the parent is taken care of or even has enough to eat. A duty can be created, however, if the adult child is the legal agent of the parent or there has been a contract formed where the adult child has promised to care for the parent in return for some type of consideration. In about 28 states, **"filial responsibility" laws** exist. These statutes create a duty to financially provide for one's aged and infirm parents if one is able to do so. In some states, a defense

---

[28] MASS. GEN. CODE, Ch. 268, § 40.

can be offered that the parent abandoned the child before the age of majority. Despite the fact that these state statutes exist, they are rarely enforced; in 11 of these states, no one has ever been prosecuted.[29] Consider other relationships that may have inherent duties:

- Does Person A have a duty to warn Person B of the imminent threat made by Person C to Person B? (Generally, there is no duty unless there is a special relationship between A and B.)
- Do psychiatrists have a duty to warn others if there is an imminent and clear threat that a patient is going to harm someone? (Generally, yes, if the threat is specific and the patient has a history of violence.)
- Do brothers and sisters have duties to each other to ensure that a sibling does not end up homeless or hungry? (Legally there is no duty unless created by contract.)

3. Contractual Duties

Where a person has a contractual duty to protect or care for others and fails to carry out that contractal duty, he or she may be criminally liable for not performing that duty. For example, in the case of *People v. Montecino,* a nurse was held liable for failing to care for a patient she had been hired to care for.[30] Another example is the failure of a railroad gateman who was employed to lower the gates to protect the cars and pedestrians from passing trains, with the resulting death of the driver of a car. The gateman was criminally responsible for failing to carry out his contractual obligation.[31] In an example of a verbal contractual duty, a grandmother who took care of a grandchild violated the duty of reasonable care when she became so intoxicated that she let the child smother. In that case, the court held the grandmother guilty of manslaughter.[32]

Other examples of contractual duties exist between the following actors:

- Lifeguards to swimmers
- Child care providers to those in their care
- Police officer to citizen
- Adult child to parent (if they are a legal agent, i.e., have power of attorney)
- Doctor to patient

In these cases, gross negligence in failing to perform one's duties may give rise to a finding of criminal culpability if there is a death or serious injury. Of course, the

---

[29]   See *Caring for Our Parents in an Aging World: Sharing Public and Private Responsibility for the Elderly,* 5 N.Y.U.J. Legis. and Pub. Pol'y 563 (2001).
[30]   66 Cal. App. 2d 85, 152 P.2d 5 (1944).
[31]   State v. Harrison, 107 N.J. 213, 152 A. 867 (1931).
[32]   Cornell v. State, 159 Fla. 687, 32 So. 2d 610 (1947).

omission or failure to act must be the direct cause of the death or serious injury in order for there to be criminal culpability.

LEGAL NEWS: MICHAEL JACKSON'S DOCTOR CONVICTED

In November 2011, Conrad Murray was convicted of involuntary manslaughter in the death of Michael Jackson. Evidence showed that the doctor routinely gave the singer propofol as a sleeping aid despite the fact that medical standards indicated the drug should be used only in hospital settings under strict guidelines. The judge, in sentencing Murray to four years in prison, stated that he failed in his legal duties as a physician to a patient in his standard of care.

Retrieved December 20, 2011 from http://www.cnn.com/2011/11/29/justice/california-conrad-murray-sentencing/index.html.

---

4. Failure to Continue Care Duties

If a person who has no statutory, relationship, or contractual obligation to render aid assumes this obligation, that person must not put the helpless person in such a position as to prevent others from rendering aid. For instance, unless a state has a Good Samaritan law, there is no statutory duty to stop and render assistance if one sees a traffic accident. However, if a driver does stop and begins to help, then they must continue until such time as others have arrived. If one sees a person in distress on the street, there is no duty to render aid, however, if a passerby helps the person in distress to a park bench or helps them to a doorway or in any other way moves them away from where they might receive assistance from others, then the duty to continue care has been created. The rationale is that abandoning one's effort would leave the victim in a worse condition than before.

Consider two different scenarios.

Situation 1. Defendant socializes with Victim in bar; Victim is extremely drunk and becomes incoherent; Victim tells Defendant that he has ingested a large amount of drugs as well as alcohol; Defendant leaves Victim in bar and goes home.

Situation 2. Defendant socializes with Victim in bar; Victim is extremely drunk and becomes incoherent; Victim tells Defendant that he has ingested a large amount of drugs as well as alcohol; Defendant assists Victim to his or her house where Victim passes out on floor. Defendant goes to bed. Victim dies from drug overdose or alcohol poisoning.

In Situation 2, the defendant may be charged with involuntary manslaughter because when the defendant moved the victim from a place where others might help, he or she created a continuance of care duty. Therefore, if gross negligence or recklessness was proven (i.e., that the defendant should have known to call for medical assistance), the defendant may be criminally culpable.

B. *Knowledge and Impossibility*

Before a person can be held responsible for an omission, knowledge of one's duty and an opportunity to perform and failure to perform the act must be shown. The majority view is that, although one may be under a legal duty to act, an omission will not render the defendant criminally liable unless he or she has knowledge of the facts creating the duty. For example, a person charged with "failure to stop" after causing an accident must be aware that the accident had occurred. The responsibility of showing knowledge falls upon the prosecution.[33]

On the other hand, lack of knowledge *of the law* does not provide an excuse. For example, a defendant's claim that he did not know that he had to report an accident as required by law would not be a defense. However, if a statute punished for the *willful* (intentional) failure to return an income tax report, then knowledge of the law must be proved. The reasoning is that there can be no *willful* violation if there is no knowledge.[34]

Also, there can be no criminal prosecution if the failure to act is based upon impossibility. There is no criminal act, or criminal failure to act, when the defendant's omission was due to the fact that he lacked the means or ability to perform. Evidence should be introduced to show that the defendant had the ability to take action. However, failure due to impossibility is not a defense if a person could have gotten help, even if that person was not able to perform the duty; for example, failure to seek aid for a person who needs medical care.[35]

C. *Summary*

In order for an omission to create criminal culpability, there must be a duty. Duties are created through statute, relationship, contract, or through undertaking to care for a person in distress. Simple ignorance of the law defining the duty is not sufficient to relieve one of liability. However, a failure to act cannot create criminal liability unless there is

- knowledge of facts that give notice to the person that they have a duty to perform, and
- an ability to perform one's duty.

§ 2.5   Criminal State of Mind—*Mens Rea*

Recall that in order for there to be a crime, there must be an act (*actus reus*), a criminal state of mind (***mens rea***), causation, and concurrence. We turn now to the requisite mental state in order for a person to be criminally culpable. The criminal state of

---

[33]   People v. Henry, 23 Cal. App. 2d 155, 72 P.2d 915 (1937).
[34]   United States v. Murdock, 290 U.S. 389, 54 S. Ct. 223, 78 L. Ed. 381 (1933).
[35]   People v. Beardsley, 150 Mich. 206, 113 N.W. 1128 (1907).

mind generally must unite with the overt act, or there must be a union or joint operation of the criminal act and intention. The criminal intent need not have existed for any length of time before the act, as long as it existed at the instant of the act.[36]

A. Common Law

The common law evolved through the slow accumulation of individual case decisions. The definitions of crimes, therefore, were not conceived in any organized or comprehensive way. Each crime possessed a *mens rea*, but the language used in old English cases and early state statutes and cases in this country was not uniform; thus, for instance, the necessary intent for homicide might have been malicious, premeditated, depraved indifference, depraved heart, wanton disregard, or some other term. Each statute utilized specific language to describe the different levels of *mens rea* for different levels of culpability, but there was no uniformity in the language used, nor even consistency in the meaning of words, such as "wanton disregard" from one state to the next.

The *mens rea* requirement for crimes traditionally falls into one of three categories: specific intent, general intent, or negligence. In the case of *People v. Hood*, the majority of the Supreme Court of California acknowledged that "Specific and general intent have been notoriously difficult terms to define and apply."[37] However, they are still relevant to the understanding of criminal culpability and serve to distinguish different levels of culpability.

1. Specific Intent

Specific intent refers to an intention to commit some act to accomplish a result that is known to be illegal. If the statute defining a crime includes specific intent as an ingredient of criminality, such intent must be established as any other element of the crime. One way to think about specific intent is that the offender intended to do the act AND intended the consequence of the act (even if the consequence, apart from the act, was only to break the law).

In the case of *State v. LeBlanc*, the defendant was convicted of second-degree murder and attempted first-degree murder of a police officer from an incident where he shot at two police detectives while running away from them, killing one. On appeal, the defendant argued that the trial court erred in charging the jury that it could convict the defendant of attempted first-degree murder upon proof that the defendant specifically intended either to kill Detective Mims or inflict great bodily harm upon him. The reviewing court agreed that this instruction was incorrect, as the *gravamen* of attempted murder is a specific attempt to kill, not simply to inflict great bodily harm. Included in the decision is this definition of specific intent:

---

[36] United States v. Lester, 363 F.2d 68 (6th Cir. 1967), *cert. denied*, 385 U.S. 1002 (1967); State v. Morgan, 22 Utah 162, 61 P. 527 (1900).
[37] 1 Cal. 3d 444, 462 P.2d 370 (1969).

> Specific intent is that state of mind which exists when the circumstances indicate that the offender actively desires the prescribed consequences to follow from his act or failure to act. ... Specific intent need not be proven as a fact, but may be inferred from the circumstances of the transaction and the actions of the defendant.[38]

In distinguishing between specific intent and general intent, a Michigan court indicated that specific intent requires a particular criminal intent beyond the act done, while a general intent crime requires merely the intent to perform a proscribed physical act.[39] First-degree or capital murder, for instance, is often defined as a specific intent crime because the prosecutor must prove not only that the offender *intended to do the act* that resulted in a death (i.e., shoot, stab, hit the victim), but that the offender *intended the result* (death). On the other hand, second-degree murder is a general intent crime because the prosecutor must prove only that the defendant intended to do the act that resulted in the death of the victim. Another specific intent crime is burglary (breaking and entering *with intent* to commit a felony inside). If it cannot be proven that the defendant intended to commit a felony after entry, then the crime committed is only breaking and entering or trespassing. Possession of drugs is a general intent crime, but possession *with intent* to distribute is a specific intent crime. All crimes of attempt are specific intent because the prosecutor must show that the acts were committed *with the intent* to achieve the unconsummated substantive crime.

2. General Intent

General intent is present when a person consciously chooses to do a prohibited act. The only state of mind required is the intent to commit the act constituting the crime. The person charged need not have intended to violate the law, nor have been aware that the law made the act criminal. If specific intent is not required as an element of the crime, general intent may be inferred from the fact that the defendant engaged in the prohibited conduct.

Criminal intent may be found by the jury upon consideration of the "words, conduct, demeanor, motive and all other circumstances connected with the act for which the accused is prosecuted."[40] In defining general intent, a New York court stated that in a prosecution for a general intent crime, the government needs to prove only that the defendant intended to do what the law forbids; it is not necessary for the prosecution to prove that the defendant intended the precise result that occurred.[41]

Thus, think of specific intent as premeditated murder and general intent as other "garden variety" murders in which there is no proof that the offender intended the result. It is the difference, for instance, between a murder in which the offender planned the act, made preparations, laid in wait for the victim, and then cold-bloodedly killed

---

[38]   State v. LeBlanc, 719 So. 2d 592 (La. 1998).
[39]   People v. Whitney, 228 Mich. App. 230, 578 N.W.2d 329 (1998).
[40]   Miller v. State, 233 Ga. App. 814, 506 S.E.2d 136 (1998).
[41]   United States v. Francis, 975 F. Supp. 288 (S.D.N.Y. 1997).

the victim, versus a situation in which the offender grabbed a nearby gun and shot the victim during an argument. The offender could say that he never meant to kill the victim; he was only trying to scare or injure him. In most cases, this is a general intent murder and not the lesser crime of manslaughter because a grave injury was almost certain to occur. The prosecutor can prove that the offender meant to do the act (shooting), and we will hold him responsible for the almost certain effect of his act, but his criminal culpability will be limited to a general intent homicide rather than specific intent homicide (first degree). To reiterate: specific intent is when the actor intends the act and intends the consequence; and general intent requires only that the actor intends the prohibited act.

3. Negligence

In common law, **negligence** is the failure to perform a duty when such conduct is reckless and indifferent to the consequences. It must be more, or of a greater degree, than "ordinary negligence." Criminal negligence is not established simply by the fact that the defendant failed to exercise due care; the negligence must involve a higher probability of harm than is necessary for purposes of imposing civil liability. Because they are so similar, many statutes and cases combine recklessness and negligence as one category of criminal culpability; however, the Model Penal Code distinguishes these two levels of *mens rea*.

B. *Model Penal Code*

The Model Penal Code includes the following section on culpability:

§ 2.02 General Requirements of Culpability[42]

(1) Minimum Requirements of Culpability
   Except as provided in § 2.05, a person is not guilty of an offense unless he acted purposely, knowingly, recklessly or negligently, as the law may require, with respect to each material element of the offense.
(2) Kinds of Culpability Defined
   (a) Purposely
       A person acts purposely with respect to a material element of an offense when:
       (i) if the element involves the nature of his conduct or a result thereof, it is his conscious object to engage in conduct of that nature or to cause such a result; and
       (ii) if the element involves the attendant circumstances, he is aware of the existence of such circumstances or he believes or hopes that they exist.
   (b) Knowingly
       A person acts knowingly with respect to a material element of an offense when:

---

[42] MODEL PENAL CODE § 2.02 (1985).

(i) if the element involves the nature of his conduct or the attendant circumstances, he is aware that his conduct is of that nature or that such circumstances exist; and

(ii) if the element involves a result of his conduct he is aware that it is practically certain that his conduct will cause such a result.

(c) Recklessly

A person acts recklessly with respect to a material element of an offense when he consciously disregards a substantial and unjustifiable risk that the material element exists or will result from his conduct. The risk must be of such a nature and degree that, considering the nature and purpose of the actor's conduct and the circumstances known to him, its disregard involves a gross deviation from the standard of conduct that a law-abiding person would observe in the actor's situation.

(d) Negligently

A person acts negligently with respect to a material element of an offense when he should be aware of a substantial and unjustifiable risk that the material element exists or will result from his conduct. The risk must be of such a nature and degree that the actor's failure to perceive it, considering the nature and purpose of his conduct and the circumstances known to him, involves a gross deviation from the standard of care that a reasonable person would observe in the actor's situation.

Some argue that one of the greatest contributions of the Model Penal Code is that all the myriad definitions of *mens rea* were condensed into only four enumerated mental states. In all states that have adopted the Model Penal Code, statutes clearly specify that the actor must have acted purposely, knowingly, recklessly, or negligently. To reiterate, the definitions of these terms are as follows:

- *Purposely:* when the actor intends the act and intends to cause the result
- *Knowingly:* when the actor is aware of the nature of his conduct and is aware of the practical certainty of the result of his conduct
- *Recklessly*: when the actor knows of but consciously disregards an unjustifiable risk (and the action involves a gross deviation from a reasonable standard of conduct)
- *Negligently:* when the actor is unaware of but *should have been* aware of an unjustifiable risk (and the action involves a gross deviation from a reasonable standard of conduct)

In states that do not use the Model Penal Code's structure for defining criminal culpability, different terms may mean the same thing. For instance, "wantonly," as used in the Kentucky Code, is defined as when an individual is aware of and consciously disregards a substantial and unjustifiable risk and that creates a gross deviation from the standard of conduct.[43] This is, of course, very similar to the MPC definition of "reckless," but in the Kentucky code, "reckless" is the term used to refer to failing to perceive a risk. The MPC uses similar terminology to refer to negligence. Furthermore, some states, even if they have adopted the MPC definitions, still refer to specific intent and general intent. We can see from the definitions above that specific intent

---

[43]   KY. REV. STAT. §. 501.020 (2002).

roughly equates to the *mens rea* of "purposely" and general intent to the *mens rea* of "knowingly."

C. Transferred Intent

One other concept important to criminal *mens rea* is the principle of **transferred intent**. Under the common law and most modern applications of criminal culpability, the offender is culpable to the level of his or her intent, not to the actual target of his actions.[44] This can be remembered as "bad aim" intent because the classic example is that if Defendant intends to kill Victim A, but misses and kills Victim B instead, he will be guilty of first-degree murder (for B's death) and Attempted Murder (for trying to kill A). The intent to kill was transferred to the actual victim. Arson is another crime where one might see the applicability of transferred intent. If Offender Joe intends to burn down his mother-in-law's house but is mistaken as to the address and burns another's house instead, the crime is still arson.

This applies only within the limits of the same crime, however. For example, Defendant's intent to commit arson by burning down Victim A's house would not translate into culpability for murder if B's property was burned by mistake and B was killed during the fire (although the defendant would be guilty of arson and, perhaps, felony murder). While a defendant can be convicted when he or she has both the *mens rea* and commits the *actus reus* required for a given offense, he or she cannot be convicted if the *mens rea* relates to one crime and the *actus reus* to another. The Model Penal Code endorses the principle of transferred intent in Section 2.03(2)(a), which provides when an act purposely causes a particular result, that element is established if the actual result differs only in that a different person or different property is harmed.

The defendant will only be culpable to the extent of his original intent. Thus, for instance, if he drunkenly intends to push (assault) Victim A, but mistakenly pushes Victim B instead and B falls down, hits his head, and dies, then the death is still only manslaughter—not homicide. The drafters of the Model Penal Code, in providing for this principle, included a provision that the elements of "purposely" or "knowingly" causing a particular result are not established when the actual result is not within the original purpose or contemplation of the actor.[45]

D. Summary

Mens rea can be defined as criminal state of mind. It is not just intent, although that is one level of *mens rea*. The four different levels of criminal states of mind that are recognized in the Model Penal Code and many state criminal codes are *purposely*, *knowingly*, *recklessly*, and *negligently*. The level of *mens rea* is related to the seriousness of the crime and the degree of punishment. Although we hold negligent offenders responsible for their actions, we do not believe they are as culpable as those who

---

[44]   People v. Scott, 927 P.2d 238 (1996).

[45]   See MODEL PENAL CODE § 2.03 (1985), and the other included exceptions.

commit their crime with premeditation. Specific intent can be roughly equated to *purposely*, and general intent can be roughly equated to *knowingly*. Transferred intent is a doctrine whereby the offender is charged with the crime that he intended regardless of who is actually harmed.

§ 2.6 Causation

Recall the equation that identifies the elements of any crime (*Actus Reus + Mens Rea + Causation + Concurrence = Crime*). We have discussed the criminal act (*actus reus*), and the requisite mental state (*mens rea*). Now we will turn our attention to causation. In order for one who is accused of a crime to be convicted of that crime, the prosecution must show that the act of the defendant constituted a substantial factor in bringing about the result. Those who wrote the Model Penal Code and those who have drafted federal and state legislation have faced a difficult problem of defining causation. The following provision is included in the Model Penal Code.[46]

> § 2.03 Causal Relationship Between Conduct and Result; Divergence Between Result Designed or Contemplated and Actual Result, or Between Probable and Actual Result
>
> (1) Conduct is the cause of a result when:
>   (a) it is an antecedent but for which the result in question would not have occurred; and
>   (b) the relationship between the conduct and result satisfied any additional causal requirements imposed by the Code or by the law defining the offense.

A. Proximate Causation

In order for a person to be guilty of a crime, his or her act or omission (performed with the requisite mental state) must have *caused* the result that creates the crime. On the other hand, the law does not hold one liable for everything that happens as a result of one's actions. The concept of "**proximate causation**" is a common sense approach to cut off liability even though one's actions may have actually caused the result or contributed to the result.

A person's action will be defined as the proximate cause of the result when there are no intervening superseding factors that come between the actions and the end result. Intervening and superseding factors are defined as those that are *unforeseeable* or *unnatural*, and will break the causal chain. If the intervening factors are *foreseeable* or *natural*, then the causal chain is not broken.

In most situations, events that can naturally occur as a result of the defendant's actions will not break the causal chain. For example, where the defendant struck

---

[46] MODEL PENAL CODE § 2.03(1) (1985).

the deceased, who was a hemophiliac, once on the jaw with his fist, which resulted in a hemorrhage from which the deceased died 10 days later, the defendant was properly convicted of manslaughter.[47] The court in *State v. Frazier* explained that it is immaterial that the defendant did not know that the deceased was in a feeble condition, or that he did not reasonably anticipate that the result would be death. This conclusion stems from a legal doctrine that the offender "takes his victim as he finds him"—meaning that if the victim is a hemophiliac and bleeds to death from a cut or hit that would not have killed another person it is still a natural result or if the victim has a "glass jaw" and is seriously injured from a blow that would not have harmed another, it is still a natural result of the assault. The defendant is legally culpable even when the victim does not care for himself and may contribute to his own death, for instance, when a victim refuses medical assistance and, because of the refusal, dies.

In the following situations, the defendant's actions were considered to be the proximate cause of the resulting death:

- The defendant struck the victim, knocking him unconscious, and while unconscious, the victim vomited and choked to death.[48]
- The defendant wounded the victim and, after he was taken to the hospital, the victim pulled out supporting tubes while he was in a semiconscious condition.[49]
- The defendant inflicted knife wounds on the victim who ultimately died from a pulmonary embolism.[50]

On the other hand, if there is a **superseding intervening factor**—an independent act or occurrence that supersedes the defendant's act as the legally significant causal factor—the defendant's conduct will not be the legal cause of the result. To constitute a superseding cause, the independent occurrence must be

- intervening,
- unforeseeable (or unnatural), and
- the sole direct cause of the result.

In general, whether something is considered unforeseeable or unnatural relates to the likelihood of it happening as well as whether it is an intentional or volitional act of another. For instance, consider the following two situations:

- A defendant shoots a victim who is taken to the hospital, contracts an infection during surgery, and dies.
- A defendant shoots a victim who is taken to the hospital and is killed by a homicidal nurse.

---

[47] State v. Frazier, 339 Mo. 966, 98 S.W.2d 707 (1936).
[48] People v. Geiger, 10 Mich. App. 339, 159 N.W.2d 383 (1968).
[49] United States v. Hamilton, 182 F. Supp. 548 (D.D.C. 1960).
[50] Pittman v. State, 528 N.E.2d 67 (Ind. 1988).

In both situations, one could say that the defendant's actions "caused" the death of the victim because the victim would not have been in the hospital *but for* the acts of the defendant. However, the second situation is an example of when a superseding intervening cause breaks the causal chain for the defendant. The defendant is still guilty of aggravated assault or attempted murder, but not homicide because the homicidal nurse is an unforeseeable, unnatural intervening event. Part of the reason this case is considered one of superseding intervening factors is that the acts of the nurse are the volitional acts of a third party that the defendant in no way controls. Case decisions in this area are not always consistent. What some courts may find to be superseding intervening factors may be considered foreseeable and natural by other courts.

In one case, a victim is taken to a hospital after being injured by the defendant, and the injury would not normally be serious, but the victim contracts scarlet fever from a doctor and dies of the disease.[51] In this case, the court ruled that injury was not the proximate cause of death; however, other courts have held that any fatal infection or disease acquired in a hospital where the victim is taken after an assault will *not* break the causal chain.

In another case, the defendant, who had stolen a car, led the police on a high-speed car chase and two police helicopters collided due to the careless action of one of the pilots.[52] The court ruled that the defendant's actions were the proximate cause of the subsequent deaths of police officers. In this case, even though there was evidence that one of the helicopter pilots operated the helicopter improperly, the court held that the driver's actions contributed more substantially to the end result. In general, offenders who engage in high-speed car chases with police are held criminally culpable for any accidental deaths that occur as a result of the chase.[53]

Case decisions have held that intentional or criminally negligent actions on the part of a third actor *will* break the causal chain. The central question is foreseeability. In referring to the intervening cause principle, the court explained

> An independent intervening variable will not be superseding in three instances: (1) where it is merely a contributing cause to the defendant's direct cause; (2) where the result was intended; or (3) where the resulting harm was reasonably foreseeable when the act was done. ... As to the third exception, the consequence need not have been a strong probability; a possible consequence which might reasonably have been contemplated is enough. ... The precise consequence need not have been foreseen; it is enough that the defendant should have foreseen the possibility of some harm of the kind which might result from his act.[54]

---

[51] Bush v. Commonwealth, 78 Ky. 268 (1880).

[52] People v. Acosta, 284 Cal. Rptr. 117 (Cal. Ct. App. 1991). *See also* Ewing v. State, 719 N.E.2d 1221 (Ind. 1999).

[53] *See* People v. Harris, 52 Cal. App. 3d 419, 125 Cal. Rptr. 40 (1975), in which the Court of Appeals reversed the dismissal of a vehicular manslaughter prosecution in a case in which a police car pursuing a defendant in a high-speed chase collided with another vehicle, killing one of its passengers. *See also* People v. Pike, 197 Cal. App. 3d 732, 243 Cal. Rptr. 54 (1988), in which the Court of Appeals affirmed a vehicular manslaughter conviction that arose when two police cars pursuing the defendant in a high-speed chase collided, resulting in the death of one of the officers.

[54] People v. Acosta, 284 Cal. Rptr. 117, 137 (Cal. Ct. App. 1991).

B. Summary

The main thing to remember about causation is that the law is only concerned with "proximate causation" or legal causation. This is when there is no break in the causal chain between the offender's action and the result. If there is a superseding intervening factor, then the causal chain is broken and the offender is not responsible for the ultimate result (although he would still be responsible for his action). It helps to think of it as a time line:

Offender's action > events that are foreseeable and/or natural > result = proximate causation/culpable

Offender's action > events that are unforeseeable and/or unnatural > result = not proximate/not culpable

§ 2.7 Concurrence—Criminal Act and State of Mind

We will now turn to "**concurrence**," the last element in the crime equation. Although this principle is not as well known, and becomes an issue in relatively few cases, it should be mentioned. If the crime is one that requires a particular *mens rea*, such as intent, knowledge, or negligence, in addition to the act or omission, the physical act and the state of mind must occur at the same time. For example, in some states, the crime of first-degree burglary is committed when the person "*knowingly* enters or remains unlawfully in a dwelling *with the intent* to commit a crime." Under the principle of concurrence, the *intent* to steal must be concurrent with the *act* of entry or with unlawfully remaining in the dwelling.[55] If the intent to steal does not exist at the time of the entry, then burglary has not occurred. In criminal law, the intent will not relate to the entry. Of course, the person might be found guilty of breaking and entering if one cannot prove the elements of burglary.

Consider this example: A is planning to murder B, a business partner. He has bought a gun, identified where and when would be the best time to ambush B without getting caught, and has even planned which day to do the crime. While driving to the location of his planned crime, he uses his cell phone to send a text message to B to make sure B is there. While looking down to text, ironically, he runs over B killing him. Is he guilty of first-degree murder? He had the intent to kill and his actions resulted in the death of B, but there was no concurrence between his *mens rea* and his *actus reus*. He might be charged with some form of negligent manslaughter or vehicular manslaughter, but, even though he had intent to murder, it must be concurrent with the act to constitute first-degree murder.

---

[55] Jackson v. State, 102 Ala. 167, 15 So. 344 (1894).

§ 2.8   Attendant Circumstances

Before concluding this discussion of the principles of criminal liability, mention must be made of the fact that, in some crimes, proof must be offered to show that certain circumstances existed at the time of the act in question. For example, the common law crime of burglary requires that the entry be made at night, the crime of receiving stolen property requires that the goods received be stolen goods, and bigamy requires proof of a previous marriage. Also, statutory rape requires that the victim be underage, and perjury requires that the person be sworn. In these cases, evidence must be offered to prove that certain circumstances specified by the criminal statute existed at the time the act occurred. Thus, evidence must be introduced in a statutory rape case to show that the victim was under the statutory age. Further, all states have adopted "threshold" dollar levels in theft statutes delineating the line between felonies and misdemeanors, and these dollar figures must be proven. In many instances, these attendant circumstances are listed as elements of the crime.

§ 2.9   Strict Liability

As indicated in § 2.5, *mens rea* (i.e., purposeful, knowing, reckless, or negligent) is considered an essential element of any crime. However, **strict liability** crimes do not require any level of *mens rea*. The legislature may either forbid or require an act without regard to the mental state of the actor. The following provision describing this type of liability is from the Model Penal Code.[56]

§ 2.05 When Culpability Requirements Are Inapplicable to Violations and to Offenses Defined by Other Statutes; Effect of Absolute Liability in Reducing Grade of Offenses to Violation

(1) The requirements of culpability prescribed by §§ 2.01 and 2.02 do not apply to:
    (a) offenses which constitute violations, unless the requirement involved is included in the definition of the offense or the Court determines that its application is consistent with effective enforcement of the law defining the offense; or
    (b) offenses defined by statutes other than the Code, insofar as a legislative purpose to impose absolute liability for such offenses or with respect to any material element thereof plainly appears.
(2) Notwithstanding any other provision of existing law and unless a subsequent statute otherwise provides:
    (a) when absolute liability is imposed with respect to any material element of an offense defined by a statute other than the Code and a conviction is based upon such liability, the offense constitutes a violation; and
    (b) although absolute liability is imposed by law with respect to one or more of the material elements of an offense defined by a statute other than the Code, the culpable commission of the offense may be charged and proved, in which event negligence with respect to such elements constitutes

---

[56]   *See generally* MODEL PENAL CODE §§ 2.01, 2.02, 2.05 (1985).

> sufficient culpability and the classification of the offense and the sentence that may be imposed therefore upon conviction are determined by § 1.04 and Article 6 of the Code.

The rationale for strict liability crimes is that, if the prosecution were required to prove the mental element, convictions would be so difficult to achieve that the existence of the criminal statute would not deter the conduct. The legislature might reason that it is important to reduce harmful conduct at all costs, even at the risk of convicting innocent-minded persons as a result. The actor may be criminally liable even though he or she does not know the act is criminal or even does not know that the law exists.[57]

Although such liability is usually limited to the so-called "regulatory" or "public welfare offenses" or to violations that carry only a relatively small penalty and do not involve moral stigma, the rationale for not requiring criminal intent has been held to apply in some *mala in se* crimes. The crimes of bigamy and statutory rape are the classic examples of traditional crimes that incorporate an element of strict liability. In some states, a person can be convicted of bigamy even though that person reasonably believed that he or she was unmarried at the time of the second marriage.[58] Also, a man can be convicted of statutory rape even though he reasonably believed the female with whom he had intercourse was above the age of consent.[59]

The courts have been more likely to find strict liability in narcotics cases. For example, in the case of *State v. Hermann*, a Wisconsin court found that the state is not required to prove that the defendant, charged with an illegal drug transaction, knew that he was within 1,000 feet of a school when committing the felony in order for the defendant to be sentenced to the mandatory minimum prison term of at least three years. Referring to the purpose of the statute, the court explained, "When the legislature's primary goal is to regulate, to accomplish a social good, or to obtain a high standard of care, proof of a criminal state of mind often is eliminated to achieve the desired result."[60] The court reasoned that, because the statute was designed to deter drug distribution in and around schools, even the potential for a lengthy incarceration does not make a strict liability statute unconstitutional. New Jersey and other states have statutes that holds individuals responsible for deaths that occur when the death is the direct result of ingesting a dangerous controlled substance manufactured or distributed by the defendant.[61] The defendant is strictly liable and does not need any *mens rea* in regard to the death, only the drug crime. In *Dean v. United States*, the case included for this chapter in Part II, the issue is sentencing rather than criminal culpability for a crime, but the discussion is

---

[57] Landen v. United States, 299 F. 75 (6th Cir. 1924); United States v. Park, 499 F.2d 839 (4th Cir. 1974).
[58] People v. Vogel, 46 Cal. 2d 798, 299 P.2d 850 (1956).
[59] State v. Superior Court, 104 Ariz. 440, 454 P.2d 982 (1969).
[60] State v. Hermann, 474 N.W.2d 906 (Wis. 1991).
[61] N.J. GEN. STAT. Ch. 35 § 9.

enlightening as to the Supreme Court's views on the relationship between intent and strict liability.

Generally, when an offense is *mala prohibita*, the courts find little problem with enforcing the statute when intent or knowledge are not required. On the other hand, courts have had some difficulty with statutory crimes when the penalty was more severe. For instance, in *Lambert v. California*,[62] the Supreme Court overturned the defendant's conviction under a California statute that required convicted felons to register. As written, the failure to register was a strict liability crime; however, the Supreme Court held that "fair notice" demanded at least a warning to show some level of *mens rea* because the failure to know of the requirement was not unreasonable.

> **CASE NOTE:** *Dean v. United States*, 556 U.S. ___ (2009)
> What was the holding of the Court?
> What was the appellant's argument as to why Dean should not have been given the 10-year sentence for discharge of a firearm?
> What were the two arguments in the dissent as to why the Court should not interpret the sentencing statute to include strict liability in the discharge of a firearm?

Where the criminal statutes do not specify any level of *mens rea*, the courts have sometimes held that the statute means what it says and impose criminal liability with no proof of any level of *mens rea*. On the other hand, in some instances, the courts have read into the statutes some requirements of *mens rea*. In reaching a compromise on the issue, the Model Penal Code provides that culpability is an element of all offenses, except in specific classes of crimes.[63] Under the Model Penal Code, the maximum penalty for violation of a strict liability crime is a fine. State statutes will designate the requirements for criminal liability. For example, the Ohio Criminal Code provides

> When the section defining an offense does not specify any degree of culpability, and plainly indicates a purpose to impose strict criminal liability for the conduct described in such sections, then culpability is not required for a person to be guilty of the offense. When the section neither specifies culpability nor plainly indicates a purpose to impose strict liability, recklessness is sufficient culpability to commit the offense.[64]

§ 2.10　Vicarious Liability

In previous sections, it was noted that, in order for a crime to be committed, there must be a concurrence of *actus reus* and *mens rea*. In Section 2.9, which discusses the strict liability exception, it was pointed out that, in a few crimes, a person may be held liable without any *mens rea*. There are other crimes that do not require the *actus reus* OR the *mens rea*. **Vicarious liability** is liability for crimes committed by another person, imposed simply because of the relationship between the parties. It is unnecessary

---

[62]　355 U.S. 225 (1957).
[63]　*See* MODEL PENAL CODE §§ 2.02(1), 2.05 (1985).
[64]　OHIO REV. CODE ANN. § 2901.21(B) (Anderson 2002).

to show that the defendant acted in any way or participated in the offense; it need only be established that the crime was committed by another person and that the defendant stood in the required relationship as stated by statute.

In most instances, vicarious liability applies when one conducting a business is made liable without personal fault for the conduct of someone else, generally an employee. For example, some criminal statutes specifically impose criminal liability upon the employer if his or her agent sells articles at short weight. Some statutes provide that persons under the age of 14 shall not be employed at certain jobs.[65] These statutes are generally misdemeanor in character, and are construed to impose vicarious liability upon the employer even though the employer was not aware that his or her agent acted in violation of the statute. Statutes imposing criminal liability upon an innocent employer for the illegal conduct of his or her employee are generally upheld as constitutional.[66] In *United States v. Park*, for example, the president of a corporation was held criminally liable for the actions of his employees, who allowed food to be stored in a warehouse contaminated by rats.[67] However, if the statute, as interpreted, imposes a jail sentence as well as a fine, there is a good possibility that the courts will find that this violates due process guarantees.[68]

LEGAL NEWS: BAR OWNERS CRIMINALLY LIABLE

In April 2011, the owner of a Pennsylvania bar pled guilty to reckless endangerment. The charge stemmed from an incident three years earlier when a young woman was served alcohol while visibly intoxicated and then was escorted to her car by the bar's bouncer. She crashed the car, killing herself and two passengers. The bar's owner was vicariously liable for the actions of the bartender and bouncer because of failing to properly train employees.

Retrieved December 20, 2011 from http://www.abc27.com/story/14411448/middletown-tavern-owners-ordered-to-pay-12500-in-crash-that-killed-3.

Some cities have passed ordinances and states have statutes that hold parents responsible for the criminal acts of their children. Of course, parents are civilly responsible for their children's torts, but these statutes make them criminally responsible as well. For instance, a Salt Lake city ordinance holds parents responsible for failure to control their children when the child becomes involved in the juvenile system. The parent may be

---

[65]   KY. REV. STAT. § 339.220 (2001).
[66]   In re Marley, 29 Cal. 2d 525, 175 P.2d 832 (Cal. Ct. App. 1946).
[67]   United States v. Park, 421 U.S. 658 (1975).
[68]   Pennsylvania v. Koczwara, 397 Pa. 575, 155 A.2d 825 (1959).

sentenced to counseling or community service.[69] California's statute was passed as an anti-gang statute, and holds parents responsible when they do not "exercise reasonable care, supervision, protection, and control" over their children. Parents can be fined or even jailed for the offense. The statute was upheld by the California Supreme Court against a challenge that it was vague and intruded on family privacy rights.[70] Other laws hold parents responsible when their child uses a gun that they did not secure in a way that made it inaccessible. In general, parental responsibility laws are acceptable as long as the punishment is reasonable and there is evidence of negligent supervision.

§ 2.11   Lesser Included Offenses

All states and the federal courts adhere to the concept that defendants may be convicted of "lesser included offenses." That is, when a defendant has been charged with the crime of "X," consisting of elements A, B, and C, a verdict of guilty may be returned for the crime of "Y" as long as all of the elements of "Y" are included within the original crime charged. In this example, because the crime of "X" consists of the elements of A, B, and C, the defendant could be found guilty of any "lesser included offense" that consisted of any combination of these elements (A and B, A and C, or B and C). Specific examples of lesser included offenses are (1) manslaughter, a lesser included offense of murder in that all the elements of manslaughter are included within the elements of murder, and (2) trespass, a lesser included offense of burglary in that burglary contains all the elements of trespass (plus other elements).[71]

If a defendant is convicted of a crime of a higher degree, that defendant cannot be convicted of a lesser included offense arising from the same act or omission. Applying this principle, a New York court held that where the defendant was convicted of criminal possession of a controlled substance in the third and fourth degrees, his conviction of criminal possession of a controlled substance in the seventh degree, based upon possession of the same cocaine, had to be reversed.[72]

§ 2.12   Summary

At common law, and by statute in some states, participants in crimes are either principals or accessories. Principals are further divided into principals in the first degree and principals in the second degree. A principal in the first degree is one who

---

[69]   Salt Lake City Ordinance 11.60.020-060.

[70]   *Gang Member's Mother Denies 'Failure' Charge*, L.A. TIMES, May 20, 1989, at 2. Adam Culbreath, *Parental Liability Law Upheld in California*, YOUTH LAW NEWS, Sept.-Oct. 1993, at 12.

[71]   For a discussion of the laws regarding lesser included offenses, *see* United States v. Quintero, 21 F.3d 885 (9th Cir. 1994) and United States v. Browner, 889 F.2d 549 (5th Cir. 1989).

[72]   People v. Jones, 680 N.Y.S.2d 764 (App. Div. 1998).

actually commits the act that causes the crime to occur, while a principal in the second degree does not actually commit the crime, but instead aids or encourages the principal party to commit the crime, and is present at the scene.

An accessory also may be guilty of a criminal offense even though he or she did not actually participate in the crime and was not present when the crime occurred. Accessories are categorized as accessories before the fact and accessories after the fact. An accessory before the fact is one who counsels, procures, or commands the principal to commit a criminal act, but who is too far away to aid in the act. An accessory after the fact is one who gives comfort or assists another, after the crime has occurred, knowing that the other has committed a felony, in order to hinder the perpetrator's apprehension, prosecution, or conviction.

Most modern statutes and the Model Penal Code dispense with the distinctions between principals and accessories, and hold persons legally accountable if they commit the act, solicit the commission of offense, aid in commission, or, in some instances, fail to take proper efforts to prevent it. Modern statutes do distinguish the accessory after the fact and treat the crime as a lesser offense.

In order for a person to be convicted of a crime, the prosecution must show that the person charged committed a prohibited act or failed to act when he or she had the legal obligation to do so. This principle, referred to as *actus reus*, may involve an actual physical movement or may consist of verbal acts. However, one cannot be punished for evil intent without an act, nor for a violation of a statute that makes status alone a violation. Although in the usual case an affirmative act is required to support a conviction, in some instances, liability can rest upon the failure to act if there was a legal responsibility to do so through statute, relationship, contract or continuance of care obligations.

The second requirement for conviction of a crime is that the act, except as otherwise provided by statute, must be accompanied by a criminal state of mind (i.e., purposeful, knowing, reckless, or negligent). This criminal state of mind is referred to as *mens rea*.

The third requirement is that the alleged unlawful act or omission must be so integrated with and related to the ultimate result that it can be said to have proximately caused the result. In other words, the prosecution must show that the conduct was the proximate cause of the crime. Finally, the physical act and state of mind must be in concurrence. That is, the prosecution must show that the intent or *mens rea* existed at the time the act was perpetrated.

There are a few crimes that do not require all of the elements discussed above. In strict liability crimes, *mens rea* is not required. In "vicarious liability" crimes, there is no requirement for either *mens rea* or *actus reus* because this type of liability occurs through a relationship with others who do prohibited acts. For instance, a business owner may be liable for the conduct of someone else, generally an employee. These statutes have been upheld, because the penalty is a fine rather than a jail sentence.

REVIEW QUESTIONS

1. List and define the four different parties to a crime under common law.
2. Explain the two parties recognized by the Model Penal Code.
3. Explain the changes that were made in accomplice liability in the MPC from common law (hint: foreseeable acts and convicted principals).
4. Describe criminal facilitation statutes and why they were created.
5. Describe the elements of *actus reus* (i.e., voluntariness, status).
6. What were the holdings of *Robinson v. California* and *Powell v. Texas*?
7. Explain how words and possession can form the *actus reus* of a crime.
8. Describe when an omission can form the basis of liability (mention the four types of duty and provide examples).
9. Describe Good Samaritan laws.
10. Describe "filial responsibility" laws.
11. Explain the importance of knowledge and impossibility in relation to liability for an omission.
12. Describe the four levels of *mens rea* under the Model Penal Code.
13. Distinguish between specific intent and general intent.
14. Explain the doctrine of transferred intent.
15. Describe the concept of proximate causation. When is culpability cut off even though the defendant's act was the "but for" cause of the ultimate result?
16. Explain the concept of concurrence.
17. Define "attendant circumstances" and provide examples.
18. Explain the concept of strict liability.
19. Explain the concept of vicarious liability.
20. List and define all five elements necessary for any crime.

Capacity and Defenses

3

Chapter Outline

Cases

Infancy (Juvenile Culpability): *Graham v. Florida*, 560 U.S. __ (2010)
Test of Insanity: *Clark v. Arizona*, 548 U.S. 735 (2006)

§ 3.1   Introduction

One purpose of criminal law is to establish and define standards of human conduct. A general legal principle is that all persons have the power to choose between right and wrong and to do or refrain from doing that which the law commands. Notwithstanding this general principle, courts in England and other countries recognized early that there are situations in which persons, for one reason or another, do not have the capacity to distinguish between right and wrong, or do not have the capacity to form the mental intent that may be required as an element of some crimes. There are generally "classes" of people who cannot, by definition, form the necessary criminal intent; for instance, infants or the insane. There are others who, while not a member of an "incompetent" class, may experience circumstances such that they should not be held responsible for their actions.

In this chapter, most of the common defenses claimed by defendants who are accused of crime are considered. They include incapacity to commit crimes due to infancy or mental impairment, duress or compulsion, necessity, defense of self or others, entrapment, alibi, ignorance or mistake, statute of limitation defenses, and others.

§ 3.2   Infancy or Immaturity

A crime is not committed if the mind of the person doing the act is incapable of forming a culpable *mens rea*; therefore, an infant is exempt from criminal responsibility for his or her acts if sufficient mental capacity is lacking. **Infancy**, in this case, means only that the child does not have the capacity to determine right and wrong; the age of infancy is set by case law or statute.

A. Common Law

At common law, a child under the age of 7 was conclusively presumed to be incapable of having the necessary criminal intent and could not commit a crime. Even if the child confessed to the act, and even if the state introduced evidence to indicate that the child knew the difference between right and wrong, there could be no conviction for that crime. A child between the ages of 7 and 14 was *presumed* not to have the capacity to commit the crime; however, the presumption was rebuttable. That is, the prosecution could introduce evidence to show that, in fact, the child did possess the necessary mental capacity to entertain the criminal intent.[1]

The common law definitions and distinctions are still followed in a few states and have had a significant bearing on statutes in other states. Today, most state statutes have specifically defined the jurisdiction of juvenile courts and detailed the procedures necessary to "waive" jurisdiction to adult courts.

B. Model Penal Code

The Model Penal Code establishes the age at which the juvenile court shall have exclusive jurisdiction and briefly states the procedure to be followed in transferring a case from the juvenile court to the criminal court. Section 4.10 of the Model Penal Code provides

§ 4.10 Immaturity Excluding Criminal Conviction; Transfer of Proceedings to Juvenile Court[2]

(1) A person shall not be tried for or convicted of an offense if:
  (a) at the time of the conduct charged to constitute the offense he was less than sixteen years of age, in which case the juvenile court shall have exclusive jurisdiction; or
  (b) at the time of the conduct charged to constitute the offense he was sixteen or seventeen years of age, unless:
    (i) the Juvenile Court has no jurisdiction over him or
    (ii) the Juvenile Court has entered an order waiving jurisdiction and consenting to the institution of criminal proceedings against him.

This section proposes that no one less than 16 years old at the time of the alleged offense may be tried for or convicted of the offense in criminal court. However, if the juvenile was 16 or more years of age, but less than 18 at the time of the offense, the juvenile court, after a hearing, may enter an order waiving jurisdiction and the case will be transferred to adult criminal court.

C. State Statutes, Codes, and Cases

Under the laws that exist in most states today, infancy is a defense. Juveniles may avail themselves of the infancy defense and come under the jurisdiction of the juvenile court in most instances. However, there is no recognized constitutional right to be

---

[1]   Angelo v. People, 96 Ill. 209 (1880).
[2]   MODEL PENAL CODE § 4.10 (1985).

treated as a juvenile. That right is granted by the legislature, which may restrict or qualify that right as it sees fit, as long as no arbitrary or discriminatory classification is involved.[3]

At present, all states have established juvenile court systems that deal with juveniles who have been charged with criminal violations. However, even in states that have enacted juvenile justice laws, the question of capacity is often raised. For example, in the case of *State v. Q.D.,*[4] the Supreme Court of Washington was called upon to determine whether the state statutory presumption of infant incapacity applied in juvenile proceedings. A Washington statute provides, in part:

> Children under the age of 8 are incapable of committing crime. Children of 8 and under 12 years of age are presumed to be incapable of committing crime, but this presumption may be removed by proof that they have sufficient capacity to understand the act or neglect and to know that it was wrong.[5]

In the majority of states, criminal acts committed by juveniles are generally adjudicated in juvenile court. Exceptions, however, are made when certain more serious crimes are committed, in which case the juvenile court may waive jurisdiction. In some states, certain crimes are statutorily diverted to adult courts, even when committed by juveniles. Statutory diversion is becoming more common than waivers.

In 2010, the Supreme Court heard the case *Graham v. Florida*, excerpted in Part II of this text. In this case, the issue of whether or not juveniles should be subject to life without parole was addressed, not whether or not youthfulness negated culpability for a particular crime. The case is included here, however, to show how the Supreme Court majority views the diminished culpability of juveniles for their crime. It is instructive to note how the Court looks to emerging psychological and biological findings regarding brain development to determine principles of law.

D. Summary

Under the common law and under state statutes in all 50 states, infancy may be a defense to criminal culpability. In common law and in most states today, there is an age under which a child is believed to be incapable of forming criminal intent, which is usually around age 7 or 8. There is also an age range where the presumption

CASE NOTE
Graham v. Florida
560 U.S. __ (2010)

What was the holding of the Supreme Court?
Explain why the Court felt a life without parole sentence met the definition of cruel and unusual.
Did international opinion influence the Court's decision? If so, how?

---

[3]   Miles v. State, 594 A.2d 1208 (Md. Ct. App. 1991).
[4]   State v. Q.D., 685 P.2d 557 (Wash. 1984).
[5]   REV. CODE WASH. § 9A.04.050.

of incompetence is rebuttable, that is, the state may show (by clear and convincing evidence) that the child knows right from wrong and can understand the proceedings. In these cases, the child may be held responsible for their actions. Juvenile court may adjudicate proceedings against children who are found competent, or the case may be transferred to adult court, depending on the statutory authority of the state. Current cases indicate that courts continue to be persuaded that juveniles must be treated differently from adults under the law in that they are less culpable and more amenable to reform.

§ 3.3   Mental Impairment or Insanity

In some criminal cases, the defendant claims that he is entitled to an acquittal because at the time of the crime he was so impaired by mental illness as to be "insane" within the meaning of the criminal law definition. **Insanity** is a legal term, not a medical term. It refers to any mental illness that meets the legal threshold for incapacity. Mental incapacity or insanity may be used by one accused of crimes at several points in the criminal process. The following describe the various ways mental incapacity may become an issue in a criminal proceeding.

- "Competency": Mental incapacity may be used to argue **incompetency** to stand trial; specifically, that the defendant's mental state is such that he is unable to understand the proceedings against him or help in his own defense.
- "Insanity": Insanity is a type of mental incapacity; specifically, that the defendant's mental state was such at the time of the crime that he should not be held responsible for his crime. Insanity and incompetency to stand trial are different findings and the standards for determining each are different.[6]
- "Diminished capacity/responsibility": The defendant's mental state at the time of the crime (or at the time of sentencing) may be taken into consideration even though the legal standard of insanity was not reached.

LEGAL NEWS: INCOMPETENT TO STAND TRIAL

In January 2011 the nation was horrified when Jared Lee Loughner opened fire in a crowd gathered to hear Representative Gabrielle Giffords in Phoenix, Arizona. He was quickly identified and caught. The total death toll was 6 with another 13 injured, including Representative Giffords. He was charged with 49 crimes in

---

[6]   United States v. Santos, 131 F.3d 16 (1st Cir. 1997), which held that the standards of competency and insanity are different and the finding of competency to stand trial is not prejudicial to an insanity defense or admissible at the trial.

relation to the incident. In May of 2011, he was declared unfit to stand trial by a federal judge. He will undergo months of intensive therapy with the goal to bring him to a level of mental competence to stand trial. Until that occurs, he will be held in a mental facility.

Retrieved December 21, 2011 from http://www.outsidethebeltway.com/jared-lee-loughner-gabrielle-giffords-shooter-unfit-to-stand-trial/.

A. *Common Law*

The practice of recognizing the defense of mental impairment is long-standing and was present in common law rulings. Basically, courts held that if the defendant had no understanding or memory to know what he was doing was wrong, he was like an infant or wild beast and, therefore, not culpable. Most authorities indicate that the modern insanity defense began with the *M'Naghten* case.[7] In this case, Daniel M'Naghten was charged with murder. The facts indicate that M'Naghten suffered delusions that he was being persecuted by the Prime Minister of Great Britain, Sir Robert Peel. On January 20, 1843, M'Naghten shot and killed Peel's assistant, Edward Drummond, believing him to be Peel. At the trial, the medical evidence showed that M'Naghten was in a seriously disordered medical condition at the time of the incident. The jury returned a verdict of not guilty after being instructed to convict if the defendant was in a sound state of mind at the time, but that he would be entitled to a verdict in his favor if he "had not the use of his understanding so as to know he was doing a wrong or wicked act." The resulting uproar led the House of Lords to inquire of the 15 judges of the Queen's Bench as to the proper test to be applied in such cases.[8]

The doctrine announced by Lord Chief Justice Tindal of the Common Pleas Court had three important aspects and thus the court's declaration is properly labeled *M'Naghten's* **Rules**. First, and most importantly, the general rule was set down that a jury should acquit a defendant if it found that the accused "was laboring under such a defect of reason, from disease of the mind, as not to know the nature and quality of the act he was doing, or, if he did know it, that he did not know he was doing what was wrong." Second, the judges also addressed the issue of partial insanity, the situation in which a person, otherwise sane, is laboring under some insane delusion involving the situation in question. In such a case of "partial delusion," the judges declared, acquittal would depend upon whether the act would

---

[7]　Smith, *Insanity Plea in Mississippi*, 10 MISS. C. L. REV. 147 (1990).

[8]　M'Naghten's Case, 8 Eng. Rep. 718 (1843), discussed in Leland v. Oregon, 343 U.S. 790, 725 S. Ct. 1002, 966 L. Ed. 1302 (1952).

have been right if the situation had actually been as the person believed it to be. Third, the judges opined that a "medical man" might, in some cases, give his opinion to the jury as to the state of the accused's mind at the time of the offense.

M'Naghten's Rules were quickly adopted throughout Anglo-American jurisdictions, and the so-called "right and wrong test" became the bedrock of the insanity defense. This test has been and still is followed in many jurisdictions. Briefly stated, the test asks "Was the defendant, at the time of committing the act, laboring under such a defect of reason, from disease of the mind, as not to know the nature and quality of the act he was doing; or, if he did know it, he did not know what he was doing was wrong?"

B. Model Penal Code

The drafters of the Model Penal Code prepared the following provision to address mental incapacity.

Model Penal Code § 4.01[9]

(1) A person is not responsible for criminal conduct if at the time of such conduct as a result of mental disease or defect he lacks substantial capacity either to appreciate the criminality of his conduct or to conform his conduct to the requirements of the law.
(2) The terms "mental disease or defect" do not include an abnormality manifested only by repeated criminal or otherwise antisocial conduct.
Under the provisions of the Model Code, a defendant is entitled to acquittal by reason of insanity if the evidence shows that, because of a mental disease or defect, he
(a) lacked substantial capacity to appreciate the criminality of his conduct; or
(b) lacked substantial capacity to conform his conduct to the requirements of the law.

The Model Penal Code has attempted to incorporate the various tests used by state statutes to determine whether insanity should excuse criminal conduct. Although the Model Code approach has been looked upon favorably by many jurisdictions, most states have not adopted the formula.

C. State Statutes, Codes, and Cases

Insanity is an "**affirmative defense**." In order to raise the issue, a defendant need only present evidence that is sufficient to raise a reasonable doubt as to his or her sanity before the burden of proof shifts to the state. The level of proof necessary is usually a preponderance, but some jurisdictions have raised the defendant's burden of proof to clear and convincing. If the defendant meets this burden of proof, then the burden shifts to the state and the prosecution must introduce evidence to prove sanity beyond a

---

[9] MODEL PENAL CODE § 4.01 (1985).

reasonable doubt. In the case of *State v. Doyle*, for instance, the reviewing court indicated that because the state introduced no evidence at all on the issue of sanity, it failed to meet this burden.[10]

1. Tests of Insanity

What is the modern test for "insanity"? There is considerable disagreement among the states as to what standard should be used to determine whether a mental disorder or impairment is sufficient to render the defendant legally not guilty because of insanity. States have widely varying statutes and some states have abolished the insanity defense, except as it is relevant to *mens rea*. The more common tests are discussed here.

a. M'Naghten's Rule (Right-Wrong Test)

most used ↓

This test, as described above, is often referred to as the right-wrong test and is still used in the majority of jurisdictions. To establish criminal incapacity under this test, a defendant must introduce at least some evidence to show that, as a result of his mental condition, he (a) did not know the nature and quality of his act OR (b) did not know that the act was wrong.

The more than 100-year-old *M'Naghten* Rule (referring to the first of the *M'Naghten* Rules described earlier) is criticized in modern times because psychiatrists and psychologists arguably have more to say about the defendant's mental state than can be succinctly explained by simple "yes" or "no" answers to the questions of the rule. In Minnesota, for instance, where the *M'Naghten* Rule is followed, the court held that the *M'Naghten* insanity defense did not require consideration of the defendant's volition and capacity to control behavior.[11] Because of the difficulty in applying the *M'Naghten* Rule, other rules have developed in the United States.

b. Irresistible Impulse Rule

The **irresistible impulse rule** was added to the right-wrong test in some states, but has been rejected in most states and in England and Canada. In states where this rule is followed, it is added to the basic *M'Naghten* test. The theory is that if a person acts under an irresistible impulse, from disease of the mind, he is incapable of restraining himself, though he may know that he is doing wrong.[12] To state this differently, a person may know, at the time the act was committed, the nature and quality of the act he was doing, and (or) that what he was doing was wrong, but because of a mental disease, he may have lost power to choose between right and wrong and to avoid doing the act.[13] In another case, the court made this point about the irresistible impulse rule:

---

[10]   State v. Doyle, 117 Ariz. 349, 572 P.2d 1187 (1977).
[11]   State v. Schreiber, 558 N.W.2d 474 (Minn. 1997).
[12]   People v. Lowhone, 292 Ill. 32, 126 N.E. 620 (1920).
[13]   Parsons v. State, 81 Ala. 577, 2 So. 854 (1887).

The jury must be satisfied that at the time of committing the act, the accused, as a result of disease of the mind:

(a) did not know the nature and quality of the act or
(b) did not know that it was wrong or
(c) was incapable of preventing himself from doing it.[14]

However, the irresistible impulse test was never adopted by a majority of states and has been rejected even by some states that had previously utilized it. One major criticism of the test is that it is hard to know whether or not the impulse was irresistible—the only thing that is known for sure is that the defendant did not resist it.

c. *Durham Rule* *least used*

In 1954, a District of Columbia court concluded that the proper solution was to discard all tests of insanity and have the jury determine (a) whether the defendant had a mental disease or defect at the time of the alleged crime and, if so, (b) whether the harmful act was the *product* of his insanity.[15] This is known as the ***Durham* Rule**. Apparently the court took the position that the right-wrong test and the irresistible impulse test had not been displaced but were merely supplemented by the "product" test, and that it was proper for the jury to be instructed as to all three.[16]

The objective of the court was to simplify the test and to make it possible to use more modern methods of determining mental impairment or disease. This rule has been criticized because it provides no criteria to guide the jury, but hands the case to them for a verdict to be returned on the basis of intuition or conjecture, rather than law.[17] Many of the critics also believe that the test is too broad and leaves too much to the jury with inadequate guidance. Today the rule has only a limited following and has, in fact, been abandoned by the District of Columbia.[18]

d. *American Law Institute (ALI) Test (Model Penal Code)*

Described earlier, this test expands the definition by allowing more testimony other than whether or not the defendant knew what he was doing or what he was doing was wrong. The test determines whether the defendant lacked "substantial capacity" to conform his behavior to the law. It allows the expert witness to discuss how the act was a product of the mental illness, and also allows for the defense of irresistible impulse. However, as stated above, it has not been adopted in the majority of jurisdictions.

---

[14]   State v. White, 58 N.M. 324, 270 P.2d 727 (1954).
[15]   Durham v. United States, 214 F.2d 862 (D.C. Cir. 1954).
[16]   Douglas v. United States, 239 F.2d 52 (D.C. Cir. 1956).
[17]   United States v. Smith, 5 C.M.A. 314, 17 C.M.R. 3 (1954).
[18]   United States v. Brawner, 471 F.2d 969 (D.C. Cir. 1972).

2. Recent Issues and Applications

Andrea Yates drowned her five children in 2001 and was convicted of second-degree murder. She pled insanity and there was ample evidence that she was mentally ill: she had been under psychiatric care and had taken antipsychotic medications in the past, and her doctor testified she suffered from extreme postpartum depression and delusions. Five different mental health experts testified she did not know right from wrong or that she thought she was doing right by sending the children to God before she ruined their chances of getting into heaven. The state's psychiatrist, however, provided testimony that she met the legal definition of sanity. Texas, like many states, has a version of the *M'Naghten* Rule. Defense attorneys agreed that she knew what she was doing when she drowned her children; however, they argued she did not know that it was wrong because she was under the delusion that she was protecting them. However, the state argued that she knew it was wrong because she called the police afterwards. Yates thought she was saving her children, but because she demonstrated knowledge of the wrongfulness of her action (by calling police), she was found sane.

Does the wrongfulness of the act refer to rational, legal knowledge, or "moral" knowledge? If someone in a delusional state thought they were saving the world by killing someone, but they knew that killing was against the law, they could be found sane, not insane, because most jurisdictions instruct the jury that the knowledge requirement relates to *legal* or *societal* definitions, not *moral* definitions. There have been some jurisdictions that allowed for an exception to this general rule when the defendant believed they were following a rule of God. The exception is consistent with the concept that the wrongfulness must be based on societal definitions arguably because the defendant would believe that God's commands would be supported by society.[19]

LEGAL NEWS: POSTPARTUM PSYCHOSIS

Andrea Yates was retried in Houston in June of 2006. Her conviction was overturned on appeal because of the testimony of a state psychiatrist that there was a *Law and Order* television program episode about a woman who drowned her baby and was acquitted. The implication of the testimony was that Yates mimicked the crime in hopes that she would be acquitted. However, there was no such television show and the psychiatrist was either mistaken or intentionally misled the jury. Without the testimony, the new jury still was faced with the difficult question of whether she was insane. They decided she was. She was sent to a mental hospital after acquittal and remains there as of 2011. Her defense attorney, George Parham, has set up a foundation to further knowledge and provide assistance to those suffering from postpartum depression.

Retrieved December 21, 2011 from http://abclocal.go.com/ktrk/story?section=news/local&id=8201721.

---

[19]　State v. Crenshaw, 659 P.2d 488 (Wash. 1983).

While most states follow, or have adapted, the *M'Naghten* Rules or the Model Penal Code, some states and the federal government have formulated alternatives. After John Hinckley attempted to assassinate Ronald Reagan in 1981 and won an acquittal by reason of insanity, Congress passed the Insanity Defense Reform Act,[20] which abolished the irresistible impulse test and increased the burden of proof on the defendant to prove insanity by "clear and convincing" evidence rather than by a preponderance of the evidence.

About 13 states now have adopted the "guilty but mentally ill" concept, which preserves the traditional insanity defense but provides an alternative to it. A jury can choose between a verdict of "not guilty by reason of insanity," which results in acquittal, or a verdict of "guilty but mentally ill," which will result in a sentence for the same term provided for a regular guilty verdict. The sentence, however, would be served in a state mental hospital.[21] Between 1979 and 1983 three states—Idaho, Montana, and Utah—passed legislation that restricted the admission of psychiatric evidence to the issue of *mens rea*, abolishing insanity as a separate affirmative defense.[22] What this means is that if the defendant knows what he is doing, whether or not they know it is wrong is irrelevant to the finding of guilt. Thus, someone who is in an active psychotic state and literally does not know that he is killing someone lacks any level of *mens rea* (purposeful, knowing, reckless, or negligent), but the defendant who kills because voices tell him to do so or a woman who kills her child because she is "saving" the infant from the Devil, will be found guilty.[23] In *Clark v. Arizona*, provided in Part II, a teenager killed a police officer, believing that he was an alien. In Arizona, he could not use mental illness to argue a lower level of *mens rea*, and a finding of insanity resulted in a "guilty but insane" verdict.

CASE NOTE: *Clark v. Arizona*, 548 U.S. 735 (2006)
What were the issues in this case?
What level of proof is necessary for the defendant to utilize the defense of insanity under Arizona's law?
What was the Supreme Court holding?

In general, these changes in statutes have been upheld against constitutional challenges. For instance, an Indiana court upheld the state statute that permits the jury to find the defendant guilty but mentally ill, agreeing that the statute did not violate the equal protection clause and the statute had a rational relationship to a legitimate state interest in securing convictions and obtaining treatment for defendants who suffer from mental illness.[24] In *Ake v. Oklahoma*, the Supreme Court held that it was "highly doubtful" that due process required a state to have the insanity defense available to criminal defendants.[25] In the case of *State v. Searcy*,

[20] 18 U.S.C.A. §17 (1988). *See* Chapter 13.
[21] 730 ILL. COMP. STAT. § 515-2 (1999); MICH. COMP. LAWS § 768.36 (1999).
[22] IDAHO CODE § 18-207 (1990); MONT. CODE ANN. § 46-14-102 (1989); UTAH CODE ANN. § 76-2-305 (1990).
[23] *See*, for instance, State v. Herrera, 895 P.2d 359 (Utah 1995).
[24] Gambill v. State, 675 N.E.2d 668 (Ind. 1997).
[25] 470 U.S. 68, 105 S.Ct. 1087, 84 L.Ed. 2d 53 (1985).

the Idaho Supreme Court upheld the constitutionality of the state statute that had abolished insanity as an affirmative defense. The court noted that previous U.S. Supreme Court cases have given the states broad discretion to determine the burden of proof to impose on the defendants raising the insanity defense.[26]

Today, very few states (Idaho, Kansas, Montana, and Utah) have completely discarded the traditional insanity defense. Even in those states, evidence of mental illness might be used to rebut the state's evidence of *mens rea* because mental illness may preclude a finding that the defendant was capable of the requisite premeditation or intent. There is considerable debate that continues over this difficult legal issue. The basic question is to what extent do we hold people responsible for their actions when it is clear that they suffer from mental disease or defect.

3. Incompetency to Stand Trial

The issue of mental impairment may first arise when determining whether the defendant is capable of making a proper defense, aiding his or her attorney, or securing evidence at the time of the trial. The test for incompetency was set forth in the case of *Dusky v. United States*, as follows:

> Whether he (accused) has sufficient present ability to consult with his lawyer with a reasonable degree of rational understanding and whether he has a rational as well as factual understanding of the proceedings against him.[27]

In the case of *Dunn v. Commonwealth*, a Kentucky court approved the test as follows:

> The test is whether he has substantial capacity to comprehend the nature and consequences of the proceeding pending against him and to participate rationally in his defense. It is not necessary that this determination be made by a jury.[28]

Although these standards are worded differently, most state requirements are basically the same—if an individual cannot help in his or her own defense, they cannot be forced to stand trial.[29] The typical result is that they are held in a mental facility until such time that they are proven competent. Case decisions have indicated that the Supreme Court continues to uphold the idea that a trial cannot proceed if the defendant is unable to understand the proceedings against him or her.[30] It is possible, however, that the defendant may be found competent to stand trial, and then, at trial, be found legally insane.

It should also be noted that there may be other reasons why a defendant is found incompetent to stand trial. The defendant may be mentally handicapped and not have sufficient cognitive abilities to understand the consequences of

---

[26] State v. Searcy, 789 P.2d 914 (Idaho 1990).
[27] Dusky v. United States, 362 U.S. 402, 80 S. Ct. 788, 4 L. Ed. 2d 824 (1960).
[28] Dunn v. Commonwealth, 573 S.W.2d 651 (Ky. 1978).
[29] Cooper v. Oklahoma, 515 U.S. 348 (1996).
[30] *Id.*

criminal prosecution. The defendant may have amnesia and may not be able to help in his or her own defense. It is also possible that the defendant is either injured or ill to the extent that they are unable to assist in their defense. In these cases, the prosecution cannot go forward.

LEGAL NEWS: ELIZABETH SMART'S CAPTOR RULED COMPETENT AND SANE

Brian David Mitchell kidnapped 14-year-old Elizabeth Smart in 2002 and held her captive for 9 months before she was rescued. He said he was a prophet and God commanded him to take her as his wife. He and his wife held the girl captive and threatened to kill her if she tried to escape. Mitchell raped her every day and Wanda Barzee, his wife, cooperated in the continued captivity. After they were caught both Mitchell and Barzee were initially determined to be incompetent to stand trial. Psychiatric testimony indicated that Mitchell was a paranoid schizophrenic who heard "revelations from God." They were held for years while the court process played out. Several subsequent hearings continued to rule that Mitchell was incompetent. In 2009, the U.S. attorney filed federal charges of kidnapping and, in a federal competency hearing, Mitchell was finally ruled competent to stand trial after a psychiatric nurse at the forensic facility where he was being held testified that she believed he was faking his symptoms, jail staff members testified he behaved normally until he was taken into the courtroom at which time he would begin to sing (eventually forcing the judge to remove him), and other experts testified that he was not psychotic or delusional. During his trial in 2010 defense attorneys sought to persuade the jury that he was insane. Psychologists and psychiatrists testified on both sides regarding his mental state and whether his revelations and religious beliefs were evidence of insanity or manipulation. The jury returned a guilty verdict and he was sentenced to life in prison. Wanda Barzee was also eventually found competent, convicted, and sentenced to 15 years.

Retrieved December 21, 2011 from http://articles.cnn.com/2010-11-20/justice/Utah-Mitchell-Defense_1_insanity-defense-insanity-claim-mental-illness?_s=PM:CRIME.

D. Diminished Capacity

When someone does not meet the test for legal insanity, it is possible that their mental state affects the level of their *mens rea*. In this case, their culpability (and capacity) is not absent, but merely diminished. Thus, it may be found that they were unable to form the intent required for specific intent crimes, or that they could not form the *mens rea* required for murder, and thus manslaughter would be the appropriate finding. Diminished capacity is not a clear concept and states have different approaches as to how it can be brought in, as well as what types of evidence can be used for proof. As you read in *Clark v. Arizona*, the state of Arizona does not allow evidence of mental illness to be used to reduce the *mens rea* of homicide from specific intent to manslaughter. Some states allow such evidence only in homicide cases, others allow it only for specific intent crimes, while other states do not allow the defense at all (i.e., Arizona, Florida, D.C.). The so-called "Twinkie Defense" was coined in the 1979 trial of Dan White, a former San Francisco county supervisor who killed Mayor George Moscone and Supervisor Harvey Milk. Some aspects of this case were shown in the 2008 movie *Milk*, which focused on one of the victims, known today for being one of the first openly gay politicians. Defense attorneys presented evidence that White lived on a diet of soda, candy bars, and Twinkies, and the diet created biochemical changes in his brain that reduced his ability to reason and control his behavior. There was also evidence that he suffered from manic depression. None of the evidence was sufficient to prove insanity; however, his defense was successful in reducing his culpability from first-degree murder to voluntary manslaughter. The following presents a sampling of some of the types of diminished capacity defenses. Some of the "syndromes" below are not recognized in some states.

1. Premenstrual Syndrome (PMS) and Postpartum Depression Syndrome (PPD)

Premenstrual syndrome (PMS) affects a small percentage of the population, but in its most extreme forms, it has been associated with a form of psychosis. In England, it has been used successfully to acquit a defendant who killed her husband. It has had less success in this country as an accepted defense.[31]

Another syndrome that affects only women is postpartum depression (PPD). As discussed earlier, Andrea Yates suffered from this hormonal imbalance that, in its most severe form, can cause psychosis.

2. Intoxication

About one-third of states have statutorily barred the use of voluntary intoxication as a defense to any crime, and the Supreme Court, in *Montana v. Egelhoff*,[32] upheld these statutes. The following excerpt from the case illustrates the reasoning of the Court:

> We consider in this case whether the bue process clause is violated by Montana Code Annotated § 45-2-203, which provides, in relevant part, that voluntary intoxication "may not be taken into consideration in determining the existence of a mental state which is an element of [a criminal] offense." . . . In July 1992, while camping out in the Yaak region of northwestern Montana to pick mushrooms, respondent made friends with Roberta Pavola and John Christenson, who were doing the same. On Sunday, July 12, the three sold the mushrooms they had collected and spent the rest of the day and evening drinking, in bars and at a private party in Troy, Montana. Some time after 9 p.m., they left the party in Christenson's 1974 Ford Galaxy station wagon. The drinking binge apparently continued, as respondent was seen buying

---

[31]   *Premenstrual Syndrome: A Criminal Defense*, 59 NOTRE DAME l. REV. 263 (1983).
[32]   Montana v. Egelhoff, 518 U.S. 37 (1996).

beer at 9:20 p.m. and recalled "sitting on a hill or a bank passing a bottle of Black Velvet back and forth" with Christenson. . . . At about midnight that night, officers of the Lincoln County, Montana, sheriff's department, responding to reports of a possible drunk driver, discovered Christenson's station wagon stuck in a ditch along U.S. Highway 2. In the front seat were Pavola and Christenson, each dead from a single gunshot to the head. In the rear of the car lay respondent, alive and yelling obscenities. His blood-alcohol content measured .36 percent over one hour later. On the floor of the car, near the brake pedal, lay respondent's .38 caliber handgun, with four loaded rounds and two empty casings; respondent had gunshot residue on his hands.

Respondent was charged with two counts of deliberate homicide, a crime defined by Montana law as "purposely" or "knowingly" causing the death of another human being. . . . A portion of the jury charge, uncontested here, instructed that "[a] person acts purposely when it is his conscious object to engage in conduct of that nature or to cause such a result," and that "[a] person acts knowingly when he is aware of his conduct or when he is aware under the circumstances his conduct constitutes a crime; or, when he is aware there exists the high probability that his conduct will cause a specific result." . . .

Respondent's defense at trial was that an unidentified fourth person must have committed the murders; his own extreme intoxication, he claimed, had rendered him physically incapable of committing the murders, and accounted for his inability to recall the events of the night of July 12. Although respondent was allowed to make this use of the evidence that he was intoxicated, the jury was instructed, pursuant to Mont. Code Ann. § 45-2-203 (1995), that it could not consider respondent's "intoxicated condition . . . in determining the existence of a mental state which is an element of the offense." . . . The jury found respondent guilty on both counts, and the court sentenced him to 84 years' imprisonment.

The Supreme Court of Montana reversed. It reasoned (1) that respondent "had a due process right to present and have considered by the jury all relevant evidence to rebut the State's evidence on all elements of the offense charged,". . . , and (2) that evidence of respondent's voluntary intoxication was "clearly . . . relevant to the issue of whether [respondent] acted knowingly and purposely,". . . .

The cornerstone of the Montana Supreme Court's judgment was the proposition that the due process clause guarantees a defendant the right to present and have considered by the jury "*all relevant evidence* to rebut the State's evidence on all elements of the offense charged." . . . [but] As we have said: "The accused does not have an unfettered right to offer [evidence] that is incompetent, privileged, or otherwise inadmissible under standard rules of evidence."

. . . By the laws of England, wrote Hale, the intoxicated defendant "shall have no privilege by this voluntary contracted madness, but shall have the same judgment as if he were in his right senses.". . . . According to Blackstone and Coke, the law's condemnation of those suffering from *dementia affectata* was harsher still: Blackstone, citing Coke, explained that the law viewed intoxication "as an aggravation of the offence, rather than as an excuse for any criminal misbehaviour.". . . . This stern rejection of inebriation as a defense became a fixture of early American law as well. . . .

The historical record does not leave room for the view that the common law's rejection of intoxication as an "excuse" or "justification" for crime would nonetheless permit the defendant to show that intoxication prevented the requisite *mens rea*. Hale, Coke, and Blackstone were familiar, to say the least, with the concept of *mens rea*, and acknowledged that drunkenness "deprive[s] men of the use of reason," . . . It is inconceivable that they did not realize that an offender's drunkenness might impair his ability to form the requisite intent; and inconceivable that their failure to note this massive exception from the general rule of disregard of intoxication was an oversight. Hale's statement that a drunken offender shall have the same judgment "as if he were in his right senses" must be understood as precluding a defendant from arguing that, because of his intoxication, he could not have possessed the *mens rea* required to commit the crime. And the same must be said of the exemplar of the common-law rule cited by both Hale and Blackstone,... : "If a person that is drunk kills another, this shall be Felony, and he shall be hanged for it, and yet he did it through Ignorance, for when he was drunk he had *no Understanding* nor Memory; but inasmuch as that Ignorance was occasioned by his own Act and Folly, and he might have avoided it, he shall not be privileged thereby" (emphasis added). ...

Over the course of the 19th century, courts carved out an exception to the common law's traditional across-the-board condemnation of the drunken offender, allowing a jury to consider a defendant's intoxication when assessing whether he possessed the mental state needed to commit the crime charged, where the crime was one requiring a "specific intent." ... by the end of the 19th century, in most American jurisdictions, intoxication could be considered in determining whether a defendant was capable of forming the specific intent necessary to commit the crime charged. ...

[However] It is not the State which bears the burden of demonstrating that its rule is "deeply rooted," but rather respondent who must show that the principle or procedure *violated* by the rule (and allegedly required by due process) is "'so rooted in the traditions and conscience of our people as to be ranked as fundamental.'" ... Thus, even assuming that when the Fourteenth Amendment was adopted the rule Montana now defends was no longer generally applied, this only cuts off what might be called an *a fortiori* argument in favor of the State. The burden remains upon respondent to show that the "new common-law" rule — that intoxication may be considered on the question of intent — was so deeply rooted at the time of the Fourteenth Amendment (or perhaps has become so deeply rooted since) as to be a fundamental principle which that Amendment enshrined.

That showing has not been made. Instead of the uniform and continuing acceptance we would expect for a rule that enjoys "fundamental principle" status, we find that fully one-fifth of the States either never adopted the "new common-law" rule at issue here or have recently abandoned it. ...

... Disallowing consideration of voluntary intoxication has the effect of increasing the punishment for all unlawful acts committed in that state, and thereby deters drunkenness or irresponsible behavior while drunk.

The rule also serves as a specific deterrent, ensuring that those who prove incapable of controlling violent impulses while voluntarily intoxicated go to prison. And finally, the rule comports with and implements society's moral perception that one who has voluntarily impaired his own faculties should be responsible for the consequences. ...

There is, in modern times, even more justification for laws such as § 45-2-203 than there used to be. Some recent studies suggest that the connection between drunkenness and crime is as much cultural as pharmacological — that is, that drunks are violent not simply because alcohol makes them that way, but because they are behaving in accord with their learned belief that drunks are violent. ... This not only adds additional support to the traditional view that an intoxicated criminal is not deserving of exoneration, but it suggests that juries — who possess the same learned belief as the intoxicated offender — will be too quick to accept the claim that the defendant was biologically incapable of forming the requisite *mens rea*. Treating the matter as one of excluding misleading evidence therefore makes some sense.

In sum, not every widespread experiment with a procedural rule favorable to criminal defendants establishes a fundamental principle of justice. Although the rule allowing a jury to consider evidence of a defendant's voluntary intoxication where relevant to *mens rea* has gained considerable acceptance, it is of too recent vintage, and has not received sufficiently uniform and permanent allegiance, to qualify as fundamental, especially since it displaces a lengthy common law tradition which remains supported by valid justifications today.

Other states do allow intoxication to be used to rebut the state's evidence that the defendant had the *mens rea* to commit the crime. Generally, such a defense only reduces culpability by reducing the level of *mens rea* from intentional to reckless or negligent. For instance, it may be possible to show extreme intoxication negated the ability to form intent for first-degree murder, burglary, or robbery. This means, for instance, that the defendant might prove that he was extremely intoxicated, and therefore could not have formed the intent to murder.

Even in states that bar voluntary intoxication evidence, if the defendant can show that his intoxication was not voluntary, i.e., that he unknowingly ingested alcohol, then such evidence could be presented to show that he was incapable of forming the *mens rea* required for the crime.

3. Posttraumatic Stress Disorder

This phrase was first created in association with Vietnam veterans; however, the condition had different names in earlier wars (such as "shell-shocked" from World War II). Generally, the diagnosis is used for individuals who suffer from traumatic incidents or long periods of severe stress. Their symptoms may include flashbacks, dreams, sensory hallucinations and, in some cases, their delusions may cause them to commit crimes. Today, the diagnosis is used not just for returning soldiers, but for anyone who has experienced trauma and is experiencing some or all of the symptoms described above.

LEGAL NEWS: VETERANS TREATMENT COURTS

Some jurisdictions (starting with Buffalo, New York in 2008) have created "Veterans Treatment Courts." The specialized court dockets follow the drug court model. These courts handle cases where veterans are defendants. They have special expertise and resources to deal with issues such as PTSD that have been determined to be the cause of many problems of returning veterans who become involved in the justice system. Typically such courts only deal with nonviolent crimes.

For more information, go to http://www.ptsd.va.gov/public/pages/keeping-PTSD-vets-out-JS.asp.

4. Battered Woman Syndrome

Battered woman syndrome has been described as a type of posttraumatic stress disorder because the victim has been subjected to a long period of severe stress that causes her, in some cases, to do extreme acts. However, it has also been described as a type of duress, as a type of self-defense, and as a type of temporary insanity. We describe the syndrome more fully in the section on duress.

E. *Summary*

From the foregoing, it is obvious that the questions relating to mental impairment as a defense to crime have not been resolved. At present it is safe to say that the majority of the states still follow the *M'Naghten* Rule with possibly some modifications. The other tests that are not used by a majority of the states are the irresistible impulse rule, the *Durham* Rule, and the Model Penal Code (ALI) test. The three situations in which mental impairment is considered during adjudication are a determination of incompetency at time of trial (determining whether or not the defendant can assist in his or her own trial), a verdict of sanity or insanity (the decision is whether or not the defendant was insane at the time of the offense), and a determination at sentencing that the defendant had diminished capacity (to be used a mitigating factor). Diminished capacity defenses are used when the defendant is not legally insane, but his or her mental condition does call into question whether the required *mens rea* for the crime could be formed.

§ 3.4   Duress or Compulsion

What would ordinarily be a criminal act may be excused at law if the act is committed under **duress** or compulsion. Except in the case of homicide, an act that would otherwise constitute a crime may be excused when committed under duress or compulsion that is imminent, and produces a well-grounded apprehension of death or serious bodily harm.[33]

There are conditions to the application of this defense in criminal cases. The coercion must be of such a nature as to induce a well-grounded apprehension of death or serious bodily harm and there must be no reasonable escape without committing the crime.[34] Also, a threat of future injury is not enough to justify committing a crime. If there is a possibility of seeking help and avoiding the necessity of taking action, this avenue must be pursued. However, the theory that there must be

---

[33]   United States v. Anthony, 145 F. Supp. 323 (M.D. Pa. 1956); Jackson v. State, 558 S.W.2d 816 (Mo. Ct. App. 1977).

[34]   State v. St. Clair, 262 S.W.2d 25 (Mo. 1953); Jackson v. State, 504 S.W.2d 488 (Tex. Crim. App. 1974).

a "gun to the head" is not a required condition to the application of this defense, as long as a threat is real.[35]

A. Common Law

The common law recognized duress or compulsion as a defense for some crimes, but not all. It did not recognize any compulsion, even the threat of instant death, as sufficient to excuse the intentional killing of an innocent person.[36] The common law rule is still recognized and has been incorporated in some state statutes. For example, the common law rule was applied in the case of *Harris v. State* in 1977.[37] In this case, the court refused an instruction submitted by the defense that "if defendant was not intending any wrong, was swept along by a party of persons whom he did not resist, he would not be responsible for any wrong done if he was compelled to do the said wrong." The reviewing court stated that the instruction was properly refused when the defendant was indicted for murdering a prison guard during a riot. The court explained that the instruction was an incorrect statement of law for two reasons: first, the common law never allowed the compulsion defense for the taking of the life of an innocent person, and second, the defendant knew that the riot was about to occur and could have escaped from the cell block before it took place.

B. Model Penal Code

According to the comments following the Model Penal Code, at the time the Model Code was considered, 20 states had legislation dealing with the defense of duress in criminal cases. The Model Code recognizes some of the provisions of the state statutes in existence and also some of the common law exceptions.

§ 2.09 Duress[38]

(1) It is an affirmative defense that the actor engaged in the conduct charged to constitute an offense because he was coerced to do so by the use of, or a threat to use, unlawful force against his person or the person of another, that a person of reasonable firmness in his situation would have been unable to resist.

(2) The defense provided by this Section is unavailable if the actor recklessly placed himself in a situation in which it was probable that he would be subjected to duress. The defense is also unavailable if he was negligent in placing himself in such a situation whenever negligence suffices to establish culpability for the offense charged.

(3) It is not a defense that a woman acted on the command of her husband, unless she acted under such coercion as would establish a defense under this Section. (The presumption that a woman acting in the presence of her husband is coerced is abolished.)

(4) When the conduct of the actor would otherwise be justifiable under § 3.02, this Section does not preclude such defense.

---

35   People v. Unger, 33 Ill. App. 3d 770, 338 N.E.2d 442 (Ill. Ct. App. 1975).
36   Arp v. State, 97 Ala. 5, 12 So. 301 (1893).
37   352 So. 2d 460 (Ala. Crim. App. 1977).
38   MODEL PENAL CODE § 2.09 (1985).

Under the Model Code, the defense of duress is not established simply by the fact that the defendant was coerced; he must have been coerced in circumstances under which a person of reasonable firmness in his situation would likewise have been unable to resist. Subsection (2) of the Model Code deprives the actor of the duress defense if he recklessly places himself in a situation in which it was probable that he would be subject to duress.

C. State Statutes, Codes, and Cases

As stated before, duress is not available as a defense to murder.[39] In order for duress or compulsion to be recognized as a defense to criminal charges, the compulsion must come from an outside source and be of such a degree as to overcome the will of the actor. Applying this rationale, a North Dakota court affirmed a lower court's decision that the defendant's claim that he was compelled to commit robberies in order to provide money for his family for food and shelter did not constitute "duress" as a defense to robbery charges.[40]

Some state statutes deny the defense of duress to an individual who intentionally or wantonly places himself in a situation in which coercion is likely to be applied. For example, if a person joins criminal activity voluntarily and seeks exoneration for some act committed by him or her in the course of the activity by asserting that a companion threatened him or her with death, the defense of duress is not available.

In a Connecticut case, the court concluded that the defense of duress does not justify carrying a pistol without a permit.[41] A Missouri appeals court refused to allow the defense of duress alleged by a prisoner who claimed that his acts were forced by other prisoners. The court declared that the defense of duress is not available to a prisoner who could, but did not, seek the alternative of protective custody.[42]

Duress excuses criminal behavior where the defendant shows that the acts were the product of threats inducing a reasonable fear of immediate death or serious bodily injury. Where it is properly shown, duress is a complete defense to a crime.[43] The defense of duress requires that the perceived threat or use of unlawful force be against the actor or another person; it does not encompass threats made to or force used against a third party of which the actor was unaware.[44]

The threat must be imminent. In *State v. Rosillo*,[45] the defendant committed perjury because of threats to his and his family's life, but the threats were determined not to constitute an imminent threat, and, therefore, the defense of duress was rejected in his prosecution for perjury. In its application to the affirmative defense of duress, an "imminent threat" has two components of immediacy: first, the person making the

---

[39]   Wright v. State, 402 So.2d 493 (Fla. Dist. Ct. App. 1981).
[40]   State v. Gann, 244 N.W.2d 746 (N.D. 1976).
[41]   State v. Hopes, 602 A.2d 23 (Conn. 1992).
[42]   State v. Hope, 935 S.W.2d 85 (Mo. 1996).
[43]   Arnold v. Commonwealth, 560 S.E.2d 915 (Va. 2002).
[44]   Pujh v. State, 89 S.W.3d 909 (Ark. 2002).
[45]   282 N.W.2d 872 (Minn.1979).

threat must intend and be prepared to carry out the threat immediately, and second, carrying out the threat must be predicated on the threatened person's failure to commit the charged offense immediately.[46] Applying this standard, a court held that the alleged threat that the defendant and his family would be killed if the defendant did not rob a bank, made four days before the robbery, did not qualify as an "imminent threat" required for the affirmative defense of duress, even if the defendant believed no law enforcement agency could protect him, absent any showing that persons who made the threat intended or were prepared to carry it out immediately, or that they even gave the defendant any time frame for committing the robbery.

LEGAL NEWS: DURESS AS A CRIMINAL DEFENSE

Peter Daniel Schoernig was tried in 2009 for the 2006 murder of Guy Farmer. The murder took place on the farm of Donald Sherman, also charged with the murder. Schoernig testified, in his defense, that his actions were the result of duress, claiming that he was in fear for his life during the time of Farmer's murder. Evidently, Sherman was a methamphetamine manufacturer and distributor. Farmer was believed to have stolen some of Sherman's chemicals used in the manufacture of methamphetamine. According to Schoernig's testimony Sherman called in two men referred to as "torturers" or "enforcers" who systematically beat Farmer's kneecaps and chest with hammers over the course of two days. They also burned his feet and genitals with a blowtorch. He was eventually poisoned with narcotics and his body was dumped in a nearby mine shaft. Schoernig, while admitting to not doing anything to help Farmer, and retying him at some point during the torture when he was able to free himself, defended himself by saying that his life was threatened too and he was hit in the face by one of Sherman's "torturers" and believed that if he tried to leave or help Farmer he would be killed. The jury convicted Schoernig of first-degree murder and sentenced him to 25 years to life in prison.

Retrieved December 21, 2011 from http://auburnjournal.com/detail/126373.html and http://placeropolis.com/detail/140431.html.

---

1. Battered Spouse/Woman Syndrome

Beginning in the late 1980s, the "**battered woman defense**" was developed as a type of duress defense. If an individual is defending oneself, the traditional affirmative defense/justification of "self-defense" can be used. However, in some cases of domestic violence, the victim does not use violence against the abuser during a violent episode, but rather during a time when the batterer is either asleep or otherwise incapacitated (i.e., intoxicated). By doing so, the victim/attacker precludes the use of

---

[46]   Anguish v. State, 991 S.W.2d 883 (Tex. 1999).

self-defense because one element of the justification is that the threat be "imminent." *The Burning Bed* was a movie that presented the case of Francine Hughes, a woman who set her husband on fire while he was sleeping. In subsequent cases, women killed their abusers in similar situations; however, it is a myth that most battered women kill their abusers during times when the abuser is asleep or unable to defend himself. In fact, one study indicated that 75 percent of all cases in the sample involved killings during active confrontations.[47]

The battered woman syndrome/defense, as created and championed by Lenore Walker, a clinical social worker, argues that the victim in a consistent, serious pattern of abuse becomes "helpless" to escape, similar to victims of concentration camps. The victims attempt to escape the abuse, only to have their abuser threaten their children or their parents. Law enforcement seems unable to help and, therefore, the victim comes to feel there is no escape. At some point, some victims "snap" and, believing there is no way out of their abuse, kill the abuser. They may do so during a time when he is incapacitated because they are simply too frightened of him to fight back when he is threatening them.[48]

In the 1990s, in response to the increasing number of cases involving this issue, and in deference to the public's demand that these defendant-victims be accorded some relief, many legislative bodies codified new defenses, or amended existing ones, to permit defendant-victims to introduce evidence of their abuse as part of their defense. The new statutes came to be known in some jurisdictions as the "battered spouse syndrome" defense and in other jurisdictions as the "battered woman syndrome" defense.[49] Regardless of the name, defendant-victims were now, statutorily, permitted some leeway in linking their abusive past to a defense in a criminal trial.

In the majority of jurisdictions, the statutes did not create a new statutory defense, but rather permitted the introduction of evidence that the defendant-victim suffered from the syndrome in cases in which the defendant-victim was relying on the traditional and long-recognized defenses of self-defense, duress, necessity, or defense of others.[50] Most statutes permitted such evidence to be introduced through the expert testimony of a psychologist or psychiatrist.

As one court noted in describing the nature of the Ohio statute:

> A woman's status as a battered woman does not alter the evidentiary burden in establishing a self-defense claim in a homicide prosecution; but evidence of that status may be offered to assist the jury in determining whether the defendant acted out of a reasonable belief that she was in imminent danger of death or great bodily harm and that the use of force was the only means of escaping that danger.[51]

---

[47] Holly Maguigan, *Battered Women and Self Defense: Myths and Misconceptions in Current Reform Proposals*, 14 U. PA. l. REV. 379 (1992).

[48] LENORE WALKER, THE BATTERED WOMAN. New York: Harper Collins, 1979.

[49] *See*, for instance, MO. REV. STAT. § 563.033 (1996); OHIO REV. CODE ANN. § 2901.06 (Anderson 1994).

[50] State v. Riker, 123 Wash. 2d 351, 869 P.2d 43 (1994).

[51] State v. Daws, 104 Ohio App. 3d 448, 662 N.E.2d 805 (1994), *appeal allowed*, 71 Ohio St. 3d 1406, 641 N.E.2d 203 (1995), appeal dismissed as improvidently allowed, 74 Ohio St. 3d 1284, 659 N.E.2d

Generally, the defense is unavailable when a woman hires a third party to kill her abuser.[52]

In more recent years, the defense has fallen out of favor even in those states that had initially recognized it. Arguably, the defense is not needed if traditional elements of self-defense or duress are present, and posttraumatic stress disorder is a less gender-specific explanation for the defendant's behavior. Generally, the defense is still used, however, to show why an abused spouse or intimate partner does not leave his or her abuser.

A very different situation is when the battered woman uses duress as a defense to crimes other than assaulting or killing her abuser. In these cases, the defendant argues that her fear of the batterer compelled her to commit crimes. These are more similar to standard duress claims and, thus, the same elements apply. Battered woman syndrome testimony may be allowed to show the reasonableness of her belief of imminent harm, a necessary component of a duress defense.[53] In *People v. Romero*, a California court overturned a robbery conviction and remanded for a new trial, ordering the court to consider evidence that the defendant was a battered spouse of her codefendant and helped him commit the robberies under duress.[54]

LEGAL NEWS: *DIXON V. UNITED STATES*, 548 U.S. 1 (2006)

In *Dixon v. U.S.* (2006), the defendant used a duress defense to explain why she purchased guns for her abusive boyfriend. She alleged she was afraid of him because he threatened to kill her and her children if she did not do as he asked. She also testified that she was a victim of a pattern of abuse, including four or five beatings the week of the gun purchase. She was convicted of a federal charge of receiving guns while under indictment (for an unrelated charge). She appealed, arguing that the burden of proof should have been on the prosecutor to disprove her duress (through battering), because proving *mens rea* is an essential element of due process. The Fifth Circuit followed precedent by holding the defendant to a preponderance level of proof in the affirmative defense of duress. Despite the fact that the majority of jurisdictions did place the burden on the prosecutor to disprove duress, once raised as a defense, the Supreme Court agreed, holding that it was not a violation of due process to require the defendant to bear the burden of proof.

1282 (1996). For a superb discussion of the law regarding this issue, see Laurie Kratky Dore, *Downward Adjustment and the Slippery Slope: The Use of Duress in Defense of Battered Offenders*, 56 OHIO STATE L.J. 665-766 (1995).

[52] People v. Yaklich, 833 P.2d 758, 762 (Col. Ct. App. 1991).

[53] United States v. Willis, 38 F.3d 170 (5th Cir. 1994); United States v. Marenghi, 893 F. Supp. 85 (D. Me. 1995). United States v. Willis, 38 F.3d 170 (5th Cir. 1994).

[54] People v. Romero, 15 Cal. App. 4th 1519 (1992).

D. *Summary*

The defense of duress has been an accepted defense since the common law, but it is very limited in its application. The defendant must be in imminent fear of bodily harm by another with no escape, the crime cannot be homicide (or probably any serious personal violent crime), and the defendant must not have been reckless in putting themselves in harm's way. The battered woman defense is a special type of duress defense but is not universally recognized.

§ 3.5   Necessity (Choice of Evils)

Duress and **necessity** are somewhat similar defenses; however, while duress always involves fear of harm or intimidation, necessity is a broader defense that justifies criminal actions if the harm that will result from compliance with the law is greater than that which will result from violation of it. The traditional view is that the pressure or the factors that made the violation necessary must come from the physical forces of nature rather than from human beings. For instance, if one is trapped in a snowstorm on a mountaintop and the choice is to freeze to death or break into someone's cabin, the law allows the person to choose the criminal action (as long as there is compensation to the victim). However, the necessity defense, as is true with duress, will not allow one to sacrifice an innocent to save oneself or one's property. The classic necessity case is *Regina v. Dudley and Stephens*.[55] In this case, Dudley and Stephens were tried for the murder of another sailor. All three had been adrift in an open boat for 20 days and were starving. They killed and ate the victim because he was the youngest and the weakest and were rescued four days later. The court found that they would have most probably died if they had not committed the act and that the boy would have died before them; however, they were convicted because necessity was not recognized as a defense to murder. They were sentenced to death but the Crown commuted their sentence to six months' imprisonment.[56] A similar early case in the United States involved ship crewmen who threw 14 male passengers out of a lifeboat when it began taking on water to save other passengers and themselves. The court held that the defense of necessity was not applicable to their actions and their convictions of manslaughter were upheld.[57]

A. *Common Law*

The defense of necessity should be and has been very strictly applied. Under the common law, one may be justified by necessity in violating the law and causing harm in order to avoid a greater harm caused by complying with the law. However, this defense

---

[55]   14 Q.B.D. 273 (1884).

[56]   A similar American case was United States v. Holmes, 26 F. Cas. 360 (C.C.E.D. Pa. 1842).

[57]   United States v. Holmes, 26 F. Cas. 360 (C.C.E.D. Pa. 1842).

was not recognized unless the defendant acted with the intention of avoiding the greater harm, and it was for the court, not the defendant, to weigh the relative harmfulness of the two alternatives.

B. Model Penal Code

Section 3.02 of the Model Penal Code includes the recommended model statute relating to necessity under the title "Choice of Evils."

§ 3.02 Choice of Evils[58]

(1) Conduct that the actor believes to be necessary to avoid a harm or evil to himself or to another is justified, provided that:
    (a) the harm or evil sought to be avoided by such conduct is greater than that sought to be prevented by the law defining the offense charged; and
    (b) neither the Code nor other law defining the offense provides exceptions or defenses dealing with specific situations involved; and
    (c) a legislative purpose to exclude the justification claim does not otherwise plainly appear.

Under this provision of the Model Code, as in the common law and other statutes, the evil sought to be avoided must be greater than that sought to be prevented by the law defining the offense. Also, the legislature must not have previously foreclosed the choice that was made by resolving the conflict of values at stake. It is broader than the common law necessity defense in that it does not demand an immediate harm, nor is the emergency limited to natural forces or physical harm. Some examples in the commentary include property may be destroyed to prevent the threat of fire, a speed limit may be violated in pursuing a suspected criminal, and an ambulance may pass a traffic light.[59] The Model Penal Code expands the common law parameters of the necessity defense, but it is not universally accepted by the states.

C. State Statutes, Codes, and Cases

Some states apply the common law rule in dealing with the necessity defense issue. In about half of the states, statutes have been enacted to more specifically define the necessity defense. In Virginia[60] the court explained that the essential elements of the common law necessity defense include a reasonable belief that the action was necessary to avoid imminent threatened harm, lack of adequate means to avoid the threatened harm, and a direct causal relationship that may be reasonably anticipated between the action taken and avoidance of harm.

In Indiana, the court explained the elements of the necessity defense.[61] In order to prevail on a claim of necessity, the defendant must show the following:

---

[58]   MODEL PENAL CODE § 3.02 (1985).

[59]   *See* the Model Penal Code for a discussion of the rationale for this defense and a list of the states that have adopted all or part of the Model Penal Code.

[60]   Long v. Commonwealth, 478 S.E.2d 424 (Va. Ct. App. 1996).

[61]   Dozier v. State, 709 N.E.2d 27 (Ind. 1999).

- The act charged as criminal must have been done to prevent a significant evil.
- There must have been no adequate alternative to the commission of the act.
- The harm caused by the act must not be disproportionate to the harm avoided.
- The accused must entertain a good faith belief that this act was necessary to prevent greater harm.
- Such belief must be objectively reasonable under all the circumstances.
- The accused must not have substantially contributed to the creation of the emergency.

After stating these requirements, the Indiana court opined that reasonable options other than carrying a handgun to school were available to a juvenile, who claimed he did so in order to protect himself from threatened retaliation by members of his former gang.

In an Illinois case, the court comprehensively explained the conception of legal necessity. The defense of necessity does not negate any element of the crime, but represents the public policy decision not to punish someone, despite proof of the crime.[62] The court continued by stating that to invoke the defense of necessity, the defendant must show the immediacy of peril and that violating the law was the only reasonable action available to him under the circumstances; the situation must have been an emergency, must have threatened physical harm, and must have left the defendant with no legal alternative.

Examples of successful and unsuccessful uses of the necessity defense include the following:

- a convicted felon who is barred from possession of firearms grabs a gun from an aggressor to prevent him from using it (successful)[63]
- someone who steals food out of economic necessity (unsuccessful)[64]
- a defendant who kidnaps another to save them from a religious cult (unsuccessful)[65]
- defendants who leave their children in the car while they work when it is below freezing weather because they don't have a babysitter (unsuccessful)[66]

Recently there have been new and intriguing applications of the necessity defense, most of which have met with little success in the courts.

1. Marijuana as a Medical Necessity

A growing number of people argue that marijuana is the only effective treatment for symptoms of medical conditions such as glaucoma, cancer (nausea), multiple sclerosis (pain), and AIDS (pain). In medical necessity cases, the defendants argue that medical necessity overcomes criminal drug laws and provides a defense to conviction for possession (if not distribution).[67] Although many states

---

[62] People v. Galambos, 128 Cal. Rptr. 844 (2002).
[63] United States v. Paolello, 951 F.2d 537 (3d Cir. 1991).
[64] State v. Moe, 24 P.2d 638 (Wash. 1933).
[65] People v. Brandyberry, 812 P.2d 674 (Colo. Ct. App. 1991).
[66] People v. Turner, 619 N.E.2d 781 (1993).
[67] Jenks v. State, 582 So.2d 676 (Fla. Dist. Ct. App. 1991); State v. Hanson, 468 N.W.2d 77 (Minn. Ct. App. 1991), State v. Ownbey, 996 P.2d 510 (Ore. App. 2000), State v. Poling, 531 S.E.2d 678 (W. Va. 2000), United States v. Randall, 104 Daily Wash. L. Rptr. 2249 (D.C. Super. Ct. 1976).

have statutes recognizing medical necessity, the Supreme Court has not recognized a medical necessity defense that overcomes the 1970 Controlled Substances Act; therefore a person may conform to state law but still be in violation of federal drug laws.[68] Proponents argue that the sole Supreme Court case involved distribution, not possession, and that it is possible the Court would be more sympathetic to a case of a seriously ill individual who possessed marijuana for their medical needs. More than a dozen states have legalized the medical use of marijuana; therefore, this issue will continue to be contentious.[69]

2. Escape from Prison to Avoid Injury

In a few cases, inmates have used duress or necessity as a defense to prison escape. In *People v. Lovercamp,*[70] the inmate successfully argued that his escape was to avoid an immediate rape, but the court offered a very narrow holding that required the threat to be imminent, that there be no alternatives, and that the inmate immediately turn himself in. A different court refused to allow the defense in another case because the inmate did not immediately turn himself in to authorities.[71] Courts seem to disagree on whether the proper defense to escape prison conditions is necessity or duress; however, it is clear that whatever form the defense takes, it is limited to rare circumstances.[72]

3. Civil Disobedience to Prevent Government Wrongs

Can a protestor argue necessity when they violate a law or a city ordinance in their opposition to government policy? They can, but they are rarely successful, because there are, arguably, other alternatives to committing a crime for one who is attempting to stop some governmental action.[73] In cases of direct acts of civil disobedience, the defendant violates a law that they believe to be unconstitutional (such as civil rights demonstrators who broke Jim Crow laws in the south). In cases of indirect civil disobedience, the demonstrator breaks some unrelated law (typically trespass, obstruction of justice, or failure to disperse) in the course of protesting a government action. In no case has indirect civil disobedience been successfully defended with the necessity defense.

---

[68]   United States v. Oakland Cannabis Buyer's Cooperative, 532 U.S. 483 (2001).

[69]   The following states have statutes that recognize medical exceptions to legal prohibitions against marijuana possession or use: AK, CA, CO, HA, MD, ME, MT, NV, OR, VT, WA.

[70]   43 Cal. App. 3d 823 (1974).

[71]   State v. Reese, 272 N.W.2d 863 (1978).

[72]   *See*, in addition to already cited cases, People v. Unger, 362 N.E.2d 319 (1977); Spakes v. State, 913 S. W.2d 597 (Tex. Crim. App. 1996); People v. Harmon, 220 N.W.2d 212 (Mich. Ct. App. 1974); State v. Kinslow, 799 P.2d 844 (Ariz. 1990)k.

[73]   Cohen, J. 2007. Civil disobedience and the necessity doctrine. 6 *Pierce Law Review* 111-175.

D. Summary

In distinguishing between the defenses of compulsion or duress and necessity, an Illinois court advised that compulsion is a defense distinct from necessity; compulsion implies a complete deprivation of free will and absence of choice, while necessity involves choice between two or more admitted evils.[74] Both tend to be limited to property offenses and cannot be used to justify harming an innocent victim.

§ 3.6 Self-Defense

An act that might otherwise be a crime is not punishable if the act was committed in **self-defense**. The general rule is that a person is privileged to use force as reasonably appears necessary to defend himself or herself against an apparent threat of unlawful and immediate violence from another.

A. Common Law

The right to protect oneself, one's family, and one's "castle" is a time-honored right that existed before the common law and was recognized by it. The right to defend oneself in places other than one's home is a natural outgrowth of the "castle" defense.

---

[74] People v. Roberson, 780 N.E.2d 1144 (Ill. 2002).

Availability of this defense to a criminal charge depended, under common law, upon a showing that

- the defendant believed physical force to be necessary for self-protection, or protection of another;
- his or her belief was based upon reasonable grounds;
- the threat of danger was imminent; and
- the force used was not in excess of that believed necessary to repel the unlawful attack.

B. Model Penal Code

The Model Penal Code includes a comprehensive section relating to the use of force and self-protection.

§ 3.04 Use of Force in Self-Protection[75]

(1) Use of Force Justifiable for Protection of the Person. Subject to the provisions of this Section and of Section 3.09, the use of force upon or toward another person is justifiable when the actor believes that such force is immediately necessary for the purpose of protecting himself against the use of unlawful force by such other person on the present occasion.

Under this section, the use of force upon or toward another person is justifiable when the actor believes that such force is immediately necessary for the purpose of protecting himself against the use of unlawful force by such other person on the present occasion. The actor's actual belief is sufficient to support the defense. The use of force is not justified to resist an arrest that the actor knows is being made by a police officer although the arrest is unlawful. Also, the use of deadly force is not justified if the actor can avoid the necessity of using such force with complete safety by taking certain alternative steps such as retreating, surrendering possession of the thing to a person asserting the claim of a right thereto, or complying with the demand that he abstain from action that he has no duty to take.

C. State Statutes, Codes, and Cases

The elements relating to self-defense are somewhat different from state to state. It is important to be familiar with the case decisions in any particular jurisdiction that refine the basic elements of self-defense.

1. Fear of Physical Harm to Self or Another

Self-defense is most often claimed as a defense in homicide or assault cases. To establish self-defense, a defendant must show some evidence that unlawful force was threatened against him, the danger of serious harm was imminent, he was not the aggressor, he fully believed that danger existed, force was necessary to avert the danger, and the type and amount of force used was necessary.

---

[75]   MODEL PENAL CODE § 3.04 (1985).

2. Reasonableness of Fear

The jury is required to determine whether the defendant's perception of the need for self-defense, or the degree of force that was used, was reasonable.[76] For example, in an aggravated assault case, the court found that it was reversible error to refuse to allow the defendant to show that there had been a long-standing dispute with the victim and the victim's brother over a $400 debt.[77] In this case, the victim was outside in a car while his brother went to the defendant's door to collect a debt. The defendant came outside and fired three shots at the victim. Days before the incident, the victim had broken the defendant's nose. The trial court had refused to admit evidence that the victim's brother had waved a gun at the defendant and threatened to shoot him nine months before the incident. This refusal, according to the court, was error and the conviction was reversed. The court pointed out that the testimony bore on the issue of self-defense; and although the victim himself had not communicated the threat, it was relevant to prove the hostility of both the brothers.

On the one hand, if the test applied is an objective "reasonable man" test, the jury must find that a reasonable person, placed in the defendant's situation, would have experienced fear. On the other hand, a subjective test allows the jury to determine whether the defendant experienced fear, whether or not such fear was reasonable. Even in states that use an objective reasonableness standard, there is some opinion that there should be a "reasonable woman" standard that is different from a reasonable man standard allowing for differences in size and strength between the sexes.[78]

A Connecticut court, in a comprehensive statement, held that subjective-objective inquiry into the defendant's belief regarding the necessary degree of force to repel the victim's alleged attack requires the jury to make two separate affirmative determinations for the defendant's claim of self-defense to succeed: (1) the jury must determine whether, on the basis of all evidence presented, the defendant in fact believed that he needed to use deadly physical force, as opposed to some lesser degree of force, to repel the victim's alleged attack; and (2) if the jury determines that the defendant in fact believed that the use of deadly force was necessary, the jury must make a further determination as to whether that belief was reasonable, from the perspective of a reasonable person in the defendant's circumstances.[79]

If the defendant's fear was unreasonable but honest, he is not entitled to the absolute defense of self-defense; however, some states may allow a finding that his culpability is reduced from homicide to manslaughter.[80] This finding is not a recognition

---

[76]   People v. Brown, 578 N.E.2d 1168 (Ill. 1991); People v. Willis, 577 N.E.2d 1215 (Ill. 1991); Holbrook v. Commonwealth, 813 S.W.2d 811 (Ky. 1991).

[77]   Manofsky v. State, 354 So. 2d 1249 (Fla. Dist. Ct. App. 1978).

[78]   State v. Wanrow, 559 P.2d 548 (Wash. 1977).

[79]   State v. Adams, 52 Conn. App. 643, 727 A.2d 780 (1999).

[80]   In re Christian S., 872 P.2d 574 (1994); Swann v. United States, 648 A.2d 928 (1994); State v. Campos, 921 P.2d 1266 (N.M. 1996).

of self-defense per se, but rather a finding that the *mens rea* elements of murder are missing.

3. Imminence of Danger

Under the statutes and case law, the person claiming self-defense must show evidence that he or she reasonably perceived an "imminent" danger. If the danger is to take place some time in the future and can be avoided, then the defense will not prevail.

The most famous self-defense case is *People v. Goetz*.[81] In that case, Goetz shot and wounded four African-American teenagers in a subway car in New York due to a fear that they were about to rob him. The only words that passed between him and his victims were when they asked him for money. He perceived the request as a precursor to a robbery; they testified that they were not planning to rob anyone, although two were carrying screwdrivers, which they admitted they used to break into coin boxes. He was indicted, appealed his indictment, and the Court of Appeals of New York upheld the indictment, but a jury acquitted him of aggravated assault and attempted murder, although he was convicted for unlawful possession of a weapon. In 1996, Goetz lost a civil suit against him by one of the youths who was paralyzed by the shooting.

4. Proportionality of Force Used

The amount of force that may be justifiable must be reasonably related to the threatened harm that the user seeks to avoid. One may justifiably use deadly force against another in self-defense only if the person using the force reasonably believes that the other is about to inflict unlawful death or serious bodily harm, and that it is necessary to use the deadly force to prevent it.[82]

5. "Clean Hands"

Another element of self-defense that is fairly consistent throughout the states is that the defendant is barred from using self-defense if he started the incident that led to the imminent danger. Generally, those who start a "bar room brawl" will not be able to use self-defense to excuse their culpability unless they can show that they made a substantial effort to get away or stop the fracas. This is known as the "clean hands" doctrine.

In a 1997 case, a South Carolina court interpreted the requirements by stating that to establish self-defense, the defendant must prove (1) he was without fault in bringing on the difficulty; (2) he actually believed he was in imminent danger of losing his life or sustaining serious bodily injury; (3) a reasonably prudent person of ordinary firmness

---

[81]   497 N.E.2d 41 (N.Y. 1986).

[82]   State v. Philbrick, 402 A.2d 59 (Me. 1979).

and courage would have entertained the same belief; and (4) he had no other probable means of avoiding the danger.[83]

6. Duty to Retreat

State courts have disagreed on the obligation to attempt to retreat before responding with force or deadly physical force to repel the attack. In an early case, Justice John M. Harlan is quoted as stating that "he was not obligated to retreat, nor to consider whether he could safely retreat, but was entitled to stand his ground and meet attack upon him with a deadly weapon."[84] And in a Kentucky case, the court held that, "it is the tradition that a Kentuckian never runs. He does not have to."[85] A South Carolina court noted that a person attacked on his own premises, without fault, has the right to claim immunity from the law of retreat.[86]

On the other hand, some courts look upon the duty to retreat with more favor. A Louisiana court, in discussing the duty to retreat, stated that while there is no unqualified duty to retreat from an altercation, the possibility of escape is a recognized factor in determining whether a defendant had a reasonable belief whether deadly force was necessary to avoid the danger, to support a claim of self-defense on a homicide charge.[87]

Some courts have made it quite clear that there is a duty to retreat before using deadly force in self-defense. In other states, "Stand your Ground" laws have expanded the legal right to use lethal force. In 2012 Florida's law was the center of controversy in the shooting of Trayvon Martin, a teenager shot by a neighborhood watch volunteer who followed him as he was walking through the neighborhood and ended up shooting him. His release without charges set up a national outcry and investigation by federal authorities. The case is unresolved as this book goes to press.[88] The Florida statute allows an individual to use force up to lethal force when he or she has a reasonable fear of being harmed. There is no duty to retreat.[89]

Even in states that recognize a duty to retreat, the "castle exception" indicates that one is not obligated to retreat if the threat occurs within the parameters of one's own home. Thus, an intruder who poses an imminent threat of bodily harm may be met with force without having to retreat out of the home or within the home to a different room.[90]

---

[83] State v. Long, 480 S.E.2d 62 (S.C. 1997).

[84] Beard v. United States, 158 U.S. 550 (1895).

[85] Gibson v. Commonwealth, 34 S.W.2d 936 (Ky. 1931).

[86] State v. Long, 480 S.E.2d 62 (S.C. 1997).

[87] State v. Barnes, 729 So. 2d 44 (La. 1999).

[88] See, for instance, http://www.usatoday.com/news/nation/story/2012-04-05/trayvon-martin-poll/54047512/1.

[89] Fla. Stat. 776.012.

[90] State v. Marsh, 593 N.E.2d 35 (Ohio Ct. App. 1990); Gainer v. State, 391 A.2d 856 (Md. Ct. Spec. App. 1978); State v. Thomas, 673 N.E.2d 1339 (Ohio 1997).

7. "Make My Day" Laws and Defense of Property

Named after Clint Eastwood's famous quote in the "Dirty Harry" movie, these laws allow the use of deadly force to protect one's home. Recall that, under common law, individuals had a right to use deadly force to prevent entry. Generally, statutory definitions of the right of self-defense restricted its use to fear of grievous bodily harm. The Model Penal Code allowed the use of deadly force in order to prevent serious crimes (such as arson, burglary, robbery, or theft) if the force was immediately necessary and the other person had previously used deadly force against the defendant or another person or there was substantial risk of injury. "Make my Day" statutes expand self-defense in that an individual is privileged to use deadly force against a home intruder in situations where the user of lethal force does not feel an immediate threat from the person who made the unlawful entry, as long as there is a reasonable belief that a crime is intended. Colorado's law, for instance, states that

> ... any occupant of a dwelling is justified in using any degree of physical force, including deadly physical force, against another person when that person has made an unlawful entry into the dwelling, and when the occupant has a reasonable belief that such other person has committed a crime in the dwelling in addition to the uninvited entry, or is committing or intends to commit a crime against a person or property in addition to the uninvited entry, and when the occupant reasonably believes that such other person might use any physical force, no matter how slight, against any occupant ...[91]

Case law has generally prohibited the use of spring guns or devices that would harm someone attempting an illegal entry because they are not capable of distinguishing a burglar from a firefighter or other person who may have a justification for entry. Another reason such devices are illegal is that the homeowner is only privileged to use deadly force in cases where there is a serious risk to self; in some cases of children breaking in with no weapons, no such risk presents itself and, therefore, the use of lethal force is unwarranted. Recently, however, more than a dozen states have passed "stand my ground" laws that allow the use of lethal force to protect against all felonies that involve one's home or automobile, including property crimes.

Utah Statute
76-2-405. Force in defense of habitation

(1) A person is justified in using force against another when and to the extent that he reasonably believes that the force is necessary to prevent or terminate the other's unlawful entry into or attack upon his habitation; however, he is justified in the use of force which is intended or likely to cause death or serious bodily injury only if:
   (a) the entry is made or attempted in a violent and tumultuous manner, surreptitiously, or by stealth, and he reasonable believes that the entry is attempted or made for the purpose of assaulting or offering personal violence to

---

[91] COLO. REV. STAT. §18-1-704.

any person, dwelling, or being in the habitation and reasonably believes that the force is necessary to prevent the assault or offer of personal violence; or

(b) he reasonably believes that the entry is made or attempted for the purpose of committing a felony in the habitation and that the force is necessary to prevent the commission of the felony. . . .

Texas Statute
Sec. 9.31. SELF-DEFENSE

(a) Except as provided in Subsection (b), a person is justified in using force against another when and to the degree the actor reasonably believes the force is immediately necessary to protect the actor against the other's use or attempted use of unlawful force. The actor's belief that the force was immediately necessary as described by this subsection is presumed to be reasonable if the actor:

(1) knew or had reason to believe that the person against whom the force was used:

    (A) unlawfully and with force entered, or was attempting to enter unlawfully and with force, the actor's occupied habitation, vehicle, or place of business or employment;

    (B) unlawfully and with force removed, or was attempting to remove unlawfully and with force, the actor from the actor's habitation, vehicle, or place of business or employment; . . . .

LEGAL NEWS: DEFENSE OF PROPERTY

In a 2008 case, a South Texas man was prosecuted for murder after he caught four boys ranging in age from 11 to 15 burglarizing a mobile home on his property. A victim of several burglaries, the homeowner had a shotgun and ordered the boys to their knees. He then shot one of the boys in the back and ordered the others to take the body outside. The homeowner said the boy was lunging at him; the boys said that he shot the victim and then kicked him. The murder trial of the homeowner resulted in an acquittal, largely because Texas has a "defense of property statute" that allows a homeowner to use deadly force to protect his or her property.

In a more recent case, Juan Romero, a convenience store clerk, shot and killed Jorge Vielma after the man grabbed a 12 pack of beer and ran out of the store with it. Romero argued he had the right to shoot to protect property. Testimony at trial indicated Vielma was shot outside the store as he was running to get in a car driven by friends. He died in the car and the others abandoned it; his body was found the next day. Romero was also charged with tampering with evidence because after police responded a short time later to a report of shots fired, he told them he hadn't seen anything. He was eventually convicted of manslaughter and is serving an eight-year probation sentence.

Source: "Verdict: Prosecutor Said Case About When Deadly Force is Justified." *Austin American-Statesman*, September 28, 2008: B1, B6. Also, see http://www.statesman.com/news/local/manslaughter-not-murder-for-shooting-of-beer-thief-1196649.html.

8. Right to Resist Unlawful Force by Police

Self-defense is often claimed by a defendant who is charged with assaulting a law enforcement officer. In a Rhode Island case, the court held that a defendant has a right to defend himself when police use excessive force against him in placing him under arrest.[92] Whether the defendant has a right of self-defense against the police naturally depends upon whether there was excessive force in effecting the arrest. If the arresting officer uses reasonable force, the privilege of self-defense is inapplicable. However, some states and the federal statutes provide that an arrestee does not have the right to defend himself even when the police use excessive force.[93]

The reverse situation is what level of force police officers are privileged to use in effecting an arrest. Police officers' legal authority to use any type of force lies in the common law self-defense principles. Generally, police officers are justified in using deadly force for the same reason civilians are—self-defense. Under common law, officers had the right to use deadly force against "fleeing felons," but that right has been rejected under modern law. In *Tennessee v. Garner*, the Supreme Court held that officers could not use deadly force to capture fleeing felons who did not pose a risk to the officers or others. In *Grahm v. Connor*, the Supreme Court defined the reasonableness test to determine if the use of force by police officers is legal, that is, would a reasonable officer in those circumstances consider the force used to be necessary to effect an arrest, or to protect self or others.[94] If it is determined that his or her actions were not reasonable, then an officer can be charged with a crime, ranging from homicide to assault to official oppression.

D. *Summary*

Self-defense has been recognized since common law. Generally, people have the legal right to defend themselves or others against an imminent danger. The general elements of self-defense are that the fear must be of bodily harm and reasonable, and the danger must be imminent. Also, the defendant cannot have instigated the danger, and in some states, there is a duty to retreat before resorting to force.

§ 3.7   Entrapment

In the early 1980s, members of Congress caught in the ABSCAM scandal claimed that the government had *created* rather than *uncovered* criminal conduct. Seven defendants, including four former members of the House of Representatives, failed to convince the court that they were victims of entrapment or that the agents responsible for ABSCAM acted "outrageously." The U.S. Court of Appeals for the Third Circuit

---

[92]   State v. Hurteau, 810 A.2d 222 (R.I. 2002).
[93]   Title 18 § 111. *See* United States v. Lopez, 710 F.2d 1071 (5th Cir. 1983).
[94]   Tennessee v. Garner, 471 U.S. 1 (1985); Graham v. Connor, 490 U.S. 386 (1989).

agreed that the action by the U.S. government agents did not amount to **entrapment**. In the case before that court, the facts were as follows. The investigators, posing as representatives of an Arab sheik, told the defendants that the sheik was interested in building a hotel in Philadelphia, but that he wanted to make sure of having friends in high places to take care of any problems that might develop. A defendant, Schwartz, accepted a $30,000 payment from the agents and Congressman Jannotti received $10,000. The court found that the evidence presented at the trial, particularly the videotapes showing the defendant taking the payments, supported a jury's finding of predisposition.[95]

In subsequent years, governmental actions in undercover drug operations and in investigating and apprehending purveyors of obscenity have come under scrutiny most often. The entrapment defense argues that even if the defendant *committed* the crime, he or she should not be punished because government agents *created* the crime.

A. Common Law

Entrapment, as a defense to criminal culpability, is not a legacy of the common law. The defense of entrapment was first recognized by the U.S. Supreme Court in *Sorrells v. United States* in 1932. In the *Sorrells* case, Chief Justice Hughes noted that merely to afford an opportunity or facilities for the commission of the offense does not defeat the prosecution. The majority continued with the following:

> However, a different question is presented when the criminal design originates with the officials of the government and they implant in the mind of an innocent person the disposition to commit the alleged offense and induce its commission in order that they may prosecute.[96]

The views of the U.S. Supreme Court were solidified in *Sherman v. United States* in 1958.[97] *Sorrels* and *Sherman,* taken together, were said to create an entrapment "test" that looked to government action to determine whether entrapment occurred. If government agents played too large a role, for instance, by providing essential ingredients or creating the idea of the crime and providing all the materials for it, then they have "entrapped" the defendant and the defendant carries less culpability than the government agents for the crime.

This so-called objective test was supplanted by the "subjective test" in *United States v. Russell.*[98] In *Russell*, the Supreme Court changed the focus of the test from government actions to the "predisposition" of the offender. If the offender was predisposed to commit the crime, then it did not matter what the government did. Only when the offender was a true innocent who had no predisposition could entrapment serve as a

---

[95]   United States v. Jannotti, 673 F.2d 578 (3d Cir. 1982).
[96]   287 U.S. 435, 53 S. Ct. 210, 77 L. Ed. 413 (1932).
[97]   356 U.S. 369, 78 S. Ct. 819, 2 L. Ed. 2d 848 (1958).
[98]   411 U.S. 423 (1973).

defense under this new test of entrapment. In *Jacobsen v. United States*,[99] the Supreme Court had to decide if Jacobsen had a predisposition to purchase obscene publications or whether the government agents created the idea.

Justice White delivered the opinion of the Court

On September 24, 1987, petitioner Keith Jacobson was indicted for violating a provision of the Child Protection Act of 1984 (Act), . . . which criminalizes the knowing receipt through the mails of a "visual depiction [that] involves the use of a minor engaging in sexually explicit conduct. . . .". . . . Petitioner defended on the ground that the Government entrapped him into committing the crime through a series of communications from undercover agents that spanned the 26 months preceding his arrest. . . .

Because the Government overstepped the line between setting a trap for the "unwary innocent" and the "unwary criminal,". . . , and as a matter of law failed to establish that petitioner was independently predisposed to commit the crime for which he was arrested, we reverse the Court of Appeals' judgment affirming his conviction. . . .

In February 1984, petitioner, a 56-year-old veteran-turned-farmer who supported his elderly father in Nebraska, ordered two magazines and a brochure from a California adult bookstore. The magazines, entitled Bare Boys I and Bare Boys II, contained photographs of nude preteen and teenage boys. The contents of the magazines startled petitioner, who testified that he had expected to receive photographs of "young men 18 years or older.". . . .

The young men depicted in the magazines were not engaged in sexual activity, and petitioner's receipt of the magazines was legal under both federal and Nebraska law. Within three months, the law with respect to child pornography changed; Congress passed the Act illegalizing the receipt through the mails of sexually explicit depictions of children. In the very month that the new provision became law, postal inspectors found petitioner's name on the mailing list of the California bookstore that had mailed him Bare Boys I and II. There followed over the next 2½ years repeated efforts by two Government agencies, through five fictitious organizations and a bogus pen pal, to explore petitioner's willingness to break the new law by ordering sexually explicit photographs of children through the mail. . . .

By March 1987, 34 months had passed since the Government obtained petitioner's name from the mailing list of the California bookstore, and 26 months had passed since the Postal Service had commenced its mailings to petitioner. Although petitioner had responded to surveys and letters, the Government had no evidence that petitioner had ever intentionally possessed or been exposed to child pornography. The Postal Service had not checked petitioner's mail to determine whether he was receiving questionable mailings from persons — other than the Government — involved in the child pornography industry. . . .

At this point, a second Government agency, the Customs Service, included petitioner in its own child pornography sting, "Operation Borderline," after receiving his name on lists submitted by the Postal Service. . . . The Postal Service also continued its efforts in the Jacobson case, writing to petitioner as the "Far Eastern Trading Company Ltd." . . . . . [finally] petitioner ordered Boys Who Love Boys, . . . , a pornographic

---

[99] Jacobson v. U. S., 503 U.S. 540 (1992).

magazine depicting young boys engaged in various sexual activities. Petitioner was arrested after a controlled delivery of a photocopy of the magazine.

When petitioner was asked at trial why he placed such an order, he explained that the Government had succeeded in piquing his curiosity:

"Well, the statement was made of all the trouble and the hysteria over pornography and I wanted to see what the material was. It didn't describe the — I didn't know for sure what kind of sexual action they were referring to. . . ."

In petitioner's home, the Government found the Bare Boys magazines and materials that the Government had sent to him in the course of its protracted investigation, but no other materials that would indicate that petitioner collected, or was actively interested in, child pornography. . . .

In their zeal to enforce the law, however, Government agents may not originate a criminal design, implant in an innocent person's mind the disposition to commit a criminal act, and then induce commission of the crime so that the Government may prosecute. . . . Where the Government has induced an individual to break the law and the defense of entrapment is at issue, as it was in this case, the prosecution must prove beyond reasonable doubt that the defendant was disposed to commit the criminal act prior to first being approached by Government agents. . . .

. . . Had the agents in this case simply offered petitioner the opportunity to order child pornography through the mails, and petitioner — who must be presumed to know the law — had promptly availed himself of this criminal opportunity, it is unlikely that his entrapment defense would have warranted a jury instruction. . . .

But that is not what happened here. By the time petitioner finally placed his order, he had already been the target of 26 months of repeated mailings and communications from Government agents and fictitious organizations. Therefore, although he had become predisposed to break the law by May 1987, it is our view that the Government did not prove that this predisposition was independent and not the product of the attention that the Government had directed at petitioner since January 1985. . . .

. . . On the other hand, the strong arguable inference is that, by waving the banner of individual rights and disparaging the legitimacy and constitutionality of efforts to restrict the availability of sexually explicit materials, the Government not only excited petitioner's interest in sexually explicit materials banned by law but also exerted substantial pressure on petitioner to obtain and read such material as part of a fight against censorship and the infringement of individual rights. . . .

Petitioner's ready response to these solicitations cannot be enough to establish beyond reasonable doubt that he was predisposed, prior to the Government acts intended to create predisposition, to commit the crime of receiving child pornography through the mails. . . . The evidence that petitioner was ready and willing to commit the offense came only after the Government had devoted 2 1/2 years to convincing him that he had or should have the right to engage in the very behavior proscribed by law. . . .

Law enforcement officials go too far when they "implant in the mind of an innocent person the *disposition* to commit the alleged offense and induce its commission in order that they may prosecute." . . . Like the *Sorrells* Court, we are "unable to conclude that it was the intention of the Congress in enacting this statute that its processes of detection and enforcement should be abused by the instigation by government officials of an act on the part of persons otherwise innocent in order to lure them to its commission and to punish them." . . . When the

Government's quest for convictions leads to the apprehension of an otherwise law-abiding citizen who, if left to his own devices, likely would have never run afoul of the law, the courts should intervene.

Because we conclude that this is such a case and that the prosecution failed, as a matter of law, to adduce evidence to support the jury verdict that petitioner was predisposed, independent of the Government's acts and beyond a reasonable doubt, to violate the law by receiving child pornography through the mails, we reverse the Court of Appeals' judgment affirming the conviction of Keith Jacobson.

B. *Model Penal Code*

The Model Penal Code utilized elements of both the objective and subjective entrapment tests. It designates two ways in which a public law enforcement official or person acting in cooperation with such an official can perpetrate an entrapment. The first is by making representations known to be false for the purpose of inducing a belief that the conduct is not prohibited by law (this would be a type of objective test but one that is very specific). The second is by employing methods of persuasion that create a substantial risk that such offense would be committed by persons other than those who are ready to commit it (this is a predisposition test). However, the Model Penal Code has an exception that denies the defense in situations in which the defendant causes or threatens bodily injury to someone other than the person perpetrating the entrapment.

§ 2.13 Entrapment

(1) A public law enforcement official or a person acting in cooperation with such an official perpetrates an entrapment if for the purpose of obtaining evidence of the commission of an offense, he induces or encourages another person to engage in conduct constituting such offense by either:
    (a) making knowingly false representations designed to induce the belief that such conduct is not prohibited; or
    (b) employing methods of persuasion or inducement that create a substantial risk that such an offense will be committed by persons other than those who are ready to commit it.
(2) Except as provided in Subsection (3) of this Section, a person prosecuted for an offense shall be acquitted if he proves by the preponderance of evidence that his conduct occurred in response to an entrapment. The issue of entrapment shall be tried by the Court in the absence of the jury.
(3) The defense afforded by this Section is unavailable when causing or threatening bodily injury is an element of the offense charged and the prosecution is based on conduct causing or threatening such injury to a person other than the person perpetrating the entrapment.

C. *State Statutes, Codes, and Cases*

While many states choose to rely upon the entrapment defense as defined by state and federal appellate courts, some states have enacted statutes that codify the defense. One such statute is that of Colorado.

Colo. Rev. Stat. § 18-1-709[100]

The commission of acts which would otherwise constitute an offense is not criminal if the defendant engaged in the proscribed conduct because he was induced to do so by a law enforcement official or other person acting under his direction, seeking to obtain that evidence for the purpose of prosecution, and the methods used to obtain that evidence were such as to create a substantial risk that the acts would be committed by a person who, but for such inducement, would not have conceived or engaged in conduct of the sort induced. Merely affording a person an opportunity to commit an offense is not entrapment even though representations or inducements calculated to overcome the offender's fear of detection are used.

This statute and other state statutes make it clear that merely affording the person an opportunity to commit an offense is not entrapment.[101] The line between police conduct that amounts to entrapment and merely affording an opportunity for the defendant to commit the offense is often a fine one. In showing the willingness of the defendant to engage in criminal conduct, especially in conduct involving illegal drugs, the question arises as to whether evidence of prior use of illegal drugs is admissible. The general rule is that a defendant's previous unlawful involvement with a controlled substance can be given consideration when evaluating his predisposition to commit other narcotics offenses. In *State v. Eib*, evidence was introduced to show that the appellant sold cocaine on two different occasions to a Kansas City police officer, after the transactions were negotiated by a police informant. After arrangements were made by the informant, the appellant handed the officer cocaine, which was contained in clear plastic bags, and received $300 for the cocaine. On appeal, the defendant claimed that the sale was the result of entrapment by the officer and the informant. The reviewing court, however, noted that "to show entrapment, the defendant must show both unlawful mental inducement to engage in unlawful conduct and his lack of predisposition." The reviewing court, in determining what evidence is admissible to show predisposition, held that a "defendant's unlawful involvement with a controlled substance can be given consideration when evaluating his previous position to commit other narcotics offenses." The court continued by stating that "more specifically the defendant's prior use of other illegal drugs constitutes substantial evidence of predisposition in cases involving the sale of narcotics."[102]

It has been argued that the predisposition test bars a defendant from ever utilizing the entrapment defense if they have prior convictions. For instance, if a former drug addict is enticed to sell drugs to an undercover officer, can he ever argue that he was not predisposed to drug use and sales? The distinction between what is or is not entrapment has been articulated in many cases:

- To rely upon the entrapment defense, the defendant must, as a threshold matter, present evidence that the government conduct created a substantial risk that the

---

[100]   Colo. Rev. Stat. § 18-1-709 (2002). *See also* § 18-1-710, which provides that entrapment is an affirmative defense.

[101]   Bailey v. People, 630 P.2d 1062 (Colo. 1987); Sayre v. State, 533 So. 2d 464 (Miss. 1988).

[102]   State v. Eib, 716 S.W.2d 304 (Mo. 1986).

offense would be committed by a person other than one ready to commit it, and if the defendant succeeds in meeting this burden, the government must prove beyond a reasonable doubt that the defendant was predisposed to commit the offense.[103]

- The essence of the offense of entrapment occurs where the evil intent and the criminal design of the offense originate in the mind of the government agent, and the defendant would not have committed an offense of that character except for the urging of the agent.[104]

- Entrapment may be found on the basis of reprehensible police conduct if the furnishing of the opportunity for a target to commit an offense requires the police to commit certain criminal, dangerous, or immoral acts.[105]

Entrapment is an affirmative defense, which means that the defendant must affirmatively raise the defense and offer some level of proof before the state is required to offer evidence or rebut the alleged entrapment.[106]

The federal government and most states follow some version of the subjective predisposition test. However, a minority of states continue to apply the objective test, a few combine the tests and require that the defendant prove both elements (government activity and lack of predisposition), and at least one state (New Mexico) requires the defendant to prove either one or the other.[107]

LEGAL NEWS: PREDISPOSITION TO TERRORISM

The most recent cases where the entrapment defense has been offered are when individuals are accused of plotting terroristic bombings. One such case is that of Mohamed Osman Mohamud, a Somali-born U.S. citizen, who is charged with planning to bomb the annual Christmas-tree lighting ceremony in Portland in 2010. He and several others over the last several years have been caught in sting operations when FBI agents pretend to be like-minded individuals in jihad-oriented chat rooms. The targets are then offered opportunities to take affirmative steps to commit acts of terror and are arrested when they do. Because of the subjective test of entrapment, the prosecution simply has to prove predisposition on the part of the offender, which is easy to do if they were found in jihad chat rooms. Critics argue that the government is creating terrorists in that these men would not have committed any crime but for the interaction of the agents provocateurs. The opposing argument is, of course, that it is better to find out who is willing to do such acts of violence while government agents have control, rather than after the fact.

For more information, go to http://www.npr.org/2010/12/02/131758291/entrapment-defense-hasn-t-worked-in-terror-cases.

---

[103]   United States v. Purneda-Gonzalez, 953 F.2d 190 (5th Cir. 1992).

[104]   State v. Schuman, 226 Wis. 2d 398, 595 N.W.2d 86 (1999).

[105]   People v. Connolly, 232 Mich. App. 425, 591 N.W.2d 340 (1998).

[106]   McGowan v. State, 671 N.E.2d 872 (Ind. 1996).

[107]   *See* State v. Little, 435 A.2d 517 (N.H. 1981); England v. State, 887 S.W.2d 902 (Tex. Crim. App. 1994); State v. Vallegjos, 945 P.2d 957 (N.M. 1997).

D. Summary

Entrapment is an affirmative defense. Once the defendant has made out a *prima facie* case to raise the issue of entrapment, the government bears the burden of proving beyond a reasonable doubt that the defendant was not entrapped. In most states, once the defendant offers some proof of entrapment, the government must establish that the defendant had a predisposition, independent of government action, to commit the crime.

§ 3.8   Ignorance or Mistake

There are two types of mistakes—mistake about the legality of an action ("I didn't know it was against the law") and mistake about an essential fact ("I didn't know the goods were stolen"). Mistake of law is rarely successful as a defense; mistake of fact (if honest and reasonable) is likely to excuse criminal culpability if it negates an element of the offense.

A. Common Law

Generally ignorance of the law or *mistake of the law* is no excuse for violating it. Mistake about the law is disallowed as a defense because of practical considerations. It would be very difficult to prove, in every situation, that the person charged with a violation of the law knew the law.

Under common law, if there is an honest and reasonable *mistake of fact*, such ignorance or mistake of fact may exempt a person from criminal liability, unless the mistake arose from want of proper care on the part of the accused. The question as to whether a person acts in good faith, honestly, and without fault or negligence is determined by the circumstances as they appear to the person when the mistake is made and the effect that the surrounding circumstances might reasonably be expected to have on his or her mind in forming the intent, criminal or otherwise, upon which he or she acted.[108] The mistake-of-fact defense requires a showing that the mistaken belief is not the result of negligence or fault of the defendant.[109]

If there is a mistake of fact, a person will be relieved of criminal liability only if his or her belief is of such a nature that the conduct would have been lawful had the facts been as he or she reasonably supposed them to be. The classic example of a mistake of fact defense is when someone mistakenly takes another's coat from a restaurant. Taking possession of the property of another is ordinarily theft, but since the *mens rea* of theft is *intentionally* taking the property of another, the mistake negates the *mens rea* requirement.

---

[108]   United States v. Squires, 440 F.2d 859 (2d Cir. 1971); United States v. Jewell, 532 F.2d 697 (9th Cir.), *cert. denied*, 426 U.S. 951, 96 S. Ct. 3173, 49 L. Ed. 2d 1188 (1976); Jones v. State, 439 S.E.2d 645 (Ga. 1994).

[109]   Johnson v. State, 831 So. 2d 1171 (Miss. 2002).

B. Model Penal Code

The Model Penal Code views mistakes of fact as relevant to a finding of *mens rea*.

Section 2.04. Ignorance or Mistake[110]

(1) Ignorance or mistake as to a matter of fact or law is a defense if:
    (a) the ignorance or mistake negatives the purpose, knowledge, belief, recklessness or negligence required to establish a material element of the offense; or
    (b) the law provides that the state of mind established by such ignorance or mistake constitutes a defense.
(2) Although ignorance or mistake would otherwise afford a defense to the offense charged, the defense is not available if the defendant would be guilty of another offense had the situation been as he supposed. In such case, however, the ignorance or mistake of the defendant shall reduce the grade and degree of the offense of which he may be convicted to those of the offense of which he would be guilty had the situation been as he supposed.
(3) A belief that conduct does not legally constitute an offense is a defense to a prosecution for that offense based upon such conduct when:
    (a) the statute or other enactment defining the offense is not known to the actor and has not been published or otherwise reasonably made available prior to the conduct alleged; or
    (b) he acts in reasonable reliance upon an official statement of the law, afterward determined to be invalid or erroneous, contained in (i) a statute or other enactment; (ii) a judicial decision, opinion or judgment; (iii) an administrative order or grant of permission; or (iv) an official interpretation of the public officer or body charged by law with responsibility for the interpretation, administration or enforcement of the law defining the offense.
(4) The defendant must prove a defense arising under Subsection (3) of this Section by a preponderance of evidence.

Because the Model Penal Code is much more specific in the *mens rea* required for each crime, mistakes are easier to deal with. If the defendant's honest mistake negates the required *mens rea*, then it is a defense. If a defendant is mistaken, for instance, in a victim's consent to sexual intercourse, but he is reckless in his belief that she consents, then he is still guilty if the requisite *mens rea* is purposeful, knowing, or reckless. If the defendant is mistaken in her honest belief that the property she acquires is not stolen, then she cannot be guilty of receipt of stolen property because the requisite *mens rea* is purposeful.

The Model Penal Code also covers the situation of undercover operations and drug dealers or smugglers who are mistaken in their belief about the substance they are dealing with. If a drug dealer purchases or sells to anyone a substance that he believes to be a drug, or smuggles in a substance he believes to be a drug, but the substance is really powdered sugar, sheetrock, or some other noncontraband, then Subsection (2) applies because the defendant would have been committing a crime if the circumstances had been as he thought they were.

---

[110]   MODEL PENAL CODE § 2.04 (1985).

C. State Statutes, Codes, and Cases

1. Mistake of Law

In general, state statutes have followed common law in that ignorance of the law is no excuse. However, when specific intent (instead of general intent) is the *mens rea* of the crime charged, then ignorance of the law negates the existence of such intent.[111] For instance, for laws that make it a crime to intentionally violate an open meetings law, then the general intent to meet is not sufficient, and there must be evidence that the defendant knew of the law and intended to violate it.

There also is a small exception to this general rule when the law in question is so obscure that a "reasonable person" would not be expected to know of it. The Supreme Court has held that if the law is so technical or obscure that it threatens to ensnare innocent people, then it violates due process protections.[112] Examples of successful and unsuccessful mistake-of-law defenses include the following:

- Defendant erroneously believed a type of gambling was not prohibited by a state's gambling laws (unsuccessful defense).
- Defendant erroneously believed that seatbelts were not required for passengers (unsuccessful defense).
- Defendant depended on Attorney General's written opinion that his actions were not in violation of the law (successful defense).

2. Mistake of Fact

Some states have codified the mistake-of-fact defense. For example, the Georgia statute provides

> A person shall not be found guilty of a crime if the act or omission to an act constituting the crime was induced by misapprehension of fact which, if true, would have justified the act or omission.[113]

In interpreting this statute, the Court of Appeals of Georgia decided that the defendant's testimony that he knew the arresting officers were police officers, but he did not believe that they had a warrant for his arrest, did not constitute a valid mistake-of-fact defense to the charge of obstruction of an officer.[114] The court said that this was a misapprehension of law rather than fact. Examples of successful and unsuccessful mistake-of-fact defenses include the following:

- Defendant erroneously believed that the horse he took from the field was his (successful).

---

[111] United States v. Ehrlichman, 376 F. Supp. 29 (D.D.C. 1974). *See also* D.F. v. State, 682 So. 2d 149 (Fla. 1996).
[112] Bryan v. United States, 524 U.S. 184, 118 S. Ct. 1939, 141 L. Ed. 2d 197 (1998).
[113] GA. CODE ANN. § 16-3-5 (1996).
[114] Woolfolk v. State, 413 S.E.2d 242 (Ga. 1991). *See also* State v. Brumback, 671 N.E.2d 1064 (Ohio Ct. App. 1996).

- Defendant erroneously believed that the woman he was having sex with had consented (perhaps successful if belief is reasonable).
- Defendant erroneously believed that house he was burning down belonged to his mother-in-law (unsuccessful because it does not negate any element of the *mens rea* of arson).

D. Summary

In general, mistakes of law are generally not a defense unless the crime requires specific intent. Mistakes of fact may be a defense if they negate an element of the crime.

§ 3.9   Alibi

It has been argued that **alibi** is not really an excuse or justification as are all the other defenses described in this chapter since in these cases, the defendant admits he committed the crime but that he had a justification or excuse. In alibi defenses, on the other hand, the defendant argues that he did not commit the offense.

A. Common Law

Because in the defense of alibi the defendant is arguing that he was at another place at the time of the crime, the defense has been recognized from the time of common law. The argument that still continues is whether it is an affirmative defense (which involves shifting burdens of proof on the part of the prosecutor and defendant), or is simply a negation of an element of the crime.

B. Model Penal Code

The Model Penal Code does not include any provisions for alibi defenses under either Section 2 (General Principles of Liability) or Section 3 (General Principles of Justification).

C. State Statutes, Codes, and Cases

The defense of alibi is universally recognized, but safeguards have been established to avoid the abuse of this defense. For example, it is not enough for the accused to say that he was not at the scene of the crime; he must show that he was at another specified place at the time the crime was committed.[115]

The Latin term *alibi* means "elsewhere." It is a defense that places the defendant, at the relevant time, in a different place from the location involved in the crime as to render it impossible for the defendant to be the guilty party. In the context of a criminal

---

[115]   Commonwealth v. McQueen, 178 Pa. Super. 38, 112 A.2d 820 (1955).

prosecution, *alibi* denotes an attempt by the defendant to demonstrate that he or she did not commit the crime because, at the time, he or she was in another place so far away or in a situation preventing the defendant from doing the act charged against him or her.[116]

Although the state retains the burden to prove each element of the crime charged, it need not offer evidence directly showing that the alibi was fabricated; it is sufficient if, by the introduction of evidence inconsistent with the proffered alibi, the prosecution is able to establish the factual predicates necessary to support a conviction.[117]

While some courts indicate that alibi is an affirmative defense that attempts to negate elements of the crime charged, others insist that alibi is not an affirmative defense, but that the fact of the defendant's presence elsewhere is an affirmative fact logically operative to negate his presence at the time and place of the crime.[118]

In explaining the alibi defense, one court, quoting other cases, commented that:

> In the context of a criminal prosecution, "alibi" denotes an attempt by the defendant to demonstrate he "did not commit the crime because at the time he was in another place so far away, or in a situation preventing his doing the thing charged against him . . . Strictly speaking, *alibi evidence* is merely rebuttal evidence directed to that part of the state's evidence which tends to identify the defendant as the person who committed the alleged crime."

In acknowledging that the alibi defense is not truly an independent affirmative defense, the court noted that it is simply evidence in support of the defendant's plea of not guilty and should not be treated merely as evidence tending to disprove one of the essential factors in the case of the prosecution.[119]

If the defendant is successful in convincing the judge or jury that he or she was at another place and that he or she therefore could not have committed the crime, the "alibi" defense is a complete defense and precludes the possibility of guilt. However, there is no obligation on the part of the trial court to believe the alibi testimony over positive identification of the accused, even though the alibi testimony may be given by a greater number of witnesses.[120]

The defendant may claim the defense of alibi at the trial even though he or she did not tell the police or district attorney that he or she had an alibi defense. In one case, the defendant was convicted of robbery, attempted robbery, assault, and criminal possession of a weapon. At the trial, the defendant presented an alibi defense. The district attorney encouraged the jury to infer that the alibi defense was a recent fabrication because the defendant was silent about the alibi from the time of his arrest until trial.

---

[116] Commonwealth v. Warrington, 326 A.2d 427 (Pa. 1974); State v. El-Tabech, 405 N.W.2d 585 (Neb. 1987). *See also* Commonwealth v. Mikell, 729 A.2d 566 (Pa. 1999).

[117] State v. Watkins, 806 A.2d 1072 (Conn. 2002).

[118] State v. Armstad, 283 S.W.2d 577 (Mo. 1955).

[119] Villarreal v. State, 821 S.W.2d 682 (Tex. Ct. App. 1991).

[120] People v. Woodson, 41 Cal. Rptr. 487 (1964); State v. Martin, 2 Ariz. App. 510, 410 P.2d 132 (1966). People v. Smallwood, 166 Ill. Dec. 978, 586 N.E.2d 636 (1991).

The appellate division reversed the defendant's conviction, pointing out that a defendant has no obligation, when in custody, to tell either the police or the district attorney that he has an alibi defense.[121]

D. *Summary*

The only real issue in the defense of alibi is whether it is a true affirmative defense or simply an argument as to the lack of one of the elements of the crime. All states recognize the defense of alibi but the defendant must, in order to present a prima facie case of alibi, cover the time of the crime exactly. Further, the jury or judge is free to weigh the credibility of the alibi evidence against other evidence, as is true in all aspects of trial evidence. This is the only defense where the defendant's position is one of actual innocence.

§ 3.10   Time Limitations (Statute of Limitations)

A defendant charged with a crime may claim that he should not be tried for that offense because the time limitation for prosecution has expired. This is often referred to as the **statute of limitations** defense. The rationale for the time limitations is that the defendant should have some substantial safeguards against an erroneous conviction because of the staleness of the evidence and because the defendant is entitled to a speedy trial. Therefore, when the defendant claims that the statutory period has expired, the guilt or innocence of the defendant is not an issue. If the statutory period has expired, the defendant is entitled to an acquittal as a matter of right.

Generally speaking, a statute of limitations begins to run as soon as the offense is completed. While determining the date of the crime ordinarily is not difficult, in some instances this can cause a problem, especially in drug-related cases in which several offenses are committed over a period of time.

As a general rule, the time begins to run when the crime is committed and runs until the prosecution is commenced. Depending upon the provisions of the statute, the running of the time is stopped by the filing of an indictment or information or at the time a complaint is laid before a magistrate and a warrant of arrest is issued.[122]

It is obvious that justice would not be served if the defendant conceals himself or otherwise makes it impossible for an investigation to take place or for the prosecution to commence. To overcome this possibility, statutes have been enacted that provide that if the person who has committed the offense is absent from the state, or so conceals himself that process cannot be served upon him, or conceals the fact of the crime, the time of the absence or concealment is not to be included in computing the period of limitations. This is often referred to as tolling the statute of limitations.

---

[121]   People v. Smoot, 59 A.D.2d 898, 399 N.Y.S.2d 133 (N.Y.A.D. 1977).
[122]   Jarrett v. State, 49 Okla. Crim. 162, 292 P. 888 (1930).

A. Common Law

Since statutes of limitation are identified by statute, common law is not relevant to this defense.

B. Model Penal Code

The Model Penal Code includes a time limitation for all offenses, including felonies and misdemeanors, with the exception of murder. In the case of murder, the prosecution may be commenced at any time. This recommended statute specifies four periods of limitation:

- six years for felonies of the first degree
- three years for less serious felonies
- two years for misdemeanors
- six months for petty misdemeanors and violations.

The Model Penal Code also includes a subsection that defines when an offense is commenced for statute of limitations purposes and indicates specifically when the statute of limitations does not run.[123]

C. State Statutes, Codes, and Cases

Most jurisdictions have enacted statutes to limit the time for the commencement of some criminal proceedings. These statutes vary in their terms and almost always provide that a prosecution for murder may be commenced at any time. Some statutes provide that the prosecution for *any* felony is not subject to a period of limitations and may be commenced at any time. An example of the latter provision is that of Kentucky. The Kentucky statute provides

K.R.S. 500.050 Time Limitations[124]

(1) Except as otherwise expressly provided, the prosecution of a felony is not subject to a period of limitation and may be commenced at any time.
(2) Except as otherwise expressly provided, the prosecution of an offense other than a felony must be commenced within one year after it is committed.
(3) For the purpose of this Section, an offense is committed either when every element occurs, or if a legislative purpose to prohibit a continuing course of conduct plainly appears, at the time in the course of conduct of the defendant's complicity therein is terminated.

The statute of limitations exists primarily to ensure against the inevitable prejudice and injustice to a defendant occasioned by delay in prosecution. The statute of limitations strikes a balance between an individual's interest in being placed on notice to formulate a defense for a crime charged, and the state's interest in having sufficient

---

[123]　MODEL PENAL CODE § 1.06 (1985).
[124]　KY. REV. STAT. § 500.050 (Baldwin 2002).

time to investigate and develop its case. One court noted that any exceptions to the limitation period must be construed narrowly and in a light most favorable to the accused.[125] The state bears the burden of showing that there has been a just and legal cause for the interruption of the "tolling" of the time period, for instance, by the defendant's flight and/or concealment from the jurisdiction.[126] In these cases, the government must prove, by a preponderance of the evidence, that the accused acted with the intent to avoid arrest or prosecution.[127]

§ 3.11   Other Defenses

1. Acting under the Authority or Direction of Others

Those who are charged with crimes often seek to justify their actions by explaining that they acted because they were ordered to do so. This defense is very difficult to demonstrate, especially when one argues they acted upon an order by a military authority. However, the general law is that, except insofar as the element of duress or compulsion may be present, the fact that one undertakes a crime or performs a criminal act under the authority or direction of a supervisor, one nevertheless is responsible for that act.[128]

An exception to the general law is recognized where a statute provides that a layperson acting on the orders of a peace officer is immune from prosecution for violations so committed. This defense applies only if the person accused is acting directly under the order of the police officer who is at that time carrying out his or her assigned responsibilities.[129]

2. Immunity

At least in some states, a witness who is granted immunity by the prosecutor may claim this as a defense if charged with a crime for which the immunity was granted. For example, if the prosecutor agrees not to prosecute the defendant if he or she cooperates with the police, despite the prosecutor's knowledge that the defendant was apparently involved in a bank robbery as the driver of the getaway car, this establishes an enforceable agreement not to prosecute. Defendants who are granted immunity are entitled to use this as a defense to any subsequent prosecutions.[130]

3. Constitutional Challenges

As discussed in Chapter 2, defendants may seek to avoid conviction by claiming that statutes were unconstitutional as being vague or overbroad, or that evidence

---

[125]   Roberts v. State, 712 N.E.2d 23 (Ind. 1999).
[126]   State v. McCord, 727 So.2d 1262 (La. 1999).
[127]   Ross v. United States Marshal for the Eastern District of Oklahoma, 168 F.3d 1190 (10th Cir. 1999).
[128]   Canales v. State, 496 S.W.2d 614 (Tex. Crim. App. 1973).
[129]   People v. Benford, 53 Cal.2d 1, 345 P.2d 928 (1959).
[130]   People v. Jackson, 480 N.W.2d 283 (Mich. 1991). *See also* United States v. Barone, 781 F. Supp. 1072 (E.D. Pa. 1991); United States v. Van Trourout, 100 F.3d 590 (1996).

is inadmissible due to an illegal search or seizure, improper techniques in obtaining a confession, or violation of the right to counsel.[131] Double jeopardy is also prohibited by the Constitution. This is a defense that the criminal act has already been prosecuted and the state or federal government is barred from further prosecution. However, double jeopardy bars prosecution for the same offense and lesser included offenses, but not a different but related offense; thus, a defendant who is acquitted for murder might be retried for kidnapping because kidnapping is not a lesser included offense of murder. Furthermore, double jeopardy does not bar prosecutions by different jurisdictions; therefore, for instance, defendants who were acquitted of racial murders during the Civil Rights era were retried for the same deaths by federal courts for federal crimes.

4. Outrageous Government Conduct

One particular constitutional challenge falls under due process protections. A defense claim that has received more attention in recent years has been labeled "outrageous government conduct" or "egregious law enforcement conduct." The argument made is that the indictment should be dismissed on the grounds that the government's outrageous conduct violated the due process clause of the Constitution. The courts have hesitated to recognize this doctrine. In *State v. Romero*, the court cautioned that the doctrine of outrageous government conduct is a most narrow defense, and thus protection afforded by the due process clause of the Fifth Amendment applies only when the government activity in question violates some protected right of the defendant.[132]

To support dismissal of an indictment on grounds of outrageous government conduct, the defendant must prove that the government's conduct was so excessive, flagrant, scandalous, intolerable, and offensive as to violate due process.[133] Applying the "outrageous conduct" defense claim, a federal appeals court held that the government did not engage in outrageous conduct as would violate due process, even if the government induced the defendants to attempt to rob an armored car and allowed the informant to let the defendants use his apartment to store guns and ammunition, to organize a time to unload the firearms, to supply ammunition, and to drive the defendants to the robbery scene, and even if the government put lives at risk by allowing an informant to store automatic weapons in his home and to give the defendants access to them.[134]

5. Vindictive Prosecution

Another defense that has received attention is the defense of "vindictive prosecution." Prosecutorial vindictiveness requires objective evidence that a

---

[131] *See* Kanovitz & Kanovitz, Constitutional Law (10th ed. 2006) and Klotter, Walker, and Hemmens, Legal Guide for Police (7th ed. 2005).
[132] State v. Romero, 926 P.2d 717 (Mont. 1996).
[133] United States v. Edmonds, 103 F.3d 822 (9th Cir. 1996).
[134] United States v. Rodriguez, 54 F.3d 739 (3d Cir. 2002), *cert. denied*, 537 U.S. 1179, 123 S. Ct. 1010, 154 L. Ed. 3d 926 (2002).

prosecutor's actions were designed to punish a defendant for asserting his legal rights.[135] A showing of actual prosecutorial vindictiveness is exceedingly difficult to make; however, a presumption of vindictiveness may be established in cases in which a reasonable likelihood of vindictiveness exists. When considering the vindictive prosecution defense, a federal court decided that the prosecution of an attempted reentry case was not vindictive even when the prosecutor did not seek to add charges until after the alien made it clear that he was going to trial rather than plead guilty; the prosecutor's office had a system of expediting such cases by initially charging only reentry offenses, with additional charges being sought after the file was scrutinized more closely.[136]

§ 3.12   Summary

The courts have recognized that there are situations in which persons who commit acts that would ordinarily be crimes may introduce evidence to show they do not have the capacity to form the criminal intent that is required as an element of some crimes, or to demonstrate other legitimate defenses.

An infant is exempt from criminal responsibility for his or her act if he or she lacks sufficient mental capacity to entertain the criminal act. Also, most states provide a method of treating juvenile offenders that is distinct from that of treating adult offenders.

Under the common law, and by statutes and court decisions in all states, mental incapacity or insanity may be alleged by one accused of crimes at several points in criminal procedure. Several tests have been used by the courts over the years to determine whether the mental disorder or impairment is sufficient to eliminate the ability of the defendant to form any level of *mens rea* that would create criminal culpability. These include the

- *M'Naghten* Rules
- irresistible impulse rule
- *Durham* Rule
- Model Penal Code (ALI) test

The law in this area continues to evolve and several states have changed their statutes to restrict the use of this defense. The issue of insanity or mental impairment may also arise when determining whether the defendant is competent to stand trial. The elements for this determination are whether the defendant is capable of making a proper defense, aiding his attorney, or securing evidence at the time of the trial.

What would ordinarily be a criminal act may be excused at law if the act is committed under duress or compulsion. In order to excuse an act that would ordinarily be a

---

[135]   State v. Tilson, 794 A.2d 465 (R.I. 2002).
[136]   United States v. Gonzales, 52 F.3d 330 (9th Cir. 2002).

crime, the compulsion or coercion must be present, imminent, or impending. Closely related to duress and compulsion is the defense of necessity. The general rule is that "a criminal offense may be justified or excused if done under necessity." Neither of these defenses will excuse harming an innocent victim.

Self-defense requires the force used by the defendant to be reasonable to defend against an apparent threat of unlawful and immediate violence from another. In order to successfully claim this defense, the defendant must show that

- he believed physical force to be necessary for self-protection against an unlawful attack,
- his belief was based upon reasonable grounds,
- the force used was believed necessary to avoid imminent danger, and
- the force used was not in excess of that believed necessary to repel the unlawful attack.

The statutes and cases differ as to what force is justified, and under what circumstances.

Entrapment is a defense in a criminal case. If the criminal design originates in the mind of the police and not with the accused, entrapment is a proper defense. The rationale for the entrapment defense is that no person should be convicted of a crime that he or she was induced to commit by the very government that is prosecuting him or her for committing the crime.

Although ignorance or mistake of the law is no excuse, an honest and reasonable mistake of fact that negates one element of the crime may result in no criminal culpability unless the mistake arises from a want of proper care on the part of the accused.

Other defenses include alibi, statute of limitations, authorization by an authority, constitutional challenges that the law itself was unconstitutional (as overbroad or vague), and procedural due process challenges (procedural violations, outrageous government conduct, and vindictive prosecution).

REVIEW QUESTIONS

1. What was the age at which a child could not be held culpable for their acts under common law? What were the ages where the presumption of incompetence was rebuttable? What about the Model Penal Code?

2. What are the three ways (or times in the process) in which one's mental capacity are considered during criminal adjudication and punishment?

3. Describe the four tests of insanity. Which is the most frequently used?

4. Explain changes in some state laws regarding the defense of insanity. What is the verdict of guilty but insane?

5. Describe the test for incompetency.

6. Explain the diminished capacity defense. Describe some examples.

7. Explain how intoxication might be used as a diminished capacity defense. Describe whether such a defense is successful in all states.

8. Describe the elements to the defense of duress.

9. Describe the battered woman defense.

10. Describe the elements of the defense of necessity. Provide examples of successful and unsuccessful uses.

11. Describe the six elements of self defense.

12. What are "Make my Day" laws and how are they different from traditional self-defense.

13. Did the entrapment defense exist under common law? Describe the objective versus subjective tests of entrapment.

14. Explain the mistake-of-law and mistake-of-fact defenses. Which is almost never a defense to criminal culpability?

15. Describe the defense of alibi.

16. Describe the defense of statute of limitations.

17. Describe the defense of "acting under the authority of others."

18. Describe the defense of immunity.

19. Describe some constitutional challenges that may be used as defenses.

20. Describe the defenses of outrageous governmental conduct and vindictive prosecution.

Preparatory Activity Offenses

4

Chapter Outline

Section

Cases

Attempt: *Commonwealth of Pennsylvania v. Henley*, 504 Pa. 408 (1984)
Conspiracy: *Bolden v. Nevada*, 124 P.3d 191, 121 Nev. Adv. Rptr 86 (2005).

§ 4.1 Introduction

The most common preparatory activity crimes are "attempt," "conspiracy," and "solicitation." Legislative bodies have provided penalties for these preparatory acts to reach those who have not actually perpetrated a substantive crime, but have been involved in preparing to commit a crime.

In this chapter, the three most often charged preparatory activity crimes (attempt, solicitation, and conspiracy) are defined and explained.

§ 4.2 Attempt

An **attempt** to commit a crime has been defined as an act done with intent to commit a crime, beyond mere preparation, but falling short of its actual commission.[1] It is also defined as "any overt act done with intent to commit the crime which and except for the interference of some cause preventing the carrying out of the intent, would have resulted in the commission of the crime."[2]

The distinction between "intent" and an "attempt" to do a thing is that the former implies the purpose only, while the latter implies both the purpose and an actual effort to carry that purpose into execution. Because the purpose of the law concerning criminal intent is to permit the courts to adjudge a penalty in cases in which conduct falls short of a completed substantive crime, an attempt to commit a crime is, as a general rule, an indictable offense that is separate and distinct from the substantive crime.[3]

---

[1]   State v. Reis, 230 N.C. 272, 52 S.E.2d 880 (1949).
[2]   State v. Leach, 36 Wash. 2d 641, 219 P.2d 972 (1950).
[3]   People v. Crane, 302 Ill. 217, 134 N.E. 99 (1922).

A. Common Law

In early days, no crime was committed until the defendant carried out the *actus reus* of a substantive crime. Later, common law decisions and early court cases recognized attempts as crimes separate from the substantive crime, but considered them misdemeanors. Eventually, statutes were created that ascribed the same level of seriousness to the attempt as the crime attempted.

Because the elements of the offense of attempt are often unclear and difficult to prove, many courts have framed their own definitions. These indicate the requirements that are necessary to prove this offense. One court coined a short definition: "An attempt to commit a crime is an act done with intent to commit that crime, carried beyond mere preparation to commit it, but falling short of its actual commission."[4]

The criminal law is not designed to impose liability for bad thoughts alone. While one might consider committing a specific crime, such thoughts do not create criminal culpability unless there is an overt act to go along with the intent. The overt act must also be sufficiently proximate to the intended crime. While mere preparation to commit an offense does not constitute an attempt, preparation plus an overt act going beyond mere preparation, toward commission of the crime, does constitute the offense.[5] Unless the statutory elements are different, the traditional elements of an "attempt" to commit a crime generally are

1. a specific intent to commit a crime,
2. an overt act toward its commission,
3. the apparent possibility of commission, and
4. failure of consummation.

1. Specific Intent

Although there seems to be a minority opinion that only general intent is necessary for the crime of attempt,[6] the better approach is that because the substantive crime has not been consummated, it is incumbent on the prosecutor to show the higher level of intent. Generally, prosecutors must show **specific intent**, that is, proof must be offered that the offender intended to do the act (the overt act that was in furtherance of the crime) and intended the outcome (that is, the ultimate crime). However, specific intent can be inferred from circumstantial evidence.

---

[4]   State v. Goodman, 322 S.E.2d 408 (N.C. 1984).

[5]   Fleming v. State, 374 So. 2d 954 (Fla. 1979); Gilley v. Commonwealth, 280 Ky. 306, 133 S.W.2d 67 (1939).

[6]   *See* Smith v. United States, 813 A.2d 216 (D.C. 2002), in which the court held that the only intent required to commit the crime of "attempt" is an intent to commit the offense allegedly attempted.

2. Tests for Overt Act

Different courts have used different tests to decide whether an act has been committed that is sufficiently beyond preparation to constitute the **overt act** requirement. The tests can be remembered as

- "any" act,
- substantial step,
- act beyond mere preparation, and
- all but the last step.

The "any act" test would be the easiest for the prosecutor to prove and the "all but the last step" test would be the hardest. The **"substantial step"** test is the most common language employed. Courts note that an overt act to prove attempt requires conduct that is strongly corroborative of the actor's criminal purpose. The overt act consists of conduct constituting a "substantial step" toward commission of the crime and consists of conduct that is strongly corroborative of the firmness of the defendant's criminal intent. Mere preparation does not constitute a "substantial step."[7] Some examples of when courts have decided that the defendant completed the overt acts necessary to constitute attempt include

- lying in wait and shooting at the victim (attempted murder);
- pouring gasoline in the victim's house (attempted arson); and
- grabbing the victim, dragging her off the sidewalk into an alley, and tearing at her clothes (attempted rape).

Other scenarios probably would not be sufficient to constitute attempt. Would the following acts constitute attempt? If so, under what test?

- downloading bomb instructions from the Internet (attempted arson/terroristic act)
- entering the house of a former girlfriend with rope, a knife, tape, and a camera (attempted rape)
- standing outside a bank with a gun (attempted bank robbery)

3. Apparent Ability: Impossibility as a Defense

Because one of the elements of attempt is the apparent ability to complete the substantive crime, can a person be guilty of attempt if it is impossible to succeed in the commission of the crime? For example, can a man be guilty of attempted murder when, with intent to commit murder, he shoots a body, but unbeknownst to the offender, the person was already dead?

The courts have differed in their response to situations in which the defendant could not have succeeded in the attempt to commit a crime. There is agreement that

---

[7]   State v. Group, 781 N.E.2d 980 (Ohio 2002); United States v. Buffington, 815 F.2d 292 (9th Cir. 1987).

its consummation must be *apparently possible* and there must be at least an *apparent ability* to commit it. Further, the act itself, if consummated, must be a crime. The general rule is that **factual impossibility** does not constitute a defense. For example, when a defendant attempted to steal money from the victim's pocket and did everything he could to commit theft, but the crime failed only because the pocket was empty, impossibility was not a defense.[8]

The courts have held that it is not necessary that there be a actual ability to complete the crime—only an apparent ability. Therefore

> if there is an apparent ability to commit the crime in the way attempted, the attempt is indictable, although, unknown to the person making the attempt, the crime cannot be committed, because the means employed are in fact unsuitable, or because of extrinsic facts, such as the non-existence of some essential object or an obstruction by the intended victim or by a third person.[9]

Think of it this way: if the offender had been successful in achieving what he attempted to do and the result would have been a crime, then the existence of factual impossibility will not excuse the attempt. Some situations will illustrate factual impossibilities that do not create a defense for the offender. In the following cases, the offender would still be guilty of the attempted crime:

- attempt to shoot someone but the gun was unloaded or inoperable (unknown to the offender)
- attempt to solicit murder but asks an undercover police officer
- attempt to commit rape but intended victim is not in bed
- attempt to kill someone but victim was already dead
- attempt to commit theft but safe is empty
- attempt to rob bank but bank is closed and offender cannot get in the door
- attempt to solicit sex from a minor in an Internet chat room, but "minor" is really a police officer

---

LEGAL NEWS: SOLICITING CHILDREN ONLINE

Law enforcement has increasingly become adept at using the Internet as well as potential offenders who solicit children for sex in Internet chat rooms. Adult officers pretend to be children and engage adult predators in online conversations. Usually such conversations begin in chat rooms that cater to those who are predisposed to such behavior. When the adult solicits sex from the minor he or she has already committed the crime of solicitation. If they arrange to meet the child somewhere and are arrested after they attempt to make the meeting, they are arrested for attempted molestation or whatever the state charge is for sex with a minor. Even though it would have been impossible for the act to have taken place

---

[8]   People v. Fiegelman, 33 Cal. App. 2d 100, 91 P.2d 156 (1933).
[9]   22 C.J.S. *Criminal Law* § 123 (1989).

> because the "minor" was, in fact, a police officer, this is an example of factual impossibility or hybrid legal impossibility and, so, is not a defense to the crime of attempt.
>
> _____
>
> For more information, go to http://www.sdcda.org/preventing/protecting-children-online/real-cases.html.

However, **legal impossibility** may be a defense. If it is not a crime to do what the person is attempting to do, then the attempt is not indictable. For example, if the defendant thought that bringing dried fruit rolls into the country violated customs laws and hid them in her luggage, she has not attempted smuggling because what she thought she was doing is not a crime. Even if she was caught with dried fruit rolls, she would not be guilty of attempted smuggling even though she thought she was breaking a law. Other examples of pure legal impossibility are

- attempting to commit solicitation of prostitution but doing so in a Nevada county where prostitution is legal;
- attempting to break a speeding law by going 65 but not being aware that the speed limit was 65; and
- attempting to commit a gambling violation but gambling in a way that is legal in that state.

Contrast this situation with a person who thinks he is smuggling cocaine (but it turns out to be baking powder). The defendant is correct in the belief that smuggling cocaine is illegal, but is incorrect that what he is hiding is cocaine. While some would define this as another example of factual impossibility and others incorrectly define it as legal impossibility because smuggling baking powder is not criminal, the more accurate characterization is to define it as "hybrid legal impossibility." Other examples of hybrid legal impossibility include a case in which the defendant attempted to bribe someone he mistakenly believed to be a juror but the person was not a juror. The court held that no attempt had been committed because even if the person had accepted the money, the elements of bribery were not present.[10] Other instances of this type of hybrid legal impossibility follow (along with the court opinions where they were considered):

_____

[10]   State v. Taylor, 345 Mo. 325, 133 S.W.2d 336 (1939).

- not attempted poaching by shooting a stuffed deer (because if the offender was successful it would still be shooting a stuffed deer)[11]
- not attempted possession of marijuana by smoking a substance that is not illegal (because no matter what the offender thought he was doing, it was not an illegal substance)
- not attempted receipt of stolen goods when goods were not stolen (because it was not illegal to receive and could not be made so by offender's mistaken belief)[12]
- not attempted subornation of perjury when issue was not material to case (because even if offender thought he was committing crime, the immateriality of the issue meant it could never be a crime)[13]

The distinction between true legal impossibility and hybrid legal impossibility is this: In true legal impossibility the person believes some act is against the law but it is not. Examples might be the fruit roll smuggler above, or other situations in which a person believes there is a law against their behavior, but there is not. In hybrid legal impossibility, the defendant is *correct* in their belief that the act is against the law, but *incorrect* as to an essential element of the law. An essential element of bribing jurors, for instance, is that it is a juror who is offered the bribe. The difference between factual and hybrid legal impossibility is that in factual impossibility, the mistake is not concerning an element of the crime. An attempted murder when the gun has no bullets is factual impossibility because the mistake is not an element of the crime, but attempted poaching by shooting a stuffed deer is hybrid legal impossibility because the poaching laws specify deer, not deer facsimiles. Finally, a mistake in thinking that there is a law regarding hunting in a certain area when the law does not exist at all is an example of legal impossibility.

Mistaken Belief	Example
1. Mistaken belief not related to element of crime of a true crime = factual impossibility.	1. D shoots and hits V (with intent to kill V), but V is already dead; if D had been successful, it would have been murder = factual (no defense to attempt charge).
2. Mistaken belief that action is a crime but there is no crime = legal impossibility.	2. D buys lottery ticket (with intent to commit a gambling crime), but lottery is legal (no crime); if D had been successful in buying the ticket, he would have bought a legal lottery ticket = legal (no criminal attempt).
3. Mistaken belief related to element of a true crime = legal hybrid impossibility.	3. D shoots at deer (with intent to hunt out of season), but deer is fake; if D had been successful in shooting at what he thought was a deer, he would have been guilty of a crime = legal hybrid (no defense to attempted illegal hunting now in most jurisdictions).

---

[11]   State v. Guffey, 262 S.W.2d 152 (Mo. Ct. App. 1953).
[12]   People v. Jaffe, 185 N.Y. 497, 78 N.E. 169 (N.Y. 1906). See also United States v. Monasterski, 567 F.2d 677 (E.D. Mich. 1987).
[13]   People v. Teal, 196 N.Y. 372, 89 N.E. 1086 (1909).

These distinctions are difficult to make; sometimes even judges and juries are confused about the difference between the two. The current trend is to disallow the defense of hybrid legal impossibility; therefore, the cases discussed above would be decided differently by today's courts. No doubt partially due to the difficulties in distinguishing the forms of impossibility, the Model Penal Code has chosen to eliminate the defense of legal impossibility entirely.

4. Failure of Consummation: Abandonment as a Defense

Obviously, if the crime is completed, the defendant would be prosecuted for the substantive crime; thus, attempts are those situations in which, for whatever reason, the crime was not completed. **Abandonment** or withdrawal is a defense if the attempt to commit a crime is freely and voluntarily abandoned before the final execution of the crime, and if there is no outside cause prompting the abandonment. To state this differently, if a person voluntarily abandoned his or her proposed plan of crime before actual commission of the crime, and he or she does so voluntarily, he or she cannot be held guilty of an attempt.[14]

Abandonment is no defense if failure to complete the crime is due to **extraneous intervening circumstances**. For example, failure to complete the crime because of a threatened arrest or appearance of the police is not the free and voluntary abandonment necessary to constitute the defense.[15] Abandonment is not a defense when it is due to factual impossibility, for instance, if a person attempted to rob a bank but arrived as the door was locked. Even if the offender walked away, he might still be indicted for attempt because his abandonment was due to the extrinsic factor of the locked door. Only if the abandonment is a voluntary decision on the part of the offender, and not due to external reasons, will it serve as a defense.

B. *Model Penal Code*

The Model Penal Code uses the "substantial step" test to determine whether an overt act has been committed sufficient to create criminal culpability. There are also specific examples of what constitutes a substantial step. The Code deviates from the traditional approach because it does not recognize the defense of legal impossibility. Attempt is defined in terms of conduct that would constitute the crime if circumstances were as the defendant believed them to be. This opens the door to attempted smuggling when the smuggler is carrying nondrugs; attempted receipt of stolen property when the property is really recovered property in an undercover sting operation; and attempted murder when the hired hit man is really a police officer. The Code does, however, follow traditional statutes in that abandonment is recognized as a defense only if it is free, voluntary, and unrelated to extrinsic circumstances.

---

[14]   People v. Montgomery, 47 Cal. App. 2d 1, 117 P.2d 437 (1941).
[15]   People v. Walker, 33 Cal. 2d 250, 201 P.2d 6 (1948), *cert. denied*, 336 U.S. 940, 69 S. Ct. 744, 93 L. Ed. 1098 (1949).

§ 5.01 Criminal Attempt[16]

(1) **Definition of Attempt.** A person is guilty of an attempt to commit a crime if, acting with the kind of culpability otherwise required for commission of the crime, he:
  (a) purposely engages in conduct which would constitute the crime if the attendant circumstances were as he believes them to be; or
  (b) when causing a particular result is an element of the crime, does or omits to do anything with the purpose of causing or with the belief that it will cause such result without further conduct on his part; or
  (c) purposely does or omits to do anything which, under the circumstances as he believes them to be, is an act or omission constituting a substantial step in a course of conduct planned to culminate in his commission of the crime.
(2) **Conduct Which May Be Held Substantial Step Under Subsection (1)(c).** Conduct shall not be held to constitute a substantial step under Subsection (1)(c) of this Section unless it is strongly corroborative of the actor's criminal purpose. Without negating the sufficiency of other conduct, the following, if strongly corroborative of the actor's criminal purpose, shall not be held insufficient as a matter of law:
  (a) lying in wait, searching for or following the contemplated victim of the crime;
  (b) enticing or seeking to entice the contemplated victim of the crime to go to the place contemplated for its commission;
  (c) reconnoitering the place contemplated for the commission of the crime;
  (d) unlawful entry of a structure, vehicle or enclosure in which it is contemplated that the crime will be committed;
  (e) possession of materials to be employed in the commission of the crime, which are specially designed for such unlawful use or which can serve no lawful purpose of the actor under the circumstances;
  (f) possession, collection or fabrication of materials to be employed in the commission of the crime, at or near the place contemplated for its commission, where such possession, collection or fabrication serves no lawful purpose of the actor under the circumstances;
  (g) soliciting an innocent agent to engage in conduct constituting an element of the crime.
(3) **Conduct Designed to Aid Another in Commission of a Crime.** A person who engages in conduct designed to aid another to commit a crime which would establish his complicity under § 2.06 if the crime were committed by such other person, is guilty of an attempt to commit the crime, although the crime is not committed or attempted by such other person.
(4) **Renunciation of Criminal Purpose.** When the actor's conduct would otherwise constitute an attempt under Subsection (1)(b) or (1)(c) of this Section, it is an affirmative defense that he abandoned his effort to commit the crime or otherwise prevented its commission, under circumstances manifesting a complete and voluntary renunciation of his criminal purpose. The establishment of such defense does not, however, affect the liability of an accomplice who did not join in such abandonment or prevention.

Within the meaning of this Article, renunciation of criminal purpose is not voluntary if it is motivated, in whole or in part, by circumstances, not present or apparent at the inception of the actor's course of conduct, which increase the probability of detection or apprehension or which make more difficult the accomplishment of the criminal purpose. Renunciation is not complete if it is motivated by a decision to postpone the criminal conduct until a more advantageous time or to transfer the criminal effort to another but similar objective or victim.

---

[16]   MODEL PENAL CODE § 5.01 (1985).

C. State Statutes, Codes, and Cases

Many states have created general attempt offenses that replace scores of statutes creating special attempt crimes. Some state statutes still include separate provisions for punishment for "attempted rape," "attempted arson," and "attempted burglary," but the more recent approach is to consolidate all of the statutes into a single attempt provision uniformly relating the penalty for criminal attempt to the penalty for the crime attempted. An example of such a statute is that of Kentucky, which provides

§ 506.010—Criminal attempt[17]

(1) A person is guilty of criminal attempt to commit a crime when, acting with the kind of culpability otherwise required for commission of the crime, he:
   (a) Intentionally engages in conduct which would constitute the crime if the attendant circumstances were as he believes them to be; or
   (b) Intentionally does or omits to do anything which, under the circumstances as he believes them to be, is a substantial step in a course of conduct planned to culminate in his commission of the crime.
(2) Conduct shall not be held to constitute a substantial step under Subsection (1)(b) unless it is an act or omission which leaves no reasonable doubt as to the defendant's intention to commit the crime which he is charged with attempting.
(3) A person is guilty of criminal attempt to commit a crime when he engages in conduct intended to aid another person to commit that crime, although the crime is not committed or attempted by the other person, provided that his conduct would establish complicity under KRS 502.020 if the crime were committed by the other person.
(4) A criminal attempt is a:
   (a) Class C felony when the crime attempted is a violation of KRS 521.020 or 521.050;
   (b) Class B felony when the crime attempted is a Class A felony or capital offense;
   (c) Class C felony when the crime attempted is a Class B felony;
   (d) Class A misdemeanor when the crime attempted is a Class C or D felony;
   (e) Class B misdemeanor when the crime attempted is a misdemeanor.

Section 506.020 of the Kentucky Penal Code offers the defense of renunciation. As with most modern codes, this makes voluntary renunciation a defense to criminal attempt. It provides that renunciation is not voluntary within the meaning of this provision if motivated by a "belief that circumstances exist that pose a particular threat of apprehension or detection." This is interpreted to mean that if an offense is not completed due to the interference of a police officer, the defense of renunciation would not be available.[18]

In an attempt case, one can expect the defense to emphasize that (1) the intent element has not been proved; (2) there was no overt act; and (in some cases) (3) the defendant voluntarily "abandoned the intent prior to committing an overt act in furtherance of the plan."

---

[17] KY. REV. STAT. § 506.010 (Baldwin 2002).
[18] Luttrell v. Commonwealth, 554 S.W.2d 75 (Ky. 1977).

In the case of *State v. Miller*, the defendant shot a victim during a robbery attempt and then ran away without taking the victim's money. He was convicted of murder and attempted armed robbery. The attempted robbery was appealed, arguing that there was insufficient evidence of attempted armed robbery, either because there was no action beyond preparation and, even if there was, the defendant abandoned the attempt, which negated his culpability.[19] The appeals court first pointed out that the elements of attempt to commit any crime are (1) intent to commit the substantive offense; and (2) an overt act done for a purpose that goes beyond mere preparation; but (3) falls short of a completed offense. The court held that prior statements the defendant made indicating his desire to rob the victim, in addition to his actions, which entailed sneaking up on the victim and firing his gun into the victim's head, were sufficient to prove specific intent and an overt act. He was not entitled to an abandonment defense because, under North Carolina law, once an overt act is committed, even a defendant who voluntarily abandons the effort with no outside interference is guilty of attempt (this is different from many other states that do recognize the defense of abandonment in these circumstances).

To prove the "intent" element, the prosecution must offer evidence to show a specific intent to commit a specific offense. In *People v. Ritson*, the defendant was convicted of attempted kidnapping, among other charges. He sexually solicited two young boys in a park and when they refused, he drove to a shopping center and stopped next to a 12-year-old boy who was alone, opened the car door, and told him to "get the hell in the car." The boy ran to his mother and Ritson was eventually arrested and charged. He challenged the conviction, arguing that there was insufficient evidence of attempted kidnapping. The appellate court found the facts, taken together with the prior incident, indicated an attempt to complete the elements of kidnapping which included taking, holding, or detaining someone by instilling fear.[20]

One might wonder when a person might be charged with attempted murder in addition to or instead of aggravated assault. In most cases, it has to do with the severity of the injuries received by the victim and/or other evidence that proves intent to kill. If someone stabs or hits a victim, that, in itself, may not convince a jury of the intent to kill. Even a drive-by shooting may not be sufficient proof of intent to kill. On the other hand, if the defendant stabbed the victim multiple times, or beat the victim severely, or shot the victim intentionally, then the actions alone may constitute sufficient proof of intent.

Even when the defendant's intent is clear, his or her actions, in order to support an attempt conviction, must cross the line between mere preparation and an unequivocal demonstration that the crime will take place unless interrupted by independent circumstances. That is, there must be an overt act. In *State v. Green*, the defendant picked out a woman, seemingly at random, and decided to kill her. When she parked her van in a

---

[19] State v. Miller, 477 S.E.2d 915 (N.C. 1996). *See also* State v. Williams-Rusch, 928 P.2d 169 (Mont. 1996).

[20] People v. Ritson, 74 Cal. Rptr. 2d 698 (1998). *See also* People v. Saous, 661 N.Y.2d 488 (1997).

store parking lot and went in, he hid inside her van and planned to stab her and "drink her blood." When she came back, she surprised the defendant by pulling open the sliding door of the van instead of getting in the driver's seat. When she angrily demanded he get out, he did so docilely and made up a story as to why he had climbed inside. Passersby restrained him and he was subsequently convicted of attempted aggravated murder. The defendant argued that he had not completed a substantial step toward the completion of the crime but the appellate court disagreed and upheld the conviction.[21]

In *People v. Sabo*, the defendant hired "John Doe" to kill the victim, but instead Doe went to the police. They arranged for him to accept the assignment and Sabo gave him a plan to carry to out the murder, a photograph of the intended victim, and a down payment of $10,000 with a promise of $15,000 more once the deed was done. Conversations regarding the murder were recorded and the police even created a photograph that showed what appeared to be the dead victim. Sabo did not accept the photograph as proof and demanded that the body be found in a public place and the victim's family hold a funeral for the intended victim before he would pay the remaining money. He was arrested shortly after and indicted for attempted murder, criminal solicitation, and criminal conspiracy. Sabo challenged his indictment by arguing that attempt is defined by New York law as coming "dangerously close" to the completion of the crime. Since the apparent "hit man" was actually working with police, there was no way that the crime would have ever been committed. (Was this a defense of factual or legal impossibility?) However, New York law did not recognize either factual or legal impossibility as a defense, and therefore the indictment was not quashed. The court noted that in this case, the acts Sabo took did come "dangerously close" to completion because the crime itself would have been committed but for timely interference.[22] In *Pennsylvania v. Henley*, a case included in Part II of this text, the court also ruled on a case of legal or factual impossibility.

> **CASE NOTE: *Commonwealth of Pennsylvania v. Henley*, 504 PA 408 (1984)**
> What was the issue?
> What is the Pennsylvania's court holding in regard to the defense of "legal impossibility"?
> Was this a case of factual, legal, or hybrid legal impossibility?

D. Summary

The offense of criminal attempt is especially important to enforcement officials. It is often overlooked and no action is taken when the intended offense is not consummated. However, legislatures in all jurisdictions have recognized that a person who goes as far as possible in implementing a criminal purpose manifests dangerousness sufficient to warrant some sanctions. The rationale for including attempt as an offense is that other crimes might be prevented by taking action against the person who has indicated this criminal purpose.

---

21 State v. Green, 122 Ohio App. 3d 566, 702 N.E.2d 462 (1997).
22 People v. Sabo, 687 N.Y.S.2d 513 (1998).

Attempt
(A/R) an overt act toward the completion of a crime (beyond mere preparation; usually the test is "substantial step"); apparent ability; noncompletion of the crime (M/R) specific intent (to do the intended crime)

§ 4.3   Criminal Solicitation

A. Common Law

The common law crime of **solicitation** is defined as "to solicit another to commit a felony." The rationale for making solicitation of another a separate offense is similar to the rationale for making attempt a crime: the criminal culpability of the solicitor is as great as it would be if the proposal were accepted and the underlying offense completed. The offense of solicitation was punishable at common law without regard for the nature of the substantive crime solicited; that is, criminal solicitation of murder had the same potential sanction as criminal solicitation of larceny.[23]

Commenting on the common law, an Oregon court stated that at common law, a person was guilty of solicitation if that person requested, commanded, or importuned another to commit a felony or serious misdemeanor. If the solicited person agreed to commit the crime, each party was guilty of conspiracy. The court pointed out that solicitation was a well-established crime when the first American guarantees of free expression were adopted.[24] The offense is complete even though the person solicited refuses to commit the crime.[25] The elements of solicitation are

1. an intent to promote or facilitate the commission of a particular criminal offense; and
2. some overt act, such as the initiatory act of solicitation, request, command, or encouragement.

B. Model Penal Code

Under the Model Penal Code, it is necessary to show "intent" (the mental element) plus asking another to engage in specific conduct. The Model Code includes a specific defense of **renunciation**, provided the renunciation is complete and voluntary. "Solicitation" is defined as an offer or invitation to another to commit a crime; it does not, by itself, constitute an attempt, but may escalate into an attempt to commit a crime after the offeror commits a direct, unequivocal act toward committing the crime.

---

[23]   Commonwealth v. Randolph, 146 Pa. 83, 23 A. 388 (1882).
[24]   State v. Grimes, 735 P.2d 1277 (Or. 1987).
[25]   People v. Burt, 45 Cal. 2d 311, 288 P.2d 503 (1955).

§ 5.02 Criminal Solicitation[26]

(1) Definition of Solicitation. A person is guilty of solicitation to commit a crime if with the purpose of promoting or facilitating its commission he commands, encourages or requests another person to engage in specific conduct which would constitute such crime or an attempt to commit such crime or which would establish his complicity in its commission or attempted commission.

(2) Uncommunicated Solicitation. It is immaterial under Subsection (1) of this Section that the actor fails to communicate with the person he solicits to commit a crime if his conduct was designed to effect such communication.

(3) Renunciation of Criminal Purpose. It is an affirmative defense that the actor, after soliciting another person to commit a crime, persuaded him not to do so or otherwise prevented the commission of the crime, under circumstances manifesting a complete and voluntary renunciation of his criminal purpose.

C. State Statutes, Codes, and Cases

Although solicitation was recognized as an offense at common law, it was not made a statutory offense in all states. The offense of solicitation was punishable at common law as a misdemeanor without regard to the nature of the substantive crime solicited; however, recently enacted statutes provide a penalty structure that gears the penalty to the crime solicited.

In some states, there are specific solicitation statutes attached to certain crimes, such as murder. In Illinois, the statute provides "A person commits solicitation when, with intent that an offense be committed, other than first-degree murder, he commands, encourages or requests another to commit that offense."[27] Under the Illinois Code, specific intent is required for a conviction of the crime of solicitation, but the intent may be inferred from surrounding circumstances and acts of the defendant.[28] In addition to the element of specific intent, the prosecution must show that the defendant commanded, encouraged, or asked another to commit a specific crime. The offense is complete when the principal offense is commanded, requested, or encouraged with the specific intent that the principal offense be committed.[29]

The Nevada statute provides

(1) Every person who counsels, hires, commands or otherwise solicits another to commit kidnapping or arson is guilty of a gross misdemeanor if no criminal act is committed as a result of that solicitation.

(2) Every person who counsels, hires, commands or otherwise solicits another to commit murder, if no criminal act is committed as a result of the solicitation, shall be punished by imprisonment in the state prison for not less than one year nor more than ten years, and may be further punished by a fine of not more than $10,000.00.[30]

---

[26]   Model Penal Code § 5.02 (1985).

[27]   720 Ill. Comp. Stat. 5/8-1 (2003).

[28]   People v. Lewis, 84 Ill. App. 3d 556, 406 N.E.2d 11 (1980).

[29]   People v. McCommon, 79 Ill. App. 3d, 399 N.E.2d 224 (1979).

[30]   Nev. Rev. Stat. § 199.500 (1995).

In *Moran v. Schwarz*, the defendant was charged with a violation of this statute. The defendant was accused of having solicited two men to kill a man named Thomas Susman in exchange for money and jewelry, and having provided them with information about Susman so they could carry out the murder.[31] The defendant appealed his conviction, arguing that he changed his mind about the murder and abandoned his plan. The Nevada appellate court rejected this defense, stating that, in Nevada, the harm was "in the asking," and the crime of solicitation was complete at that point.

Similarly, a Virginia court held that criminal solicitation involves an attempt of the accused to incite another to commit a criminal offense; it is immaterial whether the solicitation is of any effect and whether the crime solicited is in fact committed, because the *actus reus* of the offense is the incitement.[32]

Other states have more general solicitation statutes. For instance, Florida's statute states

777.04 Attempts, solicitation, and conspiracy.—

(1) A person who attempts to commit an offense prohibited by law and in such attempt does any act toward the commission of such offense, but fails in the perpetration or is intercepted or prevented in the execution thereof, commits the offense of criminal attempt, ranked for purposes of sentencing as provided in subsection (4). Criminal attempt includes the act of an adult who, with intent to commit an offense prohibited by law, allures, seduces, coaxes, or induces a child under the age of 12 to engage in an offense prohibited by law.

(2) A person who solicits another to commit an offense prohibited by law and in the course of such solicitation commands, encourages, hires, or requests another person to engage in specific conduct which would constitute such offense or an attempt to commit such offense commits the offense of criminal solicitation, ranked for purposes of sentencing as provided in subsection (4).

(3) A person who agrees, conspires, combines, or confederates with another person or persons to commit any offense commits the offense of criminal conspiracy, ranked for purposes of sentencing as provided in subsection (4).

(4) (a) Except as otherwise provided in . . . , the offense of criminal attempt, criminal solicitation, or criminal conspiracy is ranked for purposes of sentencing under chapter 921 and determining incentive gain-time eligibility under chapter 944 one level below the ranking under . . . the offense attempted, solicited, or conspired to. If the criminal attempt, criminal solicitation, or criminal conspiracy is of an offense ranked in level 1 or level 2 under . . . such offense is a misdemeanor of the first degree, . . . (b) If the offense attempted, solicited, or conspired to is a capital felony, the offense of criminal attempt, criminal solicitation, or criminal conspiracy is a felony of the first degree, . . . if the offense attempted, solicited, or conspired to is a life felony or a felony of the first degree, the offense of criminal attempt, criminal solicitation, or criminal conspiracy is a felony of the second degree, . . .

Many of the recently enacted statutes include specific provisions regarding the defense of renunciation or incapacity. The wording of the renunciation provision is usually similar to the wording of § 5.02(3) of the Model Penal Code. Generally, the incapacity provision of the statutes provides for a defense if the accused would not

---

[31]   Moran v. Schwarz, 826 P.2d 952 (Nev. 1992).

[32]   Branche v. Commonwealth, 25 Va. App. 480, 489 S.E.2d 692 (1997).

be guilty of the principal offense committed because of some individual incapacity the accused might have, such as being underage; but it would not be a defense for the accused that the person solicited would not be guilty of the principal offense, because of some legal incapacity or immunity.

D. *Summary*

The crime of solicitation under common law was a misdemeanor and carried the same punishment regardless of the seriousness of the crime solicited. Today, states often tie solicitation to the specific crime, or they have gradations of solicitation depending on the seriousness of the crime. While some states offer the defense of renunciation, others do not, holding the position that the crime "is in the asking."

> Solicitation
> (A/R) request, solicit, encourage, incite another to commit a specified crime
> (M/R) specific Intent

§ 4.4   Conspiracy

Conspiracy is basically an agreement between individuals to commit a crime. The rationale for making conspiracy a crime is that society, having the power to punish for dangerous behavior, cannot be powerless against those who work to bring about that behavior.[33] As one court indicated, the law punishes for conspiracy because it does not deem it prudent to wait until the criminal plan has reached fruition.[34]

A. *Common Law*

Conspiracy was an offense at English common law, defined as an agreement between two or more persons to accomplish a criminal or unlawful purpose, or some purpose, not in itself criminal or unlawful, by criminal or unlawful means. However, there must be some act in addition to the conspiring. It has also been defined as "an agreement among conspirators, an act of conspiring together; and it necessarily implies acting in concert, undertaking some joint action."[35] A conspiracy to commit an offense and the actual commission of the offense are separate crimes and may be punished separately.[36]

---

[33]   Scales v. United States, 367 U.S. 203, 81 S. Ct. 1469, 6 L. Ed. 2d 782 (1961).

[34]   United States v. Cryan, 490 F. Supp. 1234 (D.N.J. 1980).

[35]   Miller v. United States, 382 F.2d 583 (9th Cir. 1967); United States v. Heck, 449 F.2d 778 (9th Cir. 1974).

[36]   United States v. Jenkins, 313 F.3d 549 (10th Cir. 2002).

1. An Intentional Agreement

One court defined conspiracy in the following manner:

> "Conspiracy" consists in a corrupt agreement between two or more persons to do an unlawful act, existence of which agreement may be established by direct proof, or by inference, as a deduction from acts and conduct, which discloses a common design on their part to act together for accomplishment of an unlawful purpose.[37]

2. Between Two or More

There must be at least two persons agreeing to do an act; that is, the conspiracy is a joint undertaking or a combination, agreement, or understanding, tacit or otherwise, between two or more persons for the purpose of committing the unlawful act. Under the **Wharton Rule**, in crimes that require at least two people (bigamy, adultery, incest), a conspiracy charge cannot be based solely on the agreement of only the two people necessarily involved in the crime. The Wharton Rule has been rejected in some states.

3. To Commit a Criminal Act or Commit a Lawful Act in an Unlawful Manner

Because the essence of the crime of "conspiracy" is the agreement rather than the commission of the objective substantive crime, conspiring to commit a crime is an offense separate and distinct from commission of the crime that is the objective of the conspiracy.[38] It is not double jeopardy to bring criminal actions against a defendant under the conspiracy statute as well as the substantive crime statute.

4. Some Overt Act by One of the Parties

As in the crime of attempt, it must be shown that one of the conspirators committed an overt act in furtherance of the conspiracy. The overt act must at least start to carry the conspiracy into effect or reach far enough toward the accomplishment of the desired result to amount to the commencement of the consummation.[39] The **Pinkerton Rule**, from an early federal criminal case, states that any coconspirator is culpable for all natural and foreseeable acts committed by coconspirators within the scope of the conspiracy. In the case, Justice Douglas held that each coconspirator is responsible for any of the acts of other conspirators, except for those described here:

> [a] different case would arise if the substantive offense committed by one of the conspirators was not in fact done in furtherance of the conspiracy, did not fall within the scope of the unlawful project, or was merely a part of the ramifications

---

[37]   Kennemore v. State, 149 S.E.2d 791 (Ga. 1966).

[38]   United States v. Cantu, 557 F.2d 1173 (5th Cir. 1977).

[39]   Hall v. United States, 109 F.2d 976 (10th Cir. 1940); State v. Porro, 377 A.2d 909 (N.J. 1977).

of the plan which could not be reasonably foreseen as a necessary or natural consequence of the unlawful agreement.[40]

Even with the limitation of probable and foreseeable, the rule that all conspirators are responsible for acts they did not originally agree to has been rejected by some states and the Model Penal Code. The more general rule is that coconspirators are culpable for all crimes that are part of the criminal enterprise agreed upon.

5. Withdrawal as a Defense

Traditionally, withdrawal from the criminal conspiracy did not constitute a defense to the crime, but most courts now recognize that if a defendant effectively withdraws from the criminal conspiracy, it is a defense. The majority of federal courts confronted with the issue have held that it is the defendant who bears the burden of proving withdrawal. However, in a 1981 case, the U.S. Court of Appeals for the Seventh Circuit concluded that due process requires the government to disprove withdrawal beyond a reasonable doubt once the defendant has met the burden of going forward with evidence of withdrawal.[41] In order to prove withdrawal, evidence must be introduced to show that the defendant disavowed or defeated the purpose of the conspiracy.

B. *Model Penal Code*

Under the Model Penal Code, the offense is committed if there is an agreement with another person or persons to engage in such conduct that constitutes a crime or an attempt or solicitation to commit such crime; or where the agreement is to aid such other person or persons in the planning or commission of such crime or of an attempt or solicitation to commit such crime.

§ 5.03 Criminal Conspiracy[42]

(1) Definition of Conspiracy. A person is guilty of conspiracy with another person or persons to commit a crime if with the purpose of promoting or facilitating its commission he:
  (a) agrees with such other person or persons that they or one or more of them will engage in conduct which constitutes such crime or an attempt or solicitation to commit such crime; or
  (b) agrees to aid such other person or persons in the planning or commission of such crime or of an attempt of solicitation to commit such crime.
(2) Scope of Conspiratorial Relationship. If a person guilty of conspiracy, as defined by Subsection (1) of this Section, knows that a person with whom he conspires to commit a crime has conspired with another person or persons to commit the

---

[40]   Pinkerton v. United States, 328 U.S. 640, 647 (1946).
[41]   United States v. Bradsby, 628 F.2d 901 (5th Cir. 1980); Krasn v. United States, 614 F.2d 1229 (9th Cir. 1980); United States v. Read, 658 F.2d 1225 (7th Cir. 1981).
[42]   MODEL PENAL CODE § 5.03 (1985).

same crime, he is guilty of conspiring with such other person or persons, whether or not he knows their identity, to commit such crime.

(3) Conspiracy With Multiple Criminal Objectives. If a person conspires to commit a number of crimes, he is guilty of only one conspiracy so long as such multiple crimes are the object of the same agreement or continuous conspiratorial relationship.

(4) Joinder and Venue in Conspiracy Prosecutions.

    (a) Subject to the provisions of paragraph (b) of this Subsection, two or more persons charged with criminal conspiracy may be prosecuted jointly if:

        (i) they are charged with conspiring with one another; or

        (ii) the conspiracies alleged, whether they have the same or different parties, are so related that they constitute different aspects of a scheme of organized criminal conduct.

    (b) In any joint prosecution under paragraph (a) of this Subsection:

        (i) no defendant shall be charged with a conspiracy in any county [parish or district] other than one in which he entered into such conspiracy or in which an overt act pursuant to such conspiracy was done by him or by a person with whom he conspired; and

        (ii) neither the liability of any defendant nor the admissibility against him of evidence of acts or declarations of another shall be enlarged by such joinder; and

        (iii) the Court shall order a severance or take a special verdict as to any defendant who so requests, if it deems it necessary or appropriate to promote the fair determination of his guilt or innocence and shall take any other proper measures to protect the fairness of the trial.

(5) Overt Act. No person may be convicted of conspiracy to commit a crime, other than a felony of the first or second degree, unless an overt act in pursuance of such conspiracy is alleged and proved to have been done by him or by a person with whom he conspired.

(6) Renunciation of Criminal Purpose. It is an affirmative defense that the actor, after conspiring to commit a crime, thwarted the success of the conspiracy, under circumstances manifesting a complete and voluntary renunciation of his criminal purpose.

(7) Duration of Conspiracy. For purposes of § 1.04(4):

    (a) conspiracy is a continuing course of conduct which terminates when the crime or crimes which are its object are committed or the agreement that they be committed is abandoned by the defendant and by those with whom he conspired; and

    (b) such abandonment is presumed if neither the defendant nor anyone with whom he conspired does any overt act in pursuance of the conspiracy during the applicable period of limitation; and

    (c) if an individual abandons the agreement, the conspiracy is terminated as to him only if and when he advises those with whom he conspired of his abandonment or he informs the law enforcement authorities of the existence of the conspiracy and of his participation therein.

The Model Code handles the overt act element by providing that an overt act is a requirement in cases other than a felony of the first or second degree. It is an affirmative defense that the actor, after conspiring to commit a crime, thwarted the success of the conspiracy, under circumstances manifesting a complete and voluntary renunciation of criminal purpose. It is interesting to note that the Model Penal Code also only requires an agreement "by" the defendant rather than between the parties. This makes it possible to convict a person of conspiracy with a person who has been acquitted or a police officer who has pretended to be a conspirator.

C. State Statutes, Codes, and Cases

Many of the more recently revised codes follow the Model Penal Code at least in part. An example of a state statute that takes a somewhat different approach is that of Indiana.

§ 35-41-5-2. Conspiracy.[43]

(a) A person conspires to commit a felony when, with intent to commit the felony, he agrees with another person to commit the felony. However, a conspiracy to commit murder is a Class A felony.

(b) The state must allege and prove that either the person or the person with whom he agreed performed an overt act in furtherance of the agreement.

(c) It is no defense that the person with whom the accused person is alleged to have conspired:
(1) Has not been prosecuted;
(2) Has not been convicted;
(3) Has been acquitted;
(4) Has been convicted of a different crime;
(5) Cannot be prosecuted for any reason; or
(6) Lacked the capacity to commit the crime.

The Indiana statute specifically provides that the prosecution must present evidence to prove an overt act in furtherance of the agreement and states that it shall be no defense that the person who performed the act has not been prosecuted, has not been convicted, has not been acquitted, has been convicted of a different crime, cannot be prosecuted for any reason, or lacked the capacity to commit the crime. This takes away some of the indefiniteness that sometimes makes it difficult to prosecute for a conspiracy. Because of the wording of the statute, the Indiana courts have found that it is no defense to a charge of conspiracy that one of the conspirators was an undercover police agent. The Indiana Court of Appeals also made it clear that in proving a conspiracy, it is not necessary to prove that the object of the conspiracy has been carried out.[44]

In the Indiana case of *Sawyer v. State*, a conspiracy conviction that resulted from a sting operation was appealed. In the sting operation, an employee of the prosecutor's office and an FBI agent met with the defendant and expressed an interest in buying a tavern. During this meeting, the FBI agent, using an assumed name, told the defendant that he would buy the tavern, but only if he had a guarantee that there would be no zoning problems. The defendant then suggested that he knew of a person who could be very valuable in obtaining the zoning variance that had been requested and denied. At a later

---

[43] IND. CODE ANN. § 35-41-5-2 (Burns 2002).

[44] Williams v. State, 274 Ind. 578, 412 N.E.2d 1211 (1980); Lee v. State, 397 N.E.2d 1047 (Ind. Ct. App. 1979), *cert. denied*, 449 U.S. 983, 101 S. Ct. 399, 66 L. Ed. 2d 245 (1980). *See also* State v. Nichols, 481 S.E.2d 118 (S.C. 1997) and Buell v. State, 668 N.E.2d 251 (Ind. 1996).

meeting, the defendant accepted $1,000.00 for his part in this deal. He was charged with conspiracy to commit bribery and bribery. The defendant was acquitted of the bribery charge because the person who was to have obtained the zoning variance was not a public servant. However, he was convicted of conspiring to commit bribery.

The appellate court confirmed the conspiracy conviction, holding that "Although it may have been impossible for Sawyer to have committed bribery, impossibility generally is not a defense to a charge of conspiracy." The court continued by explaining that the crime of conspiracy focuses on the intent with which the defendant agrees with another person. It is irrelevant that the defendant's conduct could not constitute bribery; what is relevant is the intent and belief Sawyer had when he agreed with the others to "confer, offer or agree to confer" money to another in exchange for the other party's influence in resolving the zoning matter. The evidence was sufficient to support the conspiracy conviction.[45] A case involving conspiracy to receive stolen property with property that turned out not to be stolen ended in a similar holding.[46]

The Alaska statute follows the traditional elements of conspiracy. Portions of it are as follows:

AS 11.31.120. Conspiracy

(a) An offender commits the crime of conspiracy if, with the intent to promote or facilitate a serious felony offense, the offender agrees with one or more persons to engage in or cause the performance of that activity and the offender or one of the persons does an overt act in furtherance of the conspiracy.

(b) If an offender commits the crime of conspiracy and knows that a person with whom the offender conspires to commit a serious felony offense has conspired or will conspire with another person or persons to commit the same serious felony offense, the offender is guilty of conspiring with that other person or persons to commit that crime whether or not the offender knows their identities.

(c) In a prosecution under this section, it is not a defense that a person with whom the defendant conspires could not be guilty of the crime that is the object of the conspiracy because of

   (1) lack of criminal responsibility or other legal incapacity or exemption;

   (2) belonging to a class of persons who by definition are legally incapable in an individual capacity of committing the crime that is the object of the conspiracy;

   (3) unawareness of the criminal nature of the conduct in question or of the criminal purpose of the defendant; or

   (4) any other factor precluding the culpable mental state required for the commission of the crime.

   .... [remaining provisions omitted]

The Alaska statute goes on to state that a person can be liable for the completed crime and a conspiracy charge if the crime is brought to fruition. It also provides a renunciation defense.

---

[45]   Sawyer v. State, 583 N.E.2d 795 (Ind. Ct. App. 1991).
[46]   United States v. Bobo, 586 F.2d 355 (5th Cir. 1978).

In 2003, the United States Supreme Court considered a conspiracy appeal. The defendant argued that he could not be guilty of conspiracy because undercover agents were running the alleged drug operation at the time that he agreed to participate. The Court opined that conspiracy poses a threat to the public over and above the threat of the commission of the relevant substantive crime, both because the partnership in crime makes more likely the commission of other crimes and because it decreases the probability that the individuals involved will depart from the path of criminality. After stating that the essence of a conspiracy is an agreement to commit an unlawful act, the Court continued by explaining that the agreement to commit an unlawful act, which constitutes the essence of a conspiracy, is a distinct evil that may exist and may be punished whether or not the substantive crime ensues. They also held that the government's involvement that acted to defeat the conspiracy does not automatically end the potential culpability of subsequent conspirators.[47]

Generally, state statutes require that the state prove intent and an overt act. A California court held that a conviction of conspiracy requires proof that the defendant and another person had the specific intent to agree or conspire to commit an offense, as well as a specific intent to commit the elements of that offense, together with proof of the commission of an overt act by one or more of the parties to such agreement in furtherance of the conspiracy.[48] Intent is generally proven in a conspiracy prosecution by circumstantial evidence because direct evidence of the accused's state of mind is rarely available.[49] Commenting on the proof necessary to convict in a conspiracy case, a Pennsylvania court included a statement that conspiracy can be proven by the relation, conduct, or circumstances of the parties.[50]

In a Nevada case, the court warned that mere knowledge or approval of, or acquiescence in, the object and purpose of the conspiracy *without agreement* to cooperate in achieving the object or purpose does not make one a party to the conspiracy.[51] Any one of the conspirators may commit the overt act toward achievement of the goal; it does not have to be performed by the defendant. In a more recent case, a Nevada court dealt with the Pinkerton Rule that held each coconspirator culpable for

CASE NOTE: *Bolden v. Nevada*, 124 P.3d 191 (2005)

Bolden was charged and convicted of a list of crimes; what were those crimes and which were the object of the appeal? What was the specific issue the court addressed in this part of the holding? What was the court's opinion regarding the Pinkerton Rule? Why were the crimes of burglary and kidnapping distinguished from the crime of robbery?

---

47 United States v. Jimenez Recio, 537 U.S. 270, 123 S. Ct. 819, 154 L. Ed. 2d 744 (2003).
48 People v. Athar, 129 Cal. Rptr. 2d 351 (2002).
49 United States v. Oberdick, 810 A.2d 296 (Conn. 2002).
50 Commonwealth v. Baskerville, 681 A.2d 195 (Pa. 1996).
51 Doyle v. State, 921 P.2d 901 (Nev. 1996).

all the natural and foreseeable acts of each coconspirator.[52] This case, *Bolden v. Nevada*, is excerpted in Part II of the text.

In some states, the statute includes a provision regarding the defense of renunciation.[53] Under these statutes, it is a defense if the facts manifest a voluntary and complete renunciation of the criminal purpose and the defendant prevented the commission of the crime. However, renunciation is not voluntary if motivated by the belief that circumstances exist that pose a particular threat of apprehension or detection.

D. Summary

Conspiracy was a crime at common law and is a crime in all states. While it is not a crime to think about committing a crime, and it is not a crime to discuss committing a crime, once that discussion changes to an agreement among the parties and at least one party commits at least one overt act, the crime of conspiracy has occurred.

> Conspiracy
> (A/R) agreement by one party with another, to commit a criminal act or a lawful act in a criminal manner, and an overt act by at least one of the parties
> (M/R) specific intent

§ 4.5   Summary

Persons may be guilty of an offense if their acts or conduct are part of the preparation for the commission of substantive crimes even though those crimes are not consummated. The rationale of the lawmakers is that conduct that clearly indicates the dangerousness of a defendant or a predisposition toward criminality should not go unpunished even though the intended criminal act is not completed. These preparatory activity crimes usually consist of "attempt," "solicitation," and "conspiracy."

One may be punished for attempt if the prosecution can show intent to commit a crime plus performance of some overt act toward the commission of the crime. To constitute attempt, the defendant's conduct must be more than merely preparatory, but it is not necessary to show that the ultimate step toward commission of the substantive crime occurred. The fact that it is impossible to commit the crime is not necessarily a defense; however, its consummation must be at least apparently possible. Also, abandonment or withdrawal is a defense if the intent to commit the crime is freely and voluntarily abandoned before the act was put in progress for final execution and if no outside cause prompted the abandonment.

---

[52]   Bolden v. Nevada, 124 P.3d 191 (2005).
[53]   *See*, for instance, KY. REV. STAT. § 506.060 (Baldwin 2002); or KY. REV. STAT. 161.430 (Baldwin 1995); TEX PENAL CODE § 15.04 (2002).

The crime of solicitation consists of an intent to promote or facilitate the commission of a particular criminal offense and some overt act, such as the initiatory act of solicitation, request, command, or encouragement. At common law, the offense of solicitation was punishable as a misdemeanor without regard to the nature of the substantive crime solicited. However, some recently enacted statutes provide a penalty structure that is geared toward the penalty for the crime solicited.

The crime of conspiracy was an offense under the English common law and is an offense in all states. The rationale for making conspiracy a crime is that society, having the power to punish for dangerous behavior, cannot be powerless against those who work to bring about that behavior.

Conspiracy has been defined as an agreement or combination of two or more persons to do a criminal or unlawful act or to accomplish a criminal or unlawful purpose, followed by an overt act. Withdrawal from a conspiracy may be a defense—that is, the defendant may introduce evidence to show that he disavowed or defeated the purpose of the conspiracy before the agreement was carried out. The majority rule seems to be that the defendant bears the burden of proving withdrawal from a conspiracy.

REVIEW QUESTIONS

1. What were the three preparatory offenses discussed in this chapter?
2. Under common law was attempt a felony or a misdemeanor?
3. What does it mean to say that attempt is a specific intent crime?
4. What are the four traditional elements of attempt?
5. What are the four tests to prove the "overt act" element?
6. Distinguish between factual and legal impossibility.
7. Explain hybrid legal impossibility and whether or not the majority of states allow this as a defense to culpability in attempt cases.
8. Explain when abandonment might be used as a defense to a charge of attempt.
9. What test does the MPC use to prove "overt act"? Does the MPC recognize legal impossibility as a defense? Does the MPC allow abandonment (or renunciation) as a defense?
10. Under common law was solicitation to murder a more serious crime than solicitation to commit forgery?
11. What are the traditional elements of solicitation? Is it a specific intent crime?
12. Can one renunciate a solicitation as a defense?

13. What are the traditional elements of the crime of conspiracy?

14. Is it a defense to a charge of conspiracy that the defendant is really in league with government informants who have no intention of carrying out the crime?

15. Describe the Wharton Rule.

16. Describe the Pinkerton Rule. Is it still the law in most states?

17. Is a defense of abandonment available for the charge of conspiracy?

18. The MPC requires an overt act in only some types of conspiracies - which are they?

19. Is conspiracy a specific intent crime?

20. Can someone be convicted of conspiracy if other conspirators are never charged with a crime?

Offenses against Persons— Excluding Sex Offenses

5

Chapter Outline

Cases

asportation	kidnapping
assault	malice aforethought
assisted suicide	mayhem
battery	murder
depraved heart murder	negligent homicide
excusable homicide	premeditation
felony-murder doctrine	provocation
feticide	transferred intent
hate crime	unlawful imprisonment
homicide	voluntary manslaughter
involuntary manslaughter	year-and-a-day rule
justifiable homicide	

§ 5.1 Introduction

Crimes are usually classified according to the social harm they cause. In Chapters 5 through 11, crimes are placed in categories that roughly approximate most state penal codes. The United States Code, which defines federal crimes, will be reviewed in Chapters 12 and 13.

Although the terminology is often "offenses against the person" and "offenses against the habitation," what is really meant is "an offense against the state in the form of harm to the person" as well as "an offense against the state in the form of harm to the habitation." When charged with an "offense against property," the defendant is prosecuted in the interest of the state, and not in the interest of the individual whose property was involved, although, of course, the individual who owns the property is concerned. In this book, the discussion regarding state crimes is divided into these segments:

1. offenses against persons, excluding sex crimes (Chapter 5);
2. offenses against persons, sex crimes (Chapter 6);
3. offenses against property—destruction and intrusion offenses (Chapter 7);
4. offenses involving theft and deception (Chapter 8);
5. offenses against the public health and morals (Chapter 9);

6. offenses against the public peace, including drugs (Chapter 10); and
7. offenses against justice administration (Chapter 11).

In this chapter (after first defining and explaining homicide in general), the specific crimes of murder, manslaughter, suicide, assault and battery, kidnapping and related offenses, and other crimes against the person are explained. The discussion for every crime will follow the same organization:

- a discussion of common law;
- the presentation of the Model Penal Code; and
- a discussion of current state statutes and any special issues or circumstances.

§ 5.2   Homicide

Not all deaths are homicides. The elements of homicide come to us from the common law.

A. *Common Law*

In early common law, any intentional killing was homicide, even if it was suicide. However, in later years, **homicide** was generally defined as the unlawful killing of a human being *by another* human being. Homicide has also been defined as "the unlawful killing of a human being under any circumstances, by the act, agency, or omission of another."[1] The use of "another" was added to separate homicide from suicide, although suicide or attempted suicide was still an ecclesiastical offense.

According to the most modern definitions, suicide is not a homicide, and may or may not be a crime, depending on the statutory provisions of the jurisdiction. Applying this definition, it is not homicide for a man to kill an animal or for an animal to kill a man.[2] It is a homicide if an animal is used as a means of killing another person. In such a case, the law attributes the killing of the human to the person who set in motion the means of causing death.

1. Year-and-a-Day Rule

Under common law, death was defined as the cessation of cardiac and respiratory functions. One causation issue occurred when the death resulted long after the injury. The law developed a rule to resolve the issue called the **"year-and-a-day" rule**. At common law, as early as 1763, the courts recognized the "year-and-a-day" rule.[3] This rule, as stated, for instance, in *State v. Orrell* (1826), was

---

[1]   Kinsey v. State, 49 Ariz. 201, 65 P.2d 1141 (1937). *See* WHARTON, HOMICIDE § 1 (3d ed.).
[2]   Kinsey v. State, 49 Ariz. 201, 65 P.2d 1141 (1937).
[3]   STATUTES OF GLOUCESTER, EDW. I., c IX (1763).

If death did not take place within a year and a day of the time of receiving the wound, the law draws the conclusion that it was not the cause of death; and neither the court nor jury can draw a contrary one.[4]

The reason for applying the rule in murder prosecutions was the uncertainty of medical science in determining the cause of death, and that when a defendant's life was at stake, the rule of law ought to be certain. Of course, the offender could be prosecuted and tried for other offenses, such as assault or attempted murder.

2. *Mens Rea*

The common law recognized that, in order to be murder, the killing had to be done with **malice aforethought**; however, this *mens rea* was not uniform, as malice did not necessarily imply the person had to have evil intent, nor did aforethought necessarily mean premeditation. The idea of malice aforethought encompassed many different descriptions, including "abandoned and malignant heart," "willful or reckless," and "intent to inflict grievous bodily harm." Common law terms were not uniform in distinguishing different levels of culpability. The Model Penal Code addressed this issue.

B. Model Penal Code

The Model Penal Code's greatest contribution to jurisprudence is that it specifically defined the levels of *mens rea* that relate to the different degrees of homicide. The level of *mens rea* determines the type of homicide: murder, manslaughter, or negligent homicide. The basic elements of homicide are the same as in common law.

§ 210.1 Criminal Homicide[5]

(1) A person is guilty of criminal homicide if he purposely, knowingly, recklessly or negligently causes the death of another human being.
(2) Criminal homicide is murder, manslaughter or negligent homicide.

C. State Statutes, Codes, and Cases

Some states have adopted much of the wording of the Model Penal Code, but have retained the distinction between first and second degrees of murder.[6] Other states have divided manslaughter into degrees.[7] The *actus reus* of homicide is always an act that results in the death of another. The *mens rea* determines the type of homicide.

---

[4]   State v. Orrell, 12 N.C. 139 (1826).
[5]   MODEL PENAL CODE § 210.1 (1985).
[6]   Examples are Ariz., Ark., Conn., Fla., Ind., Mont., N.H., N.M., N.Y., Pa., Tex., Utah, and Wash.
[7]   Examples are Conn., Ga., Ill., Ind., Iowa, Kan., Ky., Minn., N.M., N.Y., Or., S.D., Tex., and Wash.

1. *Actus Reus*: Causation (Year-and-a-Day Rule)

All states have addressed either by statute or through case law the idea that the defendant's actions had to have a substantial role in the death of the victim. Except for other avenues of culpability (i.e., party liability or felony murder), the defendant's actions had to be the substantial cause of the victim's death. Consider the situation where the defendant pushed a victim in a verbal altercation and the victim, coincidentally, happens to die at that moment from a blood clot in the brain. Although the push was an assault, it was not a substantial factor in the death, and, therefore, there was no homicide.

Advancements in medical science have necessitated modifications of the common law year-and-a-day rule, although some state courts have concluded that it is up to the legislature to change the rule.[8] In the case of *State v. Hefler*, the Supreme Court of North Carolina took judicial notice of the rapid development and proliferation of the arts and sciences of medicine and crime detection, and concluded that the law was an anachronism.[9]

In *Rogers v. Tennessee*, a defendant appealed his conviction of second-degree murder. His victim died of a kidney infection 15 months after the defendant stabbed the man in the heart. The defendant/appellant argued that the year-and-a-day rule was part of the law of Tennessee, having been carried over to statutory law from the common law; he argued that not applying it to him would be a violation of due process and an unconstitutional ex post facto application of law. The Supreme Court upheld the Tennessee court decision that affirmed his conviction and held that it was not a violation of due process because it was not unexpected (and therefore there was notice) that the rule would be abandoned. Justice O'Connor, writing for the majority, said

> The year and a day rule is widely viewed as an outdated relic of the common law. Petitioner does not even so much as hint that good reasons exist for retaining the rule, and so we need not delve too deeply into the rule and its history here. . . . For this reason, the year and a day rule has been legislatively or judicially abolished in the vast majority of jurisdictions recently to have addressed the issue . . . the fact that a vast number of jurisdictions have abolished a rule that has so clearly outlived its purpose is surely relevant to whether the abolition of the rule in a particular case can be said to be unexpected and indefensible by reference to the law as it then existed.[10]

Today, about half of all states have abolished the year-and-a-day rule because of medical advances. Homicide prosecutions in those states can take place years after the event as long as the prosecution has medical evidence that death resulted, substantially, from the original injury.

---

8   State v. Young, 390 A.2d 556 (N.J. 1978); State v. Gabehart, 836 P.2d 102 (N.M. Ct. of App. 1992).
9   State v. Hefler, 310 S.E.2d 310 (N.C. 1984).
10 Rogers v. Tennessee, 532 U.S. 451, 453 (2001).

2. *Actus Reus*: Defining Death

Under common law, death was defined as the cessation of respiratory functions. As medical science is now able to maintain cardiorespiratory systems even after the brain stops functioning, brain-death statutes have been substituted for the common law in determining when a person is dead.[11]

According to the National Conference of Commissioners on Uniform State Laws and the American Law Institute, the Uniform Determination of Death Act (1980) codifies the existing common law basis of determining death—total failure of the cardiorespiratory system—and extends the common law determination of death to include irreversible loss of all brain function. The entire brain must cease to function, irreversibly. The "entire brain" includes the brain stem, as well as the neocortex. The concept of "entire brain" distinguishes determination of death under this Act from "neocortical death" or "persistent vegetative state."

In deciding who makes the determination of death, a Washington court held that it is for the law, rather than medicine, to define the standard of death, and although the law adopts the brain-death standard, it is for the medical profession to determine the applicable criteria, in accordance with accepted medical standards, for deciding whether brain death has occurred. In *In re Welfare of Bowman*, the court reiterated that an individual who has sustained either (1) irreversible cessation of circulation and respiratory functions, or (2) irreversible cessation of all functions of the entire brain, including the brain stem, is "dead."[12]

The Terry Schiavo case was a sad example of the difficulties of determining death and the problems that arise when someone is in a permanent vegetative state with minimal brain functioning. In this case, Schiavo was diagnosed as being in a permanent vegetative state and had been for 15 years. However, she was not "brain dead" according to the definitions above. According to Florida law, her husband and her doctors had the legal authority to remove her feeding tubes, thus allowing her to die. The legal wrangling that resulted occurred because her parents did not want that to happen. The legal questions that were litigated included the following: Who had legal authority to decide whether to remove the feeding tubes? In what circumstances must medical authorities prolong life despite lack of neocortical functioning? The fact is that medical science can keep a person's body "alive" long after the body would die naturally. States have had to deal with this fact by statutorily defining death and defining the authority to stop life-prolonging procedures. Without statutory authority, removing feeding tubes from someone in a vegetative state may be murder.

---

[11]   Uniform Determination of Death Act, 120 U.L.A., 1987 Pocket Part 287.

[12]   In re Welfare of Bowman, 94 Wash.2d 407, 617 P. 2d 731 (1980). *See also* People v. Eulo, 482 N.Y.S. 436 (1984).

3. Exception to Double Jeopardy

What happens if a victim dies as a result of an assault after the perpetrator has already been charged and convicted of a lesser crime (assault or attempted murder)? One would assume that the prohibition of double jeopardy would prevent such a prosecution but that is not necessarily the case. In an exception to double jeopardy recognized by some state statutes, a second prosecution may commence because of a finding that the more serious crime of homicide includes additional elements to the lesser crime of assault. In *New York v. Latham*, the defendant had pled guilty to attempted murder in the second degree after he stabbed his ex-fiancée. She was, at the time, completely paralyzed after having suffered a stroke as a result of the stabbing. Seven weeks after he was sentenced, she died and an indictment for depraved indifference murder was returned. The state statute authorized a "delayed death" exception to the double jeopardy protections in federal and state constitutions. The court held that double jeopardy is not violated by a second prosecution because the attempted homicide charge does not contain the *actus reus* of causing the death of another, while a homicide charge does require a death. Therefore, the two prosecutions are not based on the same offense and are not violative of double jeopardy.[13] Note that if the state has abolished the year-and-a-day rule, the second prosecution may come long after the first conviction.

4. Summary

Although the law of homicide has been changed greatly by statute, one can get an overall concept of the common law relating to homicide if the elements of the various crimes are summarized and distinguished.

Murder—first degree (aggravated or premeditated)
1. Unlawful killing
2. One person by another
3. With malice aforethought
4. With deliberation, purpose, design, or premeditation

Murder
1. Unlawful killing
2. One person by another
3. With malice aforethought

Felony murder
1. Unlawful killing
2. One person by any other or foreseeable cause
3. During an inherently dangerous felony

Voluntary manslaughter
1. Unlawful killing
2. One person by another

---

13   New York v. Latham, 83 N.Y.2d 233, 631 N.E.2d 83 (1994).

3. Intentional killing but with adequate provocation and committed in the heat of passion

Involuntary manslaughter
1. Unlawful killing
2. One person by another
3. During unlawful act or lawful act done in a criminally negligent manner

Misdemeanor manslaughter
1. Unlawful killing
2. One person by any other or foreseeable cause
3. During the commission of a misdemeanor

§ 5.3   Murder

A. Common Law

At common law, and traditionally in the United States, **murder** is defined as a homicide committed with malice aforethought. Because the prosecutor is required to introduce evidence to prove each of the specific elements, each element is discussed here.

1. Unlawful Killing

In homicide, a killing is unlawful unless it comes under the **justifiable homicide** or excusable category. Homicide is justifiable if it is either commanded or authorized by law, for example, the killing of an enemy on the field of battle as an act of war and within the rules of war. Another example is the execution of a sentence of death pronounced by a competent tribunal. **Excusable homicide** is committed by one doing a lawful act without intention to hurt, or in self-defense. If death occurs by accident while the person causing the death is engaged in a lawful act and performing it with due care, the homicide is excusable.[14]

The distinction between justifiable and excusable homicide was important at early common law, because excusable homicide resulted in forfeiture of goods. However, the distinction is less important today, because neither entails any criminal responsibility. Today, the two terms are often used synonymously.

2. A Human Being

In the absence of a statute, a person cannot be convicted of murder unless the person whose death occurred was born alive. This means that under common law if a defendant beat a pregnant woman with the express purpose of killing her fetus, the crime was only assault (of the woman), not murder or attempted

---

[14]   United States v. Meacher, 37 F. 875 (1888); People v. Lyons, 110 N.Y. 618, 17 N.E. 391 (1888).

murder (of the fetus). As one court stated, "there is no murder without homicide, and no homicide without birth alive."[15] However, almost half of the states have amended their statutes to define murder as the "unlawful killing of a human being, or a fetus . . ."[16] or created a new **feticide** statute to cover the killing of an unborn.[17] In crafting new laws or applying old ones, care must be taken to avoid coming into conflict with Supreme Court decisions that prohibit laws that "unreasonably intrude" upon a woman's right to choose an abortion.[18] Laws typically distinguish by stage of pregnancy and/or intent and mindset of the woman.[19] In many states, the right to an abortion is narrowly defined, and anything that falls outside of the statutory limits could be charged as a homicide.

LEGAL NEWS: FETICIDE LAWS

According to the National Conference of State Legislatures, at least 38 states have fetal homicide laws. The states include **Alabama, Alaska, Arizona, Arkansas, California, Colorado, Florida, Georgia, Idaho, Illinois, Indiana, Iowa, Kansas, Kentucky, Louisiana, Maine, Maryland, Massachusetts, Michigan, Minnesota, Mississippi, Nebraska, Nevada, North Carolina, North Dakota, Ohio, Oklahoma, Pennsylvania, Rhode Island, South Carolina, South Dakota, Tennessee, Texas, Utah, Virginia, Washington, West Virginia,** and **Wisconsin.**

For more information, go to http://www.ncsl.org/default.aspx?tabid=14386.

---

3. By Another Human Being

Proof that the killing was committed by another human being requires that evidence be produced to show that the person accused committed the act or put into motion the means that resulted in the death. In modern law, suicide is not homicide, but attempted suicide might be. We will discuss these concepts in a later section.

4. With Malice Aforethought

Early common law required at least an attempt to kill, plus an element of hatred, spite, or ill will, in order to bring the killing within the malice definition. Also, at first, judges required that the prosecution prove that the defendant actually had a previously

---

[15]   Keeler v. Superior Court, 80 Cal. Rptr. 865 (Cal. Ct. App. 1969).
[16]   CAL. PENAL CODE § 187 (2002).
[17]   State v. Beale, 376 S.E.2d 1 (N.C. 1989).
[18]   Kelley Shannon, *Execute Doctors for Abortions?* AUSTIN AMERICAN-STATESMAN, August 30, 2005 at B3.
[19]   Pam Easton, *Man Convicted for Causing Miscarriage Taunted Girlfriend.* FORT WORTH STAR TELE-GRAM, June 18, 2005 at A1.

thought-out intent to kill, though spite probably was never actually necessary.[20] Gradually, judges in England came to recognize that a murder may be committed even though there was no premeditated intent to kill. The older authorities resorted to an "implied intent" rationale in which no intent, in fact, existed. Later the courts spoke more factually and frankly, agreeing that murder may be committed under some circumstances without the intent to kill.[21] In fact, even though early statutes required "malice aforethought," the defendant did not need to have ill will toward the victim, nor was there a necessity that the intent to kill was anything more than a split-second before the act as long as there is a showing of intent to kill. "Malice" may be found even though the killing is a "mercy killing."[22] In this case, there may be no malicious intent as originally defined, but the intent to kill is there and that is sufficient to support a murder conviction.

5. Felony Murder

In England, a doctrine gradually developed that came to be known as the **felony-murder doctrine**. Under early English law, one who, in the commission or attempted commission of any felony, caused another's death, could be found guilty of murder. Blackstone's view was that "If one intends to do another a felony, and undesignedly kills a man, this is also murder."[23]

The justification for this rule is that it places upon the person committing or attempting a felony the hazard of possible guilt of murder if he or she creates a substantial risk that could result in the loss of life. According to this reasoning, common experience points to the presence of a substantial human risk from the perpetration of some felonies.

B. Model Penal Code

The Model Penal Code has had great influence on the revision of the state laws. In the Model Penal Code, murder is not differentiated into first and second degree as it is in many state codes.

§ 210.2 Murder[24]

(1) Except as provided in § 210.3(1)(b), criminal homicide constitutes murder when:
    (a) it is committed purposely or knowingly; or
    (b) it is committed recklessly under circumstances manifesting extreme indifference to the value of human life. Such recklessness and indifference are

---

[20] *See generally*, MORELAND, THE LAW OF HOMICIDE (1952); Perkins, *The Law of Homicide*, 36 J. CRIM. L. & CRIMINOLOGY 391 (1946).

[21] People v. Hartwell, 341 Ill. 155, 173 N.E. 112 (1930). *See also* State v. Russell, 106 Utah 116, 145 P.2d 1003 (1944).

[22] Commonwealth v. Noxon, 319 Mass. 495, 66 N.E.2d 814 (1946).

[23] Regina v. Serne, 16 (Cox) CC 311 (1887).

[24] MODEL PENAL CODE § 210.2 (1985).

presumed if the actor is engaged or is an accomplice in the commission of, or an attempt to commit, or flight after committing or attempting to commit robbery, rape or deviate sexual intercourse by force or threat of force, arson, burglary, kidnapping or felonious escape.

(2) Murder is a felony of the first degree [but a person convicted of murder may be sentenced to death, as provided in § 210.6].

The Model Penal Code makes no reference to such terms as "malice aforethought" and "premeditation," but instead substitutes a different grading structure. Under § 210.2 (1)(a), a person may be found guilty of murder if the killing was done purposely or knowingly. Purposeful murders are those that are premeditated and with specific intent. Knowing murders are those where the person may not have specifically intended to murder, but their actions were such that a death was almost certain to result; for instance, shooting a gun at someone to "only injure" them or scare them would be an example of this type of murder.[25]

Under Subsection (b), criminal homicide also constitutes murder when it is "committed recklessly under circumstances manifesting extreme indifference to the value of human life." The idea is that the action is so egregious that the person must have intended the result or, when undertaking an act of gross recklessness, simply did not care if someone would be killed. It is sometimes referred to as "wanton disregard" or depraved heart murder. Playing Russian Roulette would be an example of this type of murder.[26] There is such a high probability of someone being killed or injured by this activity that the law holds the surviving player responsible for a type of murder.

The recklessness displayed in this type of murder is different from the *mens rea* of recklessness found in involuntary manslaughter. Consider the difference: Speeding or drinking and driving may be considered reckless (you knew of the risk and did it anyway), and if a death results, you would no doubt be charged with some form of vehicular or involuntary manslaughter. However, it is quite another thing to drive a car up onto a sidewalk through a crowd of people, or shoot a gun into a crowded bar. Even though you may not have intended to kill someone, you would probably be charged with murder rather than manslaughter because of your "wanton disregard," "extreme indifference," or "depraved indifference" to human life. In effect, the law will hold you to the natural and foreseeable consequences of your act and because it is extremely probable that someone will be killed, the law will hold you to the same degree of culpability as if you intended someone to die.

The different levels of *mens rea* offered by the Model Penal Code were defined and described in an earlier chapter. Purposeful is when the actor has a conscious objective to conduct the act and cause the result and is aware of the existence of any attendant circumstances of the crime. Knowing is when the actor is aware of any material element of the crime and/or that his conduct is of the nature prohibited. Recklessness is when the

---

[25]   Myrick v. State, 199 Ga. 244, 34 S.E.2d 36 (1945).
[26]   Commonwealth v. Malone, 354 Pa. 180, 47 A.2d 445 (1946).

actor is aware of a substantial and unjustifiable risk and engages in an action despite that knowledge. Negligence is when the actor engages in action while unaware of a substantial and unjustifiable risk, but should have known of the risk.

The Model Penal Code does not distinguish between first-degree and second-degree murder, and provides that murder is a felony of the first degree. The Model Penal Code does not use the term "felony murder," but provides that murder committed in the perpetration, or an attempt to perpetrate, other crimes will be murder in the first degree. It does, however, limit the culpability only to certain designated crimes (those that have been determined to be "inherently dangerous").

C. State Statutes, Codes, and Cases

Some states have modified the common law relating to murder, others have adopted the Model Penal Code in substance, while still others have taken parts of the Model Penal Code and retained parts of their previously written statutes. Some states include provisions that retain the felony-murder doctrine.

New Mexico's revised statute deviates from the common law, and uses different language from the Model Penal Code. This statute provides

§ 30-2-1 Murder

(A) Murder in the first degree is the killing of one human being by another without lawful justification or excuse, by any of the means with which death may be caused:
    (1) by any kind of willful, deliberate and premeditated killing;
    (2) in the commission of or attempt to commit any felony; or
    (3) by any act greatly dangerous to the lives of others, indicating a depraved mind regardless of human life.
    Whoever commits murder in the first degree is guilty of a capital felony.
(B) Unless he is acting upon sufficient provocation, upon a sudden quarrel or in the heat of passion, a person who kills another human being without lawful justification or excuse commits murder in the second degree if in performing the acts which cause the death he knows that such acts create a strong probability of death or great bodily harm to that individual or another.

    Murder in the second degree is a lesser included offense of the crime of murder in the first degree.

    Whoever commits murder in the second degree is guilty of a second degree felony . . .[27]

1. First-Degree Murder

In most states, legislatures decided very early that the crime of murder should be divided into two categories for the purpose of fixing the penalty. First-degree murder encompasses the intent to commit murder, accompanied by premeditation and

---

[27]   N.M. STAT. ANN. § 30-2-1 (Michie 2002).

deliberation. In some states, the first-degree category of murder includes murder by lying in wait, by poison, or by torture. The distinguishing factors in first-degree murder are premeditation and deliberation. When these terms are used, the prosecution must show not only that there was malice, but also must prove **premeditation** or deliberation. Premeditation means that one in fact did reflect, at least for a short period, before the act of killing.[28]

In most states that require proof of deliberation and premeditation to sustain a finding of first-degree murder, the evidence must establish that a human being was unlawfully killed, that the defendant did the killing, and that the killing was done in an intentional, deliberate, and premeditated way. In defining premeditation, a Florida court noted that premeditation, as an element of first-degree murder, is a fully formed conscious purpose to kill, which exists in the mind of the perpetrator for a sufficient length of time to permit reflection, and in pursuance of which an act of killing ensues. Premeditation does not have to be contemplated for any particular period before the act, and may occur in moments before the act.[29] In some states, other forms of murder are also designated by statute as first degree. An example would be the killing of a peace officer.

2. Second-Degree Murder

If premeditation or intent (or the particular *mens rea* requirements specified by statute) cannot be proven, then the murder would be prosecuted as second degree. Recall the concepts of specific intent and general intent. First-degree murder is a specific intent crime (one intends the act and intends the consequence), and second-degree murder is a general intent crime (one intends the act but not necessarily the consequence). In other words, the prosecutor does not have to prove that the defendant intended that his act would result in the death of the victim. An individual who beats a victim, shoots at a victim, pushes a victim out of a boat and the victim drowns, or in any other way commits dangerous acts that put the victim in peril, may argue that he or she never intended for the victim to die; however, if death or grievous bodily harm is the natural and foreseeable consequence of the defendant's actions and the defendant intended to do the actions, then a second-degree murder conviction can be sustained.

3. Depraved Heart or Depraved Indifference Murder

Under common law and the Model Penal Code, when an offender does an act that shows a complete disregard (or depraved indifference) for human life and there is a probable certainty of injury, that offender may be found guilty of **depraved heart**

---

[28]   State v. Bowser, 214 N.C. 249, 199 S.E. 31 (1938). *See also* State v. Hutchins, 303 N.C. 321, 279 S. E.2d 788 (1981). In State v. Hutchins, the North Carolina Supreme Court reaffirmed that premeditation and deliberation may be inferred from circumstantial evidence. The court also determined that no fixed period is required for these mental processes to occur.

[29]   Loehrke v. State, 722 So.2d 867 (Fla. 1998).

murder even if they had no intent to kill. One example is a person shooting into a crowded bar but not aiming at anyone or intending anyone to die. Other acts that might create this higher level of culpability include drag racing and playing Russian Roulette.

In a federal case in 1983, the court explained that the malice required for a conviction of first- or second-degree murder does not require subjective intent to kill, but may be established by evidence of conduct that is reckless, wanton, and a gross deviation from reasonable standards of care, of such a nature that the jury is warranted in inferring that the defendant was aware of a serious risk of death or serious bodily harm.[30]

In some cases, homicides resulting from drunk driving may be prosecuted as depraved indifference murders rather than involuntary homicides. The degree of drunkenness and extent of prior offenses are factors that go into a prosecutor's decision to charge.[31]

4. Transferred Intent

The doctrine of **transferred intent** holds an offender responsible even when the end result is not what was intended. If there is an *actus reus* and a *mens rea*, then the *mens rea* need not be directed toward the person killed. For example, if one intends to kill one person or group of persons, but instead kills someone else, this is sufficient to bring the crime within the category of murder.[32] Recall from a previous chapter that this is sometimes referred to as "bad aim" intent. If A intended to kill B and shot at him, but killed C instead, A would still be properly charged with first-degree murder even though the killing was accidental.

5. Felony Murder

Under the common law, any killing that occurred during the course of a felony could be a "felony murder," which was the same degree of seriousness as murder with "malice aforethought." The Model Penal Code continued the felony-murder doctrine, but limited it to specific felonies that were "inherently dangerous." Most state statutes also restrict felony-murder culpability to only certain felonies; however the felony-murder doctrine may include victims that range from the target of the underlying felony, to passersby, onlookers, public safety officials responding to the felony, and even codefendants killed by police officers. Some state courts, however, evidently would prefer to abolish the doctrine.

In discussing the constitutionality of the felony-murder rule, the Supreme Court of New Mexico discerned that "[f]ew legal doctrines have been as maligned and yet have

---

[30]   United States v. Shaw, 701 F.2d 367 (5th Cir.), *reh'g denied*, 714 F.2d 544 (5th Cir.), *cert. denied*, 104 S. Ct. 1419 (1983).

[31]   Pears v. State, 672 P.2d 903 (Alaska App. 1983).

[32]   Banks v. State, 85 Tex. Crim. 165, 211 S.W. 217 (1919).

shown as great a resiliency as the felony-murder rule."[33] The court pointed out that this rule has been described as "astonishing," "monstrous," and an insupportable "legal fiction." The court quoted from another case in holding that there is "no logical or practical basis for its existence in modern law." While not declaring the felony-murder statute to be invalid, the Supreme Court of New Mexico first imposed the requirement that, in order to charge a felony murder for a killing in the commission or attempted commission of a felony, the felony must be either a first-degree felony or the lesser-degree felony must be inherently dangerous or committed under circumstances that are inherently dangerous. In addition, to prove that the defendant caused the killing, "there must be proof that the defendant intended to kill (or was knowingly heedless that death might result from his conduct)."[34]

An example of a statute that uses some of the terminology of the Model Penal Code but also contains provisions concerning felony murder is that of Indiana.[35] Note that the Indiana statute has added provisions concerning the killing of a human being while committing crimes related to drugs and carjacking. It provides

35-42-1-1. Murder—A person who:

(1) Knowingly or intentionally kills another human being;
(2) Kills another human being while committing or attempting to commit arson, burglary, child molesting, consumer product tampering, criminal deviate conduct, kidnapping, rape, robbery, or carjacking;
(3) Kills another human being while committing or attempting to commit:
  (A) Dealing in or manufacturing cocaine, a narcotic drug, or methamphetamine [IC 35-48-4-1];
  (B) Dealing in a schedule I, II, or III controlled substance [IC 35-48-4-2];
  (C) Dealing in a schedule IV controlled substance [IC 35-48-4-3]; or
  (D) Dealing in a schedule V controlled substance; or
(4) Knowingly or intentionally kills a fetus that has attained viability (as defined in IC 16-18-2-365);
Commits murder, a felony.

The courts have found several ways of justifying the felony-murder rule. For example, one court indicated that the general rationale behind the felony-murder rule is that the intent to commit the felony substitutes for the malice aforethought.[36] The felony-murder statutes have been held valid as a proper exercise of the legislature's authority to prescribe serious punishment for killings committed with the requisite criminal intent. If the killing occurred during the commission or the attempted commission of inherently dangerous felonies as described in the respective codes, the statutes are constitutional and enforceable.

---

[33] State v. Harrison, 90 N.M. 439, 564 P.2d 1321 (1977).
[34] State v. Ortega, 112 N.M. 554, 817 P.2d 1196 (1991).
[35] IND. CODE ANN. § 35-42-1-1 (Burns 2002).
[36] State v. Cheatham, 134 Idaho 565, 6 Pa.3d 815 (2000).

The felony-murder rule can produce harsh results. For example, a defendant left a loaded gun on a table and, unaware that his friend had turned the firing chamber, fired at and killed his friend. His lack of intent would negate any intentional murder charge; however, instead of involuntary manslaughter, he was successfully charged with felony murder based on the felonies of aggravated assault and possession of a firearm during the commission of a felony.[37]

Offenders may be held responsible for accidental deaths that occur during the course of a felony—the decedent might be the targeted victim, a bystander, crime partner, or even a police officer or public safety official. For instance, an arsonist would very likely be charged with felony murder if a firefighter died in the fire. In *People v. Stamp*, a robbery victim died of a heart attack during the robbery. The conviction was upheld even though there was evidence that with the victim's heart problems, he might have died soon anyway.[38] In another case, the victim died of cardiac arrest while pursuing a purse snatcher.[39] The purse snatcher was convicted of felony murder and sentenced to 30 years imprisonment.

A felony that results in a death may be charged as felony murder, while a misdemeanor that results in a death may be charged as misdemeanor manslaughter. Generally, deaths that result from drunk driving are charged as involuntary manslaughter, vehicular manslaughter, negligent manslaughter, or misdemeanor manslaughter. If state statutes define a DWI as a felony (in many states the second or third offense does increase the charge to a felony), and allows for that type of felony to be used as the underlying felony for felony murder, then a death that occurs because of a DWI may be charged as felony murder (which is first degree and carries the heaviest sanctions).

During the 1980s, the U.S. Supreme Court considered the constitutionality of felony-murder convictions in state courts when they resulted in death sentences. In *Enmund v. Florida*, the defendant was convicted, along with his codefendant, of first-degree robbery and the murder of two elderly people in their farmhouse. Both were sentenced to death.[40] The defendant claimed that, because he was not present at the killings, and he was only the driver of the car parked at the side of the road near the farmhouse at the time of the killings, the imposition of the death sentence was inconsistent with the Eighth and Fourteenth Amendments. The Supreme Court of the United States agreed. The majority pointed out that only a small minority of states (nine) allowed the death penalty to be imposed solely because the defendant somehow participated in the robbery in the course of which a murder was committed, but did not take or intend to take life, or intend that lethal force be employed. The Court also indicated that, while robbery is a serious crime deserving serious punishment, it is not a crime that is so grievous an affront to humanity that the only

---

[37]   Dunagan v. State, 269 Ga. 590, 502 S.E.2d 726 (1998).
[38]   People v. Stamp, 82 Cal. Rptr. 598 (Ct. App. 1969).
[39]   State v. McClain, 623 A.2d 280 (N.J. Super. Ct. App. Div. 1993).
[40]   Enmund v. Florida, 458 U.S. 782, 102 S. Ct. 3368, 73 L. Ed. 2d 1140 (1982).

CASE NOTE: *Tison v. Arizona*, 481 U.S. 137 (1987)
What was the holding of the case? Exactly how were the actions of the Tison brothers different from the defendant in *Enmund v. Florida*? What is the limit on the culpability of crime partners when a death occurs during a crime?

adequate response may be the penalty of death. The court concluded that putting the defendant to death to avenge two killings that he did not commit or intend to commit or cause would not measurably contribute to the retribution end of ensuring that the criminal gets his or her just desserts.

However, in the case of *Tison v. Arizona* in 1987, the U.S. Supreme Court affirmed the defendant's conviction of capital murder under Arizona's felony-murder and accomplice-liability statutes.[41] This case is provided in Part II of the text. The defendants had challenged their death sentence in a state post-conviction proceeding, alleging that the *Enmund v. Florida* case discussed earlier required a finding of "intent to kill." They argued that the finding in the *Enmund* case included situations in which the defendant intended, contemplated, or anticipated that lethal force would or might be used, or that life would or might be taken in accomplishing the underlying felony.

Upon retrial, the Tison brothers were again convicted and sentenced to death.

LEGAL NEWS: SOPRANOS STAR AQUITTED OF FELONY MURDER

Lillo Brancato Jr., an actor in the popular drama series *The Sopranos* about organized crime, was acquitted of felony murder in December 2008. The trial stemmed from his participation in a 2005 attempted burglary during which a police officer was shot by his crime partner. The jury declined to convict him on the more serious felony-murder charge, arguably because they believed him when he argued that he did not know that his crime partner had a gun, nor could he have reasonably foreseen that there would be a killing during the burglary attempt.

Source: Fahim, K. (2008). "Weighing Guilt When the Man on Trial Did No Killing." New York Times, December 24, 2008:B1.

Note that an alternative theory to culpability is the law of parties. Recall that under many states' laws today, anyone who participates as an accessory to a crime is as guilty as every other party, so if the murder is part of the criminal transaction, then every codefendant is equally responsible, regardless of who pulled the trigger. However, this theory of culpability is more restricted than felony murder and would not include culpability for inadvertent deaths. In summary, while the felony-murder rule has some restrictions in

---

[41]   Tison v. Arizona, 481 U.S. 137, 107 S. Ct. 1676, 95 L. Ed. 2d 127 (1987).

application, a defendant may be found guilty of murder even if he or she does not "intend to kill" or participate in the act that results in the killing. Defendants may be found guilty and may even receive the death penalty if the court finds a reckless disregard for human life in combination with major participation in the felony resulting in the death.

D. *Summary*

Murder is often divided into first- and second-degree in modern statutes. The difference between the two levels of murder is based on the *mens rea*. The degree of the murder will affect the level of punishment. The *actus reus* and *mens rea* of murder are summarized in the following:

First Degree
(A/R) unlawful killing of one by another human
(M/R) intentional, premeditated

Second Degree
(A/R) unlawful killing of one by another human
(M/R) "without premeditation" or "with callous disregard" or "wanton disregard" or "depraved indifference"

Felony Murder
(A/R) unlawful killing or foreseeable death + A/R of underlying felony
(M/R) intentional (of the underlying felony) + (in some states) callous disregard and/or major participation

§ 5.4   Voluntary Manslaughter

A. *Common Law*

The common law did not distinguish between voluntary and involuntary manslaughter even though they did recognize that some killings did not have the same level of culpability as others. Generally, manslaughter (instead of murder) was found when there was (a) provocation, (b) a mistaken justification (i.e., invalid self-defense), or (c) diminished mental capacity. The more common reference to common law manslaughter is what we now call voluntary manslaughter. **Voluntary manslaughter** is the intentional killing of one human being by another without justification or excuse, but committed under the influence of passion induced by great provocation. If there is absence of malice and the killing is due to the influence of sudden passion, the crime is reduced from murder to manslaughter.

In order for a killing that otherwise would be murder to be considered manslaughter, the following conditions must exist:

1. there must have been adequate provocation,
2. the killing must have been in the heat of passion,

3. it must have been a sudden passion, i.e., the killing must have followed the provocation before there has been a reasonable opportunity for the passion to cool, and

4. there must have been a causal connection between the provocation, the passion, and the fatal act.

B. Model Penal Code

The Model Penal Code does not distinguish between voluntary and involuntary manslaughter, but it retains the concept that reducing the crime from murder to manslaughter is justified when there is sufficient mental or emotional disturbance.

Note that the first example of manslaughter in (1)(a) is "reckless." In many state statutes, this type of manslaughter is separated and defined as involuntary manslaughter, leaving voluntary manslaughter to be defined by the remaining definitional elements in the MPC.

§ 210.3[42]

(1) Criminal homicide constitutes manslaughter when
    (a) it is committed recklessly; or
    (b) a homicide which would otherwise be murder is committed under the influence of extreme mental or emotional influence for which there is reasonable explanation or excuse. The reasonableness of such explanation or excuse shall be determined from the viewpoint of the person in the actor's situation under the circumstances as he believes them to be.
(2) Manslaughter is a felony of the second degree.

C. State Statutes, Codes, and Cases

Two of the elements of manslaughter are exactly the same as those of murder:

1. an unlawful killing of
2. one person by another.

The difference is that the *mens rea* is either reckless (involuntary) or under some extreme provocation (voluntary). The most distinguishable element of voluntary manslaughter is the sudden passion aroused by extreme provocation. It is this element that separates these killings from second-degree murders. Other definitions of voluntary manslaughter from cases include

- "manslaughter is the unlawful killing of a human being without malice aforethought, either express or implied."[43]

---

[42]   MODEL PENAL CODE § 210.3 (1985).
[43]   State v. Lillibridge, 454 A.2d 237 (R.I. 1982).

- "manslaughter is the unlawful killing of a human being without malice and without premeditation and deliberation."[44]
- [manslaughter includes an] "absence of malice; that while the killing may be with the design to effect death, the offense is reduced to manslaughter by circumstances of great and sudden provocation."[45]

An example of a statute that generally follows the Model Penal Code, but has a different provision concerning voluntary manslaughter, is that of Ohio, which provides

> No person while under the influence of sudden passion or in a sudden fit of rage, either of which is brought on by serious provocation occasioned by the victim that is reasonably sufficient to incite him into using deadly force, shall knowingly cause the death of another.[46]

The Indiana statute defining voluntary manslaughter includes the terms *knowingly* and *intentionally*, but also reduces the crime from murder to voluntary manslaughter if the killing of another person occurs while acting under "sudden heat." That statute provides

> Voluntary manslaughter. (a) A person who knowingly or intentionally kills another human being while acting under sudden heat commits voluntary manslaughter, a Class B felony. However, the offense is a Class A felony if it is committed by means of a deadly weapon. (b) The existence of sudden heat is a mitigating factor that reduces what otherwise would be murder under section 1(1) of this chapter to voluntary manslaughter.[47]

The Indiana statute makes it clear that voluntary manslaughter is a knowing or intentional killing committed while acting under "sudden heat." Some states do not recognize voluntary manslaughter but similar provocation and passion may reduce first-degree murder charges to second-degree murder.

1. Provocation

Provocation necessary to reduce the crime from murder to manslaughter must be of such a nature as to be recognized at law as adequate for that purpose. Provocation must be of a nature calculated to inflame the passions of an ordinary reasonable person under the circumstances. Under common law, words alone could never be provocation enough to justify a voluntary homicide finding. Consider the following cases in which the court decided whether the provocation was sufficient to induce passion:

- a bare claim of "fear" (no)[48]
- staggering blows to the face of the person (yes)[49]

---

[44]   State v. Cousins, 223 S.E.2d 338 (N.C. 1976).

[45]   State v. Nelson, 103 N.H. 478, 175 A.2d 814 (1961).

[46]   Ohio Rev. Code Ann. § 2903.03(A) (Anderson 1999).

[47]   Ind. Stat. Ann. § 35-42-1-3 (Burns 2002).

[48]   Moore v. State, 694 S.W.2d 529 (Tex. Crim. Ct. App. 1985).

[49]   Stewart v. State, 75 Ala. 436 (1885).

- the infliction of pain and bloodshed (yes)[50]
- the killing or assaulting of a relative (yes)[51]
- finding one's spouse engaged in sexual relations (yes)[52]

The latter situation is the most commonly described example of voluntary homicide; so much so that it has sometimes been called the "paramour defense." However, case law indicates that it was a defense more successfully used by men than women.

The court holdings are not consistent in their finding that discovering one's spouse *in flagrante delicto* is sufficient provocation to inflame the passion of a reasonable person. Generally, the slayer must discover the deceased in the very act of intercourse or immediately before or after intercourse, and the killing must have followed immediately on detection and must have been committed under the influence of passion engendered by the discovery.[53]

While the common law rule was that words alone are insufficient provocation, there are some exceptions in state cases. If the words are informational, i.e., they convey a fact that constitutes reasonable provocation rather than morally insulting or abusive words, this could be sufficient provocation. For instance, if the victim taunts the killer with the fact that they just murdered his or her child, it may be sufficient provocation to reduce a murder conviction to manslaughter. It has been held by some courts that a husband who kills his wife's lover immediately after she confesses adultery, and before the lapse of reasonable cooling-off time, is guilty of manslaughter only.[54]

LEGAL NEWS: PROVOCATION

In 2002, Clara Harris, a Houston woman, confronted her husband and his lover in a hotel lobby. She screamed at and assaulted the woman and was pulled away and ejected from the hotel by employees. Immediately afterward, she killed her husband by running over him three times in the parking lot. In a strange coincidence, the private investigator she hired happened to videotape the incident because they had been following her husband. The jury decided that she did commit the act in sudden passion, but under Texas law, that only reduced first-degree murder to second-degree murder. She was sentenced to 20 years in prison. The case became the basis for a 2004 television movie called *Suburban Madness*. She lost her appeal but is eligible for parole in 2013.

Source: http://topics.nytimes.com/top/reference/timestopics/people/h/clara_harris/index.html.

---

[50]   State v. Michael, 74 W.Va. 613, 82 S.E. 611 (1914).
[51]   Commonwealth v. Paese, 220 Pa. 371, 69 A. 891 (1908).
[52]   State v. Thornton, 730 S.W.2d 309 (Tenn. 1987).
[53]   State v. Young, 52 Or. 227, 96 P. 1067 (1908).
[54]   Haley v. State, 123 Miss. 87, 85 So. 129 (1920).

2. Heat of Passion

Not only must there be provocation, but the provocation must have led to "heat of passion" or "hot blood." That is, the emotional state must have dominated the slayer at the time of the homicidal act, and it must have been directed toward the person slain, and not to another person. It is difficult to separate the provocation from the resulting heat and passion. In determining whether the act that caused the death was impelled by heat of passion, all of the surrounding circumstances and conditions are to be taken into consideration. In order to reduce the crime to manslaughter, the provocation must be such as would naturally and reasonably arouse the passions of an ordinary person beyond his or her power of control.

One court indicated that the passion of the killer must have been such as to negate deliberation. That is, the degree of mental disturbance must have been such as to deprive the killer of the power to form a design to kill with a deliberate mind. Another court noted that the passion of the killer must have been such as to render his or her mind incapable of cool reflection and to overcome and dominate or suspend the exercise of judgment and self-control.[55]

Manslaughter may also occur when a person kills another in the heat of sudden combat, if upon reasonable provocation. Reasonable provocation is the provocation that would inflame a reasonable and law-abiding person to the point at which he or she would be capable of killing another. Even with these general definitions, it is difficult to define the point at which the degree of passion is sufficient to reduce the crime from murder to manslaughter. In order to meet the heat of passion test, "the defendant must have in fact been deprived of his self-control under the stress of such provocation and must have committed the crime while so deprived."[56]

3. No "Cooling Off"

Even if there was sufficient provocation to reduce the crime from murder to manslaughter, and there were sufficient facts to constitute passion or "hot blood," a manslaughter instruction is not justified if the passion cooled before the commission of the homicidal act. If it appears that the defendant reflected, deliberated, or cooled off for any period before the fatal act, the killing is murder, being attributable to malice or revenge and not to mental disturbance.

What constitutes "cooling-off time" depends upon the nature and circumstances of provocation, the extent to which the passion has been aroused, and the nature of the act causing the provocation. Therefore, no precise time can be laid down as a rule within which the passions must be held to have subsided and reason to have resumed its control. In some instances, the court is authorized to say, as a *matter of law*, that the cooling-off time is sufficient if an unreasonable period has elapsed between the provocation and

---

[55] White v. State, 44 Tex. Crim. 346, 72 S.W. 173 (1902). State v. McLawhorn, 270 N.C. 622, 155 S. E.2d 198 (1967); State v. Coop, 223 Kan. 302, 573 P.2d 1017 (1978).

[56] State v. King, 37 N.J. 285, 181 A.2d 158 (1962).

the killing, while in other situations this determination becomes a difficult problem and is one that must be decided by the jury. In the *State v. Thornton* case, the Court held that the defendant was entitled to a provocation defense. Thornton had observed a car in the driveway of his wife's home, peeked in the window and saw her "date," let the air out of his tires and went home to retrieve a camera and a gun, came back, and after observing them through the window for over an hour, entered the house and shot the man. The Court seems to decide the case based on the wife's behavior as much as the estranged husband's state of mind:[57]

> In several previous decisions from this Court and in the almost unanimous course of judicial authority from other states, the encountering by a spouse of the situation which occurred here has been held, as a matter of law, to constitute sufficient provocation to reduce a charge of homicide from one of the degrees of murder to manslaughter absent actual malice, such as a previous grudge, revenge, or the like. Every case, of course, must be decided upon its own facts, but the facts in the present case were entirely undisputed. Appellant's wife testified at the trial and admitted her unfaithfulness to her husband and simply sought to excuse it upon the view that she was separated from him, and that she had told him earlier on the evening of the homicide that she had met someone else and planned to "date" him. In fact she had met McConkey on the evening of Saturday, April 30, 1983, and had had intimate sexual relations with him on that night and on each of the succeeding three nights, including the night of May 3 just before appellant burst into the bedroom and found both of them nude and in bed together. . . .
>
> She testified that she thought that when she told her husband that she might want to "date" someone else, that this, in modern society, indicated that she intended to have sexual relations. In that manner she sought to mitigate her infidelity and misconduct toward a husband who had never been unfaithful to her insofar as disclosed by the record.
>
> The marriage of the parties was in some difficulty, apparently as a result of dissatisfaction of Mrs. Thornton. She had advised her husband in March 1983 that she wanted to be separated from him for a time, and he had voluntarily taken an apartment about two miles away from their home. He visited the home almost daily, however, and there has been no suggestion that he was ever guilty of violence, physical misconduct or mistreatment toward his wife or son.
>
> . . . When he arrived at the home he saw an automobile parked in the driveway. He did not recognize the car as being one belonging to any of his wife's friends. Accordingly he parked around the corner and walked back to the house. Observing from the rear of the house, he saw his wife and McConkey in the kitchen with the child. He observed as Mrs. Thornton washed some laundry for McConkey and as they were eating dinner. Thereafter they sat and read. They drank wine and smoked some marijuana, and appellant saw them kissing.
>
> He decided to go home to get his camera, but before doing so he let the air out of one of the tires on McConkey's car. He went to his apartment, and obtained his camera and an old pistol which had belonged to his father. He visited a convenience store in an attempt to find film for the camera, and finally obtained some at a drugstore. He then returned to the marital residence, arriving at about 9:30 p.m. He testified that he intended to take pictures for the purpose of showing them to the

---

[57]   State v. Thornton, 730 S.W.2d 309 (Tenn. 1987); State v. Flory, 40 Wyo. 184, 276 P. 458 (1929).

marriage counselor on the next day and possibly also for use in evidence if divorce proceedings did ensue.

Appellant spent more than an hour in the backyard of his home observing his wife and McConkey in the den and kitchen. Thereafter they left the den area, but appellant remained behind the house, thinking that McConkey was about to leave. When he went around the house, however, he found that McConkey's car was still in the driveway and saw the drapes in the front guest bedroom downstairs had been closed. He listened near the window and heard unmistakable sounds of sexual intercourse. He then burst through the front door and into the bedroom where he found the nude couple and attempted to take some pictures. At that point he testified that he thought McConkey was attempting to attack him. In all events he drew his pistol and fired a single shot, striking McConkey in the left hip. Appellant did not harm either his wife or child, although Mrs. Thornton said that he did make some threats against her. He went upstairs and brought down the little boy, who had been awakened and who was crying. He assisted in giving directions to enable an ambulance to bring aid to McConkey, and he remained at the house until the police arrived.

Appellant testified that he simply lost control and "exploded" when he found his wife in bed with the victim. He testified that he had armed himself because McConkey was much larger than he, and he felt that he needed protection if there was trouble when he returned to the residence with the camera.

Appellant testified that he did not intend to kill McConkey, but simply to shoot him in order to disable him and also because of his outrage at the situation which he had found.

The facts of the present case are far stronger than any of the foregoing. Appellant actually discovered his wife *in flagrante delicto* with a man who was a total stranger to him, and at a time when appellant was trying to save his marriage and was deeply concerned about both his wife and his young child. He did not fire a shot or in any way harm the victim until he actually discovered the victim and his wife engaged in sexual intercourse in appellant's own home. In our opinion the passions of any reasonable person would have been inflamed and intensely aroused by this sort of discovery, given the factual background of this case. Even though he was not legally insane so as to relieve him of all criminal responsibility for the tragic death which occurred, in our opinion this was a classic case of voluntary manslaughter and no more.

We are of the opinion that the necessary elements of malice and premeditation were not demonstrated in this case and that the appellant acted under legally sufficient provocation. The conviction of murder in the first degree is set aside, and the cause will be remanded to the trial court for sentencing of the defendant for voluntary manslaughter and for such other disposition as may be appropriate in view of the time already served by the appellant. Costs of the appeal are taxed to the State. All other costs will be fixed by the trial court.

In an early case, a defendant contended that information given him by his wife as to rape and incest committed upon her by the deceased so aroused his passions and deprived him of self-control that voluntary manslaughter rather than murder should be the conviction. The state contended that because at least one day, and probably longer, had elapsed after the defendant had been informed of the acts of the deceased, his blood had cooled and he was no longer "in the heat of passion" necessary to sustain a voluntary homicide finding. However, the court agreed with the defendant's contention and explained that the crime of the deceased, if true, was most heinous and was calculated to create a most violent passion in the mind of the defendant, and it hardly could be expected that it would, as a matter of law, subside within so short a time.[58]

On the other hand, in the case of *Weaver v. State*, the court found that one day was a sufficient cooling-off period. The defendant had killed the victim one day after becoming angry while overhearing the victim planning to kill the defendant's brother. The defendant invited the victim to his place to get money from his safe, and shot him in the head while the victim was reaching into the safe. The evidence also indicated that the defendant took great pains to clean up the area afterward. The court decided that the defendant had not displayed the "sudden heat" necessary to reduce the charge from murder to voluntary manslaughter.[59]

Thus, there is no definite time for the cooling-off period that would negate the passion required before a defendant can have a murder charge reduced to voluntary manslaughter. Many courts submit this question to the jury under proper instructions.

4. A Causal Connection

In order for a homicide to be reduced from murder to manslaughter, the defendant must show that the heat of passion resulted from justifiable provocation and that the heat of passion caused the act that resulted in death. If the heat of passion element existed prior to the provocation, there is no justification for reducing the crime to manslaughter. If there was adequate provocation, but the order of provocation and the heat of passion are reversed, i.e., the provocation was not the cause of the heat of passion, there can be no reduction.[60]

There must be a causal link between the provocation, the passion, and the act. For example, if one has, for some time, intended to kill the victim to get even for mistreatment over a period of years, but immediately before he is about to carry out his intent to kill the victim, he finds the victim in bed with his daughter, it would be difficult to justify a reduction from murder to manslaughter.

5. Burden of Proof

Note that, in general, the provocation and passion elements are mitigating factors to a murder charge rather than elements to a crime. That is, prosecutors will typically charge a defendant with second-degree murder and it is up to the defendant to make some showing of provocation and passion in order to reduce a murder conviction

---

[58]   State v. King, 37 N.J. 285, 181 A2d 158 (1962).

[59]   Weaver v. State, 583 N.E.2d 136 (Ind. 1991). See also People v. Spurlin, 156 Cal. App. 3d 199 (1984) and State v. Landry, 449 So. 2d 1320 (La. Ct. App. 1986).

[60]   Rex v. Thomas, 7 Car. P. 817, 173 Eng. Rep. 356 (1837); State v. Speors, 76 Wyo. 82, 300 P.2d 555 (1956).

to one of voluntary manslaughter. Once a defendant places provocation and passion in issue, the state then bears the burden of negating the presence of sudden heat beyond a reasonable doubt.[61] Determining whether provocation of the defendant is sufficient to excite a sudden, violent, and irresistible passion in a reasonable person, thereby reducing the offense from murder to manslaughter, is a question for the jury.[62]

D. Summary

Voluntary manslaughter shares the same elements as murder but has special circumstances.

> Voluntary Manslaughter
> (A/R) unlawful killing of one by another human
> (M/R) intentionally, knowingly but without "malice"—may be defined as "without premeditation"
> (Attendant circumstances)—provocation sufficient to incite a reasonable person to passion that undermines reason with no cooling-off period, and death was the direct cause of the provocation

§ 5.5   Involuntary Manslaughter

A. Common Law

Under the common law and MPC, manslaughter covered both the situation where there was provocation and passion, and reckless behavior that resulted in a death. The type of manslaughter that involves recklessness is now called involuntary manslaughter. The distinguishing factor of **involuntary manslaughter** is that it is unintentional. If the act was intended, then it could not come within the involuntary manslaughter category. The elements of involuntary manslaughter are

1. an unlawful killing of one person by another that is
2. unintentional *but* occurs
   a. during commission of a lawful act performed with gross negligence or
   b. because of failure to perform a legal duty or
   c. during the commission of a crime that is not a felony (misdemeanor manslaughter).

A killing may be unlawful if death results from gross, wanton, or culpable negligence. A distinction is made between simple or ordinary negligence and criminally culpable negligence or recklessness.[63] For instance, if a doctor is negligent, he or

---

[61]   Evans v. State, 727 N.E.2d 1072 (Ind. 2000).
[62]   Moses v. State, 270 Ga. 127, 508 S.E.2d 661 (1998); Carsner v. State, 970 P.2d 28 (Idaho 1998).
[63]   Maryland v. Chapman, 101 F. Supp. 335 (D.Md. 1951).

she may be sued in the civil court system for medical malpractice. However, the degree of negligence required to prove involuntary manslaughter is much higher than simple negligence and goes up to the level of recklessness. The mistake must be egregious, not merely careless. Examples of recklessness that may result in charges of involuntary homicide are bar owners who lock the fire doors (with the consequence that patrons subsequently die in a fire), target shooting when there is awareness that other people are about, and driving in an extremely reckless manner.

The second situation is when a killing occurs because of a failure to perform a legal duty. If a person is required by law to do an act but, in disregarding that duty, causes the death of another, he or she can be guilty of involuntary manslaughter.[64] For instance, consider the scenario where a childcare provider sees a child seriously injured by another child and does nothing about it, tells no one, and covers up the incident; if the child dies from an untreated head injury, the provider could be found guilty of involuntary manslaughter.

The third situation is when the defendant has committed a crime, but not an inherently dangerous felony, and a death results. Recall that if a death occurs while a person is engaged in certain felonies, the crime could be murder under the felony-murder doctrine. However, if death occurs during a felony that is not inherently dangerous or during a misdemeanor, the crime is involuntary manslaughter.[65] To constitute involuntary manslaughter, the prosecution must show that there is a causal connection between the unlawful act and the death; that is, the unlawful act was the cause of the death. For instance, in *People v. Crucoani*, the defendant assisted a person who was injecting heroin into his arm. The defendant was charged with involuntary manslaughter for his acts when the victim died of a drug overdose.[66]

The difference between second-degree "depraved indifference" murder and involuntary manslaughter is the degree or egregiousness of the recklessness. For instance, driving while drunk and killing someone may be charged as involuntary homicide, but driving with an extremely high intoxication level, after having successive arrests for DWI, and driving up onto a sidewalk in a school zone, killing several children, may be charged as second-degree (depraved indifference) murder. Doing target practice in your backyard in a rural area and accidentally killing a neighbor would probably be charged as involuntary manslaughter, but shooting into a crowded bar could be charged as depraved indifference murder. The difference is that in second-degree depraved indifference murder, there is a virtual certainty of the action resulting in a death or serious injury.

---

[64]   Jones v. United States, 308 F.2d 307 (D.C. Cir. 1962).
[65]   People v. Penny, 44 Cal.2d 861, 285 P.2d 926 (1955).
[66]   People v. Crucoani, 70 Misc. 2d 528, 334 N.Y.2d 515 (1972).

B. Model Penal Code

The Model Penal Code includes "reckless" as one type of manslaughter, but also has a provision regarding **negligent homicide**. This provision is as follows:

§ 210.4 Negligent Homicide[67]

(1) Criminal homicide constitutes negligent homicide when it is committed negligently.
(2) Negligent homicide is a felony of the third degree.

The standard of negligence required for violations of § 210.4 requires proof of substantial fault and limits penal sanctions to cases in which there are gross deviations from ordinary standards of conduct. Note that negligent manslaughter defines an even lower level of *mens rea* than required for involuntary manslaughter. Consider the following levels of less-than-intentional *mens rea*:

> depraved indifference - second-degree murder
> recklessness, gross negligence - involuntary manslaughter
> criminal negligence - negligent homicide
> negligence - civil negligence (no criminal culpability)

The lines between each of these levels of culpability are fluid and court cases among the states vary in what level of culpability would attach to any specific type of behavior.

LEGAL NEWS: NEGLIGENT HOMICIDE?

Every year there are cases where distracted parents leave infants or toddlers in a car and the baby dies because of excessive heat. In 2010, one such case in Williamson County, Texas occurred when Kesen Hu (34) left his infant son in his car seat when he went in to work. The baby died several hours later in the Texas heat. He was indicted by a grand jury on two felony counts of criminally negligent homicide and endangering a child; each carried up to two years behind bars. His attorneys argued that because he had forgotten that the child was in the car seat (he was not used to taking the child to day care and he was distracted by a telephone call), he did not meet the *mens rea* of endangerment, which involves at least negligence (should have known of risk). He pled guilty to endangering a child and received two years probation. The following year the almost exact occurrence took place across the county line in Travis County (Austin) when a father forgot his infant daughter in his truck. He was not indicted.

Retrieved December 23, 2011 from http://www.statesman.com/news/local/austin-father-not-indicted-over-daughters-death-in-1761176.html.

---

[67]   Model Penal Code § 210.4.

C. State Statutes, Codes, and Cases

Jurisdictions may include, in their criminal statutes, involuntary manslaughter, negligent homicide, or both.[68] Still others have added special statutes to meet the needs of a society in which many homicides involve automobiles. For example, the Ohio Criminal Code includes the crimes of negligent homicide, aggravated vehicular homicide, and vehicular homicide. These are in addition to the crimes of aggravated murder, murder, voluntary manslaughter, and involuntary manslaughter. The Ohio Criminal Code provides

§ 2903.05 Negligent homicide[69]

(A) No person shall negligently cause the death of another or the unlawful termination of another's pregnancy by means of a deadly weapon or dangerous ordinance as defined in section 2923.11 of the Revised Code.

§ 2903.06 Aggravated vehicular homicide; vehicular homicide; vehicular manslaughter

(A) No person, while operating or participating in the operation of a motor vehicle, motorcycle, snowmobile, locomotive, watercraft, or aircraft, shall cause the death of another or the unlawful termination of another's pregnancy in any of the following ways:
   (1) As the proximate result of committing a violation of division (A) of section 4511.19 of the Revised Code or of a substantially equivalent municipal ordinance;
   (2) Recklessly;
   (3) Negligently;
   (4) As the proximate result of committing a violation of any provision of any section contained in Title 45 of the Revised Code that is a minor misdemeanor or of a municipal ordinance that, regardless of the penalty set by ordinance for the violation, is substantially equivalent to any provision of any section contained in Title 45 of the Revised Code that is a minor misdemeanor.
(B) (1) Whoever violates division (A)(1) or (2) of this section is guilty of aggravated vehicular homicide . . .
   (2) Whoever violates division (A)(3) of this section is guilty of vehicular homicide . . .
   (3) Whoever violates division (A)(4) of this section is guilty of vehicular manslaughter . . .

Note that the difference between "aggravated vehicular homicide" and "vehicular homicide" is that "recklessly" is used in the former and "negligently" in the latter.

Involuntary manslaughter in North Carolina is defined as (1) an unlawful act not amounting to a felony nor naturally dangerous to human life; or (2) a culpably negligent act or omission.[70] An Illinois court commented that, in general, a defendant acts recklessly for purposes of the offense of involuntary manslaughter when he or she is aware

---

[68]   Statutory schemes may be found in ALASKA STAT. § 11.41.120 (1995); CAL. PENAL CODE § 192 (West 1996); D.C. CODE ANN. § 22-2405 (1995); MD. CODE ANN., Crim. Law § 387, 388, 388A (1992); MASS. GEN. LAWS ANN. ch. 265, § 13 (West 1995); MICH. COMP. LAWS § 750.321 (1995).

[69]   OHIO REV. CODE ANN. § 2903 *et seq.* (Anderson 1999).

[70]   Keel v. French, 162 F.3d 263 (4th Cir. 1998).

that his or her conduct might result in death or great bodily harm, although that result is not substantially certain to occur.[71]

Involuntary manslaughter, or second-degree manslaughter, is often referred to as the "catch-all" in the law of homicide. It includes all unlawful homicides that are not covered under one of the other categories.

- Manslaughter in the second degree or "involuntary manslaughter" is the unlawful killing of a human being without malice, either express or implied, and without intent to kill or inflict injury causing death, committed accidentally in the commission of some unlawful act not felonious, or in the improper or negligent performance of an act lawful in itself.[72]
- "Manslaughter in the second degree" occurs where it plainly appears that neither death nor great bodily harm was intended but death was accidentally caused by some unlawful act or act strictly lawful in itself but done in an unlawful manner and without due caution.[73]
- Involuntary manslaughter [occurs] if one person recklessly causes the death of another and reckless means when one "consciously disregards a substantial and unjustifiable risk that circumstances exist or that a result will follow, and such disregard constitutes a gross deviation from the standard of care that a reasonable person would exercise in this situation"[74]

In *Commonwealth v. Welansky*, the defendant was convicted of involuntary manslaughter when the night club he owned caught fire and several people were killed. His culpability stemmed from findings that he provided inadequate exits.[75] A somewhat similar fact situation occurred in a more recent case in 2006 when the pyrotechnics used in a band's performance caused a tragic fire in a Rhode Island nightclub in 2003, killing 100 people and injuring another 200.[76]

LEGAL NEWS: THE RHODE ISLAND NIGHTCLUB FIRE

In 2003, 100 people died and 200 were injured when the pyrotechnics set off by band manager Daniel Biechele ignited flammable soundproofing foam that lined the walls and ceiling of the club. The fire burned so hot that fire marshals testified most of the victims died instantly. Others were killed or injured at the door in a stampede that blocked many from escaping the blaze. The two club owners,

---

[71] People v. Kolzow, 703 N.E.2d 424 (Ill. 1998).

[72] Callahan v. State, 343 So. 2d 551 (Ala. Ct. App. 1977).

[73] Pitts v. State, 122 So.2d 542 (Ala. Ct. App. 1960).

[74] State v. Miller, 981 S.W.2d 623 (Mo. 1998).

[75] Commonwealth v. Welansky, 55 N.E.2d 402 (Mass. 1944).

[76] Eric Tucker, *Band Manager to Plead Guilty in R.I. Nightclub Fire*. Boston.Com News. Retrieved June 29, 2006 from http://www.boston.com/news/local/rhode_island/articles/2006/01/31/band_ manager_reach_plea_agreement_in_nightculb_fire_case/.

Jeffrey and Michael Derderian, and Daniel Biechele were indicated on 100 counts of involuntary manslaughter with criminal negligence and 100 counts of involuntary manslaughter in violation of a misdemeanor. Biechele pled guilty and received four years in prison, eleven years suspended, and three years probation. Michael Derderian also received a four-year sentence for installing the foam. Jeffrey Derderian received probation and 500 hours of community service. Biechele won the support of family members of the dead when he sent letters of apology to every victim's family. Some of them came to his parole hearing and he was released early on parole in 2008.

For more information, go to http://www.cbsnews.com/stories/2008/03/19/national/main3951445.shtml.

1. Burden of Proof and Instructions to Jury

Frequently, a person charged with murder requests an instruction on the lesser included offense of involuntary manslaughter. If there is any evidence, however slight, as to whether the offense is murder or involuntary manslaughter, an instruction as to the law of both offenses should be given. However, if there is no evidence whatsoever to indicate negligence rather than intent, then an instruction on involuntary manslaughter is not required.[77]

D. *Summary*

The major concept to remember about involuntary manslaughter is that the level of *mens rea* is either recklessness or negligence.

Involuntary Manslaughter
(A/R) killing of one by another human while doing an unlawful act or a lawful act in a criminally negligent or reckless manner
(M/R) reckless, negligence

Misdemeanor Manslaughter
(A/R) killing during the commission of a felony or misdemeanor that is not inherently dangerous
(M/R) the *mens rea* required for the underlying crime

Negligent Homicide (MPC)
(A/R) unlawful killing of one by another human being while doing an act in a criminally negligent manner
(M/R) criminal negligence

---

[77] Boone v. State, 234 Ga. App. 373, 506 S.E.2d 884 (1998); Commonwealth v. Souza, 429 Mass. 478, 702 N.E.2d 1167 (1998).

§ 5.6   Suicide and Assisted Suicide

A. Common Law

Suicide is defined as intentional self-destruction. Although suicide is not strictly a homicide, because there is no killing of one person by another person, it is often considered in relation to the law of homicide. At common law suicide was a felony and was known as *felo de se* or felon of oneself—unless the person was a minor.[78] At early common law, suicide was punished by an ignominious burial and the forfeiture of goods and chattels to the king. If two persons mutually agreed to commit suicide, and the means employed to produce death was effective only as to one, the survivor was guilty of the murder of the one who died.[79]

B. Model Penal Code

The Model Penal Code does not define suicide as a crime; however, there is the crime of solicited or **assisted suicide**.

> § 210.5 Causing or Aiding Suicide[80]
>
> (1) Causing Suicide as Criminal Homicide. A person may be convicted of criminal homicide for causing another to commit suicide only if he purposely causes such suicide by force, duress or deception.
> (2) Aiding or Soliciting Suicide as an Independent Offense. A person who purposely aids or solicits another to commit suicide is guilty of a felony of the second degree if his conduct causes such suicide or an attempted suicide, and otherwise of a misdemeanor.

Section 210.5 provides that a person is guilty of criminal homicide if, with the requisite culpability, he or she causes the death of another by "causing another to commit suicide." Only when the person actively participates in inducing the suicide will criminal penalties result. The second subsection of § 210.5 more closely defines an act that was a crime under the common law. This section creates a separate offense of aiding or soliciting suicide, even though suicide itself is not a crime. To prove a violation in this case, the prosecutor must introduce evidence to show that the accused "purposely" aided or solicited another to commit suicide. Thus, conduct not seriously intended to aid or persuade another to take his own life may not be punishable under this section.

---

[78]   Commonwealth v. Mink, 123 Mass. 422 (1877); Grace v. State, 44 Tex. Crim. 193, 69 S.W. 529 (1902).

[79]   Burnett v. People, 204 Ill. 208, 68 N.E. 505 (1903).

[80]   Model Penal Code § 210.5 (1985).

C. State Statutes, Codes, and Cases

Even though the early common law took the position that suicide was a crime, the great majority of states today do not criminalize suicide. However, in most states it is a crime to help another to commit or attempt suicide.[81] The laws making it a crime to aid, advise, or encourage another to commit suicide have taken several forms. California law provides "Every person who deliberately aids, or advises, or encourages another to commit suicide is guilty of a felony."[82] The New York law includes the offense as part of the manslaughter statutes. This law provides that "A person is guilty of manslaughter in the second degree when . . . (3) he intentionally causes or aids another to commit suicide."[83] The most famous opponent to assisted suicide laws was Dr. Jack Kevorkian. He flagrantly violated Michigan's assisted suicide law until he was convicted and sentenced to prison for 10 to 25 years in the early 1990s.[84] He served eight years before being paroled in 2007. He died at the age of 83 in 2011.

The state statutes have been challenged on constitutional grounds. Several of these cases have reached the United States Supreme Court. In the case of *Washington v. Glucksberg,*[85] three terminally ill patients, four physicians, and nonprofit organizations brought an action against the state of Washington for a declaratory judgment that the statute banning assisted suicide violated the due process clause of the United States Constitution. They held that the Washington law that criminalized causing or aiding a suicide did not violate the due process clause. The Supreme Court explained that an examination of our nation's history, legal traditions, and practices demonstrates that Anglo-American common law has punished or otherwise disapproved of assisted suicide for more than 700 years.

> **CASE NOTE: *Washington et al. v. Glucksberg et al.*, 521 U.S. 702 (1997)**
> What was the issue in this case?
> Why did the Court decide that choosing where and when to die was not a fundamental liberty interest?
> How can someone who is competent and terminally ill commit suicide in states that do not have Death with Dignity Acts?

In the case of *Vacco v. Quill,*[86] physicians brought an action challenging the constitutionality of the New York statute that made it a crime to aid a person in committing suicide or attempting to commit suicide. In this case, the New York statute outlawing assisted suicide was challenged as a violation of the equal protection clause of the United States Constitution. The argument was that, because New York law treated competent, terminally ill persons who wish to hasten their deaths by self-administering prescribed drugs differently from those who wish to do so by directing the removal of life-support

---

81   Vacco v. Quill, 521 U.S. 793, 117 S. Ct. 2293, 139 L. Ed. 2d 834 (1997). (See this case for a list of states that prohibit assisted suicide.) *See also* Kevorkian v. Arnett, 939 F. Supp. 725 (C.D. Cal. 1996).

82   CAL. PENAL CODE § 401 (1999).

83   N.Y. PENAL LAW § 125.15 (McKinney 1997).

84   People v. Kevorkian, 527 N.W.2d 714 (Mich. 1994).

85   Washington v. Glucksberg, 521 U.S. 702, 117 S. Ct. 2258, 138 L. Ed. 2d 792 (1997).

86   Vacco v. Quill, 521 U.S. 793, 117 S. Ct. 2293, 139 L. Ed. 2d 834 (1997).

systems, there was a violation of the equal protection clause. The United States Supreme Court disagreed with this argument, concluding that the two groups were not similarly situated. The United States Supreme Court found that the overwhelming majority of state legislatures have drawn a clear line between assisting suicide and withdrawal or permitting the refusal of unwanted life-saving medical treatment by prohibiting the former and permitting the latter. The case includes citations from many state courts.

On the other hand, the most recent Supreme Court decision regarding assisted suicide involved Oregon's "Death with Dignity" statute,[87] which allows physicians, in certain limited situations, to assist a patient by prescribing controlled substances in order to end their life.[88] Because this case (Gonzales v. Oregon) deals with federal drug laws it will be discussed and offered as a case reading in Chapter 13. In this case, the federal government sought a ruling that the physician's prescription of drugs to end one's life was not a legitimate medical use and, therefore, doctors could be guilty under the Controlled Substances Act of 1970. The Supreme Court did not rule directly on Oregon's Death with Dignity Act, but did hold that it exceeded the authority of the Attorney General to determine what was a legitimate medical purpose. At this point, the Oregon law has not been overturned and is still good law. It should be noted that doctors can only prescribe fatal drugs for a strictly limited group of people. If anyone administers the drugs to the individual, they may still be guilty of some form of homicide.

LEGAL NEWS: DEATH WITH DIGNITY ACTS

Washington state has now joined Oregon in its passage of a "right-to-die" statute. In November 2008, 59 percent of Washington voters passed a statute allowing physician-assisted suicide. The statute, known as the Death with Dignity Act, went into effect in March 2009. Patients who are over 18, mentally competent, and with less than six months to live can now ask their doctors for a prescription for lethal medicine that they then can self-administer. Doctors and pharmacists opposed to the practice are not obligated to participate.

In 2009 the Montana Supreme Court ruled in *Baxter v. Montana*, that a doctor who assisted a competent, terminally ill patient, could not be prosecuted for murder, but did not make the broader ruling that there was a right to assisted suicide. In 2011 Montana legislators defeated a proposed bill that would make physician assisted suicide legal. There has also been a bill proposed that would invalidate the Montana Supreme Court's holding in *Baxter v. Montana*; however, that bill has not as of this writing been put to a vote.

Source: Kapralos, K. (2008). "Physician-Assisted Suicide Law Goes into Effect in March." Everett Herald, November 10, 2008:A1. Also see http://www.lifenews.com/2011/02/11/montana-defeats-bill-allowing-regulating-assisted-suicide/.

---

[87]   OR. REV. STAT. § 127.880 *et seq.*
[88]   Gonzales v. Oregon, 126 S.Ct. 904, 163 L.Ed.2d 748 (2006).

D. *Summary*

Although there are no current statutes or case law that criminalize suicide, most states do have laws that prohibit one party from assisting another in committing suicide and the Supreme Court has upheld such laws, finding that there is no constitutional right to die. Since *Gonzales v. Oregon*, however, the door is open for states to pass their own laws that allow for assisted suicide by physicians in certain limited circumstances when a patient is terminally ill.

Assisting Suicide (or other statutes)
(A/R) cause (through duress or force), solicit, assist, aid, advise suicide of another
(M/R) purposeful

§ 5.7   **Assault and Battery**

A. *Common Law*

At common law, assault and battery were two separate crimes. In many jurisdictions and in the Model Penal Code, the crimes are classified under the designation of "assault" without use of the word "battery." However, under common law they were distinguished in the following manner.

1. Assault

An **assault** was any unlawful offer or attempt to injure another, with an apparent present ability to effectuate the attempt under circumstances creating a fear of imminent peril. To constitute an assault, no touching was necessary, but there must have been an unlawful threat to do bodily harm to another with the apparent present ability to accomplish the deed if not prevented. An example would be a person who points a loaded firearm at another to cause injury or induce fear.[89] Note that the intent to cause injury or fear can be proven by circumstantial evidence, but assault was a specific intent crime, meaning that the defendant must have intent to make the threat and have the intent that his or her action would cause fear or apprehension.

2. Battery

Under common law, **battery** was the unlawful touching of the person of another by the aggressor or by some substance put in motion by him. A battery has been defined as the "consummation of the assault," and the "unlawful application of force to the person of another."[90] "Battery" is the actual use of force and occurs when the violence is accomplished.[91] Unlike assault, battery is a general intent crime because all that is necessary is the intent to perform the unlawful touching.

---

[89]   State v. Heitman, 618 S.W.2d 902 (Mo. Ct. App. 1981).
[90]   State v. Hefner, 199 N.C. 778, 155 S.E. 879 (1930).
[91]   Commonwealth v. Hill, 237 Pa. Super. 543, 353 A.2d 870 (1975).

B. Model Penal Code

The Model Penal Code eliminates the common law categories of assault and battery. It merges several kinds of misconduct under the generic offense of assault. Offenses are graded according to the gravity of harm intended or caused and the dangerousness of the means used. Under the Model Penal Code, assault is limited to cases involving either the *fact* or *prospect* of physical injury.

§ 211.1 Assault[92]

(1) Simple Assault. A person is guilty of assault if he:
  (a) attempts to cause or purposely, knowingly or recklessly causes bodily injury to another; or
  (b) negligently causes bodily injury to another with a deadly weapon; or
  (c) attempts by physical menace to put another in fear of imminent serious bodily harm.
Simple assault is a misdemeanor unless committed in a fight or scuffle entered into by mutual consent, in which case it is a petty misdemeanor.
(2) Aggravated Assault. A person is guilty of aggravated assault if he:
  (a) attempts to cause serious bodily injury to another, or causes such injury purposely, knowingly or recklessly under circumstances manifesting extreme indifference to the value of human life; or
  (b) attempts to cause or purposely or knowingly causes bodily injury to another with a deadly weapon.
Aggravated assault under paragraph (a) is a felony of the second degree; aggravated assault under paragraph (b) is a felony of the third degree.

C. State Statutes, Codes, and Cases

Some states have followed the reasoning of the drafters of the Model Penal Code. Others have separate provisions relating to assaults on police officers and other designated categories of persons.[93] Still others take a different approach and define degrees of assault, or provide more or less serious penalties according to the offender's degree of guilty mind, the means used to commit the offense, and the actual harm to persons involved. An example of the latter is Ohio, where six categories of assault and menacing deal with offenses formerly characterized as different kinds of assault, battery, and menacing threats. The six categories are felonious assault, aggravated assault, assault, negligent assault, aggravated menacing, and menacing.[94]

1. Elements of Assault

Most states have now combined assault and battery under one statute. In those states that have combined assault and battery, to constitute an actionable assault, the following elements must be proved beyond a reasonable doubt: an attempt or offer;

---

[92]   Model Penal Code § 211.1 (1985).

[93]   N.H. Rev. Stat. Ann. § 632-A:2 (1994); N.J. Rev. Stat. § 2 C:12-1 (1995); Pa. Cons. Stat. 18 § 2701(b) (2) (1995).

[94]   Ohio Rev. Code Ann. §§ 2903.11, 2903.12, 2903.13, 2903.14, 2903.21, 2903.22 (Anderson 1999).

with force and violence; to do some immediate physical injury to the person of another; and with the apparent present or immediate ability *or* any unlawful touching.

1. *Attempt or offer.* The force intended to be applied must be put into motion. Mere preparation does not amount to an assault; there must be some act that could apparently produce injury.

2. The *force or violence* offered must be unlawful, but it may be in any degree. For example, when a defendant attempted to apply force to the victim's person and grab money held fast in the victim's hand, this action constituted the necessary force to constitute assault.[95]

3. The attempt or offer must be *directed toward another person.* There need not be any touching or striking of the person, but there must be an offer to use force to injure another.[96] The prosecution must show that the person is placed in reasonable apprehension of receiving an immediate battery; there must be a showing of force or menace of violence that would be sufficient to put a person of reasonable firmness in fear of immediate bodily harm.[97]

4. It is necessary is to show "*apparent present ability*" to effectuate the harm. Assault does not occur unless the individual is placed in reasonable fear of *imminent* bodily harm, but if the victim is placed in reasonable fear of bodily harm, by conduct of the defendant, and the defendant had the apparent ability to carry out the threatening nature of his act, it is not necessary that the prosecution show that the defendant had the *actual* ability to carry out the act. For example, one may be found guilty of assault by pointing an unloaded firearm at another when the person threatened does not know that the gun is not loaded.[98]

5. (*Or*) *An unlawful application of force to the person of another.* The application of force must be unlawful (i.e., a police officer has the right to use force to subdue an arrestee).[99] The force may be direct or indirect, as by exposing a helpless person to the inclemency of the weather.[100] Any touching, if it is unlawful, may constitute the force necessary for a battery.[101] The force must be to the person of another and be unpermitted; for example, the defendant putting his hand into the victim's pants and upon the victim's penis.[102] But it is unnecessary that the victim's body or even his or her clothing be touched, because touching anything connected with his or her person is sufficient. For example, the intentional snatching of a patron's dinner plate from him by the manager of a hotel's club in a loud and offensive manner was sufficient to constitute battery.[103]

---

[95]   People v. LeFlore, 96 Mich. App. 557, 293 N.W.2d 628 (1980).
[96]   Albright v. State, 214 So. 2d 887 (Fla. Dist. Ct. App. 1968).
[97]   State v. Harding, 22 N.C. App. 66, 205 S.E.2d 544 (1974).
[98]   Allen v. Hannaford, 138 Wash. 223, 244 P. 700 (1926).
[99]   Trougn v. Fruchtman, 58 Wis. 2d 569, 207 N.W.2d 297 (1973).
[100]   Pallis v. State, 123 Ala. 12, 26 So. 339 (1899).
[101]   Scruggs v. State, 161 Ind. App. 666, 317 N.E.2d 807 (1974).
[102]   Brenneman v. State, 458 S.W.2d 677 (Tex. Crim. App. 1970).
[103]   Fisher v. Carrousel Motor Hotel, 424 S.W.2d 627 (Tex. 1967).

While touching with one's hands may constitute application of force to another person, not every touch is a criminal battery. Generally, the courts have required that the act be done in a wrongful or intentionally angry, resentful, rude, or insolent manner to make the act a battery. If the touching is the result of an unavoidable accident in the pursuit of a lawful act, this is a valid defense to a charge of battery.[104]

2. Issues of *Actus Reus* and *Mens Rea*

As discussed above, typically statutes now use one word—assault—for what was assault and battery. Many state statutes divide the crime of assault into simple and aggravated assault. The difference between the two can be either the degree of harm and/or the status of the victim. For instance, statutes have designated as aggravated assault those that were performed with a weapon, assaults against peace officers or children, and those that were conducted with extreme indifference to human life. The application of these statutes may create issues in the definition of *actus reus* or *mens rea*. For instance, in statutes that make the assault of a "peace officer" a more serious crime (aggravated assault), consider the following questions:

- Who is considered a peace officer to constitute the *actus reus*? (A juvenile probation officer was included in the definition.)[105]
- What is the *mens rea* required in regard to the knowledge that the victim is a police or peace officer? (If the defendant *should have known*, that is sufficient *mens rea*.)[106]

To provide more serious penalties for assaults that are considered especially troublesome, legislation designates specific types of assaults. Consider some of the following specific types of assault, which can be found in state statutes:

- assault with a deadly weapon[107]
- assault with a caustic or flammable chemical[108]
- assaults with tasers or stun guns[109]
- assaults on an unborn child[110]

It should be noted that assault crimes may not only serve as original charges, but also they may be used as a lesser included offense of murder or attempted murder. If, for example, the evidence against a murder defendant leaves room for doubt as to whether his or her act was the cause of death, an assault instruction is appropriate when all of the elements of assault are present.

---

[104] Crabtree v. Dawson, 83 S.W. 557 (Ky. 1904).
[105] In re David H., 967 P.2d 134 (Ariz. 1998).
[106] Dawsey v. State, 234 Ga. App. 540, 507 S.E.2d 786 (1998); *see also* State v. Chang, 587 N.W.2d 459 (Iowa 1998).
[107] S.D. CODIFIED LAWS ANN. § 22-18-11 (Michie 1995).
[108] CAL. PENAL CODE § 244 (West 1995).
[109] CAL. PENAL CODE § 244.5 (West 1995).
[110] S.D. CODIFIED LAWS ANN. 22-18-1.3 (Michie 1995).

3. Assault via HIV/AIDS

With the number of human immunodeficiency virus/acquired immunodeficiency syndrome (HIV/AIDS) cases growing steadily, it was inevitable that criminal courts would be asked to resolve issues involving defendants who knew they were HIV positive. In *Smallwood v. State*,[111] the court upheld a defendant's conviction for assault with intent to commit murder where the defendant, who knew he was HIV positive, attempted to rape the victim without wearing a condom. Other courts reviewing HIV/AIDS as an aggravated condition or factor have reached similar conclusions.[112]

In a Michigan case, a statute making it a crime for one who is aware that he or she has AIDS, or has tested positive for HIV, to fail to inform a sexual partner that he or she is infected was challenged on the grounds that it violated the First Amendment to the Constitution. The court upheld the conviction under the statute, finding that the statute did not violate the First Amendment right against compelled expression, because the state had an overwhelming interest in compelling the disclosure in order to stop the spread of HIV/AIDS.[113]

4. Definition of Weapon (in Aggravated Assault)

Where the state statute includes the crime of assault with a dangerous weapon, the prosecution must show that a dangerous weapon was, in fact, involved. In a Michigan case, the defendant was charged with and convicted of felonious assault against two small girls. He had no weapon, but used his hands to hold both victims, with one hand being placed over the lower face of one victim to quiet her as well as to restrain her. On appeal, the defendant contended that he could not be convicted of felonious assault, because he had no dangerous weapon. The state claimed that the pair of hands should be considered dangerous weapons. The reviewing court held that the statute is not limited to the dangerous weapons specifically listed, but bare hands cannot be considered weapons. The court based its decision to some extent on the fact that another statute defined assault not involving dangerous weapons, reasoning that if bare hands were construed as "dangerous weapons," the distinction between categories of assault would be meaningless.[114]

While a person's hand is not generally considered a dangerous weapon under a statute that prohibits assault with a deadly instrument, the courts have found that other

---

[111]   Smallwood v. State, 661 A.2d 747 (Md. Ct. App. 1995).

[112]   Scroggins v. State, 198 Ga. App. 29, 401 S.E.2d 13 (1990), condition was a "deadly weapon"; State v. Deal, 459 S.E.2d 93 (S.C. 1995), HIV status was "aggravating circumstance"; State v. Smith, 262 N.J. Super. 487, 621 A.2d 493 (App. Div. 1993), "aggravated assault"; Commonwealth v. Brown, 413 Pa. Super. 421, 605 A.2d 429 (1992), "serious bodily injury" was upheld. *See also* State v. Bird, 81 Ohio St. 3d 582, 692 N.E.2d 1013 (1998), in which the court upheld the conviction of an HIV-infected defendant for felonious assault when the defendant spit in a police officer's face.

[113]   People v. Jensen, 231 Mich. App. 439, 586 N.W.2d 748 (1998).

[114]   People v. Van Diver, 80 Mich. App. 352, 263 N.W.2d 370 (Mich. Ct. App. 1978). *See also* People v. Nealy, 681 N.Y.S.2d 29 (1998).

instruments can be considered dangerous weapons under certain circumstances. For example, an Alabama court found that intentionally putting an automobile in motion and violently and intentionally driving it against a police officer is "an assault with a deadly instrument," in violation of the statute.[115]

In the case of *State v. Torres*, the court of appeals of North Carolina agreed with the lower court that four large metal rings worn by the defendant were properly the basis for a conviction on a charge of assault with a deadly weapon.[116] In this case, the defendant was involved in a fistfight in the parking lot of a Durham County high school. The defendant was wearing four large silver rings ornamented with a skull or pirate head. The victim suffered a broken jaw, and the rings on the hand of the defendant were found to be covered with blood at the time of the arrest. The defendant was charged with using metal, raised-design rings on his fingers as deadly weapons to assault and inflict serious injury. The reviewing court refused to find error on the part of the trial court in allowing this as evidence of a deadly weapon under the North Carolina statute. Other courts have defined dangerous weapons to include the following:

- sulphuric acid[117]
- automobile[118]
- imitation or "blank" pistol[119]

5. Sporting Events

Why aren't boxers arrested for assault? The answer lies in the concept of consent. Recall that one of the elements of common law battery was *unpermitted* touching. Consent is recognized as a defense when one of the elements of a crime is "against the will" of the victim. This is obvious in sexual assault, and is applicable, to some degree, in assault as well. As case law has developed, the rule is that sporting events give individuals the right to engage in a certain amount of sanctioned force against other players. However, if players violate the rules and normal practices of the game, then they can be charged with assault and battery. For instance, boxing necessarily involves hitting each other (which would otherwise be assault), but it does not allow biting; thus, when Mike Tyson bit off a part of his opponent's ear, that act was not consented to and could be defined as assault. If baseball players intentionally throw a bat at someone, that could be assault; and if football players intentionally injure another player in a "late hit," that could be charged as assault.

While sports events are a type of consent to simple assault, there is no general right to consent to aggravated assault (injury). That is, victims cannot agree to be killed

---

[115]   Kelly v. State, 362 So.2d 1292 (1978).
[116]   State v. Torres, 335 S.E.2d 34 (N.C. Ct. App. 1985).
[117]   Bishop v. United States, 349 F.2d 220 (D.C. Cir. 1965).
[118]   Powell v. United States, 485 A.2d 596 (D.C. Ct. App. 1984), *cert. denied*, 474 U.S. 981, 106 S. Ct. 420, 88 L. Ed. 2d 339 (1985).
[119]   Harris v. United States, 333 A.2d 397 (D.C. Ct. App. 1975).

(recall the assisted suicide section above), or even whipped or otherwise injured.[120] While case law is mixed in this area, generally courts have held that, for public policy reasons, a defendant cannot use the defense that the victim asked to be hurt.

6. Mayhem

Under common law, there was a specific type of battery called "**mayhem**." This was described as maliciously depriving another of the use of his limbs so as to make him unable to defend himself against adversaries. Later, it included other forms of injury that included any kind of dismemberment or disfigurement. There is no specific provision for mayhem under the Model Penal Code, although a few current state statutes still distinguish this crime. For instance, Idaho's statute specifies that a person guilty of mayhem "maliciously deprives a human being of a member of his body, or disables, disfigures or renders it useless, or cuts or disables the tongue, puts out an eye, slits the nose, ear or lips, . . ."[121]

LEGAL NEWS: MODERN MAYHEM

The most famous mayhem case in the United States is probably that of Lorena Bobbitt, who cut off her husband's penis when he was sleeping. Her defense was that her husband had raped her and she was a victim of domestic violence. She claimed temporary insanity and was committed to a mental health facility for 45 days for observation.

Source: http://www.cbsnews.com/stories/2008/06/25/earlyshow/leisure/celebspot/main4207517.shtml.

---

7. Domestic Violence

Although it may seem different, domestic violence is, under the law, assault. The level of assault (simple or aggravated) will be determined by the extent of injuries and whether or not a weapon was used. Note the following Texas statute for assault specifically notes that it includes a spouse.

> Sec. 22.01. ASSAULT. (a) A person commits an offense if the person:
> (1) intentionally, knowingly, or recklessly causes bodily injury to another, including the person's spouse;
> (2) intentionally or knowingly threatens another with imminent bodily injury, including the person's spouse; or
> (3) intentionally or knowingly causes physical contact with another when the person knows or should reasonably believe that the other will regard the contact as offensive or provocative. [remainder of statute omitted]

---

[120]   State v. Fransua, 510 P.2d 106 (1973).
[121]   IDAHO CODE § 18-5001 (1995).

Under common law, there were some interpretations that indicated men had the power to discipline their wives and children; today, no one would seriously argue that assault is different somehow when one is threatening or hitting a family member. Difficulties arise, however, in prosecuting such cases when victims are unwilling to cooperate.

LEGAL NEWS: DOMESTIC ASSAULT

A recent news item presented findings from a study on domestic violence. According to a telephone survey of 9,000 women and 7,400 men, one out of four women have been attacked by boyfriends or husbands. While some argue that the methodology of the study might lead to inflated numbers, others say they are not surprised. Attacks included choking, beating, stabbing, shooting, punching, and hair-pulling.

Retrieved December 22, 2011 from http://abclocal.go.com/kgo/story?section=news/heath& id=8467766.

D. Summary

There is a wide variety of statutes in the assault and battery area; however, the general elements are fairly standard and merely combine the common law crimes of assault and battery as indicated below.

Assault
(A/R) attempt, threaten or offer, with unlawful force, to inflict immediate bodily injury accompanied with apparent present ability, or offensive touching
upon another
(M/R) purposely, knowingly, recklessly, or negligently (depending on level or particular type of assault)

§ 5.8   Kidnapping and Related Offenses

A. Common Law

At common law, "**kidnapping**" was defined as the forcible abduction and carrying away of a man, woman, or child from his or her own country into another.[122] Other older definitions of kidnapping include the following:

• willfully seizing, confining, or luring another, with the intent to cause him or her, without authority of law, to be secretly confined or imprisoned within the state; to be sent out of the state; to be sold as a slave or to be in any way held to service; or to be kept or detained against his or her will.[123]

---

[122]   Tate v. State, 32 Md. App. 613, 363 A.2d 622 (1976).
[123]   State v. Croatt, 227 Minn. 185, 34 N.W.2d 716 (1948).

- forcibly detaining another against his will to unlawfully obtain ransom, or unlawfully restraining another and forcibly moving the person imprisoned to another place.[124]

The essence of kidnapping is the intentional taking of a person and detaining that person against his or her will. The traditional elements of kidnapping are

1. unlawful imprisonment by
   a. detaining another
   b. by force or fraud
   c. without his or her consent and
   d. without legal cause, and
2. moving him or her to another place (asportation)
3. to unlawfully obtain ransom.

1. Unlawful Imprisonment

One of the elements of kidnapping under the common law and under some statutes is **unlawful imprisonment**, which means unlawfully restraining, unlawfully removing, or unlawfully confining a person against their will. For instance, a court held the act of holding the person for a proscribed purpose necessarily implies an unlawful physical and mental restraint where the detention is for an appreciable period, is against the person's will, and is done with a willful intent to confine the victim.[125]

If all of the elements for the crime of kidnapping are not present (such as the demand for ransom or asportation), a person may be guilty of unlawful imprisonment. For example, a person is guilty of unlawful imprisonment under some statutes when he or she knowingly and unlawfully restrains another under circumstances that expose that person to a risk of serious physical injury. The elements of unlawful imprisonment under this statute are

1. knowingly and
2. unlawfully
3. restraining another,
4. under circumstances that expose the victim to a risk of physical injury.

B. Model Penal Code

Under the Model Penal Code, kidnapping is a felony of the first degree unless the actor voluntarily releases the victim alive and in a safe place, in which case it is a felony of the second degree. Removal or confinement of a person is unlawful within the meaning of this section if it is accomplished by force, threat, or

---

[124] Gwooch v. United States, 82 F.2d 534 (10th Cir. 1936).
[125] Chatwin v. United States, 326 U.S. 455, 66 S. Ct. 233, 90 L. Ed. 198 (1946).

deception, or, in the case of a person who is under the age of 14 or incompetent, if it is accomplished without the consent of a parent, guardian, or other person responsible for his or her general supervision. The penalty for kidnapping under the Model Penal Code is determined by the treatment of the victim and the circumstances surrounding the kidnapping.

§ 212.1 Kidnapping[126]

A person is guilty of kidnapping if he unlawfully removes another from his place of residence or business, or a substantial distance from the vicinity where he is found, or if he unlawfully confines another for a substantial period in a place of isolation, with any of the following purposes:

(a) to hold for ransom or reward, or as a shield or hostage; or
(b) to facilitate commission of any felony or flight thereafter; or
(c) to inflict bodily injury on or to terrorize the victim or another; or
(d) to interfere with the performance of any governmental or political function.

The wording of the Model Penal Code is cast in terms of removal of the victim "from" a location, rather than transporting him "to" another place as was used in some pre-Model Code statutes. To avoid confusion and technical interpretations, the word "vicinity" is used, rather than "place." Also, "substantial" removal is required to preclude kidnapping convictions based on trivial changes of location having no bearing on the evil at hand. The Model Penal Code definition includes unlawful confinement of another "for a substantial period in a place of isolation." This eliminates the "asportation" element that was included in the common law definitions, but still leaves questions as to what is "substantial" and what amounts to "a place of isolation."

The Model Penal Code includes the offenses of Felonious Restraint, False Imprisonment, Interference with Custody, and Criminal Coercion as offenses related to kidnapping.[127] These and other specifically defined offenses were added in many states to make it possible for the state to take action when a wrongful act is committed, but the wrong is not serious enough to come within the technical definition of kidnapping. Generally, these less serious offenses, as defined by statute, have a penalty attached that is of a lower degree than the penalty for kidnapping.

C. State Statutes, Codes, and Cases

Even though federal law enforcement is believed to always be involved in kidnappings, the crime was first and primarily a state crime. Only in 1934, with the Charles Lindbergh Jr. kidnapping, did Congress pass a federal kidnapping law. Today, unless there are interstate elements, kidnapping remains a state crime. State statutory provisions have greatly enlarged the scope of kidnapping and, in some instances, added other offenses that directly relate to kidnapping, but do not require that all elements be

---

[126]   Model Penal Code § 212.1 (1985).
[127]   Model Penal Code §§ 212.2-212.5 (1985).

proved. As the following definitions indicate, the terms used in defining kidnapping vary from jurisdiction to jurisdiction.

- "must have falsely imprisoned his victim by acquiring complete dominion and control over him for some appreciable period of time and must have carried him beyond the immediate vicinity of the place of such false imprisonment."[128]
- "Kidnapping constitutes the carrying away of a person for a purpose such as ransom or the committing of a bodily felony ... elements of kidnapping are (1) taking or seizure of a human being, (2) asportation or movement of the seized individual, (3) by means of unlawful force or fraud, (4) and for the purpose of ransom, reward or committing a felony."[129]
- "to take and carry away any person by unlawful force or fraud and against his will."[130]

An example of a state statute that differs from the Model Penal Code in various ways is that of New York. In addition to the offenses of "unlawful imprisonment" in the first and second degree, the New York law provides heavier penalties for the offenses of kidnapping in the second degree and kidnapping in the first degree.[131]

§ 135.05 Unlawful imprisonment in the second degree

A person is guilty of unlawful imprisonment in the second degree when he restrains another person.

Unlawful imprisonment in the second degree is a Class A misdemeanor.

§ 135.10 Unlawful imprisonment in the first degree

A person is guilty of unlawful imprisonment in the first degree when he restrains another person under circumstances which expose the latter to a risk of serious physical injury.

Unlawful imprisonment in the first degree is a Class E felony.

§ 135.20 Kidnapping in the second degree

A person is guilty of kidnapping in the second degree when he abducts another person.

Kidnapping in the second degree is a Class B felony.

§ 135.25 Kidnapping in the first degree

A person is guilty of kidnapping in the first degree when he abducts another person and when:

1. His intent is to compel a third person to pay or deliver money or property as ransom, or to engage in other particular conduct, or to refrain from engaging in particular conduct; or

---

[128]   State v. Roberts, 286 N.C. 265, 210 S.E.2d 396 (1974).
[129]   Lovell v. State, 92 Nev. 128, 546 P.2d 1301 (1976).
[130]   State v. Ayers, 198 Kan. 467, 426 P.2d 21 (1967).
[131]   N.Y. PENAL LAW §§ 135.05-135.30 (McKinney 1999).

2. He restrains the person abducted for a period of more than twelve hours with intent to:
   (a) Inflict physical injury upon him or violate or abuse him sexually;
   (b) Accomplish or advance the commission of a felony; or
   (c) Terrorize him or a third person; or
   (d) Interfere with the performance of a governmental or political function; or
3. The person abducted dies during the abduction or before he is able to return or to be returned to safety. Such death shall be presumed, in a case where such person was less than sixteen years old or an incompetent person at the time of the abduction, from evidence that his parents, guardians or other lawful custodians did not see or hear from him following the termination of the abduction and prior to trial and received no reliable information during such period persuasively indicating that he was alive. In all other cases, such death shall be presumed from evidence that a person whom the person abducted would have been extremely likely to visit or communicate with during the specific period were he alive and free to do so did not see or hear from him during such period and received no reliable information during such period persuasively indicating that he was alive.
   Kidnapping in the first degree is a Class A-I felony.

§ 135.30 Kidnapping; defense

In any prosecution for kidnapping, it is an affirmative defense that:
(a) the defendant was a relative of the person abducted, and
(b) his sole purpose was to assume control of such person.

The elements of the crime of kidnapping depend upon the wording of the respective statutes. In general, most of the elements of common law kidnapping can be found in most state statutes so we will discuss the traditional elements. In most statutes all of the following elements are present:

1. Detaining Another

Some states require that the victim's confinement be substantial. In the case of *State v. Denmon*, a New Jersey court held that the determination of whether a victim's confinement is substantial, and thus supports a kidnapping charge, is not determined by its duration; rather, the jury should look at the enhanced risk of harm resulting from the confinement and isolation of the victim.[132]

2. By Force or Fraud

The "force" element of kidnapping may be accomplished either by actual physical coercion or force to the body of such a person, or by coercion of the will of the person by threats, fear, intimidation, deception, or other inducement that deprives the victim of the will to resist.[133]

---

[132]   State v. Denmon, 347 N.J. Super. 457, 790 A.2d 921 (2002).
[133]   State v. Brown, 181 Kan. 375, 312 P.2d 832 (1957).

3. Without Consent

A defendant cannot be convicted of kidnapping if the alleged victim consented to the restraint or consented to go with the defendant. However, the initial consent is converted into an unlawful detention if the defendant refuses to allow the person to leave. For example, when hitchhikers consented to be given a ride to their home, but instead, over their objection and under threats of death, they were driven to a far distant place where one of them was raped, the court found that, even if the original taking was not forcible or fraudulent, the unlawful detention commenced when the defendant refused to drive the hitchhikers home and drove away from the area.[134] In addition, minors generally cannot give consent so even if they go willingly, it would still be considered kidnapping. Finally, if someone is misled as to the true nature of the situation (i.e., the kidnapper tells the victim that their child is injured and they will take them to the injured child), under the law they have not given consent because consent requires that one knowingly and voluntarily offered their assent; in the case of deception there can be no consent.

4. Without Legal Cause

A police officer who restrains another is not guilty of kidnapping when, acting in his or her official capacity, he or she detains a person pursuant to a warrant issued by a court, or is otherwise carrying out his or her official duties. But if the officer does not act in good faith and the entire transaction indicates an unlawful purpose, the officer technically could be held for kidnapping.[135] This is especially true when a peace officer goes into another state and, without authority, apprehends a person and returns him or her to the state where the officer has jurisdiction.

5. Asportation

Under the common law, and under some statutes, an element of kidnapping is **asportation**: this is the taking, leading, carrying away, or transportation of the victim. The degree of movement from one place to another depends upon the wording of the statute. If, for example, the statute requires that the person be removed from the state, then the prosecution must show that the person was, in fact, moved from the state. However, if the statute provides that "a person is guilty if he unlawfully removes one from his place of residence or business, or a substantial distance from the vicinity where he is found," then all that is necessary is to show that the unlawful removal took place. In this regard, one court upheld a kidnapping conviction when the accused, under the pretense of being a good faith passenger, forced a taxi driver at gunpoint to

---

[134]   Matter of Appeal in Maricopa County Juvenile Action, 25 Ariz. App. 377, 543 P.2d 806 (1975).
[135]   People v. Fick, 89 Cal. 144, 26 P. 759 (1891).

drive him to another destination. The appellant had argued that the taxicab driver was not carried from any "place" because the moving vehicle was not a place.[136]

In the case of *State v. Morris*, a Minnesota court determined that the removal of a victim the distance of only 150 feet, and detention for five minutes in the process of committing indecent assault, constituted "kidnapping" and it was proper to charge kidnapping as a separate offense.[137] In another case, the court determined that the word "kidnapping," as used in the statute of that state, means the unlawful taking and carrying away of a person by force and against his or her will. That court agreed that it is the fact, not the distance, of forcible removal of the victim that constitutes the kidnapping; any carrying away is sufficient and the distance is immaterial.[138]

In interpreting the North Carolina statute that requires the victim to be "removed," the state court determined that the "removal" of the victims from the main room of stores was independent of the robberies committed, and therefore the defendant could be convicted of kidnapping in addition to robbery. In this case, the victims were moved from the main area of stores into bathrooms or offices, and rooms to which victims were ordered to go did not contain safes, cash registers, or locked boxes that held the property that was taken.[139]

In interpreting the "removal" provision of the state's statutes, a Georgia court concluded that the offense of kidnapping does not require a showing that the movement of the victim was made in a clandestine or surreptitious manner and that the slightest movement of a victim will establish the asportation requirement for kidnapping.[140]

In a case decided by the District of Columbia Court of Appeals, it was held that under the District of Columbia statute there is no requirement that the victim be removed any particular distance or held for any particular length of time; all that is required is "seizing," "confining," or the like, and holding or detaining for ransom or reward "or otherwise."[141]

6. For Ransom or Other Unlawful Purpose (not parental kidnapping)

Under common law and the Model Penal Code, the purpose for the detainment had to be unlawful, i.e., for ransom or other nefarious purpose. Some states have eliminated this requirement or, through case law, defined any reason as unlawful, i.e., to get an ex-girlfriend to agree to marry; to induce action on the part of the victim; or to frighten a parent by taking their child.

---

[136]   Epperson v. State, 211 Ind. 237, 6 N.E.2d 538 (1937).

[137]   State v. Morris, 281 Minn. 119, 160 N.W.2d 715 (1968).

[138]   State v. Dix, 14 N.C. App. 328, 188 S.E.2d 737 (1972).

[139]   State v. Joyce, 410 S.E.2d 516 (N.C. 1991). *See also* Elozar v. State, 825 So.2d 490 (2002).

[140]   Cosby v. State, 234 Ga. App. 723, 507 S.E.2d 551 (1998). *See also* Duncan v. State, 253 Ga. App. 239, 558 S.E.2d 783 (2002), which held that any unlawful asportation, however slight, will support a kidnapping conviction.

[141]   West v. United States, 599 A.2d 788 (D.C. Ct. App. 1991).

In more recent times, the courts have had to deal with the issue of parental kidnappings that occur when a parent who does not have legal custody of a child refuses to return the child to the custodial parent, and/or abducts the child. Because of the difficulties of applying traditional kidnapping statutes to such behavior, and the reluctance of juries to find guilt when the kidnapper is a parent, many states have created new statutes that define the behavior as a crime separate from kidnapping. One such statute is Oregon's "Custodial Interference" statute.

Oregon Revised Statute 163.245-Custodial Interference in the Second Degree

A person commits the crime of custodial interference in the second degree if, knowing or having reason to know that the person has no legal right to do so, the person takes, entices or keeps another person from the other person's lawful custodian or in violation of a valid joint custody order with intent to hold the other person permanently or for a protracted period.

Oregon Revised Statute 163.257-Custodial Interference in the First Degree

A person commits the crime of custodial interference in the first degree if the person violates ORS 163.245 and:
(a) Causes the person taken, enticed or kept from the lawful custodian or in violation of a valid joint custody order to be removed from the state; or
(b) Exposes that person to a substantial risk of illness or physical injury.

An Ohio statute designed to prevent child stealing and enticing a child away is titled "Interference with Custody." It provides:

(A) No person, knowing he is without privilege to do so or being reckless in that regard, shall entice, take, keep, or harbor a person identified in Division (A)(1), (2), or (3) of this section from his parent, guardian, or custodian:
   (1) A child under the age of eighteen, or a mentally or physically handicapped child under the age of twenty-one;
   (2) A person committed by law to an institution for delinquent, unruly, neglected, abused, or dependent children;
   (3) A person committed by law to an institution for the mentally ill or mentally retarded.[142]

The Ohio statute provides a defense for enticing a child away if there is a reasonable belief that it is necessary for the child's protection, and also provides a defense to harboring a child if the actor notifies the authorities of the child's whereabouts in a timely fashion.

LEGAL NEWS: COUNTRY SINGER TAKES CHILD

In December of 2011, country singer Mindy McCready went into hiding with her five-year-old son, violating a custody order awarding the child to the singer's mother. She was found with the child unharmed and has stated publicly she

---

142   OHIO REV. CODE ANN. § 2919.23 (Anderson 2002).

> was protecting him from abuse he suffered at her mother's home, a charge the boy's maternal grandmother vehemently denies. It is not clear whether or not criminal charges will be filed against her.
>
> ---
>
> Retrieved December 23, 2011 from http://www.foxnews.com/entertainment/2011/12/02/police-take-custody-singer-mindy-mccreadys-son/.

D. Summary

Kidnapping has maintained the elements of common law for the most part; however, case law has greatly reduced the asportation requirement. The common law requirement that the reason for the kidnapping be for ransom or another unlawful purpose has also been expanded, either by case law or statute. The most recent issue concerning the law of kidnapping is how to deal with parental kidnappings, especially those in which the parent has at least some arguably noble purpose in protecting their child from an abusive custodial parent. States must honor the custodial orders of other states and, therefore, parents must be deterred from taking the law into their own hands by seizing the child. Everyone can agree, however, that these cases are different from kidnappings for ransom.

Kidnapping
(A/R) detaining another, with force or fraud, without consent, asportation, for ransom or other unlawful purpose
(M/R) purposefully, knowingly

§ 5.9 Hate Crimes (Bias Crimes)

A. Common Law

There was no such crime under common law. The concept of hate crimes is purely statutory.

B. Model Penal Code

The impetus for and creation of the first hate crime statutes occurred well after the development and dissemination of the Model Penal Code.

C. State Statutes, Codes, and Cases

Several well-publicized incidents involving victims who were targeted because they were African-American, Jewish, or homosexual in the late 1980s and early 1990s resulted in the creation of criminal statutes that came to be known as "hate crime" statutes. **Hate crime** statutes are similar to traditional criminal statutes prohibiting acts such as assault, battery, or vandalism; however, the hate crime statutes require an additional element—that the victim (or property) was selected as a target because of the victim's membership in a protected group. One author described these crimes as crimes that have been "committed not out of animosity toward the victim as an individual, but out of hostility toward the group to which the victim belongs."[143]

1. Construction

Hate crime statutes generally have two components: prohibited acts and protected groups. The prohibited acts addressed by a hate crime statute may either be listed by name (assault, battery, aggravated assault, misdemeanor theft, criminal trespass to residence, misdemeanor criminal damage to property, criminal trespass to vehicle, criminal trespass to real property, or mob action) or the statute may simply refer to particular crimes by category or statute number.[144]

Specific groups that are protected by hate crime statutes vary from jurisdiction to jurisdiction. Generally, however, most statutes include the following categories: age, race, color, creed, religion, ancestry, gender, sexual orientation, physical or mental disability, or national origin.

Hate crimes also vary by the nature of the penalty. In some jurisdictions, the determination that a particular crime qualifies as a hate crime serves to enhance, or increase, the sentence of the underlying criminal offense,[145] while in other jurisdictions a hate crime is a separate and distinct criminal offense carrying a separate penalty.[146]

California's statute is as follows:

422.6 (a)[147]

No person, whether or not acting under color of law, shall by force or threat of force, willfully injure, intimidate, interfere with, oppress, or threaten any other person in the free exercise or enjoyment of any right or privilege secured to him or her by the Constitution or laws of this state or by the Constitution or laws of the United States because of the other person's race, color, religion, ancestry, national origin, disability, gender, or sexual orientation, or because he or she perceives that the other person has one or more of those characteristics.

---

[143]   Elizabeth A. Pendo, *Recognizing Violence Against Women: Gender and Hate Crime Statistics*, 17 HARV. WOMEN'S L.J. 157 (1994).

[144]   720 ILL. COMP. STAT. § 5/12-7.1 (West 1994); WIS. STAT. § 939.645(1)(b).

[145]   Wisc. Stat. § 939.645.

[146]   I.L.C.S. § 12-7.1. Hate Crime.

[147]   CAL. PENAL CODE 422(a).

Forty-nine states have adopted some form of hate crime legislation.[148] Further, at the federal level, legislation has been enacted that requires states to keep track of hate crime statistics.[149] Bias crime statutes are almost as varied in their scope, linguistic particulars, and the circumstances of creation as the jurisdictions that have enacted them. There is no formal or historic feature that a law must have in order to be properly called a "hate crime statute."

2. Judicial Review of Hate Crimes

Care must be taken when drafting hate crime legislation to not criminalize speech (or symbolic speech) that is constitutionally protected. Two recent decisions by the U.S. Supreme Court have clarified the relationship between actions that can constitutionally be criminalized by a hate crime statute and actions that must be tolerated as protected free speech.[150]

In *R.A.V. v. St. Paul*, juveniles burned a cross on the lawn of an African-American family. They were convicted of violating a city ordinance that prohibited actions based on "bias-motivated hatred." In striking down that particular hate crime ordinance, the Supreme Court noted that the ordinance was "content-based" toward particular forms of speech rather than facially neutral, prohibiting all speech or actions likely to provoke a fight. In other words, rather than criminalizing all actions or words likely to invoke a violent response ("fighting words"), the St. Paul ordinance singled out, by content, specific activities to criminalize:

> Whoever places on public or private property, a symbol, object, appellation, characterization or graffiti, including, but not limited to, a burning cross or Nazi swastika, which one knows or has reasonable grounds to know arouses anger, alarm or resentment in others on the basis of race, color, creed, religion or gender commits disorderly conduct and shall be guilty of a misdemeanor.

In Virginia v. Black, the Virginia law against cross burning was struck down only to the extent that the cross burning itself was considered *prima facie* evidence of intimidation. The Supreme Court held the state must prove intent to intimidate for it to be a hate crime.

The Court's rulings in these two cases indicate that hate crime legislation will be upheld as being valid as long as the statute or ordinance criminalizes traditionally prohibited acts ("fighting words") and such legislation does not single out specific actions based on the speech-related content.

---

[148]   Marlene Z. Stanger, *Hate Crime Legislation: Panacea or Protractor of Societal Ills?* 3 San Diego Just. J. 419 (1995).

[149]   Federal Hate Crimes Statistics Act of 1990, 28 U.S.C. § 534(b)(1).

[150]   R.A.V. v. St. Paul, 505 U.S. 377 (1992); Virginia v. Black, 538 U.S. 343 (2003).

In Wisconsin v. Mitchell, the defendant, who was black, specifically selected a white victim to assault. The defendant was convicted under the Wisconsin statute that mandated an enhanced sentence when a defendant "[i]ntentionally selects the person against whom the crime . . . is committed . . . because of the [victim's] race. . .". In upholding the validity of the Wisconsin statute, the Court distinguished R.A.V. v. St. Paul because the Wisconsin statute was "content-neutral" in that ". . .the statute . . . is aimed at conduct unprotected by the First Amendment."[151] Several state courts have come to similar conclusions in upholding the validity of their hate crime statutes.[152]

LEGAL NEWS: HATE CRIMES

In 2010, 1,949 law enforcement agencies reported 6,628 hate crime incidents involving 7,699 offenses. There were 6,624 single-bias incidents that involved 7,690 offenses, 8,199 victims, and 6,001 offenders. Of these, 47.3 percent were racially motivated; 20.0 percent were motivated by religious bias; 19.3 percent resulted from sexual-orientation bias; 12.8 percent stemmed from ethnicity/national origin bias; and 0.6 percent were prompted by disability bias.

For more information, go to http://www.fbi.gov/about-us/investigate/civilrights/hate_crimes.

D. *Summary*

Hate or bias crimes are recent additions to the law. They add specific penalties or enhanced penalties when crimes are perpetrated against members of protected groups.

> Hate or Bias Crimes
> (A/R) certain specified (illegal) acts, i.e., murder, assault, vandalism, kidnapping; against specific victims (members of protected groups)
> (M/R) intentional

---

[151]   Wisconsin v. Mitchell, 508 U.S. 476 (1993).

[152]   The court specifically referenced the findings in *Crimes Motivated By Hatred: The Constitutionality and Impact of Hate Crime Legislation in the United States*, 1 SYRACUSE J. LEGIS. & POL'Y 29 (1995). See also Anthony M. Dillof, *Punishing Bias: An Examination of the Theoretical Foundation of Bias Crime Statutes*, 91 NW. U. L. REV., Spring 1997; Steven G. Gey, *What if Wisconsin v. Mitchell Had Involved Martin Luther King, Jr.? The Constitutional Flaws of Hate Crime Enhancement Statutes*. 65 GEO. WASH. L. REV., August 1997; Frederick M. Lawrence, *Federal Bias Crime Law Symposium*, 80 B.U. L. REV., Vol. 1185 (2000) (this article is followed by other articles that consider the pros and cons of federalizing hate crimes); Christopher Chorba, *The Danger of Federalizing Hate Crimes*, 87 VA. L. REV. 319 (2001).

§ 5.10 Summary

Crimes that are considered under the heading "Offenses against Persons" are homicide, suicide, assault and battery, kidnapping and related offenses, mayhem, hate crimes, and "other crimes against the person." The most serious of these are in the homicide category. Homicide is defined as the killing of a human being by another human being. Not all homicides are illegal. At the top of the scale of crimes relating to homicide is murder in the first degree. At the other end of the scale are excusable and justifiable homicides, which are not subject to punishment under the law.

The common law crime of murder is defined as "the unlawful killing of a human being by another human being with malice aforethought." At common law, and in some states, there are no degrees of murder. However, in most states, the crime of murder is divided into two categories: first degree and second degree. The distinguishing factors of first-degree murder are premeditation and deliberation.

Manslaughter is defined as the unlawful killing of a human being, done without malice, express or implied, either in a sudden quarrel or unintentionally while in the commission of an unlawful act. Manslaughter is usually divided into two categories: voluntary, when the homicidal act is intentional but passion-produced and occasioned by some provocation; and involuntary, when it results from the commission of certain unlawful acts not accompanied by any intention to take life.

Suicide is not a homicide, because there is no killing of one person by another person. While some of the early courts took the position that suicide was a crime, even if no punishment could be inflicted, today suicide is not considered a crime. However, a person may be guilty of criminal homicide if, with the requisite culpability, he or she causes the death of another by causing that person to commit suicide. Also, under some statutes, a person may be guilty of a separate offense of aiding or soliciting suicide even when suicide itself is not a crime.

Although assault and battery were two separate common law crimes, under the modern statutes, they are usually combined into one crime of assault. The common definition of assault is "an unlawful offer or attempt to injure another, with apparent present ability to effectuate the attempt under circumstances creating a fear of imminent peril" or "the unlawful touching of the person of another by the aggressor or by some substance put in motion by him," which was the common law definition of battery.

Kidnapping is "the forcible detaining of another against his will to unlawfully obtain ransom, or unlawfully restraining another and forcibly moving the person imprisoned to another place." The essence of kidnapping is the intentional taking of a person and compelling him or her to be detained against his or her will. Kidnapping is considered a very serious crime and under the Model Penal Code is designated a felony in the first degree, unless the actor voluntarily releases the person alive and in a safe place, in which case it is a felony in the second degree. Parental kidnapping laws are a recent addition to penal codes.

Recently, hate crime laws have been added to the group of laws under the category of "Offenses against Persons." Hate or bias crimes have been defined as crimes that have been committed not out of animosity toward the victim as an individual, but out of hostility toward the group to which the victim belongs. Specific groups that are protected by hate crime statutes vary from jurisdiction to jurisdiction. Generally, however, most statutes include the following categories: age, race, color, creed, religion, ancestry, gender, sexual orientation, physical or mental disability, or national origin. They have been upheld as long as they do not infringe on constitutional rights of free speech.

REVIEW QUESTIONS

1. What are the different types of homicide and what are the elements of each?
2. Distinguish first-degree from second-degree murder and voluntary from involuntary manslaughter.
3. What are assisted suicide laws? How many states have them?
4. What is the "year-and-a-day rule"?
5. What are the three types of homicide defined in the Model Penal Code?
6. How does current law define death? How does current law define a person?
7. Distinguish justifiable and excusable homicide.
8. Discuss the concepts of "delayed death" exceptions to double jeopardy.
9. Describe transferred intent.
10. Describe the felony-murder doctrine. Explain what type of deaths could be attributable to the defendants in felony-murder cases.
11. Can someone be executed for felony murder even though they didn't intend anyone to be killed? Explain.
12. Describe the types of provocation necessary to prove voluntary manslaughter and those that would not provide a defense. What are the other elements of voluntary manslaughter?

13. Distinguish between depraved heart (or depraved indifference) murder, involuntary manslaughter, and negligent homicide.
14. How short is the "cooling-off" period during which time a person is believed to be less culpable for the killing of another?
15. Distinguish assault and battery under the common law. How does the MPC change these traditional definitions? Provide the elements of assault.
16. When can consent be used as a defense to assault?
17. What is the crime of mayhem?
18. Distinguish between unlawful imprisonment and kidnapping. What are the elements of each?
19. What are the elements and defenses to parental kidnapping statutes?
20. Describe hate crime statutes. Describe when such statutes would be ruled unconstitutional and when they would be ruled constitutional.

Offenses against Persons— Sex Related

6

Chapter Outline

Cases

carnal knowledge	sexual abuse
deviate sexual intercourse	sexual assault
importuning	sexual contact
indecent exposure	sexual misconduct
lewdness	sexual predator laws
marital exemption	sodomy
rape	statutory rape
rape shield laws	utmost resistance standard
seduction	voyeurism

§ 6.1   Introduction

Although most sex-related offenses are also offenses against the person, they are considered separately for several reasons. Some sexual acts were considered serious offenses in the past, but not today. For example, adultery and fornication were classified as felonies at common law and by some early statutes.[1] Today they are minor misdemeanors if they are crimes at all. On the other hand, some acts that were not considered serious crimes in the past or were neglected by the law now receive greater attention, for instance, acquaintance rape, sexual harassment, and HIV/AIDS transmission. Some sex-related crimes are consensual and, therefore, are not "offenses against the person." In this chapter, nonconsensual sex crimes are considered and in Chapter 9 other sex-related crimes, such as adultery, prostitution, incest, and obscenity offenses are discussed.

The specific offenses defined and explained in this chapter are rape; sodomy and related crimes; sexual abuse (sexual assault); lewdness (indecent exposure); and other crimes such as seduction, importuning, voyeurism, sexual misconduct, and intercourse with a person in custody.

---

[1]   State v. Young, 52 Or. 227, 96 P. 1067 (1908).

§ 6.2 Rape

A. *Common Law*

The common law definition of **rape** is "the act of having unlawful carnal knowledge by a man of a woman, forcibly and against her will."[2] In reflecting on the common law, as compared to statutory law, one court indicated that common law rape is the act of a man having unlawful carnal knowledge of a female over the age of 10 years by force without the consent and against the will of the victim.[3]

Thus, the common law elements of rape are the following: unlawful; carnal knowledge (sexual intercourse); by force or fear; without consent or against the will; of a woman.

1. Unlawful

Under common law, unlawful was defined as "not authorized by law," and interpreted to be intercourse between those who are not husband and wife. Under the common law, and as defined by most early statutes, rape was an act of sexual intercourse with a female, not the wife of the perpetrator.[4]

The rationale for the concept that forced intercourse between husband and wife was lawful was that the matrimonial consent that the wife gave when she assumed the marital relationship could not be revoked. A seventeenth-century jurist, Matthew Hale, formulated the concept that by "their mutual matrimonial consent and contract the wife hath given of herself in this kind unto her husband, which she cannot retract."[5]

The first American case to recognize the **marital exemption** was decided in 1857 by the Supreme Judicial Court of Massachusetts, which included a comment that "it would always be a defense to rape to show marriage to the victim."[6] Decisions to the same effect by other courts followed, usually with no rationale or authority cited, other than Hale's implied consent view. In New York, a 1922 decision noted the marital exemption in the penal laws, and stated that it existed "on account of the matrimonial consent which the wife has given, and which she cannot retract."[7]

2. Carnal Knowledge (or Sexual Intercourse)

Carnal knowledge is synonymous with sexual intercourse. Regardless of the definition used, according to all early authorities, to complete the crime of rape there must be some penetration, although the least penetration is sufficient. According to one court, the slightest penetration of the vulva is sufficient to constitute rape and emission

---

[2]　State v. Tuttle, 67 Ohio St. 440, 66 N.E. 524 (1903).
[3]　Hazel v. State, 221 Md. 464, 157 A.2d 922 (1960).
[4]　Adams v. State, 5 Okla. Crim. 347, 114 P. 347 (1911).
[5]　1 Hale, History of the Pleas of the Crown 619 (1800).
[6]　Commonwealth v. Fogerty, 74 Mass. 489 (1857).
[7]　People v. Meli, 193 N.Y.S. 365 (1922).

is not necessary. However, the prosecution must prove beyond a reasonable doubt that penetration in fact occurred.[8]

3. Force or Fear

The force that is a necessary element in the commission of the common law crime of rape includes actual physical force in compelling submission of the female and also includes threatened force or violence for the purpose of preventing resistance. This element may be met by showing that there was actual force or that the force was constructive. *Forcibly* does not necessarily mean *violently*. In one case, the court determined that

> . . . the force must be such as may reasonably be supposed adequate to overcome physical resistance of the woman upon whom rape is charged to have been committed, taking into consideration the relative strength of the parties and other circumstances of the case, such as outcries and giving alarm.[9]

The offense is complete even if no actual force is used, if it can be shown by the evidence that the woman is made to yield through fear and does not consent voluntarily to the act of sexual intercourse.

The force necessary to constitute rape may also be constructive. For example, if the female is mentally unconscious from drink or is asleep, or from other causes is in a state of insensibility, the act is committed without conscious and voluntary permission, therefore, force is "constructive." The unlawful imposition constitutes the necessary force if the man knows that the woman is in a state of unconsciousness.[10] Note that such a condition also negates the ability to give consent, another element of the crime.

Without force, actual or constructive, there can be no rape. If the prosecution can show that actual force was used, or he can show that the victim submitted as a result of terror or fear caused by threats or intimidation, or if the force is constructive in that the woman is unconscious, this is sufficient to meet the "force" requirement in proving the crime of rape.

4. Without Consent or against the Will

This element, which is sometimes stated in terms such as "without her consent," has been interpreted to mean that the sexual act must be committed against the will of the woman without her voluntary consent. Intercourse accomplished by force is without consent; however, voluntary consent given at any time prior to the penetration deprives the subsequent intercourse of its criminal character, regardless of

---

[8]   State v. Pollock, 57 Ariz. 414, 114 P.2d 249 (1941).
[9]   Powell v. Commonwealth, 179 Va. 703, 20 S.E.2d 536 (1942).
[10]   Commonwealth v. Stephens, 143 Pa. Super. 394, 17 A.2d 919 (1941).

how reluctantly it may have been given or how much force theretofore had been employed.[11]

It is not necessary that the victim resist physically if the evidence indicates that she physically feared the defendant and expressed her unwillingness to engage in intercourse. On the other hand, early cases also sometimes discussed the "**utmost resistance standard**." This was the idea that a woman should want to resist at all costs any attempt of rape. If she did not appear to have suffered any injury, there was an inclination to use that as evidence that consent was granted. Some cases have led to seemingly unfair findings, such as a case in which a woman had been in a physically abusive relationship with the assailant but had left him. He threatened her and her mother if she did not accompany him and then took her to a house and told her she was going to have sex with him. Even though she told him she did not want to, she did not physically resist, arguably because she was afraid of him. The appellate court overturned the conviction because although the victim had not consented, there was no showing of force or threats to overcome the resistance of the victim.[12] It is this narrow and tortured reading of the difference between consent and force that has spurred a reexamination of the definitions of traditional elements of rape.

As mentioned earlier, if the woman is wholly insensible she is incapable of consenting. Therefore, unlawful intercourse with a woman who had fainted was held to be rape in a Georgia case.[13] When a man has reduced a woman to a state of insensibility through alcohol, she is unable to give consent; however, cases have held that inducing a woman to drink intoxicating beverages or to use drugs to "excite her passions," leaving her at the same time capable of comprehending the nature of the act, does not amount to rape, because there has been consent.[14]

Also, where consent is obtained by fraud, there is no legal consent. For example, where a doctor had sexual intercourse with a woman under the fraudulent pretense of medical treatment, this was rape because there was no voluntary consent.[15] However, some case decisions indicate that the deception must be in regard to the sexual intercourse, not some other fact. In other words, if a doctor convinces a patient that what is happening is not sexual intercourse, but is a medical treatment instead, it is rape; but if a doctor lies to a patient and says that sexual intercourse is necessary to make her healthy and she consents, it is not rape.[16]

---

[11]   Reynolds v. State, 27 Neb. 90, 42 N.W. 903 (1889); Whittaker v. State, 50 Wis. 518, 7 N.W. 431 (1880).

[12]   State v. Alston, 312 S.E.2d 470 (N.C. 1984).

[13]   Lancaster v. State, 168 Ga. 470, 148 S.E. 139 (1929).

[14]   State v. Lung, 21 Nev. 209, 28 P. 235 (1891).

[15]   State v. Ely, 114 Wash. 185, 194 N.W. 988 (1921).

[16]   Boro v. Superior Court, 210 Cal. Rptr. 122 (Ct. App. 1985).

5. Of a Female

Under common law, only women could be raped, and only men could rape (although a male victim would be protected under the laws of assault and battery). The history of this crime originates in the man's dominion over his female relatives (both spouse and child). The rape was seen as an offense against her, but also against him. It was, in a sense, an affront to his property rights because any resulting pregnancy might be the seed of the rapist instead of his, confusing the rightful lines of inheritance.

6. *Mens Rea*

The *mens rea* of common law rape was intentional. The perpetrator also has to know that the victim is not consenting to sexual intercourse.

7. Common Law Statutory Rape

Under the early English cases, it was not rape to have sexual intercourse with a female child if she consented. However, later English statutes included sections that provided that females under 12 years of age were incapable of consent, and to have sexual intercourse with a female child under this age was considered rape, even though there was consent.[17] This has come to be known as **statutory rape**. In the United States, the age of consent was fixed by statute in practically all states; some states set the age at 14, some at 16, and some at 18.

B. *Model Penal Code*

The Model Penal Code clarified the required elements of the crime of rape, and graded different types of sex offenses.

§ 213.1 Rape and Related Offenses[18]

(1) Rape. A man who has sexual intercourse with a female not his wife is guilty of rape if:
    (a) he compels her to submit by force or by threat of imminent death, serious bodily injury, extreme pain or kidnapping, to be inflicted on anyone; or
    (b) he has substantially impaired her power to appraise or control her conduct by administering or employing without her knowledge drugs, intoxicants or other means for the purpose of preventing resistance; or
    (c) the female is unconscious; or
    (d) the female is less than 10 years old.
Rape is a felony of the second degree unless:
    (i) in the course thereof the actor inflicts serious bodily injury upon anyone, or
    (ii) the victim was not a voluntary social companion of the actor upon the occasion of the crime and had not previously permitted him sexual liberties, in which case the offense is a felony of the first degree.

---

[17]   75 C.J.S. *Rape* § 13 (1952).
[18]   MODEL PENAL CODE § 213.1 (1985).

(2) Gross Sexual Imposition. A male who has sexual intercourse with a female not his wife commits a felony of the third degree if:
- (a) he compels her to submit by any threat that would prevent resistance by a woman of ordinary resolution; or
- (b) he knows that she suffers from a mental disease or defect which renders her incapable of appraising the nature of her conduct; or
- (c) he knows that she is unaware that a sexual act is being committed upon her or that she submits because she mistakenly supposes that he is her husband.

These provisions encompassed many of the acts that were made illegal under the common law and various state statutes, and brought them together in a more uniform way. Similar to common law, the MPC defines rape in such a way that only men can rape and only women (and not the wife of the rapist) can be raped. Also, penetration is required.

C. State Statutes, Codes, and Cases

State statutes follow the MPC in grading different degrees of rape based on characteristics of the victim and/or the violation. The specific elements within each grading system vary from state to state. Parts of the Kentucky Code are included here.

Kentucky Code § 510.040—Rape in the first degree

(1) A person is guilty of rape in the first degree when:
- (a) he engages in sexual intercourse with another person by forcible compulsion; or
- (b) he engages in sexual intercourse with another person who is incapable of consent because he:
    - (1) is physically helpless; or
    - (2) is less than twelve (12) years old.

(2) Rape in the first degree is a Class B felony unless the victim is under twelve (12) years old or receives a serious physical injury in which case it is a Class A felony. (Enact. Acts 1974, Ch. 406, § 84)

§ 510.050—Rape in the second degree

(1) A person is guilty of rape in the second degree when, being eighteen (18) years old or more, he engages in sexual intercourse with another person less than fourteen (14) years old.

(2) Rape in the second degree is a Class C felony. (Enact. Acts 1974, Ch. 406, § 85)

§ 510.060—Rape in the third degree

(1) A person is guilty of rape in the third degree when:
- (a) he engages in sexual intercourse with another person who is incapable of consent because he is mentally retarded or mentally incapacitated; or
- (b) being twenty-one (21) years old or more, he engages in sexual intercourse with another person less than sixteen (16) years old.

(2) Rape in the third degree is a Class D felony.

The Wyoming statute describes first-degree sexual assault as follows:

Wyoming Code. 6-2-302. Sexual assault in the first degree

(a) Any actor who inflicts sexual intrusion on a victim commits a sexual assault in the first degree if:

   (i) The actor causes submission of the victim through the actual application, reasonably calculated to cause submission of the victim, of physical force or forcible confinement;

   (ii) The actor causes submission of the victim by threat of death, serious bodily injury, extreme physical pain or kidnapping to be inflicted on anyone and the victim reasonably believes that the actor has the present ability to execute these threats;

   (iii) The victim is physically helpless, and the actor knows or reasonably should know that the victim is physically helpless and that the victim has not consented; or

   (iv) The actor knows or reasonably should know that the victim through a mental illness, mental deficiency, or developmental disability is incapable of appraising the nature of the victim's conduct.

As state statutes are different, we will use the traditional elements of rape from the common law to illustrate the changes that have taken place in the definition and prosecution of rape.

1. Unlawful

Recall that under the common law, it was legally impossible to rape one's wife. This was called the marital exemption or marital immunity. Even as recently as 1984, the Model Penal Code and about 40 states retained some form of marital exemption for rape. Today some state courts have judicially determined that a man can be convicted of rape of his wife if other factors are proved and some states have changed their statutes and omitted the words "not his wife" from the statutory definition of rape, eliminating the rape exemption entirely.[19]

In a 1981 New Jersey case, the husband of the victim broke into his wife's apartment and forced her to have sexual intercourse. The trial court granted a motion to dismiss the rape charges because the couple was married and the rape took place before the statute was passed by the New Jersey legislature. However, the couple were separated at the time of the rape and had been living apart for more than a year. In addition to the rape, the victim was choked, beaten, and held against her will for several hours. The New Jersey Supreme Court, after discussing the changes in the divorce laws and other legal developments, reasoned that the corollary of a spouse's right to make a unilateral decision to end the marriage is "a wife can refuse sexual

---

[19] For a discussion of the various statutory and judicial variations of the marital exemption, *see Old Wine in New Bottles: The "Marital" Rape Allowance*, 72 N.C. l. REV. 261 (1993) and *Legal Rape: The Marital Exemption*, 24 J. MARSHALL l. REV. 393 (1991). *See also* TEX. PENAL CODE ANN. § 22.011 (c)(2) (West 1994).

intercourse with her husband during the period of separation prior to divorce." The court continued, stating

> If a wife has a right to refuse intercourse, or deny consent, then a husband's forceful carnal knowledge of his wife clearly includes all three elements of the crime of rape. He cannot defend by asserting that there was no lack of consent because he was still legally married to the victim.[20]

Thus, the holding was that even though new laws cannot be applied retroactively, due process and equal protection required that at least in cases in which the couple were separated and no longer shared the "marital bed," the marital exemption did not apply to excuse criminal culpability when sexual intercourse was achieved through force and without a wife's consent.

In the case of *People v. Liberta*, the Court of Appeals of New York, after carefully considering the "marital exemption rule," declared the rule to be unconstitutional. The court declared that there is no rational basis for distinguishing marital rape and nonmarital rape. The court reasoned that

> [t]he various rationales which have been asserted in defense of the exemption are either based upon archaic notions about the consent and property rights incident to marriage or are simply unable to withstand even the slightest scrutiny. We, therefore, declare the marital exemption for rape in the New York statute to be unconstitutional.[21]

In the case of *People v. M.D.*, the Illinois Supreme Court declared the Illinois marital exemption statute (completely prohibiting prosecution for sexual abuse and permitting only very limited prosecution for sexual assault) unconstitutional in that it violated public policy, equal protection, and due process.[22]

No state recognizes the marital exemption today:

- Some totally abolished the marital rape exemption for any kind of sexual contact or persuasion.
- Some abolished the exemption for forcible rape but not for lesser sexual assault crimes.
- Some expanded the exemption to persons within a marriage-like relationship even though they are not married.[23]

2. Carnal Knowledge (or Sexual Intercourse)

Most states still have some requirement of penetration; however, the penetration may be by an object rather than a penis, and the slightest penetration will suffice. Some state criminal statutes define the term "sexual intercourse" to include penetration of the

---

[20]   State v. Smith, 85 N.J. 193, 426 A.2d 38 (1981).
[21]   People v. Liberta, 474 N.E.2d 567 (N.Y. 1984).
[22]   595 N.E.2d 702 (Ill. 1992).
[23]   National Center for Victims of Crime. Retrieved December 30, 2011 from http://www.ncvc.org/ncvc/main.aspx?dbName=DocumentViewer&DocumentID=32701.

sex organs, or in some cases the anus, by foreign objects manipulated by third parties.[24] A majority of the states have specifically eliminated the requirement of "emission" (or "ejaculation") by statute. However, where an assailant experiences an emission or ejaculation, absent evidence of some penetration, the crime of rape is not complete, although the offense of attempted rape will most likely be found.[25] The slightest penetration can constitute rape; however, repeated penetrations during the act, if a continuous process, constitute but one crime.[26]

Some courts have judicially created a broad definition of the term "sexual intercourse" to include homosexual acts as well as heterosexual acts. The federal statutes employ the term "sexual act" rather than "sexual intercourse" and define the term to include biological sexual intercourse, oral sex (cunnilingus and fellatio), and penetration by hands, fingers, and objects.[27]

The crime of rape requires sexual intercourse with a living victim. However, if a criminal statute prohibits "deviate sexual intercourse" and if the statute further defines the term to include sexual intercourse with a corpse, an assailant will be guilty of that substantive offense, in addition to attempted rape. A New Jersey court held that because the victim was alive when the defendant was choking her and when the codefendant began removing her clothing, the defendant could be convicted of sexual assault, even if the victim was dead by the time the sexual penetration actually occurred.[28]

3. Force or Fear

Modern statutes, as did the common law, overlap the concepts of force and consent. When the term "compulsion" is used, the term is defined as physical force that overcomes earnest resistance, or any threat, express or implied, that overcomes earnest resistance by placing a person in fear of immediate death or physical injury to self or fear that another person will be harmed.

In determining the presence or absence of forcible compulsion for purposes of the offense of rape, the issue is whether the victim perceived the aggressor's force or imminent threat of force as compelling her compliance. In the case cited, the court pointed out that it is the victim's perspective, not the assailant's, from which the presence or absence of forcible compulsion is to be determined. This is a subjective test that looks to the victim's perception of the circumstances surrounding the incident in question.[29]

---

[24]   KY. REV. STAT. § 510.010(8) (1994).
[25]   Miller v. State, 82 P.2d 317 (Okla. 1938); Smith v. State, 601 So.2d 201 (Ala. 1992).
[26]   Beasley v. State, 94 Okla. Crim. 353, 236 P.2d 263 (1952).
[27]   18 U.S.C. § 2245.
[28]   State v. Jones, 705 A.2d 805 (N.J. 1998). *See also* People v. Rowland, 841 P.2d 897 (Cal. 1992); People v. Kelly, 822 P.2d 385 (Cal. 1992). *See* N.D. CENT. CODE § 12.1-20-02(1) (1989).
[29]   Ruth v. State, 706 N.E.2d 257 (Ind. 1999).

4. Without Consent or against the Will

Recall that, under common law, if the woman consented (even if duress preceded the consent), then no rape was said to have occurred. A woman's consent to sexual intercourse is void if it is given in fear of personal violence. However, the line between force, duress, and persuasion is sometimes not an easy one to make. The victim of a sexual assault is not required to physically resist the assault and the courts agree that "no means no"; however, it is incumbent on the victim to make it clear to the attacker that she is unwilling.[30] Courts allow an inference from "torn clothing, bruises, and body position" to overcome the claim of the defendant that it was consensual.[31]

Modern courts continue to struggle with the concept of consent. The general rule is that if the victim consents to sexual intercourse prior to penetration and withdraws consent following penetration, there is no rape.[32] However, this does not preclude the perpetrator from being found guilty of another crime, such as assault, if warranted by the evidence.

The biggest change in the prosecution of rape has not been in the definitions or elements, but rather in the application or interpretation of the definitions to cases. The "utmost resistance" standard, for instance, has been discounted and abolished. A New York court refused to give an instruction that "to be guilty of rape in the first degree the victim must oppose the perpetrator to the utmost limit of her power by genuine active resistance." The trial judge instead explained that "the degree of force required to place somebody in fear will vary with the person involved."[33]

The idea that a woman can withhold consent even in circumstances of "date rape" is more accepted. Some case decisions today would have probably been decided differently 50 years ago. For instance, in *People v. Reed*, the defendant was convicted of rape and three counts of deviate sexual assault.[34] On appeal, he claimed that the complainant consented to the sexual activities and explained that she had consented to a nude massage in order to relieve muscle tension and, by her actions, consented to the sexual intercourse. The reviewing court reasoned that, although the complainant's consent to a nude massage with no apprehension of sexual involvement was naïve, it might reasonably be explained by the fact that defendant, who was 30 years older than she, introduced himself as an acquaintance of her best friend, and indicated that he was a doctor and psychologist. The court found that this was rape and there was no consent to the sexual intercourse.

A variety of opinions relate to the use of liquor or drugs in obtaining consent. There is no doubt that unlawful sexual intercourse by a man with a woman whom he has

---

[30]   State v. O'Bryan, 572 N.W.2d 870 (Wis. 1997).
[31]   People v. Miller, 620 N.Y.S.2d 179 (1994).
[32]   People v. Burroughs, 19 Cal. Rptr. 344, 200 Cal. App. 2d 629 (1962); People v. Vela, 218 Cal. Rptr. 161, 172 Cal. App. 3d 237 (1985).
[33]   People v. Yanik, 400 N.Y.S.2d 778, 371 N.E.2d 497 (1977), *on remand*, 404 N.Y.S.2d 633, 63 App. Div. 574 (1978); *see also* State v. Ricks, 34 N.C. App. 734, 239 S.E.2d 602 (1977).
[34]   373 N.E.2d 538 (Ill. 1978).

reduced to a state of insensibility by intoxicating liquor or drugs is rape. However, anything less than insensibility on the victim's part would still render her capable of consent. The statutory definition that includes any type of insensibility addresses situations such as occurred in a New York case in which the victim was undergoing nitrous oxide treatment at her dentist's office and was mentally alert, but physically unable to resist sexual intercourse by the dentist.[35] In a Kansas case, the court held that the victim did not consent where the evidence supported that the victim was both psychologically and physiologically impaired due to the effects of her medical condition and medications.[36]

In one case that illustrates the difficulty the law has with the concept of consent, the rape victim requested that her assailant wear a condom before engaging in sexual intercourse. The victim had obtained the condom from a package of condoms she kept in the trunk of her vehicle. At trial, the assailant raised the defense of consent, based on the actions of the victim in keeping condoms in her vehicle and her request that one be used during intercourse; however, the assailant did not prevail on his claim.[37]

LEGAL NEWS: CONDOMS = CONSENT?

Another "condom rape case" was that of Xan Wilson in Austin, Texas. She was assaulted by the defendant, who broke into her home. Faced with an inevitable rape, she pleaded with her attacker to wear a condom because she was afraid she would be infected with HIV/AIDS. Because of her request that he wear a condom, the grand jury declined to indict him under the belief that she consented. After a firestorm of publicity, he was subsequently indicted by a different grand jury, prosecuted, convicted, and sentenced to 40 years' imprisonment.

Source: *Austin American-Statesman*, June 10, 1993 at B1.

---

5. Of a Female

States have made rape statutes gender-neutral, using terms such as "person" or "actor," so as to make it possible to convict a person of a sex crime regardless of whether that person is male or female. Under a Michigan statute, for instance, a person is guilty of criminal sexual conduct in the first degree if she or he engages in sexual penetration with another person and if other circumstances exist. The terms "male" and "female" are not used and either may be guilty of criminal sexual conduct. Today, virtually all

---

[35]   People v. Wankowitz, 564 N.Y.S.2d 488 (1991).

[36]   State v. Requena, 41 P.3d 862 (Kan. 2001).

[37]   State v. Davis, 824 S.W.2d 936 (Mo. 1992). For a complete discussion of the issue, *see Condom or Not, Rape is Rape: Rape Law in the Era of AIDS—Does Condom Use Constitute Consent?* 19 DAYTON L. REV. 227 (1993).

rape statutes, both forcible and statutory, are gender-neutral and use the term "person" when referring to the assailant. Thus, both males and females may be found guilty of rape.[38]

6. *Mens Rea*

The defendant must know he/she is forcing sexual intercourse on an unwilling victim (and one must know that the victim is unwilling). It is a general intent crime.

7. Statutory Rape

The act of having intercourse with a female under the age of consent became commonly known as "statutory rape." Where the female is under the age of statutory consent, as stated by the respective statutes, it makes no difference whether the act was accomplished against her will, or without her consent, or even with her consent.[39]

The state is not required to show evidence that the act was accomplished against the will of the minor, or without her consent or by force. However, failure to introduce evidence to establish that the victim was under the age specified by the statute when the offense occurred will require reversal of the conviction. In *State v. Dixon*, the court held that failure to introduce testimony establishing the victim's age requires reversal.[40]

Unless statutes specifically provide for the defense of mistake, a defendant will not be permitted to argue that he or she thought the victim was of the age permitted by the statutes. However, some states have enacted statutory provisions that permit the defense of mistake regarding the age of the victim if evidence establishes that "at the time he engaged in the conduct constituting the offense he did not know of the facts or conditions."[41] Other states require a defendant to base the mistake specifically on the statements of the victim and, absent such explicit statements, will not permit a defense of mistake based on the victim's appearance.[42] Another form of statutory relief involves statutes that declare that no offense is committed when the underage victim and the defendant were legally married at the time of the sexual intercourse.[43]

Some states have mitigated the severity of statutory rape by making exceptions to strict liability or making exceptions for when the age difference between the two parties is not large. For instance, the Texas Criminal Code has a statute called "Indecency with a Child" that prohibits sex acts with a child younger than 17 that is not the defendant's spouse. However, the statute also provides that

---

[38] MICH. COMP. LAWS §§ 750.520(a)-750.520(c) (2002).
[39] Fields v. State, 203 Ark. 1046, 159 S.W.2d 745 (1942).
[40] State v. Dixon, 70 S.W.3d 540 (Mo. 2002).
[41] KY. REV. STAT. § 510.030 (2002); *see also* ALASKA STAT. § 11.41.445 (1994) and State v. Guest, 583 P.2d 836 (Alaska 1978).
[42] State v. Bennett, 672 P.2d 772 (Wash. 1983).
[43] KY. REV. STAT. § 510.035 (Baldwin 2002).

> It is an affirmative defense to prosecution for this crime that the actor: (1) was not more than three years older than the victim and of the opposite sex; and (2) did not use duress, force, or a threat against the victim at the time of the offense.[44]

However, even in these states, victims below a certain age will maintain the mantle of protection of strict liability with no defense of mistake or age. For instance, in Pennsylvania, a defendant may use mistake of age as a defense when he or she is within four years of the age of the victim; however, sex with a victim under the age of 13 is a strict liability crime.[45]

When both parties are under the age of majority (21 or 18), typically the crime is graded as less serious. Statutes covering this behavior, such as Kentucky's sexual misconduct statute, are described later in this chapter. In general, today's statutory rape statutes are gender-neutral. Historically, statutory rape was reserved for the protection of girls. The reason for the law was to protect the virginity of young women. Even fairly recently, the Supreme Court has held that it is a legitimate state purpose to protect against pregnancies of young girls and that is sufficient to distinguish young men and young women in order to justify different treatment.[46] However, many states use the term "person" or "someone" in their statutory rape laws and, thus, women can be guilty of statutory rape as well.

LEGAL NEWS: 12-YEAR-OLDS INELIGIBLE FOR STATUTORY RAPE

The U.S. Supreme Court denied *certiorari* in an Ohio case involving a 12-year-old boy who traded sex with an 11-year-old boy for video games. The 12-year-old was charged under Ohio's statutory rape law, which made it a crime to engage in sex with a person under the age of 13. In the appeal of his conviction, the Ohio Supreme Court ruled that it was unconstitutional to charge a 12-year-old with statutory rape because it would not be clear who the victim and who the perpetrator was in any case. The Supreme Court held open the possibility of charges if there was force or imposition. The United States Supreme Court declined to hear the appeal from state attorneys who charged that the Ohio Supreme Court decision took away too much discretion from prosecutors.

Retrieved December 20, 2011 from http://www.newarkadvocate.com/article/20111213/NEWS01/112130303/U-S-Supreme-Court-won-t-review-statutory-rape-case.

---

[44]   TEXAS PENAL CODE ANN. §21.11 (West 1999).
[45]   Commonwealth v. Dennis, 784 A.2d 179 (Pa. 2001).
[46]   Michael M. v. Superior Court of Sonoma County, 450 U.S. 464; 101 S. Ct. 1200; 67 L. Ed. 2d 437 (1981).

8. Rape Shield Statutes and Decisions

Traditionally, defense attorneys would attempt to impugn the chastity and veracity of the rape victim in order to create reasonable doubt that the sexual intercourse was without consent. Many states, after carefully considering the desirability of protecting the rape victim, enacted legislation that became known as **rape shield laws**. The rationale behind such statutes is that evidence of a rape victim's prior sexual activity is of dubious probative value and relevance, and is highly embarrassing and prejudicial. Those who argued for such statutes assert that the protection offered by the statutes would encourage victims of sexual assault to report the crimes without fear of having their sexual history exposed to the public.

Today, most state statutes and the federal code include provisions restricting testimony on the victim's prior sexual behavior to that genuinely relevant to the defense. In 1978 Federal Rule of Evidence 412, the Rape Shield Statute, was created. Rule 412 prohibits the introduction at trial of reputation or opinion evidence of a rape victim's sexual history. The rule also prohibits introduction of sexual history evidence not in reputation or opinion form, subject to three exceptions:

1. The first exception concerns evidence that a rape defendant has a constitutional right to have introduced.
2. The second exception is for evidence of the victim's behavior with persons other than the defendant that the defendant offers to show that he was not the source of semen or injury.
3. The third exception is for the past sexual behavior of the victim with the defendant himself, which the defendant offers to show consent.

Even if the evidence fits into one of the latter two categories, it is admissible only if the trial judge finds, after an *in camera* (in chambers) hearing, that it is both relevant and more probative than prejudicial.

Most states follow the basic contours of Federal Rule of Evidence 412. Many states, however, do not expressly provide an exception for constitutionally required evidence. Other states ban sexual history evidence subject to an exception only for specific instances of conduct with the defendant.

Although the rape shield statutes generally serve the two basic purposes of protecting the privacy of the rape victims and encouraging rape victims to come forward, the courts have also given consideration to the rights of the defendant. For example, in a 1986 case, the defendant, appealing a rape conviction, argued that the lower court erred in refusing to allow him to introduce evidence that he had a previous sexual relationship with the victim. The single issue was whether the trial court erred, as a matter of law, in ruling that any evidence of a prior sexual relationship between the defendant and the victim was inadmissible. The issue related not only to the question of consent on the part of the victim, but to the whole question of her credibility as a witness. At trial the victim had said that she had never had intercourse with the defendant, and the defendant offered to introduce evidence to prove that she had had a previous sexual relationship with the defendant. The reviewing court agreed with the defendant that, under these circumstances, evidence should have been admitted. The court determined that the evidence should be admissible if its probative value outweighs its inflammatory or prejudicial nature, and it is material to an issue of fact. In reversing the decision of the lower court, the reviewing court agreed that "clearly, the testimony was material and relevant to the question of consent; and this court finds its probative value outweighed any resulting prejudice."[47]

A different court ruled that a rape defendant was not entitled to present evidence regarding the victim's alleged sexual relations with another party on the date of the alleged rape, in an effort to establish that he was not the perpetrator of the rape. The court ruled that evidence of the victim's past sexual behavior is admissible only to establish a source of semen, pregnancy, disease, or injury.[48]

The "interests of justice" exception to the rape shield law has been offered as a defense in numerous federal and state courts. In a Minnesota case, the court precisely stated that the rape shield statute serves to emphasize the general irrelevance of a victim's sexual history, not to remove relevant evidence from the jury's consideration. The court continued by stating that the rape shield law is a legislative limitation on a citizen's Sixth Amendment right to confront and cross-examine opposing witnesses and the law must be scrutinized to determine whether it provides or prevents a fair and orderly trial.[49]

In a case that considered the application of the rape shield statute where the female was under the age of consent, a Wisconsin court established some specific guidelines. In that case, the court held that to admit evidence of a child complainant's past sexual misbehavior under the judicial exception to the rape shield law, the defendant must show that the proffered evidence meets the following five criteria and then balance the parties' interests to determine whether the evidence is admissible:

1. the prior acts must have clearly occurred;
2. the prior acts must closely resemble those of the present case;
3. the prior acts must be clearly relevant to a material issue;
4. the evidence must be necessary to a defendant's case; and
5. the probative value of the evidence must outweigh its prejudicial effect.[50]

Rape shield laws have been challenged as being unconstitutional because they violate the defendant's right of confrontation. In a Texas case, the defendant appealed his conviction of aggravated rape, claiming that the rape shield law in that state violated his right of confrontation and his due process rights. The rape shield law in Texas provided, in part, that

---

47   Bixler v. Commonwealth, 712 S.W.2d 366 (Ky. 1986).
48   Levy v. State, 724 So.2d 405 (Miss. Ct. App. 1998).
49   State v. Carroll, 639 N.W.2d 623 (Minn. 2002).
50   State v. Dunlap, 250 Wis. 2d 466, 640 N.W.2d 112 (2002).

Evidence of specific instances of a victim's sexual conduct, opinion evidence of the victim's sexual conduct, and reputation evidence of the victim's sexual conduct may be admitted ... only if, and only to the extent that, the judge finds that the evidence is material to a fact at issue in the case and that its inflammatory or prejudicial nature does not outweigh its probative value.

The Texas statute establishes procedures for introduction of evidence, provides for an *in camera* hearing, and requires that the record be sealed. The reviewing court, in upholding the constitutionality of the rape shield law, reasoned that the right to confront and cross-examine is not absolute and may, in appropriate cases, bow to accommodate other legitimate interests in the criminal law process. In applying that reasoning to the rape shield law, the court indicated that, although statutory, the rape victim shield law is analogous to judge-made rules of evidence that prevent the admissibility of opinion evidence, hearsay testimony, and convictions of very old standing, if the probative value of the evidence is outweighed by the possibility of jury prejudice.[51]

LEGAL NEWS: EXPANDED DEFINITION OF RAPE

In January 2012, U.S. officials announced that the definition of rape used for collection of crime statistics for the Uniform Crime Reports would be expanded. This is the first change in 80 years and comes after many states have already changed their rape statutes to include other forms of sexual assault. The expansion of the definition of rape will now include men as well as women and any victim who is unable to give consent or who is violated with an object. Until now, the FBI's definition counted only forcible vaginal penetration of a woman as "rape." The new definition expands rape to include oral and anal sex acts against women as well as men. It also says if a victim cannot give consent for any reason (i.e., alcohol or drug use or under the age of consent), the crime is a rape even if force is not used.

The FBI reported in 2010 that there were almost 85,000 forcible rapes under the old definition, and that the forcible rape rate declined 5.1 percent in the first half of 2011 compared to the same period of the previous year.

Source: Heavey, J. and J. Pelofsky, 2012. U.S. Widens Definition of Sex Crimes. Reuters News Service. Retrieved January 6, 2012 from http://www.courant.com/health/sns-rt-us-usa-crime-rapetre805197-20120106,0,232128.story.

D. Summary

Because there have been several changes from common law definitions of rape, and because state statutes vary so widely in their definitions and interpretations of the elements of rape, the summary provided here should be viewed as a rough

---

[51]   Allen v. State, 700 S.W.2d 924 (Tex. Crim. App. 1985).

generalization of what might be the case in any particular state. The most dramatic changes have been

- the elimination of marital exemption or immunities,
- the development of rape victim shield laws,
- the expansion of the definition of penetration to include objects, and
- the definition of rape as a gender-neutral crime.

Statutory rape is also quite different from state to state and some states allow for the mistake of age defense.

Rape
(A/R) unlawful sexual intercourse, with force or threat of force, without consent
(M/R) intentional/knowing

Statutory Rape
(A/R) unlawful sexual intercourse with a minor (statutorily defined; some states specify the perpetrator must be over 18 or an age that is statutorily defined)
(M/R) strict liability (except in those states that allow for mistake of age defense in which case it would be knowing or reckless)

§ 6.3　Sodomy and Related Crimes

A. Common Law

In England, **sodomy** at first was subject only to punishment by the ecclesiastical authorities. However, early English statutes made sodomy a criminal offense, and it was this offense under the common law that was used as a basis for the laws in the United States. While the original English enactments proscribed only anal intercourse between males, the coverage was extended so as to punish fellatio and cunnilingus, as well as anal intercourse and bestiality. In some states, the crime was designated by statute as a "crime against nature."[52]

The term "sodomy" has been defined in many ways by many jurisdictions. In its broadest terms, sodomy is the "carnal copulation by human beings with each other against nature, or with a beast." The broad definition includes bestiality, buggery, cunnilingus, and fellatio.[53] A definition, included in an early case, is

A person who carnally knows in any manner any animal or bird, or carnally knows any male or female person by the anus, or with the mouth, or voluntarily submits to such carnal knowledge, or attempts sexual intercourse with a dead body, is guilty of sodomy.[54]

From the foregoing, it becomes clear that some sodomy crimes are consensual. These offenses are considered in this chapter because the trend in modern statutes has been to require the presence of force or imposition.

---

[52]　Johnsen, *Sodomy Statutes—A Need for Change*, 13 S.D. L. REV. 384 (1968).
[53]　81 C.J.S. *Sodomy* § 1 (1985).
[54]　State v. Schwartz, 215 Minn. 476, 10 N.W.2d 370 (1943).

B. Model Penal Code

Rather than using the term "sodomy," the drafters of the Model Penal Code took a different approach, defining the offense as "deviate sexual intercourse by force or imposition." It is immediately apparent that the words "by force or imposition" change the common law concept of sodomy. The Model Penal Code exempts from criminal sanction deviate sexual intercourse between consenting adults that would have been defined as illegal under common law. Under the Model Code, **deviate sexual intercourse** is not criminal if both participants consent and each is of sufficient age and mental capacity to give consent and they conduct their relations in private and create no public nuisance.

§ 213.2 Deviate Sexual Intercourse by Force or Imposition[55]

(1) By Force or Its Equivalent. A person who engages in deviate sexual intercourse with another person, or who causes another to engage in deviate sexual intercourse, commits a felony of the second degree if:
   (a) he compels the other person to participate by force or by threat of imminent death, serious bodily injury, extreme pain or kidnapping, to be inflicted on anyone; or
   (b) he has substantially impaired the other person's power to appraise or control his conduct, by administering or employing without the knowledge of the other person drugs, intoxicants or other means for the purpose of preventing resistance; or
   (c) the person is unconscious; or
   (d) the other person is less than 10 years old.
(2) By Other Imposition. A person who engages in deviate sexual intercourse with another person, or who causes another to engage in sexual intercourse, commits a felony of the third degree if:
   (a) he compels the other person to participate by any threat that would prevent resistance by a person of ordinary resolution; or
   (b) he knows that the other person suffers from a mental disease or defect which renders him incapable of appraising the nature of his conduct; or
   (c) he knows that the other person submits because he is unaware that a sexual act is being committed upon him.

C. State Statutes, Codes, and Cases

Because there are many statutory crimes in the general sodomy category, it is difficult to enumerate elements. A few early statutes included these definitions:

- Sodomy is carnal copulation with members of the same sex or with an animal or unnatural carnal copulation with a member of the opposite sex.[56]
- [Sodomy] is a carnal copulation between two human beings per anus or by a human being in any manner with a beast.[57]

---

[55] MODEL PENAL CODE § 213.2 (1985).
[56] People v. Durham, 74 Cal. Rptr. 262, 449 P.2d 198 (1969).
[57] Pruitt v. State, 463 S.W.2d 191 (Tex. Crim. App. 1971).

Under many statutes, and at common law, penetration was an essential element of the crime of sodomy. Where penetration is an element, any penetration, however slight, is sufficient to constitute the element. For example, in the case of *People v. Hickock*, the complaining witness had been hypnotized to a point at which she was unable to move, but retained consciousness and had her teeth tightly clenched when the accused placed his penis inside her lips. In this case, the court said that this was a penetration sufficient to allow conviction under the statute providing that "any person participating in the act of copulating the mouth of one person with the sexual organ of another is punishable by imprisonment not exceeding fifteen years."[58] Although there has been some conflict in interpretation, the general rule is that emission is not required as an element of the offense. This was made clear by some statutes that specifically provide that emission is not essential and that penetration is sufficient to constitute the crime. A Texas statute, for instance, defined "Deviate Sexual Intercourse" as any contact between any part of the genitals of one person and the mouth or anus of another person. The Texas Court of Appeals interpreted this statute to require only "any contact," not penetration.[59]

All statutes similar to the Model Penal Code provide sanctions where the person engages in deviate intercourse with another person where the deviate sexual intercourse results *from force or imposition*. Some state statutes, however, provided that a person was guilty of sodomy when he or she engaged in deviate sexual intercourse with another person of the same sex *even if no force or imposition was involved*. These statutes have been challenged as violating the constitutional right to privacy.

In the 1986 case of *Bowers v. Hardwick*, the United States Supreme Court, by a five-to-four majority, upheld the constitutionality of the Georgia sodomy law, agreeing with the Georgia court that the United States Constitution does not confer a fundamental right upon homosexuals to engage in homosexual sodomy.[60] However, by 2001, only 18 states still retained sodomy laws that criminalized same-sex consensual activity.[61]

In 2003, the Supreme Court overturned the *Bowers* decision in *Lawrence et al. v. Texas*.[62] In this case, Houston police entered Lawrence's apartment while responding to a reported weapons disturbance and saw him and another adult man engaging in a private consensual act. The men were arrested and convicted of deviate sexual intercourse in violation of the Texas sodomy statute. The majority held that the Texas statute violated the due process clause of the Fourteenth Amendment. This case is included in Part II of this text.

Statutes that prohibit such activity through the use of force or imposition, against children, or against animals are not affected by the *Lawrence* decision.

---

[58]   96 Cal. App. 2d 621, 216 P.2d 140 (1950).

[59]   Donoho v. State, 628 S.W.2d 485 (Tex. 1982).

[60]   Bowers v. Hardwick, 478 U.S. 186 (1986).

[61]   Marc S. Spindelman, *Reorienting Bowers v. Hardwick*, 79 N.C. L. Rev. 359 (2001).

[62]   Lawrence et al. v. Texas, 539 U.S 558 (2003).

Case Note: *Lawrence et al. v. Texas*, 539 U.S. 558 (2003)
What was the holding of this case?
What constitutional right was said to have been violated?
What is the state's interest in maintaining laws regarding private sexual activity between consenting adults?

D. Summary

Historically, sodomy laws covered all forms of "deviate" sexual activity which, in the broadest definition, was any form of sexual activity that was not sexual intercourse between a man and a woman that could lead to procreation. Sodomy laws were gradually restricted so that such forms of sexual activity between men and women were decriminalized, and with the decision of *Lawrence v. Texas,* consensual sex between same-sex adults has been decriminalized. However, states still have the power to criminalize such activity when it is accompanied by force or imposition (so that, for instance, in some states, a rapist may be charged with both rape and sodomy). Further, sex between humans and animals is still illegal in most states although it may be defined under other statutes. Our general summary of elements below may or may not represent your state's sodomy law.

Sodomy
(A/R) deviate sexual activity (defined as when the sexual organ of one person comes into contact with, or penetrates, the mouth or anus of another person); by force; or without consent
(M/R) intentional, knowing

§ 6.4 Sexual Abuse and Child Molestation

A. Common Law

Under common law, rape required penetration; therefore, anything short of penetration was generally dealt with under battery prosecutions. Today, such conduct is covered under more general sexual assault statutes or other names for sexual assault, such as indecent assaults or deviate sexual assault.

B. Model Penal Code

In the Model Penal Code, forms of sexual touching that do not include penetration are called **sexual assault**. This crime is treated as a sexual offense rather than included under the crime of assault.

§ 213.4 Sexual Assault[63]

A person who has sexual contact with another not his spouse, or causes such other to have sexual conduct with him, is guilty of sexual assault, a misdemeanor, if:

(1) he knows that the contact is offensive to the other person; or

---

[63]   MODEL PENAL CODE § 213.4 (1985).

(2) he knows that the other person suffers from a mental disease or defect which renders him or her incapable of appraising the nature of his or her conduct; or

(3) he knows that the other person is unaware that a sexual act is being committed; or

(4) the other person is less than 10 years old; or

(5) he has substantially impaired the other person's power to appraise or control his or her conduct, by administering or employing without the other's knowledge drugs, intoxicants or other means for the purpose of preventing resistance; or

(6) the other person is less than [16] years old and the actor is at least [four] years older than the other person; or

(7) the other person is less than 21 years old and the actor is his guardian or otherwise responsible for general supervision of his welfare; or

(8) the other person is in custody of law or detained in a hospital or other institution and the actor has supervisory or disciplinary authority over him.

"Sexual contact" as used in the Model Code is defined to include "any touching of the sexual or other intimate parts of the person for the purpose of arousing or gratifying sexual desire." The prosecution must show that the "purpose" of the touching was to arouse or gratify sexual desire. Also, the prosecution must prove the touching of the sexual or other intimate parts of the person.

C. State Statutes, Codes, and Cases

State statutes have also provided sanctions for offensive sexual contacts that are not protected by rape laws because there is no penetration. Various statutes were given titles such as "indecent or immoral practices with another," **"sexual abuse,"** or "sexual imposition."[64] Other states have provided punishment under the general laws relating to assault and battery.[65]

Some states have followed the Model Code in establishing only one degree of sexual abuse, but grade the offense as a lesser felony. However, in some statutes, the offenses of sexual assault or sexual abuse are graded according to the degree of force and the age or mental condition of the victim. An example of a statute that graduates the penalty based upon age is that of New York.[66]

§ 130.55 Sexual abuse in the third degree

A person is guilty of sexual abuse in the third degree when he or she subjects another person to sexual contact without the latter's consent; except that in any prosecution under this Section, it is an affirmative defense that (a) such other person's lack of consent was due solely to incapacity to consent by reason of being less than seventeen years old, and (b) such other person was more than fourteen years old, and (c) the defendant was less than five years older than such other person.

Sexual abuse in the third degree is a Class B misdemeanor.

---

[64]   N.Y. PENAL LAW §§ 130.55-130.60 (McKinney 1994); KY. REV. STAT. §§ 510.110-510.130 (2001); OHIO REV. CODE ANN. § 2907.06 (Anderson 2002).

[65]   MASS. ANN. LAWS ch. 265 (Law. Co-op. 1992).

[66]   N.Y. PENAL LAWS § 130.55 (McKinney 2002), and following commentaries.

§ 130.60 Sexual abuse in the second degree

A person is guilty of sexual abuse in the second degree when he or she subjects another person to sexual contact and when such other person is:
(1) incapable of consent by reason of some factor other than being less than seventeen years old; or
(2) less than fourteen years old.
Sexual abuse in the second degree is a Class A misdemeanor.

"Sexual contact" as used in these sections means "any touching of the sexual or other intimate parts of a person for the purpose of arousing or gratifying sexual desire." In interpreting the term "sexual contact," as used in the New York statute, the New York courts decided that kissing the victim against her will and inserting his tongue into her mouth was "sexual contact" within the meaning of the sexual abuse statute, because the mouth is an intimate part of the body.[67] Another New York court found that allegations that the defendant "fondled" the 16-year-old complainant's leg and upper thigh were sufficient to allege that the defendant fondled "intimate parts" of the complainant, necessary to the charge of third degree sexual abuse.[68]

A New York court held that, to establish the crime of third-degree sexual abuse, the statute does not require that actual gratification occur, but only that the touching be for that purpose. Therefore, the intentional and sexually motivated touching of a person's covered buttocks, whether by a coworker, social acquaintance, or other, unquestionably qualifies as "sexual contact" under sexual abuse in the third degree statute, and is properly punishable by criminal sanction.[69]

In interpreting the Indiana statute titled "sexual battery," the court held that to convict a defendant of sexual battery, the state was required to prove that the defendant

1. with intent to arouse or satisfy his own sexual desires;
2. touched the victim;
3. when the victim was compelled to submit to touching by force or threat of force.

The court explained that the force used to compel the victim to submit to touching, as an element of the crime of sexual battery, need not be physical or violent, but may be implied from the circumstances. The court further noted that courts considered the victim's perspective, not the assailant's, when determining whether the presence or absence of forceful compulsion necessary to a conviction for sexual battery existed.[70] Because the state statutes differ and state court interpretations of statutes differ, it is essential that both the statute and case decisions be studied to determine whether a crime has been committed.

---

[67] People v. Rivera, 525 N.Y.S.2d 118 (1988). *See also* People v. Brown, 674 N.Y.S.2d 149 (1998).
[68] People v. Morvelli, 544 N.Y.S.2d 442 (1989).
[69] People v. Sumpter, 737 N.Y.S.2d 219 (2001).
[70] Bailey v. State, 764 N.E.2d 728 (Ind. 2002).

1. Child Sexual Abuse

States provide special coverage for taking indecent liberties with children. Sometimes called child molestation, state statutes criminalize touching of children for sexual gratification. Consent of the child is never a defense. An example of this is a Kentucky statute passed in 1962, which provided

> Any person of the age of seventeen years or over who carnally abuses the body, or indulges in any indecent or immoral practices with the body or organs of any child under the age of 15 years, or who induces, procures or permits a child under the age of 15 years to indulge in immoral, sexual or indecent practices with himself or any person shall be guilty of a felony, punishable on conviction thereof by imprisonment in the penitentiary for not less than one year nor more than ten years.[71]

States are not uniform in which statutes define crimes involving sexual abuse of children. States may address these crimes with statutory rape, sexual abuse, child abuse, injury to a child, or other statutes. For instance, under the Massachusetts law, such behavior is defined as indecent assault and battery on a child. Note that there is a special section for those who sexually abuse a child as a mandated reporter.

Massachusetts G.L. Chapter 265

> Section 13B. Whoever commits an indecent assault and battery on a child under the age of 14 shall be punished by imprisonment in the state prison for not more than 10 years, or by imprisonment in the house of correction for not more than 2 ½ years. A prosecution commenced under this section shall neither be continued without a finding nor placed on file.
>
> In a prosecution under this section, a child under the age of 14 years shall be deemed incapable of consenting to any conduct of the defendant for which such defendant is being prosecuted.
>
> Section 13B1/2. Whoever commits an indecent assault and battery on a child under the age of 14 and:
> (a) the indecent assault and battery was committed during the commission or attempted commission of the following offenses:— (1) armed burglary as set forth in section 14 of chapter 266; (2) unarmed burglary as set forth in section 15 of said chapter 266; (3) breaking and entering as set forth in section 16 of said chapter 266; (4) entering without breaking as set forth in section 17 of said chapter 266; (5) breaking and entering into a dwelling house as set forth in section 18 of said chapter 266; (6) kidnapping as set forth in section 26 of chapter 265; (7) armed robbery as set forth in section 17 of said chapter 265; (8) unarmed robbery as set forth in section 19 of said chapter 265; (9) assault and battery with a dangerous weapon or assault with a dangerous weapon, as set forth in sections 15A and 15B of said chapter 265; (10) home invasion as set forth in section 18 C of said chapter 265; or (11) posing or exhibiting child in state of nudity or sexual conduct as set forth in section 29A of chapter 272; or
> (b) at the time of commission of said indecent assault and battery, the defendant was a mandated reporter as is defined in section 21 of chapter 119, shall be punished by imprisonment in the state prison for life or for any term of years, but not less than

---

[71] KY. REV. STAT. § 435.105 (1975).

10 years. The sentence imposed on such person shall not be reduced to less than 10 years, or suspended, nor shall any person convicted under this section be eligible for probation, parole, work release, or furlough or receive any deduction from his sentence for good conduct until he shall have served 10 years of such sentence. Prosecutions commenced under this section shall neither be continued without a finding nor placed on file.

In a prosecution under this section, a child under the age of 14 years shall be deemed incapable of consenting to any conduct of the defendant for which such defendant is being prosecuted.

Various statutes describe as illegal a wide variety of acts involving children if the purpose is for sexual gratification, including touching the child or having the child touch the perpetrator for sexual gratification, taking pictures of the child for sexual gratification, or having the child disrobe or do other acts singly or with other children for purposes of sexual gratification.

LEGAL NEWS: JERRY SANDUSKY

In 2011 Jerry Sandusky, an esteemed former assistant football coach at Pennsylvania State University, was alleged to be a serial child rapist and molester. Grand jury findings illustrated a sequence of relationships with 8- to 14-year-old boys who he had met through The Second Mile, a charity program he founded and fundraised for that targeted troubled youth. Nine victims came forward to testify that they had been touched, and, in some cases, made to perform oral sex on Sandusky or were subjected to it from him. In Pennsylvania, the charges would be involuntary deviate sexual intercourse and indecent assault.

Another part of the story was that a graduate assistant had seen Sandusky raping a young boy in the showers of the university in 2002. This assistant had told Joe Paterno, the head coach, who, in turn, told the university athletic director; the vice president for business and finance was also alerted. None of these men reported the incident to the police although they prohibited Sandusky from bringing children on to the campus. In their testimony they recalled that the graduate assistant had said that Sandusky and the boy were only "horsing around" and they didn't remember he described it as sexual intercourse, but their testimony was deemed "not credible" by the grand jury. Not reporting child abuse by mandated reporters is a violation of 23 Pa.C.S.§6311 (Child Protective Services Law). This alleged victim has never been identified.

For more information about the grand jury report, go to http://www.nytimes.com/interactive/2011/11/06/sports/ncaafootball/20111106-pennstate-document.html.

A difficult issue arises when the sexual behavior is between two teens. Statutes are not uniform. While some states recognize a defense if the two parties are close in age, other states do not.

For example, New Jersey law states that the age of consent is 16, but children as young as 13 can legally engage in sexual activity with someone as long as that individual is less than four years older than the victim. However, in 12 states, "the legality is based solely on the difference between the ages of the two parties." For instance, in the District of Columbia, sexual intercourse with a minor under the age of 16 is illegal only if the defendant is four or more years older than the victim. Although extremely uncommon, some states like Washington allow the statutory age differentials to vary depending on the age of the victim such that intercourse with a teen who is between the ages of 14 and 16 is illegal if the accused is four or more years older than the victim. However, the law allows this age differential to decrease to three years in situations where the victim is less than 14 and decrease even further to a two-year age difference where the victim is under 12 years old. Thus, depending on the state, exceptions to criminal culpability are made if both parties are minors and the activity is consensual.[72]

> **Case Note: *Norris v. Morgan*, 622 F.3d 1276 (9th Cir. 2010)**
> What was the issue and holding of the case? What factors were used to determine if life without parole was too harsh for a repeat child molester?

2. Sexual Offender Registration Laws

Since the early 1990s, sex offender registration laws have been created in all states in response to sexual crimes against children. In 1994, the Jacob Wetterling Crimes Against Children and Sexually Violent Offender Registration Act required all states to implement sex offender registries. This law required sex offenders to register their addresses with authorities, sometimes for life. States that did not comply risked losing federal funds. In 1996, Megan's Law was passed because of the tragic rape and murder of seven-year-old Megan Kanka by a sex offender who lived in her neighborhood. President Clinton signed Megan's Law on May 17, 1996, which required states to set up sex offender registries and provide information to community members regarding whether sex offenders were living in the community if they wanted access to federal funding. Typically it is a violation of parole or probation and/or a new crime if a sex offender does not register. Public dissemination of sex offender registries allows anyone to see who has a sex offender label.

Some observers note that laws against sexual offenders have become too extreme. State laws now require all types of sexual offenders to register, including those convicted of statutory rape, which may have stemmed from a consensual relationship between young people, or those who possessed obscene materials not involving children. The laws do not limit registration requirements to sexual predators; in some states these laws include all those who have committed any sex crime and/or crimes involving children. Further, laws drastically restrict where sex offenders may live and travel.

---

[72]   L. Walters, *How to fix sexting problem: An analysis of the legal and policy considerations for sexting legislation.* 9 FIRST AMEND. L. REV. 98, 108 (2010).

Some argue that making them unable to reintegrate back into the community may increase the risk of recidivism rather than protect child victims.[73] Supreme Court holdings have held that requiring offenders to register, even if they committed their crime before the registration laws went into effect, was not a violation against ex post facto laws because these are defined as civil requirements, not criminal punishment.[74]

D. Summary

Sexual assault or sexual abuse laws did not exist under common law. They have been created to protect victims against offensive sexual contact that does not meet the definition of rape. Sexual acts against children that do not meet the definition of statutory rape fall under such laws or states have created laws specifically to address child victims.

Sexual Assault
(A/R) any touching; of the sexual or other intimate parts of a person; for the purpose of arousing or gratifying sexual desire; without consent; or toward a child (defined by statute); or a person unable to give consent (i.e., unconscious or incompetent)
(M/R) intentional and knowing

§ 6.5   Lewdness (Indecent Exposure)

A. Common Law

At common law, particular acts and forms of lewdness constituted criminal offenses. The word "**lewdness**" means open and public indecency. Usually in order to amount to an indictable crime, the offense must have been committed in a public place and seen by persons lawfully in that place. However, the early statutes provided a broader interpretation. Under these statutes, it was not necessary to allege or prove that such act was committed in a public place or in the presence of many people.

In the 1845 case of *State v. Willard*, the statute prohibited "open and gross lewdness":

If any man or woman, married or unmarried, shall be guilty of open and gross lewdness or lascivious behavior, he shall be imprisoned in the common jail not more than two years, or fined not exceeding $300.[75]

However, the court could find no particular definition in the statute as to what constituted lewdness, saying that "the indelicacy of the subject forbids it, and does not require of the court to state what particular conduct will constitute the offense." In this case, the respondent entered the house of a woman and "exposed his private parts and persistently urged her to have sexual intercourse with him." The court said there was no question that this was "lewdness" within the meaning of the statute and was "open within the meaning of the statute," defining openness to mean "undisguised, not

[73] A. Agan. *Sex offender registries: Fear without function.* 54 J. LAW & ECONOMICS 207 (2011).
[74] Connecticut Dept. of Public Safety v. Doe, 538 U.S. 1 (2003).
[75] State v. Willard, 18 Vt. 574, 46 Am. Dec. 170 (1845); the statute is quoted in the case.

concealed, and opposite to private, concealed, and unseen." Interestingly, in another early case, disrobing in a "house of ill fame" and intercourse therein did not warrant conviction for lewdness.[76]

Under the common law and early statutes, the elements that were required to convict a person of lewdness were intentionally, indecently, and offensively exposing the sex organs, in the presence of another, in an offensive manner.

B. Model Penal Code

Prior to the drafting of the Model Penal Code, indecent exposure and related crimes were covered under a multitude of statutes and given such titles as "Lewd and Lascivious Behavior," "Public Lewdness," and even "Appearing on the Highway in Bathing Garb." To make the offense more definite and the terms less likely to be misinterpreted, the Model Penal Code defines **indecent exposure** more narrowly.

§ 213.5 Indecent Exposure[77]

A person commits a misdemeanor if, for the purpose of arousing or gratifying sexual desire of himself or of any person other than his spouse, he exposes his genitals under circumstances in which he knows his conduct is likely to cause affront or alarm.

It requires, specifically, the exhibition of the genitals (a display of the buttocks or breasts is not prohibited under this statute). Second, the Model Code requires that the actor have a purpose to arouse or gratify the sexual desire of himself or another not his spouse. Third, the offense requires the actor to know that his conduct is likely to affront or alarm another. This would exclude from the scope of the crime the member of a nudist colony and even the nude dancer who performs only for those desiring such entertainment.

LEGAL NEWS: TOPLESS CAR WASHES NOT INDECENT

When several women short of money decided to set up a "topless car wash" enterprise in Moscow, Idaho in 2009, there was no law that prevented them from doing so. An earlier city ordinance prohibiting women from going topless was struck down as vague and revealing breasts does not meet the legal definition of indecency. The car wash business was short-lived, however, when their landlord evicted them and the city council scrambled to write a new ordinance preventing anyone else from competing with established car wash business owners by offering topless car washes.

———

Source: http://www.cbsnews.com/2100-201_162-514852.html.

---

[76] State v. Gardner, 174 Iowa 748, 156 N.W. 747 (1916).
[77] MODEL PENAL CODE § 213.5 (1985).

C. State Statutes, Codes, and Cases

Some statutes retain the terminology used before the Model Penal Code was written, and prohibit essentially the same conduct. Some use the terminology of the Model Code, but prohibit display of "sex organs" or other specifically named areas of the body, such as breasts.[78] Where a statute contains language such as "in a vulgar or indecent manner," or "with an immoral purpose," or "indecently," the prosecution must offer evidence to prove these elements as defined by the statute or by cases interpreting the statute.

An example of an indecent exposure statute is the Texas statute,[79] which provides

Indecent Exposure

(a) A person commits an offense if he exposes his anus or any part of his genitals with intent to arouse or gratify the sexual desire of any person, and he is reckless about whether another is present who will be offended or alarmed by the act.

(b) An offense under this class is a Class B misdemeanor.

The Texas statute does not proscribe exposure of the buttocks or the female breasts as these two areas of the anatomy are not traditionally included within the term "genitals." The intent must be to arouse or gratify the sexual desire of any person. Also, the Texas statute reduces *mens rea* from knowing to reckless in the actor's belief that anyone present would be offended or alarmed. The standard for determining offensiveness is objective; that is, it is not whether the defendant knows others would be offended or whether those present were actually offended, but rather, whether it would offend an ordinary person. Applying this standard, the court held in *Hefner v. State* that it was irrelevant whether the officer to whom the defendant exposed his penis was offended; the issue was whether the defendant was reckless about whether another was present who would be offended.[80]

LEGAL NEWS: BREASTFEEDING INDECENT?

Breastfeeding in public has been a perennial point of contention between those who argue it is natural and should be considered acceptable anywhere, even if the breast is fully exposed, and those who argue that exposing the breast, if not illegal, is unacceptable in public. In December 2008, the popular computer social networking site, Facebook, was the target of a mass protest for their policy of removing pictures of breastfeeding when too much of the breast was

---

[78]　For example, ARIZ. REV. STAT. ANN. § 13-1402 (1994), prohibits exposure of genitals, anus, and the areola or nipple of a female breast.

[79]　TEX. PENAL CODE § 21.08 (Vernon 1999).

[80]　Hefner v. State, 934 S.W.2d 855 (Tex. 1996); *see also* Young v. State, 976 S.W.2d 771 (Tex. 1998).

exposed. The issue has prompted at least nine states to pass a law specifically protecting the act in public. Montana, for instance, has a statute that says the following:

The Montana Legislature finds that breastfeeding a baby is an important and basic art of nurturing that must be protected in the interests of maternal and child health and family values. A mother has a right to breastfeed the mother's child in any location, public or private, where the mother and child are otherwise authorized to be present, irrespective of whether or not the mother's breast is covered during or incidental to the breastfeeding. The act of breastfeeding may not be considered a nuisance, indecent exposure, sexual conduct or obscenity. (Montana Code Annotated: 50-19-501)

UPDATE: The issue remains contentious. In December 2011, a mother was threatened with arrest for indecent exposure when she was breastfeeding her infant in a public building in Washington, DC. The security officer demanded she go into the women's bathroom to feed her baby.

Source: Devlin, V. (2009). "Complaints on Breastfeeding Lead to Lesson on Breastfeeding Law." Accessed January 2, 2009 from www.missoulian.com/articles/2009/01/02/news/local/znews06.txt; also see http://newsone.com/nation/newsonestaff4/breastfeeding-mother-indecent-exposure, accessed January 2, 2012.

A Michigan court held that an act of masturbation in a public restroom between adult males was "grossly indecent" within the meaning of the state's indecency statute. In the Michigan statute, the crime is a felony.[81]

D. *Summary*

Under common law, the elements of lewdness were intentionally, indecently, and offensively exposing the sex organs, in the presence of another, in an offensive manner. The Model Penal Code added that the exposure should be for the purpose of sexual arousal. Some statues reduce the *mens rea* to reckless in the actor's belief whether others would be offended and employ an objective standard as to offensiveness. In general, exposure of breasts or buttocks are not considered genitals but may be specifically added to the definition in the statute or be the subject of additional city ordinances.

Public Lewdness (Indecent Exposure)
(A/R) exposure of genitals; in a public place; for the purpose of sexual arousal; in a manner that is offensive (based on a reasonable person)
(M/R) reckless

---

[81]   People v. Bono, 641 N.W.2d 278 (Mich. 2002).

§ 6.6　Other Sex-Related Offenses against the Person

There are other statutes in various states that relate to sex offenses. Some of these are discussed briefly here.

A. Seduction

The crime of **seduction** is an example of how the law reflects societal norms and sexual stereotypes. Seduction was "the act of a man inducing a woman to commit unlawful sexual intercourse with him by means of enticement, persuasion, solicitations, promises, bribes or other means without the employment of force, therefore overcoming her reluctance and her scruples."[82] Under the provisions of some early statutes, as interpreted, consent of the woman seduced to the intercourse was no defense and, in some jurisdictions, unless so provided by statute, marriage to the accused after the seduction was no defense. Generally, the woman who was seduced had to be both unmarried and chaste at the time.[83] Under common law, the elements of seduction were inducement that overcomes the female's reluctance and scruples; unlawful sexual intercourse; by means of arts, persuasion, solicitations, promises, or bribes. Also, generally, the woman had to be unmarried and chaste.

The Model Penal Code continued to recognize seduction as a crime, but restricted its coverage. It applies to a male who induces a female to participate in intercourse "by a promise of marriage which the actor does not mean to perform." It does not cover other types of deception that might give rise to liability.

States have either eliminated this statute or have limited its scope to civil damages. Some states include the term "statutory sexual seduction" in their definition of statutory rape, to cover the aspect of voluntary sexual intercourse by minors. However, a few states still retain the traditional elements of the crime of seduction, such as South Carolina.

South Carolina. SECTION 16-15-50

Seduction under promise of marriage.[84] A male over the age of sixteen years who by means of deception and promise of marriage seduces an unmarried woman in this State is guilty of a misdemeanor and, upon conviction, must be fined at the discretion of the court or imprisoned not more than one year. There must not be a conviction under this section on the uncorroborated testimony of the woman upon whom the seduction is charged, and no conviction if at trial it is proved that the woman was at the time of the alleged offense lewd and unchaste. If the defendant in any action brought under this section contracts marriage with the woman, either before or after the conviction, further proceedings of this section are stayed.

---

[82]　Mackey v. Commonwealth, 255 Ky. 466, 74 S.W.2d 915 (1934); Spangler v. Commonwealth, 188 Va. 436, 50 S.E.2d 265 (1948).

[83]　Smith v. State, 13 Ala. App. 388, 69 So. 402 (1915). State v. Dacke, 59 Wash. 238, 109 P. 1050 (1910).

[84]　S.C. CODE ANN. § 16-15-50 (1995).

B. *Importuning/Sexual Solicitation of a Minor*

In most states, there are statutes prohibiting solicitation of sexual activity to minors. This is sometimes called **importuning**. For example, the Ohio Revised Code[85] provides

(a) No person shall solicit a person under thirteen years of age to engage in sexual activity with the offender, whether or not the offender knows the age of such person.

(b) No person shall solicit a person of the same sex to engage in sexual activity with the offender, when the offender knows such solicitation is offensive to the other person, or is reckless in that regard.

(c) No person shall solicit another, not the spouse of the offender, to engage in sexual conduct with the offender, when the offender is eighteen years of age or older and four or more years older than the other person, and the other person is over twelve but not over fifteen years of age, whether or not the offender knows the age of the other person.

This and similar statutes are designed to prohibit soliciting a person under age 13 to engage in sexual activity, or soliciting a person age 13 to 15 to engage in sexual conduct, when the solicitor is 18 years or older and four or more years older than the person solicited.

Recently, Internet chat rooms have been the focus of both sexual predators of children and police officers who seek to catch them before any children are harmed. Police officers pretend to be children and engage in cyber-conversations with individuals who show a sexual interest. When the defendant solicits the "child" and sets up a meeting, he is arrested. The defense of those caught is typically that they didn't believe the "child" was truly underage, or that they did not plan to have sex with the child. Generally, the fact that the "child" was a police officer is a case of factual impossibility and the charges are both sexual solicitation (the asking), and attempted sexual contact. Some states have chosen to create specific statutes for online solicitation, such as Texas, as follows.

Texas. Sec. 33.021. ONLINE SOLICITATION OF A MINOR. [86]

(a) In this section:
    (1) "Minor" means:
        (A) an individual who represents himself or herself to be younger than 17 years of age; or
        (B) an individual whom the actor believes to be younger than 17 years of age.
        (2) "Sexual contact," "sexual intercourse," and "deviate sexual intercourse" have the meanings assigned by Section 21.01.

---

[85] OHIO REV. CODE ANN. § 2907.07 (Anderson 1999).

[86] Acts 2007, 80th Leg., R.S.,"http://www.legis.state.tx.us/tlodocs/80R/billtext/html/SB00006F.HTM" \t "new" 1291, Sec. 7, eff. September 1, 2007.

(3) "Sexually explicit" means any communication, language, or material, including a photographic or video image, that relates to or describes sexual conduct, as defined by Section 43.25.

(b) A person who is 17 years of age or older commits an offense if, with the intent to arouse or gratify the sexual desire of any person, the person, over the Internet, by electronic mail or text message or other electronic message service or system, or through a commercial online service, intentionally:
    (1) communicates in a sexually explicit manner with a minor; or
    (2) distributes sexually explicit material to a minor.

(c) A person commits an offense if the person, over the Internet, by electronic mail or text message or other electronic message service or system, or through a commercial online service, knowingly solicits a minor to meet another person, including the actor, with the intent that the minor will engage in sexual contact, sexual intercourse, or deviate sexual intercourse with the actor or another person.

(d) It is not a defense to prosecution under Subsection (c) that:
    (1) the meeting did not occur;
    (2) the actor did not intend for the meeting to occur; or
    (3) the actor was engaged in a fantasy at the time of commission of the offense.

(e) It is a defense to prosecution under this section that at the time conduct described by Subsection (b) or (c) was committed:
    (1) the actor was married to the minor; or
    (2) the actor was not more than three years older than the minor and the minor consented to the conduct.

(f) An offense under Subsection (b) is a felony of the third degree, except that the offense is a felony of the second degree if the minor is younger than 14 years of age or is an individual whom the actor believes to be younger than 14 years of age at the time of the commission of the offense. An offense under Subsection (c) is a felony of the second degree.

(g) If conduct that constitutes an offense under this section also constitutes an offense under any other law, the actor may be prosecuted under this section, the other law, or both.

C. Voyeurism

Traditionally, "peeping toms" were those who, for sexual gratification, peered in windows at unsuspecting victims, watching while homeowners undressed or engaged in private behavior. Today's technology greatly expands the opportunities for voyeurs who may now use camera phones, "spy cameras," and small video recorders to secretly invade the privacy of individuals in stores, locker rooms, bathrooms, and a range of other places. Many state statutes are written generally enough that they cover newer forms of **voyeurism**. The Ohio Revised Code[87] includes a section providing the following:

(A) No person, for the purpose of sexually arousing or gratifying himself or herself, shall commit trespass or otherwise surreptitiously invade the privacy of another, to spy or eavesdrop upon another.

(B) Whoever violates this Section is guilty of voyeurism, a misdemeanor of the third degree.

---

[87]   OHIO REV. CODE ANN. § 2907.08 (Anderson 2002).

This section prohibits not only trespassing, but any invasion of privacy, to eavesdrop or spy on another for the purpose of obtaining a vicarious sexual thrill. Other states have passed related laws, such as a Florida statute which is directed specifically at merchants and does not mention sexual gratification.

> 877.26 Direct observation, videotaping, or visual surveillance of customers in merchant's dressing room, . . .
>
> (1) It is unlawful for any merchant to directly observe or make use of video cameras or other visual surveillance devices to observe or record customers in the merchant's dressing room, fitting room, changing room, or restroom when such room provides a reasonable expectation of privacy. However, a merchant may directly observe a customer from outside such room if the observation is within the scope of the merchant's duties and the observation does not otherwise violate 810.14 or 810.145 or if the customer invites or consents to the presence of the merchant in the room . . .

LEGAL NEWS: "UPSKIRTING" CRIMES

State legislatures have responded to **upskirting** violations with new statutes. The term refers to individuals who take pictures of victims without their knowledge, sometimes using "spy" cameras or other technology. In Texas, a math teacher was arrested under the law punishing such behavior for taking pictures of high school girls' backsides, but another individual who took pictures of specific body parts of people at a state fair was released with no charges filed. Legal observers note that the law may be difficult to enforce except in the most flagrant cases since it is, in some ways, too broad (it covers photography that might be considered art or have no sexual purpose), and too limiting (some photographs may be for sexual purposes but not be covered by the law).

L. Heinauer. *Arrest stokes photo law debate*. Austin American Statesman, December 17, 2006, B1, B7.

D. Sexual Misconduct

In some states statutory rape laws do not distinguish between perpetrators who are much older than the underage victim and those who are nearer in age; however, many states do restrict such laws to those who are more than four years (or some other statutorily defined number of years) older than the victim. In these states, the young people may still be guilty of the crime of **sexual misconduct**. Some statutes have been challenged when they provide too harsh a penalty for minors engaged in consensual sex. For instance, the Florida Supreme Court overturned the conviction of a 16-year-old who had consensual sex with another 16-year-old. The Florida statute that was voided specified that "any person" who had sexual contact with a minor was guilty of the offense.[88] Today, the statute requires the person be 24 years of age or older.

---

[88]   B.B. v. Florida, 659 So.2d 256 (1995).

LEGAL NEWS: UNDERAGE SEX

Genarlow Wilson spent two years in a Georgia prison after he was convicted of a sexual crime for having consensual oral sex with a 15-year-old even though he was only 17 years old at the time. His 2003 conviction earned him a mandatory 10-year sentence and the ensuing scandal prompted the Georgia legislature to revise the law so that consensual sex by underage participants became only a misdemeanor, but they did not make the law retroactive. Upon appeal, the Georgia Supreme Court ruled that Wilson's 10-year sentence was cruel and unusual and ordered an immediate release on October 26, 2007. He had already served 2 years of his 10-year sentence by the time of his release.

Source: WSB Atlanta (2007). "Genarlow Wilson Speaks at Ebeneezer Baptist Church." Retrieved online from http://www.wsbtv.com/news/14429689/detail.html on December 28, 2008.

E. Intercourse with a Person in Custody

The Model Penal Code includes a provision that provides a penalty when a person engages in sexual intercourse or deviate sexual relations, or causes another to engage in such relationship, if the person with whom he has sexual intercourse or causes another to have sexual intercourse with is in custody of law enforcement officials or detained in a hospital or other institution and the actor has supervisory or disciplinary authority over him. This provides a penalty for one who engages in intercourse with a person under his supervisory or disciplinary authority, and is designed to deter abuse of custodial authority.[89]

All states except Vermont now have laws criminalizing sex, even consensual sex, between prisoners and correctional officials or civilian employees of the corrections system. The legal premise of such laws is that persons under confinement are not in a position to give free and knowing consent to someone who holds power over them. Congress passed the Prison Rape Elimination Act in 2003, which mandated the Federal Bureau of Statistics to collect the numbers of rapes that occur in prison. Unfortunately, one of the findings that has emerged is that a substantial percentage of sexual assaults in prison, especially in prisons for women, are perpetrated by correctional personnel.[90]

F. Sex Offenses Involving Human Immunodeficiency Virus (HIV) and Acquired Immune Deficiency Syndrome (AIDS)

In addition to civil statutes and administrative regulations, which authorize tort liability for transmission of HIV, a number of states have enacted substantive HIV/AIDS-specific statutes. An example is that of Illinois:

---

[89]   MODEL PENAL CODE § 213.3 (1985).
[90]   Beck, A. and Harrison, P. (2007). *Sexual Victimization Reported in State and Federal Prisons, Reported by Inmates, 2007*. Washington, DC: B.J.S., U.S. Dept. of Justice.

§ 12-16.2 Criminal Transmission of HIV[91]

(a) A person commits criminal transmission of HIV when he or she, knowing that he or she is infected with HIV:
 (1) engages in intimate contact with another;
 (2) transfers, donates, or provides his or her blood, tissue, semen, organs, or other potentially infectious body fluids for transfusion, transplantation, insemination, or other administration to another; or
 (3) dispenses, delivers, exchanges, sells, or in any other way transfers to another any nonsterile intravenous or intramuscular drug paraphernalia.

Under this statute, the defendant does not have to have sexual intercourse; "intimate sexual contact" is defined as exposing the body of the victim to bodily fluid in a manner that could result in the transmission of HIV. The victim does not have to acquire HIV in order for the defendant to be convicted. It is an affirmative defense that the person exposed knew that the infected person was infected with HIV, knew that the action could result in infection with HIV, and consented to the action with the knowledge.

Both the Illinois statute and a similar Michigan statute were challenged as being unconstitutional, but the court determined that the statute was not unconstitutionally overbroad or vague and did not violate the First Amendment.[92]

A Florida appeals court held that a defendant who had been charged with sexual offenses involving transmission of body fluids could be required to submit to HIV testing upon the request of the victim or the victim's parent.[93]

In jurisdictions where specific HIV/AIDS-related criminal statutes have not been enacted, individuals transferring, or attempting to transfer, body fluids, knowing they are HIV-positive or infected with AIDS, have been convicted of battery, aggravated assault, and even attempted murder under existing criminal statutes.[94]

§ 6.7   Summary

In this chapter, nonconsensual sex crimes were considered; the most serious sex crime is rape. Rape is defined as the act of unlawful carnal knowledge by a man of a woman, forcibly and against her will. While some courts in the past have admitted evidence concerning the complainant's past sexual activities on the issue of whether

---

[91]   720 ILL. COMP. STAT. 5/12-16.2 (2002). *See also* N.D. CENT. CODE § 12.1-20-17(2) (1989).
[92]   People v. Russell, 630 N.E.2d 794 (Ill. 1994); People v. Jensen, 231 Mich. App. 439, 586 N.W.2d 748 (1998).
[93]   Isom v. State, 722 So. 2d 237 (Fla. 1998).
[94]   See the discussion of HIV/AIDS cases in Chapter 3; *see also* Smallwood v. State, 680 A.2d 512 (Md. 1995).

the carnal knowledge was against the will of the female, the modern trend is to limit the use of evidence relating to such sexual activities.

In general, modern rape statutes may be characterized as either "forcible rape" (sexual intercourse by force or threat of force), or "statutory rape" (sexual intercourse with victims incapable of giving consent because of age or mental incapacity). Within the latter category, most states have adopted statutes that increase punishment according to the age of the victim, with younger victims (typically under the age of 12) receiving the greatest protection. Modern statutes differ from common law in that the crime is gender-neutral, may include other acts in addition to sexual penetration by genitals, and eliminates the so-called marital exemption.

A second sex crime in the category of offenses against the person is sodomy. Sodomy has been defined as "carnal copulation by human beings with each other against nature or with a beast." Rather than using the term *sodomy*, the drafters of the Model Penal Code took a different approach, defining the offense as "deviate sexual intercourse by force or imposition." The Model Code never did and modern statutes cannot prohibit such sexual intercourse between consenting adults. The Supreme Court ruled it an unconstitutional invasion of privacy, as long as both have the age and mental capacity to render consent and if they conduct their relations in private and create no public nuisance.

The third sex crime considered is sexual abuse (or assault). Under various titles, states provided penalties for unlawfully subjecting another person to sexual contact (without penetration) without the other's consent. The crime is covered in the Model Penal Code under the term "sexual assault." The MPC only established one degree of sexual abuse, grading it a lesser felony. In other states, the offenses of "sexual assault" or "sexual abuse" are graded according to the degree of force and the age or mental condition of the victim. Other statutes also may cover sexual conduct involving children, including child molestation, deviate sexual assault, or others.

At common law, particular acts and forms of lewdness constituted a criminal offense. The word "lewdness" means open and public indecency. Under the Model Penal Code, a person commits the crime of indecent exposure if, for the purpose of arousing or gratifying the sexual desire of himself or any other person other than his spouse, he exposes his genitals under circumstances in which he knows his conduct is likely to cause affront or alarm. Some of the more recently revised statutes use the terms in the Model Penal Code, but extend the coverage to exposure of other specifically named areas of the body.

Other acts subject to penalty are the following:

- Seduction: the act of a man inducing a woman to commit unlawful sexual intercourse with him by means of enticement, persuasions, solicitations, promises, bribes, or other means without the employment of force, thereby overcoming her reluctance and her scruples.
- Importuning or sexual solicitation of a minor: solicitation of sexual activity from an underage person.
- Voyeurism: trespass or invasion of privacy of another to spy or eavesdrop for the purpose of sexual gratification.

- **Sexual misconduct:** sexual intercourse between a defendant under 18 and a victim under 16 (in some states) who is incapable of giving consent because of age.
- **Intercourse with a person in custody:** any correctional official who has sexual intercourse with a person in custody whether or not such intercourse was consensual.
- **Transmission of HIV and AIDS:** intentional sexual contact with knowledge of the possibility of transmitting the HIV virus.
- **Sexual registry laws:** the requirement that sexual offenders, as specified by statute, register as a sex offender.

As statutes relating to sexual offenses against the person now vary from state to state, these statutes must be consulted to determine the particular statute applicable.

REVIEW QUESTIONS
---

1. What are the six elements of common law rape? Is rape a specific intent or general intent crime?
2. What was the utmost resistance standard?
3. Define statutory rape.
4. What was the common law marital exemption for rape? Does it still exist?
5. What are the categories of victims who cannot give consent and, therefore, any sexual intercourse is considered rape?
6. What are the current changes to the traditional *mens rea* of statutory rape?
7. What are rape shield laws? What are the exceptions?
8. What are the four major changes in rape/sexual assault laws from the common law?
9. Define common law sodomy and how current laws are different from common law sodomy.
10. Describe the case holding that ruled that laws against consensual sodomy violated the right to privacy.
11. What is sexual assault or sexual abuse (as distinguished from rape)?
12. Define the types of statutes that might be used to punish child molestation and describe Megan's Law.
13. What is the *actus reus* and *mens rea* for lewdness (indecent exposure)?
14. Define the crime of sexual solicitation of a minor.
15. Define the crime of seduction.
16. Define the crime of voyeurism.
17. Which laws would be used to address perpetrators who take pictures of individuals in a state of undress without their consent?
18. Define the crime of sexual misconduct.
19. Define the crime of intercourse with a person in custody.
20. Define the crime of intentional transmission of HIV/AIDS.

Offenses against Property— Destruction and Intrusion Offenses

7

Chapter Outline

Cases

Trespass: *Pruneyard Shopping Center v. Robins*, 447 U.S. 74 (1980)
Burglary: *People v. Ramos*, 52 Cal. App. 4th 300, 60 Cal. Rptr. 523 (1997)

arson	curtilage
breaking and entering	dwelling
burglary	malicious mischief
burning	trespass
criminal mischief	vandalism

§ 7.1   Introduction

In studying the history of criminal law and procedure, one recognizes that, in most societies, offenses that interfere with the sanctity of a person's home are considered more serious than other property offenses, and are treated accordingly. This is especially true in countries that have followed traditional English law, in which the concept that a person's home is his "castle" was recognized very early, and honored throughout many generations. Therefore, although certain crimes, such as arson and burglary, are essentially offenses against property, they are considered two of the most serious crimes. In addition, malicious mischief and trespass are included in this chapter. These two offenses are not normally as serious as arson and burglary, but share the characteristics of destruction and intrusion.

The process followed in discussing these and other property destruction and intrusion crimes is first to define the common law crime, and the Model Penal Code, and then discuss the statutory and code changes that have taken effect in most states.

§ 7.2   Arson

A. Common Law

Because of the great danger to human life resulting from the burning of a dwelling house, **arson** at common law was considered to be a heinous felony punishable by death. The primary purpose of the laws relating to arson was to preserve the security of the habitation, to protect dwellers within the building from injury or death by fire, and to protect the possessory interest in the house. It was considered one of the most serious common law felonies and, according to Sir William Blackstone, was frequently more destructive than murder itself because of the inability to control fire.[1]

---

[1]   1 Blackstone, Commentaries 220-228.

At common law, arson was defined in the following ways:

- the willful and malicious burning of another's dwelling house or of an outbuilding within its curtilage
- the willful and malicious burning of a dwelling house of another person[2]

Common law arson has the following four elements: burning; a dwelling house (or any building within the curtilage); of another person; maliciously.

1. Burning

In order to constitute the traditional crime of arson, there must be a **burning**—that is, there must have been some consuming of the material with which the house is built. It was sufficient for common law arson if any part of the dwelling house itself was burned, no matter how small, and no matter how insignificant to the structural integrity of the building. For example, a spot on the floor that was charred was held sufficient to constitute this element of the crime of arson. There need not be a blaze and it is immaterial how soon the fire was extinguished or whether it was put out or went out by itself. While it was necessary that there be some "combustion," "ignition," or "charring" to constitute burning, this element was not present if there was only damage caused by smoke.[3]

2. Dwelling House or Outbuilding Used in Connection Therewith

Because the essence of the offense at common law was the danger to the lives of persons who dwelt in or occupied the house, or the buildings used in connection therewith, it was necessary that the dwelling be occupied. However, it is not necessary that the house be actually inhabited at the time of the burning, provided that it was usually inhabited and the owner only temporarily absent.[4]

At least under some interpretations, a building that was not itself a dwelling house could be the subject of arson if it were within the **curtilage** of a dwelling house. This was defined as the space adjoining a dwelling and habitually used for family purposes. Some examples of buildings that were considered under the definition of "dwellings" under the common law arson were a barn, a stable, a cow-house, a sheep-house, a dairy-house, and a milk-house, all of which were located within the curtilage of a dwelling house.[5]

---

[2] State v. White, 291 N.C. 118, 229 S.E.2d 152 (1976).
[3] Commonwealth v. Van Schaack, 16 Mass. 104 (1819); State v. Braathen, 77 N.D. 309, 43 N.W.2d 202 (1950); State v. Wyatt, 48 N.C. App. 709, 269 S.E.2d 717 (1980); State v. Hall, 93 N.C. 571 (1885); Honey v. State, 112 Tex. Crim. 439, 17 S.W.2d 50 (1929).
[4] State v. Wyatt, 48 N.C. App. 709, 269 S.E.2d 717 (1980).
[5] 1 Hawkins, Pleas of the Crown, 105-106 (1716).

3. The House Must Belong to or Be Occupied by Another

The common law definition requires that the house burned be possessed by another. Accordingly, it was arson for the legal owner of the house to burn his own house, which was in the possession of another, for instance, a renter. Conversely, it was not arson at common law for a person to burn his own dwelling, which was occupied by him.

As insurance on the dwelling became common and houses sometimes were burned in order to collect insurance, additional statutes were enacted to supplement the common law crime of arson. Under these statutes, it is unlawful to burn insured property with the specific intent to injure, prejudice, or defraud the insurer.[6]

4. The Burning Must Be Done Maliciously

Perhaps the most difficult task of a prosecutor in proving the common law crime of arson is to show that the burning was willful or malicious. Mere accident, carelessness, or simple negligence is not enough to constitute the common law crime of arson. If the prosecutor introduces evidence to show that the person intentionally started the fire that resulted in the burning, this is a clear-cut case. However, it is more difficult to prove malice when the acts amounted to a wanton burning without justification or excuse. In the latter situation, the requirements of arson could be met if evidence indicated that the actor performed an intentional act that created a very high risk of the burning of a dwelling house. Also, there is sufficient intent or malice to constitute the crime of arson if there exists general malice or an intent to burn a structure; a particular intent or malice against a particular person or thing is not required.[7]

B. *Model Penal Code*

Under the Model Penal Code, arson is enlarged to include exploding as well as burning and buildings other than dwellings. The crime of arson is graded partly according to the kind of property destroyed or imperiled and partly according to the danger to persons. The most serious type of arson is a felony in the second degree and is most similar to common law arson. Under this definition, arson occurs when a person starts a fire or causes an explosion, either to destroy a building or occupied structure of another, or his or her own or another's property to collect insurance for such loss.

> § 220.1 Arson and Related Offenses[8]
>
> (1) Arson. A person is guilty of arson, a felony of the second degree, if he starts a fire or causes an explosion with the purpose of:
> (a) destroying a building or occupied structure of another; or

---

6   Edwards v. Commonwealth, 204 Ky. 515, 264 S.W. 1083 (1924).
7   Colbert v. State, 125 Wis. 423, 104 N.W. 61 (1905); Hough v. State, 929 S.W.2d 484 (Tex. 1996).
8   MODEL PENAL CODE § 220.1 (1985).

    (b) destroying or damaging any property, whether his own or another's, to collect insurance for such loss. It shall be an affirmative defense to prosecution under this paragraph that the actor's conduct did not recklessly endanger any building or occupied structure of another or place any other person in danger of death or bodily injury.

(2) Reckless Burning or Exploding. A person commits a felony of the third degree if he purposely starts a fire or causes an explosion, whether on his own property or another's, and thereby recklessly:

    (a) places another person in danger of death or bodily injury; or

    (b) places a building or occupied structure of another in danger of damage or destruction.

(3) Failure to Control or Report Dangerous Fire. A person who knows that a fire is endangering life or a substantial amount of property of another and fails to take reasonable measures to put out or control the fire, when he can do so without substantial risk to himself, or to give a prompt fire alarm, commits a misdemeanor if:

    (a) he knows that he is under an official, contractual, or other legal duty to prevent or combat the fire; or

    (b) the fire was started, albeit lawfully, by him or with his assent, or on property in his custody or control.

The other two crimes defined in the Model Penal Code are "Reckless Burning or Exploding" and "Failure to Control or Report a Dangerous Fire." These obviously have been added to provide a penalty for an act that results in a burning or explosion when some of the technical requirements of the crime of arson are missing.

C. State Statutes, Codes, and Cases

Similarly to the Model Penal Code, most state statutes protect property other than dwellings and provide a penalty for burning of property that was not within the common law *mens rea* requirements. Further, states now grade arson by severity. These statutes establish degrees of arson determined by

1. the value of the property,
2. the use of the property, such as a dwelling house,
3. whether the place is inhabited, and
4. the level of *mens rea*

Also, statutes have been enacted to punish those who *attempt* to commit the crime of arson. The modern state statutes have expanded not only the coverage of arson and related laws, but have simplified the wording so as to make definition easier. As the state statutes differ in some respects, it is essential that the statutes be checked to determine the exact elements of arson and related crimes.

An example of a statute that takes into consideration the type of property as well as the injury inflicted is that of California.[9]

---

[9]   CAL. PENAL CODE § 451 (2002). See also CAL. PENAL CODE § 451.1 (2002).

A person is guilty of arson when he or she willfully and maliciously sets fire to or burns or causes to be burned or who aids, counsels, or procures the burning of, any structure, forest land, or property.

(a) Arson that causes bodily injury is a felony punishable by imprisonment in the state prison for five, seven, or nine years.

(b) Arson that causes an inhabited structure or inhabited property to burn is a felony punishable by imprisonment in the state prison for three, five, or eight years.

(c) Arson of a structure or forest land is a felony punishable by imprisonment in the state prison for two, four, or six years.

(d) Arson of property is a felony punishable by imprisonment in the state prison for 16 months, two, or three years. For purposes of this paragraph, arson of property does not include one burning or causing to be burned his or her own personal property unless there is an intent to defraud or there is injury to another person or another person's structure, forest land, or property.

Vermont also distinguishes types of arson. First-degree arson covers dwelling houses (occupied or vacant), and any adjoining buildings. Second-degree arson covers any other buildings or property. Third-degree arson covers personal property. Fourth-degree arson is when the offender attempts to burn a structure but is unsuccessful.[10] In many states, the courts refer to the common law in determining definitions and elements; thus, we will revisit the common law elements.

1. Burning

Modern definitions of burning are consistent with case decisions under the common law in that any type of burning is sufficient to prove this element of the crime. For example, the "burning" element was satisfied when a New York court found evidence that indicated the building suffered blistering from the fire.[11]

2. Dwelling House (or Outbuilding within the Curtilage)

Recall that one of the issues under the common law was what type of building met the definition of **dwelling**. In general, the building had to be a dwelling house, but it need not have someone living in it at the time. In the 1993 case of *Barnes v. State,* a Wyoming court explained that an occupied structure within the meaning of the arson statute meant one that was intended to be occupied and usually was occupied. However, a 1995 Michigan court held that when the house was unoccupied and dilapidated to the extent that it was deemed abandoned, it was no longer considered a dwelling house.[12]

Some court decisions have refined and restricted the meaning of dwelling to include only those dwellings currently inhabited. In interpreting the term "inhabited structure" as used in the California statute, a California court declared that the offense

---

[10]   13 VT. CODE R. § 502-05 (West 2007).

[11]   People v. Calderon, 682 N.Y.S.2d 38 (App. Div. 1998).

[12]   Barnes v. State, 858 P.2d 522 (Wyo. 1993); People v. Reeves, 528 N.W.2d 160 (Mich. 1995).

of setting a fire to an inhabited structure requires someone to be using the structure as a dwelling at the time of the fire and not merely that the structure's purpose is to serve as a dwelling.[13] A North Carolina court reiterated that "it is an essential element of the crime of arson that the burned house be inhabited."[14] Of course, in these states, burning other types of buildings would be prosecuted as a less serious type of arson.

3. Of Another

Generally, setting fire to your own dwelling is not considered arson; however, statutes may include it as such when the purpose is for insurance proceeds. Case law in this area typically deals with the definition of ownership. Even if the burning does not come into the definition of arson, there may be other laws broken, especially if such conduct is defined as reckless or negligent.

4. Malicious Intent

Under common law, the act of burning had to be "malicious," meaning intentional. In referring to the malice element, a Mississippi court held that where statutes make malice and willfulness an ingredient of the crime of arson, a particular intent or malice against a person or thing is not essential; it is sufficient to show that the accused acted on a malicious motive and that he set the fire willfully rather than negligently or accidentally.[15]

In order to obtain a conviction for intentional arson, the prosecutor must show both the act (*actus reus*) and the intent (*mens rea*) to set fire to a structure (this is the concept of concurrence). If the actor intended to set fire to a dwelling but only managed to set fire to property, then that is attempted arson and perhaps some lesser form of unlawful fire covered in the statute, but not typically first-degree arson. Likewise, if the actor intended to set fire to property and accidentally caused a dwelling to burn, then the *mens rea* is missing.

LEGAL NEWS: WILDFIRES AND ARSON

Most wildfires are caused by lightning. One source estimates that only 7 percent of California's wildfires are set intentionally. However a much larger number are set by humans accidentally. Intentional fires that might burn thousands of acres and cause millions of dollars in damage could not have been prosecuted under common law arson, but statutes have been created to cover such actions and the crimes can be felonies with defendants facing jail time for starting fires. Even those who set fires accidentally may be charged with felonies for

---

[13]   People v. Jones, 245 Cal. Rptr. 85 (1988) The fact that some furniture was left in the house after the tenants were evicted was not determinative.

[14]   State v. Britt, 510 S.E.2d 683 (N.C. 1999).

[15]   Barnes v. State, 721 So. 2d 1130 (Miss. 1998).

> recklessly starting a fire, such as two workmen who were welding and sparked a blaze that cost $1.5 million. The individuals and their employer face civil suits to recover damages, but, also, the men have been charged with a crime since the *mens rea* is reckless, not intentional. Even a 10-year-old boy who was playing with matches and set off a different wildfire might have been charged under the state's laws (but, ultimately, the prosecutor chose not to).
>
> _____
>
> For more information, see http://articles.latimes.com/2007/dec/02/local/me-firestart2/2.

Recall that some states grade the offense of arson depending on whether the building was inhabited. An intent to set fire to a home when people are inside is the most serious grade of arson; however, some states also include a type of "wanton disregard" as equivalent to intentional. For instance, in Missouri, if the actor sets fire to a dwelling in "conscious disregard of the substantial risk" that a person might be inside the building or in proximity thereto, that is also considered the highest level of *mens rea*.[16]

Some states have expanded the definition of arson to include lesser levels of *mens rea* and then graded the offense based on the level. Obviously, purposefully or intentionally is the highest level of *mens rea*. Statutes also, however, have lower grades of arson that include reckless and negligent fires. An example of a statute that punishes for *negligent* burning is that of Alaska. There, the law provides that a person commits the crime of criminal negligent burning if, with criminal negligence, he or she damages the property of another by fire or explosion.[17]

5. Burning of Personal Property

While common law arson was only defined as setting fire to dwellings, modern law covers all types of property, albeit in an inconsistent fashion from state to state. The Model Penal Code categorized the burning of personal property valued at less than $5,000.00 as a misdemeanor. Most state statutes, however, define any burning of personal property valued at more than $250 as a felony. Also, 29 states allow for imprisonment of more than one year for setting fire to personal property valued at more than $2,000. Further, Massachusetts and Hawaii do not even define burning of personal property as a lesser crime, but include it under their arson statute.[18]

Thus, modern statutes may be different from the common law, but they are based on common law definitions. In *Michigan v. Reeves*, the defendant was charged with felony murder for his part in starting a fire that burned down an abandoned house,

_____

[16]   MO. REV. STAT. § 569.040 (2002).
[17]   ALASKA STAT. § 11-46-430 (1995).
[18]   Statistics cited in United States v. Hathaway, 757 F. Supp. 324 (D. Vt. 1991).

killing a firefighter who responded. The Court of Appeals reversed the conviction, finding that the felony murder statute was based on common law arson, not modern statutes that expand the type of buildings that can be the targets in arson. The Supreme Court of Michigan heard the appeal and agreed.[19]

> We granted the prosecution's application for leave to appeal to determine whether the word "arson" in the felony murder statute includes the burning of other real property . . . . In the present case, the defendants set fire to a dilapidated abandoned house. Our task is to determine whether the house was a dwelling house so that the burning of it would constitute the crime of arson. . . . The legislature intended that the crime of arson and the definition of dwelling house be defined as at common law. . . . We hold that the house burned in the present case was not a dwelling house. Therefore, the defendants could not be charged with arson. . . . . A review of the history of the felony murder statute and the crime of arson reveals the legislative intent to retain the common-law definition of arson for purposes of constructing the felony murder statute. The common-law definition of arson referred only to the burning of another's dwelling house and appurtenances. At common law, the structure burned must be a habitable dwelling. The house at issue in the present case was not a dwelling house. . . . .

D. Summary

First-degree arson is considered a very serious crime because it threatens human life. The highest level of *mens rea* (intent), and the greatest likelihood that someone will be harmed (occupied dwelling house) are elements of first-degree arson. Other forms of arson include other types of buildings and lower levels of *mens rea* (recklessness). We will conclude this section by using the common law elements of arson with the understanding that these elements are most similar to first-degree arson. Any particular state, however, may include other forms of structures (other than dwellings) and/or other forms of *mens rea* (other than malicious).

> Arson
> (A/R) setting fire to; dwelling; of another
> (M/R) malicious (intentional)

§ 7.3 Malicious Mischief (Criminal Mischief)

A. Common Law

Although there is some doubt concerning whether **malicious mischief** was a crime at common law in England, a number of very early cases enforced it as a common law crime.[20] The crime commonly known as malicious mischief is difficult to define, because the name is applied to acts varying widely as to terms, phraseology, and purpose. Generally, it has been defined as the willful and unlawful injury to or destruction of the property of another with the malicious intent to injure the owner.

---

[19] Michigan v. Reeves, 528 N.W.2d 160 (1995).
[20] State v. Watts, 48 Ark. 56, 2 S.W. 342 (1886); State v. Manuel, 72 N.C. 201, 21 Am. Rep. 455 (1875).

It is distinguished from arson in that forms of destruction other than fire are included and statutes cover personal property as well as dwellings. The elements of the crime of malicious mischief vary, but the common elements are described as follows. Failure to prove every element constitutes a complete defense.[21]

1. Malice

Malice is generally held to be an essential ingredient of the offense of malicious mischief. The name itself implies that malice must be proved. Malice can be thought of as *intent to do harm.*

2. Injury or Destruction

At common law, either an injury to or destruction of property suffices as the *actus reus* of the offense.[22] Modern statutes require that the damage be measured by monetary damages and reach some minimum level.

3. Property of Another

While in some jurisdictions malicious mischief may be committed as to personal property only, in others, real property as well as personal property can be the subject of the offense. In any event, it is necessary to prove that the property belonged to another person.

B. *Model Penal Code*

The Model Penal Code section is titled "Criminal Mischief" rather than "Malicious Mischief." The Model Code takes the approach of consolidating the form of malicious mischief provisions of various statutes and even the common law into a single comprehensive offense.

§ 220.3 Criminal Mischief[23]

(1) Offense Defined. A person is guilty of criminal mischief if he:
   (a) damages tangible property of another purposely, recklessly, or by negligence in the employment of fire, explosives, or other dangerous means listed in § 220.2(1); or
   (b) purposely or recklessly tampers with tangible property of another so as to endanger person or property; or
   (c) purposely or recklessly causes another to suffer pecuniary loss by deception or threat.
(2) Grading. Criminal mischief is a felony of the third degree if the actor purposely causes pecuniary loss in excess of $5,000, or a substantial interruption or impairment of public communication, transportation, supply of water, gas or power, or

---

[21] State v. Minor, 17 N.D. 454, 117 N.W. 528 (1908).
[22] State v. Watts, 48 Ark. 56, 2 S.W. 342 (1886).
[23] MODEL PENAL CODE § 220.3 (1985).

[handwritten margin note: vol act has been committed w/o legal excuse or justification.]

other public service. It is a misdemeanor if the actor purposely causes pecuniary loss in excess of $100, or a petty misdemeanor if he purposely or recklessly causes pecuniary loss in excess of $25. Otherwise criminal mischief is a violation.

Section (1)(a) reaches purposeful or reckless damage to the tangible property of another, as well as negligent damage caused by dangerous instrumentalities. Section (1)(b) expands the traditional offense to include tampering with another's property so as to endanger the person or property, and § (1)(c) adds a penalty for purposely or recklessly damaging personal property and causing another to suffer pecuniary loss by deception or threat. As in the traditional offense of malicious mischief, the Model Code offense differs from the theft, forgery, and fraud provisions in that the focus is not upon the misappropriation of property, but rather upon its destruction.

C. State Statutes, Codes, and Cases

Legislation in many states expands upon the common law crime of malicious mischief in defining particular types of malicious mischief. While the original crime related only to *personal* property, some legislation enlarged the definition to include malicious injury or destruction of *real* property (real estate), including trees, mines, coal, and even tobacco plants. The legislatures apparently responded to needs as they arose in particular jurisdictions. The grade of the offense of malicious mischief and the amount of punishment are ordinarily prescribed by the statute. These are usually determined on the basis of the amount of injury or damage inflicted, or by the value of the property injured or destroyed.

Some of the state statutes have followed the Model Penal Code approach of consolidating the former malicious mischief provisions into a single comprehensive offense or an integrated series of related offenses. Other codes integrate a series of related offenses into a single crime. Still others retain parts of the old approach to criminal mischief.

An example of a statute that consolidates former malicious mischief and similar crimes into two sections is that of Missouri.

§ 569.100 Property damage in the first degree[24]

(1) A person commits the crime of property damage in the first degree if:
    (a) He knowingly damages property of another to an extent exceeding seven hundred and fifty dollars; or
    (b) He damages property to an extent exceeding one thousand dollars for the purpose of defrauding an insurer.
(2) Property damage in the first degree is a Class D felony.

---

[24]   MO. REV. STAT. § 569.100 (2002).

§ 569.120 Property damage in the second degree

(1) A person commits the crime of property damage in the second degree if:
    (a) He knowingly damages property of another; or
    (b) He damages property for the purpose of defrauding an insurer.
(2) Property damage in the second degree is a Class B misdemeanor.

As with the common law and the Model Penal Code, the Missouri statute requires property to be damaged. The *mens rea* is *knowing* (which can be thought of as general intent—the prosecutor must prove the actor knew he was doing an act that would cause the damage). In the Missouri statute, a person may be convicted of the offense even if they damage their own property if it is for the purpose of defrauding an insurer (but the required cost of damage is higher). In interpreting § 569.100 of the Missouri statutes, the Missouri courts agreed that although there must be some evidence of injury to property to sustain a conviction for property damage, the damage need only be slight. The damage can be to an automobile.[25]

1. Malice

In general, the *mens rea* for malicious mischief is "malicious," which can be equated to general intent. As we saw earlier, Missouri defined the *mens rea* requirement as *knowing* rather than *intentional*. On the other hand, Massachusetts requires that the defendants' conduct be motivated by cruelty, hostility, or revenge.[26] Reckless or criminally negligent actions that result in the destruction of personal or real property of another are covered in state statutes as less serious forms of criminal mischief or by other statutes.

2. Injury or Destruction

In a Montana case, the defendant was found guilty of violating the criminal mischief statute after a police car was blown up by explosives. Evidence that a particular brand of safety fuse and dynamite had been used, that the defendant had access to such safety fuses and dynamite through his employer, that the employer was missing large amounts of blasting caps and fuses, and that the defendant confided to a friend that he had blown up the police car was sufficient to justify conviction.[27]

The amount of damage determines the degree, or the class, of the crime. If the amount of damage is an element of the crime, then evidence must be introduced to indicate that the damage resulted from the acts of the defendant. This may be shown by cost of repair, by diminution in value, or by replacement costs.

---

[25]   In the Interest of V.H., 655 S.W.2d 833 (Mo. 1983); State v. Walker, 755 S.W.2d 404 (Mo. 1988).
[26]   Commonwealth v. Lauzier, 760 N.E.2d 1256 (Mass. 2002).
[27]   State v. Wolfe, 821 P.2d 339 (Mont. 1991).

3. Property of Another

One of the continuing issues in the prosecution of malicious mischief is when property is shared. In this case, typically the actor who damages shared property will be guilty of a crime. For instance, evidence was sufficient to support a conviction for second-degree malicious mischief when a police officer testified that the defendant's wife reported that the defendant broke a mirror, a birdcage, and other household items after an argument, and that she estimated the total amount of damage to be $620.66.[28]

4. Related Statutes

Vandalism and **criminal mischief** cover similar types of behaviors. The Model Penal Code does not have a separate crime of vandalism, nor was there such a crime under common law. An example of a vandalism statute is that of Ohio, which provides

§ 2909.05 Vandalism.[29]

(A) No person shall knowingly cause serious physical harm to an occupied structure or any of its contents.

(B) (1) No person shall knowingly cause serious physical harm to property that is owned or possessed by another, when either of the following applies:

   (a) The property is used by its owner or possessor in his profession, business, trade, or occupation, and the value of the property or the amount of physical harm involved is five hundred dollars or more;

   (b) Regardless of the value of the property or the amount of damage done, the property or its equivalent is necessary in order for its owner or possessor to engage in the owner's or possessor's profession, business, trade, or occupation.

This section of the Ohio statute contains the usual provisions prohibiting vandalism. This would be the crime charged for breaking windows in a home, destroying furniture, or causing other damage, making it temporarily unusable or requiring a substantial amount of time, effort, or money to repair the damage. This section also embraces a relatively new concept: that of knowingly causing serious harm to property used in or necessary to the occupation of its owner or possessor. Examples of this type of violation include rifling and scattering case files of an attorney, damaging the samples of a traveling salesperson, or destroying a plumber's tools. Other states have vandalism statutes that cover public buildings and/or churches.[30]

D. Summary

Although the elements of malicious mischief are fairly simple, the specific definition and interpretation of them may vary widely from state to state.

---

[28] State v. Coria, 48 P.3d 980 (Wash. 2002).

[29] OHIO REV. CODE ANN. § 2909.05 (Anderson 2002).

[30] 18 Pa. Cons. Stat. Ann. 3307(a) 2001.

Malicious Mischief (Criminal Mischief)
(A/R) injury or destruction; of property; of another
(M/R) malicious (knowing)

§ 7.4   Trespass (Criminal Trespass)

The next three sections deal with three sequentially more serious crimes: trespass, breaking and entering, and burglary. It is helpful to think of these crimes as building blocks with elements added to the *actus reus* and *mens rea* for each successively more serious crime.

A. Common Law

At common law, **trespass** had a much different meaning than the generally used definition today. In its broadest sense, it encompassed any misfeasance, transgression, or offense that damaged another's person, health, reputation, or property.[31] However, at common law, trespass referred to the remedy, not the offense. An *action of trespass* was the proper remedy to recover damages when the injury consisted of damage to personal property or real property. Where the trespass was an intrusion upon the real property of another, the writ was known as *trespass quare clausum fregit*.[32] Generally, the *action in trespass* was a civil action to recover damages.

At common law, every man's land was deemed to be enclosed, so that every unwarrantable entry on such land necessarily carried with it some damages for which the trespasser was civilly liable. Civil action in trespass is for money damages, and because every unauthorized entry onto the land of another infers some damages, nominal damages were recoverable even though there was no substantial damage to the property. When there was damage to realty from the trespass, actual damages were awarded.

While at common law most of the trespass actions were civil actions, certain acts of trespass that were accompanied by a breach of the peace were regarded as crimes. However, it seems clear from a study of the cases that every trespass that was the subject of a civil action was not an indictable offense. Where criminal trespass actions were authorized at common law, the definition of trespass was more precise, and the mere invasion of private property without a disturbance of the peace was not considered a crime.[33]

B. Model Penal Code

The Model Penal Code represents the modern view that entry onto another's property with notice that was one is not invited or permitted is a crime.

---

[31]   Cox v. Strickland, 120 Ga. 104, 47 S.E. 912 (1904).
[32]   3 Street, Foundations of Legal Liability 229 *et seq.* (1980).
[33]   State v. Wheeler, 3 Vt. 344, 23 Am. Dec. 212 (1830).

§ 221.2 Criminal Trespass[34]

(1) Buildings and Occupied Structures. A person commits an offense if, knowing that he is not licensed or privileged to do so, he enters or surreptitiously remains in any building or occupied structure, or separately secured or occupied portion thereof. An offense under this Subsection is a misdemeanor if it is committed in a dwelling at night. Otherwise it is a petty misdemeanor.

(2) Defiant Trespasser. A person commits an offense if, knowing that he is not licensed or privileged to do so, he enters or remains in any place as to which notice against trespass is given by:
    (a) actual communication to the actor; or
    (b) posting in a manner prescribed by law or reasonably likely to come to the attention of intruders; or
    (c) fencing or other enclosure manifestly designed to exclude intruders.
    An offense under this subsection constitutes a petty misdemeanor if the offender defies an order to leave that is personally communicated to him or her by the owner of the premises or another authorized person. Otherwise it is a violation.

(3) Defenses. It is an affirmative defense to prosecution under this Section that:
    (a) a building or occupied structure involved in an offense under Subsection (1) was abandoned; or
    (b) the premises were at the time open to members of the public and the actor complied with all lawful conditions imposed on access to or remaining in the premises; or
    (c) the actor reasonably believed that the owner of the premises, or other person empowered to license access thereto, would have licensed him to enter or remain.

Under the provisions of the Model Penal Code, the prosecution must first show that the actor knowingly intruded into a place where he knew he was not licensed or privileged to be. As indicated in subsection (1), the trespass is aggravated if committed at night. If at night, it is a misdemeanor, while at any other time it is a petty misdemeanor. Subsection (2) deals with the person who enters or remains on property after some form of notice has been communicated. Communication may be actual or by posting or fencing. This provision carries over some of the provisions of previous statutes.

It is noted also that the grading of the offense is determined partly by whether the surreptitious entry is into an occupied building or "any place as to which notice against trespass is given." Model Code § 221.2 also lists affirmative defenses.

C. *State Statutes, Codes, and Cases*

State statutes make certain acts of trespass punishable as crimes, but they have been construed somewhat strictly. For example, where a statute states that the charge will be valid only after a person has been ordered to depart, the prosecution must introduce evidence to show that there was such an order. Criminal trespass, as it has developed, usually covers only impermissible entries into a structure or "premises";

---

[34]   Model Penal Code § 221.2 (1985).

however, the definitions are very broad and have been interpreted to include warehouses, docks, wharfs, and the curtilage of structures.

During the 1960s and early 1970s, many trespassing statutes were found to be unconstitutional as conflicting with the First Amendment when they were applied to public buildings.[35] However, in the case of *Hudgens v. National Labor Relations Board*, handed down in 1976, the Supreme Court decided that shopping center owners are not constitutionally compelled to allow the use of property for demonstrations by members of the public.[36] Also, generally, private property is not constitutionally available for picketing, handbilling, marching, and other such activities unless the owner is willing to voluntarily submit to this use. It should also be noted, however, that the Supreme Court has held, in *Pruneyard Shopping Center v. Robins*, that state constitutions may recognize greater First Amendment rights of demonstrators than the federal Constitution.[37] This case provided in Part II of this textbook deals with a California case.

> **Case Note: *Pruneyard Shopping Center v. Robins* 447 U.S. 74 (1980)**
> Whose First Amendment rights were evaluated in this case?
> Why did the Supreme Court decide that the shopping center must allow reasonable accommodations to those seeking petition signatures?

The Texas Penal Code provides

§ 30.05 Criminal Trespass[38]

(a) A person commits an offense if he enters or remains on property or in a building of another without effective consent and he:
   (1) had notice that the entry was forbidden; or
   (2) received notice to depart but failed to do so.
(b) For purposes of this Section:
   (1) "Entry" means the intrusion of the entire body.
   (2) "Notice" means:
      (A) oral or written communication by the owner or someone with apparent authority to act for the owner;
      (B) fencing or other enclosure obviously designed to exclude intruders or to contain livestock;
      (C) a sign or signs posted on the property or at the entrance to the building, reasonably likely to come to the attention of intruders, indicating that entry is forbidden;
      (D) the placement of identifying purple paint marks on trees or posts on the property, provided that the marks are:
         (i) vertical lines of not less than eight inches in length and not less than one inch in width;
         (ii) placed so that the bottom of the mark is not less than three feet from the ground or more than five feet from the ground; and

---

[35] *See* Kanovitz & Kanovitz, Constitutional Law (10th ed. 2006).
[36] 424 U.S. 507, 96 S. Ct. 1029, 47 L. Ed. 2d 196 (1976).
[37] Pruneyard Shopping Center v. Robins, 447 U.S. 74 (1980).
[38] Tex. Penal Code Ann. § 30.05 (Vernon 2002); Daniels v. State, 633 S.W.2d 899 (Tex. 1982).

          (iii) placed at locations that are readily visible to any person approaching the property and no more than:
             (a) 100 feet apart on forest land; or
             (b) 1,000 feet apart on land other than forest land; or
       (E) the visible presence on the property of a crop grown for human consumption that is under cultivation, in the process of being harvested, or marketable if harvested at the time of entry.
     (3) "Shelter center" has the meaning assigned by Section 51.002(1), Human Resources Code.
   (c) It is a defense to prosecution under this Section that the actor at the time of the offense was a fire fighter or emergency medical services personnel, as that term is defined by Section 773.003, Health and Safety Code, acting in the lawful discharge of an official duty under exigent circumstances.
   (d) An offense under this section is a Class B misdemeanor unless it is committed in a habitation or a shelter center or unless the actor carries a deadly weapon on or about his person during the commission of the offense, in which event it is a Class A misdemeanor.

Under Texas law, the elements of the offense of criminal trespass are the following: (1) a person; (2) without effective consent; (3) enters or remains on property or in the building of another; (4) knowingly, intentionally, or recklessly; (5) when he or she had notice that entry was forbidden or received notice to depart but failed to do so. Where the trespass is on land or into a building, there is no violation unless notice was given that the entry was forbidden and the actor entered without "effective consent." Subsection (b)(2) establishes five methods of giving notice.

The Texas Code has been challenged on two constitutional grounds: the First Amendment to the Constitution and the "void for vagueness" issue. One Texas court found that the statute, as enforced, did not violate the First Amendment to the Constitution, when the defendant was charged with trespassing after distributing anti-abortion booklets to high school students while he was standing on the sidewalk inside the school campus.[39]

A second Texas appeals court held that the use of the undefined term "remain," in this section, which defines the crime as entering or remaining on property of another without effective consent, does not render the section vague, because the term "remain" can be construed according to its ordinary usage, as meaning to "stay," and thus a stay of any length of time after entry satisfies the "remain" requirement.[40]

The statutes in some states have strict requirements that must be met before a criminal action can be brought against a person for trespass. California prohibits "entering upon uncultivated or unenclosed lands where signs forbidding trespass are displayed" at intervals not less than three to the mile along all exterior boundaries and at all trails and roads entering the land.[41]

---

[39]   Reed v. State, 762 S.W.2d 640 (Tex. 1988).
[40]   Hernandez v. State, 783 S.W.2d 764 (Tex. 1990).
[41]   CAL. PENAL CODE ch. 720. § 5/21-3 (2002).

There is no trespass when the possessor has consented to the entry. But for the purposes of criminal trespass, a parent-owner of premises has a superior interest in the home to that of an unemancipated minor residing there and the parent's withdrawal of authority to enter the home supersedes any authority a minor may have to invite others to enter the home.[42] Actual notice generally is not required when an enclosure manifestly is designed to exclude intruders such as, for example, a home. In addition, a few states add a fourth element: a specific intent to enter for some unlawful purpose, which makes trespass similar to burglary.[43]

LEGAL NEWS: OCCUPY WALL STREET, SEATTLE, OAKLAND, ...

In 2011 similar protests began around the country by those who objected to the Wall Street "bailout" that was supposed to avert an economic collapse due to the activities of derivatives trading. Protesters camped out in parks and in front of city hall in New York City, Portland, Seattle, Oakland, Austin, and other cities across the country. Although public officials allowed the protests to continue for several weeks, eventually most cities forced the protesters to move using trespass, no-camping, or other city ordinances. It is not a violation of First Amendment rights to put reasonable limits on rights to protest and, if individuals disobey these regulations, trespass occurs, even if the location is a public park or public building.

D. Summary

The common law definition of trespass was more often related to a civil action taken to recover damages for unwarranted entry onto one's property. However, there were occasions when the trespass could be a crime. The modern crime of trespass generally include the elements listed below; however, many statutes require notice (posted signs) to prove the "without consent" element. Further, Supreme Court cases have restricted the ability to define and prosecute trespass when the entry is to a "public" place.

Trespass
(A/R) entry onto property (land or building); owned by another; without consent
(M/R) knowing

---

[42] People v. Long, 669 N.E.2d 1237 (Ill. 1996).
[43] GA. CODE ANN. § 16-7-21(b) (2002).

§ 7.5 Breaking and Entering

A. Common Law

There was no separate crime of **breaking and entering** under common law, although these elements were part of the *actus reus* of burglary, or the act might have been punished under trespass.

B. Model Penal Code

The Model Penal Code does not have a separate crime defined as breaking and entering; however, trespass covers the circumstances in which an offender enters the home or building of another, knowing they do not have permission to do so. This comprises the "entry" element of breaking and entering, but some states are more specific in their distinction between trespass and breaking and entering.

C. State Statutes, Codes, and Cases

All of the states have enacted legislation to provide punishment for offenses that do not meet the definition of common law burglary. Some statutes provide a penalty for breaking and entering, which is considered more serious than simple trespass but less serious than burglary.

§ 2911.13 Breaking and Entering.[44]

(A) No person by force, stealth, or deception, shall trespass in an unoccupied structure, with purpose to commit therein any theft offense as defined in § 2913.01 of the Revised Code, or any felony.

(B) No person shall trespass on the land or premises of another, with purpose to commit a felony.

(C) Whoever violates this Section is guilty of breaking and entering, a felony of the fifth degree.

The purpose of this Ohio statute is to establish a violation when all of the elements of burglary are not present. An offense similar to burglary is defined, except that the structure involved is unoccupied rather than occupied. This is classified as a felony of the fifth degree, the rationale being that there is comparatively less risk of personal harm.

Other state statutes add additional aggravating factors. For example, in Oregon, being armed with a burglar's tool is an aggravating factor. In Puerto Rico, a higher penalty is available when force is used to enter. [45]

The rationale of having a breaking and entering crime separate from burglary and separate from trespass is that trespass is often a misdemeanor and covers entry onto

---

[44] OHIO REV. CODE ANN. §§ 2911.11 (Anderson 1999).

[45] OR. REV. STAT. § 164.225 (1999); P.R. LAWS ANN. tit. 33 § 4277 (1992).

land (not homes), and entry or remaining in a building without any degree of force required to enter (i.e., through an open door or remaining in a place beyond the parameters of one's permission to do so). Breaking and entering implies a greater property intrusion. It covers situations in which the offender took steps to actually break through the property's boundary protections (i.e., by getting through a window or door). The only thing, in fact, that is different between breaking and entering and burglary is the inability to prove the specific intent to commit a crime inside the dwelling.

D. Summary

Breaking and entering did not exist under common law and is not a separate crime under the Model Code; however, some states have chosen to distinguish breaking and entering from simple trespass to cover situations that are more serious than trespass, but do not meet the technical definition of burglary. While many states utilize the elements of breaking and entering as a more serious grade of trespass, the general elements are as follows.

> Breaking and Entering
> (A/R) breaking and entering; of a building; of another
> (M/R) general intent

§ 7.6   Burglary

A. Common Law

One of the most serious crimes in practically every society is the crime of **burglary**. Burglary is considered more serious than crimes such as larceny, due to the possible injuries to people within the dwelling and the fact that the courts and legislative bodies have long looked upon the home as deserving special protection. According to one court, the crime is against possession and is primarily intended to protect the sanctity of one's home, especially at night when peace, solitude, and safety are most desired and expected. From early times, burglary was considered a felony and at one time was punishable by death.[46]

The term *burglary* is a combination of the Saxon term "burg," meaning *house*, and "laron," meaning *theft*.[47] Burglary was defined in one early case in the following way:

> "Burglary" is the breaking into a house in the night season with intent to commit a felony, and if a house is so entered, it is burglary, whether the felony be executed or not, and regardless of the kind of felony intended or the manner in which the felony may be frustrated, or the value of the property taken, or any other circumstance which is not intrinsic.[48]

---

[46]   State v. Brooks, 277 S.C. 111, 283 S.E.2d 830 (1981); State v. Allison, 169 N.C. 375, 85 S.E. 129 (1915).

[47]   Anderson v. State, 48 Ala. 665, 17 Am. Rep. 36 (1872).

[48]   Conrad v. State, 75 Ohio St. 52, 78 N.E. 957 (1906).

The common law crime of "burglary" was an offense against the habitation, and the essential elements were the following: a breaking; and entry; of a dwelling house; of another; in the nighttime; with intent to commit a felony therein.

1. Breaking

In order to meet this element, the prosecution must prove that some *breaking [in]* of the structure, either actual or constructive, occurred. Breaking consists of putting aside a part of the house that obstructs the entrance and is closed, or in penetrating an opening that is as much closed as the nature of the case admits. The law puts a premium upon a reasonable degree of care in acting to prevent burglaries by closing doors, windows, and other openings. Therefore, under the common law, an entry through an open door or window would not complete this element, even if there was intent to commit a felony.[49]

The early courts did, however, recognize "constructive breaking." To constitute this element, the breaking could be by an entry effected through fraud, or by threat or intimidation. An example is where the defendant pretended that he had business with the owner of the house and gained entry.[50]

2. Entry

An entry is also necessary to constitute the crime of burglary. A breaking without entry is not burglary, but an entry, however slight after breaking, is sufficient; for example, where a head, a hand, an arm, a foot, or even a finger is thrust within the house.[51] In the case of *People v. Peddinger*, the breaking of the window of a service station by the defendant and insertion of an arm into the building was sufficient "entry" in a burglary prosecution.[52] And in the case of *People v. Davis*, the court held that it is not the size of the hole that determines whether an entry was made, but whether a hand or instrument was actually inserted into the hole for the purpose of committing the felony.[53]

3. Dwelling House

At common law, and under many statutes, breaking and entering, to constitute burglary, must be of a dwelling house. The dwelling house has been defined as any kind of structure used as a place of habitation and occupied by persons other than the defendant. Temporary absence of the occupant will not deprive the dwelling house of its character as such. It is not necessary to prove that the owner or occupant or some

---

[49]   Adair v. State, 19 Ala. App. 174, 95 So. 827 (1923); State v. Petit, 32 Wash. 129, 72 P. 1021 (1903); People v. Webber, 138 Cal. 145, 70 P. 1089 (1902).

[50]   Davis v. Commonwealth, 132 Va. 521, 110 S.E. 356 (1922); Johnson v. Commonwealth, 85 Pa. 54, 27 Am. Rep. 622 (1877); Nichols v. State, 68 Wis. 416, 32 N.W. 543 (1887).

[51]   Penman v. State, 163 Ind. App. 583, 325 N.E.2d 478 (1975).

[52]   94 Cal. App. 297, 271 P. 132 (1928); *see also* Commonwealth v. Myers, 223 Pa. Super. 75, 297 A.2d 151 (1972).

[53]   People v. Davis, 3 Ill. App. 3d 738, 279 N.E.2d 179 (1972).

member of the family was in the house at the time of the burglary, but the house, although furnished as a dwelling house, loses its character as such for purposes of burglary if the occupant leaves it without the intention to return. The house must be occupied as a dwelling and not merely be suitable or intended for such purpose.[54]

Under the common law, shops, stores, and warehouses, unless they were occupied in part as a dwelling, were not covered under the law against burglary. On the other hand, stables, smokehouses, kitchens, shops, offices, or other outbuildings, if they were within the curtilage of a dwelling house, were regarded as parts of the dwelling so that it was burglary to break and enter them with felonious intent, although there may be no entry into the dwelling house itself.[55]

4. Of Another

Recall that in the case of arson, the law prohibited setting fire to the house of another, but the definition was primarily if it was *occupied* by another, not necessarily *owned* by another. So, for instance, if a landlord set fire to his own home, but others lived in it, it could be charged as arson. The definition of ownership is the same in common law burglary. The law is concerned with the protection of habitation rather than the title to property, consequently with occupancy rather than ownership. Therefore, it is not a question of whether a person actually owns the house that is broken into; possession (who is living in the house) constitutes sufficient ownership in burglary cases.[56]

5. In the Nighttime

At common law, breaking and entering a dwelling house in the daytime was not burglary. According to some decisions, nighttime begins when daylight ends, or when the countenance ceases to be reasonably discernible by the light of the sun, and ends at dawn, or as soon as the countenance becomes discernible.[57]

6. With Intent to Commit a Felony Inside

Burglary is a "specific intent" crime. Breaking and entering of a dwelling of another is not enough to define the act as burglary under common law or modern statutes. The intent to break and enter is not sufficient—there must also be proof that the defendant intended to break and enter with the intent to commit a felony inside. Specific intent may be inferred from the facts. The prosecution must prove that the intent to commit a felony inside existed in the mind of the perpetrator at the moment of entry.[58]

---

[54] Smith v. State, 80 Fla. 315, 85 So. 911 (1920); Henderson v. State, 80 Fla. 491, 86 So. 439 (1920); Carrier v. State, 227 Ind. 726, 89 N.E.2d 74 (1949).

[55] Henderson v. United States, 172 F.2d 289 (D.C. Cir. 1949); State v. Gatewood, 169 Kan. 679, 221 P.2d 392 (1950).

[56] Wilson v. State, 247 Ala. 84, 22 So. 2d 601 (1945).

[57] Ashford v. State, 36 Neb. 38, 53 N.W. 1036 (1893).

[58] People v. Markus, 147 Cal. Rptr. 151, 82 Cal. App. 3d 477 (1978).

The intent must be concurrent with the breaking and entering but may be formed at the moment the breaking occurs. The early courts determined that if the intent does not exist until after the house was entered, there could be no burglary under the common law definition.[59]

Burglary is generally committed with the intent to steal, which is a felony, but the indictment may allege breaking and entering with intent to commit other felonies, such as murder or rape. In any event, the prosecution must introduce evidence to show specific intent on the part of the perpetrator to commit a specific felony. If there was intent to commit a felony inside, and a breaking and entry occurs, then even if the actor abandons the effort once inside, the crime of burglary is complete.[60]

B. Model Penal Code

The Model Penal Code retains much of the common law concept of burglary but simplifies the definition. Instead of a dwelling house, any building can be burglarized. Also, the strict definitions of breaking and entering have been reduced to entry with the intent to commit a crime inside.

§ 221.1 Burglary[61]

(1) Burglary Defined. A person is guilty of burglary if he enters a building or occupied structure, or separately secured or occupied portion thereof, with purpose to commit a crime therein, unless the premises are at the time open to the public or the actor is licensed or privileged to enter. It is an affirmative defense to prosecution for burglary that the building or structure was abandoned.

(2) Grading. Burglary is a felony of the second degree if it is perpetrated in the dwelling of another at night, or if, in the course of committing the offense, the actor:
  (a) purposely, knowingly or recklessly inflicts or attempts to inflict bodily injury on anyone; or
  (b) is armed with explosives or a deadly weapon.
    Otherwise, burglary is a felony of the third degree. An act shall be deemed "in the course of committing" an offense if it occurs in an attempt to commit the offense or in flight after the attempt or commission.

(3) Multiple Convictions. A person may not be convicted both for burglary and for the offense which it was his purpose to commit after the burglarious entry or for an attempt to commit that offense, unless the additional offense constitutes a felony of the first or second degree.

In subsection (2), the factors that accompany the entry and determine the grade of the offense are considered. The common law reasoning that entry at night is more serious than entry in the daytime is carried over into the Model Code. The Model Code does not provide an offense for one who surreptitiously remains on the premises, and apparently the common law definition as to what amounts to entry still prevails.

---

[59] Jackson v. State, 102 Ala. 167, 15 So. 344 (1894).
[60] Schwartz v. State, 114 S.W. 809, 55 Tex. Crim. 36 (1909).
[61] MODEL PENAL CODE § 221.1 (1985).

Under the Model Code, an "occupied structure" is any structure, vehicle, or place adapted for overnight accommodation of persons, or for carrying on business therein, whether or not a person is actually present. Therefore, it is not necessary to allege that the building was occupied. However, the final sentence of subsection (1) provides a defense that would bar prosecution for burglary of abandoned or derelict buildings unsuited and, in fact, unused for human occupancy.

The phrase "purpose to commit a crime therein" differs from that used in common law definitions in that "purpose" is substituted for "intent" and "crime" is substituted for "felony." The word *crime* is defined as "an offense for which a sentence of imprisonment is authorized."

Apparently to forestall any arguments concerning the possibility of double jeopardy, subsection (3) of the Model Code precludes accumulation of penalties for burglary and for the intended offense in all circumstances, except where the offense is itself a felony of the first or second degree. For example, consecutive sentences may be given when a person is convicted of burglary and the purpose was to commit rape, and the elements of rape are also proved by the prosecution. "At night" is defined in the Model Penal Code as "the period thirty minutes past sunset and thirty minutes before sunrise."

C. State Statutes, Codes, and Cases

Generally, state statutes follow the Model Penal Code and are not too different from the common law except that they are more inclusive of the types of offenses that could be covered under a burglary definition. The state of Ohio provides for three related statutes: breaking and entering (which we discussed in the previous section), burglary, and aggravated burglary.

Ohio. § 2911.12 Burglary[62]

(A) No person, by force, stealth or deception, shall do any of the following:
   (1) Trespass in an occupied structure or in a separately secured or separately occupied portion of an occupied structure, when another person other than an accomplice of the offender is present, with purpose to commit in the structure or in the separately secured or separately occupied portion of the structure any criminal offense.
   (2) Trespass in an occupied structure or in a separately secured or separately occupied portion of an occupied structure that is a permanent or temporary habitation of any person when any person other than an accomplice of the offender is present or likely to be present with purpose to commit in the habitation any criminal offense.
   (3) Trespass in an occupied structure or in a separately secured or separately occupied portion of an occupied structure, with purpose to commit in the structure or separately secured or separately occupied portion of the structure any criminal offense.

---

[62]   OHIO REV. CODE ANN. §§ 2911.12 (Anderson 1999).

    (4) Trespass in a permanent or temporary habitation of any person when any person other than an accomplice of the offender is present or likely to be present.

(B) As used in this section, "occupied structure" has the same meaning as in § 2909.01 of the Revised Code.

(C) Whoever violates this section is guilty of burglary. A violation of division (A)(1) or (2) of this section is a felony of the second degree. A violation of division (A)(3) of this section is a felony of the third degree. A violation of division (A)(4) of this section is a felony of the fourth degree.

Note that instead of the nighttime element of common law, the Ohio statute defines burglary and entry when someone else is likely to be present. In interpreting the "likely to be present" provision, the court held that there is no evidence that a person is "likely to be present," for purposes of the statute proscribing burglary, where a burglary occurs during the regular working hours of the homeowner and there is no evidence that the homeowner was in or out or that he or she was likely to return at varying times.[63] The more serious grade of burglary is "aggravated burglary."

§ 2911.11 Aggravated Burglary.[64]

(A) No person, by force, stealth, or deception, shall trespass in an occupied structure as defined in § 2909.01 of the Revised Code, or in a separately secured or separately occupied portion thereof, with purpose to commit therein any theft offense as defined in § 2913.01 of the Revised Code, or any felony, when any of the following apply:

    (1) The offender inflicts, or attempts or threatens to inflict physical harm on another;

    (2) The offender has a deadly weapon or dangerous ordnance as defined in § 2923.11 of the Revised Code on or about his person or under his control;

(B) Whoever violates this Section is guilty of aggravated burglary, a felony of the first degree.

Other state statutory definitions of burglary include the following:

- A person commits the crime of burglary if he knowingly enters or remains unlawfully in a building with the intent to commit a felony therein.[65]
- In order to commit the felony of burglary, a suspect must enter a conveyance or structure without consent and with intent to commit an offense inside.[66]
- To convict a person of the crime of burglary, the state must prove two elements: (1) unlawful breaking and entering; and (2) intent to commit some crime once entry has been gained.[67]

---

[63] State v. Cantin, 726 N.E.2d 565 (Ohio 1999).
[64] OHIO REV. CODE ANN. §§ 2911.13 (Anderson 1999).
[65] Dyson v. State, 722 So. 2d 782 (Ala. 1997).
[66] Nickell v. State, 722 So. 2d 924 (Fla. 1998).
[67] Harrison v. State, 722 So. 2d 681 (Miss. 1998).

Statutes generally criminalize some of the activities that were not covered under common law burglary. We will consider some of these changes below.

1. Breaking

In a number of states, the necessity for "breaking" was omitted and entry alone was sufficient if the required intent was also present.

2. Entry

State statutes also provide a penalty for one who remains unlawfully on premises as well as for one who enters unlawfully. For instance, in one case a police officer was convicted of burglary because he stole several items when investigating a warehouse theft. His presence in the warehouse was defined as unlawfully remaining in the building after his official duties were completed.[68] Similarly to common law, any part of the body is sufficient to be defined as entry. A court in a New York case agreed that testimony that the defendant reached a gloved hand through a broken window to reach an inside doorknob was sufficient to establish an entry in a prosecution for violating a burglary statute. A California court agreed that for purposes of the burglary statute, entry that is just barely inside the premises, even if the area penetrated is small, is sufficient.[69]

3. Dwelling House

Statutes enlarged the scope of the dwelling requirement to include businesses and other buildings, warehouses, shops, offices, barns, and stables. In some states, even if the statute specifies dwelling, it need not be occupied. In one case, the court decided that if the structure initially qualifies under the statutory definition of a dwelling, and its character is not substantially changed to the extent that it becomes unsuitable for lodging by people, it remains a dwelling irrespective of actual occupancy.[70] In Florida, houses under construction are "dwellings" within the meaning of the burglary statute, which define the dwelling as a building of any kind that has a roof over it and was designed to be occupied by people lodging therein at night.[71] In Mississippi, a house was a "dwelling" for purposes of the burglary statute, even though the owner lived there only four months out of the year, because the owner received her mail there and kept her personal property there, indicating her clear intent to return to the house.[72] On the other hand, in California, evidently a house loses its character as a dwelling immediately

---

[68]   People v. Czerminski, 464 N.Y.S.2d 83 (App. Div. 1983).
[69]   People v. Clark, 649 N.Y.S.2d 568 (1996); People v. Valencia, 120 Cal. Rptr. 2d 131, 46 P.3d 970 (2002).
[70]   Perkins v. State, 672 N.E.2d 417 (Ind. 1996).
[71]   Gonzalez v. State, 724 So.2d 126 (Fla. 1998).
[72]   Wilkerson v. State, 724 So.2d 1089 (Miss. 1998).

Case Note: *People v. Ramos 52 Cal. App.4th 300, 60 Cal. Rptr. 2d 523 (1997)*
What were the issue and holding of the case?
Define "dwelling" according to the California statute.
Of what could he be charged and convicted?

upon the death of the occupant. As we see in *People v. Ramos*, a case included in Part II, a burglar can then be charged only with a less serious degree of burglary. [73]

4. Of Another

Generally, modern statutes are interpreted in the same way as the common law. Possession is more important than title. An Ohio court, for instance, concluded that when the defendant took a child from its mother's home after the defendant moved out, he could be convicted of burglary. [74] In this definition of ownership, a landlord could burglarize his own house if he had rented it to someone else, and a man could burglarize his own house if he was legally separated from his spouse and the court had awarded her the use of the family home, or even if she had been exercising custody or control of that dwelling.

5. In the Nighttime

In almost all states, statutes have been enacted to punish those who commit the act in the daytime, as well as at night. In statutes that retain the requirement of nighttime (perhaps, for instance, to define an aggravating factor), they have generally defined nighttime as the period between sunset and sunrise.

6. With Intent to Commit Felony (or Crime) Inside

State statutes differ in regard to the intent to commit a crime element. In some states, the intent to commit a felony is not required, and the intent to commit a misdemeanor is sufficient. The Texas statute requires "an attempt to commit any felony or theft."[75] To obtain a burglary conviction, a state must prove that the defendant intended to commit an independent crime other than trespass after an illegal entry into a building. However, it is not element of burglary that the victim's property be taken. For example, a New York court held that burglary requires only the intent to commit a crime inside the dwelling.[76] Intent to commit a crime in the building can be inferred from circumstances of the breaking and entering. In the case described in the following Legal

---

[73] People v. Ramos, 52 Cal. App. 4th 300, 60 Cal. Rptr. 523 (1997).
[74] State v. Hill, 75 Ohio St. 3d 195, 661 N.E.2d 1068 (1996).
[75] TEX. PENAL CODE ANN. § 30.02 (1999); White v. State, 630 S.W.2d 340 (Tex. 1982).
[76] Briecke v. New York, 936 F. Supp. 78 (E.D.N.Y. 1996).

News box, the circumstances generally support a burglary charge, but if the intent was to commit theft, why did he curl up for a nap under a desk?

LEGAL NEWS: SPECIFIC INTENT?

On June 16, 2006 it was reported that Michael Pickens, the son of billionaire T. Boone Pickens, was found sleeping under a desk of a fly-fishing shop by the owner who had just discovered that the shop had been broken into and that $3,000 worth of merchandise had been placed in a cooler. He was under indictment for securities fraud violations at the time of the incident. The police charged him with burglary.

Source: Retrieved on June 29, 2006 from http://www.msnbc.msn.com/id/13368639/.

---

7. Other Issues

In some states, the defendant may be charged with and convicted of a higher degree of burglary, such as aggravated burglary, if the entrance was by force; if the defendant purposely, knowingly, or recklessly inflicted or attempted to inflict bodily injury; or if the person entering the premises was armed. Some states have added the crime of "burglary of a motor vehicle." Breaking into a car to steal it or steal the contents inside does not meet the *actus reus* of burglary because it is not a structure, nor does it meet the definition of larceny if the perpetrator is caught before a theft can occur. Therefore states have either enlarged their definition of burglary to include automobiles, or they have created this statutory crime.

D. Summary

Although there are differences in wording and interpretation of the elements of burglary among the states, in general, the elements are the same as the common law except that in the majority of states: (a) a dwelling has been generously defined and can include businesses or other buildings; and (b) burglary can occur during the daytime.

Burglary
(A/R) breaking and entering (or remaining in; and sometimes no breaking); of a dwelling or building; of another; with intent to commit a felony (or crime) inside
(M/R) specific intent

§ 7.7   Causing or Risking Catastrophe

A. Common Law

This crime did not exist under the common law.

B. *Model Penal Code*

The Model Penal Code defines as criminal behavior that which causes or has a high likelihood of causing a "catastrophe" (which is also defined in the statute).

§ 220.2 Causing or Risking Catastrophe[77]

(1) Causing Catastrophe
   A person who causes a catastrophe by explosion, fire, flood, avalanche, collapse of a building, release of poisonous gas, radioactive material, or other harmful force or substance, or by any other means of causing potentially widespread injury or damage, commits a felony of the second degree if he does so purposely or knowingly, or a felony of the third degree if he does so recklessly.
(2) Risking Catastrophe
   A person is guilty of a misdemeanor if he recklessly creates a risk of catastrophe in the employment of fire, explosives or other dangerous means listed in Subsection (1).

   Under the provisions of subsection (1), if a person purposely or knowingly causes a catastrophe by one of the specified means or by any other means of causing potentially widespread injury or damage, the offense is a second degree felony. However, if the action is reckless rather than purposeful or knowing, the offense is a third degree felony.

The crime is divided into two sections; the first covering situations in which a catastrophe did occur; and the second covers situations in which the offender risked a catastrophe by his behavior, but it did not occur. The *mens rea* is either intentional, knowing, or reckless.

C. *State Statutes, Codes and Cases*

Several states have statutes similar to the Model Penal Code that provide a penalty for the specific wrong of causing or risking a catastrophe.[78] The purpose of such statutes is to punish those who purposely, knowingly, or recklessly bring about a catastrophe.

D. *Summary*

The elements of the crime have been suggested by the Model Penal Code, and thus we will use it to specify the elements.

Causing or Risking Catastrophe
(A/R) cause or risk catastrophe by explosion, fire, flood, avalanche, collapse of a building, release of poisonous gas, radioactive material, or other harmful force or substance
(M/R) purposely, knowingly, recklessly

---

[77]   Model Penal Code § 220.2.
[78]   Among the states having statutes of this type are Alaska, Ark., Me., Mo., N.J., N.D., Pa., Utah, Vt., and W. Va.

§ 7.8   Summary

Under common law, offenses against the home were considered extremely serious offenses. Arson and burglary are two examples of common law crimes that received the death penalty in early England and the colonies. Common law arson was defined as the willful and malicious burning of the dwelling house of another. Modern statutes, however, provide punishment for burning structures other than dwellings and provide a penalty when a person burns his or her own house or property in order to defraud an insurer.

Another property destruction crime is malicious mischief, sometimes designated "criminal mischief." It is generally defined as the willful and unlawful injury to or destruction of the property of another with malicious intent to injure the owner. The more recent codes consolidate many of the former malicious mischief provisions that were enacted to meet the needs of society at the time into a single comprehensive offense or an integrated series of related offenses. Vandalism is a similar crime and may be used in addition to or instead of criminal mischief in a state's penal code.

At common law, trespass was the civil remedy to recover damages when the injury consisted of damage to personal property or real property. However, in addition, certain acts of trespass were considered crimes. Trespass can be defined as an unlawful intrusion upon the real property of another without the other's consent. Many states have enacted specific trespass statutes to prohibit willful and unlawful entry upon the premises of another for certain purposes. All states currently have provisions prohibiting entering or remaining on property without the consent of the owner. Some require that notice be given that entry is forbidden, and some require that a specific intent to enter for some unlawful purpose be proved. In some statutes, one requirement is that a fence be constructed or that the trespasser be ordered off the property before any action can be taken.

Another crime that was and is considered very serious is burglary. At common law, the crime consisted of breaking and entering into the dwelling house of another in the night with the intent to commit a felony therein. Most states today have enlarged the definition to include other types of buildings and to include the intent to commit a misdemeanor therein. Also, many statutes do not require the breaking and entering to occur at night. The grade of the crime is determined by such factors as the time the crime was perpetrated (day or night), whether bodily injury was inflicted or attempted purposely or knowingly, and whether the person was armed or unarmed. Most states today provide a penalty for breaking and entering structures, including homes and other buildings, when the intent to commit a crime inside cannot be proven.

Other state statutes provide penalties for offenses of which property damage is the main thrust. For instance, the Model Penal Code suggested the crime of "Causing or Risking a Catastrophe."

REVIEW QUESTIONS

1. What are the four elements of the common law crime of arson?
2. Define *dwelling*. Is an abandoned house a dwelling? What is meant by *curtilage*? Define *burning*.
3. When can one be convicted of arson for burning one's own house down?
4. How did the MPC change the common law definitions of arson?
5. In modern statutes, is it a crime to burn down structures other than dwellings? What factors affect the seriousness of various types of burning?
6. Define *malicious mischief* (provide the *mens rea* as well) and distinguish it from larceny and arson. Give some examples of criminal mischief.
7. Describe the crime of vandalism.
8. Would destroying shared property (i.e., a husband or wife destroys marital property) support a charge of criminal mischief or vandalism?
9. The crime of burglary can be thought of as the most serious of a sequence of property intrusions—what is the sequence?
10. Explain *trespass quare clausum fregit*.
11. What are the elements of modern criminal trespass? What is the *mens rea* required by most trespass statutes?
12. In the 1976 case of *Hudgens v. National Labor Relations Board*, the Supreme Court of the United States was asked to determine the constitutionality of a trespass statute protecting a shopping center (which arguably is also a type of public place). What was the decision of the Court in regard to the constitutionality of such a statute?
13. The modern crime of breaking and entering is often available when which element of burglary cannot be proven?
14. The common law crime of burglary was very technical. In order to find a person guilty of burglary, it was necessary to prove many elements. What are the elements of the common law crime of burglary?
15. Under the common law, only one type of building was protected under burglary statutes—what was it? How is it defined?
16. What constitutes *breaking* under common law burglary definitions?
17. What constitutes *entry* under most burglary statutes? Is reaching into a building through an open window considered *breaking*?
18. Under the common law, an indictment for burglary must allege a specific intent to commit a particular felony. What is meant by specific intent, as used in burglary cases?
19. The Model Penal Code, in defining the offense of burglary, carries over some of the concepts of the common law. However, the grade of the crime of burglary is determined by several factors. What are those factors? At what point must the intent exist?
20. Define the crime of "causing or risking a catastrophe."

Offenses Involving Theft and Deception

8

Chapter Outline

Cases

Robbery: *Lattimore v. United States*, 684 A.2d 357 (D.C. App. 1996).
Extortion: *Ohio v. Cunningham*, No. 08-CA-09 (Ohio App., October 3, 2008)

asportation	forgery
caption	joyriding
carjacking	identity theft
cheats	larceny
commercial bribery	legal efficacy
computer-related crimes	puffery
conversion	real property
criminal simulation	receipt of stolen property
embezzlement	robbery
extortion	theft by deception
false advertising	theft of services
false pretenses	trespass
fiduciary relationship	uttering

§ 8.1   Introduction

All societies have laws or rules that are designed to protect property against theft. In the United States, theft offenses make up the great majority of crimes, and criminal justice personnel spend much of their time investigating crimes that relate to theft. Although statutes have changed the common law, it is essential that the history of theft crimes be studied in order to understand the terminology and the elements that make up the various crimes relating to theft.

At early common law in England, larceny was the only form of theft that was criminally punishable. Because the offense became more and more narrowly construed, many forms of deception were not commonly regarded as criminal. Citizens relied upon civil law to correct wrongs that did not come within the technical definition of larceny. However, as commerce increased, the criminal law was expanded to punish other forms of theft, such as embezzlement, theft by false pretenses, and extortion. In England, various types of cheating were made crimes under the early common law. For example, in 1511, it was a crime to add oil or water to woolcloth or to overstretch cloth. In 1541, a statute was enacted in England that made it a crime to counterfeit letters or privy tokens or to receive money or goods in other men's names. On the other hand, early courts and legislatures hesitated to make simple dishonesty in business a crime, reasoning that a certain amount of dishonesty in business was expected.

Even after adding the new crimes, the technicalities made application of the laws involving theft very difficult. Today, many states have abolished the separate offenses of larceny, embezzlement, and related theft crimes, and combined them into new, comprehensive theft statutes. As the law developed in England and in the United States, criminal statutes were enacted to make it a crime to commit various types of cheating and fraud. The extensive use of checks and other commercial paper made it necessary that specific statutes be developed to punish the making of false documents or altering documents with the intent to defraud. Crimes continue to be defined as technology and business practices create the opportunities for new ways to victimize.

§ 8.2 Larceny

A. *Common Law*

Larceny was defined at common law as the felonious taking, by trespass and carrying away by any person, of the personal goods or things of another from any place, without the owner's consent and with the felonious intent to permanently deprive the owner of his or her property and to convert it to the taker's own use or to the use of some person other than the owner.[1]

To constitute the common law crime of larceny, the property taken must be personal property, as distinguished from **real property** (real estate and what is part of the realty), and the property must belong to another. It must be taken by trespass from the possession of another and carried away from the place it occupies. In addition, the taking and removal must be accompanied by the intent to deprive the owner of the property. The following elements constitute the common law crime of theft or larceny.

1. Trespass (Unlawful)

To constitute larceny, there must be a taking of the property against the will of one who has actual or constructive possession of it. This intrusion upon the personality of another is referred to as "**trespass**." Obviously the use of the term is not the same as the modern-day crime of trespass, nor is it the same as the crime of trespass of premises. It is related to the writ of *trespass de bonis asportatis* (trespass for goods carried away), which was the civil law approach to retrieving stolen goods.

As one court stated, larceny, as it developed at common law, is best defined as the taking and removal, by trespass, of personal property, which the trespasser knows to belong to another, with the felonious intent to deprive him of his ownership therein.[2] In larceny, it is not necessary that the trespass be accompanied by violence if the taker secures physical custody of the property and has it in his power to take it away and appropriate it.

---

[1] Fitch v. State, 135 Fla. 361, 185 So. 435 (1938).
[2] State v. Grant, 135 Vt. 222, 373 A.2d 847 (1977).

2. Taking (Caption)

A taking occurs when the offender secures dominion over the property. There can be no taking (**caption**) or dominion if the defendant, in an attempt to steal another's property, fails to gain possession of it. In a 1978 case, the North Carolina Supreme Court determined that, in order to satisfy the taking element in larceny, the accused must have the goods in his or her possession and under his or her control, even if only for an instant.[3] Stated in different terms, to constitute larceny, there must be a severance of the possession of the owner and an actual possession by the wrongdoer.[4]

3. Carrying Away (Asportation)

To constitute carrying away or **asportation**, the property must be moved from the place where it was. The distance moved may be very minor. In the North Carolina case cited earlier, the defendant had moved an air conditioner in a motel room approximately four inches from its base and toward the door. The reviewing court agreed that this movement was sufficient to establish asportation. If there is a complete severance of the chattel from the possession of the person from whom it was taken, and the goods are actually carried away at least a short distance, this is sufficient to constitute taking and asportation, even if possession of the taker is immediately interrupted.[5]

4. Personal Property

At common law, and in some states today, larceny is limited to theft of goods and chattels. Under this definition, it is not larceny to carry away real property such as trees, crops, minerals, and fixtures that are part of realty. According to the definition of larceny, unless a statute modifies the common law, one cannot be found guilty of larceny if items such as stocks, bonds, checks, and promissory notes were the subject of the taking. The statutes in most states today have expanded the scope of larceny by modifying the definition of property, or by including additional offenses that prohibit the taking of specific items of real property as well as intangibles and negotiable instruments.

5. Of Another

To constitute larceny, the property taken must be property of another person. That is, it must be owned by or in the possession of someone other than the thief. It is not essential that the thief know who the owner is; it is sufficient if he knows that the property is not his own and takes it in order to deprive the true owner of the property. As one court indicated, it is not that the property belongs to or is owned by a specific person or entity, but rather that it is the property of someone other than the thief.[6] All that is

---

3   State v. Carswell, 296 N.C. 101, 249 S.E.2d 427 (1978).
4   Mouldin v. State, 376 So. 2d 788 (Ala. Ct. App. 1979).
5   Hutchinson v. State, 427 P.2d 112 (Okla. Crim. App. 1967).
6   State v. Leicht, 124 N.J. Super. 127, 305 A.2d 78 (1973).

necessary is that the prosecution include a description of the property for purposes of identification and to show ownership in a person or persons other than the accused.

6. With Intent to Steal

The *mens rea* for larceny is intent to permanently deprive the owner of his or her property. This element may be difficult to prove. If the defense introduces evidence to show that the property was taken for temporary use only, the jury could find that the suspect lacked the intent to steal as required for the crime of larceny. Further, to constitute larceny, the intent to steal must exist at the time of the taking; that is, the taker must have a conscious purpose to steal that which did not belong to him at the time he took the property and carried it away.[7]

B. *Model Penal Code*

In the Model Penal Code, all theft offenses are consolidated into a single offense. Traditional offenses designated as larceny, embezzlement, obtaining property by false pretenses, cheating, blackmail, extortion, fraudulent conversion, receiving stolen property, and others are not separated into individual statutory offenses.

After first explaining that the theft offenses are consolidated, the grading of theft offenses is detailed, affirmative defenses are enumerated, and for a purpose that is not sufficiently explained, reference is made to the fact that interspousal immunity is abolished except in narrowly specified circumstances.

> § 223.1 Consolidation of Theft Offenses; Grading; Provisions Applicable to Theft Generally[8]
>
> (1) Consolidation of Theft Offenses. Conduct denominated theft in this Article constitutes a single offense. An accusation of theft may be supported by evidence that it was committed in any manner that would be theft under this Article, notwithstanding the specification of a different manner in the indictment or information, subject only to the power of the Court to ensure fair trial by granting a continuance of other appropriate relief where the conduct of the defense would be prejudiced by lack of fair notice or by surprise.
> (2) Grading of Theft Offenses.
>   (a) Theft constitutes a felony of the third degree if the amount involved exceeds $500, or if the property stolen is a firearm, automobile, airplane, motorcycle, motorboat, or other motor-propelled vehicle, or in the case of theft by receiving stolen property, if the receiver is in the business of buying or selling stolen property.
>   (b) Theft not within the preceding paragraph constitutes a misdemeanor, except that if the property was not taken from the person or by threat, or in breach of a fiduciary obligation, and the actor proves by a preponderance of the evidence that the amount involved was less than $50, the offense constitutes a petty misdemeanor.
>   (c) The amount involved in a theft shall be deemed to be the highest value, by any reasonable standard, of the property or services which the actor

---

[7] Reid v. Florida Real Estate Comm'n, 188 So. 2d 846 (Fla. Dist. Ct. App. 1966).
[8] MODEL PENAL CODE § 223.1 (1985).

stole or attempted to steal. Amounts involved in thefts committed pursuant to one scheme or course of conduct, whether from the same person or several persons, may be aggregated in determining the grade of the offense.

(3) Claim of Right. It is an affirmative defense to prosecution for theft that the actor:
    (a) was unaware that the property was that of another; or
    (b) acted under an honest claim of right to the property or service involved or that he had a right to acquire or dispose of it as he did; or
    (c) took property exposed for sale, intending to purchase and pay for it promptly, or reasonably believing that the owner, if present, would have consented.

(4) Theft from Spouse. It is no defense that theft was from the actor's spouse, except that misappropriation of household and personal effects, or other property normally accessible to both spouses, is theft only if it occurs after the parties have ceased living together.

§ 223.2 Theft by Unlawful Taking or Disposition

(1) Movable Property. A person is guilty of theft if he unlawfully takes, or exercises unlawful control over, movable property of another with purpose to deprive him thereof.

(2) Immovable Property. A person is guilty of theft if he unlawfully transfers immovable property of another or any interest therein with purpose to benefit himself or another not entitled thereto.

Section 223.2 of the Model Code does not use the term larceny, but has the same elements as common law larceny (as indicated in the parentheses that follow the elements outlined next). The elements of theft under the Model Penal Code are

- unlawful (the idea of trespass)
- taking, or unlawfully exercising control over (caption and asportation)
- movable property (expanded definition of property)
- of another
- with the purpose to deprive him thereof (intent to permanently deprive)

As mentioned earlier, the concept of property has been expanded under the Model Penal Code. "Movable property" is defined in Section 223.0 as "property, the location of which can be changed, including things growing on, affixed to, or found in land, and documents, although the rights represented thereby have no physical location." "Property of another" includes property in which any person other than the actor has an interest even if the actor also has an interest in the property, and regardless of the fact that the other person might be precluded from civil recovery because the property was used in an unlawful transaction or was subject to forfeiture as contraband. In other words, you can still be guilty of theft if you steal your partner's share of a marijuana crop even though it is illegal contraband.

The Model Penal Code also provides a definition of "deprive":

(a) to withhold property of another permanently or for so extended a period as to appropriate a major portion of its economic value, or with intent to restore only upon payment of reward or other compensation, or
(b) to dispose of the property so as to make it unlikely that the owner will recover it.[9]

---

[9]   Model Penal Code § 223.0(1) (1985).

With these definitions, it is readily apparent that the coverage of this statute is more comprehensive than the coverage of traditional larceny statute. For example, while the traditional statute applied only to personal property, this section includes a penalty for taking either personal or real property, including intangible property.

C. State Statutes, Codes, and Cases

Definitions by state courts differ, but the general elements are fairly consistent. Some examples will point out the differences and similarities:

- To constitute "larceny," there must be an unlawful acquisition of property with intention to convert it to the taker's use and an appropriation by one who took it.[10]
- "Larceny" is the wrongful taking and carrying away of personal property of another from any place, with a felonious intent to convert it to the taker's own use without consent of the owner.[11]
- Generally, "larceny" is the felonious taking and carrying away of personal property of another with intent on the part of the taker to convert it to his own use or to deprive the owner thereof.[12]

Many states have followed the Model Penal Code and consolidated most of the theft offenses into one statute. That is, what formerly was larceny, embezzlement, false pretenses and, in some instances, other statutory crimes are consolidated into one comprehensive provision. An example of a statute that consolidates many theft crimes is that of Kentucky.

§ 514.030—Theft by unlawful taking or disposition; penalties[13]

(1) Except as otherwise provided in KRS217.181 or 218A.1418, a person is guilty of theft by unlawful taking or disposition when he unlawfully:
   (a) Takes or exercises control over movable property of another with intent to deprive him thereof; or
   (b) Obtains immovable property of another or any interest therein with intent to benefit himself or another not entitled thereto.
(2) Theft by unlawful taking or disposition is a Class A misdemeanor unless the value of the property is three hundred dollars ($300) or more, in which case it is a Class D felony; or unless:
   (a) The property is a firearm (regardless of the value of the firearm), in which case it is a Class D felony; or
   (b) The property is anhydrous ammonia (regardless of the value of the ammonia), in which case it is a Class D felony unless it is proven that the person violated this section with the intent to manufacture methamphetamine in violation of KRS218A.1432, in which case it is a Class B felony for the first offense and a Class A felony for each subsequent offense.

---

[10] State v. Smith, 2 Wash. 2d 118, 98 P.2d 647 (1939).
[11] State v. Jackson, 251 Iowa 537, 101 N.W.2d 731 (1960).
[12] Webb v. State, 55 Ala. App. 195, 314 So. 2d 114 (1975).
[13] KY. REV. STAT. § 514.030 (2001).

Under the provisions of this statute and other similar statutes and codes, the elements are taking or exercising control, over the movable property of another, with intent to deprive; or obtaining immovable property of another or any interest therein or with intent to benefit him or to benefit another not entitled to the property. "Deprive," as used in this statute, is similar to the Model Penal Code's definition: it means to "withhold property of another permanently, or for so extended a period as to appropriate a major portion of its economic value or with intent to restore only upon payment of reward or other compensation, or to dispose of the property so as to make it unlikely that the owner will recover it."

Some state statutes enumerate the types of personal property that are subject to larceny. For instance, part of the Michigan statute provides

750.356. Larceny[14]

Sec 356.(1) A person who commits larceny . . . by stealing any of the following property of another person is guilty of a crime as provided in this section:
   (a) Money, goods, or chattels.
   (b) A bank note, bank bill, bond, promissory note, due bill, bill of exchange or other bill, draft, order, or certificate.
   (c) A book of accounts for or concerning money or goods due, to become due, . . . or to be delivered.
   (d) A deed or writing containing a conveyance of land or other valuable contract in force.
   (e) A receipt, release, or defeasance.
   (f) A writ, process, or public record.

Unlike Kentucky, which has a consolidated theft statute, Michigan covers theft in several larceny-related statutes, including "larceny from motor vehicles or trailers; stealing firearms of another; theft of motor vehicle fuel; and larceny of a rented motor vehicle, trailer or other tangible property."

States have had to expand the definition of property either by statute, as in the Michigan example, or by case law, because the types of valuable items today could hardly have been imagined by those who developed the common law. For instance, consider the following: a password to a bank account, electric power, cable service, food stamps, an algorithm, a telephone authorization code. Are these property and can their theft give rise to a conviction for larceny? State case law varies in the application of property to these and other items.

The degree of punishment is determined by the *value* of the property as well as the *number* of previous theft convictions. As a general rule, the value of property is determined by applying the fair market value. Even if there is no legal market value for the personal property, value may be determined by other methods. For example, a Michigan case held that in a prosecution for larceny of more than $100 arising out of the defendant's theft of a deer carcass from a third person, expert testimony was properly allowed to establish the value of the carcass, even though no legal market existed for deer carcasses.[15]

---

[14]   MICH. COMP. LAWS § 750.356 (2002).
[15]   People v. Brown, 445 N.W.2d 801 (Mich. 1989).

D. Summary

The Model Penal Code and many states have consolidated theft statutes into one crime; however, even these statutes require proof of specific elements for each individual crime whether it is larceny, embezzlement, or theft by false pretenses. The general elements for larceny are indicated below.

> Larceny
> (A/R) unlawful; taking; of property; of another; without permission
> (M/R) intent to permanently deprive (specific intent)

§ 8.3   Robbery

A. Common Law

Larceny is a lesser included crime of **robbery**. All the elements of larceny exist, with a couple added elements. The elements that distinguish robbery from larceny are

1. the taking of property *from the person or presence* of the victim, and
2. the taking is accompanied by means of *force or threat of force*.

There are valid arguments for treating the crime of robbery as an offense against the person; however, because the primary objective of the actor is to take the personal property of another, it is included in this chapter along with other thefts.

LEGAL NEWS: O.J.'S ROBBERY

O.J. Simpson was convicted of robbery and kidnapping in October 2008 for his role in a botched attempt to retrieve sports memorabilia. He and five other men, one of whom used a weapon, held the victims in a room and demanded the return of items that Simpson argued were his. The jury found that the state had proven all the elements of not only robbery, but also kidnapping. O.J. supporters argued that the jury was influenced by his acquittal almost 15 years ago in the death of his wife and Ronald Goldman.

Source: Friess, S. (2008). "Simpson's Path: Celebrity to Pariah to Afterthought." *Austin American-Statesman*, October 5, 2008:A1, A12.

Where the common law offense of robbery still exists, and in states where the term is not defined by statute, robbery consists of eight elements: the six elements of larceny plus two additional elements that are unique to robbery. These eight elements are listed and briefly described (or reviewed) here.

1. Trespass (from Possession and against the Will)

Historically, one of the elements of robbery and larceny was that the thief took the property out of another's possession and against the will of one who had actual or constructive possession of it. However, it is not necessary that the victim of a robbery also be the owner of the goods taken, because robbery is an offense against the person who has either actual or constructive possession of the goods.[16]

2. Taking (Caption)

Taking is defined as securing dominion or absolute control over the property. At common law, this was called "caption." Before the crime of robbery or larceny is complete, the prosecution must offer evidence to show that the actor had actual physical caption; that is, he or she had dominion over the property and left no control in the owner or possessor. If the accused has not gained complete control of the property, there can be no caption or taking, even if he thinks he has the property in his possession.[17] In this case, the correct charge would be attempted robbery.

3. Carrying Away (Asportation)

The offense of robbery is not necessarily complete at the moment the stolen property is in the robber's possession, because robbery also includes the element of asportation. There must be such a carrying away or asportation as to supersede the possession of the owner for an appreciable time. If the prosecution can show that the person charged with robbery removed the property from the place it originally occupied, even for an instant and even to a small degree, this is sufficient asportation to constitute the offense.[18]

4. Personal Property

In proving this element, all that is necessary is that it is shown that the property is personal, as compared to real property. Generally, the type and value of the property taken are immaterial insofar as the offense of robbery is concerned. While the property must have some value, proof of a specific monetary value is not required.[19]

5. Of Another

To constitute robbery, evidence must be introduced to show that the ownership or right of possession of the property taken is vested in a person other than the taker. It is not necessary that the ownership of the property taken be in the person who was robbed;

---

[16]　People v. Estes, 147 Cal. App. 3d 23, 194 Cal. Rptr. 909 (1983).

[17]　People v. Maier, 75 Cal. 383, 17 P. 431 (1888).

[18]　People v. Melendez, 25 Cal. App. 2d 490, 77 P.2d 870 (1938); Neal v. State, 214 Ind. 328, 14 N.E.2d 590 (1938).

[19]　People v. Nolan, 250 Ill. 351, 95 N.E. 140 (1911).

it is sufficient if he or she had exclusive possession of it at the time. For example, robbery was a proper charge when the defendant took money from the person of a filling station attendant, even though he was not the actual owner of the stolen property. This element is present, therefore, if the property is taken from a bailee, an agent, an employee, or other representative of the owner.[20]

6. With Intent to Steal

One of the most difficult elements to prove in the crimes of robbery and larceny is intent (*animus furandi*). Unless a statute changes the definition of the offense, robbery and larceny require specific intent. That is, evidence must be introduced to prove, beyond a reasonable doubt, that the accused intended to appropriate the property to a use inconsistent with the rights of the person from whom it was taken. Therefore, when the taking is under an honest, though mistaken, claim of ownership, or claim of a lawful right to possess the property, the crime is not robbery or larceny.[21]

The definition of robbery requires that there be intent to steal the personal property of another. This intent must be to deprive the owner, wholly and permanently, of his or her property. This element has resulted in some very technical distinctions. For example, in Arizona, a charge of robbery failed when the attempt was to collect a bona fide debt.[22] However, this defense is not available to a defendant when the amount he or she claims is uncertain. Therefore, in another case, the conviction for robbery was upheld even though the defendant claimed that he was seeking return of monies lost in an illegal card game. In this case, the appellate court held that the jury could have drawn an inference from the evidence that the defendant did not, in good faith, intend to take only money that he had lost, but additional money.[23] In discussing specific intent, a distinction has been made between reclaiming specific personal property and taking money claimed to be owed. Referring to a previous case, one court used the example that although a debtor may owe $100, and $100 is in the debtor's pocket, it is not the same $100 that belongs to the creditor, and the creditor may not take the money even if he or she intends to apply it to the debt.[24]

7. From the Person or Presence of Another

One of the elements that distinguishes robbery from larceny and justifies a more severe penalty is the aggravating element of taking from the person. Robbery requires more than a simple trespassory taking. The taking must be from the person or presence of the victim, as well as from his or her possession. Property is taken from the person if

---

[20] Lanahan v. State, 176 Ark. 104, 2 S.W.2d 55 (1928); People v. Cabassa, 249 Mich. 543, 229 N.W. 442 (1930).

[21] Moyers v. State, 185 Ga. 446, 197 S.E. 846 (1938).

[22] State v. Lewis, 121 Ariz. 155, 589 P.2d 29 (1978).

[23] People v. Lain, 57 Cal. App. 2d 123, 134 P.2d 284 (1943).

[24] Edwards v. State, 49 Wis. 2d 105, 181 N.W.2d 383 (1970).

it is taken from his or her hand, pocket, clothing, or from a package in his or her hand. However, it is not required that the property be taken directly from the person. This element is complete if the property is taken from his or her presence, which includes the area under the victim's immediate control. "Presence" is not so much a matter of being within the view of the victim as it is a matter of proximity and control. The test is that the property taken in the robbery must be close enough to the victim and sufficiently under his control that, had the latter not been subjected to violence or intimidation by the robber, he or she could have prevented the taking.[25]

8. By Violence or Intimidation

The second additional element that distinguishes robbery from larceny is that the taking must involve some violence or intimidation. This has been explained in several ways. For example, one court indicated that "the taking must be against the will of the possessor accompanied by means of force or fear."[26] The particular means of force, or manner in which fear is imparted, is immaterial in determining this element of robbery.

Violence is present, even if the force is very slight, if it is sufficient to achieve the purpose of the accused. The following may be sufficient to prove force was used:

- struggling with the victim;
- use of an intoxicant or drugs to make the victim compliant; or
- intimidating/threatening the victim with or without a weapon.

B. Model Penal Code

In the Model Code, robbery is considered under a separate heading from the consolidated theft statute because of the special elements of danger commonly associated with forcible theft from the person. Although only one robbery offense is defined, it includes aggravated behavior occurring in the course of committing a theft. For purposes of punishment, a grading scheme is included in the Model Penal Code. Robbery is a felony of the second degree, except that it is a felony of the first degree if, in the course of committing the theft, the actor attempts to kill anyone, or purposely inflicts, or attempts to inflict, serious bodily injury.

> § 222.1 Robbery[27]
>
> (1) Robbery Defined. A person is guilty of robbery if, in the course of committing a theft, he:
>   (a) inflicts serious bodily injury upon another; or
>   (b) threatens another with or purposely puts him in fear of immediate serious bodily injury; or

---

[25] People v. Braverman, 340 Ill. 525, 173 N.E. 55 (1930).

[26] In re Massie, 283 P.2d 573 (Okla. Crim. App. 1955).

[27] MODEL PENAL CODE § 222.1 (1985).

(c) commits or threatens immediately to commit any felony of the first or second degree.

　　An attempt shall be deemed "in the course of committing a theft" if it occurs in an attempt to commit theft, or in flight, after the attempt or commission.

(2) Grading. Robbery is a felony of the second degree, except that it is a felony of the first degree if in the course of committing the theft the actor attempts to kill anyone, or purposely inflicts or attempts to inflict serious bodily injury.

"In the course of committing a theft" includes an attempt to commit theft or flight after the attempt or commission. In addition to the infliction or threatened infliction of serious bodily harm, which is the usual statutory provision, the Model Code provides an alternative. Even if there is no actual threat against the personal safety of the victim, the offender can be found guilty of robbery if, in the course of committing the theft, he commits or threatens to commit any other felony of the first or second degree.

The traditional requirement of "taking from the person" has not been included in Model Penal Code. Also, the Model Code, following the lead of some of the pre-Model Code statutory provisions of the various states, has eliminated the "intent to permanently deprive" requirement.

C. *State Statutes, Codes, and Cases*

State statutes have modified the technical requirements of robbery under the common law. These changes make it possible to prosecute persons for crimes in which the technical elements, such as asportation, may not be present.

1. Taking and Asportation

The taking requirement is obviously still very much an element of modern statutes and case law concerning robbery. Taking requires custody and control, but not necessarily physical possession. For instance, if the robber obtains keys to a car through the threat of force, he, not the victim, has constructive control over the car and the robbery would be complete. Some state statutes still include the common law element of asportation; however, case law has virtually eliminated the requirement of proof because any distance, however, slight, will be defined as asportation. The case *Lattimore v. United States* in Part II of this text illustrates this point.

Case Note: *Lattimore v. United States*, 684 A.2d 357 (D.C. App. 1996)
What was the issue in this case?
Did the court require asportation?
What distance meets the definition of asportation?

2. Personal Property of Another

As with larceny, the definition of property has been expanded from the common law definition to include intangibles, negotiable instruments, and other items of value.

3. With Intent to Permanently Deprive

Recall that, under common law, in order to be convicted of robbery, specific intent must be proven. That is, it must be proven that the defendant intended the actions (i.e., putting the victim in fear) and intended the consequence (to acquire the personal property and to permanently deprive the victim of the property). Because the intent element has been difficult to prove, resulting in the miscarriage of justice, states have modified this element in their statutes. For example, in Florida, the legislature expanded the scope of robbery by eliminating the requirement of specific intent. The Florida Supreme Court upheld a conviction of robbery under the statute that defines robbery as the "taking of money or other property from the person or custody of another by force."[28] This means that there is no need to prove that the defendant meant to permanently deprive the victim, only that there was a taking.

4. Using Force or Threat of Force from Their Person or in Their Presence

Although it is not necessary to prove *both* force and intimidation, both *may* be used together to constitute robbery, if acted upon by the victim and the property is given to the defendant. Both state and federal courts have been called upon to decide whether "pocket picking," without the knowledge of the victim, is robbery. Generally speaking, pocket picking is not robbery, because the element of violence or intimidation is not present. However, if there is a struggle by the owner to maintain possession, this element will be present and the actions could amount to robbery. For example, in a 1978 case, a defendant, attempting to snatch the pocketbook of a woman standing on a subway platform, was met with resistance, and the ensuing struggle resulted in the woman being hit by the train. The court reasoned that, although purse-snatching, when unaccompanied by resistance on the part of the victim, generally is not sufficient to constitute robbery, there was, in this case, sufficient evidence to support a jury finding that the victim resisted by clinging to her purse, and that the overcoming of this resistance through the use of overwhelming momentum of the train, constituted attempted robbery.[29]

In other cases, juries and courts are called upon to determine whether there has been sufficient intimidation or threat of force to constitute robbery. For instance, in a Texas case, the defendant/appellant entered a convenience store, selected a piece of bubble gum, and placed the gum and a dime on the front counter. When the clerk, who was the only person in the store, opened the register to ring up the sale, the appellant placed his hands inside the register drawer. The clerk grabbed the appellant's wrist and said, "What are you doing?" The frightened clerk released her grip on the appellant, who quickly grabbed two $10 bills and a $20 bill and then ran out of the store. The defendant was convicted of robbery and appealed, claiming that the evidence was insufficient to prove the complaining witness was put in fear of imminent bodily injury or death.

[28] Bell v. State, 354 So.2d 1266 (Fla. Dist. Ct. App. 1978).
[29] People v. Santiago, 62 App. Div. 2d 572, 405 N.Y.S.2d 752 (1978).

The reviewing court, citing previous cases, held that "fear must arise from the conduct of the accused rather than the mere temperamental timidity of the victim," and "in order to prove the offense of robbery, there must have been actual or threatened violence to the person, or intimidation of such a nature that the threatened or injured party was put in fear." The court then noted that the jury believed that the appellant's actions were calculated to and did invoke the requisite fear. While admitting that the question was a close one, the court found that the appellant's "menacing glance" and "clenched fists" constituted intentionally threatening conduct sufficient to cause fear of imminent bodily injury sufficient to part with property. In making the decision, the court took into consideration the fact that the defendant was 5 feet, 10 inches tall and was "huskily built," while the clerk was a "not very tall" woman in her late thirties.[30]

Another issue in determining whether robbery has occurred is when the force was applied. Some states require that the force occur before or at the same time as the taking of property; otherwise, it is not robbery. For instance, consider a scenario where a shoplifter takes property from a store, runs out of the store, and struggles with a security guard, knocking the guard to the ground. In some states, this would be prosecuted as larceny and assault because the robbery statute requires the force be used to obtain the property. Other states, however, have statutes that describe the use of force as occurring at any time during the taking and, in these states, force used in escape would meet the definition of robbery.

5. Examples of Statutes

Many states, including Texas, differentiate degrees of robbery based upon the seriousness of the injury that has been caused. Aggravated robbery is a more serious crime with more serious punishment. If the bodily injury is "serious," or if a deadly weapon is used, then the offense is aggravated robbery and is graded as a felony in the first degree.

§ 29.02 Robbery[31]

(a) A person commits an offense if, in the course of committing theft as defined in Chapter 31 of this Code and with intent to obtain or maintain control of the property, he:
  (1) intentionally, knowingly, or recklessly causes bodily injury to another; or
  (2) intentionally or knowingly threatens or places another in fear of imminent bodily injury or death.
(b) An offense under this Section is a felony of the second degree.

§ 29.03 Aggravated Robbery

(a) A person commits an offense if he commits robbery as defined in § 29.02 of this code, and he:

---

[30] Wilmeth v. State, 808 S.W.2d 703 (Tex. 1991). *See also* Commonwealth v. Lashway, 634 N.E.2d 930 (Mass. 1994).

[31] TEX. PENAL CODE ANN. § 29.02-29.03 (Vernon 2002).

(1) causes serious bodily injury to another;

(2) uses or exhibits a deadly weapon; or

(3) causes bodily injury to another person or threatens or places another person in fear of imminent bodily harm or death, if the other person is:

    (A) 65 years of age or older; or

    (B) a disabled person

(b) An offense under this section is a felony of the first degree.

(c) In this section, "disabled person" means an individual with a mental, physical, or developmental disability who is substantially unable to protect himself from harm.

In many states, increased penalties result when there are aggravating factors, such as the use of a "deadly weapon." A Texas court found that a weapon is "deadly" if it is capable of causing serious bodily injury in the manner of its use, without regard to whether the actual result is infliction of serious bodily injury.[32] Another Texas court found that, although a knife could be a deadly weapon, a pocketknife with a two-inch blade was not a deadly weapon and thus the defendant could not be convicted of aggravated robbery.[33]

In Illinois, the statute includes the term "armed robbery" to designate the more serious crime, providing that a person commits armed robbery if the robbery is committed while the person is armed with a dangerous weapon. Armed robbery in Illinois is a Class A felony.[34] In determining what is a dangerous weapon, an Illinois court decided that a utility knife used in an armed robbery was a "dangerous weapon" when it had a six-inch grip with a one-inch, heavy-duty, single-edge, sharp blade, and where the blade was in a fully exposed position when used. However, a sharp fingernail is not a dangerous weapon as used in this statute, because no portion of the human anatomy is legally a dangerous weapon. Pepper spray that the defendant sprayed on the victims during a bank robbery was a "dangerous weapon," so as to sustain an armed robbery conviction, where the spray temporarily incapacitated the victims and the effects did not wear off completely until several hours after the robbery.[35]

State courts have also dealt with the issue of the use of toy guns. Note that it is a different question as to whether a toy gun constitutes the force or threat of force necessary as an element of the crime of robbery (it does because the threat is from the viewpoint of the victim), and whether a toy gun is a "dangerous weapon" that would increase the severity of the offense to an aggravating category (case decisions are mixed). While a toy gun may not constitute aggravated robbery, an unloaded gun

---

[32] Bosier v. State, 771 S.W.2d 221 (Tex. 1989). *See also* People v. Holder, 577 N.Y.S.2d 1022 (1991), which held that a knife brandished by the defendant's accomplice was a "dangerous instrument" supporting a first-degree robbery conviction in New York.

[33] Birl v. State, 763 S.W.2d 860 (Tex. 1988).

[34] Ill. Ann. Stat. ch. 720 § 5/18-2 (Smith-Hurd 1999).

[35] People v. Westefer, 522 N.E.2d 1381 (Ill. 1988); People v. Bias, 475 N.E.2d 253 (Ill. 1985); People v. Ellis, 419 N.E.2d 727 (Ill. 1981). People v. Elliott, 299 Ill. App. 3d 766, 702 N.E.2d 643 (1998).

has been defined as a dangerous weapon because, according to the court, it can be used to bludgeon the victim.[36]

Recall that, under party liability principles, those who participate in the offense of armed robbery or aggravated robbery may be convicted even if they were not present when the robbery took place. For instance, in one case, the defendant was convicted of armed robbery because he drove two men to the victim's home, dropped them off, waited nearby, and picked them up as they fled the victim's home after robbing and shooting him.[37] In another case, a federal court agreed with the lower court that evidence was sufficient to support the defendant's conviction for aiding and abetting an armed bank robbery although the defendant was not in the bank at the time the robberies occurred, as the defendant drove the vehicle for the codefendants, and there was evidence that the use of firearms was discussed during the planning stage of the crime and the defendant was in a position to observe the actual use of firearms in at least some of the robberies.[38]

LEGAL NEWS: SPECIFIC FORMS OF ROBBERY

"Home invasions" and "carjackings" are types of robberies, although home invasions are sometimes mistakenly categorized as burglaries and carjackings are mistakenly categorized as auto theft. The intentional use of force or threat of force to accomplish the theft is what sets these crimes apart and, arguably, makes the crimes much more serious than the theft alternatives. Some states have addressed carjackings and home invasions by special statutes, such as Florida's home-invasion robbery statute (Florida Statutes § 775.021).

D. *Summary*

Remember that robbery is larceny with the addition of two elements: the taking must be from the person or the presence of the victim, and there is a use of force or threat of force. The major changes between the common law and modern statutes are that it is not necessary to prove specific intent to permanently deprive, nor is it necessary in most states to show that the property was moved any appreciable distance. In general, the crime of robbery is more straightforward today, with fewer technical problems in prosecuting it. Many states have identified a more serious form of robbery when the victim is injured, when deadly weapons are used, or other elements are present.

---

[36] McLaughlin v. United States, 476 U.S. 16 (1986).
[37] State v. Martinez, 47 P.3d 115 (Utah 2002).
[38] United States v. Gordon, 290 F.3d 539 (3d Cir. 2002).

Robbery
(A/R) taking, property, of another, without permission, in presence or from person, with force or threat of force
(M/R) intentional (specific intent)

§ 8.4 Embezzlement

At common law, if there was no "trespass," because the property came into the possession of the taker lawfully even though he later appropriated the property against the owner's desire, then the person who committed the wrong would often go unpunished. To fill this void, the English Parliament in 1799 and later, states, by legislative action, enacted laws creating the crime of embezzlement. In **embezzlement**, the perpetrator acquires possession of the property lawfully, but converts it to his or her own use. As the chief distinction between larceny and embezzlement lies in the manner of acquiring possession of the property, emphasis is on this distinction. To reiterate, in embezzlement, the property comes lawfully into the possession of the taker but is later fraudulently or unlawfully appropriated by him.

A. Common Law

As stated earlier, there was no crime of embezzlement under the common law. Early as well as recent decisions agree that the offense of embezzlement did not exist at common law and is purely a statutory offense.[39]

B. Model Penal Code

Recall that the Model Penal Code consolidated all theft offenses; therefore, embezzlement is one type of theft as described. In addition, Section 223.8 of the Model Penal Code provides for a specific type of embezzlement:

§ 223.8 Theft by Failure to Make Required Disposition of Funds Received

A person who purposely obtains property upon agreement, or subject to a known legal obligation, to make specified payment or other disposition, whether from such property or its proceeds or from his own property to be reserved in equivalent amount, is guilty of theft if he deals with the property obtained as his own and fails to make the required payment or disposition. The foregoing applies notwithstanding that it may be impossible to identify particular property as belonging to the victim at the time of the actor's failure to make the required payment or disposition. An officer or employee of the government or of a financial institution is presumed:

(i) to know any legal obligation relevant to his criminal liability under this Section, and
(ii) to have dealt with the property as his own if he fails to pay or account upon lawful demand, or if an audit reveals a shortage or falsification of accounts.

---

[39]   Fortney v. Commonwealth, 162 S.W.2d 193 (Ky. 1942).

Under the Model Code, the conduct proscribed consists essentially of two elements: (1) obtaining property upon an agreement and/or subject to a known legal obligation to make a specified payment or other disposition; and (2) dealing with the property as one's own and failing to make the required payment or disposition. Examples of this type of crime would be a mortgage holder who accepted payments but did not apply them to principle or an insurance broker who accepted premiums from clients but did not send them to the insurance companies leaving the unsuspected clients uninsured.

C. State Statutes, Codes, and Cases

Although there is a considerable difference in the scope and wording of the statutes of various states defining embezzlement, both regarding the person liable and the kind of property protected, all statutes, as well as the courts, include *wrongful appropriation* or **conversion** as a common element. Some definitions by various courts will help in developing a definition of the offense of embezzlement.

• The crime of "embezzlement" builds on the concept of conversion, but adds two further elements; first, embezzled property must have been in lawful possession of the defendant at the time of its appropriation, and second, "embezzlement" requires knowledge that the appropriation is contrary to the wishes of the owner of the property.[40]
• "Embezzlement" is the wrongful appropriation or conversion of property where the original taking was lawful or with consent of the owner.[41]

To sustain a conviction of "embezzlement," it must be shown that the accused was the "agent" or "bailee" of the victim and had, at one time, lawfully possessed the victim's property but then intentionally converted the victim's property to his own use. The four elements of embezzlement are as follows:

1. Fraudulent Intent

There must be intent on the part of the defendant to unlawfully convert the property. Generally, the fraudulent intent required as an element may be found from the acts of the defendant in using or disposing of the property. As an example, when an official of a union had control of union property, directed the sale of the property, and appropriated part of the proceeds to his own use, he was guilty of embezzlement, because the intent was clear from the actions of the official.[42] Some state statutes require evidence of an intent to "permanently" deprive the owner of the property.

In a Michigan case, the court explained that proving fraudulent intent by showing lack of consent of the owner is necessary only when the perpetrator hides the property

---

[40]   United States v. Stockton, 788 F.2d 210 (4th Cir. 1986).
[41]   Jones v. State, 79 So.2d 273 (Miss. 1955).
[42]   People v. Swanson, 174 Cal. App. 2d 453, 344 P.2d 832 (1959).

but has not yet converted it. In all other cases, conversion will go to prove lack of consent of the true owner. [43]

2. Appropriation or Conversion

The essence of the crime of embezzlement is that the wrongdoer has the money or other property of another person that comes into his hands legally but is not used as intended by the owner. To constitute wrongful appropriation or conversion, there must be a serious act of interference with the owner's rights. While damage to the property does not amount to conversion or appropriation, selling it, pledging it, giving it away, delivering it to one not entitled to it, claiming it against the owner, unreasonably withholding possession of it from the owner, or spending it (in the case of money) is conversion. To prove this element, the prosecution must establish that the accused converted funds to his own use or to the benefit of another; mere receipt of funds and failure to account for them is not enough.[44]

3. By One in Lawful Possession

To constitute embezzlement, there must be an actual and lawful possession or custody of property of another by virtue of some trust, duty, agency, or employment of the accused, otherwise it is larceny. The very essence of the crime of embezzlement is that the property was converted by one who was entrusted with the property or into whose hands it lawfully came. A common example is conversion by a bank employee who embezzles, purloins, or willfully misapplies bank funds that have come into his or her possession through his or her employment. However, agents, executors, and administrators may also be charged with violating embezzlement statutes.

Even an attorney may be guilty of embezzling the money of his or her client that comes into his or her possession during the course of business. For instance, in the case of *Commonwealth v. Turrell*, an attorney was charged with violation of the Pennsylvania embezzlement statute, which contains almost exactly the same wording as the Model Penal Code. The attorney had accepted funds to hold "for his client" but commingled those funds with his own. The court held that the attorney's commingling of the client's funds transmitted to the attorney for payment to a designated third party in itself does not constitute a crime. However, when the payment was due and the attorney failed to transmit the funds in his possession, the attorney evinced an intent not to make the required payment, thereby meeting the definition of embezzlement.[45]

---

[43]   People v. Wood, 451 N.W.2d 563 (Mich. 1990).

[44]   State v. Randecker, 1 Wash. App. 834, 464 P.2d 447 (1970).

[45]   Commonwealth v. Turrell, 584 A.2d 882 (Pa. 1990).

4. Property of Another

In some statutes, the property that is the subject of theft (and embezzlement) is limited to personal property. In others, "property" includes both real and personal property. And in still others, "property" is defined as personal property and real property that has been "severed." In general, recall that modern statutes have expanded the restrictive common law definition of property in theft statutes.

As in the case of larceny, to constitute embezzlement, the property must be "property of another." In order to prove a violation of an embezzlement statute, the prosecution must prove that the property was that of a person other than the accused. The traditional rule is that a person cannot be guilty of converting his or her own property. Therefore, if both possession and title of the property have been passed to the defendant prior to the alleged conversion, the defendant cannot properly be convicted of embezzlement. Further, the defendant must know that the property is owned by another because the *mens rea* is to intentionally convert another's property.[46]

5. Examples of Statutes

Some states still have not consolidated the crimes of embezzlement and larceny. An example of such a statute is that of Michigan, which provides

750.174. Embezzlement[47]

Sec. 174. (1) A person who as the agent, servant, or employee of another person, governmental entity within this state, or other legal entity or who as the trustee, bailee, or custodian of the property of another person, governmental entity within this state, or other legal entity fraudulently disposes of or converts to his or her own use, or takes or secretes with the intent to convert to his or her own use without the consent of his or her principal, any money or other personal property of his or her principal that has come to that person's possession or that is under his or her charge or control by virtue of his or her being an agent, servant, employee, trustee, bailee, or custodian, is guilty of embezzlement.

The Michigan statute includes an elaborate penalty section based on the value of the property stolen and the number of prior convictions. In addition to this general embezzlement statute, Michigan law includes other embezzlement statutes that provide penalties for embezzlement of specific types of property.

D. *Summary*

Embezzlement is a crime that did not exist under the common law. Embezzlement was created to cover situations in which the defendant was entrusted with the property of another but converted it to his own use. Many states followed the Model Penal Code and incorporated embezzlement into a general theft statute; however, embezzlement

---

46   Commonwealth v. Austin, 393 A.2d 36 (Pa. 1978).
47   MICH. COMP. LAWS § 750.174 (2002).

still exists as a separate statute in other states. The separate elements of embezzlement are noted below.

> Embezzlement
> (A/R) conversion or appropriation, of property of another, lawfully obtained
> (M/R) intent to deprive lawful owner (specific intent)

§ 8.5   Obtaining Property by False Pretenses

A. *Common Law*

Recall that the crime of embezzlement did not exist under the common law. The same is true for obtaining property by **false pretenses**. Common law larceny covered only situations in which the defendant intruded upon the personality of the rightful owner by a "taking." Common law did not define as crimes situations in which the perpetrator obtains title and possession of the property by means of deception.

In 1757, the British Parliament created the crime of false pretenses to protect victims of unscrupulous criminals who used deception to obtain property. It defined as criminal the person who obtains property of another "knowingly and designedly, by false pretense or pretenses, with intent to cheat or defraud any person or persons of the same."[48] The essence of the crime of obtaining money or property by false pretenses is that the victim transfers the title to the property to the wrongdoer under the influence of false pretenses.

B. *Model Penal Code*

The Model Penal Code designates the crime we have been calling "false pretenses" as **"theft by deception."** Even though the words are different, many of the elements that existed under the traditional statutes continue as requirements in the Model Code. For example, under the Model Code, the actor must purposely obtain the property of another and must purposely deceive. These are substitutes for "knowledge" and "intent" as used in some pre-Model Code statutes.

> § 223.3 Theft by Deception[49]
>
> A person is guilty of theft if he purposely obtains property of another by deception. A person deceives if he purposely:
>
> (1) creates or reinforces a false impression, including false impressions as to law, value, intention or other state of mind; but deception as to a person's intention to perform a promise shall not be inferred from the fact alone that he did not subsequently perform the promise; or
>
> (2) prevents another from acquiring information which would affect his judgment of a transaction; or

---

[48]   W. LaFave and A. Scott, Criminal Law (1986), p. 739.

[49]   Model Penal Code § 223.3 (1985).

(3) fails to correct a false impression which the deceiver previously created or reinforced, or which the deceiver knows to be influencing another to whom he stands in a fiduciary or confidential relationship; or

(4) fails to disclose a known lien, adverse claim or other legal impediment to the enjoyment of property which he transfers or encumbers in consideration for the property obtained, whether such impediment is or is not valid, or is or is not a matter of official record.

The Model Penal Code clarifies some of the questions that existed prior to the time that it was adopted. For example, "deception," as used in the Model Code, includes not only creating a false impression, but reinforcing a false impression that the victim may have entertained prior to the intervention by the actor. The term "deceive" does not, however, include falsity as to matters having no pecuniary significance. The crime also does not criminalize what is known as **puffery**, which refers to exaggerations or statements unlikely to deceive ordinary persons in the group addressed. Many salespeople, for instance, may make exaggerated claims of the product's effects (i.e., perfumes or aftershaves that will make one irresistible to the opposite sex). If one buys the product based on such claims, it does not mean that the salesperson is guilty of theft by deception because a "reasonable" person would not believe the exaggerations.

It is not necessary to show that there was a pecuniary loss by the victim. In interpreting Section 405(2) of the Utah statute, which was modeled after this section of the Model Penal Code, a Utah court found that this subsection does not support the contention that pecuniary loss must be an element of the crime of theft by deception. In this case, the Supreme Court of Utah upheld a conviction of theft by deception where the defendant made false representations that he would invest the victim's money in gold and would clear the title to the land used to secure the transaction.[50]

C. State Statutes, Codes, and Cases

While the courts, prior to the Model Penal Code, reached some consensus in defining the offense of false pretenses, the wording of the definitions differed. Some examples will point out these differences and similarities.

- A "false pretense" may consist of any act, word, symbol, or token calculated and intended to deceive, and it may be made either expressly or by implication.[51]
- A "false pretense" may be defined as the false representation of a subsisting fact, whether by oral or written words or conduct, that is calculated to deceive, intended to deceive, and that does, in fact, deceive, and by means of which one person obtains value from another without compensation.[52]

---

[50] State v. Roberts, 711 P.2d 235 (Utah 1985). The case lists 12 states that have adopted the language of § 223.3 of the Model Penal Code.
[51] Fuller v. State, 221 Miss. 227, 72 So.2d 454 (1954).
[52] State v. Carlson, 171 N.C. 818, 89 S.E. 30 (1916).

The elements of the crime of obtaining money or property under false pretenses (or simply "false pretenses") are, generally, as follows:

1. Obtaining Money, Goods, or Things of Value of Another

Generally, this element is defined in broad terms either by statute or case decisions. In some states, specific articles were enumerated in the statute, while others used such terms as "valuable thing" or "other property." One approach is to consider property that can be obtained by false pretenses in the same class of property that is the subject of larceny. However, some statutes broadened this to include such things as promissory notes, bills of exchange, checks, and other securities. After discussing the definition of "things of value," one court noted that the crime of false pretenses is committed when a chattel, money, or a valuable security is obtained from another by making a false representation with intent to defraud and with knowledge of its falsity.[53]

2. By False Representation

The general rule is that the representation must be false as to facts, past or present. In many early statutes, a statement that something would happen in the future or a mere promise to do something was not considered sufficient. However, a number of states and the general modern trend indicate that "false promises" could equate to false pretenses.[54]

The crime also does not cover other misdeeds where no false misrepresentations have been made. Where a defendant received $600 from a homeowner for work that could have been done for $25, this was not false pretenses, even though ethically indefensible.[55] The court advised that an essential element of the crime is a fraudulent misrepresentation and, in this case, there was no evidence of any misrepresentation. Obviously, the defendant needs to know that he is misrepresenting a fact. If he believes what he is saying, there is no misrepresentation, even if it is untrue.

3. With Intent to Defraud the Owner

The mental element of the crime of false pretenses has two essential phases:

- that the defendant knew the representations which he made to be untrue, and
- that he made them with intent to defraud.

The prosecution has the responsibility to prove *knowledge of the falsity of the statements* on the part of the defendant.

The prosecution must introduce evidence to show that the defendant knew that his or her representation was untrue *and* he or she made it with the intent to defraud. A Texas court explained that there must be *intent* to cheat or defraud, but that this

---

[53] Baumgartner v. State, 319 A.2d 592 (Md. 1974).

[54] ILL. ANN. STAT. 720 § 5/15-4(e) (Smith-Hurd 1995).

[55] People v. Marks, 163 N.W.2d 506 (Mich. Ct. App. 1968).

may be inferred from false representations.[56] However, it is not necessary to prove an intent to permanently deprive in many state statutes.[57]

4. Examples of State Statutes

In some states, the traditional crime of false pretenses is incorporated into the theft statute. For example, in the state of Ohio, theft by deception is a part of § 2913.02. This section provides

(A) No person, with purpose to deprive the owner of property or services, shall knowingly obtain or exert control over either the property or the services in any of the following ways:

(1) Without the consent of the owner or the person authorized to give consent;
(2) Beyond the scope of the express or implied consent of the owner or person authorized to give consent;
(3) By deception;
(4) By threat.[58]

Under the provisions of this statute, the elements of the crime are similar to traditional larceny elements, except that control over the property is obtained by deception rather than by taking.

Another approach was taken when the Kentucky General Assembly drafted a similar provision. This section provides

§ 514.040—Theft by deception.[59]

(1) A person is guilty of theft by deception when he obtains property or services of another by deception with intent to deprive him thereof. A person deceives when he intentionally:

(a) creates or reinforces a false impression, including false impressions as to law, value, intention or other state of mind; or
(b) prevents another from acquiring information which would affect his judgment of a transaction; or
(c) fails to correct a false impression which the deceiver previously created or reinforced or which the deceiver knows to be influencing another with whom he stands in a fiduciary or confidential relationship; or
(d) fails to disclose a known lien, adverse claim or other legal impediment to the enjoyment of property which he transfers or encumbers in consideration for the property obtained, whether such impediment is or is not valid or is or is not a matter of official record; or
(e) issues or passes a check or similar sight order for the payment of money, knowing that it will not be honored by the drawee.

---

[56]   Cowan v. State, 41 Tex. Crim. 617, 56 S.W. 751 (1900).
[57]   State v. Grimes, 46 P.3d 801 (Wash. 2002).
[58]   OHIO REV. CODE ANN. § 2913.02 (Anderson 2002).
[59]   KY. REV. STAT. § 514.040 (2001).

The key word that distinguishes this crime from others is "deception." Deception, as used in the statute, is broadly defined and specifically includes creating or reinforcing a false impression, preventing another from acquiring information that would affect his judgment of a transaction, failing to correct a false impression, failing to disclose a known lien or other adverse claim and, finally, issuing or passing a check or other order for the payment of money, knowing that it will not be honored by the drawee.

In an interesting Georgia case, a police officer-defendant was charged with eight counts of misdemeanor theft by deception based on allegations that he had obtained wages from two employers (one being the city police department) through the creation of a false impression of fact by working for both of them during the same period. A Georgia appellate court overturned his conviction, stating that if he did not have a contract that specifically said that he could not work for another party during his employment hours, then it was not larceny by deception.[60]

The Georgia Court of Appeals stated that the offense of theft by deception is defined in O.C.G.A. § 16-8-3 as follows:

(a) A person commits the offense of theft by deception when he obtains property by any deceitful means or artful practice with the intention of depriving the owner of the property.
(b) A person deceives if he intentionally: (1) Creates or confirms another's impression of an existing fact or past event which is false and which the accused knows or believes to be false; . . .
(c) "Deceitful means" and "artful practice" do not, however, include falsity as to matters having no pecuniary significance.

The charge of theft of property by deception is appropriate if a contractor fails to perform promised work where the evidence indicates that the promise was made *with the intention* not to perform. In the case of *Baker v. State*, the defendant failed to perform his contractual promise to remodel a person's home. The court found that this was a violation of the statute and that the jury could infer the necessary intent to defraud from the defendant's evasive conduct, delaying tactics, admission that he had spent the victim's money without purchasing materials, and repeated requests for additional money.[61]

LEGAL NEWS: EBAY ESCAPADES

A news item in 2004 described a teenager who received more than $4,500 from eBay purchasers who thought they were buying a video card from him. Twenty victims paid their money and received nothing. This case is representative of the growth of Internet purchasing and Internet crime. It is high-tech larceny by trick or false pretenses. The 19-year-old faces 40 years in prison and $20,000 in fines.

Retrieved on June 29, 2006 from www.usatoday.com/tech/news/2004-03-12-teen-ebay-scamx._htm.

---

[60]   Wilburn v. State, 410 S.E.2d 321 (Ga. Ct. App. 1991).
[61]   Baker v. State, 588 So. 2d 945 (Ala. Crim. App. 1991).

D. *Summary*

False pretenses differs from larceny and embezzlement in that the rightful owner of the property freely hands over title (or money) to the offender, but the transfer occurs because of the deceptive statements of the offender. While not a crime at common law, the offense was defined early as the type of dishonest act that needed to be punished by criminal law. However, it should be clear that "false pretenses" or "theft by deception" does not cover merely unethical business practices, i.e., charging more than the average cost for a product or service to a naïve customer; making vague or ridiculous promises of what might happen when one buys a product, and so on. The general elements of the crime are indicated below.

> Obtaining Property by False Pretenses
> (A/R) obtaining money, goods, or things of value of another; by false representation; knowing the same to be false
> (M/R) intent to defraud (specific intent)

§ 8.6   Extortion

A. *Common Law*

The traditional definition of **extortion** was obtaining money or other things of value by the misuse of official power or position.[62] Extortion was a misdemeanor and could only be committed by officials when they misused their position. The elements of extortion were expanded by early statutes to include what we now think of as blackmail. Note that robbery is defined as obtaining property through force or threats of force; but the common law was silent in situations where threats were other than physical injury, such as threats to one's reputation. Further, robbery requires a present or immediate threat of force, thus, if the threat is not immediate it is not robbery. Put another way, if an actor says, "give me your money or I will shoot you," it is robbery, but if he says, "give me your money or I will hurt you and your family next week" it is not robbery. Therefore, early statutes expanded common law to include these traditional elements:

1. Obtaining money or property. As in theft, usually the property must be personal property.
2. By threats or coercion. The threat may be either oral or written, and may even be by innuendo or suggestions, but it must be such as would ordinarily create alarm.
3. To perform certain enumerated acts. Specific acts that must be threatened by the perpetrator are often enumerated. One that was common to most statutes is "to injure the person or property of the individual threatened."

---

[62]   Kirby v. State, 57 N.J.L. 320, 31 A. 213 (1894).

B. Model Penal Code

Recall that the Model Penal Code consolidated all theft statutes. Extortion is considered a type of theft. The Model Penal Code provides that a person is guilty of theft if he purposely obtains property of another by threatening to do one of the seven specific acts enumerated. The list of acts in the Model Code is similar to some used in states prior to the time the Model Code was written. The Model Code does contain a residual provision (subsection (7)) that was not included in most state legislation and makes the Model Code more comprehensive in its application.

§ 223.4 Theft by Extortion[63]

A person is guilty of theft if he purposely obtains property of another by threatening to:

(1) inflict bodily injury on anyone or commit any other criminal offense; or
(2) accuse anyone of a criminal offense; or
(3) expose any secret tending to subject any person to hatred, contempt or ridicule, or to impair his credit or business repute; or
(4) take or withhold action as an official, or cause an official to take or withhold action; or
(5) bring about or continue a strike, boycott or other collective unofficial action, if the property is not demanded or received for the benefit of the group in whose interest the actor purports to act; or
(6) testify or provide information or withhold testimony or information with respect to another's legal claim or defense; or
(7) inflict any other harm which would not benefit the actor.

It is an affirmative defense to prosecution based on subsections (2), (3), or (4) that the property obtained by threat of accusation, exposure, lawsuit, or other invocation of official action was honestly claimed as restitution, or indemnification for harm done in the circumstances to which such accusation, exposure, lawsuit, or other official action relates, or as compensation for property or lawful services. This means that a person does not commit extortion if they threaten legal action unless the opposing party pays some rightful claim (i.e., for property damage); however, it would be extortion if a person threatened to either offer or withhold testimony in a legal action unless an amount of money was paid.

C. State Statutes, Codes, and Cases

Modern statutes have expanded the crime of extortion to include what is generally called "blackmail." Extortion was originally limited to obtaining money or things of value through misuse of official power, whereas blackmail referred to obtaining money or property by a private individual. However, as more comprehensive statutes were written, the term blackmail became equivalent to and synonymous with extortion within the nontechnical meaning of the term. The crime of extortion under these statutes may be committed by a public officer under color of his or her office, or by a private individual. Generally, a person is guilty of extortion (or blackmail) if he or she obtains the property of another by threats or coercion. The elements are further discussed next.

---

[63]   MODEL PENAL CODE § 223.4 (1985).

1. Obtaining Money or Property of Another

As in theft, the definition of property has been expanded in modern statutes, but usually involves money or something of value.

2. By Threats or Coercion

The threat may be either oral or written, and may even be by innuendo or suggestions, but it must be such as would ordinarily create alarm. Obviously, it must be communicated to the victim in order to constitute extortion.

3. To Perform Certain Enumerated Acts (or Not to Perform Duties Required by One's Office)

Specific acts that must be threatened by the perpetrator are often defined under the law. The statutes vary as to the type of threats that will suffice for the crime. Some examples of the types of threats that have been held to be actionable are threats to

- unlawfully injure the person or property of the individual threatened or someone else,
- accuse the individual threatened or someone else of a crime, or
- expose any secret affecting the individual threatened or some other person.

4. The Threat Causes the Victim to Surrender Property

Case Note: *Ohio v. Cunningham*, No. 08-CA-09 (Ohio App., October 3, 2008)
What was the issue and holding of the case?
What was the specific threat?
What is the meaning of the term "benefit"?

To constitute extortion, there must be a causal connection between the threats and the victim surrendering the property. That is, it must be shown that the threat was the controlling factor in the victim's decision to part with the property. However, case law also indicates that the extorter may be seeking a "benefit" that is intangible. Note that in *Ohio v. Cunningham*, presented in Part II of the text, the case concerns a threat in order to get the child-victim to recant her testimony of a sexual offense.

5. Examples of State Statutes

Missouri's statute is an example of how extortion is dealt with in a consolidated theft statute.

§ 570.030 Stealing[64]

(1) A person commits the crime of stealing if he or she appropriates property or services of another with the purpose to deprive him thereof, either without his or her consent or by means of deceit or coercion . . .

---

[64]   MO. ANN. STAT. § 570.030 (Vernon 2002).

"Coercion" is defined under the Missouri statute as

§ 570.010(3) "Coercion" means a threat, however communicated

(a) To commit any crime; or
(b) To inflict physical injury in the future on the person threatened or another; or
(c) To accuse any person of any crime; or
(d) To expose any person to hatred, contempt or ridicule; or
(e) To harm the credit or business repute of any person; or
(f) To take or withhold action as a public servant, or to cause a public servant to take or withhold action; or
(g) To inflict any other harm which would not benefit the actor.

A threat of accusation, lawsuit, or other invocation of official action is not coercion if the property sought to be obtained by virtue of such threat was honestly claimed as restitution or indemnification for harm done in the circumstances to which the accusation, exposure, lawsuit, or other official action relates, or as compensation for property or lawful service.

In New York, the crime of extortion is also a part of the larceny statute. The part relating to extortion provides

§ 155.05 Larceny; defined[65]

(1) A person steals property and commits larceny when, with intent to deprive another of property or to appropriate the same to himself or to a third person, he wrongfully takes, obtains or withholds such property from an owner thereof.
(2) Larceny includes a wrongful taking, obtaining or withholding of another's property, with the intent prescribed in subdivision (1) of this Section, committed in any of the following ways: . . .
(e) By extortion.
A person obtains property by extortion when he compels or induces another person to deliver such property to himself or to a third person by means of instilling in him a fear that, if the property is not so delivered, the actor or another will:
    (i) Cause physical injury to some person in the future; or
    (ii) Cause damage to property; or
    (iii) Engage in other conduct constituting a crime; or
    (iv) Accuse some person of a crime or cause criminal charges to be instituted against him; or
    (v) Expose a secret or publicize an asserted fact, whether true or false, tending to subject some person to hatred, contempt or ridicule; or
    (vi) Cause a strike, boycott or other collective labor group action injurious to some person's business; except that such a threat shall not be deemed extortion when the property is demanded or received for the benefit of the group in whose interest the actor purports to act; or
    (vii) Testify or provide information or withhold testimony or information with respect to another's legal claim or defense; or
    (viii) Use or abuse his position as a public servant by performing some act within or related to his official duties, or by failing or refusing to perform an official duty, in such manner as to affect some person adversely; or

---

[65]   N.Y. PENAL LAW § 155.05 (McKinney 1995).

    (ix) Perform any other act which would not in itself materially benefit the actor but which is calculated to harm another person materially with respect to his health, safety, business, calling, career, financial condition, reputation or personal relationships.

According to the provisions of this part of the statute, in addition to the intent element, the prosecution must show that the wrongful taking was by compelling or inducing another to deliver property to the person making the threat or to a third person by means of instilling fear. This last element (instilling fear) limits the application of the statute.

An issue that arises is how to distinguish extortion from expressing a legal right to demand compensation or seek redress for a wrong. It is not extortion when an aggrieved party threatens to sue; however, it is extortion when someone threatens to come forward with damaging information unless money is paid. The difference is in criminal intent. This issue was present when a young woman threatened to expose actor and comedian Bill Cosby as her biological father unless he paid her a large sum of money. He reported the threat to the authorities and Autumn Jackson was convicted of the federal extortion statute (we will read this case in Chapter 13, which covers federal crimes).

The court commented that the New York and federal extortion statutes applied to the defendant's conduct of sending an unsigned contract to the publisher to print the defendant's claim that she was the victim's child born out of wedlock, along with a demand for $40 million dollars from the victim, whose reputation was threatened, and that this was the precise kind of private transaction, motivated purely by selfish desire for gain, that the extortion statutes validly punish. Subsequently, the case was brought to trial and Jackson was convicted. Upon appeal, the circuit court agreed that the jury instructions should have included the definitional element of "wrongfulness" as a part of the definition of extortion; however, because it was ruled as harmless error, the conviction was ultimately upheld.[66]

Other courts have rendered decisions that explain or limit the scope of the extortion statutes, for instance, to require a reasonable belief that the threat can be carried out. In a North Carolina case, the court agreed that "a threat made in such a manner and with such circumstances that a reasonable person would believe the threat would be carried out" was the proper instruction.[67]

D. *Summary*

In modern statutes extortion can be committed either by a public official or a private citizen. Extortion occurs when a threat is made to perform an act (or not perform an act) that is made in order to obtain property from the victim unlawfully. If the perpetrator is an official, it is usually in relation to their duties or discretionary power; for

---

[66] United States v. Jackson, 180 F.3d 55 (2d Cir. 1999); United States v. Jackson, 196 F.3d 383 (2d Cir. 1999).

[67] State v. Cunningham, 474 S.E.2d 772 (N.C. 1996).

instance, an officer of the court will threaten that prosecution will occur if money is not paid. If the perpetrator is an individual it usually involves a threat of injury—either physical or to the victim's reputation. Extortion does not occur when an individual has a legal right to demand just compensation and threatens legal action if compensation is not paid.

> Extortion
> (A/R) obtain money or thing of value; by threats or coercion to perform or not perform enumerated acts; and property is given in response to threat
> (M/R) intent (specific intent)

§ 8.7   Receiving Stolen Property

A. Common Law

Apparently, under the early English laws, there was no separate and distinct offense of **receipt of stolen property**, but the receiver was subject to indictment and punishment as an accessory to the theft itself. However, the English courts and legislative bodies soon recognized the necessity of creating a substantive crime that was indictable and punishable as an offense separate and distinct from the larceny.[68]

In an effort to reduce the theft of property by punishing those who received the stolen property, the drafters of legislation in this country enacted statutes very early that provided for the prosecution and punishment of those who knowingly aided the takers of property by purchasing the fruits of the crime. Some of the earlier offenses designated the crime of receiving stolen property a misdemeanor, but it was soon recognized that a light penalty was not enough to deter the "fence" (receiver of stolen property). Later statutes made the crime a felony.

Although the terms of the early statutes varied, they generally included the elements of

- receiving stolen property,
- knowing it to have been stolen,
- with the intent to deprive the owner of it.

The gravamen of the offense is the felonious receiving of stolen property belonging to another knowing that it has been stolen.[69]

B. Model Penal Code

The Model Penal Code retains the general provisions of the pre-Model Code statutes, with some exceptions that were the result of case decisions under the previous statutes. For example, the MPC recognizes a defense that the property was "received,

---

[68]   Kirby v. United States, 174 U.S. 47, 19 S. Ct. 574, 43 L. Ed. 890 (1894).
[69]   Curl v. People, 53 Colo. 578, 127 P. 751 (1912); Yeargain v. State, 57 Okla. Crim. 136, 45 P.2d 1113 (1935).

retained, or disposed of with purpose to restore it to the owner." The Model Code also uses the words "retains," or "disposes" rather than the single word "receives," as used in previous statutes.

§ 223.6 Receiving Stolen Property[70]

(1) Receiving. A person is guilty of theft if he purposely receives, retains, or disposes of movable property of another knowing that it has been stolen, or believing that it has probably been stolen, unless the property is received, retained, or disposed of with purpose to restore it to the owner. "Receiving" means acquiring possession, control of title, or lending on the security of the property.

(2) Presumption of Knowledge. The requisite knowledge or belief is presumed in the case of a dealer who:
    (a) is found in possession or control of property stolen from two or more persons on separate occasions; or
    (b) has received stolen property in another transaction within the year preceding the transaction charged; or
    (c) being a dealer in property of the sort received, acquires it for a consideration which he knows is far below its reasonable value.

In the Model Penal Code, the property that may be received, retained, or disposed of is limited to "movable property." Movable property is defined as "property, the location of which can be changed, including things growing on, affixed to, or found in land, and documents, although the rights represented thereof have no physical location." Subsection (2) of the Model Code differs from some older statutes in that it details instances in which the requisite knowledge or belief is presumed to exist. This makes it easier to prove the elements of the crime and is apparently aimed also at making it less difficult to prosecute a fence who receives stolen property.

C. State Statutes, Codes, and Cases

Although all states have statutory provisions that prohibit receiving stolen property and provide a penalty for those who violate the statute, there are differences in the wording of the various statutes. Some, for example, use the word "receiving," which is the traditional term, while others define the prohibited conduct as "obtaining control over stolen property" or "criminal possession of stolen property." In fact, New York has five degrees of receiving stolen property.[71] As to culpability, some states require that the receiver "know that the property is stolen;" some provide that the receiver must "know or believe that the property has probably been stolen;" and others use the phrase "reasonable grounds for believing the property is stolen." As in other criminal cases, to prove the crime of receiving stolen property, the state must prove each element beyond

---

[70]   MODEL PENAL CODE § 223.6 (1985).

[71]   N.Y. PENAL LAW §§ 165.40-165.55 (McKinney 2002). *See* People v. Chapman, 682 N.Y.S.2d 5 (1998).

a reasonable doubt to the exclusion of every reasonable hypothesis of innocence. The elements of the crime differ to some extent from state to state, but some elements are common to most state statutes; these elements are the following:

- receipt of property;
- the property was actually stolen;
- the receiver knew at the time that such property had been stolen; and
- felonious intent on the part of the receiver.

1. Receipt of the Property

This has been interpreted to mean that the person has control over the property—not necessarily physical possession. Taking the property into constructive possession is sufficient, for example, where it was agreed that the property would be put in a place where the receiver would have access to it. Nor is it necessary that the receiver receive the stolen property directly from the thief. If he receives it from an innocent agent of the thief, it is the same as a direct conveyance, and if he knows the goods are stolen, he is guilty of receiving.[72] If the statute requires the state to prove that the object received had value, evidence to that effect must be introduced.

2. The Property Must Have Been Stolen

To constitute the crime, the goods must have been stolen and the character of the goods, as stolen goods, must exist at the time they are received. This element is not present if they are, in fact, not stolen goods, even though the receiver may have believed them to be stolen. The state must also show that the property had been the subject of a robbery or theft by another person. Failure of the state to introduce evidence to show that some other person stole the personal property requires reversal of the conviction.[73]

What happens when the receiver is the target of a sting operation and it is really an undercover police officer who is delivering or selling the property to the receiver? In this case, the property is not stolen because it is in police custody. Even if it had been stolen, once recovered by police, it is arguably not stolen property any longer, but rather recovered property. Some courts have held that the defendant cannot be convicted of receipt of stolen property in these circumstances (although, arguably, they may be guilty of attempt).[74] This is a case of either factual or hybrid legal impossibility. It is possible that some courts may not even allow for a conviction of attempted stolen property if they interpret it as a type of legal impossibility (the property's character will make it such that it could never be a crime to receive it). On the other hand, the majority

---

[72]   Sanderson v. Commonwealth, 12 S.W. 136 (Ky. 1889); Commonwealth v. White, 123 Mass. 430, 25 Am. Rep. 116 (1877).
[73]   State v. Price, 980 S.W.2d 143 (Mo. 1998).
[74]   United States v. Monasterski, 567 F.2d. 677 (1987).

opinion is that it is either an attempted receipt, or statutes can be rewritten to revise the nature of the property to include "apparently stolen" property.

3. The Recipient Must Know That It Was Stolen

One of the most difficult elements to prove is the knowledge of the stolen character of the goods. Knowledge at the time the goods were received that they have been stolen is absolutely essential. In proving this element, the jury may infer knowledge from the circumstances. For example, evidence that the defendant had in his possession a wallet containing six stolen credit cards and the complainant's checkbook was legally sufficient to support this element.[75] Guilty knowledge can be established from circumstantial evidence that would, in the opinion of the fact finder, lead a reasonable person to believe the property was stolen. But mere possession of a stolen thing does not rise to a presumption that the possessor knew it was stolen.[76]

One court explained that guilty knowledge that property is stolen, as required to support a conviction for receiving stolen property, may be proved by direct evidence or by any surrounding facts or circumstances from which such knowledge may be inferred. The court continued by stating that evidence of the unexplained possession of recently stolen goods by one charged with unlawfully receiving them is a strong circumstance to be considered with all the evidence on the question of guilty knowledge, and may be sufficient to warrant conviction when it is coupled with attempts at concealment.[77]

4. The Recipient Must Have Felonious Intent

In order to be criminally liable, the prosecution must prove felonious intent. For example, one who receives goods, knowing them to have been stolen, is not guilty if his purpose is to return them to their owner or merely to detect the thief.[78]

5. Examples of State Statutes

A Louisiana court designated the elements that must be proved, stating that in order to convict the defendant of illegal possession of stolen goods valued at more than $500, the state must prove beyond a reasonable doubt that the defendant (1) intentionally possessed, procured, received, or concealed; (2) anything of value; (3) that has been the subject of any robbery or theft; (4) where circumstances indicate that the offender knew or had good reason to believe that the thing was the subject of one of these offenses; and that (5) the value of the stolen items exceeds $500.[79]

---

[75]   People v. Chapman, 682 N.Y.S.2d 5 (1998).
[76]   Cunningham v. State, 475 S.E.2d 924 (Ga. 1996).
[77]   State v. R.W., 721 So.2d 743 (La. 1998). *See also* Avett v. State, 928 S.W.2d 326 (Ark. 1996).
[78]   Washington v. State, 726 So.2d 209 (Miss. 1998).
[79]   State v. Alexander, 720 So.2d 82 (La. 1998).

A Virginia appeals court enumerated the elements of the offense of receiving stolen property with this summary:

> Conviction of the defendant for receiving property required proof that the automobile was: (1) previously stolen by another; (2) received by the defendant; (3) with knowledge of the theft; and (4) a dishonest intent.[80]

6. Dealing in Stolen Property

Some states have chosen to utilize separate statutes for those individuals who traffic in stolen goods. Florida's statute, for instance, targets a person who "traffics in, or endeavors to traffic in, property that he knows or should know was stolen . . ." and includes those who organize, plan, finance, direct, manage or supervise the theft of property.[81]

D. *Summary*

The crime of receiving stolen property did not exist under the common law; instead, the perpetrator was charged as an accessory to the theft. However, statutes were created as early as the 1800s that made the crime of receiving stolen property a separate and distinct crime. These statutes are directed toward the "fence"—the individual who makes it more convenient for the thief to receive money for the property he steals. Today, there are strict controls on businesses such as pawnshops and flea market vendors to attempt to regulate the sale of stolen merchandise. These businesses are required to keep invoices and other paperwork and allow police access to inspect these records. When stolen goods are identified, failure to keep these records may go to prove knowledge that the goods were stolen.

> Receipt of Stolen Goods
> (A/R) receipt (possession or constructive possession) of stolen goods
> (M/R) knowledge (that goods are stolen); intent (felonious, i.e., no intent to return goods to owner)

§ 8.8   Other Crimes Involving Theft

Although contemporary statutes in the various states are more uniform than they were 15 or 20 years ago, there are still specific acts that are offenses in some states but not in others. In this section, some of the statutes that have not been discussed previously are included as examples of statutes that may or may not be found in the states.

---

[80]   Bynum v. Commonwealth, 477 S.E.2d 750 (Va. 1996).
[81]   Fla. Stat. Ann. § 812.019 (West 1999).

A. *Operating a Motor Vehicle without the Owner's Consent*

After the use of the automobile became common, there was a problem with the laws of theft when the individual did not keep the automobile but merely "borrowed" it and left it somewhere for the owner to find. Because one of the elements of larceny is "intent to permanently deprive the owner," "**joyriding**" could not be defined as larceny.

The Model Penal Code addresses the unauthorized use of vehicles and is broad enough to include any motor-driven vehicle. The MPC recognizes an affirmative defense that the actor *reasonably* believes that the owner would have consented to the operation had he or she known of it.

§ 223.9 Unauthorized Use of Automobiles and Other Vehicles[82]

A person commits a misdemeanor if he operates another's automobile, airplane, motorcycle, motorboat, or other motor-propelled vehicle without consent of the owner. It is an affirmative defense to prosecution under this Section that the actor reasonably believed that the owner would have consented to the operation had he known of it.

In some states, the larceny statutes were modified to include unlawfully taking, driving, or operating a motor vehicle without the knowledge and consent of the owner, with the punishment being the same as for larceny. Other specific statutes were designed to punish a person who temporarily took possession of automobiles and other motor vehicles for the purpose of temporarily depriving the owner of the use of the vehicle.

While each state has a statute or code dealing with theft of vehicles, they differ in scope and even the penalty attached. Some include any vehicle, while others restrict the coverage to propelled vehicles. Some require that the person charged know that he does not have the consent of the owner, while in other states it is an affirmative defense if the defendant reasonably believes that the owner would have consented.

An example of a state statute that is broad enough in scope to include the unauthorized use of any vehicle and also requires that the prosecution show that the person operating the vehicle knew that he did not have consent is that of New York. The statute provides

§ 165.05 Unauthorized use of a vehicle in the third degree[83]

A person is guilty of unauthorized use of a vehicle in the third degree when:

(1) Knowing that he does not have the consent of the owner, he takes, operates, exercises control over, rides in or otherwise uses a vehicle. A person who engages in any such conduct without the consent of the owner is presumed to know that he does not have such consent; or

(2) Having custody of a vehicle pursuant to an agreement between himself or another and the owner thereof whereby he or another is to perform for compensation a specific service for the owner involving the maintenance, repair or use of

---

82　MODEL PENAL CODE § 223.9 (1985).
83　N.Y. PENAL LAW § 165.05 (McKinney 2002).

such vehicle, he intentionally uses or operates the same, without the consent of the owner, for his own purposes in a manner constituting a gross deviation from the agreed purpose; or

(3) Having custody of a vehicle pursuant to an agreement with the owner thereof whereby such vehicle is to be returned to the owner at a specified time, he intentionally retains or withholds possession thereof, without the consent of the owner, for so lengthy a period beyond the specified time as to render such retention or possession a gross deviation from the agreement.

For purposes of this Section, "a gross deviation from the agreement" shall consist of, but not be limited to, circumstances wherein a person who, having had custody of a vehicle for a period of fifteen days or less pursuant to a written agreement, retains possession of such vehicle for at least seven days beyond the period specified in the agreement and continues such possession for a period of more than two days after service or refusal of attempted service of a notice in person or by certified mail at an address indicated in the agreement, stating:

(i) the date and time at which the vehicle was to have been returned under the agreement;

(ii) that the owner does not consent to the continued withholding or retaining of such vehicle and demands its return; and that continued withholding or retaining of the vehicle may constitute a class A misdemeanor punishable by a fine of up to one thousand dollars or by a sentence to a term of imprisonment for a period of up to one year or by both such fine and imprisonment.

In addition to providing a penalty where a person knowingly takes or operates a vehicle without the consent of the owner, the New York statute includes a provision that subjects short-term car renters to criminal liability for failure to return a rental car on time. The elements of unauthorized use of a vehicle under paragraph (1) of the New York statute are taking, operating, exercising control over, or riding in or otherwise using a vehicle, without the consent of the owner, or knowledge that the owner has not consented.

In interpreting the phrase "exercises control over," one court reasoned that a juvenile's momentary presence in a stripped car did not constitute exercise of dominion over the vehicle and did not constitute "unauthorized use of a vehicle" as used in the statute. In this case, the police officer had indicated that he saw the juvenile exiting the passenger side of the car; the juvenile claimed that he had merely reached into the car to pick up some change. There was no evidence that the car was operable.[84]

Do "taking and using without consent of the owner" statutes apply to the passengers in a car as well as the driver? One must look to the wording of the statute and to the cases interpreting the statute to make this determination. A Washington court determined that finding that the defendant rode in a vehicle knowing that it had been taken without its owner's consent was sufficiently supported by the evidence to show guilty knowledge as required to support the conviction.[85] A Maryland court also held that evidence that the person was a willing passenger in a car that he knew was stolen is

---

[84]   Matter of Ruven P., 542 N.Y.S. 272 (1989). *See also* People v. Gray, 546 N.Y.S.2d 387 (1989).

[85]   State v. Womble, 969 P.2d 1097 (Wash. 1999).

sufficient evidence of criminal intent to sustain a conviction for the unauthorized use of a motor vehicle.[86]

The crime of "joyriding" or taking a car without the owner's permission was created because traditional larceny statutes require the prosecutor to prove intent to permanently deprive the owner of the property. All states have some provision to deal with cases in which such intent cannot be proven. The elements are the following:

- possession and control of auto (sometimes mere passenger)
- without owner's permission
- knowledge of owner's lack of consent (general intent)

B. *Theft of Services*

Many states have provisions relating to the theft of designated services, such as telephone service, while others have general statutes relating to the **theft of services**. An example is that of Texas, which provides

§ 31.04 Theft of Service[87]

(a) A person commits theft of service if, with intent to avoid payment for service that he knows is provided only for compensation:

    (1) he intentionally or knowingly secures performance of the service by deception, threat, or false token;

    (2) having control over the disposition of services of another to which he is not entitled, he intentionally or knowingly diverts the other's services to his own benefit or to the benefit of another not entitled to them;

    (3) having control of personal property under a written rental agreement, he holds the property beyond the expiration of the rental period without the effective consent of the owner of the property, thereby depriving the owner of the property of its use in further rentals; or

    (4) he intentionally or knowingly secures the performance of the service by agreeing to provide compensation and, after the service is rendered, fails to make payment after receiving notice demanding payment.

(b) For purposes of this Section, intent to avoid payment is presumed if:

    (1) the actor absconded without paying for the service or expressly refused to pay for the service in circumstances where payment is ordinarily made immediately upon rendering of the service, as in hotels, campgrounds, recreational vehicle parks, restaurants, and comparable establishments;

    (2) the actor failed to return the property held under a rental agreement or failed to make payment under a service agreement within 10 days after receiving notice demanding return; or

    (3) the actor returns property held under a rental agreement after the expiration of the rental agreement and fails to pay the applicable rental charge for the property within 10 days after the date on which the actor received notice demanding payment.

(c) For purposes of Subsections (a)(4) and (b)(2), notice shall be notice in writing, sent by registered or certified mail with return receipt requested or by

---

[86]   In re Levon A., 720 A.2d 1232 (Md. 1998).

[87]   TEX. PENAL CODE ANN. § 31.04 (Vernon 2002).

telegram with report of delivery requested, and addressed to the actor at his address shown on the rental agreement or service agreement.

(d) If written notice is given in accordance with Subsection (c) of this Section, it is presumed that the notice was received no later than five days after it was sent.

(e) An offense under this Section is:

    (1) a Class C misdemeanor if the value of the service stolen is less than $20;

    (2) a Class B misdemeanor if the value of the service stolen is $20 or more but less than $500;

    (3) a Class A misdemeanor if the value of the service stolen is $500 or more but less than $1,500;

    (4) a state jail felony if the value of the service stolen is $1,500 or more but less than $20,000;

    (5) a felony of the third degree if the value of the service stolen is $20,000 or more but less than $100,000;

    (6) a felony of the second degree if the value of the service stolen is more than $100,000 but less than $200,000;

    (7) a felony of the first degree if the value of the service stolen is $200,000 or more.

Under the provisions of this statute and similar statutes, the elements are the following:

- receipt of services
- intent to avoid payment
- knowledge that services are provided only for compensation
- by one of the three methods indicated

LEGAL NEWS: THEFT OF AN EDUCATION

A homeless mother in Connecticut has been charged with grand larceny because she enrolled her son at an elementary school using a false address. School authorities who filed the complaint say she has "stolen" $15,686 worth of services—the cost of a year of school in the town where she sent her son to school.

Retrieved January 5, 2011 from http://www.newser.com/story/117295/tanya-mcdowell-case-homeless-mom-faces-jail-for-enrolling-son-in-school.html.

C. Theft of Property Lost, Mislaid, or Delivered by Mistake

One might argue that keeping property that is found, or that was delivered by mistake, should not be a crime. However, in most jurisdictions, the lawmakers have determined that failure to take reasonable measures to restore lost, mislaid, or misdelivered property to the owner with the intent to deprive the owner of the property should be a crime, even though this was not a crime at common law. An example of a statute that punishes for theft of property lost, mislaid, or delivered by mistake is that of Kentucky. It provides

§ 514.050. Theft of Property Lost, Mislaid, or Delivered by Mistake[88]

(1) Except as provided in KRS 365.710, a person is guilty of theft of property lost, mislaid, or delivered by mistake when:
  (a) he comes into control of the property of another that he knows to have been lost, mislaid, or delivered under a mistake as to the nature or amount of the property or the identity of the recipient; and
  (b) with intent to deprive the owner thereof, he fails to take reasonable measures to restore the property to a person entitled to have it.
(2) Theft of property lost, mislaid, or delivered by mistake is a Class A misdemeanor unless the value of the property is $300, in which case it is a Class D felony.

Under the Kentucky statute and like statutes, the elements of the offense are

- control of property by suspect
- property of another
- knowledge that property had been lost, mislaid, or mistakenly delivered
- intent to deprive the owner of the property
- failure to take reasonable measures to restore the property to the person entitled to it

This list of crimes involving theft is not intended to be exhaustive. There are many other crimes involving theft that are included in various federal, state, and local laws.

§ 8.9 Forgery and Related Offenses

One of the most common crimes in our society today is **forgery**. After some hesitation to enact fraud statutes, lawmakers and merchants recognized that there was a strong social interest in maintaining trust in the genuineness of checks and other commercial paper. If false instruments are prevalent in a community or society, commerce is affected because people will have less trust that these documents are genuine.

A. Common Law

At early common law, forgery belonged to the class of misdemeanors called **cheats**, and was regarded as a misdemeanor, not a felony. Later, it was designated a felony in both English and American statutes. One early definition of forgery is the "fraudulent making or alteration of a writing to the prejudice of another man's right."[89] Blackstone's definition included the elements currently recognized: "the false making

---

[88] KY. REV. STAT. § 514.050 (2001). See MODEL PENAL CODE § 223.5 (1985) for states that have adopted similar statutes.
[89] Ratliff v. State, 175 Tenn. 172, 133 S.W.2d 470 (1939).

or materially altering, with intent to defraud, of any writing which, if genuine, might apparently be of legal efficacy or the foundation of a legal liability."[90]

Early statutes in all states had provisions relating to forgery. These statutes, for the most part, included coverage of the common law, but sometimes extended the law to include crimes not within the scope of the common law offense, and often increased the severity of punishment.

B. Model Penal Code

The Model Code uses the term "writing" and defines writing very comprehensively. Also, the Model Code provision includes what was defined under previous provisions as "uttering a forged instrument." Instead of the term "intent to defraud," the Model Code uses "with purpose to defraud or injure anyone." Subsection (1) provides that forgery is committed if the defendant acts "with knowledge that he is facilitating a fraud or injury to be perpetrated by anyone." This makes it clear that a forger commits an offense even though he does not defraud the person to whom he sells or passes a forged writing.

§ 224.1 Forgery[91]

(1) Definition. A person is guilty of forgery if, with purpose to defraud or injure anyone, or with knowledge that he is facilitating a fraud or injury to be perpetrated by anyone, the actor:

(a) alters any writing of another without his authority; or

(b) makes, completes, executes, authenticates, issues or transfers any writing so that it purports to be the act of another who did not authorize that act, or to have been executed at a time or place or in a numbered sequence other than was in fact the case, or to be a copy of an original when no such original existed; or

(c) utters any writing which he knows to be forged in a manner specified in paragraphs (a) or (b).

"Writing" includes printing or any other method of recording information, money, coins, tokens, stamps, seals, credit cards, badges, trademarks and other symbols of value, right, privilege or identification.

(2) Grading. Forgery is a felony of the second degree if the writing is or purports to be part of an issue of money, securities, postage, or revenue stamps, or other instruments issued by the government, or part of an issue of stock, bonds, or other instruments representing interests in or claims against any property or enterprise. Forgery is a felony of the third degree if the writing is or purports to be a will, deed, contract, release, commercial instrument, or other document evidencing, creating, transferring, altering, terminating, or otherwise affecting legal relations. Otherwise forgery is a misdemeanor.

---

[90]   4 Blackstone, Commentaries 247 (1765-1869), 2 Bish. Cr. Law, § 523.

[91]   Model Penal Code § 224.1 (1985).

C. State Statutes, Codes, and Cases

Modern statutes have expanded the types of documents that can be forged and have increased the penalty of the crime. The essential elements of forgery remain unchanged from the earliest cases.

1. Fraudulent or False Writing or Alteration

It is an indispensable requirement of forgery that the writing be false. It may have been false in its inception or may have been made so by subsequent tampering with what was originally genuine.

2. Writing or Document

The subject of forgery may be a deed, a mortgage, a check, bill of exchange, order for goods or money, receipt, or even a diploma.[92] Most forgery cases that reached the courts concerned the forgery of checks or money orders. However, any writing or document may be forged and the forger prosecuted if the document is believed to have **legal efficacy**. What this means, in general, is a document that creates legal rights or obligations for any party. For instance, a New York court affirmed that a federally issued Resident Alien Card, or "green card," was covered by the state forgery law such that a defendant in possession of an allegedly forged green card could be prosecuted for criminal possession of a forged instrument.[93] In the case of *State v. Wasson*, a traffic ticket was deemed to be a writing of legal efficacy when Wasson forged his brother's signature to escape punishment.[94]

3. Intent to Defraud

Unless there is the intent to defraud, there is no crime of forgery. However, it is immaterial whether anyone is actually defrauded.[95] To put it another way, if you are, for whatever reason, doodling Brad Pitt's name on a piece of paper because you like the way it looks, that is not forgery. It is forgery when you stay in an expensive hotel and sign his name to the guest registry because you are attempting to defraud the hotel by pretending to be someone else; and it is forgery even if the hotel desk clerk knows immediately that you are not that person. While some courts describe the *mens rea* as specific intent and others call it general intent, basically what is necessary is proof that the offender meant to defraud another by the use of the material alteration or created document.

---

[92]   Hicks v. State, 176 Ga. 727, 168 S.E. 899 (1933); Saucier v. State, 102 Miss. 647, 59 So. 858 (1912).
[93]   People v. Dorneval, 684 N.Y.S.2d 434 (1998).
[94]   State v. Wasson, 964 P.2d 820 (N.M. App. 1998).
[95]   Ratliff v. State, 175 Tenn. 172, 133 S.E.2d 470 (1939); People v. Henderson, 373 N.E.2d 1338 (Ill. 1978).

4. Forgery or Alteration Is Material

While this is not spelled out in the definition itself, the courts have insisted that the forgery or the alteration be material; that is, it must have prejudicial effect. However, even a slight change in the legal meaning will be considered material and thus an alteration. In one case, the court agreed that it was not forgery to change the figures on a check to correspond with the sum recited in words (a statute provided that where there is a discrepancy, the sum expressed by the words is the sum that is payable), because the alteration did not change the legal effect of the instrument.[96] However, this action could be prosecuted as attempted forgery if the other elements of the crime were present.

5. Examples of State Statutes

Some states use the wording of the Model Penal Code; others state the violation and also define the terms used in the statute. For example, the Louisiana statute as rewritten in 2001 provides

§ 72. Forgery[97]

(A) It shall be unlawful to forge, with intent to defraud, any signature to, or any part of any writing purporting to have legal efficacy.

(B) Issuing, transferring, or possessing with intent to defraud, a forged writing, known by the offender to be a forged writing, shall also constitute a violation of the provisions of this Section.

(C) For purposes of this Section:
  (1) "Forge" means the following:
    (a) To alter, make, complete, execute, or authenticate any writing so that it purports:
      (i) To be the act of another who did not authorize that act;
      (ii) To have been executed at a time or place or in a numbered sequence other than was in fact the case; or
      (iii) To be a copy of an original when no such original existed.
    (b) To issue, transfer, register the transfer of, pass, publish, or otherwise utter a writing that is forged in accordance with the meaning of Subparagraph (1)(a).
    (c) To possess a writing that is forged within the meaning of Subparagraph (1)(a).
  (2) "Writing" means the following:
    (a) Printing or any other method of recording information;
    (b) Money, coins, tokens, stamps, seals, credit cards, badges, and trademarks; and
    (c) Symbols of value, right, privilege, or identification.

D. Whoever commits the crime of forgery shall be fined not more than five thousand dollars, or imprisoned, with or without hard labor, for not more than ten years, or both.

---

[96] People v. Lewinger, 25 Ill. 332, 96 N.E. 837 (1911).
[97] LA. REV. STAT. § 14:72 (2001).

Most forgery cases involve the forgery of checks; however, states have drafted statutes that are more comprehensive and all-inclusive. For example, the Missouri forgery statute provides that a person commits the crime of forgery if, with the purpose to defraud, that person

(1) Makes, completes, alters or authenticates any writing so that it purports to have been made by another or at another time or place in a numbered sequence other than was in fact the case or with different terms or by authority of one who did not give such authority; or

(2) Erases, obliterates or destroys any writing; or

(3) Makes or alters anything other than a writing, so that it purports to have a genuineness, antiquity, rarity, ownership or authorship which it does not possess; or

(4) Uses as genuine, or possesses for the purpose of using as genuine, or transfers with knowledge or belief that it will be used as genuine, any writing or other thing which the actor knows has been made or altered in the manner described in this section.[98]

The definition of "writing," as used in the Ohio Code, includes not only legal and commercial documents traditionally covered by forgery, but also private, noncommercial documents not formerly covered. The subject of forgery under this section may also include any symbol of value, right, privilege, or identification, such as credit cards, ID cards, trademarks, and others. The definition of "forge" includes all forms of falsification purporting to authenticate a writing.[99]

In other case decisions, courts have defined the elements of forgery:

- (Pennsylvania) "In order to obtain a forgery conviction, the Commonwealth must prove that this was a false writing, that the instrument was capable of deceiving, and that the defendant intended to defraud."[100]
- (New Mexico) "The elements of forgery include falsely making or altering a writing which purports to have legal efficacy, or knowingly issuing or transferring a forged writing."[101]
- (Georgia) "(1) knowingly making, altering or possessing any writing, (2) in such a manner that the writing as made or altered purports to have been made by authority of one who did not have such authority, and (3) uttering or delivering such writing, (4) with intent to defraud."[102]
- (Massachusetts) "only when the false making is done with specific intent to defraud is the crime of forgery established."[103]

---

[98] Mo. Rev. Stat. § 570.090 (2002).
[99] Ohio Rev. Code Ann. § 2913.31 (Anderson 1999).
[100] Commonwealth v. Fisher, 682 A.2d 811 (Pa. 1996).
[101] State v. Wasson, 125 N.M. 656, 964 P.2d 820 (1998).
[102] McClure v. State, 234 Ga. App. 304, 506 S.E.2d 667 (1998).
[103] Commonwealth v. O'Connell, 769 N.E.2d 331 (Mass. 2002). *See also* State v. Johnson, 817 So. 2d 283 (La. 2002), which held that an essential ingredient of the crime of forgery is a specific intent to defraud.

D. Related Crimes

There are many crimes related to the common law crime of forgery. We will review a few of these crimes in this section but individual states may identify and define such activities very differently.

1. Uttering a Forged Instrument

Under the common law and in some states today **uttering** and forgery are two different crimes. To utter a forged instrument is to offer it, directly or indirectly, by words or actions, as good. This, if done with intent to defraud, and with knowledge of the falsity of the instrument, was a violation at common law, and today is a crime in all states. Uttering a forged instrument is offering, as genuine, an instrument known to be false, with intent to defraud.

The traditional crime of uttering a forged instrument is included in Section 224.1 of the Model Penal Code as part of forgery. The penalty for uttering a forged instrument is the same as that provided for forgery. However, uttering can also be a distinct offense. In Michigan, which has a separate statute on uttering, to prove the elements of uttering and publishing, the prosecution introduces evidence to show that the defendant knew the instrument was false, that he or she had intent to defraud, and that he or she presented the forged instrument for payment.[104]

The elements of uttering a forged instrument generally include the following: publishing or offering (although the offer may not be successful); a forged instrument; presented as true or genuine; with knowledge that it is false; and, with intent to defraud.

The person who "utters" the forgery does not, necessarily, have to be the same person who forged the document. Thus, someone can be guilty of forgery (but not uttering), uttering (but not forgery), or both. It is essential that the prosecutor proves the utterer knew the document to be false. Also, if someone shows an item and promotes it as a fake or altered document or counterfeit, then this element is not present, nor is there intent to defraud. Proof can be circumstantial. In a Virginia case, the court found that the required knowledge element was proved when the evidence indicated that the suspect drove away from a bank window after a bank teller attempted to stall the defendant as another teller telephoned the police. This conduct, according to the court, was sufficient evidence of knowledge and intent.[105]

2. Criminal Simulation

Criminal simulation statutes are designed to prohibit forgery when the subject of the offense is not a writing but an object. For example, the Ohio statute provides

---

[104] State v. Williams, 152 Mo. 115, 53 S.W. 424 (1899); People v. Brown, 397 Ill. 92, 72 N.E.2d 859 (1947). People v. Dukes, 471 N.W.2d 651 (Mich. Ct. App. 1991); People v. Shively, 584 N.W.2d 740 (Mich. Ct. App. 1998).

[105] Ramsey v. Commonwealth, 343 S.E.2d 465 (Va. Ct. App. 1986). *See also* State v. Brown, 108 Ohio App. 3d 489, 664 N.E.2d 536 (1996).

(A) No person, with purpose to defraud, or knowing that the person is facilitating a fraud, shall do any of the following:

(1) Make or alter any object so that it appears to have value because of antiquity, rarity, curiosity, source, or authorship, which it does not in fact possess;

(2) Practice deception in making, retouching, editing, or reproducing any photograph, movie film, videotape, phonograph record, or recording tape;

(3) Falsely or fraudulently make, simulate, forge, alter, or counterfeit any wrapper, label, stamp, cork, or cap prescribed by the Liquor Control Commission under Chapters 4301. and 4303. of the Revised Code, falsely or fraudulently cause to be made, simulated, forged, altered, or counterfeited any wrapper, label, stamp, cork, or cap prescribed by the Liquor Control Commission under Chapters 4301. and 4303. of the Revised Code, or use more than once any wrapper, label, stamp, cork, or cap prescribed by the Liquor Control Commission under Chapters 4301. and 4303. of the Revised Code;

(4) Utter, or possess with purpose to utter, any object that the person knows to have been simulated as provided in Division (A)(1), (2), or (3) of this section.[106]

LEGAL NEWS: IS IT A FORGERY?

In 2007, the state of Texas announced its imminent purchase (for close to $500,000) of a letter purported to have been written by Davy Crockett shortly before he was killed at the Alamo. Upon the announcement, several experts hotly contested the authenticity of the letter, offered by Simpson Galleries in Houston, and the state backed out of the purchase when no independent expert would authenticate the letter. Experts argued that, although the letter was written on old paper and probably had been written in roughly the same period, it was not Crockett's handwriting and it contained far fewer grammatical and spelling errors than was his pattern. Some argued that it may have been a copy of a true letter by a family member for the purpose of records. In any event, the state did not purchase the letter. Even though this is a writing, it is more similar to criminal simulation than forgery because the letter has no legal efficacy (it does not create any legal obligations). Only if the seller knew the letter was not genuine and offered it with the intent to defraud would a crime be committed.

Source: Associated Press (2007). "Experts to Authenticate Purported Crokett Letter." Accessed December 30, 2008 from http://www.news8austin.com/shared/print/default.asp?ArID=191812. Also, "Texas Pays $490,000 for Fake Davy Crocket Letter?" My FineBooks blog. Accessed March 18, 2008. from http://blog.myfinebooks.com/2007/07/09/texas-pays-4900.html.

---

[106] OHIO REV. CODE ANN. § 2913.32 (Anderson 2002). *See also* KY. REV. STAT. § 516.110 (2001) and MODEL PENAL CODE § 224.2 (1985), which includes comments relating to states having similar statutes.

3. Misuse of Credit Cards

As the use of credit cards became common, states were forced to enact statutes that covered offenses involving the improper use of such cards. Some of these actions might be covered by more traditional forgery statutes, but not all of the actions involve the elements of forgery. An example is that of Ohio, which provides

(A) No person shall do any of the following:
  (1) Practice deception for the purpose of procuring the issuance of a credit card, when a credit card is issued in actual reliance thereon;
  (2) Knowingly buy or sell a credit card from or to a person other than the issuer.
(B) No person, with purpose to defraud, shall do any of the following:
  (1) Obtain control over a credit card as security for a debt;
  (2) Obtain property or services by the use of a credit card, in one or more transactions, knowing or having reasonable cause to believe that such card has expired or been revoked, or was obtained, is retained, or is being used in violation of law;
  (3) Furnish property or services upon presentation of a credit card, knowing that such card is being used in violation of law;
  (4) Represent or cause to be represented to the issuer of a credit card that property or services have been furnished, knowing that the representation is false.
(C) No person, with purpose to violate this section, shall receive, possess, control, or dispose of a credit card.[107]

Among other things, this statute prohibits the use of deception in obtaining a credit card in the first instance, buying or selling a credit card, and obtaining property or services with a credit card with knowledge that the credit card has expired or has been revoked. It also provides a penalty for the business operator who furnishes property or services and charges it to a credit card knowing that such a card is being used in violation of the law. In other states, the wording is different from that of Ohio. Some provisions require intent to defraud; others omit any intent requirements. Florida has a comprehensive credit card chapter in its criminal code. Sections include

- False statement as to financial condition or identity.
- Theft; obtaining credit card through fraudulent means.
- Fraudulent use of credit cards.
- Traffic in counterfeit credit cards.
- Expired or revoked credit cards.
- Fraud by person authorized to provide goods or services.
- Use of scanning device or reencoder to defraud; penalties.
- Possession and transfer of credit-card-making equipment.
- Receipt of money, etc., obtained by fraudulent use of credit cards.
- Alteration of credit card invoice; penalties.[108]

[107] Ohio Rev. Code Ann. § 2913.21 (Anderson 2002).
[108] Florida Statutes 2008. Title XLVI. Ch. 817. Credit Card Crimes.

4. Identity Theft

Note that what is commonly referred to as identity theft is often a combination of several crimes. First, there is a theft (offenders typically steal bank statements, credit card information or the cards themselves, or other identity information from the consumer or a business that has such information from multiple consumers), there may be a computer crime involved, then there are usually multiple crimes using the identity that might be charged as forgeries, credit card abuse, or some other theft statute depending on the state penal code. Some states have passed identity theft statutes that encompass the theft of the identity by whatever means, the possession of identity information, and the use of such for fraudulent purposes. Federal laws are more comprehensive, thus, this crime will be covered in more detail in Chapter 12.

5. Computer Crimes – State

Identity theft may involve the use of the computer in obtaining personal information or using illegally obtained personal identity information in order to defraud an unsuspecting merchant by purchasing online. As changes and advances in computer technology have developed, criminals have found new and innovative ways to use computers to assist them in committing crimes. To meet this evolving class of crimes, legislators have experimented with new laws to confront the computer criminals. Computers can be the object of a crime or an instrument of a crime. Computer hacking is when the sole interest of the criminal is to get into a company's computer records to cause havoc, but other crimes involve the computer in new forms of theft. As with identity theft, because this crime often involves federal laws and is prosecuted at the federal level, we will withhold the discussion of it until Chapter 12; however, the following legal news item shows that states also prosecute forms of computer crime.

LEGAL NEWS: STATE COMPUTER CRIMES

In 2010 a man was charged under a Texas state computer crime statute called "Break of Computer Security" punishable by up to two years behind bars. The man had recently been fired by a company that financed automobile loans. The company placed GPS locators in financed cars, which allowed it to deactivate the starter (used when owners defaulted on payments). The disgruntled ex-employee used his home computer and the password he kept from the company to access the system and deactivate the starter on dozens of cars. The result was many angry owners who demanded reimbursement for missed work and towing expenses. The man also manipulated company records, changing identification numbers and eliminating loan documents. Police tracked him through his IP address.

Source: Rosales, C. 2010. Austin car dealer stung as engines go dead. San Antonio Express News, Friday, March 19, 2010, 8b.

6. Related Offenses

Other offenses that are related to forgery are using slugs (coin replicas), fraudulent destruction, removal, or concealment of recordable instruments, and tampering with records.[109] Most states have some type of statute that prohibits knowingly tampering with records with the purpose to defraud. These statutes have different titles, but the purpose generally is the same. One example is that of Nebraska, which is titled "False Statement or Book Entry; Destruction or Secretion of Records; Penalty, Organization, Defined." A person commits a Class 5 misdemeanor if he or she

(a) willfully and knowingly subscribes to, makes or causes to be made any false statement or entry into the books of an organization; or

(b) knowingly subscribes to or exhibits false papers with intent to deceive any person or persons authorized to examine into the affairs of any such organization; or

(c) makes, states, or publishes any false statement of the amount of assets or liabilities of any such organization; or

(d) fails to make true and correct entry in the books and records of such organization of its business and transactions in the manner and form prescribed by the Department of Banking and Finances; or

(e) mutilates, alters, destroys, secretes, or removes any of the books or records of such organization, without the consent of the Director of Banking and Finance.[110]

In Ohio, the crime is called "Tampering with Records." This section prohibits tampering with all private, as well as public, records for fraudulent purposes. The rationale is that the substantial harm can, in a given case, result from tampering with a personal letter file, bank statement, or other private document, as well as from tampering with the correspondence files or records in a public office.[111]

E. Summary

Forgery has been expanded from common law to include almost any document that has "legal efficacy." It also includes the creation or alteration of documents. Some statutes have greatly enlarged the coverage of forgery to include other items in addition to documents of legal efficacy; however, in other states, these items are covered in a separate statute, sometimes called Criminal Simulation. Uttering may be a separate crime from forgery, although many state statutes include uttering in the forgery statute. In these states, uttering may be one of the alternative acts that can constitute a forgery charge. In this case, it is not considered a separate crime; however, it is not a lesser included crime in any case. The most important element of the crime of uttering is that the offender has knowledge of the forgery and intent to defraud. Credit cards and their abuse have spawned a wide range of crimes, including fraudulent obtaining and use. These statutes cover dishonest users of credit cards as well as merchants. Tampering

---

[109]   MODEL PENAL CODE § 224.3-4 (1985).

[110]   NEB. REV. STAT. § 28-612 (2002). *See also* OHIO REV. CODE ANN. § 2913.42 (Anderson 2002).

[111]   OHIO REV. CODE ANN. § 2913.45 (Anderson 2002).

with records is often a separate crime and deals with the making of false records or dishonest bookkeeping practices. Identity theft and computer crimes are growing problems and the federal government has been heavily involved in the suppression of such crimes by creating federal laws and prosecuting the activities at a federal level.

Forgery
(A/R) creation of false document or material alteration of genuine document of legal efficacy
(M/R) intent to defraud (general intent)

Uttering a Forged Document
(A/R) presenting, publishing, or offering a forged document as genuine, knowing it to be false
(M/R) intent to defraud (general intent)

§ 8.10   False Advertising

A. Common Law

False advertising, as such, was not a crime at common law. The phrase *caveat emptor* (let the buyer beware) described the situation between the consumer and merchant. In general, the consumer was expected to know that advertisers may exaggerate or even lie about their product. However, making untrue and fraudulent statements about products became so extensive that both state and municipal governments deemed it necessary for the protection of the public to prohibit the practice. As a consequence, even in the early 1900s, numerous statutes and ordinances were enacted, prohibiting false or fraudulent statements in advertising. The crime of false advertising consisted primarily of the publication and circulation of deceptive matter, and the offense was complete without regard to whether anyone was deceived or damaged.

B. Model Penal Code

The drafters of the Model Code consolidated several older crimes relating to cheating and deceptive practices into one comprehensive statute. Subsections (5), (6), and (7) deal with situations in which false or misleading statements are made for specific purposes. Under this provision, the criminality of the conduct is making "misleading" statements. The last paragraphs of the Model Code provide an affirmative defense if the defendant proves, by a preponderance of the evidence, that his or her conduct was not knowingly or recklessly deceptive.

§ 224.7 Deceptive Business Practices[112]

A person commits a misdemeanor if, in the course of business, he:

---

[112]   MODEL PENAL CODE § 224.7 (1985).

(1) uses or possesses for use a false weight or measure, or any other device for falsely determining or recording any quality or quantity; or

(2) sells, offers or exposes for sale, or delivers less than the represented quantity of any commodity or service; or

(3) takes or attempts to take more than the represented quantity of any commodity or service when as buyer he furnishes the weight or measure; or

(4) sells, offers or exposes for sale adulterated or mislabeled commodities. "Adulterated" means varying from the standard of composition or quality prescribed by or pursuant to any statute providing criminal penalties for such variance, or set by established commercial usage. "Mislabeled" means varying from the standard of truth or disclosure in labeling prescribed by or pursuant to any statute providing criminal penalties for such variance, or set by established commercial usage; or

(5) makes a false or misleading statement in any advertisement addressed to the public or to a substantial segment thereof for the purpose of promoting the purchase or sale of property or services; or

(6) makes a false or misleading written statement for the purpose of obtaining property or credit; or

(7) makes a false or misleading written statement for the purpose of promoting the sale of securities, or omits information required by law to be disclosed in written documents relating to securities.

It is an affirmative defense to prosecution under this section if the defendant proves, by a preponderance of the evidence, that his or her conduct was not knowingly or recklessly deceptive.

C. State Statutes, Codes, and Cases

In today's society, advertising has become a way of life with radio, television, and other means of conveying messages to the public. The dangers of false advertising have become more and more apparent. Generally, the contemporary statutes and codes are more comprehensive than the traditional statutes and have tended to fix responsibility on those who are in a position to know that the advertising is false or misleading. Legislatures of some states enacted comprehensive statutes. The elements of the crime, as stated in most statutes and ordinances, are the following:

1. Publication

Publication may be by advertisement or by verbal promise or statement to the intended target. It must be made in such a way as to reach the consumer or intended target.

2. False or Misleading Statement or Representation

The crime of false advertising prohibits false or misleading statements made to induce consumers to buy a product; however, the law was not intended to punish "mere puffery," which is the natural and expected exaggeration of merchants regarding their products or services. Further, the statutes do not prohibit ridiculous claims of a product's qualities. For instance, television advertisements routinely show perfumes that attract suitors or trucks that climb up sheer mountain sides, but the consumer is expected to know that this is mere exaggeration and "puffery." The law is intended to punish merchants who make serious statements that purport to be facts about the product or service, intentionally misleading the public.

3. Concerning Merchandise or Anything of Value

In general, false advertising is related to the sale of products, but it could be services or anything of value. For instance, timeshares, vacation memberships, real estate purchases, investments, and other things may be the subject of the false advertising. Even pharmaceutical companies must be careful concerning the claims made on television and other advertising regarding their product (which accounts for the extensive litany of side effects reported and frequent use of qualifying terminology in the ads).

4. For Purpose of Sale, Barter, or Exchange

The false statements or misrepresentations have to be made for the purpose of encouraging or enticing the consumer to buy the product or engage in the transaction.

5. Intent to Deceive or Mislead any Other Person

The person making the false statement must know that it is false and make the statements with intent to deceive the other party.

6. Example of State Statutes

Some states retain separate criminal provisions concerning false advertising. Consumers also have tort remedies. An example is that of Kentucky. It states

> A person is guilty of false advertising when, in connection with the promotion or the sale of or to increase the consumption of property or services, he knowingly makes or causes to be made a false or misleading statement in any advertisement addressed to the public or to a substantial number of persons.[113]

Under the provisions of Kentucky's statute, the elements of false advertising are (1) knowingly making or causing to be made a false or misleading statement, (2) for the promotion of the sale or to increase the consumption of property, with (3) an advertisement that is addressed to the public.

In addition to false advertising statutes, Kentucky also has a statute that explicitly deals with "bait advertising." The statute provides

> A person is guilty of bait advertising when in any manner, including advertising or other means of communication, he offers to the public or a substantial number of persons property or service as part of a scheme or plan with the intent not to sell or provide the advertised property or services:

---

[113]   KY. REV. STAT. § 517.030 (2001).

(a) At the price which he offered them; or

(b) In a quantity sufficient to meet the reasonable expected public demand, unless the quantity is specifically stated in the advertisement; or

(c) At all.[114]

Florida also has a specific statute directed to false advertising:

817.06 Misleading advertisements prohibited; penalty.—

(1) No person, persons, association, copartnership, or institution shall, with intent to offer or sell or in anywise dispose of merchandise, securities, certificates, diplomas, documents, or other credentials purporting to reflect proficiency in any trade, skill, profession, credits for academic achievement, service or anything offered by such person, persons, association, copartnership, corporation, or institution directly or indirectly, to the public, for sale or distribution or issuance, or with intent to increase the consumption or use thereof, or with intent to induce the public in any manner to enter into any obligation relating thereto, or to acquire title thereto, or any interest therein, or ownership thereof, knowingly or intentionally make, publish, disseminate, circulate or place before the public, or cause, directly or indirectly, to be made, published, disseminated or circulated or placed before the public in this state in a newspaper or other publication or in the form of a book, notice, handbill, poster, bill, circular, pamphlet or letter or in any other way, an advertisement of any sort regarding such certificate, diploma, document, credential, academic credits, merchandise, security, service or anything so offered to the public, which advertisement contains any assertion, representation or statement which is untrue, deceptive, or misleading.

(2) Any person, persons, association, copartnership, corporation, or institution found guilty of a violation of subsection (1) shall be guilty of a misdemeanor of the second degree, punishable as provided in 775.082 or 775.083.[115]

D. Summary

The crime of false advertising is very similar to false pretenses, described in an earlier section. In each of these crimes, there is an intent to defraud the victim through the use of false statements. The difference is that in false advertising, the attempt is usually to deceive many consumers at once through a public advertisement, while in false pretenses, one or a few victims are targeted. False advertising did not exist under the common law, which upheld the *caveat emptor* principle that the consumer needed to be cautious and protect himself against the natural dishonesty of merchants.

False Advertising
(A/R) publish, false or misleading statements, about a product or service, to encourage the sale of the product
(M/R) knowledge that the statement is false; intent to defraud

---

[114] KY. REV. STAT. § 517.040 (2001).

[115] FLORIDA STATUTES 2008, Title XLVI, Chapter 817.06 Misleading Advertisements Prohibited.

§ 8.11   Commercial Bribery

A. Common Law

At common law, bribery was a crime but was limited to the offering, giving, receiving, or soliciting of anything of value with intent to influence the recipient's action *as a public official*. Very early, it was recognized that **commercial bribery** should be a matter of concern in the criminal law as well as under tort law, and early statutes were enacted to control commercial bribery. The purpose of the statutes regarding commercial bribery was to outlaw collusion and kickbacks in commercial and business affairs.

B. Model Penal Code

The Model Penal Code provision is more comprehensive than the traditional statutes relating to commercial bribery. Under the provisions of the Model Code, a person who solicits, accepts, or agrees to accept a consideration must do so "knowingly violating or agreeing to violate a duty of fidelity" in certain specified relationships. In states that have used this terminology, the prosecution must introduce evidence to prove the "knowingly" mental element. Also, the prosecution must prove that the relationship, such as partner, agent, or employee, as specified in the Model Code, existed at the time of the transaction.

> § 224.8 Commercial Bribery and Breach of Duty to Act Disinterestedly[116]
>
> (1) A person commits a misdemeanor if he solicits, accepts or agrees to accept any benefit as consideration for knowingly violating or agreeing to violate a duty of fidelity to which he is subject as:
>   (a) partner, agent, or employee of another;
>   (b) trustee, guardian, or other fiduciary;
>   (c) lawyer, physician, accountant, appraiser, or other professional adviser or informant;
>   (d) officer, director, manager or other participant in the direction of the affairs of an incorporated or unincorporated association; or
>   (e) arbitrator or other purportedly disinterested adjudicator or referee.
> (2) A person who holds himself out to the public as being engaged in the business of making disinterested selection, appraisal, or criticism of commodities or services commits a misdemeanor if he solicits, accepts or agrees to accept any benefit to influence his selection, appraisal or criticism.
> (3) A person commits a misdemeanor if he confers, or offers or agrees to confer, any benefit the acceptance of which would be criminal under this Section.

C. State Statutes, Codes, and Cases

Very early, the courts upheld commercial bribery statutes against the challenge that they were unconstitutional. In the case of *People v. Davis*, a purchasing agent, R.H. Masey, was indicted for accepting $10 in connection with the purchase of

---

[116]   MODEL PENAL CODE § 224.8 (1985).

sponges.[117] The defendant attacked the statute as unconstitutional on the ground that it violated equal protection and freedom of contract, and that the state did not have police power to enact such statutes. The court upheld the statute, finding that the state, under its police power, did have the authority to enact such statutes for "without such a statute under the fierce competition of modern life, purchasing agents . . . can be lured all too readily into service of hopelessly conflicting interests." The court also agreed that the statute did not violate the equal protection clause of the U.S. Constitution and did not conflict with the agent's freedom of contract.

The elements of commercial bribery are basically the same as common law bribery of a public official; the difference is that the person who receives the benefit is a private party but is in a **fiduciary relationship** with an innocent victim. A fiduciary relationship means one in which the party owes the other a duty to put their interest above all others, even oneself. This could be exemplified by a CEO or CFO to his or her shareholders, a buying agent to his employer, and so on. The elements of commercial bribery are described next.

1. Giving or Offering to Give Anything of Value

As with other forms of bribery, both the person who offers and the person who accepts the offer are guilty of bribery. It is a crime to solicit bribery as well.

2. To a Private Agent, Employee, or Fiduciary

Recall that common law bribery related only to public officials. This means that commercial bribery is a statutory crime, created to cover those circumstances in which the bribe is to a private individual in return for something he or she is expected to do in the course of his or her job. Bribery involving government officials or their agents will be covered in a later chapter.

3. With Intent to Influence the Fiduciary's Action in Relation to the Principal's or Employer's Affairs

Examples of influence would be, for instance, to offer (or receive) a kickback in return for a decision to purchase goods from an individual. Another example might be if a board member of a company was offered a bribe to vote in a particular way. Another example could be to offer a bribe to a real estate appraiser to make his or her appraisal either falsely high or low.

4. Examples of State Statutes

Some states use terminology similar to that of the Model Penal Code, but add to the list of categories of persons subject to prosecution for accepting a bribe. For example, the Nebraska statute adds "Duly elected or appointed representative or trustee of a labor organization or employee of a welfare trust fund."[118]

---

[117]   People v. Davis, 33 N.Y. Crim. 460, 160 N.Y.S. 769 (1915).
[118]   NEB. REV. STAT. § 28-613(1)(e) (2002).

Other statutes take a different approach. The Louisiana statute includes this section:

§ 73. Commercial bribery[119]

Commercial bribery is the giving or offering to give, directly or indirectly, anything of apparent present or prospective value to any private agent, employee, or fiduciary, without the knowledge and consent of the principal or employer, with the intent to influence such agent's, employee's, or fiduciary's action in relation to the principal's or employer's affairs.

The agent's, employee's or fiduciary's acceptance of or offer to accept, directly or indirectly, anything of apparent present or prospective value under such circumstances shall also constitute commercial bribery.

The offender under this article who states the facts, under oath, to the district attorney charged with prosecution of the offense, and who gives evidence tending to convict any other offender under this article, may, in the discretion of the district attorney, be granted full immunity from prosecution for commercial bribery, in respect to the particular offense reported.

Whoever commits the crime of commercial bribery shall be fined not more than five hundred dollars, or imprisoned for not more than six months, or both.

The statute was challenged as being unconstitutionally vague. However, reviewing courts indicated that, because it prohibits behavior about which persons of common intelligence need not guess, it is not unconstitutionally vague.[120]

Some state statutes contain different wording and use other terms to identify the crime. Some state statutes focus on the actions of the recipient of the bribe, rather than on the actions of the person offering the bribe. For example, the California statute states "Any employee who solicits, accepts, or agrees to accept . . . ." Further, the California statute does not apply where the value of the item offered is less than $100.[121]

D. Offering or Accepting Bribes in Athletic and Sporting Events

When a New York court held that a basketball referee was outside the reach of the commercial bribery statute because basketball is not a business or trade, a new statute was created to cover this activity.[122] Most states now have a statute that covers corruption related to sporting events, athletic contests, or other publicly exhibited contests. An example is that of Massachusetts, which provides punishment by a fine of not more than $1,000 or by imprisonment for not more than two years, or both, if a person gives, promises, or offers anything of value to a professional or amateur athlete with the intent to influence him or her to lose or try to lose or cause to be lost a sport or game. This also

---

119   LA. REV. STAT. ANN. § 14:73 (2002).
120   United States v. Perrin, 580 F.2d 730 (5th Cir. 1978).
121   CAL. PENAL CODE § 641.3(a)(b) (1999).
122   People v. Levy, 283 App. Div. 383, 128 N.Y.S.2d 275 (1954).

provides penalties for fraudulent activities relating to horse racing, and specifically mentions various sports and sporting activities.[123]

In a Nebraska statute, the terminology designating this offense is "Tampering with Publicly-Exhibited Contests." The statute is broader than most in its application. It provides a penalty where a person tampers with a publicly exhibited contest as a participant or an official as well as one who offers a benefit.[124]

In Kentucky, the crime is limited to "sporting events." Here, the crime of "sports bribery" is a Class D felony, which carries a penalty of one to five years and occurs when someone

    (a) offers, confers, or agrees to confer any benefit upon a sports participant with intent to influence him not to give his best efforts in a sports contest; or

    (b) offers, confers or agrees to confer any benefit upon a sports official with intent to influence him to perform his duties improperly.[125]

E. Summary

Commercial bribery was created to cover those circumstances in which it is a private person, rather than a public official, who is offered or solicits or accepts a bribe. The types of individuals that are covered by statutes are generally listed or broad categories are given and, in general, the individuals are those who stand in a fiduciary responsibility to an innocent party—either their employer or client. Sporting and athletic events often are the subject of separate statutes because of court decisions that they are not commercial enterprises.

> Commercial Bribery
> (A/R) giving or offering to give (or taking) anything of value, to (or received by) a private agent, employee, or fiduciary
> (M/R) intent to influence the fiduciary's actions; intent to receive in return for being influenced

§ 8.12   Miscellaneous Business Offenses

In order to protect those who are involved in business activities, most states have a multitude of statutes dealing with business practices. Space prohibits any extensive coverage of such statutes here. It should be noted that almost all of these crimes are purely statutory; common law did not cover most of the types of business frauds we are protected from today. For instance, statutes exist to punish those activities that are designed to defraud creditors. These differ from state to state and must be

---

[123]   Mass. Gen. Laws Ann. ch. 271 § 39A (West 2002).

[124]   Neb. Rev. Stat. § 28-614 (2002).

[125]   Ky. Rev. Stat. § 518.040 (1995). *See also* Ky. Rev. Stat. § 518.050 (2001), Receiving Sports Bribe; Ky. Rev. Stat. § 518.060 (1999), Tampering with or Rigging Sports Contests; and Ky. Rev. Stat. § 518.070 (2001), Ticket Scalping.

thoroughly studied to determine the elements of the offenses. One example is that of Ohio, which provides that

> (A) No person, with purpose to defraud one or more of the person's creditors, shall do any of the following:
>   (1) Remove, conceal, destroy, encumber, convey, or otherwise deal with any of his property;
>   (2) Misrepresent or refuse to disclose to a fiduciary appointed to administer or manage the person's affairs or estate, the existence, amount, or location of any of the person's property, or any other information regarding such property which the person is legally required to furnish to the fiduciary.[126]

Under this section, it is an offense if a debtor, in any way, defrauds one or more of his or her creditors by hiding property, or if with the same purpose he or she fails to be truthful with a fiduciary appointed to manage his or her affairs or property, concerning the nature, extent, or whereabouts of his or her property.

Other statutes are designed to protect an individual doing business with another individual or an organization. Examples are "Fraud in Insolvency," which provides a penalty for destroying, removing, or otherwise obstructing the claims of a creditor, knowing that proceedings are to be instituted to appoint a receiver; or knowingly falsifying any writing or record; or knowingly misrepresenting or refusing to disclose the existence and identification of property subject to the proceedings. Another example of this type of statute is that relating to "Receiving Deposits in a Failing Financial Institution."[127] The purpose of this type of statute is to protect those who might unknowingly make deposits in a failing financial institution.

Thus, much of the criminal activity today involves actions that were not covered by the common law. In fact, many criminal acts would be inconceivable to earlier epochs, such as crimes connected with banking, computers, or identity theft.

§ 8.13 Summary

In the United States, most crimes are crimes against property, and the majority of the crimes against property involve theft in one way or another. Although in many states today, the specific theft crimes of larceny, embezzlement, extortion, and others are combined in a single statute, other states retain statutes that deal with each of these crimes separately.

At common law, larceny was the only form of nonaggravated theft that was criminally punishable. One definition of larceny is the felonious taking of the property of another without his or her consent and against his or her will, with the intent to convert it to the use of the taker or another. In addition to the element of trespass, other technical

---

[126] OHIO REV. CODE ANN. § 2913.45 (Anderson 2002).

[127] ME. REV. STAT. ANN. tit. 17-A, § 902 (1995); N.H. REV. STAT. ANN. § 638.9 (2001); UTAH CODE ANN. § 76-6-512 (2002).

elements are taking and carrying away of the personal property of another with intent to steal. If any of these elements is not present, there can be no larceny.

Robbery is often placed in the category of offenses against the person; however, it is covered in this chapter because it is closely related to other theft crimes. Robbery is defined as the felonious taking of money or goods of value from the person of another or in his presence against his will, by force or putting him in fear. It was a felony at common law and is a felony today in all states. The elements that distinguish it from larceny and other theft crimes are "taking from the person or presence of another," and "the taking is accompanied by means of force or putting in fear." Because of these aggravating elements, the penalty for the crime of robbery is more severe than for other theft crimes.

Although embezzlement was not a crime under early English common law, the English legislative body created a new crime to fill the gaps resulting from the technical definition of the elements of larceny. The chief distinction between larceny and embezzlement lies in the manner of acquiring possession of the property. In embezzlement, the property comes lawfully into the possession of the taker but is fraudulently or unlawfully appropriated by him or her, while in larceny there is a trespass in the unlawful taking of the property.

Another crime that was created by statute is that of obtaining property by false pretenses. This is distinguished from larceny in that the property comes into the possession of the taker not by a trespass or taking, but as a result of false pretenses with intent to defraud. It differs from embezzlement in that, in embezzlement, the property comes lawfully into the possession of the taker but he does not obtain title. In false pretenses crimes, the perpetrator obtains title and possession of the property by means of deception. The key element that distinguishes this crime from others is "deception."

Extortion involves obtaining the property of another by means of threat or coercion. Extortion was originally limited to obtaining money or things of value through the misuse of official power; however, in most states, a private individual, as well as a public official, may be found guilty of this crime.

Most states have statutes relating to "receiving stolen property." The general definition is "receiving stolen property knowing it to have been stolen with the intent to deprive the owner of it."

To protect the public against those who would deprive persons of their property, states have enacted other theft statutes. Among these are "unauthorized use of motor vehicle (joyriding)," "theft of services," and "theft of property lost, mislaid, or delivered by mistake." Sometimes the differences between the different types of theft are slight. For instance, consider someone entering a used car lot. If the person saw a car with the keys in the ignition, jumped in, and sped away with the car, this would be larceny. If he obtained permission from the clerk to test-drive the car, promising to but with no intent to return it, this would be larceny by deception. If the clerk ran after him and struggled with him through the open window, this would be robbery. If he told the clerk to let go or he would go find and kill his family, this would be extortion. If he was employed by the car dealership and was asked to move the car, but instead took it to his house with the intent to keep it, this would be embezzlement. Various federal, state, and local statutes include other theft crimes designed to protect the public against those who would, by some means, deprive owners of their property.

While various types of cheating were made crimes under the early English common law, many of the specific laws relating to forgery and commercial fraud did not develop until later. The early approach of *caveat emptor* (let the buyer beware) gave way to greater protections for the consumer and merchant from dishonest dealings. The widespread use of checks and other commercial paper, pervasive advertising, and other modern elements of commerce has led to a proliferation of statutes that criminalize dishonest practices in the marketplace.

Forgery is defined as the false making or material altering, with intent to defraud, of any writing, which, if genuine, might apparently be of legal efficacy or the foundation of a legal liability. Many modern statutes include the crime of uttering a forged instrument within the statute defining forgery. Others make this a separate offense. To utter a forged instrument is to offer it, directly or indirectly, by words or actions as good. This, if done with intent to defraud and with knowledge of the falsity of the instrument, is a violation of the law in some form in all states.

Because forgery statutes sometimes were not comprehensive enough to cover acts that should be made criminal, legislative bodies enacted other statutes such as criminal simulation, where the subject of the offense is not a writing but an object, misuse of credit cards, fraudulent destruction, removal or concealment of recordable instruments, and tampering with records. Identity theft is considered one of the fastest-growing crime problems in the United States. It usually is a combination of crimes, including forgery and credit card abuse, and often includes computer crime as well.

Numerous statutes and ordinances have been enacted that prohibit false or fraudulent statements in advertising. The crime of false advertising consists primarily in the publication and circulation of deceptive matter and the offense is complete without regard to whether anyone is deceived or damaged.

Common law bribery only concerned *public officials*, not private citizens. However, statutes have been enacted to control commercial bribery. Modern statutes encompass the bribery of general agents and employees of commercial concerns, as well as the bribery of public employees. Modern statutes also include offering or accepting bribes in athletic contests and sporting events.

A multitude of statutory crimes dealing with dishonest practices in business include defrauding creditors, and receiving deposits in failing financial institutions.

REVIEW QUESTIONS

1. What are the six elements of common law larceny? Define *caption* and *asportation*.

2. Define *robbery*. What are the eight elements of the common law offense and which two are not part of common law larceny?

3. What is trespass (as an element of both theft and robbery)?

4. One of the most difficult elements to prove in a theft or robbery case is "intent to steal." What evidence must be introduced to prove this element? What is the standard of proof?

5. Define *deadly weapon* and *dangerous weapon* as used in the aggravated robbery statutes. Is the fact that the gun was unloaded a defense? What if the gun was a toy gun—would it still be a deadly weapon?

6. What are the essential elements of the offense of embezzlement? How does embezzlement differ from larceny?

7. Were embezzlement and theft by false pretenses crimes under the common law?

8. What are the elements of "obtaining property by false pretenses"? How do these differ from the elements of larceny and embezzlement? Give some examples.

9. What are the elements of common law extortion? How are they different today?

10. Is it extortion to threaten legal action against someone? Explain why or why not. What types of threats can be used to support a charge of extortion?

11. Define the elements of the crime of "receiving stolen property." How were those who received stolen property dealt with under the common law?

12. Describe the four other crimes involving theft that are described in this chapter.

13. What are the elements of the traditional offense of forgery? Describe each. How do modern statutes differ from the common law?

14. What is the difference between the offense of forgery and uttering a forged instrument? What are the elements of uttering a forged instrument? Does the instrument have to be accepted before a crime occurs?

15. How does the offense of criminal simulation, included in the Ohio statute, differ from forgery?

16. What acts are typically included in credit card abuse statutes? What acts are typically included in identity theft?

17. What acts are prohibited by false advertising statutes? What are the usual elements of the offense of false advertising?

18. What is the difference between false advertising and obtaining property through false pretenses? Must the defendant know that the misrepresentation is a lie?

19. What is the purpose of the statutes regarding commercial bribery? How are these statutes different from common law bribery? What is a fiduciary? Give some examples of fiduciary relationships.

20. What other types of crimes exist related to business practices?

Offenses Involving Morality and Decency

9

Chapter Outline

Cases

Obscenity: *Brown v. Entertainment Merchants Assoc*, 564 U.S. __ (2011)
Partial Birth Abortion: *Gonzales v. Carhart*, 550 U.S. 124 (2007)

§ 9.1 Introduction

Some acts, such as murder, burglary, arson, and theft, are so obviously wrong that everyone, or almost everyone, can agree that punishment is necessary. Other acts may be undesirable to many members of society or even "sinful," but are not always designated as crimes. Remaining are those that are so near the borderline that they are considered crimes in some jurisdictions and not in other jurisdictions, or their definition as crimes changes over time. In this chapter, the most well-known offenses in this category are discussed. These include consensual sexual acts, including adultery, fornication, and prostitution and related offenses; offenses related to obscenity; offenses that take place within the family setting, including bigamy, polygamy, and incest; and abortion. Although drug offenses and gambling are also morality-based offenses, they will be covered in the next chapter.

§ 9.2 Adultery and Fornication

A. Common Law

Sexual intercourse out of wedlock was punished by the church as an ecclesiastical offense at early common law. In England, the common law meaning of the word **adultery** was sexual intercourse with another's wife. In 1650 adultery was made a capital crime in England, but the statute was repealed after the Restoration.[1] In this country, the offense was punishable in the common law courts when so provided by statute.[2]

---

[1] 4 BLACKSTONE, COMMENTARIES 65 (1776-1779).
[2] United States v. Clapox, 35 F. 575 (D. Or. 1888).

Although early definitions of adultery varied, at least one of the parties had to be lawfully married to another and such marriage had to be proven.[3] Under the old Roman law, it was essential to the crime of adultery that the woman be married to another. The crime was not committed where a married man had sexual intercourse with a single woman, as the gist of the offense was protecting men from adulterous wives who might become pregnant by another man. Until recently the majority of jurisdictions held that an unmarried woman who had intercourse with a married man did not commit adultery.[4] While the elements of adultery varied in early state statutes, they typically involved the following elements: voluntary sexual intercourse; between persons unmarried to each other; with one of the parties (under older laws this was the woman) being married to another.

Fornication is voluntary unlawful sexual intercourse, under circumstances not constituting adultery. While fornication was not a crime at common law, it was made a crime by early statutes in many of the states.

B. Model Penal Code

Recognizing that many of the penal statutes against fornication and adultery were unenforced, the Model Penal Code omitted any provisions relating to these offenses.

C. State Statutes, Codes and Cases

State statutes vary concerning the definition of adultery. One element is consistent: at least one of the parties must be lawfully married to another person. The three common definitions are

- Voluntary sexual intercourse between persons, one of whom is lawfully married to another, both parties being guilty.
- Intercourse by a married person with one who is not his or her wife or husband, the married person only being guilty of adultery.
- Intercourse with a married woman by one not her husband, both parties being guilty.

While many states have repealed statutes prohibiting fornication and adultery, others still contain provisions that make it a crime to participate in sexual intercourse out of wedlock. In some of these states, simple adultery—that is, one act of adultery—constitutes a criminal offense, while in others, a relationship that is continuous or "open and notorious" is required. In these states, adultery and fornication are not crimes unless the behavior is "open and notorious" and a single act would not constitute the crime.[5] An example of this type of statute is that of Mississippi.

---

[3]   People v. Stokes, 71 Cal. 263, 12 P. 71 (1886).

[4]   Lyman v. People, 198 Ill. 544, 64 N.E. 974 (1902).

[5]   For example: 720 ILL. COMP. STAT. 5/11-7 (1996) 5/17/8 (2002).

§ 97-29-1. Adultery and Fornication—Unlawful Cohabitation[6]

If any man and woman shall unlawfully cohabit, whether in adultery or fornication, they shall be fined in any sum not more than five hundred dollars each, and imprisoned in the county jail not more than six months; and it shall not be necessary, to constitute the offense, that the parties shall dwell together publicly as husband and wife, but it may be proved by circumstances which show habitual sexual intercourse.

The Mississippi Supreme Court has held that a few acts of intercourse without showing unlawful cohabitation would not constitute a violation of this statute.[7]

The historical justifications for criminalization of adultery are (1) protection of innocent spouses from potential harm, and (2) protection of public morals. However, it is clear that constitutional rights of privacy call into question the legality of any remaining statutes criminalizing adultery and/or fornication. Since *Lawrence v. Texas*,[8] the Supreme Court case that struck down the Texas statute prohibiting same-sex intercourse, it is doubtful that any of the statutes outlawing private decisions regarding voluntary adult sexual partners would withstand constitutional scrutiny if challenged.

LEGAL NEWS: THE CRIME OF ADULTERY?

One would think that laws against adultery are part of the past, along with "scarlet letters"; however, John Bushey, the city attorney for Luray, Virginia, would beg to differ. He pled guilty to adultery in 2004 for an affair with the city clerk. When he ended the affair, she reported him to the authorities and he was charged with the misdemeanor of adultery. She was not charged because she was unmarried. Despite a likely win at the appellate level, Mr. Bushey pled guilty and accepted 20 hours of community service as punishment.

Retrieved on March 22, 2006 from www.washingtonpost.com/ac2/wp-dyn/A62581-2004Sep4?language=printer.

D. *Related Crimes: Sale of Sex Toys*

It seems anachronistic, but Alabama, Virginia, Mississippi, and Texas still have laws regulating and restricting the sale of vibrators and other sex aids. Alabama, for instance, has a law that bans the sale of vibrators. Upon challenge, the Eleventh Circuit ruled that Alabama had a legitimate interest in "discouraging prurient interests in autonomous sex . . ." and held that the state could prohibit the commercial sale of

---

[6]   MISS. CODE ANN. § 97-29-1 (2002).

[7]   Brown v. State, 8 So. 257 (Miss. 1890). *See also* Spike v. State, 98 Miss. 483, 54 So. 1 (1911).

[8]   Lawrence et al. v. Texas, 539 U.S. 558 (2003).

such devices (but not the possession or use of them). It interpreted *Lawrence v. Texas* to allow the use of a rational relationship test that allowed the state to control private behavior if they could prove a legitimate state interest.[9] Texas also had a law that prohibited the commercial sale or purchase of vibrators or sex aids. "Passion parties" are the sex-aid equivalent of Tupperware parties where merchandise is offered at an event in one person's home. Undercover detectives in Austin and Fort Worth posed as married couples, purchased vibrators at one of the parties, and then arrested the organizers.[10]

The parent company sued to have the Texas law ruled unconstitutional and, in February 2008, the Fifth Circuit did so, citing *Lawrence v. Texas*. The state defended the law arguing that even if individuals had a privacy right that covered their right to use such devices, vendors had no right to sell them. The Fifth Circuit disagreed, stating that punishing vendors would present an undue burden on individuals' rights. The state also argued that *Lawrence* was based on an equal protection challenge, not substantive due process and privacy. The Fifth Circuit disagreed with this argument as well, stating that the *Lawrence* decision was clearly based on substantive due process and precedents, including *Griswold v. Connecticut*.[11] They concluded

> Because of *Lawrence*, the issue before us is whether the Texas statute impermissibly burdens the individual's substantive due process right to engage in private intimate conduct of his or her choosing. Contrary to the district court's conclusion, we hold that the Texas law burdens this constitutional right.
>
> An individual who wants to legally use a safe sexual device during private intimate moments alone or with another is unable to legally purchase a device in Texas, which heavily burdens a constitutional right. This conclusion is consistent with the decisions in *Carey* and *Griswold*, where the Court held that restricting commercial transactions unconstitutionally burdened the exercise of individual rights. Indeed, under this statute it is even illegal to "lend" or "give" a sexual device to another person. This further restricts the exercise of the constitutional right to engage in private intimate conduct in the home free from government intrusion. It also undercuts any argument that the statute only affects public conduct.
>
> The dissent relegates the burden on this right to rational basis review. The State says we have two alternatives: (1) strict scrutiny if *Lawrence* established this right as a fundamental right or (2) rational basis review if *Lawrence* did not. There has been debate about this and the Eleventh Circuit concluded that *Lawrence* did not establish a fundamental right.
>
> The Supreme Court did not address the classification, nor do we need to do so, because the Court expressly held that "individual decisions by married persons, concerning the intimacies of their physical relationship, even when not intended to produce offspring, are a form of 'liberty' protected by the due process clause of the Fourteenth Amendment. Moreover, this protection extends to intimate choices by unmarried as well as married persons." The Court also carefully delineated the types of governmental interests that are constitutionally insufficient to sustain a law that infringes on this substantive due process right. Therefore, our responsibility as an inferior

---

9   Williams v. Attorney General of Alabama, 378 F.3d 1232 (11th Cir. 2004).
10 Leonard Pitts, *Deep in the Heart of Texas They're Nuts*, CHICAGO TRIBUNE, Feb. 17, 2004, at 19.
11 Griswold v. Connecticut, 381 U.S. 479 (1965).

federal court is mandatory and straightforward. We must apply *Lawrence* to the Texas statute. [12]

Because of the disagreement between the Eleventh and Fifth Circuits, the Supreme Court may have to resolve the dispute as to whether states should be able to prohibit the sale of sex toys.

E. Summary

While many states have discarded adultery laws, they do still exist. There are variations of the definitions of adultery, however. The most common elements are described below. Fornication was the crime when neither party was married, or the crime assigned to the unmarried party in an adulterous relationship. It seems clear that *Lawrence v. Texas* will be the tool used to dismantle any remaining state statutes that seek to control individual decisions regarding sexual practices that are consensual and protected by the right of privacy.

> Adultery
> (A/R) voluntary sexual intercourse; between two persons unmarried to each other; with at least one of the parties being married to another
> (M/R) intent to have intercourse; knowing of the marriage to another
>
> Fornication
> (A/R) voluntary sexual intercourse; between two adults who are not married to each other
> (M/R) intentional

§ 9.3   Prostitution-Related Offenses

A. Common Law

At the outset, it should be noted that the term **prostitution** is not synonymous with the offense of prostitution. The term "prostitution" is defined as the practice of a female offering her body for intercourse with a man, for hire. Prostitution was not a crime at common law and is not a crime in all jurisdictions. It is more appropriate to discuss this matter in terms of "crimes relating to prostitution" rather than using prostitution, the offense, interchangeably with prostitution, the practice.

While the act or practice was not a crime at common law, the courts have recognized that states exercising reasonable police powers may enact restrictive legislation pertaining to prostitution and offenses related to prostitution. As a result, there were very early statutes relating to prostitution. These included soliciting prostitution, aiding and abetting prostitution, associating with prostitutes, keeping and operating a place or conveyance for the purpose of prostitution, receiving or offering to receive any person into any place for the purpose of prostitution, and so on.

---

[12]   Reliable Consultants, Inc. v. Earle, 517 F.3d 738 (2008), p. 744-745.

An early court included this definition of prostitution: "performance of indiscriminate sexual acts for hire and indiscriminate solicitation or agreement to perform sex acts for hire; an essential element of proof common to both grounds is the commercial nature of the sexual transaction."[13] Although the early statutes differed as to the required elements, some were common to most statutes.

1. Female

Generally, early statutes were sex-specific in that the terminology used indicated that only women could commit prostitution.

2. Offering of One's Self or One's Body

Generally there needed to be a direct or indirect offer of intercourse.

3. For Hire or for Money

Pecuniary gain has been made an element of the crime by statute in most jurisdictions. To constitute the crime of engaging in prostitution, there must be a showing of an offer for money or some profit. In one case, the court held that where the prostitution was defined by statutes as the offering, giving, or using of the body for sexual intercourse *for hire*, the term did not necessarily involve indiscriminate intercourse with more than one man.[14]

B. *Model Penal Code*

The Model Penal Code includes a fairly comprehensive section devoted to prostitution-related offenses. Note that the language, as with most modern statutes, applies to both men and women. The Model Code emphasizes the repression of commercialized sexual activity including "deviate sexual relations" as well as "sexual intercourse." It also deals with procuring, pandering, transportation, and other activities ancillary to the business of prostitution.

§ 251.2 Prostitution and Related Offenses[15]

(1) Prostitution. A person is guilty of prostitution, a petty misdemeanor, if he or she:
    (a) is an inmate of a house of prostitution or otherwise engages in sexual activity as a business; or
    (b) loiters in or within view of any public place for the purpose of being hired to engage in sexual activity.
  "Sexual activity" includes homosexual and other deviate sexual relations. A "house of prostitution" is a place where prostitution or promotion of prostitution is regularly carried on by one person under the control, management or supervision

---

13   Commonwealth v. A Juvenile, 6 Mass. App. 194, 374 N.E.2d 335 (1978).
14   Commonwealth v. Stingel, 146 Pa. 359, 40 A.2d 140 (1944).
15   MODEL PENAL CODE § 251.2 (1985).

of another. An "inmate" is a person who engages in prostitution in or through the agency of a house of prostitution. "Public place" means any place to which the public or any substantial group thereof has access.

(2) Promoting Prostitution. A person who knowingly promotes prostitution of another commits a misdemeanor or felony as provided in Subsection (3). The following acts shall, without limitation of the foregoing, constitute promoting prostitution:

    (a) owning, controlling, managing, supervising or otherwise keeping, alone or in association with others, a house of prostitution or a prostitution business; or

    (b) procuring an inmate for a house of prostitution or a place in a house of prostitution for one who would be an inmate; or

    (c) encouraging, inducing, or otherwise purposely causing another to become or remain a prostitute; or

    (d) soliciting a person to patronize a prostitute; or

    (e) procuring a prostitute for a patron; or

    (f) transporting a person into or within this state with purpose to promote that person's engaging in prostitution, or procuring or paying for transportation with that purpose; or

    (g) leasing or otherwise permitting a place controlled by the actor, alone or in association with others, to be regularly used for prostitution or the promotion of prostitution, or failure to make reasonable effort to abate such use by ejecting the tenant, notifying law enforcement authorities, or other legally available means; or

    (h) soliciting, receiving, or agreeing to receive any benefit for doing or agreeing to do anything forbidden by this Subsection.

(3) Grading of Offenses Under Subsection (2). An offense under Subsection (2) constitutes a felony of the third degree if:

    (a) the offense falls within paragraph (a), (b) or (c) of Subsection (2); or

    (b) the actor compels another to engage in or promote prostitution; or

    (c) the actor promotes prostitution of a child under 16, whether or not he is aware of the child's age; or

    (d) the actor promotes prostitution of his wife, child, ward or any person for whose care, protection or support he is responsible.

    Otherwise the offense is a misdemeanor.

(4) Presumption from Living Off Prostitutes. A person, other than the prostitute or the prostitute's minor child or other legal dependent incapable of self-support, who is supported in whole or substantial part by the proceeds of prostitution is presumed to be knowingly promoting prostitution in violation of Subsection (2).

(5) Patronizing Prostitutes. A person commits a violation if he hires a prostitute to engage in sexual activity with him, or if he enters or remains in a house of prostitution for the purpose of engaging in sexual activity. . . .

    (b) Evidence. On the issue whether a place is a house of prostitution the following shall be admissible evidence: its general repute; the repute of the persons who reside in or frequent the place; the frequency, timing and duration of visits by non-residents. Testimony of a person against his spouse shall be admissible to prove offenses under this Section.

The Model Code includes sections relating to "living off" of prostitutes and patronizing prostitutes. This makes it easier to prosecute the customers of prostitutes, who were rarely punished under previous statutes. It is interesting to note that the offense of prostitution, under the Model Code, is a petty misdemeanor, while in some instances, promoting prostitution is a felony of the third degree.

LEGAL NEWS: THE RISE AND FALL AND RISE OF ELIOT SPITZER

In March 2008 the governor of New York, Eliot Spitzer, resigned in a prostitution-related scandal. Spitzer was caught making dates with a Washington, D.C. call girl on a wiretap by the FBI, which was investigating the operation. He also attracted the attention of investigators when he withdrew large sums of money to pay the call girl. By some estimates, he paid more than $80,000 to the call girl operation for the services of one call girl. The irony of the situation was that Spitzer ran for governor on a "tough-on-crime" platform and, as a prosecutor and state attorney general, was known as a zealous opponent of prostitution. Neither state nor federal charges have been filed against him. Today, he has resurrected his career as a television commentator.

Source: Gross, S. and D. Barrett (2008). "Spitzer Tripped Up on Laws He Enforced." www.foxnews.com. March 12, 2008. Accessed January 2, 2009 from http://www.foxnews.com/printer_friendly_wires/2008Mar12/0,0465,SpitzerTheMoneyTrail,00.html.

C. State Statutes, Codes, and Cases

Every state, except Nevada, has a statute outlawing solicitation and other crimes related to prostitution. In Nevada, prostitution is legal but strictly regulated in 10 counties. Prostitutes may only operate out of brothels and must have periodic health inspections. Recently revised codes and statutes make prostitution a gender-neutral crime and include same-sex prostitution as well as heterosexual prostitution. Modern statutes include penalties not only for soliciting sexual activity for a fee, but related offenses. There is a trend to reduce the legal seriousness of simple solicitation and devote more resources to prosecution of those who promote prostitution.

An example of a statute that probably represents the approach taken in the majority of the states is that of Connecticut. This code provides punishment for prostitution, patronizing a prostitute, promoting prostitution in the first degree, promoting prostitution in the second degree, promoting prostitution in the third degree, and permitting prostitution.

§ 53a-82. Prostitution: Class A misdemeanor[16]

(a) A person is guilty of prostitution when such person engages or agrees or offers to engage in sexual conduct with another person in return for a fee.

(b) Prostitution is a Class A misdemeanor.

---

[16] CONN. GEN. STAT. §§ 53a-82-53a-89 (1999).

§ 53a-83. Patronizing a prostitute: Class A misdemeanor

(a) A person is guilty of patronizing a prostitute when:
  (1) pursuant to a prior understanding, he pays a fee to another person as compensation for such person or a third person having engaged in sexual conduct with him; or
  (2) he pays or agrees to pay a fee to another person pursuant to an understanding that in return therefore such person or a third person will engage in sexual conduct with him; or
  (3) he solicits or requests another person to engage in sexual conduct with him in return for a fee.
(b) Patronizing a prostitute is a Class A misdemeanor.

§ 53a–83a. Patronizing a prostitute from a motor vehicle: Class A misdemeanor

(a) A person is guilty of patronizing from a motor vehicle when he, while occupying a motor vehicle: (1) pursuant to a prior understanding, pays a fee to another person as compensation for such person or a third person having engaged in sexual conduct with him; or (2) pays or agrees to pay a fee to another person pursuant to an understanding that in return therefore such person or a third person will engage in sexual conduct with him; or (3) solicits or requests another person to engage in sexual conduct with him in return for a fee; or (4) engages in sexual conduct for which a fee was paid or agreed to be paid.
(b) Patronizing a prostitute from a motor vehicle is a class A misdemeanor.

§ 53a-86. Promoting prostitution in the first degree: Class B felony

(a) A person is guilty of promoting prostitution in the first degree when he knowingly:
  (1) advances prostitution by compelling a person by force or intimidation to engage in prostitution, or profits from coercive conduct by another; or
  (2) advances or profits from prostitution of a person less than sixteen years old.
(b) Promoting prostitution in the first degree is a Class B felony.

§ 53a-87. Promoting prostitution in the second degree

(a) A person is guilty of promoting prostitution in the second degree when he knowingly:
  (1) advances or profits from prostitution by managing, supervising, controlling or owning, either alone or in association with others, a house of prostitution or a prostitution business or enterprise involving prostitution activity by two or more prostitutes; or
  (2) advances or profits from prostitution of a person less than eighteen years old.
(b) Promoting prostitution in the second degree is a Class C felony.

§ 53a-88. Promoting prostitution in the third degree

(a) A person is guilty of promoting prostitution in the third degree when he knowingly advances or profits from prostitution.
(b) Promoting prostitution in the third degree is a Class D felony.

§ 53a-89. Permitting prostitution: Class A misdemeanor

(a) A person is guilty of permitting prostitution when, having possession or control of premises which he knows are being used for prostitution purposes, he fails to make reasonable effort to halt or abate such use.

(b) Permitting prostitution is a Class A misdemeanor.

These sections of the Connecticut code make clear that homosexual as well as heterosexual prostitution is prohibited. A distinction is drawn between the various kinds of prostitution-related activities, and the penalties are graded accordingly. The elements of the various crimes are fairly clear. To prove solicitation or patronizing a prostitute, evidence must be introduced to show the following:

1. Intentionally Engaging, Agreeing, or Offering to Engage

When discussing the intent element, a Texas court left no doubt that intent could be inferred by the defendant's acts, conduct, and words.[17] The court indicated that the offense could have been inferred by the jury when the facts showed that a fee had been paid, that sexual contact occurred, and that other fees were paid with the understanding, explicitly or implicitly, that similar acts, contacts, and performances would follow the continued flow of money. It should also be noted that the element of intent is not required in all states.

2. In Sexual Conduct with Another

In a New York case, the court was asked to determine whether the prostitution statutes encompassed acts between two males.[18] After reiterating that the purpose of the misdemeanor prostitution statute is to prohibit the commercial exploitation of sexual gratification or public solicitation of a sex act for a fee, the court agreed that the statute included gender-neutral language. The allegation that a male defendant agreed to engage in sexual intercourse with another male for $100 was factually and legally sufficient to support the charge of prostitution.

3. In Return for a Fee

In the case of *State v. Allen*, the Connecticut statute was challenged as being unconstitutionally vague and infringing upon the fundamental right of privacy.[19] In *Allen*, the defendant approached an undercover officer's car, opened the passenger door, and inquired if the officer had $20. Upon hearing an affirmative response, the defendant got into the car. A conversation ensued in which the defendant offered to have sex for $20. The officer then drove to a prearranged location near a school where the defendant was

---

[17]   Steinbach v. State, 979 S.W.2d 836 (Tex. 1998).

[18]   People v. Medina, 685 N.Y.S.2d 599 (1999).

[19]   State v. Allen, 37 Conn. Supp. 506, 424 A.2d 651 (1980). *See also* State v. Savio, 924 P.2d 491 (Ariz. 1996), which held that the statute was not unconstitutionally vague or overbroad.

arrested by other officers. No sexual activity was ever engaged in nor was there any transfer of money. The defendant contended that the statutory terms "sexual conduct" and "fee" were so uncertain in their meanings that they failed to apprise her that her conduct was proscribed. She claimed that the statute was unconstitutionally vague, and that her conviction thereunder violated her rights to due process of law under the Fifth and Fourteenth Amendments to the U.S. Constitution. While agreeing that the laws must give a person of ordinary intelligence a reasonable opportunity to know what is prohibited so that he or she may act accordingly, the court found no difficulty with the definition of "sexual conduct" and "fee" as appearing in the statute prohibiting prostitution. It was noted that while certain words may appear unconstitutionally vague when viewed in a vacuum, when viewed in the context of a statute they can provide fair notice of the conduct to be prohibited. In explaining that the term "sexual conduct" is sufficiently explicit, the court referred to the definition of prostitution as "normally suggesting sexual relations for hire." As to the term "sexual conduct," the opinion was that the language of § 53a-82 was sufficiently precise to give the defendant fair notice that her conduct was prohibited. The court also explained that the term "fee" was not so vague as to make persons of common intelligence guess at its meaning.

Vagueness was also the challenge to the Illinois prostitution statute. There the court held that the statute criminalizing "any" touching or fondling of sexual organs for purposes of arousal and in exchange for money was not unconstitutionally vague for failure to specify whether it also prohibited touching or fondling through the clothing, as applied to a dancer who rubbed an undercover police officer's penis through his pants during a lap dance.[20]

The crime of solicitation of prostitution may not always occur as the classic case of a prostitute soliciting customers from the street. Anytime someone offers money for sexual services, a charge of prostitution might arise. In *State v. Kittilstad*, a landlord offered to waive rent if the young men who were living with him would bring women back to the residence and have sex with them while the landlord watched. Kittilstad's convictions for soliciting prostitution were upheld, with the court defining prostitution as soliciting sex between two parties, not necessarily between the solicitor and another party.[21]

D. Summary

Almost all states have statutes relating to prostitution—**solicitation** is the most common charge and applies to the act of offering to engage in sexual conduct for a fee. In general, modern statutes have changed from early statutes in that prostitution now is gender-neutral, covers homosexual prostitution as well as heterosexual, expands the definition from sexual intercourse to sexual conduct, and tends to direct harsher

---

[20]   People v. Hill, 776 N.E.2d 828 (Ill. 2002).
[21]   State v. Kittilstad, 603 N.W.2d 732 (Wis. 1999).

punishments to promotion or to the purveyors of prostitution rather than the individual offenders.

> Solicitation of Prostitution
> (A/R) offering to, engaging in, or asking others to engage in sexual conduct, for a fee (or pecuniary gain)
> (M/R) intentional

§ 9.4 Offenses Related to Obscenity

A. Common Law

Under the early English system, matters relating to lewd or immodest acts, conduct, and language were handled by the ecclesiastical authorities. Gradually, the courts and legislative bodies assumed the responsibility for setting standards with regard to specific modes of conduct, pictorial representations of conduct, or written and oral descriptions of conduct. In attempting to define conduct that should be prohibited, the courts have, from the beginning, faced a very difficult task. There is no consensus on what should be criminalized and any such statutes must be weighed against the protections offered under the First Amendment to the Constitution (freedom of expression; freedom of press).

First, it is important to note that pornography and obscenity are not synonymous terms. While one might define pornography as depictions of sexually related conduct, **obscenity** refers to depictions of sexually related conduct that have been defined as legally impermissible. Statutes outlaw obscenity, not pornography; but that begs the question as to what constitutes obscenity. Since 1957, it has been established that obscenity is not within the ambit of constitutionally protected free speech. However, the U.S. Supreme Court spent more than a decade attempting to determine a legal test for what constitutes obscenity. We will discuss the current standard in the next section.

B. Model Penal Code

Attempting to come to grips with this difficult subject, the Model Code relies to a great extent upon the definition used in cases decided by the U.S. Supreme Court. According to the definition, the material is obscene only if its predominant appeal is to the prurient interest and it goes substantially beyond customary limits of candor in describing or representing such matters.

§ 251.4 Obscenity[22]

(1) Obscene Defined. Material is obscene, if considered as a whole, its predominant appeal is to prurient interest, that is, a shameful or morbid interest, in nudity, sex or excretion, and if in addition it goes substantially beyond customary limits of

---

[22] MODEL PENAL CODE § 251.4 (1985).

candor in describing or representing such matters. Predominant appeal shall be judged with reference to ordinary adults unless it appears from the character of the material or the circumstances of its dissemination to be designed for children or other specially susceptible audience. Undeveloped photographs, molds, printing plates and the like, shall be deemed obscene notwithstanding that processing or other acts may be required to make the obscenity patent or to disseminate it.

(2) Offenses. Subject to the affirmative defense provided in Subsection (3), a person commits a misdemeanor if he knowingly or recklessly:

    (a) sells, delivers or provides, or offers or agrees to sell, deliver or provide, any obscene writing, picture, record or other representation or embodiment of the obscene; or

    (b) presents or directs an obscene play, dance or performance, or participates in that portion thereof which makes it obscene; or

    (c) publishes, exhibits or otherwise makes available any obscene material; or

    (d) possesses any obscene material for purposes of sale or other commercial dissemination; or

    (e) sells, advertises or otherwise commercially disseminates material, whether or not obscene, by representing or suggesting that it is obscene.

A person who disseminates or possesses obscene material in the course of his business is presumed to do so knowingly or recklessly.

(3) Justifiable and Non-Commercial Private Dissemination. It is an affirmative defense to prosecution under this Section that dissemination was restricted to:

    (a) institutions or persons having scientific, educational, governmental or other similar justification for possessing obscene material; or

    (b) non-commercial dissemination to personal associates of the actor.

(4) Evidence; Adjudication of Obscenity. In any prosecution under this Section evidence shall be admissible to show:

    (a) the character of the audience for which the material was designed or to which it was directed;

    (b) what the predominant appeal of the material would be for ordinary adults or any special audience to which it was directed, and what effect, if any, it would probably have on conduct of such people;

    (c) artistic, literary, scientific, educational or other merits of the material;

    (d) the degree of public acceptance of the material in the United States;

    (e) appeal to prurient interest, or absence thereof, in advertising or other promotion of the material; and

    (f) the good repute of the author, creator, publisher or other person from whom the material originated.

After defining obscenity, the Model Code details five offenses associated with obscenity. The provision requires that the prosecution show that the defendant acted purposely, knowingly, or recklessly. However, there is a presumption that one who disseminates or possesses obscene material in the course of his or her business does so knowingly or recklessly. Subsection (3) of Section 251.4 provides an affirmative defense when material is for a scientific or educational purpose or dissemination is noncommercial and only to personal associates. The Model Penal Code also specifies the evidence that is to be admissible in obscenity situations. It concludes with "the Court shall dismiss a prosecution for obscenity if it is satisfied that the material is not obscene."

C. State Statutes, Codes, and Cases

In the case of *Miller v. California*, the United States Supreme Court dealt with the question of obscenity in an appeal from a state criminal conviction. The defense against laws against obscenity is that they violate the First Amendment. First Amendment rights are not absolute, however, and there are some forms of speech that are not protected, including obscenity. The question then becomes what separates obscene materials from other materials that might be offensive to some people. The Supreme Court announced a broad test that defined obscenity, now called the *Miller* test.

This much has been categorically settled by the Court, that obscene material is unprotected by the First Amendment.... We acknowledge, however, the inherent dangers of undertaking to regulate any form of expression. State statutes designed to regulate obscene materials must be carefully limited.... As a result, we now confine the permissible scope of such regulation to works which depict or describe sexual conduct. That conduct must be specifically defined by the applicable state law, as written or authoritatively construed. A state offense must also be limited to works which, taken as a whole, appeal to the prurient interest in sex, which portray sexual conduct in a patently offensive way, and which, taken as a whole, do not have serious literary, artistic, political, or scientific value.

The basic guidelines for the trier of fact must be: (a) whether "the average person, applying contemporary community standards" would find that the work, taken as a whole, appeals to the prurient interest, ...; (b) whether the work depicts or describes, in a patently offensive way, sexual conduct specifically defined by the applicable state law; and (c) whether the work, taken as a whole, lacks serious literary, artistic, political, or scientific value. We do not adopt as a constitutional standard the "*utterly without redeeming social value*" test of *Memoirs* v. *Massachusetts*, ...; that concept has never commanded the adherence of more than three Justices at one time.... If a state law that regulates obscene material is thus limited, as written or construed, the First Amendment values applicable to the States through the Fourteenth Amendment are adequately protected by the ultimate power of appellate courts to conduct an independent review of constitutional claims when necessary....

We emphasize that it is not our function to propose regulatory schemes for the States. That must await their concrete legislative efforts. It is possible, however, to give a few plain examples of what a state statute could define for regulation under part (b) of the standard announced in this opinion, ...:

(a) Patently offensive representations or descriptions of ultimate sexual acts, normal or perverted, actual or simulated.
(b) Patently offensive representations or descriptions of masturbation, excretory functions, and lewd exhibition of the genitals.

Sex and nudity may not be exploited without limit by films or pictures exhibited or sold in places of public accommodation any more than live sex and nudity can be exhibited or sold without limit in such public places. At a minimum, prurient, patently offensive depiction or description of sexual conduct must have serious literary, artistic, political, or scientific value to merit First Amendment protection.... For example, medical books for the education of physicians and related personnel necessarily use graphic illustrations and descriptions of human anatomy. In resolving the inevitably sensitive questions of fact and law, we must continue to rely on the jury system, accompanied by the safeguards that judges, rules of evidence, presumption of innocence, and other protective features provide, as we do with rape, murder, and a host of other offenses against society and its individual members. [23]

This so-called *Miller* **test** has been followed by both federal and state courts. The Court stated that three questions must be asked before a literary work could be considered obscene and, thus, undeserving of First Amendment protections. (1) Does the material appeal to prurient interests? (2) Does it depict "hard-core" sexual acts previously defined by state law in a patently offensive way? (3) Does it lack serious literary, artistic, political, scientific, or other value?

1. The *Miller* Test

The three questions that comprise the *Miller* test are designed to separate what is considered so contrary to public morals that it should be criminalized. In this test, the Supreme Court took into consideration that the definition of obscenity may vary from jurisdiction to jurisdiction.

*"Appeals to **prurient interests**"* means something more than the tendency to arouse normal, healthy sexual desire.[24] Works that do no more than arouse a normal, healthy interest in sex are not obscene. A work must cater to a morbid, abnormal, or disgusting interest in sex in order to satisfy the first prong of the *Miller* test. In applying the first prong of the *Miller* test, a Nebraska court held

> "Nudity" and "obscenity" are not synonymous and a nude performance does not become an obscene one, unless, taken as a whole, it appeals predominantly to the prurient interest, a shameful interest in nudity or sex beyond customary limits, it describes any patently offensive way of sexual way of sexual conduct specifically proscribed by state law, and, taken as a whole, it lacks serious or artistic value as determined by the average person applying contemporary community standards.[25]

Depicts "hard-core" sexual acts previously defined by state law in a patently offensive way. To meet the second test, evidence must be introduced to show that the work depicts patently offensive hard-core sexual acts set forth in the state obscenity laws. State obscenity laws are allowed to list the following acts: patently offensive verbal or visual depictions of ultimate sexual acts (normal or perverted, real or simulated); masturbation; lewd exhibition of the genitals; sadomasochistic sexual behavior; violent sex; bestiality; and sexual perversions.[26]

Lacks serious literary, artistic, political, scientific, or other value. In addition, the fact finder must determine that the work lacks serious literary, political, scientific, artistic, or other value. The *Miller* test requires the work to be considered as a

---

[23]   Miller v. California, 413 U.S. 15, 93 S. Ct. 2607, 37 L. Ed. 2d 419 (1973).
[24]   Brockett v. Spokane Arcades, Inc., 472 U.S. 491, 105 S. Ct. 2794, 86 L. Ed. 2d 394 (1985).
[25]   Midtown Palace, Inc., v. City of Omaha, 193 Neb. 785, 225 N.W.2d 56 (1975).
[26]   Ward v. Illinois, 431 U.S. 767, 97 S. Ct. 2085, 52 L. Ed. 2d 738 (1977).

whole. Works that have serious literary or other value may not be suppressed under the obscenity laws simply because they contain isolated objectionable pictures or passages.

2. Examples of State Statutes

The offense of obscenity, as stated and defined in the various statutes, is a distinct crime involving elements different from those of other crimes. While a state may not define obscenity in such a way that it incorporates material that does not meet the *Miller* test, it can have a more restrictive definition of obscenity so that fewer types of depictions are prohibited.[27] If statutes require other elements to constitute illegal possession or distribution of obscene materials, such as age of purchaser, time and place, motivation, or intent, these elements must be proved by the state in the prosecution.

State statutes vary in wording and in the penalties provided. Many recently revised statutes follow the Model Penal Code position, but the penalties vary. Also, elements such as "the work taken as a whole appeals to the prurient interest" vary from state to state. Some states refer to "contemporary community standards," while others refer to "state standards" as the appropriate reference point in determining whether the predominant appeal is to the prurient interest.

The Illinois statute is similar to the Model Penal Code. It provides in part

§ 11-20. Obscenity[28]

(a) Elements of the Offense.
    A person commits obscenity when, with knowledge of the nature or content thereof, or recklessly failing to exercise reasonable inspection which would have disclosed the nature or content thereof, he:
    (1) sells, delivers or provides, or offers or agrees to sell, deliver or provide any obscene writing, picture, record or other representation or embodiment of the obscene; or
    (2) presents or directs an obscene play, dance or other performance or participates directly in that portion thereof which makes it obscene; or
    (3) publishes, exhibits or otherwise makes available anything obscene; or
    (4) performs an obscene act or otherwise presents an obscene exhibition of his body for gain; or
    (5) creates, buys, procures or possesses obscene matter or material with intent to disseminate it in violation of this Section, or of the penal laws or regulations of any other jurisdiction; or
    (6) advertises or otherwise promotes the sale of material represented or held out by him to be obscene, whether or not it is obscene.
(b) Obscene Defined.
    Any material or performance is obscene if: (1) the average person, applying contemporary adult community standards, would find that, taken as a whole, it appeals to the prurient interest; and (2) the average person, applying contemporary adult community standards, would find that it depicts or describes, in a patently offensive way, ultimate sexual acts or sadomasochistic

---

[27]   People v. Ridens, 59 Ill. 2d 362, 321 N.E.2d 264 (1974).

[28]   720 ILL. COMP. STAT. § 5/11-20 (Smith-Hurd 2002). *See also* ch. 720 § 5/11-20.1 "Child Pornography."

sexual acts, whether normal or perverted, actual or simulated, or masturbation, excretory functions or lewd exhibition of the genitals; and (3) taken as a whole, it lacks serious literary, artistic, political or scientific value.

(c) Interpretation of Evidence.

Obscenity shall be judged with reference to ordinary adults, except that it shall be judged with reference to children or other specially susceptible audiences if it appears from the character of the material or the circumstances of its dissemination to be specially designed for or directed to such an audience.

Where circumstances of production, presentation, sale, dissemination, distribution, or publicity indicate that material is being commercially exploited for the sake of its prurient appeal, such evidence is probative with respect to the nature of the matter and can justify the conclusion that the matter is utterly without redeeming social importance.

In any prosecution for an offense under this Section evidence shall be admissible to show:

(1) the character of the audience for which the material was designed or to which it was directed;

(2) what the predominant appeal of the material would be for ordinary adults or a special audience, and what effect, if any, it would probably have on the behavior of such people;

(3) the artistic, literary, scientific, educational or other merits of the material, or absence thereof;

(4) the degree, if any, of public acceptance of the material in this State;

(5) appeal to prurient interest, or absence thereof, in advertising or other promotion of the material;

(6) purpose of the author, creator, publisher or disseminator.

(d) Sentence.

Obscenity is a Class A misdemeanor. A second or subsequent offense is a Class 4 felony.

In a challenge to the Illinois statute as applied to the sale of adult books, a reviewing court established some guidelines. The court held that including children in the instruction on community standards was error. However, it was not error to refuse to allow testimony that various adult bookstores and neighborhood video stores sold similar videos and magazines as evidence of acceptability of those materials by the community.[29]

Another Illinois court agreed that it is difficult to define the term "obscenity." However, the court found that the following magazine depictions were obscene:

• pictures of naked or nearly naked men, women, and transsexuals engaging in actual or imminent sexual acts, and

• pictures focused almost exclusively on the genitals of models with a sparse text describing the events taking place in the pictures.

In this case, the court held that the magazines sold from the defendant's shop to a police officer lacked any literary, artistic, political, or scientific value, and thus the trial

---

[29]　People v. Page Books, 601 N.E.2d 273 (Ill. Ct. App. 1992).

court's erroneous use of contemporary community standards in the defendant's obscenity trial was harmless.[30]

Some states use different terminology from the Model Penal Code. An example of a statute that uses terminology different from the Model Penal Code is that of California. Part of the California Code provides

> (a) every person who knowingly sends or causes to be sent, or brings, or causes to be brought, into this state for sale or distribution, or in this state possesses, prepares, publishes, produces or prints, with intent to distribute or to exhibit to others or who offers to distribute, distributes, or exhibits to others any obscene matter is for a first offense guilty of a misdemeanor.[31]

In the California statute, obscene matter is defined as "matter taken as a whole, that to the average person, applying contemporary statewide standards, appeals to the prurient interest, that, taken as a whole, depicts or describes sexual conduct in a patently offensive way, and that, taken as a whole, lacks serious literary, artistic, political, or scientific value."[32]

This section of the statute was challenged as being unconstitutionally vague, but the California Court of Appeals determined that the section defining the crime of possessing obscene material with intent to distribute it to others was not unconstitutional; it was not unconstitutionally vague, nor did it violate First Amendment protections.[33]

In 2011 the Supreme Court heard an appeal from California concerning a law seeking to bar distribution of videogames to minors based on their content of sex and violence. In *Brown v. Entertainment Merchants Association*, the Supreme Court revisited the definition of obscenity to determine whether or not the video content was protected under the First Amendment.[34] The Court concluded that it was because the law in question was both overinclusive and underinclusive.

Case Note: *Brown v. Entertainment Merchants Association et al.*, **564 U.S. __ (2011)**
What was the holding of the Court?
Why would the Court find that violent video games are protected speech?
Did it matter that the Court was not persuaded of the link between violent video games and violent behavior by youthful consumers?

The state may satisfy its burden by proving, in an obscenity case, that the defendant knew the character and content of the material in question with either direct or circumstantial evidence. Determining whether material is obscene is a question for the jury in an obscenity trial.[35]

---

[30]   People v. Sclafani, 166 Ill. App. 3d 605, 520 N.E.2d 409 (1988).
[31]   Cal. Penal Code § 311.2 (West 2003).
[32]   *Id.* at § 311 (West 2003).
[33]   People v. Wiener, 91 Cal. App. 3d 238, 154 Cal. Rptr. 110 (1979).
[34]   Brown v. Entertainment Merchants Assoc., 564 U.S. __ (2011).
[35]   Castillo v. State, 79 S.W.2d 817 (Tex. 2002); also see State v. Haltom, 653 N.W.2d 232 (Neb. 2002).

Note that the state statutes discussed define as criminal acts those that distribute or display publicly obscene materials. Mere possession is not a crime, although possession with intent to distribute or sell is. The Supreme Court has ruled that one's private possession of obscene materials is within one's privacy rights;[36] however, taking such material across state lines can be a federal crime.[37] States and the federal government also can and have made the mere possession of child pornography a crime.[38]

During the past decade, legislatures and courts have wrestled with this problem, but now that most are following the guidelines established by the U.S. Supreme Court, it appears that the decisions are reasonably consistent in holding that obscenity can be defined so as to meet the constitutional requirements and that obscenity laws, when carefully drafted, can comply with the standards required by the Constitution.

3. Child Pornography

As mentioned earlier, even mere possession of child pornography is a crime. Virtually any display of prurient nudity, sexual activity, or presence of a child in relation to sexual activity will fall within the definition of child pornography. For instance, California's statute states:[39]

> 311.1. (a) Every person who knowingly sends or causes to be sent, or brings or causes to be brought, into this state for sale or distribution, or in this state possesses, prepares, publishes, produces, develops, duplicates, or prints any representation of information, data, or image, including, but not limited to, any film, filmstrip, photograph, negative, slide, photocopy, videotape, video laser disc, computer hardware, computer software, computer floppy disc, data storage media, CD-ROM, or computer-generated equipment or any other computer-generated image that contains or incorporates in any manner, any film or filmstrip, with intent to distribute or to exhibit to, or to exchange with, others, or who offers to distribute, distributes, or exhibits to, or exchanges with, others, any obscene matter, knowing that the matter depicts a person under the age of 18 years personally engaging in or personally simulating sexual conduct, as defined in Section 311.4, shall be punished either by imprisonment in the county jail for up to one year, by a fine not to exceed one thousand dollars ($1,000), or by both the fine and imprisonment, or by imprisonment in the state prison, by a fine not to exceed ten thousand dollars ($10,000), or by the fine and imprisonment. (b) This section does not apply to the activities of law enforcement and prosecuting agencies in the investigation and prosecution of criminal offenses or to legitimate medical, scientific, or educational activities, or to lawful conduct between spouses. (c) This section does not apply to matter which depicts a child under the age of 18, which child is legally emancipated, including lawful conduct between spouses when one or both are under the age of 18. (d) It does not constitute a violation of this section for a telephone corporation, as defined by Section 234 of the Public Utilities Code, to carry or transmit messages described in this chapter or perform related activities in providing telephone services.

---

[36]   Stanley v. Georgia, 394 U.S. 557 (1969).
[37]   United States v. Orito, 413 U.S. 139 (1973).
[38]   Osborne v. Ohio, 495 U.S. 103 (1990).
[39]   Cal. Penal Code § 311.1(e) (West 2003).

The Texas Penal Code is similar in how it defines the crime of possessing or distributing child pornography.[40]

Sec. 43.26. Possession or Promotion of Child Pornography

(a) A person commits an offense if:
    (1) the person knowingly or intentionally possesses visual material that visually depicts a child younger than 18 years of age at the time the image of the child was made who is engaging in sexual conduct; and
    (2) the person knows that the material depicts the child as described by Subdivision (1).
(b) In this section:
    (1) "Promote" has the meaning assigned by Section 43.25.
    (2) "Sexual conduct" has the meaning assigned by Section 43.25.
    (3) "Visual material" means:
        (A) any film, photograph, videotape, negative, or slide or any photographic reproduction that contains or incorporates in any manner any film, photograph, videotape, negative, or slide; or
        (B) any disk, diskette, or other physical medium that allows an image to be displayed on a computer or other video screen and any image transmitted to a computer or other video screen by telephone line, cable, satellite transmission, or other method.
(c) The affirmative defenses provided by Section 43.25(f) also apply to a prosecution under this section.
(d) An offense under Subsection (a) is a felony of the third degree.
(e) A person commits an offense if:
    (1) the person knowingly or intentionally promotes or possesses with intent to promote material described by Subsection (a)(1); and
    (2) the person knows that the material depicts the child as described by Subsection (a)(1).
(f) A person who possesses visual material that contains six or more identical visual depictions of a child as described by Subsection (a)(1) is presumed to possess the material with the intent to promote the material.
(g) An offense under Subsection (e) is a felony of the second degree.

In both of these statutes, the individual must know that the performer is a child, but the jury may use circumstantial evidence to find knowledge. Another issue is whether a computer's automatic saving of images in a cache is "possession." While some courts have found that someone who looks at child pornography via the Internet but doesn't intentionally download it is still guilty of possession unless they take steps to remove it from the computer's data storage, other courts have found that only sophisticated computer users understand the cache system and, therefore, possession only occurs if the offender intentionally downloads child pornography.[41]

Recently, the issue of "sexting" has emerged and posed difficult social and legal questions. Teenagers who take naked or sexually suggestive pictures of themselves and

---

[40]   TEXAS PENAL CODE § 43.26 (Vernons 2003).
[41]   United States v. Romm, 455 F.3d 990 (9th Cir. 2006) (it is possession).

send them to other teenagers can be legally guilty of child pornography, as can the person receiving the picture unless they immediately delete it even if it is another teen. What frequently happens is that the receiver then sends the picture to several or many other teens, sometimes as part of a harassment campaign. While this type of activity was not considered the target of child pornography laws, the acts involved meet the legal definition and some teens have been prosecuted under these laws, resulting in them having to register as sex offenders as well. Some states have created new "sexting" statutes that reduce the penalties from child pornography if both parties are teens. For instance a law in Florida that went into effect in October of 2011 applies to minors who knowingly commit the following acts:

> (a) Uses a computer, or any other device capable of electronic data transmission or distribution, to transmit or distribute to another minor any photograph or video of himself or herself which depicts nudity and is harmful to minors; or
> (b) Possesses a photograph or video that was transmitted or distributed by another minor as described in paragraph (a).

A first violation would be a noncriminal violation punishable by 8 hours of community service or, if ordered by the court in lieu of community service, a $60 fine. Additionally, the court may order the minor to participate in suitable training or instruction in lieu of, or in addition to, community service or a fine. A second violation would be a second degree misdemeanor, punishable by up to 60 days in jail and a $500 fine. A minor commits a first-degree misdemeanor, punishable by up to one year in jail and a $1,000 fine, for a violation that occurs after being found to have committed a second-degree misdemeanor sexting offense. A minor commits a third-degree felony, punishable by up to 5 years imprisonment and a $5,000 fine, for a violation that occurs after being found to have committed a first degree misdemeanor sexting offense. Other states have also created sexting statutes but there are some teens who have been prosecuted under child pornography laws as the accompanying news box illustrates.

LEGAL NEWS: IN TEXTING, ARE TEENS VICTIM OR OFFENDER?

In Texas, one eighth-grader sent a picture of herself naked to a boyfriend. They broke up and he sent it to another girl who then sent it to many others; the photo then went viral. Virtually everyone in her high school saw the picture before school officials and parents became aware of it. The ex-boyfriend and the other teen who sent the photo could have been prosecuted for child pornography. They eventually plea bargained to the misdemeanor of Internet harassment.

In Iowa, Jorge Canal had to register has a sex offender because when he was 18 he sent a picture of his penis to a 14-year-old girl who asked him to do it. In Florida, Phillip Alpert was convicted of child pornography and had to register as a sex offender because he sent a naked picture of his girlfriend to dozens of people, including her parents.

> As of 2011 about half of all states have added or are in the process of creating sexting laws that reduce penalties for juveniles involved in sexting from the serious consequences that result from child pornography charges.
>
> _____
>
> Sources: http://www.mckytonlaw.com/blog/2011/07/22/florida-passes-sexting-law/; http://www.nytimes.com/2010/03/21/us/21sexting.html.; Hoffman, J. Teens' e-flirting leads to legal minefield, Austin American Statesman, March 27, 2011, A3.

Another interesting issue that has emerged in this area is whether "virtual" depictions of children engaged in sexual conduct are illegal. This issue is discussed more fully in Chapter 13 because most crimes that involve child pornography involving computers are prosecuted using federal laws. In *Ashcroft v. Free Speech Coalition*, in 2002, the Supreme Court held that computer-generated images of children engaged in acts that otherwise would be defined as child pornography do not meet the definition of obscenity and cannot be prosecuted if they do not involve real children. However, in 2003 Congress passed the Prosecutorial Remedies and Other Tools to End the Exploitation of Children Today Act of 2003 (PROTECT) that made possession or distribution of child pornography, including "virtual" pornography, illegal. In *U.S. v. Williams*, in 2008, the Court held that it was not a violation of the First Amendment to criminalize distributing or soliciting child pornography that was obscene or *what the actor believed to be* or *what he purported to be* child pornography.[42] Thus, it appears that if someone holds out the computer-generated product as merely that, it may be protected speech. This discussion will continue in Chapter 13, which discusses federal laws.

§ 9.5 Bigamy, Polygamy, and Incest

A. *Common Law*

Bigamy was not a crime at common law, but was considered an offense of ecclesiastical law with punishment in the hands of the ecclesiastical tribunals rather than the common law courts. During the reign of James I, bigamy was made a felony punishable in the civil courts. The crime of bigamy was included in an early Virginia statute and there has never been a time in any state when polygamy has not been an offense against society punishable in the criminal courts.[43]

_____

[42] Ashcroft v. Free Speech Coalition, 535 U.S. 234 (2002); U.S. v. Williams, 553 U.S. 285 (2008).

[43] *See*, for instance, State v. Sellers, 140 S.C. 66, 134 S.E. 873 (1926); Barber v. State, 50 Md. 161 (1878). 10 C.J.S. *Bigamy* § 2 (1983).

The commonly understood meaning of the term *bigamy* is having two wives or husbands at the same time. **Polygamy** has been defined as the offense of having a plurality of husbands or wives. The traditional legal definition of bigamy is willfully and knowingly contracting a second marriage where the contracting party knows that the first marriage still exists. In some states, the traditional crime was designated as either bigamy or polygamy. The definitions are very similar.

Incest was also not a crime at common law, but it was punishable as an offense in the ecclesiastical courts in England. In the United States, incest is a statutory crime, the object of which is to prohibit sexual intercourse between those within certain degrees of relationships.[44] Rape (or statutory rape) and incest are entirely different crimes; thus a man who has sex with his daughter can be convicted of both crimes. Incest is not a lesser included offense of rape. In most jurisdictions consent is irrelevant in the commission of the crime of incest.

Incest is defined as the intermarriage, or sexual relations without marriage, between a man and woman related to each other in any of the degrees of consanguinity or affinity within which marriage is prohibited. Consanguinity is defined as a blood relationship or relation of persons descended from the same stock or common ancestry. Affinity is the connection existing through marriage, between each of the married persons and the kindred of the other.

LEGAL NEWS: SAME-SEX MARRIAGE

Defenders of polygamy often draw parallels to polygamy and same-sex marriage. There are important distinctions, however. First, while there are laws that make bigamy/polygamy illegal, no such laws exist for same-sex marriage because a person can not legally obtain a marriage license unless a state passes a same-sex marriage law. Same-sex marriage needs to be defined as legal, while polygamy was defined as illegal under common law and all states. While the argument that individuals' privacy rights should include the right to marry multiple partners, the fact is that marriage is also a social and economic institution. Putting aside religious and moral arguments, the legal contract of marriage grants a variety of legal and economic rights to spouses, including social security benefits, insurance, parental rights over one's children, survivor rights of many kinds, inheritance, and so on. Arguably, having multiple legal spouses would complicate assessing such benefits in a much different way than having one spouse of the same sex.

As of 2011, eight states recognize same-sex marriages: Massachusetts, Connecticut, California, Iowa, Vermont, New Hampshire, New York, and the District of Columbia. California's voters passed a referendum changing the state's constitution to define marriage as only between a man and a woman, but

---

44   *See*, for instance, these early cases: Commonwealth v. Ashey, 248 Mass. 259, 142 N.E. 788 (1924); Signs v. State, 35 Okla. Crim. 340, 250 P. 938 (1926); State v. Hurd, 101 Iowa 391, 70 N.W. 613 (1897).

a federal district judge ruled it unconstitutional and it is currently under appeal. New York and Maryland do not allow same-sex marriages but legally recognize those from other states. Delaware, Hawaii, Illinois, New Jersey, Rhode Island, Oregon, California, Nevada, Washington, Hawaii, Maine, Wisconsin, and the District of Columbia legally recognize civil unions or domestic partnerships as having some or all the legal rights of a marriage (depending on the state).

Source: http://www.ncsl.org/default.aspx?tabid=16430.

B. Model Penal Code

The Model Penal Code defines three offenses and distinguishes between bigamy and polygamy. Although ordinary adultery is not a crime under the Code, bigamous adultery is a crime. The rationale is that bigamous cohabitation amounts to a public affront, and society demands that this act be punished.

§ 230.1 Bigamy and Polygamy[45]

(1) Bigamy. A married person is guilty of bigamy, a misdemeanor, if he contracts or purports to contract another marriage, unless at the time of the subsequent marriage:
    (a) the actor believes that the prior spouse is dead; or
    (b) the actor and the prior spouse have been living apart for five consecutive years throughout which the prior spouse was not known by the actor to be alive; or
    (c) a court has entered a judgment purporting to terminate or annul any prior disqualifying marriage, and the actor does not know that judgment to be invalid; or
    (d) the actor reasonably believes that he is legally eligible to remarry.
(2) Polygamy. A person is guilty of polygamy, a felony of the third degree, if he marries or cohabits with more than one spouse at a time in purported exercise of the right of plural marriage. The offense is a continuing one until all cohabitation and claim of marriage with more than one spouse terminates. This Section does not apply to parties to a polygamous marriage, lawful in the country of which they are residents or nationals, while they are in transit through or temporarily visiting this State.
(3) Other Party to Bigamous or Polygamous Marriage. A person is guilty of bigamy or polygamy, as the case may be, if he contracts or purports to contract marriage with another knowing that the other is thereby committing bigamy or polygamy.

The Model Code makes it clear that the partner of the married person is also guilty of bigamy or polygamy *if* he or she has knowledge that the other party was married.

---

[45]   MODEL PENAL CODE § 230.1 (1985).

Unlike some of the statutes in existence at the time the Model Penal Code was prepared, the Model Code provides specific defenses to the crime. Most of these defenses go toward the *mens rea* of the crime in that if a person has reasonable cause to believe that the first spouse is dead, then that belief becomes an affirmative defense.

The Model Penal Code defines the crime of incest as limited to blood relatives plus the relationship of parent and child by adoption, thus a relationship between a stepchild and stepparent may not be defined as incest unless there is a legal adoption.

> ### § 230.2 Incest[46]
>
> A person is guilty of incest, a felony of the third degree, if he knowingly marries or cohabits or has sexual intercourse with an ancestor or descendant, or brother or sister of the whole or half blood [or an uncle, aunt, nephew or niece of the whole blood]. "Cohabit" means to live together under the representation or appearance of being married. The relationships referred to herein include blood relationships without regard to legitimacy, and relationship of parent and child by adoption.

C. State Statutes, Codes, and Cases

There are two essential elements of the crime of bigamy: a prior marriage, and a second marriage before the first marriage is dissolved. The *mens rea* varies and in some cases, criminal intent is not essential to bigamy, nor is good faith a defense; however, in other states, a reasonable belief that the first marriage was dissolved can be an affirmative defense.

1. Prior Marriage Element

In order for a person to be convicted of the crime of bigamy, the state must prove a valid marriage entered into by the accused before the alleged bigamous marriage. If the defense can show that the prior marriage was invalid for one reason or another, there can be no conviction. However, a false assumption of the invalidity of a former marriage will not serve as a defense in some states.[47] Obviously, if the prior marriage was dissolved by death, divorce, or annulment before the second took place, there is no bigamy. But a divorce obtained by fraud or one that for some reason is ineffectual is not a defense.

2. Subsequent Marriage

Before one can be convicted of the offense of bigamy, proof must be offered to show that the person went through the form of a subsequent marriage. Such a marriage, of course, is void; nevertheless, evidence must be introduced to show that the marriage ceremony was performed.

---

[46]   Model Penal Code § 230.2 (1985).
[47]   Long v. State, 192 Ind. 524, 137 N.E. 49 (1922).

A person accused of bigamy may defend by showing the absence of one or more of the elements constituting the offense. In some recent cases, those practicing polygamy avoid legal problems by having only one legal marriage and subsequent "spiritual" marriages. Such relationships do not meet the legal tests of polygamy or bigamy because the subsequent unions do not have legal effect.

3. While First Marriage Is Still Legally Binding

Most state statutes provide that if a person is absent and not heard from for a certain number of years he or she is presumed to be dead. In some instances, the period is designated as seven years.

By some authorities, an honest belief, reasonably entertained in the exercise of care, that a divorce has been granted, is a defense to a prosecution for bigamy. The reasoning is that a person should not be held criminally liable when he has been misled without his own fault or carelessness concerning the facts. But even here it is not sufficient that the second marriage was contracted on the strength of a mere rumor of a divorce. A *bona fide* effort to ascertain the truth of the rumor is essential. A person who is contemplating a subsequent marriage may not be able to rely upon the advice of his attorney. One court held that the advice of counsel that there was no impediment to a second marriage was no defense to prosecution for bigamy.[48]

4. Examples of State Statutes

Some state statutes are strict liability offenses and some require knowledge of the ineligibility to contract the second marriage. The Alabama statute is an example of a statute that requires at least a *mens rea* of knowing.[49]

(a) A person commits bigamy when he intentionally contracts or purports to contract a marriage with another person when he has a living spouse. A person who contracts a marriage outside this state, which would be bigamous if contracted in this state, commits bigamy by cohabiting in the state with the other party to such a marriage.
(b) A person does not commit an offense under this section if:
   (1) He reasonably believes that his previous marriage is void or was dissolved by death, divorce or annulment; or
   (2) He and the prior spouse have been living apart for five consecutive years prior to the subsequent marriage, during which time the prior spouse was not known by him to be alive.
   (3) The burden of injecting the issues under this subsection is on the defendant, but this does not shift the burden of proof.
(c) Bigamy is a Class C felony.

The Georgia Code is somewhat different. It also requires a *mens rea* of knowing. This code also targets the partner of the married person.[50] The Georgia Code provides for an

---

[48] State v. Hughes, 58 Iowa 165, 11 N.W. 706 (1882).
[49] ALA. CODE § 13A-13-1 (2002).
[50] GA. CODE ANN. §§ 16-6-20, 16-6-21 (1999).

affirmative defense if the spouse has been absent for a certain period, but in this statute the period is 7 years rather than 5, as used in some statutes. If the defendant honestly believes that he has a right to make the second marriage, and it appears that this honest belief is the result of reasonable diligence to ascertain the truth, then the jury has the right to infer that the defendant had no criminal intent, and, therefore, is not guilty of a crime.

Georgia 16-6-20 Bigamy

(a) A person commits the offense of bigamy when he, being married and knowing that his lawful spouse is living, marries another person or carries on a bigamous cohabitation with another person.

(b) It shall be an affirmative defense that the prior spouse has been continually absent for a period of seven years during which time the accused did not know the prior spouse to be alive, or that the accused reasonably believed he was eligible to remarry.

Georgia 16-6-21 Marrying a bigamist

(a) An unmarried man or woman commits the offense of marrying a bigamist when he marries a person whom he knows to be the wife or husband of another.

(b) It shall be an affirmative defense that the prior spouse of the bigamist has been continually absent for a period of seven years during which time the accused did not know the prior spouse of the bigamist to be alive, or that the accused reasonably believed the bigamist was eligible to remarry.

LEGAL NEWS: POLYGAMY

In April 2008, the state of Texas removed more than 400 children and more than 100 women from a religious compound in Eldorado, Texas, after a telephone call was received by local law enforcement that young girls were being sexually abused. The Eldorado compound is part of the Fundamentalist Church of Jesus Christ of Latter-Day Saints (FLDS), a breakaway sect that separated from the Mormon church when the church disavowed polygamy. The leader of the sect, Warren Jeffs, is currently in prison after being convicted of accessory to rape for his role in commanding the marriage of a 14-year-old girl. In the Texas case, after months of investigation, most of the children were returned to their parents, although the state did find evidence that seven teenage girls were "spiritually" married to adult men and had one or more children by those men. The state is continuing to investigate whether charges of neglect can be brought against parents who allowed children to be present in a situation where they knew sexual abuse was occurring.

In November 2008, a Texas grand jury indicted several members of the FLDS for bigamy. The defense to such a charge was that the second marriages for these men were "spiritual" rather than civil. Although Texas law recognizes common law marriages of those who "purport" to be married, attorneys argued that it would be an unconstitutional violation of equal protection to enforce the law against those couples versus those who cohabit but do not purport marriage.

UPDATE: Warren Jeffs received a life sentence for rape in relation to his "spiritual marriages" to two underage girls. A dozen other members of the Eldorado ranch were charged with bigamy and the eight that went to trial received bigamy convictions (or pleaded no contest). The issue of polygamy remains a controversial one as evidenced by the 2010 reality show "Sister Wives," followed by the Utah investigation of the husband in the television show for bigamy and the family's decision to move to Nevada to escape possible charges.

Sources: Associated Press. "Polygamist Sect Calls Texas Report Fraudulent." MSNBC.com, December 28, 2008. Accessed January 2, 2009 from http://www.msnbc.msn.com/id/28408721. Associated Press. "Eight New Indictments Issued in Texas Polygamist Case." Washingtonpost.com, November 12, 2008. Accessed November 21, 2008 from http://www.washingtonpost.co/wp-dyn/content/article/2008/11/12/AR2008111202390.html. *See also* http://www.sltrib.com/sltrib/news/52788433-78/nielsen-texas-bigamy-jeffs.html.csp.

5. State Statutes: Incest

Incest statutes typically prohibit the marriage of or sexual relations between persons who are related within certain degrees, established by statute. Statutes differ as to the degree of the relationship; however, they are fairly consistent in holding that marriage or sexual relations between father and daughter, mother and son, brother and sister, uncle and niece, and aunt and nephew, are prohibited. Some statutes include first cousins but, under other statutes, prohibition of marriage between first cousins does not make their marriage or cohabitation incest.[51]

As there is a moral difference between the marriage or sexual intercourse of persons related by consanguinity (blood) and persons related only by affinity (marriage), many statutes distinguish these two. In one case, the court held that a statutory prohibition expressly relating to degrees of consanguinity will not, by implication, extend to degrees of affinity. However, other states have statutes that expressly extend to the relationship by affinity. Under these statutes, sexual intercourse between a stepfather and a stepdaughter, a stepmother and a stepson, or a brother-in-law and sister-in-law is prohibited. As a general rule, affinity ceases on the divorce or death of the blood relative through whom the relationship was created. Therefore, in the absence of a statutory provision, after such a divorce or

[51]   *See* these cases as examples: Henley v. State, 489 S.W.2d 53 (Tenn. 1972); Sizemore v. Commonwealth, 210 Ky. 637, 276 S.W. 524 (1925); State v. Couvillion, 117 La. 935, 42 So. 431 (1906).

death, it is not incest for a man to marry or have intercourse with his former wife's daughter or sister.[52]

LEGAL NEWS: WOODY ALLEN

When Woody Allen began a relationship with Soon-Yi, the adopted daughter of Mia Farrow, individuals wondered why he wasn't prosecuted for incest. Mia Farrow and Woody Allen had a long-term relationship and he had served as a father figure to the girl since she was seven. The affair came to light when Mia Farrow saw in Allen's apartment pictures of Soon-Yi posing naked. The two lived next to each other in their own apartments but had been together as a couple for 20 years, had a child together, and had adopted another child together. Regardless of the morality of the relationship between Soon-Yi and Woody Allen, it wasn't illegal. Woody Allen was not the legal father of Soon-Yi, and as indicated, relations between a stepfather and a stepdaughter are not defined as incest in many states. Supposedly the affair started after she was no longer legally a child so other laws were not broken. Farrow accused Allen of molesting their younger child but the states of New York and Connecticut never charged him, although, in their custody dispute, he had limited custodial rights with the younger children. Woody Allen and Soon-Yi married in 1997 and they have adopted two daughters.

Source: M. Meade (2000). *The Unruly Life of Woody Allen*. New York, NY: Scribner; D. Frankel (1997). "I Now Pronounce You Father and Wife." Retrieved September 21, 2006 from www.eonline.com/news/items/0,1,2286,00.html.

In the commentary following § 13A-13-3 of the Alabama Code, the reasons for the offense are enumerated. These include:

(a) The law against incest may represent a reinforcement by civil sanctions of a religious tenet.
(b) A second justification lies in the science of genetics. There is a secular utility in a prohibition against such inbreeding as would result in defective offspring by reason of the higher probability of unfavorable, recessive genes combining in the children of parents within certain blood relationships.
(c) A sociological and psychological justification is that the prohibition of incest tends to promote solidarity of the family by preventing sex rivalries and jealousies within the family unit.
(d) The utility of forbidding abuse by heads of households, especially male, of their authority and financial power over younger children, especially female.[53]

---

[52]   42 C.J.S. *Incest* § 3 (1983).
[53]   ALA. CODE § 13A-13-3 (1999).

The elements of the crime of incest are marriage or sexual intercourse, between persons within the degree of relationship proscribed by statute, with knowledge of the existence of the relationship (under some statutes).

As to the third element above, some statutes define it as a strict liability crime; therefore, in these states, knowledge of the relationship is not an element of the crime. Most current statutes, however, require knowledge as an element of the crime. An example of a state statute that requires knowledge of the relationship is that of Alabama, which provides[54]

(a) A person commits incest if he marries or engages in sexual intercourse with a person he knows to be, either legitimately or illegitimately:
   (1) His ancestor or descendant by blood or adoption; or
   (2) His brother or sister of the whole or half-blood or by adoption; or
   (3) His stepchild or stepparent, while the marriage creating the relationship exists; or
   (4) His aunt, uncle, nephew or niece of the whole or half-blood.
(b) A person shall not be convicted of incest or of an attempt to commit incest upon the uncorroborated testimony of the person with whom the offense is alleged to have been committed.
(c) Incest is a Class C felony.

The Georgia statute also requires knowledge, and includes stepchildren.

§ 16-6-22 Incest[55]

(a) A person commits the offense of incest when he engages in sexual intercourse with a person to whom he knows he is related, either by blood or by marriage as follows:
   Father and daughter or stepdaughter;
   Mother and son or stepson;
   Brother and sister of the whole blood or of the half blood;
   Grandparent and grandchild;
   Aunt and nephew; or
   Uncle and niece.
   A person convicted of the crime of incest shall be punished by imprisonment of not less than one nor more than 20 years.

The Georgia statute was challenged as violating the United States Constitution in the case of *Benton v. State*.[56] In this case, the defendant was convicted of incest along with other crimes. The 16-year-old stepdaughter of the defendant had testified at the trial that the defendant had repeatedly had forcible intercourse with her. The defendant, on appeal, asserted that the Georgia statute, which criminalizes sexual intercourse between a father and stepdaughter, unconstitutionally infringes on the right of privacy, because it bars intercourse with a non-blood-related consenting adult. The reviewing court found that the statute was not arbitrarily drawn in light of the government interest.

---

[54] ALA. CODE § 13A-13-3 (1999).
[55] GA. CODE ANN. § 16-6-22 (1999).
[56] Benton v. State, 461 S.E.2d 202 (Ga. 1995).

Classification on the basis of stepparent and stepchild bears a rational relationship to the government interest in protecting children and family unity.

In interpreting the Florida statute, a court held that the incest statute applies to half-siblings; that is, those who have only one parent in common.[57] In addition, a Connecticut court confirmed that the statute prohibiting sexual intercourse between individuals of certain degrees of kinship encompassed adopted as well as blood relatives and that an adopted child became the legal child of the parents and should be treated as if the child were the biological child of the parents.[58]

D. Summary

Bigamy and polygamy have been criminal offenses in the United States since the formation of the union and continue to be punishable under the statutes of the states. Although the statutes are consistent in providing that a previous marriage and a contract for a subsequent marriage are elements, they may differ in regard to the *mens rea* and in specifying the defenses. The statutes also differ in establishing the criminal liability of the other party to the bigamous marriage and in grading the offenses as misdemeanors or felonies. It is therefore necessary that the statutes of the respective states, as well as the decisions interpreting those statutes, be carefully researched.

Incest was not a crime under the common law but has always been a statutory crime in this country. In general, statutes prohibit marriage or sexual intercourse between relatives related by consanguinity or affinity. Most statutes require knowledge of the relationship, but some do not specify any level of *mens rea*. In general, consent or lack of consent is not an element to the crime of incest. The statutes specify what degree of relationship is prohibited and this varies from state to state.

Bigamy
(A/R) marriage, while previous marriage is still legally binding
(M/R) knowing (although in some states it may be strict liability)

Polygamy
(A/R) marriage, to more than one person, at the same time
(M/R) knowing

Incest
(A/R) sexual intercourse or marriage, between two persons related by proscribed degrees of consanguinity or affinity
(M/R) knowledge (of the relationship) (in most jurisdictions)

---

[57]   Carnes v. State, 725 So. 2d 417 (Fla. 1999).
[58]   State v. George, 785 A.2d 573 (Conn. 2001).

§ 9.6   Other Offenses within the Family

Generally, criminal law does not intrude upon the privacy of the family unit. However, as we saw in the last section, there are certain private behaviors that have been determined to be against the interests of the state and can be punished. In addition to those already discussed, not caring for children or not paying child support if one is ordered to do so by the court can be punished. We will take a brief look at some of these family-related crimes in this section.

A. *Common Law*

Modern statutes have more comprehensive laws regarding the care and support of children than did the common law. Prior to the last two centuries, the head of the household had the right to discipline his children and his wife as he saw fit, including the use of corporal punishment. Laws protecting children from physical discipline or poor working conditions did not exist at all until the nineteenth century. Of course, serious injury or death was penalized, but corporal punishment of children was not considered a matter for the criminal law until the twentieth century. The Society for the Prevention of Cruelty to Children was created in 1875 when it was discovered that although laws existed that punished individuals for beating their animals, no such laws existed to protect children. Early statutes were created to identify and punish injury to a child and, eventually, statutes also penalized abandoning children and even behaviors that put children in dangerous or unhealthy circumstances, whether or not the child was actually injured.

The concept of *parens patriae* means basically that the state will take the place of the parent when the parent is unable or unwilling to perform caregiver functions. This concept, if not part of the common law, emerged very early in the criminal codes of this country and was the basis for the creation of family courts or juvenile courts.

B. *Model Penal Code*

The Model Penal Code's Article 230 is titled "Offenses against the Family" and includes bigamy, polygamy, incest, and other family-related crimes. Other sections describe crimes of neglect and abandonment.

Section 230.4. Endangering Welfare of Children.

A parent, guardian, or other person supervising the welfare of a child under 18 commits a misdemeanor if he knowingly endangers the child's welfare by violating a duty of care, protection or support.

Section 230.5. Persistent Non-Support.

A person commits a misdemeanor if he persistently fails to provide support which he can provide and which he knows he is legally obliged to provide to a spouse, child or other dependent.

C. State Statutes

Family courts rather than criminal courts are the more likely avenue when there is an allegation of child abuse or neglect. Child abuse includes physical abuse, sexual abuse, emotional abuse, and neglect. Most child abuse falls under the category of neglect, which includes not providing adequate sustenance, supervision, or care. Generally, intervention is designed to assist parents to be better caregivers. However, if there is physical or sexual abuse or a lack of willingness to meet basic standards, then criminal prosecution is an option. States generally group family-related crimes under a section titled Family Offense, Abuse of Children, or Offenses against the Family. For instance, in the Florida statutes, Chapter 827 is titled Abuse of Children and has the following sections:

- Abuse, aggravated abuse, and neglect of a child
- Newborn infants
- Contributing to the delinquency or dependency of a child
- Nonsupport of dependents
- Sexual performance by a child
- Misuse of child support money[59]

1. Nonsupport of Dependents (and Abandonment)

All states and the Model Penal Code have laws that prohibit individuals from not taking care of dependents,[60] or abandoning them. First, there must be a duty to another (either by relationship, law, or contract). Then there must be a knowing and/or intentional omission, that is, not feeding a child or leaving them alone with no food or proper supervision. Ohio's nonsupport statute provides

> (A) No person shall abandon, or fail to provide adequate support to:
>   (1) the person's spouse, as required by law;
>   (2) the person's child who is under age eighteen, or mentally or physically handicapped child who is under age twenty-one;
>   (3) the person's aged or infirm parent or adoptive parent, who from lack of ability and means is unable to provide adequately for his or her own support;
> (B) No person shall abandon, or fail to provide support as established by a court order to, another person whom, by court order or decree, the person is legally obligated to support.[61]

The Ohio Code also includes a duty to care for aged and infirm parents. There is an affirmative defense to the charge if the actor is unable to provide adequate support, or if the parent abandoned or failed to support the accused as required by law, while the accused was under the age of 18 or was mentally or physically handicapped and under age 21. Thirty states have filial responsibility laws: Alaska, Arkansas, California,

---

[59]   Florida Statutes, 2008. Title XLVI. Crimes. Chapter 827. Abuse of Children.
[60]   Model Penal Code § 230.5 (1985).
[61]   Ohio Rev. Code Ann. § 2919.21 (Anderson 2002).

Connecticut, Delaware, Georgia, Idaho, Indiana, Iowa, Kentucky, Louisiana, Maryland, Massachusetts, Mississippi, Montana, Nevada, New Hampshire, New Jersey, North Carolina, North Dakota, Ohio, Oregon, Pennsylvania, Rhode Island, South Dakota, Tennessee, Utah, Vermont, Virginia, and West Virginia. Not all provide criminal penalties for failure to extend financial support. The most typical use of these laws is when a nursing home pursues legal action against an adult child for the care of the parent. It is still rare to find criminal prosecutions under filial support laws, however, some predict that as Medicare experiences continued cuts and the baby boom generation ages, active prosecution under such laws may become more prevalent.

Even though it is illegal to neglect or abandon your child, all states have passed a Baby Moses or "safe haven" statute (or defense to the abandonment statute) that allows a parent to abandon an infant at a fire station, hospital, or other designated location. These statutes are designed to prevent parents from leaving the infant in locations that would be dangerous to their health or, worse, killing the infant because they did not want the baby. In July 2008, the state of Nebraska was the last state to pass such a law but no age limit was specified in the statute and children as old as 18 were left at hospitals. In four months several dozen children and teenagers were abandoned to the state, causing consternation among officials who did not realize the legal loophole until parents began using the statute. While public commentary viewed the parents as uncaring, irresponsible, or evil for abandoning their older children, others and the parents themselves pointed out that the children had severe mental problems and parents were unable to care for them. In some cases, the older children were dangerous and the parents were afraid of them. The state legislature did not solve the problem of parents who could not care for their children growing up with mental and behavioral problems, but they did change the safe haven law so that, after November 2008, only infants up to 30 days could be left legally at the designated locations.[62]

California's nonsupport law identifies the crime as a misdemeanor and requires a *mens rea* of willfulness. It allows a defense for those who withhold medical care from their child when their religious beliefs prescribe prayer rather than standardized medical treatment. Whether or not a parent has custody is less relevant than a legal determination of parental responsibility.

> 270. If a parent of a minor child willfully omits, without lawful excuse, to furnish necessary clothing, food, shelter or medical attendance, or other remedial care for his or her child, he or she is guilty of a misdemeanor punishable by a fine not exceeding two thousand dollars ($2,000), or by imprisonment in the county jail not exceeding one year, or by both such fine and imprisonment. If a court of competent jurisdiction has made a final adjudication in either a civil or a criminal action that a person is the parent of a minor child and the person has notice of such adjudication and he or she then willfully omits, without lawful excuse, to furnish necessary clothing, food, shelter, medical attendance or other remedial care for his or her child, this conduct is punishable by imprisonment in the county jail not exceeding one year or in a

---

62   Associated Press (2008). "Eighteen-Year-Old Abandoned." WIBW-TV.com, November 10, 2008. Accessed January 2, 2008 from www.wibw.com/home/headlines/34205614.html.

state prison for a determinate term of one year and one day, or by a fine not exceeding two thousand dollars ($2,000), or by both such fine and imprisonment. This statute shall not be construed so as to relieve such parent from the criminal liability defined herein for such omission merely because the other parent of such child is legally entitled to the custody of such child nor because the other parent of such child or any other person or organization voluntarily or involuntarily furnishes such necessary food, clothing, shelter or medical attendance or other remedial care for such child or undertakes to do so.

Proof of abandonment or desertion of a child by such parent, or the omission by such parent to furnish necessary food, clothing, shelter or medical attendance or other remedial care for his or her child is prima facie evidence that such abandonment or desertion or omission to furnish necessary food, clothing, shelter or medical attendance or other remedial care is willful and without lawful excuse.

The court, in determining the ability of the parent to support his or her child, shall consider all income, including social insurance benefits and gifts.

The provisions of this section are applicable whether the parents of such child are or were ever married or divorced, and regardless of any decree made in any divorce action relative to alimony or to the support of the child. A child conceived but not yet born is to be deemed an existing person insofar as this section is concerned.

The husband of a woman who bears a child as a result of artificial insemination shall be considered the father of that child for the purpose of this section, if he consented in writing to the artificial insemination.

If a parent provides a minor with treatment by spiritual means through prayer alone in accordance with the tenets and practices of a recognized church or religious denomination, by a duly accredited practitioner thereof, such treatment shall constitute "other remedial care," as used in this section.[63]

2. Endangering the Welfare of a Minor

Many states have a criminal statute that covers what is considered reckless endangerment of a child. For instance, Kentucky's statute for endangering the welfare of a minor provides

> (1) a parent, guardian or other person legally charged with the care or custody of a minor is guilty of endangering the welfare of a minor when he fails or refuses to exercise reasonable diligence in the control of such child to prevent him from becoming a neglected dependent or delinquent child.[64]

These statutes typically do not require a *mens rea* of intent but do require knowing or recklessness, rather than simple negligence. They cover a wide variety of behavior including, but not limited to, allowing the child to drive, drink, be present when drug use is occurring, be present in sexually charged situations, and so on.

The Texas Criminal Code places abandonment and endangering the child in the same statute. Because of public concern, those who expose their children to methamphetamine are specifically identified in this statute. Note that the last paragraph is an

---

[63]　Cal. Penal Code § 270 (West 2003).

[64]　Ky. Rev. Stat. Ann. § 530.060 (Baldwin 1999).

example of a safe haven law that allows abandonment when the parent leaves the child at a safe location.

Sec. 22.041. Abandoning or Endangering Child.[65]

(a) In this section, "abandon" means to leave a child in any place without providing reasonable and necessary care for the child, under circumstances under which no reasonable, similarly situated adult would leave a child of that age and ability.

(b) A person commits an offense if, having custody, care, or control of a child younger than 15 years, he intentionally abandons the child in any place under circumstances that expose the child to an unreasonable risk of harm.

(c) A person commits an offense if he intentionally, knowingly, recklessly, or with criminal negligence, by act or omission, engages in conduct that places a child younger than 15 years in imminent danger of death, bodily injury, or physical or mental impairment.

(c-1) For purposes of Subsection (c), it is presumed that a person engaged in conduct that places a child in imminent danger of death, bodily injury, or physical or mental impairment if:

(1) the person manufactured, possessed, or in any way introduced into the body of any person the controlled substance methamphetamine in the presence of the child;

(2) the person's conduct related to the proximity or accessibility of the controlled substance methamphetamine to the child and an analysis of a specimen of the child's blood, urine, or other bodily substance indicates the presence of methamphetamine in the child's body; or

(3) the person injected, ingested, inhaled, or otherwise introduced a controlled substance listed in Penalty Group 1, Section 481.102, Health and Safety Code, into the human body when the person was not in lawful possession of the substance as defined by Section 481.002(24) of that code. [. . .]

(h) It is an exception to the application of this section that the actor voluntarily delivered the child to a designated emergency infant care provider under Section 262.302, Family Code.

New York also has a statute that defines endangering children as a crime. It does not specify any particular behaviors; therefore, what might be considered endangerment is based on a reasonable person concept. Generally, if the parent or guardian was negligent, authorities may first attempt to use the resources of the family court. If necessary, the state has the authority to remove the children until such time as the parent proves that they are capable of supervising and caring for the child more appropriately. However, if the behavior is extreme or the parent is noncompliant, a criminal charge of endangerment is possible.

New York. § 260.10 Endangering the welfare of a child[66]

A person is guilty of endangering the welfare of a child when:

(1) He knowingly acts in a manner likely to be injurious to the physical, mental or moral welfare of a child less than seventeen years old or directs or authorizes such

---

[65]   TEXAS PENAL CODE § 22.041 (West 2003).

[66]   New York Penal Law Section § 260.10.

child to engage in an occupation involving a substantial risk of danger to his life or health; or

(2) Being a parent, guardian or other person legally charged with the care or custody of a child less than eighteen years old, he fails or refuses to exercise reasonable diligence in the control of such child to prevent him from becoming an "abused child," a "neglected child," a "juvenile delinquent" or a "person in need of supervision," as those terms are defined in articles ten, three, and seven of the family court act.

Endangering the welfare of a child is a class A misdemeanor.

3. Injury to a Child

Physical injury to a child is assault, but many states take special note when the victim of assault is a child or one's own child or dependent. The Texas Penal Code places injury to a child in the chapter on assaultive offenses. Note that this statute is written broadly enough that it also could include behaviors that would, in other states, be prosecuted as endangerment. The statute provides a defense to those who are acting under religious beliefs and those who, by omission, fail to protect the child from the acts of another if they are also a victim.

Sec. 22.04. Injury to a Child, Elderly Individual, or Disabled Individual.[67]

(a) A person commits an offense if he intentionally, knowingly, recklessly, or with criminal negligence, by act or intentionally, knowingly, or recklessly by omission, causes to a child, elderly individual, or disabled individual:
(1) serious bodily injury;
(2) serious mental deficiency, impairment, or injury; or
(3) bodily injury. [. . .]
[. . . sections b-j omitted]

(k) It is a defense to prosecution under this section that the act or omission consisted of:
(1) reasonable medical care occurring under the direction of or by a licensed physician; or
(2) emergency medical care administered in good faith and with reasonable care by a person not licensed in the healing arts.

(l) It is an affirmative defense to prosecution under this section:
(1) that the act or omission was based on treatment in accordance with the tenets and practices of a recognized religious method of healing with a generally accepted record of efficacy;
(2) for a person charged with an act of omission causing to a child, elderly individual, or disabled individual a condition described by Subsection (a)(1), (2), or (3) that:
(A) there is no evidence that, on the date prior to the offense charged, the defendant was aware of an incident of injury to the child, elderly individual, or disabled individual and failed to report the incident; and
(B) the person:
(i) was a victim of family violence, as that term is defined by Section 71.004, Family Code, committed by a person who is also charged with an offense against the child, elderly individual, or disabled individual under this section or any other section of this title;

---

[67] Texas Penal Code § 22.04 (West 2003).

    (ii) did not cause a condition described by Subsection (a)(1), (2), or (3); and

    (iii) did not reasonably believe at the time of the omission that an effort to prevent the person also charged with an offense against the child, elderly individual, or disabled individual from committing the offense would have an effect; or

(3) that:

    (A) the actor was not more than three years older than the victim at the time of the offense; and

    (B) the victim was a child at the time of the offense.

Injuries inflicted upon a child, by intent or recklessness, are considered more serious than when the victim is an adult. While some states have chosen to provide special penalties under other crimes based on the age of the victim, others have created special statutes. In either case, the result is typically a more serious punishment. Behaviors that involve neglect, abandonment, or place the child in a situation that is dangerous to his or her health, emotional development, or morals are also subject to punishment.

States also have "mandatory reporter" laws that require certain professionals to report child abuse when they have reasonable cause to know or suspect that it is occurring or face criminal penalties. For instance, Colorado's law on child abuse identifies the following as mandatory reporters: physician, child health associate, dentist, chiropractor nurse, hospital personnel, school employee, social worker, mental health professional, veterinarian, peace officer, pharmacist, processor, clergyman advocate, commercial film and photographic print psychologist, fireman, and victim's advocate. Other states, such as Texas, under the Family Code (261.001), require all people to report child abuse when they have knowledge it is occurring. Generally prosecutions are rare and occur only when the individual is living with the child and abuser and allows it to occur.

§ 9.7 Abortion

A. Common Law

Abortion was not a crime under the common law. In fact, the fetus had virtually no legal protection because it was not defined as a person apart from the mother. However, early statutes in this country did criminalize the intentional death of a fetus. As early as 1821, the first state law dealing directly with abortion was enacted by the Connecticut legislature. By 1868, at least 36 laws enacted by state or territorial legislatures limited abortion.[68]

Abortion is the expulsion of the fetus at so early a period of uterogestation that it has not acquired the power of sustaining an independent life. Generally, the term

---

[68]   Roe v. Wade, 410 U.S. 113, 93 S. Ct. 705, 35 L. Ed. 2d 147 (1973).

"abortion" does not include the use of an intrauterine device (IUD), the so-called "morning after" pill (estrogen pregnancy prophylaxis), or birth control pills; rather, these are more commonly considered forms of birth control or contraception. The Revised Uniform Abortion Act defines "abortion" as the termination of human pregnancy with an intention other than to produce a live birth or to remove a dead embryo or fetus.

In 1973 (the year of *Roe v. Wade*) at least 36 states had laws limiting abortions. According to these statutes, purposely and unjustifiably terminating the pregnancy of another other than by a birth was a crime. For example, a Kansas statute provided that "whoever with intent to produce a miscarriage of any pregnant woman or of any woman, unlawfully administers, or causes to be given to her any drug or noxious substance whatever, or unlawfully uses any instrument or means whatever, with such intent, shall be guilty of the offense."[69]

The elements of the crime of abortion in the majority of the states prior to *Roe v. Wade* were

- an intent to produce a miscarriage;
- unlawful administration of drugs or noxious substances or using an instrument; and
- a resulting miscarriage.

In 1973, the Supreme Court decided *Roe v. Wade*.[70] In this case a woman challenged the Texas law that made it a crime to procure an abortion as defined therein or to attempt an abortion except on medical advice for the purpose of saving the life of the mother. That Supreme Court held that the Texas Criminal Abortion Statute was unconstitutional. While agreeing that the state had an interest in regulating abortions, the majority concluded that the right of personal privacy includes the right of a pregnant female to make the decision whether to terminate her pregnancy. The Court went on to explain, however, that a woman's right to terminate a pregnancy was not absolute.

The majority of the U.S. Supreme Court found that the state had a "compelling interest" that overcame the woman's privacy rights at a certain point in the pregnancy. Prior to approximately the end of the first trimester, the abortion decision and its effectuation must be left to the woman and attending physician. However, following the approximate end of the first trimester, the state may regulate abortion procedures in ways *reasonably related* to maternal health. After "viability" (the stage at which point the fetus might survive outside the womb), the state may regulate and even forbid abortion except where necessary for preservation of the life or health of the mother.

Subsequent to this decision, a number of state statutes have been passed and challenged. These subsequent decisions will be discussed in a following section.

---

[69] State v. Miller, 90 Kan. 230, 133 P. 878 (1913).
[70] Roe v. Wade, 410 U.S. 113, 93 S. Ct. 705, 35 L. Ed. 2d 147 (1973).

B. Model Penal Code

The Model Penal Code is very complex and is patterned after the *Roe v. Wade* decision. Subsection (1) prohibits the unjustified termination of the pregnancy of another. This requires an actual termination of the pregnancy. Subsection (2) defines what constitutes justifiable abortion and exceptions. Subsection (3) requires that two physicians certify in advance their belief as to the circumstances justifying the abortion, but violation of this requirement would not itself make the abortion unlawful. Subsection (4) deals with the self-abortion late in pregnancy. Subsection (5) contains a provision relating to one who represents that he is performing an abortion although he may know or believe that the woman is not pregnant, and Subsection (6) deals with the distribution of anything specifically designed to terminate a pregnancy or held out by the actor as useful for that purpose. Subsection (7) is designed to make it clear that the use of contraception devices or drugs to prevent pregnancy do not come within the ambit of the offense.

§ 230.3 Abortion[71]

(1) Unjustified Abortion. A person who purposely and unjustifiably terminates the pregnancy of another otherwise than by a live birth commits a felony of the third degree or, where the pregnancy has continued beyond the twenty-sixth week, a felony of the second degree.

(2) Justifiable Abortion. A licensed physician is justified in terminating a pregnancy if he believes there is substantial risk that continuance of the pregnancy would gravely impair the physical or mental health of the mother or that the child would be born with grave physical or mental defect, or that the pregnancy resulted from rape, incest, or other felonious intercourse. All illicit intercourse with a girl below the age of 16 shall be deemed felonious for purposes of this Subsection. Justifiable abortions shall be performed only in a licensed hospital except in case of emergency when hospital facilities are unavailable. [Additional exceptions from the requirement of hospitalization may be incorporated here to take account of situations in sparsely settled areas where hospitals are not generally accessible.]

(3) Physicians' Certificates; Presumption from Non-Compliance. No abortion shall be performed unless two physicians, one of whom may be the person performing the abortion, shall have certified in writing the circumstances which they believe to justify the abortion. Such certificate shall be submitted before the abortion to the hospital where it is to be performed and, in the case of abortion following felonious intercourse, to the prosecuting attorney or the police. Failure to comply with any of the requirements of this Subsection gives rise to a presumption that the abortion was unjustified.

(4) Self-Abortion. A woman whose pregnancy has continued beyond the twenty-sixth week commits a felony of the third degree if she purposely terminates her own pregnancy otherwise than by a live birth, or if she uses instruments, drugs or violence upon herself for that purpose. Except as justified under Subsection (2), a person who induces or knowingly aids a woman to use instruments, drugs or violence upon herself for the purpose of terminating her pregnancy otherwise

---

[71]   MODEL PENAL CODE § 230.3 (1985).

than by a live birth commits a felony of the third degree whether or not the pregnancy has continued beyond the twenty-sixth week.

(5) Pretended Abortion. A person commits a felony of the third degree if, representing that it is his purpose to perform an abortion, he does an act adapted to cause abortion in a pregnant woman although the woman is in fact not pregnant, or the actor does not believe she is. A person charged with unjustified abortion under Subsection (1) or an attempt to commit that offense may be convicted thereof upon proof of conduct prohibited by this Subsection.

(6) Distribution of Abortifacients. A person who sells, offers to sell, possesses with intent to sell, advertises, or displays for sale anything specially designed to terminate a pregnancy, or held out by the actor as useful for that purpose, commits a misdemeanor, unless:

    (a) the sale, offer or display is to a physician or druggist or to an intermediary in a chain of distribution to physicians or druggists; or

    (b) the sale is made upon prescription or order of a physician; or

    (c) the possession is with intent to sell as authorized in paragraphs (a) and (b); or

    (d) the advertising is addressed to persons named in paragraph (a) and confined to trade or professional channels not likely to reach the general public.

(7) Section Inapplicable to Prevention of Pregnancy. Nothing in this Section shall be deemed applicable to the prescription, administration or distribution of drugs or other substances for avoiding pregnancy, whether by preventing implantation of a fertilized ovum or by any other method that operates before, at, or immediately after fertilization.

C. State Statutes, Codes, and Cases

When the decision in the case of *Roe v. Wade* was announced, many state abortion statutes became invalid. Subsequently, state legislatures responded with a variety of new abortion regulations. Many of these were also challenged as violating the woman's right to privacy. The most important case decisions are described below.

1. Thornburgh v. American College of Obstetricians and Gynecologists

In 1982, Pennsylvania enacted the Abortion Control Act, which regulated the information a woman was given before obtaining an abortion, the procedure a physician followed when performing a late-term abortion, and the data that was reported to public authorities. This statute was challenged in the case of *Thornburgh v. American College of Obstetricians and Gynecologists*.[72] In this case, an action was brought challenging the constitutionality of the statute and seeking declaratory and injunctive relief. By the time the case reached the U.S. Supreme Court, the dispute centered on three sections. One section listed a set of facts that was to be recited to every woman who sought an abortion. Another section prohibited doctors from performing an abortion after the fetus was viable, except when the procedure was necessary to preserve the mother's health. The law further provided that when a physician decided that such a late abortion

---

[72]   476 U.S. 747, 106 S. Ct. 2169, 90 L. Ed. 2d 779 (1986).

was necessary, two duties were imposed upon the physician: first, the physician must try to remove the fetus alive, unless the attempt "would significantly increase the risk to the mother," and second, the physician must call a colleague into the room to take exclusive control and care for the aborted fetus.

The U.S. Supreme Court, after considering the jurisdiction question, decided that the requirement that the woman be advised that medical assistance may be available, and that the father is responsible for financial assistance in supporting the child, was unconstitutional. Also, the requirement that the physician inform the woman of the detrimental physical and psychological effects and of all the particular medical risks was also unconstitutional. The reporting requirements of the statute did not meet the constitutional requirements, nor did the provisions governing the degree of care for postviability abortions. Finally, the provisions requiring the presence of a second physician, by failing to provide a medical emergency exception for the situation in which the mother's health is endangered by delay in the second physician's arrival, was unconstitutional. The Court, after specifically reaffirming *Roe v. Wade*, made this comment:

> The states are not free under the guise of protecting maternal health or potential life, to intimidate women into continuing pregnancies. Appellants claim that the statutory provisions before us today further legitimate compelling interests of the Commonwealth. Close analysis of these provisions, however, shows that they wholly subordinate constitutional privacy interests and concerns with maternal health in an effort to deter a woman from making a decision that, with her physician, is hers to make.

The *Thornburgh* decision, which reasserted the fundamental right of women to choose abortion, was a 5-to-4 decision.

2. Webster v. Reproductive Services

In the 1988 case of *Doe v. Smith*, the U.S. Supreme Court again upheld the mother's constitutional right to abortion.[73] In this case, the Court decided that the natural father's interest in an unborn fetus, although legitimate and apparently sincere, did not outweigh the mother's constitutionally protected right to abortion. However, it was the *Webster v. Reproductive Services* case in 1989 that garnered greater attention.[74] The case concerned a challenge to a Missouri abortion statute. The preamble to the Missouri statute declared that human life began at conception and included the following provisions:

- It prohibited public employees from performing or assisting abortions not necessary to save a pregnant woman's life.
- It prohibited the use of public funds for counseling a woman to have an abortion or the use of public facilities for performing abortions, even if no public funds are involved.

---

[73]   Doe v. Smith, 486 U.S. 1308, 108 S. Ct. 2136, 100 L. Ed. 2d 909 (1988).
[74]   Webster v. Reproductive Health Services, 492 U.S. 490, 109 S. Ct. 3040, 106 L. Ed. 2d 410 (1989).

- It required doctors, who believe a woman requesting an abortion may be at least 20 weeks pregnant, to perform tests to determine whether the fetus is viable, or capable of surviving outside the womb.

While five justices upheld the state requirements, the majority took three different approaches and the dissenting justices filed two separate opinions. Writing for the plurality (Justices Kennedy, White, and Rehnquist), Justice Rehnquist found that the provision requiring doctors to determine fetal viability only required a physician to perform such tests as are necessary in accordance with the exercise of the physician's professional judgment. These judges rejected *Roe's* rigid trimester framework.

Justice O'Connor agreed that the Missouri law was constitutional, in that requiring tests to ascertain fetal viability was consistent with the state's interest in potential human life, but refused to reexamine the trimester framework set forth in *Roe*. Justice Scalia also recognized the constitutionality of the law, but criticized the plurality opinion for refusing to repudiate *Roe* outright.

The dissenting justices would have reaffirmed the *Roe* trimester framework and declared the Missouri law unconstitutional. They objected to the statute's preamble ("the life of each human begins at conception" and "unborn children have protectable interests in life, health, and well-being"). However, the majority did not find this passage objectionable, arguing that it did not, by its terms, regulate abortions or any other aspect of medical practice. The majority opinion in *Webster* upheld Missouri's regulations on abortion, including the provision that prohibited any public funds to be used for abortions.

3. Planned Parenthood v. Casey

As anticipated, these cases did not settle the arguments relating to the constitutionality of state abortion statutes. In 1992, the U.S. Supreme Court considered the constitutionality of the Pennsylvania abortion statute in *Planned Parenthood v. Casey*.[75] At issue were five provisions of the Pennsylvania Abortion Control Act as amended in 1988 and 1989.[76] The Act requires that a woman seeking an abortion notify her husband prior to the abortion procedure, and that she be provided with certain information at least 24 hours before the abortion is performed. For a minor to obtain an abortion, the Act requires the informed consent of one of the minor's parents, but provides for a judicial bypass option if the minor does not wish to or cannot obtain a parent's consent. Another provision of the Act requires that, unless certain exceptions apply, a married woman seeking an abortion must sign a statement indicating that she has notified her husband about the intended abortion. The Act exempts compliance with some of these requirements in the event of a "medical emergency" that is defined in the Act. In addition to these provisions regulating the performance of abortions, the Act imposes certain recording requirements on facilities that provide abortion services.

---

[75]   Planned Parenthood v. Casey, 505 U.S. 833, 112 S. Ct. 2791, 120 L. Ed 2d 674 (1992).

[76]   18 Pa. Cons. Stat. §§ 3203-3220 (1990).

As in previous cases, the members of the U.S. Supreme Court could find little ground for agreement. The majority refused to overturn *Roe v. Wade*. Three justices held that

1. the doctrine of *stare decisis* requires reaffirmation of *Roe v. Wade*'s essential holding recognizing a woman's right to choose an abortion before fetal viability;
2. the **undue burden test**, rather than the trimester framework, should be used in evaluating abortion restrictions before viability;
3. the medical emergency definition in the Pennsylvania statute was sufficiently broad in that it did not impose an undue burden;
4. the informed consent requirements, the 24-hour waiting period, parental consent provision, and reporting and record-keeping requirements of the Pennsylvania statute did not impose an undue burden; and
5. the spousal notification provision imposed an undue burden and was invalid.

The lack of agreement among the justices is evidenced by the fact that Justice Stevens filed an opinion concurring in part and dissenting in part; Justice Blackmun filed an opinion consenting in part, concurring in the judgment in part, and dissenting in part; Chief Justice Rehnquist filed an opinion concurring in the judgment in part and dissenting in the part in which Justices White, Scalia, and Thomas joined; and Justice Scalia filed an opinion concurring in the judgment in part and dissenting in part, in which Justices Rehnquist, White, and Thomas joined.

4. Schenck v. Pro-Choice Network of Western New York

In the 1997 case of *Schenck v. Pro-Choice Network of Western New York*,[77] the United States Supreme Court was presented with the question of whether an injunction that places restrictions on demonstrations outside an abortion clinic violates the First Amendment. The court stated that provisions imposing a "fixed buffer zone" limitation would be upheld, but that the provisions imposing "floating buffer zone" limitations violate the First Amendment. The Supreme Court reasoned that the governmental interests in ensuring public safety and order, promoting free flow of traffic on streets and sidewalks, protecting property rights, and protecting a woman's freedom to seek pregnancy-related services, in combination, were significant enough to justify an appropriately tailored preliminary injunction to secure unimpeded physical access to the clinics.

5. Stenberg v. Carhart[78] and Gonzales v. Carhart[79]

In 2000, the Court considered Nebraska's partial birth abortion law, which prohibited all second trimester abortions where the fetus is extracted from the uterus through the birth canal. Nebraska's law banned all such abortions without any definition as to

---

[77]   Schenck v. Pro-Choice Network of Western New York, 519 U.S. 357, 117 S. Ct. 855, 137 L. Ed. 2d 1 (1997).

[78]   Stenberg v. Carhart, 530 U.S. 914 (2000).

[79]   Gonzales v. Carhart, 550 U.S. 124 (2007).

whether such procedures were pre- or postviability. The law also made no exceptions for such abortions to save the life or preserve the health of the mother.

The Supreme Court struck down the law, holding that it did not meet the undue burden test because it made no allowances for medical emergencies. The case decision hinted that a partial birth abortion ban that allowed for exceptions might meet the undue burden test. In *Gonzales v. Carhart,* the Supreme Court heard an appeal regarding the federal Partial Birth Abortion Ban,[80] signed by President Bush in 2003. Both the Eighth and Ninth Circuits had overturned the federal Act, ruling that it was unconstitutional under the reasoning of *Stenberg v. Carhart.* The Supreme Court evaluated the arguments that the Act was vague and did not give physicians due notice as to whether their actions would be criminal; was overbroad in that it included behaviors that might have been inadvertent; and that it posed an undue burden on the woman's right to abortion in that it did not provide for an exception for the woman's health (only life). The Court disagreed with these arguments and upheld the federal Act in a 5 to 4 decision. The dissent, led by Justice Ginsburg, and joined by Justices Breyer, Souter, and Stevens, argued that the decision was contrary to Stenberg and prior decisions that enforced a bright-line test between previability and postviability procedures. They argued that the decision was a chipping away of the precedent of *Roe v. Wade.*

> **Case Note: *Gonzales v. Carhart*, 550 U.S. 124 (2007)**
> What is the difference between intact birth abortion and the type of procedure that the Court said was the medical alternative?
> What were the issues raised in these appeals?
> What was the holding of the Supreme Court and the rationale as to why this was not an undue burden on the woman's right to abortion?

6. Other Cases Concerning Abortion

With the undue burden test, states may pass statutes limiting, restricting, or creating procedures for abortion as long as these are not determined to be "undue burdens" on a woman's rights. A Utah statute that permitted abortions after 20 weeks gestational age in only three narrow circumstances was challenged in *Jane L. v. Bangerter.* The federal court held that this statute violated due process under *Planned Parenthood v. Casey,* because it placed an undue burden on the right to choose the abortion of a non-viable fetus. The court stated that this statute had both the impermissible purpose and impermissible effect of placing an insurmountable obstacle in the path of a woman seeking nontherapeutic abortion of a nonviable fetus after 20 weeks.[81]

After considering the provisions of a Montana abortion statute, a federal appeals court ruled that where a minor can show that (1) she is sufficiently mature to make her own decision whether to have an abortion or (2) abortion is in her best interests,

---

[80]   18 U.S.C. § 1531.
[81]   Jane L. v. Bangerter, 102 F.3d 1112 (10th Cir. 1996).

the state law must allow her to obtain that abortion without obtaining parental consent. Similarly, a federal court in Arizona agreed that the state may impose a parental consent requirement for minors seeking abortions, but must provide an anonymous and expeditious alternative.[82]

In a Missouri case, a federal circuit court declared that any constitutional right of clinics to provide abortion services is derived directly from the woman's constitutional right to choose abortion, and legislation affecting physicians and clinics that perform abortions will be found unconstitutional if it imposes an *undue burden* on women seeking abortions. The court reiterated that a statute that affects the right to abortion is an undue burden if it has the purpose or effect of placing a substantial obstacle in the path of a woman seeking an abortion.[83]

An Alabama court held that the trial court was correct in granting a minor's request for a waiver of parental consent to have an abortion when the trial judge conducted an adversarial hearing and gave both a *guardian ad litem* appointed for the minor and a *guardian ad litem* appointed for the fetus an opportunity to present evidence and to argue their respective positions.[84]

Answering a question that had come up in several courts, a West Virginia court concluded that an unwed biological father's right to establish and maintain a parental relationship with his child does not foreclose an unwed biological mother's right to terminate her pregnancy.[85]

A federal district court held that a provision of a state's abortion statute requiring that abortions performed following the twelfth week of pregnancy be performed in a hospital was an undue burden and an unnecessary infringement upon a woman's constitutional right to abortion.[86]

While *Roe v. Wade* has essentially been upheld, the Supreme Court has allowed the states additional latitude in laws that regulate abortions. Specifically, the court accepted that the following did not impose an "undue burden" on a woman's right to privacy:

* parental notification (with alternative for mature minors)
* prohibition of any public funds to pay for an abortion
* informed consent requirements
* 24-hour waiting period
* ban on "intact birth" abortions unless life of mother was at stake

Challenges to *Roe v. Wade* continue. For instance, South Dakota passed a law that requires a woman to wait three days and consult with antiabortion counselors before having an abortion. Some state legislatures are contemplating laws that would prohibit

---

[82]   Wicklund v. Salvagni, 93 F.3d 567 (9th Cir. 1996); Planned Parenthood of Southern Arizona v. Neely, 942 F. Supp. 1578 (D. Ariz. 1996).

[83]   Planned Parenthood of Mid-Missouri and Eastern Kansas, Inc., v. Dempsey, 167 F.3d 458 (8th Cir. 1999).

[84]   In re Anonymous 720 So.2d 497 (Ala. 1998).

[85]   Kessel v. Leavitt, 511 S.E.2d 720 (W. Va. 1998), *cert. denied*, 525 U.S. 1142, 119 S. Ct. 1035, 143 L. Ed. 2d 43 (1998).

[86]   Minnesota/South Dakota v. Janklow, 216 F. Supp. 2d 983 (D.S.D. 2002).

even private insurers from paying for abortions (public funds have not been available for some time). Nebraska and several states have also passed laws banning abortions after 20 weeks, even though the Supreme Court in *Casey* targeted viability as the guideline for when states may begin to impose restrictions on abortions. There is no doubt that the law regarding abortions will continue to evolve.

D. Summary

Abortion was not a crime under the common law, but very early statutes existed that criminalized intentional injury or death to a fetus. In 1973 the Supreme Court declared unconstitutional a Texas statute that prohibited abortions. That decision has been challenged many times since then but each time the majority opinion of the Supreme Court has upheld the essential holding that a woman's right to privacy is greater than the state's interest in protecting the fetus by restricting and/or prohibiting abortions, at least in the first trimester. At this point, the test is whether a state regulation or prohibition constitutes an "undue burden" on a woman's right to privacy.

§ 9.8   Summary

Some acts, such as murder, burglary, arson, and theft are so obviously wrong that punishment is provided in practically all societies. There are other acts where there is no consensus regarding punishment. Within this category are offenses designated as offenses against the public health, safety, and morals, or offenses against morality and decency.

Until recently, most states had statutes that prohibited adultery and fornication. Today, adultery and fornication statutes are largely anachronistic. The elements of adultery are voluntary sexual intercourse between parties not lawfully married to each other, with at least one of the parties being married to another person. Fornication is voluntary sexual intercourse between unmarried persons.

Soliciting prostitution is defined as offering (or requesting) sexual acts for money. Also, aiding and abetting prostitution, associating with prostitutes, and keeping and operating a place of prostitution are punishable under the statutes. The modern trend is to place less emphasis on prosecuting the prostitute, but to more aggressively enforce the laws relating to promoting prostitution.

Practically all states have laws that prohibit distributing obscene materials, but defining what is obscene is sometimes difficult. In order to comply with U.S. Supreme Court decisions, obscenity is very carefully defined in such statutes. The current definition of obscenity, provided by the Supreme Court, is called the *Miller* test. Child pornography is the target of much stricter sanctions. For instance, while laws typically do not punish mere possession of obscenity involving adult actors, the mere possession of child pornography is a crime.

Bigamy, polygamy, and incest were not crimes at common law, but were considered offenses in ecclesiastical tribunals. These later became specific crimes and were included in the early statutes of the states. The traditional legal definition of bigamy is willfully and knowingly contracting a second marriage when the contracting party knows that the first marriage still exists. Polygamy is a similar offense and the *actus reus* for polygamy also involves multiple coterminous marriages. Incest is defined as intermarriage, or sexual relations without marriage, between a man and a woman related to each other within any of the prohibited degrees of consanguinity or affinity.

There are other acts that fall within an offenses against the family category. Most, if not all, of these were not crimes under common law. Parents have a duty to provide support for their children. This means providing food, shelter, and medical care. Today, it may mean paying child support that is ordered by the court. A parent cannot abandon a child, unless their act falls within the exceptions described in safe haven laws. A parent or caregiver is committing a crime when they abuse a child, either physically, sexually, emotionally, or through neglect. Caregivers also are subject to punishment when they expose a child to dangerous or unhealthy conditions. These statutes could potentially cover a wide range of parental behaviors, but the general tendency of states is to work through family or juvenile courts if the caregivers' actions stem from inability to care for the child appropriately or through ignorance.

The term *abortion* does not necessarily imply a criminal act, because some abortions are permitted by law. The United States Supreme Court has rendered a series of decisions regarding abortion-related statutes. In the case of *Roe v. Wade*, the Supreme Court recognized a woman's right to choose an abortion before fetal viability. Following that case, a series of other cases established guidelines that must be followed by the states in enacting and enforcing statutes relating to abortions. Other courts have held that any statute that affects the right to abortion is an undue burden if it has as its purpose or effect the placing of a substantial obstacle in the path of a woman seeking an abortion.

Crimes relating to morality and decency differ from state to state, and definitions of various terms are often technical, thus it is essential to study the specific statutes, as well as cases interpreting the statutes, to understand the law of any particular state.

REVIEW QUESTIONS

1. What were the traditional elements of the offense of adultery? In some states, it was essential that one party be married. Toward which party were some early statutes directed and why?

2. How is *fornication* distinguished from *adultery*? How does the penalty for these offenses differ in various states?

3. What Supreme Court case casts doubt on the constitutionality of any statute that seeks to criminalize sex between consenting adults? Explain.

4. What is the likely result when statutes criminalizing the sale of vibrators or other sex aids are challenged? How many states still have such laws?

5. Is the term *prostitution* synonymous with the offense of prostitution? Define *prostitution*.

6. Do the prostitution statutes encompass acts between two males?

7. In the case of *Miller v. California*, the U.S. Supreme Court established some guidelines relating to obscenity. What are these guidelines?

8. How are child pornography statutes different (what behavior do they encompass that obscenity involving adults does not)? Does an offender have to "know" the actor is a child?

9. Is it illegal to create computer-generated children in sexual poses or activities? Is it illegal to distribute them as child pornography? Explain.

10. Define the terms *bigamy* and *polygamy*. Enumerate the elements of the offense of bigamy. What are the defenses?

11. Define *incest*. Is a state statute that criminalizes sexual intercourse between a father and stepdaughter constitutional? Do all states have such a statute?

12. When can a parent legally abandon a baby? Can they abandon older children?

13. What is a defense for a parent who does not provide medical care for a sick child?

14. What type of acts would fall under endangerment statutes?

15. What is the general definition of *abortion*? What did the case of *Roe v. Wade* hold?

16. Discuss the issue and holding in *Thornburgh v. American College of Obstetricians*. Under what circumstances, according to these cases, may the state regulate abortions?

17. What were the issue and holding in *Planned Parenthood v. Casey*?

18. What were the issue and holding in *Gonzales v. Carhart*?

19. What were the issue and holding in *Stenberg v. Carhart*?

20. What are the state laws or prohibitions currently in place that have not been ruled as "undue burdens" on women's rights to privacy?

Offenses against Public Peace

10

Chapter Outline

Cases

antistalking law

constructive possession

controlled substances

counterterrorism laws

deliver

disorderly conduct

dominion

drunkenness

eavesdropping

failure to identify statutes

inciting to riot

loitering

riot

rout

trafficking

unlawful assembly

vagrancy

wiretapping

§ 10.1   Introduction

In discussing the offenses against public peace, it is important to note that the U.S. Constitution, as interpreted by the courts, limits state power to enact or enforce legislation that prohibits the free exercise of individual behaviors, such as movement or speech. For example, disorderly conduct statutes have, in many instances, been declared unconstitutional as either too vague or as infringing on First Amendment rights. The balance is to have criminal laws that prohibit behavior that is dangerous and/or offensive to the majority, while allowing the greatest degree of freedom for the individual. Sometimes this balance is difficult to achieve.

In this chapter, the offenses of riot, disorderly conduct, vagrancy and loitering, and obstructing a highway or public place are discussed. Crimes of drunkenness and drug use/possession/sale can be considered crimes against public morals as well as public peace and are also considered in this chapter. Finally, *state* laws prohibiting eavesdropping and wiretapping and terrorism are discussed, although the discussion of federal laws considering these behaviors is offered in more detail in Chapter 13.

§ 10.2   Riot and Related Offenses

In riot and riot-related offenses, the number of participants must be greater than one to constitute a crime. Group behavior is potentially more dangerous to the public peace and poses special problems for the police. In most instances, at least three or more persons must be involved if the offense is to be classified as a riot. The three crimes of unlawful assembly, rout, and riot represent the traditionally recognized steps in violent mob action.

1. Unlawful Assembly

An **unlawful assembly** consists of (1) the coming together of three or more persons with a common purpose; (2) either to commit a crime by open force; or (3) to carry out their common purpose, lawful or unlawful, in such a manner as to cause persons of reasonable firmness and courage to apprehend a breach of the peace.[1]

In defining the term "unlawful assembly" and distinguishing this from the crimes of rout and riot, a West Virginia court made this comment:

> To constitute "unlawful assembly" there must be a gathering of three or more persons, to the disturbance of the public peace, with the intention of cooperating in the forcible and violent execution of some unlawful enterprise. If they take steps toward the performance of their purpose, it becomes a "rout"; and if they put their design to actual execution, it is a "riot."[2]

2. Rout

A **rout** is an unlawful assembly that has moved toward the execution of the common purpose of the persons assembled. When an unlawful assembly moves toward the accomplishment of the unlawful purpose, but no acts of violence or disorder have occurred, a rout has been committed.

3. Riot

A **riot** is either an actual beginning of the execution of an unlawful common purpose, or the execution of an unlawful purpose by an assembly that was lawful when its members first assembled; in each case, force and violence are used to engender terror.

A. *Common Law*

At common law, a "riot" was

> [a] tumultuous disturbance of the peace by three persons or more, assembling together of their own authority, with an intent mutually to assist one another against any who shall oppose them in execution of some enterprise of a private nature and afterward actually executing the same in a violent and turbulent manner, to the terror of the people, whether the act intended was, of itself, lawful or unlawful.[3]

In *Feinstein v. City of New York*, the court, referring to English common law, explained that a "riot" has been said to consist of the following elements:

---

[1]   Heard v. Rizzo, 281 F. Supp. 720 (D. Pa. 1968).
[2]   State v. Woolridge, 129 W. Va. 448, 40 S.E.2d 899 (1946).
[3]   Schoolcraft v. State, 84 Okla. Crim. 20, 178 P.2d 641 (1947).

- a number of persons, three at least;
- a common purpose;
- execution or inception of the common purpose;
- an intent to help one another by force if necessary against any person who may oppose them in the execution of their common purpose; and
- force or violence not merely used in demolishing, but displayed in such a manner as to alarm at least one person of reasonable firmness and courage.[4]

1. Inciting to Riot

"**Inciting to riot**" occurs when a person incites or encourages other persons to create or engage in a riot, as the term has been defined. In the case of *Kasper v. State*, the Supreme Court of Tennessee in 1959 affirmed that inciting to riot is a common law offense.[5]

"Inciting to riot" is a separate, distinct offense from participating in a riot. Therefore, one may incite a riot and not participate in it, or one may be involved in a riot without having incited it. However, the offense of inciting to riot may become merged with the more serious crime of riot if the actor participates during the inciting stage as well as in the execution phase of carrying out the unlawful purpose.[6]

B. *Model Penal Code*

The Model Penal Code does not carry forward the crimes of rout and unlawful assembly. Subsection (1) of Section 250.1 punishes for riot one who, under specific circumstances, participates with two or more persons in a course of disorderly conduct; thus, the Model Code includes the requirement that three persons be involved.

§ 250.1 Riot; Failure to Disperse[7]

(1) Riot. A person is guilty of riot, a felony of the third degree, if he participates with [two] or more others in a course of disorderly conduct:
  (a) with purpose to commit or facilitate the commission of a felony or misdemeanor;
  (b) with purpose to prevent or coerce official action; or
  (c) when the actor or any other participant to the knowledge of the actor uses or plans to use a firearm or other deadly weapon.
(2) Failure of Disorderly Persons to Disperse Upon Official Order. Where [three] or more persons are participating in a course of disorderly conduct likely to cause substantial harm or serious inconvenience, annoyance or alarm, a peace officer or other public servant engaged in executing or enforcing the law may order the participants and others in the immediate vicinity to disperse. A person who refuses or knowingly fails to obey such an order commits a misdemeanor.

---

[4] Feinstein v. City of New York, 283 N.Y.S. 335 (1935).
[5] Kasper v. State, 206 Tenn. 434, 326 S.W.2d 664 (1959).
[6] Commonwealth v. Apriceno, 131 Pa. Super. 158, 198 A. 515 (1938).
[7] MODEL PENAL CODE § 250.1 (1985).

The subsections spell out the circumstances under which participants may be guilty of riot. Paragraph (b) of subsection (1) applies to disorderly conduct committed with the purpose of preventing or coercing official action. Paragraph (c) covers disorderly conduct without regard to the purpose of the participation, but places the basis of liability on the actor or other participant who uses or plans to use a firearm or other deadly weapon.

C. State Statutes, Codes, and Cases

Some states' statutes and codes follow the wording of the Model Penal Code. Some specify five, rather than three, as the number of participants required to complete the crime. The range of participants required to constitute a riot ranges from two to ten in state statutes.[8] The wording also varies from state to state. For example, the New York statutes prohibit "violent and tumultuous conduct" by which the actor "intentionally or recklessly causes or creates a grave risk of causing public alarm."[9] In a prosecution for causing a riot at a federal penitentiary, a federal court defined "riot" as a "tumultuous disturbance of the peace by three persons or more, assembling together of their own authority, with an intent mutually to assist each other against any who shall oppose them, in the execution of some unlawful enterprise of a private nature and afterward actually executing the same in a violent and turbulent manner."[10]

The section of the Model Code that applies to "disorderly conduct with the purpose of preventing or coercing official action" is not common to most state statutes. Some state statutes reach the same result by including the words "substantially obstructs law enforcement or other government function." An example is the Kentucky statute, which provides

Ky. Rev. Stat. Ann. § 525.010[11]

Riot means a public disturbance involving an assemblage of five (5) or more persons which by tumultuous and violent conduct creates grave danger of damage or injury to property or persons or substantially obstructs law enforcement or other government functions.

According to that statute, a person is guilty of riot in the first degree when (a) he knowingly participates in a riot; and (b) in the course of and as a result of such a riot a person other than one of the participants suffers physical injury or substantial property damage occurs.

State statutes also cover inciting a riot. The Ohio statute includes three violations under the general heading of "Inciting, Riot, and Related Offenses." Section 2917.01 makes it an offense to incite to violence, Section 2917.02 relates to aggravated riot, and

---

8   MODEL PENAL CODE § 250.1 (1985), comments section.
9   N.Y. PENAL LAW § 240.06 (McKinney 1992).
10 United States v. Evans, 542 F.2d 805 (10th Cir. 1976).
11 KY. REV. STAT. ANN. § 525.010 (Baldwin 1999).

Section 2917.03 defines a violation titled "riot." The section of the statute that defines the offense of "riot" provides that

§ 2917.03[12]

(A) No person shall participate with four or more others in a course of disorderly conduct in violation of § 2917.11 of the Revised Code.
    (1) With purpose to commit or facilitate the commission of a misdemeanor other than disorderly conduct.
    (2) With purpose to intimidate a public official or employee into taking or refraining from official action, or with purpose to hinder, impede, or obstruct a function of government.
    (3) With purpose to hinder, impede, or obstruct the orderly process of administration or instruction at an educational institution, or to interfere with or obstruct lawful activities carried on at such institutions.
(B) No person shall participate with four or more others with purpose to do an act with unlawful force or violence, even though such act might otherwise be lawful.
(C) Whoever violates this section is guilty of riot, a misdemeanor of the first degree.

D. Summary

Riot has been a crime since common law, along with related crimes such as inciting to riot. Basically, what is necessary is at least three people who undertake either unlawful action or lawful action done in an unlawful manner (for instance, a peaceful protest that turns violent). Some states add the provision that the participants may be obstructing the orderly process of government or similar language.

Riot
(A/R) three or more persons, undertake a common action, that is unlawful or lawful but done in an unlawful manner, that is violent and tumultuous, and that obstructs orderly government
(M/R) general intent

§ 10.3   Disorderly Conduct

Disorderly conduct statutes cover a broad range of behavior. Starting in the 1970s, many state statutes were found to be unconstitutionally vague or overbroad. Today most states have attempted to comply with the requirements of the U.S. Supreme Court and structure their new statutes after the Model Penal Code. The main difference between old and new statutes is that the statutes now specify more clearly what behaviors are punishable and do not punish "free speech." Disorderly conduct is usually a misdemeanor.

---

[12]   OHIO REV. CODE ANN. § 2917.01, § 2917.02, and § 2917.03 (2002). *See* In re Jesse S., 717 N.E.2d 1143 (Ohio 1998), which held that the offense of aggravated riot requires participation by five persons and an assault by one person in concern with three others is insufficient to support a conviction.

A. *Common Law*

At common law, there was no offense known as "disorderly conduct," although misconduct that was of such a nature as to constitute a public nuisance was indictable.[13]

B. *Model Penal Code*

Section 250.2 limits disorderly conduct to specifically designated acts likely to create a public nuisance. An effort was made in drafting the proposed statute to keep within the limitations imposed by the U.S. Supreme Court. The act requires a level of culpability providing that the actor must not only engage in the proscribed conduct, but must do so with the purpose of causing public inconvenience, annoyance, or alarm, or recklessly creating a risk thereof. As the Model Code limits the definition of the word "public," police officers would not be authorized to intrude into the home to control private misbehavior simply because such misbehavior may be offensive to others in the home. Instead, the offense is limited to persons who act purposely or recklessly with respect to public annoyance or alarm.

§ 250.2 Disorderly Conduct[14]

(1) Offense Defined. A person is guilty of disorderly conduct if, with purpose to cause public inconvenience, annoyance or alarm, or recklessly creating a risk thereof, he:
(a) engages in fighting or threatening, or in violent or tumultuous behavior; or
(b) makes unreasonable noise or offensively coarse utterance, gesture or display, or addresses abusive language to any person present; or
(c) creates a hazardous or physically offensive condition by any act which serves no legitimate purpose of the actor.

"Public" means affecting or likely to affect persons in a place to which the public or a substantial group has access; among the places included are highways, transport facilities, schools, prisons, apartment houses, places of business or amusement, or any neighborhood.

(2) Grading. An offense under this Section is a petty misdemeanor if the actor's purpose is to cause substantial harm or serious inconvenience, or if he persists in disorderly conduct after reasonable warning or request to desist. Otherwise disorderly conduct is a violation.

C. *State Statutes, Codes, and Cases*

The most common constitutional challenge to various state disorderly conduct statutes was that they were vague—for instance, statutes that defined disorderly conduct as ". . . anything that is disorderly, either by words or unbecoming conduct" was

---

[13]   27 C.J.S. *Disorderly Conduct* § 1(1) (1995); In re Garafone, 193 A.2d 398 (N.J. 1963).
[14]   MODEL PENAL CODE § 250.2 (1985).

declared unconstitutional as being too vague.[15] In 1983, the U.S. Supreme Court struck down this California disorderly conduct statute:

> Every person . . . is guilty of disorderly conduct, a misdemeanor . . . who loiters or wanders upon the streets or from place to place without apparent business and who refuses to identify himself and to account for his presence when requested by any police officer to do so, if the surrounding circumstances are such to indicate to a reasonable man that the public safety demands such identification.[16]

The U.S. Supreme Court found that the statute violated the due process clause, because it vested virtually complete discretion in the hands of the police to determine whether the statute had been violated. Other disorderly conduct, vagrancy, and loitering statutes have undergone extensive change in order to enable them to withstand constitutional scrutiny. While statutes that define disorderly conduct fairly narrowly as those acts that "endanger the morals, safety, or health of the community" have been upheld, statutes that defined as a crime those acts that tended to "annoy, disturb, interfere with or obstruct, or are offensive to others" have been declared unconstitutionally overbroad and vague.[17]

Not every threatening or insulting word constitutes disorderly conduct. In order for conduct to rise to the level of disorderly conduct, such conduct must be a breach of the peace. Fighting is the most common example of disorderly conduct. If one party is the victim of a threat or battery by another, the appropriate charge is assault; however, when two parties mutually engage in fighting, the more appropriate charge is disorderly conduct. In effect, you do not have the right to consent to a fight unless it is in a licensed sport such as boxing. Public fighting is considered a breach of the peace.

LEGAL NEWS: FIGHT CLUBS

Fight clubs have emerged all across the country since the 1999 movie *Fight Club* first glorified the phenomenon. Authorities are especially alarmed at the rise of fight clubs among teens, who organize by word of mouth and texting, and then meet in alleyways or empty lots for bare-knuckle fighting, with participants sometimes numbering in the hundreds. Video recordings of these fights appear on the Internet or are sold for profit. Similar clubs have emerged among young men, often white collar, who evidently have the same "no talking" rule as the teen clubs. The rule is necessary because the clubs are illegal. Various laws are broken by all the parties involved. Promoters can be charged with conspiracy, promoting a fighting sport without a license, and accessory. Participants can be charged with disorderly conduct, criminal mischief, assault, and, if there are

---

[15]   Thompson v. Louisville, 362 U.S. 199, 80 S. Ct. 624, 4 L. Ed. 2d 654 (1960); Griffin v. Smith, 184 Ga. 871, 193 S.E. 777 (1937); State v. Koetting, 616 S.W.2d 822 (Mo. 1981).

[16]   Kolander v. Lawson, 461 U.S. 352, 103 S. Ct. 1855, 75 L. Ed. 2d 903 (1983).

[17]   27 C.J.S. *Disorderly Conduct* § 1(2) (1995). Steeley v. Ennis, 45 N.Y.S.2d 446 (1943).

more serious injuries or death, aggravated assault, involuntary manslaughter, or depraved heart murder. Even spectators can be charged with accessory to the crimes. Because of the secretive nature of the fighting, and because there is no general consensus among the public (or even enforcers of the law) that these activities should be illegal, there is little chance that the clubs will disappear anytime soon.

Source: McCarthy, M. (2006). "Illegal, Violent Teen Fight Clubs Face Police Crackdown." USA Today, July 31, 2006. Accessed January 7, 2008 from http://www.azcentral.com/families/articles/0731gns-teenfights31-ON.html.

Other acts, such as peaceful protests, may or may not be considered sufficient to justify a disorderly conduct conviction. In the activism of the civil rights era of the 1960s and 1970s, state statutes were used to punish protesters but this, in turn, led to constitutional scrutiny of the state's statute. Some representative cases are described below:

- (1971—Florida) Defendant went on stage during a performance, took over the microphone, and used obscene language toward the audience. Court upheld conviction for disorderly conduct despite the fact that the defendant's purpose was not "to create or encourage a disturbance," but to avert one.[18]
- (1973—Wisconsin) Defendant was arrested at an induction center for disorderly conduct even though there was no proven conduct that "tended to cause or provoke a disturbance." The court overturned the conviction.[19]
- (1962—Connecticut) Defendants staged a sit-in demonstration in the waiting room of a real estate firm sharing office space with lawyers and remaining there in protest against certain features of the local housing ordinances. Convictions were upheld.[20]

Generally, the use of disorderly conduct statutes to prohibit public fighting has met with little resistance from the courts; however, when used against public utterances, gestures, or displays, court holdings are inconsistent. In general, our freedom of speech is protected; however, there are certain types of speech that are not protected, including obscene speech and "fighting words." The following examples illustrate the types of speech that have been prosecuted.

[18]   City of Miami v. Powers, 247 So.2d 497 (Fla. 1971).
[19]   State v. Werstein, 60 Wis.2d 668, 211 N.W.2d 437 (1973).
[20]   State v. Petty, 24 Conn. Supp. 337, 190 A.2d 502 (1962).

- (1993—Indiana) Defendant noisily protested the arrest of someone in an alley on New Year's Eve, which caused the neighbors to come out and look. Court overturned conviction as unconstitutionally impinging on free speech.[21]
- (1994—Indiana) Defendant argued with her ex-boyfriend and his companions in a loud, screaming voice. Conviction was upheld.[22]
- (1989—Ohio) Defendant made insulting remarks to a police officer, including the assertion to the officer that he was "probably on the take." Court upheld conviction.[23]
- (1999—Massachusetts) Defendant refused a police officer's repeated requests to move her car, which was double-parked behind a school bus, while she waited for her six-year-old son to leave elementary school. Court overturned her conviction, stating that her actions served her legitimate interest in picking up her child from school.[24]

In *State v. Semple*, the 1989 Ohio case cited above, the court held that the repeated insults were sufficiently provocative to constitute "fighting words," falling within the prohibition of R.C. § 2917.11(A)(2). A dissenting judge in the *Semple* opinion disagreed, stating that he did not find that the words were (1) likely to inflict injury by their utterance, or (2) likely to provoke the average person to an immediate retaliatory breach of peace as required by U.S. Supreme Court decisions. In the next year, a similar case resulted in a different finding from the same court and the language of the dissent in *Semple* became the majority opinion.

- (1990—Ohio) Defendant yelled at a police officer "just because you've got a f____ badge you think you can f___ with people," and continued by stating "f___ you and your gun, money talks so I'll walk." Conviction was overturned and the Ohio reviewing court warned that speech must, by its very utterance, be likely to "inflict injury or provoke the average person to an immediate retaliatory breach of the peace" in order to constitute disorderly conduct.[25]
- (2002—Ohio) Defendant refused to get back into his car after a law enforcement officers' drug search found nothing, and the defendant continued to loudly question the police as to why he had been stopped. Conviction was overturned because there was no testimony of complaints about the defendant's noise level, none of the officers testified that they were inconvenienced, and patrons at a nearby restaurant did not impede traffic, but rather parked their cars to watch the scene unfold.[26]
- (1992—Indiana) Defendant cursed loudly and shouted epithets at the investigating police officer. He told the officer "to get the f___ away," that the investigation was "bull____," and the officer was "a lying motherf____." Court held these were

---

21   Price v. State, 622 N.E.2d 954 (Ind. 1993).
22   Stites v. State, 627 N.E.2d 1343 (Ind. 1994).
23   State v. Semple, 568 N.E.2d 750 (Ohio Ct. App. 1989).
24   Commonwealth v. Zettel, 46 Mass. App. 471, 706 N.E.2d 1158 (1999).
25   State v. Hampton, 583 N.E.2d 400 (Ohio Ct. App. 1990).
26   State v. Smith, 779 N.E.2d 776 (Ohio 2002).

"fighting words" and stated that "They skirt the depth of degradation despite the fact that they may be tolerated or in common usage by certain elements of our society."[27]

- (1990—Nebraska) Defendant called a police officer an "a__hole" at the end of a narcotics investigation. Court overturned conviction because insult did not constitute "fighting words."[28]
- (1999—Florida) Defendant engaged in a loud, belligerent, accusatory tirade targeting a police officer thereby exciting a gathering crowd to such a level that the second police officer developed safety concerns. The conviction was upheld.[29]

The review of case decisions indicates no consistency in what behaviors will be considered sufficient to uphold a conviction of disorderly conduct. Also, disorderly conduct statutes vary from state to state. Some are more inclusive and address various forms of misbehavior, while others serve as a catch-all for misconduct that is not dealt with more specifically under other statutes. Some statutes are very specific in their statement of the conduct that is prohibited. An example is the Ohio statute, which provides

Ohio Rev. Code Ann. § 2917.11[30]

(A) No person shall recklessly cause inconvenience, annoyance, or alarm to another, by doing any of the following:
(1) Engaging in fighting, in threatening harm to persons or property, or in violent or turbulent behavior;
(2) Making unreasonable noise or offensively coarse utterance, gesture, or display, or communicating unwarranted and grossly abusive language to any person;
(3) Insulting, taunting, or challenging another, under circumstances in which such conduct is likely to provoke a violent response;
(4) Hindering or preventing the movement of persons on a public street, road, highway, or right-of-way, or to, from, within, or upon public or private property, so as to interfere with the rights of others and by any act which serves no lawful and reasonable purpose of the offender;
(5) Creating a condition which is physically offensive to persons or which presents a risk of physical harm to persons or property, by any act which serves no lawful and reasonable purpose of the offender.

The disorderly conduct statute in Texas covers the behaviors above and a range of other behaviors that might be defined as separate crimes in other jurisdictions. For instance, the disorderly conduct statute includes the prohibited behaviors of displaying or

---

27 Robinson v. State, 588 N.E.2d 533 (Ind. Ct. App. 1992).
28 Buffkins v. City of Omaha, 922 F.2d 465 (8th Cir. 1990), *cert. denied*, 502 U.S. 898, 112 S. Ct. 273, 116 L. Ed. 2d 225 (1991).
29 Marsh v. State, 724 So.2d 666 (Fla. 1999).
30 OHIO REV. CODE ANN. § 2917.11 (Anderson 1999).

discharging firearms (firearms violations), exposing one's anus or genitals in public (public indecency), and looking in others' windows for lewd and unlawful purposes (voyeurism).[31]

D. *Summary*

Disorderly conduct did not exist under common law. Early statutes were found to be unconstitutionally broad or vague and so have been rewritten to more specifically enumerate actions that can constitute disorderly conduct. Such actions typically fall into the categories of: fighting; threatening or tumultuous behavior; unreasonable noise or obscene utterance or display; "fighting words;" or actions that create a hazardous or physically offensive condition. Obscenity or speech that can be punished has been listed as: the lewd and obscene, the profane, the libelous, and the insulting or "fighting" words—those that by their very utterance inflict injury or tend to incite an immediate breach of the peace.[32]

> Disorderly Conduct
> (A/R) fighting, offensive language (either obscenity or fighting words), or other hazardous or dangerous actions—all must tend to incite an immediate breach of the peace.
> (M/R) intent, knowing or reckless

§ 10.4   Vagrancy and Loitering

Many, if not most, of the early laws relating to **vagrancy** and **loitering** have been declared unconstitutional. Similar to the disorderly conduct statutes, state legislatures have been forced to draft statutes that are more narrowly worded so as to protect the constitutional rights of individuals. Vagrancy historically referred to the status of being homeless, penniless, and on the street or simply being an unsavory character. Loitering typically was defined as being someplace in public without purpose. The two overlap and so will be discussed together in this section.

A. *Common Law*

At common law, a person was deemed a "vagrant" who went from place to place without visible means of support, was idle and, although able to work for his maintenance, refused to do so and lived without labor or on the charity of others.[33] Another definition of a "vagrant" was "One who strolls from place to place, an idle wanderer, specifically, one who has no settled habitation, a vagabond."[34]

Early statutes in this country continued the common law definition of vagrancy and basically criminalized being a "street person" with no visible means of support.

---

[31]   TEX. PENAL CODE § 42.01 Disorderly Conduct.
[32]   Robinson v. State, 588 N.E.2d 533 (Ind. Ct. App. 1992).
[33]   People v. Banwer, 22 N.Y.S.2d 566 (1940).
[34]   Nearing v. Illinois Central R.R. Co., 383 Ill. 366, 50 N.E.2d 497 (1943).

Case Note: *Papachristou et al. v. City of Jacksonville*, 405 U.S. 156 (1972)
What was the holding of the case?
What constitutional rights were violated by this ordinance?
How could cities reform their ordinances and statutes to avoid being unconstitutional?

In *Papachristou v. City of Jacksonville,* the Supreme Court ruled on a city ordinance that defined vagrants as including rogues or vagabonds; dissolute persons who beg; common gamblers, jugglers, or those who engaged in unlawful games or play; common drunkards; common night walkers; thieves, pilferers, or pickpockets; traders in stolen property; lewd, wanton, and lascivious persons; and keepers of gambling places, among other descriptions.[35] The Supreme Court held that that such an ordinance did not give a person of ordinary intelligence fair notice that his conduct was criminal and it also allowed for arbitrary enforcement, thereby violating the due process clause. The case is provided in Part II of this text.

B. *Model Penal Code*

Recognizing that statutes that were too broad violated the due process clause of the Fourteenth Amendment and, in some instances, First Amendment protections, recent legislation is more definite and contains more limiting language. Note that the "status" of being a vagrant can never be penalized, so modern statutes must identify specific behaviors that are against the public interest. The Model Penal Code is an example.

§ 250.6 Loitering or Prowling[36]

A person commits a violation if he loiters or prowls in a place, at a time, or in a manner not usual for law-abiding individuals under circumstances that warrant alarm for the safety of persons or property in the vicinity. Among the circumstances which may be considered in determining whether such alarm is warranted is the fact that the actor takes flight upon appearance of a peace officer, refuses to identify himself, or manifestly endeavors to conceal himself or any object. Unless flight by the actor or other circumstance makes it impracticable, a peace officer shall prior to any arrest for an offense under this Section afford the actor an opportunity to dispel any alarm which would otherwise be warranted, by requesting him to identify himself and explain his presence and conduct. No person shall be convicted of an offense under this Section if the peace officer did not comply with the preceding sentence, or if it appears at trial that the explanation given by the actor was true and, if believed by the peace officer at the time, would have dispelled the alarm.

Under this code, the actor must loiter or prowl in a place, at a time, or in a manner not usual for law-abiding individuals and under circumstances that warrant alarm for the safety of persons or property in the vicinity. Section 250.6 differs from prior legislation in that it is narrowly designed to reach only "alarming" loitering. According to the commentary, typical situations covered would be

---

[35]   Papachristou et al. v. City of Jacksonville, 405 U.S. 156, 92 S. Ct. 839, 31 L. Ed. 2d 110.
[36]   MODEL PENAL CODE § 250.6 (1985).

- a known professional pickpocket who is seen loitering in a crowded railroad station;
- a person not recognized as a local resident is seen lurking in the doorway and furtively looking up and down the street to see if he is being watched;
- an unknown man is seen standing for some time in a dark alley where he has no apparent business.

Obviously, there is still some vagueness in the wording of the statute because the terms used lack specific definition. However, there are some protective provisions in the statute, especially the last sentence, which requires the police officer to evaluate any innocent explanation for the suspicious behavior.

C. State Statutes, Codes, and Cases

While some states have enacted provisions patterned closely after the Model Penal Code, others have enacted loitering statutes that are even more specific. An example of such a statute is that enacted by the Kentucky legislature, which provides

§ 525.090—Loitering[37]

(1) A person is guilty of loitering when he:
   (a) Loiters or remains in a public place for the purpose of gambling with cards, dice or other gambling paraphernalia, except that the provisions of this Section shall not apply if the person is participating in an activity defined by KRS 238.505; or
   (b) Loiters or remains in a public place for the purpose of unlawfully using a controlled substance; or
   (c) Loiters or remains in or about a school, college or university building or grounds, not having any reason or relationship involving custody of or responsibility for a pupil or student or any other specific legitimate reason for being there and not having written permission from anyone authorized to grant the same; or
   (d) Loiters or remains in any transportation facility, unless specifically authorized to do so, for the purpose of soliciting or engaging in any business, trade or commercial transactions involving the sale of merchandise or services.
(2) Loitering is a violation.

This statute preserves the traditional objectives of apprehending those who are about to commit specific crimes or whose activities are offensive to the public-at-large while limiting possible abuse of broad police authority by setting forth specific standards for determining what conduct is prohibited.

Referring to a Florida statute, which is similar to the Model Penal Code, a Florida judge cautioned that the loitering and prowling statute is not directed at mere idling.[38]

---

[37]   Ky. Rev. Stat. Ann. § 525.090 (Baldwin 2002).

[38]   E.C. v. State, 724 So. 2d 1243 (Fla. 1999). *See also* Gonzalez v. State, 828 So. 2d 496 (Fla. 2002), in which the court reiterated that the offense of loitering and prowling requires proof that (1) the defendant loitered or prowled at a place, at a time, or in a manner not usual for law-abiding individuals, and (2) such loitering and prowling were under circumstances that warranted a justifiable and reasonable alarm or immediate concern for the safety of persons or property.

The court explained that in order to prove a charge of loitering and prowling, the state must prove (1) that the defendant loitered or prowled in a place, at a time, or in a manner not usual for law-abiding individuals, and (2) the loitering and prowling were under circumstances that warranted a justifiable and reasonable alarm or immediate concern for the safety of persons or property in the vicinity. After stating the requirements, the court held that the behavior of the defendant and other juveniles in walking back and forth in front of a strip mall about eight times over a period of 40 minutes was not sufficiently alarming to raise an immediate concern for the safety of persons or property in the vicinity, and thus was insufficient to support a conviction for loitering and prowling. In a second Florida case, the court added that in order to prove that the accused was loitering and prowling in a manner not usual for law-abiding citizens, as required to support a conviction for loitering and prowling, the state must prove more than a vaguely suspicious presence.[39]

1. Failure to Identify Statutes

A more recent issue in this area is whether a state can make it a crime to refuse to identify oneself to law enforcement. This was the question asked in *Hiibel v. Sixth Judicial District of Nevada.*[40] Recall that states need to specifically identify the types of behaviors that form the basis for a loitering offense and, generally, such behavior has to be inconsistent with law-abiding behavior. One of the elements that might lead to a charge of loitering is the failure to identify oneself and the nature of one's business. Some states, however, have created separate **failure to identify statutes**. In the Nevada case, the crime occurs when a police officer, with reasonable suspicion that a crime has been or is about to be committed, requests a person's identity and they refuse to give it. Mr. Hiibel believed that the Constitution gave him the right to refuse to answer. He was wrong. The case is provided in Part II of this textbook. Other states, like Texas, require that police officers have probable cause to arrest before citizens are required to give their identity.[41]

Case Note: *Hiibel v. Sixth Judicial District of Nevada*, 542 U.S. 177 (2004)
What were the issue and holding of the case?
Which constitutional rights were offered as the source for the right to refuse to identify oneself to police?

2. Panhandling Statutes

Loitering and vagrancy statutes have been ruled unconstitutional when they have been written too broadly. Other statutes that bear constitutional scrutiny are those that criminalize panhandling (begging). Some cities have passed laws to prohibit the solicitation of money at intersections, and/or the practice of washing windshields in

---

[39] J.S.B. v. State, 729 So.2d 456 (Fla. 1999).
[40] 542 U.S. 177 (2004).
[41] TEX. PENAL CODE, § 38.02 Failure to Identify.

order to request drivers give a dollar or two in exchange. Anti-panhandling laws are extremely varied and some are fairly broad while others restrict only certain types of activities, in certain parts of the city, or during certain times of the day. Federal circuit courts have issued several opinions related to anti-panhandling statutes. The Second Circuit rejected a New York City anti-panhandling ordinance that prohibited all begging citywide, with the conclusion that begging was protected First Amendment speech and the city did not prove a strong enough governmental interest to prohibit all forms of panhandling. Furthermore, the court said that even if there was an important governmental interest, such a ban would need to be narrowly tailored, there must be alternative methods to express such speech (other avenues to acquire necessary sustenance), and the ban would have to be content-neutral.

The Seventh Circuit approved an anti-panhandling statute in Indianapolis that prohibited "aggressive" panhandling, begging at night, at bus stops, in public transportation, at intersections, in sidewalk cafés, and within 20 feet of an ATM. The court held that the statute was narrowly drawn and protected important government interests while balancing individual rights. [42]

It appears that cities can prohibit some forms of panhandling; specifically that which creates fear or anxiety in the population or to avoid public risk. So, for instance, a city could bar panhandlers from begging in intersections (because of traffic risks), in sidewalk cafés (because of private property rights), and near schools (because of concerns for safety), as well as bar "aggressive" panhandling, but broader bans would be struck down. Even if a city did not have an anti-panhandling statute, aggressive begging would fall under a public nuisance or public disturbance statute's definition.

So-called "street people" are also controlled by cities that pass anti-camping regulations that prohibit sleeping in public areas. These ordinances obviously are directed to the homeless who are compelled to sleep in alleys or on public benches. With the ordinances in place, police officers can force such people to move to shelters or move out of sight or risk arrest. There are opponents to such laws who argue that people should be free to be in public places and do what they want as long as they are not hurting others. Proponents typically argue that homeless people who sleep on the sidewalk or on public benches, and who beg for money from passersby, scare tourists, disrupt business, and threaten the economic vitality of the downtown area.

D. Summary

The common law crime of vagrancy basically criminalized poverty. Such statutes, when carried forward into modern times, carried the potential for arbitrary and capricious enforcement. The Supreme Court struck down Jacksonville's vagrancy ordinance as violative of the Fourteenth Amendment and, by doing so, invalidated any similar

---

[42] Loper v. New York City Police Department, 999 F.2d 699 (2nd Cir. 1993). Gresham v. Peterson, 225 F.3d 899 (7th Cir. 2000). For more information, go to http://www.mlive.com/news/index.ssf/2011/09/aclu_sues_grand_rapids_and_sta.html.

statutes across the country. Subsequently, loitering statutes were also struck down as being impermissibly vague unless they specified a type of action that was not "mere idling," but was consistent with unlawful behavior and raised a reasonable suspicion that criminal action was imminent. The latest category of such laws is failure to identify statutes. The Supreme Court has upheld such statutes as long as the police officer has at least reasonable suspicion to stop and detain for investigation. Anti-panhandling statutes are probably constitutional as long as they are narrowly drawn to include only those activities that alarm or threaten the population.

> Loitering
> (A/R) loitering or prowling; in a way not consistent with law-abiding behavior, that creates a reasonable alarm or concern that crime was imminent
> (M/R) intentional, knowing

§ 10.5   Drunkenness

While *being* a "drunk" cannot be a crime, being drunk in public can be. These statutes are justified under the police power of the state: the power to care for the health, morals, and welfare of the people. Statutes and ordinances have withstood constitutional challenges as long as they clearly identified behavior that was against the public good.

A. Common Law

Drunkenness was not an offense under the common law of England, but was punishable in the ecclesiastical courts.[43] Under early state statutes, a person could be punished for being under the influence of intoxicants in a private or public place, or sometimes the penalty applied only if the person appeared in an intoxicated condition in public.

In the case of *Powell v. Texas*, discussed in Chapter 1, a self-confessed alcoholic was convicted of being drunk in a public place.[44] On appeal, he contended that he was compelled to drink, and once drunk, would lose control over his behavior and that it was cruel and unusual punishment to impose criminal sanctions on him for appearing drunk in a public place. He relied on the reasoning in the case of *Robinson v. California*. In this case, the Supreme Court held that an individual could not be branded a criminal or subjected to penal sanctions, no matter how slight, simply because he occupied the status or condition of being a "known drug addict."[45]

The U.S. Supreme Court rejected the defendant's argument, explaining that although the state of Texas could not punish him for the status of being an alcoholic, the *Robinson* decision did not establish a constitutional doctrine of diminished criminal

---

[43]   2 Stephen, History of the Criminal Law in England 410 (1883).

[44]   Powell v. Texas, 392 U.S. 514, 88 S. Ct. 2145, 20 L. Ed. 2d 1254 (1968).

[45]   Robinson v. California, 370 U.S. 660, 82 S. Ct. 1417, 8 L. Ed. 2d 758 (1962).

responsibility for addicts and others similarly affected. Penalizing a person for appearing in public while intoxicated does not violate the U.S. Constitution because it punishes an act, not a status.

According to the court in the *Powell* case, being an alcoholic is no defense to the crime of public intoxication. It follows, then, that being drunk cannot be used as a defense to any crime. In general, drunkenness or even being an alcoholic cannot be used as a defense, although extreme intoxication may reduce a defendant's *mens rea* from specific intent to general intent or recklessness.

B. Model Penal Code

The Model Penal Code provides a penalty for appearing in public under the influence not only of alcohol, but also of narcotics or other drugs. It also requires that the influence be to the degree that the person charged may endanger himself or other persons or property, or annoy persons in his vicinity. The Model Code differs from some traditional statutes in that it provides a punishment for public drunkenness but not private drunkenness.

§ 250.5 Public Drunkenness; Drug Incapacitation[46]

A person is guilty of an offense if he appears in any public place manifestly under the influence of alcohol, narcotics or other drug, not therapeutically administered, to the degree that he may endanger himself or other persons or property, or annoy persons in his vicinity. An offense under this Section constitutes a petty misdemeanor if the actor has been convicted hereunder twice before within a period of one year. Otherwise the offense constitutes a violation.

C. State Statutes, Codes, and Cases

Some states subsequently enacted provisions that follow the Model Penal Code, while others have broader coverage. When the law applies only if the person is intoxicated in a public place, the prosecution must prove that the person did, in fact, appear in a public place while under the influence. According to one case, a public place does not mean a place devoted solely to the use of the public, but means a place that is in point of fact public, as distinguished from private; a place that is visited by many persons and usually accessible to the neighboring public. This includes not only public roads and streets, but various other places such as schools and places of worship.[47]

Some statutes punish intoxication in private, but with conditions attached. For example, in Ohio, a person may be punished for being intoxicated in a public place or in the presence of two or more persons. He may also be punished if he engages in

---

46   MODEL PENAL CODE § 250.5 (1985).
47   State v. Moriarty, 74 Ind. 103 (1881); Thompson v. State, 153 Miss. 593, 121 So. 275 (1929); January v. State, 66 Tex Crim. 302, 146 S.W. 555 (1912).

conduct or creates a condition that presents a risk of harm to himself or the personal property of another. As a part of the disorderly conduct section, the Ohio statute provides

Ohio Rev. Code Ann. § 2917.11[48]

(B) No person, while voluntarily intoxicated, shall do either of the following:
   (1) In a public place or in the presence of two or more persons, engage in conduct likely to be offensive or to cause inconvenience, annoyance, or alarm to persons of ordinary sensibilities, which conduct the offender, if he were not intoxicated, should know is likely to have such effect on others;
   (2) Engage in conduct or create a condition which presents a risk of physical harm to himself or another, or to the property of another.

Under the provisions of this statute, the prosecution must introduce evidence to show voluntary intoxication, plus either being in a public place or, if in a private place, that the conduct is likely to be offensive. In the alternative, the prosecution may prove voluntary intoxication, plus the person engaged in conduct or created a condition that presents a risk of physical harm to himself or another or to the property of another.

In interpreting the Ohio statute regarding voluntary intoxication, an appeals court decided that a trial court could find that the defendant was voluntarily intoxicated based on a combination of direct and circumstantial evidence. The facts indicated that a police officer testified that he smelled the odor of alcohol on the defendant's person and that the defendant was loud and "used a lot of slurring of his speech." This evidence, combined with evidence that the defendant was very antagonistic, used profanity, and was offensive, was sufficient to support a conviction under the statute.[49]

The Florida statute requires that the defendant be in a public place.

FLA. STAT. ANN. § 856.011 (2003).[50]

No person in the state shall be intoxicated and endanger the safety of another person or property, and no person in the state shall be intoxicated or drink any alcoholic beverage in a public place or in or upon any public conveyance and cause a public disturbance.

In interpreting this statute, the court held that the defendant's front porch was not a "public place" within the meaning of the statute, which prohibits intoxication or drinking of alcoholic beverages in a public place.[51] Note that if the person is intoxicated in a

---

[48]   OHIO REV. CODE ANN. § 2917.11 (Anderson 2002). *See also* FLA. STAT. ANN. § 856.011 (West 2002) and S.C. CODE ANN. § 16-17-530 (Law. Co-op. 2002).
[49]   State v. Butler, 578 N.E.2d 485 (Ohio 1989).
[50]   FLA. STAT. ANN. § 856.011 (2003).
[51]   Royster v. State, 643 So.2d 61 (Fla. 1994). *See also* Jernigan v. State, 566 So.2d 39 (Fla. 1990) for an interpretation of the Florida statute. *See* § 856.015 of the Florida statute (Open House Party), which provides a penalty if an adult knowingly allows the possession or use of an alcoholic beverage or drug by a minor.

private place, public intoxication cannot be charged in most states, but the person may be convicted of other offenses, such as assault or disorderly conduct.

> LEGAL NEWS: DRUNK IN PUBLIC (BARS)
>
> In the spring of 2006, the Texas Alcoholic Beverage Commission (TABC) operated a campaign of arresting public drunks. Undercover agents went into bars in Austin, Dallas, and the major cities of Texas and arrested people who "appeared drunk." The practice was not met with a great deal of enthusiasm on the part of the general public. One columnist quipped, "that's the reason why people go into bars." Spokespersons for the agency defended the action, arguing that bars were public places and that the campaign was designed to prevent drunk-driving incidents; however, evidently some of the arrests occurred in hotel bars and were of individuals who had rooms for the night and planned to drive nothing but the elevator. When state officials begin to receive feedback that some business conferences were being canceled and moved to other states because of a fear that their conference participants would be arrested, there was an announcement that TABC officers would be "retrained" to apply the law in a more tourist-friendly fashion.
>
> _____
>
> Retrieved July 1, 2006 from www.msnbc.msn.com/id/11965237/ and www.msnbc.msn.com/id/1230886.

1. Driving While Intoxicated/Driving Under the Influence

In some states, these terms are used for the same crime, in other states, they are two different crimes with "driving under the influence" a lesser crime than "driving while intoxicated." In all states, the definitions of "intoxication" and "influence" are set by statute and this element can be proven by Intoxilyzer tests or by officer testimony.

Individuals have the right to refuse a breath test, but state laws typically will respond to such a refusal with a mandatory confiscation of one's license. The legal rationale for such laws are that driving is a privilege and one's license creates an implied consent to submit to Intoxilyzer tests or other tests in order to continue to receive the benefits of a driver's license.[52]

More recently, many states have begun "no refusal" weekends. This campaign involves having enhanced DWI patrols, a magistrate on call, and nurses or phlebotomists on hand to draw blood. If there is probable cause that a driver is intoxicated, and the person refuses to take the breath test, they are brought before a magistrate who issues a warrant to draw blood, which is done immediately. Special squads have been called "vampire squads" in reference to the goal of obtaining blood evidence at the scene

---

[52] Felgate v. Arkansas, 63 Ark. App. 76, 974 S.W.2d 479 (Ark. App. 1998); State v. Widmaier, 157 N.J. 475, 724 A.2d 214 (1999).

or at least shortly after the stop. In some cities the magistrate and phlebotomist patrol in a police van in order to reach the scene quickly. Blood evidence is much harder to defend against in a DWI prosecution and usually results in a plea agreement rather than the motorist insisting on a jury trial. Another response to DWI has been "extreme DWI" statutes. While most states set .08 as the level at which one becomes legally impaired, some statutes set a higher blood alcohol level (i.e., .15) for an enhanced charge and attach more severe penalties.

Another issue that has been litigated in DWI or DUI prosecutions is the meaning of "in control" of the automobile. Individuals who have been found on the side of the road in the passenger seat have been convicted of DWI, as have individuals who are sitting in their car in their driveway. Even when the key to the car is not anywhere to be found, an individual may be convicted because courts have defined "in control" broadly.[53]

D. Summary

There was no common law crime of public drunkenness, but the behavior was punished in the ecclesiastical courts in early England. Early statutes in this country made it a crime punishable in the criminal court system. Alcoholism cannot be used as a defense for public intoxication, nor can drunkenness be used as a defense for any crime (although it may reduce the *mens rea* of the individual if he or she is so incoherent as to not be able to form specific intent). DUI/DWI statutes punish those who are "in control" of a motor vehicle while intoxicated with the definition of intoxication set by statute.

Public Drunkenness/Intoxication
(A/R) voluntary alcoholic intoxication (sometimes includes drugs), in a public place (sometime private with other conditions, i.e., offensive behavior); sometimes offensive behavior is required even in a public place
(M/R) intentional, reckless (*mens rea* goes to decision to drink)

§ 10.6 Drug Laws

Alcohol and drug crimes share some similarities, but also major differences. It is against the law to appear in public or operate a motor vehicle when one is intoxicated by alcohol or drug use; however, it is usually not against the law to merely possess alcohol (unless one is a minor). On the other hand, it is a crime to even possess certain types of drugs or possess certain drugs without a legal prescription. Drug laws share certain characteristics with laws against gambling and prostitution in that certain segments of the population who engage in no other types of crimes and do not consider themselves "criminal" routinely violate such laws.

We will explore federal drug laws more thoroughly in Chapter 13, but it is impossible to discuss state drug laws without reference to the federal government's role.

---

[53]   Gallagher v. Commonwealth, 205 Va. 666, 139 S.W.2d 37 (1964).

Beginning in 1970 with the Comprehensive Drug Abuse Prevention and Control Act, statutes were enacted by Congress to identify and control substances that are extremely harmful when used improperly. The Uniform Controlled Substances Act defines a large number of drugs and categorizes them by level of risk and seriousness. Most states have adopted the provisions of the Uniform Controlled Substances Act. The Act was designed to supplant the Uniform Narcotic Drug Act and the Model State Abuse Control Act, relating to depressant, stimulant, and hallucinogenic drugs, promulgated in 1966. The Act was drafted to achieve uniformity among laws of the several states and those of the federal government, and to complement federal narcotics and dangerous drug legislation. In fact, there is probably more uniformity in drug laws than in most other criminal law areas.

A. Common Law

There were no drug laws under the common law.

B. Model Penal Code

The Model Penal Code does not have any provisions for drug possession or possession with intent to sell. Drug intoxication is included with public drunkenness.

C. State Statutes, Codes, and Cases

A state, under its police power, may regulate the administration, sale, prescription, possession, and use of narcotic drugs.[54] Courts have consistently held that it is a legitimate use of police power to regulate all aspects of drug use and possession. Statutes have been upheld, for instance, in the following areas:

- Possession of paraphernalia adapted for the use of narcotic drugs and classification of marijuana as a narcotic.[55]
- Growing, possession, and use of marijuana (with some exceptions).[56]
- Being under the influence of narcotic drugs.[57]
- Inhaling glue with the intent to become intoxicated.[58]
- The use of marijuana in a private place.[59]

---

[54] Robinson v. California, 370 U.S. 660, 82 S. Ct. 1417, 8 L. Ed. 2d 758 (1962); State v. Martin, 192 La. 704, 189 So. 109 (1939).

[55] Manson v. State, 166 Tex Crim. 514, 316 S.W.2d 414 (1958); People v. Sinclair, 387 Mich. 91, 194 N. W.2d 878 (1972).

[56] People v. Fillhart, 403 N.Y.S.2d 642 (1978). Maisler v. State, 425 So.2d 107 (Fla. 1982).

[57] State v. Brown, 103 Ariz. 289, 440 P.2d 909 (1968).

[58] People v. Orozco, 266 Cal. App. 507, 72 Cal. Rptr. 452 (1968).

[59] Borras v. State, 229 So.2d 244 (Fla. 1970), *cert. denied*, 400 U.S. 808, 91 S. Ct. 70, 27 L. Ed. 2d 37 (1970).

- The sale or purchase of drugs within 1,000 feet of a school.[60]
- The use of marijuana as a sacrament for a religious ceremony.[61]

However, sometimes a state or city went too far in their attempt to criminalize drug use. A city ordinance that punished individuals from visiting "any building or place" if they knew that drugs were used, sold, or kept was ruled by one court to be "unconstitutionally broad" and was struck down. [62]

After the Supreme Court held that it was not a First Amendment violation to punish a Native American for using peyote in a religious ceremony,[63] Congress passed the Act to Amend the American Indian Religious Freedom Act (Public Law 103-344; 108 Stat. 3125) on October 6, 1994, which prohibits states from criminalizing peyote use as long as the individual was a Native American and the use was in relation to a *bona fide* religious ceremony.

1. Uniform Controlled Substances Act

The Uniform Controlled Substances Act was promulgated by the National Conference of Commissioners on Uniform State Laws to create a coordinated and codified system of drug control, similar to that utilized at the federal level. The Act sets out prohibited activities in detail, but vests the authority to administer the Act in an agency to be established by the state legislature. Because the Act authorizes the agency or person who administers it to implement, enforce, and regulate the provisions of the Act, this authority is often vested in a high-ranking state official or a committee. For example, the authority could be vested in the Office of the Attorney General, a department of health, a division of public safety, or other agency within the state responsible for regulating and enforcing the drug laws. The intent is to create reasonable flexibility within the Uniform Act so that as new substances are discovered or found to have an abuse potential, they can quickly be brought under control without constant resort to the legislature.

To make the Uniform Act consistent with the federal law, the Uniform Act follows the federal controlled substances law and lists all the **controlled substances** in five "schedules" (categories) that are identical to the federal law.

In categorizing the substances, eight criteria were followed:

- the actual or relative potential for abuse
- scientific evidence of pharmacological effects
- the state of current scientific knowledge regarding the substance
- its history and pattern of abuse
- the scope, duration, and significance of abuse

---

[60]   State v. Burch, 545 So.2d 279 (Fla. Dist. Ct. App. 1989). *See also* State v. Crawford, 727 So.2d 589 (La. 1998), which defined the meaning of "within 1,000 feet."
[61]   State v. Venet, 797 P.2d 1055 (Or. 1990).
[62]   State v. Mercherson, 488 N.W.2d 707 (Minn. Ct. App. 1989).
[63]   Employment Division v. Smith, 494 U.S. 872 (1990).

- what, if any, risks there are to the public health
- its psychic or psychological dependence liability
- whether the substance is an immediate precursor of a substance already controlled

The Uniform Controlled Substances Act deals with the manufacture and distribution of controlled substances. Much of the Act defines terms:

- "Controlled substance" means a drug, substance, or immediate precursor included in Schedules I through V of Article II.
- "Narcotic drug" means any of the following, however manufactured:
  - opium, opium derivative, and any derivative of either, including any salts, isomers, and salts of isomers of them that are theoretically possible within the specific chemical designation, but not isoquinoline alkaloids of opium;
  - synthetic opiate and any derivative of synthetic opiate, including any isomers, esters, ethers, salts, and salts of isomers, esters, and ethers of them that are theoretically possible within the specific chemical designation;
  - poppy straw and concentrate of poppy straw;
  - coca leaves, except coca leaves and extracts of coca leaves from which cocaine, ecgonine, and derivatives of ecgonine or their salts have been removed;
  - cocaine, or any salt, isomer, or salt of isomer of cocaine;
  - cocaine base;
  - ecgonine, or any derivative, salt, isomer, or salt isomer of ecgonine; and
  - compound, mixture, or preparation containing any quantity of a substance listed in this paragraph.
- "**Deliver**," unless the context otherwise requires, means to transfer a substance, actually or constructively, from one person to another, whether or not there is an agency relationship.
- "Person" means an individual, corporation, business trust, estate, trust, partnership, association, joint venture, government, or governmental subdivision or agency, or any other legal or commercial entity.

All controlled substances are categorized in Schedules I, II, III, IV, or V. Under the Uniform Controlled Substances Act, the schedules are identical with the federal law; however, this does not prevent a state from adding or removing substances from the schedule or from reclassifying the substances from one schedule to another. Also, as new substances are discovered or found to have abuse potential, they can quickly be brought under control without resort to the legislature. The purpose of the classification is to create a coordinated codified system of drug control regulation and to establish criteria for prescribing specific fines or sentences. The Controlled Substances Act does not itself designate specific fines or sentences, but leaves this up to the discretion of the individual states.

The guidelines for determining the category into which any controlled substance should be included are as follows:

- Schedule I
  - the substance has a high potential for abuse;
  - the substance has no currently accepted medical use in the United States; and
  - the substance lacks accepted safety for use under medical supervision.
- Schedule II
  - the substance has high potential for abuse;
  - the substance has currently accepted medical use in treatment in the United States, or currently accepted medical use with severe restrictions; and
  - the abuse of the substance may lead to severe psychic or physical dependence.
- Schedule III
  - the substance has a potential for abuse less than the substances listed in Schedules I and II;
  - the substance has currently accepted medical use in treatment in the United States; and
  - abuse of the substance may lead to moderate or low physical dependence or high psychological dependence.
- Schedule IV
  - the substance has a low potential for abuse relative to substances in Schedule III;
  - the substance has currently accepted medical use in treatment in the United States; and
  - abuse of the substance may lead to limited physical dependence or psychological dependence relative to the substances in Schedule III.
- Schedule V
  - the substance has low potential for abuse relative to the controlled substances included in Schedule IV;
  - the substance has currently accepted medical use in treatment in the United States; and
  - abuse of the substance may lead to limited physical dependence or psychological dependence liability relative to the controlled substances listed in Schedule IV.

Remember that controlled substances include not only "street drugs," but also pharmaceuticals that may be legal when properly prescribed and dispensed. States are free to follow or modify the suggested provisions. All states have laws that prohibit the possession, possession with intent to distribute (or traffic in), and use of controlled substances. Other statutes may also exist.

LEGAL NEWS: "SPICE" AND "BATH SALTS"

As new drugs emerge, states must react. In 2011, "bath salts" and "spice" were added to the controlled substances schedule in many states. Both drugs are synthetic substances that mimic cocaine (bath salts) and marijuana (spice). Before any ban, such drugs could be found for sale in stores and flea markets.

In South Carolina, the Board of Health and Environmental Control (the body that directs which substances should be added to the Uniform Controlled

Substances schedules) determined that the three stimulants found in bath salts and five cannabinoids found in synthetic smokable marijuana would be added to Schedule I. This made South Carolina the 38th state to make possession and sale of these substances illegal. These actions were taken in response to a jump in hospital admissions of individuals who had taken the drugs. Possession of Schedule I drugs in South Carolina may result in a prison term of up to 15 years. According to South Carolina law, the Board's action may be overturned by the state legislature passing a law, or the legislature may reinforce the Board's decision with a law outlawing the substances.

Before the inclusion of these substances in Schedule I, a dozen South Carolina counties and cities had already banned the substances from being sold. Also, the federal government had already issued a temporary ban on the sale of the substances found in bath salts (mephedrone, MDPV, and methlyone) and the five chemicals found in the synthetic marijuana. Experts note, however, that labs have, in response, slightly changed the chemical compounds so that they are not technically the same substances in the ban.

Retrieved January 10, 2012 from http://www2.wsav.com/news/2011/oct/24/sc-bans-bath-salts-synthetic-marijuana-ar-2601726/.

2. Drug Crimes

a. *Possession of a Controlled Substance Except as Authorized*

As stated above, states have the ability to punish mere possession of controlled substances such as cocaine, heroin, and marijuana. Possession statutes are comprised of two basic elements: knowledge and possession. Because knowledge is an element of the offense of possession of a controlled substance, the state has the burden of proving that a defendant's possession was knowing.[64]

The other element of the crime is possession. In many situations, the controlled substance is in the presence of, but not on the person of the defendant; or may even be at another location. Courts recognize **constructive possession**, which means that the defendant has custody or dominion over the substance, even if he does not have it on his person.[65] Of course, this begs the question as to what is "custody" or "**dominion**." The court holdings below further refine the definition of possession.

---

[64]   Jackson v. State, 832 So.2d 773 (Fla. 2002). *See also* Knight v. State, 91 S.W.3d 418 (Tex. 2002).
[65]   State v. Brider, 386 So.2d 818 (Fla. 1980).

- "Possession" or "control" within the meaning of the drug statutes means either actual physical possession with knowledge of the same or constructive possession if the accused knows of the presence of the item on or about his premises and has the ability to maintain control over it.[66]
- Possession entails (1) the accused exercised care, control, and management over the contraband, and (2) the accused knew the matter possessed was contraband.[67]
- The state must prove that the defendant exercised actual care, custody, control, or management over the contraband and he or she knew the matter possessed to be contraband.[68]
- The defendant knew of the character of the substance and its presence and exercised dominion and control over it.[69]

In some situations, the defendant is in the presence of drugs with other people, purports that they were not his drugs, or argues that he did not know they were there. The case decisions in these areas are not uniform.

- Defendant's presence as a passenger in the bed of a pickup truck in which other persons were transporting cocaine was insufficient to show that the defendant actually or constructively possessed cocaine, for purposes of trafficking.[70]
- Defendant who was found sitting on a bedroom floor, talking on the telephone, in front of a closet containing cocaine, did not have constructive possession of cocaine absent a showing that the defendant was more than a mere visitor in the house or that she could otherwise exercise dominion or control over the drug.[71]
- Defendant's mere presence at a social club where narcotics were found did not establish sufficient dominion and control by the defendant over the premises to charge him with constructive possession of 312 vials of cocaine concealed in the door of the premises.[72]
- Defendant and two other men were found seated within arm's reach of each other and cocaine along with mirror and razor blades. Other drug-related accessories were found throughout the room. The conviction was affirmed despite defendant arguing lack of possession.[73]

---

[66]   Ellis v. State, 346 So.2d 1044 (Fla. 1977). *See also* State v. Spruell, 788 P.2d 21 (Wash. 1990), which held that "actual possession" of drugs occurs when drugs are in the actual physical possession of the defendant, while "constructive possession" requires that the defendant have dominion and control over the drugs. *See also* Lawson v. State, 666 So.2d 193 (Fla. 1995).

[67]   Abshure v. State, 87 S.W.3d 822 (Ark. 2002).

[68]   Grant v. State, 989 S.W.2d 428 (Tex. 1999).

[69]   State v. Mahon, 53 Conn. App. 231, 729 A.2d 242 (1999).

[70]   Harris v. State, 501 So.2d 735 (Fla. 1987).

[71]   Brooks v. State, 501 So.2d 176 (Fla. 1987).

[72]   People v. Roveter, 549 N.Y. Supp. 2d 488 (1989).

[73]   Brown v. Commonwealth, 364 S.E.2d 773 (Va. 1988).

- Defendant was found with 53 grams of pure cocaine under the seat of a car he borrowed from a friend. The suspect denied ownership of both the car and the cocaine and denied having knowledge of the cocaine. Court upheld conviction finding that evidence was sufficient to find knowledge and constructive possession.[74]
- Defendant was a visitor in an apartment that was subject to a search warrant. Court overturned conviction, holding that the state did not prove constructive possession, specifically, statements or conduct of the accused, or other facts or circumstances that tend to show that the accused was aware of both the presence and of the character of the drugs.[75]

In order for a state to prove possession, it must show knowledge of the presence of the drug, and either physical or constructive possession. The defendant does not have to hold the drug to "possess" it; however, the state must prove custody, dominion, and control over the drug. Most states also specify the amount of drug necessary to constitute a violation. Generally, there must be at least a "measurable" amount of the drug, but drug residue, when found on drug paraphernalia, has been sufficient to uphold a conviction of possession.[76] If the amount reaches a certain limit, then there is a *prima facie* case for not just possession, but, instead, "possession with intent to distribute."

Possession with intent to deliver is a more serious crime, with more serious penalties associated with it. The state must prove both elements—possession and intent to distribute. However, intent may be proven by the mere quantity of the drug. If a drug is found in quantities that exceed "personal use," then the defendant may be convicted of the more serious crime.[77] If the defendant is successful in delivering the drug or is found after transporting a drug in preparation for delivery, the offense is trafficking.

b. Trafficking in a Controlled Substance Except as Authorized

Trafficking involves a *mens rea* of knowing (that it is a controlled substance) and specific intent to deliver. The *actus reus* is some type of delivery or transfer of a controlled substance. A Louisiana court explained that, in order to obtain a conviction for distribution of cocaine, the state must show (1) delivery or physical transfer; (2) guilty knowledge of the controlled dangerous substance at the time of the transfer; and (3) the exact identity of the controlled dangerous substance.[78]

The state may rely on evidence of constructive possession of cocaine to establish the element of transportation for the offense of trafficking in cocaine by transportation. Either proof of actual or constructive possession of cocaine is necessary to establish the element of transportation.[79]

---

[74]   Reed v. State, 367 S.E.2d 809 (Ga. 1988).
[75]   Wynn v. Commonwealth of Virginia, 362 S.E.2d 193 (Va. 1987).
[76]   Jones v. State, 589 So.2d 1001 (Fla. Dist. Ct. App. 1991).
[77]   People v. Carrasquilla, 522 N.E.2d 139 (Ill. App. Ct. 1988); State v. Lassere, 683 So.2d 922 (La. 1996); Kostelec v. State, 656 A.2d 1222 (Md. Ct. App. 1996); State v. Spencer, 683 So.2d 1326 (La. 1996).
[78]   State v. McKinney, 728 So.2d 1009 (La. 1999).
[79]   State v. Boyd, 572 S.E.2d 192 (N.C. 2002).

c. Dispensing, Prescribing, Distributing, or Administering a Controlled Substance Except as Authorized

The Uniform Controlled Substances Act and state statutes require persons who engage in, or intend to engage in, the manufacture, distribution, or dispensing of controlled substances to be registered by the state. The purpose of this part of the Act or statute is to allow the state to know who is responsible for a substance and who is dealing in the substances. This also gives those investigating violations specific authority to prosecute when the controlled substance laws have been violated. Statutes requiring pharmacists and practitioners to register, maintain records, and only prescribe, administer, and dispense controlled substances as provided in the Act have generally been held to be constitutional and are not so vague as to deny due process.[80]

A Mississippi decision indicated that "distribution" of drugs does not necessarily involve a sale. Delivery of drugs to third persons, whether or not accomplished in exchange for money or other consideration, is an act of distribution for which the law will punish the deliverer.[81] Transfer of drugs regardless of reason may satisfy state trafficking or delivery laws. For instance, some states have prosecuted mothers for delivery of drugs to their fetus as the legal news box describes.

LEGAL NEWS: DELIVERY (OF DRUGS) BEFORE DELIVERY

Tracey Ward was convicted of delivery of a controlled substance. In her case the substance was cocaine and the person she delivered it to was her unborn baby. She is one of many women who have been prosecuted under existing drug laws for using drugs while pregnant. In some states, the prosecutor's legal theory is that in the moment after birth (to ensure the definition of legal "person"), but before the umbilical cord is cut, the woman is "delivering" cocaine to her child. In Texas and other states, new statutes have been written to punish delivering drugs to a fetus, although such statutes have exceptions to cover doctors who prescribe drugs for legitimate medical purposes. The proof of delivery is in the tests that determine whether the newborn has any drugs in his or her system. In Ward's case, she pled guilty, thus averting a legal challenge of Texas's law.

Source: Betsy Blaney, "Mom Guilty of Giving Drugs to Fetus," *Austin American-Statesman*, September 8, 2004, at B6.

---

[80]   Cohn v. Department of Professional Regulation, 477 So.2d 1039 (Fla. 1985).
[81]   Martin v. State, 726 So.2d 1210 (Miss. 1998).

In defining a "constructive delivery," a Texas court reasoned that a "constructive delivery" occurs when a seller transfers a controlled substance, either belonging to him or under his control, by some other person or means, at the direction of the seller. An "actual delivery" consists of transferring real possession and control of a controlled substance from one person to another person.[82]

d. Other Crimes

States also have other statutes concerning drug use and distribution, including

- Obtaining or attempting to obtain a controlled substance by fraud, deceit, misrepresentation, or subterfuge
- Possessing, manufacturing, selling, dispensing, prescribing, distributing, or administering any counterfeit substance
- Certain advertising of controlled substances

3. Seizure and Forfeiture of Controlled Substances, Vehicles, and Drug Paraphernalia

To further discourage the manufacture, possession, or traffic in controlled substances, many states have enacted statutes that authorize seizure and forfeiture of not only controlled substances, but any vessel, vehicle, aircraft, or drug paraphernalia that has been used in or was bought with the proceeds of drug trafficking. Under the Controlled Substance Forfeiture Act, the state must simply show a "nexus" between the seized property and the unlawful activity by a preponderance of evidence. Once the state has sustained its burden, the burden shifts to the property owner to disprove the state's case or establish a statutory defense.[83]

Asset forfeiture actions may be via criminal proceedings or, more frequently through separate civil, rather than criminal, judicial proceedings that require a lower level of proof. In fact, an individual could be acquitted of the underlying criminal offense, or not even arrested at all, and still be required to forfeit property as long as the state is able to show that the property was used to facilitate an offense. The property owner need not even be aware of the criminal use since the civil forfeiture action is against the property itself, not the owner. The judicial challenges to what was perceived by some to be unfair met with mixed results in the state courts and the lower federal courts. The viability of asset forfeiture in drug cases was eventually addressed by the U.S. Supreme Court in three cases decided over the period 1989 through 1994. The holdings had consequences for any expansion of forfeiture laws in the states.

---

[82]   Marable v. State, 990 S.W.2d 421 (Tex. 1999).
[83]   Commonwealth v. McJett, 811 A.2d 104 (Pa. 2002).

- In *United States v. Halper*, the Court held that a civil sanction that could not be characterized as remedial may constitute "punishment" under the double jeopardy clause.[84]
- In *Austin v. United States*, the Court held that the "civil" distinction of forfeiture did not exempt it from Eighth Amendment scrutiny against "excessive fines." This decision limited the use of asset forfeiture when a defendant was subjected to heavy fines as part of the criminal proceedings.[85]
- In *Department of Revenue of Montana v. Kurth Ranch*, the Court held that the double jeopardy clause barred the state of Montana from imposing a civil tax for illegal drug possession on a defendant convicted and punished for the same offense in a separate criminal proceeding.[86]

In 1996, the U.S. Supreme Court revisited the issue of the relationship between the federal asset forfeiture statutes and the double jeopardy clause of the U.S. Constitution in *United States v. Usery*. The Court expressly rejected the previously employed "balancing" test (the harm suffered by the government is compared to the forfeiture imposed) in favor of the following two-part test:

1. Whether Congress intended the statutory scheme at issue to be criminal or civil
2. Whether the scheme is so punitive either in purpose or effect as to negate the intent of Congress to establish a civil asset forfeiture process

Applying this new test, the Court concluded that asset forfeiture in drug cases did not violate the double jeopardy clause in that it was not an additional penalty for the commission of a criminal act, but, rather, a separate civil action, remedial in nature and expressly sanctioned by Congress.[87] It appears that even though it is not double jeopardy, if the forfeiture is too disproportionate to the offense, it may be ruled unconstitutional.

4. Challenges to Marijuana Laws

The most contentious area of drug law has been in the regulation and punishment of marijuana use. Opponents argue that marijuana should not be a Schedule I drug and that it should not have the same severe penalties as other drugs. First, challenges based on individuals' rights to privacy over personal decisions have been raised. These challenges, although meeting some degree of success in lower state courts, are consistently rejected by appellate courts.[88] The second challenge is a medical necessity defense. This argument is that marijuana is the best medical alternative for those who are seriously ill and experiencing pain and nausea. Several states have passed medical

---

[84]   United States v. Halper, 409 U.S. 435, 109 S. Ct. 1892, 104 L. Ed. 2d 487 (1989).

[85]   Austin v. United States, 509 U.S. 602, 113 S. Ct. 2801, 125 L. Ed. 2d 488 (1993).

[86]   Department of Revenue of Montana v. Kurth Ranch, 511 U.S. 767, 114 S. Ct. 1937, 128 L. Ed. 2d 767 (1994).

[87]   United States v. Usery, 518 U.S. 267, 116 S. Ct. 2135, 135 L. Ed. 2d 549 (1996).

[88]   People v. Sinclair, 387 Mich. 91, 194 N.W.2d 878 (1972).

marijuana laws that allow the drug to be prescribed and used for legitimate medical purposes. The Supreme Court, however, has upheld the right of the federal government to enforce federal drug laws even if they directly contradict state law.[89] The challenge that federal drug laws, based on the commerce clause, did not reach marijuana that was grown and consumed entirely within one state was also rejected by the Supreme Court in *Gonzales v. Raich*.[90] As more states pass medical marijuana laws, it may be that the Supreme Court will see fit to reexamine their position on the issue.

LEGAL NEWS: MEDICAL MARIJUANA

Sixteen states and the District of Columbia have some type of medical marijuana law as of 2011. State laws do not invalidate federal drug laws, however, so an individual may be following his or her state law in possessing a small amount of marijuana with a legal prescription, but still be guilty of a federal drug crime. In 2009, the U.S. Attorney General made a statement that the Justice Department's policy would not be to pursue raids and prosecution of medical marijuana clinics; however, he was criticized for the statements by legislators who argued that he could not ignore federal laws.

States place a variety of restrictions and regulations on medical marijuana, including specifying the amount, the percentage of THC, the number of strains available, who may prescribe and for how much, who may distribute (some states leave this aspect unclear so it is illegal to possess but not to purchase), and how dispensaries may conduct business. Also, counties may pass ordinances that prohibit medical marijuana dispensaries from opening in their jurisdiction. Arizona's law, for instance, passed in 2010 allows the use of marijuana only for those suffering from cancer, HIV/AIDS, hepatitis C, and other debilitating diseases, allows only 2½ ounces every two weeks, and the prescription must be from a doctor that had treated the patient for at least a year. This would eliminate the practice in other states of marijuana dispensaries that emerged along with doctors who would write a prescription for minor or allegedly imaginary ailments. Thus, the legal arena of medical marijuana is still very unclear. In some states, medical marijuana laws were passed and states promptly put such restrictive regulations on the dispensing and use of it that few people could benefit. Advocates have, in some cases, resorted to pushing for decriminalization for everyone. It seems safe to say that the story of medical marijuana is still unfolding.

Source: For more information, go to http://medicalmarijuana.procon.org/view.resource.php?resourceID=000881. Also see A. Myers, Arizona Drafts Stringent Medical Marijuana Rules, *Austin American-Statesman*, December 18, 2010, A11. J. Dahl, In the Weeds. *The Crime Report*. Retrieved April 13, 2011 from http://www.thecrimereport.org/archive/2011-04-in-the-weeds.

---

[89]   United States v. Oakland Cannabis Buyer's Cooperative, 532 U.S. 483 (2001).
[90]   545 U.S. 1 (2004).

D. *Summary*

As one might expect, the provisions of the acts prohibiting activities related to controlled substances have been challenged many times in both federal and state courts. Such laws have been upheld as not violating the due process clauses of the Constitution; nor do the acts generally violate the right of privacy.

The Uniform Controlled Substances Act sets out prohibited activities in detail and vests the authority to administer the act in an agency to be established by the state legislature. To make the Act consistent with federal law, the Uniform Act follows the federal Controlled Substances Act and lists all of the controlled substances in five schedules that are identical to the federal law but does not prevent the state from making changes. The Act includes guidelines for determining the category into which the controlled substance generally will be included.

The Uniform Controlled Substances Act and state statutes require persons who engage in, or intend to engage in, the manufacture, distribution, or dispensing of controlled substances to be registered by the state, among other things. These acts make it unlawful for any person to manufacture, deliver, or possess, with intent to manufacture or deliver, a controlled substance and allow for the law to provide penalties determined by the classification of the substance.

Possession
(A/R) actual or constructive possession
(M/R) knowing

Possession with Intent to Deliver
(A/R) actual or constructive possession; with circumstances indicating intent is to deliver (i.e., quantity)
(M/R) knowing (goes to possession); specific intent (goes to deliver/distribute)

Trafficking
(A/R) actual or constructive possession; transfer or delivery (does not have to be for money)
(M/R) knowing (goes to possession); general intent (goes to delivering)

§ 10.7 Wiretapping and Eavesdropping

A. *Common Law*

Eavesdropping was a common law crime, the essence of which consisted of listening under walls, windows, or eaves in order to vex or annoy another by spreading slanderous rumors against him.[91] An eavesdropper was that unsavory character who snooped under the eaves to satisfy his interest in gossip. From this practice, the term *eavesdropping* developed. Modern technology has provided increasingly efficient tools to listen to the conversations of others, and legislative bodies have attempted to draft legislation to control such activity.

---

[91]   4 BLACKSTONE, COMMENTARIES 168.

The early eavesdropper listened by the naked ear under the eaves of houses or windows, or beyond their walls, seeking out private discourse. Technology has provided better vehicles for eavesdropping. Even with the advent of the telegraph, surreptitious interception of messages began. The telephone brought on a new and modern eavesdropping method known as **wiretapping**. As early as 1862, California found it necessary to prohibit the practice of eavesdropping by statute, and Illinois outlawed wiretapping by legislation in 1895. In 1905, California extended its telegraphic interception prohibition to the telephone. Most of the existing laws relating to wiretapping and eavesdropping result from decisions and legislation of the last four decades.[92] The most far-reaching legislation is federal and was enacted by Congress in 1968. Federal wiretapping laws will be addressed in Chapter 13.

A related issue to wiretapping and eavesdropping is invasion of privacy and the various ways that offenders can victimize unsuspecting individuals. Today, the use of camera phones and other devices have outstripped some states' abilities to regulate such invasions of privacy. While some new statutes have been written to cover those who use camera phones in public bathrooms or locker rooms, other states adapt existing statutes to cover such behavior, such as voyeurism statutes, invasion of privacy statutes, or laws that prohibit secret video recordings.

LEGAL NEWS: TRAGIC RESULTS

Dharun Ravi was a Rutgers University student who used his webcam to record and stream his roommate, Tyler Clementi, hugging and kissing another man. He watched the encounter from another dorm room and then wrote about it on his Twitter account. Evidently, he tried to do the same again the next evening but Clementi had disabled his computer. Clementi committed suicide and Ravi faces 15 criminal charges, including invasion of privacy, bias intimidation, and cyberbullying, which carry presumptive prison sentences. He has refused the state's offer of a plea deal that would give him probation. He also may face deportation to his native India. He was convicted March 16, 2012 and awaits sentencing as this text goes to press.

Retrieved January 10, 2011 1/10/2011 from http://gothamist.com/2011/12/09/tyler_clementis_roommate_rejects_pl.php. and http://www.nytimes.com/2011/08/13/nyregion/with-tyler-clementi-suicide-more-complex-picture-emerges.html.

B. Model Penal Code

The Model Penal Code prohibits unlawful eavesdropping or surveillance. Subsection (1) of Section 250.12 deals with unauthorized eavesdropping or surveillance in a private place and defines that term.

---

[92]   Berger v. New York, 388 U.S. 41, 87 S. Ct. 1873, 18 L. Ed. 2d 1040 (1967).

§ 250.12 Violation of Privacy[93]

(1) Unlawful Eavesdropping or Surveillance. A person commits a misdemeanor if, except as authorized by law, he:
   (a) trespasses on property with purpose to subject anyone to eavesdropping or other surveillance in a private place; or
   (b) installs in any private place, without the consent of the person or persons entitled to privacy there, any device for observing, photographing, recording, amplifying or broadcasting sounds or events in such place, or uses any such unauthorized installation; or
   (c) installs or uses outside a private place any device for hearing, recording, amplifying or broadcasting sounds originating in such place which would not ordinarily be audible or comprehensible outside, without the consent of the person or persons entitled to privacy there.

"Private place" means a place where one may reasonably expect to be safe from casual or hostile intrusion or surveillance, but does not include a place to which the public or a substantial group thereof has access.

(2) Other Breach of Privacy of Messages. A person commits a misdemeanor if, except as authorized by law, he:
   (a) intercepts without the consent of the sender or receiver a message by telephone, telegraph, letter or other means of communicating privately; but this paragraph does not extend to:
      (i) overhearing of messages through a regularly installed instrument on a telephone party line or on an extension, or
      (ii) interception by the telephone company or subscriber incident to enforcement of regulations limiting use of the facilities or incident to other normal operation and use; or
   (b) divulges without the consent of the sender or receiver the existence or contents of any such message if the actor knows that the message was illegally intercepted, or if he learned of the message in the course of employment with an agency engaged in transmitting it.

Following some of the provisions of the federal code, both paragraphs (a) and (b) of subsection (1) exempt from liability the surveillance of a private place with the consent of "the person or persons entitled to privacy." Subsection (2) provides a penalty for other interceptions of messages and for disclosure of unlawfully intercepted messages. This contains exceptions similar to those of the federal statute.

C. *State Statutes, Codes, and Cases*

Most states and the District of Columbia all have their own laws governing the use of interception devices.[94] The United States Code, which defines the federal crimes related to interception of wire, electronic, and oral communications, does not

---

[93]   MODEL PENAL CODE § 250.12 (1985).
[94]   Report of the Director of the Administrative Office of the United States Courts, Applications for Orders Authorizing or Approving the Interception of Wire, Oral, or Electronic Communications (1998).

preempt all state crimes for similar behavior. A state may impose greater restrictions than the federal statute. However, a state cannot authorize conduct that is prohibited by federal law.[95]

Many state statutes are modeled on the federal statutes; others follow the general provisions of the Model Penal Code. Many state statutes concerning the interception of communications apply only to communications that are private, or with respect to which there exists a reasonable expectation of privacy. An example of the latter is the Florida statute. It provides in part

934.03—Interception and disclosure of wire, oral, or electronic communications prohibited[96]

(1) Except as otherwise specifically provided in this chapter, any person who:
  (a) Intentionally intercepts, endeavors to intercept, or procures any other person to intercept or endeavor to intercept any wire, oral, or electronic communication;
  (b) Intentionally uses, endeavors to use, or procures any other person to use or endeavor to use any electronic, mechanical, or other device to intercept any oral communication when:
    (1) Such device is affixed to, or otherwise transmits a signal through, a wire, cable, or other like connection used in wire communication; or
    (2) Such device transmits communication by radio or interferes with the transmission of such communication;
  (c) Intentionally discloses, or endeavors to disclose, to any other person the contents of any wire, oral, or electronic communication, knowing or having reason to know that the information was obtained through the interception of a wire, oral, or electronic communication in violation of this subsection; or
  (d) Intentionally uses, or endeavors to use, the contents of any wire, oral, or electronic communication, knowing or having reason to know that the information was obtained through the interception of a wire, oral, or electronic communication in violation of this subsection; shall be punished as provided in subsection (4).

"Oral communication," as defined in the Florida statute, means any oral communication uttered by a person exhibiting an expectation that such communication is not subject to interception under circumstances justifying such exception and means any public oral communication uttered at a public meeting or any electronic communication.

A Florida court held that factors considered in determining whether the intercepted communication qualifies as "oral communication" protected under the security of communications statutes include the location in which the conversation or communications occurs, the manner in which the communication is made, and the type of communication. Thus, conversations that occur inside enclosed or secluded areas are more likely to be protected.[97]

A federal court commented that the Alabama statute prohibiting electronic eavesdropping is violated if there is (1) a willful interception, (2) of an oral communication

---

[95]   86 C.J.S. *Telecommunications* § 243.
[96]   FLA. STAT. ANN. § 934.03 (1999).
[97]   Stevenson v. State, 667 So.2d 410 (Fla. 1996).

uttered by a person exhibiting an expectation that the communication would be private, and (3) a communication made under circumstances justifying an expectation of privacy.[98]

States generally follow the federal law in making some wiretapping and eavesdropping acceptable. State statutes may allow wiretapping when at least one party consents, and always allow wiretapping by law enforcement with appropriate judicial authority. The cases below represent some of the issues.

- A New Jersey court held that an unauthorized wiretap by law enforcement officers is a constitutional violation; however, consensual interceptions do not represent the same intrusions into constitutionally protected privacy.[99]
- A North Carolina court held that the Electronic Surveillance Act prohibits nonconsensual recordings by one spouse of the other even within their family home.[100]
- A Pennsylvania court found that the police department violated the disclosure provisions of the Wiretap Act when it disclosed intercepted telephone conversations between a police officer and his estranged wife to an advocate that had been assigned to represent the police department at a disciplinary hearing, because the Wiretap Act only authorized disclosure to investigative or law enforcement officers.[101]

Some state statutes are more restrictive than the federal statute and provide criminal penalties not provided by federal law. For example, federal law allows interception of communications if one party consents. Under Massachusetts law, the warrantless interception of an oral or wire communication is prohibited absent consent by all parties, except in two statutory circumstances.[102]

LEGAL NEWS: NO PARENTAL EXCEPTION TO WIRETAPPING

A mother who, using a speakerphone, eavesdropped on her 14-year-old daughter's conversation with her boyfriend was guilty of the state's eavesdropping law. According to the Washington court, the law contained no parental exemption to the requirement that at least one of the parties must know they are being monitored. The issue arose not because the mother was prosecuted, but, rather, because the boyfriend was in jail on an armed robbery charge and the mother heard and testified regarding incriminating statements made by him to her daughter. The conviction for armed robbery was overturned because of the mother's illegal action. The mother was not prosecuted.

Retrieved December 15, 2004 from http://seattletimes.newsource.com/cgi-bin?PrintStory.pl?document_id=2002115125&zsection.

---

[98]   Ages Group, L.P. v. Raytheon Aircraft Co., Inc., 22 F. Supp. 2d 1310 (N.D. Ala. 1998), interpreting Alabama Code § 13(a)-11-31.
[99]   State v. Toth, 804 A.2d 565 (N.J. 2002).
[100] Kroh v. Kroh, 567 S.E.2d 760 (N.C. 2002).
[101] Dance v. Com. Pennsylvania State Police, 726 A.2d 4 (Pa. 1999).
[102] United States v. Sutherland, 929 F.2d 765 (1st Cir. 1991).

D. Summary

The federal government cannot usurp entirely the state's power to criminalize wiretapping. Although the states may pass their own laws regarding wiretapping, they cannot make any act legal that the federal criminal code has defined as illegal; on the other hand, they can make their statute more restrictive than the federal law and declare some acts criminal that the federal statute does not. Usually the same act may be criminal under either the state criminal code or the federal wiretapping statute, which will be discussed in Chapter 13. Some states and the Model Penal Code have included surveillance and video recording under wiretapping prohibitions when it is done without the consent or knowledge of the subjects. Other states cover these invasions of privacy under other statutes, such as voyeurism, invasion of privacy, or even disorderly conduct.

> Eavesdropping/Wiretapping
> (A/R) interception; of an oral communication; of one who has reasonable expectation of privacy in those circumstances (in some states, if at least one party consents it is lawful)
> (M/R) willful/intentional

§ 10.8   State Counterterrorism Laws

Following the terrorist attacks of September 11, 2001, many state legislatures recognized the necessity of enacting state legislation to make it less difficult to prevent terrorist attacks and to apprehend terrorists. These are called **counterterrorism laws**.

A. Common Law

There was no common law crime of terrorism.

B. Model Penal Code

The Model Penal Code does not have a provision for terrorism.

C. State Statutes, Codes, and Cases

One of the first states to pass terrorism-specific legislation was New York. The New York penal law provides penalties for those who

- provide material support for terrorism;
- engage in terroristic threats;
- engage in terrorism; or
- render assistance to a terrorist

Article 490 of the New York Penal Law on Terrorism[103] provides

---

[103]   N.Y. PENAL LAW 490.05–490.35 (McKinney 2002).

§ 490.05 Definitions

As used in this article, the following terms shall mean and include:
(1) "Act of terrorism":
    (a) for purposes of this article means an act or acts constituting a specified offense as defined in subdivision three of this section for which a person may be convicted in the criminal courts of this state pursuant to article twenty of the criminal procedure law, or an act or acts constituting an offense in any other jurisdiction within or outside the territorial boundaries of the United States which contains all of the essential elements of a specified offense, that is intended to:
        (i) intimidate or coerce a civilian population;
        (ii) influence the policy of a unit of government by intimidation or coercion; or
        (iii) affect the conduct of a unit of government by murder, assassination or kidnapping; or
    (b) for purposes of subparagraph (xiii) of paragraph (a) of subdivision one of section 125.27 of this chapter means activities that involve a violent act or acts dangerous to human life that are in violation of the criminal laws of this state and are intended to:
        (i) intimidate or coerce a civilian population;
        (ii) influence the policy of a unit of government by intimidation or coercion; or
        (iii) affect the conduct of a unit of government by murder, assassination or kidnapping
(2) "Material support or resources" means currency or other financial securities, financial services, lodging, training, safehouses, false documentation or identification, communications equipment, facilities, weapons, lethal substances, explosives, personnel, transportation, and other physical assets, except medicine or religious materials.
(3) "Specified offense" for purposes of this article means a class A felony offense other than an offense as defined in article two hundred twenty, a violent felony offense as defined in section 70.02, manslaughter in the second degree as defined in section 125.15, criminal tampering in the first degree as defined in section 145.20 of this chapter, and includes an attempt or conspiracy to commit any such offenses.
(4) "Renders criminal assistance" for purposes of sections 490.30 and 490.35 of this article shall have the same meaning as in section 205.50 of this chapter.

§ 490.10 Soliciting or providing support for an act of terrorism in the second degree

A person commits soliciting or providing support for an act of terrorism in the second degree when, with intent that material support or resources will be used, in whole or in part, to plan, prepare, carry out or aid in either an act of terrorism or the concealment of, or an escape from, an act of terrorism, he or she raises, solicits, collects or provides material support or resources.

    Soliciting or providing support for an act of terrorism in the second degree is a class D felony.

§ 490.15 Soliciting or providing support for an act of terrorism in the first degree

A person commits soliciting or providing support for an act of terrorism in the first degree when he or she commits the crime of soliciting or providing support for an act of terrorism in the second degree and the total value of material support or resources exceeds one thousand dollars.

Soliciting or providing support for an act of terrorism in the first degree is a class C felony.

§ 490.20 Making a terroristic threat

(1) A person is guilty of making a terroristic threat when with intent to intimidate or coerce a civilian population, influence the policy of a unit of government by intimidation or coercion, or affect the conduct of a unit of government by murder, assassination or kidnapping, he or she threatens to commit or cause to be committed a specified offense and thereby causes a reasonable expectation or fear of the imminent commission of such offense.
(2) It shall be no defense to a prosecution pursuant to this section that the defendant did not have the intent or capability of committing the specified offense or that the threat was not made to a person who was a subject thereof.
Making a terroristic threat is a class D felony.

§ 490.25 Crime of terrorism

(1) A person is guilty of terrorism when, with intent to intimidate or coerce a civilian population, influence the policy of a unit of government by intimidation or coercion, or affect the conduct of a unit of government by murder, assassination or kidnapping, he or she commits a specified offense.
(2) Sentencing.
    (a) When a person is convicted of a crime of terrorism pursuant to this section, and the specified offense is a class B, C, D or E felony offense, the crime of terrorism shall be deemed a violent felony offense.
    (b) When a person is convicted of a crime of terrorism pursuant to this section, and the specified offense is a class C, D or E felony offense, the crime of terrorism shall be deemed to be one category higher than the specified offense the defendant committed, or one category higher than the offense level applicable to the defendant's conviction for an attempt or conspiracy to commit the offense, whichever is applicable.
    (c) When a person is convicted of a crime of terrorism pursuant to this section, and the specified offense is a class B felony offense, the crime of terrorism shall be deemed a class A-I felony offense and the sentence imposed upon conviction of such offense shall be in accordance with section 70.00 of this chapter.
    (d) Notwithstanding any other provision of law, when a person is convicted of a crime of terrorism pursuant to this section, and the specified offense is a class A-I felony offense, the sentence upon conviction of such offense shall be life imprisonment without parole; provided, however, that nothing herein shall preclude or prevent a sentence of death when the specified offense is murder in the first degree as defined in section 125.27 of this chapter.

§ 490.30 Hindering prosecution of terrorism in the second degree

A person is guilty of hindering prosecution of terrorism in the second degree when he or she renders criminal assistance to a person who has committed an act of terrorism, knowing or believing that such person engaged in conduct constituting an act of terrorism.

Hindering prosecution of terrorism in the second degree is a class C felony.

§ 490.35 Hindering prosecution of terrorism in the first degree

A person is guilty of hindering prosecution of terrorism in the first degree when he or she renders criminal assistance to a person who has committed an act of terrorism that resulted in the death of a person other than one of the participants, knowing or believing that such person engaged in conduct constituting an act of terrorism.

Hindering prosecution of terrorism in the first degree is a class B felony.

In 2001 and 2002, the California legislature modified existing laws and added new counterterrorism statutes to the California penal code. These include sections titled the following:

§ 11418 Weapons of mass destruction; possession, transfer, use, etc.; penalties

§ 11418.1 False or facsimile weapons of mass destruction; transfer, delivery, placement, possession, etc.; penalties

§ 11418.5 Threats to use weapon of mass destruction; penalties

§ 11419 Possession of restricted biological agents; penalties; exceptions

We will deal with the Patriot Act and federal counterterrorism laws in Chapter 13. In general, federal laws are used to prosecute individuals for terroristic acts. However, states may and have passed their own laws.

D. Summary

Of course, the federal terrorism laws, such as the Patriot Act, are more often considered as the source for defining and prosecuting terrorism as a crime. However, it should be noted that states also may pass statutes criminalizing activities associated with terrorism. Not all states have such laws but those that do basically concentrate on weapons of mass destruction and threats to the general population.

§ 10.9   Other Offenses against the Public Peace

In addition to the crimes described above, state statutes and the Model Penal Code have identified a variety of other activities as crimes. These offenses "against the public peace" all have in common the aspect of victimization of the general public, at least indirectly. Also, constitutional protections, such as freedom of speech and due process, require that the statutes be written very narrowly and specify targeted behaviors rather than vague categories of undesirable behavior or people.

A. *Obstructing a Highway or Public Passage*

In order to make it possible for citizens to carry on everyday business and to avoid undue interference, statutes have been written and enforced that regulate the use of highways and other public passages. Although the statutes and ordinances regulating the use of streets and buildings have been upheld, these must comply with the safeguards of the U.S. Constitution, especially First Amendment safeguards. However, the First Amendment does not protect all speech, as the following cases indicate.

- Municipal ordinances that prohibit door-to-door sale solicitations are constitutional.[104]
- Municipalities can regulate the time, place, and manner of using public streets for the purpose of holding outdoor parades, speeches, or mass assemblies.[105]
- Municipalities can enforce greater restrictions on public gatherings around hospital districts, jail yards, fire stations, and court facilities that can be more closely protected than other public facilities.[106]

However, any restrictions that unduly limit free speech and assembly—for example, an ordinance that permits an enforcement decision to be based on consideration of the message or speech content—will be struck down as unconstitutional.[107] Recent ordinances and statutes have attempted to balance the right of the public to use streets and highways for purposes of presenting ideas and the right of the public to use the streets and highways for travel.[108]

The Model Penal Code offers a statute that covers both unlawful assemblies and individual obstructions on public thoroughfares.

§ 250.7 Obstructing Highways and Other Public Passages[109]

(1) A person, who, having no legal privilege to do so, purposely or recklessly obstructs any highway or other public passage, whether alone or with others, commits a violation, or, in case he persists after warning by a law officer, a petty misdemeanor. "Obstructs" means renders impassable without unreasonable inconvenience or hazard. No person shall be deemed guilty of recklessly obstructing in violation of this Subsection solely because of a gathering of persons to hear him speak or otherwise communicate, or solely because of being a member of such a gathering.

(2) A person in a gathering commits a violation if he refuses to obey a reasonable official request or order to move:

    (a) to prevent obstruction of a highway or other public passage; or

    (b) to maintain public safety by dispersing those gathered in dangerous proximity to a fire or other hazard.

---

[104]   Breard v. Alexandria, 341 U.S. 622, 71 S. Ct. 920, 95 L. Ed. 1233 (1951).

[105]   Cox v. New Hampshire, 312 U.S. 569, 61 S. Ct. 762, 85 L. Ed. 1049 (1941).

[106]   Adderley v. Florida, 385 U.S. 39, 87 S. Ct. 242, 17 L. Ed. 2d 149 (1967), *reh'g denied*, 385 U.S. 1020, 87 S. Ct. 698, 17 L. Ed. 2d 559 (1967).

[107]   Cox v. Louisiana, 379 U.S. 536, 85 S. Ct. 453, 13 L. Ed. 2d 471 (1965).

[108]   For a more thorough discussion, *see* Kanovitz & Kanovitz, Constitutional Law § 2.5 (10th ed. 2006).

[109]   Model Penal Code § 250.7 (1985).

> An order to move, addressed to a person whose speech or other lawful behavior attracts an obstructing audience, shall not be deemed reasonable if the obstruction can be readily remedied by police control of the size or location of the gathering.

The Model Penal Code, like other codes, has taken into consideration the possibility of constitutional challenge. Therefore, the phrase "having no legal privilege to do so" is included. Also, the language exempts from liability persons who have obtained permits or secured official permits to block off the streets. According to the comments following the statement, the result is to give the widest possible scope to picketing, protests, and other lawful assembly consistent with the need to protect reasonable public access to highways and other public passages.

Subsection (2) proscribes refusal to obey a reasonable official in order to prevent obstruction of a public passage or to disperse persons gathered in dangerous proximity to a fire or other hazard. The term "reasonable" is included so as to limit the authority of the police officer to order a person to move if the situation can be handled without stopping the speaker.

Some state codes and statutes include the provisions of the Model Penal Code. Some statutes describe the prohibited conduct more specifically. Arkansas, for example, defines obstruction as "rendering impassable."[110] In some states, the offense is made a part of the disorderly conduct statute. For example, the Ohio statute[111] provides

> (A) No person shall recklessly cause inconvenience, annoyance, or alarm to another, by doing any of the following: ...
>   (4) Hindering or preventing the movement of persons on a public street, road, highway, or right-of-way, or to, from, within, or upon public or private property, so as to interfere with the rights of others and by any act which serves no lawful and reasonable purpose of the offender.

Although the statute does not specifically exempt from liability a speaker or listener who is legally expressing ideas, it does exempt those who have a "lawful and reasonable purpose."

B. Harassment and Stalking

Although harassment targets individual victims rather than the general population as the other crimes in this chapter, it is included here because it shares similar constitutional issues. Harassment statutes and stalking statutes cover minor assaultive conduct in which the intent is to annoy or alarm a specific individual. They have been challenged as unconstitutional in that they infringe upon an individual's freedom of speech and movement. Harassment may involve driving up and down the street in front of someone's house, standing on the sidewalk, telephoning repeatedly, showing up at the victim's place of work, and so on. These behaviors are activities that are protected as freedoms up to a point, but the question is when can they become criminal? Statutes

---

[110]   ARK. STAT. ANN. § 5-71-214 (1999).
[111]   OHIO REV. CODE ANN. § 2917.11 (Anderson 2002).

must be carefully drawn to avoid impinging on constitutional rights. An example of a harassment statute is that of New Jersey. It provides

2C:33—4. Harassment

> Except as provided in subsection e., a person commits a petty disorderly persons offense if, with purpose to harass another, he:
> (a) Makes, or causes to be made, a communication or communications anonymously or at extreme inconvenient hours, or in offensively coarse language, or any other manner likely to cause annoyance or alarm;
> (b) Subjects another to striking, kicking, shoving, or other offensive touching, or threatens to do so; or
> (c) Engages in any other course of alarming conduct or of repeatedly committed acts with purpose to alarm or seriously annoy such other person.
>   A communication under subsection a. may be deemed to have been made either at the place where it originated or at the place where it was received.
> (e) A person commits a crime of the fourth degree if in committing an offense under this section, he was serving a term of imprisonment or was on parole or probation as the result of a conviction of any indictable offense under the laws of this State, any other state or the United States.[112]

The New Jersey courts, as well as federal courts, have considered the validity and meaning of the statute. Some of the court holdings in harassment appeals are presented below.

- A federal court opined that, under the statute, a person must be permitted to communicate ill-will, hatred, or bias to others, but is prohibited from acting upon such sentiments in a harassing manner.[113]
- A defendant's acts of sending a ripped-up copy of a child support order by regular and certified mail to the estranged wife was not likely to cause "annoyance" within the meaning of the harassment statute.[114]
- The fact that a defendant that positioned himself in a location where his wife could see him as she exited her house, despite an injunction prohibiting him from "having contact with" his wife, was sufficient to establish that the defendant engaged in a course of alarming conduct as required to support a harassment conviction.[115]

The Model Penal Code provides the following provision for harassment.

§ 250.4 Harassment[116]

A Person commits a petty misdemeanor if, with purpose to harass another, he:

(1) makes a telephone call without purpose of legitimate communication; or

---

[112]   N.J. STAT. ANN. 2C:33—4 (2002).
[113]   New Jersey v. Bazin, 913 F. Supp. 106 (D.N.J. 1995).
[114]   State v. B.H., 676 A.2d 565 (N.J. Super. 1996).
[115]   State v. J.T., 638 A.2d 1166 (N.J. Super. 1996).
[116]   MODEL PENAL CODE § 250.4 Harassment.

(2) insults, taunts or challenges another in a manner likely to provoke violent or disorderly response; or

(3) makes repeated communications anonymously or at extremely inconvenient
hours, or in offensively coarse language; or

(4) subjects another to an offensive touching; or

(5) engages in any other course of alarming conduct serving no legitimate purpose
of the actor.

Most states have responded to the problem of harassing behaviors by creating stand-alone statutes or incorporating harassing behavior into existing statutes such as disorderly conduct or assault. Stalking statutes are similar to harassment statutes and were created in the 1990s after the problem of stalking was publicized by the tragic Rebecca Shaeffer case in 1989.

The next year California passed the country's first anti-stalking law. Stalking statutes cover much of the same behavior as harassment statutes: lying in wait, pursue or follow, trespass, intimidate, vandalize, harass, display a weapon, and so on. The California stalking statute also defines certain Internet activity as illegal when the offender relays a credible threat that can be given through an "electronic communication device" or the threat is implied through a pattern of conduct or a "combination of verbal, written, or electronically communicated statements." Florida also has passed a cyberstalking statute.[117] The challenge of all such statutes is to be specific enough to withstand constitutional challenge. Also, of course, a victim may obtain a civil order of protection and any violation of that order would result in a contempt of court citation that may be civil or criminal, depending on the state's laws.

LEGAL NEWS: TRAGIC CONSEQUENCES OF STALKING

Harassment and "anti-stalking laws" were in the forefront of public concern after Rebecca Shaeffer was killed on the front step of her home in 1989. The young actress, a star in the television series *My Sister Sam,* was the target of an obsessive fan who stabbed her to death when she was perceived to have spurned him. California passed its anti-stalking law in 1990. Today, only Arizona and Maine have no such laws. The activities such laws prohibit include approaching, pursuing, following, trespassing, lying in wait, intimidation, contacting, and restraining. The National Institute of Justice defined stalking as a course of conduct that causes a reasonable person to fear bodily injury or death for him- or herself or members of his or her family.

Source: National Institute of Justice, U.S. Dept. of Justice. *Project to Develop a Model Anti-Stalking Code for States.* 1993, p. 43.

---

[117]   CAL. CRIM. CODE § 646.9; FLA. STAT. § 784.048 (2003).

C. Desecration of Venerated Objects

Statutes that prohibit desecration of public monuments or objects, places of worship or burial, the national or state flags, or any other patriotic or religious symbol are present in most states. These statutes are aimed at special kinds of public or quasi-public property damages that result in an affront to members of the public. The statutes are aimed more at the protection of public sensibilities than the impairment of property interests.

The Model Penal Code also presents a statute that prohibits this type of behavior.

§ 250.9 Desecration of Venerated Objects

A person commits a misdemeanor if he purposely desecrates any public monument or structure, or place of worship or burial, or if he purposely desecrates the national flag or any other object of veneration by the public or a substantial segment thereof in any public place. "Desecrate" means defacing, damaging, polluting or otherwise physically mistreating in a way that the actor knows will outrage the sensibilities of persons likely to observe or discover his actions.

The problem with such statutes, however, is that the destruction may be "speech." In cases where the destruction can be defined as a valid exercise of one's speech (i.e., burning the flag to protest the war in Iraq) and does not break any other laws (i.e., destruction of someone else's property or public property), then the Supreme Court has ruled that such statutes unconstitutionally infringe on First Amendment rights. In *Texas v. Johnson*,[118] a case discussed in Chapter 1, the Texas statute that criminalized flag burning was challenged and the Supreme Court invalidated the statute, ruling that such activity was protected speech. Congress is currently considering an amendment to the Constitution that would bar any destruction of the American flag. Proponents argue that it is important to the country to have such an amendment and there is a harm that must be prohibited in such activity. Opponents argue that many who have no intent to denigrate the flag might also be in violation of any such law if they use the flag in clothing, wrap themselves up in it during sports games, or use it for room decoration. Free speech advocates argue that if the flag stands for anything, it stands for free speech; therefore, it would be ironic to punish those who wanted to use it to express their views.

D. Other

The Model Penal Code, and many states, also provide statutes for Cruelty to Animals, Violation of Privacy, Disrupting Meetings and Processions, and False Public Alarms. These behaviors are defined as criminal under the state's police power. The purpose of all such statutes is to deter behavior that outrages or offends the feelings of substantial groups of the population. Because the various state statutes contain other

---

[118]   Texas v. Johnson, 491 U.S. 397 (1989).

offenses against the public order, they must be researched by those who are involved in the criminal justice process in order to have a thorough knowledge of the charges that are available.

§ 10.10   Summary

In order to protect the public peace, laws defining offenses, some of which are minor in character, have been enacted. These offenses are often characterized as offenses against the public peace or offenses against public order. Generally, in order to convict a person for rioting, the prosecution must prove three or more persons (1) intentionally undertake a common action; (2) that is unlawful or lawful but done in an unlawful manner; (3) that is violent and tumultuous; and (4) that obstructs orderly government. Related to riot is inciting to riot. This occurs when one incites, or encourages, other persons to create or engage in a riot as defined.

A crime that is common to all jurisdictions is disorderly conduct. What constitutes disorderly conduct depends on the terms of the statute or ordinance; however, it may be said that words and acts that tend to disturb the peace and endanger the morals, safety, or health of the community are punishable as disorderly conduct under most statutes.

Vagrancy at common law was defined as the wandering or going about from place to place by an idle person who has no lawful visible means of support and who exists on charity and does not work for a living, although able to do so. Many of the vagrancy and loitering statutes were declared unconstitutional because they were considered too vague. Modern loitering statutes are more specific and are drafted to make the person accused of the crime aware of what specific conduct is prohibited. Panhandling statutes also must be written very specifically and target only such actions that can be described as alarming or endangering citizens.

Although drunkenness was not a crime at common law, most state statutes now prohibit the appearance in any public place of a person who is manifestly under the influence of alcohol, drugs, or narcotics, if he is to the degree that he may endanger himself or other persons or property or annoy persons in his vicinity.

Drug interdiction and enforcement is a shared activity by both federal and state law enforcement. State laws all follow the Uniform Controlled Substances Act in their categorization of drugs, but enforcement provisions vary from state to state and between the federal government and states. Generally, the crimes associated with controlled substances include possession, possession with intent to deliver, and trafficking; however, there are many more, including those that penalize possession or delivery of counterfeit substances, and obtaining prescriptions under false pretenses.

Although the federal government generally enforces violations of federal laws against interception of wire or oral communications, states have also experimented with laws prohibiting eavesdropping, possession of eavesdropping devices, tampering with private communications, or divulging illegally obtained information.

States have also passed terrorism laws, especially after the terrorist attacks of September 11, 2001. Terrorism-specific state laws provide, among other things, penalties for those who provide material support for terrorism, engage in terroristic threats, engage in terrorism, or render criminal assistance to a terrorist.

In order to make it possible for citizens to carry on their everyday business and to avoid undue interference, statutes that regulate the use of highways and other passages have been written and enforced. These statutes have been challenged as being unconstitutional, but when written in accordance with constitutional guidelines, they have been upheld as a proper exercise of the police power of the state. Other offenses against the public peace include harassment (and anti-stalking laws), disrupting meetings, desecration of venerated objects, and cruelty to animals.

REVIEW QUESTIONS

1. Define the three crimes that represent the traditional steps in violent mob action. Distinguish between *rout* and *riot*.

2. Explain the difference between *riot* and *inciting to riot*. In the Model Penal Code and some of the more recently enacted state statutes regarding riots, a certain number of persons must be involved as participants to constitute the crime. What is the range of the critical numbers in the various codes?

3. Some offenses against the public peace, such as disorderly conduct, have been declared unconstitutional by the U.S. Supreme Court. What are the two grounds for challenging the constitutionality of these statutory offenses?

4. What is "disorderly conduct" as defined by the Model Penal Code? Provide examples.

5. What are the most common prohibited acts under state disorderly conduct statutes?

6. What speech is protected by the First Amendment? What speech is not protected? Does making insulting remarks to a police officer constitute disorderly conduct? Give some examples of cases in which state courts have found that certain acts constitute disorderly conduct.

7. What crimes might participants, promoters, and spectators of "fight clubs" be charged with?

8. Many of the early laws relating to vagrancy and loitering were declared unconstitutional. What was the reasoning of the Supreme Court in finding that many of these statutes violated the Constitution?

9. In the Model Penal Code definition of loitering or prowling and in most state statutes, the manner of loitering or prowling is specified. What manner of loitering or prowling is prohibited?

10. What are "stop-and-identify" statutes? What was the Supreme Court's holding regarding the

constitutionality of such statutes when they require a police officer to have reasonable suspicion that a crime has been or is about to be committed?

11. Discuss the holding of *Powell v. Texas*.

12. Is public drunkenness a violation of the law in most jurisdictions? Was it a crime under common law? Explain what is meant by public drunkenness. What factors may be taken into consideration in determining whether the statute is violated?

13. Under DWI laws, what does "in control" of the car mean? Give examples.

14. Explain the differences between the five schedules (categories) of drugs described in the Uniform Controlled Substances Act.

15. What are the issues in prosecuting possession crimes? (Define possession and the *mens rea* required.) What is the difference between possession and possession with intent to deliver? What is the difference between possession with intent to deliver and trafficking?

16. What are some other crimes associated with drugs? What are state and federal forfeiture laws? What have been some challenges to such laws?

17. What was the common law crime akin to wiretapping? Describe state wiretapping statutes and what behaviors they prohibit.

18. What is the definition of "act of terrorism" in the New York statute? Can states have their own anti-terrorism laws after the USA PATRIOT Act?

19. Does the state have the authority to enact legislation prohibiting the obstruction of highways and other public passages? What are the limitations, if any?

20. Define *harassment* as used in state statutes. List some acts that are considered harassment. Describe the crime of desecration of venerated objects. What are the potential constitutional challenges to such laws?

Offenses against Justice Administration

11

Chapter Outline

Cases

Interference with Arrest: *Houston v. Hill*, 482 U.S. 451 (1987)
Escape: *Medford v. Texas*, 990 S.W.2d 799 (Tex. Ct. App. 1999)

§ 11.1   Introduction

Some of the common law crimes that developed over the years, primarily through judicial action to protect the public, have disappeared, while new offenses have been added as new or larger agencies have been created. For example, the common law crime of barratry, designed to prevent stirring up of strife and litigation, is no longer in existence for practical purposes.[1] While these common law crimes have disappeared, others have been added. An example of a modern statute enacted to ensure that evidence is properly protected for trial is "tampering with or fabricating physical evidence." Both state and federal legislative bodies have enacted legislation to supplement traditional sanctions against those who seek to subvert the justice process.

In this chapter, the well-known offenses relating to justice administration, such as perjury and bribery, are defined and explained. In addition, statutes including obstruction of justice, escape, resisting and evading arrest, and other offenses that affect the administration of justice are discussed.

§ 11.2   Perjury and Related Offenses

A. Common Law

The necessity of guaranteeing the integrity of a sworn statement in a judicial proceeding was recognized at common law. However, common law **perjury** was limited to the false oath *in a judicial proceeding*. As the practice of requiring sworn statements in other matters developed, the offense of perjury, whether by that name or some other title

---

[1]   Common barratry is the offense of frequently inciting and stirring up suits and quarrels. Commonwealth v. Davis, 28 Mass. (11 Pick.) 432 (1831).

such as "false swearing," was extended to cover judicial or quasi-judicial proceedings as to some matter material to the issue or point in question.

Although in common parlance the terms **false swearing** and "perjury" are used interchangeably, in a strict legal sense there is a difference between them. At common law, false swearing is a separate and indictable offense, and is distinct from perjury in that the false oath in perjury must be made in a judicial proceeding, whereas in false swearing the act need not be made in such a proceeding.[2]

At common law, the offense of perjury was defined as a willful assertion as to a matter of fact, opinion, belief, or knowledge made by a witness in a judicial proceeding as a part of his evidence, either upon oath or in any form allowed by law to be substituted for an oath, whether in open court, in an affidavit, or otherwise, such assertion being known to such witness to be false, and being intended by him to mislead the court, jury, or person holding the proceedings. "Perjury" at common law was

- the willful
- giving of false testimony
- on a material point
- in a judicial proceeding
- by a person to whom a lawful oath had been administered.[3]

An essential element is that the defendant must have acted with criminal intent— he must have believed that what he swore to was false and he must have had intent to deceive.[4]

B. Model Penal Code

The Model Penal Code includes definitions of the terms statement and **materiality**. The definition of materiality does not differ substantially from prior law and refers to the idea that the statement must relate to the issue at law.

§ 241.1 Perjury[5]

(1) Offense Defined. A person is guilty of perjury, a felony of the third degree, if in any official proceeding he makes a false statement under oath or equivalent affirmation, or swears or affirms the truth of a statement previously made, when the statement is material and he does not believe it to be true.

(2) Materiality. Falsification is material, regardless of the admissibility of the statement under rules of evidence, if it could have affected the course or outcome of the proceeding. It is no defense that the declarant mistakenly believed the falsification to be immaterial. Whether a falsification is material in a given factual situation is a question of law.

---

[2]   Martin v. Miller, 4 Mo. 39 (1835); State v. Dallagiovanna, 69 Wash. 84, 124 P. 209 (1912).

[3]   *See* WHARTON, CRIMINAL LAW. 1780-1781 (12th ed. 1932); Gatewood v. State, 15 Md. App. 314, 290 A.2d 551 (1972); Bazarte v. State, 117 So.2d 227 (Fla. 1959).

[4]   State v. Laurelli, 187 F. Supp. 30 (D. Pa. 1960).

[5]   MODEL PENAL CODE § 241.1 (1985).

(3) **Irregularities No Defense.** It is not a defense to prosecution under this Section that the oath or affirmation was administered or taken in an irregular manner or that the declarant was not competent to make the statement. A document purporting to be made upon oath or affirmation at any time when the actor presents it as being so verified shall be deemed to have been duly sworn or affirmed.

(4) **Retraction.** No person shall be guilty of an offense under this Section if he retracted the falsification in the course of the proceeding in which it was made before it became manifest that the falsification was or would be exposed and before the falsification substantially affected the proceeding.

(5) **Inconsistent Statements.** Where the defendant made inconsistent statements under oath or equivalent affirmation, both having been made within the period of the statute of limitations, the prosecution may proceed by setting forth the inconsistent statements in a single count alleging in the alternative that one or the other was false and not believed by the defendant. In such case it shall not be necessary for the prosecution to prove which statement was false but only that one or the other was false and not believed by the defendant to be true.

(6) **Corroboration.** No person shall be convicted of an offense under this Section where proof of falsity rests solely upon contradiction by testimony of a single person other than the defendant.

To make the offense and definitions more clear, the Model Code also has subsections relating to retraction, inconsistent statements, and corroboration. While subornation of perjury is not specifically spelled out in the Model Code as an offense, in the comments following the statement of the provision, a comment is included explaining that this is covered under § 2.06(3)(a) of the Model Code, which provides that a person is the accomplice of another in the commission of an offense if he or she solicits the other person to commit it; therefore, under the MPC, even though no statute defines subornation of perjury as an offense, the offender would be guilty of accomplice to perjury.

In addition to the crime of perjury, the Model Penal Code includes a separate offense titled false swearing. A perjured statement that is not material to the judicial proceeding is a violation of the false swearing section of the Code. A second section deals with falsifications that do not occur in an official proceeding, but are intended to mislead a public official in the performance of his official function. Both of these are graded as misdemeanors.

C. State Statutes, Codes, and Cases

A number of states have adopted the Model Penal Code in substance. In addition, some states list the specific types of proceedings to which perjury sanctions may be applied. An example of a state code that does not follow the Model Code is that of New York, where there are three degrees of perjury:

§ 210.05 Perjury in the third degree[6]

A person is guilty of perjury in the third degree when he swears falsely.
     Perjury in the third degree is a Class A misdemeanor.

---

[6]   N.Y. PENAL LAW §§ 210.05-210.15 (McKinney 2003).

§ 210.10 Perjury in the second degree

A person is guilty of perjury in the second degree when he swears falsely and when his false statement is

(a) made in a subscribed written instrument for which an oath is required by law, and
(b) made with intent to mislead a public servant in the performance of his official functions and
(c) material to the action, proceeding or matter involved.
  Perjury in the second degree is a Class E felony.

§ 210.15 Perjury in the first degree

A person is guilty of perjury in the first degree when he swears falsely and when his false statement

(a) consists of testimony, and
(b) is material to the action, proceeding or matter in which it is made.
  Perjury in the first degree is a Class D felony.

In the New York statute, perjury is the most serious level of the crime and false swearing is the least serious. Note that materiality is not an element of perjury in the third degree; however, a court ruled that a prosecutor must have some good faith purpose behind questions he puts to a grand jury witness, beyond setting the stage for perjury prosecution.[7]

Another issue that comes up in perjury appeals is whether the question was sufficiently precise to warrant finding the answer false. A court admonished that before a person may be convicted of perjury "the burden is on the questioner to pin the witness down to the specific object of the questioner's inquiry."[8]

Each of the elements of perjury must be proven beyond a reasonable doubt. In order for conviction, the state must prove the defendant did the following:

1. Made an Intentional False Statement

In a Washington case, the court cautioned that opinions and legal conclusions are not subject to perjury convictions and that, for purposes of perjury, a false statement must relate to facts and must also be susceptible to proof as to its truth or falsity.[9]

2. That Was Material

Courts also emphasize that materiality is an essential element of the crime of perjury in the first degree and that the false statement, to be material, must reflect on a matter under consideration during the action or proceeding in which it is made.[10]

---

[7]   People v. Pomerantz, 407 N.Y.S.2d 723, 63 A.2d 457 (1978).
[8]   People v. Siggia and Partridge, 588 N.Y.S.2d 518 (1990).
[9]   In re Disciplinary Proceeding Against Huddleston, 137 Wash. 2d 560, 974 P.2d 325 (1999).
[10]   People v. Stanard, 42 N.Y.2d 74, 365 N.E.2d 857, 369 N.Y.S.2d 825, *cert. denied*, 434 U.S. 986, 98 S. Ct. 615, 54 L. Ed. 2d 481 (1977). *See also* State v. Anderson, 603 A.2d 928 (N.J. 1992); People v. Evans, 704 N.Y.S.2d 418 (2000). *See also* Luna v. Massachusetts, 224 F. Supp. 2d 302 (D. Mass.

The materiality issue arose in a New Jersey case when a police officer was convicted of perjury after falsely stating that he saw the person he arrested strike another person with a shovel. The reviewing court upheld the conviction, finding that the evidence suggested the fact that the officer did not see the person strike another person with a shovel but that the supposed shovel-wielder struck the other person with her hand. The fact that the police officer merely exaggerated was a sufficient material falsehood to sustain the perjury charge.[11]

3. In a Judicial Proceeding under Oath

As noted above, perjury often is limited to false testimony in a judicial proceeding while making false statements in other venues is either a lesser degree of perjury or is defined as false swearing.

4. For the Purpose of Misleading the Court

The *mens rea* for perjury is specific intent; that is, the defendant must intend to make the false statement *and* intend the statement to mislead the court.

5. Other Issues

Some state statutes include a corroboration or "two witness" rule.[12] This means that in order to convict someone of perjury, there must be at least two witnesses who testify as to the defendant's deception or the prosecutor must have other corroboration in addition to the testimony of only one witness.

6. False Swearing

In some states, a separate crime of false swearing is included in the statute. Generally, these statutes use somewhat the same language that is used in perjury statutes, but do not require that the false statements be made in a judicial proceeding, may not require materiality (as is required in perjury), and, in some instances, do not require intent to mislead. Where the statute includes the crime of false swearing, it is usually a lower degree offense.[13]

7. Subornation of Perjury

Subornation of perjury is the procuring of one person by another to commit the crime of perjury. This crime has two essential elements: one person must have willfully procured another to commit perjury, and the second person must have, in fact, committed the offense. If the person does not actually commit perjury, then the proper charge would be solicitation or attempted subornation.

2000), which held that under Massachusetts law materiality is one of the elements of the crime of perjury, and each element must be proven beyond a reasonable doubt.

[11] People v. Brown, 616 N.Y.S.2d 592 (1994).

[12] People v. Trotter, 83 Cal. Rptr. 2d 753 (1999).

[13] State v. Kowalczyk, 66 A.2d 175 (N.J. 1949); Plummer v. State, 84 S.E.2d 202 (Ga. 1954).

Although the crimes of perjury and subornation of perjury may be closely related in point of time and conduct, the offenses are not the same—each having elements not common to the other. One court explained that there are sufficient inherent differences between the two to warrant the lawmaking power in separating the act into its component parts, making the subornation a new and independent offense, punishable with greater or less severity than that inflicted on the perjurer.[14]

D. *Summary*

While common law restricted the definition of perjury to only false statements under oath in a judicial proceeding, modern statutes have expanded the definition of perjury or created "false swearing" to cover other forms of false statements made under oath or after swearing to the truthfulness of the statement.

Perjury
(A/R) false statement (testimony), under oath, about a material element, in a judicial proceeding
(M/R) specific intent

False swearing
(A/R) false statement (writing), after swearing
(M/R) general intent (to lie)

Subornation of perjury
(A/R) entice, encourage, reward another to commit perjury and perjury did occur
(M/R) specific intent

§ 11.3   Bribery and Related Offenses

Although history reveals that among the Romans the giving of rewards and emoluments to public officers, especially judicial officers, was tolerated, later civilizations recognized the danger of the effect of corrupt private influences upon official action. Some early cases indicate that only the bribe-taker, for example, the judge, and not the bribe-giver, could be found guilty of an offense.[15]

As a public official in the service of the people, the primary duty is to protect and further their interest and the official should not be permitted to profit through the performance of his or her public functions. To prohibit this, the offense of bribery as it relates to public officials—executive, legislative, or judicial—was created. Note that this offense is different from the commercial bribery offense described in an earlier chapter because this crime can only be committed by public officials or agents. The essence of the offense is the prostitution of a public trust, the betrayal of public interest, or the debauchment of the public conscience.[16]

---

[14]   Stone v. State, 118 Ga. 705, 45 S.E. 630 (1903) (a defendant who induced his wife to make a false affidavit was guilty of subornation of perjury); Thomas v. State, 231 S.W. 200 (1921).

[15]   PERKINS AND BOYCE, CRIMINAL LAW (3d ed. 1982).

[16]   Ex parte Winters, 10 Okla. Crim. 592, 140 P. 164 (1914).

A. Common Law

Blackstone defined **bribery** as the receiving by a judge or other officer connected with the administration of justice, of "any undue reward to influence his behavior in his office."[17] Court decisions and early statutes defined the offense more broadly, including the offering, giving, receiving, or soliciting of anything of value with the intent to influence the recipient's action as a public official, whether executive, legislative, or judicial.[18] Early common law only identified as criminal the public official who accepted the bribe; however, later opinions included both the receiver and the person who offers the bribe as criminal.[19]

The common law elements of bribery were (1) receiving or soliciting (and later, offering or giving); (2) a thing of value; (3) with intent to influence the recipient's action; and (4) the recipient is a public official.

B. Model Penal Code

The Model Penal Code follows the more recent statutory provisions in reaching both the person who offers, gives, or agrees to give a bribe in an official or political matter and the public servant or other covered individual who solicits, accepts, or agrees to accept a bribe. It applies to full-time government employees, plus consultants to government, bribery of voters and political party officials, and bribery of anyone who exercises official discretion in a judicial or administrative proceeding. This section is very broad in its scope and uses terminology that is less likely to cause problems in interpretation.

§ 240.1 Bribery in Official and Political Matters[20]

A person is guilty of bribery, a felony of the third degree, if he offers, confers or agrees to confer upon another, or solicits, accepts or agrees to accept from another:

(1) any pecuniary benefit as consideration for the recipient's decision, opinion, recommendation, vote or other exercise of discretion as a public servant, party official or voter; or

(2) any benefit as consideration for the recipient's decision, vote, recommendation or other exercise of official discretion in a judicial or administrative proceeding; or

(3) any benefit as consideration for a violation of a known legal duty as public servant or party official.

---

[17]   4 Blackstone, Commentaries 139 (1898).

[18]   Honaker v. Board of Education, 42 W. Va. 170, 24 S.E. 544 (1896); Rudolph v. State, 128 Wis. 122, 107 N.W. 466 (1906).

[19]   People v. Northey, 77 Cal. 618, 19 P. 865 (1888); United States v. Forsythe, 429 F. Supp. 715 (D. Pa. 1977); State v. Smith, 252 La. 636, 212 So.2d 410 (1968); United States v. Sisk, 476 F. Supp. 1061 (D. Tenn. 1979); People v. Ginsberg, 80 Misc.2d 921, 364 N.Y.S.2d 260 (1974).

[20]   Model Penal Code § 240.1 (1985).

It is no defense to prosecution under this section that a person whom the actor sought to influence was not qualified to act in the desired way whether because he had not yet assumed office, or lacked jurisdiction, or for any other reason.

LEGAL NEWS: GOVERNOR GOES TO PRISON

In December 2008 the country was stunned when Governor Rod Blagojevich and his chief of staff were arrested by the FBI on federal charges of bribery and criminal conspiracy. He was accused of soliciting bribes in return for the Senate seat vacated by President-elect Barack Obama. The investigation also revealed evidence that Blagojevich may also have solicited bribes in return for government contracts in large road construction projects. Although the investigation and probably charges were federal, Illinois law also addresses bribery by government officials. In the Illinois Criminal Code (720 ILCS 5 § 33-1), bribery is defined as someone who offers or solicits something of value for the performance of a public function.

> (e) He solicits, receives, retains, or agrees to accept any property or personal advantage pursuant to an understanding that he shall improperly influence or attempt to influence the performance of any act related to the employment or function of any public officer, public employee, juror or witness.

In Blagojevich's case, it appears he was soliciting campaign funds, a job for a relative, or a seat on a board or an ambassadorship for himself, in return for naming someone to the Senate seat. Even the nonmonetary items could be considered "things of value." He was potentially subject to prosecution under both federal and state statutes but was prosecuted in federal court.

UPDATE: In December of 2011, Blagojevich was sentenced to 14 years in prison for 18 corruption charges including bribery.

Sources: Long, R. and R. Pearson (2009). "Impeached Governor Blagojevich Removed from Office." *Chicago Tribune*, January 30, 2009. Accessed March 9, 2009 from http://www. chicagotribune.com/news/local/chi-blagojevich-impeachment-removal,0,5791846.story.
Davey, M. (2011). "Blagojevich Heading to Prison." *The New York Times*, December 7, 2011 Accessed January 11, 2012 from http://www.nytimes.com/2011/12/08/us/blagojevich-expresses-remorse-in-courtroom-speech.html.

C. State Statutes, Codes, and Cases

Many recently enacted state bribery statutes include most of the language of the Model Penal Code. Some, however, require specific intent. Others can be interpreted to require that the benefit be offered, or solicited upon an agreement or understanding that a specific official act will be influenced. This language indicates that an actual agreement must exist rather than simply the intent to influence.

An example of a state statute that is somewhat different from the Model Code is that of New York. It provides

§ 200.04 Bribery in the first degree[21]

A person is guilty of bribery in the first degree when he confers, or offers or agrees to confer, any benefit upon a public servant upon an agreement or understanding that such public servant's vote, opinion, judgment, action, decision or exercise of discretion as a public servant will thereby be influenced in the investigation, arrest, detention, prosecution, or incarceration of any person for the commission or alleged commission of a Class A felony defined in article two hundred twenty of the penal law or an attempt to commit any such Class A felony.
    Bribery in the first degree is a Class B felony.

A New York court has held that the legislative intent in using the words "as a public servant" in this section was to shield from corruption only the actions of a public servant that are related to or within the scope of his functions as a public servant.[22]

Bribery statutes are often categorized into sections that relate to bribery in specific situations and degrees of bribe receiving. For example, the New York statute includes, in addition to bribery in the first degree, bribery in the second degree, bribery in the third degree, bribe receiving in the third degree, bribe receiving in the second degree, and bribe receiving in the first degree.[23]

The specific charge of bribery is determined by the wording of the statute and the activity of the accused. For example, a police officer was charged with a violation of § 200.10, bribe receiving in the third degree, which provides that

A public servant is guilty of bribe receiving when he solicits, accepts or agrees to accept any benefit from another person upon an agreement or understanding that his vote, opinion, judgment, action or exercise of discretion as a public servant will thereby be influenced.

In this case, the court held that evidence was sufficient to support the police officer's conviction for bribe receiving when the officer was compensated for the introduction of a narcotics dealer to another narcotics officer who was supposed to give protection to the drug dealer. As it turned out, the other officer was assigned to the police Internal Affairs Division and made tape recordings of the transaction.[24]

In interpreting the Alabama bribery statute, an Alabama court advised that the critical inquiry in determining whether a defendant violated the bribery statute that prohibited the soliciting or accepting "something of value" is whether he or she did so

---

21   N.Y. PENAL LAW § 200.04 (McKinney 1999). *See also* §§ 200.10, 200.11, and 200.12.
22   People v. Herskowitz, 80 Misc. 2d 693, 364 N.Y.S.2d 350 (1975), *aff'd*, 41 N.Y.2d 1094, 364 N.E.2d 1127, 396 N.Y.2d 356 (1977).
23   Respectively, §§ 200-03, 200-00, 200-10, 200-11 and 200-12.
24   People v. Logan, 535 N.Y.S.2d 411 (1988).

knowingly and willfully.[25] And an Indiana appeals court noted that specific and explicit *quid pro quo* is an essential element of proof under the bribery statute.[26]

The Texas Penal Code bribery statute was considered in the case of *Rodriguez v. State*.[27] In this comprehensive decision the court stated that the essential premise of the bribery statute is that the conferring of a benefit upon a public servant and as consideration for a violation of one of his duties is an offense. Bribery focuses upon the mental state of the actor, and requires an agreement between the official and another party that some official performance will be influenced by the bribe.[28]

1. Offering, Giving, Receiving, or Soliciting

The crime is committed by one who gives a bribe as well as by one who receives it. It is also committed by one who offers a bribe or offers to accept it. One who conveys an offer to bribe, from a third person, is himself guilty, though the money is to be paid by the third person.

2. Thing of Value

Almost anything may serve as a bribe as long as it is of sufficient value in the eyes of the person bribed to influence his official conduct. It is not necessary that the thing have a value at the time it is offered or promised.[29] However, a vague offer to turn state's evidence, without anything further, was insufficient to constitute a "benefit" under the New York bribery statute.[30]

3. With Intent to Influence Public Duties

Criminal intent is a necessary element. The intent must be to corruptly influence an official in the discharge of his or her duty; and/or the intent to receive (by a public official) in return for being influenced. While the public official does not have to vote or make a favorable decision in order for the crime to be complete, these events may be used as evidence of the *mens rea* required in order for the acceptance of something of value to constitute bribery.

4. Of a Public Official

Although at one time the term *public official* was more limited, the modern tendency is to include any public officer, agent, servant, or employee. As an example, the federal law covers any "officer or employee or person acting for or on behalf of the United States, or any department or agency thereof, in any official function."[31]

---

[25]   Dill v. State, 723 So.2d 787 (Ala. 1998).

[26]   Wurster v. State, 708 N.E.2d 587 (Ind. 1999).

[27]   TEX. PENAL CODE ANN. § 36.02(A)(1) (Vernon 2001).

[28]   Rodriguez v. State, 90 S.W.3d 340 (Tex. 2001).

[29]   People v. Hockberg, 62 A.D.2d 239, 404 N.Y.S.2d 161 (1978).

[30]   People v. Cavan, 84 Misc. 2d 510, 376 N.Y.S.2d 65 (1975).

[31]   18 U.S.C. § 201.

Public official includes police officers, sheriffs, and deputy sheriffs under most state statutes.[32]

5. Conflict of Interest Statutes

To make it possible to prosecute persons who have committed acts that are similar to bribery but do not have all of the elements of bribery, legislative bodies have enacted related statutes. An example is the Pennsylvania statute, which provides

> No person shall offer or give to a public official, public employee . . . anything of monetary value, including a gift, loan, political contribution, reward, or promise of future employment based on the offeror's or donor's understanding that the vote, official action, or judgment of the public official or public employee . . . would be influenced thereby.[33]

In the case of *Commonwealth v. Heistand*, the defendant was charged with bribery, commercial bribery, and conflict of interest (403[b]). The facts indicate that the defendant's roofing company had a contract with the school district and that the defendant had an "understanding" with the facilities manager that the defendant's payment of the manager's country club membership dues would influence the manager's judgment. In fact, the defendant's company was awarded a contract after the offer was made and a second contract after the dues were paid. The defendant was convicted only of the conflict of interest charge and appealed. The reviewing court affirmed the judgment, explaining that the conflict of interest statute has a different purpose than the bribery statute. The conflict of interest statute was enacted to avoid even the appearance of impropriety by public officials.[34] Conflict of interest laws are often challenged, however, as being unconstitutional in that they are vague, and, as such, violate due process. Note that unlike bribery, prosecutors who pursue conflict of interest charges do not have to acquire evidence of an agreement between the parties, nor any action taken by the public official that would be evidence of acting for the interests of the other party. It is sufficient to show only that the public official had some economic or family relationship that could be considered a conflict of interest. It is also true that conflict of interest laws often require only disclosure of such a potential conflict and it is the nondisclosure that is punished.

LEGAL NEWS: CONFLICT OF INTEREST LAWS

In Pennsylvania a wide ranging investigation of state lawmakers resulted in charges against 25 current and former legislators. Seven pled guilty, three were convicted, two acquitted, and the others are awaiting trial. Charges include

---

[32]   Usry v. State, 90 Ga. App. 644, 83 S.E.2d 843 (1954).

[33]   65 PA. CONS. STAT. § 1103 (2002).

[34]   Commonwealth v. Heistand, 685 A.2d 1026 (Pa. Super. 1996).

conflict of interest, conspiracy, and theft because of alleged misuse of public funds for campaign purposes. Defendants are challenging the state's conflict of interest laws as being unconstitutionally vague.

Obtained January 11, 2012 from http://www.philly.com/philly/news/politics/20110728_ap_deweeselawyersfilemotioninpacorruptioncase.html.

D. *Summary*

Because the statutes vary from state to state, it is necessary to examine the respective statutes to determine the elements that must be proved and the correct statute to use in drafting the charge. In general, bribery can be committed by a person who offers or gives as well as the person who accepts or solicits. The receiver must be a public official but that term is broadly defined. The most crucial element of bribery is the *mens rea* element—there must be proof that the thing of value was given or accepted in return for a specific act related to the public official's performance of public duties. If this element cannot be proven, it may be that a conflict of interest crime has been committed (if it exists in that jurisdiction). The crime of conflict of interest punishes the mere giving or taking of items of value that may influence a public official's judgment and there is no requirement to prove an agreement regarding a specific act of the public servant in return for compensation. The following offers general elements that may be part of any particular state's penal code.

Bribery
(A/R) offer, give, solicit, receive, a thing of value, to (or by) a public official, to influence, performance of public duties
(M/R) intent to influence (or intent to receive in return for being influenced)

Conflict of Interest
(A/R) offer, give, solicit, receive; a thing of value; to (or by) a public official; that is against statutory limits
(M/R) general intent; knowing

§ 11.4　Obstructing Justice

The courts recognized early that some laws were necessary to protect the integrity of the criminal justice process. Courts and legislative bodies have also recognized the difficulty in framing legislation that would accomplish the purpose of protecting the criminal justice process, yet preserve the rights of individuals.[35]

---

[35]　58 AM. JUR. 2D *Obstructing Justice* § 1 (1989).

A. Common Law

At common law, offenses were created first by court decision and later by statutes that provided misdemeanor penalties for misdeeds that tended to distort or impede the administration of law. Although the definitions relating to the offense of **obstruction of justice** differ, there is a common theme running through these definitions. Some early definitions will assist in understanding the purpose of the offense.

- To "obstruct justice" is to interpose obstacles or impediments, or to hinder, impede, or in any manner interrupt or prevent the administration of justice.[36]
- The phrase "obstructing justice" means impeding or obstructing those who seek justice in a court, or those who have duties or powers of administering justice therein.[37]
- The state has the inherent power to punish for obstruction of justice if it is found that a person acted in such a way as to play on human frailty and to defect and to deter the court from performing its duty.[38]

B. Model Penal Code

The purpose of the Model Code was to make it possible to punish those who did not come within the technical definitions of bribery, threat, perjury, or escape, but did perform acts with the intent to subvert the justice process.

§ 242.1 Obstructing Administration of Law or Other Government Function[39]

A person commits a misdemeanor if he purposely obstructs, impairs or perverts the administration of law or other governmental function by force, violence, physical interference or obstacle, breach of official duty, or any other unlawful act, except that this Section does not apply to flight by a person charged with crime, refusal to submit to arrest, failure to perform a legal duty other than an official duty, or any other means of avoiding compliance with law without affirmative interference with governmental functions.

According to the comments following the proposed section of the Model Code, the drafters felt that it was desirable to include a residual misdemeanor offense but also recognized the necessity of not making the provision too broad in its coverage.

The offense punishes anyone who "obstructs, impairs, or perverts the administration of law, or other governmental function." It is not limited to the administration of justice, but applies to any other governmental function. In order to bring an offender within the statutory prohibition, the prosecution must show first that the person purposely obstructed or perverted the administration of law or other governmental function. The prosecution must also introduce evidence to prove that force, violence,

---

[36]   Baker v. State, 122 Ga. App. 587, 178 S.E.2d 278 (1970).

[37]   Shackelford v. Commonwealth, 185 Ky. 51, 214 S.W. 788 (1919).

[38]   State v. Sagumaker, 200 Ind. 623, 157 N.E. 769 (1927).

[39]   MODEL PENAL CODE § 242.1 (1985).

physical interference or obstacle, breach of official duty, or other unlawful act was involved in obstructing the administration of law.

C. State Statutes, Codes, and Cases

In states where the statutes have been revised, many have followed the recommendation of the Model Penal Code and consolidated obstruction of government functions into one offense. Some use other terminology, such as "willful" obstruction. Others do not require any specific means of obstruction. Some cases in which courts have upheld obstruction convictions are the following:

- Conspiracy to induce or aid one who may be required as a witness in a pending proceeding to leave the jurisdiction, in order to escape service of a subpoena or to evade such service, constituted obstruction of justice.[40]
- An attorney general's persuading a municipal judge to dispose of various criminal cases without the consent and knowledge of the district attorney.[41]
- A defendant's statement that he would kill the deputy sheriff when the threats were knowingly made in an attempt to intimidate or impede the testimony of the sheriff.[42]

Depending on whether separate statutes exist in a particular jurisdiction, obstruction charges may apply to those who hide or destroy evidence, lie on official reports, threaten jurors or prosecutors, delay or subvert the course of an official investigation, hide an offender and/or help the offender escape, or lie to investigating officers in such a way that it seriously hampers the investigation. However, "mere disagreement" or remonstrance with a police officer cannot constitute "obstruction of justice" unless the disagreement is so violent that it amounts to attempts to deter an officer from performing an arrest or official duty.[43]

An example of a code that differs somewhat from the Model Penal Code is that of Ohio. It provides

Ohio Rev. Code Ann. § 2921.31[44]

(A) No person, without privilege to do so and with purpose to prevent, obstruct, or delay the performance by a public official of any authorized act within the public official's capacity, shall do any act which hampers or impedes a public official in the performance of his lawful duties.

This statute consolidates a large number of separate sections that were included in the former law. Under this section, the means used to commit the offense are unimportant, so long as it is done without privilege and with the purpose of preventing,

---

[40] People v. Hefberd, 162 N.Y.S. 80 (1916).
[41] People v. Martin, 185 Cal. Rptr. 556 (1982).
[42] Polk v. Commonwealth, 4 Va. App. 590, 358 S.E.2d 770 (1987).
[43] McCook v. State, 145 Ga. App. 3, 243 S.E.2d 289 (1978).
[44] OHIO REV. CODE ANN. § 2921.31 (Anderson 2002).

obstructing, or delaying an official act, and actually has its intended effect. According to an Ohio court's interpretation of the statute, there must be some substantial stoppage of the officer's progress before one can say that he or she was hampered or impeded.

In *State v. Stephens*, several police officers observed a vehicle belonging to a person whose name was Hannah, for whom they had several outstanding traffic warrants, parked in front of the defendant's house. The officers walked up to the house and asked if they could speak to Hannah. The defendant told the officers she did not know Hannah and had never seen him before. One of the officers had previously seen the defendant in Hannah's company and knew that she did know him. Another officer looked through a window and observed Hannah hiding in the basement. The officers entered the house and arrested Hannah. The defendant was tried and convicted of hampering a public official in the performance of his duties, in violation of the Ohio statute.

On appeal, the conviction was reversed, the court holding that the statute, which prohibits "any act which hampers or impedes a public official in the performance of his lawful duties," did not encompass the defendant's conduct. The court indicated that the defendant's words in no way interrupted the officers' progress toward their objective and even though the defendant lied, the act did not in fact hamper or impede the officials.[45] It is entirely possible, however, that another court might have upheld this conviction.

Examples of acts that have been found to violate the obstruction statute in Ohio are

- removing a chalk mark from the tire of a vehicle placed there by a police officer in furtherance of enforcing a parking time limitation[46]
- blocking the police entrance to a residence to impede or delay a police officer in the performance of his duty[47]

However, a driver refusing to show a driver's license to a police officer upon request was not "obstruction of justice."[48] The elements of obstruction will vary from state to state, but, in general, they include the following:

1. Intentionally

The intent element of obstructing official business can be inferred, but it must be specific intent. That is, the prosecution must prove that the defendant intended to do the act that impeded, prevented, obstructed or delayed the justice process *and* that he intended that the consequence of his action would be the obstruction of the justice process.[49]

---

[45]   State v. Stephens, 57 Ohio App. 2d 229, 387 N.E.2d 252 (1978).
[46]   Sandusky v. DeTidio, 555 N.E.2d 680 (Ohio 1988).
[47]   State v. Pitts, 509 N.E.2d 1284 (Ohio 1986).
[48]   State v. McCrone, 580 N.E.2d 468 (Ohio 1989).
[49]   State v. Puterbaugh, 755 N.E.2d 359 (Ohio 2001).

2. Impede, Prevent, Obstruct, Delay

In a Florida case, the court cautioned that the police did not have probable cause to arrest the defendant for obstruction of justice arising out of the defendant's yelling the street term "ninety-nine," which means that police were in the area, while undercover officers were attempting the arrest of drug dealers, when the defendant was not the target of the drug bust and the officer was unaware if the actual target was caught.[50] However, a Washington court held that flight from officers when the officers have grounds for a *Terry* stop and a refusal to halt at their order may constitute obstruction of a public servant.[51]

Case decisions indicate that arguing with or not cooperating with police is not obstruction, but blocking or subverting their investigation by running, lying, or threatening them or others might be. Hiding or destroying evidence might be prosecuted under an obstruction statute unless the state has a specific statute that covers that type of behavior. The *actus reus* of obstruction is broad and can cover a range of different types of behaviors. In *Polk v. Virginia*, the Virginia court upheld a conviction for obstruction based on threats made to the arresting officer.[52]

> Ottie B. Polk was convicted in a bench trial of obstructing justice by threats or force in violation of Code § 18.2-460(A). He was sentenced to six months in jail, with five months suspended, and fined $100. On appeal, Polk argues that: (1) the evidence was insufficient to support his conviction because words alone will not support a conviction under Code § 18.2-460(A), and because there was no evidence of his criminal intent; and (2) he was entitled to use reasonable force to resist arrest, under the authority of *United States v. Moore* ...
>
> Shirilla testified that, at the time of the arrest, Polk threatened to sue him for false arrest and further stated: "If I lose, I'll get you some other way." Polk was handcuffed, placed in Shirilla's vehicle, and transported to the Lancaster County Sheriff's office where Shirilla served him with the failure to appear warrant. Shirilla testified that while they were awaiting the arrival of a magistrate, Polk continually repeated statements such as "I'm going to get you," and "I'm going to get even." Shirilla testified that he then read Polk his Miranda warnings and asked him: "Are you talking civil suit or are you looking for a piece of my ass?" According to Shirilla, Polk only responded: "I'm going to get you."
>
> ... Casto testified that after Shirilla left the room, Polk stated that he was going to kill him. Casto concluded that Polk was referring to Shirilla. When Shirilla returned, Casto apparently related this threat to Shirilla. Shirilla testified that based on his conversation with Casto, he obtained a warrant charging Polk with obstruction of justice.
>
> According to Shirilla, a final threat occurred after Polk had been charged with the obstruction offense. The threat occurred when Polk was issued jail clothing and was being taken to the shower. Shirilla testified that at that time he heard Polk say: "I've got five friends to help me take care of him."
>
> During the entire sequence of these events, neither Shirilla nor Casto observed Polk make any physically threatening gestures or possess any weapons. On

---

50   State v. Dennis, 684 So.2d 848 (Fla. 1996).
51   State v. Mendez, 137 Wash. 2d 208, 970 P.2d 722 (1999).
52   Polk v. Virginia, 358 S.E.2d 770 (1987).

cross-examination, Shirilla acknowledged that, except for the verbal exchanges, the arrest proceeded in a normal fashion. . . .

. . . Initially, we reject Polk's argument that words alone cannot constitute a violation under Code § 18.2-460(A) without evidence that they caused fear or apprehension in the recipient, or delay in the legal process. The plain language of Code § 18.2-460(A) provides that threats constitute a violation of the statute when they are knowingly made in an attempt to intimidate or impede law enforcement officers who are performing their duties. Thus, it is the threats made by the offender, coupled with his intent, that constitute the offense. The resulting effect of the offender's threats, such as fear, apprehension, or delay, is not an element of the crime defined in Code § 18.2-460. By the express terms of the statute, it is immaterial whether the officer is placed in fear or apprehension. The offense is complete when the attempt to intimidate is made. Where a statute contains language which has a definite and precise meaning, and is expressed in clear and concise terms which manifest the intent, courts must adopt that plain meaning. . . . We, therefore, conclude that Polk's statement that he would kill Shirilla was a threat as contemplated by the statute. . . .

. . . We turn now to consider Polk's claim that there was insufficient evidence of his criminal intent. Specifically, he argues that the evidence does not show that he actually intended to intimidate or impede Deputy Shirilla. In reviewing this claim, we examine the evidence presented in the light most favorable to the Commonwealth, and accord to the evidence all reasonable inferences fairly deducible therefrom. . . .

Intent is the purpose formed in a person's mind which may be shown by his statements or conduct. . . . We find that the trier of fact was entitled to conclude that Polk threatened to kill Shirilla, . . . , and that this threat made by Polk to Shirilla demonstrated his intent to intimidate Shirilla from completion of the post-arrest processing. For this reason, we hold that the evidence presented was sufficient to establish Polk's criminal intent.

3. A Public Official from Performing an Official Duty in the Administration of Justice

Most of the cases described above concern private individuals and their interactions with police officers. It should be noted that other public officials may be the target of the obstruction, such as prosecutors, attorneys general, and the like. Also, personnel within the criminal justice system may be subject to prosecution on charges of obstructing justice for failure to disclose evidence or to pursue an investigation. In these cases, the public official is, in effect, obstructing himself from furthering the interests of justice. In *State v. Petty,* a sheriff's nondisclosure of evidence and failure to pursue an arson investigation against the daughter of a personal friend and political associate was properly the subject of prosecution on charges of obstructing justice. The argument that he was merely exercising his discretion as a law enforcement officer did not immunize the sheriff, when a jury could find that the discretion yielded to an ulterior criminal purpose.[53]

4. Other Issues

While the state has the authority to pass laws to protect the integrity of the judicial system, such laws cannot be enforced if they violate the First Amendment. The First Amendment comprehends as "free speech" critical and challenging remarks directed at

---

[53]   State v. Petty, 5th District Court of App. Ohio 7-26-88.

Case Note: *Houston v. Hill*, **482 U.S. 451, 107 S. Ct. 2502, 96 L. Ed. 2d 398 (1987)**
What was the holding of the case?
What exactly did Mr. Hill do?
What was the wording of the ordinance?
Why was it struck down as unconstitutional?
What language of an alternative ordinance might have been successfully defended?

police when performing their duties unless the remarks are shown likely to produce a "clear and present danger of a serious substantive evil that rises far above public inconvenience, annoyance, or unrest." In *Houston v. Hill*, a municipal ordinance made it unlawful to "oppose, molest, abuse, or interrupt any policeman in the execution of his duty"; however, the ordinance was challenged on First Amendment grounds and overturned.[54] This particular ordinance is very similar to an obstruction statute, and similarly, obstruction statutes cannot be enforced in such a way as to violate free speech when the actor is merely disagreeing with a police officer but not physically obstructing him or her from performing his or her duties, nor causing an imminent public disturbance or inciting a riot.

D. *Summary*

The obstruction of justice charge is a catchall that can cover a multitude of behaviors, including interfering with an arrest, hiding evidence, or malfeasance of office on the part of a justice official. The most important point to note is that the statute or application of a statute cannot trample on constitutional rights of expression, nor can it be too vague and allow justice officials unbridled discretion. Further, specific intent must be proven.

Obstruction of Justice
(A/R) impede, prevent, delay, obstruct; justice official; from performing official functions in the administration of justice
(M/R) specific intent (intend to do the act, and intend that it obstruct justice)

§ 11.5   Escape

The offenses of escape, resisting arrest, and evading arrest are all related. Furthermore, at common law, **escape** was distinguished from a **prison break** and the offense of **rescue**. Prison break was defined as the breaking and going out of a place of confinement by one who is lawfully imprisoned. The crime was not committed unless there was an actual breaking or force was used. If there was no force, then the crime was not a prison break. Rescue was defined as the forcible delivery of a prisoner from lawful custody by one who knows that he is in custody. Rescue, at common law, could be a felony or misdemeanor, according to the crime with which the prisoner was charged.[55]

---

[54]   Houston v. Hill, 482 U.S. 451, 107 S. Ct. 2502, 96 L. Ed. 2d 398 (1987).
[55]   State v. King, 114 Iowa 413, 87 N.W. 282 (1901). *See also* Duckworth v. Boyer, 125 So.2d 844 (Fla. 1960).

A. Common Law

Escape, at common law, was broadly defined as the voluntary departure of a person, without force, from the lawful custody of an officer or from any place where he is lawfully confined.[56] The person cannot escape unless he or she has actually been arrested; neither can an escape occur when the preceding arrest was defeated by successful resistance. However, one who has been taken into custody of the law by arrest or surrender and remains in legal custody and then departs unlawfully is guilty of escape.[57]

The fact that the escape occurs as a result of the negligence of a jailer in leaving a door open is not a defense.[58] Furthermore, the crime of escape included the situation in which an officer voluntarily allows a prisoner to escape. Under this law, the officer could be held criminally liable if he unlawfully permitted the prisoner to escape.[59]

An escape was not justified or excused even if a prisoner was wrongfully held in custody and could have been released if the proper legal steps were taken.[60] However, there is no escape if there was no custody. (The proper charge in this case might be evading arrest.)

The elements of common law escape are the person must be in legal custody, and departure from the area of confinement. No intent is required other than the intent to go beyond permitted limits. Proof that the defendant was in legal custody and voluntarily departed therefrom without having been released is sufficient for a conviction in the absence of some satisfactory explanation.[61]

B. Model Penal Code

The Model Penal Code is written in clear language and includes failure to return following leave from a correctional institution granted for a specific purpose (for instance, a furlough or work release). Also, official detention is clearly defined to include arrest and detention for law enforcement purposes. The Model Code, in subsection (2) of Section 242.6, provides a penalty for a public official who permits or facilitates the escape. This is similar to provisions that existed at early common law. The punishment assigned to the offense of escape takes into consideration the crime charged and the force used in making the escape.

§ 242.6 Escape[62]

(1) Escape. A person commits an offense if he unlawfully removes himself from official detention or fails to return to official detention following temporary leave granted for a specific purpose or limited period. "Official detention" means

---

[56]   United States v. Zimmerman, 71 F. Supp. 534 (D. Pa. 1947).

[57]   Whitehead v. Keyes, 85 Mass. (3 Allen) 495 (1862).

[58]   State v. Hoffman, 30 Wash. 2d 475, 191 P.2d 865 (1948).

[59]   Houpt v. State, 100 Ark. 409, 140 S.W. 294 (1911).

[60]   People v. Hinze, 97 Cal. App. 2d 1, 217 P.2d 35 (1950).

[61]   Wiggins v. State, 194 Ind. 118, 141 N.E. 56 (1923).

[62]   MODEL PENAL CODE § 242.6 (1985).

arrest, detention in any facility for custody of persons under charge or conviction of crime or alleged or found to be delinquent, detention for extradition or deportation, or any other detention for law enforcement purposes; but "official detention" does not include supervision of probation or parole, or constraint incidental to release on bail.

(2) Permitting or Facilitating Escape. A public servant concerned in detention commits an offense if he knowingly or recklessly permits an escape. Any person who knowingly causes or facilitates an escape commits an offense.

(3) Effect of Legal Irregularity in Detention. Irregularity in bringing about or maintaining detention, or lack of jurisdiction of the committing or detaining authority, shall not be a defense to prosecution under this Section if the escape is from a prison or other custodial facility or from detention pursuant to commitment by official proceedings. In the case of other detentions, irregularity or lack of jurisdiction shall be a defense only if:

(a) the escape involved no substantial risk of harm to the person or property of anyone other than the detainee; or

(b) the detaining authority did not act in good faith under color of law.

(4) Grading of Offenses. An offense under this Section is a felony of the third degree where:

(a) the actor was under arrest for or detained on a charge of felony or following conviction of crime; or

(b) the actor employs force, threat, deadly weapon or other dangerous instrumentality to effect the escape; or

(c) a public servant concerned in detention of persons convicted of crime purposely facilitates or permits an escape from a detention facility.

Otherwise an offense under this section is a misdemeanor.

C. State Statutes, Codes, and Cases

Statutes and codes in the various states differ in wording and in establishing penalties. Some states recognize a single grade of escape with no aggravating or mitigating factors, while other states include distinct grading levels depending upon the use of force, the severity of the escapee's original crime, and the escapee's status, that is, whether he has been convicted or merely detained on suspicion. For instance, in Kentucky, three degrees of escape are defined:

§ 520.020 Escape in the First Degree[63]

(1) A person is guilty of escape in the first degree when he escapes from custody or a detention facility by the use of force or threat of force against another person.

(2) Escape in the first degree is a Class C felony.

§ 520.030 Escape in the Second Degree

(1) A person is guilty of escape in the second degree when he escapes from a detention facility or, being charged with or convicted of a felony, he escapes from custody.

(2) Escape in the second degree is a Class D felony.

---

[63] KY. REV. STAT. ANN. §§ 520.020, 520.030, 520.040 (Baldwin 1999).

§ 520.040 Escape in the Third Degree

(1) A person is guilty of escape in the third degree when he escapes from custody.

(2) Escape in the third degree is a Class B misdemeanor.

In the Kentucky statute, the degrees of "escape" are based on the type of custody and whether force was used. **Custody** means restraint by a public servant pursuant to a lawful arrest, detention, or an order of a court for law enforcement purposes, but does not include supervision of probation or parole or constraint incidental to release on bail.[64]

According to the Kentucky Court of Appeals, a defendant may be charged under the statute with escape in the second degree, a felony, despite the fact that he had been in jail and charged with misdemeanors rather than a felony. The court explained that the penalty imposed is most severe on those who effect an escape by force or threat of force.[65]

The Florida statute provides that any prisoner, confined in any prison, jail, private correctional facility, road camp, or other penal institution, whether operated by the state, a county, or a municipality, or operated under a contract with the state, a county, or a municipality, working upon the public roads, or being transported to or from a place of confinement who escapes or attempts to escape from such confinement commits a felony of the second degree, punishable as provided in § 775.082, § 775.083, or § 775.084.[66]

In Florida, the crime of escape consists of two elements: the act of leaving custody coupled with the intent to avoid lawful confinement. In *Watford v. State*, the court reasoned that when a state has established the right to custody and a conscious and intentional act of leaving, the offense is *prima facie* established. In some cases, prisoners have used the defense of necessity when charged with escape. They have argued that they needed to escape to avoid being seriously injured or killed by other inmates. While necessity would be a possible defense, the defendant must show that there were reasonable grounds to believe that the escapee is faced with real and imminent danger and the escapee must go immediately to a justice official upon escape to report the threat.[67]

While state statutes vary in their definitions and grading of escape; in general, the elements can be described as follows:

1. Voluntary Departure

Obviously, the defendant must "depart" to the extent that they are no longer in custody. If they are found hiding in the airshaft of a prison facility, the proper charge would be "attempted escape" rather than escape because they have not yet effected the departure. On the other hand, once out of custody, there is no distance requirement; so a defendant who leaves police custody after arrest may be recaptured immediately and still

---

[64]   Ky. Rev. Stat. Ann. § 520.010 (Baldwin 1999).

[65]   Commonwealth v. Johnson, 615 S.W.2d 1 (Ky. 1981).

[66]   Fl. Stat. Ann. § 944.40 (2003). *See also* Harboring or Aiding an Escapee, § 944.46; Aiding of Escape by Prisoners, § 843.09 *et seq*.

[67]   Watford v. State, 353 So.2d 1263 (Fla. Ct. App. 1978).

be charged with escape. For instance, in one case a court held that conviction for escape was proper where the defendant voluntarily departed from the city jail while in police custody and handcuffed.[68]

2. From "Custody" (Includes Detention Facilities and Failure to Return from Authorized Leave)

Custody may be jail, police custody, or any type of correctional facility. Unauthorized departure from a halfway house can be escape if the departure was willful and intentional.[69] Sometimes the statute specifically requires custody in a detention facility (rather than police custody). A Michigan court, in discussing the elements of escape in that state, held that the jail escape statute requires a showing that (1) the defendant was lawfully imprisoned in a jail or other place of confinement while awaiting legal proceedings or transfer to prison, and (2) the defendant broke or attempted to break out of the jail or place of confinement, regardless of whether the escape was actually made.[70]

A Texas appeals court stated that the elements of escape are that a person (1) escapes; (2) from custody; (3) after having been arrested for, charged with, or convicted of an offense.[71]

3. With Intent to Not Return to Custody

With the increased use of alternative procedures designed to reduce costs and address jail overcrowding, new questions are reaching the courts. For example, is a person guilty of escape if that person leaves a privately operated "detention facility" without authority? And is a person "in custody" when released prior to trial on the condition that he or she wear an electronic monitoring device at all times?

A Kentucky appeals court agreed that a person in a privately operated "detention facility" could be guilty of escape.[72] In another case, the court held that a defendant whose probation is revoked in his or her presence after a probation revocation hearing, and is informed by the judge that he or she is in custody and is to remain until a law enforcement officer can take him or her to jail, is in lawful custody for the purpose of the statute governing aggravated escape from custody.[73]

In another case, an Arizona appeals court made it clear that a defendant who was released prior to trial on felony charges on condition that he wear an electronic monitoring device and remain in his home was in "custody" so that removal of the device and unauthorized departure from his home and from the state constituted escape.[74]

---

68   State v. Brown, 29 Wash. App. 770, 630 P.2d 1378 (1981).
69   State v. Brown, 29 Wash. App. 770, 630 P.2d 1378 (1981).
70   People v. Fox, 232 Mich. App. 531, 591 N.W.2d 384 (1998).
71   Medford v. State, 990 S.W.2d 799 (Tex. Ct. App. 1999).
72   Phipps v. Commonwealth, 933 S.W.2d 825 (Ky. 1996).
73   United States v. Briggs, 48 P.3d 686 (Kan. 2002).
74   State v. Williams, 925 P.2d 1073 (Ariz. 1996).

D. Summary

An escape must begin with custody. If there is no custody, there can be no escape. However, once custody is established, then voluntary departure can constitute an escape, even if the person is not in jail or prison. Inmates of halfway houses and work-release facilities commit the crime of escape when they do not return at the expected time. Individuals in police "custody" may be charged with escape, but not if they are merely being detained for investigative purposes.

Case Note: *Medford v. State*, 990 S.W.2d 799 (Tex. Ct. App. 1999)
What was the holding of the case?
How exactly would you describe Medford's status?
At what point would the charge of escape be appropriate in this situation?
What would have been the appropriate charge for Medford?
Must officers say "you are under arrest" in order for custody to commence?

Escape
(A/R) voluntary departure, from custody, with intent not to return
(M/R) knowing (one is in custody), intent (not to return)

§ 11.6 Resisting Arrest

While a person who is not in custody cannot commit the crime of escape, someone who actively resists being put in custody might be charged with the crime of resisting arrest. Some obstruction of justice statutes include the act of **resisting arrest**. Other states have specific statutes that define the separate offense of resisting arrest.

A. Common Law

At common law, if the arrest was legal and there was resistance, the offense of resisting arrest was complete. What amounted to resistance depended on the facts of the situation. There are numerous examples of cases in which the court found that resistance occurred. The use of any weapon such as a club, pistol, or revolver is undoubtedly sufficient to constitute the resistance prohibited. However, resisting arrest does not require an attempt to cause serious bodily injury to the police officer. It is sufficient to prove that the defendant created a substantial risk of bodily injury or that the defendant put up resistance requiring the police officer to use substantial force to overcome it.[75]

In distinguishing between escape and resisting arrest, it has been held that "escape from custody" implies unlawfully freeing oneself from a completed apprehension while "resisting apprehension" means active opposition to attempts to place one in lawful custody.[76]

---

[75]   Commonwealth v. Williams, 344 Pa. Super. 108, 496 A.2d 31 (1985).
[76]   United States v. Chavez, 6 Mil. Jus. 615 (1936).

At common law, resisting arrest was an offense; however, an individual had a right to use reasonable resistance to prevent being arrested illegally.[77] If an officer did not disclose his authority and the accused did not know that he was an officer, the accused had the right to resist with whatever force was necessary.[78] However, that is generally not the case today.

B. Model Penal Code

Section 242.2 of the Model Penal Code is concerned with resistance to arrest where there is a substantial risk of bodily injury to a public servant or anyone else, or when means are employed that justify or require substantial force to overcome the resistance. Exempted from liability is one who nonviolently refuses to submit to arrest and such minor forms of resistance as running from a police officer or trying to shake free from his or her grasp.

> § 242.2 Resisting Arrest or Other Law Enforcement[79]
>
> A person commits a misdemeanor if, for the purpose of preventing a public servant from effecting a lawful arrest or discharging any other duty, the person creates a substantial risk of bodily injury to the public servant or anyone else, or employs means justifying or requiring substantial force to overcome the resistance.

Under the Model Penal Code, resisting arrest is a misdemeanor regardless of the charge against the person who resists arrest. In the commentary following the provision, it is explained that continued resistance to the arresting officer after the arrest has been made may constitute an attempt to escape in violation of § 242.6. Therefore, if the arrest is for a felony, escape from custody may be punished as a felony.

Unlike some statutes prior to the Model Penal Code and drafted since the Model Code, the Model Code does not provide a penalty for a person who resists arrest if the arrest is unlawful, unless one of the other provisions of the Model Code is violated.

C. State Statutes, Codes, and Cases

In drafting legislation, the states have differed, especially regarding resistance to an unlawful arrest. Some have been persuaded by the argument that the officer should be protected even if the arrest is unlawful and that the remedy for the person who is unlawfully arrested is a civil action against the officer.

An Ohio statute states that "No person, recklessly or by force, shall resist or interfere with a lawful arrest of the person or another."[80] Under the Ohio statute, lawful arrest is an element of the offense of resisting arrest. Where articulable suspicion, but not probable cause, to arrest exists, fleeing from a request for a *Terry*-type stop, while not

---

[77]   Fields v. State, 384 N.E.2d 1127 (Ind. Ct. App. 1979).
[78]   Presley v. State, 75 Fla. 434, 78 So. 532 (1918).
[79]   MODEL PENAL CODE § 242.2 (1985).
[80]   OHIO REV. CODE ANN. § 2921.33 (Anderson 2003).

condoned, does not constitute resisting arrest.[81] In Ohio, a judge held that the prosecution need not prove the guilt of the arrested defendant beyond a reasonable doubt in determining whether the arrest was lawful; however, for the arrest to be a "lawful arrest" as used in the resisting arrest ordinance, there must be probable cause or reasonable grounds for the arrest.[82] Another Ohio court stated the law succinctly, holding that under Ohio law, where there is no arrest, a criminal resisting arrest charge cannot be sustained. Applying this rule, an Ohio court determined that the defendant's heckling a professional baseball player did not provide a reasonable police officer with a basis to believe that it constituted a criminal offense, as was required to convict the defendant of resisting arrest.[83]

A Florida court, discussing the resisting arrest statute of that state, held that, in order to support a conviction for resisting arrest, the state must show that (1) the officer was engaged in the lawful execution of a legal duty, and (2) the action of the defendant constituted obstruction or resistance of that lawful duty.[84] In a second Florida case, the court determined that state law allows one who is illegally being arrested to resist that arrest without violence.[85] Using similar language, Pennsylvania courts have held that a valid charge of resisting arrest requires an underlying lawful arrest, which, in turn, requires the arresting officer to possess probable cause.[86]

On the other hand, other states do not allow the defense. An Indiana court has noted that, at common law, an individual had the right to use reasonable resistance to avoid an illegal arrest, but that rule no longer exists. That court advised that today a citizen may seek his or her remedy for a police officer's wrongful arrest by bringing a civil suit, while the common law right tends to promote violence. Thus, the court held, the defendant had no right to resist arrest.[87] In the case cited, the defendant was convicted of interfering with a police officer after a dispute developed when the officers ordered a tow truck to remove the defendant's vehicle from the street. The defendant contended upon appeal that he had a legal right to remove his own vehicle because, although it displayed the wrong kind of license plate, it was not otherwise illegally parked and should not have been treated as an abandoned vehicle. The court agreed that the officer had no right to have the car removed. However, the defendant had no right to resist being arrested; therefore, the conviction for resisting arrest was proper. The trend today is for states to refuse to allow individuals to resist unlawful arrests because there are other alternatives to respond, such as civil suits.[88]

---

[81]   State v. Raines, 124 Ohio App. 3d 430, 706 N.E.2d 414 (1997).

[82]   State v. Maynard, 693 N.E.2d 603 (Ohio Ct. App. 1996).

[83]   Hummel v. City of Carlisle, W.L. 31465378 (S.D. Ohio 2002); Cleveland v. Swiecicki, 775 N.E.2d 899 (Ohio 2002).

[84]   Jay v. State, 731 So.2d 774 (Fla. 1999).

[85]   Williams v. State, 727 So.2d 1050 (Fla. 1999).

[86]   Commonwealth v. Hock, 728 A.2d 943 (Pa. 1999) *and see* Commonwealth v. Maxon, 798 A.2d 761 (Pa. 2002). *See also* Vaughn v. State, 983 S.W.2d 860 (Tex. 1998).

[87]   Fields v. State, 384 N.E.2d 1127 (Ind. Ct. App. 1979).

[88]   *See* CAL. PEN. CODE §834a (West 1985); State v. Valentine, 935 P.2d 1294 (Wash. 1997).

When police use excessive force in effecting an arrest, some states allow the citizen to defend themselves against the arrest (since the illegal use of force turns it into an unlawful arrest). This right includes the use of deadly force if the individual felt their life was in danger. The right stems from the common law right of self-defense.[89] Of course, for the person to benefit from this defense, there must be a finding that the use of force by police was excessive. The elements of resisting arrest generally are as follows.

1. Resisting (Creating Risk of Bodily Injury and/or Requiring Substantial Force to Overcome)

According to one court in Texas, an arrestee can be convicted of forcefully resisting an arrest without ever successfully making physical contact with the person making the arrest. Applying this rule, the court held that "kicking at" an officer during arrest constitutes a use of force required under the penal code for the offense of resisting arrest.[90]

2. A (Lawful) Arrest

As indicated by the previous discussion, in some states, the underlying arrest must be lawful in order to support a resisting arrest charge. In other states, for public policy reasons, the common law defense that allowed resisting an unlawful arrest has been rejected. Because the states differ in regard to the elements, it is essential to be aware of the specific wording of the state statute and the decisions interpreting that statute.

D. *Summary*

While some states may cover resisting arrest in a general obstruction of justice statute, others have a separate statute that defines and penalizes resisting arrest. These statutes generally exempt nonviolent means of resistance, but punish those who create a substantial risk of harm by fighting with the police officer or otherwise creating a situation in which the police officer must use substantial force to overcome the resistance. While some states identify the lawfulness of the arrest as an element of the crime, others do not.

Resisting Arrest
(A/R) resisting, a (lawful) arrest
(M/R) knowing (one is being placed under arrest), intentional (resistance)

---

[89]   People v. White, 161 Cal. Rptr. 541 (Ct. App. 1980); Commonwealth v. French, 611 A.2d 175 (Pa. 1992).

[90]   Haliburton v. State, 80 S.W.3d 309 (Tex. 2002).

§ 11.7   Evading Arrest

Evading is the third and least serious crime in the three related crimes of escape, resisting, and evading. Not all states have a specific statute for evading arrest.

A. Common Law

No record of this crime seems to exist under the common law.

B. Model Penal Code

The Model Penal Code has a section titled "Hindering Apprehension or Prosecution" that defines as criminal those who assist another to escape or avoid capture by law enforcement; however, there is no section of "Evading Arrest." Furthermore, because the "Resisting Arrest" section described in the previous paragraphs requires a substantial risk of bodily injury or means that require the public servant to use substantial force to overcome the resistance, that section does not cover behaviors that do not involve force, such as simply running. On the other hand, if, in evading, the offender created a situation that might cause substantial injury (such as a high-speed chase), it is possible that the crime would be "resisting," not evading.

C. State Statutes, Codes, and Cases

Not all states have a separate evading arrest statute. In some states, the behavior is covered under a section of the resisting statute; in others, it might be covered under a general obstruction of justice statute. However, some states distinguish evasion and resisting. In a case in which the court distinguished between resisting arrest and avoiding arrest, a court stated that resisting arrest is a crime committed against a person; a defendant must use or threaten to use physical force or any other means that creates a substantial risk of causing physical injury to the peace officer or another to violate the statute, whereas if a defendant prevented arrest without using or threatening to use physical force or other means creating a substantial risk of physical injury, he "avoids" arrest.[91]

D. Summary

While evading arrest is not a separate crime in many states, it has been distinguished from resisting arrest.

Evading Arrest
(A/R) avoiding or fleeing, from arrest, without violence
(M/R) knowing (that arrest is attempted), intentional (flight)

---

[91]   State v. Sorkhabi, 46 P.3d 1071 (Ariz. 2002).

§ 11.8   Other Offenses against Justice Administration

All state statutes include other provisions that relate to conduct that impairs or obstructs governmental operations or public administration. The primary purpose is to preserve smooth and efficient administration of the government and to protect those who are charged with the responsibility of enforcing the laws and ordinances. Because these vary from state to state, it is obviously necessary that state statutes, and in some instances local ordinances, be studied to determine what conduct is prohibited and what elements must be proved in order to obtain a conviction when a person is charged with a violation of the ordinance or statute. Some of the offenses that are found in various state statutes are discussed here. It should be noted, however, that this list is not exhaustive.

A. *Failure to Aid a Law Enforcement Officer*

Many early statutes required persons to come to the aid of a law enforcement officer when asked to do so. In fact, at common law it was a criminal offense for any person to willfully disregard the summons of the sheriff to render assistance in apprehending a felon. Every citizen was bound to assist a known public officer in making an arrest when called upon to do so.[92] Some state statutes punished the failure to obey the call of an officer to assist in making an arrest.[93] An example of a modern statute that restates the requirement that persons come to the aid of officers is that of Ohio. It provides

Ohio Rev. Code Ann. § 2921.23[94]

(A) No person shall negligently fail or refuse to aid a law enforcement officer, when called upon for assistance in preventing or halting the commission of an offense, or in apprehending or detaining an offender, when such aid can be given without a substantial risk of physical harm to the person giving it.

This requires that a person aid the officer in apprehending an offender even though the offender has not been formally charged. It excuses the failure to render aid on the ground that there is a strong possibility that the person called upon may be hurt in the process.

B. *False Reports to Law Enforcement Authorities*

There is some evidence to the effect that giving false reports to police or other law enforcement agencies was punishable at common law, however, not all states have similar statutes. In the case of *People v. Stephens,* an Illinois court held that one who falsely reports a crime is guilty of disorderly conduct.[95]

---

[92]   Grau v. Forge, 183 Ky. 521, 209 S.W. 369 (1919); Firestone v. Rice, 71 Mich. 377, 38 N.W. 885 (1888).

[93]   Babington v. Yellow Taxi Corp., 250 N.Y. 14, 164 N.E. 726 (1928); 4 AM. JUR. *Arrest* § 129 (1936).

[94]   OHIO REV. CODE ANN. § 2921.23 (Anderson 2003).

[95]   40 Ill. App. 3d 303, 352 N.E.2d 352 (1976).

After several attempts to draft legislation that provided a penalty for giving false reports, many states now have statutes that accomplish the desired result. An example is that of Florida, which provides

§ 837.05. False reports to law enforcement authorities[96]

(1) Except as provided in subsection (2), whoever knowingly gives false information to any law enforcement officer concerning the alleged commission of any crime, commits a misdemeanor of the first degree, punishable as provided in s. 775.082 or s. 775.083.

(2) Whoever knowingly gives false information to a law enforcement officer, concerning the alleged commission of a capital felony, commits a felony of the third degree, punishable as provided in s. 775.082, s. 775.083, or s. 775.084.

States that have similar statutes are Alaska, Georgia, California, and Maryland.

Under the Kentucky statute, a person is guilty of falsely reporting an incident when he or she knowingly causes a false alarm of fire or other emergency to be transmitted.[97] Also, under this section, a person is guilty if he or she knowingly reports false information to a law enforcement agency with the intent to implicate another or initiates a report of an alleged occurrence of a fire or other emergency under circumstances likely to cause inconvenience or alarm, when he or she knows that the information reported, conveyed, or circulated is false. The major thrust of this statute is to deter those who impede investigations by furnishing fictitious leads. Such statutes are considered necessary in many jurisdictions to aid law enforcement personnel and to avoid inconvenience to members of the public as well as government agents.

C. Tampering with Witnesses

Most state statutes provide penalties for tampering with those who are to testify in trials. In some states, this is dealt with in provisions relating to obstruction of justice. This crime is closely related to obstruction of justice and subornation of perjury, both of which could be charged if the circumstances warrant.

The Model Penal Code provision relating to tampering with witnesses includes tampering with informants. It provides

§ 241.6 Tampering With Witnesses and Informants; Retaliation Against Them[98]

(1) Tampering. A person commits an offense if, believing that an official proceeding or investigation is pending or about to be instituted, he attempts to induce or otherwise cause a witness or informant to:

(a) testify or inform falsely; or

(b) withhold any testimony, information, document or thing; or

(c) elude legal process summoning him to testify or supply evidence; or

---

[96] FLA. STAT. ANN. § 837.05 (West 2003).

[97] KY. REV. STAT. ANN. § 519.040 (Baldwin 2002).

[98] MODEL PENAL CODE § 241.6 (1985).

(d) absent himself from any proceeding or investigation to which he has been legally summoned.

The offense is a felony of the third degree if the actor employs force, deception, threat or offer of pecuniary benefit. Otherwise it is a misdemeanor.

(2) Retaliation Against Witness or Informant. A person commits a misdemeanor if he harms another by any unlawful act in retaliation for anything lawfully done in the capacity of witness or informant.

(3) Witness or Informant Taking Bribe. A person commits a felony of the third degree if he solicits, accepts or agrees to accept any benefit in consideration of his doing any of the things specified in clauses (a) to (d) of Subsection (1).

This provision defines three different offenses, each of which protects against some threat to the veracity and cooperation of witnesses and informants. Subsection (1) provides that a person commits an offense if he or she attempts to induce another to testify or inform falsely or otherwise subvert the process of criminal law. Subsection (2) condemns retaliation against a witness or informant. Subsection (3) imposes a felony penalty for solicitation, acceptance, or agreement to accept any benefit in consideration of doing any of the acts enumerated in the first 10 subsections.

Many of the recently revised statutes and codes have specific provisions relating to tampering with witnesses. Some are more restrictive and some less restrictive. These, of course, must be studied in detail before any charges are made.

D. *Tampering with Evidence*

In order to ensure that evidence is preserved for presentation in court, many states have enacted legislation that prohibits tampering with evidence or fabricating physical evidence. The provisions of the statutes apply to those who attempt to impair the integrity or availability of evidence in an official proceeding or investigation, or one who purposely fabricates evidence in order to mislead the investigator. The suggested legislation as prepared by the drafters of the Model Penal Code is as follows:

§ 241.7 Tampering with or Fabricating Physical Evidence[99]

A person commits a misdemeanor if, believing that an official proceeding or investigation is pending or about to be instituted, he:

(1) alters, destroys, conceals or removes any record, document or thing with purpose to impair its verity or availability in such proceeding or investigation; or

(2) makes, presents or uses any record, document or thing knowing it to be false and with purpose to mislead a public servant who is or may be engaged in such proceeding or investigation.

The Model Penal Code punishes one who alters, destroys, conceals, or removes evidence and reaches those who "make, present, or use any record, document or thing knowing it to be false with the purpose to mislead" those engaged in investigating crimes.

---

[99]　MODEL PENAL CODE § 241.7 (1985).

Some states that have similar legislation are Connecticut, Indiana, Maine, Missouri, Montana, New Hampshire, New Jersey, Ohio, Pennsylvania, Utah, Massachusetts, and Vermont. Other states have provisions that require that the accused intend to have the evidence "introduced" in the official proceeding.

The Ohio statute provides

Ohio Rev. Code Ann. § 2921.12[100]

(A) No person, knowing that an official proceeding or investigation is in progress, or is about to be or likely to be instituted, shall do any of the following:
  (1) Alter, destroy, conceal, or remove any record, document, or thing, with purpose to impair its value or availability as evidence in such proceeding or investigation;
  (2) Make, present, or use any record, document, or thing, knowing it to be false and with purpose to mislead a public official who is or may be engaged in such proceeding or investigation, or with purpose to corrupt the outcome of any such proceeding or investigation.

Interpreting a Kentucky statute, a reviewing court agreed with the lower court opinion that evidence that an officer saw the defendant place a plastic bag containing a white powdery substance on the kitchen counter, and that this item of potential evidence disappeared from the counter after the defendant became aware of the presence of the officer and closed the front door, and before officers were granted entry through the back door, was sufficient to support a conviction of tampering with evidence.[101]

A police officer filing a report with knowledge that its contents are inaccurate because of knowing omissions and with knowledge that the report will be relied upon in a likely investigation, may be in violation of this Ohio statute.[102]

E. Other Offenses

Statutes of the various states include other offenses that relate to public justice and administration. Some include such offenses as

- compounding a crime
- impersonating a public servant
- hindering apprehension or prosecution
- bail jumping
- criminal contempt

Even when a state does not have a specific statute, the activity can usually be prosecuted under a broader statute, such as obstruction of justice.

---

[100]   OHIO REV. CODE ANN. § 2921.12 (Anderson 2003).
[101]   Burdell v. Commonwealth, 990 S.W.2d 628 (Ky. 1999).
[102]   State v. McNeeley, 548 N.E.2d 961 (Ohio 1988).

§ 11.9 Summary

As government functions developed, the need to protect them from willful interference became apparent. Legislation has been enacted to protect government agencies from interference by those outside the government and to protect the public from individuals who might take advantage of the authority granted as a result of government employment.

It was recognized early that the integrity of a sworn statement must be guaranteed to ensure the truth of statements made in judicial or quasi-judicial proceedings. To this end, the offense of perjury was created. Perjury is generally defined as the willful and corrupt false swearing or affirming after an oath has been lawfully administered in the cause of judicial or quasi-judicial proceedings as to some matter material to the issue or point in question. Subornation of perjury is the procuring of one person by another to commit the crime of perjury.

A second universally recognized offense that relates to the integrity of government administration is bribery. Bribery is defined as the offering, giving, receiving, or soliciting of anything of value with intent to influence the recipient's action as a public official. The elements of bribery are (1) offering, giving, receiving, or soliciting; (2) a thing of value; (3) with intent to influence the recipient's action; and (4) the recipient is a public official.

Early courts and legislative bodies added a crime titled obstruction of justice. Generally, these statutes and cases prohibit interference with a witness, harboring criminals, influencing a jury, suppression or destruction of evidence, and other related acts.

Escape has been broadly defined as the voluntary departure of a person without force from the lawful custody of an officer or from any place where he is lawfully confined. The elements of escape are the person is in legal custody and voluntary departure from the area of confinement. Related to escape is the offense of resisting arrest and, in some jurisdictions, evading arrest. At common law, if the arrest was legal and there was resistance, the offense of resisting arrest was complete. What amounted to resistance depended upon the facts of the situation. Under the Model Penal Code, resisting arrest is a violation when there is a substantial risk of bodily injury to a public servant or anyone else. At common law and in many states, an individual has the right to reasonable resistance to avoid an illegal arrest. That law has been changed in other states, which hold that the defendant has no right to resist an arrest, even if the arrest is illegal. The reasoning is that the common law rule tends to provoke violence and that the person wrongfully arrested has recourse by bringing a civil suit.

Other offenses against public justice and administration include failure to aid a law enforcement officer, making false reports to enforcement authorities, tampering with witnesses, and tampering with evidence. Because the state statutes differ regarding offenses against justice administration, individual state statutes should be reviewed by criminal justice personnel to determine the elements that constitute an offense in any specific state.

REVIEW QUESTIONS

1. What are the essential elements of the offense of perjury? Explain the specific intent *mens rea* of perjury.

2. Distinguish between perjury and subornation of perjury. How is false swearing different from perjury?

3. According to the common law definition of bribery, who may commit the crime? How are statutes different today?

4. Is intent an element of the offense of bribery? Explain.

5. Generally, bribery statutes apply only to public officials. What is the definition of public official as used in the contemporary statutes?

6. How does a conflict of interest statute differ from a bribery statute?

7. What are the elements of obstructing justice statutes? Under the MPC, what acts would not be sufficient to support an obstruction of justice charge?

8. Can threats to police officers, such as "I am going to get you," "I am going to get even," "I am going to kill him," and "I have got five friends to help me take care of him" be sufficient to support an obstruction of justice charge?

9. What are other examples of behaviors or actions that might form the *actus reus* of obstruction of justice?

10. What is a common challenge to the enforcement of obstruction or interfering in arrest charges? Distinguish what can and cannot be the subject of criminal prosecution.

11. Distinguish between common law escape and prison break crimes.

12. Under the Model Penal Code section relating to escape, the offense is a misdemeanor unless one of three conditions exists, in which case it is a felony. Name the three aggravating circumstances.

13. According to most state statutes, must a person be in legal custody before he or she can be convicted of escape? Define custody.

14. How does the offense of resisting arrest differ from the offense of escape? What is the common law definition of resisting arrest?

15. What is the difference between resisting arrest and avoiding/evading arrest?

16. When a person is prosecuted for resisting arrest, may the arrestee raise the unlawfulness of the arrest as a defense? Explain. Do the state laws agree on this defense? Give some examples.

17. What might a person who is the target of a police investigatory stop and runs away and/or struggles with the police officer be charged with?

18. Describe the crimes of "failure to aid a law enforcement officer" and "false reporting."

19. Describe the crimes of "tampering with witnesses" and "tampering with evidence." If a state does not have these statutes, what would the person be charged with?

20. List and describe at least three other crimes that are mentioned in the last section of this chapter.

United States Criminal Code: Offenses against Persons and Property

12

Chapter Outline

Cases

Federal Carjacking: *United States v. Cobb*, 144 F.3d 319 (4th Cir. 1998)
Honest Services Fraud: *Skilling v. U.S.*, 561 U.S. __ (2010)
Extortion: *United States v. Jackson*, 986 F. Supp. 829 (S.D.N.Y. 1997)

§ 12.1   Introduction

In the last two chapters of this text, we will introduce some aspects of federal criminal law. This discussion is not meant to be an exhaustive treatment of the federal code and only highlights, using certain laws, how the federal laws are similar to or different from state statutes.

The source of federal law is Congress. Recall that while the Constitution gives the states broad police powers, the federal government's powers are strictly enumerated in Article I, Section 8 of the Constitution. Federal criminal laws must be associated with one of these specifically enumerated powers or derive from maritime or territorial jurisdiction. Washington D.C. is under federal jurisdiction so all the types of crimes that we have covered throughout this book that occur in the District of Columbia would be federal crimes. Some crimes, such as treason and smuggling, are clearly granted by the federal government's power and duty to protect our borders. These crimes, which are clearly federal in nature, have no counterpart in state criminal laws.

Other crimes, however, that do not take place in a federal territory, nor directly relate to federal powers, are derived from a federal power. For instance, the federal government has the power to regulate interstate and foreign commerce. The **commerce clause** has been interpreted broadly to allow the federal government to pass the Civil Rights Act of 1964 (and its progeny), prohibiting discrimination on the basis of race, sex, or membership in other protected classes by businesses that participate in interstate commerce. The commerce clause is also the source for the federal government's power to pass federal criminal statutes covering kidnapping (when the victim is transported across state lines or the federal mail is used in the crime). Furthermore, most of the regulatory crimes discussed in Chapter 13 that criminalize activities of corporations in the areas of health and safety and securities transactions are derived from the power of the commerce clause. In other areas, federal laws have been created that, historically, were addressed solely by the states' police power. Proponents of the "federalization" of criminal law argue that federal law enforcement and prosecutors have the jurisdiction and resources necessary to combat crime that is increasingly national and even international in scope. Opponents of the proliferation of federal laws argue that the federal government is usurping state authority in deciding what should and what should not be criminal.

Federal crimes can be found in the **United States Code**. Most federal crimes can be found in Title 18, although they also can be found in Title 42. Many complain that the United States Code is not organized in any logical way as are the Model Penal Code and most state penal codes; rather, the U.S. Code has crimes listed alphabetically. Efforts to modernize have been unsuccessful. The number of federal crimes continues to expand. In 2008, there were close to 5,000 federal crimes. Today, a recent news report indicates that no one knows exactly how many federal crimes there are![1]

Federal crimes are prosecuted by U.S. District Attorneys in U.S. District Courts. There are 94 District Courts in the United States. These **District Courts** are organized into 12 circuits. Appeals from District Courts are heard in U.S. Courts of Appeal. There are 13 Courts of Appeal (one for each circuit and one special federal circuit). Appeals from a Court of Appeal may be heard by the Supreme Court.

Although the Supreme Court is the law of the land and governs all federal courts as well as state courts, lower-level federal courts have more limited jurisdiction. Thus, a holding from a District Court has only persuasive authority over other Districts. The same is true of **Courts of Appeals**. In fact, one of the reasons that the Supreme Court accepts a case is when there is disagreement among the Circuit Courts.

A. Constitutional Challenges

While the federal government has the power to define federal crimes, the Constitution protects us against laws that abridge our freedoms. For instance, no federal law can be vague, punish behavior after the fact (ex post facto), or infringe on freedom of expression, association, or religion. We have already discussed these protections in Chapter 1, but it should be emphasized that the original intent of the framers was to put these protections in place against unfair federal laws. Their application to state statutes came later, with the interpretation of the due process clause of the Fourteenth Amendment as protecting state citizens against state violations that offend "fundamental liberties." The most common constitutional challenges are

- vagueness and overbreadth
- ex post facto

---

[1]   J. Baker, 2008. Revisiting the Growth of Federal Crimes. The Heritage Foundation. Accessed January 12, 2012 from http://www.heritage.org/research/reports/2008/06/revisiting-the-explosive-growth-of-federal-crimes. Weiss, D. 2011. Federal Laws Multiply. *ABA Journal*, July 25, 2011. Accessed January 12, 2012 from http://www.abajournal.com/news/article/federal_laws_multiply_-jail_times_for_ misappropriating_smokey_bear_image/.

- infringements upon First Amendment rights of expression, association, religion, and privacy

Federal laws face constitutional challenges in the same way that state laws do. If a law infringes upon protected liberties, it has to show an important governmental interest. For instance, the following two news stories illustrate recent challenges to federal laws.

LEGAL NEWS: FIRST AMENDMENT CHALLENGES

The Stolen Valor Act criminalizes the action of lying about receiving a military award or medal. The purpose of the law is to prevent people from pretending to be military heroes in order to obtain valuable goods or services or even just to prevaricate for one's ego. A challenge to the law is based on the First Amendment, specifically, that such lying is protected speech that cannot be criminalized. Opponents of the law argue that the First Amendment cannot prohibit any content-based speech. The case, *United States v. Alvarez*, will be heard and decided in 2012. In *United States v. Stevens*, the Supreme Court struck down a 1999 law that made it a crime to create or sell "depictions of animal cruelty." The law was passed in order to address so-called "crusher" fetish videos where a woman's foot in a high heel was seen crushing a small kitten. The marketing of such videos ended abruptly after the law was passed. Stevens, however, was prosecuted for distributing what he called documentaries of dogfights. The court ruled that the law was fatally overbroad in that it might be used to criminalize documentaries about animal cruelty, or even hunting videos and other material that some might argue depicted cruelty to animals.

Source: For more see http://www.scotusblog.com/case-files/cases/united-states-v-stevens/.

In *United States v. Fowler*, the challenge was basically that the federal government had no jurisdiction to pass drug laws, which are the province of the police power of the state. Not surprisingly, Fowler was not successful in his challenge. As with most crimes, the commerce clause was considered the basis of the federal power to pass and enforce drug laws.[2]

… Specifically, Defendant Fowler pled guilty to possession of cocaine base under 21 U.S.C. § 844. The Fourth Circuit has not made a specific finding as to whether the intrastate possession of cocaine base invokes the Commerce Clause, Const. Art. I, § 8, cl. 3. However, such a specific finding that cocaine base affects interstate commerce is not required for the federal government to assert jurisdiction over

---

[2] 879 F. Supp. 575 (1995).

Plaintiff's claim. . . . In *Davis*, the District of Columbia Circuit ruled that "the Commerce Clause empowers Congress to regulate broad classes of activities which are found to have a substantial impact on interstate commerce.". . . . Therefore, the fact that *Atkinson* involved another controlled substance does not prevent this Court from applying the *Atkinson* holding to the case at bar. . . .

This Court also addresses whether the possession of a controlled substance unaccompanied by the intent to distribute implicates the Commerce Clause. . . . Congress possesses the power to regulate wholly intrastate activities which have an effect upon interstate commerce, . . .Congress has also explicitly declared that the intrastate possession of a controlled substance, in this case, cocaine base, affects interstate commerce. . . . These Congressional findings allow the Court to extend the Fourth Circuit's ruling in *Atkinson* to the facts of Defendant's case. . . .

Because of the possession of cocaine base affects interstate commerce, the Court had jurisdiction to prosecute, convict, and sentence Defendant. Fourth Circuit precedent, as stated in *United States v. Atkinson*, compels this Court to reach that conclusion. . . . Consequently, the Court DENIES Defendant's section 2255 motion.

§ 12.2   Principles of Criminal Liability and Capacities and Defenses

In Chapter 2, the elements of criminal liability were discussed. Similar rules of law apply regarding liability for federal crimes. In order to find culpability, the federal prosecutor must prove both the *actus reus* and *mens rea* of the crime. Recall that federal criminal law is purely statutory so the elements of the crime and principles of criminal liability must be defined statutorily.

A. Parties

Recall from Chapter 2 that modern law has, for the most part, abolished the common law designations of party liability. The federal code also abolishes the distinction between principals and accessories. Similar to the Model Penal Code and many state statutes, under federal law, anyone who commits an offense or "aids, abets, counsels, commands, induces or procures its commission" is punished as a principal.[3] In interpreting this provision of the federal code, a federal circuit court explained that, in order to sustain a conviction for aiding and abetting under the statute, the government must show that the underlying offense has occurred. The government must also demonstrate that the defendant associated with the criminal venture purposely participated in the criminal venture and sought by his or her actions to make the venture succeed. The court further noted that to participate in the criminal activity means that the defendant acted in some affirmative manner designed to aid the venture.[4]

---

[3]   18 U.S.C. § 2.

[4]   United States v. Stewart, 145 F.3d 273 (5th Cir. 1998). *See also* United States v. Hodge, 211 F.3d 74 (3d Cir. 2000), which held that the defendant can be convicted of aiding and abetting a principal in the commission of a crime even if the principal was either acquitted or not charged.

In a case decided by the Seventh Circuit Court of Appeals, the court added that the aiding and abetting standard has two prongs—association and participation. To prove association, the state must show that the defendant shared the principal's criminal intent. To show participation, there must be evidence that the defendant engaged in some affirmative conduct or overt act, designed to aid in the success of the venture. To prove this affirmative conduct or overt act, "a high level of activity need not be shown, although mere 'presence' and guilt by association are insufficient."[5]

Federal law is similar to the Model Penal Code and many state statutes in that it recognizes accessory after the fact as a separate crime. The federal statute that provides a penalty for one convicted of the offense of accessory after the fact states that

18 U.S.C. § 3

Whoever, knowing that an offense against the United States had been committed, receives, relieves, comforts or assists the offender in order to hinder or prevent his apprehension, trial or punishment, is an accessory after the fact.

A federal circuit court declared that a defendant who is accused of being an accessory after the fact must be shown to have had actual knowledge of each element of the underlying offense.[6]

B. Elements and Causation

Federal crimes, similar to state crimes, must consist of a criminal act, the requisite state of mind, causation, and concurrence. The general principles that govern *actus reus* (and omission) and *mens rea* discussed in Chapter 2 apply to federal law.

There has been concern raised recently regarding the reduced *mens rea* requirements of federal laws, along with increased numbers of federal crimes—many of which are somewhat obscure. Recall that there are probably over 5,000 federal laws (no one knows for sure) spread over all the federal statutes with many thousands more embedded in federal regulations. Many of these laws do not have a *mens rea* of "willful." Further, the "knowing" *mens rea* that is attached has been interpreted by the courts to refer to the act itself rather than knowing that the federal crime exists. So, for instance, when Gary Hancock was found guilty of a federal law that prohibited someone from owning a gun with a misdemeanor domestic violence conviction, the "knowing" went to his knowledge that he owned a gun, not knowledge of the federal law. He was convicted even though he did not know of the federal law and, in fact, he received the misdemeanor conviction before the federal law was passed. Critics argue that many federal laws passed have weak *mens rea* requirements so that, increasingly, many people may be guilty of federal crimes without even knowing they exist, much less intending to break them. Examples include an Alaskan Native American fisherman who sold 10 otters to someone he thought was Native American. The Marine Mammal Protection

---

5   United States v. Sewell, 159 F.3d 275 (7th Cir. 1998).
6   United States v. Graves, 143 F.3d 1185 (9th Cir. 1998).

Act disallowed such sale unless the buyer was Native American; and, because the law was strict liability, he faced a potential jail sentence. Another fisherman cut a whale loose from his fishing net, but because he didn't call the federal hotline and wait for rescuers, he also faced a potential jail sentence.[7] The proliferation of federal laws combined with reduced *mens rea* requirements is a problematic issue and one that is being addressed by a number of study groups and congressional committees who hope to modernize and streamline the U.S. Criminal Code.

Federal courts apply the "but for" causation test when considering the causation element of the criminal offense. To prove this element, the government must show that, *but for* the defendant's conduct, the harm would not have occurred. However, federal courts also limit "but for" causation to proximate cause. Recall that proximate causation limits criminal liability. In *United States v. Pitt-Des Moines, Inc.*,[8] the court held that, in order to prove that the defendant's conduct was the illegal cause, that is, the proximate cause, of a harm, so as to prove the causation element of the criminal offense, the government must prove that the harm was *foreseeable* and the *natural* result of the conduct. The court continued by stating that where the "but for" relationship exists between the defendant's conduct and a harm, the defendant may yet escape criminal liability for the offense containing the causation element if the harmful result is so remote or accidental in its manner of occurrence as to make it unjust to hold the defendant liable for it.

C. Capacity and Defenses

As in state courts, federal defendants may argue that they might have committed the acts that were alleged, but that they had either an excuse or justification for their actions.

1. Infancy

Title 18, Chapter 403 of the United States Code, titled "Juvenile Delinquency," defines the procedure for disposing of juvenile cases in federal court. A **juvenile** is defined as a person who has not attained his or her eighteenth birthday. It is a policy of the federal government to surrender jurisdiction in juvenile cases to the appropriate legal authorities of the state. In fact, Title 18 § 5032 specifically provides that the proceedings shall not be in a United States Court unless the Attorney General certifies through the appropriate District Court of the United States that

- the juvenile court or other appropriate court of the state does not have jurisdiction or refuses to assume jurisdiction over said juvenile with respect to such alleged act of juvenile delinquency,

---

[7] G. Fields and J. Emshwiller. 2011. As Federal Crime List Grows, Threshold of Guilt Declines. *The Wall Street Journal*, September 27, 2011. Accessed September 29, 2011 from http://online.wsj.com/article/SB10001424053111904060604576570801651620000.html.

[8] United States v. Pitt-Des Moines, Inc., 970 F. Supp. 1359 (N.D. Ill. 1997).

- the State does not have available programs and services adequate for the needs of the juveniles, or
- the offense charged is a crime of violence that is a felony or offense described in specific Sections of the federal law under Title 21, and there is a substantial federal interest in the case or the offense to warrant the exercise of federal jurisdiction.

If the juvenile is not surrendered to state authorities, the case is processed as provided in Chapter 403 of Title 18 of the U.S. Code. If the juvenile is alleged to have committed an act after his or her sixteenth birthday that, if committed by an adult, would be a felony offense that involves actual or threatened force against another, then the case may be directed to the appropriate District Court of the United States for criminal prosecution.

2. Mental Impairment

Recall from Chapter 3 that many states have reevaluated the insanity defense and some have created the "guilty but insane" conviction instead of the "not guilty by reason of insanity" finding. Federal law has also changed in this regard. Following the jury's verdict of "not guilty by reason of insanity" in the John Hinckley Jr. case,[9] Congress passed the "Insanity Defense Reform Act of 1986."[10] The federal law states

18 U.S.C. § 17

(a) Affirmative Defense. It is an affirmative defense to a prosecution under any Federal statute that, at the time of the commission of the acts constituting the offense, the defendant, as result of a severe mental disease or defect, was unable to appreciate the nature and quality or the wrongfulness of his acts. Mental disease or defect does not otherwise constitute a defense.

(b) Burden of Proof. The defendant has the burden of proving the defense of insanity by clear and convincing evidence.

One of the key factors in this federal law is that it shifts the burden of the insanity defense to the defendant. The defendant must demonstrate by clear and convincing evidence that his "severe mental disease or defect" caused him to not appreciate the nature and quality of his wrongful acts. The provisions of the Insanity Defense Reform Act, requiring a defendant to prove insanity by clear and convincing evidence, were challenged as being unconstitutional. However, in two 1986 federal cases, the courts considering the questions agreed that the provisions of the act that shifted the affirmative defense of insanity to the defendant do not violate the due process clause.[11]

---

[9]   John W. Hinckley, Jr. was charged with the attempted assassination of Ronald Reagan, then President of the United States, assault on a federal officer (a United States Secret Service agent), and the use of a firearm in the commission of a federal offense. He was found not guilty by reason of insanity and committed to the custody of St. Elizabeth's Hospital.

[10]   18 U.S.C. § 4241 *et seq.*

[11]   United States v. Freeman, 804 F.2d 1574 (11th Cir. 1986); United States v. Amos, 803 F.2d 419 (8th Cir. 1986).

Title 18 U.S.C. § 4241 sets forth the procedures for establishing the mental capacity of the defendant to stand trial. This section provides that at any time after the commencement of a prosecution for an offense and prior to the sentencing of the defendant, the defendant or the attorney for the government may file a motion for a hearing to determine the mental competency of the defendant. The court shall grant the motion, or shall order such a hearing on its own motion, if there is reasonable cause to believe that the defendant may presently be suffering from a mental disease or defect, rendering him mentally incompetent to the extent that he is unable to understand the nature and the consequences of the proceedings against him or to assist properly in his defense. The preponderance of the evidence test is applied in determining whether the defendant is suffering from a mental disease or defect.[12]

3. Duress or Compulsion

In the 1992 case of *United States v. Johnson*, the U.S. Court of Appeals for the Ninth Circuit stated that the federal criminal law had incorporated the defense of duress and that it had three elements:

- an immediate threat of death or serious bodily injury,
- a well-grounded fear that the threat will be carried out, and
- no reasonable opportunity to escape the threatened harm.[13]

The female defendants in the *Johnson* case were convicted of a variety of drug offenses. The testimony presented at the trial left no doubt that they were involved; however, they argued that their experience with the drug "kingpin" was one of severe physical abuse and that he and his associates threatened them and their family members if they did not continue to participate. The dominant issue on the appeals of the defendants was the duress defense as it interacts with sentencing. In a complicated decision, the court enumerated some general findings before making decisions on the cases; among these were the following:

- In some circumstances, gender is a factor to be considered in making an exculpatory judgment as to whether the defense of duress applies.
- In determining whether the fear was "well-grounded," the defense of duress permits the fact finder to take into account the objective situation in which the defendant was allegedly subjected to duress.
- Fear that would be irrational in one set of circumstances may be well-grounded if the experience of the defendant with those applying the threat is such that the defendant can reasonably anticipate being harmed on failure to comply.
- The defendant in this case was not entitled to an instruction on duress in the trial on charges of distribution of drugs, where the defendant made no showing that she could not have escaped the violent drug "lord" far earlier than she finally did.

---

[12]   United States v. Young, 199 F.2d 697 (S.D. Ohio 2001).
[13]   United States v. Johnson, 956 F.2d 894 (9th Cir. 1992).

In this case, the convictions were affirmed but the sentences were vacated and remanded. The court decided that the defendants were entitled to raise the claim of incomplete duress for purposes of sentencing.

As discussed in Chapter 3, in order to present the defense of duress, the defendant must establish an immediate threat of death or serious bodily injury. A federal court explained that there must be a well-grounded fear that the threat will be carried out, and lack of a reasonable opportunity to escape the threatened harm. Fear alone is not enough to establish a *prima facie* case of duress.

4. Necessity

In applying the "necessity" rule, a federal court indicated that to invoke the necessity defense, the defendants must show that they were faced with a choice of evils and chose the lesser evil; that they acted to prevent imminent harm; that they reasonably anticipated a direct causal relationship between their conduct and the conduct to be averted; and that they had no legal alternatives to violating the law.[14]

5. Self-Defense

In the case of *United States v. Branch*, the court declared that self-defense and defense of another are affirmative defenses to both murder and voluntary manslaughter, but warned that these defenses must accommodate a citizen's duty to accede to lawful government power and special protection due to federal officers who are discharging their official duties.[15] Agreeing that the evidence did not support the defendant's requested self-defense instruction on the charge of voluntary manslaughter of the Federal Bureau of Alcohol, Tobacco, and Firearms agents, the court noted that a reasonable juror could not doubt that the defendants knew that their targets were federal agents, and the defendants responded to the agents' lawful force with a deadly barrage of gunfire. When a person is identified as a law enforcement officer and uses reasonable force in the performance of his or her law enforcement duties, the use of force to resist an officer is not justified and self-defense does not apply.[16]

Under the federal code, a defendant is entitled to a jury instruction on the theory of self-defense, provided that there is a foundation in evidence, even though the evidence may be weak, insufficient, inconsistent, or of doubtful credibility.

6. Entrapment

Recall from Chapter 3 that in *Jacobson v. United States*,[17] two federal government agencies, after finding Jacobson's name on a bookstore mailing list, sent mail to him through five fictitious organizations and bogus pen pals over the course of two years to

---

[14] United States v. Schoon, 955 F.2d 1238 (9th Cir. 1991).
[15] United States v. Branch, 91 F.3d 699 (5th Cir. 1996).
[16] United States v. Sanchez-Lima, 161 F.3d 545 (9th Cir. 1998).
[17] Jacobson v. United States, 503 U.S. 540, 112 S. Ct. 1535, 118 L. Ed. 2d 174 (1992).

explore his willingness to break the law. He finally answered a letter that described concern about child pornography as hysterical nonsense and decried international censorship, and then received a catalog and ordered a magazine depicting young boys engaged in sexual activities. He was arrested after a controlled delivery of a photocopy of the magazine, but a search of his house revealed no material other than those sent by the government and the Bare Boys magazines. The majority of the U.S. Supreme Court, in a five-to-four decision, reversed the decision of the lower court and held that "it is our view that the Government did not prove that this predisposition was independent and not the product of the attention that the government had directed at the petitioner since January, 1985."

In one case, the justices of the Sixth Circuit Court of Appeals stated the entrapment rule very succinctly—to prove entrapment, the defendant must show that (1) the government induced him to commit a crime, and (2) he lacked the predisposition to engage in criminal activity.[18] The Ninth Circuit Court elaborated, stating that for a defendant to prove the defense of entrapment, he must point to undisputed evidence making it patently clear that an otherwise innocent person was induced to commit the illegal act by trickery, persuasion, or fraud of a government agent. The Court continued by explaining that the mere suggestion to commit a crime does not amount to inducement for purposes of the entrapment defense, even if the suggestion is made by a friend.[19]

Some federal courts have used such terms as **entrapment by estoppel** and "sentencing entrapment" when discussing the entrapment defense.[20] Entrapment by estoppel requires the defendant to establish (1) that a government official told him the act was legal; (2) that he relied on the advice; (3) that the reliance was reasonable; and (4) that, given the reliance, the prosecution would be unfair. "Sentencing entrapment" occurs when government agents convince offenders who are predisposed only to dealing in small quantities of drugs to deal in higher quantities for the purpose of increasing the resulting sentence of the entrapped defendant.[21]

§ 12.3 Preparatory Activity Offenses

The federal code follows the Model Penal Code and state statutes in ascribing criminal liability to acts that do not culminate in the completed crime. Recall from Chapter 4 that these crimes include attempt, solicitation, and conspiracy.

---

[18]   United States v. Cope, 312 F.3d 757 (6th Cir. 2002).
[19]   United States v. Mendoza-Prado, 314 F.3d 1099 (9th Cir. 2002). *See also* Matteo v. Superintendent, SCI Albion, 171 F.3d 877 (3d Cir. 1999).
[20]   United States v. Ellis, 168 F.3d 558 (1st Cir. 1999).
[21]   United States v. Hunt, 171 F.3d 1192 (8th Cir. 1999).

A. Attempt

The U.S. Code makes it a federal offense to attempt to commit specific acts. For instance, the U.S. Code includes penalties for attempt to commit murder or manslaughter, attempt to kill foreign officials, and attempt to escape.[22] Under Title 18 § 351 of the U.S. Code, it is a federal offense to kill or attempt to kill or kidnap any individual who is a member of Congress, a member of the Supreme Court, a member of the President's Cabinet, or other designated ranking official. Title 18 § 1751 makes it a crime punishable by imprisonment for any term of years or for life if a person is convicted of attempting to kill or kidnap the President of the United States, President-Elect, Vice President, Vice President-Elect, or members of the President's staff.

The federal statute most often used to prosecute an attempt to kill an officer or employee of the United States is Title 18 § 1114. This section—Protection of Officers and Employees of the United States—makes it possible to prosecute an offender who attempts to kill any officer or employee of the United States or of any branch of the United States government, while that officer or employee is engaged in or on account of the performance of his or her official duties. To obtain a conviction under § 1114 for attempting to kill an officer or an employee of the United States, the government is required to show that

- the defendant engaged in conduct with the intent of killing the officer or employee,
- the defendant engaged in conduct constituting a substantial step toward the attempted killing, and
- the attempted killing took place while the officer or employee was engaged in or on account of the performance of his or her official duties.[23]

Whether a federal officer is engaged in the performance of his or her official duties depends on whether the federal officer is acting within the scope of what he or she is employed to do, or is engaging in a purely personal activity. For purposes of the statute, Bureau of Alcohol, Tobacco, and Firearms agents and Bureau of Indian Affairs officers are "federal officers." However, an employee of a private company that contracts with the U.S. Postal Service to transport mail is not considered a federal employee.[24]

In federal court, to prove attempt, the government must establish an intent to commit the substantive offense and a substantial step toward its commission that is more than preparation but less than the last act necessary to commit the crime itself.[25] As one court explained, under the two-part test to determine whether a defendant is guilty of an attempted crime, the defendant must first have been acting with the kind of culpability otherwise required for the commission of the crime that he is charged with attempting,

---

[22]   18 U.S.C. § 1113; 18 U.S.C. § 1116; 18 U.S.C. § 751.
[23]   United States v. Saunders, 166 F.3d 907 (7th Cir. 1999).
[24]   United States v. Alvarez, 755 F.2d 830 (11th Cir. 1995); United States v. Oakie, 12 F.3d 1436 (8th Cir. 1993); United States v. Kirkland, 12 F.3d 199 (11th Cir. 1994).
[25]   United States v. LiCausi, 167 F.3d 36 (1st Cir. 1999).

and then the defendant must have engaged in conduct that constitutes a substantial step toward the commission of the crime.[26]

LEGAL NEWS: ATTEMPTED BOMBING

Faisal Shahazad was the naturalized American citizen from Pakistan who attempted to set off a bomb in Times Square in May 2010. The bomb did not go off and police were notified. He was pulled from a plane heading to Dubai and was indicted on 10 counts, including attempted use of a weapon of mass destruction. He pled guilty to all counts, but even if he had not, conviction was likely as he had completed the substantial steps necessary to meet the *actus reus* under federal attempt law.

Naser Jason Abdo has also been arrested for attempted use of a weapon of mass destruction. He was arrested in July 2011 a few miles away from Fort Hood in Texas. He had a handgun, an article titled "Make a bomb in the kitchen of your Mom," and the ingredients for an explosive device, including gunpowder, shrapnel, and pressure cookers. Abdo told authorities he planned to set off two bombs in a restaurant frequented by Fort Hood soldiers. If he does go to trial one of the issues will be whether or not he had completed the substantial steps necessary to meet the *actus reus* of attempt.

New York Times archive. October 5, 2010. Accessed December 21, 2011 from http://topics.nytimes.com/top/reference/timestopics/people/s/faisal_shahazad/index.html.
"Soldier said he wanted to attack Ft. Hood troops." CNN Justice, July 28, 2011. Accessed January 12, 2012 from http://articles.cnn.com/2011-07-28/justice/fort.hood.arrest_1_nidal-hasan-guns-galore-abdo?_s=PM:CRIME.

---

1. Factual and Legal Impossibility

Recall that factual impossibility is usually not a defense to any attempt charge. Legal impossibility can be a defense, but it is difficult to distinguish legal impossibility (when the act contemplated is not against the law) from hybrid legal impossibility (when the act contemplated is against the law but the act actually engaged in by the offender is not). In federal law, factual impossibility is not a defense to a charge of attempted murder. In *United States v. Carothers*, the court answered the question concerning impossibility as a defense, stating that factual impossibility is not a defense to a charge of attempted sexual exploitation of a minor.[27] In recent cases, appellants have also argued that it is legal impossibility when the "minor" solicited in Internet chat rooms is actually an undercover officer. Whether it is defined as factual or legal impossibility, offenders who solicit sex from victims they believe to be minors but are actually police officers have no defense to an attempt conviction that the act they attempted was impossible to

---

[26]   United States v. Crow, 164 F.3d 229 (5th Cir. 1999).
[27]   United States v. Carothers, 121 F.3d 659 (11th Cir. 1997).

complete, according to federal court holdings. The defense of legal impossibility has also been used by individuals who thought they were smuggling controlled substances into the country, but the substance turned out to be something else. In these cases, the federal drug statutes specifically deny the use of legal impossibility as a defense. The defendant will be convicted of attempt if the prosecutor can show the other elements of the offense.

B. Criminal Solicitation

The section of the federal statute that deals with solicitation to commit a crime of violence provides

18 U.S.C. § 373

(a) Whoever, with intent that another person engage in conduct constituting a felony that has as an element the use, attempted use, or threatened use of physical force against property or against another in violation of the laws of the United States, and under circumstances strongly corroborative of that intent, solicits, commands, induces or otherwise endeavors to persuade such other person to engage in such conduct, shall be imprisoned not more than one-half the maximum term of imprisonment or fined not more than one-half of the maximum fine prescribed for the punishment of the crime solicited, or both; or if the crime solicited is punishable by life imprisonment or death, shall be imprisoned for not more than twenty years.

(b) It is an affirmative defense to a prosecution under this section that, under circumstances manifesting a voluntary and complete renunciation of his criminal intent, the defendant prevented the commission of the crime solicited. A renunciation is not "voluntary and complete" if it is motivated in whole or in part by a decision to postpone the commission of the crime until another time or to substitute another victim or another but similar objective. If the defendant raises the affirmative defense at trial, the defendant has the burden of proving the defense by a preponderance of the evidence.

(c) It is not a defense to a prosecution under this section that the person solicited could not be convicted of the crime because he lacked the state of mind required for its commission, because he was incompetent or irresponsible, or because he is immune from prosecution or is not subject to prosecution.

According to this statute, renunciation is a defense if the defendant prevented the commission of the crime solicited, but the renunciation must be voluntary and complete. It also provides that the defendant has the burden of proving the affirmative defense by a preponderance of the evidence.

In order to convict a person of violating this statute, the prosecution must prove that the solicitation was to commit a federal offense; the fact that the individual uses interstate channels (i.e., mail or telephone) to solicit is insufficient to give rise to federal solicitation unless the crime solicited is a federal offense. However, it is only necessary that the jury find that the solicitation was to commit a federal offense; it is not necessary that a federal offense actually resulted from the solicitation.[28]

---

[28] United States v. Korav, 393 F.2d 212 (9th Cir. 1989); United States v. Razo-Leora, 961 F.2d 1140 (5th Cir. 1992).

In the case of *United States v. McNeill*, the evidence indicated that the defendant, who had been a federal prisoner at the time the alleged offense occurred, sent typewritten letters to a person outside the prison asking that the recipient of the letter physically harm the defendant's brother-in-law and kill the defendant's probation officer. The court found that this, plus other corroborative evidence, was sufficient to sustain a conviction for criminal solicitation under the federal law.[29]

C. *Conspiracy*

The U.S. Code includes a separate chapter relating to the offense of conspiracy. Section 371 of Title 18 defines the offense of conspiracy and establishes the penalty for violation.

18 U.S.C. § 371

If two or more persons conspire either to commit any offense against the United States, or to defraud the United States or any agency thereof in any manner or for any purpose and one or more such persons do any act to effect the object of the conspiracy, each shall be fined under this title or imprisoned not more than five years or both.

If, however, the offense, the commission of which is the object of the conspiracy, is a misdemeanor only, the punishment for such conspiracy shall not exceed the maximum punishment provided for each misdemeanor.

This statute can be used for any federal offense, but there are other conspiracy statutes that are specific; for instance 18 U.S.C. § 241 specifies "Conspiracy against the rights of citizens," 15 U.S.C. § 1 defines "Conspiracy in restraint of trade," and 15 U.S.C. § 2 identifies "Conspiracy to monopolize trade." Also, specific conspiracy laws related to narcotics trafficking and RICO will be discussed later.

A federal court of appeals, in a case in which the defendant was charged with a violation of Title 18 § 371 of the federal statute, summarized that to prove conspiracy the government must prove beyond a reasonable doubt that two or more people agreed to pursue an unlawful objective together, that the defendant voluntarily agreed to join the conspiracy, and that one of the members of the conspiracy performed an overt act to further the objectives of the conspiracy.[30] That same court in a previous case had held that it was not necessary to prove the elements of the crime by direct evidence, but the elements may be inferred from circumstantial evidence.[31]

In order to convict a person for a violation of the conspiracy statute, the prosecution must establish that

- two or more persons;
- conspired or combined together in an agreement;

---

[29] United States v. McNeill, 387 F.2d 448 (3d Cir. 1989).
[30] United States v. Parekh, 926 F.2d 402 (5th Cir. 1991).
[31] United States v. Schmick, 904 F.2d 936 (5th Cir. 1990).

- to accomplish an unlawful purpose;
- each had knowledge of the identity of the offense that the defendants allegedly conspired to commit; and
- at least one conspirator committed an overt act in furtherance of the conspiracy.[32]

A federal court, in discussing the elements to be proved, commented that in a conspiracy case, the government must prove that there was an agreement among the defendants to achieve some illegal purpose and that each defendant knowingly contributed efforts in furtherance of the conspiracy.[33] However, it is only necessary that one of the conspirators commit the overt act in furtherance of the agreement if the other defendants knew of the conspiracy and voluntarily participated in it.[34]

LEGAL NEWS: CONSPIRACY

In December 2008, five Muslim immigrants were convicted of conspiracy to kill American military personnel. The men, who all lived in the Philadelphia area, belonged to a loosely organized group that was infiltrated by a government agent. Although they were acquitted of attempted murder because their planning did not reach the substantial steps necessary for federal attempt, it was found that they had met the elements of conspiracy because they had conducted surveillance at several military installations before deciding on Fort Dix. Prosecutors admitted they were probably months away from an attack. Defense attorneys said there was no conspiracy, that it was all "just talk," and that the group was influenced by the two government informants. The evidence consisted largely of the informants' testimony, along with hundreds of hours of secretly recorded conversations.

Source: Mulvihill, G. "Jury: 5 Plotted to Kill Troops." *Austin American-Statesman*, December 23, 2008: A1, A12.

While generally an overt act is an essential element of the crime of conspiracy and must be alleged in the information, under the Narcotics Conspiracy Statute, the

---

[32] United States v. Rahseparian, 231 F.3d 1267 (10th Cir. 2000).

[33] United States v. Jobe, 90 F.3d 920 (5th Cir. 1996). *See also* United States v. Wilson, 103 F.3d 1402 (8th Cir. 1997).

[34] United States v. Partela, 167 F.3d 687 (1st Cir. 1999); United States v. Jackson, 167 F.3d 1280 (9th Cir. 1999). *See also* United States v. Dumes, 313 F.3d 372 (7th Cir. 2002), which held that to prove conspiracy to possess and distribute cocaine, no overt act need be charged or proven and guilt may be inferred from circumstances and conduct of the parties.

government need not prove any overt acts in furtherance of the conspiracy. This means that the government must simply have evidence of an agreement or understanding to prove a violation of this statute. Critics have argued that such laws reduce the *mens rea* requirement to such a low degree that there is a real risk of innocent people being caught up in prosecution and punishments.

1. Racketeer Influenced and Corrupt Organizations Statute (RICO)

In addition to the general conspiracy statute, conspiracy provisions are included in other federal statutes. For example, the Racketeer Influenced and Corrupt Organizations statute (**RICO**) makes it a federal offense to use or invest income derived from a pattern of racketeering activity to acquire an enterprise engaged in or affecting interstate commerce, to acquire an interest in such enterprise through a pattern of racketeering activity, to conduct the affairs of an enterprise through a pattern of racketeering activity, or to conspire to commit any of these violations.[35] The statute requires two or more of the predicate crimes (murder, kidnapping, arson, extortion, robbery, gambling, obstruction of justice, mail and wire fraud, securities fraud, bribery, sports bribery, counterfeiting, embezzlement, prostitution, bankruptcy fraud, and drug violations) within 10 years. Most states also have their own RICO statutes that punish similar activities.

This statute, with the conspiracy clause, has resulted in the conviction of those engaged in organized racketeering activities that involve kidnapping, gambling, robbery, bribery, and extortion, as well as authorizing the prosecution of officials who operate on a local level. As an example, the sheriff of Bryan County, Oklahoma, was convicted of violating this federal statute when it was found that he used his position as sheriff to extort payoffs from club operators and others in return for selective enforcement of liquor, gambling, and other laws. Evidence introduced at the trial indicated that the sheriff and a "bag man" conspired to collect payoffs after agreeing not to harass a club operator for failure to close at the required time and for directing a deputy to terminate his investigation of gambling conducted at the club.[36]

Although the RICO statute was originally conceived as a means of prosecuting organized crime figures in federal court, it has been used extensively in various types of conspiracies. For example, a court found that a RICO enterprise existed when a lawyer, a lieutenant in the Cook County Sheriff's Department, and the Chief of Police of Willow Springs, Illinois, entered into an agreement in which the police officers would refer persons arrested, ticketed, or investigated by the Willow Springs Police Department to the lawyer for legal assistance. In addition to this scheme, the three members of this conspiracy were accused of having the attorney's wife killed after she was discovered having an affair, and agreed to conceal all of their actions relating

---

35   Racketeer Influenced and Corrupt Organizations Act, 18 U.S.C. § 1961.
36   United States v. Hampton, 786 F.2d 977 (10th Cir. 1986).

to the wife's murder indefinitely.[37] The reviewing court agreed with the trial court that the jury had abundant evidence to find that the defendants had conspired to commit two or more criminal acts that constitute "racketeering activity" within the meaning of the RICO statute.

The RICO statute has also been used against those who engage in organized harassment or damage to abortion clinics or commit other crimes against those who run the clinics or use their services. However, the Supreme Court has held that the use of this statute in this type of case is improper.[38]

§ 12.4   Offenses against Persons

In many instances, there are parallel state and federal crimes. Remember that the federal government must find a source for every federal crime in one of its enumerated powers. Thus, homicide and all other crimes against persons, such as assault, in order to be a federal crime, must victimize a federal official or occur within some federal jurisdiction (for instance, the District of Columbia). Federal kidnapping convictions can only occur if the victim was taken across state lines or the mail or interstate communication was used to relay ransom demands. In short, there must be a nexus between the crime and a federal power.

A. Homicide

The United States Code defines murder as the unlawful killing of a human being with malice aforethought. Murder in the first degree includes murders that involve "poison, lying in wait, or any other kind of willful, deliberate, malicious, and premeditated killing; or committed in the perpetration of, or attempt to perpetrate, any arson, escape, murder, kidnapping, treason, espionage, sabotage, aggravated sexual abuse or sexual abuse, burglary, or robbery; or perpetrated from a premeditated design unlawfully and maliciously to effect the death of any human being other than him who is killed." All others are murders in the second degree.[39]

In determining the meaning of "human being," a federal court decided that the defendant's infliction of injuries to the fetus who was born alive but died as a result of such injuries was within the federal statutory definition of murder.[40] The more current issue is whether the death of a fetus that is killed while in the womb can be

---

[37]   United States v. Masters, 924 F.2d 1362 (7th Cir. 1991).
[38]   Scheidler v. N.O.W., 164 L. Ed. 2d 10 (2006).
[39]   18 U.S.C. § 1111 (1999).
[40]   United States v. Spencer, 839 F.2d 1341 (9th Cir. 1988), *cert. denied*, 487 U.S. 1238, 108 S. Ct. 2708, 101 L. Ed. 2d 939 (1988).

considered a crime or whether the common law rule that the fetus must be born alive to be considered a person is applied to federal law. In 2004, the Laci and Conner Law was passed, amending the United States Code and adding Title 18 § 1841, "Protection of unborn children."

18 U.S.C. § 1841

(a) (1) Whoever engages in conduct that violates any of the provisions of law listed in subsection (b) and thereby causes the death of, or bodily injury (as defined in section 1365 [18 USCS § 1365]) to, a child, who is *in utero* at the time the conduct takes place, is guilty of a separate offense under this section.

(2) (A) Except as otherwise provided in this paragraph, the punishment for that separate offense is the same as the punishment provided under Federal law for that conduct had that injury or death occurred to the unborn child's mother.

(B) An offense under this section does not require proof that—

(i) the person engaging in the conduct had knowledge or should have had knowledge that he victim of the underlying offense was pregnant; or

(ii) the defendant intended to cause the death of, or bodily injury to, the unborn child. . . .

The statute goes on to say that if the offender intended to kill the child, then the crime is to be prosecuted as a murder of a person; however, there are also three exceptions:

• any act done with the consent of the woman to effect a legal abortion;
• any act done by a medical person to save the life or for the health of the mother; and
• any act committed by the woman herself with respect to her unborn child.

The federal courts generally follow the common law concept of malice aforethought. As one federal court explained, common law malice includes three distinct mental states, any one of which is sufficient to prove murder: (1) intent to kill, (2) intent to do serious bodily harm, and (3) "depraved heart."[41]

Although deliberation and premeditation involve prior design to commit murder, no particular period is necessary for such deliberation and premeditation. Premeditation need exist only for a moment before the actual slaying and may be inferred from the brutality of the killing, the number of blows inflicted, physical disparity between the defendant and the victim, and the defendant's efforts to conceal the crime or to avoid detection.[42]

---

[41]   United States v. Quintero, 21 F.3d 885 (9th Cir. 1994); United States v. Livoti, 22 F. Supp. 2d 235 (S.D.N.Y. 1998).

[42]   Pruett v. Thompson, 771 F. Supp. 1428 (E.D. Va. 1991).

B. *Manslaughter*

The U.S. Code defines manslaughter as the unlawful killing of a human being without malice and distinguishes between voluntary and involuntary manslaughter. Voluntary manslaughter is the unlawful killing of a human being without malice upon sudden quarrel or heat of passion.[43]

In explaining this provision of the U.S. Code, a federal court noted that manslaughter occupies the middle ground between excusable, or justifiable, homicide on the one hand, and murder on the other.[44] Another court pointed out that the crime of manslaughter is, in some sense, "irrational" by definition, in that it arises out of a person's passions, but provocations to reduce murder to manslaughter must be such as would arouse reasonable and ordinary persons to kill someone.[45]

Under the federal statute, manslaughter is distinguished from murder by the absence of malice, one of murder's essential elements. Commenting upon the terminology "sudden quarrel or heat of passion" as used in the statute, the majority in the case of *United States v. Paul* stated that if a defendant killed with the mental state required for murder, but the killing occurred in the "heat of passion" caused by adequate provocation, then the defendant is guilty of voluntary manslaughter.[46]

The U.S. Code's definition of *involuntary* manslaughter is similar to the traditional definition. It defines it as the unlawful killing that occurs in the commission of an unlawful act not amounting to a felony, or in the commission of a lawful act done in an unlawful manner or without due caution or circumspection.[47] The elements necessary to prove involuntary manslaughter under the federal code are

- that the defendant inflicted injuries upon the deceased from which the deceased died;
- that the defendant acted with wanton and reckless disregard for human life;
- that the defendant was at the time committing an unlawful act not amounting to a felony;
- that the defendant knew that his conduct was a threat to the lives of others or had knowledge of circumstances that could have enabled him to reasonably foresee peril to which his act might subject others; and
- that it occurred within the special maritime or territorial jurisdiction of the United States.[48]

---

[43] 18 U.S.C. § 1112.
[44] United States v. Hart, 162 F. 192 (N.D. Fla. 1908).
[45] United States v. Collins, 690 F.2d 431, *cert. denied*, 460 U.S. 1046, 103 S. Ct. 1447, 75 L. Ed. 2d 801 (1982).
[46] United States v. Paul, 37 F.3d 496 (9th Cir. 1994).
[47] 18 U.S.C. § 1112 Manslaughter (Involuntary).
[48] United States v. Sasnett, 925 F.2d 392 (11th Cir. 1991).

In interpreting this provision of the federal statute, federal courts have held that manslaughter may result from an accidental or unintentional act and that neither intent nor malice are factors in involuntary manslaughter. As to the degree of negligence, a federal judge explained that a charge of manslaughter by negligence is not made out by proof of simple negligence that would constitute civil liability, but must amount to gross negligence, to be determined on consideration of all the facts of a particular case, and the gross negligence must be shown beyond a reasonable doubt.[49]

C. Assault and Battery

The three primary federal laws relating to assault are 18 U.S.C. § 111, "Assaulting, resisting, or impeding certain officers or employees"; 18 U.S.C. § 112, "Assaulting certain foreign diplomatic and other official personnel"; and 18 U.S.C. § 113, "Assaults within maritime and territorial jurisdiction." The federal law relating to assault that is most often enforced is 18 U.S.C. § 111. It provides

> 18 U.S.C. § 111. Assaulting, resisting, or impeding certain officers or employees
>
> (a) In general—Whoever—
>   (1) forcibly assaults, resists, opposes, impedes, intimidates, or interferes with any person designated in section 1114 of this title while engaged in or on account of the performance of official duties; or
>   (2) forcibly assaults or intimidates any person who formerly served as a person designated in section 1114 on account of the performance of official duties during such person's term of service, shall, where the acts in violation of this section constitute only simple assault, be fined under this title or imprisoned not more than one year, or both, and in all other cases, be fined under this title or imprisoned not more than three years, or both.
> (b) Enhanced penalty—Whoever, in the commission of any acts described in subsection (a), uses a deadly or dangerous weapon (including a weapon intended to cause death or danger but that fails to do so by reason of a defective component) or inflicts bodily injury, shall be fined under this title or imprisoned not more than ten years, or both.

While no intent to injure a federal officer is required, the prosecution must prove beyond a reasonable doubt that at the time of the assault the victim was engaged in the performance of his or her official duties or was attacked on account of these duties. Federal courts have held the statute covers those who attack a federal officer *because* of the officer's activities (even if not during their performance) and may be violated by a minimal physical contact, or even by threats without physical contact.[50]

The federal law relating to assault encompasses both assault and battery as defined under the common law. Therefore, physical contact is not necessary. However, the threat of force must be a present one and there must be an ability to inflict harm,

---

[49]   Thomas v. United States, 419 F.2d 1203 (D.C. Cir. 1969); United States v. Pardee, 368 F.2d 368 (4th Cir. 1966).

[50]   United States v. Hernandez, 921 F.2d 1569 (11th Cir. 1991).

not merely interfere with the performance of duty.[51] According to the interpretation by one federal court, it is not necessary that the assailant be aware that his victim is a federal officer; all that the section requires is an intent to assault, not an intent to assault a federal officer.[52]

D. Kidnapping

Several months after the kidnapping of the Lindbergh baby in March 1932, Congress enacted the first Federal Kidnapping Act, which became known as the **Lindbergh Law**. This law has since been modified by Congress and interpreted by the courts. The present federal kidnapping statute provides

18 U.S.C. § 1201 – Kidnapping

(a) Whoever unlawfully seizes, confines, inveigles, decoys, kidnaps, abducts, or carries away and holds for ransom or reward or otherwise any person, except in the case of a minor by the parent thereof, when—
  (1) the person is willfully transported in interstate or foreign commerce, regardless of whether the person was alive when transported across a State boundary if the person was alive when the transportation began;
  (2) any such act against the person is done within the special maritime and territorial jurisdiction of the United States;
  (3) any such act against the person is done within the special aircraft jurisdiction of the United States as defined in section 46501 of title 49;
  (4) the person is a foreign official, an internationally protected person, or an official guest as those terms are defined in section 1116(b) of this title; or
  (5) the person is among those officers and employees described in section 1114 of this title and any such act against the person is done while the person is engaged in, or on account of, the performance of official duties...

  shall be punished by imprisonment for any term of years or for life and, if the death of any person results, shall be punished by death or life imprisonment.

(b) With respect to subsection (a)(1), above, the failure to release the victim within twenty-four hours after he shall have been unlawfully seized, confined, inveigled, decoyed, kidnapped, abducted, or carried away shall create a rebuttable presumption that such person has been transported in interstate or foreign commerce. Notwithstanding the preceding sentence, the fact that the presumption under this section has not yet taken effect does not preclude a Federal investigation of a possible violation of this section before the 24-hour period has ended.
(c) If two or more persons conspire to violate this section and one or more of such persons do any overt act to effect the object of the conspiracy, each shall be punished by imprisonment for any term of years or for life.
(d) Whoever attempts to violate subsection (a) shall be punished by imprisonment for not more than twenty years.
(e) If the victim of an offense under subsection (a) is an internationally protected person outside the United States, the United States may exercise jurisdiction over

---

[51] United States v. Bamberger, 452 F.2d 696 (2d Cir.), *cert. denied*, 405 U.S. 1043, 92 S. Ct. 1326, 31 L. Ed. 2d 585 (1971).
[52] United States v. Feola, 420 U.S. 671, 95 S. Ct. 1255, 43 L. Ed. 2d 541 (1975).

the offense if (1) the victim is a representative, officer, employee, or agent of the United States, (2) an offender is a national of the United States, or (3) an offender is afterwards found in the United States. As used in this subsection, the United States includes all areas under the jurisdiction of the United States including any of the places within the provisions of sections 5 and 7 of this title and section 46501(2) of title 49. For purposes of this subsection, the term "national of the United States" has the meaning prescribed in section 101(a)(22) of the Immigration and Nationality Act (8 U.S.C. 1101(a)(22)).

(f) In the course of enforcement of subsection (a)(4) and any other sections prohibiting a conspiracy or attempt to violate subsection (a)(4), the Attorney General may request assistance from any Federal, state, or local agency, including the Army, Navy, and Air Force, any statute, rule, or regulation to the contrary notwithstanding . . .

A defendant may not be found guilty of kidnapping under the federal statute unless the prosecution can establish transportation in interstate commerce of an unconsenting person who was held for ransom or reward. A federal court explained that the Federal Kidnapping Act was enacted to assist the states in enforcement of state kidnapping laws by making it impossible for kidnappers to avoid apprehension merely by moving their victims across state lines.[53] To obtain a conviction for kidnapping, the government must prove four elements:

- transportation in interstate or foreign commerce;
- of an unconsenting person who is;
- held for ransom, reward, or otherwise; and
- acts knowingly and willfully.[54]

In proving that the transportation is in interstate commerce, the prosecution need only show that the victim was taken across any state line, even for a short time. A case decided in 2000 concerned the requirement that the person be willfully transported in interstate commerce. The district court dismissed the charge where the victim, acting because of false pretenses initiated by the defendant, transported himself across state lines, without accompaniment by the alleged perpetrator. The question before the court of appeals was whether the "transportation element" could be met if the defendant did not accompany the victim over state lines but arranged for the victim to cross state lines under false pretenses to discuss a purported job interview. After discussing the provisions of the Federal Kidnapping Act, the appeals court reversed the district court's decision and held that the fact that the defendant willfully caused unaccompanied travel over state lines was sufficient to confer jurisdiction. Referring to previous cases, the court noted that nothing in the policy behind the passage of the Act justifies "rewarding the kidnapper simply because he is ingenious enough to conceal his true motives from his victim."[55]

The phrase "holds for ransom or reward *or otherwise*" was challenged as being unconstitutionally void for vagueness. The court, however, held that the defendant

---

[53]   Giano v. Martino, 673 F. Supp. 92 (E.D.N.Y. 1987).

[54]   United States v. Osborne, 68 F.3d 94 (5th Cir. 1995).

[55]   United States v. Wills, 234 F.3d 174 (4th Cir. 2000).

was guilty of kidnapping in forcing a woman to ride in an automobile with him, inasmuch as he was motivated by his self-interest in convincing her to remain in a relationship with him, and thus the statute was not unconstitutionally void for vagueness.[56] In another case, the "holds for ransom or reward or otherwise" element was satisfied when the victim was taken away from her home for purposes of silencing her as a potential witness. This came within the "or otherwise" provision of the section, which required that the kidnapping be "for ransom or reward or otherwise."[57]

E. Hate Crimes

The Hate Crimes Statistics Act of 1990 (and its subsequent amendments) mandates the collection of hate crime statistics. There are also sections in the U.S. Code that can be used to prosecute those who commit crimes against an individual or group based on their race, religion, nationality, or ethnicity. The sections include 18 U.S.C. § 241 (Conspiracy against Rights), 18 U.S.C. § 245 (Interference with Federally Protected Activities), and 18 U.S.C. § 247 (Damage to Religious Property, Obstruction in Free Exercise of Religious Beliefs). The most expansive of these is 18 U.S.C. § 245, which protects individuals from crimes against them based on their race, ethnicity, or religion. In 2009, President Obama signed into law an expansion of the hate crime laws (The Matthew Shepherd and James Byrd, Jr. Prevention Act, 18 U.S.C. § 249). First, it expanded protections to individuals based on gender, sexual orientation, gender identity, and disability. Second, it removed the prerequisite that the victim was engaged in a "federally protected activity" (included in the original 1969 law were examples such as voting or going to school). It also requires hate crimes based on gender and gender identity to be counted and tracked.

LEGAL NEWS: MINISTERS SUE TO STOP ENFORCEMENT OF HATE CRIMES BILL

A panel of judges from the Sixth Circuit will hear an appeal from three Michigan ministers who allege the federal hate crimes bill signed by President Obama in 2009 is an unconstitutional infringement on their First Amendment rights. The law punishes crimes against individuals based on their sexual orientation, gender, and gender identity. They argue that they may be prosecuted under the law for sermons that condemn homosexuality. Federal officials argue that the law punishes violent acts only. A federal district court dismissed their suit and the Sixth Circuit panel will now hear the appeal.

Source: "Michigan Ministers Sue to Stop US Hate Crime Law." *CBSDetroit.com*, January 11, 2012. Accessed January 12, 2012 from http://detroit.cbslocal.com/2012/01/11/michigan-ministers-sue-to-stop-us-hate-crime-law/.

---

[56]   United States v. Walker, 137 F.3d 1217 (10th Cir. 1998).
[57]   United States v. Satterfield, 743 F.2d 827 (11th Cir. 1984), *cert. denied*, 471 U.S. 1117, 105 S. Ct. 2363, 86 L. Ed. 2d 262 (1984).

F. Sex Crimes

The nexus for sex offenses is typically the commerce clause and federal laws are triggered by transporting the victim across state lines or using the mail or wire transmissions. The other possible nexus is that the offense occurred within federal maritime or other territorial jurisdiction (i.e., the crime occurred in the District of Columbia or the victim was a federal employee or federal prisoner).

1. Rape and Sexual Abuse

The federal sexual abuse statute includes the *actus reus* of common law rape and modern sexual assault. It defines sexual assault similarly to state statutes, and the application is limited to offenses that occur within federal jurisdiction.

18 U.S.C. § 2241 – Aggravated Sexual Abuse

(a) By force or threat. Whoever, in the special maritime and territorial jurisdiction of the United States or in a Federal prison, knowingly causes another person to engage in a sexual act—
   (1) by using force against that other person; or
   (2) by threatening or placing that other person in fear that any person will be subjected to death, serious bodily injury, or kidnapping; or attempts to do so, shall be fined under this title, imprisoned for any term of years or life, or both.
(b) By other means. Whoever, in the special maritime and territorial jurisdiction of the United States or in a Federal prison, knowingly—
   (1) renders another person unconscious and thereby engages in a sexual act with that other person; or
   (2) administers to another person by force or threat of force, or without the knowledge or permission of that person, a drug, intoxicant, or other similar substance and thereby—
     (A) substantially impairs the ability of that other person to appraise or control conduct; and
     (B) engages in a sexual act with that other person;
   or attempts to do so, shall be fined under this title, imprisoned for any term of years or life, or both.
(c) With children.—Whoever crosses a State line with intent to engage in a sexual act with a person who has not attained the age of 12 years, or in the special maritime and territorial jurisdiction of the United States or in a Federal prison, knowingly engages in a sexual act with another person who has not attained the age of 12 years, or knowingly engages in a sexual act under the circumstances described in subsections (a) and (b) with another person who has attained the age of 12 years but has not attained the age of 16 years (and is at least 4 years younger than the person so engaging), or attempts to do so, shall be fined under this title, imprisoned for any term of years or life, or both. If the defendant has previously been convicted of another Federal offense under this subsection, or of a State offense that would have been an offense under either such provision had the offense occurred in a Federal prison, unless the death penalty is imposed, the defendant shall be sentenced to life in prison.
(d) State of mind proof requirement.—In a prosecution under subsection (c) of this section, the Government need not prove that the defendant knew that the other person engaging in the sexual act had not attained the age of 12 years.

If a rape occurs in a federal prison, it will be prosecuted under federal law. In a prosecution under this statute, a federal court found that the disparity in power between a jail warden and an inmate, combined with physical restraint, is sufficient to satisfy the force requirement of the statute proscribing aggravated sexual abuse within the special maritime or territorial jurisdiction of the United States.[58]

In addition to the aggravated sexual abuse statute, the federal code includes the description of a "sexual abuse" crime with lesser penalties. It provides

18 U.S.C. § 2242 – Sexual Abuse

Whoever, in the special maritime and territorial jurisdiction of the United States or in a Federal prison, knowingly—

(1) causes another person to engage in a sexual act by threatening or placing that other person in fear (other than by threatening or placing that other person in fear that any person will be subjected to death, serious bodily injury or kidnapping); or

(2) engages in a sexual act with another person if that other person is—
   (A) incapable of appraising the nature of the conduct; or
   (B) physically incapable of declining participation in, or communicating unwillingness to engage in, that sexual act; or attempts to do so, shall be fined under this title, imprisoned not more than 20 years, or both.

Two sections of the United States Code prohibit the interstate transportation of individuals for the purpose of engaging in prostitution or any other sexual activity that is a crime (18 U.S.C. § 2421); or enticing, encouraging, or otherwise fraudulently persuading an individual to cross state lines for criminal sexual activity (18 U.S.C. § 2422). This provision has been used when an offender transports the victim across state lines and then sexually assaults them because sexual assault falls under the residual category of "any other sexual activity that is a crime." In a 1985 case, a federal court of appeals agreed that transporting a female for the purpose of committing rape was within the purview of 18 U.S.C. §§ 2421 and 2422.[59]

G. Other Crimes

In addition to Sections 2241 and 2242, there are several other provisions of the United States Code that relate to sexual offenses that occur within the maritime or territorial jurisdiction of the federal government. Section 2243 ("Sexual abuse of a minor or ward") makes it a crime to knowingly engage in a sexual act with another person who has attained the age of 12 but has not attained the age of 16, or knowingly engages in a sexual act with another person who is in official detention and under the custody, supervisory, or disciplinary authority of the person so engaging. Section 2244 ("Abusive sexual contact") makes it a crime for a person to knowingly engage in or cause sexual

---

[58]   United States v. Lucas, 157 F.3d 998 (1998).
[59]   United States v. Mitchell, 778 F.2d 1271 (7th Cir. 1985).

conduct with or by another person, if to do so would violate § 2241 of Title 18, or know-ingly engage in sexual conduct with another person without that other person's permission. Section 2244 includes a provision that if the sexual contact is with an indi-vidual who has not attained the age of 12 years, the maximum term of imprisonment that may be imposed for the offense shall be twice that otherwise provided in the section.

Finding that child exploitation has become a multimillion dollar industry infil-trated by elements of organized crime, Congress in 1986 added the federal offense of "Sexual exploitation of children."

18 U.S.C. § 2251 – Sexual Exploitation of Children

It is forbidden for any person to employ, use, persuade, induce, entice, or coerce any minor to engage or assist any other person to engage in, or to transport any minor in interstate or foreign commerce with the intent that the minor engage in, any sexually explicit conduct if such person knows or has reason to know that such visual depic-tion was produced using materials that have been mailed, shipped, or transported in interstate or foreign commerce by any means, including by computer, or if such visual depiction has actually been transported in interstate or foreign commerce or mailed.

It is forbidden for any parent, legal guardian, or person having custody or control of a minor to knowingly permit such minor to engage or assist any other person to engage in sexually explicit conduct for the purpose of producing any visual depic-tion of such conduct if the parent, legal guardian, or person knows or has reason to know that such visual depiction will be transported in interstate or foreign commerce or mailed, if that visual depiction was produced using materials that have been mailed, shipped, or transported in interstate or foreign commerce by any means, in-cluding by computer, or if such visual depiction has actually been transported in in-terstate or foreign commerce or mailed.

It is forbidden for any person to knowingly make, print, or publish, or cause to be made, printed, or published, any notice or advertisement seeking or offering

• to receive, exchange, buy, produce, display, distribute, or reproduce, any visual depiction, if the production of such visual depiction involves the use of a minor en-gaging in sexually explicit conduct and such visual depiction is of such conduct, or
• to participate in any act of sexually explicit conduct by or with any minor for the purpose of producing a visual depiction of such conduct,

if such person knows or has reason to know that such notice or advertisement is or will be transported in interstate or foreign commerce by any means including by com-puter or mail.

It was held to be constitutional by a federal district court in Pennsylvania in 1987.[60]

Recall from Chapter 6 that all states have sex offender registration laws. While some states had sex offender registration laws before the federal legislation, Congress mandated that all states set up and maintain sex offender registries or lose federal money. There is also a federal sex offender registration law related to sex offenders convicted in federal courts. While the federal laws that require states to institute and

---

[60]   United States v. Fenton, 654 F. Supp. 379 (E.D. Pa. 1987). *See also* United States v. Buculei, 262 F.3d 322 (4th Cir. 2001).

maintain sex offender registrations are based on the federal government's powers under the commerce clause, the ability to require federal offenders to register as sex offenders comes from the maritime and territorial jurisdiction. For instance, a sex offender in Washington D.C. would be required to register under the federal law requiring registration because of jurisdiction. To review federal legislation:

- 1994 Jacob Wetterling Crimes Against Children and Sexually Violent Offender Registration Act—required states to track sex offenders
- 1996 Megan's Law—required that sex offender registration information be available to the public
- 1996 Pam Lychner Sex Offender Tracking and Identification Act—required the Attorney General to establish a national database of sex offenders; required those offenders in states without a minimally satisfactory sex offender registry to register with the FBI
- 1997 Jacob Wetterling Improvements Act—allowed states to add to the number of crimes for which an individual must register
- 1998 Protection of Children from Sexual Predators Act—directed the Bureau of Justice Assistance to help states comply with registration requirements
- 2006 Adam Walsh Child Protection and Safety Act—changed requirements for who should register and for how long; expanded jurisdiction of registration requirements to Indian tribes; required retroactive application for interstate travel bans

§ 12.5   Offenses against Property

As with all federal crimes, there must be a nexus between one of the federal powers and the crime. In property cases, it is typically because the crime involves a federal building or property or the crime takes place in the District of Columbia or some other federal jurisdiction.

A. Arson

Title 18 § 81 of the U.S. Code provides a penalty for those who commit arson within the special maritime and territorial jurisdiction of the United States. This section provides

18 U.S.C. § 81

Whoever, within the special maritime and territorial jurisdiction of the United States, willfully and maliciously sets fire to or burns any building, structure or vessel, any machinery or building materials or supplies, military or naval stores, munitions of war, or any structural aids or appliances for navigation or shipping, or attempts or conspires to do such an act, shall be imprisoned for not more than 25 years, fined the greater of the fine under this title or the cost of repairing or replacing any property that is damaged or destroyed, or both. If the building be a dwelling or if the life of any person be placed in jeopardy, he shall be fined under this title or imprisoned for any term of years or for life, or both.

This statute punishes arson when it is committed within the maritime and territorial jurisdiction of the United States. A federal court determined that the criminal intent necessary to satisfy the "willful and malicious" elements of the arson statute includes not only acts done with the intent of burning the buildings, but acts done with the knowledge that the burning of the building was practically certain to result.[61]

A different arson statute utilizes the commerce clause power of the federal government and assumes jurisdiction of arson when it is directed to targets that are involved in interstate or foreign commerce or in an activity affecting interstate commerce.[62] The statute provides

18 U.S.C. § 844

(i) Whoever maliciously damages or destroys, or attempts to damage or destroy, by means of fire or an explosive, any building, vehicle, or other real or personal property used in interstate or foreign commerce or in any activity affecting interstate or foreign commerce, shall be imprisoned for not less than 5 years and not more than 20 years, fined under this title, or both; and if personal injury results to any person, including any public safety officer performing duties as a direct or proximate result of conduct prohibited by this subsection, shall be imprisoned for not less than 7 years and not more than 40 years, fined under this title, or both; and if death results to any person, including any public safety officer performing duties as a direct or proximate result of conduct prohibited by this subsection, shall also be subject to imprisonment for any term of years, or to the death penalty or to life imprisonment.

This statute, which gives broad authority to federal agencies, has been challenged as overbroad and outside the federal government's power. However, the courts have been consistent in upholding the constitutionality of the statute. As one court pointed out, the federal arson statute falls within permissible regulation under Congress's commerce power, in that it protects property that is used in either interstate or foreign commerce or in any activity affecting interstate or foreign commerce.[63]

Under the statute, the government must establish that the damaged or destroyed property was used in interstate commerce or in an activity that affected interstate or foreign commerce. The phrase, "any activity affecting interstate or foreign commerce," has been interpreted exceedingly broadly. The following instances were determined to meet the nexus requirement:

• A restaurant because the restaurant purchased meat and poultry from an out-of-state supplier on a regular basis, and the insurer's headquarters were out-of-state.[64]

---

[61] United States v. M.W., 890 F.2d 239 (10th Cir. 1989); United States v. Dreamer, 88 F.3d 655 (8th Cir. 1996).

[62] 18 U.S.C. § 844(i). *See also* 18 U.S.C. § 1861.

[63] United States v. Chowdbury, 118 F.3d 742 (11th Cir. 1997). *See also* United States v. Dascenzo, 152 F.3d 1300 (11th Cir. 1998).

[64] United States v. Latouf, 182 F.3d 820 (6th Cir. 1997).

- A commercial establishment, which received supplies of natural gas via interstate commerce.[65]
- A building that was located in Iowa, owned by a Kansas resident, and served by natural gas arriving from out-of-state.[66]
- A victim's home that contained a home office of the victim's construction business containing business records and supplies.[67]

However, a federal court refused to recognize the nexus when the property was occupied and used by its owner, not for any commercial venture, but as a private residence, even though the residence received natural gas, and the mortgage and an insurance policy crossed state lines.[68]

B. Malicious Mischief

The U.S. Criminal Code, similarly to state penal codes, protects federal property from malicious mischief. It provides

18 U.S.C. § 1361. Government property or contracts

Whoever willfully injures or commits any depredation against any property of the United States, or of any department or agency thereof, or any property which has been or is being manufactured or constructed for the United States, or any department or agency thereof, or attempts to commit any of the foregoing offenses, shall be punished as follows:

If the damage or attempted damage to such property exceeds the sum of $1,000, by a fine under this title or imprisonment for not more than ten years, or both; if the damage or attempted damage to such property does not exceed the sum of $1,000, by a fine under this title or by imprisonment for not more than one year, or both.

This section of the federal code requires proof that the act was done willfully. In addition, the prosecution must show that the property falls under the definition of federal property as defined in the statute. The fact that the Navy exercised dominion and control over planes and that they had been subject to practical usage of the government was sufficient to establish a "property right" for purposes of the statute.[69] Furthermore, the government must prove the damage amount element to convict a defendant.[70]

Other federal crimes relate to damaging communication lines (18 U.S.C. § 1362) and damaging energy facilities (18 U.S.C. § 1366). Another malicious mischief statute covers other buildings under federal protection. It provides

---

[65] United States v. Disanto, 86 F.3d 1238 (1st Cir. 1996).
[66] United States v. Ryan, 23 F. Supp. 2d 1044 (S.D. Iowa 1998).
[67] United States v. Jimenez, 256 F.3d 330 (5th Cir. 2001).
[68] Jones v. United States, 529 U.S. 848, 120 S. Ct. 1904, 146 L. Ed. 2d 902 (2000).
[69] United States v. Erodhead, 714 F. Supp. 593 (D. Mass. 1989).
[70] United States v. Seaman, 18 F.3d 649 (9th Cir. 1994).

18 U.S.C. § 1363 Buildings or property within special maritime and territorial jurisdiction

Whoever, within the special maritime and territorial jurisdiction of the United States, willfully and maliciously destroys or injures or attempts to destroy or injure any structure, conveyance, or other real or personal property, shall be fined under this title or imprisoned not more than five years, or both, and if the building be a dwelling, or the life of any person be placed in jeopardy, shall be fined under this title or imprisoned not more than twenty years, or both.

C. Criminal Trespass

There are a variety of specific statutes directed to types of trespass, either prohibiting trespass on certain federal property, trespass to perform certain prohibited acts, or both. For instance, in 18 U.S.C. § 1863, the crime of "Trespass on national forest lands" is defined. In 18 U.S.C. § 1991, the crime of "Entering a train to commit a crime" is defined. The U.S. Code also has a statute directed toward trespass on military installations:

18 U.S.C. § 1382 Entering military, naval, or Coast Guard property

Whoever, within the jurisdiction of the United States, goes upon any military, naval, or Coast Guard reservation, post, fort, arsenal, yard, station, or installation, for any purpose prohibited by law or lawful regulation; or
    Whoever reenters or is found within any such reservation, post, fort, arsenal, yard, station, or installation, after having been removed therefrom or ordered not to reenter by any officer or person in command or charge thereof—
    Shall be fined under this title or imprisoned not more than six months, or both.

A federal court decided that this statute was not unconstitutional under the First Amendment when applied to defendants who were protesting against the military in light of the traditional need of the military to retain control over the scope and extent of public activity on military bases. However, the government must prove beyond a reasonable doubt that the area where the defendant was arrested constituted part of a military reservation for purposes of this statute.[71]

D. Burglary

Chapter 103 of the United States Code includes the federal offenses relating to robbery and burglary. For example, the federal code relating to breaking into a federal post office provides

18 U.S.C. § 2115

Whoever forcibly breaks into or attempts to break into any post office, or any building used in whole or in part as a post office, with intent to commit in such post office, or building or part thereof, so used, any larceny or other deprivation, shall be fined under this title or imprisoned not more than 5 years, or both.

---

[71]   United States v. Corrigan, 114 F.3d 763 (11th Cir. 1998). United States v. Zukowsky, 967 F. Supp. 269 (S.D. Ohio 1997).

In the case of *United States v. Gibson*, the Circuit Court, in discussing the elements of this offense, indicated that an offense is established when the government shows forcible entry into some part of the building and an intent to commit larceny in a part of the building used as a post office.[72]

A second federal crime, which includes some of the elements of common law burglary, provides a penalty for breaking into railway or steamboat post offices. Section 2117 of Title 18 the United States Code makes it a crime to break the seal or lock of any railroad car, vessel, aircraft, motortruck, wagon, or other vehicle or any pipeline system containing interstate or foreign shipments, or freight or express or other property, or enter any such vehicle or pipeline system with the intent in either case to commit larceny. Violators of this section may be fined as provided in the U.S. Code or imprisoned not more than 10 years, or both. An unusual provision of this statute makes it clear that a judgment of conviction or acquittal on the merits under the laws of any state shall be a bar to prosecution under this section for the same act or acts.

A more recently enacted federal statute deals with robberies and burglaries of premises registered to distribute controlled substances. Section 2118 of Title 18 the U.S. Code provides for a fine or imprisonment, or both, if one is found guilty of entering or attempting to enter, without authority, business premises or property of a person registered with the Drug Enforcement Administration, with intent to steal any material or a compound containing any quantity of a controlled substance.[73] The federal courts have recognized drugstores or pharmacies as registrants; therefore, burglary of a drugstore might be prosecuted as a federal crime rather than as a state crime.[74]

§ 12.6 Offenses of Theft and Deception

The U.S. Code includes the common law elements of larceny plus the requirement that the offense be committed within the special maritime and territorial jurisdiction of the United States.

18 U.S.C. § 661. Within special maritime and territorial jurisdiction

Whoever, within the special maritime and territorial jurisdiction of the United States, takes and carries away, with intent to steal or purloin, any personal property of another shall be punished as follows:

If the property taken is of a value exceeding $1,000, or is taken from the person of another, by a fine under this title, or imprisonment for not more than five years, or both; in all other cases, by a fine under this title or by imprisonment not more than one year, or both.

---

[72] United States v. Gibson, 444 F.2d 275 (5th Cir. 1971).

[73] 18 U.S.C. § 2118(b).

[74] United States v. Workman, 990 F. Supp. 473 (S.D. W. Va. 1998); United States v. Martin, 866 F.2d 972 (8th Cir. 1989).

Examples of thefts that come within the purview of this provision include stealing from an officer's club on a U.S. Army post in Virginia, and taking and carrying away with intent to steal a coat and purse belonging to another at a Veterans Administration Hospital.[75] In addition to the law relating to thefts on government property, federal law provides penalties for theft from interstate commerce, and thefts from organizations, governments, or agencies annually receiving in excess of $10,000 in federal assistance.[76]

A. Robbery

Many of the common law elements of robbery are carried over into the federal offense of bank robbery. They include taking, by force and violence or by intimidation, from the person or presence of another, any personal property or money or other things of value. However, the larceny portion of 18 U.S.C. § 2113(a), defining bank robbery and incidental crimes, does not require the common law elements of taking and carrying away.[77]

Title 18 § 2112 makes it a federal crime for one person to rob another of any kind of personal property belonging to the United States. Anyone found guilty of violating this statute shall be imprisoned for not more than 15 years. To be found guilty under this statute, possession or use of a deadly weapon is not required; all that is required is that the prosecution establish that the taking was by force, or threat of force, and the property taken was personal property belonging to the United States.[78]

In addition to providing a penalty for stealing or robbing another of personal property of the United States, the U.S. Code provides a penalty for bank robbery. This very comprehensive bank robbery statute was added to make it possible for federal investigators to assist in protecting the assets of banks, credit unions, and savings and loan associations. It provides in part

18 U.S.C. § 2113

(a) Whoever, by force and violence, or by intimidation, takes, or attempts to take, from the person or presence of another, or obtains or attempts to obtain by extortion, any property or money or any other thing of value belonging to, or in the care, custody, control, management, or possession of, any bank, credit union, or any savings and loan association, shall be fined under this title or imprisoned not more than 20 years, or both.

A federal court considering the constitutionality of this federal statute held that the federal bank robbery statute has the necessary nexus to interstate commerce because

---

[75] Clark v. United States, 267 F.2d 99 (4th Cir. 1959); England v. United States, 174 F.2d 466 (5th Cir. 1949).

[76] Title 18 U.S.C. § 666; United States v. Phillips, 17 F. Supp. 2d 1016 (M.D. La. 1998).

[77] United States v. Urrutia, 897 F.2d 430 (9th Cir. 1990).

[78] United States v. Torres, 809 F.2d 429 (7th Cir. 1987).

the statute's coverage is limited to banks that are members of the Federal Reserve System or insured by the Federal Deposit Insurance Corporation (FDIC).[79] The court explained that those financial institutions are instrumentalities and channels of interstate commerce, and regulation of those institutions is within the Congress's commerce clause power.

To prove the offense of bank robbery, the government must show that

- an individual or individuals;
- used force and violence or intimidation;
- to take or attempt to take;
- from the person or presence of another;
- money, property, or anything of value;
- belonging to or in the care, custody, control, management, or possession;
- of a bank, credit union, or savings and loan institution.

"Intimidation," as used in the bank robbery statute, includes the threat of force, even though the threat is a bluff. The intimidation element of the bank robbery statute is satisfied even if the defendant did not intend intimidation. A defendant was charged with the robbery of a bank in Spring Lake, North Carolina. The facts indicate that the defendant reached over a bank teller counter "as if trying to grab" the teller, vaulted over the counter, and took money from the money drawer. The defendant argued that the government failed to prove that he intended to intimidate the teller, but his actions were sufficient to sustain the conviction of robbery.[80]

An additional section of the statute also includes a penalty for entering or attempting to enter a bank, credit union, or savings and loan association with the intent to commit any felony affecting one of the financial institutions.[81] In interpreting the term "enter" as used in this statute, one federal case held that entry into the night depository located within the walls of the bank is an "entry" into a bank for purposes of this statute, which prohibits entry with intent to commit a felony.[82] Also, the removal of unprocessed deposits from the bank's night depository is a felony that "affects" a bank within the meaning of the statute prohibiting entry into a bank with intent to commit a felony affecting the bank.[83]

This statute does not apply unless the bank is a member of the Federal Reserve System, is organized or operated under the laws of the United States, or is a bank whose deposits are insured by the Federal Deposit Insurance Corporation (FDIC).

---

[79]   United States v. Harris, 108 F.3d 1107 (9th Cir. 1997). *See also* United States v. Watts, 256 F.3d 630 (7th Cir. 2001).

[80]   United States v. Jones, 732 F.2d 624 (7th Cir. 1991). *See also* United States v. Smith, 131 F.3d 185 (7th Cir. 1997). United States v. Woodrup, 86 F.3d 359 (4th Cir. 1996). *See also* United States v. Credit, 95 F.3d 362 (5th Cir. 1996).

[81]   18 U.S.C. § 2113(d).

[82]   United States v. Hanson, 751 F. Supp. 177 (D.Or. 1990).

[83]   United States v. Biajos, 292 F.3d 1068 (9th Cir. 2002)

Recognizing the increase in motor vehicle theft with its growing threat to human life and to the economic well-being of the nation, Congress enacted the "Anti-Car Theft Act" (the carjacking statute). The act provides

18 U.S.C. § 2119

Whoever, with the intent to cause death or serious bodily harm, takes a motor vehicle that has been transported, shipped, or received in interstate or foreign commerce from the person or presence of another by force or violence or by intimidation, or attempts to do so, shall—

(1) be fined under this title or imprisoned not more than 15 years, or both,

(2) if serious bodily injury (as defined in § 1365 of this title, including any conduct that, if the conduct occurred in the special maritime and territorial jurisdiction of the United States, would violate § 2241 or § 2242 of this title) results, be fined under this title or imprisoned not more than 25 years, or both, and

(3) if death results, be fined under this title or imprisoned for any number of years up to life, or both, or sentenced to death.

Following the passage of the act, several courts found no problems with its constitutionality. In U.S. v. Cobb, provided in Part II, a federal court held that the federal carjacking statute, under which the defendant was prosecuted, contained an express jurisdictional element, in that it applied only to a forcible taking of motor vehicles that had moved in interstate commerce, and the statute thus satisfied the minimal nexus required for the statute to be a valid exercise of Congress's commerce clause power.[84]

The statute, as amended, requires a specific intent element. The amendment to the carjacking statute, requiring that the defendant act with intent to cause death or serious bodily harm, converted carjacking from a general intent to a specific intent offense, thus requiring the government to prove the mental element above and beyond the special mental state required with respect to taking a vehicle.[85] As the statute and the cases reveal, there can be a conviction if the government proves forcible taking of motor vehicles that have moved in interstate commerce. The wording of the statute gives broad authority to federal agencies in carjacking cases. However, if the government fails to prove that the victim's car had ever been in interstate commerce, the defendant will be entitled to have the carjacking charge dismissed.[86]

Case Note: *United States v. Cobb*, 144 F.3d 319 (4th Cir. 1998)
What was the holding of the case?
Is it possible for a carjacking to not fall under the federal statute?

---

[84]   United States v. Cobb, 144 F.3d 319 (4th Cir. 1998). *See also* United States v. Romero, 122 F.3d 1334 (10th Cir. 1997), which held that Congress did not exceed its power under the commerce clause in enacting the federal carjacking statute.

[85]   United States v. Randolph, 93 F.3d 656 (9th Cir. 1996).

[86]   United States v. Gamble, 939 F. Supp. 569 (E.D. Mich. 1996).

In addition to these federal crimes, the federal code includes a penalty for robberies committed within the special maritime and territorial jurisdiction of the United States. This statute provides

18 U.S.C. § 2111

Whoever, within the special maritime and territorial jurisdiction of the United States, by force and violence, or by intimidation, takes from the person or presence of another anything of value, shall be imprisoned not more than 15 years.

As in other "special maritime and territorial jurisdiction" statutes, this only applies when the crime takes place within the territory defined. In the District of Columbia, robbery retains its common law elements.[87] To support a robbery conviction, the government must prove that there was

- a felonious taking;
- accompanied by asportation (or carrying away); of
- personal property of value;
- from the person of another in his or her presence;
- against his or her will;
- by violence or by putting in fear;
- *animo furandi* (the intention to steal).

B. *Embezzlement*

The federal statute combines embezzlement and theft and provides

18 U.S.C. § 641

Whoever embezzles, steals, purloins, or knowingly converts to his own use or the use of another, or without authority, sells, conveys, or disposes of any record, voucher, money, or thing of value of the United States or of any department or agency thereof, or any property made or being made under contract for the United States or any department or agency thereof; or
  Whoever receives, conceals, or retains the same with intent to convert it to his own use or gain, knowing it to have been embezzled, stolen, purloined, or converted—
  Shall be fined not more than $10,000 or imprisoned not more than ten years, or both; but if the value of such property does not exceed the sum of $1,000, he shall be fined not more than $1,000 or imprisoned not more than one year, or both.

Making it clear that the statute was to be broadly interpreted, a federal court explained that the statute prohibited conversion of any "thing of value" of the federal government.[88] Several decisions have been rendered to clarify the meaning of "thing of value of the United States." One federal court held that funds advanced to fuel subcontractors by the Small Business Administration were "property of the United States,"

---

[87] Lattimore v. United States, 684 A.2d 357 (D.C.App 1996).

[88] United States v. Collins, 56 F.3d 1416 (D.C. Cir. 1995); cert. denied, 516 U.S. 1060 (1995).

within the meaning of the embezzlement statute.[89] In another case, the fact that the marijuana that a customs officer was accused of taking was an illegal substance, and the fact that the government had paid for its destruction did not preclude the marijuana from being a "thing of value" within the statute.[90]

Title 18 § 656 defines an offense of "theft, embezzlement, or misapplication by a bank officer or employee." This provides a penalty where an employee of a federal bank or a bank that is a member of the Federal Reserve System embezzles, abstracts, purloins, or willfully misapplies any of the monies, funds, or credits of such bank. The four essential elements of the offense are

- the accused was an officer or director of the bank,
- the bank was connected in some way with a national bank or a federally insured bank,
- the accused willfully misapplied the funds of the bank, and
- the accused acted with intent to defraud the bank.

Title 18 § 666 of the federal statute is titled "Theft or bribery concerning programs receiving federal funds." Under this statute, a person may be convicted of embezzlement if the organization from which the property is embezzled is a government or agency that receives in any one-year period benefits in excess of $10,000 under a federal program involving a grant, contract, subsidy, loan, guarantee, insurance, or other form of federal assistance.

In the case of *United States v. Suarez,* the defendant was convicted under this statute of converting police evidence and victim restitution money to his own benefit.[91] Suarez had been charged with taking property, consisting of evidence and restitution payments from the Dearborn Police Department, an organization receiving federal funds for the DARE Program. On appeal, the court stated that under 18 U.S.C. § 666 the defendant need not be shown to have actually stolen any of the federal funds given to the "federal recipient" or even that his malfeasance affected these federal funds, only that the agency received federal funds. The defendant's conviction was affirmed.

C. Fraud

In Chapter 8 state fraud statutes (obtaining money by false pretenses) were discussed. The United States Code also has several section related to different types of fraud. Title 18 § 1341 of the U.S. Code is titled "Frauds and swindles." Other sections include 18 U.S.C. § 1002 (Possession of papers to defraud the United States), 18 U.S.C. § 1028 (Fraud and related activity in connection with identification documents – Identity theft), 18 U.S.C. § 1343 (Fraud by wire, radio or television), and 18 U.S.C. § 1344 (Bank fraud). The purpose of this statute is to protect the integrity of the mails by

---

[89]   United States v. Lanier, 920 F.2d 887 (11th Cir. 1991).
[90]   United States v. Gordon, 638 F.2d 886 (5th Cir. 1981).
[91]   United States v. Suarez, 263 F.3d 468 (6th Cir. 2001).

making it a crime to use them to implement fraudulent schemes of any kind, including the use of the mails to implement fraudulent schemes directed at a state agency.

Any offender who uses the U.S. mail, Internet, or wire transmissions to commit fraud could be subject to federal prosecution in addition to state prosecution. In the fall of 2008, Bernard Madoff was exposed as perpetrating one of the largest frauds, if not the largest, in history with a "Ponzi scheme." Ponzi schemes pay off early investors with the money of later investors. Victims who enter Ponzi schemes early believe that the investment is legitimate because they are getting the returns they were promised; however, the whole fraud comes apart when the offender is forced to pay out more than is coming in. Evidence indicated that Madoff's Ponzi scheme, which had been going on since probably the 1990s, resulted in at least $18 billion in losses for investors. He was sentenced to 150 years in prison for 11 federal charges, including securities fraud, wire fraud, mail fraud, money laundering, making false statements, perjury, and false filings with the Securities and Exchange Commission.

The mail and wire fraud statutes make it illegal to use the mails or any interstate electronic communication network to perpetrate a fraudulent scheme. These statutes may be invoked in any case in which there is criminal activity that involves even peripheral use of the postal system or telephone communications. The original federal mail fraud statute was enacted in 1872 and has undergone many changes since that time. The original statute only applied to illegal uses of the U.S. Postal Service; however, in September 1994, this statute was amended to include private interstate delivery services, such as Federal Express and United Parcel Service, as well as the U.S. Postal Service.

To prove **mail fraud** under § 1341, the government must show

1. a scheme to defraud;
2. committed within intent to defraud; and
3. use of the United States mail or private interstate commercial carrier to further the fraudulent scheme.

LEGAL NEWS: MEDICARE FRAUD

It is no surprise that some of the largest and most frequent criminal prosecutions for fraud at the federal level involve schemes to defraud Medicare. It was reported in December 2011 that federal agents were investigating one man who was responsible for at least 29 shell companies that had defrauded Medicare of more than $4.5 million. Another investigation uncovered a ring that used 118 shell companies, involved 44 people in 25 states, and billed more than $100 million before they were exposed. Medicare fraud rings steal or borrow patient information and then bill Medicare for phantom services; the shell companies appear to be billing companies or clinics. If they become targets of investigation, they are simply shut down and criminals open new ones. "Straw owners" are paid to have their names used to incorporate the companies in order for the ringleaders to remain anonymous. Sometimes doctors and/or patients are paid kickbacks in return for using their information, but sometimes the information is simply stolen. It is estimated that in 2010 Medicare paid out $48 billion in improper payments, nearly 10 percent of total payments. Michel De Jesus Huarte, the ringleader of one of the rings, recently pled guilty to healthcare and mail fraud and was sentenced to 22 years in prison and ordered to repay $18 million. The Healthcare Reform Act of 2010 provides $350 million to fight Medicare and Medicaid fraud; it also provides for stiffer sentences for fraud.

Source: Reuters. 2011. Special report: Phantom firms bleed millions from Medicare. Accessed January 13, 2012 from http://www.reuters.com/assets/print?aid=USTRE7BK0PY20111221.

Court decisions have indicated that the government is not required to prove that the scheme to defraud was successful. The government need only prove that a scheme existed in which the use of the mails was reasonably foreseeable and that an actual mailing occurred in furtherance of the scheme.[92]

In enacting the **wire fraud** statute, Congress relied upon the commerce clause; therefore, the wire fraud statute, unlike the mail fraud statute, requires that the communication cross state lines. However, the mail fraud statute and the wire fraud statute share the same language in relevant parts and accordingly the court applies the same analysis to both sets of offenses.

The following are some examples of frauds that have been prosecuted under these statutes[93]:

• fraudulent insurance claims
• law partners who worked with a doctor to defraud an insurance company
• use of the mails to file a fraudulent burglary claim
• a police officer who aided and abetted a fraud by skewing an arson investigation
• fraudulent investment schemes
• misrepresentations in the sale of used automobiles

---

[92]   United States v. Coppel, 24 F.3d 535 (3d Cir. 1994). See also United States v. Pierce, 224 F.3d 158 (2d Cir. 2000), which held that intent to defraud does not hinge on whether or not the appellees were successful.

[93]   See, for instance, United States v. Cavalier, 17 F.3d 90 (5th Cir. 1994); United States v. Console, 13 F.3d 641 (3d Cir. 1993); United States v. Noland, 960 F.2d 1384 (8th Cir. 1992); United States v. Figueroa, 832 F.2d 691 (1st Cir. 1987).

• owners of video gambling devices who lied about their ownership to obtain a state license

In interpreting and explaining the mail fraud statute, the justices of the Seventh Circuit Court of Appeals decided that to convict for mail fraud, the government is not required to prove that the scheme to defraud was successful, but need only prove that a scheme existed in which the use of the mails was reasonably foreseeable and that the actual mailing occurred in furtherance of that scheme.[94]

LEGAL NEWS: ABRAMOFF'S REDEMPTION?

In March 2006, it was reported that Jack Abramoff and his partner pled guilty to wire fraud and conspiracy in their purchase of a gambling riverboat in Florida. They forged a wire transfer to make it appear that they had committed money to the venture that, in reality, they did not have in order to get lenders to contribute. Abramhoff also pled guilty to mail fraud, honest services fraud, tax evasion, and conspiracy.

UPDATE: Abramoff served three and a half years and was released from prison to a federal halfway house in 2010. Today, he gives ethics speeches, for instance, to Harvard Law School and the Kentucky legislature. A 2010 movie, *Casino Jack*, was based on his life.

Source: *Austin American-Statesman*, March 30, 2006, at A18; May 6, 2006. Bykowicz, J. Abramoff as Ethics Guru Latest Chapter in Political Second Acts. Bloomberg News Online, January 3, 2012. Accessed January 12, 2012 from http://www.bloomberg.com/news/2012-01-03/abramoff-as-ethics-guru-latest-chapter-in-political-second-acts.html.

D. *Honest Services Fraud*

In 1988 Congress added 18 U.S.C. § 1346, which reads: "For the purposes of this chapter, the term 'scheme or artifice to defraud' includes a scheme or artifice to deprive another of the intangible right of honest services." This catch-all sentence has been used aggressively by federal prosecutors against public officials who have been accused of accepting illegal gifts or services as well as against private individuals who are accused of breaching their fiduciary duties to clients or their companies (such as corporate executives who utilize the company's resources for their own gain). It is somewhat similar to the state conflict of interest statutes that were discussed in Chapter 8, but the penalties are more severe, since it is a definition of fraud rather than a different, lesser crime. Similar to the discussion of conflict of interest laws, however, prosecutors used this charge when they could not prove a quid pro quo scheme of bribery.

---

94 United States v. Brisco, 65 F.3d 576 (7th Cir. 1995).

Critics contended that the definition was too broad and could be used for almost anyone, including those who leave work a little early pleading a headache to go shopping. The issue was dealt with in *Skilling v. United States,*[95] a case that is provided in Part II of this text. In this case, Jeffrey Skilling, of Enron infamy, appealed his conviction, partially on the argument that the honest services fraud charge was unconstitutionally vague. The Court combined the Skilling case along with others to rule that the honest services fraud definition must be narrowed to include only bribes and kickbacks. The cases were returned to the lower court to see if convictions could be sustained under other charges. It is worth noting that there was a strong dissent in the case by Justice Scalia and others who stated that the statute was fatally vague and could not be rehabilitated by interpreting it to mean only bribes and kickbacks. This case has raised the specter of dozens, if not hundreds, of federal convictions being appealed that were based on honest services fraud.

Case Note: Skilling v. United States, 561 U.S. __ (2010)
What was the holding of the case?
What was Skilling accused of?
What is the definition of vagueness?
Why did the Court decide the way it did?

E. Extortion

Title 18 of the U.S. Code contains seven sections dealing with extortion and threats, including 18 U.S.C. § 871 (Threats against the President and successors to the presidency), 18 U.S.C. § 873 (Blackmail), 18 U.S.C. § 874 (Kickbacks from public works employees), 18 U.S.C. § 876 (Mailing threatening communications), and 18 U.S.C. § 877 (Mailing threatening communications from foreign countries). The section that most closely resembles the traditional extortion law is § 873, titled "Blackmail." It provides

18 U.S.C. § 873

Whoever, under a threat of informing, or as a consideration for not informing, against any violation of any law of the United States, demands or receives any money or other valuable thing, shall be fined under this title or imprisoned not more than one year, or both.

The essential elements of this crime are coercion and unlawful consideration. Title 18 § 872 of the federal statute applies to extortion by officers and employees of the United States. Under this section, an officer or employee of the United States or any department or agency thereof, or representing himself to be or assuming to act as such, under color or pretense of his office or employment, who commits or attempts an act of extortion may be fined or imprisoned as provided in the statute, or both.

Recall from Chapter 8 that Autumn Jackson and her crime partners were charged with violations of 18 U.S.C. § 875 titled "Interstate communications" as well as

---

[95]   Skilling v. U.S., 561 U.S. __ (2010).

violations of the New York statute against extortion.[96] This provision punishes those who use interstate communications in ransom demands or threats, but also has a section that punishes extortion threats. This case is provided in Part II of the text.

18 U.S.C. § 875 Interstate communications

. . . (d) Whoever, with intent to extort from any person, firm, association, or corporation, any money or other thing of value, transmits in interstate or foreign commerce any communication containing any threat to injure the property or reputation of the addressee or of another or the reputation of a deceased person or any threat to accuse the addressee or any other person of a crime, shall be fined under this title or imprisoned not more than two years, or both.

18 U.S.C. § 1951 is titled "Interference with commerce by threats or violence":

(a) Whoever in any way or degree obstructs, delays, or affects commerce or the movement of any article or commodity in commerce, by robbery or extortion or attempts or conspires so to do, or commits or threatens physical violence to any person or property in furtherance of a plan or purpose to do anything in violation of this section shall be fined under this title or imprisoned not more than twenty years or both.
(b) As used in this section— . . .
  (2) The term "extortion" means the obtaining of property from another, with his consent, induced by wrongful use of actual or threatened force, violence, or fear, or under color of official right.

Note that some of the statutes described above are based on the federal government's power via jurisdiction, i.e., that the targets or offenders are federal officials, while others are based on the commerce clause, i.e., that the offenders use the mail or telephone in their threats.

> **Case Note: *United States v. Jackson*, 986 F. Supp. 829 (1997)**
> What was the holding of the case? Can an illegitimate child ever seek compensation from the biological father by threatening action without it being considered extortion?

F. Receiving Stolen Property

Title 18 § 2312 makes it a crime for a person to transport a stolen vehicle in interstate commerce. This section provides

18 U.S.C. § 2312

Whoever transports in interstate or foreign commerce a motor vehicle or aircraft, knowing the same has been stolen, shall be fined under this title or imprisoned not more than five years, or both.

---

[96] United States v. Jackson, 986 F.Supp. 829 (1997).

To be convicted of transporting stolen vehicles in interstate commerce, the government must prove that there was a stolen vehicle, that the defendant knew that it was stolen, and the defendant transported the vehicle in interstate commerce. It is not necessary to show that the defendant operated the vehicle, only that the defendant knew it was stolen and facilitated the interstate journey.[97]

The federal law relating to transportation of motor vehicles in interstate commerce was first enacted in 1919 to make it possible for federal officers to assist in reducing the number of auto thefts. The constitutionality of this section was challenged on "void for vagueness" grounds on several occasions, but was found to be valid. In order to convict a person of transporting stolen vehicles in interstate commerce, the government must prove that the vehicle was, in fact, stolen, and that the defendant transported the vehicle in interstate commerce.[98]

The federal statute that deals with receiving stolen property when the crime is committed within the special maritime and territorial jurisdiction of the United States is Title 18 § 662. This section provides

18 U.S.C. § 662

Whoever, within the special maritime and territorial jurisdiction of the United States, buys, receives, or conceals any money, goods, bank notes, or other things which may be the subject of larceny, which has been feloniously taken, stolen, or embezzled from any other person, knowing the same to have been so taken, stolen, or embezzled, shall be fined not more than $1,000 or imprisoned not more than 3 years, or both; but if the amount or value of the thing so taken, stolen, or embezzled does not exceed $100, he shall be fined not more than $1,000 or imprisoned not more than one year, or both.

After discussing the question of jurisdiction to try a person for receiving stolen property within the special jurisdiction of the United States, a court of appeals agreed that receipt or concealment of the stolen property within the confines of a military reservation was a violation of this section.[99] As in state receiving cases, in order to convict a person for the crime of receiving stolen property, the government must prove

- that the property was stolen by some person other than the defendant;
- that the defendant received the property and converted it to his own use; and
- that the defendant knew that the property that he or she received had been stolen.

A second federal statute specifies a penalty in which a person receives, conceals, stores, barters, or sells vehicles that have been moved in interstate commerce, if that person knew that the vehicle was stolen. This section provides

---

[97]　United States v. Spoone, 741 F.2d 680 (4th Cir.), cert denied, 469 U.S. 1162 (1984).
[98]　United States v. Baker, 429 F.2d 1344 (7th Cir. 1970).
[99]　United States v. Townsend, 474 F.2d 209 (5th Cir. 1973).

18 U.S.C. § 2313

(a) Whoever receives, possesses, conceals, stores, barters, sells, or disposes of any motor vehicle or aircraft, which has crossed a State or United States boundary after being stolen, knowing the same to have been stolen, shall be fined under this title or imprisoned not more than ten years, or both.

(b) For purposes of this section, the term "State" includes a State of the United States, the District of Columbia, and any commonwealth, territory, or possession of the United States.

To convict one of a violation of this section, which proscribes receiving or concealing stolen automobiles, the government must demonstrate that

- the motor vehicle or aircraft involved was stolen;
- the defendant knew that the motor vehicle or aircraft had been stolen;
- the defendant possessed, concealed, stored, received, bartered, sold, or disposed of the motor vehicle; and
- the vehicle involved was moved in interstate traffic at the time of the defendant's activities.[100]

Other federal statutes dealing with receipt of stolen goods include 18 U.S.C. § 2314 (Transportation of stolen goods); 18 U.S.C. § 2315 (Sale or receipt of stolen goods, securities, monies, or fraudulent state tax stamps); and 18 U.S.C. § 2317 (Sale or receipt of stolen lifestock).

G. Forgery

Numerous sections of the United States Code specify penalties for forgery of specific documents, including 18 U.S.C. § 473 (Bonds and obligations of certain lending agencies), 18 U.S.C. § 485 (Falsely making, forging or counterfeiting coins), 18 U.S.C. § 472 (Forgery of obligations or securities of the United States), and 18 U.S.C. § 494, which relates to falsely making, altering, or forging contractor's bonds, bids, and public records.

Title 18 § 495 provides that

18 U.S.C. § 495

Whoever falsely makes, alters, forges, or counterfeits any deed, power of attorney, order, certificate, receipt, contract or other writing for the purpose of obtaining or receiving, or of enabling any other person, either directly or indirectly, to obtain or receive from the United States or any officers or agents thereof, any sum of money; or

Whoever utters or publishes as true any such false, forged, altered, or counterfeited writing, with intent to defraud the United States, knowing the same to be false, altered, forged, or counterfeited; or

Whoever transmits to, or presents at any office or officer of the United States, any such writing in support of, or in relation to, any account or claim, with intent to

---

[100] United States v. Thomas, 676 F.2d 239 (7th Cir.), cert denied, 449 U.S. 1091 (1980).

defraud the United States, knowing the same to be false, altered, forged, or counterfeited—
    Shall be fined under this title or imprisoned not more than ten years, or both.

In interpreting this code section, the U.S. Supreme Court explained that in the absence of anything to the contrary, it is fair to assume that Congress, in using the word "forgery" in this section, which was adopted in 1823 and which remained in substantially the same form, used that word in its common law sense.[101]

After examining the provisions of Title 18 § 495 and other provisions of the federal code, the Court of Appeals for the Ninth Circuit reasoned that the forger of a treasury check endorsement may be prosecuted under the statutes penalizing those who falsely make, alter, forge, or counterfeit "other writings" with the intent of defrauding the United States (18 U.S.C. § 495) or under the statute providing specific penalties for forgery of treasury checks (18 U.S.C. § 493).[102] A defendant who qualifies for a prosecution under one section could be prosecuted under the other. The federal code provision relating to the federal crime of forgery also applies when the document is offered as genuine when known to be false.

H. False Advertising

The Federal Trade Commission is the federal agency that regulates fair advertising. Competitors or consumers may bring complaints to the FTC if they feel an advertisement is false. For instance, weight loss products that claim 10 pounds a week with no diet or exercise, or some herbal products that are "guaranteed" to lower your cholesterol will often be the targets of such claims. Generally, the FTC brings the violator into compliance through the threat of civil action rather than criminal prosecution. The FTC issues cease-and-desist orders, which usually are sufficient to stop the advertiser from running false ads. In some cases the advertiser is forced to run corrective ads; and, in some cases, the FTC will demand damages for consumers. There is also the ability of competitors to sue for damages when the false advertising affects their profits. In order for a competitor to sue, they must show that the advertisement was commercial advertising of goods and services that contained a false or misleading statement or description of the product or service or the competitor's product or service. The falsity must be material to the consumer's decision to purchase.

The Federal Trade Commission Act, 15 U.S.C. § 52(a), creates criminal liability for some forms of false advertising. It defines false advertising as a deceptive or unfair trade practice with the elements being

- the dissemination of or causing to be disseminated any false advertisement;
- by use of U.S. mails or by any means;

---

[101]   Gilbert v. United States, 370 U.S. 650 (1962).
[102]   United States v. LeCoe, 936 F.2d 398 (9th Cir. 1991).

- for the purpose of inducing or which is likely to directly or indirectly induce the purchase of food, drugs, devices, services, or cosmetics.

Recall from Chapter 9 that states also have false advertising statutes. State attorneys general will also pursue false advertising claims and, again, in almost all cases, the remedies are civil rather than criminal except for, perhaps, cases where there is actual intentional fraud; for example, vacation club claims that contain lies in order to get people to send money in return for vouchers that are not what they have been claimed to be. Similar to the earlier discussion, the FTC is concerned only with material falsities, not "puffery." Most commercials contain a certain amount of exaggeration and the consumer is expected to recognize when some claims are outrageous and presented for entertainment purposes (e.g., the man whose aftershave has women chasing after him or the truck that drives up the side of a building). Interestingly, the FTC specifically does not regulate or restrict false or misleading statements by political candidates or others during an election cycle.

I. Computer Fraud, Hacking, Illegal Downloading of Intellectual Property, and Identity Theft

As discussed in Chapter 9, the use of computers in crime has necessitated a response by legislators and law enforcement. Computers can be the object of crime (theft), the subject (vandalism and hacking), or the instrument (child pornography, fraud). If a computer is the instrument of crime (e.g., the use of a computer to commit fraud), then new crimes may not need to be defined; however, in the other instances, state and federal legislators have had to define actions as crimes that would not have been under common law (e.g., hacking). The first federal legislation became law in October 1984, when President Ronald Reagan signed into law the Counterfeit Access Device and Computer Fraud and Abuse Act of 1984. This was part of the Comprehensive Crime Control Act of 1984. The Department of Justice (DOJ) broadly defines computer crime as "any violation of criminal law that involves knowledge of computer technology for their perpetration, investigation, or prosecution."[103]

Title 18 § 1030 of the U.S. Code protects against various crimes involving "protected" computers. Protected computers include those used in interstate commerce or communications, which arguably would be most computers used by businesses. Subsection 1030(a) lists the seven specific acts of computer-related crime that the NIIPA prohibits.

- Subsection 1030(a)(1) makes it a crime to access computer files without authorization or in excess of authorization, and subsequently to transmit classified government action.

---

[103]   National Institute of Justice, Computer Crime: Criminal Justice Resource Manual (1989).

- Subsection 1030(a)(2) prohibits obtaining, without access or in excess of authorized access, information from financial institutions, the United States government, or private sector computers that are used in interstate commerce.
- Subsection 1030(a)(3) proscribes intentionally accessing a United States department or agency nonpublic computer without authorization. If the government or a government agency does not use the computer exclusively, the illegal access must affect the government's use in order to violate this law.
- Subsection 1030(a)(4) prohibits accessing a protected computer, without or beyond authorization, with the intent to defraud and obtain something of value. There is an exception if the defendant only obtained computer time with a value less than $5,000 per year.
- Subsection 1030(a)(5), which addresses computer hacking, has sustained the most substantial modifications following passage of the USA PATRIOT Act of 2001. In response to concerns about malicious computer cracking and computer terrorism, the USA PATRIOT Act reduced the *mens rea* required in order to commit the crime and now anyone who is reckless or negligent in their actions and that causes damage can be guilty of this federal crime. Furthermore, those who have authorization but intentionally cause damage may also be guilty of the crime.
- Subsection 1030(a)(6) prohibits one with intent to defraud from trafficking in passwords that would either permit unauthorized access to a government computer or affect interstate or foreign commerce.
- Finally, § 1030(a)(7) makes it illegal to transmit in interstate or foreign commerce any threat to cause damage to a protected computer with intent to extort something of value.

Whereas the 1996 Act's definition of "damage" contained certain minimum requirements, the USA PATRIOT Act amends the 1996 Act's definition of "damage" so that now § 1030(a)(5)(A) can be violated by "any impairment to the integrity or availability of data, a program, a system, or information." The effect of the amendments to § 1030(a)(5) has been to prohibit and punish crimes under this section that cause minimal damage and to increase the punishment for crimes causing significant damage.

LEGAL NEWS: STRATFOR HACKING CASE THREATENS NATIONAL SECURITY

In late 2011 it was discovered that a group called "Anonymous" hacked into the computer of Stratfor (Strategic Forecasting Inc.), a "geopolitical analysis and security intelligence company" based in Austin that provided services to a range of private corporations, the U.S. military, and other government agencies. The group was able to access the names and private information, including credit card numbers, of 75,000 of Stratfor's clients because they weren't encrypted, much to the embarrassment of the company's directors. They published the information on December 24, 2011 and experts warn that this has exposed the clients to "spear phishing," a targeted approach hackers use to infect users' computers with viruses.

Source: Hacking exposes military, FBI email. *Austin American Statesman*, January 5, 2012, B1, B5.

In interpreting 18 U.S.C. § 1030, a federal court of appeals decided that the computer fraud statute did not require the government to prove that the defendant intentionally damaged the computer files, but only that the defendant intentionally accessed the computer without authorization.[104] In this case, the defendant, a former bank employee, returned to her former work site and used a key that she kept and an old password to log onto the bank's mainframe. As a result, the bank's files were severely damaged. The defendant was convicted of violating the computer fraud statute. The court enumerated the elements that must be proved, stating that in order to have violated the statute, a defendant must have (1) accessed, (2) a federal interest computer, (3) without authorization, and (4) have altered, damaged, or destroyed information, (5) resulting in the loss to one or more others (6) of at least $1,000. In deciding this case, the court decided that the "intentionally" standard applies only to the "accesses" phase of § 1030 (a)(5)(A), and not to the "damages" phase.

In the case of *United States v. Middleton*, the defendant was convicted of intentionally causing damage to a protected computer in violation of 18 U.S.C. § 1030. The defendant worked as the personal computer administrator for an Internet service provider. Dissatisfied with his job, the defendant quit, then began to write threatening e-mails to his former employer. In addition to other violations, the defendant accessed the account of a sales representative and created two new accounts. He also changed all of the administrative passwords, altered the computer's registry, deleted the entire billing system, and deleted two internal databases. The defendant moved to dismiss the indictment, arguing that the corporation was not an "individual" within the meaning of the statute. The court disagreed, holding that the statute is broad enough to include corporations as well as natural persons and that the statute criminalizes computer crime that damages natural persons and corporations alike.[105]

The use of technology, especially computers, will continue to challenge law enforcement and require additional laws. Congress enacted the Family Entertainment and Copyright Act of 2005, which makes it a felony to use a computer to upload

---

[104] United States v. Sablan, 92 F.3d 865 (9th Cir. 1996).
[105] United States v. Middleton, 231 F.3d 1207 (9th Cir. 1991).

unreleased movies, games, or software, even if the use is purely personal.[106] More recently, a bill called Stop Online Piracy Act (SOPA) has been controversial with advocates and opponents hotly arguing whether or not the law should be passed.

LEGAL NEWS: SOPA: WILL IT KILL THE INTERNET?

In 2011 SOPA was a bitterly contested proposed new act to control online pirating of movies and music. SOPA gives the Justice Department the power to shut down "rogue" offshore websites that sell pirated materials on the Internet and force Internet websites to block content from those sites. Major Internet providers are against the legislation because they say it would unfairly blame them and force them to regulate content. Further, they say the legislation is written much too broadly and would criminalize a Youtube.com video that showed teenagers dancing because of the music playing in the background. Industry groups that represent songwriters, musicians, and Hollywood producers favor the legislation. The bill never made it out of the House Judiciary Committee in 2011 so it will take some time before the Act is passed, if ever.

Author of U.S. online piracy bill vows not to buckle. Reuters.com. January 11, 2012. Accessed January 12, 2012 from http://news.yahoo.com/author-u-online-piracy-bill-vows-not-buckle-013659789.html.

Laws related to spam, spoofing, and phishing have been passed. Computers are also used in identity theft. The prevalence of identity theft connected with the Internet has led to passage of the Fair and Accurate Credit Transactions Act (FACTA), which allows consumers one free credit report per year and the ability to freeze their credit so that identity thieves cannot obtain credit. It is estimated that 8.4 million credit card numbers are stolen each year resulting in losses of $118 billion. Hackers break into companies' websites and steal consumers' credit card numbers and security numbers and then sell the information in chatrooms and "eBay-like" websites oriented to computer criminals. It is reported that foreign criminals even have access to services that will provide them with English-speaking operatives when they need telephone calls made to banks to facilitate their criminal actions.[107] Even with laws designed to punish such actions, prosecutions are difficult because computer crime is difficult to trace and often takes place in countries that are either unwilling or unable to assist U.S. law enforcement.

---

[106] 18 U.S.C. § 875(c)
[107] Stolen Credit Cards Go For $3.50 at Amazon-like Online Bazaar. ITAC Blog. Retrieved 4/10/2012 from http://itacidentityblog.com/stolen-credit-cards-go-for-3.50-at-amazon-like-online-bazaar.

J. Tax Evasion and Money Laundering

The power to enforce tax laws is a direct power enumerated in the Constitution; therefore, there is no need for the commerce clause to be used to indirectly recognize the power to pass and enforce tax evasion laws. Tax evasion is a type of fraud. There must be an affirmative act to evade or attempt to evade and the *mens rea* is willfulness. The government must show that the individual has a tax deficiency (meaning that he or she has not paid sufficient taxes). To prove a tax deficiency the government may do so by direct means (existence of income payments that do not match what was reported), or by indirect means (evidence of lifestyle or bank account far beyond what income would support). In order to constitute the felony of tax evasion, there must be an affirmative act to evade—mere neglect to file returns is only a misdemeanor. The affirmative act to prove evasion might be filing a false return or concealing assets. This would also go to prove the *mens rea* of willfulness.

Money laundering is the process by which one conceals the existence, illegal source, or illegal application of income, and disguises that income to make it appear legitimate. Laundering criminally derived proceeds has become a lucrative, sophisticated business in the United States and is an indispensable element of organized crime's activities. Without the ability to move and hide their enormous wealth through laundering techniques, large-scale criminal activities could operate at only a small fraction of current levels, and with far less flexibility.

The federal government has attacked money laundering in different ways, beginning indirectly by imposing statutory reporting requirements. The Bank Secrecy Act made failure to report certain transactions a crime, although large cash transactions were not themselves illegal. Statutory loopholes and mixed judicial interpretations of the statute led to the Money Laundering Control Act of 1986 (MLCA).[108]

The money laundering offenses in MLCA are twofold. First, 18 U.S.C. § 1956 prohibits an individual's involvement in a financial transaction when the individual knows that the property involved in the transaction represents the proceeds of specified unlawful activities. The individual must engage in the transaction with either the intent to promote the carrying on of a specified unlawful activity, or with the knowledge that the purpose of the transaction is either to avoid a reporting requirement or to conceal the nature, location, source, ownership, or control of the specified unlawful activity proceeds.

Section 1957 prohibits an individual from engaging or attempting to engage in a monetary transaction involving property valued at more than $10,000 when the individual knows that the property is derived from specific unlawful activities. A monetary transaction is defined in the statute as a "deposit, withdrawal, transfer, or exchange, in or affecting interstate or foreign commerce or funds . . . by, through, or to a financial institution."

---

[108]   18 U.S.C. §§ 1956-1957 (1988)

There are four elements that must be established in order to obtain a conviction under 18 U.S.C. §§ 1956-1957. These elements are

- knowledge,
- the existence of a specified unlawful activity,
- a financial transaction, and
- intent.

The justices of the Tenth Circuit Court of Appeals noted that under the statute that prohibits engaging in monetary transactions with criminally derived property, the requirement that the monetary transaction in question be "in or affecting interstate or foreign commerce" is both jurisdictional and an essential element of the defense.[109] In discussing the elements required to prove a violation of § 1957, a federal court determined that the particular motive or cause that led the defendant to attempt transfer of the funds from one bank account to another was not material and thus did not preclude conviction on a charge of engaging in monetary transactions derived from unlawful activity.[110] In interpreting the money laundering statute, the courts have consistently held that the statute is not unconstitutionally vague.[111]

Another statute that makes it more difficult to hide illegally acquired funds is the **anti-structuring law**.[112] Federal law requires banks and other financial institutions to file reports with the Secretary of the Treasury whenever they are involved in a cash transaction that exceeds $10,000. It is illegal to "structure" transactions—that is, to break up a single transaction above the reporting threshold into two or more separate transactions for the purpose of evading the financial institution's reporting requirements. A person who willfully violates this anti-structuring provision is subject to criminal penalties.

To establish that a defendant willfully violated the anti-structuring law, the government must prove that the defendant acted with knowledge that the conduct was unlawful. In the case of *Ratzlaf v. United States*, the defendant ran up a debt of $160,000 playing blackjack at a Reno, Nevada, casino. The casino gave the defendant one week to pay. On the due date, the defendant returned to the casino with $100,000 in cash. After the casino official advised the defendant that all transactions involving more than $10,000 in cash must be reported to the state and federal authorities, the casino placed a limousine at the defendant's disposal and assigned an employee to accompany him to banks in the vicinity. The defendant purchased cashier's checks, each for less than $10,000 and each from a different bank. The defendant was charged with "structuring transactions" to evade the bank's obligation to report cash transactions exceeding

---

[109]   United States v. Allen, 129 F.3d 1159 (10th Cir. 1997).
[110]   United States v. Norman, 143 F.3d 375 (8th Cir. 1998).
[111]   United States v. Jackson, 988 F.2d 757 (7th Cir. 1993).
[112]   31 U.S.C. § 5313; 31 U.S.C. § 5322.

$10,000, violating 31 U.S.C. §§ 5322 and 5324. The trial judge instructed the jury that the government had to prove the defendant's knowledge of the bank's reporting obligations and its attempt to evade the obligation, but did not have to prove that the defendant knew the structuring was unlawful. The defendant was convicted, fined, and sentenced to prison. On appeal, the defendant maintained that he could not be convicted because this was not a "willful violation." The U.S. Supreme Court agreed with the defendant that the government had an obligation to prove that the defendant knew that the structuring was unlawful and reversed the conviction. The court noted that the "willfulness" requirement of the statute mandates both "knowledge of the reporting requirement" and a "specific intent to commit the crime."[113]

Congress responded to the perceived interaction of money laundering and terrorism by passing the Uniting and Strengthening America by Providing Appropriate Tools Required to Intercept and Obstruct Terrorism (USA PATRIOT Act). In this Act, the Secretary of the Treasury is given broad discretion and power to require banks and financial institutions in the United States to play a significant role in the process of uncovering money laundering. Part of the Act requires banks to take reasonable action to discover the identity of foreign account owners and the source of their funds. The Act also provides that the President should direct the Secretary of State, the Attorney General, and/or the Secretary of the Treasury to negotiate with the appropriate state officials and financial institutions of foreign nations to provide for cooperative enforcement efforts and better mechanisms for information sharing. Changes to the law have required banks to report, not just transactions over $10,000, but any "suspicious" transactions.[114]

§ 12.7 Summary

Not all sections from the chapters discussing state crimes have parallels in this chapter. It is important to understand that federal crimes are defined statutorily in the U.S. Code, they are prosecuted by federal prosecutors, and they are tried in federal courts. Offenders serve time, if convicted and sentenced to prison, in the Federal Bureau of Prisons. In order for the legislature to pass a law creating a crime, it must not violate any of the constitutional rights discussed in Chapter 1 and this chapter. Further, it must have some nexus to federal powers. Acts such as fraud that are prosecuted as federal crimes have some connection to interstate commerce, (e.g., use of interstate mail or other interstate communications), or they are committed within the maritime or territorial jurisdiction of the United States (e.g., Washington D.C.). Computers can be either the object or target of crime or the vehicle by which crimes are committed. Various federal laws have been passed to combat hacking and other computer crimes. Federal laws also encompass tax evasion and money laundering.

---

[113] Ratzlaf v. United States, 510 U.S. 135, 114 S. Ct. 655, 126 L. Ed. 2d 615 (1994).
[114] *Money Laundering*, 39 AMER. CRIM. LAW REV. 839, 861 (2002).

REVIEW QUESTIONS

1. What are the sources for federal criminal laws? Explain the federal court system.

2. What is the source for federal drug laws?

3. Explain the constitutional challenges that are used against federal laws.

4. Explain how the Insanity Defense Reform Act of 1986 changed the federal law regarding prosecution of those who alleged insanity.

5. Explain the elements necessary to use the duress claim against a federal prosecution.

6. What test of entrapment does the federal government use in *Jacobsen v. United States*?

7. Explain how the federal code defines *attempt*. Is there a general attempt statute or not? Explain factual and legal impossibility under federal law.

8. Explain the RICO conspiracy provisions; how are they different from Section 371 of Title 18?

9. What is the Laci and Conner law? What types of homicide are recognized in federal law?

10. The federal law relating to assault that is most often enforced is Title 18 §111. What are the provisions of this federal statute? How have the courts defined "while engaged in the performance of official duties"?

11. Explain the nexus between kidnapping and federal power. Explain the nexus between the rape statute and federal power. Explain what, if any, federal laws address hate crimes.

12. What two sources of power are used for federal arson statutes? Explain. Does the U.S. Code have a general trespass statute? Explain.

14. The federal code section titled "Stolen property" deals with the transportation and sale of stolen vehicles, securities, and other personal property. What must the government prove in order to convict a person of transporting a stolen vehicle in interstate commerce? How is this different from the carjacking statutes?

15. What elements must be proved in order to convict a person of bank robbery under the federal law?

16. The federal statute includes an offense titled "Theft, embezzlement or misappropriation by a bank officer or employee." What are the elements of this offense? What other ways might embezzlement become a federal crime?

17. Does the federal computer fraud statute (18 U.S.C. § 1030) require that the government prove the defendant intentionally damaged the computer files?

18. In the case of *United States v. Middleton*, what was included in the statute's term damage to the victim by computer hacking? How does the USA PATRIOT Act change that definition?

19. What behavior has become criminal through the passage of the Family Entertainment and Copyright Act of 2005? Explain.

20. What has Congress done to combat the growing problem of identity theft? Explain.

United States Criminal Code: Other Offenses

13

Chapter Outline

Cases

Virtual Child Pornography: *United States v. Williams*, 553 U.S. 285 (2008)
Marijuana and Medical Necessity: *Gonzales v. Raich*, 545 U.S. 1, 125 S. Ct. 2195
   (2005)
Cyberstalking: *United States v. Bowker*, 372 F.3d 365 (6th Cir. 2004)
Patriot Act: *Holder v. Humanitarian Law Project,* 130 S.Ct. 2705 (2010)

antitrust laws	insider trading
child pornography	obscenity
churning	Occupational Safety and Health Act
controlled substance	Patriot Act
corporate crime	*respondeat superior*
double jeopardy	RICO
environmental crime	Schedule I
Fair Labor Standards Act	states' rights
forfeiture	white-collar crime
gratuity	wiretapping

§ 13.1   Introduction

As with all the crimes in the preceding chapter, federal crimes in the areas of morality, offenses against public peace, and offenses against justice administration must have a nexus to some federal power. In addition to reviewing common law crimes, we will close this text with a short discussion of federal regulatory crimes. Crimes that are based on violations of the regulations promulgated by federal agencies (e.g., the Environmental Protection Agency or the Securities and Exchange Commission) are regulatory crimes and they are based, again, on the commerce clause of the Constitution. One of the interesting aspects of regulatory crimes is that corporations can be the guilty party, although obviously you can't put a corporation in prison.

§ 13.2   Offenses against Morality

Recall that Chapter 9 dealt with a range of behaviors that were determined to offend public morality to the extent that they were defined as criminal, including various forms of sexual activity, pornography, and abortion. Because police power lies in the state, it is largely up to the states to legislate against these activities. However, federal laws parallel state laws to punish offenses that occur under federal maritime or territorial jurisdiction, and other federal laws exist to criminalize activities with some interstate commerce nexus.

A. *Adultery, Fornication, and Prostitution*

Although Title 18 of the federal code contains no provision that directly prohibits adultery or fornication, Title 18 § 2421 includes a penalty for one who knowingly transports an individual in interstate or foreign commerce with intent that such individual engage in "any sexual activity for which any person can be charged with a criminal offense." This applies to adultery if adultery is a crime under the state law. Title 18 § 2421 was designated "White slave traffic" and has now been retitled "Transportation for Illegal Sexual Activity and Related Crimes." This section of the code was originally passed in 1910 and was amended in 1948, 1978, and 1986. The code was amended in 1948, 1978, and 1986. The 1986 version is as follows:

18 U.S.C. § 2421—Transportation generally

Whoever knowingly transports any individual in interstate or foreign commerce, or any Territory or Possession of the United States, with intent that such individual engage in prostitution, or in any sexual activity for which any person can be charged with criminal offense, or attempts to do so, shall be fined under this title or imprisoned not more than 10 years, or both.

The amended act, unlike previous versions, does not restrict application to females, although the initial law, when originally passed, was "to curb white slave traffic in interstate commerce and to eliminate traffic in women by procurers who forced victims to lead a life of debauchery."[1] In order to constitute an offense under § 2421, the prosecution must prove, among other elements, that the defendant knowingly transported an individual in interstate or foreign commerce or attempted to do so. Also, the prosecution must necessarily prove that the defendant transported such individual with intent for that person to engage in prostitution or other sexual activity for which a person can be charged with a criminal offense.[2] After examining the "purpose" element of the statute, the justices of the Second Circuit concluded that prostitution or any criminal sexual activity needs to be *one of the* dominant purposes, but need not be *the* dominant purpose of travel in order to convict.[3]

A second federal statute proscribes knowingly persuading, inducing, enticing, or coercing an individual to travel in interstate or foreign commerce to engage in prostitution or other sexual activities prohibited by law. This section provides

18 U.S.C. § 2422—Coercion and enticement

(a) Whoever knowingly persuades, induces, entices, or coerces any individual to travel in interstate or foreign commerce, or in any Territory or Possession of the

---

[1] United States v. Wheeler, 444 F.2d 385 (10th Cir. 1971).
[2] United States v. Jones, 909 F.2d 533 (D.C. Cir. 1990).
[3] United States v. Miller, 148 F.3d 207 (2d Cir. 1998); also see United States v. Kennedy, 442 F.2d 444 (10th Cir. 1971).

> United States, to engage in prostitution, or in any sexual activity for which any person can be charged with a criminal offense, or attempts to do so, shall be fined under this title or imprisoned not more than 10 years, or both.
>
> (b) Whoever, using the mail or any facility or means of interstate or foreign commerce, or within the special maritime and territorial jurisdiction of the United States knowingly persuades, induces, entices, or coerces any individual who has not attained the age of 18 years, to engage in prostitution or any sexual activity for which any person can be charged with a criminal offense, or attempts to do so, shall be fined under this title, imprisoned not more than 15 years, or both.[4]

Finding that this section of the statute is not unconstitutional, a federal court reasoned that the criminal statute that prohibits using the means of interstate commerce to persuade a minor to engage in a sexual act did not violate the First Amendment. Although the method of persuasion usually involves some form of speech, this statute did not attempt to regulate the content of the speech, but merely criminalized the conduct that incidentally involved speech.[5]

It is not **double jeopardy** to convict a defendant under both Sections 2421 and 2422, because these are separate and distinct offenses. Also, it is not improper to convict one defendant of two violations for the single act of transporting a minor female and an adult woman across the state line for purposes of prostitution.[6]

Title 18 § 2423 relates to transportation of minors with the intent that the minor engage in prostitution. The penalty for violating this provision is "not more than fifteen years" while the penalty under § 2421 is 10 years. The statute provides

> 18 U.S.C. § 2423 Transportation of minors
>
> (a) Transportation with intent to engage in criminal sexual activity. A person who knowingly transports any individual under the age of 18 years in interstate or foreign commerce, or in any Territory or Possession of the United States, with intent that the individual engage in prostitution, or in any sexual activity for which any person can be charged with a criminal offense, or attempts to do so shall be fined under this title or imprisoned not more than fifteen years, or both.

In the case of *United States v. Scisum*, the defendant appealed his conviction, arguing that the definition of "intent" was too vague.[7] The reviewing court held that the word "intent" was of common enough usage to be clear to a reasonable lay juror. The

---

[4] 18 U.S.C. § 2422. Section 2423 has similar provisions relating to transportation of minors in interstate or foreign commerce. The maximum term under this statute is 15 years.

[5] United States v. Kufrovich, 997 F. Supp. 246 (D. Conn. 1997).

[6] United States v. Taitano, 442 F.2d 467 (9th Cir.), cert. denied, 404 U.S. 852, 92 S. Ct. 92, 30 L. Ed. 2d 92 (1971); United States v. Parr, 741 F.2d 878 (5th Cir. 1984). *See also* United States v. Rashkovski, 301 F.3d 1133 (9th Cir. 2002), for cases relating to transporting Russian women to the United States in violation of this section.

[7] United States v. Scisum, 32 F.3d 1479 (10th Cir. 1994). *See also* United States v. Footman, 33 F. Supp. 2d 60 (D. Mass. 1988).

court advised, however, that the government must prove that the defendant formed intent before the defendant transported the person across state lines.

Ignorance of the victim's age provides no defense. In *United States v. Taylor*, the court indicated that if a person knowingly transports a person for the purposes of prostitution or another sex offense, the transporter assumes the risk that the victim is a minor, regardless of what the victim says or how the victim appears.[8] In another case, prohibiting transporting a minor in interstate commerce with intent that the minor engage in illegal sexual activity did not require a determination that the defendant intended to have illegal sex with the minor when he initially transported her from her state of origin, but rather that the defendant intended such illegal acts before the conclusion of his interstate journey.[9]

In addition to these statutes, Title 18 § 1384 authorizes the secretaries of the Army, Navy, and Air Force to designate areas within a reasonable distance of any military or naval camp, station, or post, where prostitution and other related offenses shall be prohibited, and provides a fine or imprisonment for failure to comply with such directive.[10]

B. Obscenity

Chapter 71 of the United States Code ("**Obscenity**") comprehensively lists and defines offenses dealing with obscenity and related issues. These statutes have been so expanded and amended that there is little that is not covered. The statutes, as written and broadly interpreted, give the federal government broad authority to investigate and prosecute crimes that are related to obscenity. The offenses described in Chapter 71 are

- Section 1460—Possession with intent to sell, and sale of, obscene matter on federal property.
- Section 1461—Mailing obscene or crime-inciting matter.
- Section 1462—Importation or transportation of obscene matters.
- Section 1463—Mailing indecent matter on wrappers or envelopes.
- Section 1464—Broadcasting obscene language.
- Section 1465—Transportation of obscene matters for sale or distribution.
- Section 1466—Engaging in the business of selling or transferring obscene matter.
- Section 1466A—Obscene visual representations of the sexual abuse of children
- Section 1467—Criminal forfeiture.
- Section 1468—Distributing obscene material by cable or subscription television.
- Section 1470—Transfer of obscene materials to minors.
- Section 2252A—Certain activities relating to material involving the sexual exploitation of minors.

---

[8] United States v. Taylor, 239 F.3d 994 (9th Cir. 2001).
[9] United States v. Cole, 262 F.3d 704 (8th Cir. 2001).
[10] 18 U.S.C. § 1384.

Section 1460 applies only where the possession or sale occurs in the special maritime and territorial jurisdiction of the United States. The other sections have more universal coverage. Title 18 § 1461 of the federal statute is the provision most often used in prosecuting at the federal level. This section mandates a fine or imprisonment for not more than five years, or both, if the defendant is convicted of using the mail to distribute obscene, lewd, lascivious, indecent, filthy, or vile articles, matter, things, devices, or substances and other materials as defined in the statute.

In interpreting this provision of the U.S. Code, federal courts follow the Supreme Court definition of "obscene" as approved in the case of *Miller v. California*, discussed in Chapter 9. Recall that in that case, obscenity was defined by answering the following questions: (1) Does the material appeal to prurient interests? (2) Does it depict "hard-core" sexual acts previously defined by state law in a patently offensive way? (3) Does it lack serious literary, artistic, political, scientific, or other value? Also recall that the Supreme Court declined to exclude violent and sexually explicit video games from First Amendment protections in *Brown v. Entertainment Merchants Assoc.*[11] Observers note that the definition of obscenity has more to do with sex than violence.

The Third Circuit Court of Appeals decided that § 1461, which prohibits knowingly using the mail for obscene materials, applies to persons who order obscene materials through the mail, even if they are for personal use. In the case of *United States v. Schein,* the defendant was convicted of mailing obscene materials. The defendant appealed, claiming that similar material had been shown at an exhibit funded by the government's National Endowment for the Arts, and that his tapes promoted sexual safety. The reviewing court rejected the defendant's arguments. Citing other cases, the court held that

- Obscene material is not protected by the First Amendment.
- The fact that the photographs of urolagnic pornography were shown at exhibits funded by the National Endowment for the Arts did not establish that videotapes containing graphic depictions of urination, masturbation, and oral and anal sex among homosexual males were not obscene.
- Merely promoting safe sex does not bring the material within the exception noted in part (c) of the *Miller* case.
- Mere availability of similar material means nothing more than other persons are engaged in similar activity.[12]

Title 18 § 1462 provides a penalty of a fine or five years' imprisonment, or both, for the first offense, and a fine and ten years' imprisonment for the second offense if the defendant is convicted of importation or transportation of obscene matters as defined in the statute.

---

[11]   Miller v. California, 413 U.S. 15 (1983); Brown v. Entertainment Merchants Assoc., 564 U.S. __ (2011).

[12]   United States v. Schein, 31 F.3d 135 (3d Cir. 1994).

Title 18 § 1463 prohibits the mailing of indecent matters on wrappers or envelopes, and § 1464 provides a penalty for one who utters any obscene, indecent, or profane language by means of radio communications. Section 1465 makes it a crime punishable by a fine or five years' imprisonment, or both, to knowingly transport, travel in, or use a facility, or means of interstate or foreign commerce or an interactive computer service in or affecting such commerce, for the purpose of sale or distribution of any obscene, lewd, lascivious, or filthy book, pamphlet, picture, film, paper, letter, writing, print, silhouette, drawing, figure, image, cast, phonograph recording, electrical transcription, or other article capable of producing sound or any matter of indecent or immoral character.

In the case of *United States v. Thomas*, the federal court made it clear that this statute, as amended, applies to computer-generated images moved from the defendants' computer bulletin board in one state to a personal computer in another state.[13]

Section 1466 makes it a crime to engage in the business of selling or transferring obscene matters. Violators shall be punished by imprisonment of not more than five years or by a fine or both. To further discourage related violations, § 1467 provides for forfeiture of obscene material as well as property, real or personal, used or intended to be used to commit or to promote the commission of such offenses. In 1988, the offense of "Distributing obscene material by cable or subscription television" was added. Section 1468 provides in part that

18 U.S.C. § 1468

[W]hoever knowingly utters any obscene language or distributes any obscene matter by means of cable television or subscription service on television, shall be punished by imprisonment for not more than two years or by fine in accordance with this title, or both.

The federal government regulates the airwaves through the powers derived under the commerce clause. The FCC (Federal Communications Commission) is the federal agency tasked with making sure that obscenity doesn't appear. However, obscenity may be in the eye of the beholder and the ability of the FCC to regulate what appears on network television is always in flux. The Supreme Court will rule in 2012 whether or not networks can be fined for allowing fleeting obscenities and nudity on the air in the case described in the news box.

LEGAL NEWS: *FCC V. FOX*

On January 10, 2012, the Supreme Court heard arguments for *FCC v. Fox*. The question presented in the case is whether the FCC is impinging on First

---

[13]   United States v. Thomas, 74 F.3d 701 (6th Cir. 1996). See also Digest of Decisions included in the United States Code.

Amendment rights by regulating and punishing "dirty words" on network television. Several instances of fines have occurred when stars use the "f-word" in awards ceremonies or when there are fleeting views of nudity on network television. This case is a challenge to the *FCC v. Pacifica* ruling in 1978 where the Supreme Court upheld the FCC's right to sanction a radio station for airing George Carlin's famous "seven dirty words" monologue. The decision hinged on the fact that broadcast media was "uniquely pervasive" and entered people's living rooms and was accessible to children. The crux of the opposing argument is nudity and vulgar language is shown routinely on cable news programming and in other venues so the idea that it can be restricted on network television has less support than it did in 1978. Justices who seemed hostile to the FCC's authority noted that it seemed arbitrary and inconsistent. Justice Elena Kagan, noting that nudity was allowed in a showing of *Schindler's List,* but not *NYPD Blue,* and swearing was allowed in a showing of *Saving Private Ryan*, but not in a blues documentary, said, "It's like nobody can use dirty words or nudity except for Steven Spielberg." The Supreme Court is expected to issue a holding in the case by summer of 2012.

For more information go to the Supreme Court website: http://www.scotusblog.com/case-files/cases/fcc-v-fox-television-stations/.

1. Child Pornography

Recall that only certain depictions of sexual conduct (e.g., deviant or explicit depictions of intercourse) are "obscene" when adults are involved. However, depictions of children may be illegal if they are merely "lascivious." Furthermore, merely possessing child pornography is a crime, whereas it is not a crime to merely possess pornography involving adult actors. Both state and federal legislatures have had difficulty constructing legislation that protects children, but also does not run afoul of the First Amendment and criminalize movies or other media that portray underage characters (even though they are adult actors) in sexual situations. The federal statute 18 U.S.C. § 2252, titled "Certain activities relating to material involving the sexual exploitation of minors," provides

18 U.S.C. § 2252

(a) Any person who—
(1) knowingly transports or ships in interstate or foreign commerce by any means including by computer or mails, any visual depiction, if—
    (A) the producing of such visual depiction involves the use of a minor engaging in sexually explicit conduct; and
    (B) such visual depiction is of such conduct;

(2) knowingly receives, or distributes, any visual depiction that has been mailed, or has been shipped or transported in interstate or foreign commerce, or which contains materials which have been mailed or so shipped or transported, by any means including by computer, or knowingly reproduces any visual depiction for distribution in interstate or foreign commerce or through the mails, if—

    (A) in the special maritime and territorial jurisdiction of the United States, or on any land or building owned by, leased to, or otherwise used by or under the control of the Government of the United States, or in the Indian country as defined in § 1151 of this title, knowingly sells or possesses with intent to sell any visual depiction; or

    (B) knowingly sells or possesses with intent to sell any visual depiction that has been mailed, or has been shipped or transported in interstate or foreign commerce, or which was produced using materials which have been mailed or so shipped or transported, by any means, including by computer, if—

        (i) the producing of such visual depiction involves the use of a minor engaging in sexually explicit conduct; and

        (ii) such visual depiction is of such conduct; or

(3) either—

    (A) in the special maritime and territorial jurisdiction of the United States, or on any land or building owned by, leased to or otherwise used by or under the control of the Government of the United States, or in the Indian country as defined in § 1151 of this title, knowingly possesses 1 or more books, magazines, periodicals, films, video tapes, or other matter which contain any visual depiction; or

    (B) knowingly possesses 1 or more books, magazines, periodicals, films, video tapes, or other matter which contain any visual depiction that has been mailed, or has been shipped or transported in interstate or foreign commerce, or which was produced using materials which have been mailed or so shipped or transported, by any means including computer, if—

        (i) the producing of such visual depiction involves the use of a minor engaging in sexually explicit conduct; and

        (ii) such visual depiction is of such conduct; shall be punished as provided in subsection (b) of this section. . .

This statute has been challenged on several constitutional grounds. The federal courts have rejected the argument that the federal government has no power under the commerce clause to punish purely private use of obscene materials. The courts have found that the government had made a sufficient showing that a defendant's possession of pornography has a sufficiently substantial effect on interstate commerce to show a nexus between the federal pornography statute and a defendant's conduct.[14] The statute has also been challenged as being in violation of the First Amendment and overbroad; however, federal courts held that the conviction for possession of child pornography that has been transported in interstate commerce met constitutional standards.[15] Note

---

[14]   United States v. Harden, 45 Fed. Appx. 237 (4th Cir. 2002). *See also* United States v. Tucker, 150 F. Supp. 2d 1263 (C.D. Utah 2001), which held that the Child Pornography Prevention Act was passed pursuant to Congress's Commerce Power, and the Act is intended to prevent the traffic in and consumption of child pornography.

[15]   United States v. Maxwell, 49 F.3d 410 (4th Cir. 2002).

that this statute covers material that would not necessarily be viewed as obscene if all the performers were adult; the fact that one or more are children is what makes the material illegal.

In *United States v. X-Citement Video*,[16] the Supreme Court dealt with the question of whether the offender had to *know* the performer was a minor, or whether the verb "know" related to knowingly transport, receive, or distribute. The Supreme Court held that "knowing" refers to the knowledge that one of the performers in the material was underage. However, in *United States v. Davis*, a court held that age is a matter on which everyone has an opinion so it is therefore particularly appropriate for a lay witness to express an opinion on the subject.[17]

In the case of *United States v. Hersh*, the circuit court held that a conviction for receipt and possession of child pornography was supported by evidence that the defendant knowingly received and possessed computer files containing images, that the images were received via the Internet and the images portrayed real minors engaged in sexually explicit conduct, and that the defendant was aware of such.[18] The act requires the introduction of evidence that shows that the visual depiction involves the use of a minor engaging in sexually explicit conduct, and such visual depiction is of such conduct.

One of the newest areas of contention is the legality of pornography that utilizes computer-generated images of children. Title 18 § 2252A of the U.S. Code covers the receipt or transmission of pornography via the Internet that uses computer-generated images of children. The argument presented is that because there are no children harmed by the production of such pornography, it is impermissibly overbroad to apply the statute to such activity. The opposing argument is that the statute not only was created to protect children, but also societal morals; in addition, children may be shown such pornography to reduce their inhibitions against sexual behavior.

One federal court dealt with the issue in *United States v. Fox* and held that it was not unconstitutional to apply the child pornography definition to computer-generated images.[19] Then in *Ashcroft v. Free Speech Coalition*,[20] the Supreme Court ruled on the question and concluded that the provision violated First Amendment freedoms because it was overbroad and not closely related to the purpose of the statute, which was to protect children. Then Congress passed the Prosecutorial Remedies and Other Tools to end the Exploitation of Children Today Act of 2003 (PROTECT Act), which added an expanded definition of pandering child pornography to the existing child pornography statute. The statute criminalizes anyone who "panders," which includes noncommercial distribution as well as commercial, for instance, someone who shares the material over the Internet. It also criminalizes a mere offer with no necessary existence of the

---

[16]   513 U.S. 64 (1994).
[17]   United States v. Davis, 41 F.3d 566 (3d Cir. 2002).
[18]   United States v. Hersh, 297 F.3d 1233 (11th Cir. 2002).
[19]   United States v. Fox, 248 F.3d 394 (5th Cir. 2001).
[20]   535 U.S. 234 (2002).

Case Note: *United States v. Williams*, 553 U.S.
285 (2008)
What was the holding of the case?
What is the purpose of child pornography
statutes?
Can you possess computer-generated child
pornography?

prohibited contraband. Finally, it covers virtual child pornography if the person who is making the offer believes it to be child pornography or purports that it is, or it involves virtual child pornography that is obscene. In *United States v. Williams*, provided in Part II of this textbook, the Supreme Court upholds the constitutionality of the Act against a First Amendment challenge.[21]

The use of computers in the distribution of obscenity and child pornography has made enforcement of criminal laws extremely difficult because the product might be made internationally and distributed instantaneously across the world. The targets of federal laws are those persons who create or distribute child pornography, but also anyone who exposes children to pornography is subject to federal laws, as 18 U.S.C. § 231 indicates:

18 U.S.C. § 231

(a) Requirement to restrict access.
    (1) Prohibited conduct. Whoever knowingly and with knowledge of the character of the material, in interstate or foreign commerce by means of the World Wide Web, makes any communication for commercial purposes that is available to any minor and that includes any material that is harmful to minors shall be fined not more than $50,000, imprisoned not more than 6 months, or both.
    (2) Intentional violations. In addition to the penalties under paragraph (1), whoever intentionally violates such paragraph shall be subject to a fine of not more than $50,000 for each violation. For purposes of the paragraph, each day of violation shall constitute a separate violation.

C. Bigamy and Incest

Title 18 of the U.S. Code contains no specific provision concerning bigamy, nor any specific provision concerning the offense of incest except in reference to offenses committed within Indian territory.[22] This section provides that the offense of incest shall be defined and punished in accordance with the laws of the state in which such offense was committed and as are in force at the time of such offense.

D. Abortion

The laws restricting and/or criminalizing abortions are state laws, therefore most of the important cases in this area have already been covered in Chapter 10. If the federal legislature ever passes a law that criminalizes abortion across the nation by making it a federal crime, it would have to find the power to do so in the commerce clause. This

---

[21]   United States v. Williams, 553 U.S. 285 (2008).
[22]   8 U.S.C. § 1153.

is unlikely. Therefore, the federal crimes relating to abortion are incidental to the act itself. The Supreme Court will play a major role, however, in deciding whether or not new state laws are unconstitutional or not.

The Freedom of Access to Clinic Entrances Act was passed to protect individuals from demonstrators at abortion clinics and family planning centers. It includes a criminal as well as a civil penalty section. This Act provides

18 U.S.C. § 248

(a) Prohibited activities.—Whoever—
   (1) by force or threat or by physical obstruction, intentionally injures, intimidates or interferes with or attempts to injure, intimidate or interfere with any person because that person is or has been, or in order to intimidate such person or any other person or any class of persons from, obtaining or providing reproductive health services;
   (2) by force or threat of force or by physical obstruction, intentionally injures, intimidates or interferes with or attempts to injure, intimidate or interfere with any person lawfully exercising or seeking to exercise the First Amendment right of religious freedom at a place of religious freedom at a place of religious worship; or
   (3) intentionally damages or destroys the property of a facility, or attempts to do so, because such facility provides reproductive health services, or intentionally damages or destroys the property of a place of religious worship.
   Shall be subject to the penalties provided in subsection (b) and the civil remedies provided in subsection (c), except that a parent or legal guardian of a minor shall not be subject to any penalties or civil remedies under this section for such activities insofar as they are directed exclusively at that minor . . .

A federal court decided that the Freedom of Access to Clinic Entrances Act is not unconstitutionally vague in violation of due process.[23] The justices of the Eighth Circuit Court of Appeals agreed that parking rental trucks at the entrances of abortion clinics could constitute a "threat of force" in violation of the Freedom of Access to Clinic Entrances Act. The court noted that the clinic staff did, in fact, perceive the trucks as a threat of force, and there was testimony that the defendant sought, by his actions, to frighten clinic patients and staff.[24]

In *Scheidler v. National Organization for Women, Inc.*,[25] an organization that supports the legal availability of abortion and two facilities that perform abortions filed a class action alleging that petitioners, individuals, and organizations that oppose legal abortion violated the Racketeer Influenced and Corrupt Organizations Act (RICO) by engaging in a nationwide conspiracy to shut down abortion clinics through "a pattern of racketeering activity" that included acts of extortion in violation of the Hobbs Act.

The District Court agreed with the respondents and awarded damages, and entered a permanent nationwide injunction against the petitioners. The Court of Appeals

[23] United States v. Balint, 201 F.3d 928 (7th Cir. 2000).
[24] United States v. Hart, 212 F.3d 1067 (8th Cir. 2000).
[25] Scheidler v. N.O.W., Inc., 126 S. Ct. 1264 (2006).

upheld the issuance of the injunction. The United States Supreme Court reversed the decision of the District Court and held that, because the acts of physical violence were not in pursuit of pecuniary gain, there was no underlying felony that could constitute the necessary racketeering required for RICO. The Court of Appeals, upon remand, ordered the case to go back to the District Court to determine whether any other acts committed by the abortion protesters, unrelated to extortion, might be considered violations of the Hobbs Act. Upon appeal back to the Supreme Court, the majority ruled that no acts of abortion protesters were properly prosecuted under the RICO statute.[26]

Other federal statutes that relate to abortion are 18 U.S.C. § 1461, which prohibits the mailing of articles or things designed, adapted, or intended to produce abortion and 18 U.S.C. § 1462, which prohibits bringing into the United States any drug, medicine, article, or thing designed, adapted, or intended to produce abortion.[27]

§ 13.3   Offenses against Public Peace

Various laws that prohibit activities that could be described as offending the public peace were described in Chapter 11. Similar federal laws must address behavior that falls within the maritime and territorial jurisdiction of the federal government or has some nexus to commerce; for instance, incitement to riot is a state crime, but traveling between states to incite a riot is a federal crime.

A. Riot and Related Offenses

Title 18 § 2101 of the U.S. Code prescribes penalties for one who travels in interstate commerce to incite a riot. It states in part that

18 U.S.C. § 2101

(a) Whoever travels in interstate or foreign commerce or uses any facility of interstate or foreign commerce, including, but not limited to, the mail, telegraph, telephone, radio, or television, with intent:
   (1) to incite a riot; or
   (2) to organize, promote, encourage, participate in, or carry on a riot; or
   (3) to commit any act of violence in furtherance of a riot; or
   (4) to aid or abet any person in inciting or participating in or carrying on a riot or committing any act of violence in furtherance of the riot; and who either, during the course of any such travel or use thereafter, performs or attempts to perform any other overt act for any purpose specified in subparagraphs (1), (2), (3) or (4)—
   shall be fined under this title or imprisoned for not more than 5 years, or both.

---

[26]   Scheidler v. N.O.W., Inc., 537 U.S. 393 (2003).
[27]   18 U.S.C. § 1461 and 18 U.S.C. § 1462.

This statute goes on to provide that a judgment of conviction or acquittal on the merits of the laws of any state shall be a bar to any prosecution hereunder for the same act or acts. Title 18 § 2102 defines the term "riot." To assure that the First Amendment provisions are not violated, the definition of the term "to incite a riot" includes a statement that this shall not be deemed to mean the mere oral or written advocacy of ideas or expression of belief, not involving advocacy of any act or acts of violence or assertion of the rightness of, or the right to commit any such act or acts. The federal riot act has been upheld as not in violation of the U.S. Constitution.[28]

In interpreting the provisions of Title 18 §§ 2101 and 2102, a federal circuit court considered two issues: (1) Are interstate telephone calls to summon others to participate in a riot proscribed by the federal anti-riot act? (2) What amounts to a "riot" for the purposes of the Act?[29] The court decided that when the defendant made an international call to summon Oneida Indians to New York and evidence of the defendant's subsequent actions demonstrated that he sought to cause an intratribal controversy, the evidence permitted a finding of "interstate commerce" as proscribed by the Act. The court also agreed that an attack by 25 people on a gas station, the break-in of a bingo hall, and an assault on two people who wanted to investigate the disturbance fit the definition of "riot" for purposes of the anti-riot act.

B. Disorderly Conduct, Vagrancy, Loitering, and Drunkenness

Title 18 of the U.S. Code contains no criminal statute relating to vagrancy or loitering, but there are several provisions for disorderly conduct near or in public buildings or close to public officials. Title 18 § 1752 provides a fine or imprisonment not exceeding six months, or both, if any person is found guilty of entering or remaining in any building or grounds designated by the Secretary of the Treasury as a temporary residence of the President or other persons protected by the Secret Service in violation of regulations. This section also makes it unlawful for any person or persons, with intent to impede or disrupt the orderly conduct of government business or official functions, to engage in disorderly or disruptive conduct in, or within a certain proximity of, any building or grounds designated as a temporary residence for the President or any other person protected by the Secret Service.[30]

In addition, Title 40 § 101 of the U.S. Code provides a penalty of not more than $500 or imprisonment for not more than six months, or both, if any person is guilty of disorderly and unlawful conduct in and about public buildings and public grounds belonging to the United States within the District of Columbia.

The U.S. Code has no specific provision relating to drunkenness or intoxication but does have a section regulating transportation of intoxicating liquor into any state, territory, or district for sale in that state, territory, or district where the state laws prohibit

---

[28] United States v. Dellinger, 472 F.2d 340 (7th Cir.), cert. denied, 410 U.S. 970, 93 S. Ct. 1443, 35 L. Ed. 2d 706 (1972).

[29] United States v. Markiewiez, 978 F.2d 786 (2d Cir.), cert. denied, 506 U.S. 1086 (1992).

[30] See 18 U.S.C. § 1752(f) for a definition of "other persons protected by the Secret Service."

the sale of intoxicating liquor.[31] The purpose of this section is to simplify enforcement by federal agents. It was designed to provide federal protection to "dry" states against violators who sought to bring alcohol into the state.[32]

C. Drug Laws

Prior to 1970, there were numerous separate federal drug control statutes on the books, each of which was aimed at a particular set of drug problems. Some of these acts relied upon the taxing power of Congress, while others relied upon the authority granted to Congress under the interstate commerce clause of the Constitution. The Narcotics Manufacturing Act of 1960, which set up a licensing system for narcotic drug manufacturers, relied upon the commerce power rather than the power to tax. In 1965, amendments to the Food, Drug and Cosmetic Act, dealing with dangerous drugs, were found to be within the power of Congress to regulate interstate commerce.[33]

The Comprehensive Drug Abuse Prevention and Control Act of 1970 created for the first time an all-encompassing scheme covering both narcotics and dangerous drugs. The provisions of this section, authorizing the Secretary of Health, Education, and Welfare to make scientific evaluations and recommendations regarding the classification of a drug, were challenged but held to be constitutional.[34] The constitutional authorization for the 1970 Act was based entirely on the commerce clause, the taxing power no longer being relied upon.

In 1984, 1986, 1988, and again in 1990, federal legislation was drafted to make it less difficult to prosecute violators and to increase the penalties. In 1986, Congress enacted a very comprehensive law titled the Anti-Drug Abuse Act of 1986. In addition to creating new offenses, the main thrust of the act was to increase the penalties for drug offenders. Also, legislation was enacted that authorized the Department of Defense to assist in enforcing the drug laws. Over objections raised by the Secretary of Defense and military officials, both houses of Congress passed bills broadening the role of the military in the drug war. Federal law enforcement officers, as well as state and local enforcement officers, are given specific powers of enforcement by the federal statute.[35]

Also, in 1986, the Congress of the United States added subtitle (H), "Money Laundering Control Act of 1986." This created a new offense for laundering of monetary instruments, with a separate penalty if a person is convicted of laundering money knowing that the property involved in the financial transaction represents the proceeds of some form of unlawful activity.[36]

---

[31] 18 U.S.C. § 1262. See also 18 U.S.C. § 1263-1264.

[32] United States v. Williams, 184 F.2d 663 (10th Cir. 1950).

[33] United States v. Walsh, 331 U.S. 432, 67 S. Ct. 1283, 91 L. Ed. 1585 (1947).

[34] United States v. Pastor, 557 F.2d 930 (2d Cir. 1977); United States v. Davis, 564 F.2d 840 (9th Cir. 1977). See also United States v. Wacker, 72 F.3d 1953 (10th Cir. 1995).

[35] 21 U.S.C. § 878.

[36] Subtitle (H), § 1351, Anti-Drug Abuse Act of 1986, Pub. L. No. 99-570.

The Anti-Drug Abuse Act of 1988 further strengthened the authority of enforcement agents to continue the war on drugs. In addition to increasing penalties for personal use of drugs, the Act included the death penalty for those convicted of drug-related killings. A new provision added a federal penalty for endangering human life while illegally manufacturing drugs and provides a mandatory life term for three-time felony drug offenders.[37]

Recall that in *United States v. Fowler*, a federal court, after reviewing previous cases, affirmed the authority of federal courts to prosecute, convict, or sentence a defendant for a crime involving the wholly intrastate possession of a controlled substance.[38] In this case, the defendant pled guilty to one count of possession of cocaine base, but later filed a motion to vacate or set aside the conviction, complaining that the United States "has no territorial jurisdiction over non-federally owned areas inside the jurisdictional boundaries of the states within the American Union." The court rejected the defendant's argument, reiterating that "the commerce clause empowers Congress to regulate broad classes of activities which are found to have a substantial impact on interstate commerce." The court continued by stating that "Congress possesses the power to regulate wholly intrastate activities which have an effect upon interstate commerce."

1. Uniform Schedule of Controlled Substances

Title 21 U.S.C. § 812 establishes five schedules of **controlled substances**, known as Schedules I, II, III, IV, and V. Such schedules are the same as those previously described in Chapter 9.[39] The criteria for determining which drug was to be placed in each schedule are set out in the statute and are similar to the criteria used in establishing the schedules for the respective states.

In 1982, a federal appeals court dealt with a challenge to the classification of marijuana as a Schedule I drug. In this case, the court found that the defendant did not meet his heavy burden of proving the irrationality of a Schedule I classification of marijuana in light of the ongoing dispute as to physical and psychological effects of marijuana, its potential for abuse, and whether it had any medical value.[40]

Schedule I:
No established medical usage, cannot be used safely, great potential for abuse — heroin, LSD, mescaline, peyote, Quaaludes, psilocybin, marijuana, hashish, etc.

Schedule II:
High potential for abuse, currently accepted medical uses — opium, morphine, codeine, cocaine, PCP, Ritalin, Preludin, etc.

---

[37]　Anti-Drug Abuse Act of 1988, §§ 6301 and 6452, 134 Cong. Rec. H 11155, Oct. 21, 1988.

[38]　United States v. Fowler, 879 F. Supp. 575 (E.D. Va. 1995).

[39]　See 21 U.S.C. § 812 as amended for a list of the drugs in each of the five schedules.

[40]　United States v. Fogarty, 692 F.2d 542 (8th Cir. 1982), cert. denied, 460 U.S. 1040, 103 S. Ct. 1434, 75 L. Ed. 2d 792 (1982). See also United States v. Green, 892 F.2d 453 (6th Cir. 1989), which held that classification of marijuana as a Schedule I controlled substance is not arbitrary or capricious or a violation of due process.

Schedule III: Some potential for abuse, accepted medical use, potential for psychological addiction	anabolic steroids, cold medicines containing codeine
Schedule IV: Low potential for abuse, medical uses	valium, librium, equanil, stimulants
Schedule V: Prescription drugs with low potential for abuse	cough and other medicines with levels of opium, morphine or codeine

The challenges to categorizing marijuana as a Schedule I drug continued. In 2001, the Supreme Court considered a case from California. In 1996, California voters passed the Compassionate Use Act of 1996, which allowed for the medical use of marijuana as a necessity exception to state possession, use, and trafficking laws. The U.S. Attorney General issued a policy announcement that the state of California could not usurp the federal government's right to enforce federal laws against marijuana and the case arose as a challenge to such enforcement. In *United States v. Oakland Cannabis Buyers' Cooperative*,[41] the Court ruled that the state of California could not create an exception to the federal drug law that placed marijuana in **Schedule I**. This case is interesting because it is also a question of **states' rights** and many conservatives who are in favor of drug laws, nevertheless, were dismayed when the Supreme Court did not protect the state's police power to create and enforce laws that, arguably, did not implicate federal interests.

In *Gonzales v. Raich*,[42] presented in Part II of this textbook, another challenge was heard against the federal drug law, with California petitioners arguing that the power of the federal government through the commerce clause did not reach the intrastate manufacture or delivery of marijuana. They lost again and the Supreme Court upheld the Attorney General's argument that federal drug laws override any state statute that recognizes a medical necessity for marijuana.

Case Note: *Gonzales v. Raich*, 545 U.S. 1, 125 S. Ct. 2195 (2005)
What was the holding in the case?
Why is marijuana categorized as a Schedule I drug?
What evidence exists that it is medically "necessary"?
What evidence exists that intrastate manufacture and delivery will affect national prices?

Interestingly, the Supreme Court upheld states' rights in *Gonzales v. Oregon*,[43] which dealt with Oregon's Death with Dignity Act. The Act allowed doctors to prescribe lethal doses of certain drugs to patients who had six months or less to live. Attorney General Ashcroft announced that, despite the state statute, such behavior violated federal law because it was not a medically accepted use of the

---

[41]   532 U.S. 483, 121 S. Ct. 1711, 149 L. Ed. 2d 722 (2001).
[42]   545 U.S. 1, 125 S. Ct. 2195 (2005).
[43]   126 S. Ct. 904, 163 L. Ed.2d 748 (2006).

controlled substance, and that any doctors who did prescribe controlled substances in the manner described would be prosecuted. In the case, which was actually brought by Ashcroft's successor, Attorney General Gonzales, the Supreme Court held that such an interpretation of the law exceeded the Attorney General's authority.

LEGAL NEWS: MEDICAL MARIJUANA

All federal drug laws remain in effect, even in those 16 states that have some form of medical marijuana laws. The Attorney General has indicated in past years that the priority of federal drug enforcement efforts will not be to enforce drug laws against medical cooperatives or dispensaries in those states, but the fact remains that they could be subject to federal laws. In mid-January 2012, news reports indicated that U.S. prosecutors cracked down on many medical marijuana dispensaries in Colorado that were located within 1,000 feet of schools, giving the proprietors 45 days to shut down or risk federal prosecution. In California, U.S. prosecutors said they would begin to enforce federal drug laws against dispensaries that they believed were fronts for large scale for-profit drug trafficking. In Montana, federal prosecutors raided greenhouses and dispensaries in 13 cities. In Washington, U.S. attorneys threatened to prosecute not only those who ran the marijuana dispensaries but also state officials who regulated the industry.

Source: K. Coffman. "Feds crack down on CO medical pot dispensaries." Reuters.com, January 13, 2012. Accessed January 13, 2012 from http://www.reuters.com/assets/print?aid=USTRE80C1MX20120113.

---

2. Possession

Title 21 § 844 of the U.S. Code as amended in 1986 provides in part

21 U.S.C. § 844

(a) It shall be unlawful for any person knowingly or intentionally to possess a controlled substance unless such substance was obtained directly, or pursuant to a valid prescription order, from a practitioner while acting in the course of his professional practice, or except as otherwise authorized by this subchapter or subchapter II of this chapter.

The statute continues with sentencing provisions and a scheme that distinguishes those with prior convictions from first-time offenders under either state or federal drug laws. Another section includes a definition of drug or narcotic offense as "any offense which proscribes the possession, distribution, manufacture, cultivation, sale, transfer or the attempt or conspiracy to possess, distribute, manufacture, cultivate, sell or transfer any substance the possession of which is prohibited under this subchapter."

To convict a person under this provision, the investigator must obtain information to show that the suspect

- knowingly or intentionally,
- possessed,
- a controlled substance.

In considering the knowledge or intent element, a federal court held that "irrespective of what the defendant's intentions were regarding the ultimate disposition of heroin he claimed to have found while performing his duties as a janitor in prison, the defendant's knowledge of the illicit nature of the substance and purposeful possession of the substance was in violation of the heroin possession statute."[44]

One does not have to have *actual* possession of the controlled substance to violate this section. A person having an association with those having physical control of the drugs so as to enable him to assure their production, without difficulty, to a customer as a matter of course, may be held to have constructive possession.[45]

Section 844(a) provides a civil penalty for possession of small amounts of certain controlled substances. According to this section, if the controlled substance is possessed for personal use in small amounts, the possessor shall be subject to a civil penalty in an amount not to exceed $10,000 for each violation. This section authorizes the Attorney General to compromise, modify, or remit, with or without conditions, any civil penalty imposed under this section. It also provides that the civil penalty under this section may not be assessed on an individual on more than two separate occasions.

Obviously, the clear meaning of what constitutes a controlled substance is exhaustively provided in the Schedule of Controlled Substances.

3. The Manufacture, Distribution, and Dispensing of Controlled Substances (Intent to Distribute)

Title 21 U.S.C. § 841 of the U.S. Code provides in part

21 U.S.C. § 841

(a) Except as authorized by this subchapter, it shall be unlawful for any person knowingly or intentionally—
   (1) to manufacture, distribute, dispense or possess with intent to manufacture, distribute or dispense a controlled substance; or
   (2) to create, distribute, dispense or possess with intent to distribute or dispense, a counterfeit substance.

---

[44]   United States v. Halloway, 744 F.2d 527 (6th Cir. 1984).
[45]   United States v. White, 660 F.2d 1178 (7th Cir. 1981).

In investigating and prosecuting violations of this section, three elements must be proved beyond a reasonable doubt:

- knowing,
- possession,
- with intent to distribute (heroin, in this case).

The Fourth Circuit Court of Appeals declared that a defendant's knowledge and intent are clearly elements that the prosecution must establish in order to prove a conspiracy to violate this section, but knowledge may be proven by extrinsic evidence.[46]

Knowledge refers to knowledge that one possesses a controlled substance; it is not necessary to know the particular controlled substance; therefore, a person can be convicted of importation of heroin and possession with intent to distribute even though he believed he was carrying cocaine rather than heroin.[47]

In a case prosecuted under 18 U.S.C. § 841, the court decided that a defendant charged with importing or possessing a drug is not required to know the type and the amount of the drug; rather, the defendant can be convicted if he believes he has some controlled substance in his possession, and the *mens rea* attaches to the possession of a controlled substance, not the type or quantity.[48] The Seventh Circuit Court of Appeals agreed, holding that the offense of possession with intent to distribute illegally controlled substances requires only that the defendant knowingly possess a controlled substance with the intent to distribute it; the drug type is not an element.[49]

In a 1999 case, the justices of the Tenth Circuit Court of Appeals summarized the requirements necessary to convict a person of violating § 841(a). In this case, the court held that a conviction for possession of cocaine with intent to distribute requires that the defendant (1) possessed a controlled substance; (2) knew he possessed a controlled substance; and (3) intended to distribute the controlled substance.[50] The court continued by affirming that "constructive possession" satisfies the first element and that the defendant has constructive possession of drugs when the defendant knowingly has ownership, dominion, or control over the narcotics and the premises where the narcotics were found. The second and third elements were not contested.

In proving the possession element, a federal court decided that the prosecution must show that the defendant had ultimate control over the drugs; it need not have been literally in hand or on the premises that he occupied but he must have a right to possess them. But mere association with those who possess drugs is not enough to justify a conviction.[51]

---

[46]   United States v. Mark, 943 F.2d 444 (4th Cir. 1991).

[47]   United States v. Samad, 754 F.2d 1091 (4th Cir. 1984); United States v. Kairouz, 751 F.2d 467 (1st Cir. 1985).

[48]   United States v. Sanchez-Hernandez, 53 F.3d 842 (9th Cir. 2002).

[49]   United States v. Martinez, 301 F.3d 860 (7th Cir. 2003).

[50]   United States v. Dozal, 173 F.3d 787 (10th Cir. 1999). *See also* United States v. Randall, 171 F.3d 195 (4th Cir. 1999).

[51]   United States v. Manzella, 791 F.2d 1263 (7th Cir. 1986).

The Seventh Circuit Court of Appeals held that a charge of possession of cocaine with intent to distribute requires proof that the defendant acted with the specific intent to commit the underlying offense. The prosecution also must prove that the defendant took a substantial step toward carrying out the intent.[52] In the case of *United States v. Vergara,* the court added that the elements may be proved by circumstantial as well as direct evidence, and possession may be shown if the heroin was possessed jointly among several defendants.[53]

As is true of other offenses, the "intent" element is often difficult to prove. The introduction of several facts sometimes makes a stronger case. For example, a conviction for possession with intent to distribute cocaine base was supported by showing that an informant told police that the defendant was dealing crack cocaine out of his home, the informant made a controlled drug buy, and 3.8 grams of crack cocaine were recovered during a search of the defendant's home.[54]

4. Other Federal Drug-Related Offenses

Title 21 U.S.C. § 859 includes a separate provision prohibiting distribution of a controlled substance to a person less than 21 years of age. This section mandates a greater penalty for those who violate this section, with a provision that a term of imprisonment under this subsection shall not be less than one year.

Title 21 U.S.C. § 860 makes it a separate violation for one to distribute or manufacture a controlled substance in, on, or within 1,000 feet of the real property comprising a public or private elementary, vocational, or secondary school or a public or private college, junior college, or university. The Second Circuit Court of Appeals noted that providing an enhanced penalty for dispensing a controlled substance within 1,000 feet of a school did not violate the commerce clause of the Constitution.[55]

Title 21 U.S.C. § 861 makes it unlawful for any person at least 18 years of age to knowingly and intentionally "employ, hire, use, persuade, induce, entice or coerce" anyone under 18 to violate the provisions of the law.

Title 21 U.S.C. § 846 defines attempt and conspiracy as they relate to drug offenses. In this conspiracy offense, no overt act is necessary; a simple agreement to commit a federal drug offense is sufficient to prove guilt and the parties are subject to the same penalties as if the crime was completed.

Title 21 U.S.C. § 848 is titled "Continuing criminal enterprise" and is similar to the RICO statute, except that it is directed specifically to someone who commits drug offenses as part of a continuing criminal enterprise. An offender may be charged with the underlying crimes, that is, possession with intent to distribute, and Section 848 (CCE).

---

[52] United States v. Cea, 914 F.2d 881 (7th Cir. 1990).

[53] United States v. Vergara, 687 F.2d 57 (5th Cir. 1981).

[54] United States v. Hawkins, 102 F.3d 973 (8th Cir. 1996). *See also* United States v. Payne, 102 F.3d 289 (7th Cir. 1996).

[55] United States v. Ekinci, 101 F.3d 838 (2d Cir. 1996).

Title 18 U.S.C. § 2118 imposes a penalty on anyone who takes or attempts to take from the person or presence of another by force or violence or by intimidation any material or compound containing any quantity of a controlled substance belonging to or in the care, custody, control, or possession of a person registered with the Drug Enforcement Administration.

5. Federal Forfeiture Statutes

Title 21 U.S.C. § 881(a) provides for the **forfeiture** of property used to facilitate drug-related offenses and for the forfeiture of proceeds from drug transactions. In 1996, the U.S. Supreme Court revisited the issue of the relationship between the federal asset forfeiture statutes and the double jeopardy clause of the U.S. Constitution. The Court expressly rejected the previously employed "balancing" test (the harm suffered by the government is compared to the forfeiture imposed) in favor of the following test: (1) whether Congress intended the statutory scheme at issue to be criminal or civil, and (2) whether the scheme is so punitive either in purpose or effect as to negate the intent of Congress to establish a civil asset forfeiture process. Applying this new test, the Court concluded that asset forfeiture in drug cases did not violate the double jeopardy clause in that it was not an additional penalty for the commission of a criminal act, but rather a separate civil action, remedial in nature and expressly sanctioned by Congress.[56]

Austin v. United States,[57] discussed in Chapter 10, was a ruling in which the Supreme Court held that a federal forfeiture was not outside the spectrum of Eighth Amendment protection, so that if it was deemed disproportional or excessive to the crime committed, the forfeiture action of the government could be overturned. Because *Austin* was not expressly overruled, legal scholars remain perplexed—the federal asset forfeiture statutes apparently do not violate the double jeopardy clause; but, where the forfeiture is too disproportionate to the offense, such statutes may violate the excessive fines clause.

D. *Wiretapping and Eavesdropping*

In 1929 and again in 1931, Congress introduced legislation designed to protect against interception of telephone communications by the use of wiretaps. However, it was not until 1934, when Congress passed the Federal Communications Act, that **wiretapping** was made illegal.[58] This act included the following provision:

18 U.S.C. § 2510

No person not being authorized by the sender shall intercept any communication or divulge or publish the existence, contents, substance, purport, effect, or meaning of such intercepted communication to any person.

---

[56] United States v. Usery, 518 U.S. 267, 116 S. Ct. 2135, 135 L. Ed. 2d 549 (1996).
[57] Austin v. United States, 509 U.S. 602, 113 S. Ct. 2801, 125 L. Ed. 2d 488 (1993).
[58] 18 U.S.C. § 2510 et seq.

LEGAL NEWS: ILLEGAL WIRETAPPING

In December 2008, a Hollywood private eye (Anthony Pellicano) was sentenced to 15 years in prison for violating federal wiretapping laws. Evidently he utilized wiretapping in his investigations of the rich and famous. He was known as the "P.I. of the stars" and did work for a long list of celebrities and business people. Some of his work involved spying on reporters who were doing stories on his clients. Charges included 78 counts of wiretapping and related crimes.

Source: Associated Press (2008). "Private Eye Gets 15 Year Term." *Austin American-Statesman*, December 16, 2008:A2.

The amended provisions of the United States Code comprehensively regulate eavesdropping and the interception of communications. Title 18 U.S.C. §§ 2510 through 2522 contain provisions that prohibit intentional interception or attempts to intercept any wire or electronic communication and includes criminal penalties for violations of the statutes and detailed provisions for exceptions. Title 18 U.S.C. § 2511 prohibits the interception and disclosure of wire, oral, or electronic communications and includes criminal as well as civil penalties. This section also has provisions for exceptions with detailed requirements for each exception. Subsection 2(c) of the statute provides that it shall not be unlawful for a person acting under color of law to intercept a wire, oral, or electronic communication where such person is a party to the communication or one of the parties to the communication has given prior consent to such interception. Subsection 2(d) provides that it shall not be unlawful under this chapter for a person not acting under color of law to intercept a wire, oral, or electronic communication where such person is a party to the communication or where one of the parties to the communication has given prior consent to such interception unless such communication is intercepted for the purpose of committing any criminal or tortious act in violation of the Constitution or laws of the United States or of any state.

The consent provisions of the statutes have been interpreted in several court cases. In a federal court case, the court held that the consent is not voluntary when it is coerced by either explicit or implied means, or by an implied threat of covert force.[59] The courts have also interpreted the consent provisions to include implied consent. In a New York federal court, the judges decided that the defendant had no reasonable expectation of privacy that warranted the suppression of tapes of telephone calls he made from pay telephones in the jail cell, where the sign in the jail booking room implied that some telephone calls, other than those to attorneys, were subject to interception and would be

---

[59]   United States v. Antoon, 933 F.2d 200 (3d Cir. 1991).

recorded.[60] The statute provides an exception that allows wiretapping and eavesdropping when a court order is properly obtained.

Although the statute does not apply to eavesdropping with the unaided ear, listening to a conversation at a distance with a highly sensitive amplifying device does violate the law.[61] While state agents must comply with both the federal minimum standards and any additional restrictions imposed by their state, federal agents need only follow federal regulations.[62]

In addition to the civil penalties, the Act provides a criminal penalty for those who violate the statute. One provision of the Act states that except as provided in paragraph (b) of subsection 2511(4) or in subsection (5), whoever violates subsection (1) shall be fined or imprisoned not more than five years, or both.[63] The penalty section of the Act continues with a detailed discussion of exceptions and modifications of penalties.

The courts continue to receive requests to interpret certain words of the statutes such as "intentionally intercepts" and the terms "use" or "disclosure." According to a federal court in Texas, criminal violation of the federal wiretap statute only requires proof of general intent, not specific intent to violate the law.[64] An individual who acted consciously, as opposed to accidentally, in taping a cordless telephone conversation of his neighbor, intentionally intercepted electronic communications in violation of the Electronic Communications Privacy Act.[65]

Note that the laws against wiretapping apply to federal agents as well as civilians. It could also apply to telecommunications companies who comply with illegal orders from federal agents. The legality of wiretapping in the investigation of terrorism has been hotly debated as the following news box relays.

LEGAL NEWS: ILLEGAL WIRETAPPING OR NOT?

In 2006, a controversy arose after it was revealed that federal officers had been using wiretaps without a warrant. A Presidential Order signed in 2002 allowed the National Security Agency to monitor international telephone calls and international e-mail messages of thousands of people inside the United States without warrants. Generally, if federal agents want to wiretap a United States citizen suspected of being involved in terrorism, they must get a warrant from the Foreign Intelligence Surveillance Court. The 1978 law that created the court has been interpreted to bar all domestic wiretapping, even for national security, unless a warrant has been issued by this court. The administration's

---

[60] United States v. Friedman, 300 F.3d 111 (2d Cir. 2002).
[61] Malpas v. State, 16 Md. App. 69, 695 A.2d 588 (1997).
[62] United States v. Pratt, 913 F.2d 983 (1st Cir. 1990), *cert. denied*, 408 U.S. 1028, 111 S. Ct. 681, 112 L. Ed. 2d 673 (1990).
[63] 18 U.S.C. § 2511 (4)(a).
[64] Peavy v. Harmon, 37 F. Supp. 2d 495 (N.D. Tex. 1999).
[65] Goodspeed v. Harman, 39 F. Supp. 2d 787 (N.D. Tex. 1999).

position was that Congress authorized the President to take any and all steps required to combat terrorism in the wake of September 11, 2001. When the practice was revealed, the wiretapping stopped. A federal court dismissed a lawsuit seeking an injunction and damages by the ACLU in 2007, concluding that the ACLU had no standing to bring the case.

Congress passed the Protect America Act in 2007, which retroactively provided immunity for the telecommunications companies involved and required warrants for future wiretapping for national security, but allowed for an emergency provision. The Protect America Act of 2007 expired in 2008, but Congress passed the FISA Amendments Act of 2008. This Act also provided immunity to telecommunications companies (both retroactively and prospectively) when they assist in investigation of terrorism, allows for destruction of records, allows warrantless wiretapping of non-U.S. citizens and U.S. citizens outside of the U.S. if they are targets of foreign intelligence investigations, and provides for a 7-day emergency period where government agents can wiretap citizens immediately while seeking a warrant. This bill will expire in December 2012.

Source: ACLU v. NSA, No. 06-20951/2140. U.S. District Court (E.D. Michigan). Decided July 6, 2007. For information about the FISA Amendments Act, go to http://www.opencongress.org/bill/110-h6304/show.

E. Other Offenses against the Public Peace

In Chapter 10, one of the other offenses against public peace described was harassment and stalking. The federal government has also responded to this issue with the passage of the Violence Against Women Act, Title IV of the Violent Crime Control and Law Enforcement Act of 1994 (Public Law 103–322, referred to as the 1994 Crime Act). Also, Congress passed the National Stalker and Domestic Violence Reduction Act, which required the federal government to collect and maintain statistics on stalking.

In the United States Code, the federal stalking law is 18 U.S.C. § 2261A, which makes it a crime to cross state lines with the intent to injure or harass another and 18 U.S.C. § 2262, which makes it a crime to cross state lines to violate a protective order.

18 U.S.C. § 2261A

"Whoever—

(1) travels in interstate or foreign commerce or within the special maritime and territorial jurisdiction of the United States, or enters or leaves Indian country, with the intent to kill, injure, harass, or place under surveillance with intent to kill, injure, harass, or intimidate another person, and in the course of, or as a result of, such

travel places that person in reasonable fear of the death of, or serious bodily injury to, or causes substantial emotional distress to that person, a member of the immediate family (as defined in section 115) of that person, or the spouse or intimate partner of that person; or

(2) with the intent—

    (A) to kill, injure, harass, or place under surveillance with intent to kill, injure, harass, or intimidate, or cause substantial emotional distress to a person in another State or tribal jurisdiction or within the special maritime and territorial jurisdiction of the United States; or

    (B) to place a person in another State or tribal jurisdiction, or within the special maritime and territorial jurisdiction of the United States, in reasonable fear of the death of, or serious bodily injury to—

        (i)   that person;

        (ii) a member of the immediate family (as defined in section 115 of that person; or

        (iii) a spouse or intimate partner of that person;

uses the mail, any interactive computer service, or any facility of interstate or foreign commerce to engage in a course of conduct that causes substantial emotional distress to that person or places that person in reasonable fear of the death of, or serious bodily injury to, any of the persons described in clauses (i) through (iii) of subparagraph (B); shall be punished as provided in section 2261(b) of this title."

The case provided in Part II of this textbook, *United States v. Bowker*, [66] is based on the federal stalking law.

§ 13.4   Offenses Related to Terrorism

> **Case Note:** *United States v. Bowker*, 372 F.3d 365 (2004)
> What was Bowker charged with?
> What was his argument as to the wording of the statutes he was charged under?
> What were the (excerpted) issues and holding of the case?

In the aftermath of the terrorist attacks on September 11, 2001, Congress enacted comprehensive legislation to vest those involved in the criminal justice system with the authority to combat terrorism. Prior to the attacks, few were aware that counterterrorism laws were in effect. Recognizing that additional legislation was required to combat terrorism, Congress enacted comprehensive legislation that made it possible for those involved in the criminal justice process to more effectively investigate and prosecute violators.

A. USA PATRIOT Act

In October 2001, the 107th Congress enacted Public Law 107-56, which is titled "Uniting and Strengthening America by Providing Appropriate Tools Required to Intercept and Obstruct Terrorism Act." This Act is known as the USA **PATRIOT Act**

---

[66]   United States v. Bowker, 372 F.3d 365 (2004).

of 2001. This lengthy act amends existing statutes concerning terrorism and adds additional provisions to the law. The numerous sections of the Act are included under 10 titles:

Title I—ENHANCING DOMESTIC SECURITY AGAINST TERRORISM
Title II—ENHANCED SURVEILLANCE PROCEDURES
Title III—INTERNATIONAL MONEY LAUNDERING ABATEMENT AND ANTITERRORIST FINANCING ACT OF 2001
Title IV—PROTECTING THE BORDER
Title V—REMOVING OBSTACLES TO INVESTIGATING TERRORISM
Title VI—PROVIDING FOR VICTIMS OF TERRORISM, PUBLIC SAFETY OFFICERS, AND THEIR FAMILIES
Title VII—INCREASED INFORMATION SHARING FOR CRITICAL INFRASTRUCTURE PROTECTION
Title VIII—STRENGTHENING THE CRIMINAL LAWS AGAINST TERRORISM
Title IX—IMPROVED INTELLIGENCE
Title X—MISCELLANEOUS

Most of the remaining discussion in this section regards the provisions of Title VIII of the Patriot Act: "Strengthening the Criminal Laws against Terrorism." Prior to the passing of the Patriot Act, Chapter 113B, titled "Terrorism," was included in the United States Code. It included criminal penalties for a series of acts relating to terrorism. Among these were

18 U.S.C. § 2332(a) Use of weapons of mass destruction
18 U.S.C. § 2332(b) Acts of terrorism transcending national boundaries
18 U.S.C. § 2332(d) Financial transactions
18 U.S.C. § 2339(A) Providing material to terrorists
18 U.S.C. § 2339(B) Providing material support or resources to designated foreign terrorist organizations

B. Definitions

Title 18 U.S.C. § 2331, as it existed prior to the Patriot Act, defined international terrorism as activities that "involve violent acts or acts dangerous to human life that are a violation of the criminal laws of the United States or of any State, or that would be a criminal violation if committed within the jurisdiction of the United States or of any State" and that appear to be intended to do one or more of the following:

(i) to intimidate or coerce a civilian population;
(ii) to influence the policy of a government by intimidation or coercion; or
(iii) to affect the conduct of a government by assassination or kidnapping; and
(C) occur primarily outside the territorial jurisdiction of the United States, or transcend national boundaries in terms of the means by which they are accomplished, the persons they appear intended to intimidate or coerce, or the locale in which their perpetrators operate or seek asylum;

Recognizing the limitations of these definitions, § 2331 of Title 18 was amended to include "by mass destruction, assassination or kidnapping" as one of the acts that constitutes terrorism. Also "domestic terrorism" was included and defined as those acts "dangerous to human life that are a violation of the criminal laws of United States or of any State" and that appear to be intended to do one of the following:

  (i)   to intimidate or coerce a civilian population;
  (ii) to influence the policy of a government by intimidation or coercion; or
  (iii) to affect the policy of a government by mass destruction, assassination, or kidnapping; and
(C) occur primarily within the territorial jurisdiction of the United States.

Title 18 U.S.C. § 2332A is titled "Use of certain weapons of mass destruction." This section provides

(a) Offense against a national of the United States or within the United States. A person who, without lawful authority, uses, threatens, or attempts or conspires to use, a weapon of mass destruction, other than a chemical weapon as that term is defined in § 3229(f), including any biological agent, toxin, or vector.
    (1) against a national of the United States while such national is outside the United States;
    (2) against any person within the United States, and the results of which use after interstate or foreign commerce, or, in the case of a threat, attempt, or conspiracy, would have affected interstate or foreign commerce; or
    (3) against any property that is owned, leased or used by the United States or by any department or agency of the United States, whether the property is within or outside the United States;
    shall be imprisoned for any term of years or for life, and if death results, shall be punished by death or imprisoned for any term of years or for life.

Section 2332B is titled "Acts of terrorism transcending national boundaries." This section provides that whoever, involving transcending national boundaries and in circumstances described in the Act,

(A) kills, kidnaps, maims, commits an assault resulting in serious bodily injury, or assaults with a dangerous weapon any person within the United States; or
(B) creates a substantial risk of serious bodily injury to any other person by destroying or damaging any structure, conveyance, or other real or personal property within the United States or by attempting or conspiring to destroy or damage any structure, conveyance, or other real or personal property within the United States;
(C) in violation of the laws of any state, or the United States, shall be punished as provided in the Act.

This section was amended by the Patriot Act to increase the violations included in the term "federal crime of terrorism" as used in the Act. John Phillip Walker Lindh was charged under this Act with conspiracy to murder nationals of the United States, including American military personnel and other government employees serving in Afghanistan following the September 11, 2001 terrorist attacks, in violation of 18 U.S.C. § 2332b. He was not convicted of violating the statute but was found guilty of other offenses.[67]

---

[67]   United States v. Lindh, 227 F. Supp. 2d 565 (E.D. Va. 2002).

Title 18 U.S.C. § 2339, "Harboring or concealing terrorists" imposes a fine as provided in the Act or imprisonment for not more than 10 years or both if a person is convicted of harboring or concealing any person who he knows or has reasonable grounds to believe has committed, or is about the commit, an offense of any of the acts included in the statute.

Title 18 U.S.C. § 2339A, "Providing material support to terrorists" provides that whoever, within the United States, provides material support or resources or conceals or disguises the nature, location, source, or ownership of material support or resources, knowing or intending that they are to be used in preparation for carrying out a violation of the sections indicated, or in preparation for, or in carrying out, the concealment or escape from the commission of such violations, shall be fined under this title, imprisoned not more than 10 years, or both. This section was amended by the Patriot Act by striking out "within the United States" and by adding sections of the law covered by the Act. The effect of deleting "within the United States" makes the provisions enforceable when the acts described occur outside the United States.

> **Case Note: Holder v. Humanitarian Law Project, 130 S.Ct. 2705 (2010)**
> What did the defendant do exactly?
> What were the (excerpted) issues and holding of the case?

Title 18 U.S.C. § 2339B, "Providing material support or resources to designated foreign terrorist organizations" was amended in part by the Patriot Act to read as follows:

(a) prohibited activities
   (1) unlawful conduct—whoever, within the United States, or subject to the jurisdiction of the United States, knowingly provides material support or resources to a foreign terrorist organization, or attempts or conspires to do so, shall be fined under this title or imprisoned not more than fifteen years, or both, and, if the death of any person results, shall be imprisoned for any term of years or for life.

This provision has led to convictions even when the defendants did not intend that their money go to terrorist activities. In *Holder v. Humanitarian Law* Project, individuals argued that the provisions of the Patriot Act violated their Fifth Amendment rights (because it was vague) and First Amendment rights. The case is provided in Part II of this text.

LEGAL NEWS: CONVICTION FOR MATERIAL SUPPORT

Two men, including a former Congressman, were sentenced to prison in January 2012 and three others were sentenced to probation under provisions of the Patriot Act that prohibited providing material support for terrorist organizations. The group was involved with a Missouri charity, the Islamic American Relief Agency, that was linked with a terrorist group in Sudan. The men convicted were not charged with knowingly providing support to terrorists. Most of the men pleaded guilty to acting as unregistered foreign agents.

Source: M. Morris, "Former congressman, Missouri charity director sentenced in terrorism case." Kansascity.com, January 11, 2012. Accessed January 12, 2012 from http://www.kansascity.com/2012/01/11/3365477/former-congressman-missouri-charity.html.

The existing chapter on terrorism was amended by the Patriot Act to include an offense designated "Terrorist attacks and other acts of violence against mass transportation systems." This comprehensive law provides penalties where one wrecks, derails, sets fire to, or disables a mass transportation vehicle or ferry. The Act also prohibits using biological weapons, impairing operations of mass transportation systems, interfering with employees, or using dangerous weapons with intent to cause injury to employees or passengers. This portion of the statute has been used against individuals who interfere with flight attendants in flight, even if that interference has nothing to do with terrorism, prompting some criticism.

The following is a list of additional terrorism-related statutes that grant jurisdiction to investigative agencies:

TITLE 18 U.S.C. § 831—PROHIBITED TRANSACTION INVOLVING NUCLEAR MATERIALS

TITLE 18 U.S.C. § 842(p)—TEACHING, DEMONSTRATING, OR DISTRIBUTION OF INFORMATION RELATIVE TO EXPLOSIVES, DESTRUCTIVE DEVICES AND WEAPONS OF MASS DESTRUCTION

TITLE 18 U.S.C. §§ 921-930—UNLAWFUL ACTIVITIES RELATING TO FIREARMS

TITLE 18 U.S.C. § 1203—ACTS FOR THE PREVENTION AND PUNISHMENT OF THE CRIME OF HOSTAGE TAKING

TITLE 18 U.S.C. § 1344—BANK FRAUD

TITLE 18 U.S.C. §§ 1541-1546—CRIMES BASED UPON IMPROPER ACQUISITION OR MISUSES OF PASSPORT, VISA, OR ENTRY DOCUMENTS

TITLE 18 U.S.C. § 1956—MONEY LAUNDERING AS IT RELATES TO TERRORISM OFFENSES

TITLE 18 U.S.C. § 1960—PROHIBITION OF ILLEGAL MONEY TRANSMITTING BUSINESS

The specific criminal laws against terrorism are included in Title VIII of the Patriot Act. Other provisions of interest to criminal justice personnel are Title II and Title V. Title II, "Enhanced Surveillance Procedures," among other things, authorizes law enforcement agencies to share investigative information. Title V, "Removing Obstacles to Investigating Terrorism," makes it less difficult to identify and locate terrorists and terrorist organizations and to acquire information to convict those who commit terrorist acts. In May 2011, Congress passed a four-year extension of the three expiring portions of the Patriot Act, despite continued criticism by civil liberties groups. The most contested provisions include Section 215, which increases the government's powers of seizure during terrorist investigations; Section 206, which allows roving wiretap authority that does not require the government to specify the target; and Section 6001, called the Lone Wolf provision, which allows secret surveillance of non-U.S. persons who are not affiliated with identified terrorist organization.

§ 13.5   Offenses against Justice Administration

Recall that the offenses in Chapter 11 concerned crimes that were directed to the obstruction or manipulation of the justice process or the administration of government. The state criminal laws prohibit such actions against state justice and administration while federal laws prohibit the same types of activities when directed toward the federal government or federal court system.

A. *Perjury and Related Offenses*

Chapter 79 of Title 18 of the U.S. Code defines three perjury-related offenses: perjury, subornation of perjury, and false declaration before a grand jury or court. The crime of perjury is defined as follows:

> 18 U.S.C. § 1621
>
> Whoever—
> (1) having taken an oath before a competent tribunal, officer, or person, in any case in which a law of the United States authorizes an oath to be administered, that he will testify, declare, depose, or certify truly, or that any written testimony, declaration, deposition, certificate by him subscribed, is true, willfully and contrary to such oaths states or subscribes any material matter which he does not believe to be true; or
> (2) in any declaration, certificate, verification, or statement under a penalty of perjury as permitted under Section 1746 of Title 28, U.S. Code, willfully subscribes as true any material matter which he does not believe to be true;
>
> is guilty of perjury and shall, except as otherwise expressly provided by law, be fined under this title or imprisoned not more than five years or both.

This section applies whether the statement or subscription is made within or outside the United States. This federal statute contains provisions that are similar to state statutes and has been found to meet constitutional standards.[68] The essential elements to prove a violation of this section are

- taking an oath in a case in which a law of the United States authorizes the oath to be administered,
- to testify willfully and contrary to such oath,
- making a false statement,

---

[68]   United States v. Masters, 484 F.2d 1251 (10th Cir. 1973).

- as to a material fact,
- which the defendant did not believe to be true.

The justices of the Eighth Circuit explained that a witness commits perjury when he or she testifies falsely under oath about a material matter, with a willful intent to deceive the fact finder.[69]

The Court of Appeals for the Ninth Circuit believed that § 1621 of the federal statute was violated by a police officer who gave false deposition testimony in a civil rights case. In this case, the police officer testified that officers who took sick leave were actually sick when in fact they were not sick. This false testimony, according to the court, would have a "tendency to influence" the jury's decision whether the department's disciplinary action for a violation of the sick leave policy was imposed for harassment and retaliation.[70]

1. Subornation of Perjury

Section 1622 of the federal statute provides

18 U.S.C. § 1622

Whoever procures another to commit any perjury is guilty of subornation of perjury, and shall be fined under this title or imprisoned not more than five years, or both.

A federal court, in interpreting the subornation provision, found that in order to constitute the offense of subornation of perjury, the offense of perjury must actually *have been committed* by another.[71] This is different than some state laws that do not require the perjury to occur before finding that the subornation has been committed. Another federal court indicated that this statute was correctly applied when an attorney was charged with subornation of perjury of a witness in violation of this section. A prosecutor who procures false testimony is also subject to a penalty under the subornation of perjury statute.[72] A federal court also found that an attorney suborned perjury of a witness in violation of 18 U.S.C. § 1622 by not advising the witness, after hearing the witness propose testimony and knowing it to be false, against testifying in that manner.[73]

2. False Swearing

In addition to the perjury statute, the United States Code criminalizes false statements under 18 U.S.C. § 1001, which states

---

[69] United States v. Molina, 172 F.3d 1048 (8th Cir. 1999). *See also* United States v. Quarrell, 310 F.3d 664 (10th Cir. 2002).
[70] United States v. Clark, 918 F.2d 843 (9th Cir. 1990).
[71] United States v. Silverman, 745 F.2d 1386 (11th Cir. 1984).
[72] United States v. Singleton, 165 F.3d 1297 (10th Cir. 1999).
[73] Tedesco v. Mishkin, 629 F. Supp. 1474 (S.D.N.Y. 1986).

18 U.S.C. § 1001

(a) Except as otherwise provided in this section, whoever, in any matter within the jurisdiction of the executive, legislative, or judicial branch of the government of the United States, knowingly and willfully—
(1) Falsifies, conceals, or covers up by any trick, scheme, or device a material fact;
(2) Makes any materially false, fictitious, or fraudulent statement or representation; or
(3) Makes or uses any false writing or document knowing the same to contain any materially false, fictitious, or fraudulent statement or entry...

B. Bribery and Related Offenses

Chapter 11 of Title 18 of the U.S. Code is titled "Bribery, Graft and Conflicts of Interest." It includes ethical standards of conduct for government employees and laws relating to many topics, including the following:

• Bribery of public officials and witnesses
• Bribery in sporting contests
• Acceptance or solicitation to obtain appointive public office
• Acceptance of loan or gratuity by financial institution examiner

1. Gratuities

Section 201(c)(1)(A) sets forth the elements of an illegal **gratuity** offense applicable to the gratuity giver, and § 201(c)(1)(B) sets forth the elements applicable to a gratuity recipient. To prove an illegal gratuity offense, the government must demonstrate (1) a thing of value; (2) was given, offered, or promised to (or demanded, sought, received, or accepted by); (3) a public official; (4) "for or because of any official act performed or to be performed by such public official." "Public official" is defined as a person who has been selected to be a public official and includes any of the following:

Members of Congress, Delegate, or Resident Commissioner, either before or after such official has qualified or an officer or employee or person acting for or on behalf of the United States, or any department, agency or branch of Government thereof, including the District of Columbia, in any official function, under or by authority of any such department, agency, or branch of government, or a juror; any person who has been nominated or appointed to be a public official, or has been officially informed that such person will be so nominated or appointed.[74]

2. Bribery

Section 201 states the following as the definition of bribery:

---

[74]   18 U.S.C. § 201.

18 U.S.C. § 201

(b) Whoever—

    (1) directly or indirectly, corruptly gives, offers or promises anything of value to any public official or person who has been selected to be a public official, or offers or promises any public official or any person who has been selected to be a public official to give anything of value to any other person or entity, with intent—

        (A) to influence any official act; or

        (B) to influence such public official or person who has been selected to be a public official to commit or aid in committing, or collude in or allow, any fraud, or make opportunity for the commission of any fraud, on the United States; or

        (C) to induce such public official or such person who has been selected to be a public official to do or omit to do any act in violation of the lawful duty of such official or person;

    (2) being a public official or person selected to be a public official, directly or indirectly, corruptly demands, seeks, receives, accepts, or agrees to receive or accept anything of value personally or for any other person or entity, in return for:

        (A) being influenced in the performance of any official act;

        (B) being influenced to commit or aid in committing, or to collude in, or allow, any fraud, or make opportunity for the commission of any fraud, on the United States; or

        (C) being induced to do or omit to do any act in violation of the official duty of such official or person;

    (3) directly or indirectly, corruptly gives, offers, or promises anything of value to any person, or offers to promise such person to give anything of value to any other person or entity, with intent to influence the testimony under oath or affirmation of such first-mentioned person as a witness upon a trial, hearing, or other proceeding, before any court, any committee of either House or both Houses of Congress, or any agency, commission, or officer authorized by the laws of the United States to hear evidence or take testimony, or with intent to influence such person to absent himself therefrom;

    (4) directly or indirectly, corruptly demands, seeks, receives, accepts, or agrees to receive or accept anything of value personally or for any other person or entity in return for being influenced in testimony under oath or affirmation as a witness upon any such trial, hearing, or other proceeding, or in return for absenting himself therefrom:

shall be fined not more than three times the monetary equivalent of the thing of value, or imprisoned for not more than fifteen years, or both, and may be disqualified from holding any office of honor, trust, or profit under the United States.

(c) Whoever—

    (1) otherwise than as provided by law for the proper discharge of official duty—

        (A) directly or indirectly gives, offers, or promises anything of value to any public official, former public official, or person selected to be a public official, for or because of any official act performed or to be performed by such public official, former public official, or person selected to be a public official; or

        (B) being a public official, former public official, or person selected to be a public official, otherwise than as provided by law for the proper discharge of official duty, directly or indirectly demands, seeks, receives, accepts, or agrees to receive or accept anything of value personally for or because of any official act performed or to be performed by such official or person;

(2) directly or indirectly, gives, offers or promises anything of value to any person, for or because of the testimony under oath or affirmation given or to be given by such person as a witness upon a trial, hearing, or other proceeding, before any court, any committee of either House or both Houses of Congress, or any agency, commission, or officer authorized by the laws of the United States to hear evidence or take testimony, or for or because of such person's absence therefrom;

(3) directly or indirectly demands, seeks, receives, accepts, or agrees to receive or accept anything of value personally for or because of the testimony under oath or affirmation given or to be given by such person as a witness upon any such trial, hearing, or other proceeding, or for or because of such person's absence therefrom;

shall be fined under this title or imprisoned for not more than two years, or both.

(d) Paragraphs (3) and (4) of subsection (b) and paragraphs (2) and (3) of subsection (c) shall not be construed to prohibit the payment or receipt of witness fees provided by law, or the payment by the party upon whose behalf a witness is called and receipt by a witness, of the reasonable cost of travel and subsistence incurred and the reasonable value of time lost in attendance at any such trial, hearing, or proceeding, or in the case of expert witnesses, a reasonable fee for time spent in the preparation of such opinion and in appearing and testifying.

(e) The offenses and penalties prescribed in this section are separate from and in addition to those prescribed in sections 1503, 1504 and 1505 of this Title.

a. Public Official

The definition of public official is fairly broad under the federal bribery statute and includes state and county officials as well. A deputy sheriff was "a public official" within the meaning of the federal bribery statute, although he was a county employee receiving no federal funds and the federal prisoners he supervised were not segregated from the state inmates.[75] In another case, a juror was considered to be a federal official for the purposes of the bribery statute.[76]

b. Official Acts

Official acts are also defined fairly broadly. The most typical acts involve decisions or votes by the public official, but can include other activities as well. A congressman engaged in "official acts," within the meaning of the federal bribery statute, when he wrote letters on behalf of a party who had paid for his vacations, using his congressional stationery, to urge federal and city officials to take action favorable to the party.[77]

---

[75] United States v. Velazquez, 847 F.2d 140 (4th Cir. 1988). *See also* Acquah v. State, 686 A.2d 690 (Md. 1996).

[76] United States v. Snell, 152 F.3d 345 (5th Cir. 1998).

[77] United States v. Biaggi, 853 F.2d 89 (2d Cir.), *cert. denied*, 489 U.S. 1052, 109 S. Ct. 1312, 103 L. Ed. 2d 581 (1988).

c. Thing of Value

A "thing of value" within the meaning of the statute is to be broadly construed to encompass intangible benefits, as long as the jury is instructed that they must determine whether the donee placed any value on the intangible gifts.[78] As an example, a defendant agricultural cooperative provided a federal official with a "thing of value" by providing for transportation and expenses of a former Secretary of Agriculture's girlfriend, so that she could be with him in Greece when he presented a speech before an agricultural group.[79] The court advised that companionship, as well as money, can be a "thing of value" to an official. Also, as used in the statute, "anything of value" covered the alleged intangible benefit of receiving favors from police in the form of an officer ignoring certain state offenses committed by the briber.[80]

LEGAL NEWS: LOUISIANA CONGRESSMAN GETS 13 YEARS

William Jefferson, the former Louisiana congressman, who was found to have $90,000 cash stashed in his freezer, was sentenced in 2009 to 13 years in prison for taking hundreds of thousands of dollars in bribes in exchange for his influence. He was convicted of 11 federal counts of bribery and racketeering. He was first accused in 2005 and was reelected in 2006, even though federal charges loomed.

Source: M. Barakat, "Bribed lawmaker gets 13 years." *San Antonio Express-News*, November 14, 2009, A9.

In *United States v. Frega*, the accused was an attorney who was prosecuted under the RICO statute as well as mail fraud and bribery. He evidently paid the equivalent of more than $100,000 to three California Superior Court judges over a 12-year period in the form of cars, car repairs, health club memberships, and at least one queen-size bed. What he received in return was favorable treatment when he had a case before the judge.[81] He argued that the gifts were given in the nature of friendship and goodwill and were not bribes. The appellate court upheld his conviction.

d. Other Applications

In interpreting Section 201(b)(4), a reviewing court ruled that an unabashedly expressed willingness of a witness to tailor her testimony to the highest bidder was sufficient to show that the defendant acted "corruptly" within the meaning of the statute.[82]

---

[78] United States v. Williams, 7 F. Supp. 2d 40 (D.D.C. 1998).
[79] United States v. Sun Diamond Growers of California, 941 F. Supp. 1262 (D.D.C. 1996).
[80] United States v. McCormick, 31 F. Supp. 2d 176 (D. Mass. 1998).
[81] United States v. Frega, 179 F.3d 793 (9th Cir. 1999).
[82] United States v. Donathan, 65 F.3d 537 (6th Cir. 1995).

The federal statute is very comprehensive and applies to those who receive or accept anything of value. It also applies not only to proceedings before any court, but also to proceedings before committees of either House of Congress or any agency, commission, or officer authorized by the laws of the United States to hear evidence, or give testimony. Cases interpreting the provisions of the statute have held that these provisions are neither unconstitutionally vague nor overbroad.[83]

Several federal courts have considered the application of the federal bribery statute where payments are made to confidential informants by law enforcement agencies. In the case of *United States v. Levenite*, a federal circuit court agreed that payment to a confidential FBI informant in a large-scale methamphetamine trafficking conspiracy who testified at criminal proceeding did not violate the statute prohibiting bribery of public officials and witnesses, because the government was explicitly authorized to pay witnesses fees as authorized by law.[84] Courts have held that the antigratuity statute, which criminalizes giving or promising anything of value in exchange for witness testimony, does not apply to the United States or to any Assistant United States Attorney acting within his or her official capacity.[85]

Although the bribery statutes have been interpreted broadly, a conviction will not stand if the defendant can show entrapment. For example, when a taxpayer offered a bribe only after an IRS agent's persistent solicitations and reminders as to the substantial amount of tax liability, the bribery charge was dismissed.[86]

C. Obstructing Justice

Chapter 73 of Title 18 of the U.S. Code has 14 sections relating to the obstruction of justice. Obstruction of justice is governed principally by 18 U.S.C. §§ 1501 through 1818, which forbid the obstruction of justice and protect the integrity of proceedings before the federal judiciary and other governmental bodies.

The section that is employed most frequently is § 1503, which provides

18 U.S.C. § 1503. Influencing or injuring officer or juror (generally)

(a) Whoever corruptly, or by threats or force, or by any threatening letter or communication, endeavors to influence, intimidate, or impede any grand or petit juror, or officer in or of any court of the United States, or officer who may be serving at any examination or other proceeding before any United States magistrate judge or other committing magistrate, in the discharge of his duty, or injures any such grand or petit juror in his person or property on account of any verdict or indictment assented to by him, or on account of his being or having been such juror, or

---

[83] United States v. Brewster, 506 F.2d 62 (D.C. Cir. 1974). *See also* United States v. McDade, 827 F. Supp. 1153 (E.D. Pa. 1993).

[84] United States v. Levenite, 277 F.3d 454 (4th Cir. 2002). *See also* United States v. Harris, 198 F.3d 957 (8th Cir. 1999).

[85] United States v. Stephenson, 183 F.3d 110 (2d Cir. 1999), *cert. denied*, 528 U.S. 1013, 120 S. Ct. 517, 145 L. Ed. 2d 400 (1999). See also United States v. Hartmon, 194 F.3d 390 (8th Cir. 1999).

[86] United States v. Sandoval, 20 F.3d 134 (5th Cir. 1994).

injures any such officer, magistrate judge, or other committing magistrate in his person or property on account of the performance of his official duties, or corruptly or by threats or force, or by any threatening letter or communication, influences, obstructs, or impedes, or endeavors to influence, obstruct, or impede, the due administration of justice, shall be punished as provided in subsection (b). If the offense under this section occurs in connection with a trial of a criminal case, and the act in violation of this section involves the threat of physical force or physical force, the maximum term of imprisonment which may be imposed for the offense shall be the higher of that otherwise provided by law or the maximum term that could have been imposed for any offense charged in such case.

(b) The punishment for an offense under this section is—
    (1) in the case of a killing, the punishment provided in sections 1111 and 1112;
    (2) in the case of an attempted killing, or a case in which the offense was committed against a petit juror and in which a class A or B felony was charged, imprisonment for not more than 20 years, a fine under this title, or both; and
    (3) in any other case, imprisonment for not more than 10 years, a fine under this title, or both.

18 U.S.C. § 1503 governs any obstruction of justice affecting jurors, officers of the court, and judges. The elements of a § 1503 offense are

- a nexus with a pending federal judicial proceeding;
- that the defendant knew of or had notice about the proceeding; and
- that the defendant acted corruptly with intent to obstruct or interfere with the proceedings or due administration of justice.[87]

While the government need not prove that the defendant had the specific purpose of obstructing justice, it must establish that the defendant's conduct possessed, at least in part, a corrupt motive. One need not succeed in obstructing justice to be convicted of a violation of § 1503. This section was challenged as being unconstitutionally vague, but the courts that have heard arguments agree that the statute does not suffer from unconstitutional vagueness.[88]

Defendants have been successfully prosecuted for knowingly, willfully, and corruptly

- attempting to impede the administration of justice in a matter under investigation by intentionally destroying documents
- giving false testimony to a grand jury concerning a third person's presence at a meeting
- corruptly influencing a grand jury witness to refuse to testify[89]

---

[87]   West Virginia v. Moore, 897 F. Supp. 276 (S.D.W.Va. 1995).
[88]   United States v. Brenson, 104 F.3d 1267 (11th Cir. 1997); United States v. Fleming, 215 F.3d 930 (9th Cir. 2000); United States v. Mitchell, 397 F.Supp. 166 (D.D.C.), cert denied, 431 U.S. 733 (1974).
[89]   United States v. McKnight, 799 F.2d 443 (8th Cir. 1986); United States v. Langella, 776 F.2d 1078 (2d Cir. 1985); United States v. Arnold, 773 F.2d 823 (7th Cir. 1985).

To show the offense of endeavoring to influence a juror in the discharge of his or her duty, the government must prove (1) that a judicial proceeding was pending; (2) that the defendant had knowledge of the judicial proceeding; and (3) that the defendant acted corruptly with the specific intent to influence, obstruct, or impede that proceeding and its due administration of justice.[90]

D. *Other Crimes*

Title 18 § 1512 of the U.S. Code includes penalties for tampering with a witness, victim, or informant. That section includes the following provisions:

> 18 U.S.C. § 1572
>
> (1) Whoever uses physical force or the threat of physical force against any person, or attempts to do so, with intent to—
>> (A) influence, delay, or prevent the testimony of any person in an official proceeding;
>> (B) cause or induce any person to—
>>> (i) withhold testimony, or withhold a record, document, or other object, from an official proceeding;
>>> (ii) alter, destroy, mutilate, or conceal an object with intent to impair the integrity or availability of the object for use in an official proceeding;
>>> (iii) evade legal process summoning that person to appear as a witness, or to produce a record, document, or other object, in an official proceeding; or
>>> (iv) be absent from an official proceeding to which that person has been summoned by legal process; or
>> (C) hinder, delay, or prevent the communication to a law enforcement officer or judge of the United States of information relating to the commission or possible commission of a Federal offense or a violation of conditions of probation, supervised release, parole, or release pending judicial proceedings; shall be punished as provided in paragraph (3).

1. Escape

Chapter 35 of Title 18 of the U.S. Code (18 U.S.C. §§ 751, 752, 755) include provisions relating to the escape of prisoners in federal custody. Title 18 U.S.C. § 751 provides

> 18 U.S.C. § 751. Prisoners in custody of institution or officer
>
> (a) Whoever escapes or attempts to escape from the custody of the Attorney General or his authorized representative, or from any institution or facility in which he is confined by direction of the Attorney General, or from any custody under or by virtue of any process issued under the laws of the United States by any court, judge or magistrate judge, or from the custody of an officer or employee of the United States pursuant to lawful arrest, shall, if the custody or confinement is by virtue of an arrest on a

---

[90]   United States v. DeLaRoss, 171 F.3d 215 (5th Cir. 1999).

charge of felony, or conviction of any offense, be fined under this title or imprisoned not more than five years, or both; or if the custody or confinement is for extradition, or for exclusion or expulsion proceedings under the immigration laws, or by virtue of an arrest or charge of or for a misdemeanor, and prior to conviction, be fined under this title or imprisoned no more than one year, or both.

The elements of the offense of escape from custody are

- the defendant is held in a statutory type of custody,
- for a felony violation, and
- leaves without authorization.[91]

To prove a violation of the statute prohibiting escape from federal custody, the government must show that an escapee knew his action would result in his leaving physical confinement without permission.[92]

In the case of *United States v. Novak*, the defendant left a work detail and was charged with escape in violation of this statute. At the trial, the parties agreed that Novak escaped from nonsecure custody on December 8, 2000, and returned voluntarily at approximately 2:30 P.M. on December 12, 2000. The time of the escape became important in determining whether the defendant was entitled to a "seven-level" downward adjustment for returning to custody voluntarily within 96 hours of his escape.[93] The court decided that escape begins when the defendant departs from local custody with the intent to evade detention, even if no one saw him wander from his work detail, rather than from the time his absence was reported.

Title 18 § 752 of the U.S. Code makes it a crime to instigate or assist an escape. Under this provision, whoever rescues or attempts to rescue, or instigates, aids, or assists the escape, or attempt to escape, of any person arrested under a warrant or other process issued under any law of the United States, shall be punished. In a prosecution for aiding and assisting the escape of a federal prisoner under this section, evidence that the defendant knew the prisoner's departure from prison was unauthorized was sufficient to sustain a conviction.[94]

Section 755 of Title 18 makes it a crime for an officer to permit an escape:

18 U.S.C. § 755

Whoever, having in his custody any prisoner by virtue of process issued under the laws of the United States by any court, judge, or magistrate judge, voluntarily suffers such prisoner to escape, shall be fined under this title or imprisoned not more than five years, or both; or if he negligently suffers such person to escape, he shall be fined under this title or imprisoned not more than one year, or both.

---

[91]   United States v. Evans, 886 F. Supp. 800 (D. Kan. 1995).
[92]   United States v. Hambrick, 299 F.3d 911 (8th Cir. 2002).
[93]   United States v. Novak, 284 F.3d 986 (9th Cir. 2002).
[94]   United States v. Nordstrom, 730 F.2d 556 (8th Cir. 1984).

As the wording indicates, this section applies only if the person accused has custody of a prisoner and either voluntarily allows the prisoner to escape or negligently permits the prisoner to escape.

2. Resisting Arrest

Title 18 § 111 makes resisting arrest a felony punishable by a fine or imprisonment of not more than eight years, or both, if a person is convicted of forcibly assaulting, resisting, opposing, impeding, or intimidating an officer in the performance of his or her official duties. If deadly force or a dangerous weapon is used, the imprisonment may be increased to 20 years.

A federal court of appeals found that this section gives a person of ordinary intelligence fair notice of what conduct is proscribed and is not unconstitutionally vague, indefinite, or ambiguous.[95]

The provision prohibiting assault against a federal officer was enacted to protect federal officers and federal functions and to provide a federal forum in which to try the alleged offender. As is the law in many states, federal officers engaged in good faith and colorable performance of their duties may not be forcibly resisted even if the person resisting is correct that the resisted action should not have been taken. The statute requires the arrestee to submit peaceably and seek legal redress thereafter. When a person is identified as a law enforcement officer, and uses reasonable force in the performance of his or her law enforcement duties, the use of force to resist that officer is not justified and self-defense does not apply.[96] The federal law making it a felony to resist arrest or intimidate an officer in the performance of his or her official duties may be violated by minimal physical contact, or even by threats, without physical contact.[97]

§ 13.6　Regulatory Crimes

The Supreme Court has agreed that Congress can delegate to a federal agency the power to make regulations that have the force of law. Thus the Federal Aviation Administration can use criminal sanctions to enforce its regulations, as can the Securities and Exchange Commission and other federal agencies.

A. *Corporate Culpability*

As federal and state agencies increase their investigative focus on **white-collar crime** and as many of the federal laws target corporations as well as individuals, the courts have found it necessary to review the laws concerning **corporate crime**. Corporate criminal liability existed well before the coining of the term white-collar crime.

---

[95]　United States v. Linn, 438 F.2d 456 (10th Cir. 1971)
[96]　United States v. Lopez, 710 F.2d 1071 (5th Cir. 1983).
[97]　United States v. Hernandez, 921 F.2d 1569 (11th Cir. 1991).

At common law, corporations could not be held liable for criminal acts. However, with the recognition by state legislatures and the courts that the imposition of corporate criminal liability is an essential part of the regulatory process, a body of law pertaining to corporate criminal liability soon developed. Without corporate liability, many crimes would be punished insufficiently because the size and structure of many corporations makes it impossible to adequately allocate responsibility to individuals. When state and federal statutes making corporations criminally liable are upheld, corporations, as well as officers and agents of the corporations, are made defendants in a number of cases.

The most fundamental hurdle for courts to overcome was the idea of holding fictional entities culpable in a legal system based on individual moral accountability. Courts gradually applied aspects of the criminal law, including sentencing, to the abstract nature of the corporation.

The Model Penal Code, discussed in earlier chapters of this book, includes a section defining the liability of corporations.[98] This comprehensive section indicates the circumstances under which a corporation may be held criminally liable, provides principles for the interpretation of statutes defining offenses for which a corporation may be liable, and deals with problems relating to the individual criminal liability of the directors, officers, and servants of corporations. In a jurisdiction following the Model Penal Code, a corporation may be criminally liable for its agent's acts when the illegal acts are codified or where "the commission of the offense was authorized, requested, commanded, performed or recklessly tolerated by the board of directors or by a high managerial agent acting on behalf of the corporation within the scope of his office or employment."

In the case of *First Federal Savings Bank of Hegewisch v. United States*, the court held that, in general, a corporation can only act through its agents, and "when they are clothed with authority to act for it, the corporation is responsible for their acts."[99] This does not mean, however, that every action an employee takes is automatically imputed to the corporation. If the employee is acting outside his or her actual or apparent authority, for example, the corporation is generally not liable for the action.

Many states have also adopted specific statutory language defining liability for criminal acts committed by "high managerial agents." In some states, the corporation may be liable for an employee's action even if the corporation's directors, officers, or other high managerial agents did not specifically approve of the employee's behavior, while in other states only the individual agents are culpable. Whether the state or federal agencies utilize ***respondeat superior*** theory for imposing criminal liability, or state and federal statutes, empirical studies demonstrate that corporations have been and will continue to be held criminally liable for acts of their agents, especially acts that are prohibited by the white-collar crime statutes.

---

[98]   MODEL PENAL CODE § 2.07 (1985).

[99]   First Federal Savings Bank of Hegewisch v. United States, 52 Fed. Cl. 774 (2002).

Title 18 § 3551 of the United States Code provides

U.S.C. § 3551

Organizations—An organization found guilty of an offense shall be sentenced in accordance with the provisions of § 3553 to—

(1) a term of probation as authorized by subchapter B; or (2) a fine as authorized by subsection (C).

A sentence to pay a fine may be imposed in addition to probation. A sanction authorized by Section 3554, 3555, or 3556 may be imposed in addition to the sentence required by this subsection.

Although the guidelines are applicable to all "organizations," they were designed with corporations in mind, and it is on corporations that they are expected to have the greatest impact. The guidelines define "organization" to include "corporations, partnerships, associations, joint stock companies, unions, trusts, pension funds, unincorporated organizations, governments and political subdivisions thereof, and nonprofit organizations."

Organizations convicted of federal felony and class A misdemeanor offenses are sentenced under the organizational guidelines. The guidelines operate under four general principles:

- the corporation must remedy any harm caused by its offense;
- a corporation run primarily for criminal purposes should receive fines high enough to divest the business of all of its assets;
- businesses run for other than criminal purposes should be fined according to the seriousness of their offenses and the culpability of the corporation; and
- the corporation shall be subject to probation if it will ensure that a company complies with sanctions or if it reduces the likelihood of future violations by the corporation.[100]

B. Environmental Crimes (EPA)

The U.S. Environmental Protection Agency (EPA) has a range of enforcement tools available—administrative, civil, and criminal—to combat **environmental crime**.

Prosecution for acts that affect the environment received little attention until recently. However, as governments have become more concerned with the protection of the quality of water, land, and air, regulations and laws have increased. While laws containing overlapping civil, criminal, and administrative penalty provisions have originated in both the federal and state legislatures, the federal government has taken the lead in controlling acts relating to the environment. In fact, in the last 40 years, environmental laws have increased in number, length, and complexity. In the paragraphs that follow, some of the prohibited acts that are most likely to come to the attention of law enforcement and criminal justice personnel are briefly discussed.

---

[100] See United States Sentencing Guidelines Manual § 8 (1998)

1. The Clean Air Act (CAA)[101]

The Clean Air Act (CAA) imposes penalties on those who knowingly violate federal or state regulations designed to achieve ambient air quality standards established by the EPA. In justifying the passage of this legislation, Congress determined that federal legislation was necessary as violations crossed boundary lines and often extended to two or more states, and that federal financial assistance and leadership is essential for the development of cooperative federal, state, and local programs to prevent and control air pollution. The CCA mandates that the EPA prescribe national air quality standards, although states are free to adopt more stringent protection. Each state then is required to adopt an implementation plan of its own for that state. If a state implementation plan is approved by the EPA, its requirements become federal law and are fully enforceable in federal court. A CAA violation occurs when a source emits pollution in excess of levels established by regulation.

Criminal sanctions apply to any person who

- violates the CAA by making false statements,
- fails to report as required,
- tampers with EPA monitoring devices, or
- fails to pay fees owed to the United States.

Criminal sanctions may be imposed on both the organizations and the individuals responsible for the actions of an organization. According to the penalty provisions, a knowing violation of any emission standard under the CAA, a knowing failure to pay fees assessed, or a knowing violation of any reporting or monitoring requirement is punishable by criminal fines, up to five years in prison, or both.

2. Safe Drinking Water Act (SDWA)[102]

The Safe Drinking Water Act (SDWA) was designed to regulate levels of harmful contaminants in public water systems and the underground injection of contaminants into ground water that supplies public drinking water. Under the provisions of the Act, the EPA is required to establish national primary drinking water regulations, and discharges must obtain permits for underground injection of contaminants. The Act also regulates the amount of lead found in drinking water coolers, and penalizes tampering with public water systems. The Act requires the EPA to establish minimum standards to prevent the contamination of underground water resources. Failure to comply with the standards could lead to civil penalties as well as criminal penalties.

As with some other environmental crime provisions, states may secure primary enforcement authority for the regulation of underground water sources if the EPA

---

[101]   42 U.S.C. §§ 7401-7671 (1994).
[102]   42 U.S.C. §§ 7401-7671 (1994).

approves the state's underground injection control program. Failure of the state to comply with this program makes it possible for the EPA to revoke the state's authority.

3. Clean Water Act (CWA)[103]

The Clean Water Act (CWA) was enacted to restore and maintain the chemical, physical, and biological integrity of the nation's waters by minimizing the effects of water pollution. The Clean Water Act is also referred to as the Federal Water Pollution Control Act. Under the terms of the Act, federal, state, and local authorities are authorized to establish programs that prohibit or regulate the discharge of pollutants into the water of the United States. In administering and enforcing the Clean Water Act, the Environmental Protection Agency and the Army Corps of Engineers share responsibility. The Corps has the nondiscretionary duty to regulate discharge of dredged or fill material by issuing permits after applying guidelines established by the EPA and has the authority to enforce permit violations. The EPA holds the ultimate responsibility for wetlands protection, has authority to seek penalties for unpermitted discharges of pollutants into United States waters and, after consulting with Corps of Engineers, can block or overrule the Corps decision to issue permits.

Under various sections of the statute, government agencies may establish effluent limitations and water quality standards, impose discharge reporting and monitoring requirements, mandate the cleanup of oil and other hazardous substances, prohibit unpermitted dredging or filling and the discharge of sewage sludge, and set up permit programs regulating discharge of pollutants and the dredging and filling of wetlands. In interpreting the Act, a federal court held that the Clean Water Act is entitled to a broad construction to implement its objective of protecting human health, welfare, and environment.[104]

Criminal penalties may be assessed against any "person" who fails to comply with the statutory requirements of the Clean Water Act. The Act established four levels of criminal penalties, depending on whether a violation was negligent, knowing, involved knowing endangerment, or involved knowing falsification of information or tampering with monitoring equipment.

The "knowledge" element of the offense reached the Circuit Court when it was asked to determine whether the government must prove that the defendant had knowledge of the law he was accused of violating, as well as knowledge of the underlying conduct that resulted in the charge. In the case of *United States v. Sinskey*, the defendants were charged with a number of Clean Water Act violations. Specifically, they were charged with participating in a "flow game"—discharging low levels of wastewater when performing monitoring tests, then discharging exceedingly high levels of ammonia and nitrogen-rich wastewater at other times. They would also submit only the best monitoring reports. At the trial, the jury was instructed that, in order to find a

---

[103]   33 U.S.C. §§ 1251-1387 (1994).
[104]   United States v. Holland, 874 F.2d 1470 (11th Cir. 1985).

knowing violation, the proof had to show that the defendant was aware of the nature of the acts, performed them intentionally, and did not act or fail to act through ignorance, mistake, or accident. The instructions further advised the jury that the government was not required to prove that the defendant knew the acts violated the permit or the Clean Water Act. On appeal, the defendant argued that the government must prove that he knew his conduct violated the permit or the Clean Water Act. The circuit court disagreed with the defendant, holding that the government is only required to prove knowledge of the underlying conduct, not knowledge of the law.[105]

LEGAL NEWS: CULPABILITY FOR THE DEEPWATER HORIZON SPILL

In 2010 the Gulf Coast experienced the worst oil spill in history, killing 11 men, injuring 17 others and releasing close to 200 million barrels of oil into the Gulf of Mexico before it was contained. The response was guided by the National Oil and Hazardous Substances Pollution Contingency Plan (NCP) and the Oil Pollution Act of 1990, which amended § 311 of the Clean Water Act. The main point of the relevant law is that the polluter is legally responsible for cleaning up the spill, regardless of fault. Thus, British Petroleum paid for cleanup and redundant containment systems offshore, in addition to setting up a $20 billion fund to compensate victims. It was reported in December of 2011 that federal prosecutors are contemplating criminal charges in relation to the spill, which should be revealed sometime in 2012.

Source: "BP oil spill: Prosecutors reportedly preparing criminal charges." HuffingtonPost.com, December 29, 2012. Accessed on January 12, 2012 from http://www.huffingtonpost.com/2011/12/29/bp-oil-spill-_n_1174542.html?view=print&comm_ref=false.

---

4. Toxic Substance Control Act (TSCA)[106]

To further the protection of the environment, Congress enacted the Toxic Substance Control Act (TSCA). The purpose of the Act is to prevent toxic substances in commerce from presenting an "unreasonable risk of injury to health or the environment," and to stem the tide of chemical substances and mixtures considered "imminent hazards." The Act also requires private industries that manufacture toxic substances to generate data with respect to the effects of the toxic chemicals.

Under the provisions of the Act, the EPA is authorized to regulate testing, premanufacturing clearance, manufacturing, and distribution of toxic substances. However, the Act also provides that enforcement agencies should not "impede unduly or create unnecessary economic barriers to technological innovation." In a federal case, the court

---

[105]   United States v. Sinskey, 119 F.3d 712 (8th Cir. 1997).
[106]   15 U.S.C. §§ 2601-2692 (1994).

made it clear that the Environmental Protection Agency must articulate an "understandable basis" to support action with respect to each substance or application of substance banned. The court stated that the EPA must make findings of unreasonable risk based upon this assessment and must balance the probability that harm will occur from activities against the effects of the proposed regulatory action on availability to society of benefits of the banned substance.[107]

Section 15(b) authorizes criminal penalties against a person who knowingly and willfully violates the TSCA. The Act provides the criminal sanctions in addition to or in lieu of any civil or administrative penalties.

5. Resource Conservation and Recovery Act (RCRA)[108]

The Resource Conservation and Recovery Act (RCRA) establishes a detailed scheme for federal regulation of all wastes, including hazardous wastes. It sets standards that govern the generation, treatment, storage, transportation, and disposal of hazardous wastes. According to Section 6902 of the Act, the objectives are to promote the protection of health and the environment and to conserve valuable material and energy resources by training and establishing practices as enumerated in the act.

Like most of the other laws establishing standards and penalties relating to the environment, this Act was promulgated by Congress pursuant to the commerce clause of the Constitution. In the case of *United States v. Rogers*, the court explained that the nexus between commercial activity and generation of solid waste was well documented, and Congress could rationally conclude that the activity affected interstate commerce.[109]

The Act provides criminal penalties for persons who knowingly treat, store, or dispose of hazardous waste without a permit, or transport hazardous waste to a facility lacking a permit. A "solid waste" is a "hazardous waste" if the EPA has listed it as such, or if the waste exhibits any of these four characteristics: ignitability, corrosivity, reactivity, or toxicity. The EPA has listed more than 700 solid wastes as hazardous, and the universe of wastes covered by the four characteristics is large and expanding.

Some of the penalties imposed for violation of the Act are quite severe. Knowingly transporting hazardous waste to a nonpermitted facility or knowingly treating, storing, or disposing of hazardous waste without a permit are subject to penalties of up to five years imprisonment and fines of $50,000 per day. Even more severe penalties result if the violators are concurrently convicted of knowingly placing another person in imminent danger of death or serious bodily injury. In these cases, individuals may be fined

---

[107]   Corrosion Proof Fittings v. EPA, 947 F.2d 1201 (5th Cir. 1991).
[108]   42 U.S.C. §§ 6901-6992k (1994).
[109]   United States v. Rogers, 685 F.Supp. 201 (D. Minn. 1987).

up to $250,000, imprisoned for up to 15 years, or both, while organizations may face fines up to $1,000,000.

6. Other Crimes

Other environment-related federal statutes include the Rivers and Harbors Act of 1899, the Comprehensive Environmental Response, Compensation and Liability Act (Superfund), which mandates the cleanup of hazardous substances at contaminated sites and imposes criminal penalties on those who violated it, and the Federal Insecticide, Fungicide and Rodenticide Act, which regulates the manufacture, registration, transportation, and sale of toxic pesticides.[110]

C. Antitrust and Securities Violations (SEC)

The Sherman Act of 1890 was enacted to prevent sabotage of the free enterprise system. The central purpose of **antitrust laws** is to prevent any acts that take away the freedom of purchasers to buy in the open market and to maintain freedom of competition.

The criminal provision of the present Sherman Act provides for criminal sanctions against any person "who shall make any contract or engage in any combination or conspiracy" in restraint of interstate commerce. This part of the Act provides

15 U.S.C. § 1

Every contract, combination in the form of trust or otherwise, or conspiracy, in restraint of trade or commerce among the several states, or with foreign nations, is declared to be illegal. Every person who shall make any contract or engage in any combination or conspiracy hereby declared to be illegal shall be deemed guilty of a felony, and, on conviction thereof, shall be punished by fine of $10,000,000, if a corporation, or, if any person, $350,000, or by imprisonment not exceeding three years, or by both said punishments, in the discretion of the court.

To prove a criminal violation, the government must establish four elements:

- two or more entities formed a combination or a conspiracy;
- the combination or conspiracy produces, or potentially produces, an unreasonable restraint of trade or commerce;
- the restrained trade or commerce is interstate in nature; and
- general intent.

According to interpretations by the federal courts, Congress did not intend the text of Sections 1 to 7 of the Antitrust Act to delineate the full meaning of their application in concrete situations; rather, Congress expected courts to give shape to their broad mandate by drawing on common law tradition.

The "conspiracy" element can be satisfied if there is "a combination or some form of concerted action between two legally distinct economic entities." The courts have

---

[110]   33 U.S.C. § 407 (1997); 42 U.S.C. §§ 9601-9675 (1994); 7 U.S.C. § 136 (1994).

made it clear that the government's success in demonstrating an interstate commerce nexus is both a critical jurisdictional fact and an element of the substantive offense under the act. In discussing the intent requirement, a reviewing court commented that the defendants can be convicted of participation in price-fixing conspiracies without any demonstration of specific intent to violate antitrust laws.[111]

Over the years there have been several other laws passed by Congress to bolster the ability of the federal government to protect free trade, including the Robinson-Patman Act, the Clayton Act, and the Federal Trade Commission Act. Some of the activities that are addressed by federal laws include

- artificially lowering the price of goods or services to force out competitors
- mergers to eliminate competition
- exclusive dealing arrangements (i.e., a manufacturer forces its distributors to not carry competing products)
- unfair or deceptive advertising
- price fixing (competitors agree to keep prices similar)
- market allocation agreements (between competitors)
- boycotts of traders
- "tying arrangements" (forcing buyers to buy a second product if they want to buy the first product)
- monopolies

1. State Antitrust Laws

Most states have statutes similar to the Sherman Act, but they are not uniform. States can enforce antitrust laws in two ways: by prosecution for violations of state antitrust laws or by suing as plaintiffs in federal court under the federal law. The Illinois Act, similar to some other states' provisions, is more detailed and leaves less interpretation to the court than the federal Antitrust Law. A federal court determined that the Illinois Antitrust Act is not preempted by federal antitrust law, but if two antitrust regimes differ, federal antitrust law may preempt state antitrust law.[112] One court, in explaining the preemption principle, noted that federal law can preempt state law in three ways: first, Congress may expressly declare that state law is preempted; second, state law is preempted if Congress intends the federal government to occupy the field exclusively; third, federal law preempts state law if the two actually conflict.[113]

---

[111]   United States v. Nippon Paper Company, 109 F.3d 1 (1st Cir. 1997).
[112]   740 ILL. COMP. STAT. 5/7 1996: Illinois ex. rel. Borris v. Panhandle Eastern Pipeline Co., 935 F.2d 1469 (7th Cir.).
[113]   Totemoff v. State, 905 P.2d 954 (Alaska 1995).

2. Securities Exchange Violations

Securities are legal documents that represent shares of ownership or debt, for instance, stocks, bonds, notes, options, and so on. The Securities Act of 1933 and the Securities and Exchange Act of 1934 required that publicly traded securities be registered and the trading of such stock be regulated, including the requirement to provide accurate information to purchasers. The Securities and Exchange Commission (SEC) is the federal agency that regulates securities trading. A number of crimes can be committed in relation to securities trading, including fraud and insider trading.

a. Securities Fraud

We have previously described the federal mail and wire fraud statute. Securities fraud shares some of the same elements but is specifically related to frauds perpetrated in the buying or selling of securities. An offender violates the law when he or she

- makes a material false statement or omission;
- knowingly, with intent to defraud;
- that causes another party damages; and
- if it is an omission, the party had a duty to disclose the information.

This would involve, for instance, a company presenting false audits that made the company appear to be more profitable than it was for the purpose of selling shares, or a broker who does not disclose negative aspects of a purchase to his or her clients in order to get them to invest. The Ponzi scheme perpetrated by Bernie Madoff also falls into this category of securities fraud. He purported that investing in his hedge fund would earn investors, on average, 10 to 12 percent returns, and investors did receive those returns, even when the market declined. However, rather than investing in stock, he used later investors' money to pay dividends to early investors, thus encouraging more and more people to give him money. When the stock market crashed in the fall of 2008, so many of Madoff's investors wanted to cash out that his whole scheme fell apart because he did not have enough assets to give investors their money. The fraud is estimated at more than $50 billion and is probably the largest Ponzi scheme in history. Some of his investors were charities who were forced into bankruptcy, and at least one investor committed suicide. An excerpt of the Criminal Complaint against him that resulted in his 144-year prison sentence reads

(1) From at least in or about December 2008 through the present, in the southern District of New York and elsewhere, BERNARD L. MADOFF, the defendant, unlawfully, willfully, and knowingly, by the use of the means and instrumentalities of interstate commerce and of the mails, directly and indirectly, in connection with the purchase and sale of securities, would and did use and employ manipulative and deceptive devices and contrivances in violation of Title 17, Code of Federal Regulations, Section 240.10b-5, by (a) employing devices, schemes, and artifices to defraud; (b) making untrue statements of material facts and omitting to state material facts

necessary in order to make the statements made, in the light of the circumstances under which they were made, not misleading, and (c) engaging in acts, practices, and courses of business which operated and would operate as a fraud and deceit upon persons, to wit, MADOFF deceived investors by operating a securities business in which he traded and lost investor money, and then paid certain investors purported returns on investment with the principal received from other, different investors, which resulted in losses of approximately billions of dollars . . .[114]

LEGAL NEWS: WALL STREET

Many people probably wonder why there have not been criminal charges raining down on those on Wall Street responsible for the economic crash of 2007, or even the foreclosure abuses that have happened since. It is a good question since there seems to be evidence that large, well known banks have used "robo-signing" contrary to banking laws in foreclosure documents. This practice involves having low-level bank employees sign documents falsely swearing to facts related to the foreclosure. Evidence of widescale illegal alterations and outright forgeries in foreclosure documents also emerged in 2010. In 2010 members of Congress requested the Justice Department to investigate but the Attorney General stated that it would be a matter best left to states. Some states have pursued charges, including New York, Massachusetts, Delaware, and California. These investigations have targeted the foreclosure abuses that took place after the economic collapse—the prospect of anyone being criminally culpable for the collapse itself seems increasingly unlikely.

Source: S. Paltrow. "Special report: The watchdogs that didn't bark." Reuters.com, December 22, 2011. Accessed December 22, 2011 from http://www.reuters.com/assets/print?aid=USTRE7BLOMC20111222.

---

b. Insider Trading

Perhaps the most frequent type of securities violation is **insider trading**. This is when someone who owns more than 10 percent of the stock in a publicly traded company buys or sells their shares based on insider information not available to the general public. Congress enacted the Insider Trading Sanctions Act of 1984, which increased penalties for this offense.

The most famous insider trading case in recent years was Martha Stewart's conviction in 2002. She sold her shares of ImClone stock days before negative information about the company caused the shares to plummet in value. She reached a plea agreement by confessing to perjury for lying to officials about her actions and paid a fine for the insider trading violation.

---

[114]   United States v. Madoff. Complaint. Violation of 15 U.S.C. Sec. 78j(b), 78ff; 17 C.F.R. Sec. 240.10b-5. Filed in Southern District of New York, Magistrate Douglas Eaton.

LEGAL NEWS: OPERATION PERFECT HEDGE

News reports in 2012 report on an FBI investigation that will result in a complicated prosecution of individuals involved in insider trading in hedge funds, with 53 charged and 50 more having pled guilty. Hedge fund managers were found to aggressively solicit insider information about the companies the hedge fund held stock in. Such information was obtained through personal friendships, business relationships, and so-called "expert consultants" who were recruited from the employee ranks of the companies targeted. Technology and pharmaceutical companies were usually the focus of such activity. Investigators described the relationships between the traders and their sources as almost like an organized crime family because it was almost impossible to break in to gain information. Relationships went back years to college days and, in some cases, were sexual relationships. The Perfect Hedge investigation obtained incriminating evidence regarding low-level employees and then used them to obtain information about others, through the use of wiretaps and secret tape recordings of conversations and interactions. They discovered that some "matchmaker" firms would set up as independent research companies, then contact employees in technology or other firms. They offered them money as "expert consultants" who would answer questions about their company. The information was then relayed to fund managers who would use the information to make decisions about buying and selling.

Source: P. Hurtado. FBI pulls off 'Perfect Hedge' to nab new insider trading class. *Bloomberg Business News*, December 20, 2011.

---

3. Sarbanes-Oxley Act of 2002

The Sarbanes-Oxley Act created new federal offenses in the area of securities violations. The new laws were passed after the Enron collapse and other major businesses such as WorldCom went bankrupt suddenly, with investors losing billions of dollars. The laws are directed toward individuals who destroy documents when they are under investigation for securities fraud or insider trading. It also requires that the chief officers of corporations certify that financial statements comply with SEC regulations, increases the penalties for fraud and conspiracy, and has a provision to protect whistleblowers in a corporation when such people expose illegal acts such as fraud or other financial improprieties.

One of the most important changes this Act has made to the enforcement of securities frauds is that the *mens rea* has been changed from *intentional* to *knowing*. This is in response to the Enron CFOs and executives, and auditing companies like Arthur Anderson, who knew the financial reports were not accurate but did nothing to prevent unsuspecting stockholders from continuing to trade in company stock. Now, such individuals are responsible for certifying the accuracy of financial statements, and whether they intentionally defraud investors or just know that a fraud is being perpetrated, they are guilty of securities fraud.

4. Other Crimes

There are other crimes that are investigated and prosecuted by the SEC. For instance, **churning** is a term used to describe when brokers buy and sell stock for clients solely to increase their own brokerage fees rather than for the benefit of the client. This violation of their fiduciary duty can be prosecuted when the government proves that the trading was excessive and the broker showed intent to defraud or exhibited a willful and reckless disregard for the investor's interests.

D. *Occupational Safety and Health Act (OSHA)*[115]

In December 1970, Congress enacted the **Occupational Safety and Health Act** (OSHA). Congress had determined that legislation was necessary due to the trend of increasing employee deaths and injuries in the late 1960s. The stated purpose of Congress was to exercise its powers to regulate commerce among the states to ensure, as far as possible, every working man and woman in the nation safe and healthful working conditions and to preserve human resources.

OSHA includes a general duty clause that requires employers to furnish their employees with a working environment free from recognized hazards. In addition, the statute requires employers to comply with specific occupational safety and health rules promulgated by the Secretary of Labor. The Act provides for both civil and criminal penalties. Criminal prosecutions have been initiated either when an employer's willful violation of a standard, rule, order, or regulation causes the death of an employee, or when an employer makes a false representation regarding compliance with the Act.

Discussing the "willful violation," a federal court noted that whether a violation was willful depends on whether it resulted from the conscious disregard of the regulation.[116] Another court held that willfulness in a criminal case may be proved by showing deliberate indifference to the fact or the law or by showing awareness of significant risk coupled with steps to avoid additional information, but in either case what must be proved beyond a reasonable doubt is actual rather than constructive knowledge.[117] In light of its broad remedial purpose, OSHA and its accompanying regulations should be liberally construed so as to afford the broadest possible protection to workers.

---

[115]   29 U.S.C. §§ 651-678.
[116]   Caterpillar, Inc. v. Herman, 154 F.3d 400 (7th Cir. 1998).
[117]   United States v. Ledish Malting Co., 135 F.3d 484 (7th Cir. 1998).

1. State Laws

The enactment of federal statutes left unanswered the question of to what extent OSHA preempted state criminal sanctions. Although states are preempted by OSHA from regulating workplace safety, the application of certain state criminal sanctions against employers is not preempted. For example, in a Texas case, the court held that applying state criminal laws to workplace conduct was not preempted by OSHA because it does not interfere with the goals of the Act.[118] Making clear that the federal government would have primary jurisdiction in these cases, the U.S. Supreme Court noted that the design of OSHA shows that Congress intended to subject employers and employees to only one set of regulations, be it federal or state, and that the only way that a state may regulate occupational and health issues that are regulated by OSHA is pursuant to an OSHA-approved state plan that displaces the federal standards.[119]

In the case of *People v. Hegedus*, an employee's supervisor was charged with involuntary manslaughter. These charges arose as a result of the death of an employee who died of carbon monoxide intoxication while working in a company-owned van. The prosecution contended that the poor condition of the van's undercarriage and exhaust system allowed exhaust fumes to leak inside the van, causing the employee's death. The defendant contended that if he were subject to any criminal liability for his acts or omissions in causing the victim's death, it was under the criminal provisions of OSHA, not under any state criminal law such as the manslaughter statute under which he was charged. The Michigan Supreme Court, in discussing the preemption issue, noted that generally, the existence of federal laws or regulations in a particular area can preempt state action in the same field where preemption is either express, implied, or the result of a conflict between state and federal law, but the extent to which federal law actually preempts state authority is a question of congressional intent. The court concluded that, in the case of OSHA violations, the state was not preempted from pursuing criminal sanctions.[120] Where Congress has not completely displaced a state regulation in a specific area, state law is nullified only to the extent that it actually conflicts with federal law.

E. *Fair Labor Standards Act*[121]

The **Fair Labor Standards Act** (FLSA) of 1938 prohibits an employer from failing to pay minimum wages or overtime compensation to an employee, failing to keep individual work records for each employee, discriminating on the basis of sex by paying different wages for equal work, or using oppressive child labor.

---

[118]   Consol v. State, 806 S.W.2d 553 (Tex. Crim. 1991).
[119]   Gade v. National Solid Waste Management Association, 505 U.S. 88 (1992).
[120]   People v. Hegedus, 443 N.W.2d 127 (Mich. 1989).
[121]   29 U.S.C. §§ 201-219.

To constitute an offense punishable by criminal sanctions under the FLSA, an employee must show that (1) the employer, (2) willfully, (3) violated the Act's provisions. A person who violates any of the provisions of § 215 of the FLSA shall, on conviction, be subject to a fine of not more than $10,000 or imprisonment of not more than six months, or both.

After some conflicting decisions concerning the application of FLSA to state and local agencies, it was determined that the Fair Labor Standards Act contains clear statements of congressional intent to abrogate state sovereign immunity, based on FLSA provisions defining "employer" to include a public agency, defining "individual employed by a public agency" as including one employed by a state, and providing for actions against a public agency in any federal or state court of competent jurisdiction.[122]

1. Minimum Wage Provisions

This section of the Fair Labor Standards Act provides that every employer shall pay to each of his employees who in any workweek is engaged in commerce or in the production of goods for commerce, or is employed in an enterprise engaged in commerce, or in the production of goods for commerce, wages as established by the Act.[123]

The FLSA has special overtime provisions to address the unique employment conditions of domestic servants, hospital workers, firefighters, police officers, and transportation workers. In interpreting the provision of the act that makes certain exceptions for firefighters and police officers, a federal court held that the practice of "averaging" firefighters' straight-time and overtime wages over a biweekly pay period does not violate the FLSA.[124] Another court applied similar reasoning in deciding that the Fair Labor Standards Act did not require firefighters to be paid extra for hours during a pay period in excess of the 95 hours for which they were paid and the 106-hour threshold at which overtime pay comes into effect, because the pay received per hour, based on 106 hours, exceeded the minimum wage.[125]

To constitute an offense punishable by criminal sanctions, an employee must show that

- the employer–employee relationship existed, and
- the employer willfully violated the Act's provisions.

The criminal penalties for a violation are outlined in § 216 of the statute. One provision states that any person who willfully violates any provisions of § 215 of the FLSA shall upon conviction thereof be subject to a fine of not more than $10,000 or to imprisonment of not more than six months, or both. The Secretary of Labor is assigned the responsibility of enforcing this provision of the Act. To carry out this responsibility, a

---

[122] Abril v. Commonwealth of Virginia, 145 F.3d 182 (4th Cir. 1998).
[123] 29 U.S.C. § 206.
[124] Mullins v. Howard County, 730 F. Supp. 667 (D. Md. 1990).
[125] Carter v. City of Charleston, 995 F. Supp. 620 (D.S.C. 1997).

special Wage and Hour Division was created in the Labor Department to allow the Administrator and the Secretary to make periodic investigations and reports in order to keep the law up-to-date and to detect violations.[126]

2. Equal Pay Provisions

The Fair Labor Standards Act prohibits discrimination on the basis of sex. These statutes provide in part that

29 U.S.C. § 206(d)

No employer having employees subject to any provisions of this section shall discriminate, within any establishment at which such employees are employed, between employees on the basis of sex by paying wages to employees in such establishment at a rate of less than the rate at which he pays wages to employees of the opposite sex in such establishment for equal work on jobs the performance of which requires equal skill, effort, and responsibility, and which are performed under similar working conditions.

In the case of *Tidwell v. Fort Howard Corp.*, the court explained that the underlying rationale of the Equal Pay Act is that individuals who are doing equal work should be paid equal wages, regardless of their sex.[127]

Interpreting this statute, a federal court determined that a female employee established a *prima facie* case under the Act that she was paid less than the male employees, even though they performed substantially equal work under similar working conditions, although the designation of the positions had different names.[128] However, another federal court found that a female employee occupied a position and performed functions that were not substantially equal to those of better paid male coworkers, because the tasks and functions the employee performed were dissimilar in level of experience required and level of complexity in performing the required functions.[129]

3. Maximum Hour Standards

In addition to the minimum wage provision and the provision prohibiting discrimination on the basis of sex by paying different wages for equal work, the FLSA includes a provision concerning maximum hours.

One section of the act provides that

29 U.S.C. § 207

Except if otherwise provided in this section, no employer shall employ any of his employees who in any workweek is engaged in commerce or in a production of goods for commerce, or is employed in an enterprise engaged in commerce or

---

[126]   29 U.S.C. § 206(d).
[127]   Tidwell v. Fort Howard Corp., 756 F. Supp. 1487 (E.D. Okla. 1991).
[128]   Tomka v. Seiler Corp., 66 F.3d 1295 (2d Cir. 1995).
[129]   Sprague v. Thorn Americas, Inc. 129 F.3d 1355 (10th Cir. 1997).

the production of goods for commerce, for a workweek longer than 40 hours unless such employee receives compensation for his employment in excess of the hours above specified at a rate of not less than one or one-half times the regular rate at which he is employed.

The section of the Fair Labor Standards Act that deals with maximum hours has exceptions and conditions. For example, employees in defined hospitals in certain conditions are exempt, employees in fire protection activities and law enforcement activities are exempt if they meet the specific provisions stated in the Act, and certain employees receiving remedial education are exempt. Although the statutes contain exceptions to the overtime requirements of the Fair Labor Standards Act, these are to be narrowly construed against the employer asserting them, and the employer carries the burden by proving by clear and affirmative evidence that it is entitled to exemption.[130]

A federal court agreed that Arizona's decision to cease counting leave time as hours worked for purposes of computing firefighters' overtime did not violate the FLSA, because Arizona's action was not undertaken in response to the extension of FLSA to state employees or as an invasion of FLSA overtime requirements.[131]

4. "Whistle-Blower" Protection

The FLSA also makes it unlawful for an employer to discharge or discriminate against an employee due to the employee's filing of an FLSA complaint.[132] This provision has become known as the "whistle-blower" statute. According to a circuit court, the purpose of this statute is not merely to vindicate the rights of the complaining party, but to foster an environment in which employees are unfettered in their decision to voice grievances without fear of economic retaliation or reprisal.[133]

F. Food and Drug Violations

The Food and Drug Administration (FDA) is the federal agency that protects consumers from unsafe or adulterated food or drugs and investigates violations of the Food, Drug, and Cosmetic Act (FDCA). The crimes that are addressed by the FDA include manufacturing, introducing, delivering, or receiving adulterated or misbranded food, drugs, or cosmetics into interstate commerce; and refusal to permit FDA food inspections. Violators may have civil or criminal penalties assessed against them. Violations are misdemeanors unless there is a showing of specific intent and/or prior violations, in which case the offense is a felony.

An adulterated food refers to one that has ingredients that are poisonous, unsanitary, or contaminated. In *United States v. Park*,[134] the president of a national food chain was held liable for violations when it was proven that food was stored in a warehouse

---

[130] 29 U.S.C. § 207.
[131] Drollinger v. Arizona, 962 F.2d 956 (9th Cir. 1992).
[132] 29 U.S.C. § 215(a).
[133] Saffels v. Rice, 40 F.3d 1546 (8th Cir. 1994).
[134] United States v. Park, 421 U.S. 658 (1975).

that allowed rodents to reach the food and rodent droppings were found in the food. The company president argued that lower-level employees, not he, were responsible for storage decisions or the lack of cleanup. The Supreme Court held that when a defendant, by his position, has either the responsibility or authority to prevent or correct a violation and does not do so, he will be held strictly liable. In early 2009, it was discovered that one company's peanut products, infected with salmonella, were distributed throughout the country. The products have been linked to several deaths. Warehouses owned by the company were determined to be unsanitary and it was discovered that the inspector did not check to see if appropriate health certificates were issued. It is too soon to say, at the time this book goes to press, whether any company officials will be prosecuted.[135]

§ 13.7   Summary

In this chapter, a wide range of federal crimes have been described. In general, federal powers to define crimes in the area of morals, public peace, justice administration, and regulatory crime must be constrained by the limits of federal power. The federal government must have some justification to pass such laws in either the commerce clause, some other enumerated federal power, or because of territorial jurisdiction.

In Chapter 9, state laws in the area of public morals were discussed; many of the state laws in this area do not exist at the federal level; for instance, laws relating to prostitution require interstate transportation in order to bring the offense into federal jurisdiction. The federal government has been active in prosecuting child pornography and obscenity in whatever medium is restricted.

In Chapter 10 we explored "Offenses against Public Peace," which included riot, disorderly conduct, drunkenness, drugs, and terrorism. The "federalization" of drug laws has dramatically changed the prosecution of drug offenders in this country from largely a state and local activity to one shared almost equally between federal law enforcement and state law enforcement. The source of the federal power to pass drug laws is the commerce clause. While we discussed state counterterrorism laws in Chapter 10, obviously the most well-known of such laws is the Patriot Act, which identifies powers and defines crimes based either on the federal government's right to defend borders or the commerce clause.

In Chapter 11 "Offenses against Justice Administration" were described, including such crimes as perjury, bribery, obstruction of justice, and escape. In this chapter, the federal versions of such laws were explored. In general, perjury, bribery, obstruction of

---

[135]   U.S. Food and Drug Administration. 2009. "Peanut Produce Recalls: Salmonella Typhimurium." Available at: http://www.fda.gov/oc/opacom/hottopics/salmonellatyph.html#update. Accessed 3/11/2009.

justice, and tampering with witnesses are similar crimes when done in state or federal venues.

The increased number of interstate violations and the complex nature of corporate crime have resulted in an expansion in the investigation of corporate crimes by federal agents. As the investigative focus on corporate crime has increased, federal laws concerning corporate criminality have received additional attention. American jurisprudence utilizes two general standards for imposing criminal liability on corporations: (1) traditional *respondeat superior* liability and (2) statutes specifically making corporations liable.

Regulatory crimes can be prosecuted against individuals or corporations. Protection of food, air, water, and worker safety are all responsibilities of federal agencies (as well as parallel state agencies). Some of the many statutes are those comprising the Clean Air Act, the Safe Drinking Water Act, the Toxic Substance Control Act, and the Resource Conservation and Recovery Act. The Securities and Exchange Commission regulates business and trading. The central policy of the antitrust laws is against agreements that take away the freedom of purchasers to buy in the open market and to maintain, in the public interest, freedom of competition. Federal agents investigate securities fraud, insider trading, and other crimes related to the buying, trading, and selling of securities.

The purpose of the Occupational Safety and Health Act (OSHA) is to ensure, as far as possible, every working man and woman safe and healthful working conditions and to preserve human resources. The Act requires employers to furnish employees with a working environment free from recognized hazards, and requires employers to comply with specific safety and health rules. The Fair Labor Standards Act (FLSA) prohibits an employer from failing to pay minimum wages or overtime compensation to an employee, failing to keep individual work records for each employee, discrimination on the basis of sex by paying different wages for equal work, or using oppressive child labor. The FLSA also makes it unlawful for an employer to discharge or discriminate against an employee due to the employee's filing of an FLSA complaint. The Food and Drug Administration polices the purity of products purchased and used by the American public. Those who adulterate or misbrand products can face both civil and criminal sanctions.

REVIEW QUESTIONS

1. When can the federal government pass laws that restrict personal decisions of whom to have sex with, or whether or not to use drugs in one's own home?

2. What are the federal statutes related to prostitution? By what authority can the federal government create such laws?

3. Explain the *Miller* test for the definition of pornography. List and describe some of the many federal laws concerning obscenity.

4. Describe the coverage of 18 U.S.C. § 2252. How is this different from obscenity statutes with adult participants? Describe the holdings of the Supreme Court cases dealing with obscenity.

5. Does the U.S. Code have an abortion statute? Explain. Describe the issue and holding of *Scheidler v. National Organization for Women*.

6. What elements are required to be found guilty of the federal crime of *riot*? What behaviors might violate federal disorderly conduct laws? Are there federal vagrancy laws? Are there federal public drunkenness laws?

7. Under what authority does the federal government enact laws regulating the use of drugs? Are such laws constitutional? Under what constitutional provisions are they challenged?

8. What is the Uniform Controlled Substances Act? What is the purpose of the Act? What controlled substances are likely to be included in Schedule I? What are the characteristics of Schedule I drugs?

9. Federal statutes that provide for forfeiture of property used to facilitate drug-related offenses and for the forfeiture of proceeds from drug transactions have been challenged, and suggestions for changes to these laws have been made. Have the courts held that these forfeiture statutes violate the double jeopardy clause of the U.S. Constitution? Explain.

10. Describe the federal wiretapping statute.

11. Explain the provisions of the USA PATRIOT Act in Title VIII that relate to criminal laws.

12. Describe the three federal perjury-related crimes.

13. Distinguish among bribery, gratuities, and conflict of interest under the federal law. What is the definition of "other public officials" for purposes of these statutes? Is payment to a confidential informant a violation of the federal statute prohibiting bribery of public officials and witnesses?

14. Describe the scope of behavior covered by the federal obstruction of justice statute. What are the elements of the federal escape statute? What are the elements of resisting arrest?

15. Were corporations criminally liable under common law? When is a corporation liable for the acts of its agents?

16. Briefly summarize the provisions of the Clean Air Act, the Safe Drinking Water Act, the Clean Water Act, and the Toxic Substance Control Act. Must the government prove the defendant had knowledge of the provisions of the Clean Water Act?

17. When was the first antitrust legislation enacted? What elements must be proved in order to obtain a conviction under the Sherman Act? What are the types of activities that constitute a violation of

this law? Do states have antitrust acts?

18. What general and specific duties does OSHA place on employers? By enacting OSHA, did Congress intend to prohibit states from enforcing laws relating to worker health and safety?

19. What is the Fair Labor Standards Act? What elements must be proven in order to constitute a violation of the minimum wage provisions? What are the provisions of the Equal Pay Act?

20. How does the "whistle-blower" provision in the Fair Labor Standards Act protect employees? Does the FLSA apply to state agencies?

PART II
Judicial Decisions

Part II: Table of Cases

sweep." ... Second, even if an enactment does not reach a substantial amount of constitutionally protected conduct, it may be impermissibly vague because it fails to establish standards for the police and public that are sufficient to guard against the arbitrary deprivation of liberty interests ....

While we, like the Illinois courts, conclude that the ordinance is invalid on its face, we do not rely on the overbreadth doctrine. We agree with the city's submission that the law does not have a sufficiently substantial impact on conduct protected by the First Amendment to render it unconstitutional. The ordinance does not prohibit speech. Because the term "loiter" is defined as remaining in one place "with no apparent purpose," it is also clear that it does not prohibit any form of conduct that is apparently intended to convey a message. By its terms, the ordinance is inapplicable to assemblies that are designed to demonstrate a group's support of, or opposition to, a particular point of view .... Its impact on the social contact between gang members and others does not impair the First Amendment "right of association" that our cases have recognized ....

On the other hand, as the United States recognizes, the freedom to loiter for innocent purposes is part of the "liberty" protected by the Due Process Clause of the Fourteenth Amendment. We have expressly identified this "right to remove from one place to another according to inclination" as "an attribute of personal liberty" protected by the Constitution .... Indeed, it is apparent that an individual's decision to remain in a public place of his choice is as much a part of his liberty as the freedom of movement inside frontiers that is "a part of our heritage" ... , or the right to move "to whatsoever place one's own inclination may direct" identified in Blackstone's Commentaries ....

There is no need, however, to decide whether the impact of the Chicago ordinance on constitutionally protected liberty alone would suffice to support a facial challenge under the overbreadth doctrine .... For it is clear that the vagueness of this enactment makes a facial challenge appropriate. This is not an ordinance that "simply regulates business behavior and contains a scienter requirement." ... It is a criminal law that contains no *mens rea* requirement, ... , and infringes on constitutionally protected rights, ... When vagueness permeates the text of such a law, it is subject to facial attack.

Vagueness may invalidate a criminal law for either of two independent reasons. First, it may fail to provide the kind of notice that will enable ordinary people to understand what conduct it prohibits; second, it may authorize and even encourage arbitrary and discriminatory enforcement .... Accordingly, we first consider whether the ordinance provides fair notice to the citizen and then discuss its potential for arbitrary enforcement.

IV

"It is established that a law fails to meet the requirements of the Due Process Clause if it is so vague and standardless that it leaves the public uncertain as to the conduct it prohibits ...." ....
The Illinois Supreme Court recognized that the term "loiter" may have a common and accepted meaning, ... , but the definition of that term in this ordinance—"to remain in any one place with no apparent purpose"—does not. It is difficult to imagine how any citizen of the city of Chicago standing in a public place with a group of people would know if he or she had an "apparent purpose." If she were talking to another person, would she have an apparent purpose? If she were frequently checking her watch and looking expectantly down the street, would she have an apparent purpose?

Since the city cannot conceivably have meant to criminalize each instance a citizen stands in public with a gang member, the vagueness that dooms this ordinance is not the product of uncertainty about the normal meaning of "loitering," but rather about what loitering is covered by the ordinance and what is not. The Illinois Supreme Court emphasized the law's failure to distinguish between innocent conduct and conduct threatening harm. Its decision followed the precedent set by a number of state courts that have upheld ordinances that criminalize loitering combined with some other overt act or evidence of criminal intent. However, state courts have uniformly invalidated laws that do not join the term "loitering" with a second specific element of the crime.

The city's principal response to this concern about adequate notice is that loiterers are not subject to sanction until after they have failed to comply with an officer's order to disperse. "Whatever problem is created by a law that criminalizes conduct people normally believe to be innocent is solved when persons receive actual notice from a police order of what they are expected to do." We find this response unpersuasive for at least two reasons.

First, the purpose of the fair notice requirement is to enable the ordinary citizen to conform his or her conduct to the law. "No one may be required at peril of life, liberty or property to speculate as to the meaning of penal statutes." . . . . Although it is true that a loiterer is not subject to criminal sanctions unless he or she disobeys a dispersal order, the loitering is the conduct that the ordinance is designed to prohibit. If the loitering is in fact harmless and innocent, the dispersal order itself is an unjustified impairment of liberty. If the police are able to decide arbitrarily which members of the public they will order to disperse, then the Chicago ordinance becomes indistinguishable from the law we held invalid in *Shuttlesworth v. Birmingham,* . . . Because an officer may issue an order only after prohibited conduct has already occurred, it cannot provide the kind of advance notice that will protect the putative loiterer from being ordered to disperse. Such an order cannot retroactively give adequate warning of the boundary between the permissible and the impermissible applications of the law.

Second, the terms of the dispersal order compound the inadequacy of the notice afforded by the ordinance. It provides that the officer "shall order all such persons to disperse and remove themselves from the area." . . . . This vague phrasing raises a host of questions. After such an order issues, how long must the loiterers remain apart? How far must they move? If each loiterer walks around the block and they meet again at the same location, are they subject to arrest or merely to being ordered to disperse again? As we do here, we have found vagueness in a criminal statute exacerbated by the use of the standards of "neighborhood" and "locality." . . . . We remarked in *Connally* that "both terms are elastic and, dependent upon circumstances, may be equally satisfied by areas measured by rods or by miles." . . . .

Lack of clarity in the description of the loiterer's duty to obey a dispersal order might not render the ordinance unconstitutionally vague if the definition of the forbidden conduct were clear, but it does buttress our conclusion that the entire ordinance fails to give the ordinary citizen adequate notice of what is forbidden and what is permitted. The Constitution does not permit a legislature to "set a net large enough to catch all possible offenders, and leave it to the courts to step inside and say who could be rightfully detained, and who should be set at large." . . . . This ordinance is therefore vague "not in the sense that it requires a person to conform his conduct to an imprecise but comprehensible normative standard, but rather in the sense that no standard of conduct is specified at all." . . . .

V

The broad sweep of the ordinance also violates "'the requirement that a legislature establish minimal guidelines to govern law enforcement.'" . . . . There are no such guidelines in the ordinance. In any public place in the city of Chicago, persons who stand or sit in the company of a gang member may be ordered to disperse unless their purpose is apparent. The mandatory language in the enactment directs the police to issue an order without first making any inquiry about their possible purposes. It matters not whether the reason that a gang member and his father, for example, might loiter near Wrigley Field is to rob an unsuspecting fan or just to get a glimpse of Sammy Sosa leaving the ballpark; in either event, if their purpose is not apparent to a nearby police officer, she may—indeed, she "shall"—order them to disperse.

Recognizing that the ordinance does reach a substantial amount of innocent conduct, we turn, then, to its language to determine if it "necessarily entrusts lawmaking to the moment-to-moment judgment of the policeman on his beat." . . . . As we discussed in the context of fair notice, . . . , the principal source of the vast discretion conferred on the police in this case is the definition of loitering as "to remain in any one place with no apparent purpose."

As the Illinois Supreme Court interprets that definition, it "provides absolute discretion to police officers to determine what activities constitute loitering." . . . We have no authority to construe the language of a state statute more narrowly than the construction given by that State's highest court. "The power to determine the meaning of a statute carries with it the power to prescribe its extent and limitations as well as the method by which they shall be determined." . . .

Nevertheless, the city disputes the Illinois Supreme Court's interpretation, arguing that the text of the ordinance limits the officer's discretion in three ways. First, it does not permit the officer to issue a dispersal order to anyone who is moving along or who has an apparent purpose. Second, it does not permit an arrest if individuals obey a dispersal order. Third, no order can issue unless the officer reasonably believes that one of the loiterers is a member of a criminal street gang.

Even putting to one side our duty to defer to a state court's construction of the scope of a local enactment, we find each of these limitations insufficient. That the ordinance does not apply to people who are moving—that is, to activity that would not constitute loitering under any possible definition of the term—does not even address the question of how much discretion the police enjoy in deciding which stationary persons to disperse under the ordinance. Similarly, that the ordinance does not permit an arrest until after a dispersal order has been disobeyed does not provide any guidance to the officer deciding whether such an order should issue. The "no apparent purpose" standard for making that decision is inherently subjective because its application depends on whether some purpose is "apparent" to the officer on the scene.

Presumably an officer would have discretion to treat some purposes—perhaps a purpose to engage in idle conversation or simply to enjoy a cool breeze on a warm evening—as too frivolous to be apparent if he suspected a different ulterior motive. Moreover, an officer conscious of the city council's reasons for enacting the ordinance might well ignore its text and issue a dispersal order, even though an illicit purpose is actually apparent.

It is true, as the city argues, that the requirement that the officer reasonably believes that a group of loiterers contains a gang member does place a limit on the authority to order dispersal. That limitation would no doubt be sufficient if the ordinance only applied to loitering that had an apparently harmful purpose or effect, or possibly if it only applied to loitering by persons reasonably believed to be criminal gang members. But this ordinance, for reasons that are not explained in the findings of the city council, requires no harmful purpose and applies to non-gang members as well

as suspected gang members. It applies to everyone in the city who may remain in one place with one suspected gang member as long as their purpose is not apparent to an officer observing them. Friends, relatives, teachers, counselors, or even total strangers might unwittingly engage in forbidden loitering if they happen to engage in idle conversation with a gang member.

Ironically, the definition of loitering in the Chicago ordinance not only extends its scope to encompass harmless conduct, but also has the perverse consequence of excluding from its coverage much of the intimidating conduct that motivated its enactment. As the city council's findings demonstrate, the most harmful gang loitering is motivated either by an apparent purpose to publicize the gang's dominance of certain territory, thereby intimidating nonmembers, or by an equally apparent purpose to conceal ongoing commerce in illegal drugs. As the Illinois Supreme Court has not placed any limiting construction on the language in the ordinance, we must assume that the ordinance means what it says and that it has no application to loiterers whose purpose is apparent. The relative importance of its application to harmless loitering is magnified by its inapplicability to loitering that has an obviously threatening or illicit purpose.

Finally, in its opinion striking down the ordinance, the Illinois Supreme Court refused to accept the general order issued by the police department as a sufficient limitation on the "vast amount of discretion" granted to the police in its enforcement . . . . That the police have adopted internal rules limiting their enforcement to certain designated areas in the city would not provide a defense to a loiterer who might be arrested elsewhere. Nor could a person who knowingly loitered with a well-known gang member anywhere in the city safely assume that they would not be ordered to disperse no matter how innocent and harmless their loitering might be.

VI

In our judgment, the Illinois Supreme Court correctly concluded that the ordinance does not provide sufficiently specific limits on the enforcement discretion of the police "to meet constitutional standards for definiteness and clarity." . . . . We recognize the serious and difficult problems testified to by the citizens of Chicago that led to the enactment of this ordinance. "We are mindful that the preservation of liberty depends in part on the maintenance of social order." . . . . However, in this instance the city has enacted an ordinance that affords too much discretion to the police and too little notice to citizens who wish to use the public streets.

[Footnotes and citations omitted. Concurring and dissenting opinions omitted.]

OTIS McDONALD ET AL.
v.
CITY OF CHICAGO, ILLINOIS ET AL.

SUPREME COURT OF THE UNITED STATES

130 S.CT. 3020 (2010)

Two years ago, in *District of Columbia v. Heller,* 554 U.S. ___, 128 S.Ct. 2783, 171 L.Ed.2d 637 (2008), we held that the Second Amendment protects the right to keep and bear arms for the purpose of self-defense, and we struck down a District of Columbia law that banned the possession of handguns in the home. The city of Chicago (City) and the village of Oak Park, a Chicago suburb, have laws that are similar to the District of Columbia's, but Chicago and Oak Park argue that their laws are constitutional because the Second Amendment has no application to the States. We have previously held that most of the provisions of the Bill of Rights apply with full force to both the Federal Government and the States. Applying the standard that is well established in our case law, we hold that the Second Amendment right is fully applicable to the States.

I

Otis McDonald, Adam Orlov, Colleen Lawson, and David Lawson (Chicago petitioners) are Chicago residents who would like to keep handguns in their homes for self-defense but are prohibited from doing so by Chicago's firearms laws.

A City ordinance provides that "[n]o person shall . . . possess . . . any firearm unless such person is the holder of a valid registration certificate for such firearm." . . . The Code then prohibits registration of most handguns, thus effectively banning handgun possession by almost all private citizens who reside in the City. . . . Like Chicago, Oak Park makes it "unlawful for any person to possess . . . any firearm," a term that includes "pistols, revolvers, guns and small arms . . . commonly known as handguns." . . .

Chicago enacted its handgun ban to protect its residents "from the loss of property and injury or death from firearms." . . . The Chicago petitioners and their *amici,* however, argue that the handgun ban has left them vulnerable to criminals. Chicago Police Department statistics, we are told, reveal that the City's handgun murder rate has actually increased since the ban was enacted and that Chicago residents now face one of the highest murder rates in the country and rates of other violent crimes that exceed the average in comparable cities.

Several of the Chicago petitioners have been the targets of threats and violence. For instance, Otis McDonald, who is in his late seventies, lives in a high-crime neighborhood. He is a community activist involved with alternative policing strategies, and his efforts to improve his neighborhood have subjected him to violent threats from drug dealers. . . . Colleen Lawson is a Chicago resident whose home has been targeted by burglars. "In Mrs. Lawson's judgment, possessing a handgun in Chicago would decrease her chances of suffering serious injury or death should she ever be threatened again in her home." Mc-Donald, Lawson, and the other Chicago petitioners own handguns that they store outside of the city limits, but they would like to keep their handguns in their homes for protection.

After our decision in *Heller,* the Chicago petitioners and two groups filed suit against the City in the United States District Court for the Northern District of Illinois. They sought a declaration that the handgun ban and several related Chicago ordinances violate the Second and Fourteenth Amendments to the United States Constitution. Another action challenging the Oak Park law was filed in the same District Court by the National Rifle Association (NRA) and two Oak Park residents.

In addition, the NRA and others filed a third action challenging the Chicago ordinances. All three cases were assigned to the same District Judge.

II

Petitioners argue that the Chicago and Oak Park laws violate the right to keep and bear arms for two reasons. Petitioners' primary submission is that this right is among the "privileges or immunities of citizens of the United States" and that the narrow interpretation of the Privileges or Immunities Clause adopted in the *Slaughter-House Cases,* . . . should now be rejected. As a secondary argument, petitioners contend that the Fourteenth Amendment's Due Process Clause "incorporates" the Second Amendment right.

Chicago and Oak Park (municipal respondents) maintain that a right set out in the Bill of Rights applies to the States only if that right is an indispensable attribute of *any* "civilized" legal system. . . . If it is possible to imagine a civilized country that does not recognize the right, the municipal respondents tell us, then that right is not protected by due process. . . . . And since there are civilized countries that ban or strictly regulate the private possession of handguns, the municipal respondents maintain that due process does not preclude such measures. . . . . In light of the parties' far-reaching arguments, we begin by recounting this Court's analysis over the years of the relationship between the provisions of the Bill of Rights and the States.

The Bill of Rights, including the Second Amendment, originally applied only to the Federal Government. In *Barron ex rel. Tiernan v. Mayor of Baltimore,* . . . (1833), the Court, in an opinion by Chief Justice Marshall, explained that this question was "of great importance" but "not of much difficulty.". In less than four pages, the Court firmly rejected the proposition that the first eight Amendments operate as limitations on the States, holding that they apply only to the Federal Government. . . .

The constitutional Amendments adopted in the aftermath of the Civil War fundamentally altered our country's federal system. The provision at issue in this case, § 1 of the Fourteenth Amendment, provides, among other things, that a State may not abridge "the privileges or immunities of citizens of the United States" or deprive "any person of life, liberty, or property, without due process of law."

Four years after the adoption of the Fourteenth Amendment, this Court was asked to interpret the Amendment's reference to "the privileges or immunities of citizens of the United States." The *Slaughter-House Cases,* involved challenges to a Louisiana law permitting the creation of a state-sanctioned monopoly on the butchering of animals within the city of New Orleans. Justice Samuel Miller's opinion for the Court concluded that the Privileges or Immunities Clause protects only those rights "which owe their existence to the Federal government, its National character, its Constitution, or its laws." . . . The Court held that other fundamental rights—rights that predated the creation of the Federal Government and that "the State governments were created to establish and secure"— were not protected by the Clause. . . .

In drawing a sharp distinction between the rights of federal and state citizenship, the Court relied on two principal arguments. First, the Court emphasized that the Fourteenth Amendment's Privileges or Immunities Clause spoke of "the privileges or immunities of *citizens of the United States,*" and the Court contrasted this phrasing with the wording in the first sentence of the Fourteenth Amendment and in the Privileges and Immunities Clause of Article IV, both of which refer to *state* citizenship. Second, the Court stated that a contrary reading would "radically chang[e] the whole theory of the relations of the State and Federal governments to each other and of both these governments to the people," and the Court refused to conclude that such a change had been made "in the absence of language which expresses such a purpose too clearly to admit of doubt." . . . Finding the phrase "privileges or immunities of citizens of the United States" lacking by this high standard, the Court reasoned that the phrase must mean something more limited.

Under the Court's narrow reading, the Privileges or Immunities Clause protects such things as the right.

> "to come to the seat of government to assert any claim [a citizen] may have upon that government, to transact any business he may have with it, to seek its protection,

to share its offices, to engage in administering its functions . . . [and to] become a citizen of any State of the Union by a *bona-fide* residence therein, with the same rights as other citizens of that State." . . .

Finding no constitutional protection against state intrusion of the kind envisioned by the Louisiana statute, the Court upheld the statute. Four Justices dissented. Justice Field, joined by Chief Justice Chase and Justices Swayne and Bradley, criticized the majority for reducing the Fourteenth Amendment's Privileges or Immunities Clause to "a vain and idle enactment, which accomplished nothing, and most unnecessarily excited Congress and the people on its passage." . . .

Today, many legal scholars dispute the correctness of the narrow *Slaughter-House* interpretation. . . . [some discussion has been omitted]

Three years after the decision in the *Slaughter-House Cases,* the Court decided *Cruikshank,* the first of the three 19th-century cases on which the Seventh Circuit relied. . . . In that case, the Court reviewed convictions stemming from the infamous Colfax Massacre in Louisiana on Easter Sunday 1873. Dozens of blacks, many unarmed, were slaughtered by a rival band of armed white men. Cruikshank himself allegedly marched unarmed African-American prisoners through the streets and then had them summarily executed. Ninety-seven men were indicted for participating in the massacre, but only nine went to trial. Six of the nine were acquitted of all charges; the remaining three were acquitted of murder but convicted under the Enforcement Act of 1870, 16 Stat. 140, for banding and conspiring together to deprive their victims of various constitutional rights, including the right to bear arms.

The Court reversed all of the convictions, including those relating to the deprivation of the victims' right to bear arms. The Court wrote that the right of bearing arms for a lawful purpose "is not a right granted by the Constitution" and is not "in any manner dependent upon that instrument for its existence." . . . . "The second amendment," the Court continued, "declares that it shall not be infringed; but this . . . means no more than that it shall not be infringed by Congress." Our later decisions . . . reaffirmed that the Second Amendment applies only to the Federal Government." . . .

As previously noted, the Seventh Circuit concluded that *Cruikshank, Presser,* and *Miller* doomed petitioners' claims at the Court of Appeals level. Petitioners argue, however, that we should overrule those decisions and hold that the right to keep and bear arms is one of the "privileges or immunities of citizens of the United States." In petitioners' view, the Privileges or Immunities Clause protects all of the rights set out in the Bill of Rights, as well as some others, . . . but petitioners are unable to identify the Clause's full scope, . . . Nor is there any consensus on that question among the scholars who agree that the *Slaughter-House Cases'* interpretation is flawed. . . .

We see no need to reconsider that interpretation here. For many decades, the question of the rights protected by the Fourteenth Amendment against state infringement has been analyzed under the Due Process Clause of that Amendment and not under the Privileges or Immunities Clause. We therefore decline to disturb the *Slaughter-House* holding.

At the same time, however, this Court's decisions in *Cruikshank, Presser,* and *Miller* do not preclude us from considering whether the Due Process Clause of the Fourteenth Amendment makes the Second Amendment right binding on the States. . . . None of those cases "engage[d] in the sort of Fourteenth Amendment inquiry required by our later cases." As explained more fully below, *Cruikshank, Presser,* and *Miller* all preceded the era in which the Court began the process of "selective incorporation" under the Due Process Clause, and we have never previously addressed the question whether the right to keep and bear arms applies to the States under that theory.

Indeed, *Cruikshank* has not prevented us from holding that other rights that were at issue in that case are binding on the States through the Due Process Clause. In *Cruikshank,* the Court held that the general "right of the people peaceably to assemble for lawful purposes," which is protected by the First Amendment, applied only against the Federal Government and not against the States. . . . . Nonetheless, over 60 years later the Court held that the right of peaceful assembly was a "fundamental righ[t] . . . safeguarded by the due process clause of the Fourteenth Amendment." . . . We follow the same path here and thus consider whether the right to keep and bear arms applies to the States under the Due Process Clause.

In the late 19th century, the Court began to consider whether the Due Process Clause prohibits the States from infringing rights set out in the Bill of Rights. . . . Five features of the approach taken during the ensuing era should be noted.

First, the Court viewed the due process question as entirely separate from the question whether a right was a privilege or immunity of national citizenship. . . . [some discussion has been omitted]

Second, the Court explained that the only rights protected against state infringement by the Due Process Clause were those rights "of such a nature that they are included in the conception of due process of law." . . . While it was "possible that some of the personal rights safeguarded by the first eight Amendments against National action [might] also be safeguarded against state action," the Court stated, this was "not because those rights are enumerated in the first eight Amendments." . . .

The Court used different formulations in describing the boundaries of due process. For example, in *Twining,* the Court referred to "immutable principles of justice which inhere in the very idea of free government which no member of the Union may disregard." . . . In *Snyder v. Massachusetts* . . . the Court spoke of rights that are "so rooted in the traditions and conscience of our people as to be ranked as fundamental." And in *Palko,* the Court famously said that due process protects those rights that are "the very essence of a scheme of ordered liberty" and essential to "a fair and enlightened system of justice." . . .

Third, in some cases decided during this era the Court "can be seen as having asked, when inquiring into whether some particular procedural safeguard was required of a State, if a civilized system could be imagined that would not accord the particular protection." . . .

Fourth, the Court during this era was not hesitant to hold that a right set out in the Bill of Rights failed to meet the test for inclusion within the protection of the Due Process Clause. The Court found that some such rights qualified. . . . (freedom of speech and press); . . . (assistance of counsel in capital cases); . . . (freedom of assembly); . . . (free exercise of religion). . . .

. . . [some discussion has been omitted]

. . . the Court eventually moved in that direction by initiating what has been called a process of "selective incorporation," *i.e.,* the Court began to hold

that the Due Process Clause fully incorporates particular rights contained in the first eight Amendments. . . .

The decisions during this time abandoned three of the previously noted characteristics of the earlier period. The Court made it clear that the governing standard is not whether *any* "civilized system [can] be imagined that would not accord the particular protection." . . . Instead, the Court inquired whether a particular Bill of Rights guarantee is fundamental to *our* scheme of ordered liberty and system of justice. . . .

. . . [some discussion has been omitted]

Finally, the Court abandoned "the notion that the Fourteenth Amendment applies to the States only a watered-down, subjective version of the individual guarantees of the Bill of Rights," stating that it would be "incongruous" to apply different standards "depending on whether the claim was asserted in a state or federal court." . . . Instead, the Court decisively held that incorporated Bill of Rights protections "are all to be enforced against the States under the Fourteenth Amendment according to the same standards that protect those personal rights against federal encroachment." . . .

. . . [some discussion has been omitted]

With this framework in mind, we now turn directly to the question whether the Second Amendment right to keep and bear arms is incorporated in the concept of due process. In answering that question, as just explained, we must decide whether the right to keep and bear arms is fundamental to *our* scheme of ordered liberty, or as we have said in a related context, whether this right is "deeply rooted in this Nation's history and tradition," . . .

Our decision in *Heller* points unmistakably to the answer. Self-defense is a basic right, recognized by many legal systems from ancient times to the present day, and in *Heller,* we held that individual self-defense is "the *central component*" of the Second Amendment right. . . . Explaining that "the need for defense of self, family, and property is most acute" in the home, we found that this right applies to handguns because they are "the most preferred firearm in the nation to 'keep' and use for protection of one's home and family," . . .

Heller makes it clear that this right is "deeply rooted in this Nation's history and tradition." . . . . *Heller* explored the right's origins, noting that the 1689 English Bill of Rights explicitly protected a right to keep arms for self-defense, and that by 1765, Blackstone was able to assert that the right to keep and bear arms was "one of the fundamental rights of Englishmen," . . .

Blackstone's assessment was shared by the American colonists. As we noted in *Heller*, King George III's attempt to disarm the colonists in the 1760's and 1770's "provoked polemical reactions by Americans invoking their rights as Englishmen to keep arms." . . .

The right to keep and bear arms was considered no less fundamental by those who drafted and ratified the Bill of Rights. . . . Antifederalists and Federalists alike agreed that the right to bear arms was fundamental to the newly formed system of government. . . . But those who were fearful that the new Federal Government would infringe traditional rights such as the right to keep and bear arms insisted on the adoption of the Bill of Rights as a condition for ratification of the Constitution. . . . This is surely powerful evidence that the right was regarded as fundamental in the sense relevant here.

. . . [some discussion has been omitted]

By the 1850 s, the perceived threat that had prompted the inclusion of the Second Amendment in the Bill of Rights—the fear that the National Government would disarm the universal militia—had largely faded as a popular concern, but the right to keep and bear arms was highly valued for purposes of self-defense. . . .

After the Civil War, many of the over 180,000 African Americans who served in the Union Army returned to the States of the old Confederacy, where systematic efforts were made to disarm them and other blacks. . . .

. . . [some discussion has been omitted]

Union Army commanders took steps to secure the right of all citizens to keep and bear arms, but the 39th Congress concluded that legislative action was necessary. Its efforts to safeguard the right to keep and bear arms demonstrate that the right was still recognized to be fundamental.

The most explicit evidence of Congress' aim appears in § 14 of the Freedmen's Bureau Act of 1866, which provided that "the right . . . to have full and equal benefit of all laws and proceedings concerning personal liberty, personal security, and the acquisition, enjoyment, and disposition of estate, real and personal, *including the constitutional*

right to bear arms, shall be secured to and enjoyed by all the citizens . . . without respect to race or color, or previous condition of slavery." . . . Section 14 thus explicitly guaranteed that "all the citizens," black and white, would have "the constitutional right to bear arms."

The Civil Rights Act of 1866, . . . which was considered at the same time as the Freedmen's Bureau Act, similarly sought to protect the right of all citizens to keep and bear arms. Section 1 of the Civil Rights Act guaranteed the "full and equal benefit of all laws and proceedings for the security of person and property, as is enjoyed by white citizens." This language was virtually identical to language in § 14 of the Freedmen's Bureau Act, 14 Stat. 176-177 ("the right . . . to have full and equal benefit of all laws and proceedings concerning personal liberty, personal security, and the acquisition, enjoyment, and disposition of estate, real and personal"). And as noted, the latter provision went on to explain that one of the "laws and proceedings concerning personal liberty, personal security, and the acquisition, enjoyment, and disposition of estate, real and personal" was "the constitutional right to bear arms." . . .

Congress, however, ultimately deemed these legislative remedies insufficient. Southern resistance, Presidential vetoes, and this Court's pre-Civil-War precedent persuaded Congress that a constitutional amendment was necessary to provide full protection for the rights of blacks. Today, it is generally accepted that the Fourteenth Amendment was understood to provide a constitutional basis for protecting the rights set out in the Civil Rights Act of 1866. . . .

. . . [some discussion has been omitted]

Even those who thought the Fourteenth Amendment unnecessary believed that blacks, as citizens, "have equal right to protection, and to keep and bear arms for self-defense." . . .

Evidence from the period immediately following the ratification of the Fourteenth Amendment only confirms that the right to keep and bear arms was considered fundamental. . . .

The right to keep and bear arms was also widely protected by state constitutions at the time when the Fourteenth Amendment was ratified. In 1868, 22 of the 37 States in the Union had state constitutional provisions explicitly protecting the right to keep and bear arms. . . . A clear majority of the States in 1868, therefore, recognized the right to keep and bear arms as being among the foundational rights necessary to our system of Government.

In sum, it is clear that the Framers and ratifiers of the Fourteenth Amendment counted the right to keep and bear arms among those fundamental rights necessary to our system of ordered liberty.

Despite all this evidence, municipal respondents contend that Congress, in the years immediately following the Civil War, merely sought to outlaw "discriminatory measures taken against freedmen, which it addressed by adopting a non-discrimination principle" and that even an outright ban on the possession of firearms was regarded as acceptable, "so long as it was not done in a discriminatory manner." . . . This argument is implausible.

. . . [some discussion has been omitted]

Municipal respondents' remaining arguments are at war with our central holding in *Heller*: that the Second Amendment protects a personal right to keep and bear arms for lawful purposes, most notably for self-defense within the home. Municipal respondents, in effect, ask us to treat the right recognized in *Heller* as a second-class right, subject to an entirely different body of rules than the other Bill of Rights guarantees that we have held to be incorporated into the Due Process Clause.

Municipal respondents' main argument is nothing less than a plea to disregard 50 years of incorporation precedent and return (presumably for this case only) to a bygone era. Municipal respondents submit that the Due Process Clause protects only those rights "'recognized by all temperate and civilized governments, from a deep and universal sense of [their] justice.'" . . .

This line of argument is, of course, inconsistent with the long-established standard we apply in incorporation cases. . . . And the present-day implications of municipal respondents' argument are stunning. For example, many of the rights that our Bill of Rights provides for persons accused of criminal offenses are virtually unique to this country. If *our* understanding of the right to a jury trial, the right against self-incrimination, and the right to counsel were necessary attributes of *any* civilized country, it would follow that the United States is the only civilized Nation in the world.

. . .

Municipal respondents maintain that the Second Amendment differs from all of the other provisions of the Bill of Rights because it concerns the right to possess a deadly implement and thus has implications for public safety. . . . And they note that there is intense disagreement on the question whether the private possession of guns in the home increases or decreases gun deaths and injuries. . . .

The right to keep and bear arms, however, is not the only constitutional right that has controversial public safety implications. All of the constitutional provisions that impose restrictions on law enforcement and on the prosecution of crimes fall into the same category. . . .

We likewise reject municipal respondents' argument that we should depart from our established incorporation methodology on the ground that making the Second Amendment binding on the States and their subdivisions is inconsistent with principles of federalism and will stifle experimentation. Municipal respondents point out—quite correctly—that conditions and problems differ from locality to locality and that citizens in different jurisdictions have divergent views on the issue of gun control. Municipal respondents therefore urge us to allow state and local governments to enact any gun control law that they deem to be reasonable, including a complete ban on the possession of handguns in the home for self-defense.

There is nothing new in the argument that, in order to respect federalism and allow useful state experimentation, a federal constitutional right should not be fully binding on the States. This argument was made repeatedly and eloquently by Members of this Court who rejected the concept of incorporation and urged retention of the two-track approach to incorporation. Throughout the era of "selective incorporation," Justice Harlan in particular, invoking the values of federalism and state experimentation, fought a determined rearguard action to preserve the two-track approach. . . .

Time and again, however, those pleas failed. Unless we turn back the clock or adopt a special incorporation test applicable only to the Second Amendment, municipal respondents' argument must be rejected. Under our precedents, if a Bill of Rights guarantee is fundamental from an American perspective, then, unless *stare decisis* counsels otherwise, that guarantee is fully binding on the States and thus *limits* (but by no means eliminates) their ability to devise solutions to social problems that suit local needs and values. As noted by the 38 States that have appeared in this case as *amici* supporting petitioners, "[s]tate and local experimentation with reasonable firearms regulations will continue under the Second Amendment."

... [some discussion has been omitted]

Municipal respondents assert that, although most state constitutions protect firearms rights, state courts have held that these rights are subject to "interest-balancing" and have sustained a variety of restrictions. ... In *Heller,* however, we expressly rejected the argument that the scope of the Second Amendment right should be determined by judicial interest balancing, and this Court decades ago abandoned "the notion that the Fourteenth Amendment applies to the States only a watered-down, subjective version of the individual guarantees of the Bill of Rights," ...

... [some discussion has been omitted]

It is important to keep in mind that *Heller,* while striking down a law that prohibited the possession of handguns in the home, recognized that the right to keep and bear arms is not "a right to keep and carry any weapon whatsoever in any manner whatsoever and for whatever purpose." ... We made it clear in *Heller* that our holding did not cast doubt on such longstanding regulatory measures as "prohibitions on the possession of firearms by felons and the mentally ill," "laws forbidding the carrying of firearms in sensitive places such as schools and government buildings, or laws imposing conditions and qualifications on the commercial sale of arms ... We repeat those assurances here. Despite municipal respondents' doomsday proclamations, incorporation does not imperil every law regulating firearms.

Municipal respondents argue, finally, that the right to keep and bear arms is unique among the rights set out in the first eight Amendments "because the reason for codifying the Second Amendment (to protect the militia) differs from the purpose (primarily, to use firearms to engage in self-defense) that is claimed to make the right implicit in the concept of ordered liberty." ... Municipal respondents suggest that the Second Amendment right differs from the rights heretofore incorporated because the latter were "valued for [their] own sake." But we have never

previously suggested that incorporation of a right turns on whether it has intrinsic as opposed to instrumental value, and quite a few of the rights previously held to be incorporated—for example the right to counsel and the right to confront and subpoena witnesses—are clearly instrumental by any measure. Moreover, this contention repackages one of the chief arguments that we rejected in *Heller*; that is, that the scope of the Second Amendment right is defined by the immediate threat that led to the inclusion of that right in the Bill of Rights. In *Heller,* we recognized that the codification of this right was prompted by fear that the Federal Government would disarm and thus disable the militias, but we rejected the suggestion that the right was valued only as a means of preserving the militias. ... On the contrary, we stressed that the right was also valued because the possession of firearms was thought to be essential for self-defense. As we put it, self-defense was "the *central component* of the right itself." ...

We turn, finally, to the two dissenting opinions. Justice STEVENS' eloquent opinion covers ground already addressed, and therefore little need be added in response. ... He would hold that "[t]he rights protected against state infringement by the Fourteenth Amendment's Due Process Clause need not be identical in shape or scope to the rights protected against Federal Government infringement by the various provisions of the Bill of Rights." ...

As we have explained, the Court, for the past half-century, has moved away from the two-track approach. If we were now to accept Justice STEVENS' theory across the board, decades of decisions would be undermined. ...

The relationship between the Bill of Rights' guarantees and the States must be governed by a single, neutral principle. ...

... [some discussion has been omitted]

Justice BREYER's dissent makes several points to which we briefly respond. To begin, while there is certainly room for disagreement about *Heller*'s analysis of the history of the right to keep and bear arms, nothing written since *Heller* persuades us to reopen the question there decided. Few other questions of original meaning have been as thoroughly explored.

Justice BREYER's conclusion that the Fourteenth Amendment does not incorporate the right to keep and bear arms appears to rest primarily on four factors: First, "there is no popular consensus" that the right is fundamental; second, the right does not protect minorities or persons neglected by those holding political power; third, incorporation of the Second Amendment right would "amount to a significant incursion on a traditional and important area of state concern, altering the constitutional relationship between the States and the Federal Government" and preventing local variations; and fourth, determining the scope of the Second Amendment right in cases involving state and local laws will force judges to answer difficult empirical questions regarding matters that are outside their area of expertise. Even if we believed that these factors were relevant to the incorporation inquiry, none of these factors undermines the case for incorporation of the right to keep and bear arms for self-defense.

First, we have never held that a provision of the Bill of Rights applies to the States only if there is a "popular consensus" that the right is fundamental, and we see no basis for such a rule. But in this case, as it turns out, there is evidence of such a consensus. . . . .

Second, petitioners and many others who live in high-crime areas dispute the proposition that the Second Amendment right does not protect minorities and those lacking political clout. The plight of Chicagoans living in high-crime areas was recently highlighted when two Illinois legislators representing Chicago districts called on the Governor to deploy the Illinois National Guard to patrol the City's streets. . . . If, as petitioners believe, their safety and the safety of other law-abiding members of the community would be enhanced by the possession of handguns in the home for self-defense, then the Second Amendment right protects the rights of minorities and other residents of high-crime areas whose needs are not being met by elected public officials.

Third, Justice BREYER is correct that incorporation of the Second Amendment right will to some extent limit the legislative freedom of the States, but this is always true when a Bill of Rights provision is incorporated. Incorporation always restricts experimentation and local variations, but that has not stopped the Court from incorporating virtually every other provision of the Bill of Rights. . . .

Finally, Justice BREYER is incorrect that incorporation will require judges to assess the costs and benefits of firearms restrictions and thus to make difficult empirical judgments in an area in which they lack expertise. As we have noted, while his opinion in *Heller* recommended an interest-balancing test, the Court specifically rejected that suggestion. . . .

* * *

In *Heller,* we held that the Second Amendment protects the right to possess a handgun in the home for the purpose of self-defense. Unless considerations of *stare decisis* counsel otherwise, a provision of the Bill of Rights that protects a right that is fundamental from an American perspective applies equally to the Federal Government and the States. . . . We therefore hold that the Due Process Clause of the Fourteenth Amendment incorporates the Second Amendment right recognized in *Heller.* The judgment of the Court of Appeals is reversed, and the case is remanded for further proceedings.

It is so ordered.

[Footnotes and citations have been omitted. Concurring and dissenting opinions have been omitted.]

Cases Relating to Chapter 2

Principles of Criminal Liability

POWELL
v.
TEXAS

SUPREME COURT OF THE UNITED STATES

392 U.S. 514 (1968)

Mr. Justice Marshall announced the judgment of the Court and delivered an opinion in which The Chief Justice, Mr. Justice Black, and Mr. Justice Harlan join.

In late December 1966, appellant was arrested and charged with being found in a state of intoxication in a public place, in violation of Texas Penal Code, Art. 477 (1952), which reads as follows:

"Whoever shall get drunk or be found in a state of intoxication in any public place, or at any private house except his own, shall be fined not exceeding one hundred dollars."

Appellant was tried in the Corporation Court of Austin, Texas, found guilty, and fined $20. He appealed to the County Court at Law No. 1 of Travis County, Texas, where a trial *de novo* was held. His counsel urged that appellant was "afflicted with the disease of chronic alcoholism," that "his appearance in public [while drunk was] ... not of his own volition," and therefore that to punish him criminally for that conduct would be cruel and unusual, in violation of the Eighth and Fourteenth Amendments to the United States Constitution.

The trial judge in the county court, sitting without a jury, made certain findings of fact, ... , but ruled as a matter of law that chronic alcoholism was not a defense to the charge. He found appellant guilty, and fined him $50. There being no further right to appeal within the Texas judicial system, appellant appealed to this Court; we noted probable jurisdiction ....

I

The principal testimony was that of Dr. David Wade, a Fellow of the American Medical Association, duly certificated in psychiatry. His testimony consumed a total of 17 pages in the trial transcript. Five of those pages were taken up with a recitation of Dr. Wade's qualifications. In the next 12 pages Dr. Wade was examined by appellant's counsel, cross-examined by the State, and re-examined by the defense, and those 12 pages contain virtually all the material developed at trial which is relevant to the constitutional issue we face here. Dr. Wade sketched the outlines of the "disease" concept of alcoholism; noted that there is no generally accepted definition of "alcoholism"; alluded to the ongoing debate within the medical profession over whether alcohol is actually physically "addicting" or merely psychologically "habituating"; and concluded that in either case a "chronic alcoholic" is an "involuntary drinker," who is "powerless not to drink," and who "loses his self-control over his drinking." He testified that he had examined appellant, and that appellant is a "chronic alcoholic," who "by the time he has reached [the state of intoxication] . . . is not able to control his behavior, and [who] . . . has reached this point because he has an uncontrollable compulsion to drink." Dr. Wade also responded in the negative to the question whether appellant has "the willpower to resist the constant excessive consumption of alcohol." He added that in his opinion jailing appellant without medical attention would operate neither to rehabilitate him nor to lessen his desire for alcohol.

On cross-examination, Dr. Wade admitted that when appellant was sober he knew the difference between right and wrong, and he responded affirmatively to the question whether appellant's act of taking the first drink in any given instance when he was sober was a "voluntary exercise of his will." Qualifying his answer, Dr. Wade stated that "these individuals have a compulsion, and this compulsion, while not completely overpowering, is a very strong influence, an exceedingly strong influence, and this compulsion coupled with the firm belief in their mind that they are going to be able to handle it from now on causes their judgment to be somewhat clouded."

Appellant testified concerning the history of his drinking problem. He reviewed his many arrests for drunkenness; testified that he was unable to stop drinking; stated that when he was intoxicated he had no control over his actions and could not remember them later, but that he did not become violent; and admitted that he did not remember his arrest on the occasion for which he was being tried. . . . . .

. . . In the first place, the record in this case is utterly inadequate to permit the sort of informed and responsible adjudication which alone can support the announcement of an important and wide-ranging new constitutional principle. We know very little about the circumstances surrounding the drinking bout which resulted in this conviction, or about Leroy Powell's drinking problem, or indeed about alcoholism itself. The trial hardly reflects the sharp legal and evidentiary clash between fully prepared adversary litigants which is traditionally expected in major constitutional cases. The State put on only one witness, the arresting officer. The defense put on three—a policeman who testified to appellant's long history of arrests for public drunkenness, the psychiatrist, and appellant himself.

Furthermore, the inescapable fact is that there is no agreement among members of the medical profession about what it means to say that "alcoholism" is a "disease." One of the principal works in this field states that the major difficulty in articulating a "disease concept of alcoholism" is that "alcoholism has too many definitions and disease has practically none." This same author concludes that *"a disease is what the medical profession recognizes as such."* In other words, there is widespread agreement today that "alcoholism" is a "disease," for the simple reason that the medical profession has concluded that it should attempt to treat those who have drinking problems. There the agreement stops. Debate rages within the medical profession as to whether "alcoholism" is a separate "disease" in any meaningful biochemical, physiological, or psychological sense, or whether it represents one peculiar manifestation in some individuals of underlying psychiatric disorders.

Nor is there any substantial consensus as to the "manifestations of alcoholism." E. M. Jellinek, one of the outstanding authorities on the subject, identifies five different types of alcoholics which predominate in the United States, and these types display a broad range of different and occasionally inconsistent symptoms. Moreover, wholly distinct types, relatively rare in this country, predominate in nations with different cultural attitudes regarding the consumption of alcohol. Even if we limit our consideration to the range of alcoholic symptoms more typically found in this country, there is substantial disagreement as to the manifestations of the "disease" called "alcoholism." Jellinek, for example, considers that only two of his five alcoholic types can truly be said to be suffering from "alcoholism" as a "disease," because only these two types attain what he believes to be the requisite degree of physiological dependence on alcohol. He applies the label "gamma alcoholism" to "that species of alcoholism in which (1) acquired increased tissue tolerance to alcohol, (2) adaptive cell metabolism . . . , (3) withdrawal symptoms and 'craving,' i.e., physical dependence, and (4) loss of control are involved." A "delta" alcoholic, on the other hand, "shows the first three characteristics of gamma alcoholism as well as a less marked form of the fourth characteristic—that is, instead of loss of control there is inability to abstain." Other authorities approach the problems of classification in an entirely different manner and, taking account of the large role which psycho-social factors seem to play in "problem drinking," define the "disease" in terms of the earliest identifiable manifestations of any sort of abnormality in drinking patterns.

[Further discussion of cultural elements of drinking omitted.]

. . . . It is one thing to say that if a man is deprived of alcohol his hands will begin to shake, he will suffer agonizing pains and ultimately he will have hallucinations; it is quite another to say that a man has a "compulsion" to take a drink, but that he also retains a certain amount of "free will" with which to resist. It is simply impossible, in the present state of our knowledge, to ascribe a useful meaning to the latter statement. This definitional confusion reflects, of course, not merely the undeveloped state of the psychiatric art but also the conceptual difficulties inevitably attendant upon the importation of scientific and medical models into a legal system generally predicated upon a different set of assumptions.

[Some discussion omitted.]

. . . . The picture of the penniless drunk propelled aimlessly and endlessly through the law's "revolving door" of arrest, incarceration, release and re-arrest is not a pretty one. But before we condemn the present practice across-the-board, perhaps we ought to be able to point to some clear promise of a better world for these unfortunate people. Unfortunately, no such promise has yet been forthcoming. If, in addition to the absence of a coherent approach to the problem of treatment, we consider the almost complete absence of facilities and manpower for the implementation of a rehabilitation program, it is difficult to say in the present context that the criminal process is utterly lacking in social value. This Court has never held that anything in the Constitution requires that penal sanctions be designed solely to achieve therapeutic or rehabilitative effects, and it can hardly be said with assurance that incarceration serves such purposes any better for the general run of criminals than it does for public drunks.

Ignorance likewise impedes our assessment of the deterrent effect of criminal sanctions for public drunkenness. The fact that a high percentage of American alcoholics conceal their drinking problems, not merely by avoiding public displays of intoxication but also by shunning all forms of treatment, is indicative that some powerful deterrent operates to inhibit the public revelation of the existence of alcoholism. Quite probably this deterrent effect can be largely attributed to the harsh moral attitude which our society has traditionally taken toward intoxication and the shame which we have associated with alcoholism. Criminal conviction represents the degrading public revelation of what Anglo-American society has long condemned as a moral defect, and the existence of criminal sanctions may serve to reinforce this cultural taboo, just as we presume it serves to reinforce other, stronger feelings against murder, rape, theft, and other forms of antisocial conduct.

[Some discussion omitted.]

. . . . Appellant claims that his conviction on the facts of this case would violate the Cruel and Unusual Punishment Clause of the Eighth Amendment as applied to the States through the Fourteenth Amendment. The primary purpose of that clause has always been considered, and properly so, to be directed at the method or kind of punishment imposed for the violation of criminal statutes; the nature of the conduct made criminal is ordinarily relevant only to the fitness of the punishment imposed . . . .

Appellant, however, seeks to come within the application of the Cruel and Unusual Punishment Clause announced in *Robinson v. California,* . . . (1962), which involved a state statute making it a crime to "be addicted to the use of narcotics." This Court held there that "a state law which imprisons a person thus afflicted [with narcotic addiction] as a criminal, even though he has never touched any narcotic drug within the State or been guilty of any irregular behavior there, inflicts a cruel and unusual punishment . . . ." . . .

On its face the present case does not fall within that holding, since appellant was convicted, not for being a chronic alcoholic, but for being in public while drunk on a particular occasion. The State of Texas thus has not sought to punish a mere status, as California did in *Robinson;* nor has it attempted to regulate appellant's behavior in the privacy of his own home. Rather, it has imposed

upon appellant a criminal sanction for public behavior which may create substantial health and
safety hazards, both for appellant and for members
of the general public, and which offends the moral
and esthetic sensibilities of a large segment of the
community. This seems a far cry from convicting
one for being an addict, being a chronic alcoholic,
being "mentally ill, or a leper . . . ." . . . .

Robinson so viewed brings this Court but a very
small way into the substantive criminal law. And
unless *Robinson* is so viewed it is difficult to see
any limiting principle that would serve to prevent
this Court from becoming, under the aegis of
the Cruel and Unusual Punishment Clause, the
ultimate arbiter of the standards of criminal responsibility, in diverse areas of the criminal law,
throughout the country.

It is suggested in dissent that *Robinson* stands
for the "simple" but "subtle" principle that "[crim-
inal] penalties may not be inflicted upon a person
for being in a condition he is powerless to
change." . . . . In that view, appellant's "condition"
of public intoxication was "occasioned by a compulsion symptomatic of the disease" of chronic
alcoholism, and thus, apparently, his behavior
lacked the critical element of *mens rea.* Whatever
may be the merits of such a doctrine of criminal
responsibility, it surely cannot be said to follow
from *Robinson.* The entire thrust of *Robinson*'s interpretation of the Cruel and Unusual Punishment
Clause is that criminal penalties may be inflicted
only if the accused has committed some act, has
engaged in some behavior, which society has an
interest in preventing, or perhaps in historical
common law terms, has committed some *actus
reus.* It thus does not deal with the question of
whether certain conduct cannot constitutionally
be punished because it is, in some sense, "involuntary" or "occasioned by a compulsion."

Likewise, as the dissent acknowledges, there
is a substantial definitional distinction between
a "status," as in *Robinson,* and a "condition,"
which is said to be involved in this case. Whatever may be the merits of an attempt to distinguish between behavior and a condition, it
is perfectly clear that the crucial element in this
case, so far as the dissent is concerned, is
whether or not appellant can legally be held responsible for his appearance in public in a state
of intoxication. The only relevance of *Robinson*

to this issue is that because the Court interpreted
the statute there involved as making a "status"
criminal, it was able to suggest that the statute
would cover even a situation in which addiction
had been acquired involuntarily . . . . That this
factor was not determinative in the case is
shown by the fact that there was no indication
of how Robinson himself had become an addict.

Ultimately, then, the most troubling aspects of
this case, were *Robinson* to be extended to meet
it, would be the scope and content of what could
only be a constitutional doctrine of criminal responsibility. In dissent it is urged that the decision
could be limited to conduct which is "a characteristic and involuntary part of the pattern of the disease as it afflicts" the particular individual, and
that "[it] is not foreseeable" that it would be
applied "in the case of offenses such as driving
a car while intoxicated, assault, theft, or
robbery." . . . That is limitation by fiat. In the first
place, nothing in the logic of the dissent would
limit its application to chronic alcoholics. If Leroy
Powell cannot be convicted of public intoxication, it
is difficult to see how a State can convict an individual for murder, if that individual, while exhibiting
normal behavior in all other respects, suffers from
a "compulsion" to kill, which is an "exceedingly
strong influence," but "not completely overpowering." Even if we limit our consideration to chronic
alcoholics, it would seem impossible to confine the
principle within the arbitrary bounds which the dissent seems to envision.

It is not difficult to imagine a case involving
psychiatric testimony to the effect that an individual suffers from some aggressive neurosis which
he is able to control when sober; that very little alcohol suffices to remove the inhibitions which normally contain these aggressions, with the result
that the individual engages in assaultive behavior
without becoming actually intoxicated; and that
the individual suffers from a very strong desire
to drink, which is an "exceedingly strong influence" but "not completely overpowering." Without being untrue to the rationale of this case,
should the principles advanced in dissent be accepted here, the Court could not avoid holding
such an individual constitutionally unaccountable
for his assaultive behavior.

Traditional common-law concepts of personal
accountability and essential considerations of

federalism lead us to disagree with appellant. We are unable to conclude, on the state of this record or on the current state of medical knowledge, that chronic alcoholics in general, and Leroy Powell in particular, suffer from such an irresistible compulsion to drink and to get drunk in public that they are utterly unable to control their performance of either or both of these acts and thus cannot be deterred at all from public intoxication. And in any event this Court has never articulated a general constitutional doctrine of *mens rea.*

We cannot cast aside the centuries-long evolution of the collection of interlocking and overlapping concepts which the common law has utilized to assess the moral accountability of an individual for his antisocial deeds. The doctrines of *actus reus, mens rea,* insanity, mistake, justification, and duress have historically provided the tools for a constantly shifting adjustment of the tension between the evolving aims of the criminal law and changing religious, moral, philosophical, and medical views of the nature of man. This process of adjustment has always been thought to be the province of the States.

Nothing could be less fruitful than for this Court to be impelled into defining some sort of insanity test in constitutional terms. Yet, that task would seem to follow inexorably from an extension of *Robinson* to this case. If a person in the "condition" of being a chronic alcoholic cannot be criminally punished as a constitutional matter for being drunk in public, it would seem to follow that a person who contends that, in terms of one test, "his unlawful act was the product of mental disease or mental defect," . . . , would state an issue of constitutional dimension with regard to his criminal responsibility had he been tried under some different and perhaps lesser standard, *e.g.,* the right-wrong test of *M'Naghten's Case.* The experimentation of one jurisdiction in that field alone indicates the magnitude of the problem . . . . But formulating a constitutional rule would reduce, if not eliminate, that fruitful experimentation, and freeze the developing productive dialogue between law and psychiatry into a rigid constitutional mold. It is simply not yet the time to write into the Constitution formulas cast in terms whose meaning, let alone relevance, is not yet clear either to doctors or to lawyers.

Affirmed.

[Footnotes and citations omitted. Concurring and dissenting opinions omitted.]

CHRISTOPHER MICHAEL DEAN, PETITIONER
v.
UNITED STATES

SUPREME COURT OF THE UNITED STATES

556 U.S. ___ (2009)

CHIEF JUSTICE ROBERTS delivered the opinion of the Court.

Accidents happen. Sometimes they happen to individuals committing crimes with loaded guns. The question here is whether extra punishment Congress imposed for the discharge of a gun during certain crimes applies when the gun goes off accidentally.

Title 18 U. S. C. §924(c)(1)(A) criminalizes using or carrying a firearm during and in relation to any violent or drug trafficking crime, or possessing a firearm in furtherance of such a crime. An individual convicted of that offense receives a 5-year mandatory minimum sentence, in addition to the punishment for the underlying crime. §924(c)(1)(A)(i). The mandatory minimum increases to 7 years "if the firearm is brandished" and to 10 years "if the firearm is discharged." §§924(c)(1)(A)(ii), (iii). In this case, a masked man entered a bank, waved a gun, and yelled at everyone to get down. He then walked behind the teller counter and started removing money from the teller stations. He grabbed bills with his left hand holding the gun in his right. At one point, he reached over a teller to remove money from her drawer. As he was collecting the money, the gun discharged, leaving a bullet hole in the partition between two stations. The robber cursed and dashed out of the bank. Witnesses later testified that he seemed surprised that the gun had gone off. No one was hurt. . . .

Police arrested Christopher Michael Dean and Ricardo Curtis Lopez for the crime. Both defendants were charged with conspiracy to commit a robbery affecting interstate commerce, in violation of 18 U. S. C. §1951(a), and aiding and abetting each other in using, carrying, possessing, and discharging a firearm during an armed robbery, in violation of §924(c)(1)(A)(iii) and §2. . . . At trial, Dean admitted that he had committed the robbery, and a jury found him guilty on both the robbery and firearm counts. The District Court sentenced Dean to a mandatory minimum term of 10 years in prison on the firearm count, because the firearm "discharged" during the robbery. . . . .

Dean appealed, contending that the discharge was accidental, and that the sentencing enhancement . . . requires proof that the defendant intended to discharge the firearm. The Court of Appeals affirmed, holding that separate proof of intent was not required. . . . . That decision created a conflict among the Circuits over whether the accidental discharge of a firearm during the specified crimes gives rise to the 10-year mandatory minimum. . . . .We granted certiorari to resolve that conflict. . . .

II

Section 924(c)(1)(A) provides:

"[A]ny person who, during and in relation to any crime of violence or drug trafficking crime . . . uses or carries a firearm, or who, in furtherance of any such crime, possesses a firearm, shall, in addition to the punishment provided for such crime of violence or drug trafficking crime—

"(i) be sentenced to a term of imprisonment of not less than 5 years; "(ii) if the firearm is brandished, be sentenced to a term of imprisonment of not less than 7 years; and "(iii) if the firearm is discharged, be sentenced to a term of imprisonment of not less than 10 years."

. . . The parties disagree over whether §924(c)(1)(A)(iii) contains a requirement that the defendant intend to discharge the firearm. We hold that it does not.

"We start, as always, with the language of the statute." . . . The text of subsection (iii) provides that a defendant shall be sentenced to a minimum of 10 years "if the firearm is discharged." It does not require that the discharge be done knowingly or intentionally, or otherwise contain words of limitation. As we explained in *Bates v. United States*, 522 U. S. 23 (1997), in declining to infer an "'intent to defraud'" requirement into a statute, "we ordinarily resist reading words or elements into a statute that do not appear on its face." . . .

. . . [some discussion omitted]

Congress's use of the passive voice further indicates that subsection (iii) does not require proof of intent. The passive voice focuses on an event that occurs without respect to a specific actor, and therefore without respect to any actor's intent or culpability. It is whether something happened—not how or why it happened—that matters. The structure of the statute also suggests that subsection (iii) is not limited to the intentional discharge of a firearm. Subsection (ii) provides a 7-year mandatory minimum sentence if the firearm "is brandished." Congress expressly included an intent requirement for that provision, by defining "brandish" to mean "to display all or part of the firearm, or otherwise make the presence of the firearm known to another person, *in order to intimidate* that person." . . . . The defendant must have intended to brandish the firearm, because the brandishing must have been done for a specific purpose. Congress did not, however, separately define "discharge" to include an intent requirement. "[W]here Congress includes particular language in one section of a statute but omits it in another section of the same Act, it is generally presumed that Congress acts intentionally and purposely in the disparate inclusion or exclusion." . . .

Dean argues that the statute is not silent on the question presented. Congress, he contends, included an intent element in the opening paragraph of §924(c)(1)(A), and that element extends to the sentencing enhancements. Section 924(c)(1)(A) criminalizes using or carrying a firearm "during and in relation to" any violent or drug trafficking crime. In *Smith v. United States*, 508 U. S. 223 (1993), we stated that the phrase "in relation to" means "that the firearm must have some purpose or effect with respect to the drug trafficking crime; its presence or involvement cannot be the result of accident or coincidence." . . . . Dean argues that the adverbial phrase thus necessarily embodies an intent requirement, and that the phrase modifies all the verbs in the statute—not only use, carry, and possess, but also brandish and discharge. Such a reading requires that a perpetrator knowingly discharge the firearm for the enhancement to apply. If the discharge is accidental, Dean argues, it is not "in relation to" the underlying crime.

The most natural reading of the statute, however, is that "in relation to" modifies only the nearby verbs "uses" and "carries." The next verb—"possesses"—is modified by its own adverbial clause, "in furtherance of." The last two verbs—"is brandished" and "is discharged"—appear in separate subsections and are in a different voice than the verbs in the principal paragraph. There is no basis for reading "in relation to" to extend all the way down to modify "is discharged." The better reading of the statute is that the adverbial phrases in the opening paragraph—"in relation to" and "in furtherance of"—modify their respective nearby verbs, and that neither phrase extends to the sentencing factors.

But, Dean argues, such a reading will lead to absurd results. The discharge provision on its face contains no temporal or causal limitations. In the absence of an intent requirement, the enhancement would apply "regardless of when the actions occur, or by whom or for what reason they are taken." . . . It would, for example, apply if the gun used during the crime were discharged " weeks (or years) before or after the crime." . . . .

We do not agree that implying an intent requirement is necessary to address such concerns. As the Government recognizes, sentencing factors such as the one here "often involve . . . special features of the manner in which a basic crime was carried out." . . . The basic crime here is using or carrying a firearm during and in relation to a violent or drug trafficking crime, or possessing a firearm in furtherance of any such crime. Fanciful hypotheticals testing whether the discharge was a "special featur[e]" of how the "basic crime was carried out," . . . , are best addressed in those terms, not by contorting and stretching the statutory language to imply an intent requirement.

Dean further argues that even if the statute is viewed as silent on the intent question, that silence compels a ruling in his favor. There is, he notes, a presumption that criminal prohibitions include a requirement that the Government prove the defendant intended the conduct made criminal. In light of this presumption, we have "on a number of occasions read a state-of-mind component into an offense even when the statutory definition did not in terms so provide." . . . . "[S]ome indication of congressional intent, express or implied, is required to dispense with *mens rea* as an element of a crime." . . . . Dean argues that the presumption is especially strong in this case, given the structure and purpose of the statute. In his view, the three subsections are intended to provide harsher penalties for increasingly culpable conduct: a 5-year minimum for using, carrying, or possessing a firearm; a 7-year minimum for brandishing a firearm; and a 10-year minimum for discharging a firearm. Incorporating an intent requirement into the discharge provision is necessary to give effect to that progression, because an accidental discharge is less culpable than intentional brandishment. . . .

It is unusual to impose criminal punishment for the consequences of purely accidental conduct. But it is not unusual to punish individuals for the unintended consequences of their *unlawful* acts. . . . . The felony-murder rule is a familiar example: If a defendant commits an unintended homicide while committing another felony, the defendant can be convicted of murder. . . . . The Sentencing Guidelines reflect the same principle. . . . .

Blackstone expressed the idea in the following terms:

> "[I]f any accidental mischief happens to follow from the performance of a *lawful* act, the party stands excused from all guilt: but if a man be doing anything *unlawful*, and a consequence ensues which he did not foresee or intend, as the death of a man or the like, his want of foresight shall be no excuse; for, being guilty of one offence, in doing antecedently what is in itself unlawful, he is criminally guilty of whatever consequence may follow the first misbehaviour." 4 W. Blackstone, Commentaries on the Laws of England 26–27 (1769).

Here the defendant is already guilty of unlawful conduct twice over: a violent or drug trafficking offense and the use, carrying, or possession of a firearm in the course of that offense. That unlawful conduct was not an accident. . . .

The fact that the actual discharge of a gun covered under §924(c)(1)(A)(iii) may be accidental does not mean that the defendant is blameless. The sentencing enhancement in subsection (iii) accounts for the risk of harm resulting from the manner in which the crime is carried out, for which the defendant is responsible. . . . . An individual who brings a loaded weapon to commit a crime runs the risk that the gun will discharge accidentally. A gunshot in such circumstances—whether accidental or intended—increases the risk that others will be injured, that people will panic, or that violence (with its own danger to those nearby) will be used in response. Those criminals wishing to avoid the penalty for an inadvertent discharge can lock or unload the firearm, handle it with care during the underlying violent or drug trafficking crime, leave the gun at home, or—best yet—avoid committing the felony in the first place.

JUSTICE STEVENS contends that the statute should be read to require a showing of intent because harm resulting from a discharge may be punishable under other provisions, such as the Sentencing Guidelines (but only if "bodily injury" results). . . . . But Congress in §924(c)(1)(A)(iii) elected to impose a mandatory term, without regard to more generally applicable sentencing provisions. Punishment available under such provisions therefore does not suggest that the statute at issue here is limited to intentional discharges.

And although the point is not relevant under the correct reading of the statute, it is wrong to assert that the gunshot here "caused no harm." . . . By pure luck, no one was killed or wounded. But the gunshot plainly added to the trauma experienced by those held during the armed robbery. . . .

Dean finally argues that any doubts about the proper interpretation of the statute should be resolved in his favor under the rule of lenity. . . . . "The simple existence of some statutory ambiguity, however, is not sufficient to warrant application of that rule, for most statutes are ambiguous to some degree." . . . . "To invoke the rule, we must conclude that there is a grievous ambiguity or uncertainty in the statute." . . . . In this case, the statutory text and structure convince us that the discharge provision does not contain an intent requirement. Dean's contrary arguments are not enough to render the statute grievously ambiguous.

Section 924(c)(1)(A)(iii) requires no separate proof of intent. The 10-year mandatory minimum applies if a gun is discharged in the course of a violent or drug trafficking crime, whether on purpose or by accident. The judgment of the Court of Appeals for the Eleventh Circuit is affirmed.

It is so ordered.

JUSTICE STEVENS, dissenting.

Accidents happen, but they seldom give rise to criminal liability. Indeed, if they cause no harm they seldom give rise to any liability. The Court today nevertheless holds that petitioner is subject to a mandatory additional sentence—a species of criminal liability—for an accident that caused no harm. For two reasons, 18 U. S. C. §924(c)(1)(A)(iii) should not be so construed. First, the structure of §924(c)(1)(A) suggests that Congress intended to provide escalating sentences for increasingly culpable conduct and that the discharge provision therefore applies only to intentional discharges. Second, even if the statute did not affirmatively support that inference, the common law presumption that provisions imposing criminal penalties require proof of *mens rea* would lead to the same conclusion. . . . . Accordingly, I would hold that the Court of Appeals erred in concluding that petitioner could be sentenced under §924(c)(1)(A)(iii) absent evidence that he intended to discharge his gun.

It is clear from the structure and history of §924(c)(1)(A) that Congress intended §924(c)(1)(A)(iii) to apply only to intentional discharges. The statute's structure supports the inference that Congress intended to impose increasingly harsh punishment for increasingly culpable conduct. The lesser enhancements for carrying or brandishing provided by clauses (i) and (ii) clearly require proof of intent. Clause (i) imposes a 5-year mandatory minimum sentence for using or carrying a firearm "during and in relation to" a crime of violence or drug trafficking offense, or possessing a firearm "in furtherance" of such an offense. As we have said before, the provision's relational terms convey that it does not reach inadvertent conduct. . . . ("The phrase 'in relation to' . . . at a minimum, clarifies that the firearm must have some purpose or effect with respect to the drug trafficking crime; its presence or involvement cannot be the result of accident or coincidence"). Similarly, clause (ii) mandates an enhanced penalty for brandishing a firearm only upon proof that a defendant had the specific intent to intimidate. See §924(c)(4). In that context, the most natural reading of clause (iii), which imposes the greatest mandatory penalty, is that it provides additional punishment for the more culpable act of intentional discharge.

The legislative history also indicates that Congress intended to impose an enhanced penalty only for intentional discharge. In *Bailey v. United States*, 516 U. S. 137, 148 (1995), the Court held that "use" of a firearm for purposes of §924(c)(1) required some type of "active employment," such as "brandishing, displaying, bartering, striking with, and, most obviously, firing or attempting to fire." Congress responded to *Bailey* by amending §924(c)(1), making it an offense to "posses[s]" a firearm "in furtherance of" one of the predicate offenses and adding sentencing enhancements for brandishing and discharge . . . . Given the close relationship between the *Bailey* decision and Congress' enactment of the brandishing and discharge provisions, those terms are best read as codifying some of the more culpable among the "active employments" of a firearm that the Court identified in *Bailey*.

Even if there were no evidence that Congress intended §924(c)(1)(A)(iii) to apply only to intentional discharges, the presumption that criminal provisions include an intent requirement would lead me to the same conclusion. Consistent with the common-law tradition, the requirement of *mens rea* has long been the rule of our criminal jurisprudence. . . . . The concept of crime as a "concurrence of an evil-meaning mind with an evil-doing hand . . . took deep and early root in American soil." . . . . Legislating against that backdrop, States often omitted intent elements when codifying the criminal law, and "courts assumed that the omission did not signify disapproval of the principle but merely recognized that intent was so inherent in the idea of the offense that it required no statutory affirmation." . . . . Similarly, absent a clear statement by Congress that it intended to create a strict liability offense, a *mens rea* requirement has generally been presumed in federal statutes. . . . With only a few narrowly delineated exceptions for such crimes as statutory rape and public welfare offenses, the presumption remains the rule today. . . . .

Although mandatory minimum sentencing provisions are of too recent genesis to have any common-law pedigree, . . . , there is no sensible reason for treating them differently from offense elements for purposes of the presumption of *mens rea*. Sentencing provisions of this type have substantially the same effect on a defendant's liberty as aggravated offense provisions. Although a sentencing judge has discretion to issue sentences under §924(c)(1)(A) within the substantial range bounded on one end by the 5-, 7-, or 10-year mandatory minimum sentence and on the other by the statutory maximum sentence, judges in practice rarely exercise that discretion. . . .

If anything, imposition of a mandatory minimum sentence under §924(c)(1)(A) will likely have a greater effect on a defendant's liberty than will conviction for another offense because, unlike sentences for most federal offenses, sentences imposed pursuant to that section must be served consecutively to any other sentence. See §924(c)(1)(D)(ii).

As the foregoing shows, mandatory minimum sentencing provisions are in effect no different from aggravated offense provisions. The common-law tradition of requiring proof of *mens rea* to establish criminal culpability should thus apply equally to such sentencing factors. Absent a clear indication that Congress intended to create a strict-liability enhancement, courts should presume that a provision that mandates enhanced criminal penalties requires proof of intent. This conclusion is bolstered by the fact that we have long applied the rule of lenity—which is similar to the *mens rea* rule in both origin and purpose—to provisions that increase criminal penalties as well as those that criminalize conduct. . . . Accordingly, I would apply the presumption in this case and avoid the strange result of imposing a substantially harsher penalty for an act caused not by an "evil-meaning mind" but by a clumsy hand. The majority urges the result in this case is not unusual because legislatures commonly "punish individuals for the unintended consequences of their *unlawful* acts," but the collection of examples that follows this assertion is telling. The Court cites the felony-murder rule, 18 U. S. C. §1111, and Sentencing Guidelines provisions that permit increased punishment based on the seriousness of the harm caused by the predicate act, ... These examples have in common the provision of enhanced penalties for the infliction of some additional harm. By contrast, §924(c)(1)(A)(iii) punishes discharges whether or not any harm is realized. Additionally, in each of the majority's examples Congress or the Sentencing Commission made explicit its intent to punish the resulting harm regardless of the perpetrator's *mens rea*. Section 924(c)(1)(A)(iii) contains no analogous statement. For these reasons, §924(c)(1)(A)(iii) is readily distinguishable from the provisions the majority cites.

Contrary to the majority's suggestion, the existence of provisions that penalize the unintended consequences of felonious conduct underscores the reasonableness of reading §924(c)(1)(A)(iii) to require proof of intent. When harm results from a firearm discharge during the commission of a violent felony or drug trafficking offense, the defendant will be punishable pursuant to USSG §2B3.1(b)(3) (increasing the offense level for robbery according to the resulting degree of bodily injury), the felony-murder rule, or a similar provision. That a defendant will be subject to punishment for the harm resulting from a discharge whether or not he is also subject to the enhanced penalty imposed by §924(c)(1)(A)(iii) indicates that the latter provision was intended to serve a different purpose—namely, to punish the more culpable act of intentional discharge.

In sum, the structure and history of §924(c)(1)(A) indicate that Congress meant to impose the more substantial penalty provided by clause (iii) only in cases of intentional discharge. Were the statute unclear in that regard, I would reach the same conclusion by applying the presumption that Congress intended to include a *mens rea* requirement. Mandatory sentencing provisions are not meaningfully distinguishable from statutes defining crimes to which we have previously applied the presumption; the rule of *Morissette* and *Staples* and not the felony murder rule should therefore guide our analysis. Because there is insufficient evidence to rebut the presumption in this case, I respectfully dissent.

[Footnotes and citations omitted. Other dissenting opinions omitted.]

Cases Relating to Chapter 3

Capacity and Defenses

**TERRANCE JAMAR GRAHAM,
PETITIONER**

v.

FLORIDA.

**SUPREME COURT OF THE UNITED
STATES**

560 U.S. __ (2010)

*JUSTICE KENNEDY delivered the opinion of
the Court.*

The issue before the Court is whether the
Constitution permits a juvenile offender to be
sentenced to life in prison without parole for a
non-homicide crime. The sentence was imposed
by the State of Florida. Petitioner challenges the
sentence under the Eighth Amendment's Cruel
and Unusual Punishments Clause, made applicable to the States by the Due Process Clause of
the Fourteenth Amendment. . . .

I

Petitioner is Terrance Jamar Graham. He was
born on January 6, 1987. Graham's parents were
addicted to crack cocaine, and their drug use persisted in his early years. Graham was diagnosed
with attention deficit hyperactivity disorder in
elementary school. He began drinking alcohol
and using tobacco at age 9 and smoked marijuana
at age 13.

In July 2003, when Graham was age 16, he and
three other school-age youths attempted to rob a
barbeque restaurant in Jacksonville, Florida. One
youth, who worked at the restaurant, left the back
door unlocked just before closing time. Graham
and another youth, wearing masks, entered
through the unlocked door. Graham's masked accomplice twice struck the restaurant manager in
the back of the head with a metal bar. When the
manager started yelling at the assailant and
Graham, the two youths ran out and escaped in a
car driven by the third accomplice. The restaurant
manager required stitches for his head injury. No
money was taken.

Graham was arrested for the robbery attempt.
Under Florida law, it is within a prosecutor's discretion whether to charge 16- and 17-year-olds
as adults or juveniles for most felony crimes. . . .
Graham's prosecutor elected to charge Graham
as an adult. The charges against Graham were
armed burglary with assault or battery, a first-
degree felony carrying a maximum penalty of
life imprisonment without the possibility of
parole, . . . ; and attempted armed-robbery, a second-degree felony carrying a maximum penalty
of 15 years' imprisonment, . . .

. . . *[some discussion omitted]*

The trial court accepted the plea agreement. The
court withheld adjudication of guilt as to both
charges and sentenced Graham to concurrent
3-year terms of probation. Graham was required
to spend the first 12 months of his probation in
the county jail, but he received credit for the time
he had served awaiting trial, and was released on
June 25, 2004.

Less than 6 months later, on the night of
December 2, 2004, Graham again was arrested.
The State's case was as follows: Earlier that

evening, Graham participated in a home invasion robbery. His two accomplices were Meigo Bailey and Kirkland Lawrence, both 20-year-old men. According to the State, at 7 p.m. that night, Graham, Bailey, and Lawrence knocked on the door of the home where Carlos Rodriguez lived. Graham, followed by Bailey and Lawrence, forcibly entered the home and held a pistol to Rodriguez's chest. For the next 30 minutes, the three held Rodriguez and another man, a friend of Rodriguez, at gunpoint while they ransacked the home searching for money. Before leaving, Graham and his accomplices barricaded Rodriguez and his friend inside a closet.

The State further alleged that Graham, Bailey, and Lawrence, later the same evening, attempted a second robbery, during which Bailey was shot. Graham, who had borrowed his father's car, drove Bailey and Lawrence to the hospital and left them there. As Graham drove away, a police sergeant signaled him to stop. Graham continued at a high speed but crashed into a telephone pole. He tried to flee on foot but was apprehended. Three handguns were found in his car.

When detectives interviewed Graham, he denied involvement in the crimes. He said he encountered Bailey and Lawrence only after Bailey had been shot. One of the detectives told Graham that the victims of the home invasion had identified him. He asked Graham, "Aside from the two robberies tonight how many more were you involved in?" Graham responded, "Two to three before tonight." . . . . The night that Graham allegedly committed the robbery, he was 34 days short of his 18th birthday.

On December 13, 2004, Graham's probation officer filed with the trial court an affidavit asserting that Graham had violated the conditions of his probation by possessing a firearm, committing crimes, and associating with persons engaged in criminal activity. The trial court held hearings on Graham's violations about a year later, in December 2005 and January 2006. The judge who presided was not the same judge who had accepted Graham's guilty plea to the earlier offenses.

. . . [some discussion omitted]

The trial court found Graham guilty of the earlier armed burglary and attempted armed robbery charges. It sentenced him to the maximum sentence authorized by law on each charge: life imprisonment for the armed burglary and 15 years

for the attempted armed robbery. Because Florida has abolished its parole system, . . . , a life sentence gives a defendant no possibility of release unless he is granted executive clemency.

Graham filed a motion in the trial court challenging his sentence under the Eighth Amendment. The motion was deemed denied after the trial court failed to rule on it within 60 days. The First District Court of Appeal of Florida affirmed, concluding that Graham's sentence was not grossly disproportionate to his crimes. . . .

We granted certiorari.

II

. . . The Cruel and Unusual Punishments Clause prohibits the imposition of inherently barbaric punishments under all circumstances. . . .

For the most part, however, the Court's precedents consider punishments challenged not as inherently barbaric but as disproportionate to the crime. . . . The Court's cases addressing the proportionality of sentences fall within two general classifications. The first involves challenges to the length of term-of-years sentences given all the circumstances in a particular case. The second comprises cases in which the Court implements the proportionality standard by certain categorical restrictions on the death penalty.

[Discussion of proportionality and categorical line of cases omitted.]

The present case involves an issue the Court has not considered previously: a categorical challenge to a term-of-years sentence. The approach in cases such as *Harmelin* and *Ewing* is suited for considering a gross proportionality challenge to a particular defendant's sentence, but here a sentencing practice itself is in question. This case implicates a particular type of sentence as it applies to an entire class of offenders who have committed a range of crimes. As a result, a threshold comparison between the severity of the penalty and the gravity of the crime does not advance the analysis. Here, in addressing the question presented, the appropriate analysis is the one used in cases that involved the categorical approach, specifically *Atkins, Roper*, and *Kennedy*.

. . . [some discussion omitted]

The analysis begins with objective indicia of national consensus. . . . Six jurisdictions do not allow life without parole sentences for any juvenile offenders. . . . Seven jurisdictions permit life without parole for juvenile offenders, but only for homicide crimes. . . . Thirty-seven States as well as the District of Columbia permit sentences of life without parole for a juvenile non-homicide offender in some circumstances. . . . Federal law also allows for the possibility of life without parole for offenders as young as 13. . . . Relying on this metric, the State and its *amici* argue that there is no national consensus against the sentencing practice at issue.

This argument is incomplete and unavailing. "There are measures of consensus other than legislation." . . . . Actual sentencing practices are an important part of the Court's inquiry into consensus. . . . . Here, an examination of actual sentencing practices in jurisdictions where the sentence in question is permitted by statute discloses a consensus against its use. Although these statutory schemes contain no explicit prohibition on sentences of life without parole for juvenile non-homicide offenders, those sentences are most infrequent. According to a recent study, nationwide there are only 109 juvenile offenders serving sentences of life without parole for non-homicide offenses. . . . .

. . . *[some discussion omitted]*

. . . Thus, adding the individuals counted by the study to those we have been able to locate independently, there are 129 juvenile non-homicide offenders serving life without parole sentences. A significant majority of those, 77 in total, are serving sentences imposed in Florida. . . .

. . . The available data, nonetheless, are sufficient to demonstrate how rarely these sentences are imposed even if there are isolated cases that have not been included in the presentations of the parties or the analysis of the Court.

. . . *[some discussion omitted]*

The evidence of consensus is not undermined by the fact that many jurisdictions do not prohibit life without parole for juvenile nonhomicide offenders. The Court confronted a similar situation in *Thompson*, where a plurality concluded that the death penalty for offenders younger than 16 was unconstitutional. A number of States then allowed the juvenile death penalty if one considered the statutory scheme. As is the case here, those States authorized the transfer of some juvenile offenders to adult court; and at that point there was no statutory differentiation between adults and juveniles with respect to authorized penalties. The plurality concluded that the transfer laws show "that the States consider 15-year-olds to be old enough to be tried in criminal court for serious crimes (or too old to be dealt with effectively in juvenile court), *but tells us nothing about the judgment these States have made regarding the appropriate punishment for such youthful offenders*." . . .

The same reasoning obtains here. Many States have chosen to move away from juvenile court systems and to allow juveniles to be transferred to, or charged directly in, adult court under certain circumstances. Once in adult court, a juvenile offender may receive the same sentence as would be given to an adult offender, including a life without parole sentence. But the fact that transfer and direct charging laws make life without parole possible for some juvenile non-homicide offenders does not justify a judgment that many States intended to subject such offenders to life without parole sentences.

. . . *[some discussion omitted]*

B

Community consensus, while "entitled to great weight," is not itself determinative of whether a punishment is cruel and unusual. . . . The judicial exercise of independent judgment requires consideration of the culpability of the offenders at issue in light of their crimes and characteristics, along with the severity of the punishment in question. . . . In this inquiry the Court also considers whether the challenged sentencing practice serves legitimate penological goals. . . . .

Roper established that because juveniles have lessened culpability they are less deserving of the most severe punishments. . . . As compared to adults, juveniles have a "'lack of maturity and an underdeveloped sense of responsibility'"; they "are more vulnerable or susceptible to negative influences and outside pressures, including peer pressure"; and their characters are "not as well formed." . . . These salient characteristics mean that "[i]t is difficult even for expert psychologists to differentiate between the juvenile offender whose crime reflects unfortunate yet transient immaturity, and the rare juvenile offender whose crime reflects irreparable corruption." . . . Accordingly, "juvenile offenders cannot with reliability be classified among the worst offenders." . . . A juvenile is not absolved of responsibility for his actions, but his transgression "is not as morally reprehensible as that of an adult." . . . .

No recent data provide reason to reconsider the Court's observations in *Roper* about the nature of juveniles. As petitioner's *amici* point out, developments in psychology and brain science continue to show fundamental differences between juvenile and adult minds. For example, parts of the brain involved in behavior control continue to mature through late adolescence. . . . . Juveniles are more capable of change than are adults, and their actions are less likely to be evidence of "irretrievably depraved character" than are the actions of adults. . . . . It remains true that "[f]rom a moral standpoint it would be misguided to equate the failings of a minor with those of an adult, for a greater possibility exists that a minor's character deficiencies will be reformed." These matters relate to the status of the offenders in question; and it is relevant to consider next the nature of the offenses to which this harsh penalty might apply.

[Discussion of the seriousness of homicide versus nonhomicide crimes omitted.]

As for the punishment, life without parole is "the second most severe penalty permitted by law." . . . The State does not execute the offender sentenced to life without parole, but the sentence alters the offender's life by a forfeiture that is irrevocable. It deprives the convict of the most basic liberties without giving hope of restoration, except perhaps by executive clemency—the remote possibility of which does not mitigate the harshness of the sentence. . . .

. . . *[some discussion omitted]*

Life without parole is an especially harsh punishment for a juvenile. Under this sentence a juvenile offender will on average serve more years and a greater percentage of his life in prison than an adult offender. A 16-year-old and a 75-year-old each sentenced to life without parole receive the same punishment in name only. . . . This reality cannot be ignored.

The penological justifications for the sentencing practice are also relevant to the analysis. . . . Criminal punishment can have different goals, and choosing among them is within a legislature's discretion. . . . A sentence lacking any legitimate penological justification is by its nature disproportionate to the offense. With respect to life without parole for juvenile nonhomicide offenders, none of the goals of penal sanctions that have been recognized as legitimate—retribution, deterrence, incapacitation, and rehabilitation, . . . —provides an adequate justification.

Retribution is a legitimate reason to punish, but it cannot support the sentence at issue here. Society is entitled to impose severe sanctions on a juvenile nonhomicide offender to express its condemnation of the crime and to seek restoration of the moral imbalance caused by the offense. But "[t]he heart of the retribution rationale is that a criminal sentence must be directly related to the personal culpability of the criminal offender." . . . And as *Roper* observed, "[w]hether viewed as an attempt to express the community's moral outrage or as an attempt to right the balance for the wrong to the victim, the case for retribution is not as strong with a minor as with an adult." The case becomes even weaker with respect to a juvenile who did not commit homicide. *Roper* found that "[r]etribution is not proportional if the law's most severe penalty is imposed" on the juvenile murderer. The considerations underlying that holding support as well the conclusion that retribution does not justify imposing the second most severe penalty on the less culpable juvenile nonhomicide offender.

Deterrence does not suffice to justify the sentence either. *Roper* noted that "the same characteristics that render juveniles less culpable than adults suggest . . . that juveniles will be less susceptible to deterrence." Because juveniles' "lack of maturity and underdeveloped sense of responsibility . . . often result in impetuous and ill-considered actions and decisions," . . . they are less likely to take a possible punishment into consideration when making decisions. This is particularly so when that punishment is rarely imposed. That the sentence deters in a few cases is perhaps plausible, but "[t]his argument does not overcome other objections." . . . . Even if the punishment has some connection to a valid penological goal, it must be shown that the punishment is not grossly disproportionate in light of the justification offered. Here, in light of juvenile nonhomicide offenders' diminished moral responsibility, any limited deterrent effect provided by life without parole is not enough to justify the sentence.

Incapacitation, a third legitimate reason for imprisonment, does not justify the life without parole sentence in question here. Recidivism is a serious risk to public safety, and so incapacitation is an important goal. . . . But while incapacitation may be a legitimate penological goal sufficient to justify life without parole in other contexts, it is inadequate to justify that punishment for juveniles who did not commit homicide. To justify life without parole on the assumption that the juvenile offender forever will be a danger to society requires the sentencer to make a judgment that the juvenile is incorrigible. The characteristics of juveniles make that judgment questionable. "It is difficult even for expert psychologists to differentiate between the juvenile offender whose crime reflects unfortunate yet transient immaturity, and the rare juvenile offender whose crime reflects irreparable corruption." . . .

. . . *[some discussion omitted]*

Finally there is rehabilitation, a penological goal that forms the basis of parole systems. . . . The concept of rehabilitation is imprecise; and its utility and proper implementation are the subject of a substantial, dynamic field of inquiry and dialogue. . . . . It is for legislatures to determine what rehabilitative techniques are appropriate and effective.

A sentence of life imprisonment without parole, however, cannot be justified by the goal of rehabilitation. The penalty forswears altogether the rehabilitative ideal. By denying the defendant the right to reenter the community, the State makes an irrevocable judgment about that person's value and place in society. This judgment is not appropriate in light of a juvenile nonhomicide offender's capacity for change and limited moral culpability. A State's rejection of rehabilitation, moreover, goes beyond a mere expressive judgment. As one *amicus* notes, defendants serving life without parole sentences are often denied access to vocational training and other rehabilitative services that are available to other inmates. . . . For juvenile offenders, who are most in need of and receptive to rehabilitation, . . . the absence of rehabilitative opportunities or treatment makes the disproportionality of the sentence all the more evident.

In sum, penological theory is not adequate to justify life without parole for juvenile nonhomicide offenders. This determination; the limited culpability of juvenile non-homicide offenders; and the severity of life without parole sentences all lead to the conclusion that the sentencing practice under consideration is cruel and unusual. This Court now holds that for a juvenile offender who did not commit homicide the Eighth Amendment forbids the sentence of life without parole. This clear line is necessary to prevent the possibility that life without parole sentences will be imposed on juvenile nonhomicide offenders who are not sufficiently culpable to merit that punishment. Because "[t]he age of 18 is the point where society draws the line for many purposes between childhood and adulthood," those who were below that age when the offense was committed may not be sentenced to life without parole for a nonhomicide crime. . . .

. . . The Eighth Amendment does not foreclose the possibility that persons convicted of nonhomicide crimes committed before adulthood will remain behind bars for life. It does forbid States from making the judgment at the outset that those offenders never will be fit to reenter society.

C

. . . *[some discussion omitted]*

The case-by-case approach to sentencing must, however, be confined by some boundaries. The dilemma of juvenile sentencing demonstrates this. For even if we were to assume that some juvenile nonhomicide offenders might have "sufficient psychological maturity, and at the same time demonstrat[e] sufficient depravity," to merit a life without parole sentence, it does not follow that courts taking a case-by-case proportionality approach could with sufficient accuracy distinguish the few incorrigible juvenile offenders from the many that have the capacity for change. *Roper* rejected the argument that the Eighth Amendment required only that juries be told they must consider the defendant's age as a mitigating factor in sentencing. The Court concluded that an "unacceptable likelihood exists that the brutality or coldblooded nature of any particular crime would overpower mitigating arguments based on youth as a matter of course, even where the juvenile offender's objective immaturity, vulnerability, and lack of true depravity should require a sentence less severe than death." . . . Here, as with the death penalty, "[t]he differences between juvenile and adult offenders are too marked and well understood to risk allowing a youthful person to receive" a sentence of life without parole for a nonhomicide crime "despite insufficient culpability."

Another problem with a case-by-case approach is that it does not take account of special difficulties encountered by counsel in juvenile representation. As some *amici* note, the features that distinguish juveniles from adults also put them at a significant disadvantage in criminal proceedings. Juveniles mistrust adults and have limited understandings of the criminal justice system and the roles of the institutional actors within it. They are less likely than adults to work effectively with their lawyers to aid in their defense. . . . Difficulty in weighing long-term consequences; a corresponding impulsiveness; and reluctance to trust defense counsel seen as part of the adult world a rebellious youth rejects, all can lead to poor decisions by one charged with a juvenile offense. . . . . These factors are likely to impair the quality of a juvenile defendant's representation. . . . A categorical rule avoids the risk that, as a result of these difficulties, a court or jury will erroneously conclude that a particular juvenile is sufficiently culpable to deserve life without parole for a nonhomicide.

Finally, a categorical rule gives all juvenile nonhomicide offenders a chance to demonstrate maturity and reform. The juvenile should not be deprived of the opportunity to achieve maturity of judgment and self-recognition of human worth and potential. In *Roper*, that deprivation resulted from an execution that brought life to its end. Here, though by a different dynamic, the same concerns apply. Life in prison without the possibility of parole gives no chance for fulfillment outside prison walls, no chance for reconciliation with society, no hope. Maturity can lead to that considered reflection which is the foundation for remorse, renewal, and rehabilitation.

. . . [some discussion omitted]

D

There is support for our conclusion in the fact that, in continuing to impose life without parole sentences on juveniles who did not commit homicide, the United States adheres to a sentencing practice rejected the world over. This observation does not control our decision. The judgments of other nations and the international community are not dispositive as to the meaning of the Eighth Amendment. But "'[t]he climate of international opinion concerning the acceptability of a particular punishment'" is also "'not irrelevant.'" . . .

Today we continue that longstanding practice in noting the global consensus against the sentencing practice in question. A recent study concluded that only 11 nations authorize life without parole for juvenile offenders under any circumstances; and only 2 of them, the United States and Israel, ever impose the punishment in practice. . . . But even if Israel is counted as allowing life without parole for juvenile offenders, that nation does not appear to impose that sentence for nonhomicide crimes; all of the seven Israeli prisoners whom commentators have identified as serving life sentences for juvenile crimes were convicted of homicide or attempted homicide. . . .

Thus, as petitioner contends and respondent does not contest, the United States is the only Nation that imposes life without parole sentences on juvenile nonhomicide offenders. We also note, as petitioner and his *amici* emphasize, that Article 37 (a) of the United Nations Convention on the Rights of the Child, Nov. 20, 1989, 1577 U. N. T. S. 3 (entered into force Sept. 2, 1990), ratified by every nation except the United States and Somalia, prohibits the imposition of "life imprisonment without possibility of release . . . for offences committed by persons below eighteen years of age." . . . . As we concluded in *Roper* with respect to the juvenile death penalty, "the United States now stands alone in a world that has turned its face against" life without parole for juvenile nonhomicide offenders.

. . . [some discussion omitted]

The Court has treated the laws and practices of other nations and international agreements as relevant to the Eighth Amendment not because those norms are binding or controlling but because the judgment of the world's nations that a particular sentencing practice is inconsistent with basic principles of decency demonstrates that the Court's rationale has respected reasoning to support it.

The Constitution prohibits the imposition of a life without parole sentence on a juvenile offender who did not commit homicide. A State need not guarantee the offender eventual release, but if it imposes a sentence of life it must provide him or her with some realistic opportunity to obtain release before the end of that term. The judgment of the First District Court of Appeal of Florida affirming Graham's conviction is reversed, and the case is remanded for further proceedings not inconsistent with this opinion.

It is so ordered.

[Notes and citations omitted. Concurring and dissenting opinions omitted.]

CLARK
v.
ARIZONA

SUPREME COURT OF THE UNITED STATES

548 U.S. 735 (2006)

Justice Souter delivered the opinion of the Court.

The case presents two questions: whether due process prohibits Arizona's use of an insanity test stated solely in terms of the capacity to tell whether an act charged as a crime was right or wrong; and whether Arizona violates due process in restricting consideration of defense evidence of mental illness and incapacity to its bearing on a claim of insanity, thus eliminating its significance directly on the issue of the mental element of the crime charged (known in legal shorthand as the *mens rea*, or guilty mind). We hold that there is no violation of due process in either instance.

. . . In the early hours of June 21, 2000, Officer Jeffrey Moritz of the Flagstaff Police responded in uniform to complaints that a pickup truck with loud music blaring was circling a residential block. When he located the truck, the officer turned on the emergency lights and siren of his marked patrol car, which prompted petitioner Eric Clark, the truck's driver (then 17), to pull over. Officer Moritz got out of the patrol car and told Clark to stay where he was. Less than a minute later, Clark shot the officer, who died soon after but not before calling the police dispatcher for help. Clark ran away on foot but was arrested later that day with gunpowder residue on his hands; the gun that killed the officer was found nearby, stuffed into a knit cap.

Clark was charged with first-degree murder under Ariz. Rev. Stat. Ann. §13-1105(A)(3) (West Supp. 2005) for intentionally or knowingly killing a law enforcement officer in the line of duty. In March 2001, Clark was found incompetent to stand trial and was committed to a state hospital for treatment, but two years later the same trial court found his competence restored and ordered him to be tried. Clark waived his right to a jury, and the case was heard by the court.

At trial, Clark did not contest the shooting and death, but relied on his undisputed paranoid schizophrenia at the time of the incident in denying that he had the specific intent to shoot a law enforcement officer or knowledge that he was doing so, as required by the statute. Accordingly, the prosecutor offered circumstantial evidence that Clark knew Officer Moritz was a law enforcement officer. The evidence showed that the officer was in uniform at the time, that he caught up with Clark in a marked police car with emergency lights and siren going, and that Clark acknowledged the symbols of police authority and stopped. The testimony for the prosecution indicated that Clark had intentionally lured an officer to the scene to kill him, having told some people a few weeks before the incident that he wanted to shoot police officers. At the close of the State's evidence, the trial court denied Clark's motion for judgment of acquittal for failure to prove intent to kill a law enforcement officer or knowledge that Officer Moritz was a law enforcement officer.

In presenting the defense case, Clark claimed mental illness, which he sought to introduce for two purposes. First, he raised the affirmative defense of insanity, putting the burden on himself to prove by clear and convincing evidence, §13-502(C) (West 2001), that "at the time of the commission of the criminal act [he] was afflicted with a mental disease or defect of such severity that [he] did not know the criminal act was wrong," §13-502(A). Second, he aimed to rebut the prosecution's evidence of the requisite *mens rea*, that he had acted intentionally or knowingly to kill a law enforcement officer. . . . .

The trial court ruled that Clark could not rely on evidence bearing on insanity to dispute the *mens rea*. The court cited *State v. Mott*, . . . (1997), which "refused to allow psychiatric testimony to negate specific intent," . . . , and held that "Arizona does not allow evidence of a defendant's mental disorder short of insanity . . . to negate the *mens rea* element of a crime,"

As to his insanity, then, Clark presented testimony from classmates, school officials, and his family describing his increasingly bizarre behavior over the year before the shooting. . . . A psychiatrist testified that Clark was suffering from paranoid schizophrenia with delusions about "aliens" when he killed Officer Moritz, and he concluded that Clark was incapable of luring the officer or understanding right from wrong and that he was thus insane at the time of the killing. In rebuttal, a psychiatrist for the State gave his opinion that Clark's paranoid schizophrenia did not keep him from appreciating the wrongfulness of his conduct, as shown by his actions before and after the shooting (such as circling the residential block with music blaring as if to lure the police to intervene, evading the police after the shooting, and hiding the gun).

. . . The judge then issued a special verdict of first-degree murder, expressly finding that Clark shot and caused the death of Officer Moritz beyond a reasonable doubt and that Clark had not shown that he was insane at the time. The judge noted that though Clark was indisputably afflicted with paranoid schizophrenia at the time of the shooting, the mental illness "did not . . . distort his perception of reality so severely that he did not know his actions were wrong." . . .

Clark moved to vacate the judgment and sentence, arguing, among other things, that Arizona's insanity test and its *Mott* rule each violate due process. As to the insanity standard, Clark claimed (as he had argued earlier) that the Arizona Legislature had impermissibly narrowed its standard in 1993 when it eliminated the first part of the two-part insanity test announced in *M'Naghten's Case*, . . . The court denied the motion.

The Court of Appeals of Arizona affirmed Clark's conviction, treating the conclusion on sanity as supported by enough evidence to withstand review for abuse of discretion, and holding the State's insanity scheme consistent with due process. . . . As to the latter, the Court of Appeals reasoned that there is no constitutional requirement to recognize an insanity defense at all, the bounds of which are left to the State's discretion. Beyond that, the appellate court followed *Mott*, reading it as barring the trial court's consideration of evidence of Clark's mental illness and capacity directly on the element of *mens rea*. The Supreme Court of Arizona denied further review.

We granted certiorari to decide whether due process prohibits Arizona from thus narrowing its insanity test or from excluding evidence of mental illness and incapacity due to mental illness to rebut evidence of the requisite criminal intent. . . . We now affirm.

. . . When the Arizona Legislature first codified an insanity rule, it adopted the full *M'Naghten* statement. . . . In 1993, the legislature dropped the cognitive incapacity part, leaving only moral incapacity as the nub of the stated definition. . . . Under current Arizona law, a defendant will not be adjudged insane unless he demonstrates that "at the time of the commission of the criminal act [he] was afflicted with a mental disease or defect of such severity that [he] did not know the criminal act was wrong," . . .

. . . Even a cursory examination of the traditional Anglo-American approaches to insanity reveals significant differences among them, with four traditional strains variously combined to yield a diversity of American standards. The main variants are the cognitive incapacity, the moral incapacity, the volitional incapacity, and the product-of-mental-illness tests. The first two emanate from the alternatives stated in the *M'Naghten* rule. The volitional incapacity or irresistible-impulse test, which surfaced over two centuries ago (first in England, then in this country), asks whether a person was so lacking in volition due to a mental defect or illness that he could not have controlled his actions. And the product-of-mental-illness test was used as early as 1870, and simply asks whether a person's action was a product of a mental disease or defect. Seventeen States and the Federal Government have adopted a recognizable version of the *M'Naghten* test with both its cognitive incapacity and moral incapacity components. One State has adopted only *M'Naghten's* cognitive incapacity test, and 10 (including Arizona) have adopted the moral incapacity test alone. Fourteen jurisdictions, inspired by the Model Penal Code, have in place an amalgam of the volitional incapacity test and some variant of the moral incapacity test, satisfaction of either (generally by showing a defendant's substantial lack of capacity) being enough to excuse. Three States combine a full *M'Naghten* test with a volitional incapacity formula. And New Hampshire alone stands by the product-of-mental-illness test. The alternatives are multiplied further by variations in the prescribed insanity verdict: a significant number of these jurisdictions supplement the traditional "not guilty by reason of insanity" verdict with an alternative of "guilty but mentally ill." Finally, four States have no affirmative insanity defense, though one provides for a "guilty and mentally ill" verdict. These four, like a number of others that recognize an affirmative insanity defense, allow consideration of evidence of mental illness directly on the element of *mens rea* defining the offense.

With this varied background, it is clear that no particular formulation has evolved into a baseline for due process, and that the insanity rule, like the conceptualization of criminal offenses, is substantially open to state choice. . . . There being such fodder for reasonable debate about what the cognate legal and medical tests should be, due process imposes no single canonical formulation of legal insanity.

. . . Nor does Arizona's abbreviation of the *M'Naghten* statement raise a proper claim that some constitutional minimum has been shortchanged. Clark's argument of course assumes that Arizona's former statement of the *M'Naghten* rule, with its express alternative of cognitive incapacity, was constitutionally adequate (as we agree). That being so, the abbreviated rule is no less so, for cognitive incapacity is relevant under that statement, just as it was under the more extended formulation, and evidence going to cognitive incapacity has the same significance under the short form as it had under the long.

Though Clark is correct that the application of the moral incapacity test (telling right from wrong) does not necessarily require evaluation of a defendant's cognitive capacity to appreciate the nature and quality of the acts charged against him, . . . his argument fails to recognize that cognitive incapacity is itself enough to demonstrate moral incapacity. . . . In practical terms, if a defendant did not know what he was doing when he acted, he could not have known that he was performing the wrongful act charged as a crime. . . .

We are satisfied that neither in theory nor in practice did Arizona's 1993 abridgment of the insanity formulation deprive Clark of due process.

. . . Clark's second claim of a due process violation challenges the rule adopted by the Supreme Court of Arizona in *State v. Mott*, . . . This case ruled on the admissibility of testimony from a psychologist offered to show that the defendant suffered from battered women's syndrome and therefore lacked the capacity to form the *mens rea* of the crime charged against her. . . . The state court held that testimony of a professional psychologist or psychiatrist about a defendant's mental incapacity owing to mental disease or defect was admissible, and could be considered, only for its bearing on an insanity defense; such evidence could not be considered on the element of

mens rea, that is, what the State must show about a defendant's mental state (such as intent or understanding) when he performed the act charged against him. . . .

Understanding Clark's claim requires attention to the categories of evidence with a potential bearing on *mens rea*. First, there is "observation evidence" in the everyday sense, testimony from those who observed what Clark did and heard what he said; this category would also include testimony that an expert witness might give about Clark's tendency to think in a certain way and his behavioral characteristics. . . .

Second, there is "mental-disease evidence" in the form of opinion testimony that Clark suffered from a mental disease with features described by the witness. As was true here, this evidence characteristically but not always comes from professional psychologists or psychiatrists who testify as expert witnesses and base their opinions in part on examination of a defendant, usually conducted after the events in question. . . .

Third, there is evidence we will refer to as "capacity evidence" about a defendant's capacity for cognition and moral judgment (and ultimately also his capacity to form *mens rea*). This, too, is opinion evidence. Here, as it usually does, this testimony came from the same experts and concentrated on those specific details of the mental condition that make the difference between sanity and insanity under the Arizona definition. . . .

. . . It is clear that *Mott* itself imposed no restriction on considering evidence of the first sort, the observation evidence. We read the *Mott* restriction to apply, rather, to evidence addressing the two issues in testimony that characteristically comes only from psychologists or psychiatrists qualified to give opinions as expert witnesses: mental-disease evidence (whether at the time of the crime a defendant suffered from a mental disease or defect, such as schizophrenia) and capacity evidence (whether the disease or defect left him incapable of performing or experiencing a mental process defined as necessary for sanity such as appreciating the nature and quality of his act and knowing that it was wrong).

Mott was careful to distinguish this kind of opinion evidence from observation evidence generally and even from observation evidence that an expert witness might offer, such as descriptions of a defendant's tendency to think in a certain way or his behavioral characteristics; the Arizona court made it clear that this sort of testimony was perfectly admissible to rebut the prosecution's evidence of *mens rea*, . . . Thus, only opinion testimony going to mental defect or disease, and its effect on the cognitive or moral capacities on which sanity depends under the Arizona rule, is restricted. . . . *[The majority then held that Clark did not argue that the trial court erroneously applied the Mott rule by disregarding observational evidence, but, rather, objected to the Mott rule itself.]*

In sum, the trial court's ruling, with its uncertain edges, may have restricted observation evidence admissible on *mens rea* to the insanity defense alone, but we cannot be sure. But because a due process challenge to such a restriction of observation evidence was, by our measure, neither pressed nor passed upon in the Arizona Court of Appeals, we do not consider it. . . . What we do know, and now consider, is Clark's claim that Mott denied due process because it "*preclude[d] Eric from contending that . . . factual inferences*" of the "mental states which were necessary elements of the crime charged" "*should not be drawn* because the behavior was explainable, instead, as a manifestation of his chronic paranoid schizophrenia." . . . We consider the claim, as Clark otherwise puts it, that "Arizona's prohibition of 'diminished capacity' evidence by criminal defendants violates" due process . . .

. . . The first presumption is that a defendant is innocent unless and until the government proves beyond a reasonable doubt each element of the offense charged. . . . Before the last century, the *mens rea* required to be proven for particular offenses was often described in general terms like "malice," . . . , but the modern tendency has been toward more specific descriptions, as shown in the Arizona statute defining the murder charged against Clark: the State had to prove that in acting to kill the victim, Clark intended to kill a law enforcement officer on duty or knew that the victim was such an officer on duty. . . . As applied to *mens rea* (and every other element), the force of the presumption of innocence is measured by the force of the showing needed to overcome it, which is proof beyond a reasonable doubt that a defendant's state of mind was in fact what the charge states. . . .

. . . The presumption of sanity is equally universal in some variety or other, being (at least) a presumption that a defendant has the capacity to form the *mens rea* necessary for a verdict of guilt and the consequent criminal responsibility. . . . The force of this presumption, like the presumption of innocence, is measured by the quantum of evidence necessary to overcome it; unlike the presumption of innocence, however, the force of the presumption of sanity varies across the many state and federal jurisdictions, and prior law has recognized considerable leeway on the part of the legislative branch in defining the presumption's strength through the kind of evidence and degree of persuasiveness necessary to overcome it, . . .

There are two points where the sanity or capacity presumption may be placed in issue. First, a State may allow a defendant to introduce (and a factfinder to consider) evidence of mental disease or incapacity for the bearing it can have on the government's burden to show *mens rea*. . . . If it is shown that a defendant with mental disease thinks all blond people are robots, he could not have intended to kill a person when he shot a man with blond hair, even though he seemed to act like a man shooting another man. In jurisdictions that allow mental-disease and capacity evidence to be considered on par with any other relevant evidence when deciding whether the prosecution has proven *mens rea* beyond a reasonable doubt, the evidence of mental disease or incapacity need only support what the factfinder regards as a reasonable doubt about the capacity to form (or the actual formation of) the *mens rea*, in order to require acquittal of the charge. . . .

The second point where the force of the presumption of sanity may be tested is in the consideration of a defense of insanity raised by a defendant. Insanity rules like *M'Naghten* . . . are attempts to define, or at least to indicate, the kinds of mental differences that overcome the presumption of sanity or capacity and therefore excuse a defendant from customary criminal responsibility, . . . even if the prosecution has otherwise overcome the presumption of innocence by convincing the factfinder of all the elements charged beyond a reasonable doubt. The burden that must be carried by a defendant who raises the insanity issue, again, defines the strength of the sanity presumption. A State may provide, for example, that whenever the defendant raises a claim of insanity by some quantum of credible evidence, the presumption disappears and the government must prove sanity to a specified degree of certainty (whether beyond reasonable doubt or something less). . . . Or a jurisdiction may place the burden of persuasion on a defendant to prove insanity as the applicable law defines it, whether by a preponderance of the evidence or to some more convincing degree, . . . In any case, the defendant's burden defines the presumption of sanity, whether that burden be to burst a bubble or to show something more.

. . . As Clark recognizes, however, the right to introduce relevant evidence can be curtailed if there is a good reason for doing that. "While the Constitution . . . prohibits the exclusion of defense evidence under rules that serve no legitimate purpose or that are disproportionate to the ends that they are asserted to promote, well-established rules of evidence permit trial judges to exclude evidence if its probative value is outweighed by certain other factors such as unfair prejudice, confusion of the issues, or potential to mislead the jury." . . . And if evidence may be kept out entirely, its consideration may be subject to limitation, which Arizona claims the power to impose here. State law says that evidence of mental disease and incapacity may be introduced and considered, and if sufficiently forceful to satisfy the defendant's burden of proof under the insanity rule it will displace the presumption of sanity and excuse from criminal responsibility. But mental-disease and capacity evidence may be considered only for its bearing on the insanity defense, and it will avail a defendant only if it is persuasive enough to satisfy the defendant's burden as defined by the terms of that defense. The mental-disease and capacity evidence is thus being channeled or restricted to one issue and given effect only if the defendant carries the burden to convince the factfinder of insanity; the evidence is not being excluded entirely, and the question is whether reasons for requiring it to be channeled and restricted are good enough to satisfy the standard of fundamental fairness that due process requires. We think they are. . . .

To begin with, the diagnosis may mask vigorous debate within the profession about the very contours of the mental disease itself. . . . Next, there is the potential of mental-disease evidence to mislead jurors (when they are the factfinders) through the power of this kind of evidence to suggest that a defendant suffering from a recognized mental disease lacks cognitive, moral, volitional, or other capacity, when

that may not be a sound conclusion at all. . . . There are, finally, particular risks inherent in the opinions of the experts who supplement the mental-disease classifications with opinions on incapacity: on whether the mental disease rendered a particular defendant incapable of the cognition necessary for moral judgment or *mens rea* or otherwise incapable of understanding the wrongfulness of the conduct charged. Unlike observational evidence bearing on *mens rea*, capacity evidence consists of judgment, and judgment fraught with multiple perils: a defendant's state of mind at the crucial moment can be elusive no matter how conscientious the enquiry, and the law's categories that set the terms of the capacity judgment are not the categories of psychology that govern the expert's professional thinking. . . . In sum, these empirical and conceptual problems add up to a real risk that an expert's judgment in giving capacity evidence will come with an apparent authority that psychologists and psychiatrists do not claim to have. We think that this risk, like the difficulty in assessing the significance of mental-disease evidence, supports the State's decision to channel such expert testimony to consideration on the insanity defense, on which the party seeking the benefit of this evidence has the burden of persuasion.

It bears repeating that not every State will find it worthwhile to make the judgment Arizona has made, and the choices the States do make about dealing with the risks posed by mental-disease and capacity evidence will reflect their varying assessments about the presumption of sanity as expressed in choices of insanity rules. The point here simply is that Arizona has sensible reasons to assign the risks as it has done by channeling the evidence . . .

Arizona's rule serves to preserve the State's chosen standard for recognizing insanity as a defense and to avoid confusion and misunderstanding on the part of jurors. For these reasons, there is no violation of due process under *Chambers* and its progeny, and no cause to claim that channeling evidence on mental disease and capacity offends any " 'principle of justice so rooted in the traditions and conscience of our people as to be ranked as fundamental,' " . . .

The judgment of the Court of Appeals of Arizona is, accordingly, affirmed.

[Notes and citations omitted. Concurring and Dissenting opinions omitted.]

Cases Relating to Chapter 4

Preparatory Activity Offenses

COMMONWEALTH OF PENNSYLVANIA, APPELLEE
v.
SAMUEL HENLEY, APPELLANT

SUPREME COURT OF PENNSYLVANIA

504 Pa. 408, 474 A.2d 1115 (1984)

PAPADAKOS, Justice.

This is the appeal of Samuel Henley (Appellant) from the en banc Opinion and Order of the Superior Court . . . which reversed a Philadelphia Common Pleas Order sustaining Appellant's demurrer to the evidence charging him with attempting to receive stolen property.

The facts are not in dispute and can be easily summarized. Appellant is the owner of the Henley Brothers Jewelry Store located at 740 Samson Street in the City of Philadelphia. On December 22, 1980, an informant, wired with a tape recording device, was given five (5) specially coated chains by the police, and sent to Appellant's jewelry store. The informant entered the store and offered to sell the five (5) gold chains to Appellant. He represented to Appellant that the chains were stolen. Appellant, believing them to be stolen, purchased the chains for $30.00, took possession of them, and expressed a willingness to buy more stolen goods in the future. This conversation was recorded. The informant then left the store, met with the detective who had accompanied him, played the tape recording, and turned over the $30.00.

The detective then entered the store and arrested Appellant, charging him with the crime of theft by receiving stolen goods and receiving stolen property as a business. . . . These charges were later amended to attempted theft by unlawful taking or disposition, . . . and he was tried on this charge at a non-jury trial on November 18, 1981.

At the conclusion of the Commonwealth's case, Appellant demurred to the evidence, arguing that the chains were not stolen property because they were in police custody, and that, therefore, he could not be found guilty of an attempt to receive stolen property which was not stolen. The trial court found this defense of legal impossibility persuasive and granted the demurrer.

The Commonwealth appealed to the Superior Court, which reversed and remanded for trial, concluding that the defense of legal impossibility had been abolished in Pennsylvania. Because this issue was one of first impression, we granted allocatur.

Impossibility defenses were usually classified as either legal or factual in nature. "Factual impossibility denotes conduct where the objective is proscribed by the criminal law but a circumstance unknown to the actor prevents him from bringing it about. The classic example is the thief who picks an empty pocket." . . . Legal impossibility was said to occur where the intended acts would not amount to a crime even if completed. A frequently cited case standing for this proposition is *People v. Jaffe*, . . . The *Jaffe* Court held that where an element of the completed crime required the goods be stolen, the fact that the goods were not stolen was a defense to the completed act. Consequently, an attempt to do an act which would not be criminal if completed could not itself be criminal regardless of the actor's intent. . . .

Factual impossibility has never been recognized as a defense to an attempt charge by any American Court, . . . and this Court specifically rejected factual impossibility as a defense to an attempt charge. . . .

Legal impossibility had been recognized in many jurisdictions as a defense to attempt charges, and this Court cited the *Jaffe* case approvingly . . . , indicating that the defense of legal impossibility was available as a defense to attempt charges in this Commonwealth.

The reasoning in the *Jaffe* line of cases has come under considerable criticism in the last twenty-five years, and in response to the criticism the defense has been uniformly rejected by the highest courts of most states where the issue has been raised. Additionally, many states have passed legislation which specifically abrogated the defense. The suggested abrogation of the impossibility defense through legislation was first introduced to most state legislatures via the Model Penal Code. . . .

Our Legislature was keenly aware of the necessity to consolidate, amend, and revise the penal laws of the Commonwealth, and as early as 1963 began preparing legislation for a new crimes code.

[Discussion of legislative action in preparing new Criminal Attempt statute, which Court then provides.]

Section 901 Criminal Attempt

(a) Definition of attempt–a person commits an attempt when, with intent to commit a specific crime, he does any act which constitutes a substantial step toward commission of that crime.
(b) Impossibility–it shall not be a defense to a charge of attempt that because of a misapprehension of the circumstances it would have been impossible for the accused to commit the crime attempted. . . .

Because of variance in the language of the Model Penal Code and our Crimes Code, appellant argues that the Legislature intended to reject the provision of the Model Penal Code and to retain the legal impossibility defense to inchoate crimes. We disagree. The mere fact that our Legislature

improved upon the language in its Criminal Attempt Section over that found in the Model Penal Code cannot by itself support the conclusion that the Legislature intended to reject the provisions of the Model Penal Code and thus, to retain the legal impossibility defense.

Our Crimes Code is clear in defining the two (2) elements of the offense of attempt by providing: (1) that the actor intend to commit an offense; and (2) that the actor take a substantial step toward completion of the offense. The Code then specifically provides that impossibility is not a defense if the completed offense could have occurred had the circumstances been as the accused apprehended them to be. Read as a whole, the provisions of Section 901(a) and (b) of our Crimes Code parallel the provisions of the Model Penal Code and other states' crimes codes (which are all based on the provisions of the Model Penal Code) in their intent if not in their terminology.

Those sections have all been interpreted as eliminating the defense of legal impossibility because of statutory language to the effect that impossibility (factual or legal) is not a defense if the completed offense could have occurred had the circumstances been as the accused believed them to be. Our Code's provisions are strikingly similar except that our statute speaks to the accused's misapprehension.

The choice in terminology between "beliefs" and "misapprehensions," however, is of no consequence since both terms would require the actor mentally or intellectually to perceive, comprehend, or accept a reality, phenomenon, or set of occurrences without regard to actual extrinsic circumstances. The use of either term then is interchangeable, and the Legislature could just as easily have used words referring to the actor's "beliefs" instead of his "apprehensions" or "misapprehensions" of the circumstances. . . .

We are thoroughly aware of the unsound basis for the legal impossibility defense and we hasten to add that the application of either of the impossibility defenses "is so fraught with intricacies and artificial distinctions that the defense has little value as an analytical method for reaching substantial justice." . . .

The effort to compartmentalize factual patterns into these judicially created categories of factual or legal impossibilities is but an illusory test leading to contradictory and sometimes absurd results, because courts are left to evaluate an actor's beliefs or apprehensions in the light of the actual facts. Our statute abandons this out-dated approach with its former distinctions of legal and factual impossibilities and instead evaluates the actor's conduct according to his mental frame of reference alone.

Thus, if one forms intent to commit a substantive crime, then proceeds to perform all the acts necessary to commit the crime, and it is shown that completion of the substantive crime is impossible, the actor can still be culpable of attempt to commit the substantive crime. A defense based on the old legal or factual impossibility argument clearly is no longer available. Under the new Code, an intent to commit an act which is not characterized as a crime by the laws of the subject jurisdiction cannot be the basis of a criminal charge and conviction even though the actor believes or misapprehends the intended act to be proscribed by the criminal laws. An example of this is where a fisherman believes he is committing an offense in fishing on a certain lake without a license when a fishing license is, in fact, not required in the subject jurisdiction. Since the conduct here would be perfectly legal, the actor could not be held accountable for any attempted crime. In all other cases, the actor should be held responsible for his conduct. Our reading of Section 901(b) would do just that.

Since the defense of legal impossibility has been abrogated, it was not available to Appellant and the demurrer was improperly granted. This matter must, therefore, be remanded to the Court of Common Pleas for trial.

The Order of the Superior Court is affirmed.

ANTHONY THOMAS BOLDEN, APPELLANT

v.

SUPREME COURT OF NEVADA

124 P.3d 191; 2005 Nev. LEXIS 103; 121 Nev. Adv. Rep. 86

December 15, 2005, Decided

Opinion

Appellant Anthony Thomas Bolden and four other masked men broke into Silvia Rascon's apartment and committed a number of crimes against the occupants. A jury convicted Bolden of burglary while in possession of a deadly weapon, home invasion while in possession of a deadly weapon, first-degree kidnapping with use of a deadly weapon, second-degree kidnapping with use of a deadly weapon, two counts of robbery with use of a deadly weapon, and conspiracy to commit robbery and/or kidnapping. In this appeal, Bolden alleges that the district court committed error during jury selection under *Batson v. Kentucky* and that the State failed to present sufficient evidence to support the jury's verdicts with respect to all the charged offenses, failed to prove that the kidnapping charges were not incidental to the robbery charges, and failed to present sufficient evidence in support of the deadly weapon enhancements.

Although we reject Bolden's specific contentions, in resolving his sufficiency of the evidence challenge, we have found it necessary to determine whether the jury could have properly based its verdicts for the specific intent crimes of burglary and kidnapping on the State's theory of vicarious coconspirator liability. We conclude that the jury was not properly instructed on this theory of vicarious coconspirator liability and that the error cannot be held harmless under the circumstances of this case. Therefore, we reverse Bolden's conviction with respect to the counts concerning the specific intent crimes of burglary and first- and second-degree kidnapping, and we remand this matter for further proceedings consistent with this opinion. We affirm Bolden's conviction of the remaining counts.

Facts

On December 7, 2002, at approximately 2 a.m., Bolden and four other masked men kicked in the door of Silvia Rascon's apartment. Rascon, her three children and a friend were present. The men apparently broke into the apartment looking for drugs and money. With the aid of knives, box cutters or other sharp objects, one or more of the men separately moved Rascon and her oldest daughter from room to room for the purposes of locating items to steal and sexually molesting the daughter. Police arrived and apprehended all of the intruders, three of whom had exited the residence in possession of property stolen from Rascon and her family. Police found Bolden inside the apartment, hiding under a bedroom mattress. Ironically, these men were misinformed concerning the presence of either drugs or considerable financial lucre.

The State charged Bolden and his compatriots with burglary, home invasion, first-degree kidnapping of Rascon, second-degree kidnapping of Rascon's daughter, robbery of Rascon, robbery of Rascon's son, and conspiracy to commit robbery and/or kidnapping. All of the charges, save the conspiracy count, were accompanied by deadly weapon enhancements. This timely appeal followed. . . .

Bolden contends that the State failed to present sufficient evidence to convict him on any of the charges. In short, he claims that the entire body of proof against him established no more than his mere presence during the events in question. In this, the district court instructed the jury that "mere presence" of the defendant, or his "knowledge that a crime is being committed," is insufficient to establish guilt without proof that the defendant was "a participant and not merely a knowing spectator."

More specifically, Bolden asserts that the State failed to prove his participation in a conspiracy; failed to prove the intent elements of the home invasion, robbery, burglary, first-degree kidnapping and second-degree kidnapping charges; failed to prove that the kidnapping charges were not incidental to the robbery charges; and failed to present sufficient evidence in support of the deadly weapon enhancements.

The relevant inquiry in reviewing the sufficiency of the evidence supporting a jury's verdict is "'whether, after viewing the evidence in the light most favorable to the prosecution, any rational trier of fact could have found the essential elements of the crime beyond a reasonable doubt.'" Moreover, "circumstantial evidence alone may support a conviction." In resolving Bolden's contentions, we have reviewed the evidence supporting the jury's findings of guilt with respect to each of the charged offenses. Additionally, with respect to the nonconspiracy offenses, we have reviewed the evidence supporting the jury's verdicts under the three separate theories of guilt alleged by the State for those offenses.

Conspiracy to commit robbery and/or kidnapping

The State alleged that Bolden and the other defendants met with each other and willfully, unlawfully, and feloniously conspired and agreed to commit robbery and/or kidnapping. Additionally, the State alleged that in furtherance of the conspiracy the defendants in fact committed the crimes of robbery and kidnapping. Nevada law defines a conspiracy as "an agreement between two or more persons for an unlawful purpose." "A person who knowingly does any act to further the object of a conspiracy, or otherwise participates therein, is criminally liable as a conspirator . . . ." "Evidence of a coordinated series of acts furthering the underlying offense is sufficient to infer the existence of an agreement and support a conspiracy conviction." "However, absent an agreement to cooperate in achieving the purpose of a conspiracy, mere knowledge of, acquiescence in, or approval of that purpose does not make one a party to conspiracy."

Here, the evidence presented at trial established that Bolden and his cohorts forcibly entered the Rascon apartment armed with switchblades, box cutters or other sharp objects and robbed the occupants. Some of the men moved two of the victims around in the residence for purposes that were both incidental and not incidental to the robberies themselves. The State presented overwhelming circumstantial and direct evidence that Bolden participated in the joint enterprise to acquire drugs and money; that he entered into an agreement to rob the Rascon family; that he was not merely a spectator in the Rascon apartment, as he claims; and that when the police arrived, Bolden was found hiding under a mattress. To the extent that Bolden contends that the evidence fails to support his participation in the conspiracy, his contention is without merit. The State presented more than sufficient evidence to support Bolden's conviction for conspiracy to commit robbery and/or kidnapping.

The burglary, home invasion, robbery, and kidnapping charges

With respect to the burglary, home invasion, robbery and kidnapping charges, the State alleged three alternative theories of criminal liability: (1) that Bolden directly committed the offenses, (2) that he aided and abetted his cohorts, or (3) that he was vicariously responsible for all of the acts of his cohorts done in aid of the conspiracy. When alternate theories of criminal liability are presented to a jury and all of the theories are legally valid, a general verdict can be affirmed even if sufficient evidence supports only one of the theories. When any one of the alleged theories is legally erroneous, however, reversal of a general verdict is required—except under the very narrowly defined circumstances discussed below–regardless of the legal and factual sufficiency of the other theories. Accordingly, we turn to an analysis of the legal and evidentiary support for each of the State's theories of liability.

Aiding and abetting and direct participation

Bolden contends that the jury convicted him primarily upon an aiding and abetting theory. A person aids and abets the commission of a crime if he aids, promotes, encourages or instigates, by act or advice, the commission of such crime with the intention that the crime be committed. Relying upon our decision in *Sharma v. State*, Bolden argues that the State failed to prove that he specifically intended to aid and abet the crimes committed at the Rascon residence.

In *Sharma*, we held,

> In order for a person to be held accountable for the specific intent crime of another under an aiding or abetting theory of principal liability, the aider or abettor must have knowingly aided the other person with the intent that the other person commit the charged crime.

Bolden's reliance on *Sharma* is misplaced for several reasons. First, robbery and home invasion are not specific intent crimes. Second, the State proceeded on two additional alternate theories of criminal liability, direct participation as a principal and perpetration of the offenses in furtherance of a conspiracy. Third, the State presented sufficient evidence for the jury to convict Bolden under all of its theories of culpability. Fourth, per *Sharma*, the district court correctly instructed the jury concerning the State's aiding and abetting theory:

> All persons concerned in the commission of a crime who either directly and actively commit the act constituting the offense or who knowingly and with criminal intent aid and abet in its commission or, whether present or not, who advise and encourage its commission, with the intent that the crime be committed, are regarded by the law as principals in the crime thus committed and are equally guilty thereof.

As noted above, Bolden was one of five masked men who entered a private residence by force, committed the robberies, and moved two of the victims around in the residence. The State provided ample circumstantial evidence of direct participation in, and the specific intent to aid and abet, all of the nonconspiracy crimes committed that morning. Bolden was not, as he now reasons, "merely present" or a "mere spectator." We therefore conclude that substantial evidence supports the State's direct participation and aiding and abetting theories of home invasion, burglary, robbery and kidnapping.

Coconspirator liability

Our conclusion that there is sufficient evidentiary and legal support for Bolden's conviction of the charged crimes as a principal and as an aider and abettor does not end our inquiry. Bolden's sufficiency argument, coupled with his reliance on this court's holding in *Sharma*, calls into question the legal viability of the State's remaining theory of vicarious coconspirator liability. As noted above, if any one of the theories of criminal liability alleged by the State is legally erroneous, reversal of a verdict that fails to specify the precise theory upon which the verdict is based is generally required regardless of the legal and factual sufficiency of the other theories. Despite our conclusion that Bolden's conviction of the nonconspiracy crimes is legally and factually sufficient under the State's theories of principal and aiding and abetting liability, we must now determine whether there is a valid legal and factual basis supporting Bolden's conviction of the nonconspiracy crimes under the State's theory of vicarious coconspirator liability.

In this respect, the district court gave the following instruction:

> Each member of a criminal conspiracy is liable for each act and bound by each declaration of every other member of the conspiracy if the act or the declaration is in furtherance of the object of the conspiracy.
>
> The act of one conspirator pursuant to or in furtherance of the common design of the conspiracy is the act of all conspirators. Every conspirator is legally responsible for an act of a co-conspirator that follows as one of the probable and natural consequences of the object of the conspiracy even if that was not intended as part of the original plan and even if he was not present at the time of commission of such act. . . .

In *Garner v. State*, this court approved the above-quoted "probable and natural consequences" doctrine, which exposes conspirators to criminal liability for any act so long as the act was committed in furtherance of the conspiracy as a natural or probable consequence of the unlawful agreement. However, *Garner* restricted the doctrine considerably by holding that "this rule does not constitute a per se basis for holding an accomplice to one crime liable for a related crime by the principal simply because the related crime was foreseeable." To do so, we concluded, "would be 'to base criminal liability only on a showing of negligence rather than criminal intent.'" Consequently, *Garner* concluded that if "the relationship between the defendant's acts and the charged crime is too attenuated, the State must provide 'some showing of specific intent to aid in, or specific knowledge of, the crime charged.'" *Garner*, however, did not discuss vicarious coconspirator and accomplice liability as discrete concepts.

As previously noted, in *Sharma v. State,* this court overruled *Garner* to the extent that a defendant could be held accountable for the specific intent crime of another, under an aiding or abetting theory of liability, without proof that he specifically intended to aid the other in the commission of the charged crime. We stated,

> [The natural and probable consequences] doctrine has been harshly criticized by most commentators ... as both incongruous and unjust because it imposes accomplice liability solely upon proof of foreseeability or negligence when typically a higher degree of *mens rea* is required of the principal. It permits criminal liability to be predicated upon negligence even when the crime involved requires a different state of mind. Having reevaluated the wisdom of the doctrine, we have concluded that its general application in Nevada to specific intent crimes is unsound precisely for that reason: it permits conviction without proof that the accused possessed the state of mind required by the statutory definition of the crime. ... As the Supreme Court of New Mexico observed in rejecting the doctrine for similar reasons, the doctrine thus allows a defendant to be convicted for crimes the defendant may have been able to foresee but never intended. ... Because the natural and probable consequences doctrine permits a defendant to be convicted of a specific intent crime where he or she did not possess the statutory intent required for the offense, we hereby disavow and abandon the doctrine. It is not only inconsistent with more fundamental principles of our system of criminal law, but is also inconsistent with those Nevada statutes that require proof of a specific intent to commit the crime alleged.. ... Accordingly, we ... hold that in order for a person to be held accountable for the specific intent crime of another under an aiding or abetting theory of principal liability, the aider or abettor must have knowingly aided the other person with the intent that the other person commit the charged crime.

Thus, *Sharma* addressed the natural and probable consequences doctrine only with respect to a theory alleging that a defendant could be held criminally liable for the specific intent crime of another under an aiding and abetting theory of principal liability. The question left unanswered in *Garner* and *Sharma*, but presented in this case, is whether a theory of vicarious coconspirator liability based upon the natural and probable consequences doctrine is a legally viable theory in this state.

Nearly 60 years ago in *Pinkerton v. United States*, the United States Supreme Court defined coconspirator liability in terms of reasonable foreseeability and reaffirmed the concept that a conspiracy and the completion of the substantive offense are two distinct criminal acts. The Court concluded,

> ... If [the overt act] can be supplied by the act of one conspirator, we fail to see why the same or other acts in furtherance of the conspiracy are likewise not attributable to the others for the purpose of holding them responsible for the substantive offense.

A different case would arise if the substantive offense committed by one of the conspirators was not in fact done in furtherance of the conspiracy, did not fall within the scope of the unlawful project, or was merely a part of the ramifications of the plan which could not be reasonably foreseen as a necessary or natural consequence of the unlawful agreement.

. . . The Nevada Legislature has not adopted the *Pinkerton* rule, but a number of states have addressed the issue by judicial decision. Several states have embraced the rule and permit defendants to be held liable for the criminal acts of a coconspirator so long as the crime was foreseeable and committed in furtherance of the conspiracy. Nonetheless, the *Pinkerton* rule has garnered significant disfavor. Concerns respecting the ramifications of the rule arose shortly after the opinion issued:

In the final analysis the *Pinkerton* decision extends the wide limits of the conspiracy doctrine to the breaking-point and opens the door to possible new abuses by over-zealous public prosecutors. While membership in a conspiracy may well be evidence for the jury's consideration in holding others than the direct actor guilty, it should not be sufficient, in the absence of some further showing of knowledge, acquiescence, aid or assistance, to convict one conspirator for another's criminal act.

. . . The drafters of the Model Penal Code have similarly rejected the *Pinkerton* view, commenting that the "law would lose all sense of just proportion" if by virtue of his crime of conspiracy a defendant was "held accountable for thousands of additional offenses of which he was completely unaware and which he did not influence at all."

The Washington Supreme Court has rejected *Pinkerton* as an inaccurate reflection of state law. A Washington criminal statute provides liability for criminal conspiracy but is silent respecting vicarious liability for coconspirators. The Washington court concluded that vicarious liability of coconspirators, if any, must be based on a state accomplice liability statute, which requires knowledge of the crime charged. Therefore, the court held that liability based on foreseeability alone is incompatible with its state law.

The Arizona Supreme Court has also rejected the *Pinkerton* rule, holding that conspiratorial liability does not extend to separate criminal acts of coconspirators when a particular coconspirator is not an accomplice or principal to those crimes, even though he may be guilty of conspiracy. That court noted that its holding "simply prevents a conspirator, who is not also an accomplice, from being held liable for a potentially limitless number of criminal acts which, though later determined to be 'foreseeable,' are at the time of their commission totally beyond the conspirator's knowledge and control." . . .

The natural and probable consequences doctrine under Nevada law

Nevada case law addressing the principles of conspiracy is limited to the following concepts. As we noted above, a conspiracy is generally defined as "an agreement between two or more persons for an unlawful purpose." "A person who knowingly does any act to further the object of a conspiracy, or otherwise participates therein, is criminally liable as a conspirator . . . ." "Evidence of a coordinated series of acts furthering the underlying offense is sufficient to infer the existence of an agreement and support a conspiracy conviction." "However, absent an agreement to cooperate in achieving the purpose of a conspiracy, mere knowledge of, acquiescence in, or approval of that purpose does not make one a party to conspiracy."

We have never expressly adopted the *Pinkerton* rule and our discussion of coconspirator liability has been limited. . . . In *McKinney v. Sheriff*, McKinney challenged the sufficiency of the evidence supporting an indictment for murder, which was committed during the course of a robbery. McKinney argued that he was unaware of and did not participate in the murder and thus there was no probable cause to support the murder charge. In rejecting his claim, this court stated that the fact that McKinney's cohorts deviated from their agreed-upon plan by committing the murder did not absolve McKinney of liability. "Where the purpose of the conspiracy is to commit a dangerous felony, each member runs the risk of having the venture end in homicide . . . . Hence each is guilty of murder if one of them commits homicide in the perpetration . . . of an agreed-upon robbery. . . ."

. . . [O]ur overarching concern in *Sharma* centered on the fact that the natural and probable consequences doctrine regarding accomplice liability permits a defendant to be convicted of a specific intent crime where he or she did not possess the statutory intent required for the offense. We are of the view that vicarious coconspirator liability for the specific intent crimes of another, based on the natural and probable consequences doctrine, presents the same problem addressed in *Sharma*, and we conclude that *Sharma's* rationale applies with equal force under the circumstances of the instant case. To convict Bolden of burglary and kidnapping, the State was required to prove under Nevada law that he had the specific intent to commit those offenses. Holding otherwise would allow the State to sidestep the statutory specific intent required to prove those offenses.

The overriding factor in our decision to reject the natural and probable consequences doctrine for coconspirator liability respecting specific intent crimes is the absence of a statutory basis for it. Our statutes lack a comprehensive statutory definition or explanation of coconspirator liability. Nevada distinguishes parties as principals or accessories and by statute outlines the criminal liability of both. NRS 195.010 classifies parties as principals and accessories. NRS 195.020 defines criminal liability as a principal:

> Every person concerned in the commission of a felony, gross misdemeanor or misdemeanor, whether he directly commits the act constituting the offense, or aids or abets in its commission, and whether present or absent; and every person who, directly or indirectly, counsels, encourages, hires, commands, induces or otherwise procures another to commit a felony, gross misdemeanor or misdemeanor is a principal, and shall be proceeded against and punished as such. The fact that the person aided, abetted, counseled, encouraged, hired, commanded, induced or procured, could not or did not entertain a criminal intent shall not be a defense to any person aiding, abetting, counseling, encouraging, hiring, commanding, inducing or procuring him.

Additionally, NRS 199.480 sets forth the penalties for conspiracy offenses. These statutes are silent respecting the parameters of coconspirator vicarious liability. . . .

In the absence of statutory authority providing otherwise, we conclude that a defendant may not be held criminally liable for the specific intent crime committed by a coconspirator simply because that crime was a natural and probable consequence of the object of the conspiracy. To prove a specific intent crime, the State must show that the defendant actually possessed the requisite statutory intent.

Although we refuse to adopt the natural and probable consequences doctrine in general, our decision is limited to vicarious coconspirator liability based on that doctrine for specific intent crimes only. The mental state required to commit a general intent crime does not raise the same concern as that necessary to commit a specific intent crime. General intent is "the intent to do that which the law prohibits. It is not necessary for the prosecution to prove that the defendant intended the precise harm or the precise result which eventuated." On the other hand, specific intent is "the intent to accomplish the precise act which the law prohibits." To hold a defendant criminally liable for a specific intent crime, Nevada requires proof that he possessed the state of mind required by the statutory definition of the crime. Although we affirm Bolden's conviction for the general intent crimes of home invasion and robbery, we conclude that in future prosecutions, vicarious coconspirator liability may be properly imposed for general intent crimes only when the crime in question was a "reasonably foreseeable consequence" of the object of the conspiracy. We caution the State that this court will not hesitate to revisit the doctrine's applicability to general intent crimes if it appears that the theory of liability is alleged for crimes too far removed and attenuated from the object of the conspiracy.

We conclude that the district court understandably but erroneously instructed the jury that Bolden could be found guilty of the specific intent crimes of burglary and first- and second-degree kidnapping as long as the commission of those offenses was a natural and probable consequence of the conspiracy, and even if Bolden never intended the commission of those crimes. We further conclude, however, that the error is applicable only with respect to Bolden's conviction of the specific intent crimes of burglary and kidnapping and does not require reversal of his conviction of the general intent crimes of home invasion and robbery. . . .

[Other points of error deleted.]

Conclusion

Although sufficient evidence supports Bolden's convictions for the specific intent offenses of burglary and kidnapping under the State's alternative theories of direct participation and aiding and abetting liability, we must reverse these convictions because under the particular facts of this case, the jury's general verdict precludes us from concluding with absolute certainty that the jury did not find Bolden guilty of these offenses based on the State's alleged theory of coconspirator liability. We affirm Bolden's remaining convictions. Accordingly, we affirm Bolden's conviction in part, reverse it in part, and remand this matter for further proceedings consistent with this opinion.

[Footnotes deleted.]

Cases Relating to Chapter 5

Offenses against Persons—Excluding Sex Offenses

WASHINGTON ET AL.

v.

GLUCKSBERG ET AL

SUPREME COURT OF THE UNITED STATES

ARGUED JANUARY 8, 1997; DECIDED JUNE 26, 1997

521 U.S. 702 (1997)

Chief Justice Rehnquist delivered the opinion of the Court.

The question presented in this case is whether Washington's prohibition against "caus[ing]" or "aid[ing]" a suicide offends the Fourteenth Amendment to the United States Constitution. We hold that it does not.

It has always been a crime to assist a suicide in the State of Washington. In 1854, Washington's first Territorial Legislature outlawed "assisting another in the commission of self-murder." Today, Washington law provides: "A person is guilty of promoting a suicide attempt when he knowingly causes or aids another person to attempt suicide." . . . "Promoting a suicide attempt" is a felony, punishable by up to five years' imprisonment and up to a $10,000 fine. . . . At the same time, Washington's Natural Death Act, enacted in 1979, states that the "withholding or withdrawal of life-sustaining treatment" at a patient's direction "shall not, for any purpose, constitute a suicide." . . .

Petitioners in this case are the State of Washington and its Attorney General. Respondents

Harold Glucksberg, M.D., Abigail Halperin, M. D., Thomas A. Preston, M.D., and Peter Shalit, M.D., are physicians who practice in Washington. These doctors occasionally treat terminally ill, suffering patients, and declare that they would assist these patients in ending their lives if not for Washington's assisted-suicide ban. In January 1994, respondents, along with three gravely ill, pseudonymous plaintiffs who have since died and Compassion in Dying, a nonprofit organization that counsels people considering physician-assisted suicide, sued in the United States District Court, seeking a declaration that Wash. Rev. Code § 9A.36.060(1) (1994) is, on its face, unconstitutional. . . .

The plaintiffs asserted "the existence of a liberty interest protected by the Fourteenth Amendment which extends to a personal choice by a mentally competent, terminally ill adult to commit physician-assisted suicide." Relying primarily on *Planned Parenthood of Southeastern Pa. v. Casey,* 505 U. S. 833 (1992), and *Cruzan v. Director, Mo. Dept. of Health,* 497 U. S. 261 (1990), the District Court agreed, . . . and concluded that Washington's assisted-suicide ban is unconstitutional because it "places an undue burden on the exercise of [that] constitutionally protected liberty interest." . . . The District Court also decided that the Washington statute violated the Equal Protection Clause's requirement that "'all persons similarly situated . . . be treated alike.'" . . .

A panel of the Court of Appeals for the Ninth Circuit reversed, emphasizing that "[i]n the two hundred and five years of our existence no constitutional right to aid in killing oneself has ever been asserted and upheld by a court of final jurisdiction." . . . The Ninth Circuit reheard the case en banc, reversed the panel's decision, and affirmed the District Court. . . . Like the District Court, the en banc Court of Appeals emphasized our *Casey* and *Cruzan* decisions. . . . The court also discussed what it described as "historical" and "current societal attitudes" toward suicide and assisted suicide, and concluded that "the Constitution encompasses a due process liberty interest in controlling the time and manner of one's death— that there is, in short, a constitutionally-recognized 'right to die.'" After "[w]eighing and then balancing" this interest against Washington's various interests, the court held that the State's assisted-suicide ban was unconstitutional "as applied to terminally ill competent adults who wish to hasten their deaths with medication prescribed by their physicians." . . . The court did not reach the District Court's equal protection holding. . . . We granted certiorari, and now reverse.

We begin, as we do in all due process cases, by examining our Nation's history, legal traditions, and practices. . . . The States' assisted-suicide bans are not innovations. Rather, they are long-standing expressions of the States' commitment to the protection and preservation of all human life. . . . Moreover, the majority of States in this country have laws imposing criminal penalties on one who assists another to commit suicide . . . .

More specifically, for over 700 years, the Anglo-American common-law tradition has punished or otherwise disapproved of both suicide and assisting suicide . . . In the 13th century, Henry de Bracton, one of the first legal-treatise writers, observed that "[j]ust as a man may commit felony by slaying another so may he do so by slaying himself." . . . The real and personal property of one who killed himself to avoid conviction and punishment for a crime were forfeit to the King; however, thought Bracton, "if a man slays himself in weariness of life or because he is unwilling to endure further bodily pain . . . [only] his movable goods [were] confiscated." . . . Thus, "[t]he principle that suicide of a sane person, for whatever reason, was a punishable felony was . . . introduced into English common law." Centuries later, Sir William Blackstone, whose Commentaries on the Laws of England not only provided a definitive summary of the common law but was also a primary legal authority for 18th- and 19th-century American lawyers, referred to suicide as "self-murder" and

"the pretended heroism, but real cowardice, of the Stoic philosophers, who destroyed themselves to avoid those ills which they had not the fortitude to endure . . . ." . . . . *[some discussion omitted]*

For the most part, the early American Colonies adopted the common-law approach. . . . .

Over time, however, the American Colonies abolished these harsh common-law penalties. William Penn abandoned the criminal-forfeiture sanction in Pennsylvania in 1701, and the other Colonies (and later, the other States) eventually followed this example. . . .

That suicide remained a grievous, though non-felonious, wrong is confirmed by the fact that colonial and early state legislatures and courts did not retreat from prohibiting assisting suicide. Swift, in his early 19th-century treatise on the laws of Connecticut, stated that "[i]f one counsels another to commit suicide, and the other by reason of the advice kills himself, the advisor is guilty of murder as principal." . . . This was the well-established common-law view, . . .

The earliest American statute explicitly to outlaw assisting suicide was enacted in New York in 1828, . . . and many of the new States and Territories followed New York's example. . . . By the time the Fourteenth Amendment was ratified, it was a crime in most States to assist a suicide. . . .

Though deeply rooted, the States' assisted-suicide bans have in recent years been reexamined and, generally, reaffirmed. Because of advances in medicine and technology, Americans today are increasingly likely to die in institutions, from chronic illnesses. . . . Public concern and democratic action are therefore sharply focused on how best to protect dignity and independence at the end of life, with the result that there have been many significant changes in state laws and in the attitudes these laws reflect. Many States, for example, now permit "living wills," surrogate health-care decisionmaking, and the withdrawal or refusal of life-sustaining medical treatment. . . . At the same time, however, voters and legislators continue for the most part to reaffirm their States' prohibitions on assisting suicide.

The Washington statute at issue in this case, . . . was enacted in 1975 as part of a revision of that State's criminal code. Four years later, Washington passed its Natural Death Act, which specifically stated that the "withholding or withdrawal of life-sustaining treatment . . . shall not, for any purpose, constitute a suicide" and that "[n]othing in this chapter shall be construed to condone, authorize, or approve mercy killing . . . ." . . . In 1991, Washington voters rejected a ballot initiative which, had it passed, would have permitted a form of physician assisted suicide. Washington then added a provision to the Natural Death Act expressly excluding physician-assisted suicide. . . .

California voters rejected an assisted-suicide initiative similar to Washington's in 1993. On the other hand, in 1994, voters in Oregon enacted, also through ballot initiative, that state's "Death With Dignity Act," which legalized physician-assisted suicide for competent, terminally ill adults. Since the Oregon vote, many proposals to legalize assisted-suicide have been and continue to be introduced in the States' legislatures, but none has been enacted. And just last year, Iowa and Rhode Island joined the overwhelming majority of states explicitly prohibiting assisted suicide. . . . Also, on April 30, 1997, President Clinton signed the Federal Assisted Suicide Funding Restriction Act of 1997, which prohibits the use of federal funds in support of physician-assisted suicide. . . . *[some discussion omitted]*

Thus, the States are currently engaged in serious, thoughtful examinations of physician-assisted suicide and other similar issues. . . . *[some discussion omitted]*

Attitudes toward suicide itself have changed since Bracton, but our laws have consistently condemned, and continue to prohibit, assisting suicide. Despite changes in medical technology and notwithstanding an increased emphasis on the importance of end-of-life decisionmaking, we have not retreated from this prohibition. Against this backdrop of history, tradition, and practice, we now turn to respondents' constitutional claim.

The Due Process Clause guarantees more than fair process, and the "liberty" it protects includes more than the absence of physical restraint. . . . The Clause also provides heightened protection against government interference with certain fundamental rights and liberty interests. . . . In a long line of cases, we have held that, in addition to the specific freedoms protected by the Bill of Rights, the "liberty" specially protected by the Due Process Clause includes the rights to marry; to have children; to direct the education and upbringing of one's children; to marital privacy; to use contraception; to bodily integrity, and to abortion. We have also assumed, and strongly suggested, that the Due Process Clause protects the traditional right to refuse unwanted life saving medical treatment.

But we "ha[ve] always been reluctant to expand the concept of substantive due process because guide posts for responsible decision making in this unchartered area are scarce and open-ended." . . . By extending constitutional protection to an asserted right or liberty interest, we, to a great extent, place the matter outside the arena of public debate and legislative action. We must therefore "exercise the utmost care whenever we are asked to break new ground in this field," . . . , lest the liberty protected by the Due Process Clause be subtly transformed into the policy preferences of the Members of this Court, ...

Our established method of substantive-due-process analysis has two primary features: First, we have regularly observed that the Due Process Clause specially protects those fundamental rights and liberties which are, objectively, "deeply rooted in this Nation's history and tradition," . . . . Second, we have required in substantive-due-process cases a "careful description" of the asserted fundamental liberty interest. . . . . Our Nation's history, legal traditions, and practices thus provide the crucial "guide posts for responsible decisionmaking," that direct and restrain our exposition of the Due Process Clause. As we stated recently in *Flores,* the Fourteenth Amendment "forbids the government to infringe . . . 'fundamental' liberty interests *at all,* no matter what process is provided, unless the infringement is narrowly tailored to serve a compelling state interest." . . .

Justice Souter, relying on Justice Harlan's dissenting opinion . . . would largely abandon this restrained methodology, and instead ask "whether [Washington's] statute sets up one of those 'arbitrary impositions' or 'purposeless restraints' at odds with the Due Process Clause of the Fourteenth Amendment," . . . In our view, however, the development of this Court's substantive-due-process jurisprudence, . . . has been a process whereby the outlines of the "liberty" specially protected by the Fourteenth Amendment—never fully clarified, to be sure, and perhaps not capable of being fully clarified—have at least been carefully refined by concrete examples involving fundamental rights found to be deeply rooted in our legal tradition. This approach tends to rein in the subjective elements that are necessarily present in due process judicial review. In addition, by establishing a threshold requirement—that a challenged state action implicate a fundamental right—before requiring more than a reasonable relation to a legitimate state interest to justify the action, it avoids the need for complex balancing of competing interests in every case.

Turning to the claim at issue here, the Court of Appeals stated that "[p]roperly analyzed, the first issue to be resolved is whether there is a liberty interest in determining the time and manner of one's death," or, in other words, "[i]s there a right to die?," Similarly, respondents assert a "liberty to choose how to die" and a right to "control of one's final days," and describe the asserted liberty as "the right to choose a humane, dignified death," and "the liberty to shape death," As noted above, we have a tradition of carefully formulating the interest at stake in substantive due-process cases. For example, although *Cruzan* is often described as a "right to die" case, . . . we were, in fact, more precise: We assumed that the Constitution granted competent persons a "constitutionally protected right to refuse lifesaving hydration and nutrition." . . . The Washington statute at issue in this case prohibits "aid[ing] another person to attempt suicide," . . . , and, thus, the question before us is whether the "liberty" specially protected by the Due Process Clause includes a right to commit suicide which itself includes a right to assistance in doing so.

We now inquire whether this asserted right has any place in our Nation's traditions. Here, . . . we are confronted with a consistent and almost universal tradition that has long rejected the asserted right, and continues explicitly to reject it today, even for terminally ill, mentally competent adults. To hold for respondents, we would have to reverse centuries of legal doctrine and practice, and strike down the considered policy choice of almost every State. . . .

Respondents contend, however, that the liberty interest they assert *is* consistent with this Court's substantive-due process line of cases, if not with this Nation's history and practice. Pointing to *Casey* and *Cruzan,* respondents read our jurisprudence in this area as reflecting a general tradition of "self-sovereignty," . . . and as teaching that the "liberty" protected by the Due Process Clause includes "basic and intimate exercises of personal autonomy," . . . According to respondents, our liberty jurisprudence, and the broad, individualistic principles it reflects, protects the "liberty of competent, terminally ill adults to make end-of-life decisions free of undue government interference." . . . The question presented in this case, however, is whether the protections of the Due Process Clause include a right to commit suicide with another's assistance. With this "careful description" of respondents' claim in mind, we turn to *Casey* and *Cruzan.*

In *Cruzan,* we considered whether Nancy Beth Cruzan, who had been severely injured in an automobile accident and was in a persistive vegetative state, "ha[d] a right under the United States Constitution which would require the hospital to withdraw life-sustaining treatment" at her parents' request. . . . We began with the observation that "[a]t common law, even the touching of one person by another without consent and without legal justification was a battery." We then discussed the related rule that "informed consent is generally required for medical treatment." After reviewing a long line of relevant state cases, we concluded that "the common-law doctrine of informed consent is viewed as generally encompassing the right of a competent individual to refuse medical treatment." Next, we reviewed our own cases on the subject, and stated that "[t]he principle that a competent person has a constitutionally protected liberty interest in refusing unwanted medical treatment may be inferred from our prior decisions." Therefore, "for purposes of [that] case, we assume[d] that the United States Constitution would grant a competent person a constitutionally protected right to refuse life saving hydration and nutrition." . . . . We concluded that, notwithstanding this right, the Constitution permitted Missouri to require clear and convincing evidence of an incompetent patient's wishes concerning the withdrawal of life-sustaining treatment. . . .

. . . [some discussion omitted]

The right assumed in *Cruzan,* however, was not simply deduced from abstract concepts of personal autonomy. Given the common-law rule that forced medication was a battery, and the long legal tradition protecting the decision to refuse unwanted medical treatment, our assumption was entirely consistent with this Nation's history and constitutional traditions. The decision to commit suicide with the assistance of another may be just as personal and profound as the decision to refuse unwanted medical treatment, but it has never enjoyed similar legal protection. Indeed, the two acts are widely and reasonably regarded as quite distinct. . . .

Respondents also rely on *Casey*. There, the Court's opinion concluded that "the essential holding of *Roe v. Wade*. . . should be retained and once again reaffirmed." . . . We held, first, that a woman has a right, before her fetus is viable, to an abortion "without undue interference from the State"; second, that States may restrict post viability abortions, so long as exceptions are made to protect a woman's life and health; and third, that the State has legitimate interests throughout a pregnancy in protecting the health of the woman and the life of the unborn child. In reaching this conclusion, the opinion discussed in some detail this Court's substantive-due-process tradition of interpreting the Due Process Clause to protect certain fundamental rights and "personal decisions relating to marriage, procreation, contraception, family relationships, child rearing, and education," and noted that many of those rights and liberties "involv[e] the most intimate and personal choices a person may make in a lifetime." . . .

. . . *[some discussion omitted]*

By choosing this language, the Court's opinion in *Casey* described, in a general way and in light of our prior cases, those personal activities and decisions that this Court has identified as so deeply rooted in our history and traditions, or so fundamental to our concept of constitutionally ordered liberty, that they are protected by the Fourteenth Amendment. . . . That many of the rights and liberties protected by the Due Process Clause sound in personal autonomy does not warrant the sweeping conclusion that any and all important, intimate, and personal decisions are so protected, . . . and *Casey* did not suggest otherwise.

The history of the law's treatment of assisted suicide in this country has been and continues to be one of the rejection of nearly all efforts to permit it. That being the case, our decisions lead us to conclude that the asserted "right" to assistance in committing suicide is not a fundamental liberty interest protected by the Due Process Clause. . . .

[Paragraphs describing the state's interest in protecting life omitted.]

The State also has an interest in protecting the integrity and ethics of the medical profession. . . . the American Medical Association, like many other medical and physicians' groups, has concluded that "[p]hysician-assisted suicide is fundamentally incompatible with the physician's role as healer." . . .

Next, the State has an interest in protecting vulnerable groups—including the poor, the elderly, and disabled persons—from abuse, neglect, and mistakes. . . . We have recognized, however, the real risk of subtle coercion and undue influence in end-of-life situations. . . .

. . . The State's assisted-suicide ban reflects and reinforces its policy that the lives of terminally ill, disabled, and elderly people must be no less valued than the lives of the young and healthy, and that a seriously disabled person's suicidal impulses should be interpreted and treated the same way as anyone else's. . . .

Finally, the State may fear that permitting assisted suicide will start it down the path to voluntary and perhaps even involuntary euthanasia. . . . it turns out that what is couched as a limited right to "physician-assisted suicide" is likely, in effect, a much broader license, which could prove extremely difficult to police and contain. Washington's ban on assisting suicide prevents such erosion.

. . . *[some discussion omitted]*

We need not weigh exactly the relative strengths of these various interests. They are unquestionably important and legitimate, and Washington's ban on assisted suicide is at least reasonably related to their promotion and protection. We therefore hold that Wash. Rev. Code § 9A.36.060(1) (1994) does not violate the Fourteenth Amendment, either on its face or "as applied to competent, terminally ill adults who wish to hasten their deaths by obtaining medication prescribed by their doctors." . . .

Throughout the Nation, Americans are engaged in an earnest and profound debate about the morality, legality, and practicality of physician-assisted suicide. Our holding permits this debate to continue, as it should in a democratic society. The decision of the en banc Court of Appeals is reversed, and the case is remanded for further proceedings consistent with this opinion.

It is so ordered.

[Concurring and dissenting opinions omitted. Footnotes and citations omitted.]

TISON
v.
ARIZONA

ARGUED NOVEMBER 3, 1986; DECIDED APRIL 21, 1987

481 U.S. 137 (1987)

JUSTICE O'CONNOR delivered the opinion of the Court.

The question presented is whether the petitioners' participation in the events leading up to and following the murder of four members of a family makes the sentences of death imposed by the Arizona courts constitutionally permissible although neither petitioner specifically intended to kill the victims and neither inflicted the fatal gunshot wounds. We hold that the Arizona Supreme Court applied an erroneous standard in making the findings required by *Enmund v. Florida*, 458 U. S. 782 (1982), and, therefore, vacate the judgments below and remand the case for further proceedings not inconsistent with this opinion.

Gary Tison was sentenced to life imprisonment as the result of a prison escape during the course of which he had killed a guard. After he had been in prison a number of years, Gary Tison's wife, their three sons Donald, Ricky, and Raymond, Gary's brother Joseph, and other relatives made plans to help Gary Tison escape again. . . . The Tison family assembled a large arsenal of weapons for this purpose. Plans for escape *were* discussed with Gary Tison, who insisted that his cellmate, Randy Greenawalt, also a convicted murderer, be included in the prison break. The following facts are largely evidenced by petitioners' detailed confessions given as part of a plea bargain according to the terms of which the State agreed not to seek the death sentence. The Arizona courts interpreted the plea agreement to require that petitioners testify to the planning stages of the breakout. When they refused to do so, the bargain was rescinded and they *were* tried, convicted, and sentenced to death.

On July 30, 1978, the three Tison brothers entered the Arizona State Prison at Florence carrying a large ice chest filled with guns. The Tisons armed Greenawalt and their father, and the group, brandishing their weapons, locked the prison guards and visitors present in a storage closet. The five men fled the prison grounds in the Tisons' Ford Galaxy automobile. No shots were fired at the prison.

After leaving the prison, the men abandoned the Ford automobile and proceeded on to an isolated house in a white Lincoln automobile that the brothers had parked at a hospital near the prison. At the house, the Lincoln automobile had a flat tire; the only spare tire was pressed into service. After two nights at the house, the group drove toward Flagstaff. As the group traveled on back roads and secondary highways through the desert, another tire blew out. The group decided to flag down a passing motorist and steal a car. Raymond stood out in front of the Lincoln; the other four armed themselves and lay in wait by the side of the road. One car passed by without stopping, but a second car, a Mazda occupied by John Lyons, his wife Donnelda, his 2-year-old son, Christopher, and his 15-year-old niece, Theresa Tyson, pulled over to render aid.

As Raymond showed John Lyons the flat tire on the Lincoln, the other Tisons and Greenawalt emerged. The Lyons family was forced into the backseat of the Lincoln. Raymond and Donald drove the Lincoln down a dirt road off the highway and then down a gas line service road farther into the desert; Gary Tison, Ricky Tison, and Randy Greenawalt followed in the Lyons' Mazda. The two cars were parked trunk to trunk and the Lyons family was ordered to stand in front of the Lincoln's headlights. The Tisons transferred their belongings from the Lincoln into the Mazda. They discovered guns and money in the Mazda which they kept, and they put the rest of the Lyons' possessions in the Lincoln.

Gary Tison then told Raymond to drive the Lincoln still farther into the desert. Raymond did so, and, while the others guarded the Lyons and Theresa Tyson, Gary fired his shotgun into the radiator, presumably to completely disable the vehicle. The Lyons and Theresa Tyson were then escorted to the Lincoln and again ordered to stand in its headlights. Ricky Tison reported that John Lyons begged, in comments "more or less directed at everybody," "Jesus, don't kill me." Gary Tison said he was "thinking about it." John Lyons asked the Tisons and Greenawalt to "[g]ive us some water - . . . just leave us out here, and you all go home." Gary Tison then told his sons to go back to the Mazda and get some water. Raymond later explained that his father "was like in conflict with himself . . . . What it was, I think it was the baby being there and all this, and he wasn't sure about what to do."

The petitioners' statements diverge to some extent, but it appears that both of them went back towards the Mazda, along with Donald, while Randy Greenawalt and Gary Tison stayed at the Lincoln guarding the victims. Raymond recalled being at the Mazda filling the water jug "when we started hearing the shots." Ricky said that the brothers gave the water jug to Gary Tison who then, with Randy Greenawalt went behind the Lincoln, where they spoke briefly, then raised the shotguns and started firing. In any event, petitioners agree they saw Greenawalt and their father brutally murder their four captives with repeated blasts from their shotguns. Neither made an effort to help the victims, though both later stated they were surprised by the shooting. The Tisons got into the Mazda and drove away, continuing their flight. Physical evidence suggested that Theresa Tyson managed to crawl away from the bloodbath, severely injured. She died in the desert after the Tisons left.

Several days later the Tisons and Greenawalt were apprehended after a shootout at a police roadblock. Donald Tison was killed. Gary Tison escaped into the desert where he subsequently died of exposure. Raymond and Ricky Tison and Randy Greenawalt were captured and tried jointly for the crimes associated with the prison break itself and the shootout at the roadblock; each was convicted and sentenced.

The State then individually tried each of the petitioners for capital murder of the four victims as well as for the associated crimes of armed robbery, kidnapping, and car theft. The capital murder charges were based on Arizona felony-murder law providing that a killing occurring during the perpetration of robbery or kidnapping is capital murder, . . . , and that each participant in the kidnapping or robbery is legally responsible for the acts of his accomplices. . . . Each of the petitioners was convicted of the four murders under these accomplice liability and felony-murder statutes.

Arizona law also provided for a capital sentencing proceeding, to be conducted without a jury, to determine whether the crime was sufficiently aggravated to warrant the death sentence. . . . The statute set out six aggravating and four mitigating factors. . . . The judge found three statutory aggravating factors:

(1) the Tisons had created a grave risk of death to others (not the victims);
(2) the murders had been committed for pecuniary gain;
(3) the murders were especially heinous.

The judge found *no* statutory mitigating factor. Importantly, the judge specifically found that the crime was *not* mitigated by the fact that each of the petitioners' "participation was relatively minor." . . . . Rather, he found that the "participation of each [petitioner] in the crimes giving rise to the application of the felony murder rule in this case was very substantial." . . . The trial judge also specifically found, that each "could reasonably have foreseen that his conduct . . . would cause or create a grave risk of . . . death." . . . He did find, however, three non-statutory mitigating factors:

(1) the petitioners' youth—Ricky was 20 and Raymond was 19;
(2) neither had prior felony records;
(3) each had been convicted of the murders under the felony-murder rule.

Nevertheless, the judge sentenced both petitioners to death.

On direct appeal, the Arizona Supreme Court affirmed. . . .

Petitioners then collaterally attacked their death sentences in state postconviction proceedings alleging that *Enmund v. Florida*, 458 U. S. 782 (1982), which had been decided in the interim, required reversal. A divided Arizona Supreme Court, interpreting *Enmund* to require a finding of "intent to kill," declared in Raymond Tison's case "the dictate of *Enmund* is satisfied," writing:

"Intend *[sic]* to kill includes the situation in which the defendant intended, contemplated, or anticipated that lethal force would or might be used or that life would or might be taken in accomplishing the underlying felony. . . .

[citing the Arizona Supreme Court]"In the present case the evidence does not show that petitioner killed or attempted to kill. The evidence does demonstrate beyond a reasonable doubt, however, that petitioner intended to kill. Petitioner played an active part in preparing the breakout, including obtaining a getaway car and various weapons. At the breakout scene itself, petitioner played a crucial role by, among other things, holding a gun on prison guards. Petitioner knew that Gary Tison's murder conviction arose out of the killing of a guard during an earlier prison escape attempt. Thus petitioner could anticipate the use of lethal force during this attempt to flee confinement; in fact, he later said that during the escape he would have been willing personally to kill in a 'very close life or death situation,' and that he recognized that after the escape there was a possibility of killings."

. . . *[some discussion omitted]*

"From these facts we conclude that petitioner intended to kill . . . ."

In Ricky Tison's case the Arizona Supreme Court relied on a similar recitation of facts to find intent. . . .

In *Enmund v. Florida,* this Court reversed the death sentence of a defendant convicted under Florida's felony-murder rule. Enmund was the driver of the "getaway" car in an armed robbery of a dwelling. The occupants of the house, an elderly couple, resisted and Enmund's accomplices killed them. The Florida Supreme Court found the inference that Enmund was the person in the car by the side of the road waiting to help his accomplices escape sufficient to support his sentence of death:

. . . *[some discussion omitted]*

This Court, citing the weight of legislative and community opinion, found a broad societal consensus, with which it agreed, that the death penalty was disproportional to the crime of robbery-felony murder "in these circumstances." . . .

. . . Furthermore, the Court found that Enmund's degree of participation in *the murders* was so tangential that it could not be said to justify a sentence of death. It found that neither the deterrent nor the retributive purposes of the death penalty were advanced by imposing the death penalty upon Enmund. The *Enmund* Court was unconvinced "that the threat that the death penalty will be imposed for murder will measurably deter

one who does not kill and has no intention or purpose that life will be taken." . . .

That difference was also related to the second purpose of capital punishment, retribution. . . . Thus, in Enmund's case, "the focus [had to] be on *his* culpability, not on that of those who committed the robbery and shot the victims, for we insist on 'individualized consideration as a constitutional requirement in imposing the death sentence.'" . . .

. . . *[some discussion omitted]*

Petitioners argue strenuously that they did not "intend to kill" as that concept has been generally understood in the common law. We accept this as true. Traditionally, "one intends certain consequences when he desires that his acts cause those consequences or knows that those consequences are substantially certain to result from his acts." . . . As petitioners point out, there is no evidence that either Ricky or Raymond Tison took any act which he desired to, or was substantially certain would, cause death.

. . . *[some discussion omitted]*

This definition of intent is broader than that described by the *Enmund* Court. Participants in violent felonies like armed robberies can frequently "anticipat[e] that lethal force . . . might be used . . . in accomplishing the underlying felony." Enmund himself may well have so anticipated. Indeed, the possibility of bloodshed is inherent in the commission of any violent felony and this possibility is generally foreseeable and foreseen; it is one principal reason that felons arm themselves. The Arizona Supreme Court's attempted reformulation of intent to kill amounts to little more than a restatement of the felony-murder rule itself. Petitioners do not fall within the "intent to kill" category of felony murderers for which *Enmund* explicitly finds the death penalty permissible under the Eighth Amendment.

On the other hand, it is equally clear that petitioners also fall outside the category of felony murderers for whom *Enmund* explicitly held the death penalty disproportional: their degree of participation in the crimes was major rather than minor, and the record would support a finding of the culpable mental state of reckless indifference to human life.

. . . *[some discussion omitted]*

These facts not only indicate that the Tison brothers' participation in the crime was anything but minor; they also would clearly support a finding that they both subjectively appreciated that their acts were likely to result in the taking of innocent life. The issue raised by this case is whether the Eighth Amendment prohibits the death penalty in the intermediate case of the defendant whose participation is major and whose mental state is one of reckless indifference to the value of human life. *Enmund* does not specifically address this point. We now take up the task of determining whether the Eighth Amendment proportionality requirement bars the death penalty under these circumstances.

. . . [some discussion omitted]

A critical facet of the individualized determination of culpability required in capital cases is the mental state with which the defendant commits the crime. Deeply ingrained in our legal tradition is the idea that the more purposeful is the criminal conduct, the more serious is the offense, and, therefore, the more severely it ought to be punished. The ancient concept of malice aforethought was an early attempt to focus on mental state in order to distinguish those who deserved death from those who through "Benefit of . . . Clergy" would be spared. . . . In *Enmund v. Florida,* the Court recognized again the importance of mental state, explicitly permitting the death penalty in at least those cases where the felony murderer intended to kill and forbidding it in the case of a minor actor not shown to have had any culpable mental state.

A narrow focus on the question of whether or not a given defendant "intended to kill," however, is a highly unsatisfactory means of definitively distinguishing the most culpable and dangerous of murderers. Many who intend to, and do, kill are not criminally liable at all—those who act in self defense or with other justification or excuse. Other intentional homicides, though criminal, are often felt undeserving of the death penalty—those that are the result of provocation. On the other hand, some nonintentional murderers may be among the most dangerous and inhumane of all—the person who tortures another not caring whether the victim lives or dies, or the robber who shoots someone in the course of the robbery, utterly indifferent to the fact that the desire to rob may have the unintended consequence of killing the victim as well as taking the victim's property. This reckless indifference to the value of human life may be every bit as shocking to the moral sense as an "intent to kill." Indeed it is for this very reason that the common law and modern criminal codes alike have classified behavior such as occurred in this case along with intentional murders. . . . For example, the Model Penal Code treats reckless killing, 'manifesting extreme indifference to the value of human life,' as equivalent to purposeful and knowing killing"). *Enmund* held that when "intent to kill" results in its logical though not inevitable consequence—the taking of human life—the Eighth Amendment permits the State to exact the death penalty after a careful weighing of the aggravating and mitigating circumstances. Similarly, we hold that the reckless disregard for human life implicit in knowingly engaging in criminal activities known to carry a grave risk of death represents a highly culpable mental state, a mental state that may be taken into account in making a capital sentencing judgment when that conduct causes its natural, though also not inevitable, lethal result.

The petitioners' own personal involvement in the crimes was not minor, but rather, as specifically found by the trial court, "substantial." Far from merely sitting in a car away from the actual scene of the murders acting as the getaway driver to a robbery, each petitioner was actively involved in every element of the kidnaping-robbery and was physically present during the entire sequence of criminal activity culminating in the murder of the Lyons family and the subsequent flight. The Tisons' high level of participation in these crimes further implicates them in the resulting deaths. Accordingly, they fall well within the overlapping second intermediate position which focuses on the defendant's degree of participation in the felony.

Only a small minority of those jurisdictions imposing capital punishment for felony murder have rejected the possibility of a capital sentence absent an intent to kill, and we do not find this minority position constitutionally required. We will not attempt to precisely delineate the particular types of conduct and states of mind warranting imposition of the death penalty here. Rather, we simply hold that major participation in the felony committed, combined with reckless indifference to human life, is sufficient to satisfy the *Enmund* culpability requirement. The Arizona courts have clearly found that the former exists; we now vacate the judgments below and remand for determination of the latter in further proceedings not inconsistent with this opinion.

It is so ordered.

[Concurring and dissenting opinions omitted. Footnotes and citations omitted.]

Cases Relating to Chapter 6

Offenses against Persons—Sex Related

JOHN GEDDES LAWRENCE
AND TYRON GARNER
v.
TEXAS

COURT OF APPEALS OF TEXAS

539 U.S. 558 (2003)

Justice Kennedy delivered the opinion of the Court.

Liberty protects the person from unwarranted government intrusions into a dwelling or other private places. In our tradition the State is not omnipresent in the home. And there are other spheres of our lives and existence, outside the home, where the State should not be a dominant presence. Freedom extends beyond spatial bounds. Liberty presumes an autonomy of self that includes freedom of thought, belief, expression, and certain intimate conduct. The instant case involves liberty of the person both in its spatial and more transcendent dimensions.

I

The question before the Court is the validity of a Texas statute making it a crime for two persons of the same sex to engage in certain intimate sexual conduct.

In Houston, Texas, officers of the Harris County Police Department were dispatched to a private residence in response to a reported weapons disturbance. They entered an apartment where one of the petitioners, John Geddes Lawrence resided. The right of the police to enter does not seem to have been questioned. The officers observed Lawrence and another man, Tyron Garner, engaging in a sexual act. The two petitioners were arrested, held in custody over night, and charged and convicted before a Justice of the Peace.

The complaints described their crime as "deviate sexual intercourse, namely anal sex, with a member of the same sex (man).". . . . The applicable state law is Tex. Penal Code Ann. § 21.06(a) (2003). It provides: "A person commits an offense if he engages in deviate sexual intercourse with another individual of the same sex." The statute defines "deviate sexual intercourse" as follows:

(A) "any contact between any part of the genitals of one person and the mouth or anus of another person; or
(B) "the penetration of the genitals or the anus of another person with an object." § 21.01(1).

The petitioners exercised their right to a trial *de novo* in Harris County Criminal Court. They challenged the statute as a violation of the Equal Protection Clause of the Fourteenth Amendment and of a like provision of the Texas Constitution. Tex. Const., Art. 1, § 3a. Those contentions were rejected. The petitioners, having entered a plea of *nolo contendere*, were each fined $200 and assessed court costs of $141.25. . . .

The Court of Appeals for the Texas Fourteenth District considered the petitioners' federal constitutional arguments under both the Equal Protection and Due Process Clauses of the Fourteenth Amendment. After hearing the case *en banc* the court, in a divided opinion, rejected the constitutional arguments and affirmed the convictions. . . . The majority opinion indicates that the Court of Appeals considered our decision in *Bowers v. Hardwick*, . . . (1986), to be controlling on the federal due process aspect of the case. *Bowers* then being authoritative, this was proper.

We granted certiorari, . . . to consider three questions:

1. "Whether Petitioners' criminal convictions under the Texas "Homosexual Conduct" law—which criminalizes sexual intimacy by same-sex couples, but not identical behavior by different-sex couples—violate the Fourteenth Amendment guarantee of equal protection of laws?
2. "Whether Petitioners' criminal convictions for adult consensual sexual intimacy in the home violate their vital interests in liberty and privacy protected by the Due Process Clause of the Fourteenth Amendment?
3. "Whether *Bowers v. Hardwick*, . . . , should be overruled?" . . .

The petitioners were adults at the time of the alleged offense. Their conduct was in private and consensual.

II

We conclude the case should be resolved by determining whether the petitioners were free as adults to engage in the private conduct in the exercise of their liberty under the Due Process Clause of the Fourteenth Amendment to the Constitution. For this inquiry we deem it necessary to reconsider the Court's holding in *Bowers*.

There are broad statements of the substantive reach of liberty under the Due Process Clause in earlier cases, including *Pierce v. Society of Sisters*, . . . (1925), and *Meyer v. Nebraska*, . . . (1923); but the most pertinent beginning point is our decision in *Griswold v. Connecticut*, . . . (1965).

In *Griswold* the Court invalidated a state law prohibiting the use of drugs or devices of contraception and counseling or aiding and abetting the use of contraceptives. The Court described the protected interest as a right to privacy and placed emphasis on the marriage relation and the protected space of the marital bedroom. . . .

After *Griswold* it was established that the right to make certain decisions regarding sexual conduct extends beyond the marital relationship. In *Eisenstadt v. Baird*, . . . (1972), the Court invalidated a law prohibiting the distribution of contraceptives to unmarried persons. The case was decided under the Equal Protection Clause, . . . ; but with respect to unmarried persons, the Court went on to state the fundamental proposition that the law impaired the exercise of their personal rights. . . . It quoted from the statement of the Court of Appeals finding the law to be in conflict with fundamental human rights, and it followed with this statement of its own:

> "It is true that in *Griswold* the right of privacy in question inhered in the marital relationship. . . . If the right of privacy means anything, it is the right of the *individual*, married or single, to be free from unwarranted governmental intrusion into matters so fundamentally affecting a person as the decision whether to bear or beget a child." . . .

The opinions in *Griswold* and *Eisenstadt* were part of the background for the decision in *Roe v. Wade*, . . . (1973). As is well known, the case involved a challenge to the Texas law prohibiting abortions, but the laws of other States were affected as well. Although the Court held the woman's rights were not absolute, her right to elect an abortion did have real and substantial protection as an exercise of her liberty under the Due Process Clause. The Court cited cases that protect spatial freedom and cases that go well beyond it. *Roe* recognized the right of a woman to make certain fundamental decisions affecting her destiny and confirmed once more that the protection of liberty under the Due Process Clause has a substantive dimension of fundamental significance in defining the rights of the person.

In *Carey v. Population Services Int'l*, . . . (1977), the Court confronted a New York law forbidding sale or distribution of contraceptive devices to persons under 16 years of age. Although there was no single opinion for the Court, the law was invalidated. Both *Eisenstadt* and *Carey*, as well as the holding and rationale in *Roe*, confirmed that the reasoning of *Griswold* could not be confined to the protection of rights of married adults. This was the state of the law with respect to some of the most relevant cases when the Court considered *Bowers* v *Hardwick.*

The facts in *Bowers* had some similarities to the instant case. A police officer, whose right to enter seems not to have been in question, observed Hardwick, in his own bedroom, engaging in intimate sexual conduct with another adult male. The conduct was in violation of a Georgia statute making it a criminal offense to engage in sodomy. One difference between the two cases is that the Georgia statute prohibited the conduct whether or not the participants were of the same sex, while the Texas statute, as we have seen, applies only to participants of the same sex. Hardwick was not prosecuted, but he brought an action in federal court to declare the state statute invalid. He alleged he was a practicing homosexual and that the criminal prohibition violated rights guaranteed to him by the Constitution. The Court, in an opinion by Justice White, sustained the Georgia law. Chief Justice Burger and Justice Powell joined the opinion of the Court and filed separate, concurring opinions. Four Justices dissented. . . .

The Court began its substantive discussion in *Bowers* as follows: "The issue presented is whether the Federal Constitution confers a fundamental right upon homosexuals to engage in sodomy and hence invalidates the laws of the many States that still make such conduct illegal and have done so for a very long time.". . . . That statement, we now conclude, discloses the Court's own failure to appreciate the extent of the liberty at stake. To say that the issue in *Bowers* was simply the right to engage in certain sexual conduct demeans the claim the individual put forward, just as it would demean a married couple were it to be said marriage is simply about the right to have sexual intercourse. The laws involved in *Bowers* and here are, to be sure, statutes that purport to do no more than prohibit a particular sexual act. Their penalties and purposes, though, have more far-reaching consequences, touching upon the most private human conduct, sexual behavior, and in the most private of places, the home. The statutes do seek to control a personal relationship that, whether or not entitled to formal recognition in the law, is within the liberty of persons to choose without being punished as criminals.

This, as a general rule, should counsel against attempts by the State, or a court, to define the meaning of the relationship or to set its boundaries absent injury to a person or abuse of an institution the law protects. It suffices for us to acknowledge that adults may choose to enter upon this relationship in the confines of their homes and their own private lives and still retain their dignity as free persons. When sexuality finds overt expression in intimate conduct with another person, the conduct can be but one element in a personal bond that is more enduring. The liberty protected by the Constitution allows homosexual persons the right to make this choice.

Having misapprehended the claim of liberty there presented to it, and thus stating the claim to be whether there is a fundamental right to engage in consensual sodomy, the *Bowers* Court said: "Proscriptions against that conduct have ancient roots.". . . . In academic writings, and in many of the scholarly *amicus* briefs filed to assist the Court in this case, there are fundamental criticisms of the historical premises relied upon by the majority and concurring opinions in *Bowers*. . . . We need not enter this debate in the attempt to reach a definitive historical judgment, but the following considerations counsel against adopting the definitive conclusions upon which *Bowers* placed such reliance.

At the outset it should be noted that there is no longstanding history in this country of laws directed at homosexual conduct as a distinct matter. Beginning in colonial times there were prohibitions of sodomy derived from the English criminal laws passed in the first instance by the Reformation Parliament of 1533. The English prohibition was understood to include relations between men and women as well as relations between men and men. . . . Nineteenth-century commentators similarly read American sodomy, buggery, and crime-against-nature statutes as criminalizing certain relations between men and women and between men and men. . . . The absence of legal prohibitions focusing on homosexual conduct may be explained in part by noting that according to some scholars the concept of the homosexual as a distinct category of person did not emerge until the late 19th century. . . . Thus early American sodomy laws were not directed at homosexuals as such but instead sought to prohibit nonprocreative sexual activity more generally. This does not suggest approval of homosexual conduct. It does tend to show that this particular form of conduct was not thought of as a separate category from like conduct between heterosexual persons.

Laws prohibiting sodomy do not seem to have been enforced against consenting adults acting in private. A substantial number of sodomy prosecutions and convictions for which there are surviving records were for predatory acts against those who could not or did not consent, as in the case of a minor or the victim of an assault. As to these, one purpose for the prohibitions was to ensure there would be no lack of coverage if a predator committed a sexual assault that did not constitute rape as defined by the criminal law. Thus the model sodomy indictments presented in a 19th-century treatise, . . . addressed the predatory acts of an adult man against a minor girl or minor boy. Instead of targeting relations between consenting adults in private, 19th-century sodomy prosecutions typically involved relations between men and minor girls or minor boys, relations between adults involving force, relations between adults implicating disparity in status, or relations between men and animals.

To the extent that there were any prosecutions for the acts in question, 19th-century evidence rules imposed a burden that would make a conviction more difficult to obtain even taking into account the problems always inherent in prosecuting consensual acts committed in private. Under then-prevailing standards, a man could not be convicted of sodomy based upon testimony of a consenting partner, because the partner was considered an accomplice. A partner's testimony, however, was admissible if he or she had not consented to the act or was a minor, and therefore incapable of consent. . . . The rule may explain in part the infrequency of these prosecutions. In all events that infrequency makes it difficult to say that society approved of a rigorous and systematic punishment of the consensual acts committed in private and by adults. The longstanding criminal prohibition of homosexual sodomy upon which the *Bowers* decision placed such reliance is as consistent with a general condemnation of nonprocreative sex as it is with an established tradition of prosecuting acts because of their homosexual character.

The policy of punishing consenting adults for private acts was not much discussed in the early legal literature. We can infer that one reason for this was the very private nature of the conduct.

Despite the absence of prosecutions, there may have been periods in which there was public criticism of homosexuals as such and an insistence that the criminal laws be enforced to discourage their practices. But far from possessing "ancient roots," . . . , American laws targeting same-sex couples did not develop until the last third of the 20th century. The reported decisions concerning the prosecution of consensual, homosexual sodomy between adults for the years 1880–1995 are not always clear in the details, but a significant number involved conduct in a public place. . . .

It was not until the 1970s that any State singled out same-sex relations for criminal prosecution, and only nine States have done so. . . . Over the course of the last decades, States with same-sex prohibitions have moved toward abolishing them. . . .

In summary, the historical grounds relied upon in *Bowers* are more complex than the majority opinion and the concurring opinion by Chief Justice Burger indicate. Their historical premises are not without doubt and, at the very least, are overstated.

It must be acknowledged, of course, that the Court in *Bowers* was making the broader point that for centuries there have been powerful voices to condemn homosexual conduct as immoral. The condemnation has been shaped by religious beliefs, conceptions of right and acceptable behavior, and respect for the traditional family. For many persons these are not trivial concerns but profound and deep convictions accepted as ethical and moral principles to which they aspire and which thus determine the course of their lives. These considerations do not answer the question before us, however. The issue is whether the majority may use the power of the State to enforce these views on the whole society through operation of the criminal law. "Our obligation is to define the liberty of all, not to mandate our own moral code." . . .

Chief Justice Burger joined the opinion for the Court in *Bowers* and further explained his views as follows: "Decisions of individuals relating to homosexual conduct have been subject to state intervention throughout the history of Western civilization. Condemnation of those practices is firmly rooted in Judeo-Christian moral and ethical standards." . . . As with Justice White's assumptions about history, scholarship casts some doubt on the sweeping nature of the statement by Chief Justice Burger as it pertains to private homosexual conduct between consenting adults. . . . In all events we think that our laws and traditions in the past half century are of most relevance here. These references show an emerging awareness that liberty gives substantial protection to adult persons in deciding how to conduct their private lives in matters pertaining to sex. . . .

This emerging recognition should have been apparent when *Bowers* was decided. In 1955 the American Law Institute promulgated the Model Penal Code and made clear that it did not recommend or provide for "criminal penalties for consensual sexual relations conducted in private.". . . . It justified its decision on three grounds: (1) The prohibitions undermined respect for the law by penalizing conduct many people engaged in; (2) the statutes regulated private conduct not harmful to others; and (3) the laws were arbitrarily enforced and thus invited the danger of blackmail. . . . In 1961 Illinois changed its laws to conform to the Model Penal Code. Other States soon followed. . . .

In *Bowers* the Court referred to the fact that before 1961 all 50 States had outlawed sodomy, and that at the time of the Court's decision 24 States and the District of Columbia had sodomy laws. . . . Justice Powell pointed out that these prohibitions often were being ignored, however. Georgia, for instance, had not sought to enforce its law for decades. . . .

The sweeping references by Chief Justice Burger to the history of Western civilization and to Judeo-Christian moral and ethical standards did not take account of other authorities pointing in an opposite direction. A committee advising the British Parliament recommended in 1957 repeal of laws punishing homosexual conduct. . . . Parliament enacted the substance of those recommendations 10 years later. . . .

Of even more importance, almost five years before *Bowers* was decided the European Court of Human Rights considered a case with parallels to *Bowers* and to today's case. An adult male resident in Northern Ireland alleged he was a practicing homosexual who desired to engage in consensual homosexual conduct. The laws of Northern Ireland forbade him that right. He alleged that he had been questioned, his home had been searched, and he feared criminal prosecution.

The court held that the laws proscribing the conduct were invalid under the European Convention on Human Rights. . . . Authoritative in all countries that are members of the Council of Europe (21 nations then, 45 nations now), the decision is at odds with the premise in *Bowers* that the claim put forward was insubstantial in our Western civilization.

In our own constitutional system the deficiencies in *Bowers* became even more apparent in the years following its announcement. The 25 States with laws prohibiting the relevant conduct referenced in the *Bowers* decision are reduced now to 13, of which 4 enforce their laws only against homosexual conduct. In those States where sodomy is still proscribed, whether for same-sex or heterosexual conduct, there is a pattern of nonenforcement with respect to consenting adults acting in private. The State of Texas admitted in 1994 that as of that date it had not prosecuted anyone under those circumstances. . . .

Two principal cases decided after *Bowers* cast its holding into even more doubt. In *Planned Parenthood of Southeastern Pa. v. Casey,* . . . (1992), the Court reaffirmed the substantive force of the liberty protected by the Due Process Clause. The *Casey* decision again confirmed that our laws and tradition afford constitutional protection to personal decisions relating to marriage, procreation, contraception, family relationships, child rearing, and education. . . . In explaining the respect the Constitution demands for the autonomy of the person in making these choices, we stated as follows:

> "These matters, involving the most intimate and personal choices a person may make in a lifetime, choices central to personal dignity and autonomy, are central to the liberty protected by the Fourteenth Amendment. At the heart of liberty is the right to define one's own concept of existence, of meaning, of the universe, and of the mystery of human life. Beliefs about these matters could not define the attributes of personhood were they formed under compulsion of the State." . . .

Persons in a homosexual relationship may seek autonomy for these purposes, just as heterosexual persons do. The decision in *Bowers* would deny them this right.

The second post-*Bowers* case of principal relevance is *Romer v. Evans, . . .* (1996). There the Court struck down class-based legislation directed at homosexuals as a violation of the Equal Protection Clause. *Romer* invalidated an amendment to Colorado's constitution which named as a solitary class persons who were homosexuals, lesbians, or bisexual either by "orientation, conduct, practices or relationships," . . . , and deprived them of protection under state antidiscrimination laws. We concluded that the provision was "born of animosity toward the class of persons affected" and further that it had no rational relation to a legitimate governmental purpose. . . .

As an alternative argument in this case, counsel for the petitioners and some *amici* contend that *Romer* provides the basis for declaring the Texas statute invalid under the Equal Protection Clause. That is a tenable argument, but we conclude the instant case requires us to address whether *Bowers* itself has continuing validity. Were we to hold the statute invalid under the Equal Protection Clause some might question whether a prohibition would be valid if drawn differently, say, to prohibit the conduct both between same-sex and different-sex participants.

Equality of treatment and the due process right to demand respect for conduct protected by the substantive guarantee of liberty are linked in important respects, and a decision on the latter point advances both interests. If protected conduct is made criminal and the law which does so remains unexamined for its substantive validity, its stigma might remain even if it were not enforceable as drawn for equal protection reasons. When homosexual conduct is made criminal by the law of the State, that declaration in and of itself is an invitation to subject homosexual persons to discrimination both in the public and in the private spheres. The central holding of *Bowers* has been brought in question by this case, and it should be addressed. Its continuance as precedent demeans the lives of homosexual persons.

The stigma this criminal statute imposes, moreover, is not trivial. The offense, to be sure, is but a class C misdemeanor, a minor offense in the Texas legal system. Still, it remains a criminal offense with all that imports for the dignity of the persons charged. The petitioners will bear on their record the history of their criminal convictions. Just this Term we rejected various challenges to state laws requiring the registration of sex offenders. . . . We

are advised that if Texas convicted an adult for private, consensual homosexual conduct under the statute here in question the convicted person would come within the registration laws of at least four States were he or she to be subject to their jurisdiction. . . . This underscores the consequential nature of the punishment and the state-sponsored condemnation attendant to the criminal prohibition. Furthermore, the Texas criminal conviction carries with it the other collateral consequences always following a conviction, such as notations on job application forms, to mention but one example.

The foundations of *Bowers* have sustained serious erosion from our recent decisions in *Casey* and *Romer*. When our precedent has been thus weakened, criticism from other sources is of greater significance. In the United States criticism of *Bowers* has been substantial and continuing, disapproving of its reasoning in all respects, not just as to its historical assumptions. . . . The courts of five different States have declined to follow it in interpreting provisions in their own state constitutions parallel to the Due Process Clause of the Fourteenth Amendment, . . .

To the extent *Bowers* relied on values we share with a wider civilization, it should be noted that the reasoning and holding in *Bowers* have been rejected elsewhere. The European Court of Human Rights has followed not *Bowers* but its own decision in *Dudgeon* v *United Kingdom*. . . . Other nations, too, have taken action consistent with an affirmation of the protected right of homosexual adults to engage in intimate, consensual conduct. . . . The right the petitioners seek in this case has been accepted as an integral part of human freedom in many other countries. There has been no showing that in this country the governmental interest in circumscribing personal choice is somehow more legitimate or urgent.

The doctrine of *stare decisis* is essential to the respect accorded to the judgments of the Court and to the stability of the law. It is not, however, an inexorable command. . . . In *Casey* we noted that when a Court is asked to overrule a precedent recognizing a constitutional liberty interest, individual or societal reliance on the existence of that liberty cautions with particular strength against reversing course. . . . The holding in *Bowers*, however, has not induced detrimental reliance comparable to some instances where recognized individual rights are involved. Indeed, there has been no individual or societal reliance on *Bowers* of the sort that could counsel against overturning its holding once there are compelling reasons to do so. *Bowers* itself causes uncertainty, for the precedents before and after its issuance contradict its central holding.

The rationale of *Bowers* does not withstand careful analysis. In his dissenting opinion in *Bowers* Justice Stevens came to these conclusions:

> "Our prior cases make two propositions abundantly clear. First, the fact that the governing majority in a State has traditionally viewed a particular practice as immoral is not a sufficient reason for upholding a law prohibiting the practice; neither history nor tradition could save a law prohibiting miscegenation from constitutional attack. Second, individual decisions by married persons, concerning the intimacies of their physical relationship, even when not intended to produce offspring, are a form of "liberty" protected by the Due Process Clause of the Fourteenth Amendment. Moreover, this protection extends to intimate choices by unmarried as well as married persons." . . .

Justice Stevens' analysis, in our view, should have been controlling in *Bowers* and should control here.

Bowers was not correct when it was decided, and it is not correct today. It ought not to remain binding precedent. *Bowers v. Hardwick* should be and now is overruled.

The present case does not involve minors. It does not involve persons who might be injured or coerced or who are situated in relationships where consent might not easily be refused. It does not involve public conduct or prostitution. It does not involve whether the government must give formal recognition to any relationship that homosexual persons seek to enter. The case does involve two adults who, with full and mutual consent from each other, engaged in sexual practices common to a homosexual lifestyle. The petitioners are entitled to respect for their private lives. The State cannot demean their existence or control their destiny by making their private sexual conduct a crime. Their right to liberty under the Due Process Clause gives them the full right to engage in their conduct without intervention of the

government. "It is a promise of the Constitution that there is a realm of personal liberty which the government may not enter.". . . . The Texas statute furthers no legitimate state interest which can justify its intrusion into the personal and private life of the individual.

Had those who drew and ratified the Due Process Clauses of the Fifth Amendment or the Fourteenth Amendment known the components of liberty in its manifold possibilities, they might have been more specific. They did not presume to have this insight. They knew times can blind us to certain truths and later generations can see that laws once thought necessary and proper in fact serve only to oppress. As the Constitution endures, persons in every generation can invoke its principles in their own search for greater freedom.

The judgment of the Court of Appeals for the Texas Fourteenth District is reversed, and the case is remanded for further proceedings not inconsistent with this opinion.

It is so ordered.

[Footnotes and citations omitted. Concurring and dissenting opinions omitted.]

BRACH EDWARD NORRIS, PETITIONER-APPELLANT, v. RICHARD MORGAN, SUPERINTENDENT OF WASHINGTON STATE PENITENTIARY, RESPONDENT-APPELLEE.

UNITED STATES COURT OF APPEALS FOR THE NINTH CIRCUIT

622 F.3D 1276; 2010 U.S. APP LEXIS 19812

BERZON, Circuit Judge:

Brach E. Norris was convicted by a jury of child molestation in the first-degree. Norris had also had been convicted of child molestation ten years earlier. The State of Washington's "two strikes" law for repeat sex offenders provides for a mandatory sentence of life in prison without the possibility of parole, and Norris was so sentenced. Invoking the Eighth Amendment's prohibition against cruel and unusual punishment, Norris challenges his sentence as grossly disproportionate to his offense.

The Washington Court of Appeals denied Norris's claim, holding his life-without-parole sentence not grossly disproportionate to his crime. On habeas review, we decide whether the Washington Court of Appeals's decision denying Norris's claim "was contrary to, or involved an unreasonable application of, clearly established federal law." . . . . We conclude that the decision was not contrary to clearly established federal law. Additionally, while finding the issue a close one, we conclude that Norris's Eighth Amendment claim would fail even on de novo review, and thus need not determine whether the state appellate court decision involved an unreasonable application of clearly established federal law. We affirm.

. . . [Some discussion omitted]

At approximately 2:00 p.m. on March 5, 2001, Mark Hyndman and three of his four children, including his stepdaughter, C.D., then five years old, went to a McDonald's restaurant in Spokane, Washington, for a late lunch. After they finished eating, Hyndman's children went to play in an enclosed play-room inside the restaurant. As he sat outside the playroom and watched his children play, Hyndman noticed Norris, then 42-years old, sitting alone inside the playroom and making facial expressions at Hyndman's children while they threw balls against netting on the structure in the playroom. He also saw Norris get up and walk back and forth inside the playroom a few times, repeatedly looking up into the tubes on the structure on which some of the children were playing. Hyndman eventually went into the playroom and sat down so he could watch his children more closely.

Norris approached Hyndman and began talking to him. Hyndman, smelling alcohol on Norris's breath, moved away slightly and continued to watch his children. Hyndman's children were in different areas of the playroom at this time—the youngest was playing with some balls, and the others were playing on the slide next to Norris.

At some point, Hyndman, who had been watching his youngest child play with the balls, turned around and saw Norris bend, reach down with one hand, and touch C.D., who had just come down the slide, between the legs. Hyndman immediately grabbed Norris by the shirt and shoved him against a wall inside the playroom. He then shoved Norris outside the playroom, through the McDonald's lobby, and outside the restaurant, yelling to the McDonald's employees to call the police and that Norris had just inappropriately touched his daughter. Once outside, Norris broke free from Hyndman's grasp and ran away, but Hyndman pursued him on foot. Norris eventually ducked behind an air conditioning unit adjacent to a nearby building, but three police officers arrived soon thereafter and took him into custody.

A few days later, Washington charged Norris with one count of child molestation in the first-degree in violation of Revised Code of Washington § 9A.44.083(1). At trial, Hyndman testified that he saw Norris "reach[ ] down to fondle [C.D.]" as she was trying to pull herself off the edge of the slide, touching her genitalia over her clothing and moving his fingers between her legs. Hyndman stated that the touch occurred "very quickly"—a couple of seconds at most—and in "a real sweeping quick motion," after which Norris "stood right up as if nothing had ever happened." C.D. also testified at trial, stating that while she was playing on the slide at the McDonald's a man touched her on her "privates," "[t]he front one." She also stated that the man had "wiggled" his hand and that she felt his fingers. C.D. could not identify Norris as the man who touched her but indicated that the man who touched her was the same person Hyndman had fought with at the McDonald's. On cross-examination, C.D. testified that the man had not hurt her.

Norris testified in his own defense. He offered an innocent explanation for his conduct, stating that while he was talking to Hyndman he heard a noise, turned to see C.D. on the edge of the slide, and instinctively grabbed her ankle and then placed his hand further up her body—he could not remember exactly where—to steady her, believing that she was going to fall. Norris also testified that he had just gotten off work, drunk two beers, and stopped at the McDonald's to pass the time until his bus came.

At the end of the trial, the trial judge instructed the jury that "[a] person commits the crime of child molestation in the first-degree [in violation of Wash. Rev. Code § 9A.44.083(1)] when he or she has sexual contact with a person who is less than 12 years old . . . ," where "sexual contact" is defined as "any touching of the sexual or other intimate parts of a person done for the purpose of gratifying sexual desires of either party or a third party." The jury convicted Norris of first-degree child molestation.

Before the sentencing hearing, Norris, who had previously been convicted of first-degree child molestation in 1991, filed a motion challenging the application of Washington's two strikes law to his present conviction as cruel and unusual punishment under the federal Constitution's Eighth Amendment. Addressing *Andrade v. Attorney General of the State of California*, . . . (2003), the trial court noted that "the [Eighth] Amendment does not require strict proportionality between the crime and sentence, but rather it forbids . . . extreme sentences that are grossly disproportionate to the crime . . . ." The court then applied a four-factor test adopted by the Washington Supreme Court . . . taking into account (1) the nature of the crime, (2) the legislative purpose behind the sentencing scheme; (3) the sentence Norris would receive for the same crime in other jurisdictions; and (4) the sentence Norris would receive for similar crimes in Washington.

The trial court first applied the Fain factors to repeat first-degree child molesters in the abstract and concluded that, "in general[,] as far as an objective look at the sentencing scheme for this case [,] . . . application of [the] two strikes law is not cruel and unusual punishment under the Eighth Amendment." The trial court next considered whether application of the two strikes law to Norris's specific offense constituted cruel and unusual punishment. The court explained:

> I think the question becomes . . . is this a child molestation in the first degree [that] is classified as a violent crime and the answer is yes[;] all the elements of child molestation in the first degree were demonstrated beyond a reasonable doubt, and the jury made a finding of guilty in this case.
>
> Unlike the Andrade case where we started out from the get-go with a nonserious, nonviolent, non-threatening charge of shoplifting or theft, we don't start out on that

level in this case. We start out with exactly the type of crime that the . . . two strikes law is intending to prevent.

> Secondly, not only do we have a prior conviction for [ ] Norris, it happens to be a prior conviction of exactly the same offense, child molestation . . . in the first degree. . . . That matter also involved a young[ ] . . . female child as this matter did.
>
> One of the major thrusts of the [POAA] is to prevent recidivism. This is a repeat offense. It has many of the earmarks of the prior offense as best I can determine from what I reviewed in the [presentence report].
>
> [A]nother issue I find disturbing in this particular case is this case took place in an open, very public area. There was another adult nearby. It indicates to me a complete lack of impulse control on Norris'[s] part and . . . risk[-]taking in a public place; in other words, the risk that [Norris is] going to be caught causes me concern about his behavior and the kind of behavior that the two strikes law is intend[ed] to prevent, [e.g.,] repeat behavior.
>
> . . . . [Some of the excerpt has been omitted]
>
> . . . . This is not a shoplifting case. This is a case of a commission of an offense that is specifically prohibited by a very tailored, limited two strikes law to sex offenders.

The trial court concluded that "the application of the [POAA] for two strikes [to Norris's most recent child molestation conviction] did not violate the [Eighth Amendment]," and sentenced Norris to a term of life imprisonment without the possibility of parole.

On direct review, the Washington Court of Appeals affirmed in an unpublished opinion. . . .

Addressing the first Fain factor, the Washington Court of Appeals concluded that Norris had "committed a most serious, violent, sex offense against a child." It acknowledged Norris's "argu[ment] that the touch was 'de minimis,' and was 'a brief one-second touch over clothing' that did not involve violence" but rejected it, reasoning that "the [Washington] Legislature has classified first degree molestation as a 'most serious,' 'violent,' 'sex offense,' " and "Norris . . . was convicted of first degree child molestation." Turning to the second factor, the court stated that the legislative purpose behind the two strikes law was two-fold: "to provide mandatory sentences for repeat offenders to deter such crimes and to protect society." And, as Norris "had previously committed the same crime," "violated the conditions of his parole by interacting with young children, without required supervision," and "now . . . molested another young girl, in a public place, with her stepfather close by, watching him and the children," the court held that "Norris's sentence [was consistent with the purposes of the [two strikes law]." Additionally, the Washington Court of Appeals held that Norris's sentence was comparable to the sentence he would have received for committing similar crimes in the State—the fourth Fain factor—because "[s]everal other similar offenses, such as first or second degree rape and first or second degree rape of a child[,] would similarly qualify an offender for life in prison if the offender had a prior first degree molestation conviction."

In examining other jurisdictions' sentencing schemes under the third Fain factor, the Washington Court of Appeals did note that "[m]ost states that have 'two strikes' laws require sex offenses with some degree of penetration and infliction of serious bodily harm." In addition, according to the state appellate court, only "[a] small[ ] number of states would impose a sentence of life in prison without parole for a second offense after a similar prior offense. For example, Georgia, Montana, New Mexico, South Carolina, and Wisconsin all have two strikes laws for some types of sexual offenses." Nonetheless, . . . the court concluded that the third factor was "not dispositive" in this case.

The Washington Court of Appeals also drew a distinction between property crimes and crimes against persons . . .

Based on this analysis, the Washington Court of Appeals concluded that Norris's life-without-parole sentence was not grossly disproportionate to his crime. The Washington Supreme Court denied discretionary review, without comment.

Norris filed a pro se petition for a writ of habeas corpus in the United States District Court for the Eastern District of Washington. Applying federal law, the district court concluded that Norris's life-without-parole sentence did not violate the Eighth Amendment . . .

Having reviewed the record and the opinion of the [state appellate court], th[is] Court concludes that the [state court] did not apply the law concerning gross disproportionality in an objectively unreasonable manner. The [state court] reached the same conclusion that this Court reached in applying Ninth Circuit law.

After rejecting Norris's other claims, the district court denied his habeas petition.

Norris timely filed a notice of appeal and applied for a certificate of appealability. We certified one issue for appeal: "whether appellant's sentence of life in prison without the possibility of parole violates the Eighth Amendment's bar against cruel and unusual punishment." We also ordered appointment of counsel for Norris on appeal.

This petition is governed by the Antiterrorism and Effective Death Penalty Act of 1996 (AEDPA), Pub. L. No. 104-132, 110 Stat. 1214. Under AEDPA, a federal habeas court may grant a habeas petition if, inter alia, the state court's adjudication of the merits of the petitioner's claim "resulted in a decision that was contrary to, or involved an unreasonable application of, clearly established Federal law, as determined by the Supreme Court of the United States." . . .

. . . [some discussion omitted]

Ewing and *Andrade* were the last pertinent Supreme Court Eighth Amendment opinions before the state appellate court decision denying relief to Norris became final, so *Andrade's* statement about what federal law was clearly established controls our analysis here.

The gross disproportionality principle necessarily has a core of clearly established meaning . . .

[Discussion of gross proportionality omitted.]

We turn now to the case before us and ask if the state court adjudication of Norris's claim was "contrary to, or involved an unreasonable application of" the proportionality principle when it concluded that Norris's sentence was not grossly disproportionate to his crime under Washington's two strikes law.

. . . [some discussion omitted]

The State argues that the state courts' reliance on the Fain factors cannot be contrary to clearly established Supreme Court caselaw because the Supreme Court has not ruled on the question whether a sentence of life without the possibility of parole for a repeat sex offender violates the Eighth Amendment's bar against cruel and unusual punishment. This contention—that there is no clearly established Supreme Court law unless the Supreme Court has addressed the precise circumstances presented to us in a federal habeas petition—has been repeatedly rejected. . . .

Norris argues that the Washington Court of Appeals's failure to address the *Solem* factors and use of the Fain factors exclusively was contrary to clearly established Supreme Court caselaw. As previously discussed, however, the Supreme Court, shortly before the Washington Court of Appeals's decision became final, made clear in *Andrade* that the only relevant clearly established law in an Eighth Amendment challenge such as this one was the gross disproportionality principle, and stressed that its "precise contours" were "unclear." . . .

In the alternative, Norris argues that the Washington Court of Appeals's use of the Fain factors was an unreasonable application of the proportionality principle to the facts of this case. . . . Applying the proportionality analysis developed in Fain and its progeny, the Washington Court of Appeals held Norris's life-without-parole sentence not grossly disproportionate to his crime because the nature of his crime, first-degree child molestation, is defined by Washington statute as a "violent" and "most serious" offense; his sentence served the legislative purposes behind the two strikes law of incapacitation and deterrence for recidivist sex offenders; and he would have received the same sentence under the two strikes law for committing similar crimes.

. . . [some discussion omitted]

With respect to the harshness of his sentence, Norris argues that a sentence of life imprisonment without the possibility of parole is extremely harsh, and the State so concedes, as it must. . . . It "share[s] some characteristics with death sentences that are shared by no other sentences," and "deprives the convict of the most basic liberties without giving hope of restoration, except perhaps by executive clemency—the remote possibility of which does not mitigate the harshness of the sentence." Although the offender's life is spared, he is condemned to die in "a living tomb,

there to linger out what may be a long life . . . without any of its alleviation or rewards—debarred from all pleasant sights and sounds, and cut off from all earthly hope."

. . . In Washington, only one crime—first-degree aggravated murder, —is punishable by life imprisonment without the possibility of parole for a first offense. Life without parole is otherwise reserved for criminals sentenced under Washington's two or three strikes laws. . . .

The question therefore is whether Norris's harsh sentence of life imprisonment without the possibility of parole is justified by the gravity of his most recent offense and criminal history. Although the issue is close, we hold that it is.

In evaluating the gravity of Norris's most recent offense, the State of Washington, like the state courts in this case, relies heavily on the fact that Norris's offense, first-degree child molestation, is defined by state statute as a "most serious," and "violent" offense . . . We recognize that the statutory classification of crimes, like "the fixing of prison terms for [those] crimes[,] involves a substantive penological judgment that, as a general matter, is 'properly within the province of legislatures, not courts.' " . . .

Norris's most recent offense, first-degree child molestation, is a class A felony punishable by up to life imprisonment with the possibility of parole. Additionally, because of Norris's criminal history and the statutory "seriousness level" of his offense, even if his offense had not been his second strike and he thus had not been sentenced pursuant to the POAA, Norris would have been subject under Washington's sentencing guidelines to a term of imprisonment between 98 and 130 months. Nonetheless, Norris argues that his conduct was not "so serious" as to justify a life-without-parole sentence because it involved only a momentary touching of a young child between the legs on the outside of her clothing—"represent[ing] perhaps the most minimal conduct which could possibly have satisfied the statute"—and, according to Norris involved neither violence nor the threat of it. The State disputes Norris's description of his conduct as de minimis, arguing that it involved "a purposeful touch with the purpose of sexual gratification," and was done "under the very eyes of the parent, in a public restaurant frequent[ed] by children, indicat[ing] a severe lack of impulse control." The State also notes that child molestation is a crime against a person and therefore inherently involves a degree of force.

. . . In addition, while Norris attempts to downplay his culpability by labeling his conduct "de minimis," it nonetheless comprised a completed crime, not merely an attempted one. Moreover, the circumstances surrounding Norris's most recent offense include his entering a playroom inside a McDonald's alone after drinking alcohol and interacting with a stranger's children, in the presence of the children's parents, despite having been convicted previously of first-degree child molestation. As the state courts reasonably determined, this behavior exhibits a lack of impulse control and so supports the conclusion that Norris cannot be trusted to refrain from similar behavior in the future.

Furthermore, "[t]he impact of [child molestation] on the lives of [its] victims is extraordinarily severe." . . . [W]e and our sister circuits have [therefore] consistently held that sexual offenses [by older adults] against younger children constitute 'crimes of violence.' "

Moreover, and critically, the question in this case is not whether Norris's most recent first-degree child molestation offense would by itself justify the harsh sentence he received. Because Norris was sentenced as a recidivist under the two strikes law, "in weighing the gravity of [his] offense, we must place on the scales not only his current felony," but also criminal history.

. . . The circumstances under which Norris committed his previous first-degree child molestation offense are not sufficiently developed in the record for us to determine the gravity of that offense. But even assuming that Norris's previous offense involved the least offensive conduct that could support a conviction under the child molestation statute, that offense, . . . is "directly related to [his] triggering offense, evincing a clear pattern of recidivism." . . . .

To be sure, as we previously discussed, Norris's sentence of life imprisonment without the possibility of parole is harsh and forsakes any rehabilitative ideal. "By denying [Norris] the right to reenter the community, [Washington has] ma[de] an irrevocable judgment about [his] value and place in society." But regardless whether we agree with the propriety of this judgment, we cannot conclude that it is constitutionally infirm in light of the gravity of Norris's offense and criminal history. Norris's sentence "reflects a rational legislative judgment, entitled to deference," that sex offenders who have committed a serious or violent sex offenses and who continue to commit such sex offenses must be permanently incapacitated. . . .

We conclude that Norris's sentence is not grossly disproportionate to his crime and so does not violate the Eighth Amendment's prohibition against cruel and unusual punishment.

AFFIRMED.

[Footnotes and citations omitted.]

Cases Relating to Chapter 7

Offenses against Property—Destruction and Intrusion Offenses

PRUNEYARD SHOPPING CENTER
v.
ROBINS

APPEAL FROM THE SUPREME COURT OF CALIFORNIA

447 U.S. 74

MR. JUSTICE REHNQUIST delivered the opinion of the Court.

We postponed jurisdiction of this appeal from the Supreme Court of California to decide the important federal constitutional questions it presented. Those are whether state constitutional provisions, which permit individuals to exercise free speech and petition rights on the property of a privately owned shopping center to which the public is invited, violate the shopping center owner's property rights under the Fifth and Fourteenth Amendments or his free speech rights under the First and Fourteenth Amendments.

I

Appellant PruneYard is a privately owned shopping center in the City of Campbell, Cal. It covers approximately 21 acres—5 devoted to parking and 16 occupied by walkways, plazas, sidewalks, and buildings that contain more than 65 specialty shops, 10 restaurants, and a movie theater. The PruneYard is open to the public for the purpose of encouraging the patronizing of its commercial establishments. It has a policy not to permit any visitor or tenant to engage in any publicly expressive activity, including the circulation of petitions, that is not directly related to its commercial purposes. This policy has been strictly enforced in a nondiscriminatory fashion. The PruneYard is owned by appellant Fred Sahadi.

Appellees are high school students who sought to solicit support for their opposition to a United Nations resolution against "Zionism." On a Saturday afternoon they set up a card table in a corner of PruneYard's central courtyard. They distributed pamphlets and asked passersby to sign petitions, which were to be sent to the President and Members of Congress. Their activity was peaceful and orderly, and, so far as the record indicates, was not objected to by PruneYard's patrons.

Soon after appellees had begun soliciting signatures, a security guard informed them that they would have to leave because their activity violated PruneYard regulations. The guard suggested that they move to the public sidewalk at the PruneYard's perimeter. Appellees immediately left the premises and later filed this lawsuit in the California Superior Court of Santa Clara County. They sought to enjoin appellants from denying them access to the PruneYard for the purpose of circulating their petitions.

The Superior Court held that appellees were not entitled under either the Federal or California Constitution to exercise their asserted rights on the shopping center property. It concluded that there were "adequate, effective channels of communication for [appellees] other than soliciting on the private property of the [PruneYard]." The California Court of Appeal affirmed.

The California Supreme Court reversed, holding that the California Constitution protects "speech and petitioning, reasonably exercised, in shopping centers even when the centers are privately owned." . . . It concluded that appellees were entitled to conduct their activity on Prune-Yard property. In rejecting appellants' contention that such a result infringed property rights protected by the Federal Constitution, the California Supreme Court observed:

"It bears repeated emphasis that we do not have under consideration the property or privacy rights of an individual homeowner or the proprietor of a modest retail establishment. As a result of advertising and the lure of a congenial environment, 25,000 persons are induced to congregate daily to take advantage of the numerous amenities offered by the [shopping center there]. A handful of additional orderly persons soliciting signatures and distributing handbills in connection therewith, under reasonable regulations adopted by defendant to assure that these activities do not interfere with normal business operations . . . would not markedly dilute defendant's property rights." . . .

The California Supreme Court thus expressly overruled its earlier decision in *Diamond v. Bland,* . . . , which had reached an opposite conclusion. Before this Court, appellants contend that their constitutionally established rights under the Fourteenth Amendment to exclude appellees from adverse use of appellants' private property cannot be denied by invocation of a state constitutional provision or by judicial reconstruction of a State's laws of private property. We postponed consideration of the question of jurisdiction until the hearing of the case on the merits. We now affirm.

II

We initially conclude that this case is properly before us as an appeal under 28 U.S.C. § 1257 (2). It has long been established that a state constitutional provision is a "statute" within the meaning of § 1257(2). . . . Here the California Supreme Court decided that Art. 1, §§ 2 and 3, of the

California Constitution gave appellees the right to solicit signatures on appellants' property in exercising their state rights of free expression and petition. In so doing, the California Supreme Court rejected appellants' claim that recognition of such a right violated appellants' "right to exclude others," which is a fundamental component of their federally protected property rights. Appeal is thus the proper method of review.

III

Appellants first contend that *Lloyd Corp. v. Tanner,* . . . (1972), prevents the State from requiring a private shopping center owner to provide access to persons exercising their state constitutional rights of free speech and petition when adequate alternative avenues of communication are available. *Lloyd* dealt with the question whether, under the Federal Constitution, a privately owned shopping center may prohibit the distribution of handbills on its property when the handbilling is unrelated to the shopping center's operations. The shopping center had adopted a strict policy against the distribution of handbills within the building complex and its malls, and it made no exceptions to this rule. Respondents in *Lloyd* argued that, because the shopping center was open to the public, the First Amendment prevents the private owner from enforcing the handbilling restriction on shopping center premises. In rejecting this claim, we substantially repudiated the rationale of *Food Employees v. Logan Valley Plaza* . . . which was later overruled in *Hudgens v. NLRB* . . . . We stated that property does not "lose its private character merely because the public is generally invited to use it for designated purposes," and that " [t]he essentially private character of a store and its privately owned abutting property does not change by virtue of being large or clustered with other stores in a modern shopping center."

Our reasoning in *Lloyd,* however, does not, *ex proprio vigore,* limit the authority of the State to exercise its police power or its sovereign right to adopt in its own Constitution individual liberties more expansive than those conferred by the Federal Constitution. . . . In *Lloyd, supra,* there was no state constitutional or statutory provision that had been construed to create rights to the use of private property by strangers, comparable to those found to exist by the California Supreme Court here. It is, of course, well established that a State, in the exercise of its police power, may adopt reasonable restrictions on private property so long as the restrictions do not amount to a taking without just compensation or contravene any other federal constitutional provision. . . . *Lloyd* held that, when a shopping center owner opens his private property to the public for the purpose of shopping, the First Amendment to the United States Constitution does not thereby create individual rights in expression beyond those already existing under applicable law.

IV

Appellants next contend that a right to exclude others underlies the Fifth Amendment guarantee against the taking of property without just compensation and the Fourteenth Amendment guarantee against the deprivation of property without due process of law.

It is true that one of the essential sticks in the bundle of property rights is the right to exclude others. . . . And here there has literally been a "taking" of that right to the extent that the California Supreme Court has interpreted the State constitution to entitle its citizens to exercise free expression and petition rights on shopping center property. But it is well established that "not every destruction or injury to property by governmental action has been held to be a 'taking' in the constitutional sense." . . . . Rather, the determination whether a state law unlawfully infringes a landowner's property in violation of the Taking Clause requires an examination of whether the restriction on private property "forc[es] some people alone to bear public burdens which, in all fairness and justice, should be borne by the public as a whole." . . . This examination entails inquiry into such factors as the character of the governmental action, its economic impact, and its interference with reasonable investment-backed expectations . . .

Here the requirement that appellants permit appellees to exercise state-protected rights of free expression and petition on shopping center property clearly does not amount to an unconstitutional infringement of appellants' property right under the Taking Clause. There is nothing to suggest that preventing appellants from prohibiting this sort of activity will unreasonably impair the value or use of their property as a shopping center. The PruneYard is a large commercial complex that covers several city blocks, contains numerous separate business establishments, and is open to the public at large. The decision of the California Supreme Court makes it clear that the PruneYard may restrict expressive activity by adopting time, place, and manner regulations that will minimize any interference with its commercial functions. Appellees were orderly, and they limited their activity to the common areas of the shopping center. In these circumstances, the fact that they may have "physically invaded" appellants' property cannot be viewed as determinative.

This case is quite different from *Kaiser Aetna v. United States. Kaiser Aetna* was a case in which the owners of a private pond had invested substantial amounts of money in dredging the pond, developing it into an exclusive marina, and building a surrounding marina community. The marina was open only to fee-paying members, and the fees were paid in part to "maintain the privacy and security of the pond." The Federal Government sought to compel free public use of the private marina on the ground that the marina became subject to the federal navigational servitude because the owners had dredged a channel connecting it to "navigable water."

The Government's attempt to create a public right of access to the improved pond interfered with Kaiser Aetna's "reasonable investment backed expectations." We held that it went "so far beyond ordinary regulation or improvement for navigation as to amount to a taking . . . ." Nor, as a general proposition, is the United States, as opposed to the several States, possessed of residual authority that enables it to define "property" in the first instance. A State is, of course, bound by the Just Compensation Clause of the Fifth Amendment, . . . , but here appellants have failed to demonstrate that the "right to exclude others" is so essential to the use or economic value of their property that the state-authorized limitation of it amounted to a "taking."

There is also little merit to appellants' argument that they have been denied their property without due process of law. . . .

[Some discussion omitted.]

V

Appellants finally contend that a private property owner has a First Amendment right not to be forced by the State to use his property as a forum for the speech of others. They state that, in *Wooley v. Maynard*, . . . , this Court concluded that a State may not constitutionally require an individual to participate in the dissemination of an ideological message by displaying it on his private property in a manner and for the express purpose that it be observed and read by the public. This rationale applies here, they argue, because the message of *Wooley* is that the State may not force an individual to display any message at all.

Wooley, however, was a case in which the government itself prescribed the message, required it to be displayed openly on appellee's personal property that was used "as part of his daily life," and refused to permit him to take any measures to cover up the motto even though the Court found that the display of the motto served no important state interest. Here, by contrast, there are a number of distinguishing factors. Most important, the shopping center, by choice of its owner, is not limited to the personal use of appellants. It is instead a business establishment that is open to the public to come and go as they please. The views expressed by members of the public in passing out pamphlets or seeking signatures for a petition thus will not likely be identified with those of the owner. Second, no specific message is dictated by the State to be displayed on appellants' property. There consequently is no danger of governmental discrimination for or against a particular message. Finally, as far as appears here, appellants can expressly disavow any connection with the message by simply posting signs in the area where the speakers or handbillers stand. Such signs, for example, could disclaim any sponsorship of the message and could explain that the persons are communicating their own messages by virtue of state law.

. . . [some discussion omitted]

We conclude that neither appellants' federally recognized property rights nor their First Amendment right have been infringed by the California Supreme Court's decision recognizing a right of appellees to exercise state-protected rights of expression and petition on appellants' property.

The judgment of the Supreme Court of California is therefore

Affirmed.

THE PEOPLE, PLAINTIFF AND RESPONDENT
v.
EDMOND JAMES RAMOS, DEFENDANT AND APPELLANT

52 Cal. App. 4th 300; 60 Cal. Rptr. 2d 523 (1997)

January 27, 1997, Decided
VOGEL (Miriam A.), J.

Is a dead man "temporarily absent" from his house? Since we doubt that he will ever return, we think not. We therefore reduce Edmond James Ramos's conviction of first degree burglary to second degree burglary and remand for resentencing.

Facts

On November 23, 1994, Virgil Wagner died at home from natural causes. His daughter-in-law, Marilyn Ball, was notified of his death, and when she went to Wagner's house two days later, she found that a microwave and a VCR were missing. Although Ball locked the house when she left, there were at least two more unauthorized entries into the house and other items were taken. When the police investigated, they found Ramos's fingerprints inside Wagner's house. When he was arrested, Ramos told the police that he went to Wagner's house on November 23, knocked on the front door and, when no one answered, walked around to the back of the house. Since it appeared that no one was home, Ramos decided to go in and take something he could sell to obtain money to buy drugs. Ramos broke a window, entered the house, walked by Wagner's bedroom, looked in and saw a body on the bed. The body did not move, so Wagner entered the bedroom to get a closer look. When he saw Wagner's stiff body and his face "turned to the left with the eyes open," Ramos ran out the door, grabbing the VCR on his way.

Ramos was charged with five counts of first degree burglary. At trial, the People presented evidence of the November 23 entry plus others occurring before and after Wagner's death. During argument, the prosecutor conceded the later entries were second degree burglaries but argued that the November 23 entry was a first degree burglary because the house was "occupied" until Wagner's remains were removed. The jury convicted Ramos of three counts, finding the November 23 entry was a first degree burglary and two other entries (after Wagner's death) were second degree burglaries. Ramos appeals.

Discussion

(1) Ramos contends the evidence is insufficient to support his first degree burglary conviction because it shows that Wagner was dead at the time Ramos entered his house on November 23. We agree.

To prove first degree burglary of an inhabited dwelling, the People must present evidence that the house is "currently being used for dwelling purposes, whether occupied or not." What this means is that a dwelling is inhabited if the occupant is absent but intends to return and to use the house as a dwelling . . . . To put it plainly, a dead body is not using a house for a "dwelling" and there is no way to say that a dead man is going to return or that he has an "intent" of any kind. It follows that, at the time of Ramos's entry on November 23, the house was not occupied within the meaning of section.

We reject as metaphysical sophistry the Attorney General's suggestion that the house was inhabited because Wagner "went to sleep, fully intending to remain in his house." By the time Ramos got there, Wagner was dead and, to the best of our knowledge, unable to entertain any intent of any kind. The house was no longer occupied . . . . "a house left unoccupied by its occupant's death is not an 'occupied' dwelling"; . . . the inhabitant's death renders a dwelling uninhabited "since someone must 'live' in a dwelling for it to be 'inhabited' . . . "

It follows that Ramos's first degree burglary conviction must be reduced to second degree burglary.

Disposition

The judgment is modified by reducing Ramos's conviction of first degree burglary to second degree burglary and, as modified, is affirmed and remanded to the trial court for resentencing, with directions to not impose the two 5-year enhancements pursuant to section 667, subdivision (a), to reconsider Ramos's presentence conduct credits, to exercise the discretion granted . . . and, after resentencing, to issue a corrected abstract of judgment.

[Footnotes and concurring opinions deleted.]

Cases Relating to Chapter 8

Offenses Involving Theft and Deception

GERALD LATTIMORE, WILLIAM LATTIMORE, AND JAMES HUNT
v.
UNITED STATES

DISTRICT OF COLUMBIA COURT OF APPEALS

684 A.2d 357 (1996)

Newman, Senior Judge:

Gerald Lattimore was convicted, after a jury trial, of armed robbery and possession of a firearm during a crime of violence. William Lattimore and James Hunt were convicted by the same jury of armed robbery. On this appeal, they argue there was insufficient evidence to prove the elements of armed robbery and urge reversal. We affirm.

I

On June 11, 1993, at approximately 9:55 P.M., Genaro Villegas and his sister-in-law, Alipia Sanchez, left the Rhode Island Avenue Metro station headed for his home. As they were walking by the bus area, four men accosted them. Gerald Lattimore struck Villegas, pointed a revolver into his side and demanded money. Hunt held Villegas while William Lattimore patted him down and fully searched him. William Lattimore pulled a wallet from Villegas' pocket, opened it, looked inside, and threw it back. Villegas opened the wallet and gave William Lattimore his payroll check of $431. William Lattimore took the check, looked at it, and threw it back at Villegas.

Angered that their victim had no money, Gerald Lattimore struck Villegas across the face and on the side of his face with the handle of his gun while Hunt continued to restrain him and William Lattimore further searched him. During the entire confrontation, a fourth suspect restrained Sanchez and prevented her from seeking help. This suspect was never apprehended.

Because of a recent string of robberies, Metro Transit Officer Paul Ludwig was stationed at the back of the parking lot, approximately sixty yards from the bus area. When he observed the confrontation between the bandits and the victims, Ludwig called for backup and rode his mountain bike to the scene. When Ludwig announced himself, the bandits turned and ran. Ludwig apprehended James Hunt approximately four yards from the scene. William Lattimore was apprehended on Bryant Street, approximately two and a half blocks from the scene and approximately three minutes after the robbery. Out of breath, William immediately remarked he was not the one with the gun. Gerald Lattimore was arrested a few minutes later further down on Bryant Street. No weapon was ever recovered.

At trial, Sanchez and Officer Ludwig each positively identified all three appellants as Villegas' assailants. Villegas, who suffered multiple injuries requiring stitches and a four-day hospitalization, testified as to the confrontation but could not identify any of the individual appellants or describe any distinguishing characteristics.

II

Appellants do not dispute the facts, but argue that they are legally insufficient to sustain their respective armed robbery convictions. Rather, they contend that the government failed to prove some of the elements of armed robbery, namely "taking," "asportation" or "carrying away," and "intent to steal." . . . . Specifically, they allege that, because none of Villegas' property was in fact taken from the scene of the incident, nor possessed by appellants for a significant period of time, the evidence is only sufficient to support an attempted robbery charge or assault with intent to commit robbery. . . . We disagree.

To determine whether evidence is sufficient to sustain a conviction, we view the evidence in the light most favorable to the government, giving due deference to "the jury's prerogative to weigh the evidence, determine witnesses' credibility, and draw reasonable inferences from the evidence presented.". . . . The evidence need not compel a finding of guilt or negate every possible inference of innocence. . . . Thus, if a trier of fact could find the essential elements of the crime beyond a reasonable doubt, we must affirm the convictions. . . . Conversely, we must reverse "if 'there is no evidence upon which a reasonable mind might fairly conclude guilt beyond a reasonable doubt.'" . . .

In the District of Columbia, robbery retains its common law elements. . . . Thus the government must prove larceny and assault. . . . To support a robbery conviction, the government must prove that there was "(1) a felonious taking, (2) accompanied by an asportation [or carrying away], of (3) personal property of value, (4) from the person of another or in his presence, (5) against his will, (6) by violence or by putting him in fear, (7) *animo furandi* [the intention to steal]." . . . Additionally, to prove armed robbery, the government must establish that, at the time of the offense, the defendant was armed with a firearm. . . .

Because robbery is comprised of larceny and assault, . . . , we examine what constitutes a "taking" and "asportation" of property in larceny. It is not disputed that an assault against Villegas took place; therefore, if the evidence supports a taking, asportation, and the requisite intent, the evidence will sufficiently support appellants' armed robbery convictions.

An individual has committed larceny if that person "without right took and carried away property of another with the intent to permanently deprive the rightful owner thereof.". . . . It does not matter that the person possessed the property for only a brief amount of time or that the person was apprehended before removing the goods from the owner's premises. . . .

In the present case the fact that the Lattimores and Hunt never kept any of Villegas' property does not purge their original taking and asportation of his property. . . . During the confrontation appellants acquired at gunpoint Villegas' wallet and paycheck valued at $431. Both items were clearly within their complete and exclusive control as they had the opportunity to keep (or permanently remove from Villegas' person) the wallet and check if they so chose. Their complete and exclusive control is demonstrated as they physically held the items in their hands while restraining and threatening to shoot Villegas. Moreover, they retained their control over Villegas (and any of his property) by pistol-whipping Villegas after finding nothing of value on him. It is irrelevant whether they personally took the wallet and check out of his pocket or whether Villegas handed them both items for a jury could properly find that Villegas was reacting to their threats and demands for money.

An individual may hold onto the property for only a brief amount of time and still commit a larceny. . . . Here it does not matter that the appellants might have held the check and the wallet for only a brief amount of time before throwing both back at Villegas. A jury could properly find that they took the items with the intention of permanently depriving Villegas of his property. The fact that the property did not meet their needs or that they did not depart from the crime scene with any property does not absolve them of their original taking and asportation. In fact, "the slightest moving of an object from its original location may constitute an asportation." . . .

Because the government established that there was a taking and asportation in conjunction with proof of the appellants' intent to take Villegas' property, the government has sufficiently proven the crime of larceny. Combined with the assault in this case, the government also has established the elements of robbery. . . . Finally, because at the time of the robbery appellants were armed with a firearm, there is sufficient evidence to support their armed robbery convictions,. . . .

Affirmed.

[Footnotes and citations omitted. Concurring and dissenting opinions omitted.]

STATE OF OHIO, PLAINTIFF-
APPELLEE
v.
ROBERT CUNNINGHAM,
DEFENDANT-APPELLANT

APPELLATE CASE NO. 08-CA-09

COURT OF APPEALS OF OHIO,
SECOND APPELLATE DISTRICT,
CLARK COUNTY

2008 OHIO 5164; 2008 OHIO APP.
LEXIS 4354

Opinion

BROGAN, J.

A jury found Robert Cunningham guilty of
child enticement, extortion, coercion, and menacing by stalking, and he was sentenced to prison. In
this appeal, he directly challenges only his child
enticement and extortion convictions. He contends
that the child enticement statute under which he
was convicted is unconstitutional, that there is
insufficient evidence to support a finding of extortion, and that the prosecutor committed misconduct during closing arguments. We recently held
unconstitutional the child enticement statute used
to convict him, so we will vacate that conviction.
But the remainder of the trial court's judgment will
be affirmed.

H.D., a twelve-year old girl, was the victim of
Robert Cunningham's crimes for the second time
in as many years. In 2005, he was convicted of gross
sexual imposition for sexually assaulting her and
another young girl. He was classified as a
sexually-oriented offender and received probation.
He was ordered not to have any contact with his
two victims or unsupervised contact with other
minors. In May 2007, his probation ended early based in part on his probation officer's belief that he
had consistently obeyed the rules of his probation.

Some time in 2006, H.D. received an envelope
in the mail. She thought that it was from her grandmother because her return address sticker was
on it. Upon opening it, however, she quickly discovered that Cunningham had written the letter inside. More disguised letters followed, some with

money, most telling her how much he longed to
see her again. Some of these letters she hid away
in a dresser drawer; others she threw out. Cunningham admonished her in several letters not to tell
anyone that he was writing to her. For a time,
she didn't.

One day, in May 2007, H.D. was walking home
from school, as she usually did, with her cousin.
They suddenly heard a voice behind them.
"H.D.," they heard someone call. Turning around,
they were surprised to see Cunningham driving
along behind them. He pulled alongside them and
stopped. They walked up to his car and he
talked to H.D. for several minutes. She encountered him this way several more times. Sometimes,
he gave her money. Once, he asked her to come to
his house, and he wanted her to bring a friend.
Many times he asked her to get in his car so that
he could drive her home, but H.D. never did. He
would also instruct her, "don't tell your grandma
or anybody that you saw me or I saw you."

H.D. soon discovered that he also wanted her to
do something. Every time he talked to her he
demanded that she tell everyone that her testimony
that had helped convict him two years earlier was a
lie. She refused so he threatened her. He passed her
notes that he had written. "When you're done reading it, give it back to me," he would tell her. He
wrote the notes, as he later admitted to police, as
threats to pressure her into recanting. When he
was arrested, police found in his wallet several
notes, which he had not yet shown H.D., many
of which contained threats, spelled out in X-rated
language, that if she did not tell people that she had
lied, he would expose her past sexual activity to
her parents. He also threatened to expose this
when she resisted talking to him. He held up an envelope for her to see and threatened that if she
would not see him, he would use it to send a letter
to her parents. Although H.D. did not know what
the letter said, based on the notes that she had read
and what she knew that he knew she felt fairly certain what it was that he was threatening to expose.
Cunningham was successful in making her afraid.
Her stepmother, Sarah, noticed a change come
over H.D. when confronted with issues dealing
with him. She was just not herself. She "gets upset,
very nervous, sort of shameful," Sarah noticed.
"[S]he just kind of coils back into herself."

The last time H.D. encountered him before he
was arrested was while she walked home from

school with a group of friends. As they neared one of their houses, Cunningham pulled alongside them and began trying to talk to H.D. When Katie (the mother of the friend whose house they were near) stepped outside her house, she saw the group placing themselves between H.D. and Cunningham's car. Thinking that they were fighting, she marched up to the group in time to hear Cunningham say to H.D., "It's okay, honey. You can get in." Grasping the situation, she quickly grabbed a panicked and scared looking H.D. and brought her into her home. H.D.'s stepmother, Sarah, soon received a phone call from a distressed-sounding Katie. Sarah arrived to find her stepdaughter visibly upset. Once they were home, Sarah and H.D. talked about what had happened. Eventually, she showed Sarah the hidden letters from Cunningham. The following day Sarah called the police, and Cunningham was eventually arrested.

The grand jury indicted him on charges of child enticement with a specification of a prior offense, extortion, coercion, and menacing by stalking with two specifications—a prior offense and a minor victim. A one-day jury trial was held in December 2007. All of the available letters and notes that Cunningham had written were shown—many read—to the jury. Despite Cunningham's objections, the trial judge admitted each into evidence. The following day closing arguments were made by both sides. While reminding the jury of the evidence against Cunningham, the prosecutor read, a second time, portions of a particularly graphic note. Later that same day, the jury returned from its deliberations and delivered its verdict: guilty, guilty, guilty, guilty.

The trial court sentenced Cunningham to seven and one-half years in prison—one year for child enticement, eighteen months for menacing by stalking, and five years for extortion. Cunningham now appeals his child enticement and extortion convictions based on four alleged errors.

. . . [some discussion omitted]

For his second assignment of error, Cunningham contends that the jury improperly found him guilty of extortion because the State failed to present legally-sufficient evidence for each essential element. 'Sufficiency' is a term of meaning that legal standard which is applied to determine . . . whether the evidence is legally sufficient to support the jury verdict as a matter of law." . . . That is, tautology-free, "whether [a] rational finder of fact, viewing the evidence in a light most favorable to the state, could have found the essential elements of [extortion] proven beyond a reasonable doubt." . . . We will marshal the evidence that the State presented to determine whether it is sufficient to support the essential elements.

The pertinent portion of the extortion statute, the portion used to find Cunningham guilty, reads: "No person, with purpose to obtain any valuable thing or valuable benefit or to induce another to do an unlawful act, shall do any of the following: . . . Expose or threaten to expose any matter tending to subject any person to hatred, contempt, or ridicule, or to damage any person's personal or business repute, or to impair any person's credit." Cunningham contests the sufficiency of the State's evidence for three essential elements. He contends that there is insufficient evidence to prove, first, that he sought to obtain a "valuable thing or valuable benefit"; second, that he sought an "unlawful act"; and third, that he threatened to expose a "matter tending to subject any person to hatred, contempt, or ridicule, or to damage any person's personal . . . repute.". . .

. . . [some discussion omitted]

Cunningham does not challenge the State's evidence per se but raises a question of law: how the phrase "valuable thing or valuable benefit" ought to be construed. He asserts that it must be construed to mean that the State must prove a "valuable thing or valuable benefit" that is tangible. If it were construed to include intangibles, he argues, nothing would distinguish extortion from the separate statutory offense of coercion as the elements and evidence would be the same for both. In his case, he points out, he was found guilty of extortion for trying to pressure H.D., using threats, into saying that she lied. He was also found guilty of coercion for trying to coerce her, using threats, to say that she lied. In short, he was found guilty of two offenses based on the same conduct (threatening H.D.) that sought the same intangible thing (her recantation).

The question raised, then, is one of statutory meaning, which is the court's job to determine. Our duty is to give effect to the Legislature's intended meaning.

. . . [some discussion omitted]

The meaning of "valuable thing and valuable benefit" is clear and unambiguous. Common usage of the words "thing" and "benefit" includes reference to intangibles. . . . Moreover, prior cases have found intangibles encompassed by the meaning of "thing" and "benefit." . . .

Moreover, even when viewed in the context of the criminal code, "thing" and "benefit" retain their common meanings. Cunningham's assertion that this interpretation results in identical offenses is wrong, and is based on a misreading of his cited authorities. Far from supporting his conclusion they actually support ours. He primarily relies on the Model Penal Code and the U.S. Supreme Court's use of it . . . The correct reading of these [cases], however, reveals that neither the Code nor *Scheidler* restricts "property" to tangible property. On the contrary, *Scheidler* expressly rejected the notion. Indeed, the Court did not exclude the possibility under the Hobbs Act "that liability might be based on obtaining something as intangible as another's right to exercise exclusive control over the use of a party's business assets."

. . . Said the Court, citing the Model Code, while coercion and extortion certainly overlap to the extent that extortion necessarily involves the use of coercive conduct to obtain property, there has been and continues to be a recognized difference between these two crimes." The recognized difference to which *Scheidler* refers is extortion's requirement that one "obtains [the] property of another."

Similarly, under Ohio law, while coercive conduct is necessary for extortion, it is not sufficient. Although the same coercive conduct can underlie both offenses, the purpose and effect of the conduct differs. The language of these two offenses bears this out. On the one hand, coercion requires proof of a "purpose to coerce another into taking or refraining from action concerning which the other person has a legal freedom of choice." The effect is to deprive another of the freedom to act. Extortion, on the other hand, requires proof of a "purpose to obtain any valuable thing or valuable benefit or to induce another to do an unlawful act." The effect of extortion is to coerce another in order to obtain something to which the extorter has no right. The important distinction, then, is extortion's additional evidentiary requirement of an intent to obtain something. It matters not that the thing sought is intangible.

Cunningham sought to obtain an intangible "valuable benefit" from H.D. Despite his assertions to the contrary, we are unconvinced that he was seeking to obtain her recantation for its own sake. Rather, we think that he wanted to obtain the valuable benefits that her recantation would bring—benefits such as the ability to deny that he had committed a crime, which would help restore his reputation and permit him to challenge his conviction. That he sought these benefits, and not simply the recantation, is a permissible inference that a reasonable juror could, and most likely would, draw from the evidence.

A rational juror, then, viewing the evidence offered in support of this element in the light most favorable to the State, and drawing all reasonable inferences, could find that Cunningham threatened H.D. into recanting because he wanted to obtain the "valuable benefits" that the recantation would bring. Therefore, we find that the evidence in support of this element is legally sufficient.

. . . Cunningham next asserts that the evidence is not sufficient to find that he made threats to induce another to do an "unlawful act." It would not be unlawful, he argues, for H.D. to recant. To prove extortion, the State needed to show the alleged extorter threatened another with the purpose either to obtain a valuable thing or benefit, or alternatively, to induce another to do an "unlawful act." Because "valuable benefit" and "unlawful act" are disjunctives, the evidence need show only one. We just determined that there is sufficient evidence to find that Cunningham threatened H.D. because he wanted to obtain "valuable benefits." As a result, we do not have to determine also whether recanting would be an "unlawful act."

. . . Finally, Cunningham asserts that there is insufficient evidence that the "matter" that he threatened to expose would tend to subject H.D. to "hatred, contempt, or ridicule, or to damage" her reputation. Here, he does challenge the State's evidence directly. He argues that the State presented no evidence that the envelope with which he threatened H.D. contained tell of such a matter. Therefore, he concludes, without knowing what was inside, the jury could not have properly concluded that it concerned a matter that could be characterized in the way required by the extortion statute.

Although Cunningham raises only an issue of fact, we begin with an issue of law, namely, the meaning of "matter." Again, we need not engage the rules of statutory construction because the meaning of "matter" is clear and unambiguous. Turning to the dictionary for guidance on common usage, we find the word "matter" pertinently defined as a "subject of concern, feeling, or action." ... A matter, then, refers to a vaguely specified concern. Cunningham admitted to police that he had written the notes intending to pressure H.D. into recanting. All of the available notes that he had written were admitted into evidence and were before the jury. The common subject that links them together is H.D.'s sexual relationships. We suspect that few would disagree that a young girl would be concerned to prevent others from knowing this information. Further, it is not hard to accept the notion that exposure of this subject could subject a young girl to the opprobrium of others and consequent damage to her reputation. Cunningham must have thought so; otherwise, how would his threats create the fear in her that he needed to force her to recant?

Cunningham's argument that H.D. did not know the precise content of the envelope is unavailing because the exact language is immaterial. Regardless of the exact words used, a reasonable juror could find that the matter that he threatened to expose was one that would tend to damage her reputation. Therefore, there is sufficient evidence to meet this element.

The purpose behind Cunningham's threats was broader than just to coerce a particular course of action. He also used fear in an attempt to get something to which he was not entitled. We hold that when viewing the evidence in the light most favorable to the State, and drawing all reasonable inferences, a reasonable juror could find evidence to support each of the contested elements of the crime of extortion. Accordingly, we overrule Cunningham's second assignment of error. . . .

[Other issues are omitted.]

[Footnotes and citations omitted.]

Cases Relating to Chapter 9

Offenses Involving Morality and Decency

**BROWN, GOVERNOR OF
CALIFORNIA, ET AL.
v.
ENTERTAINMENT MERCHANTS
ASSOCIATION ET AL.**

**SUPREME COURT OF THE UNITED
STATES**

**CERTIORARI TO THE UNITED
STATES COURT OF APPEALS FOR
THE NINTH CIRCUIT**

**ARGUED NOVEMBER 2, 2010—
DECIDED JUNE 27, 2011**

564 U. S. ____

SCALIA, J., delivered the opinion of the Court, in
which KENNEDY, GINSBURG, SOTOMAYOR, and
KAGAN, J.J., joined. ALITO, J., filed an opinion concurring in the judgment, in which ROBERTS, C. J.,
joined. THOMAS, J., and BREYER, J., filed dissenting
opinions.

JUSTICE SCALIA delivered the opinion of the
Court.

We consider whether a California law imposing
restrictions on violent video games comports with
the First Amendment.

I. California Assembly Bill 1179 (2005), Cal.
Civ. Code Ann. §§1746–1746.5 (West 2009)
(Act), prohibits the sale or rental of "violent video
games" to minors, and requires their packaging to
be labeled "18." The Act covers games "in which
the range of options available to a player includes
killing, maiming, dismembering, or sexually
assaulting an image of a human being, if those acts
are depicted" in a manner that "[a] reasonable person, considering the game as a whole, would find
appeals to a deviant or morbid interest of minors,"
that is "patently offensive to prevailing standards
in the community as to what is suitable for minors," and that "causes the game, as a whole, to
lack serious literary, artistic, political, or scientific
value for minors." §1746(d)(1)(A). Violation of
the Act is punishable by a civil fine of up to
$1,000. . . . [some discussion omitted]

Respondents, representing the video-game
and software industries, brought a preenforcement challenge to the Act in the United States
District Court for the Northern District of
California. That court concluded that the Act violated the First Amendment and permanently
enjoined its enforcement. . . . The Court of Appeals affirmed, . . . [some discussion omitted]

II. California correctly acknowledges that video
games qualify for First Amendment protection.
The Free Speech Clause exists principally to protect discourse on public matters, but we have long
recognized that it is difficult to distinguish politics
from entertainment, and dangerous to try. "Everyone is familiar with instances of propaganda
through fiction. What is one man's amusement,
teaches another's doctrine." . . . . Like the protected books, plays, and movies that preceded
them, video games communicate ideas—and even
social messages—through many familiar literary

devices (such as characters, dialogue, plot, and music) and through features distinctive to the medium (such as the player's interaction with the virtual world). That suffices to confer First Amendment protection. Under our Constitution, "esthetic and moral judgments about art and literature . . . are for the individual to make, not for the Government to decree, even with the mandate or approval of a majority." . . . And whatever the challenges of applying the Constitution to ever-advancing technology, "the basic principles of freedom of speech and the press, like the First Amendment's command, do not vary" when a new and different medium for communication appears. . . .

> The most basic of those principles is this: "[A]s a general matter, . . . government has no power to restrict expression because of its message, its ideas, its subject matter, or its content." *Ashcroft v. American Civil Liberties Union*, 535 U. S. 564, 573 (2002) . . . There are of course exceptions. "'From 1791 to the present,' . . . the First Amendment has 'permitted restrictions upon the content of speech in a few limited areas,' and has never 'include[d] a freedom to disregard these traditional limitations.'" *United States v. Stevens*, 559 U. S. ___, ___ (2010) (slip op., at 5) . . . These limited areas—such as obscenity, *Roth v. United States*, 354 U. S. 476, 483 (1957), incitement, *Brandenburg v. Ohio*, 395 U. S. 444, 447–449 (1969) *(per curiam)*, and fighting words, *Chaplinsky v. New Hampshire*, 315 U. S. 568, 572 (1942)—represent "well-defined and narrowly limited classes of speech, the prevention and punishment of which have never been thought to raise any Constitutional problem," . . .

Last Term, in *Stevens*, we held that new categories of unprotected speech may not be added to the list by a legislature that concludes certain speech is too harmful to be tolerated. *Stevens* concerned a federal statute purporting to criminalize the creation, sale, or possession of certain depictions of animal cruelty. . . . The statute covered depictions "in which a living animal is intentionally maimed, mutilated, tortured, wounded, or killed" if that harm to the animal was illegal where the

"the creation, sale, or possession t[ook] place," . . . . A saving clause largely borrowed from our obscenity jurisprudence, see *Miller v. California*, . . . (1973), exempted depictions with "serious religious, political, scientific, educational, journalistic, historical, or artistic value," § 48(b). We held that statute to be an impermissible content-based restriction on speech. There was no American tradition of forbidding the *depiction of* animal cruelty—though States have long had laws against *committing* it.

The Government argued in *Stevens* that lack of a historical warrant did not matter; that it could create new categories of unprotected speech by applying a "simple balancing test" that weighs the value of a particular category of speech against its social costs and then punishes that category of speech if it fails the test. *Stevens* . . . . We emphatically rejected that "startling and dangerous" proposition. *Ibid.* "Maybe there are some categories of speech that have been historically unprotected, but have not yet been specifically identified or discussed as such in our case law." . . . . But without persuasive evidence that a novel restriction on content is part of a long (if heretofore unrecognized) tradition of proscription, a legislature may not revise the "judgment [of] the American people," embodied in the First Amendment, "that the benefits of its restrictions on the Government outweigh the costs." . . .

That holding controls this case. As in *Stevens*, California has tried to make violent-speech regulation look like obscenity regulation by appending a saving clause required for the latter. That does not suffice. Our cases have been clear that the obscenity exception to the First Amendment does not cover whatever a legislature finds shocking, but only depictions of "sexual conduct" . . .

Stevens was not the first time we have encountered and rejected a State's attempt to shoehorn speech about violence into obscenity. In *Winters*, we considered a New York criminal statute "forbid[ding] the massing of stories of bloodshed and lust in such a way as to incite to crime against the person," . . . The New York Court of Appeals upheld the provision as a law against obscenity. "[T]here can be no more precise test of written indecency or obscenity," it said, "than the continuing and changeable experience of the community as to what types of books are likely to bring about the corruption of public morals or other analogous injury to the public order." . . . That is of course the same expansive view of governmental power to abridge the freedom of speech based on interest-balancing that we rejected in *Stevens*. Our opinion in *Winters*, which concluded that the New York statute failed a heightened vagueness standard applicable to restrictions upon speech entitled to First Amendment protection, . . . , made clear that violence is not part of the obscenity that the Constitution permits to be regulated. The speech reached by the statute contained "no indecency or obscenity in any sense heretofore known to the law."

Because speech about violence is not obscene, it is of no consequence that California's statute mimics the New York statute regulating obscenity-for-minors that we upheld in *Ginsberg v. New York* . . . (1968). That case approved a prohibition on the sale to minors of *sexual* material that would be obscene from the perspective of a child. We held that the legislature could "adjus[t] the definition of obscenity 'to social realities by permitting the appeal of this type of material to be assessed in terms of the sexual interests . . . ' of . . . minors. " . . . . And because "obscenity is not protected expression," the New York statute could be sustained so long as the legislature's judgment that the proscribed materials were harmful to children "was not irrational." . . .

The California Act is something else entirely. It does not adjust the boundaries of an existing category of unprotected speech to ensure that a definition designed for adults is not uncritically applied to children. California does not argue that it is empowered to prohibit selling offensively violent works *to adults*—and it is wise not to, since that is but a hair's breadth from the argument rejected in *Stevens*. Instead, it wishes to create a wholly new category of content-based regulation that is permissible only for speech directed at children.

That is unprecedented and mistaken. "[M]inors are entitled to a significant measure of First Amendment protection, and only in relatively narrow and well-defined circumstances may government bar public dissemination of protected materials to them." . . . . No doubt a State possesses legitimate power to protect children from harm, . . . , but that does not include a free-floating power to restrict the ideas to which children may be exposed. "Speech that is neither obscene as to youths nor subject to some other legitimate proscription cannot be suppressed solely to protect the young from ideas or images that a legislative body thinks unsuitable for them." . . .

California's argument would fare better if there were a longstanding tradition in this country of specially restricting children's access to depictions of violence, but there is none. Certainly the *books* we give children to read—or read to them when they are younger—contain no shortage of gore. Grimm's Fairy Tales, for example, are grim indeed. As her just deserts for trying to poison Snow White, the wicked queen is made to dance in red hot slippers "till she fell dead on the floor, a sad example of envy and jealousy." . . . Cinderella's evil stepsisters have their eyes pecked out by doves. . . . . And Hansel and Gretel (children!) kill their captor by baking her in an oven. . . .

High-school reading lists are full of similar fare. Homer's Odysseus blinds Polyphemus the Cyclops by grinding out his eye with a heated stake. . . . ("Even so did we seize the fiery-pointed brand and whirled it round in his eye, and the blood flowed about the heated bar. And the breath of the flame singed his eyelids and brows all about, as the ball of the eye burnt away, and the roots thereof crackled in the flame"). In the Inferno, Dante and Virgil watch corrupt politicians struggle to stay submerged beneath a lake of boiling pitch, lest they be skewered by devils above the surface. . . . . And Golding's Lord of the Flies recounts how a schoolboy called Piggy is savagely murdered *by other children* while marooned on an island. . . . [some discussion omitted]

This is not to say that minors' consumption of violent entertainment has never encountered resistance. In the 1800's, dime novels depicting crime and "penny dreadfuls" (named for their price and content) were blamed in some quarters for juvenile delinquency. . . . . When motion pictures came along, they became the villains instead. "The days when the police looked upon dime novels as the most dangerous of textbooks in the school for crime are drawing to a close . . . . They say that the moving picture machine . . . tends even more than did the dime novel to turn the thoughts of the easily influenced to paths which sometimes lead to prison." . . . . For a time, our Court did permit broad censorship of movies because of their capacity to be "used for evil," . . . , but we eventually reversed course, ... Radio dramas were next, and then came comic books. . . . . Many in the late 1940's and early 1950's blamed comic books for fostering a "preoccupation with violence and horror" among the young, leading to a rising juvenile crime rate. . . . . But efforts to convince Congress to restrict comic books failed. . . . And, of course, after comic books came television and music lyrics.

California claims that video games present special problems because they are "interactive," in that the player participates in the violent action on screen and determines its outcome. The latter feature is nothing new: Since at least the publication of The Adventures of You: Sugarcane Island in 1969, young readers of choose-your-own adventure stories have been able to make decisions that determine the plot by following instructions about which page to turn to. . . . As for the argument that video games enable participation in the violent action, that seems to us more a matter of degree than of kind. As Judge Posner has observed, all literature is interactive. "[T]he better it is, the more interactive. Literature when it is successful draws the reader into the story, makes him identify with the characters, invites him to judge them and quarrel with them, to experience their joys and sufferings as the reader's own." . . .

JUSTICE ALITO has done considerable independent research to identify, . . . video games in which "the violence is astounding," . . . . "Victims are dismembered, decapitated, disemboweled, set on fire, and chopped into little pieces . . . . Blood gushes, splatters, and pools." . . . . JUSTICE ALITO recounts all these disgusting video games in order to disgust us—but disgust is not a valid basis for restricting expression. And the same is true of JUSTICE ALITO's description, . . . , of those video games he has discovered that have a racial or ethnic motive for their violence—"'ethnic cleansing' [of] . . . African Americans, Latinos, or Jews." To what end does he relate this? Does it somehow increase the "aggressiveness" that California wishes to suppress? Who knows? But it does arouse the reader's ire, and the reader's desire to put an end to this horrible message. Thus, ironically, JUSTICE ALITO's argument highlights the precise danger posed by the California Act: that the *ideas* expressed by speech—whether it be violence, or gore, or racism—and not its objective effects, may be the real reason for governmental proscription.

III. Because the Act imposes a restriction on the content of protected speech, it is invalid unless California can demonstrate that it passes strict scrutiny—that is, unless it is justified by a compelling government interest and is narrowly drawn to serve that interest. The State must specifically identify an "actual problem" in need of solving, . . . , and the curtailment of free speech must be actually necessary to the solution . . . . That is a demanding standard. "It is rare that a regulation restricting speech because of its content will ever be permissible." . . . [some discussion omitted]

California cannot meet that standard. At the outset, it acknowledges that it cannot show a direct causal link between violent video games and harm to minors. Rather, relying upon our decision in *Turner Broadcasting System, Inc. v. FCC,* . . . (1994), the State claims that it need not produce such proof because the legislature can make a predictive judgment that such a link exists, based on competing psychological studies. But reliance on *Turner Broadcasting* is misplaced. That decision applied *intermediate scrutiny* to a content-neutral regulation. . . . . California's burden is much higher, and because it bears the risk of uncertainty, . . . , ambiguous proof will not suffice.

The State's evidence is not compelling. California relies primarily on the research of Dr. Craig Anderson and a few other research psychologists whose studies purport to show a connection between exposure to violent video games and harmful effects on children. These studies have been rejected by every court to consider them, and with good reason: They do not prove that violent video games *cause* minors to *act* aggressively (which would at least be a beginning). Instead, "[n]early all of the research is based on correlation, not evidence of causation, and most of the studies suffer from significant, admitted flaws in methodology." . . . . They show at best some correlation between exposure to violent entertainment and minuscule real-world effects, such as children's feeling more aggressive or making louder noises in the few minutes after playing a violent game than after playing a nonviolent game.

Even taking for granted Dr. Anderson's conclusions that violent video games produce some effect on children's feelings of aggression, those effects are both small and indistinguishable from effects produced by other media. In his testimony in a similar lawsuit, Dr. Anderson admitted that the "effect sizes" of children's exposure to violent video games are "about the same" as that produced by their exposure to violence on television. . . . . And he admits that the *same* effects have been found when children watch cartoons starring Bugs

Bunny or the Road Runner, . . . , or when they play video games like Sonic the Hedgehog that are rated "E" (appropriate for all ages), . . . , or even when they "vie[w] a picture of a gun," . . . .

Of course, California has (wisely) declined to restrict Saturday morning cartoons, the sale of games rated for young children, or the distribution of pictures of guns. The consequence is that its regulation is wildly underinclusive when judged against its asserted justification, which in our view is alone enough to defeat it. Underinclusiveness raises serious doubts about whether the government is in fact pursuing the interest it invokes, rather than disfavoring a particular speaker or viewpoint. . . . . Here, California has singled out the purveyors of video games for disfavored treatment—at least when compared to booksellers, cartoonists, and movie producers—and has given no persuasive reason why.

The Act is also seriously underinclusive in another respect—and a respect that renders irrelevant the contentions of the concurrence and the dissents that video games are qualitatively different from other portrayals of violence. The California Legislature is perfectly willing to leave this dangerous, mind-altering material in the hands of children so long as one parent (or even an aunt or uncle) says it's OK. And there are not even any requirements as to how this parental or avuncular relationship is to be verified; apparently the child's or putative parent's, aunt's, or uncle's say-so suffices. That is not how one addresses a serious social problem.

California claims that the Act is justified in aid of parental authority: By requiring that the purchase of violent video games can be made only by adults, the Act ensures that parents can decide what games are appropriate. At the outset, we note our doubts that punishing third parties for conveying protected speech to children *just in case* their parents disapprove of that speech is a proper governmental means of aiding parental authority. Accepting that position would largely vitiate the rule that "only in relatively narrow and well-defined circumstances may government bar public dissemination of protected materials to [minors]." . . . But leaving that aside, California cannot show that the Act's restrictions meet a substantial need of parents who wish to restrict their children's access to violent video games but cannot do so. The video-game industry has in place a

voluntary rating system designed to inform consumers about the content of games. The system, implemented by the Entertainment Software Rating Board (ESRB), assigns age-specific ratings to each video game submitted: EC (Early Childhood); E (Everyone); E10+ (Everyone 10 and older); T (Teens); M (17 and older); and AO (Adults Only—18 and older). . . . . The Video Software Dealers Association encourages retailers to prominently display information about the ESRB system in their stores; to refrain from renting or selling adults only games to minors; and to rent or sell "M" rated games to minors only with parental consent. . . . In 2009, the Federal Trade Commission (FTC) found that, as a result of this system, "the video game industry outpaces the movie and music industries" in "(1) restricting target marketing of mature-rated products to children; (2) clearly and prominently disclosing rating information; and (3) restricting children's access to mature-rated products at retail." . . . . This system does much to ensure that minors cannot purchase seriously violent games on their own, and that parents who care about the matter can readily evaluate the games their children bring home. Filling the remaining modest gap in concerned-parents' control can hardly be a compelling state interest.

And finally, the Act's purported aid to parental authority is vastly overinclusive. Not all of the children who are forbidden to purchase violent video games on their own have parents who *care* whether they purchase violent video games. While some of the legislation's effect may indeed be in support of what some parents of the restricted children actually want, its entire effect is only in support of what the State thinks parents *ought* to want. This is not the narrow tailoring to "assisting parents" that restriction of First Amendment rights requires.

California's effort to regulate violent video games is the latest episode in a long series of failed attempts to censor violent entertainment for minors. While we have pointed out above that some of the evidence brought forward to support the harmfulness of video games is unpersuasive, we do not mean to demean or disparage the concerns that underlie the attempt to regulate them—concerns that may and doubtless do prompt a good deal of parental oversight. We have no business passing judgment on the view of the California Legislature that violent video games (or, for that matter, any other forms of speech) corrupt the young or harm their moral development. Our task is only to say whether or not such works constitute a "well-defined and narrowly limited clas[s] of speech, the prevention and punishment of which have never been thought to raise any Constitutional problem," . . . (the answer plainly is no); and if not, whether the regulation of such works is justified by that high degree of necessity we have described as a compelling state interest (it is not). Even where the protection of children is the object, the constitutional limits on governmental action apply. California's legislation straddles the fence between (1) addressing a serious social problem and (2) helping concerned parents control their children. Both ends are legitimate, but when they affect First Amendment rights they must be pursued by means that are neither seriously underinclusive nor seriously overinclusive. . . . As a means of protecting children from portrayals of violence, the legislation is seriously underinclusive, not only because it excludes portrayals other than video games, but also because it permits a parental or avuncular veto. And as a means of assisting concerned parents it is seriously overinclusive because it abridges the First Amendment rights of young people whose parents (and aunts and uncles) think violent video games are a harmless pastime. And the overbreadth in achieving one goal is not cured by the underbreadth in achieving the other. Legislation such as this, which is neither fish nor fowl, cannot survive strict scrutiny.

We affirm the judgment below.

It is so ordered.

[Citations and footnotes omitted. Concurring and dissenting opinions omitted.]

ALBERTO R. GONZALES, ATTORNEY GENERAL, PETITIONER
v.
LEROY CARHART, ET AL.
AND
ALBERTO R. GONZALES, ATTORNEY GENERAL, PETITIONER
v.
PLANNED PARENTHOOD FEDERATION OF AMERICA, Inc., ET AL.

550 U.S. 124; 127 S. Ct. 1610 (2007)

Justice Kennedy delivered the opinion of the Court.

These cases require us to consider the validity of the Partial-Birth Abortion Ban Act of 2003 (Act), 18 U.S.C. § 1531 (2000 ed., Supp. IV), a federal statute regulating abortion procedures. In recitations preceding its operative provisions the Act refers to the Court's opinion in *Stenberg v. Carhart*, . . . (2000), which also addressed the subject of abortion procedures used in the later stages of pregnancy. Compared to the state statute at issue in *Stenberg*, the Act is more specific concerning the instances to which it applies and in this respect more precise in its coverage. We conclude the Act should be sustained against the objections lodged by the broad, facial attack brought against it.

In No. 05-380 (Carhart) respondents are LeRoy Carhart, William G. Fitzhugh, William H. Knorr, and Jill L. Vibhakar, doctors who perform second-trimester abortions. These doctors filed their complaint against the Attorney General of the United States in the United States District Court for the District of Nebraska. They challenged the constitutionality of the Act and sought a permanent injunction against its enforcement. *Carhart v. Ashcroft*, . . . (2004). In 2004, after a 2-week trial, the District Court granted a permanent injunction that prohibited the Attorney General from enforcing the Act in all cases but those in which there was no dispute the fetus was viable - . . . The Court of Appeals for the Eighth Circuit affirmed . . . . We granted certiorari.

In No. 05-1382 (Planned Parenthood) respondents are Planned Parenthood Federation of America, Inc., Planned Parenthood Golden Gate, and the City and County of San Francisco. The Planned Parenthood entities sought to enjoin enforcement of the Act in a suit filed in the United States District Court for the Northern District of California . . . . The City and County of San Francisco intervened as a plaintiff. In 2004, the District Court held a trial spanning a period just short of three weeks, and it, too, enjoined the Attorney General from enforcing the Act . . . . The Court of Appeals for the Ninth Circuit affirmed . . . . We granted certiorari.

The Act proscribes a particular manner of ending fetal life, so it is necessary here, as it was in , to discuss abortion procedures in some detail. Three

United States District Courts heard extensive evidence describing the procedures. In addition to the two courts involved in the instant cases the District Court for the Southern District of New York also considered the constitutionality of the Act. It found the Act unconstitutional, . . . , and the Court of Appeals for the Second Circuit affirmed, . . . The three District Courts relied on similar medical evidence; indeed, much of the evidence submitted to the Carhart court previously had been submitted to the other two courts . . . . We refer to the District Courts' exhaustive opinions in our own discussion of abortion procedures.

Abortion methods vary depending to some extent on the preferences of the physician and, of course, on the term of the pregnancy and the resulting stage of the unborn child's development. Between 85 and 90 percent of the approximately 1.3 million abortions performed each year in the United States take place in the first three months of pregnancy, which is to say in the first trimester . . . . The most common first-trimester abortion method is vacuum aspiration (otherwise known as suction curettage) in which the physician vacuums out the embryonic tissue. Early in this trimester an alternative is to use medication, such as mifepristone (commonly known as RU-486), to terminate the pregnancy . . . . The Act does not regulate these procedures.

Of the remaining abortions that take place each year, most occur in the second trimester. The surgical procedure referred to as "dilation and evacuation" or "D&E" is the usual abortion method in this trimester . . . . Although individual techniques for performing D&E differ, the general steps are the same.

A doctor must first dilate the cervix at least to the extent needed to insert surgical instruments into the uterus and to maneuver them to evacuate the fetus . . . . The steps taken to cause dilation differ by physician and gestational age of the fetus . . . . A doctor often begins the dilation process by inserting osmotic dilators, such as laminaria (sticks of seaweed), into the cervix. The dilators can be used in combination with drugs, such as misoprostol, that increase dilation. The resulting amount of dilation is not uniform, and a doctor does not know in advance how an individual patient will respond. In general the longer dilators remain in the cervix, the more it will dilate. Yet the length of time doctors employ osmotic dilators varies. Some may keep dilators in the cervix for two days, while others use dilators for a day or less . . . .

After sufficient dilation the surgical operation can commence. The woman is placed under general anesthesia or conscious sedation. The doctor, often guided by ultrasound, inserts grasping forceps through the woman's cervix and into the uterus to grab the fetus. The doctor grips a fetal part with the forceps and pulls it back through the cervix and vagina, continuing to pull even after meeting resistance from the cervix. The friction causes the fetus to tear apart. For example, a leg might be ripped off the fetus as it is pulled through the cervix and out of the woman. The process of evacuating the fetus piece by piece continues until it has been completely removed. A doctor may make 10 to 15 passes with the forceps to evacuate the fetus in its entirety, though sometimes removal is completed with fewer passes. Once the fetus has been evacuated, the placenta and any remaining fetal material are suctioned or scraped out of the uterus. The doctor examines the different parts to ensure the entire fetal body has been removed. . . .

Some doctors, especially later in the second trimester, may kill the fetus a day or two before performing the surgical evacuation. They inject digoxin or potassium chloride into the fetus, the umbilical cord, or the amniotic fluid. Fetal demise may cause contractions and make greater dilation possible. Once dead, moreover, the fetus' body will soften, and its removal will be easier. Other doctors refrain from injecting chemical agents, believing it adds risk with little or no medical benefit. . . .

The abortion procedure that was the impetus for the numerous bans on "partial-birth abortion," including the Act, is a variation of this standard D&E . . . . The medical community has not reached unanimity on the appropriate name for this D&E variation. It has been referred to as "intact D&E," "dilation and extraction" (D&X), and "intact D&X." . . . For discussion purposes this D&E variation will be referred to as intact D&E. The main difference between the two procedures is that in intact D&E a doctor extracts the fetus intact or largely intact with only a few passes. There are no comprehensive statistics indicating what percentage of all D&Es are performed in this manner.

Intact D&E, like regular D&E, begins with dilation of the cervix. Sufficient dilation is essential for the procedure. To achieve intact extraction some doctors thus may attempt to dilate the cervix to a greater degree. This approach has been called "serial" dilation .... Doctors who attempt at the outset to perform intact D&E may dilate for two full days or use up to 25 osmotic dilators ....

In an intact D&E procedure the doctor extracts the fetus in a way conducive to pulling out its entire body, instead of ripping it apart ....

Intact D&E gained public notoriety when, in 1992, Dr. Martin Haskell gave a presentation describing his method of performing the operation .... In the usual intact D&E the fetus' head lodges in the cervix, and dilation is insufficient to allow it to pass .... Haskell explained the next step as follows:

"'At this point, the right-handed surgeon slides the fingers of the left [hand] along the back of the fetus and "hooks" the shoulders of the fetus with the index and ring fingers (palm down).

"'While maintaining this tension, lifting the cervix and applying traction to the shoulders with the fingers of the left hand, the surgeon takes a pair of blunt curved Metzenbaum scissors in the right hand. He carefully advances the tip, curved down, along the spine and under his middle finger until he feels it contact the base of the skull under the tip of his middle finger.

"'[T]he surgeon then forces the scissors into the base of the skull or into the foramen magnum. Having safely entered the skull, he spreads the scissors to enlarge the opening.

"'The surgeon removes the scissors and introduces a suction catheter into this hole and evacuates the skull contents. With the catheter still in place, he applies traction to the fetus, removing it completely from the patient.'" ...

This is an abortion doctor's clinical description. Here is another description from a nurse who witnessed the same method performed on a 26 1/2-week fetus and who testified before the Senate Judiciary Committee:

"'Dr. Haskell went in with forceps and grabbed the baby's legs and pulled them down into the birth canal. Then he delivered the baby's body and the arms— everything but the head. The doctor kept the head right inside the uterus ....

"'The baby's little fingers were clasping and unclasping, and his little feet were kicking. Then the doctor stuck the scissors in the back of his head, and the baby's arms jerked out, like a startle reaction, like a flinch, like a baby does when he thinks he is going to fall.

"'The doctor opened up the scissors, stuck a high-powered suction tube into the opening, and sucked the baby's brains out. Now the baby went completely limp ....

"'He cut the umbilical cord and delivered the placenta. He threw the baby in a pan, along with the placenta and the instruments he had just used.'" ...

Dr. Haskell's approach is not the only method of killing the fetus once its head lodges in the cervix, and "the process has evolved" since his presentation ... Another doctor, for example, squeezes the skull after it has been pierced "so that enough brain tissue exudes to allow the head to pass through." ... Still other physicians reach into the cervix with their forceps and crush the fetus' skull .... Others continue to pull the fetus out of the woman until it disarticulates at the neck, in effect decapitating it. These doctors then grasp the head with forceps, crush it, and remove it ....

Some doctors performing an intact D&E attempt to remove the fetus without collapsing the skull .... Yet one doctor would not allow delivery of a live fetus younger than 24 weeks because "the objective of [his] procedure is to perform an abortion," not a birth .... The doctor thus answered in the affirmative when asked whether he would "hold the fetus' head on the internal side of the [cervix] in order to collapse the skull" and kill the fetus before it is born .... Another doctor testified he crushes a fetus' skull not only to reduce its size but also to ensure the fetus is dead before it is removed. For the staff to have to deal with a fetus that has "some viability to it, some movement of limbs," according to this doctor, "[is] always a difficult situation." . . .

D&E and intact D&E are not the only second-trimester abortion methods. Doctors also may abort a fetus through medical induction. The doctor medicates the woman to induce labor, and contractions occur to deliver the fetus. Induction, which unlike D&E should occur in a hospital, can last as little as 6 hours but can take longer than 48. It accounts for about 5 percent of second-trimester abortions before 20 weeks of gestation and 15 percent of those after 20 weeks. Doctors turn to two other methods of second-trimester abortion, hysterotomy and hysterectomy, only in emergency situations because they carry increased risk of complications. In a hysterotomy, as in a cesarean section, the doctor removes the fetus by making an incision through the abdomen and uterine wall to gain access to the uterine cavity. A hysterectomy requires the removal of the entire uterus. These two procedures represent about .07% of second-trimester abortions . . . .

After Dr. Haskell's procedure received public attention, with ensuing and increasing public concern, bans on "'partial birth abortion'" proliferated. By the time of the decision, about 30 States had enacted bans designed to prohibit the procedure . . . . In 1996, Congress also acted to ban partial-birth abortion. President Clinton vetoed the congressional legislation, and the Senate failed to override the veto. Congress approved another bill banning the procedure in 1997, but President Clinton again vetoed it. In 2003, after this Court's decision in, Congress passed the Act at issue here . . . . On November 5, 2003, President Bush signed the Act into law. It was to take effect the following day . . . .

The Act responded to in two ways. First, Congress made factual findings. Congress determined that this Court in "was required to accept the very questionable findings issued by the district court judge," . . . , but that Congress was "not bound to accept the same factual findings," Congress found, among other things, that "[a] moral, medical, and ethical consensus exists that the practice of performing a partial-birth abortion . . . is a gruesome and inhumane procedure that is never medically necessary and should be prohibited."

Second, and more relevant here, the Act's language differs from that of the Nebraska statute struck down in . . . . The operative provisions of the Act provide in relevant part:

"(a) Any physician who, in or affecting interstate or foreign commerce, knowingly performs a partial-birth abortion and thereby kills a human fetus shall be fined under this title or imprisoned not more than 2 years, or both. This subsection does not apply to a partial-birth abortion that is necessary to save the life of a mother whose life is endangered by a physical disorder, physical illness, or physical injury, including a life-endangering physical condition caused by or arising from the pregnancy itself. This subsection takes effect 1 day after the enactment.

"(b) As used in this section—

"(1) the term 'partial-birth abortion' means an abortion in which the person performing the abortion—

"(A) deliberately and intentionally vaginally delivers a living fetus until, in the case of a head-first presentation, the entire fetal head is outside the body of the mother, or, in the case of breech presentation, any part of the fetal trunk past the navel is outside the body of the mother, for the purpose of performing an overt act that the person knows will kill the partially delivered living fetus; and

"(B) performs the overt act, other than completion of delivery, that kills the partially delivered living fetus; and

"(2) the term 'physician' means a doctor of medicine or osteopathy legally authorized to practice medicine and surgery by the State in which the doctor performs such activity, or any other individual legally authorized by the State to perform abortions: Provided, however, That any individual who is not a physician or not otherwise legally authorized by the State to perform abortions, but who nevertheless directly performs a partial-birth abortion, shall be subject to the provisions of this section.

. . .

"(d)(1) A defendant accused of an offense under this section may seek a hearing before the State Medical Board on whether the physician's conduct was necessary to save the life of the mother whose life was endangered by a physical disorder, physical illness, or physical injury, including a life-endangering physical condition caused by or arising from the pregnancy itself.

"(2) The findings on that issue are admissible on that issue at the trial of the defendant. Upon a motion of the defendant, the court shall delay the beginning of the trial for not more than 30 days to permit such a hearing to take place.

"(e) A woman upon whom a partial-birth abortion is performed may not be prosecuted under this section, for a conspiracy to violate this section, or for an offense under section 2, 3, or 4 of this title based on a violation of this section." . . .

The Act also includes a provision authorizing civil actions that is not of relevance here . . . . [some discussion omitted]

The District Court in Carhart concluded the Act was unconstitutional for two reasons. First, it determined the Act was unconstitutional because it lacked an exception allowing the procedure where necessary for the health of the mother. Second, the District Court found the Act deficient because it covered not merely intact D&E but also certain other D&Es.

The Court of Appeals for the Eighth Circuit addressed only the lack of a health exception. The court began its analysis with what it saw as the appropriate question—"whether 'substantial medical authority' supports the medical necessity of the banned procedure." . . . This was the proper framework, according to the Court of Appeals, because "when a lack of consensus exists in the medical community, the Constitution requires legislatures to err on the side of protecting women's health by including a health exception." The court rejected the Attorney General's attempt to demonstrate changed evidentiary circumstances since and considered itself bound by *Stenberg's*

conclusion that a health exception was required . . . . It invalidated the Act.

The District Court in Planned Parenthood concluded the Act was unconstitutional "because it (1) pose[d] an undue burden on a woman's ability to choose a second trimester abortion; (2) [was] unconstitutionally vague; and (3) require[d] a health exception as set forth by . . . *Stenberg*."

The Court of Appeals for the Ninth Circuit agreed. Like the Court of Appeals for the Eighth Circuit, it concluded the absence of a health exception rendered the Act unconstitutional. The court interpreted *Stenberg* to require a health exception unless "there is consensus in the medical community that the banned procedure is never medically necessary to preserve the health of women." Even after applying a deferential standard of review to Congress' factual findings, the Court of Appeals determined "substantial disagreement exists in the medical community regarding whether" the procedures prohibited by the Act are ever necessary to preserve a woman's health.

The Court of Appeals concluded further that the Act placed an undue burden on a woman's ability to obtain a second-trimester abortion. The court found the textual differences between the Act and the Nebraska statute struck down in *Stenberg* insufficient to distinguish D&E and intact D&E. As a result, according to the Court of Appeals, the Act imposed an undue burden because it prohibited D&E.

Finally, the Court of Appeals found the Act void for vagueness. Abortion doctors testified they were uncertain which procedures the Act made criminal. The court thus concluded the Act did not offer physicians clear warning of its regulatory reach. Resting on its understanding of the remedial framework established by this . . . , the Court of Appeals held the Act was unconstitutional on its face and should be permanently enjoined.

II

. . . Whatever one's views concerning the *Casey* joint opinion, it is evident a premise central to its conclusion—that the government has a legitimate and substantial interest in preserving and promoting fetal life—would be repudiated were the Court now to affirm the judgments of the Courts of Appeals.

Casey involved a challenge to *Roe v. Wade*, . . . (1973). . . . [some discussion omitted]

To implement its holding, *Casey* rejected both *Roe's* rigid trimester framework and the interpretation of *Roe* that considered all previability regulations of abortion unwarranted . . . . On this point *Casey* overruled the holdings in two cases because they undervalued the State's interest in potential life. . . . [some discussion omitted]

We assume the following principles for the purposes of this opinion. Before viability, a State "may not prohibit any woman from making the ultimate decision to terminate her pregnancy." It also may not impose upon this right an undue burden, which exists if a regulation's "purpose or effect is to place a substantial obstacle in the path of a woman seeking an abortion before the fetus attains viability." On the other hand, "[r]egulations which do no more than create a structural mechanism by which the State, or the parent or guardian of a minor, may express profound respect for the life of the unborn are permitted, if they are not a substantial obstacle to the woman's exercise of the right to choose." *Casey*, in short, struck a balance. The balance was central to its holding. We now apply its standard to the cases at bar.

III

We begin with a determination of the Act's operation and effect. A straightforward reading of the Act's text demonstrates its purpose and the scope of its provisions: It regulates and proscribes, with exceptions or qualifications to be discussed, performing the intact D&E procedure.

Respondents agree the Act encompasses intact D&E, but they contend its additional reach is both unclear and excessive. Respondents assert that, at the least, the Act is void for vagueness because its scope is indefinite. In the alternative, respondents argue the Act's text proscribes all D&Es. Because D&E is the most common second-trimester abortion method, respondents suggest the Act imposes an undue burden. In this litigation the Attorney General does not dispute that the Act would impose an undue burden if it covered standard D&E.

We conclude that the Act is not void for vagueness, does not impose an undue burden from any overbreadth, and is not invalid on its face.

A

The Act punishes "knowingly perform[ing]" a "partial-birth abortion." It defines the unlawful abortion in explicit terms.

First, the person performing the abortion must "vaginally delive[r] a living fetus." The Act does not restrict an abortion procedure involving the delivery of an expired fetus. The Act, furthermore, is inapplicable to abortions that do not involve vaginal delivery (for instance, hysterotomy or hysterectomy). The Act does apply both previability and postviability because, by common understanding and scientific terminology, a fetus is a living organism while within the womb, whether or not it is viable outside the womb. We do not understand this point to be contested by the parties.

Second, the Act's definition of partial-birth abortion requires the fetus to be delivered "until, in the case of a head-first presentation, the entire fetal head is outside the body of the mother, or, in the case of breech presentation, any part of the fetal trunk past the navel is outside the body of the mother." The Attorney General concedes, and we agree, that if an abortion procedure does not involve the delivery of a living fetus to one of these "anatomical 'land-marks'"—where, depending on the presentation, either the fetal head or the fetal trunk past the navel is outside the body of the mother—the prohibitions of the Act do not apply.

Third, to fall within the Act, a doctor must perform an "overt act, other than completion of delivery, that kills the partially delivered living fetus." For purposes of criminal liability, the overt act causing the fetus' death must be separate from delivery. And the overt act must occur after the delivery to an anatomical landmark. This is because the Act proscribes killing "the partially delivered" fetus, which, when read in context, refers to a fetus that has been delivered to an anatomical landmark.

Fourth, the Act contains scienter requirements concerning all the actions involved in the prohibited abortion. To begin with, the physician must have "deliberately and intentionally" delivered the fetus to one of the Act's anatomical landmarks. If a living fetus is delivered past the critical point by accident or inadvertence, the Act is inapplicable. In addition, the fetus must have been delivered "for the purpose of performing an overt act that the [doctor] knows will kill [it]." If either intent is absent, no crime has occurred. This follows from the general principle that where scienter is required no crime is committed absent the requisite state of mind . . . . [some discussion omitted]

B

Respondents contend the language described above is indeterminate, and they thus argue the Act is unconstitutionally vague on its face. As generally stated, the void-for-vagueness doctrine requires that a penal statute define the criminal offense with sufficient definiteness that ordinary people can understand what conduct is prohibited and in a manner that does not encourage arbitrary and discriminatory enforcement." . . . The Act satisfies both requirements.

The Act provides doctors "of ordinary intelligence a reasonable opportunity to know what is prohibited." . . . Indeed, it sets forth "relatively clear guidelines as to prohibited conduct" and provides "objective criteria" to evaluate whether a doctor has performed a prohibited procedure . . . . Unlike the statutory language in *Stenberg* that prohibited the delivery of a "'substantial portion'" of the fetus—where a doctor might question how much of the fetus is a substantial portion—the Act defines the line between potentially criminal conduct on the one hand and lawful abortion on the other . . . . Doctors performing D&E will know that if they do not deliver a living fetus to an anatomical landmark they will not face criminal liability.

This conclusion is buttressed by the intent that must be proved to impose liability. The Court has made clear that scienter requirements alleviate vagueness concerns . . . . The Act requires the doctor deliberately to have delivered the fetus to an anatomical landmark. Because a doctor performing a D&E will not face criminal liability if he or she delivers a fetus beyond the prohibited point by mistake, the Act cannot be described as "a trap for those who act in good faith . . .

Respondents likewise have failed to show that the Act should be invalidated on its face because it encourages arbitrary or discriminatory enforcement. Just as the Act's anatomical landmarks provide doctors with objective standards, they also "establish minimal guidelines to govern law enforcement." The scienter requirements narrow the scope of the Act's prohibition and limit prosecutorial discretion. It cannot be said that the Act "vests virtually complete discretion in the hands of [law enforcement] to determine whether the [doctor] has satisfied [its provisions]." . . . Respondents' arguments concerning arbitrary enforcement, furthermore, are somewhat speculative. This is a preenforcement challenge, where "no evidence has been, or could be, introduced to indicate whether the [Act] has been enforced in a discriminatory manner or with the aim of inhibiting [constitutionally protected conduct]." . . . The Act is not vague.

C

We next determine whether the Act imposes an undue burden, as a facial matter, because its restrictions on second-trimester abortions are too broad. A review of the statutory text discloses the limits of its reach. The Act prohibits intact D&E; and, notwithstanding respondents' arguments, it does not prohibit the D&E procedure in which the fetus is removed in parts.

1

The Act prohibits a doctor from intentionally performing an intact D&E. The dual prohibitions of the Act, both of which are necessary for criminal liability, correspond with the steps generally undertaken during this type of procedure. First, a doctor delivers the fetus until its head lodges in the cervix, which is usually past the anatomical landmark for a breech presentation. This step satisfies the overt-act requirement because it kills the fetus and is distinct from delivery . . . . The Act's intent requirements, however, limit its reach to those physicians who carry out the intact D&E after intending to undertake both steps at the outset.

The Act excludes most D&Es in which the fetus is removed in pieces, not intact. If the doctor intends to remove the fetus in parts from the outset, the doctor will not have the requisite intent to incur criminal liability. A doctor performing a standard D&E procedure can often "tak[e] about 10-15 'passes' through the uterus to remove the entire fetus." . . . Removing the fetus in this manner does not violate the Act because the doctor will not have delivered the living fetus to one of the anatomical landmarks or committed an additional overt act that kills the fetus after partial delivery.

A comparison of the Act with the Nebraska statute struck down in *Stenberg* confirms this point. The statute in *Stenberg* prohibited "'deliberately and intentionally delivering into the vagina a living unborn child, or a substantial portion thereof, for the purpose of performing a procedure that the person performing such procedure knows will kill the unborn child and does kill the unborn child.'" . . . The Court concluded that this statute encompassed D&E because "D&E will often involve a physician pulling a 'substantial portion' of a still living fetus, say, an arm or leg, into the vagina prior to the death of the fetus." . . . The Court also rejected the limiting interpretation urged by Nebraska's Attorney General that the statute's reference to a "procedure" that "'kill[s] the unborn child'" was to a distinct procedure, not to the abortion procedure as a whole.

Congress, it is apparent, responded to these concerns because the Act departs in material ways from the statute in *Stenberg*. It adopts the phrase "delivers a living fetus," instead of "'delivering . . . a living unborn child, or a substantial portion thereof,'" . . . The Act's language, unlike the statute in *Stenberg*, expresses the usual meaning of "deliver" when used in connection with "fetus," namely, extraction of an entire fetus rather than removal of fetal pieces . . . . The Act thus displaces the interpretation of "delivering" dictated by the Nebraska statute's reference to a "substantial portion" of the fetus . . . . In interpreting statutory texts courts use the ordinary meaning of terms unless context requires a different result . . . . Here, unlike in *Stenberg*, the language does not require a departure from the ordinary meaning. D&E does not involve the delivery of a fetus because it requires the removal of fetal parts that are ripped from the fetus as they are pulled through the cervix.

The identification of specific anatomical landmarks to which the fetus must be partially delivered also differentiates the Act from the statute at issue in *Stenberg*. The Court in *Stenberg* interpreted "'substantial portion'" of the fetus to include an arm or a leg. The Act's anatomical landmarks, by contrast, clarify that the removal of a small portion of the fetus is not prohibited. The landmarks also require the fetus to be delivered so that it is partially "outside the body of the mother." To come within the ambit of the Nebraska statute, on the other hand, a substantial portion of the fetus only had to be delivered into the vagina; no part of the fetus had to be outside the body of the mother before a doctor could face criminal sanctions.

By adding an overt-act requirement Congress sought further to meet the Court's objections to the state statute considered in *Stenberg* . . . . The Act makes the distinction the Nebraska statute failed to draw (but the Nebraska Attorney General advanced) by differentiating between the overall partial abortion and the distinct overt act that kills the fetus. The fatal overt act must occur after delivery to an anatomical landmark, and it must be something "other than [the] completion of delivery." This distinction matters because, unlike intact D&E, standard D&E does not involve a delivery followed by a fatal act.

The canon of constitutional avoidance, finally, extinguishes any lingering doubt as to whether the Act covers the prototypical D&E procedure. "[T]he elementary rule is that every reasonable construction must be resorted to, in order to save a statute from unconstitutionality." . . . It is true this longstanding maxim of statutory interpretation has, in the past, fallen by the wayside when the Court confronted a statute regulating abortion. The Court at times employed an antagonistic "canon of construction under which in cases involving abortion, a permissible reading of a statute [was] to be avoided at all costs." . . . *Casey* put this novel statutory approach to rest . . . . *Stenberg* need not be interpreted to have revived it. We read that decision instead to stand for the uncontroversial proposition that the canon of constitutional avoidance does not apply if a statute is not "genuinely susceptible to two constructions." . . . In *Stenberg* the Court found the statute covered D&E. Here, by contrast, interpreting the Act so that it does not prohibit standard D&E is the most reasonable reading and understanding of its terms.

2

Contrary arguments by respondents are unavailing . . . .

[Argument that doctors may mistakenly violate law omitted. Court says scienter requirement

prevents doctors who perform intact D&E unintentionally from being prosecuted.]

IV

Under the principles accepted as controlling here, the Act, as we have interpreted it, would be unconstitutional "if its purpose or effect is to place a substantial obstacle in the path of a woman seeking an abortion before the fetus attains viability." The abortions affected by the Act's regulations take place both previability and postviability; so the quoted language and the undue burden analysis it relies upon are applicable. The question is whether the Act, measured by its text in this facial attack imposes a substantial obstacle to late-term, but previability, abortions. The Act does not on its face impose a substantial obstacle, and we reject this further facial challenge to its validity.

A

The Act's purposes are set forth in recitals preceding its operative provisions. A description of the prohibited abortion procedure demonstrates the rationale for the congressional enactment. The Act proscribes a method of abortion in which a fetus is killed just inches before completion of the birth process. Congress stated as follows: "Implicitly approving such a brutal and inhumane procedure by choosing not to prohibit it will further coarsen society to the humanity of not only newborns, but all vulnerable and innocent human life, making it increasingly difficult to protect such life." The Act expresses respect for the dignity of human life.

Congress was concerned, furthermore, with the effects on the medical community and on its reputation caused by the practice of partial-birth abortion. The findings in the Act explain:

> "Partial-birth abortion ... confuses the medical, legal, and ethical duties of physicians to preserve and promote life, as the physician acts directly against the physical life of a child, whom he or she had just delivered, all but the head, out of the womb, in order to end that life."

. . .

The government may use its voice and its regulatory authority to show its profound respect for the life within the woman. A central premise of the opinion was that the Court's precedents after *Roe* had "undervalue[d] the State's interest in potential life." The plurality opinion indicated "[t]he fact that a law which serves a valid purpose, one not designed to strike at the right itself, has the incidental effect of making it more difficult or more expensive to procure an abortion cannot be enough to invalidate it." This was not an idle assertion. The three premises of *Casey* must coexist. The third premise, that the State, from the inception of the pregnancy, maintains its own regulatory interest in protecting the life of the fetus that may become a child, cannot be set at naught by interpreting *Casey's* requirement of a health exception so it becomes tantamount to allowing a doctor to choose the abortion method he or she might prefer. Where it has a rational basis to act, and it does not impose an undue burden, the State may use its regulatory power to bar certain procedures and substitute others, all in furtherance of its legitimate interests in regulating the medical profession in order to promote respect for life, including life of the unborn.

The Act's ban on abortions that involve partial delivery of a living fetus furthers the Government's objectives. No one would dispute that, for many, D&E is a procedure itself laden with the power to devalue human life. Congress could nonetheless conclude that the type of abortion proscribed by the Act requires specific regulation because it implicates additional ethical and moral concerns that justify a special prohibition. Congress determined that the abortion methods it proscribed had a "disturbing similarity to the killing of a newborn infant," and thus it was concerned with "draw[ing] a bright line that clearly distinguishes abortion and infanticide," The Court has in the past confirmed the validity of drawing boundaries to prevent certain practices that extinguish life and are close to actions that are condemned. . . . [some discussion omitted]

It is objected that the standard D&E is in some respects as brutal, if not more, than the intact D&E, so that the legislation accomplishes little. What we have already said, however, shows ample justification for the regulation. Partial-birth abortion, as defined by the Act, differs from a standard D&E because the former occurs when the fetus is partially outside the mother to the point of one of the Act's anatomical landmarks. It was reasonable for Congress to think that partial-birth abortion, more than standard D&E, "undermines the public's perception of the appropriate role of a physician during the delivery process, and perverts a process during which life is brought into the world." There would be a flaw in this Court's logic, and an irony in its jurisprudence, were we first to conclude a ban on both D&E and intact D&E was overbroad and then to say it is irrational to ban only intact D&E because that does not proscribe both procedures. In sum, we reject the contention that the congressional purpose of the Act was "to place a substantial obstacle in the path of a woman seeking an abortion."

B

The Act's furtherance of legitimate government interests bears upon, but does not resolve, the next question: whether the Act has the effect of imposing an unconstitutional burden on the abortion right because it does not allow use of the barred procedure where "necessary, in appropriate medical judgment, for the preservation of the . . . health of the mother." . . . The prohibition in the Act would be unconstitutional, under precedents we here assume to be controlling, if it "subject[ed] [women] to significant health risks." . . . In *Ayotte* the parties agreed a health exception to the challenged parental-involvement statute was necessary "to avert serious and often irreversible damage to . . . Here, by contrast, whether the Act creates significant health risks for women has been a contested question. The evidence presented in the trial courts and before Congress demonstrates both sides have medical support for their position.

Respondents presented evidence that intact D&E may be the safest method of abortion, for reasons similar to those adduced in *Stenberg*. Abortion doctors testified, for example, that intact D&E decreases the risk of cervical laceration or uterine perforation because it requires fewer passes into the uterus with surgical instruments and does not require the removal of bony fragments of the dismembered fetus, fragments that may be sharp. Respondents also presented evidence that intact D&E was safer both because it reduces the risks that fetal parts will remain in the uterus and because it takes less time to complete. Respondents, in addition, proffered evidence that intact D&E was safer for women with certain medical conditions or women with fetuses that had certain anomalies . . . .

These contentions were contradicted by other doctors who testified in the District Courts and before Congress. They concluded that the alleged health advantages were based on speculation without scientific studies to support them. They considered D&E always to be a safe alternative . . . .

There is documented medical disagreement whether the Act's prohibition would ever impose significant health risks on women . . . . The three District Courts that considered the Act's constitutionality appeared to be in some disagreement on this central factual question. The District Court for the District of Nebraska concluded "the banned procedure is, sometimes, the safest abortion procedure to preserve the health of women." The District Court for the Northern District of California reached a similar conclusion . . . . The District Court for the Southern District of New York was more skeptical of the purported health benefits of intact D&E. It found the Attorney General's "expert witnesses reasonably and effectively refuted [the plaintiffs'] proffered bases for the opinion that [intact D&E] has safety advantages over other second-trimester abortion procedures." . . . In addition it did "not believe that many of [the plaintiffs'] purported reasons for why [intact D&E] is medically necessary [were] credible; rather [it found them to be] theoretical or false." The court nonetheless invalidated the Act because it determined "a significant body of medical opinion . . . holds that D&E has safety advantages over induction and that [intact D&E] has some safety advantages (however hypothetical and unsubstantiated by scientific evidence) over D&E for some women in some circumstances.

The question becomes whether the Act can stand when this medical uncertainty persists. The Court's precedents instruct that the Act can survive this facial attack. The Court has given state and federal legislatures wide discretion to pass legislation in areas where there is medical and scientific uncertainty . . . .

This traditional rule is consistent with *Casey*, which confirms the State's interest in promoting respect for human life at all stages in the pregnancy. Physicians are not entitled to ignore regulations that direct them to use reasonable alternative procedures. The law need not give abortion doctors unfettered choice in the course of their medical practice, nor should it elevate their status above other physicians in the medical community. In *Casey* the controlling opinion held an informed-consent requirement in the abortion context was "no different from a requirement that a doctor give certain specific information about any medical procedure." The opinion stated "the doctor-patient relation here is entitled to the same solicitude it receives in other contexts." . . .

Medical uncertainty does not foreclose the exercise of legislative power in the abortion context any more than it does in other contexts. The medical uncertainty over whether the Act's prohibition creates significant health risks provides a sufficient basis to conclude in this facial attack that the Act does not impose an undue burden.

The conclusion that the Act does not impose an undue burden is supported by other considerations. Alternatives are available to the prohibited procedure. As we have noted, the Act does not proscribe D&E. One District Court found D&E to have extremely low rates of medical complications. Another indicated D&E was "generally the safest method of abortion during the second trimester." . . . In addition the Act's prohibition only applies to the delivery of "a living fetus." If the intact D&E procedure is truly necessary in some circumstances, it appears likely an injection that kills the fetus is an alternative under the Act that allows the doctor to perform the procedure.

The instant cases, then, are different from *Planned Parenthood of Central Mo. v. Danforth*, . . . (1976), in which the Court invalidated a ban on saline amniocentesis, the then-dominant second-trimester abortion method. The Court found the ban in *Danforth* to be "an unreasonable or arbitrary regulation designed to inhibit, and having the effect of inhibiting, the vast majority of abortions after the first 12 weeks." Here the Act allows, among other means, a commonly used and generally accepted method, so it does not construct a substantial obstacle to the abortion right.

In reaching the conclusion the Act does not require a health exception we reject certain arguments made by the parties on both sides of these cases. On the one hand, the Attorney General urges us to uphold the Act on the basis of the congressional findings alone. Although we review congressional factfinding under a deferential standard, we do not in the circumstances here place dispositive weight on Congress' findings. The Court retains an independent constitutional duty to review factual findings where constitutional rights are at stake . . . . [some discussion omitted]

As respondents have noted, and the District Courts recognized, some recitations in the Act are factually incorrect . . . . Whether or not accurate at the time, some of the important findings have been superseded. Two examples suffice. Congress determined no medical schools provide instruction on the prohibited procedure. The testimony in the District Courts, however, demonstrated intact D&E is taught at medical schools . . . . Congress also found there existed a medical consensus that the prohibited procedure is never medically necessary. The evidence presented in the District Courts contradicts that conclusion . . . . Uncritical deference to Congress' factual findings in these cases is inappropriate.

On the other hand, relying on the Court's opinion in *Stenberg*, respondents contend that an abortion regulation must contain a health exception "if 'substantial medical authority supports the proposition that banning a particular procedure could endanger women's health.'" . . . As illustrated by respondents' arguments and the decisions of the Courts of Appeals, *Stenberg* has been interpreted to leave no margin of error for legislatures to act in the face of medical uncertainty . . . .

A zero tolerance policy would strike down legitimate abortion regulations, like the present one, if some part of the medical community were disinclined to follow the proscription. This is too exacting a standard to impose on the legislative power, exercised in this instance under the Commerce Clause, to regulate the medical profession. Considerations of marginal safety, including the balance of risks, are within the legislative competence when the regulation is rational and in pursuit of legitimate ends. When standard medical options are available, mere convenience does not suffice to displace them; and if some procedures have different risks than others, it does not follow that the State is altogether barred from imposing reasonable regulations. The Act is not invalid on its face where there is uncertainty over whether the barred procedure is ever necessary to preserve a woman's health, given the availability of other abortion procedures that are considered to be safe alternatives.

V

The considerations we have discussed support our further determination that these facial attacks should not have been entertained in the first instance. In these circumstances the proper means to consider exceptions is by as-applied challenge. The Government has acknowledged that preenforcement, as-applied challenges to the Act can be maintained. This is the proper manner to protect the health of the woman if it can be shown that in discrete and well-defined instances a particular condition has or is likely to occur in which the procedure prohibited by the Act must be used. In an as-applied challenge the nature of the medical risk can be better quantified and balanced than in a facial attack.

The latitude given facial challenges in the First Amendment context is inapplicable here. Broad challenges of this type impose "a heavy burden" upon the parties maintaining the suit. What that burden consists of in the specific context of abortion statutes has been a subject of some question . . . . We need not resolve that debate.

As the previous sections of this opinion explain, respondents have not demonstrated that the Act would be unconstitutional in a large fraction of relevant cases. We note that the statute here applies to all instances in which the doctor proposes to use the prohibited procedure, not merely those in which the woman suffers from medical complications. It is neither our obligation nor within our traditional institutional role to resolve questions of constitutionality with respect to each potential situation that might develop. "[I]t would indeed be undesirable for this Court to consider every conceivable situation which might possibly arise in the application of complex and comprehensive legislation." For this reason, "[a]s-applied challenges are the basic building blocks of constitutional adjudication." . . .

The Act is open to a proper as-applied challenge in a discrete case . . . . No as-applied challenge need be brought if the prohibition in the Act threatens a woman's life because the Act already contains a life exception.

* * *

Respondents have not demonstrated that the Act, as a facial matter, is void for vagueness, or that it imposes an undue burden on a woman's right to abortion based on its overbreadth or lack of a health exception. For these reasons the judgments of the Courts of Appeals for the Eighth and Ninth Circuits are reversed.

It is so ordered.

[Citations and footnotes omitted. Concurring and dissenting opinions omitted.]

Cases Relating to Chapter 10

Offenses against Public Peace

PAPACHRISTOU ET AL.
v.
CITY OF JACKSONVILLE

SUPREME COURT OF THE UNITED STATES

405 U.S. 156 (1972)

Mr. Justice Douglas delivered the opinion of the Court.

This case involves eight defendants who were convicted in a Florida municipal court of violating a Jacksonville, Florida, vagrancy ordinance. Their convictions were affirmed by the Florida Circuit Court in a consolidated appeal, and their petition for certiorari was denied by the District Court of Appeal on the authority of *Johnson v. State*, . . . The case is here on a petition for certiorari, which we granted. . . . For reasons which will appear, we reverse.

At issue are five consolidated cases. Margaret Papachristou, Betty Calloway, Eugene Eddie Melton, and Leonard Johnson were all arrested early on a Sunday morning, and charged with vagrancy—"prowling by auto."

Jimmy Lee Smith and Milton Henry were charged with vagrancy—"vagabonds."

Henry Edward Heath and a codefendant were arrested for vagrancy—"loitering" and "common thief."

Thomas Owen Campbell was charged with vagrancy—"common thief."

Hugh Brown was charged with vagrancy— "disorderly loitering on street" and "disorderly conduct—resisting arrest with violence."

The facts are stipulated. Papachristou and Calloway are white females. Melton and Johnson are black males. Papachristou was enrolled in a job-training program sponsored by the State Employment Service at Florida Junior College in Jacksonville. Calloway was a typing and shorthand teacher at a state mental institution located near Jacksonville. She was the owner of the automobile in which the four defendants were arrested. Melton was a Vietnam war veteran who had been released from the Navy after nine months in a veterans' hospital. On the date of his arrest he was a part-time computer helper while attending college as a full-time student in Jacksonville. Johnson was a tow-motor operator in a grocery chain warehouse and was a lifelong resident of Jacksonville.

At the time of their arrest the four of them were riding in Calloway's car on the main thoroughfare in Jacksonville. They had left a restaurant owned by Johnson's uncle where they had eaten and were on their way to a nightclub. The arresting officers denied that the racial mixture in the car played any part in the decision to make the arrest. The arrest, they said, was made because the defendants had stopped near a used-car lot which had been broken into several times. There was, however, no evidence of any breaking and entering on the night in question.

Of these four charged with "prowling by auto" none had been previously arrested except Papachristou who had once been convicted of a municipal offense.

Jimmy Lee Smith and Milton Henry (who is not a petitioner) were arrested between 9 and 10 a. m. on a weekday in downtown Jacksonville, while waiting for a friend who was to lend them a car so they could apply for a job at a produce company. Smith was a part-time produce worker and part-time organizer for a Negro political group. He had a common-law wife and three children supported by him and his wife. He had been arrested several times but convicted only once. Smith's companion, Henry, was an 18-year-old high school student with no previous record of arrest.

This morning it was cold, and Smith had no jacket, so they went briefly into a dry cleaning shop to wait, but left when requested to do so. They thereafter walked back and forth two or three times over a two-block stretch looking for their friend. The store owners, who apparently were wary of Smith and his companion, summoned two police officers who searched the men and found neither had a weapon. But they were arrested because the officers said they had no identification and because the officers did not believe their story.

Heath and a codefendant were arrested for "loitering" and for "common thief." Both were residents of Jacksonville, Heath having lived there all his life and being employed at an automobile body shop. Heath had previously been arrested but his codefendant had no arrest record. Heath and his companion were arrested when they drove up to a residence shared by Heath's girl friend and some other girls. Some police officers were already there in the process of arresting another man. When Heath and his companion started backing out of the driveway, the officers signaled to them to stop and asked them to get out of the car, which they did. Thereupon they and the automobile were searched. Although no contraband or incriminating evidence was found, they were both arrested, Heath being charged with being a "common thief" because he was reputed to be a thief. The codefendant was charged with "loitering" because he was standing in the driveway, an act which the officers admitted was done only at their command.

Campbell was arrested as he reached his home very early one morning and was charged with "common thief." He was stopped by officers because he was traveling at a high rate of speed, yet no speeding charge was placed against him.

Brown was arrested when he was observed leaving a downtown Jacksonville hotel by a police officer seated in a cruiser. The police testified he was reputed to be a thief, narcotics pusher, and generally opprobrious character. The officer called Brown over to the car, intending at that time to arrest him unless he had a good explanation for being on the street. Brown walked over to the police cruiser, as commanded, and the officer began to search him, apparently preparatory to placing him in the car. In the process of the search he came on two small packets which were later found to contain heroin. When the officer touched the pocket where the packets were, Brown began to resist. He was charged with "disorderly loitering on street" and "disorderly conduct—resisting arrest with violence." While he was also charged with a narcotics violation, that charge was *nolled*.

Jacksonville's ordinance and Florida's statute were "derived from early English law," . . . , and employ "archaic language" in their definitions of vagrants. . . . The history is an oftentold tale. The breakup of feudal estates in England led to labor shortages which in turn resulted in the Statutes of Laborers, designed to stabilize the labor force by prohibiting increases in wages and prohibiting the movement of workers from their home areas in search of improved conditions. Later vagrancy laws became criminal aspects of the poor laws. The series of laws passed in England on the subject became increasingly severe. But "the theory of the Elizabethan poor laws no longer fits the facts," . . . . The conditions which spawned these laws may be gone, but the archaic classifications remain.

This ordinance is void for vagueness, both in the sense that it "fails to give a person of ordinary intelligence fair notice that his contemplated conduct is forbidden by the statute," . . . , and because it encourages arbitrary and erratic arrests and convictions. . . .

Living under a rule of law entails various suppositions, one of which is that "[all persons] are entitled to be informed as to what the State commands or forbids." . . .

Lanzetta is one of a well-recognized group of cases insisting that the law give fair notice of the offending conduct. . . . In the field of regulatory statutes governing business activities, where the acts limited are in a narrow category, greater leeway is allowed. . . .

The poor among us, the minorities, the average householder are not in business and not alerted to the regulatory schemes of vagrancy laws; and we assume they would have no understanding of their meaning and impact if they read them. Nor are they protected from being caught in the vagrancy net by the necessity of having a specific intent to commit an unlawful act. . . .

The Jacksonville ordinance makes criminal activities which by modern standards are normally innocent. "Nightwalking" is one. Florida construes the ordinance not to make criminal one night's wandering, . . . We know, however, from experience that sleepless people often walk at night, perhaps hopeful that sleep-inducing relaxation will result.

Luis Munoz-Marin, former Governor of Puerto Rico, commented once that "loafing" was a national virtue in his Commonwealth and that it should be encouraged. It is, however, a crime in Jacksonville.

"Persons able to work but habitually living upon the earnings of their wives or minor children"—like habitually living "without visible means of support"—might implicate unemployed pillars of the community who have married rich wives.

"Persons able to work but habitually living upon the earnings of their wives or minor children" may also embrace unemployed people out of the labor market, by reason of a recession or disemployed by reason of technological or so-called structural displacements.

Persons "wandering or strolling" from place to place have been extolled by Walt Whitman and Vachel Lindsay. The qualification "without any lawful purpose or object" may be a trap for innocent acts. Persons "neglecting all lawful business and habitually spending their time by frequenting . . . places where alcoholic beverages are sold or served" would literally embrace many members of golf clubs and city clubs.

Walkers and strollers and wanderers may be going to or coming from a burglary. Loafers or loiterers may be "casing" a place for a holdup. Letting one's wife support him is an intra-family matter, and normally of no concern to the police. Yet it may, of course, be the setting for numerous crimes.

The difficulty is that these activities are historically part of the amenities of life as we have known them. They are not mentioned in the Constitution or in the Bill of Rights. These unwritten amenities have been in part responsible for giving our people the feeling of independence and self-confidence, the feeling of creativity. These amenities have dignified the right of dissent and have honored the right to be nonconformists and the right to defy submissiveness. They have encouraged lives of high spirits rather than hushed, suffocating silence.

They are embedded in Walt Whitman's writings, especially in his "Song of the Open Road." They are reflected, too, in the spirit of Vachel Lindsay's "I Want to Go Wandering," and by Henry D. Thoreau.

This aspect of the vagrancy ordinance before us is suggested by what this Court said in 1876 about a broad criminal statute enacted by Congress: "It would certainly be dangerous if the legislature could set a net large enough to catch all possible offenders, and leave it to the courts to step inside and say who could be rightfully detained, and who should be set at large." . . .

While that was a federal case, the due process implications are equally applicable to the States and to this vagrancy ordinance. Here the net cast is large, not to give the courts the power to pick and choose but to increase the arsenal of the police. In *Winters v. New York*, . . . , the Court struck down a New York statute that made criminal the distribution of a magazine made up principally of items of criminal deeds of bloodshed or lust so massed as to become vehicles for inciting violent and depraved crimes against the person. The infirmity the Court found was vagueness—the absence of "ascertainable standards of guilt" . . . in the sensitive First Amendment area. Mr. Justice Frankfurter dissented. But concerned as he, and many others, had been over the vagrancy laws, he added:

"Only a word needs to be said regarding *Lanzetta v. New Jersey*, ... The case involved a New Jersey statute of the type that seek to control 'vagrancy.' These statutes are in a class by themselves, in view of the familiar abuses to which they are put. . . . Definiteness is designedly avoided so as to allow the net to be cast at large, to enable men to be caught who are vaguely undesirable in the eyes of police and prosecution, although not chargeable with any particular offense. In short, these 'vagrancy statutes' and laws against 'gangs' are not fenced in by the text of the statute or by the subject matter so as to give notice of conduct to be avoided." . . .

Where the list of crimes is so all-inclusive and generalized as the one in this ordinance, those convicted may be punished for no more than vindicating affronts to police authority:

"The common ground which brings such a motley assortment of human troubles before the magistrates in vagrancy-type proceedings is the procedural laxity which permits 'conviction' for almost any kind of conduct and the existence of the House of Correction as an easy and convenient dumping-ground for problems that appear to have no other immediate solution." . . .

Another aspect of the ordinance's vagueness appears when we focus, not on the lack of notice given a potential offender, but on the effect of the unfettered discretion it places in the hands of the Jacksonville police. Caleb Foote, an early student of this subject, has called the vagrancy-type law as offering "punishment by analogy." . . . Such crimes, though long common in Russia, are not compatible with our constitutional system. We allow our police to make arrests only on "probable cause," a Fourth and Fourteenth Amendment standard applicable to the States as well as to the Federal Government. Arresting a person on suspicion, like arresting a person for investigation, is foreign to our system, even when the arrest is for past criminality. Future criminality, however, is the common justification for the presence of vagrancy statutes. . . . Florida has, indeed, construed her vagrancy statute "as necessary regulations," *inter alia*, "to deter vagabondage and prevent crimes." . . .

A direction by a legislature to the police to arrest all "suspicious" persons would not pass constitutional muster. A vagrancy prosecution may be merely the cloak for a conviction which could not be obtained on the real but undisclosed grounds for the arrest. . . . But as Chief Justice Hewart said in *Frederick Dean*, . . . (1924):

"It would be in the highest degree unfortunate if in any part of the country those who are responsible for setting in motion the criminal law should entertain, connive at or coquette with the idea that in a case where there is not enough evidence to charge the prisoner with an attempt to commit a crime, the prosecution may, nevertheless, on such insufficient evidence, succeed in obtaining and upholding a conviction under the Vagrancy Act, 1824."

Those generally implicated by the imprecise terms of the ordinance—poor people, nonconformists, dissenters, idlers—may be required to comport themselves according to the lifestyle deemed appropriate by the Jacksonville police and the courts. Where, as here, there are no standards governing the exercise of the discretion granted by the ordinance, the scheme permits and encourages an arbitrary and discriminatory enforcement of the law. It furnishes a convenient tool for "harsh and discriminatory enforcement by local prosecuting officials, against particular groups deemed to merit their displeasure." . . . It results in a regime in which the poor and the unpopular are permitted to "stand on a public sidewalk . . . only at the whim of any police officer." . . . . Under this ordinance,

"If some carefree type of fellow is satisfied to work just so much, and no more, as will pay for one square meal, some wine, and a flophouse daily, but a court thinks this kind of living subhuman, the fellow can be forced to raise his sights or go to jail as a vagrant." . . .

A presumption that people who might walk or loaf or loiter or stroll or frequent houses where liquor is sold, or who are supported by their wives or who look suspicious to the police are to become future criminals is too precarious for a rule of law. The implicit presumption in these generalized vagrancy standards—that crime is being nipped in the bud—is too extravagant to deserve extended treatment. Of course, vagrancy statutes are useful to the police. Of course, they are nets making easy the roundup of so-called undesirables. But the rule of law implies equality and justice in its application. Vagrancy laws of the Jacksonville type teach that the scales of justice are so tipped that evenhanded administration of the law is not possible. The rule of law, evenly applied to minorities as well as majorities, to the poor as well as the rich, is the great mucilage that holds society together.

The Jacksonville ordinance cannot be squared with our constitutional standards and is plainly unconstitutional.

Reversed.

[Footnotes and citations omitted. Concurring and dissenting opinions omitted.]

LARRY D. HIIBEL
v.
SIXTH JUDICIAL DISTRICT COURT OF NEVADA, HUMBOLDT COUNTY

SUPREME COURT OF THE UNITED STATES

542 U.S. 177 (2004)

Justice Kennedy delivered the opinion of the Court.

The petitioner was arrested and convicted for refusing to identify himself during a stop allowed by *Terry v. Ohio*, . . . (1968). He challenges his conviction under the Fourth and Fifth Amendments to the United States Constitution, applicable to the States through the Fourteenth Amendment.

I

The sheriff's department in Humboldt County, Nevada, received an afternoon telephone call reporting an assault. The caller reported seeing a man assault a woman in a red and silver GMC truck on Grass Valley Road. Deputy Sheriff Lee Dove was dispatched to investigate. When the officer arrived at the scene, he found the truck parked on the side of the road. A man was standing by the truck, and a young woman was sitting inside it. The officer observed skid marks in the gravel behind the vehicle, leading him to believe it had come to a sudden stop.

The officer approached the man and explained that he was investigating a report of a fight. The man appeared to be intoxicated. The officer asked him if he had "any identification on [him]," which we understand as a request to produce a driver's license or some other form of written identification. The man refused and asked why the officer wanted to see identification. The officer responded that he was conducting an investigation and needed to see some identification. The unidentified man became agitated and insisted he had done nothing wrong. The officer explained that he wanted to find out who the man was and what he was doing there. After continued refusals to comply with the officer's request for identification, the man began to taunt the officer by placing his hands behind his back and telling the officer to arrest him and take him to jail. This routine kept up for several minutes:

the officer asked for identification 11 times and was refused each time. After warning the man that he would be arrested if he continued to refuse to comply, the officer placed him under arrest.

We now know that the man arrested on Grass Valley Road is Larry Dudley Hiibel. Hiibel was charged with "willfully resist[ing], delay[ing], or obstruct[ing] a public officer in discharging or attempting to discharge any legal duty of his office" in violation of Nev. Rev. Stat. (NRS) § 199.280 (2003). The government reasoned that Hiibel had obstructed the officer in carrying out his duties under § 171.123, a Nevada statute that defines the legal rights and duties of a police officer in the context of an investigative stop. Section 171.123 provides in relevant part:

"1. Any peace officer may detain any person whom the officer encounters under circumstances which reasonably indicate that the person has committed, is committing or is about to commit a crime.

. . . . .

"3. The officer may detain the person pursuant to this section only to ascertain his identity and the suspicious circumstances surrounding his presence abroad. Any person so detained shall identify himself, but may not be compelled to answer any other inquiry of any peace officer."

Hiibel was tried in the Justice Court of Union Township. The court agreed that Hiibel's refusal to identify himself as required by § 171.123 "obstructed and delayed Dove as a public officer in attempting to discharge his duty" in violation of § 199.280. . . . Hiibel was convicted and fined $250. The Sixth Judicial District Court affirmed, rejecting Hiibel's argument that the application of § 171.123 to his case violated the Fourth and Fifth Amendments. On review the Supreme Court of Nevada rejected the Fourth Amendment challenge in a divided opinion. . . . Hiibel petitioned for rehearing, seeking explicit resolution of his Fifth Amendment challenge. The petition was denied without opinion. We granted certiorari. . . . [some discussion omitted]

II

NRS § 171.123(3) is an enactment sometimes referred to as a "stop and identify" statute. . . .

Stop and identify statutes often combine elements of traditional vagrancy laws with provisions intended to regulate police behavior in the course of investigatory stops. The statutes vary from State to State, but all permit an officer to ask or require a suspect to disclose his identity. A few States model their statutes on the Uniform Arrest Act, a model code that permits an officer to stop a person reasonably suspected of committing a crime and "demand of him his name, address, business abroad and whither he is going." . . . . Other statutes are based on the text proposed by the American Law Institute as part of the Institute's Model Penal Code. . . . The provision, originally designated § 250.12, provides that a person who is loitering "under circumstances which justify suspicion that he may be engaged or about to engage in crime commits a violation if he refuses the request of a peace officer that he identify himself and give a reasonably credible account of the lawfulness of his conduct and purposes." § 250.12 . . . . In some States, a suspect's refusal to identify himself is a misdemeanor offense or civil violation; in others, it is a factor to be considered in whether the suspect has violated loitering laws. In other States, a suspect may decline to identify himself without penalty.

Stop and identify statutes have their roots in early English vagrancy laws that required suspected vagrants to face arrest unless they gave "a good Account of themselves," . . . , a power that itself reflected common-law rights of private persons to "arrest any suspicious night-walker, and detain him till he give a good account of himself . . . ". In recent decades, the Court has found constitutional infirmity in traditional vagrancy laws. In *Papachristou v. Jacksonville,* . . . (1972), the Court held that a traditional vagrancy law was void for vagueness. Its broad scope and imprecise terms denied proper notice to potential offenders and permitted police officers to exercise unfettered discretion in the enforcement of the law. . . .

The Court has recognized similar constitutional limitations on the scope and operation of stop and identify statutes. In *Brown v. Texas,* . . . (1979), the Court invalidated a conviction for violating a Texas stop and identify statute on Fourth Amendment grounds. The Court ruled that the initial stop was not based on specific, objective facts establishing reasonable suspicion to believe the suspect was involved in criminal activity. . . . Absent that factual basis for detaining the defendant, the Court held, the risk of "arbitrary and abusive police practices" was too great and the stop was impermissible. . . . Four Terms later, the Court invalidated a modified stop and identify statute on vagueness grounds. . . . The California law in *Kolender* required a suspect to give an officer "credible and reliable" identification when asked to identify himself. . . . The Court held that the statute was void because it provided no standard for determining what a suspect must do to comply with it, resulting in "virtually unrestrained power to arrest and charge persons with a violation." . . .

The present case begins where our prior cases left off. Here there is no question that the initial stop was based on reasonable suspicion, satisfying the Fourth Amendment requirements noted in *Brown* Further, the petitioner has not alleged that the statute is unconstitutionally vague, as in *Kolender.* Here the Nevada statute is narrower and more precise. The statute in *Kolender* had been interpreted to require a suspect to give the officer "credible and reliable" identification. In contrast, the Nevada Supreme Court has interpreted NRS § 171.123(3) to require only that a suspect disclose his name. . . . As we understand it, the statute does not require a suspect to give the officer a driver's license or any other document. Provided that the suspect either states his name or communicates it to the officer by other means—a choice, we assume, that the suspect may make—the statute is satisfied and no violation occurs. . . .

III

Hiibel argues that his conviction cannot stand because the officer's conduct violated his Fourth Amendment rights. We disagree.

Asking questions is an essential part of police investigations. In the ordinary course a police officer is free to ask a person for identification without implicating the Fourth Amendment. "[I]nterrogation relating to one's identity or a request for identification by the police does not, by itself, constitute a Fourth Amendment seizure." . . . .

Beginning with *Terry v. Ohio,* . . . (1968), the Court has recognized that a law enforcement officer's reasonable suspicion that a person may be involved in criminal activity permits the officer to stop the person for a brief time and take additional steps to investigate further. . . . To ensure that the resulting seizure is constitutionally reasonable, a *Terry* stop must be limited. The officer's action must be "justified at its inception, and . . . reasonably related in scope to the circumstances which justified the interference in the first place." . . . . For example, the seizure cannot continue for an excessive period of time, . . . or resemble a traditional arrest, ...

Our decisions make clear that questions concerning a suspect's identity are a routine and accepted part of many *Terry* stops. . . .

Obtaining a suspect's name in the course of a *Terry* stop serves important government interests. Knowledge of identity may inform an officer that a suspect is wanted for another offense, or has a record of violence or mental disorder. On the other hand, knowing identity may help clear a suspect and allow the police to concentrate their efforts elsewhere. Identity may prove particularly important in cases such as this, where the police are investigating what appears to be a domestic assault. Officers called to investigate domestic disputes need to know whom they are dealing with in order to assess the situation, the threat to their own safety, and possible danger to the potential victim.

Although it is well established that an officer may ask a suspect to identify himself in the course of a *Terry* stop, it has been an open question whether the suspect can be arrested and prosecuted for refusal to answer. . . . Petitioner draws our attention to statements in prior opinions that, according to him, answer the question in his favor. In *Terry,* Justice White stated in a concurring opinion that a person detained in an investigative stop can be questioned but is "not obliged to answer, answers may not be compelled, and refusal to answer furnishes no basis for an arrest." . . . . The Court cited this opinion in dicta in *Berkemer v. McCarty,* . . . (1984), a decision holding that a routine traffic stop is not a custodial stop requiring the protections of *Miranda v. Arizona,* . . . (1966). In the course of explaining why *Terry* stops have not been subject to *Miranda,* the Court suggested reasons why *Terry* stops have a "nonthreatening

character," among them the fact that a suspect detained during a *Terry* stop "is not obliged to respond" to questions. . . . According to petitioner, these statements establish a right to refuse to answer questions during a *Terry* stop.

We do not read these statements as controlling. The passages recognize that the Fourth Amendment does not impose obligations on the citizen but instead provides rights against the government. As a result, the Fourth Amendment itself cannot require a suspect to answer questions. This case concerns a different issue, however. Here, the source of the legal obligation arises from Nevada state law, not the Fourth Amendment. Further, the statutory obligation does not go beyond answering an officer's request to disclose a name. . . . As a result, we cannot view the dicta in *Berkemer* or Justice White's concurrence in *Terry* as answering the question whether a State can compel a suspect to disclose his name during a *Terry* stop.

The principles of *Terry* permit a State to require a suspect to disclose his name in the course of a *Terry* stop. The reasonableness of a seizure under the Fourth Amendment is determined "by balancing its intrusion on the individual's Fourth Amendment interests against its promotion of legitimate government interests." . . . . The Nevada statute satisfies that standard. The request for identity has an immediate relation to the purpose, rationale, and practical demands of a *Terry* stop. The threat of criminal sanction helps ensure that the request for identity does not become a legal nullity. On the other hand, the Nevada statute does not alter the nature of the stop itself: it does not change its duration, . . . , or its location, ... A state law requiring a suspect to disclose his name in the course of a valid *Terry* stop is consistent with Fourth Amendment prohibitions against unreasonable searches and seizures.

Petitioner argues that the Nevada statute circumvents the probable cause requirement, in effect allowing an officer to arrest a person for being suspicious. According to petitioner, this creates a risk of arbitrary police conduct that the Fourth Amendment does not permit. . . . These are familiar concerns; they were central to the opinion in *Papachristou,* and also to the decisions limiting the operation of stop and identify statutes in *Kolender* and *Brown.* Petitioner's concerns are met by the requirement that a *Terry* stop must be justified at its inception and "reasonably related in scope to the circumstances which justified" the initial stop. . . . Under these principles, an officer may not arrest a suspect for failure to identify himself if the request for identification is not reasonably related to the circumstances justifying the stop. The Court noted a similar limitation in *Hayes*, where it suggested that *Terry* may permit an officer to determine a suspect's identity by compelling the suspect to submit to fingerprinting only if there is "a reasonable basis for believing that fingerprinting will establish or negate the suspect's connection with that crime." . . . . It is clear in this case that the request for identification was "reasonably related in scope to the circumstances which justified" the stop. . . . The officer's request was a common-sense inquiry, not an effort to obtain an arrest for failure to identify after a *Terry* stop yielded insufficient evidence. The stop, the request, and the State's requirement of a response did not contravene the guarantees of the Fourth Amendment.

IV

Petitioner further contends that his conviction violates the Fifth Amendment's prohibition on compelled self-incrimination. The Fifth Amendment states that "[n]o person . . . shall be compelled in any criminal case to be a witness against himself." To qualify for the Fifth Amendment privilege, a communication must be testimonial, incriminating, and compelled. . . .

Respondents urge us to hold that the statements NRS § 171.123(3) requires are nontestimonial, and so outside the Clause's scope. We decline to resolve the case on that basis. "[T]o be testimonial, an accused's communication must itself, explicitly or implicitly, relate a factual assertion or disclose information." . . . . Stating one's name may qualify as an assertion of fact relating to identity. Production of identity documents might meet the definition as well. As we noted in *Hubbell*, acts of production may yield testimony establishing "the existence, authenticity, and custody of items [the police seek]." . . . . Even if these required actions are testimonial, however, petitioner's challenge must fail because in this case disclosure of his name presented no reasonable danger of incrimination.

The Fifth Amendment prohibits only compelled testimony that is incriminating. . . . A claim of Fifth Amendment privilege must establish

> "reasonable ground to apprehend danger to the witness from his being compelled to answer. . . . [T]he danger to be apprehended must be real and appreciable, with reference to the ordinary operation of law in the ordinary course of things,—not a danger of an imaginary and unsubstantial character, having reference to some extraordinary and barely possible contingency, so improbable that no reasonable man would suffer it to influence his conduct." . . .

As we stated in *Kastigar v. United States,* . . . (1972), the Fifth Amendment privilege against compulsory self-incrimination "protects against any disclosures that the witness reasonably believes could be used in a criminal prosecution or could lead to other evidence that might be so used." Suspects who have been granted immunity from prosecution may, therefore, be compelled to answer; with the threat of prosecution removed, there can be no reasonable belief that the evidence will be used against them. . . .

In this case petitioner's refusal to disclose his name was not based on any articulated real and appreciable fear that his name would be used to incriminate him, or that it "would furnish a link in the chain of evidence needed to prosecute" him. . . . As best we can tell, petitioner refused to identify himself only because he thought his name was none of the officer's business. Even today, petitioner does not explain how the disclosure of his name could have been used against him in a criminal case. While we recognize petitioner's strong belief that he should not have to disclose his identity, the Fifth Amendment does not override the Nevada Legislature's judgment to the contrary absent a reasonable belief that the disclosure would tend to incriminate him.

The narrow scope of the disclosure requirement is also important. One's identity is, by definition, unique; yet it is, in another sense, a universal characteristic. Answering a request to disclose a name is likely to be so insignificant in the scheme of things as to be incriminating only in unusual circumstances. . . . In every criminal case, it is known and must be known who has been arrested and who is being tried. . . . Even witnesses who plan to invoke the Fifth Amendment privilege answer when their names are called to take the stand. Still, a case may arise where there is a substantial allegation that furnishing identity at the time of a stop would have given the police a link in the chain of evidence needed to convict the individual of a separate offense. In that case, the court can then consider whether the privilege applies, and, if the Fifth Amendment has been violated, what remedy must follow. We need not resolve those questions here.

The judgment of the Nevada Supreme Court is affirmed.

[Footnotes and citations omitted. Concurring and dissenting opinions omitted.]

Cases Relating to Chapter 11

Offenses against Justice Administration

CITY OF HOUSTON, TEXAS
v.
HILL

SUPREME COURT OF THE UNITED STATES

482 U.S. 451 (1987)

Justice Brennan delivered the opinion of the Court.

This case presents the question whether a municipal ordinance that makes it unlawful to interrupt a police officer in the performance of his or her duties is unconstitutionally overbroad under the First Amendment.

I

Appellee Raymond Wayne Hill is a lifelong resident of Houston, Texas. At the time this lawsuit began, he worked as a paralegal and as executive director of the Houston Human Rights League. A member of the board of the Gay Political Caucus, which he helped found in 1975, Hill was also affiliated with a Houston radio station, and had carried city and county press passes since 1975. He lived in Montrose, a "diverse and eclectic neighborhood" that is the center of gay political and social life in Houston. . . .

The incident that sparked this lawsuit occurred in the Montrose area on February 14, 1982. Hill observed a friend, Charles Hill, intentionally stopping traffic on a busy street, evidently to enable a vehicle to enter traffic. Two Houston police officers, one of whom was named Kelley, approached Charles and began speaking with him. According to the District Court, "shortly thereafter" Hill began shouting at the officers "in an admitted attempt to divert Kelley's attention from Charles Hill." . . . Hill first shouted: "Why don't you pick on somebody your own size?" After Officer Kelley responded: "Are you interrupting me in my official capacity as a Houston police officer?" Hill then shouted: "Yes, why don't you pick on somebody my size?" . . . Hill was arrested under Houston Code of Ordinances, § 34-11(a), for "willfully or intentionally interrupt[ing] a city policeman . . . by verbal challenge during an investigation." . . . Charles Hill was not arrested. Hill was then acquitted after a nonjury trial in Municipal Court.

Code of Ordinances, City of Houston, Texas, § 34-11(a) (1984), reads:

> "Sec. 34-11. Assaulting or interfering with policemen. "(a) It shall be unlawful for any person to assault, strike or in any manner oppose, molest, abuse or interrupt any policeman in the execution of his duty, or any person summoned to aid in making an arrest."

Following his acquittal in the Charles Hill incident, Hill brought the suit in the Federal District Court for the Southern District of Texas, seeking (1) a declaratory judgment that § 34-11(a) was unconstitutional both on its face and as it had been applied to him, (2) a permanent injunction against any attempt to enforce the ordinance, (3) an order expunging the records of his arrests under the ordinance, and (4) damages and attorney's fees under 42 U. S. C. §§ 1983 and 1988.

At trial, Hill introduced records provided by the city regarding both the frequency with which arrests had been made for violation of the ordinance and the type of conduct with which those arrested had been charged. He also introduced evidence and testimony concerning the arrests of several reporters under the ordinance. Finally, Hill introduced evidence regarding his own experience with the ordinance, under which he has been arrested four times since 1975, but never convicted.

The District Court held that Hill's evidence did not demonstrate that the ordinance had been unconstitutionally applied. The court also rejected Hill's contention that the ordinance was unconstitutionally vague or overbroad on its face. The ordinance was not vague, the court stated, because:

> "the wording of the ordinance is sufficiently definite to put a person of reasonable intelligence on fair notice of what actions are forbidden. In particular, the Court finds that the use of words such as 'interrupt' are sufficiently clear by virtue of their commonly-understood, everyday definitions. Interrupt commonly means to cause one to cease, such as stopping someone in the middle of something. The Plaintiff, for example, clearly 'interrupted' the police officers regarding the Charles Hill incident." . . .

The court also held that the statute was not overboard because "the ordinance does not, at least facially, proscribe speech or conduct which is protected by the First Amendment." . . . .

A panel of the Court of Appeals reversed. . . . The city's suggestion for rehearing *en banc* was granted, and the Court of Appeals, by a vote of 8-7, upheld the judgment of the panel. . . . The Court of Appeals agreed with the District Court's conclusion that the ordinance was not vague, and that it "plainly encompasse[d] mere verbal as well as physical conduct." . . . . Applying the standard established in *Broadrick v. Oklahoma*, . . . (1973), however, the Court of Appeals concluded that the ordinance was substantially overbroad. It found that "[a] significant range of protected speech and expression is punishable and might be deterred by the literal wording of the statute." . . . .

The Court of Appeals also reviewed the evidence of the unconstitutional application of the ordinance which Hill had introduced at trial. The court did not disturb the District Court's ruling that the statute had not been unconstitutionally applied to Hill or to the reporters. It did conclude, however, that other evidence not mentioned by the District Court revealed "a realistic danger of, and a substantial potential for, the unconstitutional application of the ordinance." . . . . This evidence showed that the ordinance "is officially regarded as penalizing the mere interruption of a policeman while in the line of duty," . . . , and has been employed to make arrests for, *inter alia*, "arguing," "talking," "interfering," "failing to remain quiet," "refusing to remain silent," "verbal abuse," "cursing," "verbally yelling," and "talking loudly, walking through scene." . . .

The city appealed, claiming that the Court of Appeals erred in holding the ordinance facially overboard and in not abstaining until the ordinance had been construed by the state courts. We noted probable jurisdiction, . . . and now affirm.

II

The elements of First Amendment overbreadth analysis are familiar. Only a statute that is substantially overbroad may be invalidated on its face. . . . Criminal statutes must be scrutinized with particular care, . . . ; those that make unlawful a substantial amount of constitutionally protected conduct may be held facially invalid even if they also have legitimate application. . . .

The city's principal argument is that the ordinance does not inhibit the exposition of ideas, and that it bans "core criminal conduct" not protected by the First Amendment. . . . In its view, the application of the ordinance to Hill illustrates that the police employ it only to prohibit such conduct, and not "as a subterfuge to control or dissuade free expression." . . . Since the ordinance is "content-neutral," and since there is no evidence that the city has applied the ordinance to chill particular speakers or ideas, the city concludes that the ordinance is not substantially overbroad.

We disagree with the city's characterization for several reasons. First, the enforceable portion of the ordinance deals not with core criminal conduct, but with speech. As the city has conceded, the language in the ordinance making it unlawful for any person to "assault" or "strike" a police officer is pre-empted by the Texas Penal Code. . . . The city explains, . . . , that "any species of physical assault on a police officer is encompassed within the provisions [§§ 22.01, 22.02] of the Texas Penal Code," and under § 1.08 of the Code, "[no] governmental subdivision or agency may enact or enforce a law that makes any conduct covered by this code an offense subject to a criminal penalty." . . . . Accordingly, the enforceable portion of the ordinance makes it "unlawful for any person to . . . in any manner oppose, molest, abuse or interrupt any policeman in the execution of his duty," and thereby prohibits verbal interruptions of police officers.

Second, contrary to the city's contention, the First Amendment protects a significant amount of verbal criticism and challenge directed at police officers. "Speech is often provocative and challenging. . . . [But it] is nevertheless protected against censorship or punishment, unless shown likely to produce a clear and present danger of a serious substantive evil that rises far above public inconvenience, annoyance, or unrest." . . . In *Lewis v. City of New Orleans*, . . . (1974), for example, the appellant was found to have yelled obscenities and threats at an officer who had asked appellant's husband to produce his driver's license. Appellant was convicted under a municipal ordinance that made it a crime "'for any person wantonly to curse or revile or to use obscene or opprobrious language toward or with reference to any member of the city police while in the actual performance of his duty.'" . . . . We vacated the conviction and invalidated the ordinance as facially overbroad. Critical to our decision was the fact that the ordinance "punishe[d] only spoken words" and was not limited in scope to fighting words that "'by their very utterance inflict injury or tend to incite an immediate breach of the peace.'" . . . Moreover, in a concurring opinion in *Lewis*, Justice Powell suggested that even the "fighting words" exception recognized in *Chaplinsky v. New Hampshire*, . . . (1942), might require a narrower application in cases involving words addressed to a police officer, because "a properly trained officer may reasonably be expected to 'exercise a higher degree of restraint' than the average citizen, and thus be less likely to respond belligerently to 'fighting words.'" . . .

The Houston ordinance is much more sweeping than the municipal ordinance struck down in *Lewis*. It is not limited to fighting words nor even to obscene or opprobrious language, but prohibits speech that "in any manner . . . interrupt[s]" an officer. The Constitution does not allow such speech to be made a crime. The freedom of individuals verbally to oppose or challenge police action without thereby risking arrest is one of the principal characteristics by which we distinguish a free nation from a police state.

The city argues, however, that even if the ordinance encompasses some protected speech, its sweeping nature is both inevitable and essential to maintain public order. The city recalls this Court's observation in *Smith v. Goguen*, . . . (1974):

> "There are areas of human conduct where, by the nature of the problems presented, legislatures simply cannot establish standards with great precision. Control of the broad range of disorderly conduct that may inhibit a policeman in the performance of his official duties may be one such area requiring as it does an on-the-spot assessment of the need to keep order."

The city further suggests that its ordinance is comparable to the disorderly conduct statute upheld against a facial challenge in *Colten v. Kentucky*, . . . (1972).

This Houston ordinance, however, is not narrowly tailored to prohibit only disorderly conduct or fighting words, and in no way resembles the law upheld in *Colten*. Although we appreciate the difficulties of drafting precise laws, we have repeatedly invalidated laws that provide the police with unfettered discretion to arrest individuals for words or conduct that annoy or offend them. As the Court observed over a century ago, "it would certainly be dangerous if the legislature could set a net large enough to catch all possible offenders, and leave it to the courts to step inside and say who could be rightfully detained, and who should be set at large." *United States v. Reese*, . . . (1876).

[Further discussion of similar cases omitted.]

Houston's ordinance criminalizes a substantial amount of constitutionally protected speech, and accords the police unconstitutional discretion in enforcement. The ordinance's plain language is admittedly violated scores of times daily, . . . , yet only some individuals — those chosen by the police in their unguided discretion — are arrested. Far from providing the "breathing space" that "First Amendment freedoms need . . . to survive," . . . , the ordinance is susceptible of regular application to protected expression. We conclude that the ordinance is substantially overbroad, and that the Court of Appeals did not err in holding it facially invalid.

III

The city has also urged us not to reach the merits of Hill's constitutional challenge, but rather to abstain for reasons related to those underlying our decision in *Railroad Comm'n v. Pullman Co.* , . . . (1941). In its view, there are certain limiting constructions readily available to the state courts that would eliminate the ordinance's overbreadth.

[Discussion of state's request for court to consider "abstention" and allow a limited construction of the statute omitted.]

IV

Today's decision reflects the constitutional requirement that, in the face of verbal challenges to police action, officers and municipalities must respond with restraint. We are mindful that the preservation of liberty depends in part upon the maintenance of social order. . . . But the First Amendment recognizes, wisely we think, that a certain amount of expressive disorder not only is inevitable in a society committed to individual freedom, but must itself be protected if that freedom would survive. We therefore affirm the judgment of the Court of Appeals.

It is so ordered.

[Footnotes and citations omitted. Concurring and dissenting opinions omitted.]

BILLY DOYLE MEDFORD
v.
THE STATE OF TEXAS

COURT OF APPEALS OF TEXAS

990 S.W.2d 799 (1999)

Opinion by Judge Dea Ann Smith.
Appellant Billy Doyle Medford appeals from the trial court's denial of his motion to suppress evidence and his subsequent conviction for the offenses of felony escape and possession of cocaine in an amount less than one gram. . . . The jury found that appellant had five prior felony convictions as alleged in the enhancement paragraphs of the indictment. Pursuant to the habitual felony offender statute, the jury assessed punishment for the cocaine possession at 20 years' imprisonment and life imprisonment for the escape conviction. The trial court ordered the sentences to run concurrently. In this appeal, Medford claims that the trial court erred in denying his motion to suppress evidence and by submitting to the jury improper definitions of "custody" and "under arrest" in the escape charge; he also challenges the sufficiency of the evidence to support his escape conviction. We will affirm in part and reverse and render in part the trial-court judgment.

[Discussion concerning all issues other than escape conviction omitted.]

Legal Sufficiency of the Evidence

In his fourth point of error, appellant challenges the legal sufficiency of evidence to convict him of escape. In conducting a legal sufficiency review, we determine whether, after viewing the evidence in the light most favorable to the verdict, any rational trier of fact could have found the essential elements of the crime beyond a reasonable doubt. . . . The elements of escape are that a person (1) escape (2) from custody (3) after having been arrested for, charged with or convicted of an offense. . . .

Appellant argues that the evidence adduced at trial did not legally establish that he escaped from custody while he was under arrest for an offense.

"Escape" is statutorily defined for purposes of chapter 38 of the Penal Code as "unauthorized departure from custody," and "custody" is defined as "under arrest by a peace officer or under restraint by a public servant pursuant to an order of a court." . . . Thus, in order to sustain appellant's conviction, we must find that Medford had been placed under restraint or taken into custody at the time he fled from officers Price and Baladez.

The State argues that actual, physical restraint is not a prerequisite to a showing of custody, citing *Harrell v. State*, . . . (Tex. Crim. App. 1987). The State also posits that an "oral pronouncement of arrest by a police officer to a suspect, with or without any evidence of physical restraint, is sufficient to establish the element of custody, if a reasonable person in the suspect's position would have believed he was not free to leave." For this proposition, the State relies on *Morris v. State*, . . . (*Tex. Crim. App.* 1987) and *Gilbert v. State*, . . . (Tex. App. — Fort Worth 1990, . . .). For reasons we will discuss, we believe that neither proposition is a valid statement of the law as applied to this case.

The issue in *Harrell* was whether a prisoner transferred to a hospital out of medical necessity retained the legal status of arrestee for purposes of determining whether he was in "custody" under section 38.06(a). Before entering the hospital, Harrell was told that he was still under arrest and in custody, and that if he ran away from the hospital he would be treated as if he had escaped from jail. Harrell ignored that admonition and drove to Florida with another patient and a local woman. . . .

The Court of Criminal Appeals upheld Harrell's conviction for escape. The court stated: "We now hold that actual, physical 'hands-on' restraint is not a prerequisite to a showing of custody in the context of the offense of escape. Rather, it is important to look at the legal status of the individual at the time of the escape." . . . .

Examining Harrell's legal status, the court held that Harrell remained under arrest while at the hospital. . . . Because Harrell was still "in custody"

regardless of his physical location, it held that the court of appeals had erred in focusing on the fact that Harrell was not under any kind of physical restraint while at the hospital. . . .

As the Harrell court recognized, the issue of what constitutes an initial arrest was not before the court in that case. . . . However, that is precisely the issue in the present case: whether a person who has been stopped for questioning and who then flees prior to being handcuffed has escaped from "custody" under section 38.06(a). Because Harrell only instructs that physical restraint is not a necessary prerequisite to continuing custody after an arrest and conviction, that rule is inapplicable to the present case.

We next examine the proposition that a person is under arrest or in custody for the purpose of escape if a reasonable person in the position of the arrestee would have believed that he was not free to leave. In *Morris*, the defendant was appealing his conviction for theft; he had not been charged with escape. The court of appeals found that, after being arrested but before being searched, the appellant committed the felony offense of escape by running from the police officer who arrested him. . . . The intermediate court concluded that since Morris's escape in the presence of the police officer provided probable cause for the second arrest, the evidence seized subsequent thereto was properly admitted. . . .

A divided Court of Criminal Appeals affirmed. The three-judge plurality looked to *United States v. Mendenhall*, . . . (1980), which held that a person has been "seized" within the meaning of the Fourth Amendment only if, in view of all the circumstances surrounding the incident, a reasonable person would have believed that he was not free to leave. . . . The plurality then applied the Mendenhall test for "seizure" to the issue of whether a person is "in custody" for purposes of committing the offense of escape. . . . However, as the dissent observed:

> When we treat an offense based on a statutorily defined element of "custody," resort to decisions construing the meaning of "seizure" in the Fourth Amendment is not

likely to solve the problem. . . . Whether a person was "seized" is merely a threshold inquiry in determining a claim that an intrusion upon his liberty or privacy occurred without particularized and objective justification required in the circumstances to render the "seizure" reasonable. Therefore, a "seizure" for purposes of the Fourth Amendment does not necessarily equate with "custody" within the meaning of [the escape statute]. So, federal decisions relied on by the majority do not dictate our construction of a state statute in which the critical component is "custody," not "seizure." . . . .

Two courts of appeals have cited *Morris* and used the *Mendenhall* test to determine that an appellant committed the offense of escape. . . . However, a majority of the Court of Criminal Appeals has never embraced the view advanced by the *Morris* plurality. This Court has discussed *Morris* and questioned the soundness of equating seizure for Fourth Amendment purposes with the statutory definition of "arrest" in the context of escape or resisting arrest. . . . We have also held that the term "custody" in the escape context clearly implies a degree of physical limitation, restraint, or control. . . .

Common sense does not support the idea that a person is "in custody," in the context of the offense of escape, when a reasonable person would not feel free to leave. As appellant's counsel urged at oral argument, a reasonable person might not feel free to leave if a police officer telephoned him at home and instructed him to remain there. Adopting the State's definition of "custody" would lead to the conclusion that a person in that situation would commit the offense of escape simply by departing his home. This result is not compelled either by the statutory definition of "custody" or by controlling case law.

We also find *Morris* distinguishable on its facts. In *Morris*, the detention took place in the controlled space of a probation officer's office; the appellant sat in a chair and was questioned by the arresting officer after being told he was under arrest. Morris decided to flee only after discussing the impact of his arrest on his probation. The arresting officer did not handcuff Morris because he did not have handcuffs with him and

presumably he did not feel the need to subdue Morris any further when Morris was sitting in a chair in the probation office, surrounded by the police officer and the probation officer. The factual circumstances of Morris are similar to those in Harrell because in both cases, the appellant had been placed under arrest and was in a situation in which enough control was being exerted over him that further physical restraint was not believed to be necessary. In the present case, however, custody had not clearly been established when Medford fled, since Officer Price was unsuccessful in his attempt to handcuff Medford immediately after a Terry encounter that took place on a public street.

For these reasons, we believe that *Gilbert v. State*, ... was wrongly decided. In *Gilbert*, the appellant and a young female passenger were observed in a parked car by police officers Solomon and Riddle in an area in which vehicles were prohibited. Both officers ordered the driver to stop after the car began to pull away. As Officer Solomon approached the vehicle, he saw the female passenger pulling up her panties and blue jeans; she exclaimed to Solomon, "he made me do it" and told the officer that she was eleven years old. Officer Solomon then directed Gilbert to stand by the car, where he was ordered into a spread-eagle position, searched, and advised that he was under arrest. However, Gilbert refused to be handcuffed and fled into a nearby park. . . .

The Fort Worth Court of Appeals upheld Gilbert's conviction for escape. . . . The court adopted the Morris plurality's rule that a person is under arrest or in custody for purposes of the escape statute if a reasonable person in the defendant's position would have believed that they were not free to leave. . . . The Gilbert court also repeated the statement from Harrell that "actual, physical 'hands-on' restraint is not a prerequisite to a showing of custody in the context of the offense of escape." . . . . Because a reasonable person in Gilbert's position at the time Officer Solomon was attempting to handcuff him would not have believed that he was free to leave, the court reasoned, Gilbert was in custody and sufficient evidence existed to support his conviction for escape. . . .

Extending the Gilbert court's reasoning, Gilbert would have apparently been in "custody" at the moment the police officers approached his car and advised him to stop — even if they only shouted the warning across a parking lot — since a reasonable person in that situation would presumably not feel free to leave. However, this is precisely the type of situation contemplated by the offense of evading arrest. . . . We decline to expand *Harrell* beyond its facts or follow the *Morris* plurality in borrowing Fourth Amendment case law to define "custody" in the context of escape.

We believe that a better analysis is found in *Snabb v. State*, ... In *Snabb*, an airport security officer saw the defendant, whom he knew to be intoxicated, attempting to drive out of the parking lot. After pursuing Snabb on foot, the officer and his partner succeeded in stopping her. The officer told Snabb that she was under arrest and ordered her to gather her possessions, lock her car, and come with him. Snabb refused to cooperate and ran away in disregard of his command to stop, but was quickly apprehended. Based on this evidence, Snabb was convicted of escaping from the officer's custody following arrest. . . .

The court of appeals reversed, noting that "the offense of escape occurs after having been arrested, not before the arrest is complete. . . . The court cited to *Smith v. State*, . . . , which held:

> An arrest of a person carries with it an element of detention, custody or control of the accused. The mere fact that an officer makes the statement to an accused that he is under arrest does not complete the arrest. There must be custody or detention and submission to such arrest.

. . . . Applying this standard, the court found that Snabb had not been arrested when she fled. While she apparently committed the offense of evading arrest, she had not been charged with that crime. Because the evidence was insufficient to show that Snabb had escaped from an arrest or from custody, the court ordered her acquittal. . . .

Two resisting arrest cases are also helpful to our determination of whether Medford was arrested or in custody when he fled. In *White v. State*, . . . , the arresting officer had drawn his pistol, placed the defendant in a spread-eagle position against a horse trailer, and was preparing to handcuff him when White turned around and kicked the officer

in the groin. . . . The court affirmed White's conviction for resisting arrest and noted that the arrest was taking place at the time of the appellant's action. . . . The facts of *Schrader v. State*, . . . are similar. In that case, two peace officers were preparing to arrest Schrader in a restaurant parking lot for public intoxication after ejecting him from the restaurant. Schrader accompanied one officer to a point near the restaurant while the other officer called to determine if there were any outstanding warrants for Schrader's arrest. After learning that there was an outstanding arrest warrant, the officer informed Schrader that he was under arrest and attempted to handcuff him. Schrader resisted by hitting, kicking, and biting one of the officers in a brief struggle. . . .

On appeal, Schrader argued that his assault on the officers while they were attempting to handcuff him could not constitute resisting arrest because his arrest was complete when he submitted to their authority in the parking lot. Instead, he claimed, the assault was an attempt to escape from custody. . . . This Court rejected Schrader's attempt to define the phrase "effecting an arrest" using Fourth Amendment standards. First, we noted the different purposes behind the Fourth Amendment and the resisting arrest statute: the former was designed to protect citizens' privacy interests, while the latter was enacted to protect police officers attempting to carry out their duties. See id. While agreeing that Schrader's arrest was "complete" with his detention in the parking lot, for some purposes of the law, we held that the officers were still effecting his arrest when he assaulted them at the point near the restaurant. . . .

At Medford's trial, there was some dispute about whether Officer Price had made contact with appellant's arm when he attempted to handcuff him. Officer Price testified at the suppression hearing that his right arm was free when he reached for the handcuffs with his left hand; he described Medford as being "within touching distance" at the moment Medford fled. However, at trial he testified that his left hand was on Medford's left arm as he reached for his handcuffs. Price further testified that as he grabbed Medford's left wrist in an attempt to secure him, Medford "went down and lunged and ran south . . . "

This account of an actual touching or grabbing differs from that given by Officer Baladez, who testified both at the suppression hearing and at trial that Medford started to put his hands to his side (free of any touching) when he fled, lunging between Baladez and the police car.

Viewing this evidence in the light most favorable to the verdict, as we must, we must accept as true Officer Price's testimony that he was touching Medford's wrist or arm just before Medford fled. However, we cannot say that the State carried its burden of establishing that Medford had been placed under restraint or taken into custody; by his own account, Officer Price attempted to gain physical control of Medford but was unsuccessful. While Medford apparently committed the offense of evading arrest, . . . , the State elected not to charge him with that offense. By its pleading charging Medford with escape, the State assumed the burden of proving a completed arrest. Because the evidence viewed in a light most favorable to the prosecution shows that Officer Price never succeeded in securing custody and control of appellant, the State did not satisfy that burden. We find the evidence of escape legally insufficient and sustain appellant's fourth point of error.

[Discussion of other points of error omitted.]

[Footnotes and citations omitted. Concurring and dissenting opinions omitted.]

Cases Relating to Chapter 12

U.S. Criminal Code: Offenses against Persons and Property

UNITED STATES OF AMERICA
v.
WILLIAM NATHANIEL COBB

UNITED STATES COURT OF APPEALS FOR THE FOURTH CIRCUIT

144 F.3d 319 (1998)

Wilkinson, Chief Judge:

William Nathaniel Cobb was convicted of carjacking, 18 U.S.C. § 2119, use of a firearm during a crime of violence, 18 U.S.C. § 924(c), and bank fraud, 18 U.S.C. § 1344. Cobb appeals the district court's denial of his motion to dismiss the carjacking and firearm counts. He argues that the federal carjacking statute, which also defined the crime of violence for his firearm conviction, exceeds Congress' authority under the Commerce Clause. Because we find the carjacking statute to lie within the bounds of Congress' commerce power, we affirm the judgment of the district court.

I

On the morning of October 6, 1995, Amanda Yezerski departed Charleston, South Carolina in her Mercury Cougar for Savannah, Georgia. Along the way she stopped in Summerville, South Carolina to retrieve cash from an automatic teller machine (ATM) and to fill her car with gas. While pumping gas at a service station, Yezerski saw the defendant loitering in the area. Once she finished at the pump, Yezerski walked around to the driver's side of her car and again noticed Cobb through her peripheral vision. Before she was able to shut her door and drive away, Cobb cornered Yezerski against her car. Yezerski observed that Cobb was carrying a tote bag with a gun partially protruding from it. He demanded her car and told her not to scream. Yezerski did scream, however, and Cobb pulled her from the car and squeezed past her into the driver's seat himself. When she reached into the car in an attempt to retrieve her keys, Cobb started the car. He then proceeded to pull Yezerski's body partially into the car, such that her legs were left dangling out the open door. Cobb then exited the gas station and drove across a multilane highway into a store parking lot, where he pushed Yezerski from the car and drove away. At the point Yezerski began screaming at the gas station, another woman who had stopped there became aware of the carjacking in progress. That woman, Tuesday Crosby, jumped into her truck and pursued the carjacker. When Cobb exited the store parking lot after pushing Yezerski from the car, Crosby followed him onto the interstate. She ended her pursuit, however, when Cobb extended his arm out the car window and pointed a gun in Crosby's direction. Cobb then moved into the emergency lane and sped off.

Cobb escaped with both Yezerski's Mercury Cougar and purse, which held her cash, debit card, ATM card, and checkbook. Evidence showed that Cobb used Yezerski's debit card to purchase clothing, that he and another woman successfully forged one of Yezerski's checks, and that Cobb made at least five unsuccessful attempts to withdraw money using the stolen ATM card.

Cobb was eventually arrested and indicted by a grand jury on one count of carjacking, 18 U.S.C. § 2119, one count of use of a firearm during that carjacking, 18 U.S.C. § 924(c), and five counts of bank fraud, 18 U.S.C. § 1344. Cobb moved to dismiss the first two counts of the indictment, arguing that the federal carjacking statute was an unconstitutional exercise of Congress' power under the Commerce Clause. The district court denied Cobb's motion and a trial was held in May 1996. The jury found Cobb guilty on all counts of the indictment. The district court sentenced Cobb to a total imprisonment term of 248 months. Cobb now appeals the district court's denial of his motion to dismiss.

II

At the time Cobb committed the acts charged in the indictment, the federal carjacking statute provided:

Whoever, with the intent to cause death or serious bodily harm takes a motor vehicle that has been transported, shipped, or received in interstate or foreign commerce from the person or presence of another by force and violence or by intimidation, or attempts to do so, shall—

(1) be fined under this title or imprisoned not more than 15 years, or both,

(2) if serious bodily injury (as defined in section 1365 of this title) results, be fined under this title or imprisoned not more than 25 years, or both, and

(3) if death results, be fined under this title or imprisoned for any number of years up to life, or both, or sentenced to death.

. . . Arguing against the weight of all seven circuits that have considered the question, . . . , Cobb challenges Congress' authority to enact this criminal statute. He contends that, in light of the Supreme Court's decision in *United States v. Lopez*, . . . (1995), section 2119 is beyond the reach of Congress' commerce power and therefore unconstitutional.

Cobb's challenge is without merit. The *Lopez* Court's articulation of the scope of Congress' commerce power is by now familiar. The Court recognized Congress' authority to (1) "regulate the use of the channels of interstate commerce;" (2) "regulate and protect the instrumentalities of interstate commerce, or persons or things in interstate commerce;" and (3) regulate "those activities that substantially affect interstate commerce." . . . When determining whether the Gun-Free School Zones Act of 1990 fit within the third category, the Court found that 18 U.S.C. § 922(q) lacked a "jurisdictional element which would ensure, through case-by-case inquiry, that the firearm possession in question affects interstate commerce." . . . . Because section 2119 does contain just such a jurisdictional element, and because the statute falls within Congress' power to regulate the instrumentalities of interstate commerce, we reject Cobb's constitutional challenge.

A.

The *Lopez* Court acknowledged that Congress could include a jurisdictional element in criminal statutes to ensure that each instance of criminalized conduct also has "an explicit connection with or effect on interstate commerce." . . . . The Court cited its prior interpretation of the former felon-in-possession statute in *United States v. Bass*, . . . (1971), as an example of such a jurisdictional requirement. In *Bass*, the Court suggested that the government could satisfactorily prove a nexus with interstate commerce by demonstrating "that the firearm received has previously traveled in interstate commerce." . . . . The Court confirmed that this reading was correct in *Scarborough v. United States*, . . . (1977), holding that the government need only prove "that the firearm have been, at some time, in interstate commerce." . . . .

In *United States v. Wells*, . . . (4th Cir. 1996), we rejected a Lopez challenge to 18 U.S.C. § 922(g), which criminalizes the shipment, transport, possession, or receipt of a firearm by a specific class of persons. Section 922(g) permits the government to prove a commerce nexus by showing that the defendant received a firearm "which has been shipped or transported in interstate or foreign commerce." . . . . We turned aside the constitutional challenge, holding that the jurisdictional element both distinguished the case from *Lopez* and satisfied the requirements of the Commerce Clause . . . .

The federal carjacking statute also contains an express jurisdictional element. Section 2119 applies only to the forcible taking of motor vehicles that have been "transported, shipped, or received in interstate or foreign commerce." Thus, in Cobb's case the government was forced to prove—and did prove—that Yezerski's Mercury Cougar was manufactured in Ohio and shipped in interstate commerce to South Carolina. Like our decision in Wells, therefore, we find that section 2119's jurisdictional element "distinguishes *Lopez* and satisfies the minimal nexus required for the Commerce Clause." . . . . Additionally, we note that our holding is in accord with the decisions of four other circuits that have similarly relied on section 2119's jurisdictional element in finding the statute a valid exercise of Congress' authority under the Commerce Clause. . . .

B.

Section 2119 is also a valid exercise of Congress' power to regulate an instrumentality of interstate commerce—cars. In *Lopez*, the Court confirmed that Congress can protect such instrumentalities, "even though the threat may come only from intrastate activities." . . . . The Court has also held that interstate roads, . . . , and toll roads and drawbridges connecting interstate roads, . . . , are instrumentalities of interstate commerce because they are essential to the carriage of persons and goods moving in interstate commerce. As the Third Circuit has observed, "Instrumentalities differ from other objects that affect interstate commerce because they are used as a means of transporting goods and people across state lines. Trains and planes are inherently mobile; highways and bridges, though static, are critical to the movement of automobiles." Bishop, ...

Undoubtedly, if planes and trains qualify as instrumentalities of interstate commerce, so too do automobiles. The fact that not every car, train, or plane trip has an interstate destination has never been thought to remove these means of transport from the category of an instrumentality of commerce. Cars, like trains and aircraft, are both inherently mobile and indispensable to the interstate movement of persons and goods. We therefore hold that section 2119 is a valid exercise of Congress' power to regulate and protect an instrumentality of interstate commerce. In this respect, our conclusion is in accord with the decisions of four other circuits. . . .

III

For the foregoing reasons, we affirm the judgment of the district court.

[Footnotes and citations omitted. Concurring and dissenting opinions omitted.]

JEFFREY SKILLING
V.
UNITED STATES

SUPREME COURT OF THE UNITED STATES

NO. 08–1394. ARGUED MARCH 1, 2010—DECIDED JUNE 24, 2010

561 U.S. __

JUSTICE GINSBURG delivered the opinion of the Court.

In 2001, Enron Corporation, then the seventh highest revenue-grossing company in America, crashed into bankruptcy. We consider in this opinion two questions arising from the prosecution of Jeffrey Skilling, a longtime Enron executive, for crimes committed before the corporation's collapse. First, did pretrial publicity and community prejudice prevent Skilling from obtaining a fair trial? Second, did the jury improperly convict Skilling of conspiracy to commit "honest-services" wire fraud, 18 U. S. C.§§371, 1343, 1346?

Answering no to both questions, the Fifth Circuit affirmed Skilling's convictions. We conclude, in common with the Court of Appeals, that Skilling's fair-trial argument fails; Skilling, we hold, did not establish that a presumption of juror prejudice arose or that actual bias infected the jury that tried him. [*This discussion is omitted from this excerpt.*] But we disagree with the Fifth Circuit's honest-services ruling. In proscribing fraudulent deprivations of "the intangible right of honest services," §1346, Congress intended at least to reach schemes to defraud involving bribes and kickbacks. Construing the honest-services statute to extend beyond that core meaning, we conclude, would encounter a vagueness shoal. We therefore hold that § 1346 covers only bribery and kickback schemes. Because Skilling's alleged misconduct entailed no bribe or kickback, it does not fall within § 1346's proscription. We therefore affirm in part and vacate in part.

Founded in 1985, Enron Corporation grew from its headquarters in Houston, Texas, into one of the world's leading energy companies. Skilling launched his career there in 1990 when Kenneth Lay, the company's founder, hired him to head an Enron subsidiary. Skilling steadily rose through the corporation's ranks, serving as president and chief operating officer, and then, beginning in February 2001, as chief executive officer. Six months later, on August 14, 2001, Skilling resigned from Enron. Less than four months after Skilling's departure, Enron spiraled into bankruptcy. The company's stock, which had traded at $90 per share in August 2000, plummeted to pennies per share in late 2001. Attempting to comprehend what caused the corporation's collapse, the U. S. Department of Justice formed an Enron Task Force, comprising prosecutors and FBI agents from around the Nation. The Government's investigation uncovered an elaborate conspiracy to prop up Enron's short-run stock prices by overstating the company's financial well-being. In the years following Enron's bankruptcy, the Government prosecuted dozens of Enron employees who participated in the scheme. In time, the Government worked its way up the corporation's chain of command: On July 7, 2004, a grand jury indicted Skilling, Lay, and Richard Causey, Enron's former chief accounting officer. These three defendants, the indictment alleged, "engaged in a wide-ranging scheme to deceive the investing public, including Enron's shareholders, . . . about the true performance of Enron's businesses by:

(a) manipulating Enron's publicly reported financial results; and (b) making public statements and representations about Enron's financial performance and results that were false and misleading." . . .

Skilling and his coconspirators, the indictment continued, "enriched themselves as a result of the scheme through salary, bonuses, grants of stock and stock options, other profits, and prestige." . . .

Count 1 of the indictment charged Skilling with conspiracy to commit securities and wire fraud; in particular, it alleged that Skilling had sought to "depriv[e] Enron and its shareholders of the intangible right of [his] honest services." . . . The indictment further charged Skilling with more than 25 substantive counts of securities fraud, wire fraud, making false representations to Enron's auditors, and insider trading.

In November 2004, Skilling moved to transfer the trial to another venue; he contended that hostility toward him in Houston, coupled with extensive pretrial publicity, had poisoned potential jurors. To support this assertion, Skilling, aided by media experts, submitted hundreds of news reports detailing Enron's downfall; he also presented affidavits from the experts he engaged portraying community attitudes in Houston in comparison to other potential venues. [*Change of venue discussion omitted.*]

. . . The Court of Appeals also rejected Skilling's claim that his conduct did not indicate any conspiracy to commit honest-services fraud. "[T]he jury was entitled to convict Skilling," the court stated, "on these elements": "(1) a material breach of a fiduciary duty . . . (2) that results in a detriment to the employer," including one occasioned by an employee's decision to "withhold material information, i.e., information that he had reason to believe would lead a reasonable employer to change its conduct." . . . The Fifth Circuit did not address Skilling's argument that the honest-services statute, if not interpreted to exclude his actions, should be invalidated as unconstitutionally vague. Arguing that the Fifth Circuit erred in its consideration of these claims, Skilling sought relief from this Court. We granted certiorari, . . . and now affirm in part, vacate in part, and remand for further proceedings. . . .

We next consider whether Skilling's conspiracy conviction was premised on an improper theory of honest services wire fraud. The honest-services statute, §1346, Skilling maintains, is unconstitutionally vague. Alternatively, he contends that his conduct does not fall within the statute's compass.

A.

To place Skilling's constitutional challenge in context, we first review the origin and subsequent application of the honest-services doctrine.

Enacted in 1872, the original mail-fraud provision, the predecessor of the modern-day mail- and wire-fraud laws, proscribed, without further elaboration, use of the mails to advance "any scheme or artifice to defraud." ... In 1909, Congress amended the statute to prohibit, as it does today, "any scheme or artifice to defraud, *or for obtaining money or property by means of false or fraudulent pretenses, representations, or promises.*" § 1341 (emphasis added); .... Emphasizing Congress' disjunctive phrasing, the Courts of Appeals, one after the other, interpreted the term "scheme or artifice to defraud" to include deprivations not only of money or property, but also of intangible rights.

In an opinion credited with first presenting the intangible-rights theory, *Shushan v. United States,* ... (1941), the Fifth Circuit reviewed the mail-fraud prosecution of a public official who allegedly accepted bribes from entrepreneurs in exchange for urging city action beneficial to the bribe payers. "It is not true that because the [city] was to make and did make a saving by the operations there could not have been an intent to defraud," the Court of Appeals maintained. ... "A scheme to get a public contract on more favorable terms than would likely be got otherwise by bribing a public official," the court observed, "would not only be a plan to commit the crime of bribery, but would also be a scheme to defraud the public." ....

The Fifth Circuit's opinion in *Shushan* stimulated the development of an "honest-services" doctrine. Unlike fraud in which the victim's loss of money or property supplied the defendant's gain, with one the mirror image of the other, ... the honest-services theory targeted corruption that lacked similar symmetry. While the offender profited, the betrayed party suffered no deprivation of money or property; instead, a third party, who had not been deceived, provided the enrichment. For example, if a city mayor (the offender) accepted a bribe from a third party in exchange for awarding that party a city contract, yet the contract terms were the same as any that could have been negotiated at arm's length, the city (the betrayed party) would suffer no tangible loss. ... Even if the scheme occasioned a money or property *gain* for the betrayed party, courts reasoned, actionable harm lay in the denial of that party's right to the offender's "honest services." ...

"Most often these cases ... involved bribery of public officials," ... , but courts also recognized private-sector honest-services fraud. In perhaps the earliest application of the theory to private actors, a District Court, reviewing a bribery scheme, explained:

> "When one tampers with [the employer-employee] relationship for the purpose of causing the employee to breach his duty [to his employer,] he in effect is defrauding the employer of a lawful right. The actual deception that is practiced is in the continued representation of the employee to the employer that he is honest and loyal to the employer's interests." *United States v. Procter & Gamble Co.,* 47 F. Supp. 676, 678 (Mass. 1942).

Over time, "[a]n increasing number of courts" recognized that "a recreant employee"—public or private—"c[ould] be prosecuted under [the mail-fraud statute] if he breache[d] his allegiance to his employer by accepting bribes or kickbacks in the course of his employment," ... ; by 1982, all Courts of Appeals had embraced the honest-services theory of fraud, ... In 1987, this Court, in *McNally v. United States,* stopped the development of the intangible-rights doctrine in its tracks. *McNally* involved a state officer who, in selecting Kentucky's insurance agent, arranged to procure a share of the agent's commissions via kickbacks paid to companies the official partially controlled. ... The prosecutor did not charge that, "in the absence of the alleged scheme[,] the Commonwealth would have paid a lower premium or secured better insurance." Instead, the prosecutor maintained that the kickback scheme "defraud[ed] the citizens and government of Kentucky of their right to have the Commonwealth's affairs conducted honestly." ...

We held that the scheme did not qualify as mail fraud. "Rather than constru[ing] the statute in a manner that leaves its outer boundaries ambiguous and involves the Federal Government in setting standards of disclosure and good government for local and state officials," we read the statute "as limited in scope to the protection of property rights." ... "If Congress desires to go further," we stated, "it must speak more clearly." ... Congress responded swiftly. The following year, it enacted a new statute "specifically to cover one of the 'intangible rights' that lower courts had protected ... prior to *McNally:* 'the intangible right of honest services.'" . . . In full, the honest-services statute stated:

> "For the purposes of th[e] chapter [of the United States Code that prohibits, *inter alia*, mail fraud, §1341, and wire fraud, § 1343], the term 'scheme or artifice to defraud' includes a scheme or artifice to deprive another of the intangible right of honest services." §1346.

Congress, Skilling charges, reacted quickly but not clearly: He asserts that §1346 is unconstitutionally vague. To satisfy due process, "a penal statute [must] define the criminal offense [1] with sufficient definiteness that ordinary people can understand what conduct is prohibited and [2] in a manner that does not encourage arbitrary and discriminatory enforcement." . . . The void-for-vagueness doctrine embraces these requirements.

According to Skilling, §1346 meets neither of the two due process essentials. First, the phrase "the intangible right of honest services," he contends, does not adequately define what behavior it bars. . . . Second, he alleges, §1346's "standardless sweep allows policemen, prosecutors, and juries to pursue their personal predilections," thereby "facilitat[ing] opportunistic and arbitrary prosecutions." . . .

In urging invalidation of §1346, Skilling swims against our case law's current, which requires us, if we can, to construe, not condemn, Congress' enactments. . . . Alert to §1346's potential breadth, the Courts of Appeals have divided on how best to interpret the statute. Uniformly, however, they have declined to throw out the statute as irremediably vague.

We agree that §1346 should be construed rather than invalidated. First, we look to the doctrine developed in pre-*McNally* cases in an endeavor to ascertain the meaning of the phrase "the intangible right of honest services." Second, to preserve what Congress certainly intended the statute to cover, we pare that body of precedent down to its core: In the main, the pre-*McNally* cases involved fraudulent schemes to deprive another of honest services through bribes or kickbacks supplied by a third party who had not been deceived. Confined to these paramount applications, §1346 presents no vagueness problem. . . .

There is no doubt that Congress intended §1346 to refer to and incorporate the honest services doctrine recognized in Court of Appeals' decisions before *McNally* derailed the intangible-rights theory of fraud. . . . Congress enacted §1346 on the heels of *McNally* and drafted the statute using that decision's terminology. . . . As the Second Circuit observed in its leading analysis of §1346: "The definite article 'the' suggests that 'intangible right of honest services' had a specific meaning to Congress when it enacted the statute—Congress was recriminalizing mail- and wire-fraud schemes to deprive others of *that* 'intangible right of honest services,' which had been protected before *McNally*, not *all* intangible rights of honest services whatever they might be thought to be."

Satisfied that Congress, by enacting §1346, "meant to reinstate the body of pre-*McNally* honest-services law," . . . we have surveyed that case law. In parsing the Courts of Appeals decisions, we acknowledge that Skilling's vagueness challenge has force, for honest-services decisions preceding *McNally* were not models of clarity or consistency. . . . While the honest-services cases preceding *McNally* dominantly and consistently applied the fraud statute to bribery and kickback schemes—schemes that were the basis of most honest-services prosecutions—there was considerable disarray over the statute's application to conduct outside that core category. In light of this disarray, Skilling urges us, as he urged the Fifth Circuit, to invalidate the statute *in toto*. . . . It has long been our practice, however, before striking a federal statute as impermissibly vague, to consider whether the prescription is amenable to a limiting construction. . . .

Although some applications of the pre-*McNally* honest-services doctrine occasioned disagreement among the Courts of Appeals, these cases do not cloud the doctrine's solid core: The "vast majority" of the honest-services cases involved offenders who, in violation of a fiduciary duty, participated in bribery or kickback schemes. . . . Indeed, the *McNally* case itself, which spurred Congress to enact §1346, presented a paradigmatic kickback fact pattern. . . . Congress' reversal of *McNally* and reinstatement of the honest-services doctrine, we conclude, can and should be salvaged by confining its scope to the core pre-*McNally* applications.

As already noted, the honest-services doctrine had its genesis in prosecutions involving bribery allegations. . . . In view of this history, there is no doubt that Congress intended §1346 to reach *at least* bribes and kickbacks. Reading the statute to proscribe a wider range of offensive conduct, we acknowledge, would raise the due process concerns underlying the vagueness doctrine. . . . we now hold that §1346 criminalizes *only* the bribe and-kickback core of the pre-*McNally* case law. . . . *McNally*, as we have already observed, involved a classic kickback scheme: A public official, in exchange for routing Kentucky's insurance business through a middleman company, arranged for that company to share its commissions with entities in which the official held an interest. . . . This was no mere failure to disclose a conflict of interest; rather, the official conspired with a third party so that both would profit from wealth generated by public contracts. . . . Reading §1346 to proscribe bribes and kickbacks—and nothing more—satisfies Congress' undoubted aim to reverse *McNally* on its facts.

Nor are we persuaded that the pre-*McNally* conflict-of-interest cases constitute core applications of the honest services doctrine. Although the Courts of Appeals upheld honest-services convictions for "some schemes of nondisclosure and concealment of material information," . . . they reached no consensus on which schemes qualified. In light of the relative infrequency of conflict-of-interest prosecutions in comparison to bribery and kickback charges, and the inter-circuit inconsistencies they produced, we conclude that a reasonable limiting construction of §1346 must exclude this amorphous category of cases.

. . . Holding that honest-services fraud does not encompass conduct more wide-ranging than the paradigmatic cases of bribes and kickbacks, we resist the Government's less constrained construction absent Congress' clear instruction otherwise. . . .

In sum, our construction of §1346 "establish[es] a uniform national standard, define[s] honest services with clarity, reach[es] only seriously culpable conduct, and accomplish[es] Congress's goal of 'overruling' *McNally*." "If Congress desires to go further," we reiterate, "it must speak more clearly than it has."

Interpreted to encompass only bribery and kickback schemes, §1346 is not unconstitutionally vague. Recall that the void-for-vagueness doctrine addresses concerns about (1) fair notice and (2) arbitrary and discriminatory prosecutions. . . . A prohibition on fraudulently depriving another of one's honest services by accepting bribes or kickbacks does not present a problem on either score.

As to fair notice, "whatever the school of thought concerning the scope and meaning of" § 1346, it has always been "as plain as a pikestaff that" bribes and kickbacks constitute honest-services fraud, . . . , and the statute's *mens rea* requirement further blunts any notice concern, . . . Today's decision clarifies that no other misconduct falls within §1346's province. . . .

As to arbitrary prosecutions, we perceive no significant risk that the honest-services statute, as we interpret it today, will be stretched out of shape. Its prohibition on bribes and kickbacks draws content not only from the pre-*McNally* case law, but also from federal statutes proscribing—and defining—similar crimes. . . . A criminal defendant who participated in a bribery or kickback scheme, in short, cannot tenably complain about prosecution under §1346 on vagueness grounds.

It remains to determine whether Skilling's conduct violated §1346. Skilling's honest-services prosecution, the Government concedes, was not "prototypical." The Government charged Skilling with conspiring to defraud Enron's shareholders by misrepresenting the company's fiscal health, thereby artificially inflating its stock price. It was the Government's theory at trial that Skilling "profited from the fraudulent scheme . . . through the receipt of salary and bonuses, . . . and through the sale of approximately $200 million in Enron stock, which netted him $89 million." . . . The Government did not, at any time, allege that Skilling solicited or accepted side payments from a third party in exchange for making these misrepresentations. . . . It is therefore clear that, as we read §1346, Skilling did not commit honest-services fraud.

Because the indictment alleged three objects of the conspiracy—honest-services wire fraud, money-or-property wire fraud, and securities fraud—Skilling's conviction is flawed. . . . This determination, however, does not necessarily require reversal of the conspiracy conviction; we recently confirmed, . . . that errors of the *Yates* variety are subject to harmless-error analysis. The parties vigorously dispute whether the error was harmless. . . . We leave this dispute for resolution on remand.

For the foregoing reasons, we affirm the Fifth Circuit's ruling on Skilling's fair-trial argument, vacate its ruling on his conspiracy conviction, and remand the case for proceedings consistent with this opinion.

It is so ordered. (Citations and footnotes omitted. Concurring and dissenting opinions omitted.)

UNITED STATES OF AMERICA
v.
AUTUMN JACKSON, JOSE MEDINA, AND BORIS SABAS

UNITED STATES DISTRICT COURT

986 F. Supp. 829 (1997)

Barbara S. Jones, United States District Judge:
Pending is a motion by defendant Autumn Jackson, in which co-defendant Yosi Medina joins, to dismiss the Superseding Indictment pursuant to Federal Rule of Criminal Procedure 12(b)(2). Specifically, Jackson argues that 18 U.S.C. § 875(d) ("§ 875(d)") and § 155.05.2(e)(v) of the New York Penal Law ("§ 155.05") are unconstitutionally overbroad and vague on their face and as applied in this case. For the reasons set forth below, the Court denies the motion.

Background

On February 27, 1997, the Grand Jury returned a superseding indictment charging Jackson, Medina, and co-defendant Boris Sabas, a/k/a "Boris Shmulevich," in three counts.

Count One charged that from late 1996 until January 18, 1997, in violation of 18 U.S.C. § 371, the defendants and others conspired to (1) transmit in interstate commerce communications threatening to injure the reputation of the actor Bill Cosby with the intent to extort money from him, in violation of 18 U.S.C. § 875(d), and (2) travel in and use interstate commerce facilities with the intent to carry on extortion in violation of 18 U.S.C. §

875(d) and § 155.05 of the New York Penal Law, in violation of the Travel Act, 18 U.S.C. § 1952(a)(3).

Count Two charged that, from late 1996 to January 18, 1997, the defendants transmitted in interstate commerce communications containing threats to injure the reputation of Bill Cosby with the intent to extort money from him, in violation of 18 U.S.C. § 875(d).

Count Three charged that the defendants violated the Travel Act by using facilities and traveling in interstate commerce with the intent to carry on extortion in violation of 18 U.S.C. § 875(d) and Section 155.05 of the New York Penal Law.

During a thirteen day trial that began July 7, 1997 and concluded July 25, 1997, the Government introduced evidence in the form of testimony, tape-recorded conversations, and documents. This proof established that from late 1996 to January 18, 1997, the defendants engaged in a campaign to threaten to publicize in tabloid newspapers that Jackson was Cosby's daughter out-of-wedlock and that he was mistreating her if Cosby did not pay Jackson millions of dollars. The Government established that the defendants conveyed this threat to Cosby through his attorneys, his television network CBS, and his sponsors, including Eastman Kodak Company. The campaign culminated with Jackson's January 16, 1997 demand to Cosby's attorney that if Cosby did not pay her $40 million, she would take her damaging story to The Globe. This threat was accompanied by an unsigned copy of a contract between Jackson, Medina and The Globe for the sale of Jackson's story about Cosby.

On July 25, 1997, the jury found Jackson and Medina guilty of all three counts of the Superseding Indictment and found Sabas guilty of Counts One and Three.

Discussion

I. Overbreadth

Jackson asserts both a facial and an as applied overbreadth challenge to §§ 875(d) and 155.05.

A. Facial Overbreadth

As an initial matter, only a statute that is substantially overbroad may be invalidated on its face. Accordingly, in addressing a facial overbreadth challenge, a court's first task is to ascertain whether the enactment reaches a substantial amount of constitutionally protected conduct. . . . An act's overbreadth "must not only be real, but substantial as well, judged in relation to the statute's plainly legitimate sweep." .... The overbreadth doctrine is "strong medicine," and should be used "sparingly and only as a last resort." ....

Jackson argues that §§ 875(d) and 155.05, on their face and as interpreted by this Court, sweep constitutionally protected speech—"non-violent communications uttered in a good-faith effort to resolve legitimate financial disputes or accomplish legitimate political, social or economic goals" ... — within their ambit. Her claim is incorrect, as the statutes do not cover such protected speech.

First, it is well settled that the punishment of certain threats does not offend the First Amendment. In this connection, courts have upheld similar statutes in the face of overbreadth challenges by narrowly interpreting the term "threats." Consistent with the First Amendment, Congress can proscribe threats that, according to their language and context, convey a gravity of purpose and likelihood of execution that render them beyond the pale of constitutional protection. .... A "true threat"—which "on its face and in the circumstances in which it is made is so unequivocal, unconditional, immediate and specific as to the person threatened, as to convey a gravity of purpose and imminent prospect of execution"—may be punished because it, itself, affronts the important social interests of "justice" and "equal rights under the law." ...

Accordingly, this Court has interpreted the "threats" punishable by §§ 875(d) and 155.05 as only those that are unequivocal, unconditional, and specific. For example, in this case the jury was instructed that:

> a threat is an avowed present determination to injure, at once or in the future. The mere hope, desire, or wish to injure someone's reputation is insufficient to constitute a threat. In order to find that the defendant you are considering threatened to injure Bill Cosby's reputation, you must find that a reasonable person would have understood the defendant's statement as a serious expression of intent, determination, or purpose to injure the reputation of another person.

To determine whether or not the defendant you are considering threatened to injure Bill Cosby's reputation, you should consider the circumstances under which the statement was made, including the kind of statement made, the place where it was made, to whom it was made, how it was spoken, whether it was said plainly and unconditionally or in jest, and its context with respect to surrounding conversation. You may also consider the language the defendant used and the reaction of the person to whom the communication was addressed ....

Second, the "threats" prohibited by §§ 875(d) and 155.05 are not expressions of ideas or advocacy that typically implicate the First Amendment. Rather, § 875(d) is confined to (1) threats to injure the reputation of another, that are (2) made with the intent to extort money or things of value. Similarly, § 155.05 prohibits (1) threats to expose a secret tending to subject some person to hatred, contempt or ridicule, that are (2) made with intent to deprive another of property. This limited scope takes the statutes "out of the realm of social or political conflict where threats to engage in behavior that may be unlawful may nevertheless be part of the marketplace of ideas, broadly conceived to embrace the rough competition that is so much the staple of social or political discourse." ...

Jackson also argues that only threats to perform independently unlawful actions, such as kidnapping or physical injury, can be constitutionally proscribed. This argument is wrong. Courts have rejected constitutional challenges to statutes similar to § 875(d) that proscribe threats to injure reputation as a means of obtaining money or property ....

The cases cited by Jackson in her Reply Memorandum, in which state courts have struck down various state coercion statutes, do not dictate a different result. Although in *State v. Robertson*, ... (Or. 1982), the court sustained an overbreadth challenge to Oregon's coercion statute, it did so because the statute impermissibly extended the principal of extortion to cover threats made in a public setting designed to inform and perhaps involve others in the issues posed by the demand. Robertson, ... Further, the Robertson court confirmed that extortion statutes are, and historically have been, constitutionally valid because they punish threats made to obtain property for "selfish gain" or personal benefit from a victim in a private, bilateral transaction akin to robbery....

Similarly, the criminal extortion statutes struck down in *Whimbush v. People*, ... (Colo. 1994), and *State v. Weinstein*, ... (Ariz. 1995) and the coercion statute invalidated in *City of Seattle v. Ivan*, ... (Wash. 1993) failed to require an intent to extort money or thing of value. In fact, the statutes in *Robertson* and *Ivan* had no express intent element at all.

Jackson also complains that § 875(d) fails to define the requisite "intent to extort money or thing of value" and that the Court interpreted that intent element too broadly. The facial validity of statutes providing no greater specification or definition of intent, however, has been often upheld . . . .

With respect to the Court's interpretation of the intent element, the Court first notes that while § 875(d) may criminalize extortionate threats to injure reputation that are common, their frequency does not necessarily render them constitutionally protected or legal. Moreover, the Court narrowly defined "intent to extort money or thing of value" by instructing the jury that "to extort means to obtain money or a thing of value from another by use of threats to reputation." . . .

Jackson further argues that the Court's refusal to graft a "specific intent" requirement onto § 875(d) (i.e., a requirement that the statute requires a "guilty mind") and to allow for a "claim of right" defense under it renders the statute unconstitutionally overbroad. While Jackson may disagree with the Court's rulings on statutory interpretation, she fails to explain how these rulings affect or even implicate her First Amendment argument. Moreover, with respect to a specific intent element, the Court notes that it instructed the jury that Count One (conspiracy to violate §§ 875(d) and the Travel Act) required the Government to prove beyond a reasonable doubt that the defendants acted with bad purpose to disobey or disregard the law . . . . Similarly, the Court instructed the jury that Count Three required a finding that the defendants knew that the activity they intended to facilitate was illegal . . . .

Finally, the hypothetical situations that Jackson poses do not indicate that the statutes could be used to punish a substantial amount of constitutionally protected conduct. Several of the scenarios do not contain specific, unconditional, immediate threats or threats to injure another's reputation. In others, the postulated speakers do not necessarily have the requisite "intent to extort money or thing of customer value." In this connection, the store owner who threatens to report a non-paying to a credit reporting agency, the homeowner who threatens to report a poorly performing contractor to the Better Business Bureau, and the accident victim who threatens litigation are not engaging in "self-help." Rather, they are turning to neutral governmental or quasi-governmental intermediaries who then independently review the speaker's claim. Also, as the Government correctly points out, in these hypothetical situations the potential injury to reputation is incidental to the threat of raising the claim.

Accordingly, Jackson's facial overbreadth challenge to the statutes fails.

B. As Applied Challenge

Not surprisingly, Jackson's papers are silent with respect to the application of §§ 875(d) and 155.05 to her own speech in this case. Here, the Superseding Indictment charged and the jury rationally found beyond a reasonable doubt that Jackson and her co-conspirators communicated a "true threat" to Cosby, by faxing an unsigned contract from The Globe to print Jackson's life story along with a demand for $40 million. This was precisely the kind of private transaction, motivated purely by selfish gain, that extortion statutes have always validly punished.

Accordingly, the statutes were constitutionally applied to Jackson and her co-conspirators.

II. Void for Vagueness

The void for vagueness doctrine requires that a penal statute define the criminal offense with sufficient definiteness such that ordinary people can understand what conduct is prohibited and in a manner that does not encourage arbitrary and discriminatory enforcement . . . .

Jackson now claims that §§ 875(d) and 155.05 are unconstitutionally vague. Specifically, she argues that the statutes are impermissibly vague because (1) the statutes fail to provide or to refer to definitions for "extortion" or "intent to extort," and (2) the Court "left it up to the jury to use their 'common sense' to decide what 'extortion' means." . . .

Jackson's first argument is simply wrong. "Extortion" does have a meaning, far wider than the original common law concept, that courts have repeatedly sanctioned when interpreting statutes involving extortion . . . .

Moreover, the language of § 875(d) clearly defines the nature of the intent element: in making threats to injure another's reputation, the defendant must have acted with the intent of extorting money or a thing of value.

As for her second argument, Jackson misunderstands the Court's instructions to the jury. When instructing the jury on the elements under § 875 (d), the Court charged that:

> the final element that the Government must prove beyond a reasonable doubt is that the defendant you are considering acted with the intent to extort money or a thing of value from Bill Cosby. You should use your common sense to determine whether the defendant you are considering had the requisite intent to extort.

. . . As is plainly clear, the Court simply preserved for the jury its most basic task—the determination of intent. In fact, the Court further explained to the jury that "to extort means to obtain money or a thing of value from another by use of threats to reputation." . . .

Further, the scienter requirement—"intent to extort money or thing of value"—helps to ensure adequate notice of the proscribed conduct . . . .

Finally, law enforcers are sufficiently guided by the fact that the statutes apply only to threats to injure reputation, and only when such threats are made with the intent to extort money or a thing of value. Additionally, as stated above, the Hobbs Act and common law provide definitions of "extortion" to guide law enforcement.

The Court also notes that this is not a case where the challenged statutes contain absolutely no standard of conduct or have no core. Rather, the statutes apply to threats to injure reputation made with the intent to extort money or things of value. . . . Moreover, even if the outer boundaries of the statutes are imprecise, any such uncertainty has little relevance here, where Jackson's conduct falls squarely within the "hard core" of the statutes' proscriptions . . . .

Accordingly, the Court finds that §§ 875(d) and § 155.05 are not unconstitutionally vague, either facially or as applied.

Conclusion

For the reasons set forth above, the defendant's motion is denied.

So ordered.

[Footnotes and citations omitted. Concurring and dissenting opinions omitted.]

Cases Relating to Chapter 13

United States Criminal Code: Other Offenses

UNITED STATES, PETITIONER

v.

MICHAEL WILLIAMS

SUPREME COURT OF THE UNITED STATES

ARGUED OCTOBER 30, 2007 — DECIDED MAY 19, 2008

553 U.S. 285 (2008)

Justice SCALIA delivered the opinion of the Court.

Section 2252A(a)(3)(B) of Title 18, United States Code, criminalizes, in certain specified circumstances, the pandering or solicitation of child pornography. This case presents the question whether that statute is overbroad under the First Amendment or impermissibly vague under the Due Process Clause of the Fifth Amendment.

We have long held that obscene speech—sexually explicit material that violates fundamental notions of decency—is not protected by the First Amendment. . . . But to protect explicit material that has social value, we have limited the scope of the obscenity exception, and have overturned convictions for the distribution of sexually graphic but nonobscene material. . . . .

Over the last 25 years, we have confronted a related and overlapping category of proscribable speech: child pornography. . . . This consists of sexually explicit visual portrayals that feature children. We have held that a statute which proscribes the distribution of all child pornography, even material that does not qualify as obscenity, does not on its face violate the First Amendment. . . . Moreover, we have held that the government may criminalize the possession of child pornography, even though it may not criminalize the mere possession of obscene material involving adults. . . . .

The broad authority to proscribe child pornography is not, however, unlimited. Four Terms ago, we held facially overbroad two provisions of the federal Child Pornography Protection Act of 1996 (CPPA). . . . The first of these banned the possession and distribution of "any visual depiction" that "is, or appears to be, of a minor engaging in sexually explicit conduct," even if it contained only youthful-looking adult actors or virtual images of children generated by a computer. . . . This was invalid, we explained, because the child-protection rationale for speech restriction does not apply to materials produced without children. . . . The second provision at issue in *Free Speech Coalition* criminalized the possession and distribution of material that had been pandered as child pornography, regardless of whether it actually was that. . . . A person could thus face prosecution for possessing unobjectionable material that someone else had pandered. . . We held that this prohibition, which did "more than prohibit pandering," was also facially overbroad.

After our decision in *Free Speech Coalition,* Congress went back to the drawing board and produced legislation with the unlikely title of the Prosecutorial Remedies and Other Tools to end the Exploitation of Children Today Act of 2003, 117 Stat. 650. We shall refer to it as the Act. Section 503 of the Act amended 18 U.S.C. § 2252A to add a new pandering and solicitation provision, relevant portions of which now read as follows:

"(a) Any person who—

"(3) knowingly—

. . . . .

"(B) advertises, promotes, presents, distributes, or solicits through the mails, or in interstate or foreign commerce by any means, including by computer, any material or purported material in a manner that reflects the belief, or that is intended to cause another to believe, 1837*1837 that the material or purported material is, or contains—

"(i) an obscene visual depiction of a minor engaging in sexually explicit conduct; or

"(ii) a visual depiction of an actual minor engaging in sexually explicit conduct,

. . . . .

"shall be punished as provided in subsection (b)." § 2252A(a)(3)(B) (2000 ed., Supp. V).

Section 2256(2)(A) defines "sexually explicit conduct" as

"actual or simulated—

"(i) sexual intercourse, including genital-genital, oral-genital, anal-genital, or oral-anal, whether between persons of the same or opposite sex;

"(ii) bestiality;

"(iii) masturbation;

"(iv) sadistic or masochistic abuse; or

"(v) lascivious exhibition of the genitals or pubic area of any person."

Violation of § 2252A(a)(3)(B) incurs a minimum sentence of 5 years imprisonment and a maximum of 20 years. 18 U.S.C. § 2252A(b)(1).

The Act's express findings indicate that Congress was concerned that limiting the child-pornography prohibition to material that could be *proved* to feature actual children, as our decision in *Free Speech Coalition* required, would enable many child pornographers to evade conviction. . . . The emergence of new technology and the repeated retransmission of picture files over the Internet could make it nearly impossible to prove that a particular image was produced using real children—even though "[t]here is no substantial evidence that any of the child pornography images being trafficked today were made other than by the abuse of real children," virtual imaging being prohibitively expensive. . . .

The following facts appear in the opinion of the Eleventh Circuit, ... On April 26, 2004, respondent Michael Williams, using a sexually explicit screen name, signed in to a public Internet chat room. A Secret Service agent had also signed in to the chat room under the moniker "Lisa n Miami." The agent noticed that Williams had posted a message that read: "Dad of toddler has 'good' pics of her an [sic] me for swap of your toddler pics, or live cam." The agent struck up a conversation with Williams, leading to an electronic exchange of nonpornographic pictures of children. (The agent's picture was in fact a doctored photograph of an adult.) Soon thereafter, Williams messaged that he had photographs of men molesting his 4-year-old daughter. Suspicious that "Lisa n Miami" was a law-enforcement agent, before proceeding further Williams demanded that the agent produce additional pictures. When he did not, Williams posted the following public message in the chat room: "HERE ROOM; I CAN PUT UPLINK CUZ IM FOR REAL—SHE CANT." Appended to this declaration was a hyperlink that, when clicked, led to seven pictures of actual children, aged approximately 5 to 15, engaging in sexually explicit conduct and displaying their genitals. The Secret Service then obtained a search warrant for Williams's home, where agents seized two hard drives containing at least 22 images . . . of real children engaged in sexually explicit conduct, some of it sadomasochistic.

Williams was charged with one count of pandering child pornography under § 2252A(a)(3)(B) and one count of possessing child pornography under § 2252A(a)(5)(B). He pleaded guilty to both counts but reserved the right to challenge the constitutionality of the pandering conviction. The District Court rejected his challenge, and sentenced him to concurrent 60-month sentences on the two counts. . . . The United States Court of Appeals for the Eleventh Circuit reversed the pandering conviction, holding that the statute was both overbroad and impermissibly vague. . . .

We granted certiorari.

According to our First Amendment overbreadth doctrine, a statute is facially invalid if it prohibits a substantial amount of protected speech. The doctrine seeks to strike a balance between competing social costs. . . . On the one hand, the threat of enforcement of an overbroad law deters people from engaging in constitutionally protected speech, inhibiting the free exchange of ideas. On the other hand, invalidating a law that in some of its applications is perfectly constitutional— particularly a law directed at conduct so antisocial that it has been made criminal— has obvious harmful effects. In order to maintain an appropriate balance, we have vigorously enforced the requirement that a statute's overbreadth be *substantial,* not only in an absolute sense, but also relative to the statute's plainly legitimate sweep. . . . . Invalidation for overbreadth is "strong medicine" that is not to be "casually employed." . . .

The first step in overbreadth analysis is to construe the challenged statute; it is impossible to determine whether a statute reaches too far without first knowing what the statute covers. Generally speaking, § 2252A(a)(3)(B) prohibits offers to provide and requests to obtain child pornography. The statute does not require the actual existence of child pornography. In this respect, it differs from the statutes in *Ferber, Osborne,* and *Free Speech Coalition,* which prohibited the possession or distribution of child pornography. Rather than targeting the underlying material, this statute bans the collateral speech that introduces such material into the child-pornography distribution network. Thus, an Internet user who solicits child pornography from an undercover agent violates the statute, even if the officer possesses no child pornography. Likewise, a person who advertises virtual child pornography as depicting actual children also falls within the reach of the statute.

The statute's definition of the material or purported material that may not be pandered or solicited precisely tracks the material held constitutionally proscribable in *Ferber* and *Miller:*

obscene material depicting (actual or virtual) children engaged in sexually explicit conduct, and any other material depicting actual children engaged in sexually explicit conduct. . . .

A number of features of the statute are important to our analysis:

First, the statute includes a scienter requirement. The first word of § 2252A(a)(3)—"knowingly"—applies to both of the immediately following subdivisions, both the previously existing § 2252A(a)(3)(A) and the new § 2252A(a)(3)(B) at issue here. We think that the best reading of the term in context is that it applies to every element of the two provisions. This is not a case where grammar or structure enables the challenged provision or some of its parts to be read apart from the "knowingly" requirement. Here "knowingly" introduces the challenged provision itself, making clear that it applies to that provision in its entirety; and there is no grammatical barrier to reading it that way.

Second, the statute's string of operative verbs— "advertises, promotes, presents, distributes, or solicits"—is reasonably read to have a transactional connotation. That is to say, the statute penalizes speech that accompanies or seeks to induce a transfer of child pornography— via reproduction or physical delivery— from one person to another. For three of the verbs, this is obvious: advertising, distributing, and soliciting are steps taken in the course of an actual or proposed transfer of a product, typically but not exclusively in a commercial market. When taken in isolation, the two remaining verbs— "promotes" and "presents"—are susceptible of multiple and wide-ranging meanings. In context, however, those meanings are narrowed by the commonsense canon of *noscitur a sociis*— which counsels that a word is given more precise content by the neighboring words with which it is associated. . . . "Promotes," in a list that includes "solicits," "distributes," and "advertises," is most sensibly read to mean the act of recommending purported child pornography to another person for his acquisition. . . . Similarly, "presents," in the context of the other verbs with which it is associated, means showing or offering the child pornography to another person with a view to his acquisition. . . .

To be clear, our conclusion that all the words in this list relate to transactions is not to say that they relate to *commercial* transactions. One could certainly "distribute" child pornography without expecting payment in return. Indeed, in much Internet file sharing of child pornography each participant makes his files available for free to other participants—as Williams did in this case. "Distribution may involve sophisticated pedophile rings or organized crime groups that operate for profit, but in many cases, is carried out by individual amateurs who seek no financial reward." . . . To run afoul of the statute, the speech need only accompany or seek to induce the transfer of child pornography from one person to another.

Third, the phrase "in a manner that reflects the belief" includes both subjective and objective components. "[A] manner that reflects the belief" is quite different from "a manner that would give one cause to believe." The first formulation suggests that the defendant must actually have held the subjective "belief" that the material or purported material was child pornography. Thus, a misdescription that leads the listener to believe the defendant is offering child pornography, when the defendant in fact does not believe the material is child pornography, does not violate this prong of the statute. (It may, however, violate the "manner . . . that is intended to cause another to believe" prong if the misdescription is intentional.) There is also an objective component to the phrase "manner that reflects the belief." The statement or action must objectively manifest a belief that the material is child pornography; a mere belief, without an accompanying statement or action that would lead a reasonable person to understand that the defendant holds that belief, is insufficient.

Fourth, the other key phrase, "in a manner . . . that is intended to cause another to believe," contains only a subjective element: The defendant must "intend" that the listener believe the material to be child pornography, and must select a manner of "advertising, promoting, presenting, distributing, or soliciting" the material that *he* thinks will engender that belief—whether or not a reasonable person would think the same. (Of course in the ordinary case the proof of the defendant's intent will be the fact that, as an objective matter, the manner of "advertising, promoting, presenting, distributing, or soliciting" plainly sought to convey that the material was child pornography.)

Fifth, the definition of "sexually explicit conduct" (the visual depiction of which, engaged in

by an actual minor, is covered by the Act's pandering and soliciting prohibition even when it is not obscene) is very similar to the definition of "sexual conduct" in the New York statute we upheld against an overbreadth challenge in *Ferber*. That defined "sexual conduct" as "actual or simulated sexual intercourse, deviate sexual intercourse, sexual bestiality, masturbation, sado-masochistic abuse, or lewd exhibition of the genitals." . . . Congress used essentially the same constitutionally approved definition in the present Act. If anything, the fact that the defined term here is "sexually *explicit* conduct," rather than (as in *Ferber*) merely "sexual conduct," renders the definition more immune from facial constitutional attack. "[S]imulated sexual intercourse" (a phrase found in the *Ferber* definition as well) is even less susceptible here of application to the sorts of sex scenes found in R-rated movies—which suggest that intercourse is taking place without explicitly depicting it, and without causing viewers to believe that the actors are actually engaging in intercourse. "Sexually *explicit* conduct" connotes actual depiction of the sex act rather than merely the suggestion that it is occurring. And "simulated" sexual intercourse is not sexual intercourse that is merely suggested, but rather sexual intercourse that is explicitly portrayed, even though (through camera tricks or otherwise) it may not actually have occurred. The portrayal must cause a reasonable viewer to believe that the actors actually engaged in that conduct on camera. Critically, unlike in *Free Speech Coalition*, § 2252A(a)(3)(B)(ii)'s requirement of a "visual depiction of an actual minor" makes clear that, although the sexual intercourse may be simulated, it must involve actual children (unless it is obscene). This change eliminates any possibility that virtual child pornography or sex between youthful-looking adult actors might be covered by the term "simulated sexual intercourse."

We now turn to whether the statute, as we have construed it, criminalizes a substantial amount of protected expressive activity.

Offers to engage in illegal transactions are categorically excluded from First Amendment protection. . . . . One would think that this principle resolves the present case, since the statute criminalizes only offers to provide or requests to obtain contraband—child obscenity and child pornography involving actual children, both of which are proscribed, . . . and the proscription of which is constitutional, . . . The Eleventh Circuit, however, believed that the exclusion of First Amendment protection extended only to *commercial* offers to provide or receive contraband: "Because [the statute] is not limited to commercial speech but extends also to non-commercial promotion, presentation, distribution, and solicitation, we must subject the content-based restriction of the PROTECT Act pandering provision to strict scrutiny. . . . . " . . . [some discussion omitted]

This mistakes the rationale for the categorical exclusion. It is based not on the less privileged First Amendment status of commercial speech, . . . but on the principle that offers to give or receive what it is unlawful to possess have no social value and thus, like obscenity, enjoy no First Amendment protection. . . . Many long established criminal proscriptions—such as laws against conspiracy, incitement, and solicitation— criminalize speech (commercial or not) that is intended to induce or commence illegal activities. . . . Offers to provide or requests to obtain unlawful material, whether as part of a commercial exchange or not, are similarly undeserving of First Amendment protection. It would be an odd constitutional principle that permitted the government to prohibit offers to sell illegal drugs, but not offers to give them away for free.

To be sure, there remains an important distinction between a proposal to engage in illegal activity and the abstract advocacy of illegality. . . . The Act before us does not prohibit advocacy of child pornography, but only offers to provide or requests to obtain it. There is no doubt that this prohibition falls well within constitutional bounds. The constitutional defect we found in the pandering provision at issue in *Free Speech Coalition* was that it went *beyond* pandering to prohibit possession of material that could not otherwise be proscribed. . . .

In sum, we hold that offers to provide or requests to obtain child pornography are categorically excluded from the First Amendment. Since the Eleventh Circuit erroneously concluded otherwise, it applied strict scrutiny to § 2252A(a)(3)(B), lodging three fatal objections. We address these objections because they could be recast as arguments that Congress has gone beyond the categorical exception.

The Eleventh Circuit believed it a constitutional difficulty that no child pornography need exist to trigger the statute. In its view, the fact that the statute could punish a "braggart, exaggerator, or outright liar" rendered it unconstitutional. . . . That seems to us a strange constitutional calculus. Although we have held that the government can ban *both* fraudulent offers, . . . *and* offers to provide illegal products, the Eleventh Circuit would forbid the government from punishing *fraudulent offers to provide illegal products.* We see no logic in that position; if anything, such statements are doubly excluded from the First Amendment.

The Eleventh Circuit held that under *Brandenburg,* the "non-commercial, non-inciteful promotion of illegal child pornography" is protected, and § 2252A(a)(3)(B) therefore overreaches by criminalizing the promotion of child pornography. . . . . As we have discussed earlier, however, the term "promotes" does not refer to abstract advocacy, such as the statement "I believe that child pornography should be legal" or even "I encourage you to obtain child pornography." It refers to the recommendation of a particular piece of purported child pornography with the intent of initiating a transfer.

The Eleventh Circuit found "particularly objectionable" the fact that the "reflects the belief" prong of the statute could ensnare a person who mistakenly believes that material is child pornography. This objection has two conceptually distinct parts. First, the Eleventh Circuit thought that it would be unconstitutional to punish someone for mistakenly distributing virtual child pornography as real child pornography. We disagree. Offers to deal in illegal products or otherwise engage in illegal activity do not acquire First Amendment protection when the offeror is mistaken about the factual predicate of his offer. The pandering and solicitation made unlawful by the Act are sorts of inchoate crimes—acts looking toward the commission of another crime, the delivery of child pornography. As with other inchoate crimes— attempt and conspiracy, for example—impossibility of completing the crime because the facts were not as the defendant believed is not a defense. "All courts are in agreement that what is usually referred to as 'factual impossibility' is no defense to a charge of attempt." . . .

Under this heading the Eleventh Circuit also thought that the statute could apply to someone who subjectively believes that an innocuous picture of a child is "lascivious." (Clause (v) of the definition of "sexually explicit conduct" is "lascivious exhibition of the genitals or pubic area of any person.") That is not so. The defendant must believe that the picture contains certain material, and that material in fact (and not merely in his estimation) must meet the statutory definition. Where the material at issue is a harmless picture of a child in a bathtub and the defendant, knowing that material, erroneously believes that it constitutes a "lascivious display of the genitals," the statute has no application.

Williams and *amici* raise other objections, which demonstrate nothing so forcefully as the tendency of our overbreadth doctrine to summon forth an endless stream of fanciful hypotheticals. Williams argues, for example, that a person who offers nonpornographic photographs of young girls to a pedophile could be punished under the statute if the pedophile secretly expects that the pictures will contain child pornography. . . . That hypothetical does not implicate the statute, because the offeror does not hold the belief or intend the recipient to believe that the material is child pornography.

Amici contend that some advertisements for mainstream Hollywood movies that depict underage characters having sex violate the statute. . . . We think it implausible that a reputable distributor of Hollywood movies, such as Amazon.com, believes that one of these films contains *actual* children engaging in *actual or simulated* sex on camera; and even more implausible that Amazon.com would *intend* to make its customers believe such a thing. The average person understands that sex scenes in mainstream movies use nonchild actors, depict sexual activity in a way that would not rise to the explicit level necessary under the statute, or, in most cases, both.

There was raised at oral argument the question whether turning child pornography over to the police might not count as "present[ing]" the material. . . . . An interpretation of "presents" that would include turning material over to the authorities would of course be self-defeating in a statute that looks to the prosecution of people who deal in child pornography. And it would effectively nullify § 2252A(d), which provides an affirmative defense to the possession ban if a defendant promptly delivers child pornography to a law-enforcement agency. (The possession offense would simply be replaced by a pandering offense for delivering the material to law-enforcement officers.) In any event, the verb "present"— along with "distribute" and "advertise," as well as "give," "lend," "deliver," and "transfer"— was used in the definition of "promote" in *Ferber.* . . . Despite that inclusion, we had no difficulty concluding that the New York statute survived facial challenge. And in the period since *Ferber,* despite similar statutory definitions in other state statutes, . . . , we are aware of no prosecution for giving child pornography to the police. We can hardly say, therefore, that there is a "realistic danger" that § 2252A(a)(3)(B) will deter such activity . . .

It was also suggested at oral argument that the statute might cover documentary footage of atrocities being committed in foreign countries, such as soldiers raping young children. . . . Perhaps so, if the material rises to the high level of explicitness that we have held is required. That sort of documentary footage could of course be the subject of an as-applied challenge. The courts presumably would weigh the educational interest in the dissemination of information about the atrocities against the government's interest in preventing the distribution of materials that constitute "a permanent record" of the children's degradation whose dissemination increases "the harm to the child." . . . Assuming that the constitutional balance would have to be struck in favor of the documentary, the existence of that exception would not establish that the statute is *substantially* overbroad. The "mere fact that one can conceive of some impermissible applications of a statute is not sufficient to render it susceptible to an overbreadth challenge." . . . In the vast majority of its applications, this statute raises no constitutional problems whatever.

Finally, the dissent accuses us of silently overruling our prior decisions in *Ferber* and *Free Speech Coalition.* . . . . According to the dissent, Congress has made an end-run around the First Amendment's protection of virtual child pornography by prohibiting proposals to transact in such images rather than prohibiting the images themselves. But an offer to provide or request to receive virtual child pornography is not prohibited by the statute. A crime is committed only when the speaker believes or intends the listener to believe that the subject of the proposed transaction depicts *real* children. It is simply not true that this means "a protected category of expression [will] inevitably be suppressed," . . . . Simulated child pornography will be as available as ever, so long as it is offered and sought *as such,* and not as real child pornography. The dissent would require an exception from the statute's prohibition when, unbeknownst to one or both of the parties to the proposal, the completed transaction would not have been unlawful because it is (we have said) protected by the First Amendment. We fail to see what First Amendment interest would be served by drawing a distinction between two defendants who attempt to acquire contraband, one of whom happens to be mistaken about the contraband nature of what he would acquire. Is Congress forbidden from punishing those who attempt to acquire what they believe to be national-security documents, but which are actually fakes? To ask is to answer. There is no First Amendment exception from the general principle of criminal law that a person attempting to commit a crime need not be exonerated because he has a mistaken view of the facts.

As an alternative ground for facial invalidation, the Eleventh Circuit held that § 2252A(a)(3)(B) is void for vagueness. Vagueness doctrine is an outgrowth not of the First Amendment, but of the Due Process Clause of the Fifth Amendment. A conviction fails to comport with due process if the statute under which it is obtained fails to provide a person of ordinary intelligence fair notice of what is prohibited, or is so standardless that it authorizes or encourages seriously discriminatory enforcement. . . . . Although ordinarily "[a] plaintiff who engages in some conduct that is clearly proscribed cannot complain of the vagueness of the law as applied to the conduct of others," we have relaxed that requirement in the First Amendment context, permitting plaintiffs to argue that a statute is overbroad because it is unclear whether it regulates a substantial amount of protected speech . . . . . But "perfect clarity and precise guidance have never been required even of regulations that restrict expressive activity." . . .

The Eleventh Circuit believed that the phrases "in a manner that reflects the belief" and "in a manner . . . that is intended to cause another to believe" are "so vague and standardless as to what may not be said that the public is left with no objective measure to which behavior can be conformed." . . . The court gave two examples. First, an email claiming to contain photograph attachments and including a message that says "little Janie in the bath—hubba,

hubba!" According to the Eleventh Circuit, given that the statute does not require the actual existence of illegal material, the Government would have "virtually unbounded discretion" to deem such a statement in violation of the "reflects the belief" prong. The court's second example was an e-mail entitled "Good pics of kids in bed" with a photograph attachment of toddlers in pajamas asleep in their beds. The court described three hypothetical senders: a proud grandparent, a "chronic forwarder of cute photos with racy tongue-in-cheek subject lines," and a child molester who seeks to trade the photographs for more graphic material. . . . According to the Eleventh Circuit, because the "manner" in which the photographs are sent is the same in each case, and because the identity of the sender and the content of the photographs are irrelevant under the statute, all three senders could arguably be prosecuted for pandering. . . .

We think that neither of these hypotheticals, without further facts, would enable a reasonable juror to find, beyond a reasonable doubt, that the speaker believed and spoke in a manner that reflected the belief, or spoke in a manner intended to cause another to believe, that the pictures displayed actual children engaged in "sexually explicit conduct" as defined in the Act. The prosecutions would be thrown out at the threshold.

But the Eleventh Circuit's error is more fundamental than merely its selection of unproblematic hypotheticals. Its basic mistake lies in the belief that the mere fact that close cases can be envisioned renders a statute vague. That is not so. Close cases can be imagined under virtually any statute. The problem that poses is addressed, not by the doctrine of vagueness, but by the requirement of proof beyond a reasonable doubt. . . . .

What renders a statute vague is not the possibility that it will sometimes be difficult to determine whether the incriminating fact it establishes has been proved; but rather the indeterminacy of precisely what that fact is. Thus, we have struck down statutes that tied criminal culpability to whether the defendant's conduct was "annoying" or "indecent"—wholly subjective judgments without statutory definitions, narrowing context, or settled legal meanings. . . .

There is no such indeterminacy here. The statute requires that the defendant hold, and make a statement that reflects, the belief that the material is child pornography; or that he communicate in a manner intended to cause another so to believe. Those are clear questions of fact. Whether someone held a belief or had an intent is a true-or-false determination, not a subjective judgment such as whether conduct is "annoying" or "indecent." Similarly true or false is the determination whether a particular formulation reflects a belief that material or purported material is child pornography. To be sure, it may be difficult in some cases to determine whether these clear requirements have been met. "But courts and juries every day pass upon knowledge, belief and intent—the state of men's minds—having before them no more than evidence of their words and conduct, from which, in ordinary human experience, mental condition may be inferred." ... Thus, the Eleventh Circuit's contention that § 2252A(a)(3)(B) gives law enforcement officials "virtually unfettered discretion" has no merit. No more here than in the case of laws against fraud, conspiracy, or solicitation.

Child pornography harms and debases the most defenseless of our citizens. Both the State and Federal Governments have sought to suppress it for many years, only to find it proliferating through the new medium of the Internet. This Court held unconstitutional Congress's previous attempt to meet this new threat, and Congress responded with a carefully crafted attempt to eliminate the First Amendment problems we identified. As far as the provision at issue in this case is concerned, that effort was successful.

The judgment of the Eleventh Circuit is reversed.

It is so ordered.

[Footnotes and citations omitted. Concurring and dissenting opinions omitted.]

ALBERTO R. GONZALES, ATTORNEY GENERAL ET AL.
v.
ANGEL McCLARY RAICH ET AL.

SUPREME COURT OF THE UNITED STATES

545 U.S. 1 (2005)

Justice Stevens delivered the opinion of the Court.

California is one of at least nine States that authorize the use of marijuana for medicinal purposes. The question presented in this case is whether the power vested in Congress by Article I, § 8, of the Constitution "[t]o make all Laws which shall be necessary and proper for carrying into Execution" its authority to "regulate Commerce with foreign Nations, and among the several States" includes the power to prohibit the local cultivation and use of marijuana in compliance with California law.

I

California has been a pioneer in the regulation of marijuana. In 1913, California was one of the first States to prohibit the sale and possession of marijuana, and at the end of the century, California became the first State to authorize limited use of the drug for medicinal purposes. In 1996, California voters passed Proposition 215, now codified as the Compassionate Use Act of 1996. The proposition was designed to ensure that "seriously ill" residents of the State have access to marijuana for medical purposes, and to encourage Federal and State Governments to take steps towards ensuring the safe and affordable distribution of the drug to patients in need. The Act creates an exemption from criminal prosecution for physicians, as well as for patients and primary caregivers who possess or cultivate marijuana for medicinal purposes with the recommendation or approval of a physician. A "primary caregiver" is a person who has consistently assumed responsibility for the housing, health, or safety of the patient.

Respondents Angel Raich and Diane Monson are California residents who suffer from a variety of serious medical conditions and have sought to avail themselves of medical marijuana pursuant to the terms of the Compassionate Use Act. They are being treated by licensed, board-certified family practitioners, who have concluded, after prescribing a host of conventional medicines to treat respondents' conditions and to alleviate their associated symptoms, that marijuana is the only drug available that provides effective treatment. Both women have been using marijuana as a medication for several years pursuant to their doctors' recommendation, and both rely heavily on cannabis to function on a daily basis. Indeed, Raich's physician believes that forgoing cannabis treatments would certainly cause Raich excruciating pain and could very well prove fatal.

Respondent Monson cultivates her own marijuana, and ingests the drug in a variety of ways including smoking and using a vaporizer. Respondent Raich, by contrast, is unable to cultivate her own, and thus relies on two caregivers, litigating as "John Does," to provide her with locally grown marijuana at no charge. These caregivers also process the cannabis into hashish or keif, and Raich herself processes some of the marijuana into oils, balms, and foods for consumption.

On August 15, 2002, county deputy sheriffs and agents from the federal Drug Enforcement Administration (DEA) came to Monson's home. After a thorough investigation, the county officials concluded that her use of marijuana was entirely lawful as a matter of California law. Nevertheless, after a 3-hour standoff, the federal agents seized and destroyed all six of her cannabis plants.

Respondents thereafter brought this action against the Attorney General of the United States and the head of the DEA seeking injunctive and declaratory relief prohibiting the enforcement of the federal Controlled Substances Act (CSA), 84 Stat. 1242, 21 U.S.C. § 801 *et seq.*, to the extent it prevents them from possessing, obtaining, or manufacturing cannabis for their personal medical use. In their complaint and supporting affidavits, Raich and Monson described the severity of their afflictions, their repeatedly futile attempts to obtain relief with conventional medications, and the opinions of their doctors concerning their need to use marijuana. Respondents claimed that enforcing the CSA against them would violate the Commerce Clause, the Due Process Clause of the Fifth Amendment, the Ninth and Tenth Amendments of the Constitution, and the doctrine of medical necessity.

The District Court denied respondents' motion for a preliminary injunction . . . . Although the court found that the federal enforcement interests "wane[d]" when compared to the harm that California residents would suffer if denied access to medically necessary marijuana, it concluded that respondents could not demonstrate a likelihood of success on the merits of their legal claims . . . .

A divided panel of the Court of Appeals for the Ninth Circuit reversed and ordered the District Court to enter a preliminary injunction . . . . The court found that respondents had "demonstrated a strong likelihood of success on their claim that, as applied to them, the CSA is an unconstitutional exercise of Congress' Commerce Clause authority." . . . . The Court of Appeals distinguished prior Circuit cases upholding the CSA in the face of Commerce Clause challenges by focusing on what it deemed to be the "*separate and distinct class of activities*" at issue in this case: "the intrastate, noncommercial cultivation and possession of cannabis for personal medical purposes as recommended by a patient's physician pursuant to valid California state law." . . . . The court found the latter class of activities "different in kind from drug trafficking" because interposing a physician's recommendation raises different health and safety concerns, and because "this limited use is clearly distinct from the broader illicit drug market—as well as any broader commercial market for medicinal marijuana—insofar as the medicinal marijuana at issue in this case is not intended for, nor does it enter, the stream of commerce." . . . .

The majority placed heavy reliance on our decisions in *United States v. Lopez,* . . . (1995), and *United States v. Morrison,* . . . (2000), as interpreted by recent Circuit precedent, to hold that this separate class of purely local activities was beyond the reach of federal power. In contrast, the dissenting judge concluded that the CSA, as applied to respondents, was clearly valid under *Lopez* and *Morrison;* moreover, he thought it "simply impossible to distinguish the relevant conduct surrounding the cultivation and use of the marijuana crop at issue in this case from the cultivation and use of the wheat crop that affected interstate commerce in *Wickard v. Filburn.*" . . . .

The obvious importance of the case prompted our grant of certiorari . . . . The case is made difficult by respondents' strong arguments that they will suffer irreparable harm because, despite a congressional finding to the contrary, marijuana does have valid therapeutic purposes. The question before us, however, is not whether it is wise to enforce the statute in these circumstances; rather, it is whether Congress' power to regulate interstate markets for medicinal substances encompasses the portions of those markets that are supplied with drugs produced and consumed locally. Well-settled law controls our answer. The CSA is a valid exercise of federal power, even as applied to the troubling facts of this case. We accordingly vacate the judgment of the Court of Appeals.

II

Shortly after taking office in 1969, President Nixon declared a national "war on drugs." As the first campaign of that war, Congress set out to enact legislation that would consolidate various drug laws on the books into a comprehensive statute, provide meaningful regulation over legitimate sources of drugs to prevent diversion into illegal channels, and strengthen law enforcement tools against the traffic in illicit drugs. That effort culminated in the passage of the Comprehensive Drug Abuse Prevention and Control Act of 1970, 84 Stat. 1236.

This was not, however, Congress' first attempt to regulate the national market in drugs. Rather, as early as 1906 Congress enacted federal legislation imposing labeling regulations on medications and prohibiting the manufacture or shipment of any adulterated or misbranded drug traveling in interstate commerce. Aside from these labeling restrictions, most domestic drug regulations prior to 1970 generally came in the guise of revenue laws, with the Department of the Treasury serving as the Federal Government's primary enforcer. For example, the primary drug control law, before being repealed by the passage of the CSA, was the Harrison Narcotics Act of 1914, . . . (repealed 1970). The Harrison Act sought to exert control over the possession and sale of narcotics, specifically cocaine and opiates, by requiring producers, distributors, and purchasers to register with the Federal Government, by assessing taxes against parties so registered, and by regulating the issuance of prescriptions.

Marijuana itself was not significantly regulated by the Federal Government until 1937 when accounts of marijuana's addictive qualities and physiological effects, paired with dissatisfaction with enforcement efforts at state and local levels, prompted Congress to pass the Marihuana Tax Act, . . . (repealed 1970). Like the Harrison Act, the Marihuana Tax Act did not outlaw the possession or sale of marijuana outright. Rather, it imposed registration and reporting requirements for all individuals importing, producing, selling, or dealing in marijuana, and required the payment of annual taxes in addition to transfer taxes whenever the drug changed hands. Moreover, doctors wishing to prescribe marijuana for medical purposes were required to comply with rather burdensome administrative requirements. Noncompliance exposed traffickers to severe federal penalties, whereas compliance would often subject them to prosecution under state law. Thus, while the Marihuana Tax Act did not declare the drug illegal *per se*, the onerous administrative requirements, the prohibitively expensive taxes, and the risks attendant on compliance practically curtailed the marijuana trade.

Then in 1970, after declaration of the national "war on drugs," federal drug policy underwent a significant transformation. A number of noteworthy events precipitated this policy shift. First, in *Leary v. United States*, . . . (1969), this Court held certain provisions of the Marihuana Tax Act and other narcotics legislation unconstitutional. Second, at the end of his term, President Johnson fundamentally reorganized the federal drug control agencies. The Bureau of Narcotics, then housed in the Department of Treasury, merged with the Bureau of Drug Abuse Control, then housed in the Department of Health, Education, and Welfare (HEW), to create the Bureau of Narcotics and Dangerous Drugs, currently housed in the Department of Justice. Finally, prompted by a perceived need to consolidate the growing number of piecemeal drug laws and to enhance federal drug enforcement powers, Congress enacted the Comprehensive Drug Abuse Prevention and Control Act.

Title II of that Act, the CSA, repealed most of the earlier antidrug laws in favor of a comprehensive regime to combat the international and interstate traffic in illicit drugs. The main objectives of the CSA were to conquer drug abuse and to control the legitimate and illegitimate traffic in controlled substances. Congress was particularly concerned with the need to prevent the diversion of drugs from legitimate to illicit channels.

To effectuate these goals, Congress devised a closed regulatory system making it unlawful to manufacture, distribute, dispense, or possess any controlled substance except in a manner authorized by the CSA . . . . The CSA categorizes all controlled substances into five schedules . . . . The drugs are grouped together based on their accepted medical uses, the potential for abuse, and their psychological and physical effects on the body . . . . Each schedule is associated with a distinct set of controls regarding the manufacture, distribution, and use of the substances listed therein . . . . The CSA and its implementing regulations set forth strict requirements regarding registration, labeling and packaging, production quotas, drug security, and recordkeeping. . . .

In enacting the CSA, Congress classified marijuana as a Schedule I drug. . . . This preliminary classification was based, in part, on the recommendation of the Assistant Secretary of HEW "that marihuana be retained within schedule I at least until the completion of certain studies now underway." Schedule I drugs are categorized as such because of their high potential for abuse, lack of any accepted medical use, and absence of any accepted safety for use in medically supervised treatment . . . . These three factors, in varying gradations, are also used to categorize drugs in the other four schedules. For example, Schedule II substances also have a high potential for abuse which may lead to severe psychological or physical dependence, but unlike Schedule I drugs, they have a currently accepted medical use . . . . By classifying marijuana as a Schedule I drug, as opposed to listing it on a lesser schedule, the manufacture, distribution, or possession of marijuana became a criminal offense, with the sole exception being use of the drug as part of a Food and Drug Administration pre-approved research study . . . .

The CSA provides for the periodic updating of schedules and delegates authority to the Attorney General, after consultation with the Secretary of Health and Human Services, to add, remove, or transfer substances to, from, or between schedules . . . . Despite considerable efforts to reschedule marijuana, it remains a Schedule I drug.

III

Respondents in this case do not dispute that passage of the CSA, as part of the Comprehensive Drug Abuse Prevention and Control Act, was well within Congress' commerce power . . . . Nor do they contend that any provision or section of the CSA amounts to an unconstitutional exercise of congressional authority. Rather, respondents' challenge is actually quite limited; they argue that the CSA's categorical prohibition of the manufacture and possession of marijuana as applied to the intrastate manufacture and possession of marijuana for medical purposes pursuant to California law exceeds Congress' authority under the Commerce Clause.

In assessing the validity of congressional regulation, none of our Commerce Clause cases can be viewed in isolation. As charted in considerable detail in *United States v. Lopez*, our understanding of the reach of the Commerce Clause, as well as Congress' assertion of authority thereunder, has evolved over time. The Commerce Clause emerged as the Framers' response to the central problem giving rise to the Constitution itself: the absence of any federal commerce power under the Articles of Confederation. For the first century of our history, the primary use of the Clause was to preclude the kind of discriminatory state legislation that had once been permissible. Then, in response to rapid industrial development and an increasingly interdependent national economy, Congress "ushered in a new era of federal regulation under the commerce power," beginning with the enactment of the Interstate Commerce Act in 1887, . . . , and the Sherman Antitrust Act in 1890, ...

Cases decided during that "new era," which now spans more than a century, have identified three general categories of regulation in which Congress is authorized to engage under its commerce power. First, Congress can regulate the channels of interstate commerce . . . . Second, Congress has authority to regulate and protect the instrumentalities of interstate commerce, and persons or things in interstate commerce . . . . Third, Congress has the power to regulate activities that substantially affect interstate commerce . . . . Only the third category is implicated in the case at hand.

Our case law firmly establishes Congress' power to regulate purely local activities that are part of an economic "class of activities" that have a substantial effect on interstate commerce . . . . As we stated in *Wickard*, "even if appellee's activity be local and though it may not be regarded as commerce, it may still, whatever its nature, be reached by Congress if it exerts a substantial economic effect on interstate commerce." . . . . We have never required Congress to legislate with scientific exactitude. When Congress decides that the "total incidence" of a practice poses a threat to a national market, it may regulate the entire class . . . . In this vein, we have reiterated that when "a general regulatory statute bears a substantial relation to commerce, the *de minimis* character of individual instances arising under that statute is of no consequence." . . .

Our decision in *Wickard*, . . . , is of particular relevance. In *Wickard*, we upheld the application of regulations promulgated under the Agricultural Adjustment Act of 1938, . . . , which were designed to control the volume of wheat moving in interstate and foreign commerce in order to avoid surpluses and consequent abnormally low prices. The regulations established an allotment of 11.1 acres for Filburn's 1941 wheat crop, but he sowed 23 acres, intending to use the excess by consuming it on his own farm. Filburn argued that even though we had sustained Congress' power to regulate the production of goods for commerce, that power did not authorize "federal regulation [of] production not intended in any part for commerce but wholly for consumption on the farm." . . . Justice Jackson's opinion for a unanimous Court rejected this submission. He wrote:

> "The effect of the statute before us is to restrict the amount which may be produced for market and the extent as well to which one may forestall resort to the market by producing to meet his own needs. That appellee's own contribution to the demand for wheat may be trivial by itself is not enough to remove him from the scope of federal regulation where, as here, his contribution, taken together with that of many others similarly situated, is far from trivial." . . .

Wickard thus establishes that Congress can regulate purely intrastate activity that is not itself "commercial," in that it is not produced for sale, if it concludes that failure to regulate that class of activity would undercut the regulation of the interstate market in that commodity.

The similarities between this case and *Wickard* are striking. Like the farmer in *Wickard*, respondents are cultivating, for home consumption, a fungible commodity for which there is an established, albeit illegal, interstate market. Just as the Agricultural Adjustment Act was designed "to control the volume [of wheat] moving in interstate and foreign commerce in order to avoid surpluses . . . " and consequently control the market price, . . . a primary purpose of the CSA is to control the supply and demand of controlled substances in both lawful and unlawful drug markets . . . . In *Wickard*, we had no difficulty concluding that Congress had a rational basis for believing that, when viewed in the aggregate, leaving home-consumed wheat outside the regulatory scheme would have a substantial influence on price and market conditions. Here too, Congress had a rational basis for concluding that leaving home-consumed marijuana outside federal control would similarly affect price and market conditions.

More concretely, one concern prompting inclusion of wheat grown for home consumption in the 1938 Act was that rising market prices could draw such wheat into the interstate market, resulting in lower market prices . . . . The parallel concern making it appropriate to include marijuana grown for home consumption in the CSA is the likelihood that the high demand in the interstate market will draw such marijuana into that market. While the diversion of homegrown wheat tended to frustrate the federal interest in stabilizing prices by regulating the volume of commercial transactions in the interstate market, the diversion of homegrown marijuana tends to frustrate the federal interest in eliminating commercial transactions in the interstate market in their entirety. In both cases, the regulation is squarely within Congress' commerce power because production of the commodity meant for home consumption, be it wheat or marijuana, has a substantial effect on supply and demand in the national market for that commodity.

Nonetheless, respondents suggest that *Wickard* differs from this case in three respects: (1) the Agricultural Adjustment Act, unlike the CSA, exempted small farming operations; (2) *Wickard* involved a "quintessential economic activity"—a commercial farm—whereas respondents do not sell marijuana; and (3) the *Wickard* record made it clear that the aggregate production of wheat for use on farms had a significant impact on market prices. Those differences, though factually accurate, do not diminish the precedential force of this Court's reasoning.

The fact that Wickard's own impact on the market was "trivial by itself" was not a sufficient reason for removing him from the scope of federal regulation . . . . That the Secretary of Agriculture elected to exempt even smaller farms from regulation does not speak to his power to regulate all those whose aggregated production was significant, nor did that fact play any role in the Court's analysis. Moreover, even though Wickard was indeed a commercial farmer, the activity he was engaged in—the cultivation of wheat for home consumption—was not treated by the Court as part of his commercial farming operation. And while it is true that the record in the *Wickard* case itself established the causal connection between the production for local use and the national market, we have before us findings by Congress to the same effect.

Findings in the introductory sections of the CSA explain why Congress deemed it appropriate to encompass local activities within the scope of the CSA . . . . The submissions of the parties and the numerous *amici* all seem to agree that the national, and international, market for marijuana has dimensions that are fully comparable to those defining the class of activities regulated by the Secretary pursuant to the 1938 statute. Respondents nonetheless insist that the CSA cannot be constitutionally applied to their activities because Congress did not make a specific finding that the intrastate cultivation and possession of marijuana for medical purposes based on the recommendation of a physician would substantially affect the larger interstate marijuana market. Be that as it may, we have never required Congress to make particularized findings in order to legislate, ... While congressional findings are certainly helpful in reviewing the substance of a congressional statutory scheme, particularly when the connection to commerce is not self-evident, and while we will consider congressional findings in our analysis when they are available, the absence of particularized findings does not call into question Congress' authority to legislate.

In assessing the scope of Congress' authority under the Commerce Clause, we stress that the task before us is a modest one. We need not determine whether respondents' activities, taken in the aggregate, substantially affect interstate commerce in fact, but only whether a "rational basis" exists for so concluding . . . . Given the enforcement difficulties that attend distinguishing between marijuana cultivated locally and marijuana grown elsewhere, . . . , and concerns about diversion into illicit channels, we have no difficulty concluding that Congress had a rational basis for believing that failure to regulate the intrastate manufacture and possession of marijuana would leave a gaping hole in the CSA. Thus, as in *Wickard*, when it enacted comprehensive legislation to regulate the interstate market in a fungible commodity, Congress was acting well within its authority to "make all Laws which shall be necessary and proper" to "regulate Commerce . . . among the several States." . . . . That the regulation ensnares some purely intrastate activity is of no moment. As we have done many times before, we refuse to excise individual components of that larger scheme.

IV

To support their contrary submission, respondents rely heavily on two of our more recent Commerce Clause cases. In their myopic focus, they overlook the larger context of modern-era Commerce Clause jurisprudence preserved by those cases. Moreover, even in the narrow prism of respondents' creation, they read those cases far too broadly.

Those two cases, of course, are *Lopez*, . . . 4, and *Morrison*, ... As an initial matter, the statutory challenges at issue in those cases were markedly different from the challenge respondents pursue in the case at hand. Here, respondents ask us to excise individual applications of a concededly valid statutory scheme. In contrast, in both *Lopez* and *Morrison*, the parties asserted that a particular statute or provision fell outside Congress' commerce power in its entirety. This distinction is pivotal for we have often reiterated that "[w]here the class of activities is regulated and that class is within the reach of federal power, the courts have no power 'to excise, as trivial, individual instances' of the class." . . .

At issue in *Lopez*, . . . , was the validity of the Gun-Free School Zones Act of 1990, which was a brief, single-subject statute making it a crime for an individual to possess a gun in a school zone . . . . The Act did not regulate any economic activity and did not contain any requirement that the possession of a gun have any connection to past interstate activity or a predictable impact on future commercial activity. Distinguishing our earlier cases holding that comprehensive regulatory statutes may be validly applied to local conduct that does not, when viewed in isolation, have a significant impact on interstate commerce, we held the statute invalid. We explained:

> "Section 922(q) is a criminal statute that by its terms has nothing to do with 'commerce' or any sort of economic enterprise, however broadly one might define those terms. Section 922(q) is not an essential part of a larger regulation of economic activity, in which the regulatory scheme could be undercut unless the intrastate activity were regulated. It cannot, therefore, be sustained under our cases upholding regulations of activities that arise out of or are connected with a commercial transaction, which viewed in the aggregate, substantially affects interstate commerce." ....

The statutory scheme that the Government is defending in this litigation is at the opposite end of the regulatory spectrum. As explained above, the CSA, enacted in 1970 as part of the Comprehensive Drug Abuse Prevention and Control Act, ... , was a lengthy and detailed statute creating a comprehensive framework for regulating the production, distribution, and possession of five classes of "controlled substances." Most of those substances—those listed in Schedules II through V—"have a useful and legitimate medical purpose and are necessary to maintain the health and general welfare of the American people." .... The regulatory scheme is designed to foster the beneficial use of those medications, to prevent their misuse, and to prohibit entirely the possession or use of substances listed in Schedule I, except as a part of a strictly controlled research project.

While the statute provided for the periodic updating of the five schedules, Congress itself made the initial classifications. It identified 42 opiates, 22 opium derivatives, and 17 hallucinogenic substances as Schedule I drugs .... Marijuana was listed as the 10th item in the third subcategory. That classification, unlike the discrete prohibition established by the Gun-Free School Zones Act of 1990, was merely one of many "essential part[s] of a larger regulation of economic activity, in which the regulatory scheme

could be undercut unless the intrastate activity were regulated." ... Our opinion in *Lopez* casts no doubt on the validity of such a program.

Nor does this Court's holding in *Morrison*, ... The Violence Against Women Act of 1994, ... , created a federal civil remedy for the victims of gender-motivated crimes of violence .... The remedy was enforceable in both state and federal courts, and generally depended on proof of the violation of a state law. Despite congressional findings that such crimes had an adverse impact on interstate commerce, we held the statute unconstitutional because, like the statute in *Lopez*, it did not regulate economic activity. We concluded that "the noneconomic, criminal nature of the conduct at issue was central to our decision" in *Lopez*, and that our prior cases had identified a clear pattern of analysis: "Where economic activity substantially affects interstate commerce, legislation regulating that activity will be sustained." ...

Unlike those at issue in *Lopez* and *Morrison*, the activities regulated by the CSA are quintessentially economic. "Economics" refers to "the production, distribution, and consumption of commodities." .... The CSA is a statute that regulates the production, distribution, and consumption of commodities for which there is an established, and lucrative, interstate market. Prohibiting the intrastate possession or manufacture of an article of commerce is a rational (and commonly utilized) means of regulating commerce in that product. Such prohibitions include specific decisions requiring that a drug be withdrawn from the market as a result of the failure to comply with regulatory requirements as well as decisions excluding Schedule I drugs entirely from the market. Because the CSA is a statute that directly regulates economic, commercial activity, our opinion in *Morrison* casts no doubt on its constitutionality.

The Court of Appeals was able to conclude otherwise only by isolating a "separate and distinct" class of activities that it held to be beyond the reach of federal power, defined as "the intrastate, noncommercial cultivation, possession and use of marijuana for personal medical purposes on the advice of a physician and in accordance with state law." .... The court characterized this class as "different in kind from drug trafficking." .... The differences between the members of a class so defined and the principal traffickers in Schedule I substances might be sufficient to justify a policy decision exempting the narrower class from the coverage of the CSA. The question, however, is whether Congress' contrary policy judgment, *i.e.*, its decision to include this narrower "class of activities" within the larger regulatory scheme, was constitutionally deficient. We have no difficulty concluding that Congress acted rationally in determining that none of the characteristics making up the purported class, whether viewed individually or in the aggregate, compelled an exemption from the CSA; rather, the subdivided class of activities defined by the Court of Appeals was an essential part of the larger regulatory scheme.

First, the fact that marijuana is used "for personal medical purposes on the advice of a physician" cannot itself serve as a distinguishing factor . . . . The CSA designates marijuana as contraband for *any* purpose; in fact, by characterizing marijuana as a Schedule I drug, Congress expressly found that the drug has no acceptable medical uses. Moreover, the CSA is a comprehensive regulatory regime specifically designed to regulate which controlled substances can be utilized for medicinal purposes, and in what manner. Indeed, most of the substances classified in the CSA "have a useful and legitimate medical purpose." . . . . Thus, even if respondents are correct that marijuana does have accepted medical uses and thus should be redesignated as a lesser schedule drug, the CSA would still impose controls beyond what is required by California law. The CSA requires manufacturers, physicians, pharmacies, and other handlers of controlled substances to comply with statutory and regulatory provisions mandating registration with the DEA, compliance with specific production quotas, security controls to guard against diversion, recordkeeping and reporting obligations, and prescription requirements . . . . Furthermore, the dispensing of new drugs, even when doctors approve their use, must await federal approval . . . . Accordingly, the mere fact that marijuana—like virtually every other controlled substance regulated by the CSA—is used for medicinal purposes cannot possibly serve to distinguish it from the core activities regulated by the CSA.

Nor can it serve as an "objective marke[r]" or "objective facto[r]" to arbitrarily narrow the relevant class as the dissenters suggest, ... More fundamentally, if, as the principal dissent contends, the personal cultivation, possession, and use of marijuana for medicinal purposes is beyond the

"'outer limits' of Congress' Commerce Clause authority," . . . , it must also be true that such personal use of marijuana (or any other homegrown drug) for recreational purposes is also beyond those "outer limits," whether or not a State elects to authorize or even regulate such use.

Justice Thomas' separate dissent suffers from the same sweeping implications. That is, the dissenters' rationale logically extends to place *any* federal regulation (including quality, prescription, or quantity controls) of *any* locally cultivated and possessed controlled substance for *any* purpose beyond the "outer limits" of Congress' Commerce Clause authority. One need not have a degree in economics to understand why a nationwide exemption for the vast quantity of marijuana (or other drugs) locally cultivated for personal use (which presumably would include use by friends, neighbors, and family members) may have a substantial impact on the interstate market for this extraordinarily popular substance. The congressional judgment that an exemption for such a significant segment of the total market would undermine the orderly enforcement of the entire regulatory scheme is entitled to a strong presumption of validity. Indeed, that judgment is not only rational, but "visible to the naked eye," . . . , under any commonsense appraisal of the probable consequences of such an open-ended exemption.

Second, limiting the activity to marijuana possession and cultivation "in accordance with state law" cannot serve to place respondents' activities beyond congressional reach. The Supremacy Clause unambiguously provides that if there is any conflict between federal and state law, federal law shall prevail. It is beyond peradventure that federal power over commerce is "superior to that of the States to provide for the welfare or necessities of their inhabitants," however legitimate or dire those necessities may be . . . . Just as state acquiescence to federal regulation cannot expand the bounds of the Commerce Clause, . . . , so too state action cannot circumscribe Congress' plenary commerce power . . . .

Respondents acknowledge this proposition, but nonetheless contend that their activities were not "an essential part of a larger regulatory scheme" because they had been "isolated by the State of California, and [are] policed by the State of California," and thus remain "entirely separated from the market." . . . . The dissenters fall prey to similar reasoning . . . . The notion that California law has surgically excised a discrete activity that is hermetically sealed off from the larger interstate marijuana market is a dubious proposition, and, more importantly, one that Congress could have rationally rejected.

Indeed, that the California exemptions will have a significant impact on both the supply and demand sides of the market for marijuana is not just "plausible" as the principal dissent concedes, . . . , it is readily apparent. The exemption for physicians provides them with an economic incentive to grant their patients permission to use the drug. In contrast to most prescriptions for legal drugs, which limit the dosage and duration of the usage, under California law the doctor's permission to recommend marijuana use is open-ended. The authority to grant permission whenever the doctor determines that a patient is afflicted with "any other illness for which marijuana provides relief," . . . , is broad enough to allow even the most scrupulous doctor to conclude that some recreational uses would be therapeutic. And our cases have taught us that there are some unscrupulous physicians who overprescribe when it is sufficiently profitable to do so.

The exemption for cultivation by patients and caregivers can only increase the supply of marijuana in the California market. The likelihood that all such production will promptly terminate when patients recover or will precisely match the patients' medical needs during their convalescence seems remote; whereas the danger that excesses will satisfy some of the admittedly enormous demand for recreational use seems obvious. Moreover, that the national and international narcotics trade has thrived in the face of vigorous criminal enforcement efforts suggests that no small number of unscrupulous people will make use of the California exemptions to serve their commercial ends whenever it is feasible to do so. Taking into account the fact that California is only one of at least nine States to have authorized the medical use of marijuana, a fact Justice O'Connor's dissent conveniently disregards in arguing that the demonstrated effect on commerce while admittedly

"plausible" is ultimately "unsubstantiated," . . . , Congress could have rationally concluded that the aggregate impact on the national market of all the transactions exempted from federal supervision is unquestionably substantial.

So, from the "separate and distinct" class of activities identified by the Court of Appeals (and adopted by the dissenters), we are left with "the intrastate, noncommercial cultivation, possession and use of marijuana." . . . . Thus the case for the exemption comes down to the claim that a locally cultivated product that is used domestically rather than sold on the open market is not subject to federal regulation. Given the findings in the CSA and the undisputed magnitude of the commercial market for marijuana, our decisions in *Wickard v. Filburn* and the later cases endorsing its reasoning foreclose that claim.

V

Respondents also raise a substantive due process claim and seek to avail themselves of the medical necessity defense. These theories of relief were set forth in their complaint but were not reached by the Court of Appeals. We therefore do not address the question whether judicial relief is available to respondents on these alternative bases. We do note, however, the presence of another avenue of relief. As the Solicitor General confirmed during oral argument, the statute authorizes procedures for the reclassification of Schedule I drugs. But perhaps even more important than these legal avenues is the democratic process, in which the voices of voters allied with these respondents may one day be heard in the halls of Congress. Under the present state of the law, however, the judgment of the Court of Appeals must be vacated. The case is remanded for further proceedings consistent with this opinion.

It is so ordered.

[Footnotes and citations omitted. Concurring and dissenting opinions omitted.]

UNITED STATES OF AMERICA
v.
ERIK BOWKER

UNITED STATES COURT OF
APPEALS FOR THE SIXTH CIRCUIT

372 F.3d 365; 2004 U.S. App. LEXIS
11536; 2004 FED App. 0178P (6th Cir.)

June 11, 2004, Decided

June 11, 2004, Filed

Opinion

CLAY, Circuit Judge.

Defendant-Appellant Erik S. Bowker appeals his convictions and sentence for one count of interstate stalking, in violation of 18 U.S.C. § 2261A(1); one count of cyberstalking, in violation of 18 U.S.C. § 2261A(2); one count of theft of mail, in violation of 18 U.S.C. § 1708; and one count of telephone harassment, in violation of 47 U.S.C. § 223(a)(1)(C). Bowker also appeals the district court's failure to rule on his motion to return seized property and the district court's enhancement of his sentence based on extreme psychological harm to the victim. For the reasons that follow, we AFFIRM Bowker's convictions and sentence, but REMAND to the district court for a ruling on Bowker's motion to return seized property. . . .

On August 28, 2001, United States Magistrate Judge George J. Limbert signed a criminal complaint charging Erik. S. Bowker ("Bowker") with one count of telephone harassment in violation of 47 U.S.C. § 223(a)(1)(C). Bowker was arrested on August 29, 2001. On September 7, 2001, the magistrate judge held a preliminary examination and detention hearing for Bowker. The magistrate judge determined that probable cause for Bowker's arrest had been established, and he ordered Bowker detained . . . .

Bowker's jury trial commenced on June 3, 2002. On June 6, 2002, the jury returned verdicts of guilty against Bowker on all counts. On September 5, 2002, the government moved for an upward departure from the sentencing guidelines based on the victim's extreme psychological harm. On September 10, 2002, the district court sentenced Bowker to 96 months' incarceration, three years of supervised release, and a $400 special assessment. In assessing the term of incarceration, the district court granted the government's motion for an upward departure. . . .

In March, 2000, Tina Knight began working as a part-time general assignment reporter at WKBN Television in Youngstown, Ohio. WKBN has a general email account for most employees, and in June, 2000, WKBN received a number of emails relating to Knight. The emails were sent from several different email addresses and purported to be from an individual variously identified as "User x," Eric Neubauer, Karen Walters, and "BB." Several of the emails attached photographs with verbal captions. One caption referred to Knight being shot with a pellet gun, and another email said, "Thanks for my daily Tina Knight fix. Thanks for helping me get my nuts off," and another said "More Tina Knight, that is what I want and need." After receiving approximately nine of these types of email, WKBN's news director took them to the station's general manager. They then contacted Special Agent Deane Hassman of the FBI. Soon thereafter, Knight was shown the emails, and she was stunned and frightened.

FBI Agent Hassman began investigating the Tina Knight emails in July, 2000. Hassman was concerned about Knight's personal safety based on the content of the emails. One of the emails that concerned Hassman stated, "I'm not the type of obsessed viewer that hides in the bushes near your home to watch you come home from work, but we shall see. That may actually be fun." Another disturbing email stated, in part, "Dear Ms. Knight. Now I'm really pissed that you were looking even cuter than normally. You fucked up a little bit and here I am watching on this black and white thrift store TV. Cute, cute, cute. I bet you were a Ho at Ohio University in Athens, doing chicks and everything. Wow."

On July 25, 2000, Hassman sent emails to the various email addresses on the correspondence pertaining to Knight. Hassman asked the sender of the emails to contact him so that he could determine the sender's intent. Within 24 to 48 hours, Hassman received a telephone call from an individual who identified himself as Erik Bowker. Hassman wanted to set up a meeting with Bowker so Hassman could positively identify the sender of the emails and also ask him to cease and desist contacting Knight. They arranged to meet at the public library in Youngstown, but Bowker never showed.

A few weeks later, Knight began receiving hand-written notes at WKBN, the majority of which were signed by "Doug Wagner." By September, the letters were arriving at the station almost every couple of days. One of the letters included the phrase, "All this week I will be playing the role of Doug Wagner." A letter dated August 9, 2000 was signed "Chad Felton"; stated, "I think you are a super babe"; and included a necklace. The return addresses on the letters were one of two P.O. Boxes registered to Erik Bowker or his mother.

Knight left her employment at WKBN in November, 2000 to take a position at WOWK CBS13 in Charleston, West Virginia. WKBN did not inform the general public of Knight's new location.

In late December, 2000, Knight's parents, who reside in Medina, Ohio, received a card and a handwritten note at their home. The card purported to be from "Kathryn Harris." The letter read, "Dear Tina Knight: I am Kathryn Harris today. I didn't want your parents asking you a lot of questions, nor did I want to attract a lot of attention to you. My letters to you are all online at yahoo.com in a standard mail account. It is all explained there so please check in and read what I have written . . . . The E-mail address is tinahatesme@yahoo.com." Agent Hassman visited the email address to check if any letters had been sent to the email address mentioned in the letter. Hassman discovered that an email had been sent December 25, 2000. At the end of the email, the name "Doug Wagner" was typed. The email read, in part, "I told you I would not contact you by mail anymore but I am sorry, I am in agony. I'm thinking about you all the time. You really are my dream girl . . . . I am blinded with affection for you. I did not ask for this. Nope, it's all your fault . . . . Please don't cat dance on my emotions by failing to respond to me at all."

In February, 2001, Bowker filed a lawsuit against Knight in the Mahoning County Common Pleas Court. Knight's social security number was stated in the complaint, which was served at Knight's home address in West Virginia. Bowker's lawsuit accused Knight of stalking him. Agent Hassman attended a status conference for the lawsuit on March 16, 2001, so that he could make face-to-face contact with Bowker. After meeting Bowker at the hearing and confirming that Bowker had been sending the unsolicited correspondence to Knight, Hassman told Bowker that the correspondence was unwelcome and might be a violation of federal law. Hassman advised Bowker that if the conduct continued, it might result in his arrest. Bowker responded that he had a First Amendment right to engage in that type of conduct. Nevertheless, during the meeting, Bowker wrote and signed a note stating, "I understand that Tina M. Knight wishes all further contact with her or any family member to stop and I agree to do so, pursuant to conversation with Deane Hassman, special agent, Federal Bureau of Investigation . . . " Bowker also agreed to voluntarily dismiss his lawsuit against Knight.

Despite Bowker's March, 16, 2001 agreement to cease and desist from any further contact with Knight, on that very same day, Bowker mailed a letter to Knight. Bowker also continued to attempt telephone contact with Knight. Between January 26 and August 29, 2001, Bowker made 146 telephone calls from his cell phone to WOWK CBS 13, where Knight worked. Bowker also made 16 calls to Knight's personal residential telephone in West Virginia between August 11 and 28, 2001. Knight's number was unlisted and unpublished. According to telephone records, each of the 16 calls placed to Knight's home were preceded by *67, which enables a caller to block identification of his telephone number on the recipient's caller identification display. Bowker also called Knight's co-worker and a neighbor.

As the telephone calls to Knight's television station persisted through the summer of 2001, Agent Hassman believed it was important to capture Bowker's voice on tape, so Hassman provided Knight with a recording device at the television station. On June 12, 2001, Knight recorded a 45 minute telephone call from Bowker who, at one point, identified himself as "Mike." During the conversation, Bowker referred to Knight's neighbors, her family members and her social security number. He also indicated he might be watching Knight with his binoculars. Knight provided the tape to the FBI and never spoke to Bowker again on the telephone.

On July 16, 2001, Knight received a letter at the television station. In the letter, Bowker referred to Knight's parents and stated several times, "You do not hang up on me." The letter also crassly referred to Knight's car, threatened to file a mechanic's lien on her car and her co-worker's car, accused Knight and her colleague of being "fuck-ups, assholes and seriously emotional and mentally unbalanced," and contained numerous sexual references. The letter stated that Bowker would be contacting Knight's neighbors, pointed out that Knight had not registered her car in West Virginia, and concluded with the words, "So bye-by, fuck you, you are an asshole and a sociopath and an embarrassment to mothers everywhere sir . . . . Adios, Eric . . . Smooch, Smooch."

On August 10, 2001, Knight received a certified letter mailed to her residence in West Virginia. Accompanying the letter were numerous photographs of Bowker at various locations in West Virginia, Knight's home state. The letter stated, in part, "Send me an E-Mail address. It keeps me long distance, you know what I mean." Knight forwarded the letter and the photographs to the FBI. Bowker's credit card statement later revealed purchases from a Kmart and a Kroger near Knight's place of employment and residence in West Virginia between June 12 and July 30, 2001.

In August 2001, Bowker left a series of messages on Knight's answering machine asking that Knight or Knight's friend call him back, which did not occur. Among other things, Bowker stated:

I don't even know why I'm nice to you ever at all, you and your fucked-up friend should not even be working in the media. You know you gotta mother-fucking realize there's like 50 percent men in this country and you better mother-fucking learn that you're going to have to deal with us sometime . . . .

Well, it looks like nobody is going to answer me if Tina Knight is okay, so I'm gonna take the 1:00 a.m. bus out of Columbus, Ohio and come down there and see for myself. Okay, I'll be there about 6:00 a.m. Bye.

Knight testified that these messages made her afraid to leave the house every day, and she feared that Bowker might try to rape her. She gave the answering machine recordings to the FBI.

Bowker was arrested on August 29, 2001 at a self-storage facility in Youngstown where he kept some of his possessions. Among other things recovered from the storage facility, Bowker's car, and other locations were a police scanner set to the frequency of the Youngstown Police Department, a paper with scanner frequencies from the Dunbar, West Virginia Police Department, letters bearing the name "Chad Felton, " a credit report for Tina Knight, Knight's birth certificate, a map of Dunbar, West Virginia, Greyhound bus schedules with West Virginia routes, and photos taken by Bowker during a West Virginia trip on July 11, 2001, which included pictures of Knight's place of work, her car, and CBS news trucks. The FBI also discovered that Bowker had in his possession a Discover Card credit card bill addressed to Tina Knight in West Virginia. Knight never received that statement in the mail. . . .

Bowker argues that the magistrate judge erroneously found that there was probable cause to issue a warrant for his arrest premised on an alleged violation of 47 U.S.C. § 223(a)(1)(C), which prohibits telephone harassment. He further argues that trial court committed the same error when it denied Bowker's motion to suppress evidence obtained through the arrest warrant. We reject Bowker's arguments for the reasons stated below.

. . . The Court defers to findings of probable cause made by a magistrate, and will not set aside such findings unless they were arbitrarily made. When reviewing a district court's denial of a motion to suppress, the Court reviews the district court's findings of fact for clear error and its conclusions of law de novo.

At the preliminary hearing, the government brought a one-count criminal complaint against Bowker for the crime of telephone harassment, in violation of 47 U.S.C. § 223(a)(1)(C). That section provides for a fine, imprisonment, or both for anyone, who in interstate or foreign communications:

makes a telephone call or utilizes a telecommunications device, whether or not conversation or communication ensues, without disclosing his identity and with intent to annoy, abuse, threaten, or harass any person at the called number or who receives the communications.

Incorporated into the criminal complaint was the affidavit of FBI Agent Deane Hassman, who alleged that Bowker had made numerous telephone calls to Tina Knight in which Bowker did not identify himself, including a conversation with Knight on June 12, 2001, and messages left on Knight's answering machine on August 17-19 and 25-26, 2001. Agent Hassman's affidavit also provided extensive background details on Bowker's campaign of harassment against Knight via emails, letters and telephone calls.

Bowker concedes that the magistrate judge could have found probable cause on the elements of using the telephone with the intent to annoy, abuse, threaten or harass. He argues, however, that the magistrate had no basis to find the element of failing to disclose identity during the telephone calls because Knight, the recipient of those calls, allegedly recognized his voice, making it unnecessary for him to state his name. . . . Bowker points to the fact that during the June 12, 2001 telephone conversation with Knight, she referred to Bowker as "Eric" [sic].

Bowker's argument is flawed in several respects. His argument does not address the numerous occasions when Bowker called Knight and no conversation ensued and no messages were left or her answering machine. The evidence before the magistrate showed that Bowker used a caller identification blocking feature to place these calls, thereby concealing his identity. Since the telephone harassment law prohibits calls made with the intent to harass or annoy "whether or not conversation or communication ensues," there was probable cause to find that Bowker had concealed his identity in those instances. Knight's alleged ability to identify Bowker's voice was irrelevant. . . .

Even assuming that Knight was able to identify Bowker's voice, the magistrate judge properly found probable cause to believe that Bowker had not disclosed his identity during the June 12, 2001 conversation in which he misidentified himself as "Mike" and in August, 2001, when he left messages on Knight's answering machine without providing any name at all. On its face, the telephone harassment statute makes it illegal to place a call, with the intent to annoy, abuse threaten or harass, whenever the caller fails to identify himself. Since Bowker concedes that the magistrate judge could have found probable cause that he had the requisite intent, it was Bowker's provision of a false name and/or his failure to identify himself - not an erroneous judicial determination about the victim's recognition of his voice - that led to the issuance of his arrest warrant.

. . .

[Argument concerning failure to suppress evidence deleted.]

Bowker argues that the district court erred in failing to dismiss Counts 1 (interstate stalking), 2 (cyberstalking), and 4 (telephone harassment) of the indictment on the ground that the indictment inadequately alleged the elements of the offenses charged, and on the ground that the statutes that the indictment alleged he violated are unconstitutionally vague and overbroad. We review the denial of a motion to dismiss de novo. For the reasons that follow, we affirm the decision of the district court.

Under the Notice Clause of the Sixth Amendment, a criminal defendant has the right "to be informed of the nature and cause of the accusation" against him . . . . "To be legally sufficient, the indictment must assert facts which in law constitute an offense; and which, if proved, would establish prima facie the defendant's commission of that crime." . . .

Count 1 (interstate stalking), Count 2 (cyberstalking), and Count 4 (telephone harassment) track the language of the relevant statutes. Count 1 alleges that, between July 10 and July 30, 2001, Bowker knowingly and intentionally traveled across the Ohio state line with the intent to injure, harass, and intimidate Tina Knight, and as a result of such travel placed Knight in reasonable fear of death or serious bodily injury, in violation of 18 U.S.C. § 2261A(1). Count 2 alleges that between December 25, 2000 and August 18, 2001 Bowker, located in Ohio, knowingly and repeatedly used the internet to engage in a course of conduct that intentionally placed Knight, then located in West Virginia, in reasonable fear of death or serious bodily injury, in violation of 18 U.S.C. § 2261A(2). Count 4 alleges that between June 12,

2001, and August 27, 2001, Bowker, located in Ohio, knowingly made telephone calls, whether or not conversation or communication ensued, without disclosing his identity and with the intent to annoy, abuse, threaten and harass Knight, in violation of 47 U.S.C. § 223(a)(1)(C). Because the indictment stated all of the statutory elements of the offenses, and because the relevant statutes state the elements unambiguously, the district court properly denied Bowker's motion to dismiss Counts 1, 2, and 4 of the indictment. The indictment's reference to the specific dates and locations of the offenses, as well as the means used to carry them out (travel, internet, telephone), provided Bowker fair notice of the conduct with which he was being charged.

... Bowker argues that the indictment was defective because it does not charge him with making direct threats against Knight and therefore should have contained a statement of facts and circumstances surrounding the alleged indirect threats he made against her, such as an explanation of the parties' relationship. ...

... All of the statutory elements of the prohibited conduct were properly alleged, including the intent to cause a reasonable fear of death or serious bodily harm. And unlike the parties involved in Landham, whose custody battle was highly relevant to the charged conduct, Bowker's relationship with Knight had no relevant bearing on the alleged illegality of his conduct. We therefore reject Bowker's challenge to the sufficiency of the indictment . . . .

According to the Supreme Court, imprecise laws can be attacked on their face under two different doctrines - overbreadth and vagueness. The "overbreadth doctrine is a limited exception to the traditional standing rule that a person to whom a statute may constitutionally be applied may not challenge that statute on the basis that it may conceivably be applied in an unconstitutional manner to others not before the court." However, "overbreadth scrutiny diminishes as the behavior regulated by the statute moves from pure speech toward harmful, unprotected conduct." "Particularly where conduct and not merely speech is involved, we believe that the overbreadth of a statute must not only be real, but substantial as well, judged in relation to the statute's plainly legitimate sweep."

Bowker has provided absolutely no argument as to how 18 U.S.C. § 2261A, which prohibits interstate stalking and cyberstalking, is facially overbroad, merely asserting that the statute "reaches large amounts of protected speech and conduct" and "potentially targets political or religious speech." We fail to see how a law that prohibits interstate travel with the intent to kill, injure, harass or intimidate has a substantial sweep of constitutionally protected conduct. The same is true with respect to the prohibition of intentionally using the internet in a course of conduct that places a person in reasonable fear of death or seriously bodily injury. It is difficult to imagine what constitutionally-protected political or religious speech would fall under these statutory prohibitions. Most, if not all, of these laws' legal applications are to conduct that is not protected by the First Amendment. Thus, Bowker has failed to demonstrate how 18 U.S.C. § 2261A is substantially overbroad.

We also reject Bowker's argument as to the purported overbreadth of the telephone harassment statute. Bowker relies on the Supreme Court's decision in *Coates v. City of Cincinnati* . . . which involved a city ordinance that made it a criminal offense for three or more persons to assemble on a sidewalk and to be "annoying" to passersby. The Court struck down the ordinance, reasoning that it was "unconstitutionally broad because it authorizes the punishment of constitutionally protected conduct."

Coates is distinguishable. First, the focus of the telephone harassment statute is not simply annoying telephonic communications. It also prohibits abusive, threatening or harassing communications. Thus, the thrust of the statute is to prohibit communications intended to instill fear in the victim, not to provoke a discussion about political issues of the day. Second, the telephone harassment statute operates in a distinctly different realm of communication than the ordinance in *Coates*, which governed the manner in which individuals could assemble and communicate in the open on public property . . . .

We acknowledge that the telephone harassment statute, if interpreted to its semantic limits, may have unconstitutional applications. For example, if Bowker had been charged with placing anonymous telephone calls to a public official with the intent to annoy him or her about a political issue, the telephone harassment statute might have been unconstitutional as applied to him . . . . But Bowker was not so charged. His calls were predominately, if not exclusively, for the purpose of invading his victim's privacy and communicating express and implied threats of bodily harm. This type of speech is not constitutionally protected . . . .

Even if an enactment does not reach a substantial amount of constitutionally protected conduct, it may be impermissibly vague because it fails to establish standards for the police and public that are sufficient to guard against the arbitrary deprivation of liberty interests." Vagueness may invalidate a criminal statute if it either (1) fails "to provide the kind of notice that will enable ordinary people to understand what conduct it prohibits" or (2) authorizes or encourages "arbitrary and discriminatory enforcement." "It is established that a law fails to meet the requirements of the Due Process Clause if it is so vague and standardless that it leaves the public uncertain as to the conduct it prohibits." . . .

The stalking and telephone harassment statutes charged in Bowker's indictment provide sufficient notice of their respective prohibitions because citizens need not guess what terms such as "harass" and "intimidate" mean. This Court's decision in *Staley v. Jones* . . . , is instructive. That case involved a habeas corpus review of a conviction for stalking under a Michigan law that defines stalking as "a willful course of conduct involving repeated or continuing harassment of another individual that would cause a reasonable person to feel terrorized, frightened, intimidated, threatened, harassed, or molested and that actually causes the victim to feel terrorized, frightened, intimidated, threatened, harassed, or molested." Michigan law defines "harassment" as "conduct directed toward a victim that includes, but is not limited to, repeated or continuing unconsented contact that would cause a reasonable individual to suffer emotional distress and that actually causes the victim to suffer emotional distress." Expressly excluded from the definition of "harassment" is "constitutionally protected activity or conduct that serves a legitimate purpose." This Court rejected the petitioner's vagueness challenge to the Michigan statute, reasoning as follows:

A person of reasonable intelligence would not need to guess at the meaning of the stalking statutes, nor would his interpretation of the statutory language differ with regard to the statutes' application, in part because the definitions of crucial words and phrases that are provided in the statutes are clear and would be understandable to a reasonable person reading the statute . . . . Also, the meaning of the words used to describe the conduct can be ascertained fairly by reference to judicial decisions, common law, dictionaries, and the words themselves because they possess a common and generally accepted meaning. We therefore conclude that the statutes are not void for vagueness on the basis of inadequate notice.

The Michigan prohibition against willful harassment that causes a reasonable person to feel fear is almost indistinguishable from the federal anti-stalking statute, which prohibits intentional harassment that causes a reasonable fear of death or serious bodily injury. In fact, the federal statute arguably is less vague because it circumscribes the type of fear a victim must feel, namely a fear of death or serious bodily injury, whereas the Michigan law does not.

Bowker attempts to distinguish the Michigan statute by pointing to the fact that Michigan law defines the word "harassment," whereas federal law does not. The harassment definition under Michigan law, however, contains nothing not already reflected in the federal statute's general prohibition. The Michigan definition of harassment requires conduct directed toward a victim, but this requirement is implicitly reflected in the federal statute's requirement that a perpetrator intend to harass a victim. Michigan's harassment definition also requires that the conduct cause a reasonable individual to suffer emotional distress, but the federal statute requires conduct that causes a fear of death or serious bodily injury. There simply is no principled basis to distinguish the language of the federal statute from the Michigan statute which this Court upheld in *Staley*.

We also reject Bowker's argument that the stalking and telephone harassment statutes' failure to define words like "harass" and "intimidate" render them void for vagueness. As noted by the Court in

Staley, the meaning of these words "can be ascertained fairly by reference to judicial decisions, common law, dictionaries, and the words themselves because they possess a common and generally accepted meaning." Indeed, the Michigan anti-stalking statute, which the *Staley* Court upheld, does not appear to define the word "intimidate," a word that Bowker claims is too vague in the federal law. For this reason as well, we reject Bowker's vagueness challenge to the federal law . . . .

We further reject Bowker's argument that the federal stalking and telephone harassment statutes authorize or encourage arbitrary or discriminatory enforcement. Although the statutes provide no guidelines on terms like harass and intimidate, the meanings of these terms "can be ascertained fairly by reference to judicial decisions, common law, dictionaries, and the words themselves because they possess a common and generally accepted meaning." Thus, Bowker has not demonstrated that these statutes fail to provide "sufficiently specific limits on the enforcement discretion of the police to meet constitutional standards for definiteness and clarity."

Only Bowker's vagueness challenge to part of the telephone harassment statute, merits further discussion. As noted above, that statute prohibits using a telephone, without disclosing identity, with the intent to annoy, abuse, threaten, or harass any person at the number called. Bowker argues that the term "annoy" is unconstitutionally vague, relying on the Supreme Court's decision in *Coates* . . .

We agree that the word "annoy," standing alone and devoid of context and definition, may pose vagueness concerns. But that is not the case with the telephone harassment statute. The statute reads "annoy, abuse, threaten, or harass." The Supreme Court has observed that canons of construction ordinarily suggest that terms connected by a disjunctive be given separate meanings, unless the context dictates otherwise." Here, the statutory language must be read in the context of Congressional intent to protect innocent individuals from fear, abuse or annoyance at the hands of persons who employ the telephone, not to communicate, but for other unjustifiable motives. This context suggests that the words annoy, abuse, threaten or harass should be read together to be given similar meanings. Any vagueness associated with the word "annoy" is mitigated by the fact that the meanings of "threaten" and "harass" can easily be ascertained and have generally accepted meanings.

Even assuming, arguendo, that Bowker's vagueness argument theoretically has merit, he cannot rely on it to invalidate the indictment or his conviction for telephone harassment, because the statute clearly applies to the conduct he allegedly committed . . . .

Here, Bowker engaged in an anonymous campaign of threatening and harassing conduct directed toward Knight through use of the telephone (as well as the mails and the computer) that clearly fell within the statute's prohibition. This type of conduct lies at the core of what the telephone harassment statute was designed to prohibit. FBI Agent Hassman specifically warned Bowker that he might be arrested if he persisted in his course of telephone harassment, but Bowker ignored that warning. Moreover, the fact that Bowker engaged in this campaign with an intent to threaten or harass mitigates any concern that he may have been punished for merely having a communication over the telephone. . . . The appellant cannot claim confusion about the conduct proscribed where, as here, the statute precisely specifies that the actor must intend to perform acts of harassment in order to be culpable. Thus, Bowker vagueness challenge fails. The district court did not err in denying his motion to dismiss Counts 1, 2, and 4 of the indictment.

. . .

[Remaining arguments omitted.]

B. Interstate Stalking Count

Count 1 of the indictment charges Bowker with interstate stalking, in violation of 18 U.S.C. § 2261A(1). The government was required to prove:

(1) that the defendant traveled in interstate or foreign commerce;
(2) with the intent to kill, injure, harass, or intimidate another person; and
(3) in the course of, or as a result of, such travel places that person in reasonable fear of the death of, or serious bodily injury to, that person, a member of the immediate family of that person, or the spouse or intimate partner of that person.

Bowker argues that the government did not prove, pursuant to the interstate stalking count, that the "result of" Bowker's travel from Ohio to West Virginia in July, 2001, was to put Knight in reasonable fear of her life or bodily injury, because Knight did not learn of Bowker's travels until August 2001, after he had completed his travel. This argument is specious. Knight learned of Bowker's travel to West Virginia because he sent her numerous photographs informing her that he had been in the state the preceding month. Accompanying the photographs was the statement, "Take the photos out to read the backs of them. Send me an E-mail address. It keeps me long distance, you know what I mean." The clear implication of this statement was that Bowker would continue to communicate with Knight, unless she provided him with her email address. The jury was entitled to infer that this statement, combined with the photographs of Bowker at various locations in West Virginia, was intended to intimidate Knight by showing her that Bowker had traveled to her state and would do so in the future. The statute did not require the government to show that Bowker actually intended to harass or intimidate Knight during his travels, only that the result of the travel was a reasonable apprehension of fear in the victim. Since Knight testified that she was afraid that Bowker might rape her, and her fear seemed reasonable, the government proved all of the elements of the interstate stalking count.

C. Cyberstalking Count

Count 2 of the indictment charges Bowker with cyberstalking, in violation of 18 U.S.C. § 2261A (2). The government was required to prove:

(1) Bowker intentionally used the mail or any facility of interstate or foreign commerce;
(2) Bowker engaged in a course of conduct with the intent to place Knight in reasonable fear of death of, or serious bodily injury to, herself, her spouse or intimate partner, or a member of her immediate family; and
(3) Bowker's course of conduct actually placed Knight in reasonable fear of death of, or serious bodily injury to, herself.

The evidence shows that Bowker's intended to instill in Knight a fear of death or serious bodily harm through use of the mails and other facilities of interstate commerce, required elements of the

cyberstalking count. During a June 12, 2001 telephone conversation with Knight, Bowker told her: You don't know where I'm at. I might be in your house in Dunbar, West Virginia]; you don't know that . . . . I know all of your neighbors. . . . And I have access to all that information, just like anybody else does who knows where to find it. I have an enormous amount of things about you that I'm not going to disclose unless I have to. I'm not going to tell anybody about it except if you lie to me. I might not say anything to you at the time, but that might come back, you know . . . . I know the names of all your relatives and where they live . . . . I know your brothers' wives['] names, their ages, their Social Security numbers and their birth dates . . . and their property values . . . . Maybe I live on 20th Street in Dunbar . . . . Maybe I watch you with binoculars all the time and maybe I don't." A July 16, 2001 letter that Bowker sent to Knight at the television station had both sexual and threatening connotations . . . .

In August 2001, Bowker left a series of messages on Knight's answering machine asking that Knight or Knight's friend call him back, which did not occur. These messages contained statements that Knight reasonably could perceive to be threats to her personal safety . . . . Since Knight testified that these intentionally intimidating, threatening, and harassing interstate communications made her afraid to leave the house every day and that Bowker might try to rape her, the government proved all of the elements of the cyberstalking count.

D. Telephone Harassment Count

Count 4 of the indictment charged Bowker with telephone harassment, in violation of 47 U.S.C. § 223(a)(1)(C). The government had to prove that:

(1) Bowker made interstate telephone calls to Knight;
(2) Bowker did not disclose his identity in the telephone calls; and
(3) in the telephone calls, whether or not conversation or communication ensued, Bowker intended to annoy, abuse, threaten, or harass Knight or any person at the called number.

Bowker's primary argument against his conviction for telephone harassment is that Knight allegedly was aware of Bowker's identity when she received his calls. The statute, however, does not preclude criminal responsibility merely because the recipient may suspect, or have a very good idea of, the caller's identity. Rather, assuming that Bowker called Knight with the requisite intent to annoy, abuse, threaten, or harass, the only issue is whether Bowker disclosed his identity in those calls. It is clear that in all of the at-issue telephone calls, Bowker never affirmatively identified himself as Erik Bowker. In fact, he denied being Bowker during a conversation with Knight on June 12, 2001, and instead stated that his name was Mike. Thus, a straightforward application of the telephone harassment statute shows that the jury reasonably found the non-disclosure element to be satisfied.

. . .

[Motion for a new trial argument deleted.]

[Upward departure for extreme psychological harm to the victim argument deleted.]

[Other arguments deleted.]

Conclusion

For all the foregoing reasons, we AFFIRM Defendant Bowker's convictions and sentence. This case shall be REMANDED for the district court to conduct a hearing and to rule on Bowker's motion to return seized property.

[Footnotes and citations deleted.]

ERIC H. HOLDER, Jr., ATTORNEY GENERAL ET AL., PETITIONERS
v.
HUMANITARIAN LAW PROJECT ET AL.
HUMANITARIAN LAW PROJECT ET AL., PETITIONERS
v.
ERIC H. HOLDER, Jr., ATTORNEY GENERAL ET AL.

130 S.CT. 2705 (2010)

Chief Justice ROBERTS delivered the opinion of the Court.

Congress has prohibited the provision of "material support or resources" to certain foreign organizations that engage in terrorist activity. 18 U.S.C. § 2339B(a)(1). That prohibition is based on a finding that the specified organizations "are so tainted by their criminal conduct that any contribution to such an organization facilitates that conduct." Antiterrorism and Effective Death Penalty Act of 1996 (AEDPA), § 301(a)(7), 110 Stat. 1247, note following 18 U.S.C. § 2339B (Findings and Purpose). The plaintiffs in this litigation seek to provide support to two such organizations. Plaintiffs claim that they seek to facilitate only the lawful, nonviolent purposes of those groups, and that applying the material-support law to prevent them from doing so violates the Constitution. In particular, they claim that the statute is too vague, in violation of the Fifth Amendment, and that it infringes their rights to freedom of speech and association, in violation of the First Amendment. We conclude that the material-support statute is constitutional as applied to the particular activities plaintiffs have told us they wish to pursue. We do not, however, address the resolution of more difficult cases that may arise under the statute in the future.

I

This litigation concerns 18 U.S.C. § 2339B, which makes it a federal crime to "knowingly provid[e] material support or resources to a foreign terrorist organization." Congress has amended the definition of "material support or resources" periodically, but at present it is defined as follows:

"[T]he term 'material support or resources' means any property, tangible or intangible, or service, including currency or monetary instruments or financial securities, financial services, lodging, training, expert advice or assistance, safehouses, false documentation or identification, communications equipment, facilities, weapons, lethal substances, explosives, personnel (1 or more individuals who may be or include oneself), and transportation, except medicine or religious materials." § 2339A(b)(1); see also § 2339B(g)(4).

The authority to designate an entity a "foreign terrorist organization" rests with the Secretary of State. 8 U.S.C. §§ 1189(a)(1), (d)(4). She may, in consultation with the Secretary of the Treasury and the Attorney General, so designate an organization upon finding that it is foreign, engages in "terrorist activity" or "terrorism," and thereby "threatens the security of United States nationals or the national security of the United States." §§

1189(a)(1), (d)(4). "'[N]ational security' means the national defense, foreign relations, or economic interests of the United States." § 1189(d)(2). An entity designated a foreign terrorist organization may seek review of that designation before the D.C. Circuit within 30 days of that designation. § 1189(c)(1).

In 1997, the Secretary of State designated 30 groups as foreign terrorist organizations. . . . Two of those groups are the Kurdistan Workers' Party (also known as the Partiya Karkeran Kurdistan, or PKK) and the Liberation Tigers of Tamil Eelam (LTTE). The PKK is an organization founded in 1974 with the aim of establishing an independent Kurdish state in southeastern Turkey. . . . ; The LTTE is an organization founded in 1976 for the purpose of creating an independent Tamil state in Sri Lanka. . . . The District Court in this action found that the PKK and the LTTE engage in political and humanitarian activities. . . . . The Government has presented evidence that both groups have also committed numerous terrorist attacks, some of which have harmed American citizens. . . . . The LTTE sought judicial review of its designation as a foreign terrorist organization; the D.C. Circuit upheld that designation. . . . The PKK did not challenge its designation. . . .

Plaintiffs in this litigation are two U.S. citizens and six domestic organizations: the Humanitarian Law Project (HLP) (a human rights organization with consultative status to the United Nations); Ralph Fertig (the HLP's president, and a retired administrative law judge); Nagalingam Jeyalingam (a Tamil physician, born in Sri Lanka and a naturalized U.S. citizen); and five nonprofit groups dedicated to the interests of persons of Tamil descent. . . . , plaintiffs filed suit in federal court challenging the constitutionality of the material-support statute, § 2339B. Plaintiffs claimed that they wished to provide support for the humanitarian and political activities of the PKK and the LTTE in the form of monetary contributions, other tangible aid, legal training, and political advocacy, but that they could not do so for fear of prosecution under § 2339B. . . .

As relevant here, plaintiffs claimed that the material-support statute was unconstitutional on two grounds: First, it violated their freedom of speech and freedom of association under the First Amendment, because it criminalized their provision of material support to the PKK and the LTTE, without requiring the Government to prove that plaintiffs had a specific intent to further the unlawful ends of those organizations. . . . . Second, plaintiffs argued that the statute was unconstitutionally vague. . . .

Plaintiffs moved for a preliminary injunction, which the District Court granted in part. The District Court held that plaintiffs had not established a probability of success on their First Amendment speech and association claims. . . . . But the court held that plaintiffs had established a probability of success on their claim that, as applied to them, the statutory terms "personnel" and "training" in the definition of "material support" were impermissibly vague. . . . . [some discussion omitted]

The Court of Appeals affirmed. . . . The court rejected plaintiffs' speech and association claims, including their claim that § 2339B violated the First Amendment in barring them from contributing money to the PKK and the LTTE. . . . . But the Court of Appeals agreed with the District Court that the terms "personnel" and "training" were vague because it was "easy to imagine protected expression that falls within the bounds" of those terms. . . . [some discussion omitted]

With the preliminary injunction issue decided, the action returned to the District Court, and the parties moved for summary judgment on the merits. The District Court entered a permanent injunction against applying to plaintiffs the bans on "personnel" and "training" support. . . . . The Court of Appeals affirmed. . . .

Meanwhile, in 2001, Congress amended the definition of "material support or resources" to add the term "expert advice or assistance." . . . (Patriot Act), § 805(a)(2)(B), 115 Stat. 377. In 2003, plaintiffs filed a second action challenging the constitutionality of that term as applied to them. . . .

In that action, the Government argued that plaintiffs lacked standing and that their preenforcement claims were not ripe. . . . The District Court held that plaintiffs' claims were justiciable because plaintiffs had sufficiently demonstrated a "genuine threat of imminent prosecution," . . . , and because § 2339B had the potential to chill plaintiffs' protected expression, ... On the merits, the District Court held that the term "expert advice or assistance" was impermissibly vague. . . . . The District Court rejected, however, plaintiffs' First Amendment claims that the new term was substantially overbroad and criminalized associational speech. . . . .

The parties cross-appealed. While the cross-appeals were pending, the Ninth Circuit granted en banc rehearing of the panel's 2003 decision in plaintiffs' first action (involving the terms "personnel" and "training"). . . . The en banc court heard reargument on December 14, 2004. . . . Three days later, Congress again amended § 2339B and the definition of "material support or resources." Intelligence Reform and Terrorism Prevention Act of 2004 (IRTPA), § 6603, 118 Stat. 3762-3764.

In IRTPA, Congress clarified the mental state necessary to violate § 2339B, requiring knowledge of the foreign group's designation as a terrorist organization or the group's commission of terrorist acts. § 2339B(a)(1). Congress also added the term "service" to the definition of "material support or resources," § 2339A(b)(1), and defined "training" to mean "instruction or teaching designed to impart a specific skill, as opposed to general knowledge," § 2339A(b)(2). It also defined "expert advice or assistance" to mean "advice or assistance derived from scientific, technical or other specialized knowledge." § 2339A(b)(3). Finally, IRTPA clarified the scope of the term "personnel" by providing:

"No person may be prosecuted under [§ 2339B] in connection with the term 'personnel' unless that person has knowingly provided, attempted to provide, or conspired to provide a foreign terrorist organization with 1 or more individuals (who may be or include himself) to work under that terrorist organization's direction or control or to organize, manage, supervise, or otherwise direct the operation of that organization. Individuals who act entirely independently of the foreign terrorist organization to advance its goals or objectives shall not be considered to be working under the foreign terrorist organization's direction and control." § 2339B(h).

Shortly after Congress enacted IRTPA, the en banc Court of Appeals issued an order in plaintiffs' first action. . . . . The en banc court affirmed the rejection of plaintiffs' First Amendment claims for the reasons set out in the Ninth Circuit's panel decision in 2000. . . . . In light of IRTPA, however, the en banc court vacated the panel's 2003 judgment with respect to vagueness, and

remanded to the District Court for further proceedings. . . . . The Ninth Circuit panel assigned to the cross-appeals in plaintiffs' second action (relating to "expert advice or assistance") also remanded in light of IRTPA. . . .

The District Court consolidated the two actions on remand. . . . . The court also allowed plaintiffs to challenge the new term "service." . . . The parties moved for summary judgment, and the District Court granted partial relief to plaintiffs on vagueness grounds. . . . .

The Court of Appeals affirmed once more. . . . The court first rejected plaintiffs' claim that the material-support statute would violate due process unless it were read to require a specific intent to further the illegal ends of a foreign terrorist organization. . . . The Ninth Circuit also held that the statute was not overbroad in violation of the First Amendment. . . . . As for vagueness, the Court of Appeals noted that plaintiffs had not raised a "facial vagueness challenge." . . . The court held that, as applied to plaintiffs, the terms "training," "expert advice or assistance" (when derived from "other specialized knowledge"), and "service" were vague because they "continue[d] to cover constitutionally protected advocacy," but the term "personnel" was not vague because it "no longer criminalize[d] pure speech protected by the First Amendment." . . . .

The Government petitioned for certiorari, and plaintiffs filed a conditional cross-petition. We granted both petitions. . . .

II

Given the complicated 12-year history of this litigation, we pause to clarify the questions before us. Plaintiffs challenge § 2339B's prohibition on four types of material support—"training," "expert advice or assistance," "service," and "personnel." They raise three constitutional claims. First, plaintiffs claim that § 2339B violates the Due Process Clause of the Fifth Amendment because these four statutory terms are impermissibly vague. Second, plaintiffs claim that § 2339B violates their freedom of speech under the First Amendment. Third, plaintiffs claim that § 2339B violates their First Amendment freedom of association.

Plaintiffs do not challenge the above statutory terms in all their applications. Rather, plaintiffs claim that § 2339B is invalid to the extent it prohibits them from engaging in certain specified activities. . . . . With respect to the HLP and Judge Fertig, those activities are: (1) "train[ing] members of [the] PKK on how to use humanitarian and international law to peacefully resolve disputes"; (2) "engag[ing] in political advocacy on behalf of Kurds who live in Turkey"; and (3) "teach[ing] PKK members how to petition various representative bodies such as the United Nations for relief." . . . With respect to the other plaintiffs, those activities are: (1) "train[ing] members of [the] LTTE to present claims for tsunami-related aid to mediators and international bodies"; (2) "offer[ing] their legal expertise in negotiating peace agreements between the LTTE and the Sri Lankan government"; and (3) "engag[ing] in political advocacy on behalf of Tamils who live in Sri Lanka." . . .

Plaintiffs also state that "the LTTE was recently defeated militarily in Sri Lanka," so "[m]uch of the support the Tamil organizations and Dr. Jeyalingam sought to provide is now moot." . . . Plaintiffs thus seek only to support the LTTE "as a political organization outside Sri Lanka advocating for the rights of Tamils." . . . Counsel for plaintiffs specifically stated at oral argument that plaintiffs no longer seek to teach the LTTE how to present claims for tsunami-related aid, because the LTTE now "has no role in Sri Lanka." . . . . For that reason, helping the LTTE negotiate a peace agreement with Sri Lanka appears to be moot as well. Thus, we do not consider the application of § 2339B to those activities here.

[Discussion as to whether claim is justiciable is omitted.]

III

Plaintiffs claim, as a threshold matter, that we should affirm the Court of Appeals without reaching any issues of constitutional law. They contend that we should interpret the material-support statute, when applied to speech, to require proof that a defendant intended to further a foreign terrorist organization's illegal activities. That interpretation, they say, would end the litigation because plaintiffs' proposed activities consist of speech, but plaintiffs do not intend to further unlawful conduct by the PKK or the LTTE.

We reject plaintiffs' interpretation of § 2339B because it is inconsistent with the text of the statute. Section 2339B(a)(1) prohibits "knowingly" providing material support. It then specifically describes the type of knowledge that is required: "To violate this paragraph, a person must have knowledge that the organization is a designated terrorist organization . . . , that the organization has engaged or engages in terrorist activity . . . , or that the organization has engaged or engages in terrorism. . . ." . . . . Congress plainly spoke to the necessary mental state for a violation of § 2339B, and it chose knowledge about the organization's connection to terrorism, not specific intent to further the organization's terrorist activities.

Plaintiffs' interpretation is also untenable in light of the sections immediately surrounding § 2339B, both of which do refer to intent to further terrorist activity. See § 2339A(a) (establishing criminal penalties for one who "provides material support or resources . . . knowing or intending that they are to be used in preparation for, or in carrying out, a violation of" statutes prohibiting violent terrorist acts); § 2339C(a)(1) (setting criminal penalties for one who "unlawfully and willfully provides or collects funds with the intention that such funds be used, or with the knowledge that such funds are to be used, in full or in part, in order to carry out" other unlawful acts). Congress enacted § 2339A in 1994 and § 2339C in 2002. See § 120005(a), 108 Stat.2022 (§ 2339A); § 202(a), 116 Stat. 724 (§ 2339C). Yet Congress did not import the intent language of those provisions into § 2339B, either when it enacted § 2339B in 1996, or when it clarified § 2339B's knowledge requirement in 2004.

Finally, plaintiffs give the game away when they argue that a specific intent requirement should apply only when the material-support statute applies to speech. There is no basis whatever in the text of § 2339B to read the same provisions in that statute as requiring intent in some circumstances but not others. It is therefore clear that plaintiffs are asking us not to interpret § 2339B, but to revise it. "Although this Court will often strain to construe legislation so as to save it against constitutional attack, it must not and will not carry this to the point of perverting the purpose of a statute." . . .

Scales is the case on which plaintiffs most heavily rely, but it is readily distinguishable. That case involved the Smith Act, which prohibited membership in a group advocating the violent overthrow of the government. The Court held that a person could not be convicted under the statute unless he had knowledge of the group's illegal advocacy and a specific intent to bring about violent overthrow. . . . . This action is different: Section 2339B does not criminalize mere membership in a designated foreign terrorist organization. It instead prohibits providing "material support" to such a group. . . . Nothing about *Scales* suggests the need for a specific intent requirement in such a case. The Court in *Scales,* moreover, relied on both statutory text and precedent that had interpreted closely related provisions of the Smith Act to require specific intent. . . . . Plaintiffs point to nothing similar here.

We cannot avoid the constitutional issues in this litigation through plaintiffs' proposed interpretation of § 2339B.

IV

We turn to the question whether the material-support statute, as applied to plaintiffs, is impermissibly vague under the Due Process Clause of the Fifth Amendment. "A conviction fails to comport with due process if the statute under which it is obtained fails to provide a person of ordinary intelligence fair notice of what is prohibited, or is so standardless that it authorizes or encourages seriously discriminatory enforcement." . . . We consider whether a statute is vague as applied to the particular facts at issue, for "[a] plaintiff who engages in some conduct that is clearly proscribed cannot complain of the vagueness of the law as applied to the conduct of others." . . . We have said that when a statute "interferes with the right of free speech or of association, a more stringent vagueness test should apply." . . . "But 'perfect clarity and precise guidance have never been required even of regulations that restrict expressive activity.'" . . .

The Court of Appeals did not adhere to these principles. Instead, the lower court merged plaintiffs' vagueness challenge with their First Amendment claims, holding that portions of the material-support statute were unconstitutionally vague because they applied to protected speech—regardless of whether those applications were clear. The court stated that, even if persons of ordinary intelligence understood the scope of the term "training," that term would "remai[n] impermissibly vague" because it could "be read to encompass speech and advocacy protected by the First Amendment." . . . It also found "service" and a portion of "expert advice or assistance" to be vague because those terms covered protected speech. . . .

Further, in spite of its own statement that it was not addressing a "facial vagueness challenge," . . . the Court of Appeals considered the statute's application to facts not before it. Specifically, the Ninth Circuit relied on the Government's statement that § 2339B would bar filing an *amicus* brief in support of a foreign terrorist organization— which plaintiffs have not told us they wish to do, and which the Ninth Circuit did not say plaintiffs wished to do—to conclude that the statute barred protected advocacy and was therefore vague. . . . By deciding how the statute applied in hypothetical circumstances, the Court of Appeals' discussion of vagueness seemed to incorporate elements of First Amendment overbreadth doctrine. . . .

In both of these respects, the Court of Appeals contravened the rule that "[a] plaintiff who engages in some conduct that is clearly proscribed cannot complain of the vagueness of the law as applied to the conduct of others." . . . That rule makes no exception for conduct in the form of speech. . . . Thus, even to the extent a heightened vagueness standard applies, a plaintiff whose speech is clearly proscribed cannot raise a successful vagueness claim under the Due Process Clause of the Fifth Amendment for lack of notice. And he certainly cannot do so based on the speech of others. Such a plaintiff may have a valid overbreadth claim under the First Amendment, but our precedents make clear that a Fifth Amendment vagueness challenge does not turn on whether a law applies to a substantial amount of protected expression. . . . Otherwise the doctrines would be substantially redundant.

Under a proper analysis, plaintiffs' claims of vagueness lack merit. Plaintiffs do not argue that the material-support statute grants too much enforcement discretion to the Government. We therefore address only whether the statute "provide[s] a person of ordinary intelligence fair notice of what is prohibited." . . .

As a general matter, the statutory terms at issue here are quite different from the sorts of terms that we have previously declared to be vague. We have in the past "struck down statutes that tied criminal culpability to whether the defendant's conduct was 'annoying' or 'indecent'—wholly subjective judgments without statutory definitions, narrowing context, or settled legal meanings." . . . (holding vague an ordinance that punished "vagrants," defined to include "rogues and vagabonds," "persons who use juggling," and "common night walkers" (internal quotation marks omitted)). Applying the statutory terms in this action—"training," "expert advice or assistance," "service," and "personnel"—does not require similarly untethered, subjective judgments.

Congress also took care to add narrowing definitions to the material-support statute over time. These definitions increased the clarity of the statute's terms. See § 2339A(b)(2) ("'training' means instruction or teaching designed to impart a specific skill, as opposed to general knowledge"); § 2339A(b)(3) ("'expert advice or assistance' means advice or assistance derived from scientific, technical or other specialized knowledge"); § 2339B (h) (clarifying the scope of "personnel"). And the knowledge requirement of the statute further reduces any potential for vagueness, as we have held with respect to other statutes containing a similar requirement. . . .

Of course, the scope of the material-support statute may not be clear in every application. But the dispositive point here is that the statutory terms are clear in their application to plaintiffs' proposed conduct, which means that plaintiffs' vagueness challenge must fail. Even assuming that a heightened standard applies because the material-support statute potentially implicates speech, the statutory terms are not vague as applied to plaintiffs. . . .

Most of the activities in which plaintiffs seek to engage readily fall within the scope of the terms "training" and "expert advice or assistance." Plaintiffs want to "train members of [the] PKK on how to use humanitarian and international law to peacefully resolve disputes," and "teach PKK members how to petition various representative bodies such as the United Nations for relief." . . . A person of ordinary intelligence would understand that instruction on resolving

disputes through international law falls within the statute's definition of "training" because it imparts a "specific skill," not "general knowledge." § 2339A(b)(2). Plaintiffs' activities also fall comfortably within the scope of "expert advice or assistance": A reasonable person would recognize that teaching the PKK how to petition for humanitarian relief before the United Nations involves advice derived from, as the statute puts it, "specialized knowledge." § 2339A(b)(3). In fact, plaintiffs themselves have repeatedly used the terms "training" and "expert advice" throughout this litigation to describe their own proposed activities, demonstrating that these common terms readily and naturally cover plaintiffs' conduct. . . .

Plaintiffs respond by pointing to hypothetical situations designed to test the limits of "training" and "expert advice or assistance." They argue that the statutory definitions of these terms use words of degree—like "specific," "general," and "specialized"—and that it is difficult to apply those definitions in particular cases. . . . Whatever force these arguments might have in the abstract, they are beside the point here. Plaintiffs do not propose to teach a course on geography, and cannot seek refuge in imaginary cases that straddle the boundary between "specific skills" and "general knowledge." . . . We emphasized this point in *Scales,* holding that even if there might be theoretical doubts regarding the distinction between "active" and "nominal" membership in an organization— also terms of degree—the defendant's vagueness challenge failed because his "case present[ed] no such problem." . . .

Gentile was different. There the asserted vagueness in a state bar rule was directly implicated by the facts before the Court: Counsel had reason to suppose that his particular statements to the press would not violate the rule, yet he was disciplined nonetheless. . . . We did not suggest that counsel could escape discipline on vagueness grounds if his own speech were plainly prohibited.

Plaintiffs also contend that they want to engage in "political advocacy" on behalf of Kurds living in Turkey and Tamils living in Sri Lanka. . . . They are concerned that such advocacy might be regarded as "material support" in the form of providing "personnel" or "service[s]," and assert that the statute is unconstitutionally vague because they cannot tell.

As for "personnel," Congress enacted a limiting definition in IRTPA that answers plaintiffs' vagueness concerns. Providing material support that constitutes "personnel" is defined as knowingly providing a person "to work under that terrorist organization's direction or control or to organize, manage, supervise, or otherwise direct the operation of that organization." § 2339B(h). The statute makes clear that "personnel" does not cover *independent* advocacy: "Individuals who act entirely independently of the foreign terrorist organization to advance its goals or objectives shall not be considered to be working under the foreign terrorist organization's direction and control." . . .

"[S]ervice" similarly refers to concerted activity, not independent advocacy. . . . Context confirms that ordinary meaning here. The statute prohibits providing a service "*to* a foreign terrorist organization." § 2339B(a)(1) (emphasis added). The use of the word "to" indicates a connection between the service and the foreign group. We think a person of ordinary intelligence would understand that independently advocating for a cause is different from providing a service to a group that is advocating for that cause.

Moreover, if independent activity in support of a terrorist group could be characterized as a "service," the statute's specific exclusion of independent activity in the definition of "personnel" would not make sense. Congress would not have prohibited under "service" what it specifically exempted from prohibition under "personnel." The other types of material support listed in the statute, including "lodging," "weapons," "explosives," and "transportation," § 2339A(b)(1), are not forms of support that could be provided independently of a foreign terrorist organization. We interpret "service" along the same lines. Thus, any independent advocacy in which plaintiffs wish to engage is not prohibited by § 2339B. On the other hand, a person of ordinary intelligence would understand the term "service" to cover advocacy performed in coordination with, or at the direction of, a foreign terrorist organization.

Plaintiffs argue that this construction of the statute poses difficult questions of exactly how much direction or coordination is necessary for an activity to constitute a "service." . . . The problem with these questions is that they are entirely hypothetical. Plaintiffs have not provided any specific articulation of the degree to which *they* seek to coordinate their advocacy with the PKK and the LTTE. They have instead described the form of their intended advocacy only in the most general terms. . . .

Deciding whether activities described at such a level of generality would constitute prohibited "service[s]" under the statute would require "sheer speculation"—which means that plaintiffs cannot prevail in their preenforcement challenge. . . . It is apparent with respect to these claims that "gradations of fact or charge would make a difference as to criminal liability," and so "adjudication of the reach and constitutionality of [the statute] must await a concrete fact situation." . . .

V

A

We next consider whether the material-support statute, as applied to plaintiffs, violates the freedom of speech guaranteed by the First Amendment. Both plaintiffs and the Government take extreme positions on this question. Plaintiffs claim that Congress has banned their "pure political speech." . . . It has not. Under the material-support statute, plaintiffs may say anything they wish on any topic. They may speak and write freely about the PKK and LTTE, the governments of Turkey and Sri Lanka, human rights, and international law. They may advocate before the United Nations. As the Government states: "The statute does not prohibit independent advocacy or expression of any kind." . . . Section 2339B also "does not prevent [plaintiffs] from becoming members of the PKK and LTTE or impose any sanction on them for doing so." . . . Congress has not, therefore, sought to suppress ideas or *opinions* in the form of "pure political speech." Rather, Congress has prohibited "material support," which most often does not take the form of speech at all. And when it does, the statute is carefully drawn to cover only a narrow category of speech to, under the direction of, or in coordination with foreign groups that the speaker knows to be terrorist organizations.

For its part, the Government takes the foregoing too far, claiming that the only thing truly at issue in this litigation is conduct, not speech. Section

2339B is directed at the fact of plaintiffs' interaction with the PKK and LTTE, the Government contends, and only incidentally burdens their expression. The Government argues that the proper standard of review is therefore the one set out in *United States v. O'Brien* . . . In that case, the Court rejected a First Amendment challenge to a conviction under a generally applicable prohibition on destroying draft cards, even though O'Brien had burned his card in protest against the draft. . . . In so doing, we applied what we have since called "intermediate scrutiny," under which a "content-neutral regulation will be sustained under the First Amendment if it advances important governmental interests unrelated to the suppression of free speech and does not burden substantially more speech than necessary to further those interests." . . .

The Government is wrong that the only thing actually at issue in this litigation is conduct, and therefore wrong to argue that *O'Brien* provides the correct standard of review. *O'Brien* does not provide the applicable standard for reviewing a content-based regulation of speech, . . . and § 2339B regulates speech on the basis of its content. Plaintiffs want to speak to the PKK and the LTTE, and whether they may do so under § 2339B depends on what they say. If plaintiffs' speech to those groups imparts a "specific skill" or communicates advice derived from "specialized knowledge"—for example, training on the use of international law or advice on petitioning the United Nations—then it is barred. . . . On the other hand, plaintiffs' speech is not barred if it imparts only general or unspecialized knowledge. . . .

The Government argues that § 2339B should nonetheless receive intermediate scrutiny because it *generally* functions as a regulation of conduct. That argument runs headlong into a number of our precedents, most prominently *Cohen v. California* . . . *Cohen* also involved a generally applicable regulation of conduct, barring breaches of the peace. . . . But when Cohen was convicted for wearing a jacket bearing an epithet, we did not apply *O'Brien*. . . . Instead, we recognized that the generally applicable law was directed at Cohen because of what his speech communicated—he violated the breach of the peace statute because of the offensive content of his particular message. We accordingly applied more rigorous scrutiny and reversed his conviction. . . .

This suit falls into the same category. The law here may be described as directed at conduct, as the law in *Cohen* was directed at breaches of the peace, but as applied to plaintiffs the conduct triggering coverage under the statute consists of communicating a message. As we explained in *Texas v. Johnson*: "If the [Government's] regulation is not related to expression, then the less stringent standard we announced in *United States v. O'Brien* for regulations of noncommunicative conduct controls. If it is, then we are outside of *O'Brien*'s test, and we must [apply] a more demanding standard." . . .

B

The First Amendment issue before us is more refined than either plaintiffs or the Government would have it. It is not whether the Government may prohibit pure political speech, or may prohibit material support in the form of conduct. It is instead whether the Government may prohibit what plaintiffs want to do—provide material support to the PKK and LTTE in the form of speech.

Everyone agrees that the Government's interest in combating terrorism is an urgent objective of the highest order. . . . . Plaintiffs' complaint is that the ban on material support, applied to what they wish to do, is not "necessary to further that interest." . . . The objective of combating terrorism does not justify prohibiting their speech, plaintiffs argue, because their support will advance only the legitimate activities of the designated terrorist organizations, not their terrorism. . . .

Whether foreign terrorist organizations meaningfully segregate support of their legitimate activities from support of terrorism is an empirical question. When it enacted § 2339B in 1996, Congress made specific findings regarding the serious threat posed by international terrorism. . . . One of those findings explicitly rejects plaintiffs' contention that their support would not further the terrorist activities of the PKK and LTTE: "[F]oreign organizations that engage in terrorist activity are so tainted by their criminal conduct that *any contribution to such an organization* facilitates that conduct." § 301(a)(7) (emphasis added).

Plaintiffs argue that the reference to "any contribution" in this finding meant only monetary support. There is no reason to read the finding to be so limited, particularly because Congress expressly prohibited so much more than monetary support in § 2339B. Congress's use of the term "contribution" is best read to reflect a determination that any form of material support furnished "to" a foreign terrorist organization should be barred, which is precisely what the material-support statute does. Indeed, when Congress enacted § 2339B, Congress simultaneously removed an exception that had existed in § 2339A(a) (1994 ed.) for the provision of material support in the form of "humanitarian assistance to persons not directly involved in" terrorist activity. . . . That repeal demonstrates that Congress considered and rejected the view that ostensibly peaceful aid would have no harmful effects.

We are convinced that Congress was justified in rejecting that view. The PKK and the LTTE are deadly groups. "The PKK's insurgency has claimed more than 22,000 lives." . . . The LTTE has engaged in extensive suicide bombings and political assassinations, including killings of the Sri Lankan President, Security Minister, and Deputy Defense Minister. . . . It is not difficult to conclude as Congress did that the "tain[t]" of such violent activities is so great that working in coordination with or at the command of the PKK and LTTE serves to legitimize and further their terrorist means. . . .

Material support meant to "promot[e] peaceable, lawful conduct," . . . , can further terrorism by foreign groups in multiple ways. "Material support" is a valuable resource by definition. Such support frees up other resources within the organization that may be put to violent ends. It also importantly helps lend legitimacy to foreign terrorist groups—legitimacy that makes it easier for those groups to persist, to recruit members, and to raise funds—all of which facilitate more terrorist attacks. "Terrorist organizations do not maintain *organizational* 'firewalls' that would prevent or deter . . . sharing and commingling of support and benefits." . . . . . . "Indeed, some designated foreign terrorist organizations use social and political components to recruit personnel to carry out terrorist operations, and to provide support to criminal terrorists and their families in aid of such operations." . . .

Money is fungible, and "[w]hen foreign terrorist organizations that have a dual structure raise funds, they highlight the civilian and humanitarian ends to which such moneys could be put." . . . But

"there is reason to believe that foreign terrorist organizations do not maintain legitimate *financial* firewalls between those funds raised for civil, non-violent activities, and those ultimately used to support violent, terrorist operations." . . . Thus, "[f]unds raised ostensibly for charitable purposes have in the past been redirected by some terrorist groups to fund the purchase of arms and explosives." . . . There is evidence that the PKK and the LTTE, in particular, have not "respected the line between humanitarian and violent activities." . . .

The dissent argues that there is "no natural stopping place" for the proposition that aiding a foreign terrorist organization's lawful activity promotes the terrorist organization as a whole. . . . But Congress has settled on just such a natural stopping place: The statute reaches only material support coordinated with or under the direction of a designated foreign terrorist organization. Independent advocacy that might be viewed as promoting the group's legitimacy is not covered. . . .

Providing foreign terrorist groups with material support in any form also furthers terrorism by straining the United States' relationships with its allies and undermining cooperative efforts between nations to prevent terrorist attacks. We see no reason to question Congress's finding that "international cooperation is required for an effective response to terrorism, as demonstrated by the numerous multilateral conventions in force providing universal prosecutive jurisdiction over persons involved in a variety of terrorist acts, including hostage taking, murder of an internationally protected person, and aircraft piracy and sabotage." . . . The material-support statute furthers this international effort by prohibiting aid for foreign terrorist groups that harm the United States' partners abroad: "A number of designated foreign terrorist organizations have attacked moderate governments with which the United States has vigorously endeavored to maintain close and friendly relations," and those attacks "threaten [the] social, economic and political stability" of such governments. . . .

For example, the Republic of Turkey—a fellow member of NATO—is defending itself against a violent insurgency waged by the PKK. . . . That nation and our other allies would react sharply to Americans furnishing material support to foreign groups like the PKK, and would hardly be mollified by the explanation that the support was meant only to further those groups "legitimate" activities. From Turkey's perspective, there likely are no such activities. . . .

C

[Continued discussion of the inability to separate nonterrorist activity from terrorist activity omitted.]

Our precedents, old and new, make clear that concerns of national security and foreign relations do not warrant abdication of the judicial role. We do not defer to the Government's reading of the First Amendment, even when such interests are at stake. We are one with the dissent that the Government's "authority and expertise in these matters do not automatically trump the Court's own obligation to secure the protection that the Constitution grants to individuals." . . . . But when it comes to collecting evidence and drawing factual inferences in this area, "the lack of competence on the part of the courts is marked," . . . and respect for the Government's conclusions is appropriate.

One reason for that respect is that national security and foreign policy concerns arise in connection with efforts to confront evolving threats in an area where information can be difficult to obtain and the impact of certain conduct difficult to assess. The dissent slights these real constraints in demanding hard proof—with "detail," "specific facts," and "specific evidence"—that plaintiffs' proposed activities will support terrorist attacks. . . . . That would be a dangerous requirement. In this context, conclusions must often be based on informed judgment rather than concrete evidence, and that reality affects what we may reasonably insist on from the Government. The material-support statute is, on its face, a preventive measure—it criminalizes not terrorist attacks themselves, but aid that makes the attacks more likely to occur. The Government, when seeking to prevent imminent harms in the context of international affairs and national security, is not required to conclusively link all the pieces in the puzzle before we grant weight to its empirical conclusions. . . . This context is different from that in decisions like *Cohen*. In that case, the application of the statute turned on the offensiveness of the speech at issue. Observing that "one man's

vulgarity is another's lyric," we invalidated Cohen's conviction in part because we concluded that "governmental officials cannot make principled distinctions in this area." . . . In this litigation, by contrast, Congress and the Executive are uniquely positioned to make principled distinctions between activities that will further terrorist conduct and undermine United States foreign policy, and those that will not.

We also find it significant that Congress has been conscious of its own responsibility to consider how its actions may implicate constitutional concerns. First, § 2339B only applies to designated foreign terrorist organizations. There is, and always has been, a limited number of those organizations designated by the Executive Branch, . . . and any groups so designated may seek judicial review of the designation. Second, in response to the lower courts' holdings in this litigation, Congress added clarity to the statute by providing narrowing definitions of the terms "training," "personnel," and "expert advice or assistance," as well as an explanation of the knowledge required to violate § 2339B. Third, in effectuating its stated intent not to abridge First Amendment rights, see § 2339B (i), Congress has also displayed a careful balancing of interests in creating limited exceptions to the ban on material support. The definition of material support, for example, excludes medicine and religious materials. See § 2339A(b)(1). In this area perhaps more than any other, the Legislature's superior capacity for weighing competing interests means that "we must be particularly careful not to substitute our judgment of what is desirable for that of Congress." . . . Finally, and most importantly, Congress has avoided any restriction on independent advocacy, or indeed any activities not directed to, coordinated with, or controlled by foreign terrorist groups.

At bottom, plaintiffs simply disagree with the considered judgment of Congress and the Executive that providing material support to a designated foreign terrorist organization—even seemingly benign support—bolsters the terrorist activities of that organization. That judgment, however, is entitled to significant weight, and we have persuasive evidence before us to sustain it. Given the sensitive interests in national security and foreign affairs at stake, the political branches have adequately substantiated their determination that, to serve the Government's interest in preventing terrorism, it was necessary to prohibit providing material support in the 2729*2729 form of training, expert advice, personnel, and services to foreign terrorist groups, even if the supporters meant to promote only the groups' nonviolent ends.

We turn to the particular speech plaintiffs propose to undertake. First, plaintiffs propose to "train members of [the] PKK on how to use humanitarian and international law to peacefully resolve disputes." . . . Congress can, consistent with the First Amendment, prohibit this direct training. It is wholly foreseeable that the PKK could use the "specific skill[s]" that plaintiffs propose to impart, § 2339A(b)(2), as part of a broader strategy to promote terrorism. The PKK could, for example, pursue peaceful negotiation as a means of buying time to recover from short-term setbacks, lulling opponents into complacency, and ultimately preparing for renewed attacks. See generally A. Marcus, Blood and Belief: The PKK and the Kurdish Fight for Independence 286-295 (2007) (describing the PKK's suspension of armed struggle and subsequent return to violence). A foreign terrorist organization introduced to the structures of the international legal system might use the information to threaten, manipulate, and disrupt. This possibility is real, not remote.

Second, plaintiffs propose to "teach PKK members how to petition various representative bodies such as the United Nations for relief." . . . The Government acts within First Amendment strictures in banning this proposed speech because it teaches the organization how to acquire "relief," which plaintiffs never define with any specificity, and which could readily include monetary aid. . . . Indeed, earlier in this litigation, plaintiffs sought to teach the LTTE "to present claims for tsunami-related aid to mediators and international bodies," . . . which naturally included monetary relief. Money is fungible, . . . and Congress logically concluded that money a terrorist group such as the PKK obtains using the techniques plaintiffs propose to teach could be redirected to funding the group's violent activities.

Finally, plaintiffs propose to "engage in political advocacy on behalf of Kurds who live in Turkey," and "engage in political advocacy on behalf of Tamils who live in Sri Lanka." . . . As explained above, . . . plaintiffs do not specify their expected level of coordination with the PKK or LTTE or suggest what exactly their "advocacy" would consist of. Plaintiffs' proposals are phrased at such a high level of generality that they cannot prevail in this preenforcement challenge. . . .

In responding to the foregoing, the dissent fails to address the real dangers at stake. It instead considers only the possible benefits of plaintiffs' proposed activities in the abstract. . . . The dissent seems unwilling to entertain the prospect that training and advising a designated foreign terrorist organization on how to take advantage of international entities might benefit that organization in a way that facilitates its terrorist activities. In the dissent's world, such training is all to the good. Congress and the Executive, however, have concluded that we live in a different world: one in which the designated foreign terrorist organizations "are so tainted by their criminal conduct that any contribution to such an organization facilitates that conduct." . . . One in which, for example, "the United Nations High Commissioner for Refugees was forced to close a Kurdish refugee camp in northern Iraq because the camp had come under the control of the PKK, and the PKK had failed to respect its 'neutral and humanitarian nature.'" . . . Training and advice on how to work with the United Nations could readily have helped the PKK in its efforts to use the United Nations camp as a base for terrorist activities.

If only good can come from training our adversaries in international dispute resolution, presumably it would have been unconstitutional to prevent American citizens from training the Japanese Government on using international organizations and mechanisms to resolve disputes during World War II. It would, under the dissent's reasoning, have been contrary to our commitment to resolving disputes through "deliberative forces," . . . for Congress to conclude that assisting Japan on that front might facilitate its war effort more generally. That view is not one the First Amendment requires us to embrace.

All this is not to say that any future applications of the material-support statute to speech or advocacy will survive First Amendment scrutiny. It is also not to say that any other statute relating to speech and terrorism would satisfy the First Amendment. In particular, we in no way suggest that a regulation of independent speech would pass constitutional muster, even if the Government were to show that such speech benefits foreign terrorist organizations. We also do not suggest that Congress could extend the same prohibition on material support at issue here to domestic organizations. We simply hold that, in prohibiting the particular forms of support that plaintiffs seek to provide to foreign terrorist groups, § 2339B does not violate the freedom of speech.

VI

Plaintiffs' final claim is that the material-support statute violates their freedom of association under the First Amendment. Plaintiffs argue that the statute criminalizes the mere fact of their associating with the PKK and the LTTE, thereby running afoul of decisions like *De Jonge v. Oregon* . . . and cases in which we have overturned sanctions for joining the Communist Party, . . .

The Court of Appeals correctly rejected this claim because the statute does not penalize mere association with a foreign terrorist organization. As the Ninth Circuit put it: "The statute does not prohibit being a member of one of the designated groups or vigorously promoting and supporting the political goals of the group . . . . What [§ 2339B] prohibits is the act of giving material support . . . ." . . . . Plaintiffs want to do the latter. Our decisions scrutinizing penalties on simple association or assembly are therefore inapposite. . . .

Plaintiffs also argue that the material-support statute burdens their freedom of association because it prevents them from providing support to designated foreign terrorist organizations, but not to other groups. . . . Any burden on plaintiffs' freedom of association in this regard is justified for the same reasons that we have denied plaintiffs' free speech challenge. It would be strange if the Constitution permitted Congress to prohibit certain forms of speech that constitute material support, but did not permit Congress to prohibit that support only to particularly dangerous and lawless foreign organizations. Congress is not required to ban material support to every group or none at all.

* * *

The Preamble to the Constitution proclaims that the people of the United States ordained and established that charter of government in part to "provide for the common defence." As Madison explained, "[s]ecurity against foreign danger is . . . an avowed and essential object of the American Union." . . . We hold that, in regulating the particular forms of support that plaintiffs seek to provide to foreign terrorist organizations, Congress has pursued that objective consistent with the limitations of the First and Fifth Amendments.

The judgment of the United States Court of Appeals for the Ninth Circuit is affirmed in part and reversed in part, and the cases are remanded for further proceedings consistent with this opinion.

It is so ordered.

[Footnotes and citations omitted. Dissenting opinions omitted.]

Part III
Glossary and Table of Cases

Glossary

abandonment: a defense to a criminal charge stating that the person voluntarily abandoned his or her proposed plan of crime before actual commission of the crime; if he or she does so voluntarily, he or she cannot be guilty of attempt.

abortion: a miscarriage or premature expulsion of the fetus.

accessory after the fact: a person who, knowing a felony to have been committed by another, receives, relieves, comforts, or assists the felon, in order to enable him or her to escape from punishment, or the like.

accessory before the fact: one who orders, counsels, encourages, or otherwise aids and abets another to commit a felony and who is not present at the commission of the offense.

***actus reus*:** evil act; a deed, an act, an offense, or an omission of conduct; the wrongful act that renders one criminally liable if combined with *mens rea*.

adultery: the voluntary sexual intercourse of a married person with someone other than his or her spouse.

affirmative defense: matter constituting a defense assuming the complaint to be true e.g. insanity, self defense, entrapment; defendant has burden to put forward evidence reaching preponderance.

alibi: a defense that the offender was in a different place at the time the offense was committed.

anti-structuring laws: federal laws that prohibit breaking up deposits into amounts smaller than $10,000 to avoid reporting requirements.

antitrust: various federal and state statutes intended to protect trade and commerce from unlawful restraints and monopolies.

arson: the crime of purposely setting fire to a house or other building.

asportation: the removal of things from one place to another; the carrying away of goods; one of the circumstances requisite to constitute the offense of larceny.

assault: attempting to cause or purposely, knowingly, or recklessly causing bodily injury to another, or negligently causing bodily injury to another with a deadly weapon, or attempting by physical menace to put another in fear of imminent serious bodily injury; also called simple assault.

assisted suicide: purposely aiding or soliciting another to commit suicide.

attempt: an intent to commit a crime, combined with an act that falls short of accomplishment of the thing intended.

battered woman defense: a defense that victims of battering suffer a type of post-traumatic stress syndrome that causes them to do extreme acts; also described as a type of duress, as a type of self-defense, and as a type of temporary insanity.

battery: an unlawful touching, beating, wounding, or laying hold, however trifling, of another's person or clothes without his or her consent.

bigamy: the offense of having two husbands or two wives at the same time.

Bill of Rights: first 10 amendments to the U.S. Constitution.

breaking and entering: unlawful entry; must be without consent and must breach a threshold (e.g., closed door or window).

bribery: the offense of giving or receiving a gift or reward intended to influence a person in the exercise of a judicial, public, or fiduciary duty.

burden of proof: in the law of evidence, the necessity or duty of affirmatively proving a fact or facts in dispute on an issue raised between the parties in a cause. The obligation of a party to establish by evidence a requisite degree of belief concerning a fact in the mind of the trier of fact or the court.

burglary: breaking and entering by night into a dwelling house with the intent to commit a felony inside.

burning: some consuming of the material of a house (it must be present to constitute the traditional crime of arson).

caption: old common law term for "capture" or the idea of taking.

carjacking: armed robbery with the specific target of robbery being the automobile of the victim.

carnal knowledge: coitus; copulation; the act of a man having sexual bodily connection with a woman or child.

child pornography: depictions of sexual activity involving children or sexually suggestive depictions of children for prurient purposes.

cheats: a group of common law crimes that were misdemeanors and involved crimes against the consumer.

churning: a violation of a broker's fiduciary duty to their client when they advise the client to buy and sell stock solely to increase their own brokerage fees rather than for the benefit of the client.

commerce clause: provision of the U.S. Constitution that gives Congress exclusive powers over interstate commerce.

commercial bribery: the offense of giving or receiving a gift intended to influence a person in the exercise of his or her fiduciary responsibility.

common law: accumulation of early English case law (except for those cases from equity and ecclesiastical courts); origin of American laws.

computer-related crimes: categorized into three categories. (1) The "object" of a crime: this category primarily refers to the theft of computer hardware or software. (2) The "subject" of a crime: the computer is a subject of the attack and the site of the damage caused. (3) The "instrument" used to commit traditional crimes in a more complex manner: these traditional crimes include identity theft, child pornography, copyright infringement, and mail and wire fraud.

concurrence: a meeting or coming together; agreement or union in action; meeting of minds; union in design; in law, it refers to the contemporaneous presence of the *actus reus* and the *mens rea* for a particular crime.

conspiracy: an unlawful combination or agreement between two or more persons to carry into effect a purpose hurtful to some individual, or class, or the public at large.

constructive possession: possession that stems from dominion or control rather than physical possession.

controlled substance: various drugs or other substances classified into Schedules I, II, III, IV, and V of the Uniform Schedule of Controlled Substances.

conversion: an unauthorized assumption and exercise of the right of ownership over goods or personal chattels belonging to another, including the alteration of their condition or the exclusion of the owner's rights.

corporate crime: crimes committed by corporations either through traditional *respondeat superior* principles, or statutes that specifically make corporations liable for criminal acts.

counterterrorism laws: the Patriot Act and other federal and state statutes that address acts of terrorists and their accomplices.

Courts of Appeal: intermediate courts; in the federal system there are 13 that hear appeals from federal District Courts.

crime: a flexible term for violations of law that are punished by the state or nation because of their effect on the public.

criminal facilitation: imposing liability for providing aid to someone, knowing that he or she has committed or is about to commit an offense.

criminal law: law for the purpose of preventing harm to society; it (a) declares what conduct is criminal, and (b) prescribes the punishment to be imposed for such conduct.

criminal mischief: a species of willful and malicious injury to property made punishable by statutes in most jurisdictions.

criminal omission: liability rests upon the failure to act when there is a duty.

criminal simulation: forgery in which the subject of the offense is not a writing, but an object.

curtilage: the enclosed space of ground and buildings immediately surrounding a dwellinghouse.

custody: having the care and control of a thing or person, or dominion over the object.

deliver: to transfer care, custody, or dominion over something to a second party.

depraved heart murder: not intentional murder, but second-degree murder that stems from performing an act that had an almost virtual certainty of causing serious injury or death.

deviate sexual intercourse: a general term that can encompass sodomy as well as fellatio and cunnilingus.

disorderly conduct: conduct with purpose to cause public inconvenience, annoyance, or alarm, or recklessly creating a risk thereof: (a) engaging in fighting or threatening, or in violent or tumultuous behavior; (b) making unreasonable noise or offensively coarse utterance, gesture, or display, or addressing abusive language to a person present; or (c) creating a hazardous or physically offensive condition by an act that serves no legitimate purpose of the actor. Model Penal Code § 250.2(1).

District Courts: federal trial courts.

dominion: perfect control in right of ownership; both title and possession.

double jeopardy: common law and constitutional (Fifth Amendment) prohibition against a second prosecution after a first trial for the same offense.

drunkenness: the condition of a person whose mind is affected by the use of alcoholic beverages; intoxication; inebriation.

due process: the procedural protections designed to protect against governmental error in the deprivation of life, liberty, or property.

duress: compulsion; coercion.

***Durham* Rule:** test applied in some states for the defense of insanity; under this test, an accused is not responsible for an unlawful act if the act was the product of mental disease or defect.

dwelling: the house or other structure in which a person or persons live; a residence; abode; habitation; the apartment or building, or group of buildings, occupied by a family as a place of residence.

eavesdropping: listening under walls, windows, or eaves in order to seek out private discourse.

embezzlement: conversion to his or her own use, by an agent or employee, of money or property received by him or her for and on behalf of his or her employer.

entrapment: a defense that law enforcement officers enticed persons to commit a crime who had no preexisting disposition to do so.

entrapment by estoppel: a defense that the offender was enticed to commit a crime with the promise that there would be no prosecution.

environmental crime: illegal acts that affect the quality of water, land, and air.

escape: the voluntary departure of a prisoner from custody before he or she is released by lawful authority.

evading (arrest): physically avoiding arrest without necessarily having physical contact with a police officer (as in resisting); some states require that the offender place an officer in danger in order to find culpability for evading.

excusable homicide: the killing of a human being, either by misadventure or in self-defense.

ex post facto: made after the occurrence; every law that makes criminal an act that was innocent when done, or that inflicts a greater punishment than the law annexed to the crime when committed.

extortion: obtaining money or other things of value by threats or coercion.

extraneous intervening factors: outside factors that cause the abandonment of the final execution of a crime (the presence of these factors would negate the possibility of using abandonment as a defense).

factual impossibility: does not constitute a defense. When a defendant attempts to commit an act that is illegal and does everything to commit the crime, but fails in his or her effort to commit the actual crime because of some fact that would make it impossible to complete the crime.

Fair Labor Standards Act: an act to provide for the establishment of fair labor standards in employment in and affecting interstate commerce. 29 U.S.C. § 201 *et seq.*

false advertising: the publication of a false or misleading statement or representation concerning merchandise, with the intent to sell, barter, or exchange, with the intent to deceive or mislead.

false pretenses: a false representation of a material present or past fact that causes the victim to pass title to his property to the wrongdoer, who (a) knows his representation to be false and (b) intends thereby to defraud the victim.

false swearing: a false statement, or swearing or affirmation of the truth of a previously made false statement, made by a person under oath or equivalent affirmation when he does not believe the statement to be true, in an official proceeding or to a public servant performing his official function.

felony: a serious crime punishable by death or imprisonment in the state penitentiary, usually for more than one year.

felony-murder rule: rule that any death that occurs in the perpetration of an inherently dangerous felony could be prosecuted as murder.

feticide: destruction of the fetus; the act by which criminal abortion is produced.

fiduciary relationship: a legal, social, domestic, or personal relationship where one party is duty-bound to act in the best interests of the other party.

forfeiture: the loss of some right or property as a penalty for some illegal act.

forgery: the false making or altering of an instrument that purports on its face to be good and valid for the purposes for which it was created.

fornication: a flexible term, often defined by various state statutes as sexual intercourse by an unmarried person.

general intent: present when one consciously chooses to do a prohibited act.

Good Samaritan laws: laws that require one who sees a person in imminent and serious peril to effect a rescue, provided the attempt does not endanger oneself.

gratuity: something acquired without bargain or inducement by virtue of position or power rather than individual effort.

hate crime: certain specified (illegal) acts (e.g., murder, assault, vandalism, kidnapping) to specific victims who are members of protected groups.

homicide: committing an act that results in the death of a human being; usually defined by various state statutes.

identity theft: when an offender uses a victim's name, Social Security number, and other personal identifiers to obtain goods, services, credit, and currency.

importuning: solicitation of sexual activity.

incest: carnal knowledge of persons so related to each other that their marriage is prohibited by law (e.g., of brother and sister, father and daughter, uncle and niece).

inchoate: imperfect; partial; unfinished; begun, but not completed.

inciting to riot: occurs when one incites or encourages other persons to create or engage in a riot.

incompetency: lack of ability, capacity, or fitness to discharge the required duty; as applied to competency to stand trial, test is whether or not defendant understands proceedings and can assist attorney in presenting a defense.

infancy: at common law, a child under the age of seven; legal effect is that there is no criminal culpability; typically set by statute.

insanity: the term is a legal term rather than a medical one, and indicates a condition that renders the affected person incapable of rational thought, thereby removing criminal culpability.

insider trading: buying or selling stock based on information regarding the company that is obtained as an "insider" or from an insider of the company and not available to the general public.

involuntary manslaughter: the unlawful and unintentional killing of a human being, directly and proximately resulting from the commission of an unlawful act.

irresistible impulse rule: an insanity defense holding that notwithstanding that one accused of committing a crime may have been able to comprehend the nature and consequences of his or her act, and to know that it was wrong, he or she may be excused if he or she was forced to its exertion by an impulse that he or she was powerless to control in consequence of an actual disease of the mind.

joyriding: the temporary use of another person's automobile without permission.

justifiable homicide: may be committed intentionally, but without any evil design, and under such circumstances of necessity or duty as to render the act legal and not criminal.

juvenile: a person who has not attained his or her eighteenth birthday.

kidnapping: the forcible abduction or carrying away of a person from his or her domicile, parents, or legal protector through force or coercion with evil intent (statutes may define differently).

knowingly: in the Model Penal Code, knowledge is a lower level of *mens rea* than intentional and refers to the guilty mind that knows what they are doing is wrong but may not necessarily intend the final result.

larceny: the unlawful taking and carrying away of personal property, without permission, and with the intent to deprive the rightful owner of the same.

legal impossibility: defense of "legal impossibility" may be established only where a defendant's actions, if fully performed, would not constitute a crime.

lewdness (indecent exposure): at common law, intentionally and indecently and offensively exposing the sex organs in the presence of another in an offensive manner.

Lindbergh Law: federal law that punishes kidnapping for ransom or reward when the victim is transported from one state to another or to a foreign county (failure to release the victim within 24 hours creates a rebuttable presumption that such person has been transported in interstate or foreign commerce).

loitering: wandering or remaining in a place, at a time, or in a manner not usual for law-abiding individuals under circumstances that warrant alarm for the safety of persons or property in the vicinity.

mail fraud: statutes that make it illegal to use the mails to perpetrate a fraudulent scheme.

mala in se: acts that are wrong in and of themselves, whether prohibited by human laws or not, as distinguished from *mala prohibita*.

mala prohibita: acts that are prohibited by human laws, but not necessarily *mala in se*, or wrong in themselves.

malice aforethought: a predetermination to commit an act without legal justification or excuse.

malicious mischief (criminal mischief): the intentional and unlawful injury to or destruction of the property of another with the malicious intent to injure the owner.

marital exemption: common law and some states defined a marital exemption that stated that a married man could not rape his wife because the marriage created an irrevocable consent to sexual intercourse; no state currently recognizes this common law defense to rape.

materiality: having legal import.

mayhem: at common law, the deprivation of a member of the body proper for defense in a fight (e.g., an arm, leg, eye, or other appendage).

mens rea: criminal intent; evil intent; guilty intent.

Miller **test:** test from the case of *Miller v. California* to determine whether something is obscene.

misdemeanor: any crime or offense not amounting to a felony and not an ordinance or regulation.

M'Naghten **Rule:** test applied in some states for the defense of insanity; states that the proper standard or test for criminal responsibility is whether the accused was laboring under such a defect of reason, from disease of the mind, as to not know the nature and quality of the act he or she was doing or, if the accused did know it, he or she did not know that what he or she was doing was wrong.

money laundering: the process by which a person conceals the existence, illegal source, or illegal application of income, and disguises that income to make it appear legitimate.

murder: the willful killing of a human being with malice aforethought, either express or implied.

necessity: pressing need, overruling power, compulsion, or irresistible force; a defense (sometimes called the lesser of two evils defense) that allows an offender to claim that he or she avoided a greater evil by committing a crime.

negligence: undertaking actions that cause an unreasonable amount of risk when one should have known of the risk.

negligent homicide: the criminal offense committed by one whose negligence is the direct and proximate cause of another's death.

obscenity: conduct that is objectionable or offensive to accepted standards of decency and that tends to corrupt the public morals by its indecency and lewdness.

obstructing a highway: crime of obstructing a public thoroughfare with no authorization

obstructing justice: the offense of intentionally hindering or obstructing the arrest, conviction, and punishment of accused persons, including all proper and necessary proceedings for administering justice.

Occupational Safety and Health Act: an act to assure safe and healthful working conditions by authorizing enforcement of standards.

overt act: an element of attempt, a concrete act.

paternalistic laws: refers to the type of authority exercised by parents over their children and are those laws that punish behaviors that typically only have the capacity to injure oneself.

Patriot Act: an act passed by Congress after September 11, 2001, that expanded law enforcement investigative powers and strengthened laws against terroristic actions and those actions that might assist or contribute to terrorism.

perjury: a false statement under oath or affirmation, willfully made in regard to a material matter of fact.

phishing: form of false representation using a computer; offender sends computer messages to unknowing victims that look as though sent by actual businesses and ask for account or financial information, then uses such information to perpetrate fraud or other crimes.

Pinkerton Rule: coconspirators are culpable for all foreseeable acts in furtherance of the conspiracy that are committed by any one of the coconspirators.

police power: the Tenth Amendment to the U.S. Constitution confers upon the individual states the power to enact laws for the comfort, safety, morals, health, and prosperity of their citizens.

polygamy: plurality of wives or husbands.

premeditated: designed or intended idea formed to commit a crime or do an act before it is done.

principal in the first degree: one who, with the requisite mental state, engages in the act or omission concurring with the mental state, which causes the criminal result.

principal in the second degree: one who aids, counsels, commands, or encourages the principal in the first degree in the commission of the offense.

prison break: the common law offense of one who, being lawfully in custody, escapes from the place where he is confined, by the employment of force and violence.

procedural criminal law: that which prescribes the method of enforcing rights or obtaining redress for their invasion; machinery for carrying on procedural aspects of civil or criminal action.

prostitution: engaging in sexual activity for remuneration.

provocation: the act of inciting another to do a particular deed because of aroused rage, resentment, or fury in the latter against the former.

proximate cause: any original event that, in natural and unbroken sequence, produces a particular foreseeable result, without which the result would not have occurred.

prurient interest: a shameful or morbid interest in nudity, sex, or excretion.

puffery: refers to exaggerations or statements unlikely to deceive ordinary persons in the group addressed.

purposely: descriptive of an act of the will, of an act by intention, or of an act by design.

racketeering: an organized conspiracy to commit the crimes of extortion or coercion, or attempts to commit extortion or coercion.

rape: the act of having sexual intercourse with a woman by force and against her will.

rape shield statutes: statutes that restrict testimony about a rape victim's prior sexual behavior (or sexual history) to that genuinely relevant to the defense.

real property: land, and generally whatever is erected or growing upon or affixed to land.

receiving stolen property: purposely receiving, retaining, or disposing of movable property of another, knowing that it has been stolen, or believing that it probably has been stolen, unless the property is received, retained, or disposed with purpose to restore it to the owner. Model Penal Code § 223.6.

recklessly: carelessly, heedlessly, indifferently; a state of mind that disregards the possibility or probability of injurious consequences, or altogether, foreseeing such consequences, continues in spite of them.

renunciation: the act by which a person abandons a right acquired without transferring it to another.

rescue: act of saving or freeing.

resisting arrest: using physical force to resist being brought into custody by a law enforcement officer.

***respondeat superior*:** this maxim means that a master is liable in certain cases for the wrongful acts of his servant, or agent.

RICO: Racketeer Influenced and Corrupt Organizations Act. Addresses organized racketeering activity; punishes those separately for having a pattern of criminal activity in concert with others.

riot: a tumultuous disturbance of the peace by three or more persons assembled of their own authority and with intent to obstruct or upset governmental officials.

robbery: theft from a person, accompanied by violence or threats putting the person in fear.

rout: common law offense between unlawful assembly and riot; typically means when more than three persons have come together and committed at least one overt act against the public peace.

Schedule I drugs: drugs defined by the Uniform Schedule of Controlled Substances as drugs with no redeeming social value, little medical application, and high risk of addiction (i.e., heroin, cocaine, marijuana).

seduction: the offense of a man deceitfully inducing a woman to have unlawful sexual intercourse with him.

self-defense: a defense that the action charged as a crime was for the protection of one's person and property from injury.

sexual abuse/sexual assault: occurs when one person touches another or subjects another person to sexual contact without the other's consent.

sexual contact: touching the sexual or intimate parts of another person for the purpose of gratifying the sexual desire of either party.

sexual misconduct: in some states, sexual intercourse between a defendant under age 18 and a victim under age 16.

sexual predator laws: identify the types of crimes that lead to a sexual predator designation, and then may specify certain enhanced punishments, treatment, or, more controversially, sexual predator registration.

social contract: in political philosophy, a term applied to the theory of the origin of society associated chiefly with the names of Hobbes, Locke, and Rousseau, though it can be traced back to the Greek Sophists. Rousseau held that in the presocial state man was unwarlike and timid. Laws resulted from the combination of men who agreed, for mutual protection, to surrender individual freedom of action. Government must therefore rest on the consent of the governed.

sodomy: carnal copulation between two human beings, or between man and animal, contrary to nature.

solicitation: the offense of asking or enticing another to engage in illegal conduct for hire.

solicitation of prostitution: requesting, offering sex for hire.

specific intent: intent to commit the *actus reus* and intent to cause the result (i.e., to violate the law).

states' rights: rights not conferred on the federal government specifically in the Constitution or Articles of the Federation; according to the Tenth Amendment to the U.S. Constitution all rights not specifically identified as federal are reserved to the states.

statute of limitations: various periods of time, fixed by different state and federal statutes, within which a lawsuit must be commenced, and after the expiration of which the claimant will be forever barred from the right to bring the action.

statutory law: law created by, or depending upon, a statute, as distinguished from equitable or common law rules.

statutory rape: sexual intercourse with a female (and more currently, any child) under the age of consent.

stop-and-identify statutes: statutes that require a citizen to identify him- or herself if asked by a law enforcement officer.

strict liability: culpability that occurs without *mens rea;* in strict liability crimes, the state need not prove any level of *mens rea* on the part of the offender.

subornation of perjury: the offense of procuring another to take such a false oath as would constitute perjury in the principal.

substantial step: conduct that is strongly corroborative of the firmness of the defendant's criminal intent; a test to determine if attempt has occurred.

substantive criminal law: that part of law that creates, defines, and regulates rights.

superseding intervening factor: an act of a third person or other force, which by its intervention cuts off the culpability of the actor.

theft by deception: another term for fraud; a taking through the use of deception.

theft of services: purposely obtaining labor, professional service, transportation, telephone, or other public service, by deception or threat, or by false token or other means to avoid payment.

trafficking: selling a controlled substance.

transferred intent: doctrine holding that if the defendant shoots or strikes at A, intending to wound or kill him or her, and unforeseeably hits B instead, the defendant is guilty of the originally intended crime.

trespass: criminal trespass is entering or surreptitiously remaining in a building or occupied structure, or separately secured or occupied portion thereof, knowing that he or she is not licensed or privileged to do so. Model Penal Code § 221.2(1).

undue burden test: current test to apply to statutes that seek to curtail or place guidelines on the use of abortion; if the state law "unduly burdens" the woman's ability to choose, then it would be ruled unconstitutional.

United States Code: the code of federal laws.

unlawful assembly: a gathering of three or more persons with the intent of committing a crime with force. Often defined by various state statutes.

utmost resistance standard: requirement that a woman expend the greatest effort of which she was capable to foil a rapist, otherwise the sexual contact was not without consent; abandoned by modern courts.

uttering: to put or send (as a forged check) into circulation; to publish or put forth; to offer.

vagrancy: at common law, going from place to place without visible means of support, being idle, refusing to work, living without labor, and relying on the charity of others.

vandalism: willful and malicious acts committed with the intent to damage or destroy property of another.

vicarious liability: substituted or indirect responsibility (e.g., the responsibility of an employer for the torts committed by his employee within the scope of employment).

voluntary manslaughter: manslaughter committed voluntarily upon a sudden heat of the passions; as if, upon a sudden quarrel, two persons fight, and one of them kills the other.

voyeurism: committing trespass or otherwise surreptitiously invading the privacy of another, to spy or eavesdrop on another, for the purpose of sexually arousing or gratifying oneself.

Wharton Rule: in crimes that require at least two people (bigamy, adultery, incest), a conspiracy charge cannot be based solely on the agreement of only the two people necessarily involved in the crime.

white-collar crime: differs from traditional crimes and includes insider trading, antitrust conspiracy, restraint of trade, embezzlement, mail and wire fraud, money laundering, securities fraud, tax fraud, tax evasion, environmental crime, and employment-related crimes.

wire fraud: statutes making it illegal to use any interstate electronic communication network to perpetrate a fraudulent scheme.

wiretapping: intercepting a communication by making a connection with a telephone line. Usually defined by various statutes.

year-and-a-day-rule: if death did not take place within a year and a day of the time of receiving the wound, the law draws the conclusion that it was not the cause of death; and neither the court nor jury can draw a contrary one.

Index of Cases

Note: Page numbers followed by *np* indicate footnotes.

Index

Note: Page numbers followed by *b* indicate boxes and *t* indicate tables.